Anagram Finder

Compiled by
Market House Books Ltd

OXFORD
UNIVERSITY PRESS

OXFORD
UNIVERSITY PRESS

Great Clarendon Street, Oxford OX2 6DP

Oxford University Press is a department of the University of Oxford.
It furthers the University's objective of excellence in research, scholarship,
and education by publishing worldwide in

Oxford New York

Athens Auckland Bangkok Bogotá Buenos Aires Calcutta
Cape Town Chennai Dar es Salaam Delhi Florence Hong Kong Istanbul
Karachi Kuala Lumpur Madrid Melbourne Mexico City Mumbai
Nairobi Paris São Paulo Singapore Taipei Tokyo Toronto Warsaw

with associated companies in Berlin Ibadan

Published in the United States
by Oxford University Press Inc., New York

First published 1999

British Library Cataloguing in Publication Data
Data available

Library of Congress Cataloging in Publication Data
Data available

ISBN 0-19-860221-9

10 9 8 7 6 5 4 3 2 1

Typeset by Market House Books Ltd
Printed in Great Britain by
Mackays of Chatham plc
Chatham, Kent

PREFACE

The *Oxford Anagram Finder* is intended as a reference for people seeking anagrams as solutions for crossword puzzles. It contains over 100,000 items selected from the words in *The Concise Oxford Dictionary* and *The New Shorter Oxford English Dictionary*. The words chosen include common phrases, proper names of countries, cities, and towns, and given names for people.

The book is divided into sections for words or phrases of four letters, five letters, etc., up to twelve letters. Each word or phrase has been given an alphabetical key consisting of the letters in the word placed in alphabetical order. The keys themselves are also listed alphabetically within the section.

This arrangement allows the user to find anagrams quickly, without the usual procedure of writing the letters in random order and inspecting them to find the answer. Some examples of this are given in the following section.

The arrangement using a key for each word throws together words that are anagrams of each other. Although this is not intended as a book for browsing in, it does demonstrate some unexpected connections – how else would one know that *non-scientist* is an anagram of *inconsistent* or that *man of letters* is an anagram of *forestalment*? We believe that this book will be a valuable source for compilers of crossword puzzles as well as people looking for solutions.

GUIDE

Anagrams may occur in a number of games or puzzles in which it is necessary to find a word or phrase formed by rearranging an initial set of letters. These may be the letters of some other word or phrase or they may be random letters. For example:

Make up two words from the letters YOCITIRDAN.

To use the book, one takes the letters and arranges them in alphabetical order to give a key: in this case the key is ACDIINORTY. This is looked up in the section of ten-letter words to give the answer **dictionary** and **indicatory**.

Anagrams are often the solutions to clues in cryptic crosswords. It is usually possible to detect that the solution is an anagram by the presence of certain indicator words or phrases in the clue – 'confused', 'rearranged', 'mixed up', 'at sixes and sevens', etc. For example, take the following clue:

One who'd organized a dance (7 letters).

The word 'organized' suggests that the solution is an anagram of 'one who'd'. The letters of 'one who'd' (ONEWHOD) are taken and arranged in alphabetical order to give the key DEHNOOW. This is looked up in the section of seven-letter words to give the solution **hoedown.**

A more difficult example is the clue:

Images artist combined with musical composition (9 letters).

Here 'composition' suggests an anagram and 'artist' could be RA. The solution would then be an anagram of RA and 'musical', for which the key is AACILMRSU. This leads to the correct solution **simulacra** in the section of nine-letter words.

CONTENTS

FOUR LETTERS

AABB abba, baba
AABC caba
AABD baa'd
AABG agba
AABL alba
AABR Arab
AABS baas
AABY abay
AACN Cana
AACP capa, paca
AACR Cara
AACV cava
AACW Waac
AACZ caza
AADD adad, dada
AADG agad
AADL Adal, Alda
AADM Adam, dama
AADN Anda, Dana, nada
AADP pada
AADR Arad, raad
AADT adat, data, ta-da
AADW adaw
AADY a-day
AAER aera, area
AAES asea
AAFH haaf
AAFJ faja
AAFL alfa, fa-la
AAFN fana
AAFR afar
AAFW Waaf
AAGG gaga
AAGH agha
AAGI Gaia
AAGL agal, alga, gala
AAGM agma
AAGN naga
AAGR agar, Agra, raga
AAGS saga
AAGY Gaya
AAHH ha ha
AAHK haka
AAHM amah
AAHP paha
AAHR haar
AAHS sa-ha
AAHY ayah, Haya
AAIL Alia
AAIP Apia
AAIR aria, raia
AAJK Ajka
AAJM jama, maja
AAJR ajar, raja
AAJY Ajay
AAKK kaka
AAKM kama
AAKN kana
AAKP kapa
AAKR arak, Kara
AAKT kata, taka
AAKV kava
AAKW waka
AAKY kaya
AAKZ kaza
AALL la-la
AALM alma, lama
AALN alan, anal, Lana, nala
AALP alap, pala
AALR alar
AALS alas, sala
AALT taal, tala
AALU aula
AALV Alva, lava
AALW waal
AALX axal
AALY alay
AAMM ma'am, mama
AAMN mana, naam, Nama
AAMR maar, mara
AAMS asma, maas
AAMY maya
AANN anan, anna, naan, nana
AANO anoa
AANP napa
AANR Aran
AANS ansa, Naas
AANT anta, naat, tana
AANY Anya
AANZ azan, Zana
AAPP papa
AAPR para
AAPS sapa
AAPT atap, pata, tapa
AAPU paua
AAPW pawa
AAPY apay
AAQU aqua
AARR arra
AARS rasa, Sara
AART Arta, rata, tara
AARU aura
AARV vara
AARZ Zara
AASV vasa
AASY yaas
AASZ saza
AATT atta, ta-ta
AATU atua, taua
AATW tawa
AATX taxa
AATZ Taza
AAWW wa-wa
AAWY away
ABBE babe
ABBI Babi
ABBL blab
ABBO abob
ABBR barb, brab
ABBS Babs
ABBU babu
ABBY Abby, baby
ABCH bach
ABCK back
ABCN banc
ABCR carb, crab
ABCS scab
ABCU Cuba
ABDE abed, bade, bead
ABDL bald, blad
ABDN band
ABDO doab
ABDR bard, brad, drab
ABDU adub, baud, daub, duab
ABDW bawd
ABEK bake, beak
ABEL Abel, able, albe, bael, bale, beal, blae
ABEM beam, bema
ABEN bane, bean, nabe
ABEP peba
ABER bare, bear, brae
ABES base, sabe
ABET abet, bate, beat, beta
ABEU beau
ABEZ baze
ABFF baff
ABFL flab
ABFR barf, frab
ABFT baft
ABGI biga, Gabi
ABGL blag
ABGM gamb
ABGN bang
ABGR brag, garb, grab
ABGY gaby
ABHL blah
ABHS bash
ABHT baht, bath
ABIL Albi, bail
ABIM iamb
ABIN bani, Bina, nabi, naib
ABIR abri, rabi
ABIS bias, isba, sabi
ABIT bait, tabi
ABIW wabi
ABIZ izba
ABJL Blaj
ABJM jamb
ABJU baju, juba
ABKL balk
ABKN bank, knab
ABKR bark,

brak, krab
ABKS bask
ABKU Baku
ABLL ball
ABLM balm, lamb
ABLO bola
ABLS slab
ABLT blat, tabl
ABLW bawl
ABLY ably, blay
ABMO ambo, boma
ABMR barm, Bram
ABNR barn, bran
ABNS nabs
ABNU Buna
ABNW bawn
ABOR boar, bora
ABOS Abos, bosa
ABOT boat
ABOX abox
ABOZ Boaz, boza
ABQU quab
ABRS bras
ABRT Bart, brat, T-bar
ABRW braw, warb
ABRY bray
ABSS bass
ABST bast, bats, stab
ABSW swab
ABTT batt
ABTU abut, tabu, tuba
ABTZ batz
ACCK cack
ACCO coca
ACDE cade, dace, ecad
ACDH chad
ACDI acid, cadi, caid
ACDL clad
ACDO coda
ACDR card, drac
ACDS scad
ACDY cady
ACEF cafe, face
ACEG cage
ACEH ache, each
ACEK cake
ACEL alce, alec, lace
ACEM acme, came, mace
ACEN acne, Caen, cane
ACEP cape, pace
ACER acer, acre, care, race
ACES case
ACET cate, tace
ACEV cave
ACFF caff
ACFK fack
ACFL calf
ACFR carf
ACFT fact
ACFY facy
ACGL clag
ACGN cang
ACGR crag
ACGS scag
ACGY cagy
ACHH chah
ACHK chak, hack
ACHL chal
ACHM cham, Mach
ACHP chap
ACHR arch, char
ACHS cash, Chas
ACHT Cath, chat, tach, tcha
ACHW chaw
ACHY achy, chay
ACIL Cali, laic
ACIM mica
ACIN cain, Inca
ACIO ciao
ACIP pica
ACIR Rica
ACIS asci, saic
ACJK jack
ACJU jacu
ACKL calk, kcal, lack
ACKM mack
ACKO coak
ACKP pack
ACKR cark, rack
ACKS cask, sack
ACKT tack
ACKU cauk
ACKW cawk, wack
ACKY yack
ACKZ zack
ACLL call
ACLM calm, clam
ACLN clan
ACLO coal, cola
ACLP clap
ACLR carl
ACLT talc
ACLU caul
ACLW cawl, claw
ACLX calx
ACLY acyl, clay, lacy
ACMO coma
ACMP camp
ACMR cram, marc
ACMS scam
ACMY cyma
ACNN cann
ACNP cap'n
ACNR cran, narc
ACNS scan
ACNT cant, can't
ACNY cany, cyan
ACOP capo, paco
ACOR arco, Cora, orca
ACOS soca
ACOT coat, taco
ACOW Waco
ACOX coax, coxa
ACPR carp, crap
ACPT pact
ACPU pacu
ACPY pacy
ACRR carr
ACRS scar
ACRT cart, trac
ACRW craw
ACRY Cary, cray, racy
ACRZ czar
ACSS cass
ACST cast, scat
ACSW scaw
ACTT tact
ACUY yuca
ACVY cavy
ADDE dade, dead, Edda
ADDO adod, dado
ADDU daud, duad, udad
ADDY D-Day, dyad
ADEF deaf, fade
ADEG aged, egad, gade, gaed
ADEH hade, head
ADEI aide, idea
ADEJ jade
ADEK kade
ADEL Aled, dale, deal, Elda, lade, lead
ADEM dame, Edam, made, mead
ADEN Dane, dean, Edna
ADEO odea
ADER ared, dare, dear, read
ADES deas, sade
ADET date, tea'd
ADEV Dave, deva, vade, Veda
ADEW wade
ADEZ adze, daze
ADFF daff
ADFN fand
ADFO fado
ADFR fard
ADFT daft
ADFY fady
ADGI gadi
ADGL glad
ADGN dang
ADGO dago, goad
ADGR darg, drag, grad
ADGU gaud
ADGW dawg, Gawd
ADHJ hadj
ADHK dhak, khad
ADHL dhal
ADHN dhan, hand
ADHO Doha
ADHP Daph
ADHR dhar, hard
ADHS dash, shad
ADIK dika, kadi, kaid
ADIL Dali, dial, laid
ADIM amid, maid
ADIN Dani, dian, Dina
ADIP padi, paid
ADIQ qadi
ADIR arid, raid
ADIS Aids, dais, disa, said
ADIT adit, dita
ADIV avid, diva, Vida
ADIW wadi
ADKN dank
ADKR dark
ADKU duka
ADKW dawk
ADKY Dyak
ADLN land
ADLO Aldo, alod,

load, odal
ADLR darl, lard
ADLT dalt
ADLU auld, dual, laud, udal
ADLW wald
ADLY lady
ADMN damn
ADMO mado
ADMP damp
ADMR dram, mard
ADMU duma, maud
ADNO dona, noda
ADNP pand
ADNR darn, nard, rand
ADNS sand
ADNU duan
ADNW dawn, wand
ADNY Andy
ADOP apod, dopa
ADOR Dora, road
ADOS soda
ADOT dato, doat, toad
ADOW woad
ADPR drap, pard, prad
ADPS daps
ADQU quad
ADRS Ards, sard
ADRT dart, drat, trad
ADRU duar, dura
ADRW draw, ward
ADRY adry, dray, yard
ADSY days
ADTU daut
ADTW dawt
ADVY davy
ADWY wady
ADYZ Yazd
AEEG agee
AEEJ ajee
AEEK akee
AEEL alee, Elea
AEES ease
AEEV eave
AEFK fake, feak
AEFL fale, feal, flea, leaf
AEFM fame
AEFN fane
AEFR fare, fear, frae, Rafe
AEFS safe
AEFT Efta, fate, feat, feta
AEFV fave
AEFY Faye
AEFZ faze
AEGG gage
AEGL Gael, gale, geal, lage
AEGM egma, game, mage, mega
AEGN agen, gean, gena, nage
AEGP gape, page, peag
AEGR areg, gare, gear, Gera, rage
AEGS sage
AEGT gate, geta
AEGU ague, auge
AEGV gave, vega
AEGW wage
AEGY agey, Gaye
AEGZ gaze
AEHK hake
AEHL hale, heal, Leah
AEHM ahem, haem, hame
AEHP heap
AEHR hare, hear, rhea
AEHS seah, shea
AEHT eath, haet, hate, heat, Thea
AEHV have
AEHY ahey, haye, yeah
AEHZ haze
AEIL aiel, aile, ilea
AEIN Aine
AEIP peai
AEIR aire, Eira, eria
AEJK jake
AEJL Jael
AEJN jane, jean, Jena
AEJP jape
AEKK ekka
AEKL kale, lake, leak
AEKM kame, make
AEKN Kane, nake
AEKP peak
AEKR rake
AEKS sake
AEKT Kate, keta, take, teak
AEKV vake
AEKW wake, weak, weka
AELL Ella, leal, Lela
AELM alme, amel, Elma, lame, leam, male, meal, mela
AELN elan, laen, lane, lean, Lena, neal
AELO aloe, olea
AELP leap, pale, peal, plea
AELR earl, lare, lear, rale, real
AELS alse, Elsa, lase, sale, seal
AELT late, leat, Leta, tael, tale, teal
AELV lave, leva, vale, veal, vela
AELW wale, weal
AELX Alex, axel, axle
AELY aley, ayle
AELZ laze, zeal
AEMM emma
AEMN amen, enam, mane, mean, name, nema
AEMP mape
AEMR mare, mear, rame, ream
AEMS Ames, mase, mesa, same, seam
AEMT mate, meat, meta, tame, team
AEMW wame
AEMX Amex, exam
AEMZ maze
AENN Anne
AENO aeon, eoan
AENP nape, neap, pane, pean
AENQ Qena
AENR earn, nare, near, Rena
AENS anse, sane, sean
AENT ante, etna, neat
AENU aune
AENV aven, Evan, nave, Neva, vane, vena
AENW anew, Ewan, wane, wean
AENY ayne, yean
AENZ ezan, naze, Zane, Zena
AEOT toea
AEOZ zoea
AEPP pape
AEPR pare, pear, rape, reap
AEPS apse, spae
AEPT pate, peat, Peta, tape, tepa
AEPV pave
AEPX apex
AERR rare, rear
AERS arse, rase, sear, sera
AERT aret, rate, tare, tear
AERU urea
AERV aver, rave, Vera
AERW ware, wear
AERY aery,

ayre, eyra, yare, year
AERZ Ezra, raze
AEST east, eats, sate, seat, seta
AESU Esau, seau
AESV save, vase
AESW wase
AESX axes, saxe, seax
AESY easy, eyas
AETT Etta, tate, teat
AETV tave
AETW weta
AETX exta
AETY yate
AETZ teaz, zeta
AEUV uvea
AEUX eaux
AEVW wave
AFFF faff
AFFG gaff
AFFH haff
AFFN naff
AFFO offa
AFFP paff
AFFR raff
AFFW waff
AFFY affy
AFGL flag
AFGN fang
AFGO goaf
AFGU gufa
AFHL half
AFHS fash
AFHT haft
AFIK faik, faki
AFIL fail, fial
AFIN fain
AFIR fair, fiar
AFIT fiat
AFIW waif
AFKL flak
AFKW wakf
AFLL fall
AFLM flam
AFLN flan
AFLO foal, loaf, Olaf
AFLP flap
AFLR farl, larf
AFLT flat
AFLW flaw
AFLX falx, flax
AFLY flay
AFMO foam
AFMR farm
AFNR Fran
AFNU faun
AFNW fawn
AFOO oafo
AFOR Afro, faro
AFOS oafs, sofa
AFOY ofay
AFPR frap
AFQW waqf
AFRT fart, frat, raft
AFRU Frau
AFRY fray
AFRZ zarf
AFST fast
AFSU sauf
AFTT taft
AFTU tufa
AFTW waft
AFUX faux
AGGM magg
AGGN gang
AGGO agog
AGGU guga
AGHN ghan, hang
AGHP ghap
AGHS gash, shag
AGHT Gath, ghat
AGIL Gail, glia
AGIM magi
AGIN agin, gain, Gina
AGIO agio
AGIR gari, ragi, Riga
AGIT gait, Gita, Taig
AGIV vagi, viga
AGJO ajog, Jago
AGJT jagt
AGJU juga
AGKN kang, knag
AGKO kago
AGKS skag
AGKU gauk, kagu
AGKW gawk
AGLL gall
AGLM glam
AGLO gaol, goal, gola, Olga
AGLP galp
AGLS slag
AGLT galt, talg
AGLU aglu, Gaul, gula
AGLY Algy
AGMN G-man
AGMO ogam
AGMP gamp
AGMR gram, marg
AGMU gaum, muga
AGMY gamy
AGNO agon, gaon
AGNP gnap, pang
AGNR garn, gnar, gran, rang
AGNS sang, snag
AGNT gant, gnat, tang
AGNU aung, guan, guna
AGNV vang
AGNW gawn, gnaw, gwan, wang
AGNY yang
AGOR agro
AGOS sago
AGOT goat, toga
AGOY yoga
AGPS gasp
AGPU gaup
AGPW gawp
AGQU quag
AGRU gaur, guar
AGRY Gary, gray
AGRZ Graz
AGST gast, stag
AGSW swag
AGSY sagy
AGTT gatt
AGUY yuga
AHHS hash, shah
AHHT hath
AHIJ haji
AHIK haik
AHIL hail, Ha'il, hila
AHIM Hami
AHIN hain
AHIO ohia
AHIR hair
AHIS Shia
AHIT aith, hait, Thai
AHIU huia
AHIV Ivah
AHIY hiya
AHJJ hajj
AHKL lakh
AHKN ankh, hank, khan
AHKR hark
AHKS hask
AHKT Kath, khat
AHKU ukha
AHKW hawk
AHLL hall
AHLM halm
AHLO halo
AHLR harl
AHLS lash
AHLT halt, lath
AHLU haul, hula
AHLY hyla
AHMM Hamm
AHMO Hamo, homa
AHMR harm
AHMS mash, sham
AHMT math
AHMU huma
AHMW wham
AHNO Noah
AHNS Hans
AHNT tanh, than
AHOP opah, paho
AHOR haro, hoar, hora
AHOT oath
AHOW whoa
AHOX hoax
AHOY ahoy, hoya
AHPR harp
AHPS hasp, pash
AHPT path
AHPU hapu, puha
AHPW whap
AHRR harr
AHRS rash, Sarh
AHRT hart, rath, tahr, thar, thra
AHSS sash
AHST hast, shat, tash
AHSW shaw, wash
AHSY ashy
AHSZ Shaz
AHTT that
AHTU haut, Utah
AHTW thaw, wath, what
AHUW whau
AHYZ hazy
AIIL ilia
AIIM miai
AIIN Iain
AIIP piai
AIIX ixia
AIJL jail
AIJN Jain, Ji'an
AIJO jiao
AIJT jati
AIJV jiva
AIKK kaki
AIKL ilka, kail, kali, laik
AIKM kaim, kami
AIKN akin, kain, kina, naik
AIKP kiap, paik, Paki, pika
AIKR raik, raki, Rika
AIKS saki, sika
AIKT ikat, kati, tika

AIKV kiva, vaik
AIKZ kazi
AILL lila
AILM amil, Ilam, Ilma, Liam, Lima, mail, mali
AILN anil, lain, Lina, nail
AILO Iola
AILP pail, pali, pial
AILR aril, lair, lari, liar, lira, rail, rial
AILS Isla, lias, Lisa, sail, sial
AILT alit, alti, lait, lati, Lita, tail, tali, tial
AILV vail, vali, vial, vila
AILW liwa, wail, wali
AILX Alix, axil
AILZ Liza
AIMM imam, maim, Mima
AIMN Iman, main, mani, mina
AIMR amir, Irma, mair, Mari, Mira, rami
AIMS mias, sima
AIMT amit, mita
AIMX maxi
AIMZ zaim
AINN nain, Nina
AINO Iona, naio, naoi, noia
AINP nipa, pain, pian
AINR Iran, rain, rani, Rina
AINS anis, nasi, sain, Sian
AINT ain't, anti, nait, Nita, tian, Tina
AINV Ivan, vain, vina
AINW wain
AINZ Nazi
AIOT iota, tiao
AIOW Iowa
AIPP pipa
AIPR pair
AIPS pais, Pisa
AIPT pita
AIQR Iraq
AIQU quai
AIRS sari
AIRT airt, rait, rati, Rita, tiar
AIRV vair, vari
AIRW wari
AIRY airy, yair
AIRZ izar, zari
AISS as is, sais
AIST Asti, sati
AISV Avis, Siva, visa
AISX axis
AITT tait
AITV vita
AITW wait
AITX taxi
AITZ Ta'iz, zita
AIVV viva
AJKR jark
AJKU jauk
AJLO Loja
AJLR jarl
AJMO majo
AJMS jams
AJNN jann
AJNO Joan
AJNU Juan
AJOT jato, jota
AJPS jasp
AJPU jaup, puja
AJPW jawp
AJZZ jazz
AKLN lank
AKLO kola
AKLR Karl, lark
AKLS lask
AKLT talk
AKLU kula
AKLW lawk, walk
AKLY alky, laky
AKMN mank
AKMO amok, mako
AKMR mark
AKMS mask
AKMW mawk
AKNO Kano, kaon, koan, kona
AKNP knap
AKNR knar, kran, nark, rank
AKNS kans, sank
AKNT tank
AKNW wank
AKNY yank
AKOR karo, kora, okra
AKOS soak, Soka
AKOT Kota, okta
AKOY kayo, oaky, okay
AKPR park
AKPU kapu, puka
AKPW pawk
AKRS sark
AKRT kart
AKRU kura, raku, rauk
AKRW wark
AKRY kray, yark
AKST skat, task
AKSU Aksu, skua
AKTU kuta, tuak
AKTY Katy, kyat
ALLL lall
ALLM mall
ALLO Lola, olla
ALLP pall
ALLT tall
ALLW wall
ALLY ally, y'all
ALMM malm
ALMO Amol, loam, loma, mola, olam
ALMP lamp, palm
ALMR larm, marl
ALMS alms, slam
ALMT malt, talm
ALMU alum, maul
ALMW walm
ALMY amyl, lyam, myal
ALNO Laon, loan, Nola
ALNP plan
ALNR larn
ALNT lant
ALNU Alun, luna, ulna
ALNW lawn
ALNX lanx
ALOP opal
ALOR lora, oral
ALOS also, Laos, laso, sola
ALOT alto, lota, tola
ALOU aoul
ALOV Olav, oval, vola
ALOW alow
ALOZ lazo, Zola
ALPP Lapp, palp, plap
ALPS salp, slap
ALPT palt, plat
ALPU Palu, paul, pula
ALPW pawl
ALPY paly, play
ALRS Lars
ALRY aryl, lary, lyra, rayl
ALSS lass
ALST last, salt, slat
ALSU saul
ALSV Slav
ALSW laws, slaw
ALSY slay
ALTU Tula
ALTW walt
ALUU luau
ALUV ulva
ALUW waul
ALWW wawl
ALWY waly, yawl
ALXY laxy
ALYZ lazy
AMMO ammo, mamo
AMMR marm
AMMU maum
AMMW mawm
AMNO moan, mona, Noam, noma, Oman
AMNR mRNA
AMNT mant
AMNU maun, Muna
AMNX Manx
AMNY many, myna
AMOR maro, moar, mora, Omar, roam, Roma

AMOS Amos, moas, soma
AMOT atom, moat, mota
AMOU ouma
AMOX moxa
AMOY Amoy, mayo, moya
AMPP mapp
AMPR parm, pram, ramp
AMPS samp, spam
AMPT tamp
AMPU puma
AMPV vamp
AMRS Mars, rams
AMRT mart, tram
AMRU arum, mura
AMRV marv
AMRW warm
AMRY army, Mary, Myra, yarm
AMSS mass
AMST mast
AMSU musa
AMSW swam, wasm
AMSX Xmas
AMTT matt
AMTU muta, taum
AMTW tawm
AMTY maty
AMUX maux
AMUY Yuma
AMXY myxa
AMYZ mazy
ANNO anon, Nona
ANNR rann
ANNT nant
ANOO Oona
ANOR aron, Nora, roan, Rona
ANOS naos
ANOT Nato, nota
ANOV Avon, nova
ANOW naow
ANOX axon, noax, noxa
ANOZ zona
ANPR narp
ANPS snap, span
ANPT pant
ANPU napu, puna
ANPW pawn
ANRR narr
ANRT rant, tarn, tRNA
ANRW warn
ANRY nary, Ryan, yarn
ANSS sans
ANST Stan
ANSU anus
ANSW sawn, swan
ANSY nyas
ANTT tant
ANTU aunt, tuan, tuna
ANTW tawn, want, wa'n't
ANUY yuan
ANVY navy
ANWY yawn
ANYZ zany
AOOT tooa
AOPR proa
AOPS apso, paso, sapo, soap
AOPT atop
AOPU oupa
AOPY poya
AOQU aquo
AORR orra, roar
AORS osar, Rosa, soar, sora
AORT rota, taro, tora
AORV arvo
AORW arow
AORY oary
AORZ Zora
AOSS ossa
AOST oast, stoa, tosa
AOSY soya
AOTU auto, outa
AOTW atwo
AOTY oaty
AOVW avow
APPR parp
APPU pupa
APPY yapp
APQU quap
APRR parr
APRS pars, rasp, spar
APRT part, prat, rapt, tarp, trap
APRU prau
APRW warp, wrap
APRY pray
APSS pass
APST past, spat
APSU upas
APSW swap, wasp
APSY spay
APTU patu, puta, tapu
APUY puya, yaup
APVY pavy
APWY yawp
AQRU quar
AQTU quat
AQUY quay
ARSS rass
ARST star, tars, tsar
ARSU rusa, sura
ARTT tart
ARTW wart
ARTY arty, tray, Tyra
ARTZ tzar
ARUW waur
ARVY vary
ARWW wraw
ARWY awry, wary, wray
ARXY X-ray
ARZZ razz
ASSS sass
ASST tass
ASSU Susa
ASSY says
ASTT stat
ASTU saut
ASTV vast
ASTW swat, taws, wast
ASTY stay
ASUV Suva
ASWY sway, yaws
ATTU tatu, taut
ATTW twat, watt
ATWY tway
AVWY wavy
AWXY waxy
AWYY yawy
BBBI bibb
BBCO cobb
BBEE Bebe, Beeb
BBEL bleb
BBII bibi
BBLO blob
BBLU blub, bulb
BBMO bomb
BBOO boob, obbo
BBOS bobs
BBOU bubo
BBRU burb
BCEH Cheb
BCEI bice
BCEK beck
BCEU Cebu, cube
BCHU chub
BCIR crib
BCKO bock
BCKU buck
BCLO bloc
BCLU club
BCMO comb
BCOS scob
BCRU crub, curb
BDEI bide
BDEL bled
BDEN bend
BDEO bode, dobe
BDER bred
BDET debt
BDEU bude
BDII bidi
BDIN bind
BDIR bird, drib
BDIS dibs
BDLO bold
BDMU dumb
BDNO bond
BDNU bund
BDOO doob
BDOR bord, brod
BDOY body, Boyd, doby
BDRU burd, drub
BDSU dubs
BEEF beef, feeb
BEEH hebe
BEEL blee
BEEN been, bene, Eben
BEEP beep
BEER beer, bere, bree
BEET beet
BEGI gibe
BEGO bego
BEGR berg
BEGY gybe
BEHI Hebi
BEHR herb
BEHT Beth
BEIJ jibe
BEIK bike, kibe
BEIL bile
BEIN bein, bien, bine
BEIR bier, brei, Brie
BEIS bise
BEIT bite
BEIV vibe
BEIX ibex
BEJO jobe
BEJU jube
BEKL belk
BEKM kemb
BEKO boke
BEKR berk, kerb
BELL bell
BELO bole, lobe
BELP pleb
BELT belt
BELU bleu, blue, lube
BELW blew
BELY bley
BEMR berm
BENO bone, ebon
BENR bren
BENT bent
BEOO oboe
BEOR Boer, bore, robe
BEOS bose
BEOT bote, tobe

BEOV bove
BEOX obex
BEOY obey
BERR brer
BERS Serb
BERT Bert, bret
BERU buer, bure, rube
BERV verb
BERW brew
BERY brey, byre
BESS Bess
BEST best
BESY byes
BETU Bute, tube
BETY byte
BEUZ zebu
BEVY bevy
BFFI biff
BFFO boff
BFFU buff
BFIR frib
BFLU flub
BFMU bumf
BFOR forb
BGGI bigg
BGIL glib
BGIN bing
BGIO biog, Igbo
BGIR brig
BGIU guib
BGLO glob
BGNO bong
BGNU bung
BGOO gobo
BGOR brog
BGOY bogy, goby
BGRU burg, grub
BHIS bish
BHLU buhl
BHOO boho, hobo
BHOS bosh
BHOT both
BHOY bhoy
BHRU buhr, burh
BHSU bush
BHTU bhut
BIIR biri
BIIS ibis
BIKL bilk, blik
BIKN bink
BIKR birk, kirb
BIKS bisk
BILL bill
BILM limb
BILN blin
BILO boil
BILP blip
BILR birl
BIMN nimb
BIMR brim
BINS nibs, snib
BINT bint
BIOR biro, brio
BIOS obis
BIOT obit
BIQU quib
BIRR birr
BIRT brit
BITT bitt
BITU buit
BJOU joub
BKLO bolk
BKLU bulk
BKNO bonk, knob
BKNU bunk, knub, nubk
BKOO boko, book, kobo
BKOS bosk
BKOU bouk
BKRU burk
BKSU busk
BLLO boll
BLLU bull
BLOO bolo, bool, lobo, obol
BLOS slob
BLOT blot, bolt
BLOU boul
BLOW blow, bowl
BLRU blur, burl
BLSU slub
BLTU bult
BMNU numb
BMOO boom
BMOT tomb
BMOU umbo
BMOW womb
BMPU bump
BMRU Brum
BNNO Bonn
BNOO boon
BNOR born, Brno
BNOS bo's'n, snob
BNOU boun
BNOY bony
BNRU burn
BNRY Bryn
BNSU snub
BNTU bunt
BOOR boor, broo
BOOS boos
BOOT boot
BOOY boyo
BOOZ bozo
BOPR prob
BOPS pobs
BORS sorb
BORT bort
BORW brow
BORY orby
BOSS boss
BOSU obus
BOSW swob
BOTT bott
BOTU bout
BOTY toby
BOUY buoy
BOXY boxy
BPRU burp
BPST tbsp
BRRR brrr
BRRU burr
BRTU brut, Burt, trub, turb
BRUU buru
BRUY bury, ruby
BRUZ zubr
BSSU buss
BSTU bust, stub
BSUY busy, buys
BTTU butt
BUZZ buzz
CCEE ecce
CCHI chic, cich
CCHO choc
CCKO cock
CCKU cuck
CCOO coco
CCOR croc
CDEE cede
CDEI cedi, dice, iced
CDEK deck
CDEL cled
CDEO code, coed, deco, ecod
CDER cred
CDEU cued, duce
CDHI chid
CDIK dick
CDIO icod, odic
CDIS disc
CDIT dict
CDKO dock
CDKU duck
CDLO clod, cold
CDNO cond
CDNU cund
CDOR cord
CDOT doct
CDOU douc
CDRU crud, curd
CDSU cuds, scud
CDTU duct
CEEH eche
CEEL cele, clee
CEER cere, cree
CEET cete
CEEX exec
CEFH chef
CEFI fice
CEFK feck
CEFL clef
CEGK geck
CEGL cleg
CEHK heck
CEHL lech
CEHM mech
CEHO echo, oche
CEHR Cher
CEHT echt, etch, tech
CEHW chew
CEHY yech
CEHZ chez
CEIL ceil, ciel, lice
CEIM cime, emic, mice
CEIN cine, nice
CEIP epic, pice
CEIR Ceri, eric, rice
CEIS sice
CEIT cite, etic, tice
CEIV cive, vice
CEKK keck
CEKN neck
CEKO coke
CEKP peck
CEKR reck
CEKU cuke
CELL cell
CELM clem
CELO Cleo, cole
CELT celt, lect
CELU clue, luce
CELW clew
CEMO come
CEMR merc
CEMY cyme
CENO cone, once
CENR cern
CENT cent
CEOP cope
CEOR cero, core
CEOS cose
CEOT cote
CEOV cove, voce
CEOZ coze
CEPR perc
CEPS spec
CEPT pect
CEPU puce
CERT cert
CERU crue, cure, ecru
CERW crew
CESS cess
CEST cest, sect
CESU cues, ecus
CESY scye, syce
CETU cute
CFFO coff
CFFU cuff
CFIL flic
CFIO coif, fico, foci
CFIS fisc
CFIU fuci
CFKU fuck
CFLO floc
CFOO coof
CFOR corf
CFOT coft
CFRU curf
CFSU fusc
CGHU chug
CGLO clog
CGSU scug
CHHO hoch
CHIK hick

CHIL lich
CHIN chin, inch
CHIO icho
CHIP chip
CHIR chir, rich
CHIT chit, itch, tich
CHIU ichu
CHIV chiv
CHIW wich
CHKO hock
CHKU huck
CHLO loch
CHLY lych
CHMU chum, much
CHNO chon
CHOO coho
CHOP chop
CHOS cosh
CHOT coth, Toc H
CHOU chou, ouch
CHOW chow
CHSU cush, such
CHTU chut
CHWY wych
CIKK kick
CIKL lick
CIKM mick
CIKN nick
CIKO oick
CIKP pick
CIKR rick
CIKS sick
CIKT tick
CIKV Vick
CIKW wick
CIKY icky
CILL cill
CILO coil, coli, loci
CILP clip
CILT clit
CIMO mico
CIMR crim
CINO cion, coin, coni, icon
CINQ cinq
CINR crin
CINZ zinc
CIOP pico
CIOR coir
CIOT coit, otic
CIOX oxic
CIOZ zoic
CIPR crip
CIPS spic
CIPT pict
CIRS cris
CIRT crit
CIRU uric
CISS Ciss
CIST cist
CITU cuit
CITY city
CIUY Yuci
CJKO jock
CJKU juck
CKLO colk, lock
CKLU luck
CKMO mock
CKMU muck
CKNO conk, nock
CKOO cook
CKOP pock
CKOR cork, rock
CKOS sock
CKOT tock
CKOY yock
CKPU puck
CKRU ruck
CKSU cusk, suck
CKTU tuck
CKUY ucky, yuck
CLLO coll
CLLU cull
CLMO Colm
CLMU culm
CLMY Clym
CLOO cool, loco
CLOP clop
CLOT clot, colt
CLOU clou, coul
CLOW clow, cowl
CLOY cloy, coly
CLRU curl
CLTU cult
CLUY cyul, lucy
CMOO coom, moco
CMOP comp
CMOR corm
CMOS coms
CMRU crum
CMSU scum
CNNO conn
CNOO coon
CNOR corn
CNOU unco
CNOY cony, coyn
CNRU curn
CNSU scun
CNSY sync
CNTU cunt, tunc
COOP coop, poco
COOR croo
COOS coos
COOT coot, toco
COOZ zoco
COPR crop
COPS cops, scop
COPT Copt
COPU coup
COPW cowp
COPY copy
CORS cors
CORT torc
CORW crow
CORY croy
COSS coss
COST cost, cots, scot
COSW scow
COSY cosy
COWY cowy
COXY coxy
COYZ cozy
CPSU cusp
CRRU curr
CRSU crus, scur
CRSY scry
CRTU crut, curt
CRUX crux
CSSU cuss
CSTU cuts, scut
CSTY cyst
DDEE Dede, deed
DDEI deid, died
DDEO eddo
DDER dred, redd
DDEU dude
DDEY eddy
DDIO dido
DDIY didy
DDJU Judd
DDOO dodo
DDOS odds
DDOT Todd
DDOW dowd
DDRU rudd
DDSU sudd
DEEF feed
DEEG edge, geed
DEEH heed
DEEI Edie, idee
DEEL dele
DEEM deem, deme, Mede, meed
DEEN dene, Eden, need
DEEP deep, pede, peed
DEER deer, dere, dree, rede, reed
DEES seed
DEET teed
DEEW weed
DEEY eyed, yede
DEFL delf, fled
DEFN fend
DEFO feod
DEFR Fred
DEFT deft
DEFU feud
DEFY defy
DEGL geld, gled
DEGO doge
DEGR dreg
DEGU degu, udge
DEGY edgy
DEHI hide, hied
DEHL held
DEHN hend
DEHO hoed
DEHR herd
DEHS shed, she'd
DEHY Hedy
DEIK dike
DEIL deil, deli, eild, idle, lied
DEIM demi, dime, idem
DEIN dine, Enid, nide
DEIP pied
DEIR dire, drie, ride
DEIS dies, ides, side
DEIT diet, dite, edit, tide, tied
DEIV dive, vide
DEIW Dewi, weid, wide
DEJU Jude
DEKL keld
DEKO doek, doke
DEKR drek
DEKS desk, sked
DEKU duke
DEKY dyke
DELL dell
DELM meld
DELN lend
DELO dole, lode, olde
DELP pled
DELS seld, sled
DELT teld
DELU duel, dule, leud
DELV veld
DELW lewd, weld
DELY yeld
DEMN demn, mend
DEMO demo, dome, Edom, mode
DEMR derm, merd
DEMY demy
DENN denn
DENO done, node
DENP pend
DENR dern, nerd, rend
DENS send
DENT dent, tend
DENU dune, nude
DENV vend
DENW wend

DENY deny, dyne
DENZ Zend
DEOP dope
DEOR doer, redo, rode, roed
DEOS does, dose
DEOT dote, toed
DEOU oued
DEOV dove
DEOY yode
DEOZ doze
DEPS sped
DEPU dupe
DERU dure, rude, rued
DERV derv, Revd, verd
DERW drew
DERY drey, dyer
DESS dess
DESU sued
DESY Syed
DETU duet
DEWY dewy
DEXY dexy
DFFI diff
DFFO doff
DFFU duff
DFIN find
DFIO Fido
DFLN Nfld
DFLO fold
DFNO fond
DFNU fund
DFOO food
DFOR ford
DFOW dowf
DFRY fyrd
DGIL gild
DGIN ding
DGIR gird, grid
DGIS digs
DGIU guid
DGLO gold
DGNO dong
DGNU dung
DGOO good
DGOR drog
DGOU Doug
DGOY dogy
DGRU drug, Durg
DHIK dikh
DHIN hind
DHIS dish
DHIW whid
DHKU khud
DHLO dhol, hold, lodh
DHOO hood
DHOS dosh, shod
DHOT doth
DHOW dhow, who'd
DHOY yodh
DHOZ dzho
DHSU dush
DHTU thud
DIIL idli
DIIM midi
DIIN nidi
DIIR irid
DIIV divi
DIJO Jodi
DIJU Judi
DIKN dink, kind
DIKR dirk
DIKS disk, skid
DILL dill
DILM mild
DILN lind
DILO diol, idol, lido, Lodi, loid, olid
DILR dirl
DILS sild, slid
DILV vild
DILW wild
DILY idly, idyl, ylid
DIMN mind
DIMO modi
DIMS mids
DIMU muid
DINO Dion, nodi
DINP pind
DINR rind
DINT dint, tind
DINW wind
DINY indy
DIOO ooid
DIOT doit
DIOV void
DIOX oxid
DIOZ zoid
DIPR drip
DIQU quid
DIRT dirt
DIRU Rudi
DISS diss
DITY tidy
DIZZ dizz
DJOO dojo
DJOS jods
DJOU judo
DJOY Jody
DJUY Judy
DKLO dolk
DKNO donk
DKNU dunk
DKNY kynd
DKOR dork
DKOU kudo
DKRU durk, Kurd
DKSU dusk
DKUU kudu
DKUW dukw
DLLO doll
DLLU dull
DLMO mold
DLMU m'lud
DLNU Lund
DLOO dool
DLOP plod
DLOR lord
DLOS sold
DLOT dolt, told
DLOU loud, ludo, ould
DLOW dowl, wold
DLOY odyl, yold
DLPU plud
DLUY duly
DMOO domo, doom, mood
DMOR dorm
DMOS Mods
DMOU doum, odum
DMOY domy
DMPU dump
DMRU drum
DNOP pond
DNOT don't
DNOU udon, undo
DNOW down
DNOY yond
DNRU durn, nurd
DNSU Duns
DNTU dunt, tund
DNWY wynd
DOOP podo, pood
DOOR door, odor, ordo, rood
DOOS odso
DOOT to-do
DOOW wood
DOPR dorp, drop, prod
DOPU doup, podu
DOPY dopy
DOQU quod
DORR dorr
DORT dort, trod
DORU dour, duro
DORW drow, word
DORY dory
DOSS doss
DOST dost
DOTU dout
DOTW dowt
DOTY doty, tody
DOUY you'd
DOXY doxy
DOYZ dozy
DPSU spud
DPUU pudu
DRSU surd
DRTU turd
DRUU Ruud, Urdu
DRUY Rudy
DSSU suds
DSSY dyss
DSTU dust, stud
DTUY duty
EEFL feel, flee
EEFM feme
EEFR feer, fere, free, reef
EEFT feet
EEGH ghee
EEGK geek
EEGL glee, lege
EEGN gene
EEGO ogee
EEGR Eger, geer, gree
EEGU euge
EEHL heel, hele
EEHM heme
EEHR here
EEHT thee
EEHW whee
EEHZ Heze
EEIR Erie
EEIV Evie
EEJP jeep
EEJR jeer
EEJZ Jeez
EEKK keek
EEKL keel, leek
EEKM meek
EEKN keen, knee
EEKP keep, peek, peke
EEKR reek
EEKS seek
EEKW week
EEKZ Zeke
EELL Elle
EELM mele
EELN lene
EELP leep, peel, pele
EELR Erle, leer, lere, reel
EELS else, lees, lese, seel, sele
EELT leet, tele
EELV vele
EELW weel
EELY eely
EEMM meme
EEMN neem
EEMO omee
EEMR mere
EEMS Esme, mese, seem
EEMT meet, mete, teem
EEMU emeu
EEMZ zeme
EENN nene
EENP neep, peen
EENR erne, ne'er, Rene
EENS esne, nese, seen
EENT nete, teen
EENV even
EENW enew,

Ewen, ween
EEOV evoe
EEPP peep
EEPR peer, pree
EEPS pees, seep
EEPT Pete
EEPV veep
EEPW weep
EEPY yeep, yepe
EEQR qere
EERS Erse, seer, sere
EERT rete, teer, tree
EERV erve, ever, veer, Vere
EERW ewer, weer, were, we're, wree
EERY eyre, yere
EESS esse
EEST tees
EESX exes
EESY eyes
EETW twee, weet
EETY tyee
EEVW we've
EEZZ zeze
EFFI fief, fife
EFFJ jeff
EFFT teff
EFGL fleg
EFGS fegs
EFHI fehi
EFHT heft
EFIK fike, keif, kief
EFIL fiel, file, lief, life
EFIM imfe
EFIN fine, neif, nief
EFIR Fier, fire, rife
EFIS feis, seif
EFIT tief
EFIV five
EFIW wife
EFKR ferk, kerf
EFKY fyke
EFLL fell
EFLO floe
EFLP pelf
EFLS self
EFLT elft, felt, flet, left
EFLU flue, fuel
EFLW flew
EFLX flex
EFLY fley
EFMU fume
EFNR fern, nerf
EFNT fent
EFOR fore, froe, orfe
EFRS serf
EFRT fret, reft, tref
EFRU ufer
EFRW werf
EFSS fess
EFST fest
EFSU feus, fuse
EFTW weft
EFUZ fuze
EGGL gleg
EGGR Greg
EGGY eggy, yegg
EGHI eigh
EGHL legh
EGHU huge
EGIL glei
EGIR geir, Geri
EGIS gise
EGIT tige
EGIV give
EGKN Genk
EGKS skeg
EGKU kuge
EGLN glen, leng
EGLO gole, Lego, loge, ogle
EGLS legs
EGLT gelt, glet
EGLU glue, gule, luge
EGLW glew
EGLY gley, gyle
EGMN G-men, meng
EGMO gome
EGMR germ
EGMU geum
EGNO gone
EGNS gens
EGNT gent
EGNU genu
EGNW Gwen
EGNY gyne
EGOP pego, poge
EGOR ergo, goer, gore, ogre, rego
EGOS goes, sego
EGOT gote
EGOV gove
EGPR preg
EGPU Pegu
EGRS ergs
EGRT Gert
EGRU grue, urge
EGRW grew
EGRX grex
EGRY grey, gyre
EGST gest
EGTT gett
EGTU tegu
EGTY gyte
EGUZ guze
EGVY gyve
EHIK hike
EHIL elhi, heil
EHIN hine
EHIP hipe
EHIR heir, hire
EHIS hies
EHIT eith, heit
EHIV hive
EHKO hoke
EHKT khet
EHKU huke
EHLL hell, Hell, he'll
EHLM helm
EHLO hole
EHLP help
EHLR herl, lehr
EHLU hule
EHLY hyle
EHMO home
EHMP hemp
EHMR herm
EHMS mesh, Shem
EHMT meth, them
EHNO hone
EHNR hern
EHNS nesh
EHNT hent, then
EHNU hune
EHNW hewn, when
EHNY hyne
EHOP hope
EHOR hero, hoer
EHOS hoes, hose, shoe
EHOT Theo
EHOV hove
EHOW howe
EHOY hoey
EHPT peth
EHPW phew
EHPY hype
EHRR Herr
EHRS hers
EHRT tehr
EHRU hure
EHSS she's
EHST hest, Seth
EHSW shew
EHTT thet
EHTW thew, whet
EHTY hyte, they
EHUY Huey
EHWW whew
EHWY whey
EIJR Jeri
EIJV jive
EIKK kike
EIKL like
EIKM mike
EIKN kine
EIKP kepi, pike
EIKR Erik, Keir, keri, kier
EIKT etik, kite, tike
EIKU kuei
EIKV Kiev, kive
EIKY ikey, yike
EILM Emil, lime, mile
EILN lien, line, Neil, Nile
EILP pile
EILR leir, lire, rile
EILS Elis, Ilse, isel, isle, lies, Lise
EILT lite, teil, tile
EILU lieu
EILV evil, levi, live, veil, vile, vlei
EILW lwei, wile
EILX ilex, Leix
EILY Eily
EILZ izle
EIMM mime
EIMN mien, mine
EIMO oime, omie
EIMR emir, mire, rime
EIMS mise, semi
EIMT emit, item, mite, time
EINN nine
EINP pein, pine
EINR Erin, rein
EINS sine
EINT etin, niet, nite, t'ien, tine
EINV vein, vine
EINW wine
EINZ Inez, zein, zine
EIPP pipe
EIPR peri, pier, pire, ripe
EIPS sipe

EIPT piet, tipe
EIPW wipe
EIPZ pize
EIRS rise, seir, sire
EIRT iter, rite, tier, tire, trie
EIRV rive
EIRW weir, wire
EIST site
EISV Ives, vise
EISW wise
EISZ size
EITT tite
EITU etui
EITW wite
EITX exit
EITY yeti, yite
EIVV vive
EIVW view, wive
EJKO joke
EJKR jerk
EJKU juke
EJLL jell
EJLO Joel, jole
EJMU jume
EJNO jeon
EJNU june
EJOS joes
EJOV Jove
EJOY joey
EJPU jupe
EJRT jert
EJRU jure
EJSS jess
EJST jest
EJTU jute
EJUV juve
EJUX jeux
EKLL kell
EKLM Melk
EKLO koel
EKLP kelp, klep
EKLS elks
EKLT kelt
EKLU luke
EKLW kewl, welk
EKLY kyle, lyke, yelk
EKMO moke
EKMP kemp
EKNO keno
EKNP penk
EKNR kern, nerk
EKNT kent
EKNU nuke
EKNW knew
EKNZ knez
EKOP poke
EKOR kero, kore
EKOS soke
EKOT toke
EKOW woke
EKOY yoke
EKPR perk
EKPS skep
EKPT kept
EKPU puke
EKPY kype
EKRT trek
EKRU Kure
EKRY yerk
EKRZ zerk
EKST kest, Sekt
EKSW skew
EKSY Esky, keys, yesk
EKTY kyte, tyke
EKUY yeuk, yuke
ELLM mell, Mlle
ELLN Nell
ELLP pell
ELLS sell
ELLT tell
ELLV vell
ELLW well, we'll
ELLY Lyle, yell
ELMO melo, mole
ELMT melt
ELMU mule
ELMW mewl
ELMY elmy, lyme, yelm, ylem
ELNO enol, leno, Leon, lone, noel
ELNS lens
ELNT lent
ELNU lune
ELOO oleo
ELOP lope, pole
ELOR lore, orle, role
ELOS lose, sloe, sole
ELOT lote, tole
ELOV love, vole
ELOW lowe
ELOY yole
ELPR lerp
ELPT pelt, plet
ELPU pule
ELPW pewl, plew
ELPY yelp
ELQU quel
ELRU lure, rule
ELRY Eryl, lyre, rely
ELSS less
ELST lest, let's
ELSU lues, slue
ELSV levs
ELSW slew, wels
ELSY lyse, sley
ELTT Lett
ELTU lute, tuel, tule
ELTW welt
ELTY tyle
ELUX luxe
ELUY yule
ELVY levy
ELWY wely
EMMO memo, mome
EMMS Mmes
EMMU meum
EMMY Emmy
EMNN nemn
EMNO meno, nemo, noem, nome, omen
EMNU menu, neum
EMOP mope, poem, pome
EMOR more, omer, Orem, Rome
EMOS mose, some
EMOT mote, tome
EMOU moue
EMOV move
EMOW meow
EMOZ moze
EMPR perm, prem
EMPT empt, temp
EMRS rems
EMRT term, trem
EMRU Meru, mure
EMRV Merv
EMSS mess
EMST stem
EMSU muse
EMSW mews, smew
EMTU mute
EMTW mewt
EMTZ Metz
EMYZ zyme
EMZZ mezz
ENNO neon, none
ENOP nope, open, peon, pone
ENOR oner, Reno, rone
ENOS Enos, noes, nose, one's, sone
ENOT note, tone
ENOV oven
ENOW enow, owen, wone
ENOX exon, oxen
ENOZ zone
ENPR pern
ENPT pent
ENPU pneu
ENRT rent, tern
ENRU rune
ENRW wren
ENRY yern
ENSS ness
ENST nest, sent
ENSW news, sewn
ENSY syne
ENTT nett, tent
ENTU tune
ENTV vent
ENTW newt, went
ENTX next
ENTY nyet, tyne
ENVY envy, veny
ENWY newy
EOOR oo-er
EOOZ ooze
EOPP pepo, pope
EOPR pore, rope
EOPS epos, peso, pose
EOPT peto, poet, pote, tope
EOPX expo
EORS roes, rose, sore
EORT rote, tore
EORU euro
EORV over, rove
EORW wore
EORX oxer
EORY orey, oyer, yore
EORZ zero
EOSS osse
EOST Seto, toes
EOSX esox
EOSY oyes, yeso
EOTT tote
EOTV veto, vote
EOTW wote
EOTY eyot, toey, yote
EOTZ toze
EOUV voeu
EOVW wove
EOWY yeow, yowe
EOYZ oyez
EPPR perp, prep, repp
EPRS pres
EPRT pert, terp

EPRU Peru, Prue, puer, pure
EPRV perv
EPRX prex
EPRY prey, pyre
EPRZ prez
EPSS pess
EPST pest, sept, step
EPSU spue
EPSW spew
EPSY espy
EPTU pute
EPTW wept
EPTY pyet, type
EPVY pevy
EPWY pewy, wype
EQUY quey
ERRT terr
ERST erst, rest
ERSU Reus, rues, ruse, suer, sure, user
ERSV vers
ERTT tret
ERTU true
ERTV Trev, Tver, vert
ERTW wert
ERTY trey, tyer, tyre
ERVY very
ERWY ewry
ESSS sess
ESST Tess
ESSU sues
ESTT sett, stet, test
ESTU suet
ESTV vest
ESTW stew, west
ESTX sext
ESTY stye, yest
ESTZ zest
ESVY Yves
ESXY sexy
ETTU tute
ETTX text
ETTY Etty, yett
ETWY wyte
FFFU fuff
FFGO goff
FFGU guff
FFHU huff
FFII Fifi
FFIJ jiff
FFIK kiff
FFIM miff
FFIN niff
FFIP piff
FFIR riff
FFIT tiff
FFIV viff
FFIY iffy
FFIZ ziff
FFLU luff
FFMU muff
FFNO off'n
FFNU nuff
FFOT toff
FFPT pfft
FFPU puff
FFRU ruff
FFTU tuff
FFUU fufu
FFUW wuff
FGIO figo
FGIR frig
FGIT gift
FGIU Gifu
FGLO flog, golf
FGLU gulf
FGOO goof
FGOR frog
FGOY fogy
FGRU frug
FGUU fugu
FHII hi-fi
FHIS fish
FHOO hoof
FIIJ Fiji
FIIL fili
FIKN fink
FIKO Kofi
FIKR firk
FIKS fisk
FILL fill
FILM film, flim
FILO filo, foil, lo-fi
FILP flip
FILS fils
FILT flit, lift
FILW Wilf
FILX flix
FIMR firm, frim
FINN Finn
FINO fino, foin, info
FINR firn
FIOR Ifor
FIPU pfui
FIRT frit, rift
FIRZ friz
FIST fist, sift
FISU Sufi
FITT tift
FITW wift
FITX fixt
FITZ fitz
FIZZ fizz
FKLO folk
FKNU funk
FKOR fork
FKOU Kofu
FKSU fusk
FLLU full
FLNO flon
FLOO fool, loof
FLOP flop
FLOR flor, Rolf
FLOT flot, loft
FLOU foul
FLOW flow, fowl, wolf
FLOY Floy
FLRU furl
FLSU flus
FLSY flys
FLUX flux
FMOR form, from
FMRU frum
FMUY fumy
FNOT font
FOOP poof
FOOR roof
FOOT foot
FOOW woof
FOOY oofy
FOPR prof
FOPU pouf
FORT fort, frot
FORU four
FORW frow
FOSS foss
FOST soft
FOSU ufos
FOTT toft
FOTU tofu
FOXY foxy
FPTU puft
FQUU Qufu
FRSU surf
FRTU turf
FRUY fury
FRUZ fruz
FSSU fuss
FSTU fust
FTTU tuft
FTUY yuft
FTUZ futz
FUZZ fuzz
GGHO hogg
GGIN ging
GGIR grig
GGLU glug
GGNO gong, nogg
GGOO go-go, goog
GGOR grog
GHHI high
GHHU Hugh
GHIN hing, nigh
GHIS sigh
GHIT gith, thig
GHIW whig
GHNO hong
GHNU hung
GHOO hogo
GHOS gosh
GHOT Goth
GHOU Hugo, ough
GHOY yogh
GHRU guhr
GHSU gush
GHTU thug
GHUY hugy
GIIR giri
GIJN jing
GIKN gink, king
GILL gill
GILM glim
GILN ling
GILR girl
GILT gilt, glit
GILU Ugli
GIMN ming
GIMP gimp
GIMR grim
GIMS gism
GINP ping
GINR girn, grin, ring
GINS sign, sing, snig
GINT ting, t'ing
GINW wing
GINZ zing
GIOP gopi
GIOR giro, Igor
GIOY yogi
GIPR grip, prig
GIPS gips
GIRR girr
GIRT girt, grit, trig
GIRW wrig
GIRY gyri
GIST gist
GISW swig
GITW twig
GIVY givy
GIZZ gizz
GJNO jong
GKNO gonk
GKNU gunk
GKOO gook
GKOR grok
GKOW gowk
GKOY goky
GKRU gurk, krug
GLLU gull
GLMO glom
GLMU glum
GLNO long
GLNU lung
GLNY Glyn
GLOO gool, logo
GLOP glop
GLOS slog
GLOU Lugo
GLOW glow, gowl
GLOY logy
GLPU gulp, plug
GLRU gurl
GLSU slug
GLTU glut
GLUY ugly
GMNO mong
GMNU mung
GMOO mogo, Moog
GMOR gorm
GMOS smog
GMOU goum, mugo
GMPU gump
GMPY gymp
GMRU grum
GMSU smug
GNNO nong
GNOO goon, no go
GNOP pong
GNOS snog, song
GNOT tong
GNOU oung
GNOW gown, wong
GNOY gony, yong
GNPU pung

GNRU gurn, rung
GNSU snug, sung
GNTU tung
GNWY Gwyn
GOOP goop, pogo
GOOR goor
GOOT Togo
GOPR gorp, prog
GOPY gypo, pogy
GORS gros
GORT gort, grot, trog
GORU gour
GORW grow
GORY gory, gyro, orgy
GOSS goss
GOSY goys
GOTT togt
GOTU gout
GOTV vogt
GPSY gyps
GRTU trug
GRUU guru
GSTU gust, guts
HHIS hish
HHOO ho ho, oh-oh
HHSU hush
HHUU huhu, uh-uh
HIIL hili
HIKO hoik, hoki
HIKS kish, Sikh
HIKT kith
HILL hill
HILO hilo
HILP Phil
HILT hilt, lith
HIMP himp
HIMS shim
HIMW whim
HINO Hino
HINS hisn, shin, sinh
HINT hint, thin
HINW whin
HIOO Ohio
HIOP Hopi, ipoh
HIOT hoit, hoti
HIOW whio
HIPS pish, ship
HIPT phit, pith
HIPW whip
HIPZ phiz
HIRT thir
HIRW whir
HISS hiss
HIST hist, shit, this
HISW wish
HITW whit, with
HIWY wihy
HIWZ whiz
HIZZ hizz
HJMU jhum
HJNO john
HJOS josh
HKLO holk, kohl
HKLU hulk
HKNO honk
HKNU hunk
HKOO hook
HKOR khor
HKOS kosh
HKOW howk
HKOY hoky
HKSU husk, sukh
HLLO holl
HLLU hull
HLMO holm
HLOP holp
HLOS hols, losh
HLOT holt, loth
HLOW howl
HLOY holy
HLRU hurl
HLSU lush, Suhl
HLTU luth
HLWY hwyl
HMNY hymn
HMOO homo, Moho
HMOT moth, Thom
HMOW whom
HMOY homy
HMPU hump
HMSU mush
HMTY myth
HNOO hoon
HNOP phon
HNOR horn
HNOS nosh
HNOT thon
HNSU shun
HNTU hunt, Thun
HOOP hoop, hopo, phoo, pooh
HOOS oh-so, Osho, shoo
HOOT hoot, Otho, to-ho
HOOW whoo
HOOY yo-ho
HOPS phos, posh, shop
HOPT hopt, phot, toph
HOPU ouph
HOPW whop
HOPY hypo
HORT thro
HORU hour
HOSS hoss
HOST host, shot, tosh
HOSU huso
HOSW show
HOTU thou
HOTW thow
HPPU hupp
HPSU push
HPTU phut
HPTY hypt
HRRU hurr
HRSU rush
HRSY Rhys
HRTU hurt, Ruth, thru
HSSU huss
HSTU hust, shut, thus, tush
HSTY hyst
HSWY whys
HTTU hutt
HTUU Hutu
HUZZ huzz
IIIW iiwi
IIJX Jixi
IIKP piki
IIKR kiri
IIKT tiki
IIKW kiwi
IIKY ki-yi
IILL Lili
IILP pili
IILW wili
IIMM mimi
IIMN mini
IIMP impi
IINS nisi
IINT in it, inti
IIPP pipi
IIPT tipi
IIRS iris, Siri
IIST itis
IISW iwis
IITT titi
IITZ ziti
IIWW wiwi
IJKN jink
IJKO koji
IJLL jill
IJLT jilt
IJMP jimp
IJMS jism
IJNN jinn
IJNO join, Joni
IJNX jinx
IJST jist
IJZZ jizz
IKKL klik
IKKN kink
IKKR kirk
IKKU kuki
IKKY ikky
IKLL kill
IKLM milk
IKLN kiln, link
IKLO kilo
IKLP klip
IKLR lirk
IKLS lisk, silk
IKLT kilt
IKMN mink
IKMO moki
IKMR mirk
IKMS skim
IKNO ikon, kino, oink
IKNP pink
IKNR kirn, rink
IKNS sink, skin
IKNT knit, tink
IKNV vink
IKNW wink
IKNY inky
IKOP kopi
IKOR kori
IKOT toki
IKPS kips, skip
IKPY piky
IKRS kris, risk
IKRU kuri
IKRZ zikr
IKSS kiss, skis
IKST kist, skit
IKSW wisk
ILLL lill
ILLM mill
ILLN nill
ILLO Lilo
ILLP pill
ILLR rill
ILLS sill
ILLT it'll, lilt, till
ILLU ulli
ILLV vill
ILLW will
ILLY illy, lily, yill
ILMN limn
ILMO limo, milo, moil, olim
ILMP limp, plim
ILMR mirl
ILMS slim
ILMT milt
ILMU muli
ILMY limy
ILNN linn
ILNO lino, lion, loin, noil
ILNT lint
ILNY inly, liny
ILNZ Linz, Zlin
ILOO lolo, olio
ILOP poil
ILOR loir, Lori, roil
ILOS Lois, silo, soil, soli
ILOT ilot, loti, toil
ILOV viol
ILOY oily
ILPR pirl
ILPS lisp, slip
ILPU puli
ILPY pily
ILRT tirl
ILRV virl, vril
ILSS liss
ILST list, silt, slit

ILTT tilt
ILTW wilt
ILWY wily
IMMP mimp
IMMY immy
IMNT mint
IMNU muni
IMNX minx
IMNY miny
IMOR miro
IMOS miso
IMOT moit, omit
IMPP pimp
IMPR prim
IMPS simp
IMPU pium
IMPW wimp
IMQU quim
IMRR mirr
IMRT trim
IMRU Muir, rimu
IMRY miry, rimy
IMSS miss
IMST mist, smit
IMSW swim
IMSY misy
IMTT mitt
IMTU muti
IMTX mixt
INOP pion
INOR inro, iron, noir, nori
INOS Sion
INOT into, oint, toni
INOV vino
INOW wino
INOX noix
INOY yoni
INOZ zino, Zion
INPR pirn
INPS snip, spin
INPT pint
INPY piny
INQU quin
INRT trin
INRU ruin
INST isn't, snit
INSU unis
INTT tint
INTU unit
INTV vint
INTW twin
INTY tiny
INUX Unix

INVY viny
INWY winy
INYZ nizy
IOOZ oozi
IOPT pito, topi
IOPU poui
IOPV pivo
IORS sori
IORT riot, tiro, tori, trio
IORV Ivor
IORZ zori
IOST Otis
IOTT toit
IPPY pipy
IPPZ zipp
IPQU Puqi, quip
IPRR pirr
IPRT trip
IPRU puri
IPSS piss
IPST spit
IPSV spiv
IPSW wisp
IPSY I spy, yips
IPTT tipt
IPTU ptui, Tupi
IPTY pity
IPXY pixy
IQTU quit
IQUZ quiz
IRRT tirr
IRST stir, tris
IRTW writ
IRTX Trix
IRWY wiry
ISSV viss
ISTU suit
ISTW wist
ISWZ swiz
ITTW twit
ITTY itty
ITVY tivy
ITZZ tizz
IUWX Wuxi
IUXY Yuxi
IVYZ vizy
IZZZ zizz
JJUU juju
JKNU junk
JKOO jook
JKOU jouk
JKOY joky
JLOT jolt
JLOW jowl
JLUY july
JMOO joom, mojo
JMPU jump

JNXY jynx
JOOR joro
JORU jour
JOSS joss
JRUY jury
JSTU just
KKOO koko, kook
KKOU koku
KKUU kuku
KKUY ukky
KLMO kolm
KLNU lunk
KLOO kolo, look
KLOP klop, polk
KLOV volk
KLOY yolk
KLPU pulk
KLRU lurk
KLSU lusk, sulk
KMNO monk
KMOO moko
KMOS Omsk
KMRU murk
KMSU musk
KNNU nunk
KNOO kono, nook
KNOP knop
KNOR nork
KNOT knot, tonk
KNOW know, wonk
KNOZ zonk
KNPU punk
KNRU knur, nurk
KNSU sunk
KNTU knut, tunk
KOOP pook
KOOR koro, Kroo, rook
KOOS sook
KOOT koto, toko, took
KOPR pork
KOPY poky
KORS Orsk
KORU koru
KORW work
KORY york
KOSU souk
KOUZ zouk
KPUU puku
KRSU rusk
KRTU Kurt, turk
KRUU kuru

KSTU tusk
KUYY yuky
LLLO loll
LLLU lull
LLMO moll
LLMU mull
LLNO noll
LLNU null
LLOP poll
LLOR roll
LLOT toll
LLPU pull
LLUU lulu
LMOO loom, mool
LMOT molt
LMOU moul, omul
LMOY moly
LMPU lump, plum
LMRU murl
LMSU slum
LNNY Lynn
LNOO loon
LNOR lorn
LNOT nolt
LNOW lown
LNOY Lyon, only
LNRU nurl
LNTU lunt
LNUV vuln
LNUY luny
LNXY lynx
LOOP loop, polo, pool
LOOR orlo
LOOS Oslo, solo, sool
LOOT loot, loto, tool
LOOW wool
LOPP plop
LOPS slop
LOPT plot, polt
LOPU loup
LOPW plow
LOPY ploy, poly
LORS lors
LORU lour
LORY lory, Roly
LOSS loss
LOST lost, slot
LOSU soul
LOSW slow
LOTT tolt
LOTU lout, tolu, ulto
LOTV volt
LOWY lowy, yowl
LOXY xylo
LPPU plup, pulp
LPRU purl
LPSU plus
LPTU tulp
LPUU pulu
LRSU slur
LSTU lust, slut
LTUZ lutz
LUUZ Zulu
MMPU mump
MMSU mums
MMUU mu-mu
MNOO mono, moon
MNOR morn, norm
MNOS mons
MNOU muon
MNOW mown
MNTU munt
MOOP moop
MOOR moor, Moro, room
MOOS moos
MOOT moot, moto, tomo, toom
MOOV voom
MOOZ mozo, zoom
MOPP pomp
MOPR prom, romp
MOPU moup
MOPY mopy, yomp
MORT mort
MORW worm
MOSS moss
MOST most
MOSU muso, sumo
MOSY mosy
MOTT mott
MOTU tu-mo
MOUV ovum
MOXY myxo
MOZZ mozz
MPPU pump
MPRU rump
MPSU sump
MPTU tump
MPTY tymp
MPUW wump
MPUY yump

MRRU murr
MRTU turm
MRUU muru
MSSU muss
MSTU must, smut, stum
MSTY myst
MSUW swum
MSUY Sumy
MTTU mutt
MUZZ muzz
MXYY myxy
NNOO no-no, noon
NNOR Norn
NNOU non-U, noun
NNOW nown
NNSU sunn
NNWY wynn
NOOP noop, poon
NOOS oons, soon
NOOT onto, oont, toon
NOOW woon
NOOX Oxon
NOOZ zoon
NOPR porn
NOPS pons
NOPT pont
NOPU Puno, upon
NOPY pony
NORT torn, tron
NORU ourn
NORW worn
NOST snot
NOSU nous, onus
NOSW snow, sown
NOSY nosy
NOTT nott
NOTU unto
NOTW nowt, town, wont, won't
NOTY tony, yont
NOWY nowy
NOXY onyx
NPSU spun
NPTU punt
NPUY puny
NPXY pnyx
NRTU runt, turn
NSTU nuts, stun, tsun
NTUY tuny
OOPP oppo, poop
OOPR poor
OOPS oops
OOPT opto, topo
OOPY yoop, yopo
OORR ro-ro
OORT root, toro
OOST soot
OOSW woos
OOTT otto, toot, toto
OOTZ zoot
OOUZ ouzo
OOYY yo-yo
OOYZ oozy
OPPR prop
OPPS pops
OPQU quop
OPRR porr
OPRS pros
OPRT port, torp
OPRU pour, puro, roup
OPRW prow
OPRY opry, pory, pyro, ropy
OPSS poss
OPST post, spot, stop, tops
OPSU opus, soup
OPSW swop, wops
OPSY posy
OPTT pott
OPTU pout, toup
OPTY pyot, typo
OPUW pouw
OPXY poxy
ORRT rort, torr
ORRY Rory
ORSS Ross
ORST sort
ORSU ours, sour
ORSY rosy
ORTT tort, trot
ORTU rout, Toru, tour
ORTW trow, wort, wrot
ORTY ryot, Tory, troy, tyro
ORUV vour
ORUX roux
ORUY your, yuro
ORXY oryx, Roxy
OSST toss
OSSY Ossy
OSTT tost
OSTU oust
OSTW stow, swot, twos
OSUY yous
OTTU tout
OTUY outy
OTWY towy
OTYZ tozy
OYZZ Ozzy
PRRU purr
PRSU spur
PRSY spry
PRTU prut, purt
PSST psst, tsps
PSSU puss
PTTU putt
PTUZ putz
RRTU turr
RSSU Russ
RSTU rust
RSUU urus
RTUY yurt
SSSU suss
SSTU tuss
SSUW wuss
SUYZ Suzy
TTUU tutu

FIVE LETTERS

AAABC	abaca, Caaba
AAABK	Kaaba
AAABR	araba
AAABY	abaya
AAADN	Adana
AAAFR	afara
AAAGM	agama
AAAIS	A'asia
AAAKM	kaama
AAAKR	akara
AAALN	Alana
AAAMT	Amata
AAANS	Sana'a
AABBY	yabba
AABCC	bacca
AABCI	abaci
AABCK	aback
AABCL	cabal
AABCN	caban
AABCS	cabas
AABCT	tabac
AABCU	Bacau
AABDE	baaed
AABDN	aband
AABDR	draba
AABEM	abeam, ameba
AABER	abear
AABES	abase
AABET	abate, abeat, Beata
AABEZ	Baeza
AABFT	abaft, bafta
AABGM	gamba
AABGR	Braga
AABHI	Baha'i
AABHM	hamba
AABHR	habra
AABHS	abash, basha, sabha
AABHT	abaht
AABIL	labia
AABIN	bania
AABIR	braai
AABIW	awabi
AABJR	bajra
AABJU	Abuja
AABKS	abask
AABLM	lamba
AABLN	Alban, banal, laban, nabal, nabla
AABLO	balao
AABLR	labra
AABLS	balas, balsa, basal, sabal
AABLT	tabla
AABMM	mamba
AABMR	Abram
AABMS	Basma, samba
AABNS	basan
AABNT	Batna
AABNW	bwana, nawab
AABNZ	bazan
AABRS	sabra
AABRT	rabat
AABRU	abura, Aruba
AABRV	brava
AABRY	Araby
AABRZ	zabra
AABST	basta, sabat
AABSU	sauba
AABTT	at bat, batta
AACCL	lacca
AACCM	macca
AACCO	cacao
AACCR	accra
AACCY	yacca
AACDH	dacha
AACDU	cauda
AACEP	apace
AACER	arace, areca
AACET	acate
AACEV	cavea
AACFF	caffa
AACFI	facia
AACFN	afanc
AACFT	facta
AACGR	carga
AACGU	guaca
AACHK	kacha
AACHM	chama
AACHP	pacha
AACHR	achar, chara
AACHS	casha, Sacha
AACHU	huaca
AACIR	acari, Ciara
AACIS	Isaac
AACJL	jacal
AACJN	cajan
AACKL	alack
AACKY	yacka
AACLL	calla
AACLN	canal
AACLR	acral, Carla, Clara
AACLS	scala
AACMN	caman
AACMO	macao
AACMS	camas
AACMW	macaw
AACNN	canna
AACNT	tacan
AACNV	Cavan
AACNZ	Anzac
AACPP	cappa
AACPS	capsa
AACPU	Capua
AACPY	pacay
AACRS	sacra
AACRT	carat
AACST	tasca
AACTV	vacat
AACUV	vacua
AADDH	hadda
AADDR	adrad
AADDX	addax
AADEG	adage
AADEH	ahead
AADEL	Adela, aldea
AADER	aread
AADFR	farad
AADGG	dagga, Gadag
AADGM	Magda
AADGR	Garda
AADHI	Haida
AADHK	Dhaka
AADHL	hadal
AADHM	Ahmad
AADIM	madia
AADIN	Adina, Aidan, diana, Nadia, naiad
AADIP	apaid
AADIR	Adair, Adria
AADJM	jadam
AADKK	Akkad
AADKR	Dakar
AADKY	Dayak
AADLM	madal
AADLN	aland
AADLS	salad
AADLT	datal
AADLV	Valda
AADLW	awald
AADMM	madam
AADMN	adman, amand, daman, damna
AADMO	amado
AADMP	padma
AADMR	drama, madar
AADMU	Adamu
AADNN	danna
AADNP	panda
AADNS	sanad
AADNV	vanda
AADNW	Wanda
AADNY	dayan
AADOV	Davao
AADPT	adapt
AADRR	radar
AADRU	Audra
AADRW	award
AADRZ	Zadar, zarda
AADSY	a-days
AADSZ	sadza
AADTY	adyta
AAEFN	faena
AAEFR	afear
AAEGL	algae, galea
AAEGP	agape
AAEGR	arage
AAEGT	agate
AAEGV	agave

AAEGZ agaze
AAEHK hakea
AAEHP aheap
AAEKL akela
AAEKP apeak
AAEKW awake
AAELN Aalen
AAELP palae, palea
AAELR areal
AAELT alate, talea
AAELV avale
AAELX Alexa
AAEMR marae
AAEMT amate, A-team
AAEMZ amaze
AAENP apnea, paean
AAENR anear, arena
AAENS Seana
AAENT aetna, antae
AAEOZ zoaea
AAERR arear
AAERU aurae, Aurea
AAERW aware
AAEST saeta
AAFFJ Jaffa
AAFGS Gafsa
AAFHL halfa
AAFHR Farah
AAFIM Mafia
AAFIT tafia
AAFLN fanal
AAFLT aflat, fatal
AAFMN fanam
AAFMO afoam
AAFMR Mafra
AAFNU fauna
AAFRS saraf
AAFRT tarfa
AAFTW fatwa
AAGGN ganga
AAGGR ragga
AAGHL galah
AAGHN Ghana
AAGHR Hagar
AAGIL agila
AAGIM agami
AAGIN again, Gaian
AAGIS saiga
AAGIT gaita, taiga
AAGJN ganja
AAGKN kanga
AAGLL algal
AAGLN lagan
AAGLR argal, graal, lagar
AAGLV vagal
AAGLX galax
AAGLY gayal
AAGMM gamma, magma
AAGMN amang, manga
AAGMR grama
AAGMT tagma
AAGNP pagan, panga
AAGNR argan, grana
AAGNS sanga
AAGNT tanga
AAGNU guana
AAGNW wanga
AAGNY yagna
AAGOR agora
AAGPS agasp
AAGPU guaap
AAGRS Sagar
AAGRT targa
AAGRU guara
AAGRZ gazar
AAGST agast
AAGSV avgas
AAGTU tagua
AAGUV guava
AAHHM haham
AAHIS Aisha
AAHIW hiawa
AAHJM jamah
AAHJR rajah
AAHJT jatha
AAHKM khama
AAHKN khana
AAHKR harka
AAHKS kasha
AAHKY khaya
AAHLL Allah, halal
AAHLM almah, halma, mahal
AAHLN nahal
AAHLO aloha
AAHLP alpha
AAHLR lahar
AAHLT talha
AAHLV Alvah, halva
AAHMO haoma, Omaha
AAHMR haram, marah
AAHMS masha
AAHMU mahua
AAHMZ hamza
AAHNP hanap
AAHNS Hansa, Hasna
AAHNT thana
AAHNU an-hua
AAHNZ hazan
AAHPR Aphra
AAHPS pasha
AAHPX hapax
AAHRR arrah, arrha
AAHRS haras, Sarah
AAHRT rahat
AAHRY rayah
AAHSU Hausa
AAHSW awash, sawah
AAHTW whata
AAHWY hyawa
AAIKL laika
AAIKM makai
AAIKN inaka
AAIKP kapai
AAIKR rakia
AAIKS Sakai, sakia
AAIKT Akita, kiaat
AAIKZ Izaak
AAILM lamia
AAILN Alain, Alina, lanai, liana
AAILR laari
AAILS Ailsa, alias, asail
AAILV avail
AAILW walia
AAILX axial
AAIMN amain, Amina, amnia, anima, mania
AAIMR maria
AAIMS amasi, Masai
AAIMT matai
AAIMZ zamia
AAINP apian
AAINR arain, Arian, naira, Raina, ranai
AAINS Asian
AAINT Anita, niata, Tai'an, tania
AAINV avian
AAIPR praia
AAIPS paisa
AAIPT tapia
AAIPV pavia
AAIRS Sarai
AAIRT Arita, atria, raita, tiara
AAIRZ Zaria
AAISS assai
AAIST satai
AAITW await
AAITZ tazia
AAIZZ Aziza
AAJKR Karaj
AAJLN Jalna
AAJLP jalap
AAJMM jamma
AAJMN jaman
AAJMS samaj
AAJNN jnana
AAJNP japan
AAJNV Javan
AAJNW jawan
AAJNY yajna
AAJRV vajra
AAJRW jawar
AAKKR akkra, kakar
AAKKS kakas
AAKKY kayak, yakka
AAKLM Kamal
AAKLO Akola, koala
AAKLP kalpa
AAKLR kraal
AAKLS salak
AAKLT talak
AAKMR karma, makar
AAKMS asmak
AAKNT kanat, tanka
AAKNZ Kazan
AAKOR Okara
AAKOS asoak
AAKPP kappa
AAKPR parka
AAKPT patka
AAKPU pa-kua
AAKRT karat
AAKRY yarak
AAKST Sakta
AAKTZ zakat
AALLL Lalla
AALLM llama
AALLN Allan
AALLO Alloa
AALLP palla
AALLS salal
AALLT Talal
AALLU alula
AALLV Laval
AALLW walla
AALLY allay
AALMR alarm, malar, maral,

Marla,
ramal
AALMT Malta
AALMU ulama
AALMX malax
AALMY Malay
AALNN annal
AALNS nasal
AALNT alant,
natal
AALNU lauan,
Nuala
AALNV naval
AALNW Nawal
AALNY nyala
AALPP appal,
lappa,
papal
AALPR Paarl,
palar
AALPS palas,
palsa,
salpa
AALPT talpa
AALPU Palau,
Paula
AALPY playa
AALPZ La Paz,
plaza
AALQT talaq
AALRT altar,
ratal,
talar, tra-
la
AALRU aural,
laura
AALRV Alvar,
arval,
larva,
lavra
AALRW Alwar
AALRY alary
AALRZ lazar
AALSS Lassa,
salsa
AALST Aalst,
atlas,
salta
AALSV vasal
AALSY lasya
AALTU taula
AALTY Altay
AALUY Aulay
AALVV valva
AALWY alway
AALYY yayla
AAMMM mamma
AAMMN Amman,
namma
AAMMU mauma
AAMNN manna
AAMNS Namas,
saman
AAMNT atman,
manta
AAMNY Mayan
AAMNZ zaman
AAMOR amora,
aroma
AAMOS omasa,
Samoa
AAMOY oyama
AAMPR parma,
praam
AAMPU mapau
AAMRR marra
AAMRT Marta,
matra,
Tamar,
trama
AAMRU Maura,
Rauma
AAMRZ mazar
AAMSS amass,
Massa,
msasa
AAMST tsama
AAMSY Amyas,
Mayas
AANNN nanna
AANNO Anona
AANNT tanna
AANNV Navan
AANNW wanna
AANOR Aaron
AANOX xoana
AANPP nappa
AANPR prana
AANPS pasan,
sapan
AANPT Patan
AANPV pavan
AANQT qanat
AANRR narra
AANRS naras
AANRT antar,
antra,
ratan
AANRV varan,
varna
AANRW Anwar,
awarn
AANRY Aryan
AANRZ nazar
AANSS nassa,
sansa
AANST Santa,
Satan
AANSU sauna
AANSW Aswan
AANSY Sanya
AANTT Tanta
AANTW wanta
AANTY tanya
AANWX wanax
AAOPR Orapa
AAORR aroar
AAORT aorta
AAOST Aosta
AAPPS papas
AAPPT tappa
AAPPV vappa
AAPPW papaw
AAPRT apart
AAPRY praya
AAPST pasta,
patas,
tapas
AAPSY Pasay,
payas
AAPTT attap
AAPTW watap
AAQRT Qatar
AAQTU Aqtau
AARRS arras,
Sarra
AARRT tra-ra
AARRY array
AARSS sarsa
AARST Astra,
rasta
AARSU auras
AARSZ sarza
AARTT attar,
Tatar
AARTY tayra,
yatra
AASSY assay
AASTV avast
AASTY satay,
satya
AASWY asway
AATXY ataxy
AATYZ zayat
AATZZ tazza
ABBBY babby
ABBCO bobac,
cabob
ABBCY cabby
ABBDU dubba
ABBDY dabby
ABBEI Abbie
ABBEK kebab
ABBEL babel,
bable
ABBEN benab
ABBER barbe
ABBEY abbey
ABBGY gabby
ABBIJ jibba
ABBIR rabbi
ABBJU jubba
ABBKO bobak
ABBLO Babol
ABBLU babul,
bubal
ABBMO A-bomb
ABBNO nabob
ABBNY nabby
ABBOO baboo
ABBOT abbot
ABBTY tabby
ABBYY yabby
ABCCO bacco,
bocca
ABCCY baccy
ABCEH beach
ABCEI ceiba
ABCEL cable,
Caleb
ABCER acerb,
brace,
caber
ABCHI Chiba
ABCHR brach
ABCHT batch
ABCHU bauch
ABCIN cabin
ABCIO cobia
ABCIR cabri,
Carib
ABCIS basic
ABCJO Jacob
ABCKL black
ABCKR brack
ABCKS backs
ABCKY backy
ABCLM clamb
ABCLN blanc
ABCNO bacon,
banco
ABCNU Cuban
ABCOR carob,
coarb,
cobra
ABCOU couba
ABCOV vocab
ABCRS scrab
ABCRT bract
ABCSU scuba
ABDDE bedad
ABDDU budda
ABDDY baddy
ABDEG badge,
begad,
debag
ABDEI abide
ABDEK baked
ABDEL abled,
blade
ABDEM bemad
ABDEN Baden
ABDEO abode,
adobe
ABDER ardeb,
beard,
bread,
Breda,
debar,
Debra
ABDET bated
ABDEU daube
ABDEY beady
ABDGY by gad
ABDIL ad lib,
Blida
ABDIR bardi,
braid,
drabi,
rabid

ABDIT tabid
ABDLN bland
ABDLO dobla
ABDLU Abdul, blaud
ABDLY badly, baldy, blady
ABDNR brand
ABDNY bandy
ABDOR abord, board, broad
ABDRY bardy, Darby
ABDSU bauds
ABDWY bawdy
ABEEL abele
ABEFL fable
ABEGH begah
ABEGL bagel, gable, galbe, gleba
ABEGM gambe
ABEGN abeng, bagne, began
ABEGR barge
ABEGT begat
ABEHL belah
ABEHN Benha
ABEHO bohea, obeah
ABEHR hebra, herba, rehab
ABEHS Sheba
ABEHT bathe, beath
ABEIM abime, I-beam
ABEIN Bei'an
ABEIS Basie, beisa
ABEIZ baize
ABEJL jelab
ABEJM jambe
ABEJZ Jabez
ABEKL Blake, bleak
ABEKN baken
ABEKR baker, brake, break
ABEKY beaky
ABELL be-all, Bella, label
ABELM amble, blame, Mabel, Mable, Melba
ABELN Blane, leban
ABELP belap
ABELR abler, baler, belar, blare, blear
ABELS Basle, Blase, sable
ABELT blate, bleat, table
ABELY belay
ABELZ blaze
ABEMN maneb
ABEMR amber, brame, bream, embar
ABEMY beamy, embay, maybe, Mbeya
ABENO beano
ABENR Abner
ABENS banes
ABENT abnet
ABENU abune
ABEOV above
ABERR aberr, arber, barre
ABERS barse, saber, sabre
ABERT Berta
ABERV brave
ABERY beray, yerba
ABERZ braze, zebra
ABESS bases, basse
ABEST baste, beast, tabes
ABESU abuse, beaus
ABESW besaw
ABESY absey
ABETU beaut, butea, tubae
ABETY batey
ABEUX beaux
ABFFN Banff
ABFLM flamb
ABFRU fubar
ABGGY baggy
ABGHI bigha
ABGHN bhang
ABGIR girba
ABGMO gambo
ABGNO Gabon, obang
ABGNU ganbu
ABGNY bangy
ABGOR garbo
ABGOZ gazob
ABHIJ bhaji
ABHIS sahib
ABHIT habit
ABHKL Balkh
ABHLS blahs
ABHMO Bhamo
ABHMR brahm
ABHOR abhor
ABHOS basho
ABHRS brash
ABHST baths
ABHSU bhusa
ABHTU bahut
ABIIL alibi
ABIIM iambi
ABIIT tibia
ABIJM Jambi
ABIJO Baoji
ABIKL ikbal
ABIKT batik
ABILM limba
ABILN binal, blain
ABILO aboil
ABILQ qibla
ABILR Blair, brail, Libra
ABILS basil
ABILT Balti
ABILY Libya
ABILZ bazil
ABIMR abrim, Marib, mbira
ABIMT ambit
ABINO boina
ABINR abrin, bairn, brain, Brian
ABINS basin, sabin
ABINU nubia
ABINV bavin
ABIOT biota
ABIRR briar
ABIRT Brita
ABISS absis, basis, bassi
ABITY baity
ABJMO jambo
ABJMU jambu
ABJNO banjo
ABJOT jabot
ABKLN blank
ABKLU baulk, Kabul
ABKLY balky
ABKNR brank
ABKOR borak
ABKOY bokay
ABKRU burka
ABKRY braky
ABLLS balls
ABLLU bulla
ABLLY bally
ABLMU album
ABLMY balmy
ABLOO baloo
ABLOP Pablo
ABLOR bolar, labor, lobar
ABLOS bolas
ABLOT bloat, oblat
ABLOV vobla
ABLOW wobla
ABLRT blart
ABLRU lubra
ABLRW brawl
ABLST blast
ABLSY sably
ABLTT blatt
ABLTU tubal
ABLWY by-law
ABLYY lay-by
ABMMO mambo
ABMMU mambu
ABMNO ambon
ABMOR rambo
ABMOS sambo
ABMOT tambo
ABMOZ zambo
ABMPY pamby
ABMRU rumba, umbra
ABMRY ambry, barmy
ABMSY abysm
ABMUY mauby
ABNNS banns
ABNNU unban
ABNOO aboon
ABNOR baron, Bonar, Brona
ABNOS bason
ABNOT baton
ABNRT brant
ABNRU buran, unbar, urban
ABNRW brawn
ABNRY Bryan
ABNTU Bantu, tabun
ABNUY bunya
ABOOS boosa
ABOOT taboo
ABOOY booay, yaboo

ABOOZ	bazoo, booza
ABORR	arbor
ABORS	boras, Bosra
ABORT	abort, boart, tabor, torba
ABORV	bravo
ABORX	borax
ABORY	boyar
ABOSS	basso
ABOST	basto, boast, sabot
ABOTT	tabot
ABOTU	about, U-boat
ABOUY	bayou
ABQSU	squab
ABRRU	burra
ABRRY	barry
ABRSS	brass
ABRST	brast
ABRSU	bursa
ABRTU	turba
ABRXY	braxy
ABSSY	abyss
ABSTU	batus, tabus, tsuba, tubas
ABTTY	batty
ABUUZ	Buzau
ABUZZ	abuzz
ABWYY	byway
ACCDY	cycad
ACCEH	cache, chace
ACCEM	Mecca
ACCEU	cueca
ACCHI	chica
ACCHK	chack
ACCHO	chaco, coach
ACCHT	catch
ACCIL	licca
ACCIO	icaco
ACCIR	circa
ACCIT	cacti, ticca
ACCIW	Wicca
ACCKL	clack
ACCKO	acock
ACCKR	crack
ACCLU	Lucca
ACCMO	macco
ACCOO	cocoa
ACCOT	coact
ACCOU	couac
ACCOY	accoy
ACCUY	yucca
ACCVY	vaccy
ACDDE	decad
ACDDY	caddy
ACDEE	cadee
ACDEF	decaf, faced
ACDEG	cadge
ACDEI	cadie
ACDEL	Cadel, clade, clead, decal, laced
ACDEN	acned, dance, decan
ACDEP	caped
ACDER	acred, arced, cadre, cedar
ACDET	cadet
ACDEW	cadew
ACDEY	decay
ACDFO	Cafod
ACDGY	cadgy
ACDHO	ad hoc
ACDHR	chard, drach
ACDHS	dachs
ACDIL	alcid, calid
ACDIN	canid, nicad
ACDIR	acrid, caird, cardi, daric
ACDIS	asdic
ACDIT	dicta
ACDIZ	Cadiz
ACDKR	drack
ACDLO	acold
ACDLS	scald
ACDLU	cauld, Claud, ducal
ACDLY	yclad
ACDMO	Madoc
ACDNO	can-do
ACDNU	adunc
ACDNY	candy
ACDOR	cardo
ACDOT	octad
ACDRY	cardy, darcy
ACDSS	scads
ACDTU	ducat
ACEEK	ackee
ACEEP	peace
ACEES	cease
ACEFH	chafe
ACEFL	fecal
ACEFR	facer, farce
ACEFT	facet
ACEGL	glace
ACEGR	grace
ACEGY	cagey
ACEHL	chela, leach
ACEHN	chena, hance, nache
ACEHP	chape, cheap, peach
ACEHR	chare, rache, reach
ACEHS	chase
ACEHT	cheat, tache, teach, theca
ACEHV	chave
ACEIL	Alice, Celia, ileac
ACEIM	amice
ACEIN	naice
ACEIP	pecia
ACEIR	erica
ACEIV	Avice, cavie
ACEKL	aleck
ACEKR	crake, creak
ACEKW	wacke
ACELL	cella
ACELM	camel, clame, cleam, macle
ACELN	Ancel, ancle, canel, clean, lance
ACELP	caple, place
ACELR	carle, ceral, Clare, clear
ACELS	claes, lasce, scale
ACELT	cleat, lacet
ACELV	calve, cavel, clave
ACEMO	cameo, comae
ACEMR	cream, macer
ACENN	nance
ACENO	acone, canoe, ocean
ACENP	pecan
ACENR	caner, crane, nacre, rance
ACENS	scena
ACENT	enact
ACEOR	ocrea
ACEOX	coxae
ACEPR	caper, crape, pacer, recap
ACEPS	scape, space
ACEPT	epact
ACEPY	pacey
ACERR	carer, crare, racer
ACERS	carse, caser, sacre, scare, serac
ACERT	caret, carte, cater, crate, react, recta, trace
ACERU	eruca
ACERV	carve, caver, crave, varec
ACERX	carex
ACERY	Carey
ACERZ	craze
ACESS	casse
ACEST	caste
ACESU	cause, sauce
ACESY	Casey
ACETT	tacet
ACETU	acute
ACETX	exact
ACETZ	Aztec
ACFFH	chaff
ACFFS	scaff
ACFHT	chaft
ACFHU	chufa
ACFIL	calif
ACFIM	mafic
ACFIN	finca
ACFIV	favic
ACFKL	flack
ACFKR	frack
ACFLO	focal
ACFNR	franc
ACFNY	fancy
ACFRS	scarf
ACFRT	craft
ACFRU	furca
ACFRY	farcy

ACFTY facty
ACGHN chang, ganch
ACGHO choga
ACGHT gatch
ACGIM gamic, magic
ACGIR cigar, craig
ACGLN clang
ACGNO conga
ACGNR crang
ACGOR cargo
ACGOT cagot
ACGOU guaco
ACGRS scrag
ACHHL halch
ACHHN hanch
ACHHT hatch
ACHHY hachy
ACHIK haick
ACHIL laich
ACHIM Micah
ACHIN chain, china
ACHIR archi, chair
ACHIT aitch, Chita, tachi
ACHKL chalk
ACHKN chank
ACHKO choak
ACHKR chark
ACHKS shack
ACHKT thack
ACHKU kauch
ACHKW whack
ACHKY hacky
ACHLO chola, loach
ACHLR larch
ACHLS clash
ACHLT latch
ACHLU chula
ACHLV Vlach
ACHLW chawl
ACHMO macho, mocha
ACHMP champ
ACHMR charm, march
ACHMS chasm
ACHMT match
ACHNO nacho
ACHNP panch
ACHNR ranch
ACHNT chant, natch
ACHNU nucha
ACHNW chawn
ACHOP phoca, poach
ACHOR corah, orach, roach
ACHOS chaos
ACHOT chota, coath, tacho
ACHOU huaco
ACHOV havoc
ACHOW cahow
ACHOY choya
ACHPR parch
ACHPS chaps
ACHPT patch
ACHRR charr
ACHRS crash
ACHRT chart, ratch
ACHRY Archy, chary
ACHSU sauch
ACHSW schwa
ACHTU aucht
ACHTW watch
ACHTY Cathy, yacht
ACIIL cilia, iliac
ACIIN acini
ACIKK kiack
ACIKL alick, claik
ACILL Cilla, lilac
ACILM claim, malic
ACILN linac
ACILP plica
ACILS lacis, salic
ACILT ictal, tical
ACILU aulic, Lucia
ACILV Calvi, cavil
ACILX calix
ACIMN manic, Nicam
ACIMS camis
ACINN Incan
ACINP panic
ACINR cairn, incar
ACINT actin, antic, inact
ACINV vinca
ACIOP copia
ACIOR Cairo
ACIOT actio, coati
ACIOZ azoic
ACIPR carpi
ACIPS aspic, scapi, spica
ACIRS scari
ACIRT artic, triac
ACIRU auric, curia
ACIRV vicar, vraic
ACISU Caius
ACITT attic, tacit
ACITU Utica
ACITV vatic
ACJKY Jacky
ACJNU Cajun
ACKKN knack
ACKKY kyack
ACKLN clank
ACKLO cloak
ACKLP plack
ACKLR Clark
ACKLS slack
ACKLU caulk
ACKMS smack
ACKMU amuck
ACKNR crank
ACKNS snack
ACKOR croak
ACKOW wacko
ACKPU pucka
ACKQU quack
ACKRT track
ACKRW crawk, wrack
ACKST stack
ACKTY tacky
ACKVY vacky
ACKWY wacky
ACLLO local
ACLLS scall
ACLMO cloam
ACLMP clamp
ACLMU Calum
ACLNU Lucan
ACLOO acool
ACLOP copal
ACLOR Carlo, carol, claro, coral, Lorca
ACLOS colsa
ACLOT octal
ACLOV vocal
ACLOX coxal
ACLOY Alcoy, coaly
ACLOZ colza
ACLPS clasp, scalp
ACLPT clapt
ACLPU capul, culpa
ACLRT clart
ACLRW crawl
ACLRY Carly, Caryl, clary, Lycra
ACLSS class
ACLSU Lucas
ACLSY scaly
ACLTY talcy
ACLXY calyx
ACMMO comma
ACMNO Macon
ACMOP campo
ACMOR carom, coram, macro, Marco
ACMOS comas
ACMPR cramp
ACMPS scamp
ACMPY campy
ACMRS scram
ACMRY cymar, Marcy
ACMSU camus, scaum, sumac
ACNNO ancon, canon, Conan
ACNNY canny, nancy
ACNOP capon, pocan
ACNOR acorn, narco, racon
ACNOS ascon, Oscan
ACNOT acton, canto
ACNOW cowan
ACNOX caxon
ACNPU uncap
ACNRS scarn, scran
ACNRY carny, crany
ACNST canst, sanct, scant
ACNTY canty
ACOPR copra
ACOPS capos, posca, scopa
ACOPT capot, coapt
ACORS Oscar
ACORT actor, Croat, taroc
ACORW acrow
ACORY oracy
ACOST ascot, catso, coast, costa

ACOTT cotta
ACPPU cuppa
ACPRS craps, scarp, scrap
ACPRY crapy, parcy
ACPSU scaup
ACPSY spacy
ACPTU caput
ACRRU crura
ACRRY carry
ACRSS crass
ACRST scart, scrat
ACRSU scaur
ACRSW scraw
ACRSY carsy, Carys, scary, scray
ACRTT tract
ACRTU curat, turca
ACRTY Tracy
ACRYZ crazy
ACSSU ascus
ACSTU scuta
ACSTY Stacy
ACSUY saucy
ACTTY catty
ADDDE added
ADDDY daddy
ADDEH Hedda
ADDEJ jaded
ADDEL addle, dedal
ADDER adder, dared, dread, Dreda
ADDEV Vedda
ADDEY yedda
ADDFY faddy
ADDGI gaddi, gadid
ADDHN dhand
ADDHO hodad
ADDIO addio
ADDIV David
ADDMY Maddy
ADDNO add-on
ADDNY dandy
ADDPY paddy
ADDRY dryad
ADDTY taddy
ADDWY waddy
ADEEL Adele
ADEEM adeem, edema
ADEER eared
ADEET teaed
ADEEV deave, evade
ADEFG fadge
ADEFI fedai
ADEFL flead
ADEFM famed
ADEFN fedan
ADEFR fader, Freda
ADEFT defat, fated
ADEGL glade
ADEGM madge
ADEGP padge
ADEGR Edgar, Gerda, grade
ADEGS degas
ADEGU agued
ADEGW wadge, waged
ADEHJ jehad
ADEHK kheda
ADEHL heald
ADEHM Ahmed
ADEHN henad
ADEHR heard
ADEHS Hades, shade
ADEHT death
ADEHX hexad
ADEHY heady
ADEIK Ikeda
ADEIL Delia, ideal
ADEIM amide, maedi, media
ADEIN Andie, Diane, Edina
ADEIP pedia
ADEIR irade
ADEIS A-side, aside, desai, Sadie
ADEIU adieu
ADEIZ azide
ADEJR Jared
ADEJS dasje
ADEJV Javed
ADEKL dalek, Kelda
ADEKN knead, naked
ADEKR daker, drake
ADEKW waked
ADELL dalle, Della, ladle
ADELM Delma, medal
ADELN Alden, eland, laden, lande, naled
ADELP paled, pedal, plead
ADELR alder
ADELT dealt, delta, lated
ADELV Velda
ADELW dwale, weald
ADELY delay, leady
ADELZ Zelda
ADEMM damme
ADEMN admen, amend, maned, Medan, menad
ADEMR ad rem, armed, derma, drame, dream, madre
ADEMS mesad
ADEMU Maude
ADENO anode
ADENR denar, redan
ADENS sedan
ADENT anted, dante
ADENU Duane
ADENV vaned
ADENW awned, dewan
ADENY denay
ADEOP apode
ADEOR adore, oared, oread
ADEOT todea
ADEOZ adoze
ADEPR drape, padre
ADEPS adeps, spade
ADEPT adept
ADEPY payed
ADERR arder, darer, drear
ADERS darse, sedra
ADERT trade, tread
ADERU adure
ADERV drave
ADERW dewar, wader
ADERY deary, deray, rayed, ready
ADEST stead
ADESW sawed
ADETX taxed
ADEUV vaude
ADEVW waved
ADEWX waxed
ADFFR draff
ADFFY daffy
ADFLO Adolf
ADFNO fonda
ADFRT draft
ADFRU fraud
ADFRW dwarf
ADGGY daggy
ADGIL algid, Gilda
ADGLN gland
ADGLO Golda
ADGLY glady
ADGMO dogma
ADGNO dogan, donga, gonad
ADGNR drang, grand
ADGNU dunga
ADGNW dwang
ADGOS gadso
ADGOT toga'd
ADGOU Gouda
ADGRU guard
ADGRY gardy
ADGUY gaudy
ADGWY gawdy
ADHIJ hadji, jihad
ADHIL haldi, Hilda
ADHIM Mahdi
ADHIN ahind, Dinah
ADHIO Idaho
ADHIP aphid
ADHIS Hasid
ADHJU Judah
ADHLO ahold
ADHLU haldu, Hulda
ADHLY dhyal, Hylda
ADHMO omdah
ADHNO donah, honda
ADHNS hands
ADHNT hadn't
ADHNY handy
ADHOR hoard, Rhoda
ADHOT had to
ADHRS hards, shard
ADHRY hardy, hydra

ADHSS	shads
ADHST	hadst
ADHSU	sadhu
ADHSY	shady
ADIIL	lidia
ADIIN	India
ADIIO	oidia
ADIIR	dairi, radii
ADIKN	kadin, kinda
ADIKU	aduki
ADILN	Ladin, Linda
ADILO	dolia, idola
ADILP	plaid
ADILR	drail, laird, liard, lidar
ADILS	Aldis
ADILT	dital, tidal, Tilda
ADILU	dulia
ADILV	valid
ADILY	daily, Lydia
ADIMN	admin, Mdina
ADIMR	marid
ADIMT	admit
ADIMX	admix
ADINN	dinna
ADINO	Adoni, danio
ADINP	pinda
ADINR	dinar, drain, nadir, ranid
ADINS	disna
ADINT	daint
ADINV	divan, viand
ADIOP	podia
ADIOR	aroid, doria, radio
ADIOS	adios
ADIOT	diota
ADIOU	audio, Douai
ADIOV	avoid
ADIOZ	diazo
ADIPR	adrip, pardi, rapid
ADIPS	sapid
ADIPV	pavid, vapid
ADIRT	triad
ADIRX	radix
ADIRY	dairy, diary
ADIRZ	izard
ADIST	staid
ADISU	Saudi
ADISV	divas, visa'd
ADISW	wadis
ADISY	daisy
ADITU	audit
ADITV	davit
ADIVV	viva'd
ADJOU	Oujda
ADJSU	Judas
ADKLS	skald
ADKLY	alkyd
ADKMR	D-mark
ADKMU	dumka
ADKNR	drank
ADKOT	datok
ADKOV	vodka
ADKRW	drawk
ADKRY	darky
ADKTU	datuk
ADLLO	aldol, allod, do-all
ADLLY	dally
ADLMO	dolma, domal, modal
ADLMW	dwalm
ADLMY	madly
ADLNO	Donal, Ndola, nodal
ADLNU	laund
ADLNY	Dylan, Lynda
ADLOP	l-dopa, podal
ADLOR	Roald
ADLOT	dotal
ADLOU	aloud
ADLOW	waldo
ADLPU	plaud
ADLRU	dural
ADLRW	drawl
ADLRY	Daryl, lardy, radly, Rydal
ADLSU	Aldus, lauds, salud
ADLSY	sadly
ADLTU	adult, dault
ADLUY	yauld
ADLWY	lawdy
ADMNO	Damon, monad, nomad
ADMNU	dunam, maund
ADMNY	mandy
ADMOR	Radom
ADMRU	mudar, mudra
ADMRY	mardy
ADMSU	adsum
ADMTU	datum
ADNNO	donna, nonda
ADNNY	Danny
ADNOO	Doona
ADNOR	adorn, Doran, narod, radon, Ronda
ADNOW	adown
ADNOZ	zonda
ADNPY	pandy
ADNRR	R and R
ADNRT	drant
ADNRW	drawn
ADNRY	randy
ADNST	stand
ADNSU	Sudan
ADNSY	sandy
ADNTU	daunt
ADNWY	wandy
ADNYY	yandy
ADOOT	toado
ADOPR	adrop
ADOPT	adopt
ADOQU	quoad
ADORR	ardor
ADORS	dorsa, sarod
ADORU	douar
ADORV	vardo
ADORW	dowar
ADOTY	doaty, toady, today
ADQSU	squad
ADRRU	durra
ADRST	Strad
ADRSU	Duras, Sudra
ADRSW	sward
ADRSY	dryas
ADRTY	tardy
ADRVY	vardy
ADSTU	adust
ADUVZ	Vaduz
AEEFZ	feaze
AEEGL	eagle
AEEGR	agree, eager, eagre, ragee
AEEHV	heave, hevea
AEEIM	Aimee
AEEIR	aerie
AEEJM	meeja
AEEKN	aknee
AEEKP	pekea
AEEKR	karee
AEELN	anele, Elena
AEELR	laree
AEELS	easel, lease
AEELT	elate, taele
AEELV	leave
AEELW	aweel
AEEMN	amene, emane, enema
AEEMR	ameer
AEEMS	mease
AEEMT	metae
AEEMV	ameve, Maeve, Meave
AEENR	arene, ranee
AEENT	eaten
AEENV	veena
AEEPS	pease
AEEPY	payee
AEERS	easer, erase, saree
AEERT	eater, Taree
AEERV	reave
AEERW	waree
AEEST	setae, tease
AEESV	eaves, vease
AEETX	exeat
AEEVW	weave
AEFFG	gaffe
AEFHS	sheaf
AEFIL	Alfie, alife
AEFIR	afire, feria
AEFIT	Tiefa
AEFKL	flake
AEFKN	kenaf
AEFKR	faker, freak
AEFLL	fella
AEFLM	flame, fleam
AEFLN	flane
AEFLR	feral, flare
AEFLS	Aslef, false
AEFLT	aleft, fetal
AEFLV	favel
AEFLY	leafy
AEFLZ	fazle
AEFMR	frame
AEFNT	Fante

AEFOR afore
AEFOV fovea
AEFPR frape
AEFRR ferra
AEFRT after, frate, trefa
AEFRU feuar
AEFRW wafer
AEFRY faery, fayre, Freya
AEFST feast, festa
AEFTT fetta
AEFTW fetwa
AEFTY featy
AEFUV fauve
AEGGI Aggie
AEGGN gange
AEGGR agger, eggar
AEGGU gauge
AEGHL Helga
AEGHN Hagen
AEGHP phage
AEGHR gerah
AEGIL agile, Algie
AEGIM image
AEGIN Angie
AEGIS aegis
AEGLL egall, legal
AEGLM gamel, gleam
AEGLN angel, angle, glean, lagen
AEGLP pagle, plage
AEGLR Alger, argle, glare, greal, lager, large, regal
AEGLT aglet
AEGLV gavel
AEGLW wagel
AEGLY agley, Gayle
AEGLZ glaze
AEGMM gemma
AEGMN mange, Megan
AEGMO omega
AEGMR gamer, grame, marge
AEGMY gamey
AEGNO agone, genoa
AEGNP pagne
AEGNR anger, grane, range
AEGNS Agnes, Senga
AEGNT agent, Tegan
AEGNU augen, nugae
AEGNV vegan
AEGNY gynae
AEGOR orage
AEGOV goave
AEGPR gaper, grape, pager, parge
AEGRR rager
AEGRS garse, sarge, segar
AEGRT grate, great, Greta, targe, terga
AEGRU argue, auger
AEGRV grave
AEGRW wager
AEGRY gayer, yager
AEGRZ gazer, graze
AEGSS gases
AEGST stage
AEGSU usage
AEGSW swage
AEGTU Taegu
AEGUV vague
AEGUZ gauze
AEHHP ephah
AEHHT heath
AEHIU heiau
AEHJU Haeju
AEHKS shake
AEHKW wheak
AEHLM hamel, hemal
AEHLN Ahlen
AEHLP aleph
AEHLR haler, harle
AEHLS halse, leash, sahel, selah, shale
AEHLT athel, lathe, leath
AEHLU lehua
AEHLV halve
AEHLW whale, wheal
AEHLZ hazel, hazle
AEHMN he-man, maneh
AEHMO mahoe
AEHMR harem
AEHMS hames, shame
AEHMT mathe, Meath, thema
AEHMW whame
AEHNN henna
AEHNS ashen, hanse, Shane, Shena
AEHNT Ethan, nathe, neath, thane
AEHNV haven
AEHNY hyena
AEHOR heroa, horae
AEHPR hepar, phare, raphe
AEHPS phase, shape
AEHPY heapy
AEHRR harre
AEHRS Asher, share, shear
AEHRT earth, hater, heart, Herat, rathe
AEHRV haver
AEHRW whare
AEHST ashet, haste
AEHSU hause
AEHSV shave, sheva
AEHSW hawse
AEHTT theta
AEHTU haute
AEHTW wheat
AEHVY heavy
AEHWY wahey
AEIJK Ikeja
AEIJM Jamie
AEIJN Janie
AEIJZ jezia
AEIKL alike, alkie
AEIKP apike
AEIKR Erika
AEIKT Katie
AEIKW kiawe
AEIKZ Kezia
AEILL Allie, ileal, Leila
AEILM email
AEILN alien, aline, anile, elain, liane, linea, nelia
AEILP pilea
AEILR ariel
AEILS aisle, asile, Elias, salie
AEILT Eilat, telia
AEILV alive, Alvie, viale
AEILX axile
AEILZ Eliza
AEIMM Mamie
AEIMN amine, emina, Maine
AEIMR maire, Marie, ramie
AEIMT matie
AEIMZ maize
AEINN Annie, inane
AEINO naieo
AEINR Arnie, Raine
AEINS anise, Siena
AEINT entia, tenia, tinea
AEINV avine, naevi, naive, vinea
AEINX xenia
AEINZ azine
AEIPR perai
AEIPS paise, sepia
AEIRR airer
AEIRS Aries, arise, raise, serai
AEIRT Artie, irate, retia, terai, tiare
AEIRV aiver

AEIRZ Azeri, zaire
AEISZ seiza
AEITT tatie
AEITV Evita
AEITW tawie
AEIVW aview, waive
AEJKS jakes
AEJLO jaleo
AEJLV javel
AEJMM Jemma
AEJMR Ajmer
AEJMS James
AEJMT matje
AEJNN Jenna
AEJNR Nerja
AEJNS jeans
AEJNT Janet
AEJNU jaune
AEJNY Janey, Jayne
AEJPR japer
AEJRS esraj
AEJSY jasey
AEJTV vatje
AEKKK kakke
AEKLN ankle
AEKLR laker, rakel
AEKLS slake
AEKLT katel, ketal, latke
AEKLW kwela
AEKLY leaky
AEKMR maker
AEKNO oaken
AEKNP knape, pekan
AEKNR anker, Karen, naker, nerka
AEKNS skean, snake, sneak
AEKNT taken
AEKNV knave
AEKNW waken
AEKNY Kanye, Kenya
AEKOP opake
AEKOR Korea
AEKOW awoke
AEKPS Pakse, spake, speak
AEKPY peaky
AEKQU quake
AEKRR raker
AEKRS asker, eskar, saker
AEKRT taker
AEKRW waker, wrake, wreak
AEKRZ karez
AEKST skate, stake, steak
AEKSU ukase
AEKSW askew
AEKTW tweak
AEKWY weaky
AELLL allel
AELLM lamel
AELLN Allen, an ell
AELLP lapel, Pella
AELLS salle
AELLW we-all
AELLY alley
AELMM lemma, melam
AELMN leman, lemna
AELMO amole, maleo
AELMP ample, maple
AELMR realm
AELMS Salem, samel, Selma
AELMT metal
AELMU ulema
AELMV Melva, Velma
AELMY mealy, yealm
AELMZ Zelma
AELNO alone, anole, Leona
AELNP Nepal, panel, penal, plane
AELNR Larne, learn, neral, renal
AELNS Ansel, Elsan, nasel
AELNT anlet, laten, leant
AELNU ulnae
AELNV elvan, levan, navel, venal
AELNW wanle
AELNX nexal
AELOP peola
AELOS alose
AELOT atole
AELOV Olave
AELOZ azole
AELPP apple
AELPR lepra, parel, parle, pearl
AELPS lapse, salep, sepal
AELPT leapt, lepta, patel, pelta, petal, plate, pleat, tepal
AELQU equal, quale
AELRS arles, lares, laser, saler
AELRT alert, alter, artel, later, ratel
AELRU alure, ureal
AELRV larve, laver, ravel, velar
AELRW waler
AELRX relax
AELRY early, layer, leary, relay
AELSS salse
AELST lates, least, slate, stale, steal, stela, tales, teals, tesla
AELSU salue
AELSV Elvas, levas, salve, slave, valse
AELSW swale
AELSY asyle
AELTV tavel, valet
AELTX exalt, latex
AELUV value
AELVV valve
AELVW wavel
AELVY leavy, vealy
AEMMY mamey
AEMNO Eamon, noema
AEMNR enarm, neram, ramen, reman
AEMNS manes, manse, means, mensa
AEMNT ament, meant
AEMNU neuma
AEMNV maven
AEMNY meany, yeman
AEMOV amove
AEMPR amper
AEMRR rearm
AEMRS mares, maser, smear
AEMRT armet, mater, ramet, tamer
AEMRZ mazer
AEMST satem, steam
AEMSU amuse, musae, musea
AEMSY samey, seamy, ysame
AEMTT matte
AEMTY etyma, matey, meaty
AEMUV mauve
AEMYZ azyme, mazey
AENNP panne
AENNS senna
AENNT anent
AENNW Anwen
AENNX annex
AENOP paeon, poena
AENOT atone, neato, notae, oaten
AENOV novae
AENOW Owena
AENOZ neoza, ozena
AENPP nappe
AENPR paren
AENPS aspen

AENPT paten
AENPW pawne
AENPZ Penza
AENQU quean
AENRR reran
AENRS nares, rasen, snare
AENRT anter, antre, aren't, terna
AENRV raven, Verna
AENRY yearn
AENSS Assen, Nessa, sensa
AENST antes, nates, Nesta
AENSV avens
AENTT Netta, tante
AENTV venta
AENTW awent
AENTX Texan
AENTY yenta
AENVW navew
AENWX waxen
AENWY waney, Wayne, weany
AENWZ wanze
AENZZ zazen
AEOOZ zooea
AEOPR opera
AEOPS paseo
AEORS arose
AEORT orate
AEOSS oases
AEOTV ovate
AEOTW aweto
AEOTZ azote
AEPPR paper
AEPPS sappe
AEPPU pupae
AEPPZ zappe
AEPRR parer, raper
AEPRS asper, aspre, parse, prase, presa, spare, spear
AEPRT apert, pater, peart, Petra, prate, repat, taper, terap, trape
AEPRU pareu
AEPRV paver
AEPRY apery, payer, repay
AEPSS passe
AEPST paste, pesta, septa, spate
AEPSU pause
AEPSY peasy
AEPTT patte, tapet
AEPTU taupe
AEPTX expat
AEPTY peaty
AEQRU quare
AEQUV quave
AERRR rarer
AERRS raser, serra
AERRT terra
AERRV raver
AERRY yerra
AERSS arses, rasse
AERST aster, resat, stare, tarse
AERSV saver
AERSW sware, swear
AERSY sayer
AERTT arett, atter, tater, teart, tetra, treat
AERTV avert, tarve, trave
AERTW tawer, water
AERTX Artex, extra, taxer
AERTY teary
AERUZ azure
AERVV varve
AERVW waver
AERVY Avery
AERWX waxer
AERWY weary
AESSS asses, sasse
AESST asset, tasse, Tessa
AESSY essay
AESTT state, taste, testa
AESTV stave, vates, vesta
AESTW sweat, tawse, waste
AESTX taxes, Texas
AESTY teasy, yeast
AESUV suave
AEVWY wavey
AFFGR graff
AFFIX affix
AFFLO offal
AFFLU luffa
AFFNY Naffy
AFFQU quaff
AFFST staff
AFFTY taffy
AFGGY faggy
AFGHU faugh
AFGLU fugal
AFGNO fango
AFGOR Fargo
AFGOS Ofgas
AFGOT fagot
AFGRT graft
AFHIN hanif
AFHIR harif
AFHIT faith
AFHIZ hafiz
AFHLS flash
AFHRW wharf
AFHST shaft
AFHTT thaft
AFHTU futah
AFIKR fakir, Kafir, rafik
AFILL flail
AFILN alfin, final
AFILO folia
AFILP pilaf
AFILR filar, flair, frail
AFIMO ma foi
AFINO Fiona
AFINR infra
AFINT faint, Fanti, fiant
AFIOS Sofia
AFIRR friar
AFIRS Farsi
AFIRT afrit, frati, trifa
AFIRY fairy
AFKLN flank
AFKLS flask
AFKLY flaky
AFKNR frank
AFKOT kofta
AFKRT kraft
AFLMY flamy
AFLNW flawn
AFLOO aloof
AFLOR farol, flora
AFLOS sol-fa
AFLOT aloft, float, flota
AFLOU afoul
AFLOW aflow
AFLRY flary
AFLSU sulfa
AFLTU fault
AFLTY fatly
AFLUW awful
AFMOO mafoo
AFMOR foram, forma
AFMOX Oxfam
AFMOY foamy
AFMSU samfu
AFNNO fanon
AFNNY fanny
AFNOR Faron
AFNOY Afyon
AFNRU furan
AFNRY frayn
AFNSU snafu
AFOOT afoot
AFORV favor
AFORY foray
AFOSS fossa
AFOST fatso, softa
AFOTW Ofwat
AFRRY farry
AFRSS frass
AFRSW swarf
AFRTY rafty
AFSTU faust
AFSUV favus
AFTTY fatty
AFTWY wafty
AGGHY haggy
AGGIN aging, nigga
AGGIR aggri
AGGJY jaggy
AGGNY naggy
AGGOR aggro
AGGRY aggry, raggy
AGGSY saggy
AGHHI ahigh
AGHHL halgh
AGHHU haugh
AGHIL laigh
AGHIN anigh, hangi
AGHIZ ghazi
AGHLO golah
AGHLU laugh

AGHMO ogham, Omagh
AGHNO hogan
AGHNS gnash
AGHNT thang
AGHNW whang
AGHOR gorah
AGHOS Sohag
AGHOT Gotha
AGHPR graph
AGHRT garth
AGHST ghast
AGHSU saugh
AGHTU aught
AGHUW waugh
AGIIV vigia
AGIJR jagir, jirga
AGIKL glaik
AGIKN kiang
AGIKO Ogaki
AGILL glial
AGILN algin, align, liang, ligan, linga
AGILO logia
AGILR argil, glair, grail
AGILS sigla
AGILU ugali
AGILW wilga
AGILY gaily
AGIMM migma
AGIMN gamin
AGIMO amigo, imago
AGIMR gimar
AGIMS sigma
AGINN ingan
AGINO ngaio
AGINP pinga
AGINR agrin, grain, nigra
AGINT anti-g, giant, tangi, tiang
AGINU nigua
AGINV Gavin
AGINW awing, Wigan
AGINX axing
AGIOR orgia
AGIOS agios
AGIPR graip
AGIPS Pasig
AGIRR garri
AGIRT tragi
AGIRU guira
AGIRV virga
AGIST agist
AGISU Gaius
AGITU aguti
AGJLU jugal
AGJNO jonga
AGKLO gloak
AGKNO kango
AGKNY kyang
AGKOP gopak
AGKWY gawky
AGLLO Algol
AGLLY gally
AGLMO gloam
AGLMU algum, almug, glaum, mulga
AGLNO along, Anglo, galon, logan
AGLNR gnarl
AGLNS glans, slang
AGLOO agloo
AGLOP galop
AGLOR algor, argol, goral, largo
AGLOS Lagos
AGLOT gloat
AGLOV galvo
AGLOW aglow
AGLOY goyal
AGLPY pygal
AGLRU gular
AGLRY glary, gyral
AGLSS glass
AGLTU gault
AGLYY gayly
AGLYZ glazy, zygal
AGMMU gumma
AGMMY gammy
AGMNO among, mango, ngoma
AGMNU munga
AGMNY mangy
AGMOP gompa
AGMOR margo, mogra, Morag
AGMOT magot
AGMPR gramp
AGMRU garum
AGMSU magus, sagum
AGMTU gamut
AGMUY gaumy
AGNNO angon, gonna
AGNNW gnawn
AGNOP ponga
AGNOR angor, argon, groan, nagor, orang, organ
AGNOT nogat, tango, tonga
AGNOU guano
AGNOW gowan, wagon, wonga
AGNOY agony
AGNOZ gazon
AGNPR prang
AGNPS spang
AGNPU punga
AGNRR gnarr
AGNRT grant
AGNRU gnaur
AGNRW wrang
AGNRY angry, rangy
AGNST angst, gnast
AGNSU Angus
AGNTU gaunt
AGNTW twang
AGNTY tangy
AGNYZ ganzy
AGOOT Otago
AGOOZ gazoo
AGOPR pargo
AGORS Argos, sargo
AGORT argot, gator, gotra, groat
AGORU goura
AGOTT gotta
AGOTY goaty
AGPPY gappy
AGPRS grasp, sprag
AGPRU purga
AGPRY grapy
AGRRY Garry
AGRSS grass
AGRSU Argus, sugar
AGRUU augur
AGRVY gravy
AGSSU gauss
AGSSY gassy
AGSTU Gusta
AGSTY stagy
AGSUV vagus
AGTTU gutta
AGUYZ gauzy
AHHIT haith, hi-hat
AHHOO hoo-ha
AHHOR horah
AHHPY hypha
AHHRS harsh
AHIIT Haiti
AHIJJ hajji
AHIJR hijra
AHIKK khaki
AHIKM hakim
AHIKR khair
AHIKT kathi
AHIKU haiku
AHIKV Khiva
AHILM Hamil
AHILP phial
AHILR hilar
AHILS hilsa
AHILT Lahti, lathi, thali
AHIMR Hiram, ihram
AHIMS Amish
AHINO Hanoi
AHINR Rhian
AHINS ishan, Shani
AHINT hiant
AHINU hinau
AHIOR haori, iroha
AHIPP happi
AHIPS aphis, apish, spahi
AHIPT pahit
AHIRS Shari
AHIRU Uriah
AHIRY hairy
AHISS Shias
AHIST saith, Thais, Tisha
AHISV Shiva
AHISW washi, wisha
AHITU hutia
AHIUW Wuhai
AHJKO khoja
AHJLU jhula
AHJNO Jonah
AHJOO oojah
AHJOR johar
AHJTU thuja
AHKLU kulah
AHKLY khyal
AHKNS shank
AHKNT thank
AHKNY hanky
AHKOS shako
AHKOU kohua, oukha
AHKRS harsk, shark
AHKSY shaky
AHKTT takht
AHKTY Kathy

AHLLO	hallo,
	holla
AHLLS	shall
AHLLU	ahull
AHLMU	haulm
AHLNO	halon
AHLNP	planh
AHLNU	hulan,
	uhlan
AHLOR	horal
AHLOS	shoal
AHLOT	Athol,
	loath
AHLPR	Ralph
AHLPS	plash
AHLPY	haply,
	phyla
AHLRW	wharl
AHLSS	slash
AHLST	laths,
	shalt
AHLSW	shawl
AHLSY	shaly
AHLTU	thula
AHLTY	lathy
AHLUW	hulwa
AHMMY	hammy
AHMNO	Hamon
AHMNU	human,
	Nahum
AHMNY	Hyman,
	mynah
AHMOR	omrah
AHMOU	Houma
AHMOW	mohwa
AHMPS	pashm,
	phasm
AHMPY	phyma
AHMRS	marsh
AHMRT	tharm
AHMSS	smash
AHMST	maths
AHMSU	musha
AHMSW	shawm
AHMTU	mutha
AHNOP	napoh
AHNOR	Norah,
	Rhona
AHNOS	Shona
AHNOT	Hotan
AHNPY	hypna
AHNRU	Harun
AHNST	Hants,
	hasn't,
	shan't
AHNSU	Shaun
AHNSW	Shawn
AHNTU	ahunt,
	hantu,
	haunt
AHNTW	thawn,
	what'n
AHOOW	wahoo
AHOOY	yahoo
AHOPR	pharo
AHOPT	phota
AHORT	Thora,
	Torah
AHORY	hoary
AHORZ	Zohra,
	Zorah
AHOST	hoast,
	hosta,
	oaths,
	shoat
AHOSX	Xhosa
AHOTZ	azoth
AHPPY	happy
AHPRS	sharp
AHPRU	Hapur,
	prahu
AHPRY	harpy
AHPST	paths
AHPSW	pshaw
AHPTW	phwat
AHPTY	typha
AHPUW	whaup
AHQSU	quash
AHRRY	harry
AHRST	Rasht,
	trash
AHRSU	surah
AHRTW	thraw,
	warth,
	wrath
AHRTY	Thyra
AHRXY	hyrax
AHSST	stash
AHSSW	swash
AHSTW	swath
AHSTY	hasty
AHSWY	washy
AHTTU	tuath
AHTTY	Hatty
AHTUY	thuya
AHUZZ	huzza
AIIKL	Kaili
AIIKP	pikia
AIIKW	Iwaki
AIILM	milia
AIILO	aioli
AIILP	palii
AIIMM	Miami
AIIMN	Imani
AIIMT	Itami
AIINP	piani
AIIQR	Iraqi
AIIVV	Vivia
AIJJN	Jinja
AIJKL	kalij
AIJKN	kanji
AIJKT	Tajik
AIJLU	Julia
AIJNN	ninja
AIJNP	panji
AIJNS	Janis
AIJNW	jiwan
AIJNY	Yanji
AIJOR	Rioja
AIJOU	Ouija
AIJPW	pi jaw
AIJRV	Rajiv
AIJUV	juvia
AIJVY	Vijay
AIJYZ	jizya
AIKKM	kamik
AIKKR	kikar
AIKKT	tikka
AIKLM	malik
AIKLN	alkin,
	lakin
AIKLT	katil,
	kilta,
	talik,
	Tikal,
	tilak
AIKMN	mikan
AIKMO	maiko
AIKMU	umiak
AIKMV	mikva
AIKNO	Nokia
AIKNR	Karin
AIKNS	kisan
AIKNT	takin
AIKNU	kunai,
	nikau
AIKOP	okapi
AIKOT	taiko
AIKPP	kippa
AIKPS	Pakis
AIKPU	pikau
AIKRR	karri
AIKRS	rakis
AIKRT	kitar,
	krait,
	traik
AIKRU	kauri
AIKRV	kavir
AIKSS	sakis
AIKST	Sakti,
	Sitka
AIKTT	katti
AIKUZ	azuki
AILLL	Lilla
AILLN	all-in,
	Niall
AILLR	ralli
AILLS	allis
AILLV	villa
AILLW	Willa
AILLY	laily
AILMM	limma
AILMN	lamin,
	liman
AILMP	milpa
AILMR	armil
AILMS	Islam,
	malis,
	salmi
AILMT	Mitla,
	Tamil,
	tilma
AILMU	aumil,
	miaul
AILMV	Vilma
AILMW	Wilma
AILMX	limax
AILNO	Ilona
AILNP	plain
AILNR	larin
AILNS	nilas,
	slain,
	snail
AILNT	Latin,
	nital
AILNU	inula
AILNV	Alvin,
	anvil,
	nival,
	vinal
AILNW	inlaw
AILNY	inlay
AILOP	palio
AILOS	Laois
AILOT	talio
AILOV	oliva,
	viola
AILOX	loxia
AILPP	palpi,
	pipal
AILPR	April,
	prial
AILPS	lapis
AILPT	patil,
	plait
AILPU	pilau
AILPW	pilaw
AILQT	taliq
AILQU	quail
AILRT	trail, trial
AILRU	Lauri,
	rauli
AILRV	Avril,
	rival,
	viral
AILRX	larix
AILRY	lairy,
	riyal
AILSS	lassi,
	Silas,
	sisal
AILST	salti
AILSV	Alvis,
	silva
AILSX	salix
AILTT	atilt
AILTV	vital
AILTY	Italy,
	laity
AILUW	Laiwu
AIMMR	imram
AIMMS	miasm
AIMMX	maxim
AIMNN	Minna
AIMNO	amino,
	amnio,
	Naomi
AIMNR	Armin,
	Imran,
	inarm,

Marni, minar, ramin
AIMNS manis
AIMNT maint, matin
AIMNZ Mainz
AIMOR Maori, Mario, Moira
AIMOW miaow
AIMOX axiom
AIMOY Omiya
AIMPR prima
AIMPS sampi
AIMQU maqui
AIMRR marri
AIMRS Miras
AIMRT Marti, timar
AIMRU Iruma
AIMRZ mirza, ziram
AIMSS amiss, Assim, Miass
AIMST tamis
AIMSV mavis
AIMSW aswim, swami
AIMSX maxis
AIMSY Ismay
AIMTY amity
AINNO anion
AINNP pinna
AINNR Nairn
AINNS Annis
AINOP piano
AINOR noria, oiran
AINOS Sonia
AINOT Taino, Tonia
AINOW Owain
AINOX axion
AINPR Piran, prian
AINPS pians, sapin, Spain
AINPT inapt, paint, pinta, tap-in
AINPX pinax
AINQU quina
AINRS sarin
AINRT Nitra, train, trian, Trina
AINRU aurin
AINRV Invar, ravin
AINRW rawin
AINRY rainy
AINRZ nazir
AINSS sasin
AINST antis, saint, satin, stain, Tanis
AINSV savin, visna
AINSW swain
AINSZ Nazis
AINTT nitta, taint, tanti, Titan
AINTV vinta
AINTW twain, witan
AINUX auxin
AIOPR poria
AIOPT patio, taipo
AIORS Soria
AIORT ratio
AIORV vario
AIORX ixora
AIORY Oriya
AIOSS oasis, ossia
AIOST ostia
AIOSV aviso
AIOTW towai
AIPPP pappi, Pippa
AIPPU appui
AIPRS Paris
AIPRT atrip, parti, tapir
AIPSS apsis, aspis
AIPST tapis
AIPSV pavis
AIPTT Patti, pitta, tapit
AIPUX pauxi
AIPZZ pizza
AIQRT Tariq
AIQSU quasi
AIRRS arris
AIRRW wirra
AIRSS arsis, saris
AIRST astir, sitar, stair, stria, tarsi, trias
AIRSY Syria
AIRSZ sizar
AIRTT titar, trait
AIRTY arity
AIRVX varix
AIRVY vairy
AIRWZ wazir
AISST Astis, satis, Stasi
AISSV visas
AISTU Suita
AISTV vista
AISTW waist
AISTX taxis
AISVV vivas
AITTV vitta
AITTW atwit
AITVV vivat
AITZZ izzat
AIVVX vivax
AJKLT tjalk
AJKNR Kranj
AJKOT Tokaj
AJKTU jutka
AJLOU joual
AJLRU jarul, jural
AJMMU jumma
AJMMY jammy
AJMNU munja
AJMOR major
AJMRU jumar
AJNOS Jason, Jonas, Sonja
AJNOY yojan
AJNRU arjun
AJNTU jaunt, junta
AJNTY janty
AJOOP pooja
AJORW jowar
AJOSU sajou
AJRTU jurat
AJYZZ jazzy
AKKLU kulak
AKKMO kokam
AKKNO konak
AKKNS Kansk
AKKOO kooka
AKKOP kapok
AKKPU pukka
AKKRU kakur
AKKVY vakky
AKLLO lokal
AKLLY alkyl
AKLMU lakum
AKLNO kalon
AKLNP plank
AKLNR knarl
AKLNU kulan
AKLNY lanky
AKLOP pokal, polka
AKLOR Karol, Korla
AKLOT kotal, kotla
AKLPU pulka
AKLRY larky
AKLST stalk
AKLSW lawks
AKLTU taluk
AKLTY talky
AKLUW waulk
AKMNY manky
AKMOR korma
AKMOU oakum
AKMRS marks
AKMSU Aksum
AKMUZ muzak
AKMWY mawky
AKNOR Koran, krona
AKNOS sanko
AKNOW wakon
AKNOY koyan
AKNPR prank
AKNPS spank
AKNPU kanpu
AKNRS krans, narks, ranks, snark
AKNRT trank
AKNRU knaur
AKNRY narky
AKNST stank
AKNSU ankus
AKNSW swank
AKNSY snaky
AKNTU katun
AKNTW twank
AKNTY tanky
AKNUZ kanzu
AKOOP pooka
AKOOR Karoo
AKOOZ kazoo
AKOPP koppa
AKOPY yapok
AKORU koura
AKORW awork
AKOST oktas
AKOSY yoaks
AKOTY tokay
AKPRS spark
AKPRU kapur
AKPRY parky
AKPTU kaput
AKPWY pawky
AKQRU quark
AKQUW quawk
AKQUY quaky
AKRST karst, stark
AKRSU Kasur
AKRSY karsy, sarky
AKRTU kraut, kurta
AKRTY takyr
AKRWY rawky
AKRYZ karzy

AKSSV	kvass
AKSTY	kyats
ALLLU	lulla
ALLLY	allyl
ALLMO	molal
ALLMS	small
ALLMY	myall
ALLNO	llano
ALLNU	nulla
ALLOR	loral
ALLOS	salol
ALLOT	allot, atoll
ALLOW	allow
ALLOY	alloy, loyal
ALLPS	spall
ALLPY	pally
ALLRY	rally
ALLST	stall
ALLSU	allus
ALLSY	sally
ALLTY	tally
ALLUV	lulav
ALLWY	wally
ALLXY	laxly
ALMNO	molan, monal
ALMNU	manul
ALMNY	manly
ALMOR	molar, moral
ALMOT	matlo
ALMOY	loamy
ALMPS	plasm, psalm
ALMPU	ampul
ALMPY	amply, palmy
ALMQU	qualm
ALMRU	larum, mural
ALMRY	marly
ALMST	smalt
ALMTY	malty
ALNNO	Nolan
ALNNU	annul
ALNOP	nopal, onlap, plano
ALNOR	loran, Lorna
ALNOS	salon, solan
ALNOT	Alton, laton, notal, ontal, talon, tonal
ALNOW	lowan
ALNOX	noxal
ALNOY	onlay
ALNOZ	zonal
ALNPT	plant
ALNPU	ulpan
ALNRS	snarl
ALNRU	lunar, ulnar
ALNST	slant
ALNSU	ulnas
ALNTU	tunal
ALNTY	Lanty
ALNUY	unlay, yulan
ALNWY	Alwyn, lawny, wanly
ALNXY	xylan
ALOOP	paolo
ALOPR	parol, polar, poral
ALOPU	pulao
ALORS	solar
ALORU	Raoul
ALORV	Orval, valor, volar
ALORY	royal
ALOSS	a loss, lasso
ALOST	Alost, lotsa, salto
ALOSV	salvo
ALOTT	lotta, total
ALOTV	lovat, volta, votal
ALOTX	taxol
ALOUV	ovula
ALOVV	volva
ALPPS	palps
ALPPU	pupal
ALPPY	apply
ALPRU	plaur
ALPST	splat
ALPSY	palsy, splay
ALPTU	tapul
ALPTY	aptly, patly, platy, typal
ALPUZ	pulza
ALQRU	quarl
ALQTU	taluq
ALRRU	rural
ALRRY	larry
ALRSU	sural
ALRTU	Latur, ultra
ALRTW	trawl
ALRTY	lyart
ALRUZ	zurla
ALRWW	wrawl
ALRWY	rawly
ALSSY	lassy, lyssa
ALSTU	altus, latus, salut, sault, talus
ALSTV	vlast
ALSTY	salty, slaty
ALSUU	usual
ALSVY	salvy, sylva
ALTTY	lytta
ALTUV	vault
ALTUZ	Tuzla
ALTWY	walty
ALTWZ	waltz
ALUUV	uvula
ALUVV	vulva
ALVVY	lavvy
AMMMO	momma
AMMMY	mammy
AMMOY	myoma
AMMRS	smarm
AMMRU	mamur, marum
AMMRY	rammy
AMMSU	summa
AMMSY	sammy
AMMTY	tammy
AMNNU	unman
AMNNY	manny
AMNOR	manor, moran, Morna, norma, ramon, Roman
AMNOS	manso, mason, monas
AMNOT	manto, notam, toman
AMNOW	woman
AMNOY	anomy, Moyna, yoman
AMNOZ	Monza
AMNRU	unarm
AMNRY	Myrna
AMNSU	manus
AMNTU	tuman
AMNTY	mayn't
AMOPP	op-amp
AMOPR	pro-am
AMOPS	pasmo
AMOPU	mapou
AMORR	armor, maror, morra
AMORT	amort, morat, torma
AMORU	amour
AMORW	mowra
AMORY	mayor, moray, Moyra
AMOST	stoma
AMOTU	Omuta
AMOTY	atomy
AMOTZ	matzo
AMPRS	ramps
AMPRT	tramp
AMPRW	wramp
AMPSS	spasm
AMPST	stamp
AMPSW	swamp
AMPVY	vampy
AMRRU	murra
AMRRY	marry
AMRST	smart
AMRSU	ramus
AMRSW	swarm
AMRTY	Marty, tryma
AMRUU	aurum
AMSSY	massy
AMSTU	matsu
AMSTY	masty, mayst
AMSUW	wamus
AMSXY	xysma
AMTTY	Matty
AMTUZ	mazut
ANNNY	nanny
ANNOR	Ronna
ANNOT	Anton
ANNOY	annoy
ANNRY	ranny
ANNSU	Sunna
ANNTU	naunt
ANOOP	napoo
ANOPR	apron
ANOPT	panto
ANOPW	powan
ANOPY	yapon
ANORS	arson, orans, saron, sonar
ANORT	trona
ANORW	rowan
ANORY	rayon
ANORZ	Zoran
ANOST	santo
ANOSV	novas
ANOSX	Saxon
ANOSY	Sonya
ANOTT	tanto
ANOTU	tauon
ANOTW	towan
ANOTX	taxon
ANOTY	atony, ayont, Tonya
ANOUY	noyau
ANOWY	noway

ANPPY nappy
ANPRW prawn
ANPRY pryan, pyran
ANPST pants
ANPSW spawn
ANPSY pansy
ANPTU tupan, unapt
ANPTY panty
ANQRU Quran
ANQTU quant
ANRST trans
ANRTU Traun
ANRUU Nauru
ANRUZ zurna
ANSSU nasus, Susan
ANSSY nyssa
ANSTU astun, tansu, tunas
ANSTW wanst, wasn't
ANSTY antsy, nasty, santy, tansy
ANSUY unsay
ANSUZ Anzus
ANTTU taunt
ANTTY natty
ANTUV vaunt
ANTUY aunty
ANTWY tawny, wanty
ANVVY navvy
ANWYY yawny
AOOPP a-poop
AOOPY pooay
AOPPP poppa
AOPPR appro
AOPPZ zoppa
AOPRS prosa, psora, RoSPA, sapor, sarpo
AOPRT aport, op art, porta, Prato
AOPRU raupo
AOPRV pavor, vapor
AOPSS psoas
AOPSW Swapo
AOPSY soapy
AOPTU a-pout, Taupo
AOPTY atopy
AOPTZ topaz
AOQTU quota
AORRS rasor
AORRW arrow
AORRZ razor
AORSS saros
AORST roast
AORSV savor
AORTT tarot, troat
AORTU atour, Otaru
AORTX taxor
AORTY otary
AORVY ovary
AOSST assot, stoas, tasso
AOSSY say-so
AOSTT stoat, tasto, toast
AOSVY savoy
AOTTU outta, tatou
AOTWZ owzat
AOUYY Yuyao
AOWYZ yowza
APPPY pappy
APPRS p'raps
APPRT trapp
APPSY paspy, sappy
APPUZ zuppa
APPYY yappy
APPYZ zappy
APRRY parry
APRST parts, sprat, strap, traps
APRSY raspy, spray
APRTT pratt
APRTW wrapt
APRTY party
APRUU purau
APSTU sputa, stupa
APSTY pasty, patsy
APSWY waspy
APTTY patty
APVVY pavvy
APZZZ pzazz
AQRTU quart
AQSSU quass
AQSTU squat
AQSUW squaw
ARRSU surra
ARRTY tarry
ARRUW wurra
ARRVY varry
ARSST trass
ARSSU sarus
ARSTT start
ARSTU Sutra
ARSTW straw, swart, wrast
ARSTY artsy, satyr, stray, yrast
ARSUV varus
ARSUY saury
ARTTT tratt
ARTTU Tartu, tuart
ARTTY ratty, tarty
ARTWY warty, watry
ASSSY sassy
ASTTY tasty
ASTUY Asyut
ASTVY vasty
ASTWY wasty
ASVVY savvy
ATTTY tatty
ATTWY Wyatt
AYZZZ zazzy
BBBOY bobby
BBBUY bubby
BBCEU cubeb
BBCHU Chubb
BBCOY cobby
BBCUY cubby
BBDEY debby
BBDOU Dubbo
BBDOY dobby
BBDUY dubby
BBEEM mebbe
BBEGO begob
BBEIL Bible
BBEIR bribe
BBEMO bombe
BBEOP bebop
BBEOR berob
BBEWY webby
BBGIY gibby
BBGOY gobby
BBHMO H-bomb
BBHOY hobby
BBHUY hubby
BBIIZ zibib
BBILO bilbo
BBILY bilby, Libby
BBIMO bimbo
BBISY Sibby
BBITY Tibby
BBLOY lobby
BBLRU blurb
BBMOU bumbo
BBMOY mobby
BBNOY nobby
BBNUY nubby
BBOOY booby, yobbo
BBOPY pobby
BBSUY busby
BBTUY tubby
BCCIU cubic
BCDEI cebid
BCEEH beech
BCEEL celeb
BCEER rebec
BCEEX xebec
BCEEZ zebec
BCEHL belch
BCEHN bench
BCEHO Boche
BCEIR Brice
BCEKL bleck
BCEKR breck
BCEKY Becky
BCELL B-cell
BCELO coble
BCEMO combe
BCENO bonce
BCENU bunce
BCEOR corbe
BCEOY Boyce
BCERU Bruce
BCERY Bryce
BCHIM chimb
BCHIR birch
BCHIT bitch
BCHNU bunch
BCHOR broch
BCHOT botch
BCHTU butch
BCHUU buchu
BCIKR brick
BCIKY bicky
BCILM climb
BCILO cibol
BCIMO combi
BCIOR boric, cribo, orbic
BCIPU pubic
BCIRS scrib
BCITU cubit
BCKLO block
BCKOR brock
BCKOU bucko
BCLMO clomb
BCMOO combo, coomb
BCMOR cromb
BCMOS combs
BCMRU crumb
BCNOR bronc
BCNOU bunco
BCORU courb
BCORY Corby
BCRSU scrub
BCRUY curby
BDDIY biddy
BDDUY buddy
BDEEI beedi
BDEEL bedel, bleed, debel
BDEEM embed

BDEER brede, breed
BDEEW bedew, bewed, dweeb
BDEEY bedye
BDEGO bodge
BDEGU budge, debug
BDEIL bield
BDEIM bedim, imbed
BDEIO dobie
BDEIP bedip, biped
BDEIR bride, rebid
BDEIS B-side
BDEIT bidet, debit
BDELN blend
BDELO bodle, lobed
BDELU blued
BDEMO demob
BDENO boden
BDENS S-bend
BDENY bendy, by-end
BDEOO booed
BDEOR orbed
BDEOY dobey
BDERR brerd
BDERY Derby
BDESU debus
BDETU debut
BDFII bifid
BDGIY Digby
BDHIO dhobi
BDIIL Idlib
BDIIR bidri, Irbid
BDILN blind
BDILU build
BDINO bidon, bodin
BDIOR broid
BDIOV bovid
BDLNO blond
BDLOO blood, boldo
BDLOY Dolby
BDMOU dumbo
BDMUY dumby
BDNOU bound
BDNUU bundu
BDOOR brood, dobro, droob
BDORU bourd
BDOTU doubt
BEEEL belee
BEEES besee
BEEEV beeve
BEEFS beefs
BEEFY beefy
BEEGI beige
BEEGL glebe
BEEGM begem
BEEGR gerbe, grebe
BEEGT beget
BEEHP Phebe
BEEHR Heber
BEEHT thebe
BEEIL belie
BEEJL bejel, jebel
BEEKR breek
BEELL belle
BEELN leben, nebel, neble
BEELP bleep, plebe
BEELR rebel
BEELS lebes
BEELT betel
BEELV bevel
BEELZ bezel
BEEMR breme, ember
BEEMT tembe
BEENN benne
BEENR Berne
BEENT benet
BEEOR beroe, boree
BEEOS obese
BEERR erber
BEERT beret
BEERV bever, breve
BEERW weber
BEERY beery
BEEST beest, beset
BEETT Bette
BEETW bewet
BEEUV bevue
BEFFU buffe
BEFGO befog
BEFIR brief, fiber, fibre
BEFIT befit
BEFRU befur
BEGIL bilge, gibel
BEGIN begin, being, binge
BEGIO bogie
BEGIR giber
BEGIW bewig
BEGLO bogle, globe
BEGLU bugle, bulge
BEGMO embog
BEGMU begum
BEGNU begun
BEGOR grebo
BEGOT begot
BEGOU bogue, bouge
BEGOY bogey
BEGRU gebur
BEGRZ Brzeg
BEHRT berth
BEHRY herby
BEIJN Benji
BEIKR biker
BEILL libel
BEILM Limbe
BEILO obeli
BEILR birle, liber
BEILT blite
BEILV bevil
BEIMO biome
BEIMU imbue
BEINN Benin, benni
BEINR brine
BEINX Benxi
BEINY in-bye
BEINZ zineb
BEIOR boier
BEIOS Boise, bosie
BEIOW bowie
BEIRR brier
BEIRS birse
BEIRT biter, tribe
BEISV Bevis, vibes
BEITW bewit
BEITZ zibet
BEIVX vibex
BEJOT objet
BEKLN blenk
BEKLO bloke
BEKOR broke
BEKRU burke
BEKTY kbyte
BEKUZ Uzbek
BELLY belly
BELMO moble
BELMU umbel
BELNO noble
BELNT blent
BELOO obole
BELOR blore, borel
BELOS lesbo
BELOT botel
BELOU boule
BELOW below, bowel, elbow
BELOY obley
BELRU bluer, burel, ruble
BELRY beryl
BELSS bless
BELST blest
BELSU blues, bulse
BELSY Selby
BELTU bluet, butle
BELUY bluey
BEMOP pombe
BEMOR brome, ombre
BEMOS besom, mebos
BEMOT tembo
BEMOW embow
BEMOX embox
BEMRU brume, umber
BEMSU embus, sebum
BENNO bonne
BENNY benny
BENOR boner, borne
BENOT T-bone
BENOY ebony
BENOZ bonze
BENRT brent
BENRY Berny
BEOOZ booze
BEOPR probe
BEORR borer
BEORS brose, sober
BEORW bower
BEORX boxer
BEORY boyer
BEOST besot
BEOSU bouse
BEOSW bowse
BEOSY bosey
BEOTW bowet
BEPSU pubes
BERRY berry
BERST Brest
BERSU burse, rebus
BERTT Brett
BERTU brute, buret, rebut, tuber
BERUX exurb
BERUY buyer
BESSU buses
BESSY Bessy
BESTY Betsy
BETTU butte
BETTY Betty
BEVVY bevvy
BFFLU bluff
BFFOO boffo

BFFOU	buffo
BFFUY	buffy
BFILM	B-film
BFIOR	fibro
BFIRY	fibry
BFLYY	fly-by
BFORY	forby
BFSUY	fubsy, fusby
BGGOY	boggy
BGGUY	buggy
BGHIT	bight
BGHOU	bough
BGHRU	brugh, burgh
BGHTU	bught
BGIIL	gibli
BGILO	globi
BGIMO	imbog
BGINO	bingo, boing
BGINR	bring
BGINY	bingy
BGIOT	bigot
BGISU	Bugis, gibus
BGLOY	globy
BGLUY	bulgy
BGMOU	gumbo
BGNOO	bongo, boong
BGNRU	brung
BGNUY	bungy
BGOOR	Bogor
BGORU	bourg
BGOSU	bogus
BGRUY	rugby
BHILU	Hubli
BHIMO	himbo
BHIOS	Bisho
BHIRS	brish
BHIRT	birth
BHLSU	blush
BHMOR	rhomb
BHMPU	bumph
BHMRU	rhumb
BHMTU	thumb
BHOOT	booth
BHOOY	hoboy, oh boy
BHORT	broth, throb
BHOTY	bothy
BHRSU	brush, shrub
BHSUY	bushy
BIILM	limbi
BIILQ	qibli
BIIMN	nimbi
BIINT	binit
BIINX	bixin
BIINY	Yibin
BIIOR	oribi
BIJOU	bijou
BIKKY	bikky
BIKLN	blink
BIKNR	brink
BIKNU	kunbi
BIKRS	brisk
BIKRY	Kirby
BILLR	brill
BILLY	billy
BILMO	limbo
BILMP	blimp
BILNY	bliny
BILOR	broil
BILOS	Blois
BILRT	blirt
BILSS	bliss
BILST	stilb
BILSY	sibyl, Sybil
BILTU	built
BILTZ	blitz
BIMNY	Nimby
BIMOT	timbo
BIMOW	imbow
BINOR	inorb, robin
BINOS	bison
BINRU	Bruin, burin
BINRY	briny
BINUY	buy-in
BIORS	Boris
BIORT	orbit
BIOST	boist
BIOTU	oubit
BIPSU	pubis
BIQSU	squib
BIRTT	britt
BIRTU	bruit, tribu
BISSY	byssi
BISTT	bitts
BISTU	buist
BISTY	bitsy
BITTY	bitty
BITUY	ubity
BIVVY	bivvy
BJMOU	jumbo
BJMUY	jumby
BJNOR	Bjorn
BKLUY	bulky
BKMOU	kombu
BKNOU	bunko
BKOOR	brook
BKOSY	bosky
BKRSU	brusk
BKSUY	busky
BLLUY	bully
BLMOO	bloom
BLMPU	plumb
BLNOW	blown
BLNOY	nobly
BLNTU	blunt
BLOOP	bloop
BLOOR	brool
BLOOY	looby
BLOSU	bolus
BLOTU	boult
BLOWY	blowy
BLRTU	blurt
BLRUY	burly
BLTUY	butyl
BMOOR	bromo, broom
BMOOS	bosom
BMOOT	tombo
BMOSU	umbos
BMOTY	Bytom
BMOUX	buxom
BMPUY	bumpy
BMTUU	tumbu
BNNOY	bonny
BNNUY	bunny
BNOOR	boron
BNOOS	boson
BNORU	bourn, Bruno
BNORW	brown
BNORY	Byron, Robyn, yborn
BNOSU	bonus, bosun
BNRTU	brunt, burnt
BOORS	Sorbo
BOORT	robot
BOORU	buroo
BOOST	boost, boots
BOOSY	boosy
BOOTU	Botou
BOOTY	booty
BOOWX	oxbow
BOOYZ	boozy
BOPRY	proby
BORRU	burro
BORTU	turbo
BOSSY	bossy
BOSTU	busto, tsubo
BOTTY	botty
BPRUU	rub-up
BPSST	tbsps
BRRUU	burru
BRRUY	burry
BRSTU	burst
BSSUU	bussu
BSTUY	busty
BTTUU	butut
BTTUY	butty
CCCIO	cocci
CCEEL	Lecce
CCEER	recce
CCEHK	check
CCEHZ	Czech
CCEIL	Cecil
CCEIR	cerci, ceric, cicer
CCEKL	cleck
CCELY	cycle
CCEMU	cecum
CCEOS	cosec, secco
CCESU	cusec
CCFIU	Cufic
CCHHI	chich
CCHIK	chick
CCHIN	cinch
CCHKO	chock
CCHKU	chuck
CCHLU	culch
CCHNO	conch
CCHOO	choco
CCHOU	couch
CCHRU	curch
CCHTU	cutch
CCIIT	ictic
CCIIV	civic
CCIKL	click
CCIKR	crick
CCILO	colic
CCILY	cycli
CCIMO	comic
CCIMU	mucic
CCINO	conic
CCINT	cinct
CCINY	cynic
CCIOR	croci
CCIOS	cisco
CCIOT	octic
CCIPY	piccy
CCIRS	circs
CCKLO	clock
CCKLU	cluck
CCKOR	crock
CCKOY	cocky
CCKRU	cruck
CCOOS	cocos
CCOOZ	zocco
CCORU	occur
CCOSU	cocus
CCOUZ	Cuzco
CCUUY	cucuy
CDDUY	cuddy
CDEEI	de-ice
CDEEL	cleed
CDEER	creed
CDEEU	deuce, educe
CDEHI	chide
CDEIM	medic
CDEIR	cider, cried, dicer
CDEIS	cedis
CDEIT	edict
CDEIV	Vedic
CDEIY	dicey
CDEKR	dreck
CDEKS	decks
CDEKY	decky
CDELO	dolce
CDELU	clued, dulce

CDELY	Clyde,
	decyl
CDEMO	Medoc
CDENO	conde
CDENS	scend
CDENU	dunce
CDEOO	cooed
CDEOR	coder,
	credo,
	decor
CDEOU	douce
CDEOX	codex
CDEOY	decoy
CDERU	crude
CDERY	cyder,
	decry
CDESU	decus,
	duces
CDETU	educt
CDHIL	child
CDHIO	dioch
CDHIT	ditch
CDHNU	dunch
CDHOR	chord
CDHTU	dutch
CDHUY	duchy
CDIIN	Indic
CDIIO	iodic
CDIKY	dicky
CDILU	lucid,
	ludic
CDILY	lycid
CDIMU	mucid
CDINY	Cindy
CDIOR	Doric
CDIOS	disco,
	sodic
CDIOT	dicot
CDIOV	covid
CDIPU	Cupid,
	pudic
CDITY	dicty
CDJOU	Judoc
CDKSU	ducks
CDKUY	ducky
CDLOS	scold
CDLOU	cloud,
	could
CDLWY	Clwyd
CDNOO	codon,
	condo
CDOOR	crood
CDORS	scrod
CDORW	crowd
CDOSU	scudo
CDRUY	curdy
CEEEM	emcee
CEEFN	fence
CEEFS	feces
CEEGR	grece
CEEHK	cheek,
	keech
CEEHL	Elche,
	leche,
	leech
CEEHM	meech
CEEHN	hence
CEEHP	cheep
CEEHR	cheer
CEEHS	seech
CEEIN	niece
CEEIP	piece
CEEJL	Celje
CEEJT	eject
CEEKL	cleek
CEEKR	creek
CEELP	clepe
CEELR	creel
CEELS	secle
CEELT	elect
CEELV	cleve
CEELX	excel
CEENP	pence
CEENS	cense,
	scene
CEEOO	cooee
CEEPR	creep,
	Perce
CEERS	Crees,
	scree
CEERT	erect,
	terce
CEERW	Crewe
CEFHI	chief,
	fiche
CEFHT	fetch
CEFIM	femic
CEFKL	fleck
CEFKR	freck
CEFLT	cleft
CEFLU	fluce
CEFOR	force
CEGIN	genic
CEGIO	cogie
CEGIR	grice
CEGKO	gecko
CEGNO	genco
CEGOR	gorce
CEGOU	cogue
CEHHI	Hechi
CEHHU	heuch
CEHIL	chile
CEHIM	chime,
	hemic,
	miche
CEHIN	chine,
	niche
CEHIR	chire,
	Reich
CEHIT	ethic
CEHIV	chive
CEHJU	Cheju
CEHKL	kelch
CEHKN	kench
CEHKO	choke
CEHKR	kerch
CEHKT	ketch
CEHLM	melch
CEHLO	Chloe,
	loche
CEHLP	chelp
CEHLS	selch
CEHLT	letch
CEHLW	welch
CEHLY	chyle
CEHMN	mench
CEHMY	chyme
CEHNO	Enoch
CEHNT	tench
CEHNW	wench
CEHOO	cohoe
CEHOP	epoch
CEHOR	chore,
	ocher,
	ochre
CEHOS	chose
CEHOT	cothe
CEHOU	cohue
CEHOY	echoy
CEHPR	perch
CEHRT	chert,
	retch
CEHRU	ruche
CEHSS	chess
CEHST	chest
CEHSU	chuse
CEHTT	tetch
CEHTU	chute
CEHTV	vetch
CEHTY	techy
CEHUY	yeuch
CEHVY	chevy
CEHWY	chewy
CEIIR	icier
CEIJU	juice
CEIKL	cleik,
	ickle
CEIKP	epick
CEIKR	icker
CEILM	clime,
	melic
CEILN	cline
CEILO	locie,
	oleic
CEILP	clipe
CEILR	relic
CEILS	slice
CEILT	telic
CEILU	Lucie
CEILV	Clive,
	velic
CEIMN	mince,
	nemic
CEIMR	crime
CEIMS	mesic
CEIMT	metic
CEIMX	cimex
CEINR	cerin,
	crine
CEINS	since
CEINV	Vince
CEINW	wince
CEINY	nicey
CEIOV	voice
CEIPR	price
CEIPS	spice
CEIPU	cupie
CEIRR	crier,
	ricer
CEIRS	cries,
	crise,
	Seric
CEIRT	recti,
	trice
CEIRU	curie
CEIRX	xeric
CEITU	cutie
CEITV	civet,
	evict
CEITW	twice
CEJOY	Joyce
CEKLO	cloke
CEKLP	pleck
CEKLR	clerk
CEKLU	cleuk
CEKNS	sneck
CEKNV	V-neck
CEKOP	copek
CEKOR	coker,
	ocker
CEKOS	cokes,
	scoke,
	secko
CEKPS	speck
CEKRW	wreck
CELLO	cello
CELLT	T-cell
CELMO	celom
CELNO	clone
CELNU	uncle
CELOP	ploce
CELOR	ceorl
CELOS	close,
	socle
CELOT	clote,
	colet,
	telco
CELOV	clove
CELOW	cowle
CELOY	coley
CELOZ	cloze,
	zocle
CELPT	clept
CELPU	cupel
CELPY	clype
CELRU	cruel,
	lucre,
	ulcer
CELRY	ceryl
CELSU	clues
CELTU	culet,
	lucet
CELTY	cetyl
CELUX	culex
CEMOR	comer,
	crome
CEMOS	comes
CEMOT	comet,
	comte
CEMRY	mercy

CENNO nonce
CENOP copen, ponce
CENOR crone, oncer, recon
CENOS scone
CENOT cento, conte
CENOU Cuneo, ounce
CENOV coven
CENOX coxen, ex-con
CENOY coney
CENOZ cozen
CENST scent
CENTU cunet
CEOOR coo-er
CEOOT ocote
CEOOY cooey
CEOPR coper
CEOPS copse, scope
CEOPU coupe
CEOQU coque
CEORR corer, crore
CEORS corse, score
CEORT recto
CEORV cover, crove
CEORW cower
CEORY coyer
CEORZ croze
CEOST coset, escot, estoc, scote
CEOSV scove
CEOSW Cowes
CEOTT octet
CEOTV covet
CEOVY covey
CEOWY cowey
CEPRT crept
CEPRY Percy, pryce
CEPSS specs
CERRU curer, recur
CERRY cryer
CERSS cress
CERST crest
CERSU cruse, curse
CERSW screw
CERSY Cerys
CERTU cruet, eruct, truce
CERTY certy
CERUV curve
CERUX excur
CESSU scuse
CESTU scute
CETUY cutey
CFFHU chuff
CFFIL cliff
CFFIO coiff
CFFLO cloff
CFFOS scoff
CFFSU scuff
CFHIL filch
CFHIN finch
CFHIT fitch
CFHIU fichu
CFIIS sci-fi
CFIKL flick
CFIKU Kufic
CFILO folic
CFILT clift
CFISU ficus, Sufic
CFKLO flock
CFKOR frock
CFMOY comfy
CFORT croft
CFORY forcy
CFOSU focus
CFRSU scurf
CFSUU fucus
CGGIY ciggy
CGHLU gulch
CGHOO cohog
CGHOU cough
CGIIN icing
CGILN cling
CGILO logic
CGIMO ogmic
CGINO coign, incog
CGINU cuing
CGIOR corgi, orgic
CGIOY yogic
CGIRU Ugric
CGKLU gluck
CGLNU clung
CGNOO congo
CGORS scrog
CHHIS shchi
CHHIT hitch
CHHIW which
CHHLU hulch
CHHNU hunch
CHHOO hooch
CHHOT hotch
CHHTU hutch
CHIIL chili
CHIIP pichi
CHIKN chink
CHIKO hoick, Kochi
CHIKR chirk
CHIKT thick
CHILL chill
CHILM milch
CHILN linch
CHILO choil, choli, lochi
CHILP pilch
CHILR chirl
CHILY hylic
CHILZ zilch
CHIMO mochi, ohmic
CHIMP chimp
CHIMR chirm
CHIMT mitch
CHIMU humic, muchi
CHINO chino
CHINP pinch
CHINT nitch, tchin
CHINW winch
CHIOR choir, ichor
CHIOT toich
CHIPR chirp
CHIPS Chips
CHIPT pitch
CHIRR chirr
CHIRS Chris
CHIRT chirt, trich
CHIRU chiru
CHISU cuish
CHISZ schiz
CHITT titch
CHITW witch
CHITY itchy
CHIVY chivy, Vichy
CHIZZ chizz
CHKNU chunk
CHKOO choko, chook
CHKOS shock
CHKOW chowk
CHKOY choky
CHKSU shuck
CHKTU thuck
CHLMU mulch
CHLNU lunch
CHLNY lynch
CHLOO cholo, looch
CHLOS closh, schol
CHLOT cloth
CHLOU chulo
CHLOY lochy
CHLRU churl, lurch
CHMNU munch
CHMOO choom, mooch
CHMOP chomp
CHMOS schmo
CHMOU mouch, mucho
CHMPU chump
CHMTU mutch
CHNOT nocht, notch
CHNPU punch
CHNRU churn
CHNSY synch
CHOOP pocho, pooch
CHOPR porch
CHOPS chops
CHOPT chopt, potch
CHOPU pouch
CHORT torch
CHORY ochry
CHOSU hocus
CHOTT chott
CHOTU chout, couth, touch
CHOUV vouch
CHOUX choux
CHPSY psych
CHRRU churr
CHRSU crush, cursh
CHRTW crwth
CHSUY cushy
CHTYY Tychy
CIIKN kinic
CIIKR Ricki
CIIKV Vicki
CIILT licit
CIILV civil
CIILY icily
CIIMM mimic
CIINO ionic
CIINP pinic
CIINR ricin
CIINV vinic
CIIRR cirri
CIJKO kojic
CIJUY juicy
CIKKL klick
CIKKN knick
CIKLN clink
CIKLS slick
CIKMY micky
CIKNS snick
CIKNY Nicky
CIKOS sicko
CIKPR prick
CIKPY picky
CIKQU quick
CIKRT trick
CIKRW wrick
CIKRY Ricky
CIKST stick, ticks
CIKTW twick
CIKTY ticky
CIKVY Vicky
CILNO colin, nicol

CILNT clint
CILOT lotic,
octli
CILOU oculi
CILOW wilco
CILPT clipt
CILRU Ulric
CILRY Cyril,
lyric
CILSU sulci
CILTY lytic
CILXY cylix
CIMNO monic,
nomic
CIMNU cumin,
cu-nim,
mucin
CIMOR micro
CIMOS osmic
CIMOV vomic
CIMPR crimp
CIMRS scrim
CIMSU music
CIMTU mutic
CINNO nonic
CINOR ciron,
orcin
CINOS scion,
sonic
CINOT ontic,
tonic
CINOV covin
CINOZ zinco
CINPU Punic
CINRS scrin
CINRU incur,
runic
CINSU incus
CINTT tinct
CINTU cunit,
cutin,
incut,
tunic
CIOPS pisco
CIOPT optic,
picot,
topic
CIORT toric
CIORU curio
CIOST Stoic
CIOTX toxic
CIPRS crisp,
scrip
CIPRY pricy
CIPSY spicy
CIPTY typic
CISSU scusi
CISSY cissy
CISTU cutis,
ictus
CISUV vicus
CIVVY civvy
CJNOU junco
CKKNO knock
CKKNU knuck
CKLNO clonk
CKLNU clunk
CKLOP plock
CKLOY cloky,
locky
CKLPU pluck
CKLUY lucky
CKMOS smock
CKMOY mocky
CKMUY mucky
CKNOR cronk
CKNRU crunk
CKNSU snuck
CKOOR crook
CKOOY cooky
CKOPY pocky
CKORS corks
CKORY corky,
rocky
CKOSS socks
CKOST stock
CKRTU truck
CKSTU stuck
CKUYY yucky
CLLOY colly
CLLRU crull
CLLSU scull
CLLUY cully
CLMOP clomp
CLMOU Colum,
locum
CLMPU clump
CLMTU mulct
CLMUY cumly
CLNOO colon
CLNOW clown
CLNUY Cluny
CLOOP cloop
CLOOR color
CLOOT cloot
CLOOY cooly
CLORU clour
CLORW crowl
CLOSU locus
CLOSW scowl
CLOTU clout
CLOTY octyl
CLOYY coyly
CLPSU sculp
CLRUY curly
CMMOS scomm
CMOOP compo
CMOOS Cosmo
CMOPT compt
CMORU mucor,
mucro
CMPRU crump
CMRSU crums,
scrum
CMSUU mucus
CMTUU tucum
CNNUY cunny
CNOOR Conor,
corno,
croon
CNOOT conto
CNOOW co-own
CNOPY poncy
CNORS scorn
CNORT tronc
CNORU cornu
CNORW crown
CNORY corny,
crony
CNOSU conus
CNOTU count
CNOWY Conwy
CNRTU crunt
CNTUU uncut
COOPS scoop
COOPT co-opt
COOST scoot
COPPY coppy
COPRS corps,
scorp
COPRT cropt
COPRU croup
COPSS scops
COPSU coups,
scoup
COPUY coypu
CORRU cruor
CORSS cross
CORSU scour
CORSW scrow
CORTU court,
turco
CORWY cowry
COSST Scots
COSTT Scott
COSTU scout
CPPUY cuppy
CPRTY crypt
CPTUU cut-up
CRRUY curry
CRSTU crust,
curst
CRSUY Cyrus
CRUVY curvy
CSUZZ scuzz
CTTUY cutty
DDDIY diddy
DDDOY doddy
DDEEI Eddie
DDEEL deled
DDEER dreed,
edder
DDEEY deedy
DDEFY Dyfed
DDEGO dodge
DDEHI hided
DDEIO diode,
Dodie
DDEIR dried,
redid
DDEIS sided
DDEIT tided
DDEIV dived
DDEMO domed
DDENY neddy
DDEOY yeddo
DDERU udder
DDERY reddy,
ydred
DDETY teddy
DDGIY giddy
DDGOY dodgy
DDIKO kiddo
DDIKY kiddy
DDILO dildo
DDILY Liddy
DDIMY middy
DDINT didn't
DDINU undid
DDIRU Druid
DDIST didst
DDITY tiddy
DDIWY widdy
DDLOY oddly
DDMUY muddy
DDNOY noddy
DDNUY nuddy
DDOPR prodd
DDOPY poddy
DDORY Roddy
DDOTY toddy
DDOWY dowdy
DDPUY puddy
DDRUY ruddy
DEEEP pedee
DEEEX exede
DEEFL fleed
DEEFR defer
DEEFU feued
DEEGH hedge
DEEGK kedge
DEEGL gleed,
ledge
DEEGO geode,
ogee'd
DEEGR edger,
greed
DEEGS sedge
DEEGW wedge
DEEHR heder
DEEHW hewed
DEEIL elide
DEEIN diene
DEEIR eider
DEEIX dexie
DEEKN kneed
DEEKR Derek
DEEKY keyed
DEELN leden
DEELP depel
DEELR elder
DEELS Leeds,
lesed
DEELT Telde
DEELU elude
DEELV delve,
devel
DEEMN emend,
Mende
DEEMR merde

DEENO donee
DEENS dense, needs
DEENT de-net, teend
DEENU endue
DEENY needy
DEENZ Enzed
DEEOP epode
DEEOR erode
DEEOX exode
DEEPR dreep
DEEPS pedes, speed
DEERS drees, Seder
DEERT deter, treed
DEERY reedy
DEEST steed
DEESU suede
DEESW sewed, Swede, weeds
DEESX desex
DEESY seedy
DEETW tweed
DEEUX exude
DEEVX vexed
DEEVY deevy
DEEWY weedy
DEFGI fidge
DEFGO fodge
DEFGU fudge
DEFIL felid, Fidel, field
DEFIN fiend
DEFIR fried
DEFIT fetid
DEFIX fixed
DEFIY deify, edify
DEFJL fjeld
DEFLT delft
DEFMR fremd
DEFNU unfed
DEFPU fed up
DEGHO Hodge
DEGHY hedgy
DEGIL gelid, glide
DEGIM midge
DEGIN deign, dinge, nidge
DEGIO dogie, geoid
DEGIR de-rig, dirge, gride, ridge
DEGIT tidge
DEGIU digue, guide
DEGJU judge
DEGLO glode, lodge
DEGLU glued
DEGLY glyde, ledgy
DEGMU degum
DEGNO Ogden
DEGNR dreng
DEGNU nudge
DEGOP podge
DEGOT godet, toged
DEGOW wodge
DEGPU pudge
DEGSY sedgy
DEGTU degut
DEHII Heidi
DEHIL Delhi, hield
DEHIR hider
DEHIS shied
DEHIT Edith
DEHLO dhole, holed
DEHLP delph
DEHLU Dhule
DEHLY hydel
DEHOP ephod
DEHOR horde
DEHOT doeth
DEHPT depth
DEHRS sherd, shred
DEHTY they'd
DEIIM imide
DEIIN indie
DEIIV ivied
DEIIX dixie
DEIJO ejido, Jodie
DEIJR jerid
DEIKN inked
DEIKP piked
DEIKS skied
DEILN lined
DEILO Odile, oiled, oldie
DEILP lepid, plied
DEILR idler
DEILS delis, dilse, sidle, slide
DEILT tilde, tiled
DEILV devil, lived
DEILW dwile, wield
DEILY yield
DEIMN denim
DEIMO demoi, medio
DEIMR dimer, mired
DEIMS deism, disme
DEIMT demit
DEIMX mixed
DEINO Dione
DEINR diner
DEINS Denis, snide
DEINT detin, end it, ident, teind, tined
DEINU indue, nudie, Udine
DEINW dwine, Edwin, widen, wined
DEINX index
DEINZ dizen
DEIOV video
DEIOW dowie
DEIOX oxide
DEIPP piped
DEIPR pride, pried
DEIPS spied
DEIPT tepid
DEIPW wiped
DEIQU equid
DEIRR drier, rider
DEIRS dries
DEIRT tired, tried
DEIRV diver, drive, rived
DEIRW weird, wired, wride
DEIST deist, stied
DEISV Dives
DEISZ sized
DEITY deity
DEIVY ivyed
DEJLO jodel
DEJOR dorje
DEKKO dekko
DEKNO kendo
DEKOP poked
DEKOR droke
DEKOY yoked
DEKRY Deryk
DELLW dwell
DELMO model
DELMU ledum, muled
DELNO Eldon, loden, olden
DELOR older
DELOW dowel
DELOY yodel
DELPU duple
DELRY redly
DELSU dulse
DELTV veldt
DELTW dwelt
DELTY tyled
DEMMO modem
DEMNO demon, monde
DEMNS mends
DEMOO mooed
DEMOP moped
DEMOR drome
DEMOS demos
DEMOT moted
DEMOU odeum
DEMOW mowed
DEMRU demur
DEMSU sedum
DEMTU muted
DENNY Denny
DENOO odeon
DENOP pedon
DENOR doner, drone, ronde
DENOS nosed, sonde
DENOT noted, tendo, toned
DENOV Devon
DENOW Downe, endow, nowed
DENOY doney, doyen
DENOZ dozen, zendo, zoned
DENPS spend
DENPU upend
DENRT trend
DENRU under
DENRY Deryn, nerdy
DENSY Denys
DENTU tendu
DENUU undue
DENUW unwed
DENWY Edwyn, Wendy
DEOOR rodeo
DEOOW wooed
DEOPR doper, pedro
DEOPS Spode
DEOPT depot
DEOPX podex

DEOPY	dopey
DEORR	order
DEORS	dorse
DEORT	doter
DEORV	dover, drove, vedro
DEORW	dower
DEORX	redox
DEORZ	dozer
DEOST	doest
DEOSU	douse
DEOSW	dowse, sowed
DEOTX	detox
DEOTY	dotey
DEOVW	vowed
DEOVY	dovey
DEOXY	oxyde
DEPPU	upped
DEPRU	drupe, duper, perdu, prude
DEPRY	predy
DEPSU	pseud
DEPTY	typed
DERRY	derry, dryer
DERSS	dress
DERSU	druse
DERTU	detur, trued
DERUX	Durex
DERUZ	Druze
DETUV	duvet
DFILU	fluid
DFIMU	fumid
DFINU	fundi
DFIOR	fiord
DFIRT	drift
DFJOR	fjord
DFLOO	flood
DFLOY	Floyd
DFNOR	frond
DFNOS	fonds
DFNOU	found
DFOOR	fordo
DFOOY	foody
DFORW	F-word
DGGOO	doggo
DGGOY	doggy
DGHIT	dight
DGHOU	dough
DGIIR	rigid
DGIIT	digit
DGILU	guild
DGIMO	migod
DGINO	dingo, doing, Gidon
DGINR	dring, grind
DGINU	gundi
DGINY	dingy, dying
DGIOP	pi-dog
DGIOU	Guido
DGIRY	ridgy
DGLOY	godly, goldy
DGNOR	drong
DGNOU	gound
DGNOZ	dzong
DGNUY	gundy
DGOOO	goodo
DGOOR	Drogo, droog
DGOOY	goody
DGOPY	podgy
DGORU	gourd
DGORY	grody
DGPUY	pudgy
DHIIN	Hindi
DHIMU	humid
DHINU	Hindu
DHIOT	dhoti
DHIOY	hyoid
DHIRT	third, thrid
DHISY	dishy
DHITW	width
DHNOO	dhoon
DHNOU	hound
DHORY	hydro
DHOVZ	vozhd
DHOWY	howdy
DHRTY	dryth
DIIJL	jildi
DIILP	lipid
DIILV	livid
DIIMO	idiom, modii
DIIMR	mirid
DIIMS	midis
DIIMT	dimit, timid
DIINR	indri
DIINT	nitid
DIINV	Vidin
DIIOT	dioti, idiot
DIIRS	Idris
DIIRV	virid
DIITX	dixit
DIIVV	vivid
DIJNN	djinn
DIJNO	Dijon
DIKNR	drink
DIKNY	dinky, kindy
DILLR	drill
DILLY	dilly, idyll
DILMS	milds
DILMY	dimly
DILNY	lindy
DILOS	solid
DILOU	Loudi
DILOY	doily
DILRU	lurid
DILRY	drily, idryl
DILSY	Dilys
DILWY	wildy
DIMMU	mudim
DIMNO	mid-on
DIMOS	misdo
DIMOU	odium
DIMPS	dimps
DIMRU	mudir, murid
DIMST	midst
DIMSY	mysid
DIMTU	tumid
DINOP	poind
DINOR	nidor
DINOT	tondi
DINOW	indow
DINSU	nidus
DINWY	windy
DIOOT	ootid
DIOOV	ovoid
DIOOZ	zooid
DIOPS	dipso
DIOPY	pyoid
DIORS	Doris
DIORT	droit
DIOTT	ditto
DIOTV	divot
DIOWW	widow
DIPPY	dippy
DIPTU	putid
DIQSU	squid
DIRTU	Trudi
DIRTY	dirty
DIRUZ	durzi
DISTY	ditsy
DITTY	ditty
DITYZ	ditzy
DIVVY	divvy
DIYZZ	dizzy
DJLUY	juldy
DJNUY	jundy
DKKOO	Kodok
DKNRU	drunk
DKOOR	drook
DKORU	drouk
DKORW	drowk
DKOSU	kudos
DKOUU	Dukou
DKSUY	dusky
DKUUZ	kudzu
DLLOR	droll
DLLOY	dolly, Lloyd
DLLUY	dully
DLMOU	mould
DLMOY	moldy
DLMUY	my lud
DLNOU	nould
DLOOR	dolor, drool
DLOOS	dolos
DLOOT	toldo
DLOOW	woold
DLORU	lourd
DLORW	world
DLORY	lordy
DLOSU	dolus
DLOTY	doylt
DLOUW	would
DLOWY	dowly
DLOYY	doyly
DLPUY	duply
DLRYY	dryly
DMMOO	modom
DMMUY	dummy
DMNOO	mondo
DMNOU	mound, nodum
DMOOO	odoom
DMOOS	dooms, Sodom
DMOOU	duomo
DMOOY	doomy, moody
DMOPT	dompt
DMORY	dormy
DMOSU	domus, modus
DMPSU	dumps
DMPUY	dumpy
DMRUU	durum
DNNOU	dunno
DNNOY	Donny
DNNUY	dunny
DNOOR	donor, rondo
DNOOS	snood
DNOOT	tondo
DNOPU	pound
DNOPY	pondy
DNORU	round
DNORW	drown
DNORY	drony
DNOSU	nodus, sound
DNOSY	synod
DNOTU	donut
DNOUV	vodun
DNOUW	wound
DNOWY	downy
DNUUY	Duyun
DOOPR	droop
DOORU	douro, odour
DOOST	stood, to-dos
DOOSW	woods
DOOTU	outdo
DOOWY	woody
DOOYZ	doozy
DOPRT	dropt
DOPRU	proud, pudor
DORSS	dross
DORSW	sword
DORTU	Tudor

DORTY dorty
DORUY duroy
DORWY dowry, rowdy, wordy
DOSTU doust
DOTTY dotty
DPPUY duppy
DPRUY dry-up
DPSUY pudsy
DRSTU durst
DRTUY Trudy
DRUXY druxy
DSSUY sudsy
DSTUY dusty, study
EEEFZ feeze
EEEGS geese, seege
EEEHT te-hee
EEEHW wehee
EEEHZ heeze
EEEIR eerie
EEEKV keeve
EEELM eleme, melee
EEELP elpee
EEELV levee
EEEMS meese
EEEMX exeem, exeme
EEENV evene
EEENZ neeze
EEEPT tepee
EEEPV peeve
EEEPW pewee
EEERS see-er
EEERV reeve
EEESW weese
EEETW etwee
EEEWZ weeze
EEFFI Effie
EEFKL El Kef
EEFKR kreef
EEFLM fleme
EEFLR fleer
EEFLT fleet
EEFLY feely
EEFMM femme
EEFRR freer, frere, refer
EEFRV fever
EEFRY yfere
EEFSS fesse
EEFSU fusee
EEFUZ fuzee
EEGGN ngege
EEGGR egger
EEGHN henge
EEGHO gee-ho
EEGIL liege
EEGIN eigne, genie
EEGIS siege
EEGIV vegie
EEGKL gleek
EEGKR Greek
EEGKY geeky
EEGLM gemel
EEGLR leger
EEGLT gleet
EEGLY elegy
EEGMN engem
EEGMR merge
EEGMW gemew
EEGNR genre, green, neger
EEGNT genet
EEGNV venge
EEGNW ngwee, wenge
EEGOR goree
EEGPU gee-up
EEGRS serge
EEGRT egret, greet
EEGRV verge
EEGST egest, geste
EEGSU segue
EEHIZ heize
EEHJL jheel
EEHKT hekte, theek
EEHKW wheek
EEHLN Helen
EEHLS heels
EEHLT ethel, Lethe
EEHLV helve
EEHLW wheel
EEHMP pheme
EEHMR herem
EEHMT theme
EEHNP phene
EEHNR Herne
EEHNS sheen
EEHNT Ethne
EEHNW wheen
EEHOS see-ho
EEHPR pheer
EEHPS sheep
EEHPW wheep
EEHRS herse, sheer
EEHRT ether, there, three
EEHRW hewer, where
EEHST sheet, these
EEHTT teeth, thete
EEHTY tyhee
EEIJT eejit
EEILL Ellie
EEILM elemi, Emile
EEILS eisel, Elise, Elsie
EEILT elite
EEILV Elvie
EEILX exile
EEIMM Emmie
EEINP peine
EEINR Ernie, Irene, Reine, Renie
EEINS seine
EEINV nieve
EEINW newie
EEINX exine
EEINY ineye
EEIOR ier-oe
EEIPP Eppie
EEIPS peise
EEIRT retie
EEIRV reive
EEIRY eyrie
EEISS seise
EEIST teise
EEISV sieve
EEISX exies
EEISZ seize
EEITT Ettie
EEITV evite
EEITX exite
EEJLW jewel
EEJOR joree
EEJSS Jesse
EEJYZ jeezy
EEKKL kelek
EEKKR ekker
EEKKT tekke
EEKKU ukeke
EEKKW kweek
EEKLN kneel
EEKLS sleek
EEKLV kevel
EEKLY yelek
EEKNR Keren, kerne
EEKNS knees, Sneek
EEKNT kente
EEKOP pekoe
EEKOV evoke
EEKPR preke
EEKRS esker
EEKRU eruke
EEKRY keyer, reeky, rekey
EEKST skeet
EEKTW tweek
EELLM lemel
EELLN Ellen
EELLV level
EELMM lemme
EELMO meloe
EELMR Elmer, merel, merle
EELMS mesel
EELMT metel
EELNO leone, Noele
EELNP plene
EELNS lenes
EELNT lente
EELNV elven, nevel
EELNW newel
EELOP elope
EELPR leper, perle, repel
EELPS sleep
EELPX expel
EELRT relet
EELRV elver, lever, revel
EELRY leery
EELST leste, sleet, steel, stele
EELSV elves
EELSW Lewes
EELSY seely
EELTT ettle, tetel
EELTU elute
EELTV levet, tevel
EELTW tewel, tweel
EELTX telex
EEMMN mneme
EEMMR emmer
EEMMT emmet
EEMNO noeme
EEMNS mense, mesne, semen
EEMNU neume
EEMNY enemy, Yemen
EEMOR moree
EEMOT emote
EEMOV emove
EEMPT mtepe, Tempe
EEMQU queme
EEMRT meter, metre, terem
EEMRX remex
EEMRY emery
EEMST temse
EEMSU meuse
EENNP penne
EENNW ennew

EENPR neper, preen
EENPS penes
EENPT peent
EENQU queen
EENRS sneer
EENRT enter, terne, treen
EENRU enure
EENRV erven, nerve, never
EENRW renew
EENRY Nyree
EENSS Essen, sense
EENST teens, tense
EENSU ensue
EENSV evens, seven
EENSW sewen
EENTT tenet
EENTU tenue
EENTV event
EENTY teeny
EENUV venue
EENWY weeny
EEOPP opepe
EEOPT topee
EEOPY peeoy
EEORS erose
EEOWW wowee
EEOWY yeeow
EEOXY ox-eye
EEPPY peepy
EEPRS perse, spree
EEPRT peter, petre
EEPRU rupee
EEPRV perve, preve
EEPRY peery
EEPST peste, steep
EEPSW sweep
EEPWY weepy
EEQRU queer, quere
EEQUU queue
EERRT terre
EERRV verre
EERST ester, reset, steer, stere, teres, terse, trees
EERSU reuse
EERSV serve, sever, verse
EERSW sewer
EERSX sexer
EERSY yerse
EERTT treet, trete
EERTU tereu
EERTV evert, revet, terve
EERTW tweer
EERTX exert
EERUV revue
EERVV verve
EERVX vexer
EERVY every, veery
EERWY ewery
EESSX Essex
EESTT teste
EESTV Steve
EESTW ewest, sweet, weest
EESTZ zeste
EETTU tutee
EETTW tweet
EETTY teety
EETUX exute
EETVW wevet
EEUVV veuve
EFFFO feoff
EFFGO Geoff
EFFIR eriff, fifer
EFFNO offen
EFFOR offer
EFFRT treff
EFFRU ruffe
EFGIN feign
EFGIR grief
EFGIU fugie
EFGLM flegm
EFGLO fogle
EFGLU fugle
EFGNU funge
EFGOR forge, gofer
EFGOY fogey
EFGUU fugue
EFHIT thief
EFHLS flesh, shelf
EFHNO foehn
EFHRS fresh
EFHTT theft
EFHTW wheft
EFHTY hefty
EFIIW wifie
EFIKN knife
EFIKR kefir
EFILN elfin, nifle
EFILO folie
EFILP flipe
EFILR filer, flier, lifer, rifle
EFILS flies
EFILT filet, flite, tifle
EFILW wifle
EFILX Felix
EFIMR fermi
EFIMT metif
EFINR finer, infer
EFINT feint
EFINW finew
EFINX fixen
EFIOX foxie
EFIRR firer, frier
EFIRS fries, serif
EFIRT refit
EFIRV fiver
EFIRX fixer
EFIRY fiery, reify
EFIRZ frize
EFIST feist, fiste
EFISV fives
EFIWY wifey
EFKLS skelf
EFKLT kleft
EFKLU fluke
EFKNS fenks
EFLLY felly
EFLMU flume
EFLNO felon
EFLOR forel
EFLOT flote, Oftel
EFLPY flype
EFLRU Fleur
EFLRY ferly, flyer
EFLSS selfs
EFLSW flews
EFLTU flute
EFLTY felty, flyte, lefty
EFLYY feyly
EFMOR forme
EFMRU femur
EFMTU fumet
EFNNY fenny
EFNOR freon
EFNOT often
EFNRS ferns
EFNRY ferny
EFORR frore
EFORT fetor, forte
EFORX forex
EFORY foyer
EFORZ froze
EFOSS fosse
EFRRY ferry, fryer
EFRUZ furze
EFSTU festu, fetus
EFTTY fytte
EGGIU gigue, guige
EGGLO leggo
EGGLY leggy
EGGMY Meggy
EGGNU gunge
EGGOP pogge
EGGOR gorge, grego
EGGOT go-get
EGGOU gouge
EGGPY peggy
EGGRU gurge
EGHHI heigh
EGHHU heugh
EGHHW hewgh
EGHIL leigh
EGHIN hinge, neigh
EGHIT eight
EGHIW weigh
EGHLY hyleg
EGHNO hogen
EGHNT Ghent, thegn
EGHOT goeth, toghe
EGIIN genii
EGIJR rejig
EGIKL klieg
EGIKN eking
EGIKR grike
EGILM gleim
EGILN Elgin, ingle, linge, Nigel
EGILO logie
EGILR liger
EGILS Giles
EGILT gilet, legit
EGILU guile
EGIMM gimme
EGIMN ingem, minge
EGIMR grime
EGINN genin
EGINO genio
EGINP genip, ginep
EGINR Niger, reign
EGINS singe
EGINT tinge
EGINV given
EGINW gwine
EGINY eying, gynie

EGIOR orgie
EGIOV ogive, vogie
EGIPR gripe
EGIRS girse
EGIRT tiger
EGIRV giver, virge
EGISU egusi, guise
EGIUZ guize
EGIVY givey, vygie
EGJOT joget
EGJRU juger
EGKKO gekko
EGKLU kugel
EGKNR kreng
EGKRY gryke
EGLLY gelly
EGLMO glome, golem
EGLMU glume
EGLNO longe
EGLNT glent
EGLNU lunge
EGLOP golpe
EGLOR glore, ogler
EGLOS glose, goles
EGLOT let-go
EGLOV glove
EGLOY elogy, goyle
EGLOZ gloze
EGLPU leg-up
EGLRU gruel, Luger
EGLSU glues, gules, gusle
EGLSY Gyles
EGLUY gluey
EGLWY gwely
EGMMY gemmy
EGMNO emong, gnome
EGMOT gemot
EGMOW gemow
EGMRU grume
EGMRY germy
EGNOR goner, negro
EGNPU unpeg
EGNSU genus, negus
EGNTW Gwent
EGNTY genty
EGNUU Enugu
EGNUY yugen
EGOOS goose
EGOOY gooey
EGOPR grope, porge, prego
EGOPU pogue
EGOPY pogey
EGORR roger
EGORS esrog, gorse
EGORT ergot, etrog
EGORU orgue, rogue, rouge
EGORV grove
EGOSS gesso
EGOST goest
EGOTU togue
EGOTY goety
EGOUV vogue
EGPRU purge
EGPTU get-up
EGPTY Egypt
EGRRU urger
EGRRY Gerry
EGRSU surge
EGRTY tyger
EGRVY gyver
EGSSU guess
EGSTU guest
EGUUX gueux
EHHIT hithe
EHHOY hey-ho
EHHTY hythe
EHIKR hiker
EHIKS sheik
EHIKT Keith, kithe, theik
EHILN Linhe
EHILO helio
EHILT Ithel, lithe
EHILU Elihu
EHILW while
EHILX helix
EHIMN hemin
EHIMO homie
EHIMT meith
EHIMY Hymie
EHINR Henri
EHINS Enshi, shine
EHINT thine
EHINW whine
EHIOS hoise
EHIPT tiphe
EHIRR hirer
EHIRS shire
EHIRT herit, their
EHISS shies
EHIST heist, shite
EHISV hives
EHITT tithe
EHITW white, withe
EHKLW whelk
EHKMR Khmer
EHKOY hokey
EHKSU huske
EHKTY kythe
EHLLO hello
EHLLS shell, she'll
EHLLY helly
EHLMO holme, mohel
EHLMS melsh
EHLMW whelm
EHLNO Holne
EHLOS Sheol
EHLOT helot, hotel, thole
EHLOU Luohe
EHLOV hovel
EHLOW howel, whole
EHLOY holey, hoyle
EHLPW whelp
EHLPY phyle
EHLSW welsh
EHLTW lewth
EHLTY ethyl, lythe
EHLWW whewl
EHLWY Hywel
EHLXY hexyl
EHMMO homme
EHMNS mensh
EHMNY hymen
EHMOR homer, horme
EHMOS Moshe
EHMOT metho
EHMOY homey
EHMPY hempy
EHMRT therm
EHMRU rheum
EHMRY rhyme
EHMST meths
EHMTU humet
EHMTY thyme
EHNNY Henny
EHNOO ohone
EHNOP pheno, pheon, phone, pohen
EHNOR heron
EHNOS hosen, shone
EHNOV hoven
EHNOX hexon
EHNOY honey
EHNRY henry
EHNTT tenth
EHOOR hooer
EHOOS hoose
EHOOV hoove
EHOOY hooey
EHOOZ hooze
EHOPR ephor, hoper
EHOPT tophe
EHORS horse, shore
EHORT other, theor, throe
EHORV hover
EHORW whore
EHOSS shoes
EHOST ethos, those
EHOSU house
EHOSV shove
EHOSW whose
EHOTW theow
EHOUV houve
EHOUZ Ezhou
EHOWW ewhow
EHPRT Perth
EHPRY hyper
EHPST thesp
EHPSY Hepsy
EHPTU het up
EHRSU usher
EHRSW shrew, wersh
EHRSY shyer
EHRTW threw
EHRTZ hertz
EHTTY Hetty
EIILN lie-in
EIILP pilei
EIIMM immie
EIIMN imine
EIINS nisei
EIINT tie-in
EIINX nixie
EIIPX pixie
EIIRU uriei
EIJLU Julie
EIJMO ojime
EIJOS Josie
EIJRV jiver
EIJUV juvie
EIKLN inkle, liken
EIKLP pikel
EIKLR liker
EIKLY kylie
EIKMN minke
EIKMU ukemi
EIKNN inken
EIKNO koine
EIKNP kinep
EIKNR inker
EIKNS skein
EIKNV Kevin, knive
EIKNZ zinke

EIKOP pokie
EIKOR kiore
EIKPR piker
EIKPS kepis, spike
EIKPY epiky, pikey
EIKRR Kerri
EIKRS skier
EIKRT trike
EIKRV kevir, kiver
EIKRY Kyrie
EIKSS skies
EIKST skite
EIKSV skive
EIKSY yikes
EIKTW Kitwe
EILLL Lille
EILLM mille
EILLN Neill
EILLO Ollie
EILLR rille
EILLS Ellis, Lesli, Liesl, lisle
EILLV ville
EILMN limen
EILMP impel
EILMR limer, miler
EILMS limes, miles, slime, smile
EILMU ileum
EILMY Emily, Limey
EILNN linen
EILNO ileon, olein, onlie
EILNR liner
EILNS elsin, lenis, Niles
EILNT elint, inlet, let-in
EILNV Elvin, levin, liven, Nevil
EILNY liney
EILOO looie
EILOR Leroi, oiler, oriel
EILOT Eliot, teloi, toile
EILOU Louie
EILOV olive, voile
EILPR peril, plier
EILPS piles, spiel, spile
EILPT tiple
EILPX pixel
EILQU quile
EILRT liter, litre, relit, tiler
EILRV levir, liver, livre
EILRY Riley
EILSS lisse
EILST islet, istle, stile
EILSU ileus
EILSV Elvis, Levis, lives
EILSW lewis
EILSX lexis, silex
EILTT title
EILTU tuile, utile
EILZZ zizel
EIMMO mimeo
EIMMR immer, mimer
EIMNR miner
EIMNX mixen
EIMNZ mizen
EIMOR moire
EIMOV movie
EIMOX moxie, oxime
EIMPR prime
EIMPT tempi
EIMRS miser
EIMRT merit, miter, mitre, remit, timer
EIMRX mirex, mixer, remix
EIMSS seism, semis
EIMST metis, smite, times
EIMSW weism
EIMSY Mysie
EIMTX mixte
EINNP penni
EINNR inner, irnen
EINNS Ennis
EINNT ennit
EINNU ennui
EINNW innew
EINOP opine
EINOS eosin, noise
EINOT toe-in
EINOV envoi, ovine
EINOX oxine
EINPR piner, ripen
EINPS penis, snipe, spine
EINPT inept
EINPY piney
EINRS resin, rinse, risen, serin, siren
EINRT inert, inter, niter, nitre, Terni, trine
EINRU inure, urine
EINRV riven
EINRW winer
EINST inset, stein, tiens, tsine
EINSU insue
EINSV visne
EINSW sewin, sinew, swine
EINTU intue, unite, untie
EINTV vinet
EINTW twine
EINVW vinew
EINVX vixen
EINVY veiny
EINWY winey
EINWZ winze, wizen
EIOPR poire
EIOPS poise
EIOPZ piezo, poize
EIORS osier, Rosie
EIORU ourie
EIORV vireo
EIOSS Ossie
EIOST toise
EIOTZ zoite
EIOWY yowie
EIOWZ zowie
EIOZZ Ozzie
EIPPR piper
EIPPS Pepsi
EIPQU equip, pique
EIPRR prier
EIPRS peris, Piers, pries, prise, spire
EIPRT perit, tripe
EIPRV viper
EIPRW wiper
EIPRZ prize
EIPSS spies
EIPST piste, spite, stipe
EIPSW swipe
EIPSY yipes
EIPTT petit
EIPTU tie-up
EIPTW pewit
EIPTY piety
EIPXY pyxie
EIQRU quire
EIQSU quies
EIQTU quiet, quite
EIRRS riser
EIRRT Terri, trier
EIRRV river
EIRRW wirer, wrier
EIRST resit
EIRSV vires
EIRSW wiser
EIRSX sixer
EIRSZ sizer
EIRTT titer, titre, trite
EIRTU uteri
EIRTV rivet, tirve
EIRTW twire, write
EIRVV viver
EIRWY wirey
EISST sties
EISSU issue, Susie
EISTT testi
EISTU suite
EISTX exist, sixte
EISTY seity
EISUV Viseu
EISVV vives
EISVW wives
EITTW tewit, twite
EITVX vitex
EIUVX vieux
EIUWW wu-wei
EIVWY viewy

EJKOP kopje
EJKOR joker
EJKOY jokey
EJKRY jerky
EJLLO jello
EJLLY jelly
EJLOP polje
EJLOU joule
EJLOW jowel
EJLPU julep
EJLSU Jules
EJMMY jemmy
EJNNY jenny
EJNOT jeton
EJNOY enjoy
EJORW jower
EJRRY jerry
EJRWY Jewry
EJSSU Jesus
EJTTY jetty
EKKOP kopek
EKKOR koker
EKLLN knell
EKLLV kvell
EKLLY Kelly
EKLNT knelt
EKLOT ketol
EKLOY kyloe, lokey, yokel
EKLPY kelpy
EKLRY lerky
EKLSY kyles
EKLTY ketyl
EKLTZ keltz
EKMNS mensk
EKMOS smoke
EKMPT kempt
EKMPY kempy
EKNNY Kenny
EKNOR krone
EKNOS nokes, snoek
EKNOT tenko, token
EKNOW knowe, woken
EKNRY Kyren
EKNSY ensky
EKOPR poker, proke
EKOPS spoke
EKOPY pokey
EKORT troke
EKORW wroke
EKOST stoke
EKOSY yokes
EKPRY perky
EKPSY pesky
EKPUY pukey
EKRRY Kerry
EKRSY skyer
EKSUY Sukey
EKSYY skyey

ELLMS Mlles, smell
ELLNO nolle
ELLNU lunel
ELLNY nelly
ELLOS losel
ELLOY oleyl
ELLPS spell
ELLQU quell
ELLSW swell, Wells
ELLTU tulle
ELLTY telly
ELLVY velly
ELLWY welly
ELMMU lumme
ELMNO lemon, melon, Monel
ELMNU lumen, Melun
ELMNY Emlyn
ELMOR morel
ELMOS melos, Mosel
ELMOT metol, motel
ELMOU moule, oleum
ELMOY moley, Moyle
ELMPU plume
ELMPY emply
ELMRU lemur
ELMRY Meryl
ELMST smelt
ELMSY Myles
ELMTY melty
ELMUV mvule, velum
ELMUY muley
ELMXY xylem
ELNNY Lenny, Lynne
ELNOP pelon, pleon
ELNOR enrol, loner, Loren, Lorne, nerol
ELNOS lones
ELNOT Elton, lento, olent, tonel
ELNOV novel, Venlo
ELNOW nowel, Olwen
ELNOZ lozen
ELNWY Elwyn, newly
ELOOP Opole, Poole

ELOOS loose
ELOOY looey
ELOPR loper, plore, poler, prole
ELOPS slope
ELOPT plote
ELOPU loupe, poule
ELOPY poley
ELORR Errol
ELORS loser, sorel
ELORU loure
ELORV lover
ELORW lower, rowel
ELORY Elroy, Leroy
ELOSS loess
ELOST stole, telos
ELOSU louse, ousel, Seoul
ELOSV solve
ELOTV volet, volte
ELOTW owlet, towel
ELOTX extol
ELOUV ovule
ELOUZ ouzel
ELOVV volve
ELOVW vowel, wolve
ELOVY lovey
ELPRY lepry, reply
ELPST slept, spelt
ELPSU pulse
ELPSY slype
ELPTU let-up, plute
ELQRU querl
ELRRU lurer, ruler
ELRSY slyer
ELRTU luter
ELRTY tyler
ELRUX lurex
ELSSY lessy, lyses
ELSTY style
ELTTY letty
ELTUX exult
ELTWY tewly, wetly
ELYZZ lezzy
EMMMO momme
EMMOP pomme
EMMOT tomme
EMMSY Emmys

EMNNO nomen
EMNNU numen
EMNOR enorm, morne
EMNOS meson
EMNOT mento, monte
EMNOV venom
EMNOW women
EMNOY emony, money, moyen
EMNPT nempt
EMNRU rumen
EMNTU Tumen, unmet
EMOOR Romeo
EMOOS moose
EMOOY mooey
EMOPR moper, proem, Prome
EMOPS Epsom
EMOPT pomet, tempo
EMOPY myope
EMORR ormer, romer
EMORS meros, mores, morse
EMORT metro
EMORU merou, oumer
EMORV mover, vomer
EMORW mower
EMOSS Moses
EMOST mesto, smote
EMOSU mouse
EMOSY mosey
EMOTT motet, motte, totem
EMOTY motey
EMOZZ mezzo
EMPRS sperm
EMPRU erump
EMPST temps
EMPSU spume
EMPTT tempt
EMPTY empty
EMPUX pumex
EMRRU murre
EMRRY merry
EMRSU serum
EMRSY Emrys
EMRUX murex
EMSSY messy
EMSTU muset
ENNOO no one
ENNOS nones, onsen
ENNOT nonet,

tenno,
tenon,
tonne
ENNOX xenon
ENNPY penny
ENNRU enurn
ENNTY tenny
ENNWY Wynne
ENOOS noose,
osone
ENOOZ ozone
ENOPR preon,
prone
ENOPT tenpo
ENOPU one-up
ENOPY peony
ENORS Norse,
snore
ENORT tenor,
toner,
trone
ENORW owner,
rowen
ENOST onset,
seton,
steno,
stone
ENOSU nouse,
ouens
ENOSY nosey
ENOTU outen
ENOTY toney
ENOVW woven
ENOVY envoy
ENPRU prune
ENPST spent
ENPSY pensy
ENPTU petun
ENPTY n-type,
ypent
ENQRU quern
ENQUU nuque
ENRRU rerun
ENRST nerts,
stern
ENRSU nurse
ENRSY Nerys
ENRTU tuner
ENRTY entry
ENRVY nervy
ENRWY Newry
ENSSU Neuss
ENSTU unset
ENSUV nevus,
Venus
ENSUX nexus,
unsex
ENSWY newsy
ENTTY netty,
tenty
ENTUY tuney
ENTYZ yentz
ENVVY nevvy
EOOPS Espoo
EOOPV poove
EOOPY pooey
EOORW wooer
EOPPR pre-op
EOPPT epopt
EOPRR prore,
repro
EOPRS poser,
prose,
spore
EOPRT Porte,
poter,
repot,
tepor,
toper,
trope
EOPRU pouer
EOPRV prove
EOPRW power,
powre
EOPRY ropey
EOPSS posse
EOPST estop,
pesto,
stoep,
stope
EOPSY poesy,
posey,
sepoy
EOPXY epoxy
EOQRU roque
EOQTU quote,
toque
EORRR error
EORRT retro
EORRV rover
EORRW rower
EORST estro,
store,
torse
EORSU rouse
EORSV servo,
verso
EORSW serow,
sower,
swore,
worse
EORTT ortet,
otter,
torte,
toter
EORTU outer,
route
EORTV overt,
torve,
trove,
voter
EORTW tower,
wrote
EORTX oxter
EORUY you're
EORXX Xerox
EOSSU souse
EOSSY yesso
EOSTT set-to,
testo
EOSTU touse
EOSTV ovest,
stove
EOSTW towse
EOSUY youse
EOTTY toyte
EOUVY you've
EPPPY peppy
EPPRU upper
EPPTY p-type
EPRRU purre
EPRRY perry
EPRSS press
EPRST prest,
strep
EPRSU purse,
sprue,
super
EPRSY pryse
EPRTU erupt
EPRTW twerp
EPRUX preux
EPRXY prexy,
Pyrex
EPSTU set-up,
stupe,
upset
EPSTW swept
EPTTY petty
EPTYY typey
EQRUY query
EQSTU quest
EQTUU tuque
ERRTU truer
ERRTY retry,
terry
ERRVY verry
ERRWY wryer
ERSST tress
ERSTT trest
ERSTU trues
ERSTV verst
ERSTW strew,
trews,
wrest
ERSTY Steyr,
treys
ERSUU eurus
ERTTU tetur,
utter
ERTTY ytter
ERTUV vertu
ERTWY twyer
ERTXY extry
ESSTY styes
ESTTY testy
ESTUX exust
ESTUY suety
ESTWY westy
ESTYY yesty
ESTYZ zesty
ETTTY tetty
FFFLU fluff
FFGIL gliff
FFGIR griff
FFGOO go-off
FFGRU gruff
FFHIT fifth
FFHIW whiff
FFHOW howff
FFHUW whuff
FFHUY huffy
FFIIN finif
FFIJY jiffy
FFIKS skiff
FFILO Oliff
FFIMY miffy
FFINO in-off
FFINS sniff
FFINY niffy
FFIPS spiff
FFIQU quiff
FFIST stiff
FFITY fifty, tiffy
FFLPU pluff
FFNOO on-off
FFNSU snuff
FFOTY toffy
FFPUY puffy
FFRTU truff
FFSTU stuff
FGGOY foggy
FGGUY fuggy
FGHIT fight
FGILN fling
FGINU fungi
FGIRT grift
FGLNO flong
FGLNU flung
FGNOU fungo
FGOOR forgo,
gofor,
groof
FGOOU fogou
FGOOY goofy
FGRTU gruft
FHIIS hi-fis
FHILT filth
FHIRT firth, frith
FHIST shift
FHISY fishy
FHITW whift
FHLOS flosh
FHLSU flush
FHLTU fulth
FHOOS hoofs
FHOOW whoof
FHOOY hoofy
FHORS frosh
FHORT forth,
froth
FHOTT thoft
FHOTU fouth
FHRSU frush
FHSTU fusht
FIILX filix
FIINS finis
FIINX infix
FIITX fixit
FIKLS flisk

FIKRS frisk
FILLR frill
FILLY filly
FILMY filmy
FILNT flint
FILOO folio
FILPS splif
FILRT flirt
FILSU fusil
FILTY fitly
FIMOT motif
FIMTU mufti
FINNY finny
FINSU funis
FINTU unfit
FINTY nifty
FINUX unfix
FINUY unify
FIOST foist
FIPTU fit-up
FIRRY firry
FIRST first, frist
FIRTT fritt
FIRTU fruit
FIRTZ fritz
FIRZZ frizz
FISSU Sufis
FISTW swift
FISTY fisty
FITTY fitty
FIYZZ fizzy
FKLNU flunk
FKLOO kloof
FKLOS folks
FKLOY folky
FKLUY fluky
FKNUY funky
FKORS frosk
FKORY forky
FLLOY folly
FLLUY fully
FLMPU flump
FLNOW flown
FLOOR floor
FLORU flour, fluor, orful
FLORY flory
FLOSS floss
FLOSW fowls
FLOTU flout
FLOTY lofty
FLOWY wolfy
FLRRU flurr
FLRUY furyl
FLTUY fluty
FMOOR froom
FMORU forum
FMORY formy
FMPRU frump
FNNUY funny
FNORS frons
FNORT front
FNORW frown

FNOTU fount, futon
FOOPR proof
FOOPS spoof
FOOPY poofy
FOORS roofs
FOORT to-fro
FOORU ofuro
FOOST foots
FOOTU out of
FOOTY footy
FOOWY woofy
FOPST f-stop
FORRU furor
FORST frost
FORTY forty
FORWY frowy
FOSTY softy
FOTUY fouty
FPRUY fry-up
FRRUY furry
FRSTU frust, turfs
FRSUU Rufus
FRSUY surfy
FRTUY turfy
FRUYZ furzy
FSSUY fussy
FSTUY fusty
FSUUY Yusuf
FTTUY tufty
FUYZZ fuzzy
GGGLU glugg
GGINO going, oggin
GGIOT gigot
GGIPY piggy
GGITY tiggy
GGIWY wiggy
GGLOY loggy
GGMOY moggy
GGMUY muggy
GGNUY gungy
GGORY gorgy
GGOSY soggy
GGOTY toggy
GGPUY puggy
GGTUY tuggy
GGUVY vuggy
GHHIT hight, thigh
GHHOU hough
GHILT light
GHIMT might
GHINS Singh
GHINT night, thing
GHINW whing
GHINY hying
GHIPR griph
GHIPT pight
GHIRS girsh
GHIRT girth, grith, right

GHIST sight
GHITT tight
GHITW wight
GHLLY ghyll
GHLOU ghoul, lough
GHLPY glyph
GHMPU gumph
GHNOT thong
GHOOR ghoor
GHOPU pough
GHORU rough
GHOST ghost
GHOSU sough
GHOTU ought, tough
GHOUW wough
GHRSU grush, shrug
GHSUY gushy
GIILV vigil
GIINO Inigo
GIINP in-pig
GIJNO jingo
GIJNS jings
GIKLS glisk
GIKNY kingy
GILLR grill
GILLY gilly
GILNO lingo, log-in
GILNS sling
GILNT glint
GILNU lungi
GILNY lingy, lying
GILOO igloo
GILOS Sligo
GILOT logit
GILPU pugil
GILPY gilpy
GILRY girly
GILSS gliss
GILST glist
GILTU guilt
GILTZ glitz
GILUX gulix
GIMNY mingy
GIMOS gismo, misgo
GIMOY goyim
GIMOZ gizmo
GIMPU guimp
GIMPY pigmy
GIMRY grimy
GINNO nigon
GINNU Nguni
GINNY Ginny
GINOP gipon, pingo
GINOR groin, O-ring
GINOT ingot, tigon

GINOW owing, wongi
GINOY yogin
GINOZ ginzo, zingo
GINRU ruing, unrig
GINRW wring
GINST sting
GINSU suing
GINSV V-sign
GINSW swing
GINTW twing
GINTY tying
GINVY vying
GINWY wingy
GINYZ zingy
GIOPP gippo
GIOPR pirog
GIOPT topgi
GIORR rigor
GIORT griot
GIORU guiro
GIORV vigor, Virgo
GIOSY yogis
GIPPY gippy
GIPRS sprig
GIPSY gipsy
GIRST grist, grits
GIRSY grisy
GISTU giust, G-suit
GJMUU jugum
GJOSU jougs
GKLNO klong
GKNOO Kongo
GKNUU kungu
GKORU okrug
GLLOY golly
GLLUY gully
GLMOO gloom
GLMOU mogul
GLMPU glump
GLMUY gumly
GLNOO log-on
GLNOU gluon
GLNSU slung
GLNUY lungy
GLOOP gloop
GLOOS Logos
GLOOY gooly, ology
GLORU orgul
GLORW growl
GLORY glory
GLOSS gloss
GLOST glost
GLOTU glout
GLOUV vulgo
GLOUY ougly
GLPUY gulpy
GLRUY gurly, lurgy

GLSUY lygus
GMMUY gummy
GMNOO mongo
GMNOU mungo
GMNUY mungy
GMOOR groom
GMORY gormy
GMPRU grump
GMPYY pygmy
GNNOO ongon
GNNUY gunny
GNOOP pongo
GNOOT not-go
GNOOZ gonzo
GNOPR prong
GNOPY pongy
GNORW grown, wrong
GNORY gyron
GNOST tongs
GNOSY gonys
GNOUY young
GNPUY pungy
GNRTU grunt
GNRUW wrung
GNSTU stung, tsung
GNSUW swung
GOOPR groop, porgo
GOOPY goopy
GOORT groot
GOOSY goosy
GOOTU outgo
GOPPY gyppo
GOPRS sprog
GOPRU group
GOPRY porgy
GORRY gorry
GORSS gross
GORSY gorsy
GORTU grout
GORVY grovy
GOSTU gusto
GOSTY stogy
GOTUY gouty, guyot
GPPUY guppy
GPPYY gyppy
GPSYY gypsy
GRRUY gurry
GRSUY gyrus
GSSUY gussy
GSTUY gusty, gutsy
GTTUY gutty
HHHUU huh-uh, uh-huh
HHISW whish
HHMOU ho-hum
HHMPU humph
HHOOS hoosh
HHORU H-hour
HHSSU shush
HHSTU husht
HHSUW whush
HIILN nihil
HIIMS imshi
HIINN hinin
HIIOP opihi
HIIRS Irish, rishi
HIKLT thilk
HIKNS knish
HIKNT think
HIKRS kirsh, shirk
HIKSW whisk
HILLO hillo
HILLS shill
HILLT illth, thill
HILLY hilly
HILMU hilum
HILOT litho, thiol, tholi
HILRS Shirl
HILRT thirl
HILRW whirl
HILSU hilus
HILTT tilth
HILTY lithy
HIMOS Moshi
HIMPW whimp
HIMRT mirth
HIMST smith
HIMTY mythi, thymi
HINNT ninth
HINNY hinny
HINOR rhino
HINOS noshi
HINOV vinho
HINRT thrin
HINSY shiny
HINWY whiny
HIOPP hippo
HIOPT tophi
HIORS Roshi
HIORU houri
HIOST hoist
HIPPS hipps
HIPPY hippy
HIPQS Q-ship
HIPRT thrip
HIPSW whisp
HIPSY hi-spy
HIPTY pithy
HIQRS qirsh
HIRRS shirr
HIRRW whirr
HIRST hirst, shirt
HISSU sushi
HISSW swish, whiss
HISTW whist, wisht
HISTX sixth
HITWY whity, withy
HIWZZ whizz
HKKOU hokku
HKMOU hokum, khoum
HKNOS shonk
HKNOY honky
HKNSU hunks
HKNTU thunk
HKNUY hunky
HKOOS shook
HKOOY hooky
HKOSV kovsh
HKSUY husky
HLLOO hollo
HLLOU hullo
HLLOY holly
HLMPY lymph
HLMSU mulsh
HLOOY hooly
HLOPR Rolph
HLOPS plosh
HLOPX phlox
HLORW whorl
HLOSS slosh
HLOST sloth
HLOTU Louth
HLOTY hotly
HLOUY yuloh
HLPSU plush
HLPSY sylph
HLRUW whurl
HLRUY hurly
HLSSU slush
HLSUY lushy
HLSYY shyly
HMNOT month
HMNPY nymph
HMOOP oomph
HMOOS moosh
HMOOW whoom
HMOPR morph
HMOPW whomp
HMORU humor, mohur
HMOTU mouth
HMOTY mothy
HMPTU thump
HMPUW whump, wumph
HMPUY humpy
HMRRY myrrh
HMRTU thrum
HMSTU musth
HMSUU humus
HMSUY mushy
HMTYY thymy
HNOOP phono
HNOOR honor, Hoorn
HNOOW nohow
HNOPY phony
HNORS shorn
HNORT north, thorn
HNORY horny
HNOSW shown
HNOSY hyson
HNSTU shunt
HNSTY synth
HOOPS hoops, posho
HOOPT photo
HOOPW whoop
HOORT ortho
HOOSS shoos
HOOST hoots, shoot, sooth
HOOSW whoso, woosh
HOOTT tooth
HOPPY hoppy
HOPRT thorp
HOPSS phoss
HOPSY Sophy
HOQTU quoth
HORRY Horry
HORST horst, short
HORSU hours
HORSY horsy
HORTT troth
HORTW throw, whort, worth, wroth
HOSST shots
HOSTU shout, south, thous
HOSUY yusho
HOSWY showy
HOTTY hotty
HOTUY youth
HPSUY pushy
HQRSU qursh
HRRUY hurry
HRSTU hurst
HRSUY rushy
HRTTU truth
HSSUY hussy
HSTUU Hutus
HSUUW wushu
HUYZZ huzzy
IIIPT ipiti
IIKKN Nikki
IIKKO kikoi
IIKKR Rikki
IIKKV Vikki
IIKLM kilim
IIKNN kinin
IIKNR kirin
IIKNZ Iznik
IIKRR kirri
IIKRT kriti
IIKST tikis
IIKSW kiwis

IILLV villi
IILLW willi
IILMT limit
IILMU ilium
IILNN linin
IILNO ilion
IILNY Linyi
IILTU litui
IIMMN minim
IIMMT immit
IIMMX immix
IIMNS minis
IIMNX inmix
IIMPR primi
IIMPS impis
IIMSX mixis
IIMTZ Izmit,
Mitzi
IINNO inion
IINNS nisin
IINNT innit
IINPT tip-in
IINRV Irvin
IINRW Irwin
IINST sit-in
IINTU Inuit
IINTW inwit
IIORT torii
IIPPT pipit
IIPQU piqui
IIPRU piuri
IISTT titis
IISTV visit
IJLOU julio
IJMMY jimmy
IJNNU Injun
IJNNY jinny
IJNOT joint,
Jonti
IJNPU punji
IJOPP jippo
IJOST joist
IJOTY Jyoti
IKKNS skink
IKKNY kinky
IKKOS kiosk
IKKRU kukri
IKKUU kukui
IKLLR krill
IKLLS skill
IKLLU illuk
IKLMO milko
IKLMY milky
IKLNP plink
IKLNS links,
slink
IKLNY kylin
IKLPU pulik
IKLRS skirl
IKLSY silky
IKLXY kylix
IKMMU mukim
IKMNO ki-mon
IKMNS Minsk
IKMPS skimp
IKMRS smirk
IKMRU kumri
IKMRY mirky
IKMSU kumis
IKMTU mukti
IKNNO Konin
IKNOP pinko
IKNOR korin
IKNPR prink
IKNPS Pinsk
IKNPY pinky
IKNRT trink
IKNST skint,
stink
IKNTW twink
IKNWY winky
IKNYZ zinky
IKOOR iroko
IKPSY kipsy,
spiky
IKPTU tupik
IKQRU quirk
IKRRS skirr
IKRST skirt,
stirk
IKRSY risky
IKRTU Turki
IKRTW twirk
IKRUY Kiryu
IKSSY kissy
IKSTU kusti
IKTTY kitty
ILLMY Milly
ILLPR prill
ILLPS spill
ILLPU pulli
ILLQU quill
ILLRT trill
ILLST still
ILLSW swill
ILLSY silly, slily
ILLTW twill
ILLTY tilly
ILLWY willy
ILMMU limmu
ILMNO limon,
minol
ILMNU linum,
ulmin
ILMOO mooli
ILMPY imply
ILMSY slimy
ILMTZ miltz
ILNOR inrol,
Lorin
ILNOT in-lot
ILNPU lupin
ILNSU Sunil
ILNSY lysin
ILNTU unlit,
until
ILNTY linty
ILNUY Yulin
ILNVY vinyl
ILNYZ Lynzi
ILOOP polio
ILOOV ovoli
ILOPS polis,
spoil
ILOPT pilot
ILOPU poilu
ILOPX oxlip
ILORS loris
ILORT triol
ILORV livor
ILOST islot,
toils
ILOSU louis
ILOSY soily
ILPPU pupil
ILPPY lippy
ILPST spilt,
split
ILPSU pilus
ILPTU tulip
ILQRU quirl
ILQTU quilt
ILRSW swirl
ILRTW twirl
ILRWY wrily
ILSSY lysis
ILSTT stilt
ILSTU sluit,
tulsi
ILSTY silty, styli
ILSUU iulus
ILYZZ Lizzy
IMMNO ommin
IMMSY mimsy
IMMTY Timmy
IMNOO Minoo
IMNOR minor
IMNOS Simon
IMNOT minot
IMNOU onium
IMNSU minus
IMNTY minty
IMNYZ zymin
IMOPR impro,
primo
IMOPT Mopti
IMOPU opium
IMORT timor
IMORZ Mozir
IMOST moist
IMOTU otium
IMOTV vomit
IMPPR primp
IMPRS prism
IMPRU Purim
IMPST timps
IMPUX mix-up
IMPWY wimpy
IMRTY mitry
IMSSY missy,
mysis
IMSTU tuism
IMSTY misty,
stimy
IMVVY mivvy
INNNO ninon
INNNY ninny
INNOO onion
INNOP pinno
INNOR ronin
INNOT niton,
noint
INNOU union
INNOW no-win
INNPU unpin
INNPY pinny
INNQU Quinn
INNRU inrun,
inurn,
run-in
INNSU Sunni
INNTY tinny
INNVY vinny
INNWY winny
INOOP niopo
INOOR Orion
INOOV novio
INOOW ownio
INOPP ippon
INOPR orpin,
porin,
prion
INOPS opsin
INOPT pinto,
piton,
point,
potin
INOQU quoin
INORS rosin
INORT intro,
nitro,
torni
INORY irony
INOSV vison
INOSW Oswin
INOSY noisy
INOTT tinto
INOTX toxin
INPPU pin-up
INPPY nippy
INPRT print
INPRU unrip
INPSY spiny
INPTU input,
put-in
INPUZ unzip
INQTU quint
INSSU nisus,
sinus
INSTT stint
INSTU suint,
Tunis
INTTY nitty
INTUX Tunxi
INTUY unity
INTWY twiny
INUXY Xinyu
INUYZ Zunyi
IOOPT topoi
IOPRR prior

IOPST	opsit, pitso, posit, topis
IOPSU	pious
IOPTT	pitot
IOPTV	pivot
IOQTU	Quito, quoit
IORRS	orris
IORST	torsi
IORSV	visor
IORSZ	zoris
IORVY	ivory
IORVZ	vizor
IOSST	tisso
IOSTV	ovist, visto
IOSUX	Sioux
IOWZZ	wizzo
IPPPY	pippy
IPPTU	tip-up
IPPTY	tippy
IPPUZ	zip-up
IPPYZ	zippy
IPQUU	quipu
IPRSS	priss
IPRST	spirt, sprit, strip
IPRSU	prius, sirup
IPRSY	spiry
IPRTW	twirp
IPRVY	privy
IPSST	spits
IPSSY	pissy
IPSTU	sit-up, Tupis
IPSTY	tipsy
IPSTZ	spitz
IPSWY	wispy
IPSXY	pyxis
IPTTU	putti
IQRTU	quirt
IQSTU	quits, squit
IQSUZ	squiz
IRSTT	trist
IRSTW	wrist
IRSUV	virus
IRTUV	virtu
IRTVY	vitry
IRTYZ	ritzy
ISSSW	Swiss
ISSSY	sissy
ISTTU	Titus, Tutsi
ISTTW	twist
ISTUV	Vitus
ISTXY	sixty, xysti
ISWZZ	swizz
ITTTU	tutti
ITTTY	titty
ITTUZ	ti-tzu
ITTWY	witty
ITYZZ	tizzy
IYZZZ	zizzy
JJUUY	Jujuy
JKLOU	jokul
JKNUY	junky
JLLOO	jollo
JLLOY	jolly
JLOOS	Jools
JLOTY	jolty
JLOWY	jowly
JLSUU	julus
JLSUY	Julys
JMORU	jorum
JMPUY	jumpy
JNOPU	jupon
JNOTU	jotun, junto
JNOTY	jonty
JORRU	juror
JOSTU	joust
JTTUY	jutty
KKKOO	kokko
KKLNU	klunk
KKLSU	skulk
KKMOU	kokum
KKNSU	skunk
KKOOY	kooky
KKRSU	Kursk
KKUYY	yukky
KLLNO	knoll
KLLSU	skull
KLMOU	lokum
KLNOP	plonk
KLNPU	plunk
KLNRU	knurl
KLNSU	slunk
KLOOY	looky
KLOPS	klops
KLOYY	yolky
KLSUY	lusky, sulky
KLTUU	tukul
KLTUZ	klutz
KMOOS	smoko
KMOST	Tomsk
KMOSY	smoky
KMRUY	murky
KMSUY	musky
KNNOW	known
KNNUY	nunky
KNOOR	kroon
KNOOS	snook
KNOOY	nooky
KNOPR	pronk
KNOPS	knosp
KNORR	knorr
KNORT	tronk
KNOSY	yonks
KNOTU	knout
KNOWY	wonky
KNOYZ	zonky
KNPSU	spunk
KNPUY	punky
KNRRU	knurr
KNRTU	trunk
KNSTU	stunk
KNTUU	tunku
KOOPS	spook
KOORR	Koror
KOOSS	kosso
KOOST	stook
KOOSZ	zooks
KOOTT	totok
KOOTW	kotow
KOOTY	Kyoto, Tokyo
KOPRY	porky
KOPSV	Pskov
KORSS	kross
KORST	stork, torsk
KORWY	worky
KOSTU	tokus
KRSUU	kurus
KSTUY	tusky
LLLOY	lolly
LLMOY	molly
LLMUY	mully
LLNOU	nullo
LLNUY	nully
LLOOP	pollo
LLOOR	Rollo
LLOPY	polly
LLOQU	quoll
LLORT	troll
LLORY	Rolly
LLOSY	Lysol, Solly
LLOTY	Tolly, tolyl
LLOUY	you'll
LLOWY	lowly, wolly
LLOXY	xylol
LLRTU	trull
LLSUY	sully
LLSYY	slyly
LLUUU	ululu
LLXYY	xylyl
LMMUY	lummy
LMOOS	Olmos, osmol
LMOOT	molto
LMORU	lorum
LMOST	smolt
LMOSU	Mosul
LMOTU	moult
LMOUY	mouly
LMPPU	plump
LMPSU	slump
LMPUY	lumpy, plumy
LMRUY	murly, rumly
LNNOY	nonyl, nylon
LNOOR	Orlon
LNOOY	loony
LNOPY	pylon
LNOTU	luton
LNOWY	Olwyn
LOOOO	ooloo
LOOOV	ovolo
LOOPR	orlop
LOOPS	sloop, spool
LOOPY	loopy
LOORU	louro
LOOST	lotos, sloot, stool
LOOTT	lotto
LOOWY	wooly
LOPPU	poulp
LOPPY	loppy, polyp
LOPRW	prowl
LOPRY	proly, pylor
LOPSY	polys
LOPTU	plout, Pluto, poult
LOPTZ	plotz
LORRY	lorry
LORUY	loury
LOSSU	solus
LOSSY	lossy
LOSTU	lotus
LOSTY	stylo, tosyl
LOSUY	lousy
LOTTY	Lotty
LOTUY	outly
LOTYZ	zloty
LOUUV	voulu
LPPUY	pulpy
LPRSU	slurp
LPSUU	lupus
LRRUY	lurry
LRSUY	surly
LRTUY	truly
LRWYY	wryly
LSSUU	lusus
LSTUY	lusty
LUVVY	luvvy
MMMOY	mommy
MMMUY	mummy
MMNUY	nummy
MMOOR	mormo
MMOPY	pommy
MMORU	Murom
MMOTY	tommy
MMPSU	mumps
MMRUY	rummy
MMSUY	mumsy
MMTUY	tummy
MMUYY	yummy
MNNOU	onmun
MNOOR	moron
MNOOS	nomos
MNOOT	moton
MNOOY	moony

MNORU mourn
MNORY Myron
MNOTU mount, muton, notum
MNOTY monty
MNOUV novum
MNOWY womyn
MNPSU numps
MOOPR promo
MOORT motor
MOORV vroom
MOORY moory, roomy
MOOSS mosso
MOOTT motto
MOPPY moppy
MOPRT tromp
MOPRY rompy
MOPST stomp
MOPSU mopus
MOPSY mopsy
MORRU rumor
MORST storm
MORSW Worms
MORTU tumor
MORTY Morty
MORWY wormy
MOSSY mossy
MOSUY mousy
MOTTU totum
MOTTY motty
MPRTU trump
MPSTU stump
MPSUY spumy
MPTUY umpty
MRSTU strum
MSSUY mussy
MSTUY musty
MUYZZ muzzy
NNOOS no-nos
NNOSU nouns
NNOSY sonny
NNPUY punny
NNRUY runny
NNSUY sunny
NNTUY tunny
NOOPR ponor, porno
NOOPS snoop, spoon
NOORS Orson
NOORT Troon
NOOST snoot
NOOSW swoon
NOOTT tonto
NOOTY toyon
NOPRY porny
NOPTU punto, put-on, ton-up, Upton
NOPTY ponty
NOQRU Quorn
NORST snort
NORSW sworn
NORTU tourn
NORTY try-on
NORUY yourn
NOSSY sonsy
NOSTU nutso, snout, tonus
NOSTW wonts
NOSTY stony
NOSWY snowy, wyson
NOTWY towny
NPRSU spurn
NPRTU prunt
NPRUU run-up
NPSUU sunup
NPTUY punty
NRTUU U-turn
NRTUY runty
NSTTU stunt
NSTUY nutsy
NTTUY nutty
OOOPT potoo
OOPPY poopy
OOPRS spoor
OOPRT poort, porto, potro, proot, troop, tropo
OOPRV provo
OOPST stoop, topos
OOPSW swoop
OOPTT potto
OOPTY pooty
OOPWY woopy
OORRT rotor
OORRU Oruro
OORRZ zorro
OORST roost, torso
OORTU outro
OORTW wroot
OORTY rooty
OOSTT toots
OOSTY sooty
OOSYY yo-yos
OOTWZ wootz
OOUVY voyou
OOWYZ woozy
OPPPU pop-up
OPPPY poppy
OPPSY popsy, soppy
OPPTU top-up
OPPTY toppy
OPRSS pross
OPRST sport, strop
OPRSY prosy
OPRTY porty
OPRUY roupy
OPRXY proxy
OPSSY possy
OPSTU spout, stoup
OPSTY posty, potsy, topsy
OPSUY soupy
OPSWY Powys
OPTTU putto
OPTTY potty
OPTUW two-up
OPTUY pouty
OPYZZ pozzy
ORRSY sorry
ORRTU Truro
ORRTY rorty, torry
ORRWY worry
ORSSU sorus
ORSTU roust, torus, Tours
ORSTW strow, worst
ORSTY story
ORSUY yours
ORTTU trout, tutor
ORTUY yourt
ORUVW vrouw
OSTTU stout
OSTUY tousy
OSTWY towsy
OTTTY totty
OTWYZ towzy
PPPUY puppy
PPTUU put-up
PPUYY yuppy
PRRUY purry
PRSTU spurt, turps
PRSUU usurp
PRSUY pursy, pyrus, syrup
PRTUY purty
PSSUY pussy
PTTUY putty
RRUVY vurry
RSSTU truss
RSTTU strut, trust
RSTTY tryst
RSTUW wurst
RSTUY rusty
RSUUY usury
RTTUY rutty
SSTUY tussy
SSUWY wussy
TTTUY tutty
UWYZZ wuzzy

SIX LETTERS

AAABBD Baabda
AAABCI cabaia
AAABCL cabala
AAABCN cabana
AAABDH bahada
AAABDJ bajada
AAABDN Abadan
AAABHR habara
AAABLM Ambala
AAABLT albata, atabal, balata, Batala
AAABNN Annaba, banana
AAABNS anabas
AAABNY Abanya
AAABRZ baraza, bazaar
AAABTT batata
AAACCI acacia
AAACDN Canada
AAACJN jacana
AAACLM Calama
AAACLP alpaca
AAACMN macana
AAACMR carama, maraca
AAACNN Canaan
AAACNR arcana
AAACPT pataca
AAADDH hadada
AAADHM hamada
AAADMN Amanda
AAADMR armada, ramada
AAADNN Ananda
AAADNP panada
AAADNR Aranda
AAADPR parada
AAADRT tarada
AAAELZ azalea
AAAGHT Agatha
AAAGLM Malaga
AAAGLR argala
AAAGNN nagana
AAAGNP pa'anga
AAAGRY Yagara
AAAHIT taiaha
AAAHKM hakama
AAAHKS akasha
AAAHLL halala
AAAHLM Mahala
AAAHLW wahala
AAAHNV Havana, vahana
AAAILL alalia
AAAILM Amalia
AAAILR aralia
AAAIMN manaia
AAAINV avania
AAAITW waiata
AAAITX ataxia
AAAJLP pajala
AAAJMU ujamaa
AAAKKN kanaka
AAAKKR karaka
AAAKLM kamala
AAAKLS Alaska
AAAKMR makara
AAAKNR Ankara, karana
AAAKNT katana
AAAKPT pataka
AAAKRW Arawak
AAAKRY karaya
AAALMS masala, salaam
AAALNN alanna
AAALPP palapa
AAAMMN Manama
AAAMNP panama
AAAMNS samaan
AAAMNT ataman
AAAMRS Asmara, samara
AAAMRT Tamara, tarama
AAAMRW wamara
AAAMRY Aymara
AAAMSY Masaya, Sayama
AAAMTT matata
AAANNS ananas
AAANPT patana
AAANTT anatta
AAANTV Vantaa
AAAPPY papaya
AAAPRS apsara
AAARRT Ararat, tarara
AAARST satara
AAARTT tarata
AAARTU aurata
AAARTV avatar
AABBBO baobab
AABBCO babaco
AABBCY abbacy
AABBET abbate
AABBHN hab-nab
AABBLL lablab
AABBLO balboa
AABBLR barbal
AABBNT tabnab
AABBRR barbar, Barbra
AABBST sabbat
AABCEN cabane
AABCER bacare, bareca
AABCHS casbah
AABCIM cambia
AABCIN Bianca
AABCIR Arabic
AABCJO Jacoba
AABCMN cabman
AABCNT Cantab
AABCRS scarab
AABCSS cassab
AABCSU abacus
AABCUU aucuba
AABDER abrade
AABDEU aubade
AABDGO dagoba
AABDIN badian, Ibadan, indaba
AABDIO daboia
AABDIR abraid
AABDLL ballad
AABDLM lambda
AABDMS samba'd
AABDNR bandar
AABDOR aboard, abroad
AABDRT tabard
AABDRY bayard
AABDSS badass
AABEGT tea bag
AABEIL abelia
AABEJR jarabe
AABEKN kabane
AABEKR karabe
AABEKY kebaya
AABELN Albena
AABELR arable
AABELT ablate
AABELZ ablaze
AABEMO amoeba
AABEMT bemata
AABENT abanet, banate
AABERS abrase
AABERT rabate, trabea
AABERU bauera
AABERZ zareba
AABETU bateau
AABFIN Fabian
AABFMR barfam
AABGGR ragbag
AABGGS gasbag
AABGIM Gambia
AABGIR air bag
AABGMN bagman
AABGOZ gazabo
AABGRT ratbag
AABHIS Baha'is
AABHIW Wahabi
AABHJN bhajan
AABHKL labakh
AABHKR khabar
AABHKS kasbah, sabkha
AABHKT bhakta
AABHLR bharal
AABHMR brahma
AABHMS ambash
AABHSW bashaw
AABIKR Kariba
AABILL labial
AABILM liamba
AABILN Albina
AABILR Braila
AABILS sailab
AABILU abulia
AABIMR ambari, Bairam, rambai
AABIMZ Zambia
AABINN banian
AABINS Sabian, Sabina
AABINT Aintab
AABINZ banzai
AABIRS arabis
AABIRZ zariba
AABIST abatis
AABISW wasabi
AABJNX banjax
AABKLN Balkan
AABKMO Bamako

AABKNN kanban
AABLLN ballan
AABLLR labral
AABLMO Malabo
AABLMR rambla
AABLMS balsam, sambal
AABLNY Albany
AABLOR aboral
AABLOS sabalo
AABLOT oblata
AABLOV lavabo
AABLRU Rabaul
AABLST basalt
AABLTT blatta
AABLTU ablaut, tabula
AABMNR barman
AABMNT bantam, batman
AABMOT Ambato
AABMOY Bayamo
AABMRS sambar
AABMRZ zambra
AABMSS sambas
AABMST tsamba
AABMTY Bat Yam
AABNNT bannat
AABNNY banyan
AABORR arroba
AABORT abator, rabato
AABORZ abrazo
AABOSU oubaas
AABRRS barras
AABRTY baryta
AACCDI cicada
AACCDU caduac
AACCEL caecal
AACCHH cha-cha
AACCHM chacma
AACCIL alcaic, cicala
AACCKK ack-ack
AACCLO cloaca
AACCLP calpac
AACCLR calcar
AACCMO macaco
AACCNN cancan
AACCNR carcan, carnac
AACCPY paccay
AACCRT caract
AACDEF facade
AACDEI acedia
AACDEL alcade
AACDEN adance
AACDER arcade
AACDEU cadeau
AACDFR cafard
AACDHR chadar
AACDHT datcha
AACDHU Dachau
AACDIN Candia
AACDIR acarid, cardia
AACDJN cadjan
AACDLU caudal
AACDMP madcap
AACDNR canard, cardan
AACDOP da capo
AACDRY Arcady
AACEFL faecal
AACEFR carafe
AACEHN Aachen
AACEHP Apache
AACEHR areach
AACEHT achate, chaeta
AACEIN Nicaea
AACELN anlace, calean
AACELP palace, placea
AACELS casale
AACELT acetal
AACELY Celaya
AACEMR camera
AACENP panace
AACENR arcane
AACENT catena
AACERS Caesar
AACERT acater
AACEST sacate
AACETU acuate
AACETV caveat, vacate
AACETX exacta
AACETZ zacate
AACFIL cafila, facial
AACFIS fascia
AACFLO afocal
AACFLU facula, faucal
AACFNR Franca
AACFNT caftan
AACFRS fracas
AACFRX carfax
AACFTT fat cat
AACGGM cagmag
AACGHL chagal
AACGHN chagan
AACGIL cigala
AACGIM agamic
AACGIN cangia
AACGIR agaric
AACGIU guaiac
AACGJN cajang
AACGSU Caguas
AACHIK hackia
AACHKN achkan
AACHKR chakra, charka
AACHKW kwacha
AACHLN chalan
AACHLS calash
AACHLT caltha
AACHMN machan
AACHMR chamar
AACHNO choana
AACHNR anarch
AACHNS ashcan, nachas
AACHNZ chazan
AACHRS charas
AACHRT Cathar, charta
AACHTT attach, chatta
AACHTY Cathay
AACIIL Alicia
AACIIM Amicia
AACIJM jicama
AACIJR jicara
AACILL laical
AACILM amical, camail
AACILP apical
AACILR Alaric, racial
AACIMN caiman, mancia, maniac
AACIMR Marcia
AACINR arnica, carina, Ciaran, crania
AACINT natica
AACIOT coaita
AACIPS capias
AACIRS air sac
AACIRT Carita
AACIRV caviar
AACIRZ crazia
AACISS cassia
AACITX ataxic
AACJKL jackal
AACJOU acajou
AACKNR rackan
AACKRR arrack
AACKTT attack
AACLLU calalu
AACLMO maloca
AACLMT lactam
AACLMU macula
AACLNO canola
AACLNR carnal
AACLNT cantal
AACLNU lacuna
AACLOR Carola
AACLOT catalo
AACLPR carpal
AACLPS pascal
AACLPU paucal
AACLRS lascar, rascal, sacral, sarlac, scalar
AACLRU arcual
AACLRV carval
AACLRW acrawl
AACLSU casual, causal
AACLTU actual
AACMNR Marcan
AACMNY cayman
AACMRT amtrac, tarmac
AACNNO ancona
AACNPT catnap
AACNRT cantar
AACNRY canary
AACNST sancta
AACNSV canvas
AACNTT cattan
AACNTU canaut
AACNTV vacant
AACPPY papacy
AACPRS Caspar
AACRSU acarus
AACRSY acrasy
AACRTV cravat
AACSSV cavass
AADDEL daedal
AADDER adread
AADDIL la-di-da
AADDIN danaid, Nadiad
AADDIV Davida
AADDOU aoudad
AADEGL gelada
AADEGM damage
AADEGN agenda
AADEGZ Agadez, agazed
AADELS salade
AADELT alated
AADELV levada
AADEMM Madame
AADEMN anadem, maenad
AADEMR adream, madera
AADEMZ amazed
AADENN Andean, Deanna
AADENR Andrea
AADENS Seanad
AADENT adnate
AADENV Nevada
AADENX adnexa
AADEPR parade
AADEPS espada
AADERU radeau
AADFIR afraid
AADFNT fantad
AADGIO adagio
AADGIR Agadir
AADGLN ladang
AADGLR gradal
AADGMN gadman
AADGMR Dagmar
AADGNN Da Nang
AADGNO dogana
AADGNP padang

AADGNU Uganda
AADGOP pagoda
AADGOR daroga
AADGRU garuda, Guarda
AADHIL dahlia
AADHIN dhania
AADHIS Haidas
AADHKL Dakhla
AADHKM dakhma
AADHKN khanda
AADHKR khadar
AADHMM dhamma
AADHMN dhaman
AADHMR dharma
AADHMS samadh
AADHNN Handan
AADHNO Hadano
AADHNR dharna
AADHNY dhyana
AADHRZ hazard
AADIKV kavadi
AADILR radial
AADILS dalasi
AADIMN Damian, maidan
AADIMR Maradi
AADINR Adrian, radian
AADINS naiads
AADINT aidant
AADINV Davina, navaid
AADINX Daxian
AADIQS qasida
AADIST stadia
AADKMS damask
AADKNU Kaduna
AADKNY yakdan
AADKPU padauk
AADKRW dawark
AADLLS Dallas
AADLLY all-day
AADLMN lamdan
AADLMW wadmal
AADLMY malady
AADLNO anodal
AADLNP pandal
AADLNR Ranald, Randal
AADLNS sandal
AADLNU landau, Luanda
AADLNV vandal
AADLOP apodal
AADLOR adoral
AADLOU Douala
AADLPR pardal
AADLRT tradal
AADLRU radula
AADLSU salaud
AADLYY lay-day
AADMMN madman
AADMMR dammar
AADMNR Armand
AADMNT mandat
AADMNY man-day, Mandya
AADMOR armado
AADMOT adatom
AADMOU amadou
AADMRS madras
AADMRU maraud
AADMRZ mazard
AADMSS admass
AADMYY mayday, May Day
AADNNP pandan
AADNNR randan
AADNOP apodan
AADNPR pandar
AADNRR arrand
AADNRS sandar, Sandra
AADNRT tarand
AADNRU Arnaud
AADNRW Rwanda
AADNRZ Zandra
AADNTU adaunt
AADNTW want ad
AADOPR parado
AADOPS posada
AADPRS prasad
AADPSW padsaw
AADPYY pay day
AADQRU quadra
AADRRS sardar
AADRTU datura
AADRTY datary
AADRVW vaward
AADRWY warday
AADTTU udatta
AAEEGL galeae
AAEEGT eatage
AAEEKK ake-ake
AAEELP paleae
AAEENS Aeneas
AAEEPP paepae
AAEERS sea-ear
AAEERT aerate
AAEEYY aye-aye
AAEFGN fanega
AAEFLM aflame
AAEFLR aflare, Rafael, rafale
AAEFLV favela
AAEFMR A-frame
AAEFNR fraena
AAEFNS sea fan
AAEFNZ Faenza
AAEGGL galega
AAEGGR garage
AAEGGT gagate
AAEGGV gavage
AAEGLL Lalage
AAEGLM agleam
AAEGLN alnage, Angela, anlage, galena, lagena
AAEGLR aglare, alegar, laager
AAEGLT algate, laagte
AAEGLV lavage
AAEGMN manage
AAEGMR Gemara, marage, ramage
AAEGNT agnate, Agneta
AAEGNU Augean, aunage
AAEGOR oarage
AAEGPR parage
AAEGPV pavage
AAEGRU guarea
AAEGRV ravage
AAEGSV savage
AAEGTU gateau
AAEHKP pakeha
AAEHKS ashake
AAEHKT takahe
AAEHKY kehaya
AAEHLM haemal, Mehala
AAEHLT Althea
AAEHMS ashame
AAEHMT athame, hamate
AAEHNT aneath, Anthea, Athena
AAEHNY hyaena
AAEHPR raphae
AAEHPT apheta
AAEHRR Harare
AAEHRT Eartha
AAEHSY Ayesha
AAEHTW Etawah
AAEILM Amalie, Amelia
AAEILR aerial
AAEILX alexia
AAEIMN amaine, anemia
AAEINR Aneira, Ariane
AAEINT taenia
AAEIRS araise
AAEITV aviate
AAEITX axiate
AAEJRV jarave
AAEKLN alkane
AAEKLR karela
AAEKLS aslake
AAEKMW wakame
AAEKNW awaken
AAEKQU aquake
AAEKRT karate
AAEKRV Kerava
AAELLP paella
AAELMP Pamela
AAELMS La Mesa
AAELMT malate, tamale
AAELNN anneal
AAELNS Salena
AAELNT lanate
AAELNV Lavena
AAELOR areola
AAELPP appale, appeal
AAELPT palate, petala, platea
AAELRV larvae, Valera
AAELTT Aletta, atteal
AAELTV valeta
AAEMMM mammae
AAEMMZ mazame
AAEMNP apeman
AAEMNS seaman
AAEMNT amenta
AAEMNX axeman
AAEMRT Matera
AAEMTT attame
AAENNT annate
AAENNZ zenana
AAENOP apnoea
AAENOZ ozaena
AAENPV pavane
AAENRT Renata
AAENSU nausea
AAENTV naveta
AAEOTZ azotea
AAEPPR appear
AAEPRR parera
AAEPRS pasear, sarape
AAEPRT patera
AAEPRZ zarape
AAERRR arrear
AAERRT errata
AAERST astare
AAERTU aurate
AAERTZ zearat
AAERWX earwax
AAERWY aweary
AAESTV Avesta, savate
AAESTW asweat
AAESWY seaway
AAFFIR affair, raffia
AAFFRY affray
AAFGHN Afghan
AAFGNR farang
AAFHIT Fatiha
AAFIJT fajita
AAFIKS sifaka
AAFILM Amalfi
AAFILV Flavia
AAFIMT Fatima
AAFINR farina

AAFIRS safari
AAFITU au fait
AAFKNT kaftan
AAFLLL fal-lal
AAFLNU faunal
AAFLOS fasola
AAFLOT afloat
AAFMNR farman
AAFNNP panfan
AAFNNT fan-tan
AAFNRR Farran
AAFNSU faunas
AAGGKU gagaku
AAGGLO galago
AAGGMN gag man, mganga
AAGGNN gangan
AAGGQU quagga
AAGGRS saggar
AAGGRT ragtag, tagrag
AAGHIL alhagi
AAGHKN khanga
AAGHLZ ghazal
AAGHMR Armagh, Graham
AAGHMS gamash
AAGHNR hangar
AAGHNS sangha
AAGHST aghast
AAGIJT jagati
AAGIKN kainga
AAGILN agnail
AAGILP palagi
AAGILR argali
AAGILU aguila
AAGILV gavial
AAGIMN magian
AAGINN angina, inanga
AAGINR Grania
AAGINS sagina
AAGINT gitana
AAGINU iguana
AAGINV vagina
AAGINW Gawain
AAGIRW waragi
AAGJKN kajang
AAGJRU jaguar
AAGKLN kalgan
AAGKLU Kaluga
AAGKNW kwanga
AAGKRU kagura
AAGLLN lalang
AAGLLP plagal
AAGLMN mangal
AAGLMS malgas
AAGLNO agonal, analog, angola
AAGLNP palang
AAGLNR raglan
AAGLNT galant
AAGLNU laguna
AAGLRT tragal
AAGLST Stalag
AAGLWY Galway
AAGLXY galaxy
AAGMMN gnamma
AAGMMR gramma
AAGMMS magmas
AAGMNR granma, ragman
AAGMNS gasman, sangam
AAGMQU quagma
AAGMRY Magyar, margay
AAGNNO goanna
AAGNNP pannag
AAGNNW wangan
AAGNNY Anyang
AAGNOR angora, organa
AAGNOY Nagoya
AAGNPR parang
AAGNPW pawang
AAGNRS sangar, sarang
AAGNRY angary
AAGNST satang
AAGNTU taguan
AAGNTV vagant
AAGNUY guanay, Guyana
AAGNUZ zaguan
AAGNWY wayang
AAGORU Garoua
AAGOWY go-away
AAGPPR grappa
AAGPRS Gaspar
AAGRRY garrya
AAGRVY vagary
AAHHLV halvah
AAHHNN Hannah
AAHHPT aphtha
AAHHRR rah-rah
AAHHWW haw-haw, wah-wah
AAHHYY hya-hya
AAHIIS Isaiah
AAHIIW Hawaii
AAHIJL alhaji
AAHIKL haikal
AAHIKM kamahi
AAHIKS Akashi
AAHILR Hailar
AAHILT hiatal, tahali
AAHILW halawi
AAHIMS ahimsa
AAHINT tahina
AAHINW haniwa
AAHIOT taihoa
AAHIPR pariah, raphia
AAHIPU pai-hua
AAHIQU hiaqua
AAHIRS sharia
AAHIRV vihara
AAHIRY Raiyah
AAHITW tawhai
AAHJNR hanjar
AAHJRR jarrah
AAHKKY yakkha
AAHKKZ Kazakh
AAHKLP pakhal
AAHKLS khalsa
AAHKMO Oakham
AAHKMS kamash
AAHKNS Kashan
AAHKNU kahuna
AAHKPR khapra
AAHKPS paskha
AAHKSY yaksha
AAHLLL hallal
AAHLLP pallah
AAHLLW wallah
AAHLMM hammal
AAHLMT maltha
AAHLNP phanal
AAHLRS ashlar
AAHLRT hartal
AAHMMM hammam
AAHMNR harman
AAHMNS shaman
AAHMNT mahant
AAHMOR Amroha
AAHMPY mayhap
AAHMRS ashram, Marsha
AAHMRT Martha
AAHMST asthma
AAHNNS Anshan, sannah
AAHNNT Nathan
AAHNOV Navaho
AAHNPS ashpan
AAHNPT Pathan
AAHNPW wanhap
AAHNSS Hassan
AAHNST Santha
AAHNSU Nashua, Shauna
AAHNTV Havant
AAHNZZ hazzan
AAHOSW Oshawa
AAHOTU Tahoua
AAHPPR paraph
AAHPTY apathy
AAHRSS harass
AAHRSU Aarhus, Arusha
AAHSSU Hausas
AAHSSY sashay
AAHWWY yaw-haw
AAIIKZ zaikai
AAIIMM maimai, mia-mia
AAIJNT tinaja
AAIJRT Tarija
AAIJVY Vijaya
AAIKKK kakaki
AAIKLL alkali
AAIKLM kalmia
AAIKLN kalian
AAIKMR Marika
AAIKMT Mitaka
AAIKMY Yakima
AAIKNN Annika
AAIKNR kanari, Karina
AAIKRS askari
AAIKRU uakari
AAIKRY Kariya
AAIKSU kausia
AAILLP pallia
AAILLX axilla
AAILMN animal, lamina, Manila
AAILMP impala
AAILMS alisma, salami
AAILMU aumail
AAILMW Malawi
AAILNR narial
AAILNS Salian, salina
AAILNT antlia, Latina
AAILNV Alvina, Lavina
AAILNY inyala
AAILPR palari
AAILPS palais
AAILQU Aquila
AAILRT atrial, lariat, latria
AAILSS assail
AAILST salita
AAILSV saliva, salvia
AAILTV Latvia
AAIMMR Mariam
AAIMMS miasma
AAIMMX maxima
AAIMNR airman, Armina, Marian, marina, Ramani
AAIMNS Samian
AAIMNT Aminta
AAIMNV vimana
AAIMNX maxina
AAIMPT matapi
AAIMRS Marisa
AAIMRT amrita, Imatra, Marita, tamari
AAIMSS Masais
AAIMTT tatami
AAINNT naiant, Tainan, tannia
AAINOR Oriana
AAINOX anoxia

AAINPP papain
AAINPS paisan
AAINPT patina, taipan
AAINRS Sarina
AAINRT Tirana
AAINRU anuria
AAINRZ Zarina
AAINST istana
AAINTT attain
AAINTW atwain, Taiwan
AAINVY vinaya
AAIOPR aporia
AAIORV ovaria
AAIOTT taotai
AAIPPR appair
AAIPRS parisa
AAIPRT patria
AAIPRU au pair
AAIPRY apiary, piraya
AAIPTY atypia
AAIPZZ piazza
AAIQRT tariqa
AAIRST arista, Sarita, tarsia
AAIRTZ ziarat
AAIRVY aviary
AAIRWY airway
AAISVY Vaisya
AAITUY yautia
AAIWYZ zawiya
AAJJMR jam jar
AAJJWW jaw-jaw
AAJKMN manjak
AAJKNS sanjak
AAJMMR ram-jam
AAJMNP jampan
AAJNNO joanna
AAJNNZ Zanjan
AAJNOV Navajo
AAJNPR prajna
AAJNRU ranjau
AAJOST tasajo
AAJRSW Swaraj
AAKKMR markka
AAKKNN Kankan
AAKKNR kankar, Karnak
AAKKNU kanuka
AAKKOP kakapo
AAKKUU kau-kau
AAKLMO Akmola
AAKLNP palank
AAKLNR Karnal, Lanark
AAKLNY Kalyan
AAKLSU Lusaka
AAKMNU manuka
AAKMRT amtrak, kramat
AAKMRU karamu, kumara
AAKMTU makuta
AAKNOR anorak
AAKNRT kantar
AAKNRU karuna
AAKNSS Kansas
AAKNST askant
AAKNSU Kaunas
AAKNWZ kwanza
AAKOPR pakora
AAKRRS sarkar
AAKRSU sakura
AAKSSV kavass
AAKSSW kawass
AAKTUY yukata
AAKUYZ yakuza
AALLLN Lallan
AALLMM mallam
AALLMR Ramlal
AALLNY anally
AALLOR arolla
AALLOZ azolla
AALLPP appall, lap-lap, palpal
AALLRV larval, vallar
AALLSY sayall
AALLTT atlatl
AALLUU laulau
AALLVV valval
AALMMM mammal
AALMMS Lammas
AALMNP napalm
AALMNS Salman
AALMNU alumna, manual
AALMNW lawman
AALMNY layman
AALMOQ Aqmola
AALMOR amoral
AALMOT amatol, Motala
AALMPR palmar
AALMPS lampas, plasma
AALMRT Ratlam
AALMRU alarum, marula
AALMTY Almaty, Amytal
AALNNS annals
AALNNU annual
AALNOT atonal
AALNOV Avlona
AALNOZ azonal
AALNPR planar
AALNPT platan
AALNRT antral, tarnal
AALNRU ranula
AALNRX larnax
AALNST aslant, santal
AALNTU anlaut
AALOPR apolar
AALOPY payola
AALOVW avowal
AALPPT tappal
AALPPU papula
AALPRT pratal
AALPRU lupara, parula
AALPRY parlay
AALRST astral, tarsal
AALRSV varsal
AALRSW salwar
AALRSY salary
AALRVV valvar
AALSSV vassal
AALSUX saxaul
AALSWY always
AALTUV valuta
AALWYY waylay
AAMMNT amtman
AAMMOO maomao
AAMMRR marram
AAMMRT tammar
AAMMRY Maryam
AAMMST tsamma
AAMMTT tam-tam
AAMMUU mau-mau
AAMMUZ mazuma
AAMNNN mannan
AAMNNP pannam
AAMNOO manoao
AAMNOR oarman, Ramona
AAMNOS Samoan
AAMNOT mantoa
AAMNOZ Amazon
AAMNPS sampan
AAMNPT tampan
AAMNRS ramnas
AAMNRT mantra
AAMNST Tasman
AAMNSU Manaus
AAMNTU mantua, tamanu
AAMNTX taxman
AAMNWZ Mwanza
AAMOPR paramo
AAMORU Maroua
AAMORZ Zamora
AAMOSS samosa
AAMOTT tomata
AAMOTY Yamato
AAMPPS pampas
AAMQSU squama
AAMRSS ramass
AAMRSW aswarm
AAMRSY Ramsay
AAMRTU trauma
AAMSTX mastax
AANNOR Annora
AANNRT ran-tan
AANNRU anuran
AANNTT natant
AANOQY yaqona
AANORT torana
AANORV Novara
AANORX Roxana
AANOST sonata
AANOSV Savona
AANOTT anatto
AANPPS sappan
AANPRS parnas
AANPRT partan, tarpan, trapan
AANPRU Purana
AANPRY panary, panyar
AANPST pantas
AANPSY paysan
AANQST Qantas
AANQTU quanta
AANRRT arrant
AANRRY yarran
AANRST rasant
AANRTT rattan, tantra, tartan
AANRTU Arunta
AANRTY yantra
AANRTZ Tarzan
AANRYZ Ryazan
AANSSU Nassau
AANSTV satnav, savant
AANSTW Tswana
AANSTZ stanza
AANSYY naysay
AANTTU ataunt
AANTUV avaunt
AANWYY anyway
AAOOTT toa-toa
AAOPST sapota
AAOPTW wapato
AAORRU aurora
AAORRV varroa
AAORST aortas
AAORTT totara
AAOTTW Ottawa
AAPPWW pawpaw
AAPRST satrap
AAPRTT attrap, patart
AAPSSU Passau
AAPTTW wattap
AAPWXX paxwax
AAPZZZ pazazz
AAQRSU quasar
AAQSTU asquat
AARRST tarras
AARRTT tartar
AARRWY warray
AARSST assart
AARSSU assura
AARSTT astart, strata
AARSTY astray
AARSWW Warsaw
AARTTT rat-tat
AATWXX taxwax

ABBBEL babble
ABBCEI cabbie
ABBCIR bicarb
ABBCOR cobbra
ABBCOT bobcat
ABBCRY crabby
ABBCSY scabby
ABBDDE dabbed
ABBDEG gabbed
ABBDEJ jabbed
ABBDEL dabble
ABBDEN nabbed
ABBDER barbed, dabber
ABBDES sabbed
ABBDET tabbed
ABBDEU bedaub
ABBDIJ djibba
ABBDJO bad job
ABBEEW bawbee
ABBEGI Gabbie
ABBEGL gabble
ABBEGR gabber
ABBEIN nabbie
ABBEIR barbie, Rabbie
ABBEIY yabbie
ABBEJL jabble
ABBEJR jabber
ABBELR barbel, rabble
ABBELU bauble
ABBERR barber
ABBERT barbet, rabbet
ABBERY babery, yabber
ABBESS abbess
ABBFIY babify
ABBFLY flabby
ABBFYY babyfy
ABBGMU bumbag
ABBGOR gabbro
ABBGRY grabby
ABBHIJ jibbah
ABBHIS babish
ABBHOO haboob
ABBHSY shabby
ABBIIR bibira
ABBILL Lib-Lab
ABBILO Bilbao
ABBIMS Babism
ABBINR rabbin
ABBIRS rabbis
ABBIRT rabbit
ABBITW wabbit
ABBKNY knabby
ABBLOO babool
ABBLRU bulbar
ABBMOO bamboo
ABBMOS bambos
ABBMOX bombax
ABBMOY Bombay
ABBNOO baboon
ABBORS absorb

ABBOTU toubab
ABBRSU busbar
ABCCER baccer
ABCCIU cubica
ABCCLU buccal
ABCCNU buccan
ABCCRU buccra
ABCDEL beclad
ABCDER becard
ABCDEU abduce
ABCDHO bodach
ABCDIR bardic
ABCDTU abduct
ABCEEM became
ABCEFI biface
ABCEGI ice-bag
ABCEGO bocage
ABCEGU cubage
ABCEHL bleach
ABCEHR breach
ABCEIM amebic
ABCEIR caribe
ABCEJT abject
ABCEKN backen
ABCEKR backer
ABCEKT backet
ABCELL becall
ABCELM becalm
ABCEMR camber, cembra, crambe
ABCEMX excamb
ABCENO beacon
ABCERR bracer
ABCFIR fabric
ABCFNO confab
ABCHKU chabuk
ABCHLN blanch
ABCHNR branch
ABCHOR broach
ABCHPU hubcap
ABCHTY batchy
ABCIIM cimbia, iambic
ABCILT Baltic
ABCIMO cambio
ABCIMU cumbia
ABCISU sabicu
ABCKPU backup
ABCKRU buckra
ABCLMY cymbal
ABCLNO blanco
ABCLOT cobalt
ABCMOP mob cap
ABCMOR crambo
ABCMOT combat, tombac
ABCNOR carbon, corban
ABCNOU boucan
ABCORX boxcar
ABCORY carboy
ABCOSU basuco
ABCOUZ bazuco
ABCSSU scubas

ABDDEE beaded
ABDDEI abided, baddie
ABDDEL bladed
ABDDER badder
ABDDEY daybed
ABDDHU Buddha
ABDEEG gadbee
ABDEEH behead
ABDEEK beaked, debeak
ABDEEL beadle
ABDEER bardee
ABDEES debase, seabed
ABDEET debate
ABDEEZ bedaze
ABDEFF bedaff
ABDEGG bad egg, bagged
ABDEGL gabled
ABDEGO bodega
ABDEGR badger
ABDEHS bedash
ABDEIL baldie, diable
ABDEIR air-bed
ABDEIS biased
ABDEKR bedark, debark
ABDELM bedlam, beldam
ABDELO albedo, doable
ABDELR bedlar, bedral
ABDELS sabled
ABDELT tabled
ABDELU belaud
ABDENN banned
ABDENP bedpan
ABDENR bander, Brenda
ABDEPY pay bed
ABDERR barred
ABDERU dauber
ABDERV adverb
ABDEST bestad
ABDETT batted
ABDETU tabued
ABDFOR forbad
ABDGNO bandog
ABDGOR bodrag
ABDGOW gobdaw
ABDHOY hobday
ABDHSU dubash
ABDIIM diiamb
ABDILR bridal, ribald
ABDINR riband
ABDINT bandit
ABDIRR braird
ABDIRS disbar
ABDLLY baldly
ABDLOT bad lot

ABDLRY drably
ABDMRU rumba'd
ABDNOU abound
ABDNRU Durban
ABDNRY brandy
ABDOOR abrood
ABDORR bordar
ABDORS adsorb
ABDORY byroad
ABDOSY Abydos
ABDOTU a doubt
ABDOYY day-boy
ABDRRU durbar
ABDRSU absurd
ABDRWY bawdry
ABEEGL beagle
ABEEGR bargee
ABEEHV behave
ABEEIL bailee
ABEEIN beanie
ABEEKR beaker
ABEEKT betake
ABEELM embale, mabele
ABEELN baleen, enable
ABEELT belate
ABEEMN bemean, bename
ABEEMR beamer
ABEEMS embase
ABEENT beaten
ABEENU Beaune
ABEEOR aerobe
ABEERR bearer
ABEERS rebase
ABEERT beater, berate, rebate
ABEERV beaver
ABEERW beware
ABEERZ zereba
ABEFFL baffle
ABEFHL behalf
ABEFLL befall
ABEFLM famble
ABEFLR fabler
ABEFMO befoam
ABEFPR prefab
ABEGGN gebang
ABEGGR beggar
ABEGHI abeigh
ABEGHN behang
ABEGIN ganbei
ABEGLM gamble
ABEGLN bangle
ABEGLR garble
ABEGLT gablet
ABEGLU beluga, blague
ABEGMR Amberg, bregma
ABEGNR banger, graben
ABEGNS besang

ABEGNW begnaw
ABEGOR borage
ABEGOZ gazebo
ABEGRT braget
ABEGRZ Zagreb
ABEGTU tubage
ABEHII Beihai
ABEHIL habile
ABEHIT Bethia
ABEHKS sebkha
ABEHLM hamble
ABEHLR herbal
ABEHLU Beulah
ABEHNO hebona
ABEHNT Bethan, Theban
ABEHRT bather, bertha, breath
ABEIIL bailie
ABEIIT tibiae
ABEIJL jalebi
ABEILL alible, Belial, labile, liable
ABEILN Blaine, inable
ABEILR bailer
ABEILS abseil, Blaise, Isabel
ABEILT albeit, albite, libate
ABEILV viable
ABEILW bewail
ABEILY bailey
ABEIMS imbase
ABEINS sabine
ABEINT Benita, binate
ABEIOT boatie
ABEIRR Barrie
ABEIRS braise, rabies, Serbia
ABEIRT barite
ABEJMN enjamb
ABEJMR jamber
ABEJNT bejant
ABEJOR jerboa
ABEJRS jabers
ABEJRU abjure
ABEKLR barkle
ABEKLY blakey
ABEKMN embank
ABEKMR embark
ABEKNR banker
ABEKNT banket
ABEKRR barker
ABEKRY bakery
ABEKST basket
ABELLM emball
ABELLT ballet
ABELMM embalm
ABELMR lamber, marble, ramble
ABELMU bemaul
ABELMW wamble
ABELMY belamy
ABELNR branle
ABELNU Nabeul, nebula, unable
ABELNY by-lane
ABELOR boreal
ABELOT boatel, lobate, oblate
ABELRR barrel
ABELRT albert, balter, batler, labret, tabler
ABELRV verbal
ABELRW warble
ABELRY barely, barley, bleary
ABELRZ blazer
ABELST ablest, stable
ABELSU suable, usable
ABELSY basely
ABELTT batlet, battel, battle, tablet
ABELTU ablute, tabule
ABELTY baetyl
ABELWY bawley, bye-law
ABEMNO bemoan
ABEMNR embarn
ABEMNY byname
ABEMOY Abomey
ABEMRR marbre
ABEMRT tamber
ABEMRU merbau, umbrae
ABEMRY embrya
ABEMSU absume
ABEMYZ abzyme
ABENNR banner
ABENOR borane
ABENOT boneta
ABENRR barren
ABENRT banter, barnet
ABENRU urbane
ABENRY barney, nearby
ABENRZ brazen
ABENST absent, basnet
ABENSY Naseby
ABENTT batten
ABENTU butane
ABENTZ bezant
ABEOPR peroba
ABEORT boater, borate
ABEORZ bezoar
ABEOSS Sasebo
ABEOTT battoe
ABEOTV bovate
ABEPRT betrap
ABEPRW bewrap
ABEPTU beat-up, upbeat
ABEQRU barque
ABEQSU basque
ABERRT barret, barter
ABERST baster, bestar, breast
ABERSU abuser, bursae
ABERSZ zebras
ABERTT batter, tabret
ABERTU Aubert
ABERTX baxter
ABERTY baryte, betray
ABERUU bureau
ABERUY Aubrey
ABERWY bewray
ABERZZ Zabrze
ABESSS basses
ABESST basset
ABETTU battue
ABETTY Beatty
ABETUY beauty
ABEUXY Bayeux
ABFGLU bagful
ABFILU fibula
ABFIMS fabism
ABFLNO Fablon
ABFLRY barfly
ABGGIT baggit, gag-bit
ABGGNO gobang
ABGGOR Gro-bag
ABGHNY banghy
ABGIIL Galibi
ABGIKN baking
ABGIKT kitbag
ABGILM gimbal
ABGIMT gambit
ABGIMU ambigu
ABGIMY bigamy
ABGINO bagnio, gabion
ABGINT bating
ABGINU Bangui
ABGIOS biogas
ABGIOU Baguio
ABGKNO kobang
ABGKOO bog oak
ABGKUU bugaku
ABGLLO global
ABGLMO gambol
ABGLOR brolga
ABGLOU albugo
ABGLRU bulgar
ABGMUY May-bug
ABGNOR Bangor, brogan
ABGNPU bang-up
ABGOOT Bogota
ABGRSU Burgas
ABHIJS bhajis
ABHIKL kiblah
ABHIKT bhakti, khatib
ABHIMR mihrab
ABHINS banish
ABHIOO boohai
ABHIOP phobia
ABHLOP Bhopal
ABHLSU ablush
ABHMNO bonham
ABHMOU Huambo
ABHMRU rhumba
ABHMSU ambush
ABHNTU Bhutan
ABHOOS bhoosa
ABHORR harbor
ABHORT athrob, Hobart
ABHOST bathos
ABHOTX hatbox
ABHOXY haybox
ABHPTY bypath
ABHSSU Subhas
ABHSUW bushwa
ABHTUU Bahutu
ABIILS alibis
ABIILT tibial
ABIINY Baiyin
ABIJNT tanjib
ABIJOW Ojibwa
ABIJRU jabiru
ABIKKU kabuki
ABIKMN imbank
ABIKMO akimbo
ABIKMR imbark
ABIKRS Biskra
ABILLM limbal
ABILLR libral
ABILLY bailly
ABILMM imbalm
ABILMN in-lamb
ABILMS ablism
ABILMT timbal
ABILMU labium
ABILNO albino, Albion
ABILNR Libran
ABILNS ablins
ABILNY bylina, Libyan
ABILOR bailor

ABILOT obital
ABILRT tribal
ABILRU burial
ABILRZ brazil
ABILVY viably
ABIMMR mimbar
ABIMNN binman
ABIMNR imbarn, minbar
ABIMPT bitmap
ABIMRU barium
ABIMSU iambus
ABIMUY imbuya
ABINNT binant
ABINOR Robina
ABINOS bonsai
ABINOT Bonita, obtain
ABINRY binary, brainy
ABIORR barrio
ABIORS isobar
ABIORT aborti, tiorba
ABIOST Tobias
ABIRSU Airbus
ABIRTU rubati
ABISSU Bissau
ABJJOO jojoba
ABJLMU jumbal
ABJLNU Banjul
ABJOZZ jazzbo
ABKLNY blanky
ABKLTY by-talk
ABKLUY baulky
ABKLWY by-walk
ABKMRU barkum
ABKMSU sambuk
ABKMTU tumbak
ABKMUZ zambuk
ABKNRS branks
ABKOOR abrook
ABKORU bur oak
ABKRST Bratsk
ABKUUV Bukavu
ABLLMU lumbal
ABLLNO ballon, no-ball
ABLLOO lobola
ABLLOT ballot
ABLLOW ballow, bowall
ABLLSY ballsy
ABLMOO abloom
ABLMOP aplomb
ABLMOW mob law
ABLMOY Yambol
ABLMRU brumal, labrum, lumbar, umbral
ABLMRY marbly
ABLMTY tymbal
ABLMWY wambly
ABLNOZ blazon
ABLNSU Nablus
ABLNTU buntal
ABLOPR probal
ABLORU labour
ABLORW barlow
ABLOST oblast
ABLOTT talbot
ABLPRU burlap
ABLPYY byplay
ABLRSU bursal
ABLRSY labrys
ABLRTU brutal
ABLRUY Albury
ABLRWY byrlaw
ABLSTY stably
ABLSYY lay-bys
ABMMOO moomba
ABMNOW bowman
ABMNRU Burman
ABMNSU busman, subman
ABMNTU numbat, tubman
ABMOOS abosom
ABMOOW waboom
ABMOOZ bazoom
ABMOTV Tambov
ABMOTW wombat
ABMPRU bum rap
ABMQSU sambuq
ABMRSU rumbas, sambur, umbras
ABMRUY ambury, aumbry, bay rum
ABNOOT batoon
ABNORR Barron
ABNORT barton
ABNORY barony, baryon
ABNOST baston
ABNOSU bauson
ABNOSW bawson
ABNOTY botany
ABNRTU turban
ABNRUU auburn
ABNRUY anbury
ABNRWY brawny
ABNSTU Bantus
ABNTYZ byzant
ABOOST taboos
ABOOTT taboot
ABOOTU Baotou
ABORRU arbour
ABORRW barrow
ABORSV Brasov
ABORTU rubato, tabour
ABORTW tow bar
ABORUY Yoruba
ABOSTU abouts
ABOSWW bowsaw
ABPRTU abrupt
ABPSSY bypass, pass-by
ABPSTY bypast
ABRRSU burras, bursar
ABRSSU bursas
ABRSSY brassy
ABRTTY bratty
ABSSSU bassus
ABSUWY subway
ACCCIL calcic
ACCCLO coccal
ACCDEE accede
ACCDEN accend
ACCDII acidic
ACCDOR accord
ACCEHL cleach
ACCEHN chance
ACCEHT cachet
ACCEIL calice, celiac
ACCEIN Canice
ACCEIP ice cap, ipecac
ACCEIT accite, acetic, cat-ice
ACCEKL cackle
ACCELN cancel
ACCELS calces
ACCEMU caecum
ACCENR cancer, crance
ACCENS scance
ACCENT accent
ACCENU Cuenca
ACCEPT accept
ACCERS scarce
ACCERU accrue
ACCESS access
ACCESU accuse
ACCGNO cognac
ACCHHI chicha
ACCHIK chiack
ACCHKO chocka
ACCHLT clatch
ACCHNO concha
ACCHNR cranch
ACCHNY chancy
ACCHOU cachou
ACCHRT cratch
ACCHTU cutcha
ACCHTY catchy
ACCIIN Incaic
ACCILO accoil, calico
ACCILS scalic
ACCILT lactic
ACCINW Wiccan
ACCINY cyanic
ACCIPR capric
ACCIRR circar, ricrac
ACCIRT Arctic
ACCITT tactic, tic-tac
ACCITU cicuta
ACCIZZ ziczac
ACCKLO cockal
ACCKMO macock
ACCKNU Canuck
ACCKRT crackt
ACCKRY cracky
ACCLLO accoll
ACCLOU coucal
ACCLOY accloy
ACCLSY cyclas
ACCMOR Cormac
ACCMOY occamy
ACCOOS cocoas
ACCORS corsac
ACCORT coarct
ACCORW Cracow
ACCORY ocracy
ACCOST accost
ACCRUY curacy
ACCSTU cactus
ACCSUU caucus
ACDDEE decade
ACDDEI caddie
ACDDEL caddle
ACDDEU adduce
ACDDII diacid, diadic
ACDDIN candid
ACDDIS caddis
ACDDIT addict
ACDDIY dyadic
ACDDOW caddow
ACDDTU adduct
ACDEEF deface
ACDEEN decane
ACDEFF decaff
ACDEGR cadger, graced
ACDEGT gedact
ACDEHT detach
ACDEIM decima, medica
ACDEIN decani
ACDEIR cardie
ACDEIT dacite
ACDEIV advice
ACDEJK jacked
ACDEJT adject
ACDEKP packed
ACDEKR dacker
ACDELL Cadell
ACDELN candle, Declan
ACDELR cradle, credal
ACDELS scaled
ACDELT talced
ACDELU caudle, cedula, Claude
ACDELV calved
ACDELW clawed

ACDEMN Camden
ACDEMP decamp
ACDENN canned
ACDENO canoed, deacon
ACDENR cedarn, dancer
ACDENS ascend
ACDENT cadent, decant
ACDEOT coated
ACDEPP capped
ACDEPR redcap
ACDEPU ducape
ACDERR carder, Redcar
ACDERS sacred, scared
ACDERT cedrat, redact
ACDETT catted
ACDEUX caudex
ACDFIR fracid
ACDFNU facund
ACDGIO cogida
ACDGNO conga'd
ACDHIR diarch
ACDHMR drachm
ACDHOR chador, chorda
ACDHRT dratch
ACDIIM miacid
ACDIIP adipic
ACDIJU Judaic
ACDILP placid
ACDILS discal
ACDILU lucida
ACDILY acidly
ACDIMR marcid
ACDINO anodic
ACDINR rancid
ACDIOR cordia
ACDIOT dacoit
ACDIOZ zodiac
ACDIPR caprid
ACDIPS capsid
ACDIPU picuda
ACDIRR criard
ACDIST dicast
ACDKOU cadouk
ACDLNO dolcan
ACDLNU unclad
ACDLOR cordal
ACDLTY dactyl
ACDNNU Duncan
ACDNOR candor, Conrad
ACDNUY dauncy
ACDORS Dorcas
ACDORW Cawdor, coward
ACDORX cordax
ACEEFF efface
ACEEFN enface
ACEEFR reface
ACEEFS faeces
ACEEFT facete
ACEEFX Ceefax
ACEEGI ice age
ACEEGN encage
ACEEHK hackee
ACEEHL chelae
ACEEHN achene
ACEEHT teache, thecae
ACEEIP apiece
ACEEIX ice axe
ACEEJT ejecta
ACEELN elance, enlace
ACEELP placee
ACEELR alerce, cereal
ACEELV cleave
ACEEMN menace
ACEEMR amerce, raceme
ACEEMT mecate
ACEEMZ eczema
ACEENR careen
ACEENS Cesena, encase, seance
ACEENT cetane, tenace
ACEENV encave
ACEEOT coatee
ACEEPS escape
ACEERR career
ACEERS crease, searce
ACEERT cerate, create
ACEERV caveer, creave
ACEEVX excave
ACEFFL caffle
ACEFFT affect
ACEFHR chafer, frache
ACEFIL facile, fecial, filace
ACEFIN inface
ACEFIR fiacre
ACEFIS facies, scaife
ACEFLS falces
ACEFLU fecula
ACEFNR France
ACEFSS fasces
ACEFST fascet
ACEFSU fauces
ACEFTU faucet, fucate
ACEGHN change
ACEGHR charge, creagh
ACEGHU gauche
ACEGIL Gaelic
ACEGIN incage
ACEGIR cagier, Gracie
ACEGLN glance
ACEGLY legacy
ACEGNU cangue, uncage
ACEGNY agency
ACEGOS socage
ACEGOW cowage
ACEHIK hackie
ACEHIL heliac
ACEHIM haemic
ACEHIP paiche, piache
ACEHIR archei, Archie, cahier
ACEHIS chaise
ACEHKL hackle, lekach
ACEHKR hacker
ACEHLP chapel, pleach
ACEHLR rachel
ACEHLS cashel, chelas, laches
ACEHLT chalet
ACEHLV chavel, cheval
ACEHMN manche
ACEHMR macher
ACEHMS maches, sachem, schema
ACEHNP pechan
ACEHNR chenar, enarch
ACEHNS encash, naches
ACEHOP cheapo
ACEHOR chorea, Horace, ochrea, orache
ACEHOT choate
ACEHPR eparch, preach
ACEHPS Pesach
ACEHPT hepcat
ACEHPY peachy
ACEHQU queach
ACEHRR archer
ACEHRS chaser, eschar, search
ACEHRT charet
ACEHRV chevra
ACEHRX exarch
ACEHSS chasse
ACEHST chaste, sachet, scathe
ACEHSW cashew
ACEIJK Jackie
ACEIJN Janice
ACEIKP packie
ACEIKS sackie
ACEIKT tackie
ACEILL allice
ACEILM maleic, malice
ACEILN ancile, Celina
ACEILP epical, piacle, plaice
ACEILR Claire, lacier
ACEILT laetic
ACEIMN anemic, cinema, iceman, incame
ACEIMR Marcie, Mercia
ACEIMS camise
ACEIMT acmite
ACEIMU aecium
ACEINN Annice, canine, neanic
ACEINO caoine
ACEINR carnie, Racine
ACEINS casein, incase
ACEINV cave-in, incave
ACEINX axenic
ACEIPR pacier
ACEIPS apices
ACEIPT capite
ACEIQU caique
ACEIRR Carrie, racier
ACEIRS caries
ACEISS cassie
ACEISV vesica
ACEITV active
ACEIVV vivace
ACEJKT jacket
ACEJLO cajole
ACEJNT jacent
ACEJNU jaunce
ACEKLM mackle
ACEKLR lacker, rackle
ACEKLT tackle
ACEKLY lackey
ACEKNO nocake
ACEKNR canker
ACEKNT nacket
ACEKPR packer, repack
ACEKPT packet
ACEKRS ackers, screak

ACEKRT racket, tacker
ACEKRW wacker
ACEKRY creaky, yacker
ACEKST casket, sacket
ACEKTT tacket
ACELLO locale
ACELLR caller, cellar, recall
ACELLT callet
ACELLV clavel
ACELMP cample
ACELMR Carmel, marcel
ACELMS mascle, mescal
ACELMT camlet
ACELMU macule
ACELNN cannel
ACELNR carnel, lancer, rancel
ACELNS lances
ACELNT cantle, cental, lancet
ACELNU auncel, cuneal, lacune, launce, unlace
ACELOR Carole, coaler, coreal, oracle
ACELOS solace
ACELOT coleta, locate
ACELOV alcove, coeval
ACELPR carpel, parcel, placer
ACELPT placet
ACELPU lace-up
ACELQU calque, claque
ACELRR carrel
ACELRS sarcle, scaler, sclera
ACELRT cartel, cartle, claret, rectal
ACELRV calver, carvel, claver
ACELST castle
ACELSU casule, caules, clause
ACELSV calves
ACELSY scaley
ACELTT cattle
ACELTU cautel
ACELTY acetyl
ACELYY clayey
ACEMNO ancome
ACEMNP encamp
ACEMNR Carmen
ACEMNU acumen
ACEMOP pomace
ACEMOS cosmea
ACEMOT co-mate, tecoma
ACEMPR camper
ACEMRS scream
ACEMRY amercy, creamy
ACEMSU muscae
ACEMTU mucate
ACENNO ancone
ACENNR canner
ACENNT annect
ACENNU nuance
ACENOR cornea
ACENOS canoes
ACENOT octane
ACENPR prance
ACENPT pantec
ACENRS casern
ACENRT canter, carnet, centra, Cretan, nectar, recant, tanrec, trance
ACENRV carven, cavern, craven
ACENRY carney
ACENST ascent, secant, stance
ACENSU uncase, usance
ACENUV vaunce
ACEOPS Pascoe, scopae
ACEOPT capote, toecap
ACEORS coarse, rosace
ACEORV acover
ACEORX coaxer
ACEOST costae
ACEOSW sea cow
ACEOTU coteau
ACEOTV avocet, octave
ACEPPR capper
ACEPRR carper
ACEPRS capers, Casper, escarp, parsec, scarpe, scrape, spacer
ACEPRT carpet, peract
ACEPST aspect
ACEPSY spacey
ACEPTU teacup
ACEQSU casque
ACERRS scarer
ACERRT arrect, carter, crater, tracer
ACERRU curare
ACERRV carver, craver
ACERRY crayer
ACERSS caress, crases
ACERST caster, recast
ACERSU causer, saucer
ACERSY carsey
ACERSZ scraze
ACERTU acuter, cauter, curate
ACERTY catery, Tracey
ACESTU cuesta
ACESTX sex act
ACESTY cytase, Stacey
ACESUY causey
ACETXY extacy
ACFFHY chaffy
ACFFLS sclaff
ACFFOP off-cap
ACFFSY scaffy
ACFGIN facing
ACFHLN flanch
ACFHRT fratch
ACFILN in-calf
ACFILS fiscal
ACFIOS fiasco
ACFIPY pacify
ACFIST factis
ACFLNO falcon, flacon
ACFLOT olfact
ACFLPU capful
ACFLRU carful, fulcra
ACFMTU factum
ACFNOR franco
ACFORT factor
ACFORX carfox
ACFRRY far cry
ACFRSS scarfs
ACFRTY crafty
ACGGIO agogic
ACGGRY craggy
ACGHLS schlag
ACGHNU chaung, gaunch
ACGHOT gotcha
ACGHOU gaucho
ACGHTU caught
ACGIIM imagic
ACGILL gallic
ACGILN lacing
ACGILR garlic
ACGILS glacis
ACGILY cagily
ACGINN caning
ACGINO agonic
ACGINP pacing
ACGINR arcing, caring, racing
ACGINS casing
ACGINT acting
ACGINV caving
ACGIOR orgiac
ACGIRT tragic
ACGLNU glucan
ACGLNY glycan
ACGMNO magcon
ACGNOS congas, Gascon
ACGORT go-cart
ACGORU cougar
ACGTTU catgut
ACHHIS hachis
ACHHNU haunch
ACHHOT hotcha
ACHHOU Chaohu
ACHHTT thatch
ACHIIS ischia
ACHIIT t'ai chi
ACHIJK hijack
ACHIKN chikan
ACHIKO koi-cha
ACHIKP phakic
ACHIKU chauki
ACHIKW Hawick
ACHILO lochia
ACHILP caliph
ACHILR archil, chiral
ACHILT chital
ACHINR chinar, inarch
ACHINT canthi
ACHIPS phasic
ACHIPT haptic, pathic, phatic
ACHIQU quaich
ACHIRS Charis, rachis
ACHIST taisch
ACHISU chiaus
ACHITY cyathi
ACHIUW uchiwa
ACHKKU chukka

ACHKLO	kolach
ACHKLT	klatch
ACHKLY	chalky, hackly
ACHKOR	chokra
ACHKOW	whacko
ACHKOY	choaky
ACHKRT	thrack
ACHKRU	chukar
ACHKTU	kutcha
ACHKTW	thwack
ACHKWY	whacky
ACHLLO	cholla
ACHLNO	chalon, lochan
ACHLNP	planch
ACHLNU	launch, nuchal
ACHLOO	choola
ACHLOR	choral, lorcha
ACHLOT	cloath
ACHLRY	archly
ACHMNU	chunam, Manchu, maunch
ACHMOO	moocha
ACHMOR	chroma
ACHMRU	chumar
ACHMSU	sumach
ACHNOR	anchor, archon, rancho
ACHNOT	chaton
ACHNOU	cahoun
ACHNPU	paunch
ACHNRT	tranch
ACHNRU	raunch
ACHNRY	ranchy
ACHNSS	schans
ACHNST	snatch, stanch
ACHNTU	chaunt, nautch
ACHNTY	chanty
ACHOOT	cahoot
ACHOPR	carhop
ACHOPY	poachy
ACHORR	charro
ACHORS	Sorcha
ACHORT	trocha
ACHOUV	avouch
ACHPPY	chappy
ACHPSY	scypha
ACHPTU	chat-up
ACHPTY	patchy
ACHRRY	charry
ACHRST	scarth, starch
ACHSTU	cushat, saucht
ACHSTW	swatch
ACHSTY	chasty
ACHSUW	cushaw
ACHTTY	chatty
ACIIKN	kainic
ACIILN	anilic
ACIILS	silica
ACIILT	italic
ACIILV	clivia
ACIINN	niacin
ACIIRT	iatric, Tricia
ACIITV	viatic
ACIJNS	Jancis
ACIJOR	jicaro
ACIJQU	Jacqui
ACIKLN	calkin
ACIKMP	impack
ACIKMR	karmic
ACIKNP	ink-cap
ACIKNR	nickar
ACIKNT	catkin
ACIKOP	paiock
ACIKPX	pickax
ACIKTT	kit-cat
ACILLN	clinal, incall
ACILLS	scilla
ACILLY	lacily
ACILMT	lactim
ACILMX	climax
ACILNO	Colina, Nicola, oil can
ACILNP	caplin
ACILNR	crinal
ACILNT	tincal
ACILNU	Lucian, Lucina, uncial
ACILNV	Calvin
ACILOR	corial, lorica
ACILOS	scolia, social
ACILOT	coital
ACILOX	oxalic
ACILPR	picral
ACILPT	placit, platic
ACILRT	citral, rictal
ACILRU	curial, lauric, Ulrica, uracil
ACILRY	racily
ACILSU	caulis
ACILSV	clavis, Slavic
ACIMNO	anomic, camion, manioc, Monica
ACIMNP	incamp
ACIMNT	mantic
ACIMOR	Romaic
ACIMOS	camois, mosaic
ACIMOT	atomic, matico
ACIMOV	vomica
ACIMPS	scampi
ACIMPT	impact
ACIMRS	racism
ACIMRT	matric
ACIMRY	myrica
ACIMSS	Cassim
ACIMST	mastic
ACIMSU	musica
ACINNR	incarn
ACINNT	incant, tannic, tin can
ACINNY	cyanin
ACINOR	rancio
ACINOS	casino
ACINOT	action, atonic, cation
ACINOX	anoxic
ACINOZ	azonic
ACINPS	panisc
ACINPT	catnip
ACINRS	Cairns
ACINRT	Catrin
ACINRU	uranic
ACINST	nastic
ACINSU	acinus
ACINTT	intact
ACINTU	anicut, nautic, tunica
ACIOPR	picaro
ACIOPT	copita
ACIORS	scoria
ACIORT	aortic
ACIOST	coatis, scotia
ACIPRS	Capris, Prisca
ACIPRY	piracy
ACIPTT	tipcat
ACIQTU	acquit
ACIRRT	tricar
ACIRSS	crasis
ACIRST	crista, racist
ACIRSY	Syriac
ACIRTU	tauric
ACIRVY	vicary
ACISSS	cassis
ACISTT	static
ACISTU	tsuica
ACITUY	acuity
ACITVY	cavity
ACJKPU	jack-up
ACJKSY	jacksy
ACKLOP	polack
ACKMNO	monack
ACKMNU	muckna
ACKNOW	acknow
ACKNPU	unpack
ACKNRY	cranky
ACKNTU	untack
ACKOOR	acrook
ACKORS	corsak
ACKORT	tarock
ACKORW	crakow
ACKORY	croaky
ACLLMU	Callum
ACLLMY	calmly
ACLLNO	clonal
ACLLOO	calloo
ACLLOP	callop
ACLLOR	collar
ACLLOT	lactol
ACLLOW	callow
ACLLPU	call-up
ACLLSU	callus
ACLLSY	scally
ACLLTY	lactyl
ACLMMY	clammy
ACLMOP	copalm
ACLMOR	clamor
ACLMTU	talcum
ACLMUU	lucuma
ACLNOT	locant
ACLNOV	volcan
ACLNOY	lycaon
ACLNRY	Carlyn
ACLNUY	lunacy
ACLOOZ	zocalo
ACLOPU	copula, coupla, cupola
ACLORR	corral
ACLORS	Carlos
ACLORT	crotal
ACLORU	ocular
ACLORW	Carlow
ACLORY	calory
ACLOST	costal
ACLOSU	oscula, scuola
ACLOTW	cotwal
ACLPRY	capryl
ACLRRU	crural
ACLRSW	scrawl
ACLRTU	curtal
ACLRWY	crawly
ACLSSY	classy
ACLSTU	scutal
ACLSUV	clavus
ACMMOP	mocamp
ACMNNO	conman
ACMNOO	Monaco
ACMNOR	macron
ACMNOS	mascon
ACMNOW	cowman
ACMNSU	mancus
ACMOOP	campoo
ACMOOU	amouco
ACMOPS	Campos
ACMORR	carrom, marcor
ACMORT	marcot
ACMOST	Comsat, mascot

ACMOSU mucosa
ACMOTT tom-cat
ACMOTU motuca
ACMPSU campus
ACMRSU Marcus, sacrum
ACMSTU muscat
ACMTUU tucuma
ACMUUV vacuum
ACNNNO cannon
ACNNOT cannot, canton
ACNNOY canyon
ACNNRY cranny
ACNOOP poonac
ACNOOR caroon, corona, racoon
ACNOPT pontac
ACNOPY canopy
ACNORR rancor
ACNORT cantor, carton, contra, craton
ACNORU cornua
ACNORY crayon
ACNOSV scovan
ACNOSZ scazon
ACNOTT octant
ACNOTU noctua, toucan
ACNOYZ conyza
ACNPTU puncta
ACNRST crants
ACNSTU cantus, Tuscan
ACNSTY scanty
ACOOSS Osasco
ACOOTV octavo
ACOPRT captor
ACOPTW cow-pat
ACORRT carrot, trocar
ACORRW carrow
ACORSS across
ACORST castor, co-star, scrota
ACORTT cottar, tactor
ACORTU cuatro, turaco
ACORTV cavort
ACORYZ coryza
ACOSUV cavous
ACOTTU outact
ACPPRY crappy
ACPRSU carpus
ACPRSY scrapy
ACPRTY crypta
ACPSSU scapus
ACPSTU catsup, upcast
ACRRWY war cry
ACRSSU scarus
ACRSTU crusta, curats
ACSSTU tussac
ACSTTU tactus
ACSTTY scatty
ADDDEG gadded
ADDDEL addled, daddle
ADDDEM madded
ADDDEN addend
ADDDEP padded
ADDDER dadder
ADDDEW wadded
ADDDFY Dafydd
ADDDOO doodad
ADDEEH headed
ADDEEL leaded
ADDEEM addeem
ADDEEN deaden
ADDEFL faddle
ADDEFN feddan
ADDEFR farded
ADDEGG dagged
ADDEGR graded
ADDEHI haddie
ADDEHK keddah
ADDEHN handed
ADDEIL daidle, dialed, laddie
ADDEIM diadem, Maddie
ADDELM maddle
ADDELN dandle, landed
ADDELO loaded
ADDELP paddle
ADDELR Aldred, ladder, raddle
ADDELS saddle
ADDELW dawdle, waddle
ADDELY deadly
ADDEMM dammed
ADDEMN damned, demand, madden
ADDEMR madder
ADDENN Nanded
ADDENO dead on
ADDENR dander, darned
ADDENS dedans, sadden, sanded
ADDENU undead
ADDENW wanded
ADDEOR deodar
ADDEPP dapped
ADDEPR padder
ADDERS sadder
ADDERT traded
ADDERV verdad
ADDERW Edward
ADDFFI fidfad
ADDFOR ofdrad
ADDGIO gadoid
ADDGIP giddap
ADDGLU Dugald
ADDGMO goddam
ADDGOO ogdoad
ADDHOO doodah
ADDIMR Madrid
ADDIMY midday
ADDINR Dinard
ADDIRS disard, disdar
ADDIST distad
ADDLNO Donald
ADDMNO dodman
ADDMOO addoom, Dodoma
ADDNRU Durand
ADDOOR dorado
ADDORS dorsad
ADDORT dotard
ADEEFL leafed
ADEEFM defame
ADEEFN deafen
ADEEFT defeat
ADEEGP pedage
ADEEGR agreed
ADEEHI Haidee
ADEEHR adhere, header
ADEEHS dashee
ADEEHT heated
ADEEHV heaved
ADEEIL aedile
ADEEIM mediae
ADEEIR dearie
ADEEIT ideate
ADEEJY deejay
ADEEKP peaked
ADEELN leaden, leaned
ADEELO elodea
ADEELP leaped, pelade
ADEELR dealer, leader
ADEELS sealed
ADEELT delate, tele-ad
ADEELV leaved, levade
ADEEMN amende, demean
ADEEMO oedema
ADEEMR remade
ADEENN Deanne, ennead
ADEENR deaner, endear
ADEENV advene, Evadne
ADEEPS pesade
ADEEPT pedate
ADEERR reader, reread
ADEERS reseda
ADEERT derate
ADEERV evader
ADEERW drawee
ADEERX exedra
ADEERY yeared
ADEEST sedate
ADEFFL daffle
ADEFGG fagged
ADEFGL fladge
ADEFGN defang, fag end, fanged
ADEFIL afield, defial, failed
ADEFIN fade-in
ADEFIR Frieda
ADEFKL defalk
ADEFLO feodal
ADEFLR Alfred, fardel
ADEFLU feudal
ADEFMO foamed
ADEFNN fanned
ADEFOR fedora
ADEFRY defray
ADEFTT fatted
ADEGGG gagged
ADEGGH hagged
ADEGGJ jagged
ADEGGL daggle, lagged
ADEGGM magged
ADEGGN nagged
ADEGGR dagger, ragged
ADEGGS sagged
ADEGGT gadget, tagged
ADEGGW wagged
ADEGGZ zagged
ADEGHI hidage
ADEGHN hanged
ADEGHS dagesh
ADEGIM imaged
ADEGIR gardie
ADEGLL galled
ADEGLN angled, dangle, Glenda
ADEGLO age-old, old age
ADEGLR garled, Gerald
ADEGNR danger, gander, garden, grande
ADEGNT tag end
ADEGNU augend
ADEGNW gnawed, Gwenda

ADEGNY Deyang
ADEGOR dog-ear, O grade
ADEGOS dosage, sea dog
ADEGOT dogate, dotage, togaed
ADEGPP gapped
ADEGRR Gerard, grader, red rag, regard
ADEGRS degras
ADEGRT tadger
ADEGRU argued
ADEGRV graved
ADEGSS gassed
ADEHIL halide
ADEHIR dehair, haired
ADEHKL Khaled
ADEHKW hawked
ADEHLN Halden, handle
ADEHLR hareld, herald
ADEHMM hammed
ADEHMS em dash
ADEHNO head-on
ADEHNP daphne
ADEHNR hander, harden
ADEHNS en dash
ADEHNY Hayden
ADEHPP happed
ADEHPS shaped
ADEHPT heptad
ADEHPU head-up
ADEHRR harder
ADEHRS dasher
ADEHRT dearth, hatred, red hat, thread
ADEHSS sashed
ADEHSV shaved
ADEHSW washed
ADEHSY Hyades
ADEHTT hatted
ADEHTY deathy
ADEHYY heyday
ADEIIM Maidie
ADEIKR daiker, darkie
ADEILL allied
ADEILM mailed, medial
ADEILN Daniel, denial, lead-in, nailed
ADEILO eidola
ADEILP elapid, pleiad
ADEILR derail, dialer, redial, relaid
ADEILS aisled, deasil, deisal, ladies, sailed
ADEILT detail, dilate, tailed
ADEILU audile
ADEIMM maimed
ADEIMN Damien, maiden, median, medina
ADEIMR admire, midear
ADEIMS mesiad
ADEIMU Maudie
ADEIMV vidame, Viedma
ADEINN Dianne, Nadine
ADEINO Idonea
ADEINP pained
ADEINR indear, read-in
ADEINS Sandie, Sendai, Sinead
ADEINT detain, tienda
ADEINV evanid, invade
ADEINW dewani, Edwina
ADEIOR roadie
ADEIOT iodate
ADEIPR diaper, diapre, paired, piedra, repaid
ADEIRR arride, raider
ADEIRS raised
ADEIRT tirade
ADEIRV varied
ADEIRY Yardie
ADEISS dassie
ADEISU adieus
ADEISV advise, visaed
ADEISW wadies
ADEITV dative
ADEITX taxied
ADEIUX adieux
ADEIVV vivaed
ADEIVW adview
ADEJMM jammed
ADEJRR jarred
ADEJRU adjure
ADEJUV deja vu
ADEKKY yakked
ADEKLN Kendal
ADEKLR darkle
ADEKLT talked
ADEKMO make-do
ADEKMR demark, marked
ADEKMS masked
ADEKNR darken, Kendra
ADEKOV advoke
ADEKPR depark
ADEKPY keypad
ADEKRY darkey
ADELLN end-all
ADELLP palled
ADELLR ladler
ADELLS dalles
ADELLU allude, aludel
ADELLV devall
ADELLW walled
ADELMM lammed
ADELMN menald
ADELMP palmed
ADELMR dermal, marled, medlar
ADELMS damsel
ADELMT malted
ADELMU maudle
ADELNO loaden
ADELNR darnel, lander
ADELNS sendal
ADELNT dental
ADELNU unlade
ADELNW wandle
ADELOP pedalo
ADELOR Laredo, loader, ordeal, reload
ADELOS aldose
ADELPP dapple, lapped
ADELPR pedlar
ADELPT plated
ADELPU lead-up
ADELPW dewlap
ADELRR Darrel, larder
ADELRT dartle
ADELRU Alured, lauder
ADELRV Dervla
ADELRY dearly, D-layer
ADELST desalt
ADELSU laudes
ADELUV valued
ADELVV valved
ADELZZ dazzle
ADEMMR dammer, rammed
ADEMNN manned
ADEMNO daemon, medano, modena, nomade
ADEMNP dampen
ADEMNR randem, red man, remand
ADEMNS amends, desman
ADEMNT tandem
ADEMNU unmade
ADEMOP pomade
ADEMOR radome
ADEMOW meadow
ADEMPP mapped
ADEMPR damper
ADEMPU made up
ADEMRR marred
ADEMRT dreamt
ADEMRY dreamy
ADEMSS massed
ADEMST masted
ADEMSU medusa
ADEMTT matted
ADENNP panned
ADENNT tanned
ADENNU duenna
ADENOR orenda
ADENOT donate
ADENOU douane
ADENOY noyade
ADENPP append, napped
ADENPR pander, repand
ADENPS despan
ADENPT pedant, pentad
ADENPX expand
ADENRR darner, Darren, errand
ADENRS sander
ADENRT ardent, endart
ADENRU unread
ADENRW Andrew, wander, warden
ADENRY denary
ADENRZ zander
ADENSS dassen
ADENSU deusan, sundae
ADENTT attend, detant
ADENTU deutan
ADENTV advent
ADENTW wanted
ADENUW unawed
ADENUZ deuzan

ADENWY Dwayne
ADEOPP pea-pod
ADEOPR parode
ADEORR adorer
ADEORT doater
ADEORU Eudora
ADEOSS Odessa
ADEOSV vadose
ADEOTT dotate
ADEOTV devota
ADEOYZ azo dye
ADEPPR dapper, rapped
ADEPPS sapped
ADEPPT tapped
ADEPPY yapped
ADEPPZ zapped
ADEPRR draper
ADEPRS spread
ADEPRT depart, drapet, parted, petard
ADEPSS passed
ADEPTT patted
ADEPTU update
ADEPWY pedway
ADERRT darter, dartre, retard, tarred, trader
ADERRW drawer, redraw, reward, warder, warred
ADERRY dreary
ADERSW sawder, Seward
ADERTT ratted, tetrad
ADERTV advert
ADERTX X-rated
ADERUY Audrey
ADERVV varved
ADESSU Dessau
ADESTT tasted
ADESTV devast, staved
ADESTW wadset, wasted
ADESTY steady
ADETTT tatted
ADETTV vatted
ADETUV veduta
ADFFOR afford
ADFFOY day off, off day
ADFGIN fading
ADFGLY gadfly
ADFILY ladify
ADFINN infand
ADFINR friand
ADFIRT adrift
ADFIRY Friday
ADFLNU fundal
ADFLSU sadful
ADFLYY ladyfy
ADFMNO fandom
ADFMOU fumado
ADFNOT fantod
ADFRSW dwarfs
ADFRTY drafty
ADGGOT dog tag
ADGGRY draggy
ADGHRU durgah
ADGIKN kidang
ADGILN lading, ligand
ADGILO dialog
ADGIMR digram
ADGIMY digamy
ADGINO adoing, ganoid, Gondia
ADGINQ Daqing
ADGINR daring, gradin
ADGINT dating
ADGINW dawing
ADGIRV gravid
ADGLLO old lag
ADGLLY gladly
ADGLNY dangly
ADGLOP lapdog
ADGLOU Dougal
ADGLOY Day-Glo
ADGLSY Gladys
ADGMNO dogman
ADGMUU muduga
ADGNOO doonga, goonda
ADGNOR dragon, Gondar
ADGORU guardo
ADGRSU gradus
ADGRUY guardy
ADHHIT Hadith
ADHHIW whidah
ADHHLU Huldah
ADHHOW howdah
ADHHWY whydah
ADHIKL Khalid
ADHIKR khadir
ADHIKS kadish
ADHILT Aldith
ADHIMR dirham
ADHIMS Mahdis
ADHINS Danish, sandhi
ADHIOR hairdo
ADHIRS radish, Rashid
ADHIRY hydria, Riyadh
ADHKLO dholak
ADHKRU Dharuk
ADHLLO holla'd
ADHLMO Oldham
ADHLOP Adolph
ADHLOR Harold
ADHLOT old hat
ADHLRY hardly
ADHMNO hodman
ADHMNU numdah
ADHMOR rodham
ADHMRU Durham
ADHNNU unhand
ADHNOR hadron, hard-on, Rhonda
ADHNOY Haydon
ADHNRU dhurna
ADHNSY shandy
ADHNUU Dunhua
ADHOOV doovah
ADHORT adhort
ADHORW Howard
ADHOSW shadow
ADHPRU hard up, purdah
ADHRRU dhurra
ADIIKO aikido
ADIILM miliad
ADIILN inlaid
ADIILO Odilia
ADIILR iridal
ADIILW Diwali
ADIIMO daimio
ADIIMR mid-air
ADIINN Indian
ADIINR Indira
ADIINV avidin
ADIIPR diapir
ADIISV divisa
ADIISY saiyid
ADIJKT Tadjik
ADIJMS masjid
ADIJNO adjoin
ADIJSS jassid
ADIKKO Kodiak
ADIKMO mikado
ADIKNP ink-pad, kidnap
ADIKSU adsuki
ADIKTT diktat
ADIKUZ adzuki
ADILLP pallid
ADILLY laidly
ADILMN mandil
ADILMS dismal
ADILMY milady
ADILNN inland
ADILNO dolina, ladino, Olinda, onlaid
ADILNR aldrin
ADILNS island
ADILNT tindal
ADILNU unlaid
ADILNW Aldwin
ADILNY Lydian
ADILPU laid up
ADILPY plaidy
ADILRY aridly
ADILRZ lizard
ADILST distal
ADILUV vidual
ADILVY avidly
ADIMMT dammit
ADIMNO daimon, domain, domina
ADIMNS disman
ADIMNT mantid
ADIMOS diosma
ADIMOT diatom
ADIMOY daimyo
ADIMRS disarm
ADIMRU marudi, radium
ADIMRY myriad
ADIMSS sadism
ADIMST amidst
ADIMSY dismay
ADIMTU maudit
ADIMWY midway
ADINNO nanoid
ADINNP pindan
ADINNT Dinant
ADINNU induna
ADINNZ zindan
ADINOR Dorian, inroad, ordain
ADINOS Adonis
ADINOT dation
ADINOU audion
ADINOX dioxan
ADINPR pinard, pindar
ADINPT pandit
ADINPU unpaid
ADINRT indart
ADINRU durain, durian
ADINRW Darwin, indraw, inward
ADINSU unsaid
ADINSW windas
ADINTY dainty
ADIOPR rapido
ADIORT adroit, Dorita
ADIOSV adviso
ADIPRS sparid
ADIPSS dipsas
ADIPSX spadix
ADIQTU diquat
ADIRRS sirdar
ADIRSS Sardis
ADIRST Astrid
ADIRSU radius
ADIRVZ vizard
ADIRWZ wizard
ADIRZZ izzard
ADISST sadist

ADISSU Saudis
ADISYY sayyid
ADITTY dittay
ADJKOU judoka
ADJNOR jordan
ADJORR Jarrod
ADJSTU adjust
ADKLNO Kladno
ADKLNY dankly
ADKLOP polka'd
ADKLRY darkly
ADKNOO nakodo
ADKOPS padkos
ADKOPU padouk
ADKORX kordax
ADKOTU dotaku
ADKSTU dustak
ADLLNO olland
ADLLOR dollar
ADLLUY dually
ADLMNO almond, dolman, old man
ADLMOS dolmas
ADLMOU loadum
ADLMPY damply
ADLMTU Talmud
ADLNOP Poland
ADLNOR Arnold, Dralon, lardon, Roland, Ronald
ADLNOT dalton
ADLNOU unload
ADLNPU upland
ADLNRU lurdan
ADLNWY Aldwyn
ADLOPU load up, upload
ADLOPY polyad
ADLORS dorsal
ADLOSS dossal
ADLOSU Aldous
ADLOSW dowlas, Oswald
ADLOWY day owl
ADLRRY Darryl
ADLRWY drawly
ADMMNU damnum
ADMNOR mandor, random
ADMNOS damson
ADMNOY dynamo, Monday
ADMNPY Dympna
ADMNUY Maundy
ADMORR ramrod
ADMORT motard
ADMORU maduro
ADMTUY adytum
ADNNOU adnoun
ADNOOR nardoo
ADNOOW wandoo
ADNOPR pardon
ADNOPT dopant
ADNORT tardon
ADNORU around
ADNORW onward
ADNORX Oxnard
ADNORY donary
ADNOTT dotant
ADNOTY Dayton
ADNRST strand
ADNRSU nardus, sandur
ADNRTU draunt, durant, tundra
ADNRUW durwan
ADNSTY dynast
ADNSUY Sunday
ADNSXY sandyx
ADOORS a-doors
ADOPRU podura
ADOPRY parody
ADOPWX wax-pod
ADOQRU quadro
ADORRU ardour, dourra
ADORST dartos
ADORTW toward
ADOTUY day out
ADPRUW upward
ADRSTU dastur
ADRTWY tawdry
AEEFFR affeer, raffee
AEEFGT Getafe
AEEFGU feague, feuage
AEEFIR faerie
AEEFLM female
AEEFLY lay-fee
AEEFOV foveae
AEEFRT afreet
AEEGGM gamgee
AEEGGN engage
AEEGGR raggee, reggae
AEEGJR jaeger, jeerga
AEEGLL allege
AEEGLP peagle, pelage
AEEGLR regale
AEEGLS glease
AEEGLT eaglet, gelate, legate, teagle, telega
AEEGLU league
AEEGMM gemmae
AEEGMN manege
AEEGMR Graeme, meager, meagre
AEEGMT gamete, metage
AEEGNR enrage, genera
AEEGNS sagene
AEEGNT geneat, negate
AEEGNV avenge, geneva
AEEGNW New Age
AEEGOP apogee
AEEGOT goatee
AEEGPS pesage
AEEGPW pewage
AEEGRS agrees, grease, seegar
AEEGRT gerate
AEEGRV greave
AEEGST egesta
AEEGSW sewage
AEEHHW hee-haw
AEEHJN hajeen, hanjee
AEEHKM hakeem
AEEHLN Helena
AEEHLR healer
AEEHLT lathee
AEEHLW awheel
AEEHLX exhale
AEEHMU heaume
AEEHNP peahen
AEEHNS Sheena
AEEHNT Athene, ethane
AEEHNV heaven
AEEHNX hexane
AEEHRR hearer, rehear
AEEHRS hearse
AEEHRT aether, heater, hereat, reheat, the ear
AEEHRV heaver
AEEHSV sheave
AEEHTV theave
AEEHWY yeehaw
AEEIJN Jeanie
AEEIKW weakie
AEEILM mealie
AEEILN Aileen, aliene, Elaine, lineae, nealie
AEEIMN meanie
AEEINW weanie
AEEIRS easier
AEEJKL kaleej
AEEJLT tjaele
AEEJMN manjee
AEEJNN Jeanne
AEEJVY veejay
AEEKLN alkene, lekane
AEEKLP palkee
AEEKLR leaker
AEEKLV vakeel
AEEKMR remake
AEEKMT metake
AEEKMZ kameez
AEEKNW weaken
AEEKNY Yankee
AEEKRR karree
AEEKRT retake
AEEKRU eureka
AEELLL allele
AEELLM mallee
AEELLN allene
AEELLS sallee
AEELLV A level
AEELMN enamel, melena
AEELMP empale
AEELMR leamer, mealer
AEELMS measle
AEELNN Leanne
AEELNO loanee
AEELNP alpeen, panele
AEELNR Arlene
AEELNS enseal, Selena
AEELNT lateen, lenate, teanel
AEELNV leaven
AEELNW weanel
AEELOT oleate
AEELPR leaper, pealer, repeal
AEELPS asleep, elapse, please, sapele
AEELPT peltae
AEELPU epaule
AEELQU quelea
AEELRS leaser, resale, reseal, sealer
AEELRT earlet, elater, relate, Tralee
AEELRV laveer, leaver, reveal
AEELRY E-layer
AEELSS eassel
AEELST saltee, stelae, teasel
AEELSV leaves
AEELSW weasel
AEELSZ sleaze
AEELTU eluate

AEELTV velate, veleta
AEELTW atweel
AEELTY eyalet
AEELTZ teazel, teazle
AEELWY leeway
AEEMMM mammee
AEEMNR meaner, rename
AEEMNS enemas, enseam
AEEMNT entame
AEEMNX examen
AEEMPR ampere
AEEMPW wampee
AEEMRR reamer
AEEMRS emeras, seamer
AEEMRT teamer
AEEMSS sesame
AEEMST meseta
AEEMTT metate
AEEMTX taxeme
AEENNT neaten
AEENNX annexe
AEENPS peasen, sea pen
AEENPT nepeta
AEENPW pawnee
AEENQU Queena
AEENRR earner
AEENRS ensear, Serena
AEENRT entera
AEENRV avener, Verena
AEENRW weaner
AEENRZ Zareen
AEENST sateen, senate
AEENSU unease
AEENTW atween
AEENUV avenue
AEENWZ weazen
AEEPPR rappee
AEEPRR reaper
AEEPRS Parsee, persea, serape
AEEPRT repeat
AEEPST peseta
AEEPSW pesewa
AEEPSX apexes
AEEPVY peavey
AEEQRU quaere
AEEQTU equate
AEERRR rearer
AEERRS eraser, serrae
AEERRT errate, tearer, terrae
AEERRW warree, wearer
AEERSS essera, sarees
AEERST asteer, easter, reseat, saeter, seater, teaser, teresa
AEERSV averse, Varese
AEERTT teetar
AEERTY eatery
AEERVW weaver
AEESSW see-saw
AEESTT estate, teaset, testae
AEFFFL faffle
AEFFGL gaffle
AEFFGR gaffer
AEFFHT haffet
AEFFIN affine
AEFFIP piaffe
AEFFIW waffie
AEFFLM maffle
AEFFLR farfel, raffle
AEFFLW waffle
AEFFLY yaffle
AEFFRS saffer
AEFFRT far-fet
AEFFRY effray
AEFFRZ zaffer, zaffre
AEFFSU affuse
AEFGGR fagger
AEFGLN fangle, flange
AEFGLR reflag
AEFGMU fumage
AEFGOR forage
AEFGRY fegary
AEFHLL fellah
AEFHLN halfen
AEFHNT fat hen
AEFHRS afresh, ferash
AEFHRT father, freath
AEFIJO feijoa
AEFILL faille
AEFILN finale
AEFILR ferial
AEFILT fetial, leafit
AEFILZ filaze
AEFIMN famine, infame
AEFINN Fenian
AEFINR infare
AEFIRS fraise
AEFIST fiesta
AEFITX fixate
AEFJNT fan-jet
AEFKRY fakery, freaky
AEFLLN fallen
AEFLLP pfella
AEFLLR faller
AEFLMN flamen
AEFLNX flaxen
AEFLOR florae, loafer
AEFLOT foetal, folate
AEFLOV foveal
AEFLPR fraple
AEFLRS flaser
AEFLRT falter
AEFLRU earful, ferula
AEFLRY flayer, F-layer
AEFLSS asself
AEFLST falset, festal
AEFLSY safely
AEFLTU fluate
AEFLTY fealty, featly
AEFMNO foeman
AEFMOR femora
AEFMOS famose
AEFMRR farmer, framer
AEFNNR fanner
AEFNOT tafone
AEFNRR Farren
AEFNRU Frauen
AEFNST fasten, nefast
AEFNSU fausen, unsafe
AEFNTT fatten
AEFOSS fossae
AEFPRY perfay
AEFPTY patefy
AEFRRS Fraser
AEFRRT frater, rafter
AEFRRY rarefy
AEFRRZ Frazer
AEFRST afters, strafe
AEFRTT fatter
AEFRTU fauter
AEFRTW wafter
AEFRWY wafery
AEFSTU estufa
AEFSTY safety
AEGGGI gaggie
AEGGGL gaggle
AEGGHL haggle
AEGGHN Hegang
AEGGHW hewgag
AEGGIJ jaggie
AEGGIM maggie
AEGGIN ageing, ingage
AEGGIT Gitega
AEGGJR jagger
AEGGLN gangle, naggle
AEGGLR gargle, gregal, lagger, raggle
AEGGLT leggat
AEGGLW waggle
AEGGNR ganger, grange, nagger
AEGGNU gangue
AEGGRS sagger
AEGGRT garget
AEGGRU gauger
AEGGRW wagger
AEGGWW gewgaw
AEGHIN hangie
AEGHIO hoagie
AEGHIR hegira
AEGHIS geisha
AEGHIW aweigh
AEGHMN Meghan
AEGHMO homage
AEGHNO Eoghan
AEGHNR hanger, rehang
AEGHNW Hwange
AEGHOR gherao
AEGHRT Gareth, gather
AEGILM milage
AEGILN Ealing, genial, linage
AEGILO goalie
AEGILP paigle, pilage
AEGILR glaire
AEGILS Gisela, ligase, silage
AEGILT aiglet, ligate
AEGILV glaive, vagile
AEGIMN enigma, gamine
AEGIMP magpie
AEGIMR gamier, imager, maigre, Margie, mirage
AEGIMS ageism
AEGINR earing, gainer, graine, inrage, regain, Regina
AEGINS agnise

AEGINT eating, ingate
AEGINU guinea
AEGINV Ganvie
AEGINZ agnize
AEGIPP pipage
AEGIRS agrise
AEGIRT gaiter, tirage, triage
AEGIRV Argive, virage
AEGIRW earwig
AEGIST ageist
AEGISU aguise
AEGISV visage
AEGITU augite
AEGITY gaiety
AEGIXZ Xigaze
AEGJLN jangle
AEGJLR jargle
AEGJLT jet lag
AEGJTU jugate
AEGKST gasket
AEGLLP pegall
AEGLLT gallet
AEGLLU ullage
AEGLLY galley
AEGLMN legman, mangel, mangle
AEGLMS sal-gem
AEGLMU guemal
AEGLMV maglev
AEGLMY gamely, gleamy, mygale
AEGLNN Glenna
AEGLNO Angelo, engaol
AEGLNR angler, erlang, largen, rangle, regnal
AEGLNS gansel
AEGLNT tangle
AEGLNU langue, leguan, ulnage
AEGLNW wangle
AEGLNY angely
AEGLNZ glazen
AEGLOR galore, gaoler
AEGLOT legato
AEGLOV lovage, volage
AEGLPU plague
AEGLRT tergal
AEGLRV glaver, gravel
AEGLRY argyle
AEGLRZ glazer
AEGLSY sagely

AEGLTU tegula
AEGLTW talweg
AEGMMN gemman
AEGMMR gammer, gramme
AEGMMS smegma
AEGMNR engram, german, manger, ragmen
AEGMNS magnes
AEGMNT magnet
AEGMNY mangey
AEGMRU maugre, murage
AEGMSS megass
AEGMUY maguey
AEGMUZ zeugma
AEGNNO nonage
AEGNNT gannet
AEGNOR Gaenor, Gerona, near go, onager, orange
AEGNOS agones, geason
AEGNRR garner, ranger
AEGNRS Angers, serang
AEGNRT argent, garnet, grenat, tanger
AEGNRU nauger
AEGNRV graven
AEGNRY anergy
AEGNSY gansey
AEGNTT gatten
AEGNUX axunge
AEGOPT potage
AEGORT orgeat, toerag
AEGORU aerugo
AEGOTT togate
AEGOTU outage
AEGOTW towage
AEGOVY voyage
AEGPRS gasper, sparge
AEGPRT parget
AEGPRU Prague
AEGPRW gawper
AEGPRY grapey
AEGRRT garret, garter, grater
AEGRRU arguer
AEGRRV graver
AEGRRZ grazer
AEGRSS gasser, Grasse
AEGRST gaster, stager

AEGRSU argues, sauger
AEGRSV graves
AEGRSY greasy, gyrase
AEGRTT gatter, target
AEGRTU argute
AEGRTY gyrate
AEGRTZ grazet
AEGSSS gasses
AEGSTY gayest, stagey
AEGTYY gayety
AEHHLT health
AEHHNS Heshan
AEHHPY hyphae
AEHHRS rehash
AEHHRT hearth
AEHHST sheath
AEHHTY heathy
AEHHVY Yahveh
AEHHWY Yahweh
AEHIIW Weihai
AEHIJL Elijah
AEHIJR hejira
AEHIKN hankie
AEHIKZ Keziah
AEHILL Leilah
AEHILM hiemal
AEHILN inhale
AEHILO Aihole
AEHILR hailer, halier
AEHILS Elisha, Ilesha, sheila
AEHILT halite, laithe
AEHILW awhile
AEHIMM maihem
AEHIMN haemin, hemina
AEHIMR Hermia, mehari
AEHIMS mashie
AEHINR hairen, hernia
AEHINS ashine
AEHINT Aithne, Ianthe
AEHINV vahine
AEHINW wahine
AEHIPS saphie
AEHIRV havier
AEHIRZ hazier
AEHIST saithe
AEHITT Hattie
AEHITV thaive
AEHJPT Japhet
AEHJRS Jerash
AEHKNO Hakone
AEHKNR hanker, harken
AEHKNS shaken

AEHKPR phreak
AEHKRS shaker
AEHKRW hawker
AEHKSY ash-key
AEHLLL hallel
AEHLLM mellah
AEHLLR haller
AEHLLT lethal
AEHLMM hammle
AEHLMP pelham
AEHLMR harmel
AEHLMT hamlet, Thelma
AEHLMY hyemal
AEHLNO enhalo
AEHLNS hansel, Leshan
AEHLNT hantle, lathen
AEHLNW Helwan
AEHLOR herola
AEHLOT loathe, Olathe
AEHLPY phylae
AEHLRS lasher
AEHLRT halter, lather, thaler
AEHLRU haleru, hauler
AEHLRV halver
AEHLRW whaler
AEHLRY Harley
AEHLSS hassle
AEHLST haslet, Shelta
AEHLSV halves
AEHLSW whales
AEHLSY Ashley
AEHLTW wealth
AEHLYY Hayley
AEHMMR hammer
AEHMMY mayhem
AEHMNO mahone
AEHMNR Herman
AEHMNT anthem, Hamnet, hetman
AEHMNU humane
AEHMNW Newham
AEHMOT at-home
AEHMPR hamper
AEHMRS masher
AEHMRT mehtar
AEHMTU humate
AEHMTY maythe
AEHMTZ hametz
AEHNPP happen
AEHNPR pheran
AEHNPT hapten
AEHNRT anther, Tehran, thenar
AEHNST Athens, hasten

AEHNSU hausen
AEHNSV shaven
AEHNSW washen, whenas
AEHNTV haven't
AEHNTX Xanthe
AEHORS ashore, hoarse
AEHORX hoaxer
AEHOTW awheto
AEHPPR perhap
AEHPRR harper
AEHPRS phrase, seraph, shaper, Sherpa
AEHPRT tephra, teraph, threap
AEHPRY ephyra
AEHPSS phases
AEHPST spathe
AEHPSW peshwa
AEHPTT pettah
AEHPTY hypate
AEHRRS rasher, sharer
AEHRRT rather
AEHRSS shares
AEHRST hearst
AEHRSV shaver
AEHRSW hawser, rewash, washer
AEHRTT hatter, threat
AEHRTU huerta
AEHRTV thrave
AEHRTW wreath
AEHRTY earthy, hearty
AEHRVW wharve
AEHRVY Harvey
AEHSSU hausse
AEHSTW swathe
AEHSUU huseau
AEIILM Emilia
AEIILR Leiria
AEIILS liaise
AEIIMR mairie
AEIIMS Maisie
AEIINR Eirian
AEIIPT Taipei
AEIIRR airier
AEIISX aixies
AEIJLN enjail
AEIJLR jailer
AEIJLZ jezail
AEIJMM Jemima
AEIJNN Janine
AEIKKN kankie
AEIKKT takkie
AEIKKY keyaki
AEIKLN alkine, inleak
AEIKLS alsike
AEIKLT talkie
AEIKMR ramkie
AEIKNP kan-pei
AEIKNR Kieran
AEIKNS kinase
AEIKNT intake, kentia, take-in
AEIKNZ kaizen
AEIKPP kappie
AEIKPR parkie
AEIKRR kerria
AEIKRS kaiser
AEILLM maille, mallei
AEILLN lineal
AEILLT taille
AEILLW wallie
AEILMM lammie
AEILMN inamel, menial
AEILMP impale
AEILMR Mariel
AEILMS Malise, mesial, samiel, Sliema
AEILNN Lianne
AEILNO eolian
AEILNP alpine, Nepali, penial, pineal
AEILNR Arline, enrail, linear, nailer
AEILNS saline, Selina
AEILNT entail, latine
AEILNV alevin, alvine, Elvina, levain, valine, veinal, venial, vineal
AEILNW in-wale, lawine
AEILNX alexin, xenial
AEILOS Eloisa
AEILPP lappie
AEILPS espial, lipase
AEILPT aplite
AEILPU alpieu
AEILRR railer
AEILRS Israel, sailer, serial
AEILRT aliter, lirate, retail, tailer
AEILRU Auriel, Laurie
AEILRV Averil, Elvira
AEILRW Lawrie, wailer
AEILRY Elyria
AEILRZ lazier
AEILSS Elissa, laisse, lassie
AEILST saltie
AEILSU saulie
AEILSV valise
AEILSW alwise
AEILSX Alexis, Seixal
AEILSY easily
AEILTV lative
AEILTY tailye
AEIMMN ammine, immane
AEIMMS sammie
AEIMNN mannie
AEIMNO anomie
AEIMNP pieman
AEIMNR manier, marine, Marnie, minera, remain
AEIMNT inmate, inmeat, tamein, tamine
AEIMNX Maxine
AEIMNY Niamey
AEIMPR empair
AEIMPV impave
AEIMPY pyemia
AEIMRS samier
AEIMRT imaret, Martie, matier
AEIMRU uremia
AEIMRW Weimar
AEIMRZ mazier
AEIMST samite
AEIMTT mattie
AEIMTZ ziamet
AEIMXX maxixe
AEINNN nannie
AEINNP pinnae
AEINNR Nerina, ranine
AEINNS insane, sienna
AEINNT innate, tannie
AEINNV Vienna
AEINNW Weinan
AEINOT etaoin
AEINPR rapine
AEINPT pantie, patine, pinate, pineta
AEINRR Rainer
AEINRS arisen, arsine, sarnie
AEINRT ratine, retain, retina
AEINRV ravine
AEINRZ zanier
AEINSS sanies, sansei, sasine
AEINST santie, tisane
AEINSV savine
AEINTT tienta
AEINTU auntie, Uniate
AEINTV native
AEINTX taxine
AEINTZ zeatin
AEIOPT opiate
AEIOPZ epizoa
AEIPPR papier
AEIPPT Pepita
AEIPPW wappie
AEIPPZ papize
AEIPRR praire, rapier, repair
AEIPRS aspire, paries, praise, spirea
AEIPRT pirate, pratie
AEIPRV pavier
AEIPST pastie, patesi, pe-tsai, pietas
AEIPSV pavise
AEIPSW waspie
AEIPTT Pattie
AEIPTW tawpie
AEIPZZ peziza
AEIQTU quaite
AEIRRS raiser, sierra
AEIRRV arrive, Rivera, varier
AEIRRW warier
AEIRST satire, striae
AEIRSZ Azeris
AEIRTT attire, ratite, tertia
AEIRTW waiter

AEIRVW waiver, wavier
AEIRVX Xavier
AEIRWX waxier
AEISST siesta, tassie
AEISSU Aussie
AEISSZ assize
AEISTV sative
AEISTX taxies
AEISTY aseity
AEISVV avives
AEISVW wavies
AEITTT tattie
AEITTV vittae
AEITTW twaite
AEIVVV evviva
AEJKNN janken
AEJKNR janker
AEJMMR jammer
AEJMRT ramjet
AEJMST jetsam
AEJNNO Joanne
AEJNST sejant
AEJNUU Juneau
AEJPRS jasper
AEJPRY japery
AEJRTT trajet
AEJRVV javver
AEJRVY jarvey
AEJRZZ jazzer
AEKKNR kraken
AEKKRY yakker
AEKLNR rankle
AEKLNT anklet
AEKLNW knawel, wankle
AEKLNY alkyne
AEKLPS splake
AEKLRS leskar
AEKLRT kartel, talker
AEKLRV Kevlar
AEKLRW walker
AEKLSS Kassel
AEKLST lasket
AEKLSY kayles
AEKLTU auklet
AEKLTV vlakte
AEKLWY weakly
AEKMNP Kampen
AEKMNR Kerman
AEKMNU unmake
AEKMOS asmoke
AEKMOT matoke
AEKMPS kempas
AEKMPU make-up
AEKMPY key map
AEKMRR marker, remark
AEKMRS masker
AEKMRT market
AEKMRU kumera
AEKNNR enrank
AEKNNY Kenyan
AEKNOR Korean
AEKNOT aketon
AEKNOW awoken
AEKNRR ranker
AEKNRT ranket, tanker
AEKNRW Newark, wanker
AEKNSY sneaky
AEKOPT Topeka
AEKORS arkose, soaker
AEKPRR parker
AEKPTU take-up, uptake
AEKPUW wake-up
AEKQRU quaker
AEKQSU squeak
AEKRST skater, staker, strake, streak, tasker
AEKRSY karsey
AEKSST skates
AEKWYY keyway
AELLLU Luella
AELLMO Almelo
AELLMT mallet
AELLMY lamely, mellay
AELLNS Ansell
AELLNW enwall
AELLNY leanly
AELLOR loreal
AELLPT L-plate, pallet
AELLPX plexal
AELLPY palely
AELLRS allers
AELLRU allure, laurel
AELLRY really, yaller
AELLST estall, sallet, Stella
AELLTU luteal
AELLTW wallet
AELLTY lately
AELLUZ lazule
AELLVY valley
AELMMR rammel, rammle
AELMNN mennal
AELMNO melano
AELMNS Anselm, lemans, Le Mans, Mansel, mensal
AELMNT lament, mantel, mantle, mental
AELMNU Manuel
AELMNY laymen, Manley, meanly, namely
AELMOR morale
AELMOS almose, Salome
AELMPR ampler, emparl, lamper, palmer
AELMPS sample
AELMPU ampule
AELMRT armlet, marlet, martel
AELMRU mauler, merula
AELMRV marvel
AELMRY almery, Aylmer
AELMST samlet
AELMSU Samuel
AELMSY measly, samely
AELMTU amulet, muleta
AELMTY tamely
AELMUY mauley
AELNNP pannel
AELNNR lanner
AELNOP palone
AELNOR loaner
AELNOS lanose, salone, Sloane
AELNOT etalon, lean-to
AELNPP pen pal
AELNPR parnel, planer, plenar, replan
AELNPT pantle, planet, platen
AELNPU Plauen
AELNRS ransel
AELNRT altern, antler, learnt, rental, ternal
AELNRU Lauren, neural, unreal
AELNRV nerval, vernal
AELNRW warnel
AELNRY anerly, nearly
AELNST salten
AELNSU unseal
AELNSV snavel, snavle
AELNSY sanely
AELNTT latent, latten, talent
AELNTU eluant, lunate
AELNTV levant, valent
AELNTY neatly
AELOPP Aleppo
AELOPR parole
AELOPS aslope, El Paso
AELOPT pelota
AELOPX poleax
AELORT lorate
AELOSV loaves
AELOSW leasow
AELOTZ zealot
AELPPR lapper, rappel
AELPPS apples, sapple
AELPPT lappet
AELPPU papule
AELPQU plaque
AELPRR parrel
AELPRT palter, plater
AELPRU pleura
AELPRW pre-law, warple
AELPRY parley, pearly, player, replay
AELPSS passel
AELPST pastel, septal, staple
AELPTT patlet, pattle
AELPTU Petula, puteal
AELQRU Raquel
AELQSU lasque, squeal
AELRRT retral, terral
AELRRU laurer
AELRRY rarely
AELRSS rassle
AELRST estral, laster, rastle, salter, slater, staler, stelar
AELRSU saurel
AELRSV salver, serval,

slaver, versal
AELRSW warsle
AELRSY slayer
AELRTT latter, rattle
AELRTU lauter
AELRTV travel, varlet
AELRTW walter
AELRTY elytra, lyrate, raylet, realty
AELRUV valuer
AELRVV varvel
AELRVY Valery
AELRWX wraxle
AELRWY lawyer, warely
AELRYY yearly
AELRZZ razzle
AELSST tassel
AELSTT latest, taslet
AELSTU salute
AELSTV vestal
AELSTW wastel
AELSTY lysate
AELSUV alveus, avulse, values
AELSUX sexual
AELSVY slavey, sylvae
AELSYZ sleazy
AELTTT tattle
AELTTW wattle
AELTUV vuelta
AELTUX luxate
AELUUV uvulae
AEMMMR mammer, marmem
AEMMMT mammet
AEMMNR merman
AEMMNS sammen
AEMMRR rammer
AEMMRY yammer
AEMMRZ mamzer
AEMMST stemma
AEMMSU summae
AEMMTU maumet
AEMNNO Eamonn, one-man
AEMNNP nepman, penman
AEMNNR manner
AEMNNW new man
AEMNOP mopane
AEMNOR anomer, enamor, moaner, morena
AEMNOS nosema
AEMNOT omenta, to-name
AEMNOY yeoman
AEMNPR pre-man
AEMNPU pneuma
AEMNQU manque
AEMNRT marten
AEMNRU manure, menura, murena
AEMNSS maness, messan
AEMNST aments, stamen
AEMNSY yes-man
AEMOPT a tempo
AEMOPZ apozem
AEMORR remora, roamer
AEMORS ramose
AEMORT amoret
AEMORX xeroma
AEMOST osmate
AEMPPR mapper, pamper, preamp
AEMPRT tamper
AEMPRV revamp, vamper
AEMQRU marque
AEMQSU masque
AEMRRR marrer
AEMRRT marter
AEMRRU armure
AEMRRV marver
AEMRRW warmer
AEMRST amster, master, stream
AEMRSU Maseru
AEMRSY Ramsey, smeary
AEMRTT matter
AEMRTU mature, Mutare, temura
AEMSSU assume, Seamus, Seumas
AEMSTU Matsue, meatus, mutase
AEMSTY mayest, mystae, steamy
AEMSUU museau
AEMSYZ zymase
AEMTTU mutate
AEMUZZ mezuza
AENNNO nonane
AENNOV novena
AENNOY anyone
AENNRT tanner
AENNRV vanner
AENNRW wanner
AENNST Nantes
AENNTT tenant
AENOPV pavone
AENOPW weapon
AENOPY paeony
AENORS reason
AENORT ornate
AENORV Verona
AENORW Rowena
AENORX Roxane
AENOSS season
AENOST astone
AENOTT notate
AENOTV novate
AENOTZ zonate
AENOWY one-way
AENPPR napper, parpen, rappen
AENPRT arpent, enrapt, entrap, panter, parent, trepan
AENPRW enwrap
AENPRY napery
AENPRZ panzer
AENPTT patent, patten
AENPTU peanut
AENQTU equant
AENRRS snarer
AENRRT arrent, errant, ranter, ternar
AENRRW warner, warren
AENRRY Rayner
AENRSS sarsen
AENRST astern, sterna
AENRSV Anvers
AENRSW answer
AENRSY senary
AENRTT natter, tarten
AENRTU aunter, nature
AENRTV tavern
AENRTW wanter
AENRWY yawner
AENSST assent
AENSTU Austen, nasute, unseat
AENSTY Anstey
AENSUV naevus
AENSUY uneasy
AENSWY sawney
AENTTT attent
AENTTU attune, nutate, tauten
AENTTX extant
AENTTY tetany
AEOPPS appose
AEOPQU opaque
AEOPRR parore
AEOPRS Pesaro
AEOPRT protea
AEOPST postea
AEOPTT aptote, optate, teapot
AEOPTY teapoy
AEOPTZ poetaz, zapote
AEOQSU aquose
AEORRR roarer
AEORRS soarer
AEORSS serosa
AEORSU arouse, Roseau
AEORTT rotate
AEORTY to-year
AEORVY avoyer
AEORZZ Arezzo
AEOUVZ Zouave
AEPPRR rapper
AEPPRS sapper
AEPPRT tapper
AEPPRU pauper
AEPPRW wapper
AEPPRY papery, prepay, yapper
AEPPRZ zapper
AEPPSS papess
AEPPTT tappet
AEPPTU pupate
AEPPTY yappet
AEPQTU paquet
AEPRRS parser, rasper, sparer
AEPRRT parter, prater
AEPRRU parure
AEPRRW pre-war, rewrap, warper
AEPRRY prayer
AEPRSS passer, repass, sparse
AEPRST repast, trapes
AEPRTT patter
AEPRTU uprate
AEPRTX pre-tax
AEPRTY tepary
AEPRTZ patzer
AEPRUV rave-up
AEPRWY yawper
AEPSST stapes
AEPSSY payess
AEQRSU square

AEQRTU quarte, quatre
AEQRUU rauque
AEQRUV quaver
AEQSUY queasy
AERRRT terrar
AERRRW warrer
AERRST arrest, rarest, raster, starer
AERRSU rasure
AERRSV ravers
AERRTT ratter
AERRTY artery
AERRVY varrey
AERSST assert, essart
AERSSU assure
AERSSW wasser, wrasse
AERSTT stater, taster
AERSTV starve
AERSTW waster, waters
AERSTY estray, stayer
AERSTZ ersatz
AERSUU aureus, uraeus
AERSWY sawyer
AERTTT tatter
AERTTV trevat
AERTTY treaty, yatter
AERTUU auteur
AERTWY watery
AERVWY wavery
AESSSS assess
AESSST stases
AESSTT tasset
AESSTV staves
AESSTW saw-set
AESSTY sayest
AESTTT attest
AESTTU astute, statue
AESTWY sweaty
AESTYY yeasty
AETTWW tewtaw
AETUXY eutaxy
AFFFOR far-off
AFFGUW guffaw
AFFIKR Kaffir
AFFILP pilaff
AFFIMR affirm
AFFIOR off-air
AFFIRT tariff
AFFLOP offlap
AFFLOY lay-off, Offaly
AFFLUX afflux
AFFLWY waffly
AFFNOY Ffyona
AFFOPY pay-off
AFFORR Forfar
AFFSST staffs
AFFSSW waff SS
AFGGIO Foggia
AFGGLY flaggy
AFGGOT faggot
AFGINN fingan, infang
AFGINR faring
AFGIRU figura
AFGISY gasify
AFGITZ zaftig
AFGLNO flagon
AFGLNU fungal
AFGLRU frugal
AFGMOR fogram
AFGORR fragor
AFGOTU fugato
AFGOTY fagoty
AFGRUY argufy
AFGSTU Gustaf
AFHIIR hairif
AFHIKL khalif
AFHIKR kharif
AFHILT flaith
AFHIMS famish
AFHIOS oafish
AFHIRS sharif
AFHIRY hayrif
AFHLMU Fulham
AFHLOO loofah
AFHLSY flashy
AFHLTU hatful
AFHMOT fathom
AFHORS shofar
AFHRSW wharfs
AFHTTU futtah
AFIIJN Fijian
AFIILL filial
AFIILN finial
AFIJNN finjan
AFIKNU funkia
AFILLN infall
AFILMU famuli
AFILMY family
AFILNO Finola, in-foal
AFILNU infula
AFILNV flavin
AFILNY Finlay
AFILOR foliar
AFILRY fairly
AFILRZ frazil
AFILSY salify
AFIMNR firman
AFIMNY infamy, manify
AFIMRY ramify
AFIMSS massif
AFIMST fatism
AFIMSV favism
AFINNN finnan
AFINNT infant
AFINRU unfair
AFINRX fraxin
AFINST faints, Fantis, fiants
AFINSU fusain
AFINSY sanify
AFINTY fainty
AFINYZ Nazify
AFIPRT parfit
AFIQRU faquir
AFIRRY friary, rarify
AFIRTY artify, ratify
AFIRUY aurify
AFIRVY varify
AFISTT fatist
AFJLRU jarful
AFLLNO onfall
AFLLOR floral
AFLLOT to-fall
AFLLOW fallow
AFLLPU lapful
AFLLTY flatly
AFLLUW lawful
AFLMNU manful
AFLMOR formal
AFLMRU armful, fulmar
AFLMYY mayfly
AFLNOT fontal
AFLNPU panful
AFLNTU flaunt
AFLORS floras
AFLORV flavor
AFLOTU flauto
AFLOTY floaty
AFLPPY flappy
AFLPSU sapful
AFLRTU artful
AFLSTU flatus
AFLSTY fastly
AFLSWY sawfly
AFLTTY flatty
AFLTUY faulty
AFMORT format
AFMOSU famous
AFNNRY Franny
AFNORT afront
AFNPRY frypan, pan-fry
AFNSTU fuants
AFORRW farrow
AFORRY orfray
AFORTU far out, fautor
AFORUV favour
AFRRTY fratry
AFRSTU frusta
AGGHIS haggis
AGGHSY shaggy
AGGIIL gilgai
AGGILN laggin
AGGILO loggia
AGGILR gargil
AGGILU guglia
AGGIMN gaming, gigman
AGGIMT magtig
AGGIWW wigwag
AGGIZZ zigzag
AGGLNY gangly
AGGLOT loggat
AGGLSY slaggy
AGGLWY waggly
AGGMOT maggot
AGGNOR Gorgan
AGGNOU guango
AGGNOW waggon
AGGNOX oxgang
AGGNRU nuggar
AGGNSY snaggy
AGGPRY pygarg
AGGQUY quaggy
AGGRRU gurrag
AGHHTU haught
AGHIKU kiaugh
AGHILT alight
AGHINN nihang
AGHINV having
AGHINZ Ghazni
AGHIQU quaigh
AGHIRS garish
AGHIRT aright, graith
AGHISU aguish
AGHISZ Ghazis
AGHKRU Gurkha
AGHLLU Gullah
AGHLMO gholam
AGHLMU gumlah, Mughal
AGHLNU hangul
AGHLOS galosh
AGHLSY gashly
AGHLUY laughy
AGHMOT Gotham
AGHMRS Gramsh
AGHNNU unhang
AGHNOO Oonagh
AGHNOP P'ohang
AGHNOT gnatho
AGHNOU hougan
AGHNPU hang-up
AGHNRT Granth
AGHNRU nuragh
AGHNTU naught
AGHNUV Vaughn
AGHNUY gunyah
AGHOQU quahog
AGHOTU oughta
AGHPRY graphy
AGHRRU gurrah
AGHRRY gharry
AGHRTU raught, tughra
AGHSTU saught
AGHTTU taught
AGHTUW waught
AGIIJJ Jijiga

AGIIJN gaijin
AGIIKL Kigali
AGIILN ailing, angili, nilgai
AGIIMR agrimi
AGIINR airing, Iringa, ragini
AGIJKN kijang
AGIJSW jigsaw
AGIKMN making
AGIKNR kangri, raking
AGIKNS asking, gaskin
AGIKNT taking
AGIKNW waking
AGILLU ligula
AGILMM gimmal
AGILMN lingam, malign
AGILMO glioma
AGILMP magilp
AGILMS Glamis
AGILMU galium
AGILMY gamily
AGILNO galion, ingaol, in-goal, lingoa
AGILNP paling
AGILNS Sangli, signal
AGILNU gaulin, lingua
AGILNW lawing
AGILNY gainly, laying
AGILOR gloria
AGILOS gas oil
AGILOT galiot, latigo
AGILOV ogival
AGILRV virgal
AGILRY glairy
AGILST gaslit
AGIMNN naming
AGIMNR ingram, margin
AGIMNY maying
AGIMOS isogam
AGIMRU augrim
AGIMST stigma
AGIMWW wigwam
AGINNO ganoin
AGINNP pinang
AGINNQ Anqing
AGINNW awning
AGINOP pingao
AGINOS gosain, sagoin, Saigon
AGINOT gitano
AGINOW wongai
AGINPR paring
AGINPS pisang
AGINPV paving
AGINRR girran, raring
AGINRT gratin, rating
AGINRU airgun, Ugrian
AGINRV raving
AGINRY grainy
AGINSS assign
AGINST gainst
AGINSV saving
AGINSW aswing, saw-gin
AGINSY saying
AGINYY Yiyang
AGIORT agriot
AGIORU aurigo, giaour
AGIORV virago
AGIOTU agouti
AGIRRU guarri
AGIRST gratis
AGIRTU guitar
AGISST gassit
AGITTW witgat
AGJLMO logjam
AGJNOR jargon
AGJRTU Gujrat
AGJTTY gyttja
AGKLNO kalong
AGKLOT kgotla
AGKNOU nogaku
AGKNRU kurgan
AGKOOZ gazook
AGKORT go-kart
AGLLMU glulam
AGLLNO gallon, gollan
AGLLOP gallop
AGLLOW gallow
AGLLRY Argyll
AGLLSU gallus
AGLMOR glamor
AGLNNO longan
AGLNOO lagoon, loogan
AGLNOP galpon, pongal
AGLNOS Anglos, slogan
AGLNOU lanugo, Lugano
AGLNRU langur
AGLNRY gnarly
AGLNSY slangy
AGLNTY tangly
AGLNUU ungual, ungula
AGLOOT galoot
AGLPUY plaguy
AGLRUV vulgar
AGLRUY raguly
AGLSSY glassy
AGLSTY gastly
AGLSUV valgus
AGMMNO gammon
AGMMNU magnum
AGMMSU gummas
AGMNNO magnon, mongan
AGMNNU gunman
AGMNOO moonga
AGMNOR morgan
AGMNOT gamont, togman
AGMNOX magnox
AGMNRU granum
AGMNSU Magnus, musang
AGMOOY oogamy
AGMORS orgasm
AGMORT Margot
AGMORV vagrom
AGMORY morgay
AGMOYZ zygoma
AGMPRY grampy
AGMPTY ptygma
AGMPUZ gazump
AGNNOT Tongan
AGNNOY Yangon
AGNNPU panung
AGNNRY granny
AGNNTU tangun
AGNOOT gnatoo
AGNOQU quango
AGNORR garron
AGNORS sarong
AGNORT tangor
AGNORW awrong, growan
AGNORY Gaynor, organy, yorgan
AGNOSS gossan
AGNOTU nougat
AGNPRS sprang
AGNPRU Nagpur
AGNPUY Puyang
AGNRTY gantry
AGNRUY ray gun
AGNTTY gnatty
AGNTWY twangy
AGOORT agorot
AGOORV vorago
AGOPRU gopura
AGORST groats
AGORSU rugosa
AGORSY argosy
AGORTU ragout
AGOSTU outgas
AGOSUV vagous
AGOSYZ azygos
AGOTTU tautog
AGPSUU gaupus
AGPSUW gawpus
AGRSSU sargus
AGRSSY grassy
AGRSTU Struga, tragus
AGRSUY sugary
AGRUUY augury
AGSTUU august
AGSTUV Gustav
AHHIKS shaikh
AHHIMS Hamish, Hashim
AHHISS Shashi
AHHIUZ Zhuhai
AHHKOO hookah
AHHLPY hyphal
AHHRRU hurrah
AHHRST thrash
AHIIKL kahili
AHIIKN hinaki
AHIIKP pakihi
AHIILN Linhai
AHIILP philia
AHIILT lithia
AHIIRS airish
AHIJNS Jhansi
AHIJNU Jinhua
AHIJOS Josiah
AHIJPS japish
AHIKKS khakis
AHIKLS lakish
AHIKLT khilat
AHIKMO Kohima
AHIKNS Nashik
AHIKNT thakin
AHIKOW kowhai
AHIKPP kippah
AHIKRS Karshi, rakish, rakshi, shikar
AHIKSS shiksa
AHIKTW hawkit
AHIKTZ Itzhak
AHILLL Lillah
AHILLP phalli
AHILLT thalli
AHILLZ zillah
AHILMS lamish, mishla
AHILMT litham
AHILMU hamuli
AHILNP alphin
AHILNR rhinal
AHILNU inhaul
AHILNY hyalin, linhay
AHILOR hirola
AHILPS palish
AHILRW awhirl
AHILRY Hilary
AHILST lathis, latish, tahsil
AHILSV lavish
AHILTU thulia
AHILTW withal
AHILYZ hazily

AHIMNS hamsin
AHIMNT hit man, mithan, thamin
AHIMOR mohair
AHIMPS mishap
AHIMRS marish
AHIMRT thiram
AHINPT hatpin
AHINRS arshin
AHINSU Husain
AHINSV vanish
AHINSW washin
AHINSY Shiyan
AHINTT Tanith, tin hat
AHIOPR phoria
AHIOPS poisha, Sophia
AHIORT hot air, thoria
AHIORZ Rizhao
AHIPPS happis, papish
AHIPRS parish
AHIPRU rupiah
AHIPSS phasis
AHIRRS sirrah
AHIRRW wirrah
AHIRST Thirsa, Trisha
AHIRSV ravish
AHIRSW rawish
AHIRSZ Shiraz
AHIRTW wraith
AHIRTZ Thirza, Tirzah
AHISTU hiatus
AHISTV Vashti
AHISUU Suihua
AHJMOT Jotham
AHJOSU Joshua
AHKKPU pukkah
AHKLNU Khulna
AHKLOT khotla
AHKMNU khanum
AHKMOS moksha
AHKMOW Mohawk
AHKNPU punkah
AHKNRS shrank
AHKNTU khatun
AHKNUY hunyak
AHKORT Rohtak
AHKPRU kuphar
AHKPUU hapuku
AHKRTU kurtha, thakur
AHLLMO ollamh
AHLLMU mullah
AHLLNU nullah
AHLLOO halloo, holloa
AHLLOS hollas
AHLLOW hallow
AHLLRT thrall

AHLLUX hallux
AHLLWY whally
AHLMNY Hamlyn, hymnal
AHLMOO moolah
AHLMOS shalom
AHLMPY lympha
AHLNSU unlash
AHLOOP hoopla
AHLOPS pholas
AHLOPU houp-la
AHLORT harlot, hortal
AHLORW Harlow
AHLOSY shoaly
AHLOTY loathy
AHLPSS splash
AHLPSU lash-up, sulpha
AHLPSY plashy
AHLPTY phytal
AHLRSY rashly
AHLRTU thural
AHMMOW whammo
AHMMSY shammy
AHMMWY whammy
AHMNNU numnah
AHMNOS hansom
AHMNPY nympha
AHMOOP oompah
AHMOOT mootah
AHMOST Thomas
AHMOSU hamous
AHMOSV moshav
AHMOTU mahout
AHMOWY haymow
AHMRRU murrha
AHMRSY marshy
AHMRTW warmth
AHMSSU shamus
AHNNSU Anshun
AHNNSY shanny
AHNOOR Honora
AHNOPR harpon, orphan
AHNOPS phason
AHNOPY aphony
AHNORS Sharon, shoran
AHNORU Haroun
AHNOTW nowhat
AHNOWY anyhow
AHNPRU nuphar
AHNPSU unhasp
AHNRTW thrawn
AHNSTU sunhat
AHNSTY shanty
AHOORY hooray, yarooh
AHOPPS Paphos
AHOPRS pharos, phasor
AHOPST Pashto, pathos, potash

AHOPTT pottah, top hat
AHOQTU quotha
AHORRW harrow
AHORRY horary
AHORTT athort, throat
AHORTU author
AHORTW hot war, wroath
AHORTX thorax
AHORUV havour
AHOSSX Xhosas
AHOSTW whatso
AHOSUW Shaowu
AHOTWZ howzat
AHPSUW wash-up
AHQSSU squash
AHRRTU Arthur
AHRRUY hurray
AHRSSU hussar
AHRSTT strath
AHRSTY trashy
AHRTTW thwart
AHRTWY wrathy
AHSSTU tussah
AHSSTW swaths
AIIJLN injail
AIIKKN kinaki
AIIKLN kilian
AIIKLS Likasi
AIIKMT Kitami
AIIKPT patiki
AIIKRR rariki
AIILLM limail
AIILLN Lilian
AIILLS Lilias
AIILNP Pailin
AIILNR inrail
AIILNT intail
AIILNX Linxia
AIILOV Olivia
AIILRV virial
AIILRY airily
AIILSV Silvia
AIIMMN minima
AIIMMR Miriam
AIIMNR Mairin
AIIMNS simian
AIIMNT intima
AIIMPR impair
AIIMST samiti
AIINNN Ninian
AIINNO Ionian
AIINNZ zinnia
AIINQU quinia
AIINRS raisin
AIINST isatin
AIINSX sixain
AIINTT Titian
AIINTX Xintai
AIINVV Vivian
AIIPST pistia
AIIPTW wapiti
AIIQRS Iraqis

AIIRTV trivia
AIISSS Assisi
AIJJMM jimjam
AIJJNU Ujjain
AIJKLN kinjal
AIJLMS Majlis
AIJLNU Julian
AIJLOV jovial
AIJMNS jasmin
AIJMOR romaji
AIJNOV Jovian
AIJNSS Jansis
AIJORW jowari
AIJOSS Josias
AIJPRU pujari
AIJPSS jaspis
AIJPTU jupati
AIJRSV Jarvis
AIKKLO kokila
AIKKMM kim-kam
AIKKMO Komaki
AIKKNO konaki
AIKLLS killas
AIKLMN malkin
AIKLMS miskal
AIKLNO kaolin
AIKLNT kintal, talk-in
AIKLNW walk-in
AIKLOW kwai-lo
AIKLRU Ulrika
AIKLSU saluki
AIKLSZ Kalisz
AIKLTU likuta
AIKMMS immask
AIKMNN mankin
AIKMNW mawkin
AIKMOO oomiak
AIKMOP Maikop
AIKMPR impark
AIKMSU Kumasi
AIKNNP napkin, pankin
AIKNPR kirpan, parkin
AIKNRT kirtan
AIKNRU Kiruna
AIKOPS okapis
AIKOPT katipo
AIKORS kairos
AIKORT troika
AIKPRZ prikaz
AIKRRS karris
AIKRSS kissar
AIKRSU kauris
AIKRTU kutira
AIKTUW Kuwait
AILLMP impall
AILLMU allium
AILLNV villan
AILLNW inwall
AILLOT Lolita
AILLPR pillar
AILLRY railly
AILLSW wallis

AILLUU luluai
AILLUZ lazuli
AILLWY willya
AILLYZ lazily
AILMMS malism
AILMMU lamium
AILMNO monial, oilman
AILMNR marlin
AILMNS maslin
AILMNU alumni, lumina
AILMNV Malvin
AILMNY mainly
AILMNZ manzil
AILMOP lipoma
AILMOS Somali
AILMOT maloti
AILMPR imparl, primal
AILMRT mitral, ramtil
AILMSS missal, salmis
AILMST malist
AILMSX smilax
AILMSY mislay
AILMTU ultima
AILMTY matily
AILMUV maulvi, Valium
AILNNU annuli, unnail
AILNOP oil pan
AILNOR Lorain
AILNOS Alison
AILNOT Latino, talion
AILNPS spinal
AILNPT plaint, pliant
AILNPU paulin
AILNPY pinlay
AILNRT ratlin, trinal
AILNRU urinal
AILNST instal
AILNSU insula
AILNSV silvan
AILNTU inlaut
AILNTY litany
AILNVY vainly
AILNWY Aylwin
AILNYZ zanily
AILOOR oorali, oorial
AILOPR paroli, polari
AILOPU pailou
AILORS sailor
AILORT Rialto, tailor
AILORV virola
AILOSS assoil, loasis
AILOST ostial
AILOSU Louisa
AILOSX oxalis
AILOTX oxtail
AILPRS spiral
AILPRT tripla
AILPST pastil
AILPTU tipula
AILPWZ zip law
AILQSU quails, squail
AILRRW Wirral
AILRSW aswirl
AILRTU ritual
AILRTY traily
AILRWY warily
AILSSU asilus
AILSTX laxist
AILSUV Vaslui, visual
AILSVY Sylvia
AILSVZ vizsla
AILTXY laxity
AILVWY wavily
AILWXY waxily
AIMMMR immram
AIMMMU mummia
AIMMNO mon ami
AIMMNS manism
AIMMOS Maoism, mimosa
AIMMRY Miryam
AIMNNO amnion, Minoan, nomina
AIMNNS nanism
AIMNNT tinman
AIMNNU numina
AIMNNY minyan
AIMNOR manoir, Marion
AIMNOS maison, Simona
AIMNOT manito
AIMNPT pitman
AIMNPW impawn
AIMNPY paynim
AIMNRT Antrim, mantri, martin
AIMNRU rumina
AIMNRV Marvin
AIMNST mantis, matins, Tamsin
AIMNSU animus
AIMNSY Yasmin
AIMNSZ Nazism
AIMNTT titman
AIMOPT matipo, optima
AIMOPV vipoma
AIMOPY myopia
AIMORS Maoris
AIMOST Maoist, Taoism
AIMPPS papism
AIMPRT armpit, impart
AIMPSS passim
AIMQSU maquis
AIMRST Marist
AIMRSU Marius
AIMRTU atrium
AIMRTV Mirvat
AIMRTX matrix
AIMSSW swamis
AIMSSY missay
AIMSTU autism
AINNNT tannin
AINNOP panino
AINNOS nasion
AINNOT anoint, nation
AINNOW wanion, Winona
AINNPS inspan, pinnas
AINNPY pinnay
AINOQU quinoa
AINORS Rosina
AINORT aroint, ration
AINOSS assoin
AINOSU Siouan
AINPPT pitpan
AINPRS sprain
AINPRT intrap, patrin
AINPRU Purnia
AINPRW inwarp, inwrap
AINPST ptisan
AINPSV spavin
AINPTU Putian
AINPTY painty
AINQRT qintar
AINQTU quaint, quinta
AINQUU quinua
AINQVZ Qazvin
AINRST instar, santir, sartin, Sintra, strain
AINRSY Syrian
AINRTT nritta
AINRTU nutria
AINRTY in-tray, nritya, Tyrian
AINSTT tanist
AINSTU Austin
AINSTY sanity, satiny
AINTVY vanity
AIOORS arioso
AIOPRT portia
AIOPRV pavior
AIOPST patois
AIOPTU utopia
AIORST aorist, aristo, Rosita, satori
AIORSV savior, savoir
AIORTV viator
AIOSTT Taoist
AIOSYZ zoysia
AIPPRR riprap
AIPPRY papyri
AIPPST papist, tappis
AIPPTT pit-pat, tip-tap
AIPPTW wappit
AIPRRU Raipur
AIPRSS raspis
AIPRST rapist
AIPRSV parvis, Privas
AIPRSW ripsaw
AIPRSX praxis
AIPRTX patrix
AIPRTY parity
AIPRUY pyuria
AIPSST pastis
AIPSTW pit-saw, saw-pit
AIPZZZ pizazz
AIQSSU quaiss
AIRRTY rarity
AIRSST sistra
AIRSSU Russia
AIRSTT artist, strait, traist
AIRSTU aurist
AIRSTV travis
AIRTTT attrit
AIRTTY tityra
AIRVVY vivary
AISSST assist, stasis
AISSTW tiswas
AISSTX saxist
AISTTW atwist
AITTWX atwixt
AJKKNO konjak
AJKNSY jansky
AJKORT Rajkot
AJLOOR jarool
AJLOPY jalopy
AJMNOO jamoon, majoon
AJMORR jorram
AJMORU Majuro
AJMPSY pyjams
AJMRTU jumart
AJNORT Trojan
AJNRTU jurant
AJNTUY jaunty

AJORRW Jarrow
AJPRTU Rajput
AKKKOO kokako
AKKLMY Kalmyk
AKKNRU karkun
AKKOQU quokka
AKKPUU kukupa
AKLLNY lankly
AKLMOU lakoum
AKLNOU koulan
AKLNOW walk-on
AKLNOX klaxon
AKLNRY rankly
AKLOOT talook
AKLOPS polkas, polska
AKLORS raskol
AKLOSV Slovak
AKLOTW kotwal
AKLPUW walk-up
AKLSTY stalky
AKMNSU unmask
AKMPRU mark-up
AKMRUU kuruma
AKMSUW muskwa
AKMTUU makutu
AKNNOO kanoon
AKNOOT Nootka
AKNOPS ponask
AKNORU koruna
AKNORY ryokan
AKNPRT prankt
AKNRTY tranky
AKNRUU Nakuru
AKNSWY swanky
AKOORR Karroo
AKORSS kaross
AKOSTU katsuo
AKOTWY towkay
AKPRSS Sparks
AKPRSY sparky
AKQSUW squawk
AKRSTU tuskar
AKRTTU kuttar
AKSUUZ Suzuka
AKSWYY skyway
AKTUVZ kvutza
ALLLUY lullay
ALLMOP pollam
ALLMOS slalom
ALLMOT maltol
ALLMOW mallow
ALLMUV vallum
ALLMUW wallum
ALLNOP pollan
ALLNUU lunula
ALLOOP palolo
ALLOPR pallor
ALLOPW wallop
ALLORY orally
ALLOSW sallow
ALLOTU all-out
ALLOTW tallow
ALLOUY you-all
ALLOVY ovally
ALLOWW wallow
ALLPRU plural
ALLPSY psylla
ALLQSU squall
ALLRUY lauryl
ALLSTY lastly, saltly
ALLUVV vulval
ALMMOR mormal
ALMNOO manool
ALMNOR normal
ALMNOS salmon
ALMNOU monaul
ALMNRY Marlyn
ALMNTU Multan
ALMORS samlor
ALMORT mortal
ALMORU morula
ALMORY Malory, molary
ALMOSS molass
ALMOST almost, stomal
ALMOTW matlow
ALMOTY latomy
ALMQUY qualmy
ALMRTY martly
ALMRWY warmly
ALMSSU mussal
ALMSUY asylum
ALMTUU mutual, umlaut
ALNNOU nounal
ALNOOS saloon
ALNOOZ Alonzo
ALNOPR prolan
ALNORT latron, lontar
ALNOTU latoun, outnal
ALNOTV volant
ALNOTW Lawton
ALNOTX Laxton
ALNOTY Layton
ALNOUZ zonula
ALNPTU pultan, puntal
ALNRSY snarly
ALNRUY lunary
ALNRXY larynx
ALNSTU sultan
ALNSVY sylvan
ALNTUW walnut
ALOOPS saloop
ALOORV Orlova
ALOPPR poplar
ALOPPT applot, laptop
ALOPRR parlor
ALOPRT patrol, portal
ALOPRY pyrola
ALOPST postal
ALOQTU loquat
ALORSV salvor
ALORTU torula
ALORTY Taylor
ALORUV ovular, valour
ALORVY volary
ALOTUV voluta
ALOTUW outlaw
ALOTUY layout, outlay
ALPPSU palpus, slap-up
ALPRRU larrup
ALPRSU pulsar
ALPRSW sprawl
ALPRTY paltry, partly, raptly
ALPRUW pulwar
ALPSSU lapsus
ALRSTU lustra
ALRSUU Ursula
ALRSUW walrus
ALRTTY rattly, tartly
ALRTUW tulwar
ALRUUV uvular
ALRUVV vulvar
ALRXYY xylary
ALSSTU saltus
ALSSVY sylvas
ALSTVY vastly
ALSUVV vulvas
ALTTUY tautly
ALTUUV Tuvalu
ALTUVY vaulty
AMMMNO Mammon
AMMMOU amomum
AMMORT marmot
AMMOSU omasum
AMMOTY mamoty
AMMOXY myxoma
AMMPSU mampus
AMMPUW wampum
AMMRRU murram
AMMRSY smarmy
AMNNOR norman
AMNNOT montan
AMNNOY anonym
AMNNPU pannum
AMNOOO monoao
AMNOOR maroon, ramoon, Romano
AMNOOS Sonoma
AMNOPT tampon, topman
AMNORR marron
AMNORS ransom
AMNORT matron
AMNORY mornay, Romany
AMNOSS Samson
AMNOTU amount, man-t'ou, moutan
AMNOTV movant
AMNOTY notamy
AMNOWY Monywa
AMNPTY tympan
AMNRSU Mansur
AMNRTU antrum
AMNRTY Martyn
AMNRVY Marvyn
AMNTTU mutant
AMNTUU autumn
AMNUUZ Numazu
AMOOPT pomato
AMOORV varoom
AMOOTT tomato
AMOPST sampot
AMOPTU Maputo
AMORRT marrot, mortar
AMORRU armour
AMORRW marrow
AMORRY armory
AMORSS morass
AMORST Mostar, stroma
AMORSU ramous
AMORYY mayory
AMOSST stomas
AMOSSY massoy
AMOSUW awmous
AMOTUZ mazout
AMPRRU Rampur
AMPRTU trumpa
AMPRUW warm-up
AMPSUW wampus
AMPSWY swampy
AMRRTY martyr
AMRRUY Murray
AMRSTU struma
AMRSTY smarty
AMRSUU Saumur
ANNOOX xoanon
ANNOPR napron
ANNORT natron, non-art
ANNORY nonary
ANNOST santon, sonant
ANNOSW Wonsan
ANNOTT tonant
ANNOTW wanton
ANNOTY Antony, tannoy
ANNPSU pannus, sannup, unsnap
ANNPTU pantun
ANNRTY tranny
ANNSTU suntan
ANNTTU nutant
ANOORT ratoon
ANOOSW aswoon
ANOPPT panpot
ANOPRS aprons,

parson, sanpro
ANOPRT parton, patron, tarpon
ANOPTT optant
ANOPUY yaupon
ANORRW narrow
ANORRY Raynor
ANORST nostra, trason
ANORTT attorn, ratton
ANORTU outran
ANORTV vorant
ANORTY aroynt, notary
ANORWY Norway
ANOSST Santos
ANOSTY astony
ANOSXY saxony
ANOTVY voyant
ANOUXY noyaux
ANPPSY snappy
ANPRTU Turpan
ANPRTY pantry, prytan, trypan
ANPRUW unwrap
ANRRTU rat-run
ANRSTU Saturn
ANRSUU Uranus
ANRSYZ Syzran
ANRTTU truant
ANRTTY tyrant
ANRUWY runway, unwary
ANSTTU tutsan
ANSTWY Wystan
ANSTXY syntax
ANSYZZ snazzy
ANTUVY vaunty
AOOPST astoop
AOOPTT potato, tap-too
AOORRT orator
AOORRY arroyo
AOORTT tooart, totora
AOORTV ovator
AOOTTT tattoo
AOOTTY Toyota
AOPPRT apport, pop art
AOPPRW approw
AOPRRT parrot, raptor
AOPRRU uproar
AOPRRY porray
AOPRST pastor, portas
AOPRSU parous, sapour
AOPRUV vapour
AOPRVY vapory
AOPSST potass, topass
AOPTUY pay-out
AOQRTU quarto, quatro
AOQSTU quotas
AORRST rostra, sartor
AORRSY rosary
AORRTU Arturo
AORRTW tarrow
AORRTY rotary
AORRWY arrowy, yarrow
AORSST assort
AORSTT stator
AORSTX storax
AORSUU aurous
AORSUV savour
AORSVY savory
AORTUY outray, yaourt
AORTVY travoy, votary
AORVWY avowry
AOSTTU outsat
AOSTTY toasty
AOTUWY way-out
AOTWWY two-way
APPPSU pappus
APPRUW upwarp, wrap-up
APRRSY sparry
APRSTU raptus
APRSTY pastry
APRSWY psy-war
APSSSU passus
APSTUY stay-up
APSTUZ puszta
AQRRUY quarry
AQRTUZ quartz
ARRSTY starry
ARSSTU tarsus
ARSSTW straws
ARSTTU astrut, Stuart
ARSTUU Taurus
ARSTUX surtax
ARSTWY strawy, wastry
ARSTXY styrax
ASSTTU status
BBBDEI bibbed
BBBDEO bobbed
BBBEIL bibble
BBBEIO Bobbie
BBBEIR bibber
BBBELO bobble
BBBELU bubble
BBBEOR bobber
BBBHUU hubbub
BBBINO bobbin
BBBLOY bobbly
BBBLUY bubbly
BBCDEU cubbed
BBCELO cobble
BBCEOR cobber
BBCEOW cobweb
BBCHUY chubby
BBCLUY clubby
BBDDEI dibbed
BBDDEO dobbed
BBDDEU dubbed
BBDEEI Debbie
BBDEEW webbed
BBDEFI fibbed
BBDEFO fobbed
BBDEGO gobbed
BBDEGU bedbug
BBDEIJ jibbed
BBDEIL dibble
BBDEIN nibbed
BBDEIO dobbie
BBDEIR dibber, ribbed
BBDEJO jobbed
BBDELO lobbed
BBDEMO bombed, mobbed
BBDEOR dobber, robbed
BBDEOS sobbed
BBDEPU pubbed
BBDERU dubber, rubbed
BBDESU subbed
BBDETU tubbed
BBDGIU big bud
BBDIKU dibbuk
BBDINO dobbin
BBDINU dubbin
BBDKUY dybbuk
BBEEEE beebee
BBEEIK kebbie
BBEEKL lebbek
BBEELP pebble
BBEENN neb-neb
BBEERR Berber
BBEEYY bye-bye
BBEFIR fibber
BBEGIN Big Ben
BBEGIR gibber
BBEGIT gibbet
BBEGLO gobble
BBEGLU gubble
BBEGNU bebung, Bengbu
BBEGOT gobbet
BBEHLO hobble
BBEIIM imbibe
BBEIIS Sibbie
BBEIJO jobbie
BBEIJR jibber
BBEIKL kibble
BBEILN nibble
BBEILP pibble
BBEILR libber
BBEILT libbet
BBEIMO mobbie
BBEIMY bimeby
BBEIOR Robbie
BBEIRR briber
BBEJLO jobble
BBEJOR jobber
BBEKNU nebbuk
BBELLU bulbel
BBELMU bumble
BBELNO nobble
BBELNU nubble
BBELNY nybble
BBELOW wobble
BBELPU pubble
BBELPY pebbly, plebby
BBELRU burble, lubber, rubble
BBEMNU benumb
BBEMOR bomber, mobber
BBEORR robber
BBEOTU tubboe
BBERRU rubber
BBGGIU big bug
BBGINO gibbon
BBGINU gubbin
BBGIOU Gubbio
BBGNOO gobbon
BBGRUY grubby
BBHIOT hobbit
BBHNOO hobnob
BBIINT tibbin
BBIKOS ski-bob
BBILLU bulbil
BBILSU biblus
BBINNU nubbin
BBINOR ribbon
BBITUW wubbit
BBKNOY knobby
BBKOOS bosbok
BBLLUU bulbul
BBLNOY nobbly
BBLNUY nubbly
BBLOSY Byblos
BBLOWY by-blow, wobbly
BBLRUY rubbly
BBMOUY bumboy
BBMOXY bombyx
BBMRUY brumby
BBNNOO bon-bon
BBNOOO bonobo
BBNOSY snobby
BBNOTU nobbut
BBOOOO booboo
BBORTU burbot
BBOSUY busboy
BBRSUU suburb
BBSTUY stubby
BCCEEH chebec
BCDEEK bedeck
BCDEIO bodice
BCDEIU cue-bid
BCDEMO combed

BCDEOU obduce
BCDIOU cuboid
BCDNOU bonduc
BCDOTU obduct
BCEEHO obeche
BCEEHR breech
BCEEKR rebeck
BCEEKT becket
BCEEKZ zebeck
BCEEMO become
BCEEQU Quebec
BCEGIL Belgic
BCEGLO beclog
BCEHIN Binche
BCEHLN blench
BCEHOR broche
BCEHRU cherub
BCEIKR bicker
BCEIKU buckie
BCEILM emblic
BCEILP beclip
BCEIMO combie
BCEIOR corbie
BCEIOX icebox
BCEIPS biceps
BCEIRS scribe
BCEIRT tecbir
BCEIST bisect
BCEJOT object
BCEKLO belock
BCEKLU buckle
BCEKMO bemock
BCEKNO beckon
BCEKTU bucket
BCELMO comble
BCELMU cumble
BCELNO en bloc
BCELOR corbel
BCELRU becurl
BCEMOR comber
BCEMRU cumber
BCENOR Brecon
BCENOU bounce
BCEORS scrobe
BCEOTT obtect
BCGORU Coburg
BCGORY cyborg
BCHILO chibol
BCHIOP phobic
BCHIRT britch
BCHITY bitchy
BCHLOT blotch
BCHMOU Bochum
BCHNRU brunch
BCHNUY bunchy
BCHOOR brooch
BCHORS borsch
BCIILM limbic
BCIINO bionic, niobic
BCIINU incubi
BCIIOP biopic
BCIIOT biotic
BCIKNO kincob
BCIKRY bricky
BCILPU public
BCILRU lubric
BCIMOR bromic
BCIMSU cubism
BCINOR corbin
BCIRRU rubric
BCISTU cubist
BCLMUY cumbly
BCLTUU culbut
BCMORY corymb
BCMRSU crumbs
BCMRUY crumby
BCNOOR bronco
BCNOTU cobnut
BCNOUY bouncy
BCNRUU uncurb
BCOOWY cowboy
BDDDEE bedded
BDDDEU budded
BDDDOO odd bod
BDDEER bedder
BDDEET debted
BDDEIN bidden
BDDEIO bodied
BDDEIR bedrid, bidder
BDDELU buddle
BDDENO bonded
BDDEOR debord
BDDERU redbud
BDDISU disbud
BDDJOO odd job
BDEEEN bedene
BDEEET debtee
BDEEGG begged
BDEEHL beheld
BDEEHR herbed
BDEEIL debile, edible
BDEEIS beside
BDEEIT betide
BDEELL bedell, belled
BDEELN blende
BDEELT belted
BDEENR bender
BDEEST bested
BDEETT betted
BDEFIR fibred
BDEGGO bogged
BDEGGU bugged
BDEGIL begild
BDEGIN big end
BDEGIO bodgie
BDEGIR begird, bridge
BDEGIU budgie
BDEGLO blodge
BDEGLU bludge
BDEGOR bodger
BDEGTU budget
BDEHIN behind
BDEHLO behold
BDEHOP bed-hop
BDEHOS debosh
BDEHOT hotbed
BDEHOY dhobey
BDEHSU bushed
BDEIIM ibidem
BDEIIR birdie, Bridie
BDEILL billed
BDEILM dimble, Lib Dem, limbed
BDEILN bindle
BDEILO boiled, bolide
BDEILR bridle
BDEIMN embind
BDEIMR imbred
BDEIMU imbued
BDEINN bin-end, binned
BDEINR binder, inbred, rebind
BDEINT bident, indebt
BDEINU Beduin
BDEIOO boodie
BDEIOR boride
BDEIRR birder
BDEIRS debris
BDEIRT bedirt
BDEIRV verbid
BDEIST bedsit
BDEKNU debunk
BDELLU bedull
BDELMO embold
BDELMU dumble
BDELNO blonde, bolden
BDELNU bundle
BDELOO boodle
BDELOR belord, bordel
BDELOU double
BDELOW blowed
BDELRU deblur
BDEMMU bummed
BDEMNU numbed
BDEMOY embody
BDENNU unbend
BDENOR bonder
BDENOT obtend
BDENOY beyond
BDENRU bunder, burden, burned
BDENSU sunbed
BDEOOT booted
BDEOPP bopped
BDEOPR bedrop
BDEORR border
BDEORS desorb
BDEORT debtor
BDEORU obdure
BDESSU bussed
BDESTU bedust, bestud, busted
BDESUU subdue
BDFILO bifold
BDFIOR forbid
BDGIIN biding
BDGIIO gobiid
BDGIIR Brigid
BDGOOX dog box
BDGOOY goodby
BDHIOS dhobis
BDHIRY hybrid
BDIILO libido
BDIIMN imbind
BDIIMR midrib
BDIINN inbind
BDIITT tidbit
BDIKNO bodkin
BDILNU Dublin
BDILOY bodily
BDIMNO Bodmin
BDIMOR morbid
BDINNU unbind
BDINOU boudin
BDIORS disorb
BDIOTU outbid
BDIRTU turbid
BDKLOO kobold
BDLLOY boldly
BDLMUY dumbly
BDLNOY Blodyn
BDLOOY bloody, old boy
BDLOUY doubly
BDLRUY drubly
BDMORU Bodrum
BDNOOS dobson
BDNOOY nobody
BDNOTU obtund
BDNOUY ybound
BDOORY broody
BDORWY byword
BEEEFL feeble
BEEEHP ephebe
BEEEHT hebete
BEEEKL kelebe
BEEELT beetle
BEEEMS beseem
BEEEMT bemeet, bemete
BEEENS beseen
BEEEPR beeper
BEEEPW beweep
BEEERZ beezer, breeze
BEEESV beeves
BEEFIL befile, belief
BEEFLL befell
BEEFLY feebly
BEEFOR before
BEEFRT bereft
BEEGIL beigel
BEEGIN bingee
BEEGLY leg-bye

BEEGNO begone, engobe
BEEGNR Bergen
BEEGNU bungee
BEEGRT Egbert
BEEGRU burgee
BEEHIR Herbie
BEEHLT bethel
BEEHOP phoebe
BEEHOV behove
BEEHRR herber
BEEHRW Hebrew
BEEHRY hereby
BEEHST behest
BEEIKL belike
BEEILV belive
BEEILZ Belize
BEEIMN nembie
BEEIMR bemire, berime, bireme
BEEIMT betime
BEEINR Bernie
BEEIRT Bertie
BEEIRV brieve
BEEISS Bessie
BEEISX ibexes
BEEKOP peek-bo
BEEKOR oberek, reebok
BEEKRS breeks
BEEKRU rebuke
BEELMM emblem
BEELNO Leoben
BEELNS Belsen
BEELNU nebule
BEELOT belote
BEELOV belove
BEELPT bepelt
BEELRT belter, treble
BEELXY Bexley
BEELZZ bezzle
BEEMMR member
BEEMNR Bremen
BEEMRU embrue
BEEMSU bemuse
BEENNO boneen
BEENNT bennet
BEENOR boreen, enrobe
BEENOT been-to
BEENRU Reuben
BEENTU butene
BEEOOT bootee
BEEOPP bo-peep, peep-bo
BEEORR rebore
BEEORT bo tree
BEEORY obeyer
BEEPRU burpee
BEERRU beurre
BEERRV reverb
BEERRW brewer
BEERTT better
BEERTV brevet
BEERYZ breezy
BEESTU bustee
BEESTW bewest
BEESTY beesty
BEFFLU buffel, buffle
BEFFPU bepuff
BEFFRU buffer, rebuff
BEFFTU buffet
BEFGIT begift
BEFGOR befrog
BEFHOO behoof
BEFIKT biftek
BEFILM fimble
BEFILO foible
BEFLMU fumble
BEFLOO befool
BEFLOU befoul
BEFLRY belfry
BEFORU fourbe
BEFORY forbye
BEGGII biggie
BEGGIN biggen
BEGGIR bigger
BEGGLO boggle
BEGGRU bugger
BEGHNU behung
BEGIIL big lie
BEGIIR gibier
BEGILN bingle
BEGILO oblige
BEGILP pig-bel
BEGILR gerbil
BEGILT giblet
BEGINN benign
BEGINS besing
BEGIOO boogie
BEGIOU bougie
BEGIRT begirt
BEGIRU brigue
BEGKNU begunk
BEGLNO belong
BEGLNU blunge, bungle
BEGLOT goblet
BEGLRU bugler, burgle
BEGNOY bygone
BEGNSU besung
BEGOOR goober
BEGORU brogue
BEGOTU bouget
BEGRRU burger
BEGRSU Bruges
BEHIKT kethib
BEHILS Ishbel
BEHILT blithe, thible
BEHIOT bothie
BEHISU bushie
BEHKOR rhebok
BEHLMU humble
BEHLRU burhel
BEHLSU bushel
BEHLTY Blythe
BEHMOR hombre
BEHORT bother
BEHRTU Hubert, turbeh
BEIIKR birkie
BEIILL billie
BEIILR liberi
BEIINR brinie
BEIIRS iberis
BEIISS ibises
BEIJLR jerbil
BEIJMU jumbie
BEIKLN libken
BEIKLR bilker
BEIKOO bookie
BEIKRT tekbir
BEIKSS bekiss
BEIKST bisket
BEILLT billet
BEILMN nimble
BEILMO bemoil, emboil, emboli, mobile
BEILMR limber
BEILMW wimble
BEILMY blimey
BEILMZ zimbel
BEILNR berlin
BEILNT niblet
BEILNU nubile
BEILNY byline
BEILOR boiler, libero
BEILOS besoil, Isobel
BEILOT betoil
BEILRS birsle
BEILRW wirble
BEILRY birley
BEILSY Bisley
BEIMOV B-movie
BEIMOZ zombie
BEIMRT betrim, timber, timbre
BEIMRU erbium, imbrue
BEIMRX imbrex
BEIMST bemist
BEIMSU imbues
BEIMTU bitume
BEIMTY by-time
BEINNO Benoni, bonnie
BEINNT inbent
BEINNZ benzin
BEINOR bonier
BEINOT Benito
BEINOV bovine
BEINOX bonxie
BEINRS nebris
BEINRU Brunei
BEINRY byrnie
BEINTT bitten
BEINTU butine
BEIOPR probie
BEIORS ribose
BEIORT obiter
BEIORU ourebi
BEIORX boxier
BEIOTW bow tie
BEIPPU buppie
BEIPTY bepity
BEIQSU bisque
BEIRRU burier
BEIRRY briery
BEIRST bestir, bister, bistre
BEIRSU bruise, busier
BEIRSW brewis
BEIRTT bitter
BEIRTU Beirut, biuret
BEIRTV brevit
BEITTU buttie
BEITUY ubiety
BEITUZ itzebu
BEIVWY by-view
BEJJUU jujube
BEJLMU jumble
BEJORU objure
BEKLSU buskle
BEKNOR broken
BEKNOW beknow
BEKNRU bunker
BEKOOR booker
BEKOOT betook
BEKORR broker
BEKORS bosker
BEKOST bosket
BEKRSU busker
BELLMU bellum
BELLNO bollen
BELLOT boltel
BELLOU boulle, lobule
BELLOW bellow, bowell
BELLRU buller
BELLTU bullet
BELMMU bummel, mumble
BELMOP plombe
BELMOW embowl, womble
BELMOY emboly
BELMRU lumber, rumble
BELMSU umbles
BELMTU tumble
BELMUU ebulum
BELNNY blenny
BELNOR nobler
BELNOW blowen
BELNOZ benzol

BELNTU unbelt
BELNTY yblent
BELNUY nebuly
BELNYZ benzyl
BELOOR bolero
BELOOV Belovo
BELOOY blooey
BELOPU pueblo
BELORR borrel
BELORT bolter
BELORU rouble
BELORW blower, bowler
BELOSU blouse, boules, obelus
BELOSW blowse
BELOTT bottle
BELOWZ blowze
BELRRY blerry
BELRTU butler, turble
BELRTY trebly
BELRUY burley
BELSTU bluest, bustle, sub-let, subtle
BELSTY Beltsy
BELSUY bluesy
BELTTU buttle
BELTUU tubule
BEMMRU bummer
BEMNOT entomb
BEMNOW enwomb
BEMNRU number
BEMOOR boomer
BEMORS somber, sombre
BEMORY embryo
BEMOSS emboss
BEMPRU bumper
BEMRTY tymber
BEMSTU besmut
BENNOT bonnet
BENNSU Bunsen
BENNTU unbent
BENOOR Oberon
BENORR reborn
BENORT betorn, Breton
BENORU bourne, unrobe
BENORZ bonzer, bronze
BENOSW besnow
BENOTY betony
BENRRU burner
BENRTU brunet, bunter, burnet
BENTUY butyne
BEOORS broose
BEOORT reboot
BEOORZ boozer
BEOPPR bopper
BEOPRR prober
BEOPST bespot
BEORRS resorb
BEORRT Robert
BEORST besort, Osbert, sorbet, strobe
BEORSU bourse
BEORSW bowser, browse
BEORTT bettor
BEORTV obvert
BEORVV bovver
BEORVY over-by
BEORWY bowery, bowyer
BEORWZ browze
BEOSSS obsess
BEOSTT obtest
BEOSTU obtuse
BEOSTW bestow
BEPRSU superb
BEPRUW brew-up
BERRUY rebury
BERSTU buster
BERTTU butter
BERTUY uberty
BERTWY Wybert
BERUZZ buzzer
BESSSU busses
BESSTU subset
BFFIIN biffin
BFFINO boffin
BFFINU buffin
BFGOOW fog-bow
BFIILR fibril
BFIINR fibrin
BFIMOR biform
BFINOW bowfin
BFINOY bonify
BFKOSU obfusk
BFLOOT Botolf
BFLOTU Botulf
BFLOTY botfly
BFLOUX boxful
BFLOYY fly boy
BFLTUU tubful
BFMORY by-form
BFOORS Bofors
BGGIIN biggin
BGGIIW bigwig
BGGINU big gun
BGGLUY bluggy
BGGNOO bogong
BGGNOU bugong
BGHIIL ghibli
BGHIIN binghi
BGHILT blight
BGHIRT bright
BGHMUU humbug
BGHORU brough
BGHOTU bought
BGIIMR gimbri
BGIINT biting
BGIIRT Birgit, Brigit
BGILLY glibly
BGILNO globin, goblin, lobing
BGILNU bluing
BGINNO boning, nibong
BGINOR boring
BGINOX boxing
BGINTU tubing
BGINUU ingubu
BGINUY buying
BGIOPT big pot, big top
BGIORU gourbi
BGIORV Viborg
BGISWY wigsby
BGKNOU kubong
BGLNOO oblong
BGLOSU globus
BGLRUU bulgur, burgul
BGMNOO mbongo
BGNOOR Bongor
BGNOOY gobony
BGOORU burgoo
BGORSU Burgos
BHIIST bhisti
BHIKOS kibosh
BHIKSU bukshi
BHILSU bluish
BHIMOR rhombi
BHIOPS bishop
BHIOSY boyish
BHIRSU hubris
BHIRSY hybris
BHITWY Whitby
BHKNOU bohunk
BHKOSY kybosh
BHLLSU bullsh
BHLMUY humbly
BHLOOT blooth
BHLOSY Bolshy
BHLOTW blowth
BHLSTU blusht
BHMTUY thumby
BHOOOO boohoo
BHOTTU hot tub
BHRSUY brushy
BIIIKN bikini
BIIKTZ kibitz
BIILTV blivit
BIIMUV bivium
BIINNS sin bin
BIINOT biotin
BIINOU biniou
BIIORS oribis
BIIORV vibrio
BIITTT titbit
BIKKOO kiboko
BIKLNU bulkin
BIKMNU bumkin
BIKNSU buskin
BILLNO billon
BILLNU Lublin
BILLOW billow
BILLOX bollix
BILLOY billy-o
BILMNY nimbly
BILMSU bluism, limbus
BILNOS Lisbon
BILNYY byliny
BILORV Bovril
BILRRY blirry
BILRTY trilby
BILRUW Wilbur
BILSUY busily
BILTUU tubuli
BIMMNO mombin
BIMMOO miombo
BIMNOS bonism
BIMNOT intomb
BIMNOW inwomb
BIMNSU nimbus
BIMOSS imboss
BIMSTU submit
BINNOR inborn
BINNOU bunion
BINOOT bonito
BINORT Briton
BINORU Urbino
BINORY briony
BINOSS bisson
BINOTY bonity
BINPUY bunyip
BIOORZ borzoi
BIOOST oboist
BIOOSV ovibos
BIOPRT probit
BIOPSY biopsy
BIORRS sbirro
BIORST bistro
BIORSW browis
BIORTY orbity
BIOTTW two-bit
BIOTUW woubit
BIQSUY quisby
BIRTTU turbit
BJLMUY jumbly
BJLOOT job lot
BJMOOU boojum
BKKMUU kumbuk
BKMNUU bunkum
BKNPUU bunk-up
BKOOSY booksy
BKORWY by-work
BLLORY brolly
BLLOUX bollux
BLMNUY numbly
BLMOSY symbol
BLNOOS bolson
BLNOOT bolt-on, Bolton
BLNOTU unbolt
BLOOSU obolus
BLOOTT blotto

BLOOWY lowboy
BLOPUW blow-up
BLOWYZ blowzy
BLRRUY blurry
BLSTUY subtly
BMMRUY Brummy
BMNOOT bon mot
BMOOOS obosom
BMOORY by-room
BMOOSY bosomy
BMOOTT bottom
BMOOTY tomboy
BNNORU unborn
BNNOTU bunton
BNOORS Osborn
BNOOST Boston
BNOOTU bouton, unboot
BNOOTY botony
BNORSU suborn
BNORTU burton
BNORUW Woburn
BNORWY browny
BNORYY bryony
BNORYZ bronzy
BNOSUW sunbow
BNOTTU button
BNOTUX Buxton
BNOTUY bounty
BNRUUY unbury
BOORRW borrow
BOORSU orobus
BOOTXY toy-box
BOOTYY toyboy
BOOWWW bow-wow
BORRUW burrow
BORSTU robust
BORSTW browst
BORTTU turbot
BOTUUY buyout
BPSTUU bust-up
BSSSUY byssus
CCCDIO coccid
CCCILY cyclic
CCCOSU coccus
CCCOXY coccyx
CCDEER recced
CCDEIR Cedric, Cerdic
CCDEOT decoct
CCEEIL Cecile
CCEELR leccer
CCEELS Eccles
CCEEOR coerce
CCEHIL chicle, cliche
CCEHIM chemic
CCEHIO choice, echoic
CCEHIR chic-er
CCEHIT hectic
CCEHKY checky
CCEHLN clench
CCEHLO cloche
CCEHLT cletch
CCEHLU cleuch
CCEHNO conche
CCEHOR croche
CCEHRU cruche
CCEIIL cilice, icicle
CCEILR circle, cleric
CCEILT Celtic
CCEILY Cecily, cicely
CCEINS scenic
CCEIOR Cicero
CCEIPT pectic
CCEIRT cretic
CCEIRU erucic
CCEITY cecity
CCEKLO cockle
CCEKOP copeck
CCEKOR cocker
CCEKOT cocket
CCENOS sconce
CCEORS soccer
CCEOTX excoct
CCERSU cercus, cruces
CCFILO flocci
CCHHII chichi
CCHHIN chinch
CCHHOO chocho
CCHHRU church
CCHIKT tchick
CCHILN clinch
CCHILO cholic
CCHILT clitch
CCHILY chicly
CCHIMY chymic
CCHINO Cochin
CCHIOR choric
CCHIPU hiccup
CCHKUY chucky
CCHLNU clunch
CCHLOO clooch
CCHLSU sculch
CCHLTU clutch, cultch
CCHNOS conchs
CCHNOY conchy
CCHNRU crunch
CCHNSU scunch
CCHORS scorch
CCHORT crotch
CCHORU crouch
CCHOST scotch
CCHRTU crutch
CCHSTU scutch
CCIILN clinic
CCIILT clitic
CCIIMT mictic
CCIINO iconic
CCIINP picnic
CCIIPR picric
CCIIRT citric, critic
CCIISV civics
CCILNO clonic
CCILNY cyclin
CCILTU cultic
CCIMOS cosmic
CCIMRY Cymric
CCINOR crocin
CCINPY pycnic
CCIOPT Coptic
CCIOSS cossic
CCIPRU cupric
CCIRSU circus
CCISTY cystic
CCJOUU cucujo
CCKLOO o'clock
CCKLUY clucky
CCKMOO mocock
CCKOOP pocock
CCKOOU cuckoo
CCKOPU cock-up
CCKOSY cocksy
CCLOOS scoloc
CCLOTU occult
CCLSUY cyclus
CCNOOO cocoon
CCNORU concur
CCOOOR rococo
CCOPUY occupy
CCORSU crocus, succor
CCOSTU stucco
CCSSUU cuscus
CDDDEO codded
CDDEEI decide
CDDEEK decked
CDDEEO decode
CDDEEU deduce, deuced
CDDEHI chided
CDDEIU cuddie
CDDELO coddle
CDDELU cuddle
CDDENU cudden
CDDEOR codder, corded
CDDERU curded
CDDETU deduct
CDDHUY chuddy
CDDIIR didric
CDDLUY cuddly
CDDRUY cruddy
CDDSUY scuddy
CDEEEM emceed
CDEEER decree, recede
CDEEES secede
CDEEEX exceed
CDEEFT defect
CDEEGL cledge
CDEEHR cheder
CDEEIK deckie
CDEEIL decile, delice
CDEEIN incede
CDEEIR de-icer
CDEEIT deceit
CDEEIV device
CDEEIX excide
CDEEJT deject
CDEEKL deckle
CDEEKN necked
CDEEKO decoke
CDEEKP pecked
CDEEKR decker
CDEELL celled
CDEELT delect
CDEEMR Merced
CDEENO encode
CDEENR decern
CDEENT decent
CDEENU enduce
CDEEOO cooeed
CDEEOR decore, recode
CDEEPR decerp
CDEERS screed
CDEERU reduce
CDEERW decrew
CDEESU seduce
CDEETT detect
CDEFFU cuffed
CDEFII deific
CDEFIO coifed
CDEFNU fecund
CDEFOR forced
CDEGGO cogged
CDEGIO geodic
CDEGLU cudgel
CDEGOR codger
CDEHIL chield, childe
CDEHIN inched
CDEHIR chider, dreich, driech, herdic
CDEHLY chylde
CDEHNR drench
CDEHOU douche
CDEHRT dretch
CDEHRU ruched
CDEIIK Dickie
CDEIIL Lidice
CDEIIN incide
CDEIIR dicier
CDEIIT citied, dietic
CDEIJU juiced
CDEIKM medick
CDEIKN dicken
CDEIKP picked
CDEIKR dicker
CDEIKT ticked
CDEIKU duckie
CDEIKW wicked
CDEIKY dickey
CDEILO docile
CDEILR clerid
CDEILT delict
CDEILU Dulcie, Euclid

CDEIMO medico
CDEIMR dermic
CDEINN incend
CDEINO condie
CDEINR cinder, crined
CDEINU induce
CDEINW Wendic
CDEIOR Dorice
CDEIOV voiced
CDEIPR percid, priced
CDEIPT depict
CDEIRS scried
CDEIRT credit, direct
CDEIRV cervid
CDEIRY dry ice
CDEKLO locked
CDEKNO docken
CDEKOP pocked
CDEKOR corked, docker
CDEKOT docket
CDEKRU ducker
CDEKRY Deryck
CDEKTU tucked
CDELOO locoed
CDELOS closed
CDELOW cowled
CDELRU curdle, curled
CDELTU dulcet
CDEMOO comedo
CDEMOY comedy
CDENNO conned
CDENOR conder, corned
CDENOS second
CDENOT docent
CDENSU secund
CDEOPP copped
CDEORR record
CDEORS escrod
CDEORW crowed
CDEOST costed
CDEOSU escudo
CDEOTT cotted
CDEOTU doucet
CDEOYZ zydeco
CDEPPU cupped
CDEPSU cusped
CDERSU cursed
CDERSY descry
CDERUV curved
CDERUY decury
CDESSU cussed
CDETTU cutted
CDFIOU fucoid
CDFIOY codify
CDGOOY coydog
CDHIOP phocid
CDHIOR orchid
CDHIRY hydric
CDHITY ditchy
CDIIIR iridic
CDIIKN dickin
CDIINO indico
CDIINT indict
CDIIOT diotic
CDIIOY idiocy
CDIISV viscid
CDIKNO Dickon
CDILNO codlin
CDILNU dulcin
CDIMOR dromic
CDIMOU mucoid
CDIMOY cymoid
CDIMSU muscid
CDIMTU dictum
CDINOO conoid
CDINOR Nordic
CDINOU doucin
CDINSY syndic
CDINTU induct
CDIOOV vocoid
CDIOPS psocid
CDIORV corvid
CDIOSS cossid
CDIOTT cottid
CDIOTY cytoid, docity
CDIPSU cuspid
CDISSU discus
CDISTY cystid
CDJNOU jocund
CDKNOU undock
CDLLOY coldly
CDLOUY cloudy
CDMNOO condom
CDNOOR condor, con-rod, cordon
CDNORU uncord
CDOOOT doocot
CDOORT doctor
CDOORY corody
CDORTU ductor
CDORWY crowdy
CDSTUU ductus
CEEEFL fleece
CEEEGR Greece
CEEEHL elchee
CEEEHS cheese
CEEELV cleeve
CEEEMN ceneme
CEEEMS emcees
CEEENO Eocene
CEEENT ectene
CEEERS creese
CEEERV creeve
CEEERX exerce
CEEFFO coffee
CEEFFT effect
CEEFHL fleech
CEEFIR fierce
CEEFKT fecket
CEEFLY fleecy
CEEFNN fennec
CEEFNR fencer
CEEFRS screef
CEEFSU fescue
CEEGIR cierge, griece
CEEGLU culgee
CEEGNO congee
CEEHIL lichee
CEEHIR Cherie
CEEHIS seiche
CEEHIT techie
CEEHKL heckle
CEEHKY cheeky
CEEHLN elench
CEEHLR lecher
CEEHLW lechwe
CEEHLY lychee
CEEHMR cherem
CEEHMS scheme
CEEHNT thence
CEEHNW whence
CEEHOR cheero, choree, cohere, echoer, re-echo
CEEHOY echoey
CEEHPS speech
CEEHQU cheque
CEEHRS cheers, creesh
CEEHRT etcher
CEEHRU euchre
CEEHRW chewer
CEEHRY cheery
CEEHSS secesh
CEEHSW eschew
CEEHSY cheesy
CEEHTV chevet
CEEHTW chewet
CEEHUY yeeuch
CEEIKL Kielce
CEEILN Celine
CEEIMT emetic
CEEINP piecen
CEEINT entice
CEEINU Eunice
CEEINV evince
CEEIPR piecer, pierce, recipe
CEEIPS specie
CEEIRS cerise
CEEIRT cerite, certie, recite, tierce
CEEISX excise
CEEITX excite
CEEJNO conjee
CEEJNU cunjee
CEEJRT reject
CEEKKL keckle
CEEKLP peckle
CEEKLR lecker
CEEKLT teckel
CEEKNR necker
CEEKOO cookee
CEEKPR pecker
CEEKPT pecket
CEELLN encell
CEELMO cleome
CEELNP pencel
CEELNR crenel
CEELOR creole
CEELPR precel
CEELRS screel
CEELRT tercel
CEELRV clever
CEELRW crewel
CEELRY celery
CEELST select
CEELSU secule
CEEMNT cement
CEEMNU cumene
CEEMNY cymene
CEEMRR mercer
CEEMRT cermet
CEENOR encore
CEENOT cenote
CEENPS spence
CEENPT pecten
CEENRS censer, scerne, screen, secern
CEENRT center, centre, recent, tenrec
CEENRX excern
CEEOOS cooees
CEEOPU coupee
CEEORT cerote
CEEOTX Exocet
CEEPRS preces
CEEPRY creepy
CEEPTX except, expect
CEEPTY ectype
CEEPUY eyecup
CEERSS cesser, recess
CEERST certes, resect, secret
CEERSU cereus, ceruse, rescue, secure
CEERTT tercet
CEESSX excess
CEESTX exsect
CEESUX excuse
CEETTU cuttee
CEFFIO office
CEFFLO coffle
CEFFOR coffer
CEFHIS fiches
CEFHLN flench
CEFHLT fletch

CEFHNR French
CEFIKL fickle
CEFILO focile
CEFILS felsic
CEFINT infect
CEFIRR ferric
CEFKRU fucker
CEFLOS fo'c'sle
CEFNOR confer
CEFORR forcer
CEFORS fresco
CEFRUW curfew
CEGGIO coggie
CEGGLO coggle
CEGGPU eggcup
CEGHIO chigoe
CEGILN cingle
CEGINR cringe
CEGINU cueing
CEGIRR gricer
CEGIST gestic
CEGLRY clergy
CEGNOR conger
CEGNOT cogent
CEGNSU scunge
CEGNTY cygnet
CEGOPR precog
CEGORR grocer
CEGORU courge
CEHHIT chithe, hi-
tech
CEHHNU huchen
CEHIIK chi-ike
CEHIIN echini
CEHIIR Richie
CEHIIT Chieti
CEHIKL hickle
CEHIKT hicket
CEHIKY hickey
CEHILN lichen
CEHILS chesil,
chiles,
chisel
CEHILU chiule
CEHIMR chimer,
micher
CEHIMU echium
CEHINP phenic,
pinche
CEHINR enrich,
incher,
nicher,
richen
CEHINS chinse
CEHINT ethnic
CEHINV chevin
CEHIOR heroic
CEHIOS choise
CEHIPR ceriph,
cipher
CEHIQU chique,
quiche
CEHIRS creish,
riches,
shicer
CEHIRT cither,
thrice
CEHIST ethics
CEHITT thetic
CEHKLU huckle
CEHKNU kuchen
CEHKOR choker
CEHKOT hocket
CEHKOY chokey,
hockey
CEHKST sketch
CEHKTV kvetch
CEHLLO cholle
CEHLMS schelm
CEHLOR choler
CEHLOT clothe
CEHLOU louche
CEHLPS schlep
CEHLPY cyphel
CEHLQU quelch
CEHLRU churel
CEHLRY Cheryl
CEHMMY chemmy
CEHMNS mensch
CEHMOR chomer,
chrome
CEHMOU mouche
CEHMTU humect
CEHNOO ochone
CEHNOS chosen
CEHNOT techno
CEHNOU cohune
CEHNQU quench
CEHNRT trench
CEHNRW wrench
CEHNST stench
CEHNUU eunuch
CEHOOS choose
CEHORS cosher
CEHORT hector,
rochet,
tocher,
troche
CEHOSU chouse
CEHOSW chowse
CEHPRY chypre,
cypher
CEHPSY psyche
CEHQTU quetch
CEHQUY chequy
CEHRRY cherry
CEHRTW wretch
CEHRTY cherty
CEHSTU tusche
CEHSTY chesty,
scythe
CEHTTY chetty,
tetchy
CEHTVY vetchy
CEIIKP pickie
CEIIKS sickie
CEIILT elicit
CEIILX exilic
CEIINP picein
CEIINR irenic
CEIINS incise
CEIINT incite,
intice
CEIINV vicine
CEIISS Cissie
CEIIST iciest
CEIJKL jelick
CEIJNT inject
CEIJNU cunjie
CEIJRU juicer
CEIKKR kicker
CEIKLM melick,
mickle
CEIKLN licken,
nickel
CEIKLP pickle
CEIKLR licker
CEIKLS sickle
CEIKLT tickel,
tickle
CEIKLU luckie
CEIKMY mickey
CEIKNR nicker
CEIKNS sicken
CEIKNT ticken
CEIKNY nickey
CEIKNZ zenick
CEIKOO cookie
CEIKOS Kosice
CEIKPR picker
CEIKPT picket
CEIKRT ticker
CEIKRW wicker
CEIKRY crikey,
rickey
CEIKTT ticket
CEIKTW wicket
CEIKTY tickey
CEILLO collie,
ocelli
CEILNO Nicole
CEILNP pencil
CEILNT client,
lectin,
lentic
CEILNU Lucien,
nuclei
CEILNY nicely
CEILOO coolie
CEILOP police
CEILOR recoil
CEILOT citole
CEILOU coulie
CEILPS splice
CEILPV pelvic
CEILPY clypei
CEILQU clique
CEILRS slicer
CEILRT relict
CEILRY cilery
CEILSU sluice
CEILSV clevis
CEILTT Lettic
CEILTU luetic
CEIMMO commie
CEIMNO income
CEIMNR mincer
CEIMNU Muncie
CEIMOX Mexico
CEIMPU pumice
CEIMRS crimes
CEIMRT metric
CEIMRU cerium
CEIMSS scisme
CEIMSU cesium,
miscue
CEINNO Connie
CEINOR coiner,
orcein
CEINOS cosine,
oscine
CEINOT noetic,
notice
CEINOV novice
CEINPR pincer,
prince
CEINPT incept,
pectin
CEINQU cinque,
quince
CEINRT cretin,
crinet
CEINRU neuric
CEINRW wincer
CEINST incest,
insect,
scient
CEINSU incuse
CEINTV invect
CEINTY nicety
CEINWY wincey
CEIOOT cootie
CEIOPR copier
CEIOPT poetic
CEIORR corrie,
orrice
CEIORS corsie,
cosier
CEIORT erotic,
tercio
CEIORV voicer
CEIORW cowrie
CEIOSS cossie
CEIOST cotise,
oecist
CEIOTX exotic
CEIOZZ cozzie
CEIPPR precip
CEIPPT peptic
CEIPRR pricer
CEIPRS cripes
CEIPRY pricey
CEIPSS Pisces
CEIPST septic
CEIPSY spicey
CEIPTU cup-tie
CEIQRU cirque
CEIRRU currie
CEIRSS crises
CEIRST steric

CEIRSU cruise, crusie
CEIRSV scrive
CEIRTT tetric
CEIRTU cuiter
CEIRUV cruive
CEIRVX cervix
CEISST citess
CEISSU cuisse
CEISTU cestui, cueist
CEISTV vectis
CEJKOR jocker
CEJKOY jockey
CEJNOU jounce
CEJOOS jocose
CEKKOP kopeck
CEKLMU muckle
CEKLNO enlock
CEKLOR locker
CEKLOT locket
CEKLPU puckle
CEKLRU ruckle
CEKLSU suckle
CEKLUY yuckle
CEKMOR mocker
CEKMOT mocket
CEKMRU mucker
CEKNOR conker, reckon
CEKOOR cooker
CEKOPT pocket
CEKORR corker, rocker
CEKORT rocket
CEKOST socket
CEKPRU pucker
CEKRSU sucker, uckers
CEKRTU tucker
CEKTTU tucket
CELLOT collet
CELLOU locule
CELLOY colley
CELLRU culler
CELLTU cullet
CELMNU culmen
CELMOO coelom
CELMOP compel
CELMOY comely
CELMSU clumse, muscle
CELMUY Lyceum
CELNNU nuncle
CELNOR cornel
CELNOU leucon
CELNOV cloven
CELNRU lucern
CELNTU lucent
CELNUU nucule
CELOOR cooler
CELOOS cloose
CELOOT ocelot
CELOPP coppel, copple
CELOPU couple
CELORS closer, cresol
CELORT colter, lector
CELORU colure
CELORV clover, Velcro
CELOST closet
CELOSU coleus
CELOSV scovel
CELOSX scolex
CELOTT Toltec
CELOTU coutel
CELOUV vocule
CELOUW cue-owl
CELPRU curple
CELPTY yclept
CELPUU cupule
CELRRU curler
CELRSY cresyl
CELRTU cutler
CELRUU curule
CELRUV culver
CELRUW curlew
CELSTU scutel
CELTTU cutlet, cuttle
CELTUY cutely
CEMMRU cummer
CEMNOO come-on, oncome
CEMNOY encomy
CEMNRU crumen
CEMNTU centum
CEMOOS comose
CEMORR cremor
CEMOSU mucose
CEMOSY cymose
CEMOTU Temuco
CEMRTU rectum
CEMTTU tectum
CENNOO neo-con
CENNOR conner
CENNOT nocent
CENNOX connex
CENNRU cunner
CENOOP encoop
CENOOR ceroon
CENOPU pounce
CENOPY poncey
CENORR corner
CENORS censor
CENORT cornet, cronet
CENORU conure, noceur
CENORY Corney
CENOSU Unesco
CENOTV covent
CENOTX contex
CENOVX convex
CENOVY convey
CENOYY coynye
CENRTY centry
CENSSU census
CENSTY encyst
CEOOPR cooper
CEOORS roscoe
CEOORT cooter
CEOORV croove
CEOOTY coyote, oocyte
CEOPPR copper
CEOPRS corpse
CEOPRT copter
CEOPRU recoup
CEOQTU coquet
CEORRS scorer
CEORRT rector
CEORRV corver
CEORSS cessor, crosse, scores, scorse
CEORST corset, Cortes, coster, escort, scoter, sector
CEORSU cerous, course, crouse, source
CEORSV corves
CEORSW escrow
CEORTT cotter
CEORTU couter
CEORTV covert, vector
CEORTX cortex
CEORTY crotey
CEOSST cosset
CEOSSU Scouse
CEOSSV covess
CEOSTT cotset
CEOSTY coyest
CEOTTU cuttoe
CEPPRU cupper
CEPRRU percur
CEPRSU spruce
CEPRSY cy pres
CEPRTU pre-cut
CEPSTU pectus
CERRSU curser
CERRSY scryer
CERSTU rectus
CERSUX cruxes
CERSUZ scruze
CERSWY screwy
CERTTU cutter
CERTUV curvet
CESSTU cestus
CESSTY cystes
CESSUX excuss
CESTUY cutesy
CESTXY excyst
CFFILY cliffy
CFFINO coffin
CFFINU cuffin
CFFOTU cut-off, offcut
CFFRSU scruff
CFGINU fungic
CFHILN flinch
CFHILT flitch
CFHITY fitchy
CFHLOT flocht
CFHLSY flysch
CFIIKN finick
CFIILM filmic
CFIINN Finnic
CFIIST fistic
CFIITY citify
CFIKLY fickly
CFILOR frolic
CFIMOR formic
CFIMOT comfit
CFINNO finnoc
CFINOP poncif
CFINOX confix
CFISSU fiscus
CFISTU fustic
CFITYY cityfy
CFKLOY flocky
CFKPUU fuck-up
CFLPUU cupful
CFRSUY scurfy
CGGLOY cloggy, coggly
CGHHOU chough
CGHIIN I Ching
CGHILT glitch
CGHIOT Gothic
CGHLNU glunch
CGHLOU clough
CGHLTU glutch
CGHORU grouch
CGHRTU grutch
CGIILT tiglic
CGILNU cluing
CGILNY clingy, glycin
CGIMNO coming, gnomic
CGIMNY gymnic
CGINOP coping, picong
CGINOV coving
CGINRU curing
CGINRY crying
CGIOOT cogito
CGIORS corgis
CGLLOY glycol
CGLLYY glycyl
CGLNOU unclog
CGLOOU colugo
CGNOOU congou
CGNSUY scungy
CHHIOR chi-rho
CHHLOO lohoch
CHHNOO honcho
CHHOOS cohosh
CHHOOT hootch

CHIIKM kimchi
CHIILL chilli
CHIILN nichil
CHIILT litchi, lithic
CHIINR inrich
CHIINS nicish
CHIINT chitin
CHIIPP hippic
CHIIPT pitchi
CHIIRT trichi
CHIKNT knitch
CHIKNY Chinky
CHIKOS hoicks
CHIKOT thicko
CHIKRS kirsch
CHIKST kitsch, shtick
CHILLY chilly
CHILOR orchil
CHILOS cholis
CHILRY richly
CHIMNY hymnic
CHIMRS chrism, smirch
CHIMSS schism
CHIMTY mythic, thymic
CHINNO Chinon
CHINOP chopin, phonic
CHINOT chiton
CHINPU chin-up
CHINQU quinch
CHINRU urchin
CHINST snitch
CHINTY hincty
CHINTZ chintz
CHIOPR Orphic
CHIOPT photic
CHIORS orchis
CHIORT rhotic, trochi
CHIOST Sothic, tochis
CHIOSW cowish
CHIOSZ schizo
CHIPPY chippy
CHIPRT pritch
CHIPRY chirpy
CHIPSY physic, scyphi
CHIPTY phytic, pitchy
CHIQTU quitch
CHIRST Christ
CHISST schist
CHISTT stitch
CHISTU schuit
CHISTW switch
CHISTZ schitz
CHISUY yichus
CHITTW twitch
CHITTY chitty, titchy
CHITWY witchy
CHIVVY chivvy
CHJLOT J cloth
CHKLOO klooch
CHKNUY chunky
CHLMOO moloch
CHLMUY muchly
CHLOOS school
CHLOOT coolth
CHLOPT plotch
CHLORS schorl
CHLOST cloths
CHLOSU holcus, lochus, slouch
CHMMUY chummy
CHMOOR chromo
CHMOOS smooch
CHMSUY chymus
CHNOOP poncho
CHNOOR cohorn
CHNOOS schoon
CHNORY chrony
CHNOTY notchy
CHNPUY punchy
CHNRTU trunch
CHNTUU tuchun
CHOORT cohort
CHOOST schoot
CHOOSY choosy
CHOPPY choppy
CHOPSY psycho
CHOPUY pouchy
CHORSU chorus
CHORWY chowry
CHOSTU schout, scouth
CHOTUY touchy
CHPSTU putsch
CHSSSU schuss
CHSTUY schuyt
CHTTUY chutty
CIIIMN inimic
CIIKNW inwick
CIILMN limnic
CIILMU cilium
CIILNP inclip
CIILOP lipoic
CIILRT citril
CIIMOT miotic
CIIMSV civism
CIIMTV victim
CIINOP pionic
CIINOR ironic
CIINOS inosic
CIINQU quinic
CIINRT citrin, nitric
CIINSV viscin
CIIPST pistic
CIIRSS crisis
CIIRTV vitric
CIJKNO jonick
CIKKNS knicks
CIKKPU kick-up
CIKLNO inlock, lock-in
CIKLSY sickly
CIKLTY tickly
CIKNPU unpick
CIKNPY pyknic
CIKNTU tuck-in
CIKORR corkir
CIKOSY yoicks
CIKPPU pick-up
CIKPTU uptick
CIKRTU Turkic
CIKRTY tricky
CIKSTY sticky
CILLOU loculi
CILLSU cullis
CILMUU cumuli
CILMUY lycium
CILNOO nicolo
CILNOP clip-on
CILNOU uncoil
CILNTU incult
CILOPY policy
CILORT lictor
CILOSU coulis
CILOSV Clovis
CILOSY cosily
CILOTU coutil, toluic
CILPPY clippy
CILPUV vulpic
CILRTU citrul
CILSUU Lucius
CIMMNU cummin
CIMMOS commis
CIMMOT commit
CIMMOX commix
CIMNNO nincom
CIMNNU nincum
CIMNOR micron
CIMNOU conium
CIMOOS Cosimo
CIMOPY myopic
CIMORU corium
CIMOSS osmics
CIMOST sitcom
CIMOSU musico
CIMOTY comity, myotic
CIMPRS scrimp
CIMPRY crimpy
CIMRUU curium
CIMSTY mystic
CINNOO nonoic
CINNOU nuncio
CINNOY incony
CINNTU inunct
CINOOP coin-op
CINOOV ovonic
CINOOZ ozonic
CINOPT pontic
CINORT citron
CINORZ zircon
CINOSS cosins
CINOST tocsin
CINOSU cousin
CINOSV scovin
CINPTU puncti
CINQUY Quincy
CINSTY incyst
CIOOPT octopi
CIOORT octroi, orotic
CIOPRT protic, tropic
CIOPRY picory
CIOPST copist, optics
CIOPTT ptotic
CIOPWY wicopy
CIORTT tricot
CIORTV victor
CIOSTU coitus
CIPPSU cippus
CIPRST script
CIPRSY crispy, cypris
CIPSSU cuspis
CIRRSU cirrus
CIRSTT strict
CIRSTU citrus, Curtis, rictus, rustic
CISSTU cistus
CISSTY cystis
CISSUV viscus
CKLNOO lock-on
CKLNOU unlock
CKLNUY clunky
CKLOPU lock-up
CKLPUY plucky
CKMOPU mock-up
CKNORU uncork
CKNTUU untuck
CKOSTY stocky
CKRSTU struck, trucks
CKRSUU ruckus
CLLOOP collop
CLLOOW collow
CLLOOY coolly
CLLORS scroll
CLMNOU column
CLMOOU locoum
CLMOPY comply
CLMOUU lucumo
CLMPSU clumps
CLMPUY clumpy
CLMSUY clumsy, muscly
CLNOOS consol
CLNOOU uncool
CLNOOY colony
CLNOSU clonus, consul
CLNRUU uncurl
CLOORU colour
CLOORY colory
CLOOSS coloss

CLOSTU locust
CLOSTY costly
CLOSUU oculus
CLOSWY scowly
CLOTUW low-cut
CLPSTU sculpt
CLRTUY curtly
CLSSUU sulcus
CLSTUU cultus
CLSTUY lyctus
CMMNOO common
CMMOOT commot
CMMRUY crummy
CMMSUY scummy
CMNNOO non-com
CMOOOW moo-cow
CMOOPS compos
CMOOSS cosmos
CMOOSW Moscow
CMOSTU custom
CMOSUU mucous
CMPRSU scrump
CMSTUU scutum
CNNNOO non-con
CNNOOR Connor
CNOOPU coupon
CNOORT croton
CNOOST nostoc, oncost
CNOOSW cowson
CNOOTT cotton
CNOOTY tycoon
CNOOVY convoy
CNORSU cornus
CNOSTU Tucson
CNOTUY county
CNRSTU scrunt
CNTTUU nut-cut
COOORZ corozo
COOPRS scroop
COOPSY scoopy
COOPTU cop-out
COOPWX cowpox
COORTU octuor
COORTY octroy
COPPRY croppy
COPRSU corpus
COPRTY crypto
COPRUY croupy
COPSUY coypus
CORRSU cursor
CORSTU scruto
CORTUY outcry
COSSTU costus, custos
COSTTY scotty
COTTUU cut-out
CPRSUY Cyprus
CRRSUY scurry
CRSSUU cursus
CRSTUY crusty, curtsy
CRSUVY scurvy
CSTTUY scutty
CSUYZZ scuzzy
DDDEET tedded
DDDEEW wedded
DDDEIK kidded
DDDEIL diddle, lidded
DDDEIO doddie
DDDEIR didder, ridded
DDDELO doddle
DDDENO nodded
DDDEOP podded
DDDEOR dodder
DDDEOS sodded
DDEEER reeded
DDEEES deseed, seeded
DDEEEW weeded
DDEEFN defend
DDEEGL ledged
DDEEGR dredge
DDEEGW wedged
DDEEHL heddle
DDEEIN indeed, Neddie
DDEEIR deride
DDEEIT dieted, edited, Teddie
DDEELM meddle, melded
DDEELN ledden
DDEELP peddle
DDEELR Eldred, reddle
DDEELU delude, dueled
DDEELW welded
DDEENN denned
DDEENP depend
DDEENR redden
DDEENT dented
DDEENU denude, dudeen, duende, Dundee
DDEEPR pedder
DDEERR redder
DDEERT tedder
DDEERW wedder
DDEERY yedder
DDEFIL fiddle
DDEFLU fuddle
DDEFOR fodder
DDEFRY Freddy
DDEGGO dogged
DDEGIL gilded
DDEGIR girded
DDEGIT geddit
DDEGLU guddle
DDEGMO dodgem
DDEGNO dog-end
DDEGOR dodger
DDEGRU drudge
DDEHIN hidden
DDEHIS eddish
DDEHLU huddle
DDEHNO hodden
DDEHOO hooded
DDEIIK kiddie
DDEIIM middie
DDEIIO iodide
DDEIIV divide
DDEIKL kiddle
DDEIKR kidder
DDEILL liddle
DDEILM middle
DDEILN dindle, lidden
DDEILO doiled
DDEILP piddle
DDEILR riddle
DDEILT tiddle
DDEILW widdle
DDEIMM dimmed
DDEIMN midden, minded
DDEIMR midder
DDEIMS desmid
DDEIMU muddie
DDEINN dinned
DDEINR ridden, rinded
DDEINW winded
DDEIOT doited
DDEIOV devoid, voided
DDEIPP dipped
DDEISS dissed
DDEITU dutied
DDEJRU judder
DDEKNY kynded
DDELMO molded
DDELMU muddle
DDELNO noddle
DDELNU nuddle
DDELOO doodle
DDELOP poddle
DDELOT toddle
DDELPU puddle
DDELRU ruddle
DDELUY Dudley
DDEMNO Edmond
DDEMNU Edmund
DDEMRU mudder
DDENNO donned
DDENNU dunned
DDENOS sodden
DDENOW downed
DDENOY dynode
DDENPU pudden
DDENRU dunder, durned
DDENSU sudden
DDENUY undyed
DDEOOR doored
DDEOOS do-se-do
DDEOOW wooded
DDEOPR podder
DDEORT todder
DDEOTT dotted
DDEPRU pudder
DDERRU rudder
DDFILY fiddly
DDGIPU giddup
DDGMOO dogdom
DDGOOO do-good
DDHIOS oddish
DDHISU dudish
DDHOSY shoddy
DDIIKK dik-dik
DDIIKV kidvid
DDIIMS misdid
DDIINN din-din
DDIIOX ixodid
DDIKNO dodkin
DDILNR dirndl
DDILTY tiddly
DDIMRU dirdum
DDINNO nid-nod
DDINOO diodon
DDIOOS do-si-do
DDIOPY dipody
DDIORS sordid
DDIOTY oddity
DDKKUU duk-duk
DDLMUY muddly
DDLPUY puddly
DDMMUU dumdum
DDNOOS odds-on
DDOPRY Proddy
DEEEES seedee
DEEEFR feeder
DEEEGR degree
DEEEHL heeled
DEEEIP deepie
DEEEJR jereed
DEEEKL keeled
DEEELN needle
DEEELP peeled
DEEELT delete, teedle
DEEEMN mendee
DEEEMR redeem
DEEENP deepen
DEEENR deener
DEEENV vendee
DEEEPX expede
DEEERS reseed, seeder
DEEERV reeved
DEEERW weeder
DEEERY red-eye
DEEFGL fledge
DEEFIL defile
DEEFIN define, infeed
DEEFIR defier
DEEFLU fueled
DEEFLX deflex
DEEFNR fender
DEEFSU defuse
DEEFZZ fezzed
DEEGGI gidgee
DEEGGL gledge, legged

DEEGGP pegged
DEEGHR hedger
DEEGIR edgier
DEEGIW wedgie
DEEGLL gelled
DEEGLN legend
DEEGLP pledge
DEEGLR ledger
DEEGLS sledge
DEEGLU deluge
DEEGLY gleyde
DEEGMM gemmed
DEEGNN genned
DEEGNR gender
DEEGNU dengue
DEEGRY greedy
DEEGSU segued
DEEHIT ethide
DEEHLM helmed
DEEHLT lethed
DEEHLU huldee
DEEHLY Hedley
DEEHMM hemmed
DEEHOX hexode
DEEHRR herder
DEEHSY deeshy
DEEHTW thewed
DEEILN deline, Elined
DEEILR delire, lieder
DEEILS diesel, sedile, seidel
DEEILV veiled
DEEILY eyelid
DEEIMN medine
DEEIMP impede
DEEIMS demise
DEEINN Dennie, indene
DEEINP peneid, penide
DEEINR denier, nereid
DEEINS Denise
DEEINT eident, endite
DEEINV devein, endive, veined
DEEINZ denize
DEEIOV voidee
DEEIPR perdie
DEEIRS desire, reside
DEEIRT dieter, re-edit, tiered
DEEIRV derive
DEEIRW dewier
DEEISS seised
DEEISV devise
DEEISZ desize, seized
DEEITX exited
DEEITY tie-dye
DEEJLM El Djem
DEEJNU dejune
DEEJTT jetted
DEEKLW welked
DEEKNN kenned
DEEKNR Kenred, kerned
DEELMR melder, merled
DEELMY medley
DEELNP pendle
DEELNR eldern, lender
DEELNS lensed
DEELNU Eluned
DEELNW Delwen, wedeln
DEELNY needly
DEELOP delope
DEELPY deeply
DEELRU dueler
DEELRV delver
DEELRW welder
DEELST eldest
DEELTT letted
DEELTU teledu
DEELTW welted
DEELUX de luxe
DEEMNO omened
DEEMNR mender
DEEMNT dement
DEEMOS mesode
DEEMOT demote
DEEMPR deperm, premed
DEEMRU demure
DEEMRY remedy
DEEMTU Te Deum
DEENNP penned
DEENNT dennet, entend, needn't
DEENNY yenned
DEENOP depone
DEENOR Doreen, redone
DEENOT denote
DEENPX expend
DEENRR render
DEENRS sender
DEENRT tender, tendre
DEENRU endure
DEENRV Denver, nerved, vender
DEENST denest, sedent
DEENSU ensued
DEENSW Sweden
DEENTT detent, netted, tented
DEENTU detune
DEENTX dentex, extend
DEENUV vendue
DEEOPR podere
DEEOPS depose, speedo
DEEORS redoes
DEEORT teredo
DEEOTT Odette
DEEOTV devote
DEEOVV devove
DEEPPP pepped
DEEPPR repped
DEEPRS spreed
DEEPRU depure
DEEPSY speedy
DEEPTT petted
DEEPTU depute
DEEQUU queued
DEERRW redrew
DEERSS des res
DEERST desert
DEERSV versed
DEERTT retted
DEERTV verdet
DEERTX dexter
DEERVV revved
DEESTT detest
DEESTV devest, vested
DEETTV vetted
DEETTW wetted
DEETWY tweedy
DEFFIR differ
DEFFLU duffel, duffle
DEFFMU muffed
DEFFNO offend
DEFFNU effund
DEFFRU duffer
DEFGGI figged
DEFGGO fogged
DEFGGU fugged
DEFGIR fridge
DEFGIT fidget, gifted
DEFGLO fodgel
DEFGLY fledgy
DEFGUU fugued
DEFHOO hoofed
DEFILL filled
DEFILO defoil
DEFINN finned
DEFINR finder, friend
DEFIOO foodie
DEFIOT foetid
DEFIRT trefid
DEFIRU furied
DEFIRV fervid
DEFIST fisted
DEFITT fitted
DEFITY fedity
DEFKOR forked
DEFLMY medfly
DEFLNO enfold, fondle
DEFLOR folder
DEFLOT lofted
DEFLOU defoul
DEFLTY deftly
DEFLUX deflux
DEFMOR deform
DEFNOR fronde
DEFNOU fondue
DEFNRU refund
DEFOOR doofer, foredo, roofed
DEFOOT footed
DEFORX red fox
DEFRRU furred
DEFRTU dufter
DEFTTU tufted
DEGGGI gigged
DEGGHO hogged
DEGGHU hugged
DEGGIJ jigged
DEGGIL ligged
DEGGIN edging
DEGGIO doggie
DEGGIP pigged
DEGGIR digger, rigged
DEGGIU Duggie
DEGGIW wigged
DEGGIZ zigged
DEGGJO jogged
DEGGJU jugged
DEGGLO dog-leg, logged
DEGGLU lugged
DEGGMU mugged
DEGGNO nogged
DEGGOR dogger, gorged
DEGGOT togged
DEGGPU pugged
DEGGRU grudge, rugged
DEGGRY dreggy
DEGGSU sugged
DEGGTU tugged
DEGHIN hinged
DEGHIR dreigh, driegh
DEGHIW Hedwig
DEGIIR dirige
DEGIIW widgie
DEGILL gilled
DEGILM mid-leg
DEGILN dingle, elding, engild, gilden
DEGILO Goidel, Goldie
DEGILR gilder, girdle,

glider, regild
DEGILY edgily
DEGIMT midget
DEGINN ending, ginned
DEGINO Gideon
DEGINR dinger, engird, ringed
DEGINS design, dinges, sdeign
DEGINT nidget
DEGINW winged
DEGINY dyeing
DEGIOO goodie
DEGIOP pie-dog
DEGIOU Dougie
DEGIRR girder
DEGIRU guider
DEGIRW widger
DEGIST digest
DEGITW widget
DEGJRU judger
DEGKLU kludge
DEGLNO dongle, golden
DEGLNU gulden, lunged
DEGLNY Glynde
DEGLOP plodge
DEGLOR lodger
DEGLSU sludge
DEGMMU gummed
DEGMRU red gum
DEGMSU smudge
DEGNNU gunned
DEGNOT tonged
DEGNRU gerund, greund, nudger, runged
DEGOOR gooder
DEGOPR podger
DEGOPY pye-dog
DEGORR Rodger
DEGORT todger
DEGORU drogue
DEGOST stodge
DEGPPY gypped
DEGRTU trudge
DEGSTU degust
DEGTTU gutted
DEHHSU hushed
DEHILN inheld
DEHILS delish, shield
DEHIMN mendhi
DEHINO honied
DEHINR hinder
DEHINS shined
DEHIOO hoodie
DEHIOW howdie
DEHIOX oxhide
DEHIPP hipped
DEHIRS disher
DEHIRT dither, drieth
DEHIRU hurdie
DEHITW whited
DEHIUY Yehudi
DEHKOO hooked
DEHKSU husked
DEHLNO holden
DEHLOR holder
DEHLPU upheld
DEHLRU hurdle
DEHLTY Delyth
DEHMMU hummed
DEHMOT method, mothed
DEHMPU humped
DEHNOR dehorn, horned
DEHNOY dhoney, hoyden
DEHNSU unshed
DEHOOP hooped
DEHOOS shooed
DEHOOV hooved
DEHOPP hopped
DEHORS dehors
DEHORT dehort, red-hot
DEHORX oxherd
DEHOSW showed
DEHOTT hotted
DEHOUZ Dezhou
DEHPPY hypped
DEHRSW shrewd
DEHTTU hutted
DEIIKN dinkie
DEIIKR Kediri
DEIILL lilied
DEIILW wildie
DEIINO iodine
DEIINS Indies, inside
DEIINT indite
DEIINV divine
DEIIOS iodise
DEIIOZ iodize
DEIIPR pierid
DEIIRS irides, irised
DEIIRT tidier
DEIISS diesis
DEIISX deixis
DEIJRU juried
DEIKKN dekink
DEIKLN dinkel, kindle, linked
DEIKLO keloid
DEIKLT kilted
DEIKNY dinkey, kidney
DEIKPP kipped
DEIKRU duiker
DEIKTT kitted
DEILLM milled
DEILLU illude
DEILLV divell
DEILLW willed
DEILMN milden
DEILMO meloid, moiled
DEILMP dimple
DEILMS misled
DEILMW mildew
DEILNN linden
DEILNO doline, indole, Leonid
DEILNT dentil
DEILNW windle
DEILNZ Denzil
DEILOO doolie
DEILOP diploe, dipole, peloid, Poldie
DEILOS Isolde
DEILPP lipped
DEILPS dispel, disple
DEILPX diplex
DEILRS slider
DEILRV drivel
DEILRW wilder
DEILRY direly
DEILST idlest, listed
DEILTT titled
DEILTU dilute
DEILTY lydite
DEILWY dewily, widely, wieldy
DEILYY yieldy
DEIMMR dimmer, immerd, rimmed
DEIMMU medium
DEIMNN Minden
DEIMNO domine, emodin, monied
DEIMNP impend
DEIMNR minder, remind
DEIMNT minted
DEIMOR dormie, moider
DEIMOT domite
DEIMPU mud pie
DEIMRS dermis
DEIMRT mitred
DEIMSS demiss
DEIMST demist, misted
DEIMSU medius
DEIMTU tedium
DEINNO Dionne, ondine
DEINNP pinned
DEINNR dinner, endrin
DEINNS Dennis, sinned
DEINNT dentin, indent, intend, tinned
DEINNU undine
DEINNW enwind
DEINOP pedion
DEINOR dinero, Indore, ironed, ride-on
DEINOS donsie, no side, onside, side-on
DEINOT ditone, in-toed
DEINPP nipped
DEINPR pinder
DEINPS despin, spined
DEINPU uniped
DEINRT tinder
DEINRU indure
DEINRV driven, verdin
DEINRW indrew, rewind, winder
DEINRZ Zinder
DEINSU undies
DEINSW Widnes
DEINSY Sidney
DEINTU dunite, untied
DEIOOW woodie
DEIOOZ doozie
DEIOPP doppie
DEIOPR dopier, period
DEIOPS poised, posied
DEIOPT podite
DEIORR Dorrie
DEIORT editor, triode
DEIORV devoir, voider
DEIORW weirdo
DEIORZ dozier
DEIOTT Dottie
DEIPPP pipped
DEIPPR dipper, ripped
DEIPPS sipped
DEIPPT tipped
DEIPPY yipped
DEIPPZ zipped

DEIPQU piqued
DEIPRS spider
DEIPRT trepid, triped
DEIPSS pissed
DEIPSU upside
DEIPTT pitted
DEIRRS derris
DEIRRU durrie
DEIRRV driver
DEIRST disert, driest, stride
DEIRSV divers
DEIRTU Trudie
DEIRTV divert
DEIRWY weirdy
DEISST desist
DEISSU disuse, issued
DEISTV divest
DEITTW witted
DEJLOW jowled
DEJMPU jumped
DEJOTT jotted
DEJTTU jutted
DEKLOO looked
DEKLOY yolked
DEKMSU musked
DEKNOY donkey
DEKNOZ zedonk, zonked
DEKNRU dunker
DEKOPS spoked
DEKORW worked
DEKRUY dukery, duyker
DEKSTU tusked
DELLOU duello
DELLOW do-well
DELLWY lewdly
DELMMU dummel
DELMNO dolmen
DELMOR molder, remold
DELMOS seldom
DELMOU module
DELMOY melody
DELMPU lumped, plumed
DELNNO on-lend
DELNOO noodle
DELNOR rondel
DELNOT dolent
DELNOU louden, nodule, ulendo
DELNOZ donzel
DELNWY Delwyn
DELOOP looped, poodle
DELOOS dolose, oodles
DELOOT Toledo
DELOOW wooled
DELOPP lopped
DELOPR polder
DELOPU peludo
DELOPY deploy, podley
DELORS dorsel, resold, solder
DELORT retold, rodlet
DELORY Delroy
DELOSS doless, dossel
DELOST oldest
DELOTT Dettol, dottel, dottle, lotted
DELOYY doyley
DELOZZ dozzle
DELPRU drupel
DELPTU duplet
DELPUX duplex
DELRUY rudely
DEMMMU mummed
DEMMOT tommed
DEMMSU summed
DEMNOO mooned
DEMNOR modern, normed
DEMNOS Esmond
DEMNOT doment
DEMNOU menudo
DEMOOR doomer
DEMOPP mopped
DEMORR dormer
DEMORT Dermot
DEMORW deworm, wormed
DEMOSS mossed
DEMOST modest
DEMOSU odeums
DEMOTT domett
DEMPPU pumped
DEMPRU dumper
DEMRRU murder
DENNOR donner
DENNOT Denton, tendon
DENNOU undone
DENNPU punned
DENNRU dunner, end run
DENNSU sunned
DENNTU tunned
DENOOP podeon
DENOOS nodose, nosode
DENOOW wooden
DENOPR Pernod, ponder
DENORT rodent
DENORU enduro
DENORV vendor
DENORW downer, wonder
DENORY Rodney, yonder
DENOSS endoss
DENOST doesn't, ostend, stoned
DENOTW wonted
DENOWY Downey
DENPSU despun, send-up
DENRSU sunder
DENRTU deturn, dunter, turned
DENRTY trendy
DENRUV Verdun
DENSUU unused
DENSUW sundew
DENSYY Sydney
DENTTU nutted
DENTUX extund
DEOOPP pooped
DEOORV overdo
DEOORW wooder
DEOORZ doozer
DEOOTV devoto
DEOOYY yo-yoed
DEOPPP popped
DEOPPR Dopper
DEOPPS sopped
DEOPPT topped
DEOPRT deport, de trop, ported
DEOPRU poudre
DEOPRV proved
DEOPRW powder
DEOPST despot, posted
DEOPSU pseudo
DEOPTT potted
DEORRS dorser, orders
DEORRT dorter, retrod
DEORRU ordure
DEORRV drover
DEORRW reword
DEORSS dosser
DEORST Dorset, strode
DEORSW dowser, drowse
DEORTT detort, dotter, rotted
DEORTU derout, detour
DEORUV devour
DEORVY verdoy
DEOSTT sotted
DEOSTW dowset
DEOSUX exodus
DEOTTT totted
DEOTTU duetto
DEOTUV devout
DEOTUX tuxedo
DEPPPU pupped
DEPPSU supped
DEPPTU tupped
DEPRUU pudeur
DEPRUY dupery
DEPTTU putted
DEPTUY deputy
DERRUY rudery
DERSSU duress
DERSSY dressy
DERSTU duster
DERTTU rutted
DERTUV turved
DERTWY dewtry
DESSSU sussed
DFFIMO mid-off
DFGIIR frigid
DFGILU fulgid
DFGOOX dog-fox
DFIINY nidify
DFIIRT trifid
DFILNO infold
DFILOR florid
DFILUV fulvid
DFIMOY domify, modify
DFINNO findon
DFIOSU fusoid
DFIRTY drifty
DFKNOU fonduk
DFLNOU unfold
DFLNOY fondly
DFLOOR forold
DFLOPU upfold
DFLORU Rudolf
DFLRYY dry fly
DFNSUU fundus
DFOORX Oxford
DGGNOU dugong, gun dog
DGGOPU pug-dog
DGGRUY druggy
DGHIIN hiding
DGHINY dinghy
DGHITW Dwight
DGHOOO good-oh
DGHOOT hot dog
DGHOTU dought
DGHOUY doughy
DGIINN dining, indign, niding
DGIINO indigo
DGIINP pidgin
DGIINR Ingrid, riding
DGIINS siding
DGIINT tiding
DGIINV diving
DGILOT diglot
DGILOY dilogy

DGIMTU midgut
DGINNO on-ding
DGINOP pongid
DGINOT tin god
DGINOU guidon
DGINOW Godwin
DGINRU during, ungird
DGINRY drying
DGINSU dingus
DGINYY digyny
DGIOTW godwit
DGIRTU turgid
DGLOOY goodly
DGLOSY sly dog
DGLSUY sludgy
DGMSUY smudgy
DGNOOO no good
DGNOOR drongo, Gordon
DGNOOS godson
DGNOOW godown
DGNORU ground
DGNOSU sun-dog, sun-god
DGNRUY Grundy
DGOOPT top dog
DGORUY gourdy
DGOSTY stodgy
DGOTUU dugout
DHIIPS hispid
DHIISW widish
DHIJTU Judith
DHILNO inhold
DHILOS oldish
DHIMOS modish
DHINOO Hindoo
DHINSU Hindus
DHINSY shindy
DHIOPY hypoid
DHIORR horrid
DHIOST dhotis, dotish
DHIOSV dovish
DHIRSU rudish
DHIRSY dryish
DHKLOU dholuk
DHLOPU hold-up, uphold
DHLORY hydrol
DHLOSU should
DHLTUU Duluth
DHNOOU unhood
DHNOSU unshod
DHOOOO hoodoo
DHOORT hot rod
DHORSU shroud
DHORTU drouth
DIIISV divisi
DIILMP limpid
DIILOP lipoid
DIILOS solidi
DIILQU liquid
DIILST distil
DIILTY tidily

DIIMMS dim sim
DIIMNU indium
DIIMOS iodism
DIIMOU oidium
DIIMSS dimiss
DIIMTW dimwit
DIIMTY dimity
DIINNW inwind
DIINOT nidiot
DIINOX dioxin
DIINPT pintid
DIINRS indris
DIIOOP opioid
DIIORV viroid
DIIOTV vidiot
DIKKOP dikkop
DIKLNY kindly
DIKLTU kidult
DIKMNU dinkum
DIKNNU nudnik, unkind
DIKNOT dotkin
DIKNRY drinky
DIKOOS skidoo
DILLMY mildly
DILLNO Dillon
DILLWY wildly
DILMNY mindly
DILMOR milord
DILMOU dolium, idolum, moduli
DILMPY dimply
DILNNU dunlin
DILNOU noduli
DILNTU indult
DILNUU Ulundi
DILOPU lupoid
DILOPY dopily, ploidy
DILOSS dossil
DILOST stolid
DILOYZ dozily
DIMMNU immund
DIMMSU dim sum
DIMNOO domino, monoid
DIMNOR Nimrod
DIMNRU Nimrud
DIMNSU nudism
DIMOOR dromoi
DIMOPU podium
DIMORY yordim
DIMOSU modius, sodium
DIMOSW wisdom
DIMOXY myxoid
DIMPSY dimpsy
DINNUW unwind
DINOOR indoor
DINOPR drop-in
DINOPU dupion, unipod
DINOSW disown
DINOSY Sidony

DINOWW window
DINPTU pundit
DINPUW upwind, wind-up
DINSTU Dustin, nudist
DINTUY nudity, untidy
DIOOPS isopod
DIOORT toroid
DIOOSU odious
DIOOTX toxoid
DIOPRT torpid, tripod
DIORRT torrid
DIORSU disour
DIORTU triduo
DIOSTU studio
DIPPRY drippy
DIPRTU putrid, turpid
DIPSTU stupid
DIRSUZ durzis
DIRTUY durity
DJNNOO donjon
DJNOUY joundy
DKNOOP pondok
DKOOOO koodoo
DLLOOP dollop
DLLORY drolly, lordly
DLLOSY Lloyd's
DLLOUY loudly
DLMNUU lundum
DLMOOU modulo
DLMOSU dolmus
DLMOUY mouldy
DLMRUY drumly
DLNNOO London
DLNNOY Lyndon
DLNOOS onsold
DLNOSU unsold
DLNOTU untold
DLNUUY unduly
DLOOPS podsol
DLOOPZ podzol
DLOORU dolour
DLOOSU dolous
DLORUY dourly
DMMNUU nummud
DMNOOS Osmond
DMNOOY monody
DMNOSU osmund
DMNOUW Dunmow
DMNSUU musnud
DMOORS dromos
DMOOSY sodomy
DMORSU dorsum
DMPTUY dumpty
DNNOOT donnot
DNOOSU nodous
DNOOTW down to
DNOPSU pondus, pounds
DNORSU rounds

DNORTU rotund
DNOSUW wounds
DNOSUZ zounds
DNOUWY woundy
DNRRUY dry run
DNRSUY sundry
DNRUYY Rudnyy
DOOOOV voodoo
DOOOPW doo-wop
DOOPRY droopy
DOOSWY woodsy
DOPPRY droppy
DOPRSY dropsy
DORRTY dry rot
DORSSY drossy
DORSTU Stroud
DORSWY drowsy
DORUVY dyvour
DPSTUU dust-up
DRSTUY sturdy
DRSUYY dysury
EEEEGG gee-gee
EEEEHT tee-hee
EEEEPP pee-pee
EEEEPT teepee
EEEEPW peewee
EEEESS seesee
EEEETT teetee
EEEETV teevee
EEEEWW wee-wee
EEEFFT effete
EEEFIR feerie
EEEFLR feeler
EEEFRR reefer
EEEFRT efreet
EEEFRZ freeze
EEEGLN elenge
EEEGLT leegte
EEEGMR emerge
EEEGNP peenge
EEEGNR renege
EEEGNT gentee
EEEGNU Eugene
EEEGNV gneeve
EEEGRZ geezer
EEEGTV vegete
EEEHLN Helene
EEEHLR heeler, reheel
EEEHNT ethene
EEEHPZ pheeze
EEEHST seethe
EEEHTT teethe
EEEHWZ wheeze
EEEIKL keelie
EEEILN Eileen
EEEIMM meemie
EEEINW weenie
EEEIPR peerie
EEEIPW weepie
EEEIRR eerier
EEEITY Eyetie
EEEJTT jettee
EEEKLR keeler
EEEKLY Keeley

EEEKMN keneme, meeken
EEEKNR keener
EEEKNT ektene, ketene
EEEKPR keeper
EEEKRS seeker, sekere
EEELLT leetle
EEELMX lexeme
EEELNV eleven
EEELPR peeler
EEELRR reeler
EEELSS lessee
EEELSV sleeve
EEELTY eyelet
EEEMMS sememe
EEEMNR meneer
EEEMNT meeten
EEEMRS emerse, merese
EEEMST esteem, mestee
EEENPS pensee
EEENRS serene
EEENRT eterne
EEENRV enerve, evener, veneer
EEENSS Essene
EEENST ensete
EEENSZ sneeze
EEEOPP epopee
EEEPPR peeper
EEEPRV peever
EEEPRW weeper
EEERRV revere
EEERRW ewerer
EEERSV severe
EEERTT teeter, terete
EEERTX Exeter
EEERVW weever
EEESTT settee, testee
EEESTV steeve, vestee
EEETWZ tweeze
EEFFII fie-fie
EEFFIR effeir
EEFFLR ferfel
EEFFOT toffee
EEFFSU effuse
EEFGIR Fergie
EEFGRU refuge
EEFHIR heifer
EEFHOR hereof
EEFIIR feirie
EEFILN enfile, feline
EEFILR ferlie, relief
EEFILT leftie
EEFINR enfire, ferine, fineer, refine
EEFIRZ frieze
EEFLLO felloe
EEFLLR feller
EEFLLU leeful
EEFLMS meself
EEFLNN fennel
EEFLNS flense
EEFLRR ferrel
EEFLRT felter, reflet, trefle
EEFLRU ferule, refuel
EEFLRX reflex
EEFLRY freely
EEFLTT fettle
EEFLTW flewet
EEFLUY eyeful
EEFMTW fewmet
EEFNRS enserf
EEFNRU unfree
EEFPRR prefer
EEFPTY tepefy
EEFQRV Q fever
EEFRRR ferrer
EEFRRT ferret
EEFRST fester, freest
EEFRSU refuse
EEFRTT fetter
EEFRTU refute
EEFRTW fewter
EEFSZZ fezzes
EEGGGI geggie
EEGGIM Meggie
EEGGIN geeing
EEGGIR eggier, Reggie
EEGGIV veggie
EEGGLP peg-leg
EEGGLR legger
EEGGLT legget
EEGGLU luggee
EEGGMR Megger
EEGGMU muggee
EEGGOR George
EEGHNY hygeen
EEGHPU gee-hup
EEGILR lieger
EEGILT elegit
EEGILV veigle
EEGIMR emigre, regime
EEGINN engine
EEGINS gesine, seeing, Siegen, signee
EEGINY eyeing
EEGIRS Sergei
EEGIRT Gertie
EEGIRV grieve
EEGKLR kegler
EEGLLN leglen
EEGLMU emulge, geelum, legume
EEGLNN gennel
EEGLNO elonge
EEGLNR lenger
EEGLNT gentle
EEGLRT Gretel, reglet
EEGLTU Telegu
EEGMMN gemmen
EEGMNO genome
EEGMNR germen
EEGMNT tegmen
EEGMNU emunge
EEGMRR merger
EEGNNT gennet
EEGNOP pongee
EEGNOR engore
EEGNOX exogen
EEGNRT gerent, regent
EEGNRY energy, greeny, gyrene
EEGNST gentes, gesten
EEGNTW Tegwen
EEGRRT regret
EEGRRV verger
EEGRSS egress
EEGRST gester
EEGRSY geyser
EEGRTT getter
EEGRXY exergy
EEGSSU segues
EEHHII Heihei
EEHHNT hethen
EEHIMP imphee, Phemie
EEHINN Hennie
EEHINR herein, inhere
EEHINT Eithne, ethine, theine
EEHIPS Hepsie
EEHIRT either
EEHITV thieve
EEHITX hexite
EEHKLS shekel
EEHLLR heller
EEHLMM hemmel
EEHLMT helmet, methel
EEHLPR helper
EEHLRT lether
EEHLSV shelve
EEHLVW whelve
EEHMMR hemmer
EEHMNP hempen
EEHMNS enmesh
EEHMOR rehome
EEHMPT tempeh
EEHMUX exhume
EEHNNT thenne
EEHNNW whenne
EEHNOX hexone
EEHNPW nephew
EEHNRR Herren
EEHNRT nether, threne
EEHNSY sheeny
EEHNTY ethyne
EEHORT hereto, hetero
EEHORW howe'er, whoe'er
EEHOSX hexose
EEHOTW towhee
EEHPPR hepper
EEHPRS herpes, sphere
EEHPRT threep
EEHPSY Hepsey
EEHQTU quethe
EEHRST Esther, Hester, there's
EEHRSY heresy
EEHRTT tether
EEHRTU heurte
EEHRTW wether
EEHRTY they're, yether
EEHRVY Hervey
EEHRWY ywhere
EEHSST theses
EEHSWY weeshy
EEHTTY teethy
EEHTVY they've
EEHWYZ wheezy
EEIIKK kiekie
EEIIKR kierie
EEIILM mielie
EEIIMN meinie
EEIIMS meisie
EEIINN neinei
EEIINV nievie
EEIJNN Jennie, jinnee
EEIJNR jirene
EEIJSS Jessie
EEIKLL Kellie
EEIKLP kelpie, pelike
EEIKMN kineme
EEIKPW kewpie
EEIKRR Kerrie
EEILLN Nellie
EEILLS Leslie, Liesel
EEILLV vielle
EEILLW wellie
EEILMN meline
EEILMR Meriel
EEILMV melvie
EEILNN Lennie
EEILNO Leonie

EEILNP penile
EEILNR lierne, reline
EEILNS enisle, ensile, senile
EEILNT lenite
EEILNV enlive, enveil
EEILNW Eilwen
EEILOR loerie
EEILOS Eloise
EEILOT etoile
EEILPS Elspie
EEILPT pelite
EEILRS resile
EEILRV levier, relive, revile
EEILRY eerily
EEILTT Lettie
EEILTV Levite
EEILVW weevil
EEIMNR ermine
EEIMNY Yemeni
EEIMPR empire, epimer, premie
EEIMRR merrie
EEIMRS merise, remise
EEIMRT re-time, tremie
EEIMSS emesis
EEIMST mesite, Semite
EEINNP pinene
EEINNR nerine
EEINNT niente
EEINNV envein
EEINPR repine
EEINQU equine
EEINRS nereis, seiner, serine
EEINRT entire, nerite, triene
EEINRV envier, veiner, venire
EEINRW weiner, wiener
EEINRX Rexine
EEINSS Nessie
EEINSW newsie
EEINTT Nettie
EEINTV Venite
EEINTX extine
EEIPPY yippee
EEIPRR Pierre
EEIPRT perite
EEIPRX expire
EEIPTT petite
EEIPTW peewit
EEIQSU queise
EEIRRS sirree
EEIRRT etrier, retire
EEIRRV reiver
EEIRRW rewire
EEIRSS series
EEIRST resite
EEIRSV revise
EEIRSX sexier
EEIRSZ resize, seizer
EEIRTT ti-tree
EEIRVV revive
EEIRVW review, viewer
EEISSS seises
EEISST Tessie
EEISSV essive
EEISTV Stevie
EEISTW westie
EEJJNU jejune
EEJKRR jerker
EEJLNO Joleen, Jolene
EEJMOR Jerome
EEJMRY Jeremy
EEJNNT jennet
EEJNRY jyrene
EEJQRU jerque
EEJRST jester
EEJRSY jersey
EEJSSW Jewess
EEJSTT jet set
EEKKLR lekker
EEKKRT kretek
EEKLLR keller
EEKLMN Kenelm
EEKLMY meekly
EEKLNN kennel
EEKLNR kernel
EEKLNT kentle
EEKLNV knevel
EEKLNY keenly
EEKLPR kelper
EEKLRT kelter
EEKLSY sleeky
EEKLTT kettle
EEKLWY weekly
EEKMRS kermes
EEKNNR Kenner
EEKNOT ketone
EEKORV evoker, revoke
EEKPPU upkeep
EEKPRU peruke
EEKRRU kereru
EEKRST Kester
EEKRSW skewer
EEKRSY kersey
EELLMU Lemuel
EELLNO Noelle
EELLNT tellen
EELLOP pollee
EELLOV O level
EELLPT pellet
EELLQU quelle
EELLRS resell, seller
EELLRT retell, teller
EELLRY Ellery
EELLSV S level
EELLSY Lesley
EELMNY Emelyn
EELMOT omelet, telome
EELMPT pelmet, temple
EELMRT melter
EELMRU em rule
EELMRY merely
EELMSY seemly
EELMTT mettle
EELMTY meetly
EELNNT Lenten
EELNNV vennel
EELNOR Lenore, Loreen
EELNOV elevon
EELNPR plener
EELNPS spleen
EELNPV Pleven
EELNRT relent
EELNRU en rule, unreel
EELNSS lessen
EELNST nestle
EELNTT nettle
EELNTU eluent
EELNUV venule
EELNVY Evelyn, evenly
EELNXY xylene
EELOOS oleose
EELOPP people
EELOPR eloper
EELOPT opelet
EELOVV evolve
EELPPR lepper
EELPPU peepul
EELPRT pelter, petrel
EELPRU pelure
EELPRY yelper
EELPST pestle
EELPSV pelves
EELPSY sleepy
EELPTT pettle
EELQSU sequel
EELRRT lerret
EELRRV verrel
EELRSS lesser
EELRST Lester
EELRSV levers
EELRTT letter, lettre
EELRTW welter
EELRUV velure
EELRVY everly
EELSSS lesses
EELSSV selves, vessel
EELSSW wessel
EELSTT settle
EELSTV svelte
EELSTY sleety, steely, Yelets
EELSUV evulse
EELSWY Wesley
EELTVV velvet
EELTVW twelve
EELTWY tweely
EEMMNO moneme
EEMMOP pommee
EEMNNP penmen
EEMNOR moreen
EEMNOT toneme
EEMNPR pre-men
EEMNSS menses
EEMNTU menuet
EEMNYZ enzyme
EEMOPS empose
EEMOPT metope
EEMORT emoter, meteor, ometer, remote
EEMORV remove
EEMPRT temper
EEMPRY empery
EEMPST empest
EEMPTX exempt
EEMRRT termer
EEMRSS messer
EEMRST merest, termes
EEMRSU resume
EEMRSV vermes
EEMRTU Meerut
EEMSST tmeses
EEMSTU mustee
EEMSTX Semtex
EEMTXX Tex-Mex
EENNOO Oenone
EENNOR Noreen
EENNOT entone
EENNOV Evonne
EENNPR penner
EENNPT pennet
EENNRS Rennes
EENNRT rennet, tenner
EENNST sennet
EENNSU unseen
EENNTT entent, tenent
EENNTU entune
EENNUV uneven
EENNWY wen-yen
EENNYY yen-yen
EENOPR opener, perone, reopen

EENOPT poteen
EENOPX expone
EENORT tenore
EENORW erenow
EENORX exoner
EENOSV venose
EENOTV voteen
EENOTW townee
EENOVZ evzone
EENPRT repent, terpen
EENPRX prenex
EENPRY pyrene
EENPSY yepsen
EENQUY queeny
EENRRT renter
EENRST Ernest, nester, resent, tenser
EENRSU ensure
EENRTT netter, tenter
EENRTU neuter, retune, tenure, tureen
EENRTV venter
EENRTW weren't
EENRTX extern
EENRVY venery
EENSSU ensues
EENSTU tenues
EENSTV Steven
EENSTY teensy
EENSYZ sneezy
EENTTX extent
EENTTY teenty
EENTUX exeunt
EENTWY tweeny
EEOOST teesoo
EEOPRS repose
EEOPRU Europe
EEOPRV povere
EEOPST topees
EEOPSX expose
EEOPTU toupee
EEOPTY peyote
EEORST stereo
EEORSV soever
EEORSW Serowe
EEORTV vetoer
EEORUV oeuvre
EEOSST setose
EEPPPR pepper
EEPPST steppe
EEPRRT preter
EEPRRU purree
EEPRRY preyer
EEPRSS preses, sprees
EEPRST pester, pre-set
EEPRSU persue, peruse
EEPRSV vesper
EEPRSW spewer
EEPRTT petter
EEPRTU repute
EEPRTW pewter
EEPRTX expert
EEPRTY retype
EEPRUV prevue
EEPSTT septet
EEPSTU tupsee
EEPTTU puttee
EEQSTU queest
EEQSUU queues
EEQUXY exequy
EERRRT terrer
EERRST terser
EERRSV revers, server
EERRTT terret
EERRTU ureter
EERRTV revert
EERSTT setter, street, tester
EERSTU retuse
EERSTV verset
EERSTW wester
EERSTX exsert
EERSTY yester
EERSTZ zester
EERSVW swerve
EERSVY severy
EERTTT tetter
EERTTW wetter
EERTUY tuyere
EERTVV vervet
EERTVX vertex
EESSTT sestet, testes, tsetse
EESTTU suttee
EESTTW tweest
EESTTX sextet
EETTVY Yvette
EFFFLU fuffle
EFFGIR griffe
EFFGIY effigy
EFFGOR goffer
EFFGOT get-off
EFFGRU guffer
EFFHLU huffle
EFFHRU huffer
EFFIIR iffier
EFFIJL jiffle
EFFILP piffle
EFFILR riffle
EFFILT tiffle
EFFIMO moffie
EFFINR niffer
EFFINT infeft
EFFJRU juffer
EFFKOY off-key
EFFLMU muffle
EFFLOP poffle
EFFLOT let-off, offlet
EFFLRU ruffle
EFFLUX efflux
EFFMOR efform
EFFNOO one-off
EFFOPU pouffe
EFFORT effort
EFFORX forfex
EFFOST offset, set-off
EFFPRU puffer
EFFRSU suffer
EFFTTU tuffet
EFGGLU fuggle
EFGGOR fogger
EFGIIT giftie
EFGINR finger, fringe
EFGINU feuing
EFGIRU figure
EFGLNU engulf
EFGLOR golfer
EFGOOR forego, goofer
EFGORR forger
EFGORT forget
EFGRSU Fergus
EFGSUU fugues
EFHILS elfish
EFHIRS fisher, sherif
EFHISS fishes
EFHIST fetish
EFHLSS shelfs
EFHLSY fleshy
EFHOOR hoofer
EFHORT fother
EFIIKN knifie
EFIINT finite
EFIKLN finkle
EFIKLO folkie
EFIKNR knifer
EFIKNY knifey
EFILLR filler, refill
EFILLT fillet
EFILNN Linfen
EFILNO olefin
EFILNT finlet
EFILNY finely, lenify
EFILPP fipple
EFILPR pilfer
EFILRT filter, filtre, lifter, trifle
EFILRU ireful
EFILRV frivel
EFILSS fissle
EFILST fistle, itself, stifle
EFILSU fusile
EFILTU futile
EFILUY fulyie
EFILWY wifely
EFILZZ fizzle
EFIMRS fermis
EFINNR finner
EFINPR perfin
EFINRY finery
EFINST feints, festin, infest
EFINSU infuse
EFINTT fitten
EFINTY entify, neifty
EFIOOT footie
EFIORS froise
EFIORX foxier
EFIOST softie
EFIPRX perfix, prefix
EFIPTY tepify
EFIRST sifter, strife
EFIRSU surfie
EFIRTT fitter, titfer
EFIRTY ferity
EFIRUX fixure
EFIRVY verify
EFIRZZ fizzer
EFISTT testif
EFISTY feisty
EFLLOS folles
EFLLOT flotel
EFLLOW fellow
EFLLRU fuller
EFLMNU fulmen
EFLMSY myself
EFLNNU funnel
EFLNOT Teflon
EFLNOY felony
EFLNTU fluent, netful, unfelt
EFLOOS floose
EFLOOT footle
EFLOOZ foozle
EFLORR forrel
EFLORS Flores
EFLORT floret, lofter, torfle
EFLORW flower, fowler, wolfer
EFLORX flexor
EFLOUW woeful
EFLPRU purfle
EFLRUU rueful
EFLRUX reflux
EFLRUY fleury
EFLSTY flyest
EFLSUU useful
EFLTUY flutey

EFLTWY wet fly
EFLUZZ fuzzle
EFMNOR enform
EFMNOT foment
EFMNRU frenum
EFMORR former, reform
EFMOSU fumose
EFMRSU femurs
EFMTUY tumefy
EFNORS Fresno
EFNORZ frozen
EFNOST Sefton, soften
EFNRRU furner
EFNRYZ frenzy
EFNSTU funest
EFOORR re-roof, roofer
EFOORT foetor, footer, tofore
EFOORW woofer
EFOPRR profer
EFOPRT forpet
EFORRT Trefor
EFORRU furore
EFORRV fervor
EFORRW frower
EFORST forest, forset, fortes, foster
EFORTU fouter, foutre
EFORTW twofer
EFORWZ frowze
EFOSSY Yossef
EFOSTU foetus
EFRRSU surfer
EFRRTU Erfurt, returf
EFRSSU fusser
EFRTTY fretty
EFRTUU future
EFRTUX frutex
EFSTTU fustet
EGGGIL giggle
EGGGIO goggie
EGGGLO goggle
EGGGLU guggle
EGGGNO egg-nog
EGGHIL higgle
EGGHLU huggle
EGGHOR hogger
EGGHOT hogget
EGGHRU hugger
EGGIIP piggie
EGGIJL jiggle
EGGIJR jigger
EGGIJT jigget
EGGILN gingle, niggle
EGGILP piggle
EGGILR ligger
EGGILT giglet
EGGILU luggie
EGGILW wiggle
EGGIMO moggie
EGGINR ginger, nigger
EGGIRR rigger
EGGJLO joggle
EGGJLU juggle
EGGJOR jogger
EGGLMU muggle
EGGLNO legong
EGGLOP poggle
EGGLOR logger
EGGLOT goglet, logget, toggle
EGGLOW woggle
EGGLPU puggle
EGGLRU gurgle, lugger
EGGLTU tuggle
EGGMRU mugger
EGGMTU mugget
EGGNRU grunge
EGGNTU nugget
EGGOPR preggo
EGGORR gorger, Gregor
EGGORT gorget
EGGORU gouger
EGGPRY preggy
EGGRRU rugger
EGGRSU gurges
EGGRTU tugger
EGHHIR higher
EGHHIT eighth, height
EGHHIU Hughie
EGHIIN hieing
EGHILN hingle
EGHILS sleigh
EGHINO hoeing
EGHINT Gethin
EGHINW whinge
EGHITW weight
EGHITY eighty
EGHLMP phlegm
EGHLNT length
EGHLPU Guelph
EGHLUY hugely
EGHMMO megohm
EGHNOU enough
EGHNRU hunger, rehung
EGHOPR gopher
EGHORT ethrog
EGHOTT ghetto
EGHOTU toughe
EGHRSU gusher
EGIILL gillie
EGIILR girlie
EGIILW wilgie
EGIIMN Gemini, mingei
EGIINN ingine
EGIINP pieing
EGIINT ignite, tieing
EGIIRV virgie
EGIJLN jingle
EGIKNP Peking
EGILLN lingel, lingle
EGILLR grille
EGILLU ligule
EGILMN mingle
EGILMP megilp
EGILMT gimlet
EGILMY gleimy
EGILNN ginnel
EGILNO eloign, legion, longie
EGILNP pingle
EGILNR girnel, linger
EGILNS Glenis, single
EGILNT gentil, tingle
EGILNZ zingel
EGILOO goolie
EGILOP epilog
EGILOR gloire, logier
EGILPR pilger
EGILPT piglet
EGILRS grilse
EGILRU gluier, guiler, ligure, reguli, uglier
EGILRZ Grizel
EGILST legist
EGILTU glutei
EGIMMR gimmer, megrim
EGIMNO geonim, Imogen
EGIMNR germin, mering
EGIMOS egoism
EGIMPU guimpe
EGIMPY gympie
EGINNO oneing
EGINNR enring, ginner
EGINNS ensign
EGINNW newing
EGINOP pigeon
EGINOR ignore, region
EGINOT toeing
EGINOW wigeon
EGINPP Epping, pigpen
EGINPR pinger
EGINPU guinep
EGINRR ringer
EGINRS resign, signer, singer
EGINRT engirt
EGINRU rueing
EGINRW winger
EGINRY gyrine, ingyre
EGINRZ zinger
EGINSS gneiss
EGINST ingest, signet
EGINSU genius
EGINSW sewing, swinge
EGINTU gunite
EGINTV vigent
EGINTW twinge
EGINVX vexing
EGIOOR gooier
EGIORR gorier
EGIORS Sergio
EGIORT egriot, goiter, goitre
EGIOST egoist, stogie
EGIOTY egoity
EGIPPR grippe
EGIPPU guppie
EGIPRR griper
EGIPRS gipser
EGIPUV give-up
EGIRRV virger
EGIRSU guiser
EGIRTV grivet
EGIRUV guiver
EGISSU Gussie
EGITYZ zygite
EGJLNU jungle
EGKLNO kelong
EGKMSU muskeg
EGKNOY kyogen
EGLLTU gullet
EGLLUY gulley
EGLNNU gunnel
EGLNNY englyn
EGLNOP pelong
EGLNOR longer
EGLNOU lounge
EGLNPU plunge, pungle
EGLNRU lunger
EGLNSU gunsel
EGLNSY Glenys
EGLNTU englut, gluten
EGLNTY gently
EGLOPR proleg
EGLOPS gospel
EGLORU regulo
EGLORV glover, grovel
EGLORW glower

EGLOSU gulose
EGLOUY eulogy
EGLPRU gulper
EGLRYY greyly
EGLTTU guttle
EGLTUU Telugu
EGLTUY tulgey
EGLUZZ guzzle
EGMMRU grumme, gummer
EGMNOR germon, monger, morgen
EGMNOY myogen
EGMNTU nutmeg
EGMOOS smooge
EGMOOT mogote
EGMORU morgue
EGMOSU ugsome
EGMRSU gersum
EGMRTU tergum
EGMTUU muguet
EGNNOO non-ego
EGNNOU guenon
EGNNRU gunner
EGNOOR Oregon, orgone, orogen
EGNOOS segoon
EGNOOT gentoo
EGNOPS sponge
EGNOPW gowpen
EGNORV govern
EGNORY eryngo, groyne, yonger
EGNOTT gotten
EGNOTU tongue
EGNOXY oxygen
EGNPRU punger
EGNPUX expugn
EGNRRU gurner
EGNRTU Gunter, gurnet, urgent
EGNRTY gentry
EGNRUV guvner
EGNRUY gurney
EGNRWY Gerwyn
EGNSUU ungues
EGOORS groose
EGOORV groove, overgo
EGOOSS gooses
EGOOST stooge
EGOOSY goosey
EGOPPT pegtop
EGOPRR groper
EGOPRU groupe
EGORRS groser
EGORRV Grover
EGORRW grower, regrow
EGORSS ogress
EGORST groset
EGORSU grouse, rugose
EGORSY gyrose
EGOSTU outseg
EGOTTU get-out, goutte
EGOTYZ zygote
EGPRRU purger
EGPRSU spurge
EGRSTU gutser
EGRTTU gutter
EGRTUZ gutzer
EGRUVY guyver
EGSSTU gusset
EHHIKS sheikh
EHHIRT hither
EHHNPY hyphen
EHHRST thresh
EHHRTY hyther
EHIIJM Himeji
EHIIMN heimin
EHIINN hinnie
EHIIPP hippie
EHIIST Shiite
EHIJSW Jewish
EHIKKS kishke
EHIKNO Hikone
EHIKNS neskhi
EHIKOR hokier
EHIKPR kephir
EHIKRS shriek, shrike
EHIKSU huskie
EHILLN inhell
EHILMU helium, humlie
EHILNO helion
EHILOR holier
EHILOS isohel
EHILOT eolith
EHILPR hirple
EHILRS hirsel, hirsle, relish
EHILRT Hitler, lither
EHILSV elvish
EHILSW whiles
EHILTV thivel
EHIMMS immesh
EHIMNR menhir
EHIMNT hit men
EHIMNU inhume
EHIMOR homier
EHIMRT hermit, mither
EHIMRU humeri
EHIMST theism
EHIMSU mushie
EHIMTU humite
EHINOR heroin
EHINPX phenix
EHINRS shiner, shrine
EHINRT theirn
EHINRW whiner
EHINSW newish
EHINTW whiten, withen
EHINTY thyine
EHINTZ zenith
EHIOPS Sophie
EHIOPT ophite
EHIORS horsie, hosier
EHIORT heriot
EHIOST hostie
EHIOTT hottie
EHIPPR hipper
EHIPRS perish, pisher
EHIRRS Sherri
EHIRST hister, theirs
EHIRSV shiver, shrive
EHIRSW wisher
EHIRTT hitter, tither
EHIRTU Ruthie
EHIRTV thrive
EHIRTW wither, writhe
EHIRTZ zither
EHISST thesis
EHISTT theist
EHISTV tevish
EHISTW withes
EHITTW tewhit, thwite
EHITWY whitey
EHJOPS Joseph
EHJORS josher
EHJORT Jethro
EHKLPT klepht
EHKLRU hurkle
EHKNOR honker
EHKNRU hunker
EHKNUY hunkey
EHKOOR hooker
EHKOOY hookey
EHKORS kosher
EHKORY horkey
EHKRSU husker
EHLLOR holler
EHLLOU helluo
EHLLOW Howell
EHLLSY shelly
EHLLTY they'll
EHLMMU hummel
EHLMOP phloem
EHLMOY homely
EHLMTY methyl
EHLNOP holpen, phenol
EHLNPY phenyl
EHLOOY hooley
EHLOPP hopple
EHLORW howler
EHLOST hostel
EHLOSU housel
EHLOSV shovel
EHLOTW howlet
EHLPTY heptyl
EHLRRU hurler
EHLRSY Sheryl
EHLRTU hurtle, Luther
EHLRUV hulver
EHLRUY hurley
EHLSTU hustle, sleuth
EHLSTY shelty
EHMMRU hummer
EHMNOP phenom
EHMORT mother
EHMRRY rhymer
EHMRSU musher
EHMRUY rheumy
EHNNOP phenon
EHNNOW nowhen
EHNNRU hen-run
EHNOOR heroon
EHNOPY phoney
EHNORR horner
EHNORS senhor
EHNORT hornet, nother, throne
EHNOST honest
EHNOSW whenso
EHNOTY Thyone
EHNRSY henrys
EHNRTU hunter
EHOOOP hoopoe
EHOOPR hooper
EHOOPY phooey
EHOORT hooter
EHOORV Hoover
EHOOST soothe
EHOOSV hooves
EHOPPR hopper
EHOPPT hoppet
EHOPRT pother, thorpe
EHOPST Hospet
EHOPTT Tophet
EHORRT rhetor
EHORRW whorer
EHORST tosher
EHORSV shrove
EHORSW shower
EHORSY horsey
EHORTT hotter, tother, t'other
EHORTV throve
EHORTW throwe
EHORTX exhort
EHORTY theory
EHORTZ zeroth
EHOSUY housey
EHPRSU pusher
EHPRYZ zephyr
EHRRRU hurrer

EHRRSU rusher
EHRRSY sherry
EHRRTU hurter
EHRRWY wherry
EHRSSU rhesus
EHRSTT threst
EHRSTU thurse
EHRSTY thyrse
EHRTUW wuther
EHSSTY shyest
EIIJNR jirine
EIIKLM milkie
EIIKLT kiltie
EIIKNP pinkie
EIIKNR inkier
EIIKPS kipsie
EIILLL Lillie
EIILLM Millie
EIILLN nielli
EIILLP illipe
EIILLT illite
EIILLW willie
EIILMR limier
EIILMS simile
EIILMU milieu
EIILNN in-line
EIILNR inlier, linier
EIILNS inisle, sileni
EIILNT lintie
EIILNV inveil, live-in
EIILOR oilier
EIILOT iolite
EIILRT tirlie
EIILRV livier, virile
EIILRW wilier
EIILRX elixir
EIILSV visile
EIILZZ Lizzie
EIIMNN minnie
EIIMNT intime
EIIMRR rimier
EIIMSS missie
EIIMTX mixite
EIINNS Insein
EIINNT intine, tinnie
EIINNV invein, Vinnie
EIINNW Winnie
EIINOZ ionize
EIINPT pinite, tiepin
EIINQU inique
EIINRT intire, tinier
EIINRV Irvine
EIINRW winier
EIINSS seisin
EIINSZ seizin
EIINTV invite
EIINVV Vivien
EIIPPY yippie
EIIPRR pirrie
EIIPRS pieris
EIIPRT periti
EIIRRT irrite
EIIRRW wirier
EIIRTX Trixie
EIIRVV vivier
EIIRVZ vizier
EIISSS Sissie
EIISTV visite
EIISVV visive
EIJKNO in-joke
EIJKNR jerkin, jinker
EIJKNU junkie
EIJKOS Osijek
EIJKST jet ski
EIJLLT jillet
EIJLOT Joliet
EIJLTU Juliet
EIJNNO enjoin
EIJNOR joiner, rejoin
EIJNOS sejoin
EIJNRU injure
EIJNTY jitney
EIJOTU outjie
EIJPPR jipper
EIJRTT jitter, tri-jet
EIJSTU Jesuit
EIKKLN kinkle
EIKKNY kinkey
EIKKOS Skokie
EIKKRY yikker
EIKLLR killer
EIKLLY Ilkley, likely
EIKLMN kimnel
EIKLMR milker
EIKLNN enlink
EIKLNS silken
EIKLNT tinkle
EIKLNU unlike
EIKLNV kelvin
EIKLNW welkin, winkel, winkle
EIKLPP klippe
EIKLRT kilter, kirtle
EIKLSS kissel
EIKLTT kittel, kittle
EIKMMR kimmer
EIKMNR merkin
EIKMNS misken
EIKMOS Eskimo
EIKMRS kermis
EIKMST kismet
EIKMSU muskie
EIKMSY miskey
EIKNNO kinone
EIKNNP pinken
EIKNOO nookie
EIKNOV invoke
EIKNOY inyoke
EIKNPR Pernik
EIKNPU punkie
EIKNRS sinker
EIKNRT tinker
EIKNRW winker
EIKNSS kneiss
EIKNSV knives
EIKNTT kitten
EIKNTY kinety
EIKOOR rookie
EIKOOT kootie
EIKOPP koppie
EIKOPR pokier
EIKOST oekist
EIKOUY ukiyo-e
EIKPPR kipper
EIKRRS Kerris
EIKRSS kisser
EIKRST strike
EIKRSV skiver
EILLMO mollie
EILLMR miller
EILLMT millet
EILLMU illume
EILLNO lionel, niello
EILLNT lentil, lintel, tellin
EILLOP pollie
EILLOT Elliot
EILLPU pilule
EILLRT tiller
EILLRW willer
EILLRY Reilly
EILLST listel
EILLSU ill use
EILLTT little, tillet
EILLTU tuille
EILLTW willet
EILLTX extill
EILLVY evilly, lively, vilely
EILLWY willey
EILMMR limmer
EILMNO moline
EILMNR limner, merlin
EILMNU lumine
EILMNV Melvin
EILMNY myelin
EILMNZ menzil
EILMOT motile
EILMOY moiley
EILMPP pimple
EILMPR per mil, prelim
EILMPS simple
EILMPT limpet
EILMPW wimple
EILMPX implex
EILMRS smiler
EILMRT milter
EILMRU mulier, Muriel
EILMRV vermil
EILMRW Wilmer
EILMSS missel
EILMST mistle
EILMSU muesli
EILMSY smiley
EILMTU telium
EILMTY timely
EILMZZ mizzle
EILNNO Lonnie, online
EILNNT linnet
EILNOO loonie
EILNOP pinole
EILNOR Elinor, neroli
EILNOS insole, lesion
EILNOT entoil, lionet
EILNPP lippen, nipple
EILNPS pensil, spinel, spline
EILNPT pintle
EILNPU line-up, lupine, pinule
EILNPV plevin
EILNRT linter
EILNST enlist, listen, silent, tinsel
EILNSV snivel
EILNSY linsey, lysine
EILNTT litten
EILNTU lutein
EILNTV ventil
EILNTW wintle
EILNTY lenity
EILNUV unveil
EILOOR oriole
EILOOT lootie, oolite, toolie
EILOPS pilose, poleis
EILOPT piolet, polite
EILORS elisor
EILORT loiter, toiler
EILORU lourie
EILORV oliver, virole
EILOSU Louise
EILOTT Lottie,

toilet,
tolite
EILOTV olivet,
violet
EILOVY Yeovil
EILPPP pipple
EILPPR lipper,
ripple
EILPPT lippet,
tipple
EILPPU pile-up
EILPRS lisper,
pliers
EILPRT triple
EILPRY ripely
EILPST pistle,
stipel
EILPSU epulis,
pileus
EILPSV pelvis
EILPZZ pizzle
EILRST lister
EILRSV silver,
sliver
EILRTT litter,
tilter,
titler
EILRTU rutile
EILRTV livret
EILRVV vervil
EILRVY livery,
livyer,
verily
EILSSW wissel
EILSSY Sisley
EILSTU Iseult
EILSTW twisel
EILSVW swivel
EILSVY Sylvie
EILSWY wisely
EILSXY sexily
EILSZZ sizzle
EILTTT tittle
EILTTU lutite,
titule
EILTVY levity
EILUVV luvvie
EILVWY viewly
EIMMNU immune
EIMMOP mompei,
Pommie
EIMMOR memoir
EIMMOT immote
EIMMRS simmer
EIMMRU immure
EIMMRZ Zimmer
EIMMST semmit
EIMNNX meninx
EIMNOO Moonie
EIMNOP impone
EIMNOR merino
EIMNOS monies,
Simeon,
Simone
EIMNPT emptin,
piment,
pitmen
EIMNPU impune
EIMNRT mentri,
minter
EIMNRU murein,
murine,
nerium
EIMNRV Mervin,
vermin
EIMNRY minery
EIMNSS messin
EIMNSU insume
EIMNTT mitten
EIMNTU minuet,
minute,
mutine
EIMNTV vintem
EIMNTY enmity
EIMNUX xenium
EIMNZZ mizzen
EIMOOR roomie
EIMOPP moppie
EIMOPR mopier,
premio
EIMOPS impose,
pomeis
EIMOPT optime
EIMORS isomer,
rimose
EIMOSS mossie
EIMOST somite
EIMOSU mousie
EIMOTV evomit,
motive
EIMOTY moiety
EIMOZZ mozzie
EIMPRR primer
EIMPRS simper
EIMPRT permit
EIMPRU impure,
umpire
EIMPRX premix
EIMPST impest
EIMPTU impute,
uptime
EIMPUY yumpie
EIMRRT trimer
EIMRSS remiss
EIMRST mister,
smiter
EIMRSV verism,
vermis
EIMRSY misery
EIMSST tmesis
EIMSSU misuse
EIMSSX sexism
EIMSTY stymie
EIMSUV musive
EINNNR rennin
EINNOO ionone
EINNOP peonin
EINNOR ironen,
Ronnie
EINNOT intone
EINNOY yonnie
EINNPR pinner
EINNPT pinnet,
tenpin
EINNRS sinner
EINNRT intern,
tinner
EINNRW winner
EINNSS inness
EINNST sennit,
sinnet,
tennis
EINNTT intent,
tinnet
EINNTV invent
EINNTY ninety
EINNVY vinney
EINOOT toonie
EINOPP pepino
EINOPR orpine,
pernio,
pornie
EINOPT pointe
EINORR ironer
EINORS nosier,
senior
EINORT norite,
orient,
tonier
EINORV renvoi
EINORW inower
EINOSS enosis,
essoin,
noesis,
ossein,
sonsie
EINOST on-site
EINOSV vinose
EINOSW nowise
EINOTT tiento,
tonite
EINOTW townie
EINOTZ zonite
EINOVW inwove
EINPPR nipper
EINPPS pepsin
EINPRS sniper
EINPRT pterin,
terpin
EINPRU punier,
purine,
unripe
EINPRY pinery
EINPSS snipes
EINPST instep,
pentis,
spinet,
step-in
EINPSU puisne,
supine
EINQSU sequin
EINQTU quinte
EINQUU unique
EINQUZ quinze
EINRRS rinser
EINRST estrin,
insert,
sinter,
Strine
EINRSU insure,
ursine
EINRSV versin
EINRSY Erinys
EINRTT tinter
EINRTU triune
EINRTV invert,
vinter,
virent
EINRTW twiner,
winter
EINRTY nitery
EINRVW wivern
EINRVX vernix
EINRVY vinery
EINRWY winery
EINSSS nisses
EINSSW swines
EINSTU intuse,
tenuis
EINSTV invest,
ve-tsin
EINSTW wisent
EINSTY tinsey
EINSTZ Zenist
EINSUW unwise
EINSUX unisex
EINSWY sinewy,
winsey
EINTTW Witten
EINTTY entity
EIOOPW woopie
EIOOST otiose
EIOPPS popsie
EIOPPT pot pie,
toppie
EIOPRR ropier
EIOPRS poiser
EIOPRV Provie
EIOPRX poxier
EIOPSS possie
EIOPST postie,
potsie
EIOPTT tiptoe
EIORRS rosier
EIORRT rioter
EIORST sortie,
triose
EIORSV virose
EIORSZ seizor
EIORTT tertio,
tortie
EIOSTV soviet
EIOTVV votive
EIPPRR ripper
EIPPRS sipper
EIPPRT tipper
EIPPRU purpie
EIPPRY pipery
EIPPRZ zipper
EIPPST sippet

EIPPTT	tippet
EIPPTX	Tippex
EIPPUY	yuppie
EIPQSU	piques
EIPQTU	piquet
EIPRRS	priser
EIPRRZ	prizer
EIPRSS	pisser
EIPRST	esprit,
	priest,
	sitrep,
	sprite,
	stripe
EIPRSU	uprise
EIPRSW	swiper
EIPRTT	pitter
EIPRTV	privet
EIPRTX	extirp
EIPRTY	pyrite
EIPRXY	expiry
EIPSSS	sepsis,
	speiss
EIPSST	stipes
EIQRSU	squire
EIQRUV	quiver
EIQTUY	equity
EIRRTT	territ
EIRRTW	writer
EIRSST	resist,
	sister
EIRSSU	issuer
EIRSSY	yessir
EIRSTT	sitter,
	triste
EIRSTV	stiver,
	strive,
	trevis,
	verist
EIRSTW	wriest
EIRSVV	vivers,
	vivres
EIRTTT	titter
EIRTTV	trivet
EIRTTW	witter
EIRTUV	virtue
EIRTVY	verity
EIRUVV	viveur
EISSSU	issues
EISSTT	testis
EISSTU	tissue
EISSTX	sexist
EISTTY	tystie
EISTUX	exitus
EISTVW	swivet
EITTTX	tettix
EJKLSU	Seljuk
EJKNRU	junker
EJKNTU	junket
EJKOPS	Skopje
EJLLOY	jolley
EJLORW	jowler
EJLOST	jostle
EJLSSU	jussel
EJLSTU	justle
EJMNTU	jument
EJMPRU	jumper
EJNOTT	jetton
EJOPRT	projet
EJORSS	josser
EJORTT	jotter
EKKOPU	pukeko
EKLMOW	Welkom
EKLNOS	kelson
EKLNRU	lunker
EKLOOR	looker
EKLOPP	koppel
EKLOPT	klepto
EKLOWY	low-key
EKLRRU	lurker
EKLRSU	sulker
EKMNOS	K-meson
EKMNOY	monkey
EKMNTU	kentum
EKMOOP	mopoke
EKMOOU	okoume
EKMORS	mosker,
	smoker
EKMRUU	Kurume
EKMSTU	musket
EKNNOR	kronen
EKNNOT	enknot,
	Kenton,
	nekton
EKNNSU	sunken
EKNOPS	spoken
EKNORR	kroner
EKNORS	kernos
EKNORW	knower,
	wroken
EKNORY	yonker
EKNOUY	unyoke
EKNOYZ	zonkey
EKNPTU	unkept
EKNTTU	tunket
EKOORR	korero
EKOORT	retook
EKOPRR	porker
EKOPRT	porket
EKORRW	rework,
	worker
EKORRY	yorker
EKORST	stoker,
	stroke
EKOSST	stokes
EKPRRU	kurper
EKRRSY	skerry
EKRSTU	tusker
EKRTUY	turkey
EKRUVY	kurvey
ELLLOV	Lovell
ELLLOW	Lowell
ELLMNU	mullen
ELLMOW	mellow
ELLMRU	muller
ELLMSY	smelly
ELLMTU	mullet
ELLMUV	mulvel,
	vellum
ELLMUY	mulley
ELLNOP	pollen
ELLNOR	enroll
ELLNOS	onsell
ELLNOV	novell,
	vellon
ELLNOW	Nowell
ELLNOY	lonely
ELLNPU	pullen
ELLNSU	sullen
ELLNUU	lunule
ELLNUW	unwell
ELLOPR	poller
ELLOPS	ellops
ELLOPT	pollet
ELLOPX	pollex
ELLOPY	polley
ELLORR	Orrell,
	roller
ELLOST	tolsel
ELLOSY	solely
ELLOTW	tellow
ELLOTY	tolley
ELLOVY	lovely,
	volley
ELLOWY	yellow
ELLOWZ	Zwolle
ELLPRU	puller
ELLPTU	pullet
ELLPUY	pulley
ELLSTU	tellus
ELMMOP	pommel
ELMMOS	Moslem
ELMMPU	pummel
ELMNOR	merlon
ELMNOS	solemn
ELMNOT	loment,
	melton,
	molten
ELMNOY	lemony,
	myelon
ELMNPU	lumpen,
	plenum
ELMNSU	lumens
ELMNVY	Melvyn
ELMOOP	pomelo
ELMOOR	loomer
ELMOOS	osmole
ELMOOY	mooley
ELMOPY	employ
ELMORS	morsel
ELMORT	Merlot,
	molter
ELMOST	molest
ELMOSU	mousle
ELMOTT	mottle
ELMOTY	motley
ELMOUV	volume
ELMOXY	oxymel
ELMOZZ	mozzle
ELMPPU	peplum
ELMPRU	lumper,
	rumple
ELMPTU	plumet
ELMRTY	myrtle,
	termly
ELMSST	smelts
ELMSSU	mussel
ELMTUU	mutuel,
	mutule
ELMTUY	mutely
ELMUUV	muvule
ELMUZZ	muzzle
ELNNOS	nelson
ELNNOT	tonnel
ELNNOX	Lennox
ELNNRU	runnel
ELNNTU	nunlet,
	tunnel
ELNOOP	leopon,
	polone
ELNOOS	loosen
ELNOOW	woolen
ELNOOY	looney
ELNOPT	lepton
ELNOPY	openly
ELNORT	lentor
ELNOSS	lesson
ELNOST	stolen,
	telson
ELNOSU	ensoul
ELNOSV	sloven,
	volens
ELNOTT	tonlet
ELNOTV	volent
ELNOUZ	zonule
ELNOZZ	nozzle
ELNPRU	prunel
ELNPTU	penult
ELNPTY	pentyl,
	plenty
ELNPUX	nuplex
ELNRSU	nursle
ELNRTU	runlet,
	turnel
ELNSSU	unless
ELNSWY	Selwyn
ELNTTU	nutlet
ELNTTY	nettly
ELNUZZ	nuzzle
ELOOPR	looper
ELOOPT	pootle
ELOORS	sooler
ELOORT	looter,
	Loreto,
	retool,
	rootle,
	tooler
ELOOSU	oleous
ELOOTT	tootle
ELOPPP	popple
ELOPPR	lopper,
	propel
ELOPPS	peplos
ELOPPT	topple
ELOPPY	polype
ELOPRT	petrol
ELOPRU	pleuro,
	porule
ELOPRV	plover
ELOPRX	plexor
ELOPTT	pottle

ELOPTU poulet, tupelo
ELORRS sorrel
ELORSS lessor
ELORST ostler, sterol, torsel
ELORSV solver
ELORSY sorely
ELORTV revolt
ELORTW trowel, wortle
ELORUV louver, louvre, velour
ELORVW wolver
ELORVY overly
ELORWY owlery
ELOSST losset
ELOSSU louses
ELOSTU solute, tousle
ELOSTW Elstow
ELOSTY tylose
ELOSVW wolves
ELOSXY lyxose, xylose
ELOTTT tottle
ELOTTU let-out, outlet
ELOTUV volute
ELOTUZ touzle
ELOTWY owelty
ELOTWZ towzle
ELOTYZ tolzey
ELPPRU pulper, purple
ELPPSU supple
ELPQUU pulque
ELPRRU purler
ELPRSU pulser
ELPRTY peltry, pertly
ELPRUV pulver
ELPRUY purely
ELPSSU pussel
ELPSUX plexus
ELPTTU tuplet
ELPUZZ puzzle
ELQUUZ Queluz
ELRSSU Russel
ELRSTU luster, lustre, result, rustle, sutler, ulster
ELRSTY styler
ELRSUY surely
ELRTTU turtle
ELRTTY tetryl
ELRUWY wurley
ELRUWZ wurzel
ELSSTU tussle
ELSSTY slyest
ELSTTY stylet
EMMMOT mommet
EMMMRU mummer
EMMNNO mnemon
EMMNOO monome
EMMNOT moment
EMMNTU mentum
EMMOPR pommer
EMMOPS pommes
EMMOPY pommey
EMMORS momser
EMMORY memory
EMMORZ momzer
EMMRRU rummer
EMMRSU summer
EMMSUU museum
EMNNOT menton
EMNOOR Monroe, no more
EMNOOS monose
EMNOPY eponym
EMNORS sermon
EMNORT mentor, Merton, termon
EMNORU mourne, numero
EMNOTV movent
EMNOTY etymon
EMNOUY eunomy
EMNPSU pensum
EMNRSU mensur, rumens
EMNRVY Mervyn
EMNSSU sensum
EMNTUY Tyumen
EMOORR roomer
EMOORS morose
EMOORT mooter
EMOOSS osmose
EMOPPT moppet
EMOPRR romper
EMOPRS merops
EMOPRT metrop, pro tem, trompe
EMOPRU Euro-MP
EMOPRY empory, mopery, pomery
EMOPSY pomeys
EMOQSU mosque
EMORRT termor, tremor
EMORRW wormer
EMORSS mosser
EMORSU moeurs, mouser, oremus
EMOSSU mouses, mousse
EMOSUY mousey
EMPPRU pumper
EMPRSS sperms
EMPSTU septum, tempus
EMRRUY murrey
EMRSSS Messrs
EMRSSU serums
EMRSTU estrum, muster, stumer
EMRTTU mutter
EMRUVV muvver
EMSSTY mystes, system
EMSSUY yessum
ENNNOP pennon
ENNNOS non-ens
ENNNOT non-net
ENNOOS nonose
ENNOPT penton, ponent
ENNORT tonner
ENNORU neuron
ENNORV Vernon
ENNORW renown, wonner
ENNOST sonnet, tenson
ENNOSU non-use
ENNOTT net ton
ENNOTW newton
ENNOTZ tenzon
ENNOVY Yvonne
ENNPRU punner
ENNPTU punnet
ENNRRU runner
ENNRTU tunner
ENNRUY enurny
ENNSUW unsewn
ENOOPP oppone
ENOOPR operon
ENOORT enroot
ENOORZ ozoner
ENOOST osteon
ENOOSZ snooze
ENOOTV no-vote
ENOOTW one-two
ENOPRR perron
ENOPRS person
ENOPRU unrope
ENOPRV proven
ENOPRY pyrone
ENOPST pontes, posnet
ENOPTT potent
ENORRS snorer
ENORRY ornery
ENORSS sensor
ENORST stoner, tensor
ENORSW worsen
ENORTT rotten, torten
ENORTU tenour
ENORTY Tyrone
ENORUV unrove
ENORUZ zonure
ENOSSU onuses
ENOSTT ostent, teston
ENOSTX sexton
ENOSUV venous
ENOTTU tenuto, Teuton
ENOTTW tow-net
ENPRRU pruner
ENPRTU punter
ENPRUY penury
ENPTUW unwept
ENRRTU return, turner
ENRSTU unrest
ENRSTW strewn
ENRSTY sentry
ENRSUU unsure
ENRSUY nursey
ENRTTU nutter
ENRTUU untrue
ENRUZZ nuzzer
ENRVWY wyvern
ENSSTU sunset
ENSTUV venust
ENSUXY unsexy
ENTTWY twenty
EOOPPS oppose
EOOPPT popote
EOOPRS porose
EOOPRT pooter
EOOPTY ptooey
EOORRT rooter, torero
EOORST torose
EOORSV rooves
EOORTT tooter
EOOSYY yo-yoes
EOOTTU toe-out
EOOTTV Tetovo
EOOTVX ex-voto
EOPPPR popper
EOPPPT poppet
EOPPRR proper
EOPPRT topper
EOPPRY popery, pyrope
EOPRRS proser
EOPRRT porret, porter, pretor, report, troper
EOPRRU pourer
EOPRRV prover
EOPRST poster, presto
EOPRSU poseur, uprose
EOPRSY osprey
EOPRTT potter
EOPRTU pouter, troupe
EOPRTX export, torpex

EOPRTY poetry
EOPRTZ potzer
EOPSST posset
EOPSSU opuses, spouse
EOPSTX sexpot
EOPTTU toupet
EOQRTU roquet, torque
EORRRT terror
EORRRY orrery
EORRST resort, roster, sorter, storer
EORRSU rouser
EORRSV versor
EORRSW worser
EORRSY rosery
EORRTT retort, rotter, torret
EORRTU router, tourer
EORRTV Trevor, trover
EORRZZ rozzer
EORSST tosser, tsores
EORSSU serous
EORSTT tortes
EORSTU ouster, souter, trouse
EORSTV strove
EORSTW towser
EORSTY oyster, storey
EORSTZ zoster
EORSWW wowser
EORTTT totter
EORTTU tourte, touter
EORTTW wet rot
EORTTX extort
EORTVX vortex
EORTWY towery
EORUVY voyeur
EOSTTU outset
EPPPRY preppy
EPPPTU puppet
EPPRSU supper
EPRRSU purser
EPRRSY spryer
EPRRTU Rupert
EPRSSU pusser
EPRSUU pursue
EPRTTU putter
EPRTTY pretty
EPRTUU puture
EPRUVY purvey
EQRRUY querry
EQRTWY qwerty
ERRSTU rustre
ERRSUU usurer
ERRSUY surrey
ERRTTU turret
ERSSST stress
ERSSTU estrus, russet, tusser
ERSSTY tressy
ERSSUV versus
ERSTTU truest
ERSTUU suture, uterus
ERSTUV turves
ERSTUY surety
ERSTVY vestry
ERSTWY wryest
ERSUVY survey
ESSSUX Sussex
ESSTUX Sextus
ESTTUV vetust
FFFLUY fluffy
FFGINO offing
FFHIOS offish
FFHISU uffish
FFHIWY whiffy
FFIINT tiffin
FFIINY finify
FFILLU fulfil
FFILPS spliff
FFILTU fitful
FFIMNU muffin
FFINNU nuffin
FFINPU puffin
FFINSY sniffy
FFIOPR rip-off
FFIOPT tip-off
FFIOST soffit
FFIPSY spiffy
FFISUX suffix
FFLOTY fylfot
FFNORU run-off
FFNSUY snuffy
FFOOOO foo-foo
FFOPTU off-put
FFRRUU furfur
FFSTUY stuffy
FGGIIS fisgig
FGGIIZ fizgig
FGGORY froggy
FGHIIL higlif
FGHILT flight
FGHIRT fright
FGHORU frough
FGHOTU fought
FGIILN filing
FGIINN fining
FGIINR firing
FGIINX fixing
FGIINY ignify
FGILNU Fuling, ingulf
FGILNY flying
FGILOU fuligo
FGILUY uglify
FGINOX foxing
FGINRY fringy
FGIOTZ zoftig
FGJLUU jugful
FGKNUU kung fu
FGLMUU mugful
FGLORU fulgor
FGNSUU fungus
FGOORT forgot
FGOOSU goofus
FHIINS finish
FHIISW wifish
FHILTY filthy
FHIMSU fumish
FHIMUY humify
FHIRST shrift
FHIRTT thrift
FHISTU shufti
FHISTY shifty
FHORTU fourth
FHORTY for-thy, frothy
FHORWY forwhy
FHPRUY furphy
FIIIKL Kilifi
FIIKNR firkin
FIILLN infill
FIILLP fillip
FIILLS fillis
FIILVY vilify
FIIMNR infirm
FIIMNY minify
FIIMST misfit
FIINNP finnip
FIINOR fiorin
FIINTY finity
FIINVY vinify
FIITXY fixity
FIIVVY vivify
FIKNOR frokin
FIKNOS finsko
FIKOTX kit-fox
FIKRSY frisky
FILLOS follis
FILLPU fill-up
FILLRY frilly
FILLUW wilful
FILMOU folium
FILMRY firmly
FILMSY flimsy
FILNOR florin
FILNOW inflow
FILNSU sinful
FILNTY flinty
FILNUX influx
FILOOT foliot
FILORT firlot
FILORV frivol
FILOSS fossil
FILOXY foxily
FILPTU uplift
FILPTY fly-tip
FILRTY flirty
FILTUW witful
FIMNOR inform
FIMNOY omnify
FIMNSU munsif
FIMSSU Sufism
FINNOW finnow
FINOOS foison
FINORT forint
FINORX fornix
FINOSU fusion
FINOTT fitton
FINOTY notify, tonify
FINRRU furrin
FIOPRT forpit, profit
FIORRT forrit
FIORST fortis
FIOSSY ossify
FIOSTY foisty
FIOTTU fit-out, outfit
FIPRUY purify
FIPTYY typify
FIRTUY fruity
FIRYZZ frizzy
FJLOUY joyful
FKLNUY flunky
FKLOSY folksy
FKNOTY konfyt
FLLOOW follow
FLLOUY foully
FLMOOR formol
FLMOOS Folsom
FLMORY formyl
FLNOOW flow-on, onflow
FLNRUU unfurl, urnful
FLOOUZ zufolo
FLOOYZ floozy
FLOPPY floppy
FLOPTU potful
FLOPUU foul-up
FLORUY floury
FLOSSY flossy
FLOSTY softly
FLOTUY outfly
FLRRUY flurry
FLRSUU sulfur
FMOSUU fumous
FMPRUY frumpy
FNNRUU fun run
FNOORU unroof
FOORSS fossor
FOOTUX outfox
FORRUW furrow
FORSTU froust
FORSTW frowst
FORSTY frosty
FORSUU rufous
FORSWY frowsy
FORWYZ frowzy
GGGILY giggly
GGGORY groggy
GGHINO hoggin
GGHINU nigguh
GGHNOU gung-ho
GGIIJJ jig-jig

GGIINP piggin
GGIINV giving
GGIIRR gri-gri
GGIJLY jiggly
GGIKNO gingko, ginkgo
GGILNU gluing
GGILNY niggly
GGILOO gigolo
GGILUY gilguy
GGILWY wiggly
GGINNO nig-nog, noggin
GGINOR goring, gringo
GGINOZ Zigong
GGIOOR Gorgio
GGITWY twiggy
GGJJOO jog-jog
GGJJUU jug-jug
GGLOOO googol
GGLOOY googly
GGMMUU gum-gum
GGMOSY smoggy
GGNOOR gorgon
GGNRUY grungy
GGOOOO goo-goo
GGRRUU grugru
GHHILY highly
GHHIPU high-up
GHHITT thight
GHHOTU though
GHIIKL kilhig
GHIKNT knight
GHILPT plight
GHILST lights, slight
GHIMNO homing
GHIMTY mighty
GHINRT thring
GHINST nights, things
GHINTY nighty, thingy
GHINWY whingy
GHIOOS o-goshi
GHIOPZ phizog
GHIORS ogrish
GHIORT righto
GHIOSY goyish
GHIPTY ypight
GHIRST rights
GHIRTW wright
GHISTT tights
GHITUY thugyi
GHITWY wighty
GHLOOS golosh
GHLOPU plough
GHLOSU slough
GHMOTU mought
GHMPRU grumph
GHNNUU unhung
GHNOOP gonoph
GHNOOT ghoont
GHNORT throng
GHNOSU shogun
GHNOTU nought
GHNRUY hungry
GHNSUY gun-shy
GHNTUU hutung
GHOOPT photog
GHORTU trough
GHORTW growth
GHORUY roughy
GHOSTU sought
GHOSTY ghosty
GHOTTU tought
GHOTUY toughy
GHRRUY ghurry
GIIJNN Jining
GIIKLN liking
GIIKNP piking
GIIKNS skiing
GIIKNV Viking
GIILMN miling
GIILNN lignin, lining
GIILNT tiling
GIILNV living
GIILOR oil rig
GIILRV Virgil
GIIMNN mining
GIIMNT timing
GIIMNX mixing
GIINNN inning
GIINNT tining
GIINNV vining
GIINNY Yining
GIINOR origin
GIINOY yogini
GIINPP piping
GIINPS Siping
GIINRS rising
GIINRV Irving, virgin
GIINRW wiring
GIJLNY jingly
GIJNRU juring
GIKLNY kingly
GIKNNU unking
GIKNOS kongsi
GIKNOW Woking
GIKNOY yoking
GIKRTU tugrik
GILLOO loligo
GILLOR grillo
GILLUY uglily
GILMNU lignum
GILMRY grimly
GILMSU siglum
GILMWY Gwilym, Gwylim
GILNOO logion, olingo
GILNOR loring
GILNOS losing
GILNOT lingot, tiglon
GILNOU gluino
GILNOV loving
GILNPU plug-in
GILNRU luring, ruling
GILNSU lungis
GILNSY Glinys, Glynis, singly
GILNTU inglut, luting
GILNTY tingly
GILOOS isolog
GILOOY gooily
GILORY Gilroy, gorily
GILOST logist
GILRSY grisly
GILRUY ligury
GILTUY guilty
GILTYZ glitzy
GIMNNO mignon
GIMNOP mpingo
GIMNOR orming
GIMNOV moving
GIMNOW mowing
GIMNOY ignomy
GIMNPU impugn
GIMNRU muring
GIMOSY yogism
GIMOTU gomuti
GIMRSU simurg
GINNOO gonion
GINNOP pignon
GINNOS nosing
GINNOT tignon
GINNOZ zoning
GINNSU gunnis
GINNTU tuning
GINOOS isogon
GINOPR roping
GINOPY pongyi
GINORS grison, signor
GINORT tigron, trigon
GINOSS gnosis
GINOSW sowing
GINOTU outing
GINOTV voting
GINOTW towing
GINOUZ guinzo
GINPPU upping
GINPRS spring
GINPRY prying
GINPTU pignut
GINRST string
GINRTU truing
GINRTY trying
GINSTY stingy
GINSUU unguis
GINSUX six-gun
GINSWY swingy
GINTVY vingty
GINVWY vying w
GIOORV vigoro
GIOPSS gossip
GIOPST spigot
GIORRU rigour
GIORTU outrig, rig-out
GIORUV vigour
GIPPRY grippy
GIPSTY pigsty
GIRTTY gritty
GISUUU uguisu
GJLNUY jungly
GJNOOU goujon
GJNRUU gurjun
GKRYYZ Kyrgyz
GLLMUY glumly
GLLNOY longly
GLLOOP gollop
GLMNOO Mongol
GLMOOY gloomy
GLMOSU glomus
GLMPUY glumpy
GLMSUY smugly
GLNNOO long on
GLNOOO oolong
GLNOOT lotong
GLNPUU unplug
GLNSUY snugly
GLOOOY oology
GLOOPR prolog
GLOOSW go-slow
GLOPTU putlog
GLOSSY glossy
GLSUUV vulgus
GMNNOO gnomon
GMOOPR pogrom
GMPRUY grumpy
GMPSUY gypsum
GNNSUU unsung
GNOORT trogon
GNOORW wrongo
GNOPPU oppugn, popgun
GNOPSY spongy
GNORST strong
GNOTUU outgun
GNPRSU sprung
GNRSTU strung
GNRTUU Guntur
GNSTUU Tungus
GOOOOR gooroo
GOOPST stop-go
GOORST ostrog
GOORTT grotto
GOORTV tvorog
GOORVY groovy
GOPPRU gruppo
GORRTU turgor
GORSUY gyrous
GORTTU gut-rot, rot-gut
GORTTY grotty
GORTUY yogurt
GOSTUY gousty
GRSTUU Surgut
GRTTUU guttur
GSTTUU guttus

GSYYYZ syzygy
HHIMOS homish
HHIOPP hip hop
HHIOSW howish
HHISTW whisht
HHMMUU humhum
HHMOOU mohohu
HHMRTY rhythm
HHOOOO hoo-hoo
HHOOOY yo-ho-ho
HHOOSW whoosh
HHRSTU thrush
HIIJNS Jinshi
HIIKNO hinoki
HIIKNS inkish
HIILLS illish
HIILLT Lilith
HIILNS linish
HIILPP Philip
HIILSU Lishui
HIIMNS minish
HIIMPS impish
HIIMSS Shiism
HIIMST isthmi, mishit
HIINPS inship
HIINTW inwith, within
HIIOPT pithoi
HIIRSS rishis
HIISTT thitsi
HIISVW wivish
HIITTW with it
HIJOSU Jishou
HIJSTU Jutish
HIKMUZ muzhik
HIKNRS shrink
HIKSWY whisky
HILLNO hollin
HILLOY holily
HILLPU uphill
HILLPY Philly
HILLRS shrill
HILLRT thrill
HILLWY whilly
HILMOS holism
HILMOW whilom
HILMOY homily
HILMSU mulish
HILNPT plinth
HILNTY thinly
HILOOT oolith, tholoi
HILOPS polish
HILOST holist
HILOSW lowish, owlish
HILPST spilth
HILPSU huspil
HILRWY whirly
HILSTW whilst
HILSWY wishly
HIMMSY shimmy
HIMNOS monish
HIMNOY hominy
HIMNSU munshi
HIMOPS mopish
HIMORS hirmos, morish, Romish
HIMOTY mythoi
HIMPRS shrimp
HIMRTU thumri
HIMSTY smithy
HIMSWY whimsy
HINNSY shinny
HINNTU nuthin
HINNWY whinny
HINOOP inhoop
HINOOR orihon
HINOOS shoo-in
HINOPS siphon
HINOST Shinto, tonish
HINPSU punish, unship
HINPSX sphinx
HINPTY phytin
HINRSU inrush
HINRTU Ruthin
HINSTY shinty
HINSUV Vishnu
HIOOSV shivoo
HIOPPS popish
HIOPRT trophi
HIOPSS posish
HIOPST pithos
HIOPSY physio
HIORSS Roshis
HIORSU houris
HIOTTU hit-out
HIOTWZ howitz
HIOWZZ whizzo
HIPPSU hippus, uppish
HIPPWY whippy
HIPRST thrips
HIQSSU squish
HIRRWY whirry
HIRSTT thirst, T-shirt
HIRSTU truish
HIRSTY shirty, thyrsi
HIRTTY thirty
HISSWY swishy
HISTTY shitty
HITTUW tu-whit
HIWYZZ whizzy
HJNNOY johnny
HKLOOU holoku
HKNOOU unhook
HKNOSY shonky
HKNRSU shrunk
HKNSUU unhusk
HKOOPU hook-up
HKOOST shtook
HLLOOW hollow
HLLOPY phyllo
HLLOWY wholly
HLLSUY lushly
HLMOTY thymol
HLMPUY phylum
HLMPYY lymphy
HLNOUY unholy
HLOOSS sloosh
HLOOST Sholto, tholos
HLOPSS splosh
HLOPSY poshly
HLOPTY phytol
HLORUY hourly
HLOSSY sloshy
HLOUUZ Luzhou
HLPSUY plushy
HLSSUY slushy
HMMMUU hummum
HMMSUU hummus
HMNOPY nympho
HMNPUY hypnum
HMOOPR morpho
HMOOPW woomph
HMOOST smooth
HMOOSW whomso
HMORUU humour
HMOSTU mouths
HMOSTY mythos
HMOSUU humous
HMOTUY mouthy
HMPRTU thrump, trumph
HMPRUY murphy
HMPTUY humpty
HMRRYY myrrhy
HMRSTU thrums
HMSTUY mythus, thymus
HMTUYZ zythum
HNNOOP phonon
HNOOPT photon
HNOORT thoron
HNOORU honour
HNOOSW no-show
HNOPSU nosh-up
HNOPSY syphon
HNOPTY phyton, python, typhon
HNORSU onrush
HNORTW thrown
HNORTY thorny
HNPSUU hunsup
HNRTUU unhurt
HOOOOR hooroo
HOOOOY yoo-hoo
HOOPPR propho
HOOPST pothos
HOOPSW whoops
HOOPTT hotpot
HOORRR horror
HOORRU hurroo
HOORUZ huzoor
HOOSSW swoosh
HOOTTY toothy
HOOTUW tu-whoo
HOPPSY shoppy
HOPRSY ophrys
HOPRTY trophy
HOPSSY hyssop, phossy
HOPSTU tophus, upshot
HOQUUZ Quzhou
HORSST shorts
HORSTY hostry, Rosyth, shorty
HORTWY worthy, wrothy
HOSSTU stoush
HOSTUY youths
HOTUYY youthy
HOUUWZ Wuzhou
HPPSUU push-up
HPRSUU uprush
HPSTUU Pushtu
HPSTUY typhus
HRSTTU struth, thrust, truths
IIILLP lilipi
IIIMMN minimi
IIIPTT tipiti
IIIRST iritis
IIJNNO injoin
IIKLNN inlink
IIKNNO konini
IIKNOS inkosi
IIKNPP kippin, pipkin
IIKNSS siskin
IIKOST oikist
IIKOTT titoki
IILLMU lilium
IILLNT intill
IILLOY oilily
IILLPU illupi
IILLSW Willis
IILLWY wilily
IILMMU milium
IILNNU inulin
IILNOR Ilorin
IILNOV violin
IILNST instil
IILNTY tinily
IILOTV Tivoli
IILPST pistil
IILRWY wirily
IILTTW twilit
IILTVY vility
IIMMNU minium
IIMMNW wimmin
IIMNNO minion
IIMNNY niminy
IIMNOU ionium
IIMOPS opiism
IIMOSS miosis
IIMOTV motivi
IIMRST smriti
IIMSSS missis

IIMSTT timist
IINNOP pinion
IINNPY Pinyin
IINORS Roisin
IINORV virino, virion
IINOSV vision
IINPPP pippin
IINQTU quinti
IINSST insist
IINSTW tiswin
IINTTU intuit
IINTTW nitwit
IIOOPP piopio, poipoi
IIOOTT toi-toi
IIOOYY yoi-yoi
IIOSTT otitis
IIPPPP pip-pip
IIPPUU piupiu
IIPRRU puriri
IIPRST spirit
IIPRTU pituri
IIQTUV qiviut
IIRRTT tirrit
IJKLOY jokily
IJKMOU moujik
IJKNOS joskin
IJKOST jokist
IJLSUU Julius
IJMNOS jimson
IJNNOU unjoin
IJNORU junior
IJNOTY jointy
IJNRUY injury
IJNSTU injust, Justin
IJORRU joruri
IJRSTU jurist
IKKKRU Kirkuk
IKKLOU lukiko
IKKNNU unkink
IKKNOT tokkin
IKKORR korkir
IKKRSU kukris
IKKUUY Kikuyu
IKLLSY skilly
IKLNNU unlink
IKLNOO inlook, look-in
IKLNPU link-up, uplink
IKLNPY pinkly
IKLNSY slinky
IKLNTY tinkly
IKLOOT lookit
IKLOPU ouklip
IKLOPY pokily
IKLORY Kilroy
IKLPSY plisky
IKLSSU suslik
IKLTTU kittul
IKMNOO kimono
IKMNOR morkin
IKMPSY skimpy
IKMPTU kumpit
IKMRSY smirky
IKMSSU kumiss
IKNNOT inknot
IKNNPU punkin
IKNNSY skinny
IKNNTU unknit
IKNORW inwork
IKNOST stinko
IKNPSU piskun
IKNRSU ski run
IKNSTY stinky
IKNTWY twinky
IKOPSY pikoys
IKPRSU prusik, spruik
IKQRUY quirky
IKRSSU Russki
IKRSTY Kirsty
IKSVVY skivvy
ILLMPY limply
ILLMSY slimly
ILLNOS Llinos
ILLNOY lionly
ILLNPU pull-in
ILLOOP polloi
ILLOPW pillow
ILLORT trillo
ILLOTT tillot
ILLOWW willow
ILLPPU pilpul
ILLPSU pusill
ILLQSU squill
ILLRTU trulli
ILLSTY stilly
ILLSUV villus
ILLTTY littly
ILLTWY twilly
ILMMSU Muslim
ILMNOO nomoli
ILMNOT Milton
ILMNOU moulin
ILMNSU muslin
ILMOOV moolvi
ILMOPY imploy, mopily
ILMOSS lissom
ILMOSU limous
ILMOTU ultimo
ILMOTW Wilmot
ILMOUV moulvi
ILMOUX Limoux
ILMPPY pimply
ILMPRY primly
ILMPSY limpsy, simply
ILMPTU multip
ILMRSY lyrism
ILMRTY trimly
ILMSTU litmus
ILMTUU tumuli
ILMYZZ mizzly
ILNNOT linton
ILNOOT lotion
ILNOOV violon
ILNOPP poplin
ILNOPS slip-on
ILNOPT pontil
ILNOQU quinol
ILNORT litron
ILNORW wornil
ILNOST tonsil
ILNOSU insoul
ILNOSY nosily
ILNOTU lutino, nut oil, ultion
ILNOTW Wilton
ILNPRU purlin
ILNPST splint
ILNPUY punily
ILNRTY nitryl, nytril
ILNSTU insult, sunlit
ILOORT loriot
ILOPPY polypi
ILOPRX prolix
ILOPRY pylori, ropily
ILOPST pistol, postil, spoilt
ILOPSU pilous
ILOPTY polity
ILOQRU liquor
ILORSY rosily
ILOTTW wittol
ILPPRY ripply
ILPPSU slip-up
ILPPSY pipsyl, slippy
ILPPTU pulpit
ILPRTY triply
ILQRSU squirl
ILRSTU trisul
ILRSTY lyrist
ILRSWY swirly
ILRTTY trityl
ILRTWY twirly
ILSTTU lutist
ILSTTY slitty
ILSTUU lituus
ILSTWY wistly
IMMMOS momism
IMMNOS monism, nomism
IMMNOU omnium
IMMOOS simoom
IMMOSU osmium
IMMOTU tomium
IMMSTU mutism, summit
IMNNOW minnow
IMNNTU muntin
IMNOOR morion, Moroni, nomori
IMNOOS simoon
IMNOOT motion
IMNOSS nosism
IMNOST inmost, monist
IMNOSU musion
IMNOSY myosin, simony
IMNTUY munity, mutiny
IMOOTV motivo, vomito
IMOPRS porism
IMOPRT import, promit
IMOPRV improv
IMOPRW improw
IMOPST impost
IMORRR mirror
IMORRS morris
IMORSU rimous
IMOSSY myosis
IMOSTU ostium, timous
IMOSTY moisty
IMOTTT tomtit
IMOTVY vomity
IMPRSU primus, purism
IMPSWY Wimpys
IMQRSU squirm
IMRSTU truism
IMRSTY mistry
IMRTUV vitrum
IMSSSU missus
INNOOR iron-on
INNOOT notion
INNOOY oniony
INNOPS pinson
INNOPY pinyon
INNORS ronins
INNORT intron, nitron
INNOSU nonius, unison
INNOTW in-town
INNOWW winnow
INNRTU inturn
INNSSU Sunnis
INOOPR porion
INOOPS poison
INOOPT option, potion
INOORS orison
INOORT inroot
INOORZ zorino
INOPRS prison
INOPST piston
INOPTT tinpot
INOPTY pointy
INORRS Norris
INORSS nossir
INORSU oursin
INORSY rosiny
INORTT triton
INORTU turion
INORWW winrow

INOSTT tonist
INOSUV vinous
INOTVY novity
INPPSY snippy
INPRST sprint
INPRTU turnip
INQSTU squint
INQSUY quinsy
INRSXY syrinx
INRTVY vintry
INRTWY wintry
IOORRT torori
IOPPPT poppit
IOPPTT tiptop
IOPRRY priory
IOPRST prosit, tripos
IOPRTT tripot
IOPSST ptosis
IOPSSY pyosis
IOPSTU pistou
IORRTW worrit
IORSTU suitor
IORSUV virous
IOSSTT tsotsi
IOSTTU outsit
IOSTTV votist
IOTTUW outwit
IPPRTY trippy
IPPSSU piss-up
IPPTUY uppity
IPRRTU irrupt
IPRSST stirps
IPRSSY prissy
IPRSTU purist, spruit, tripus
IPRSTY stripy
IPRSTZ spritz
IPRTUY purity
IPSTTY spitty, typist
IPSTXY ptyxis
IPSVVY spivvy
IQRSTU squirt
IQUYZZ quizzy
IRSTWY wristy
IRTTUX tutrix
ISSTTU Tutsis
ISTTTU tuttis
ISTTWY twisty
JLLOOP jollop
JLNOOY Jolyon
JLSTUY justly
JNNOOP jonnop
JNNOOT tonjon
JNOORU journo
JNSTUU unjust
JOOSUY joyous
KKMTUU muktuk
KKNRUU kunkur
KKOOPU kokopu
KKOTUU kotuku
KKSSTT tsk tsk
KKTTUU tuk-tuk
KLMNOY monkly
KLMOOU lokoum
KLOOPU look-up
KLPSSU Slupsk
KLRTUU kultur
KLTUYZ klutzy
KMOSUX musk ox
KNNOTU unknot
KNOORR kronor
KNOORS Krosno
KNORRU kronur
KNOTTY knotty
KNPSUY spunky
KNTUUY Kuytun
KOOPSY spooky
KOORSU kouros
OOSSU kousso
KOOTWW kowtow
KRSSUY Russky
LLLOOP lollop
LLLOOT tol-lol
LLNOOR roll-on
LLNOOT tollon
LLNOPU pull-on
LLNORU unroll
LLOOTU toluol
LLOOWY woolly
LLOPRU roll-up
LLOPRY prolly
LLORST stroll
LLORTU trullo
LLORTY trolly
LLOSWY slowly
LLPPUU pull-up
LLPSUU pullus
LLSTUY lustly
LMMOUX lummox
LMMPUY plummy
LMMSUY slummy
LMMTUU multum
LMNOOT molton
LMOORU ormolu
LMOSTY mostly
LMOSUY my soul
LMOUUV ovulum
LMPPUY plumpy
LMPRUY rumply
LMTTUU tumult
LNOOPY polony
LNOOST stolon
LNOPTU pluton
LNORSY Roslyn
LNPTUU pultun
LNRUUY unruly
LNSSTU stuns'l
LOOPRY poorly
LOOSTV volost
LOOVVX volvox
LOPPPY popply
LOPPRY propyl
LOPPSY sloppy
LOPRTY portly
LOPSUU lupous
LOPTTY plotty
LOPTWY two-ply
LORSUY lusory, sourly
LORTTY trotyl
LOSTYZ zlotys
LPPRUY purply
LPPSUY supply
LPRRUY plurry
LPRSYY spryly
LRRSUY slurry
LRSTUY sultry
LRUUXY luxury
LSSTUY stylus
MMNNUU num-num
MMNOOR Mormon
MMNOSU musmon, summon
MMOOPP pompom
MMOOTT motmot, tom-tom
MMRRUU murmur
MMTTUU tum-tum
MMTUUU mutuum
MMUUUU muu-muu
MMUUYY yum-yum
MNNOUW unmown
MNOOPP pompon
MNOOPS monops
MNOORT to-morn
MNOORU unmoor
MNOOTU mouton
MNOOTW Motown
MNOTTU mutton
MNOTYZ myzont
MNSTTU mustn't
MOOOPW wompoo
MOOOSS mossoo
MOORRW morrow
MOORTY motory
MOOSTY ostomy
MOPPRT prompt
MOPSSU possum
MOPSTU upmost
MOQRUU quorum
MOQTUU quotum
MORRUU rumour
MORSTY stormy
MORSUW worsum
MORTUU tumour
MOSSTY mysost
MOSTTU utmost
MPRSUU rumpus
MPSTUU sputum
MPSTUY stumpy
MRRTUU turrum
MSTTUY smutty
NNOOTW wonton
NNOOUU nounou
NNORTU turn-on
NNORUW unworn
NNOSUW unsown
NOOORS Osorno
NOOPRR porron
NOOPRS Sopron
NOOPRT pronto, proton
NOOPST spot on
NOOPSY snoopy, spoony
NOORRY Norroy
NOORST tonsor
NOORTU unroot
NOOSST nostos
NOOSTT toston
NOOSTY snooty
NOOSYZ snoozy
NOPPTU pupton
NOPSTU unstop
NOPTUW uptown
NORRTU turron
NORSTU tornus
NORSTW strown
NORTUU outrun, run-out
NOSTTU Sutton
NOSTTY snotty
NOSTUY snouty
NPRSUU prunus
NPRTUU turn-up, upturn
OOOOPP poo-poo
OOOOTT too-too
OOPPRT troppo
OOPPST post-op
OOPPTU pop-out
OOPPVX vox pop
OOPRRT torpor
OOPRSU porous
OOPRTU uproot
OOPTTU opt-out, out-top, puttoo
OOPWWW powwow
OORRSW sorrow
OORRTT tro-tro
OORSTU torous
OORSTY rootsy
OORTWW tow-row
OOSTTY tootsy
OOWWWW wow-wow
OOWWYY yow-yow
OPPPRY proppy
OPPSSY psy-ops
OPRSTU sprout, stupor
OPRSTY prosty, sporty
OPSSTU toss-up
OPSTTY spotty
OPTTUU output
ORSTTU trouts
ORTTUY try-out, tutory
PPRRUU purpur
PPTTUU put-put
PRRSUY spurry
PRSUYY syrupy
RSTTUY trusty
SSTUXY xystus
TTTTUU tut-tut

SEVEN LETTERS

AAAABLM Alabama
AAAALNP alapana
AAABBCL cabbala
AAABBKL kabbala
AAABBLM baa-lamb
AAABBRR Barbara
AAABCIR arabica
AAABCLO bacalao
AAABCLR calabar
AAABCLV baclava
AAABCMR caramba
AAABCNR baracan
AAABCTW catawba
AAABDHM Mahabad
AAABDLM lambada
AAABDTU taubada
AAABEMN maneaba
AAABFIN Fabiana
AAABFLL falbala
AAABHJL Halabja
AAABHLR La Habra
AAABHLT Batalha
AAABHMR Abraham
AAABHMS Bahamas
AAABILN Albania
AAABILR labaria
AAABILX abaxial
AAABINR Arabian
AAABINV baviaan
AAABIST sabatia
AAABKLR Karbala
AAABKLV baklava
AAABLLT ballata
AAABLLW wallaba
AAABLMT tambala
AAABLPR palabra
AAABMMR Maramba
AAABMOS abomasa
AAABMST mastaba
AAABNNR rabanna
AAABORR araroba
AAACCDT taccada
AAACCLM malacca
AAACCLR caracal
AAACCRS Caracas,
cascara
AAACDIN Acadian
AAACDMM macadam
AAACDNR anacard
AAACDSS cassada
AAACEHN Achaean
AAACENP panacea
AAACHHL Halacha
AAACHLM Machala
AAACHLZ chalaza
AAACHRY acharya
AAACIJM Jamaica
AAACILM malacia
AAACIMR Aramaic,
cariama
AAACINT Catania
AAACJMR jacamar
AAACLMN almanac,
mancala
AAACLNN alcanna
AAACLNR Larnaca
AAACLNT Catalan
AAACLPT catalpa
AAACLRZ alcazar
AAACLSU acausal
AAACMNP campana
AAACMRS marasca,
mascara
AAACMRT matraca
AAACMST casamat
AAACNPT catapan
AAACNRT nacarat
AAACNRV caravan
AAACNST canasta
AAACNTT cantata
AAACPTZ capataz
AAACRRR Carrara
AAACRWY caraway
AAACSST cassata
AAACSSV cassava
AAACSTT catasta
AAADDFR dafadar
AAADELM alameda
AAADFRY faraday
AAADGHL Galahad
AAADGJN jangada
AAADGNR Granada
AAADHMM hammada
AAADHMN Hamadan
AAADILM almadia
AAADILX adaxial
AAADIMS saaidam
AAADINR Adriana
AAADIRT radiata
AAADJMR jamadar
AAADKNN Kannada
AAADLMN mandala
AAADMNN Adamnan
AAADMNR Ramadan
AAADMNT adamant
AAADNRS sardana
AAADNTV tandava
AAADORW Odawara
AAAEFLR Rafaela
AAAEGLT galatea
AAAEGNP apanage
AAAEHLT althaea
AAAEIMN anaemia
AAAENST anatase
AAAERWY areaway
AAAFFLL alfalfa
AAAFFMU faamafu
AAAFHLS Falasha
AAAFIRT ratafia
AAAFNRS sarafan
AAAFRWY faraway
AAAGGLN galanga
AAAGHKN Aga Khan
AAAGHNR gharana
AAAGHNT ataghan
AAAGHPR agrapha
AAAGIKN nagaika
AAAGINZ gazania
AAAGIPT patagia
AAAGISS assagai
AAAGKNO Nagaoka
AAAGKNR karanga
AAAGLMM amalgam,
malagma
AAAGLMN malanga
AAAGLMR almagra
AAAGLMS malagas
AAAGMMT magmata
AAAGMNR anagram
AAAGMNU Managua
AAAGMNZ mazagan
AAAGNPR pargana
AAAGNRR ngarara
AAAGNRT tangara
AAAGNRU guarana
AAAGNTT tangata
AAAHHKL Halakah
AAAHHLM Mahalah
AAAHHRT taharah
AAAHIKP aphakia
AAAHIKW kahawai
AAAHILM mahaila,
Mahalia
AAAHIPS aphasia
AAAHIRZ Azariah
AAAHJKW kajawah
AAAHKRT takhaar
AAAHLLU lauhala
AAAHLMR harmala

AAAHLNN Alannah
AAAHMMT mahatma
AAAHMRT Maratha
AAAHMST tamasha
AAAHNST Natasha
AAAHPPR Harappa
AAAHPRT paratha
AAAHRTW waratah
AAAHTTT tathata
AAAIIJL jai alai
AAAIJKN Kajaani
AAAIKKR karakia
AAAIKKT kaitaka
AAAILMR malaria
AAAILNT latania, Natalia
AAAILPS aplasia
AAAILPT Patiala
AAAILRT talaria
AAAIMRS Samaria
AAAINNR Arianna
AAAINTT Tatiana
AAAIPRX apraxia
AAAIPSS Aspasia
AAAIQRU aquaria
AAAJMNV Java man
AAAJMPS pajamas
AAAKKOT Takaoka
AAAKLMP Kampala
AAAKLMR Alkmaar
AAAKLNN alkanna
AAAKLNR Larkana
AAAKMOY Okayama
AAAKMRT karamat
AAAKMRY Karamay
AAAKNTY Antakya
AAAKRSW Arawaks
AAALLPT palatal
AAALLRT tra-la-la
AAALMNY Malayan
AAALMRS Marsala
AAALNNT lantana
AAALNPS pansala
AAALNPT aplanat
AAALNTT Atlanta
AAALNTY Antalya
AAALOTV taovala
AAALSTV Salavat
AAALWYY layaway
AAAMMNS mama-san
AAAMMSY samyama
AAAMMTT Matmata
AAAMNPY Mayapan
AAAMNRT maranta
AAAMPPU papauma
AAAMPRT patamar
AAAMRRS samarra
AAAMRRZ zamarra
AAAMRSS samsara
AAAMRSY Aymaras
AAAMRSZ Arzamas
AAAMRTU tamarau
AAANNRS Saranna
AAANNSV savanna
AAANRTT arnatta, tantara, tartana
AAAPPRT apparat
AAAPTTU taupata
AAAPTTY Pattaya
AAARTTT rat-a-tat
AAARTTU tuatara
AAARTXY ataraxy
AABBCEG cabbage
AABBCGY cabbagy
AABBCKR backbar
AABBDHS habdabs
AABBDIS Abbasid
AABBEGN beanbag
AABBEKL Baalbek
AABBEMN Mbabane
AABBERT barbate
AABBERU Uberaba
AABBGGR grab bag
AABBGRT gabbart
AABBHST sabbath
AABBIMU imbauba
AABBINN nibbana
AABBLOR barbola
AABBMRU rum baba
AABBNRY Barnaby
AABBRWY war baby
AABBSSU babassu
AABCCET baccate
AABCDIN Cabinda
AABCDIR Bacardi, carabid
AABCDIT cad-bait
AABCEFR cafe-bar
AABCEKR backare
AABCELN balance
AABCELP capable, pacable
AABCELR calaber
AABCELT actable
AABCEMR macabre
AABCEMS ambs-ace
AABCERR barrace
AABCERT abreact, cabaret
AABCHIR brachia
AABCHMT ambatch
AABCHNR barchan
AABCHNS Ansbach
AABCHOR abroach
AABCILM cambial
AABCIMS Cabimas
AABCIOP copaiba
AABCIST abacist
AABCITX taxicab
AABCKPY payback
AABCKRR barrack
AABCKWY way-back
AABCLMU calumba
AABCLPY capably
AABCLRY Barclay
AABCMMU macumba
AABCMOU macouba
AABCMSU sambuca
AABCORT abactor, acrobat
AABCORU carouba
AABCOST abacost, Tabasco
AABCOTT catboat
AABCOTU tacouba
AABDDET dead bat
AABDDGH Baghdad
AABDDHN dab hand, Dhanbad
AABDDIK kabaddi
AABDDIN band-aid
AABDDNO Abaddon
AABDEGM gambade
AABDEGN bandage
AABDEIS diabase
AABDELL ballade
AABDELR Albreda
AABDELT datable
AABDELW wadable
AABDEMN Bamenda
AABDEMS sambaed
AABDENU bandeau
AABDERR abrader
AABDERV bravade
AABDGHN handbag
AABDGIT dibatag
AABDGLY bag lady
AABDGMO gambado
AABDGNS sandbag
AABDHIO Obadiah
AABDHMS badmash
AABDHNT hatband
AABDHRS bardash
AABDIIS basidia
AABDIJN Abidjan
AABDIKR bidarka
AABDILR Ardabil
AABDIMR barmaid
AABDINT tabanid
AABDIOZ dazibao
AABDLLU Badulla
AABDLNS salband
AABDLRW bradawl
AABDMNR armband
AABDNNO abandon
AABDNNR Brandan
AABDNRR Barnard
AABDNRS sandbar
AABDNRT drabant
AABDNSW bandsaw
AABDORV bravado
AABDRRW drawbar
AABDRST bastard
AABDRSU absurda
AABEELT eatable
AABEEMO amoebae
AABEFFL affable
AABEFGL fleabag
AABEFGU aufgabe
AABEFLY bay leaf
AABEGGG baggage
AABEGGR garbage
AABEGIT tabagie

AABEGLR algebra
AABEGMR Bergama
AABEGMS ambages
AABEGNR angareb
AABEGRR bagarre, barrage
AABEGSS bagasse
AABEHLM mahaleb
AABEHLT hatable
AABEHRS earbash
AABEIKN ikebana
AABEILM amiable
AABEILN abelian
AABEILT labiate
AABEINU aubaine
AABEIRS airbase
AABEJLL jellaba
AABEJMU jambeau
AABEKLM makable
AABEKLT takable
AABELLL labella
AABELLM Mabella
AABELLN balneal
AABELLS sabella, salable
AABELLT ballate, tabella, tea-ball
AABELMT tamable
AABELMU lambeau
AABELNN Annabel
AABELNO abalone
AABELNS Elbasan
AABELPP papable
AABELPR parable
AABELPY payable
AABELRT Alberta, ratable
AABELST astable
AABELSV savable
AABELSY sayable
AABELTU tableau
AABELTX taxable
AABEMNS baseman
AABEMOS amoebas
AABEMRR Braemar
AABENNW wannabe
AABENRT ant-bear
AABENTY abeyant
AABERRR barrera
AABERST abreast
AABERTT tabaret
AABERTU abature
AABERTY beta ray
AABESSS sea bass
AABETUX bateaux
AABFFLY affably
AABFILU fabliau
AABFLRU fabular
AABGHMR bargham
AABGHNR bhangra
AABGHNS nash-gab
AABGHOT hag-boat
AABGHSW washbag
AABGIIL abigail
AABGILM mailbag
AABGINR bargain
AABGIRU guariba
AABGLOR Aalborg
AABGMOT tombaga
AABGMTU tumbaga
AABGNNY yangban
AABHHIW Wahhabi
AABHILM Ihiamba
AABHIMS Baha'ism
AABHINR Bahrain
AABHIST sat-bhai
AABHITT habitat, Tabitha
AABHITU habutai
AABHKRU Bukhara
AABHLMS Sambhal
AABHLTY bathyal
AABHMNR brahman
AABHMTT bath mat
AABHNOS Baoshan
AABHORU houbara
AABHOST Sabaoth
AABHSUU Bauhaus
AABIIKR Ibaraki
AABIILN Albinia
AABIILX biaxial
AABIIMN Namibia
AABIKLM kalimba
AABIKNS banksia
AABILLN Ballina
AABILLR barilla
AABILMN bimanal
AABILMY amiably
AABILNT tablina
AABILOU aboulia
AABILRR labarri
AABILRS basilar
AABIMMR marimba
AABIMST basmati
AABIMSW wambais
AABINOQ Banqiao
AABINOU ouabain
AABINOX boxiana
AABINRS Barinas, Sabrina
AABINST abstain, Bastian
AABINSY Baniyas
AABIORZ Orizaba
AABIOST taaibos
AABIRST Arabist, bartsia
AABISTT abattis
AABJNRU bunjara
AABKNRT tanbark
AABKOOZ bazooka
AABKORU kaboura
AABLLNY banally
AABLLPT patball
AABLLRW wall bar
AABLLST ballast
AABLLWY wallaby
AABLMMO malambo
AABLMPY Palm Bay
AABLMRU labarum
AABLMST lambast
AABLMSY abysmal
AABLNTT blatant
AABLRST arblast
AABLRTU tabular
AABLSSY abyssal
AABMMOS Mombasa
AABMNOT boatman
AABMNOY amboyna
AABMNST batsman
AABMORU marabou
AABMSSY ambassy
AABNNOZ bonanza
AABNOST sabaton
AABNOSY sabayon
AABNRTT trabant
AABORVY bavaroy
AABOTTY attaboy
AABQSUU sub-aqua
AABRRUV bravura
AABRSTY stay-bar
AABRSWY Barysaw
AABSSSY sassaby
AABTTTU battuta
AACCDEN Candace
AACCDES cascade, saccade
AACCDHH cha-cha'd
AACCDIR cardiac
AACCDOR Caradoc
AACCEKR carcake
AACCELO cloacae
AACCELS laccase
AACCENV vacance
AACCERS carcase
AACCEST saccate
AACCESV casevac
AACCHHM chacham
AACCHHS cha-chas
AACCHIM macchia
AACCHIN chicana
AACCHIR archaic
AACCHLN clachan
AACCHMP champac
AACCHNN cannach
AACCHRT caratch, charact
AACCILM acclaim
AACCILU acicula
AACCIOR carioca
AACCITT atactic
AACCJKR carjack
AACCKRR carrack
AACCLLO cloacal
AACCLLT catcall
AACCLOP polacca
AACCLOR Caracol
AACCLRU accrual, caracul
AACCLSU accusal
AACCMOU macauco
AACCNNY ca'canny
AACCNVY vacancy
AACCORT car coat

AACCOST accoast
AACCOTT toccata
AACCRSS carcass
AACCRVY vaccary
AACDDEL decadal
AACDDER arcaded
AACDDIN candida
AACDEEM academe
AACDEHM chamade
AACDEHR charade
AACDEHT cathead
AACDEIL alcaide
AACDELL alcalde
AACDELN candela, decanal
AACDELR caldera
AACDELS scalade
AACDELY alcayde
AACDEMN Cadmean
AACDEMY academy
AACDENS sedanca
AACDENT tacenda
AACDENV advance
AACDENZ cadenza
AACDERV cadaver
AACDERY day care
AACDETU caudate
AACDFIR faradic
AACDGOR Caradog
AACDHIM Machida
AACDHMR drachma
AACDILN calinda
AACDILR cardial, radical
AACDILU Claudia
AACDINT antacid
AACDINV vanadic
AACDIOR acaroid
AACDIRR Ricarda
AACDIRS ascarid
AACDJKW jackdaw
AACDKPY daypack
AACDKSS sad sack
AACDKSY daysack
AACDLNO calando, locanda
AACDLNS scandal
AACDLOR carload
AACDLPR placard
AACDNOR cornada
AACDOOV avocado
AACDPRU crapaud
AACDRSS csardas
AACDRSZ czardas
AACEEGR acreage
AACEEHR earache
AACEEKT teacake
AACEENT catenae
AACEETT acetate
AACEFIS fasciae
AACEFLL fallace
AACEFLT falcate
AACEFLU faculae, faecula
AACEFRR carfare
AACEGGR aggrace
AACEGKP package
AACEGKS sackage
AACEGLP placage
AACEGNR carnage, cranage
AACEGRT cartage
AACEGSV scavage
AACEHLP halpace
AACEHLR alchera, Rachael
AACEHLT elatcha
AACEHNP panache
AACEHNR Archean
AACEHPP appeach
AACEHPS apaches
AACEHPT patache
AACEHPU chapeau
AACEHRT achater, chartae, trachea
AACEHTU chateau
AACEHWY each way
AACEILZ azelaic
AACEIMN anaemic
AACEIMU camaieu
AACEINO Oceania
AACEINR acarine
AACEIRV avarice, caviare
AACEIST ectasia
AACEJKS seajack
AACEKMM ack emma
AACEKNP pancake
AACEKNS askance
AACEKOT oatcake
AACELLN canella
AACELLT lacteal
AACELLW Wallace
AACELMN manacle
AACELMR cameral, caramel, Carmela, maceral
AACELMU maculae
AACELNU lacunae
AACELNV valance
AACELNW wanlace
AACELOS sea coal
AACELOT alcoate
AACELPS Pascale
AACELPT placate
AACELRV caravel
AACELST lactase
AACELSW case law
AACELTT lactate
AACELTV clavate
AACEMNP paceman
AACEMNT manteca
AACEMNV caveman
AACEMQU macaque
AACENRS Saracen
AACENRT cateran
AACENST catenas
AACENTY cyanate
AACEOPT opacate, pea-coat
AACEOTV avocate
AACEPRT rate-cap
AACEPRY cypraea
AACERRT rat race
AACERST rasceta, sacrate
AACERSU caesura
AACERTU arcuate
AACERWY raceway
AACERZZ carezza
AACESST cassate
AACESTT sceatta
AACESUV Suceava
AACETTU actuate
AACETUV vacuate
AACFHIL chalifa
AACFILS fascial
AACFILU faucial
AACFINR African
AACFINT fanatic
AACFISS fascias
AACFLLY fallacy
AACFLPT cat flap
AACFLRT flatcar, fractal
AACFLRU facular
AACFLTU factual
AACFNRU furacan
AACFRRU farruca
AACGHNN Chang'an
AACGILL Gaillac, gallica, glacial
AACGILM magical
AACGILS scaglia
AACGINT agnatic
AACGKLL gallack
AACGLOS coal gas
AACGLOT catalog
AACGLOU coagula
AACGLRY Calgary
AACGMNS scanmag
AACGNOU guanaco
AACGNVY vagancy
AACHHLL challah
AACHHMT Chatham
AACHHRT haratch
AACHIKN kachina
AACHIKR chikara
AACHILM machila, Malachi
AACHILR achiral
AACHILY achylia
AACHIMR Amharic, machair
AACHIMS chiasma
AACHINS Sanchia
AACHIPS aphasic
AACHIPT chapati
AACHIRS arachis
AACHIRT Cathari, cithara
AACHITY chaitya
AACHKMN hackman
AACHKSW hacksaw

AACHLLN	Lachlan
AACHLMO	malcoha
AACHLMY	Malachy
AACHLPP	chappal
AACHLPS	paschal
AACHLSU	acushla
AACHMNP	chapman
AACHNOP	panocha
AACHNRV	navarch
AACHNRY	anarchy
AACHNSU	anchusa
AACHNZZ	chazzan
AACHORT	orchata
AACHRRT	catarrh
AACHRST	Cathars
AACHRSW	car wash
AACHRWY	archway
AACHRYZ	Zachary
AACIILN	lacinia
AACIINT	actinia
AACIIST	Asiatic
AACIITV	viatica
AACIJNT	Jacinta
AACIKLL	alkalic
AACIKLR	clarkia
AACIKNN	canakin
AACILLM	Camilla
AACILLN	ancilla
AACILLU	licuala
AACILMS	salmiac
AACILNR	carinal, clarain, cranial
AACILNU	Luciana
AACILOP	palacio
AACILOS	asocial
AACILOX	coaxial
AACILPR	paralic
AACILPS	spacial
AACILPT	capital, palatic, placita
AACILRR	railcar
AACILRT	talaric
AACINNT	cantina
AACINOR	ocarina
AACINPS	Capsian
AACINPT	capitan, captain
AACINRS	sarcina
AACINRT	Catrina
AACINRZ	czarina
AACINST	satanic
AACINTT	intacta
AACINTV	Vatican
AACIOPT	capitao, tapioca
AACIORT	Croatia
AACIORV	Craiova
AACIOTV	Octavia
AACIPRV	varicap
AACIQTU	aquatic
AACIRRU	curiara
AACIRSS	ascaris
AACIRST	caritas
AACISTT	astatic
AACJKMN	jackman
AACJKRT	Jack tar
AACJKSS	jackass
AACJOST	Jocasta
AACKKLP	kalpack
AACKLPV	valpack
AACKLTW	catwalk
AACKMNP	packman
AACKNRS	ransack
AACKPRR	car park
AACKPRT	pack rat
AACLLNT	callant
AACLLNU	calluna, lacunal
AACLLPU	placula
AACLLSU	clausal
AACLLVY	cavally
AACLMNO	coalman, malacon
AACLMNT	clamant
AACLMPR	arc lamp
AACLMRU	maclura, macular
AACLMSU	calamus
AACLNNU	cannula
AACLNPY	clay-pan
AACLNRU	lacunar
AACLNSU	lacunas
AACLOPT	octapla
AACLORT	coal tar, crotala
AACLOST	coastal
AACLOTT	cattalo
AACLPRT	caltrap, placart
AACLPSU	pascual, scapula
AACLPTY	play-act
AACLRST	castral
AACLRTY	lactary
AACLRVY	Calvary, cavalry
AACLSTT	salt-cat
AACLSTU	Lucasta
AACLSUV	vascula
AACLTTU	tactual
AACMNOR	camaron
AACMNRU	arcanum
AACMNTX	Manx cat
AACMORS	sarcoma
AACMORT	marcato
AACMRRT	tramcar
AACMRSS	sarcasm
AACNNOZ	canzona
AACNOST	sacaton
AACNOTZ	zacaton
AACNPRT	pancart
AACNPST	capstan
AACNRTU	curtana
AACNRTV	cravant
AACNSSV	canvass
AACORST	ostraca
AACORTU	acatour, autocar
AACPSTW	cat's-paw
AACRRSY	sacrary
AACRSST	sarcast
AACRTTT	attract
AACRTTX	tax-cart
AACRTUV	vacatur
AACRTUY	actuary
AACTUWY	cutaway
AADDDEN	addenda
AADDEFI	deaf aid
AADDEHL	lah-de-da
AADDEIL	alidade
AADDELR	Aldreda
AADDENP	deadpan, pedanda
AADDESU	saudade
AADDGNR	grandad
AADDHKR	khaddar
AADDHPR	hard pad
AADDIIK	didakai
AADDIMS	Dadaism
AADDIST	Dadaist
AADDLYY	Lady Day
AADDNVV	dvandva
AADDRST	dastard
AADEEGH	headage
AADEEIP	paedeia
AADEFGL	faldage
AADEFHT	fat-head
AADEFLR	Alfreda
AADEFNZ	fazenda
AADEGHO	go-ahead
AADEGKR	Dark Age
AADEGLN	adangle
AADEGLS	geladas
AADEGMN	agnamed, managed
AADEGNR	Grenada
AADEGNS	agendas
AADEGRT	gradate
AADEGRY	yardage
AADEHIR	airhead
AADEHKL	Khaleda
AADEHMN	headman
AADEHMS	ashamed
AADEHNZ	Zahedan
AADEHRR	haarder
AADEHRW	warhead
AADEHWY	headway
AADEIIP	paideia
AADEILR	radiale
AADEILV	vedalia
AADEIMR	madeira
AADEIMT	adamite
AADEINN	danaine
AADEINR	araneid, Ariadne
AADEINT	danaite
AADEIPS	diapase
AADEIRT	radiate
AADEIWY	die-away
AADEJMR	jemadar
AADEKKY	kayaked
AADEKMR	kamerad
AADEKPR	parkade

AADEKTZ tzedaka
AADELLN lea-land
AADELLR dare-all
AADELNR adrenal
AADELNW Danelaw
AADELRT laterad
AADELRU radulae
AADELRW raw deal
AADELRY already
AADELTU adulate
AADELTY day-tale, tea lady
AADELZZ adazzle
AADEMMN made man, man-made
AADEMNO adenoma
AADEMNT mandate
AADEMNY name-day
AADEMPR map-read
AADENNP pandean
AADENNT andante, Dantean
AADENRS Andreas
AADENRV veranda
AADENST ansated
AADENSW weasand
AADENTV Vedanta
AADEOTT toad-eat
AADEPRR parader
AADEPRS aspread
AADEPRT adapter, readapt
AADEPSS passade
AADERRW awarder
AADERSW seaward
AADFGLN langfad
AADFGLY flag day
AADFILM maladif
AADGGHR haggard
AADGGLR laggard
AADGHIS dghaisa
AADGIIR giardia
AADGIMM digamma
AADGIMR diagram
AADGIMS magadis
AADGIPR Padraig
AADGIRV gravida
AADGLLW gadwall
AADGLNO gonadal
AADGLNR garland
AADGLRU gradual
AADGMNR gramdan, grandam, grandma
AADGNPR grandpa
AADGNRT dragant
AADGNRU guarand
AADGNRY yardang
AADGOPR podagra
AADGORS rasgado
AADGRUZ zadruga
AADHHNR Dhahran
AADHHRT hard hat
AADHIMS samadhi
AADHINP daphnia
AADHINR Hadrian
AADHKNO nakhoda
AADHKNR Darkhan
AADHKNW Khandwa
AADHLRY halyard
AADHNNP nap hand
AADHNPR hardpan
AADHNRS darshan, Hansard
AADHNSW handsaw
AADHNSY sandhya
AADHNTT and that
AADHRRW Dharwar, Hardwar
AADHRWY Hayward
AADHSWY washday
AADIILR diarial
AADIINN Indiana
AADIINR diarian
AADIINV Davinia
AADIIRR air raid
AADIISV adivasi
AADIJMN jamdani
AADIKOR Kodaira
AADILMR admiral, amildar
AADILMT Matilda
AADILNP paladin
AADILNT natalid
AADILPS apsidal
AADILSS dalasis
AADILTV datival
AADILWY waylaid
AADIMNR Miranda
AADIMOR diorama
AADIMOZ diazoma
AADIMPS diapasm
AADIMRR ram-raid
AADIMRS Damaris
AADIMRU Madurai
AADINNW waniand
AADINPS anapsid
AADINPT Pandita
AADINRS sarinda
AADINRT intrada, radiant
AADINRV varanid
AADIORS Isadora
AADIRSU sudaria
AADISSV dissava
AADJNOR jornada
AADKNRT tankard
AADKRWW awkward
AADLLMR mallard
AADLLNR Randall
AADLLNW land-law
AADLLPU paludal
AADLMNN landman, landnam
AADLMNO mandola
AADLMNU ladanum
AADLNOR Ronalda
AADLNOV vandola
AADLNOY Yolanda
AADLNRY lanyard
AADLNTX land tax
AADLOPY payload
AADLPPU applaud
AADLRRU radular
AADMNNO Madonna
AADMNNS sandman
AADMNNT mandant
AADMNOR Armando, mandora, monarda, ramonda, roadman
AADMNRS mansard
AADMNRY drayman, Maynard, yardman
AADMOPP popadam
AADMOPR road map
AADMOQU madoqua
AADMORT matador
AADMRRY yardarm
AADMRZZ mazzard
AADNOPR pandora
AADNORR Andorra
AADNORT donatar, tornada
AADNORY any road
AADNOWY nowaday
AADNRST astrand, tar sand
AADNRVW vanward
AADNRWY nayward
AADNSTZ stanza'd
AADOPRR parador
AADOPRS parados
AADOPRT adaptor
AADOPRX paradox
AADOPSS passado, Posadas
AADOPSU pousada
AADORTX road tax
AADORWY roadway
AADOSTT tostada
AADQRTU quadrat
AADRRST dartars
AADRWWY wayward
AAEEFGL leafage
AAEEFLT tea leaf
AAEEGKL leakage
AAEEGLT galeate
AAEEGMN amenage
AAEEGMS megasea
AAEEGRV average
AAEEGST sage tea
AAEEHLT Alethea
AAEEHRS sea hare
AAEEHRT hetaera
AAEEINT taeniae
AAEEKLS seakale
AAEELLR real ale
AAEELMN melaena
AAEELMS malease
AAEELMT maleate
AAEELOR areolae
AAEELRZ Eleazar

AAEEMNT emanate, enemata, manatee
AAEEMTX meat-axe
AAEEPPS appease
AAEERTU aureate
AAEERTX exarate
AAEFFGR agraffe
AAEFFIR affaire
AAEFFLL falafel
AAEFFLT afflate
AAEFFNR fanfare
AAEFFTT taffeta
AAEFGLN Falange
AAEFGTW waftage
AAEFILS Falaise
AAEFMRT fermata
AAEFNST Santa Fe
AAEFRRR Ferrara
AAEFRRW warfare
AAEFRST Far East
AAEFRWY wayfare
AAEGGNR granage
AAEGGOP apagoge
AAEGGRT aggrate
AAEGHLL hallage
AAEGHLU haulage
AAEGHLY haylage
AAEGHMR Grahame
AAEGHNT Agnetha, thanage
AAEGILR Algeria, lairage, railage, regalia
AAEGIMN aenigma
AAEGINV vaginae
AAEGINW wainage
AAEGIRR arriage
AAEGISS assegai
AAEGISU ageusia
AAEGITT agitate
AAEGJTU ajutage
AAEGKNT tankage
AAEGKOS soakage
AAEGKOW Kawagoe
AAEGLLR Allegra, glareal
AAEGLLS galleas
AAEGLLT gallate, tallage
AAEGLMN gamelan
AAEGLNS lasagne
AAEGLNU aulnage
AAEGLRR realgar
AAEGLRY laygear
AAEGLST agelast, lastage
AAEGLSV salvage
AAEGMNO mangeao
AAEGMNR manager
AAEGMNT gateman, magenta, magnate
AAEGMPR rampage
AAEGMRT margate
AAEGMRW war game
AAEGMSS massage
AAEGMST mastage
AAEGMTT tag team
AAEGNNP pannage
AAEGNNT tangena, tannage
AAEGNOP apogean
AAEGNPR pergana
AAEGNPT pageant
AAEGNRR arrange
AAEGNRT granate, tanager
AAEGNTV vantage
AAEGNTW wantage
AAEGNYZ zygaena
AAEGOSS gaseosa
AAEGPRR parerga
AAEGPRT partage
AAEGPRW warpage
AAEGPSS passage
AAEGPSY paysage
AAEGQUY quayage
AAEGRRS rare gas
AAEGRRV ravager
AAEGRST sartage, tear gas
AAEGRTT regatta
AAEGSSU assuage, sausage
AAEGSTU gateaus
AAEGSTW saw-gate, wastage
AAEGTTW wattage
AAEGTUX gateaux
AAEGTWY gateway, getaway
AAEHHIL Hialeah
AAEHHLM Mehalah
AAEHILM Mehalia
AAEHILP aphelia
AAEHILS halesia
AAEHIMN Anaheim
AAEHIMP aphemia
AAEHIRT hetaira
AAEHKNT khanate
AAEHLLL heal-all
AAEHLNT ethanal
AAEHLPR phalera, Raphael
AAEHLPX hexapla
AAEHLRT trehala
AAEHMRT arthame
AAEHNPR hanaper
AAEHNPS saphena
AAEHNPT antheap, panthea
AAEHPRT pharate
AAEHRSY hearsay
AAEHSTT hastate
AAEIJTV javaite, vaatjie
AAEILLU Eulalia
AAEILLX axillae
AAEILMN laminae, Melania
AAEILMP Pamelia
AAEILMR Laramie
AAEILMS malaise
AAEILNN alanine, linnaea
AAEILNO aeolian
AAEILNR air lane, Laraine
AAEILNT laniate, Natalie
AAEILOR olearia
AAEILPR palarie
AAEILPX epaxial
AAEILRU aurelia
AAEILRV Valeria, velaria
AAEIMMT imamate
AAEIMNR Armenia
AAEIMNS amnesia
AAEIMNT amentia, animate
AAEIMNZ maizena
AAEIMPY pyaemia
AAEIMRU uraemia
AAEIMTV amative
AAEINRZ Zairean
AAEINST taenias
AAEINSV vesania
AAEIPPS apepsia
AAEIPRR pareira
AAEIPRS spiraea
AAEIPTT apatite
AAEIRRT taraire
AAEIRST atresia
AAEIRTT arietta
AAEIRTV variate
AAEISTT aetatis, satiate
AAEJKNT kajaten
AAEJNTT Janetta
AAEJOPR aparejo
AAEKKOR karaoke
AAEKLNT alkanet
AAEKMNW wakeman
AAEKMRR earmark
AAEKPRT partake
AAEKPTU pukatea
AAEKRZZ karezza
AAELLLM lamella
AAELLNV avellan
AAELLNZ zanella
AAELLPT patella
AAELLRT lateral
AAELLSV save-all
AAELLSW sea wall
AAELLTV vallate
AAELMMS melasma
AAELMMT lemmata
AAELMNS Anselma
AAELMNU alumnae, Manuela
AAELMOR maroela
AAELMOT oatmeal

AAELMPT	palmate
AAELMRS	sarmale
AAELMST	maltase
AAELMSY	amylase
AAELMTT	lametta
AAELNNP	Annaple
AAELNPU	paenula
AAELNRS	arsenal
AAELNST	sealant
AAELNSY	analyse
AAELNTT	tetanal
AAELNYZ	analyze
AAELORR	areolar
AAELORU	aureola
AAELORZ	azarole
AAELOTX	oxalate
AAELPPR	apparel
AAELPPT	palpate
AAELPPU	papulae
AAELPRV	palaver
AAELPTT	tapetal
AAELPTU	plateau
AAELQRU	laquear
AAELRST	tar-seal
AAELRTT	Arletta
AAELRTU	laurate, laureat
AAELRTV	lavaret
AAELRTZ	lazaret
AAELRVY	alveary
AAELSST	sea salt
AAELSTT	saltate
AAELSUX	asexual
AAELTUV	valuate
AAELTVV	valvate
AAEMMMR	maremma
AAEMMRS	marasme
AAEMNNT	emanant
AAEMNPP	pampean
AAEMNRS	ramenas
AAEMNRU	muraena
AAEMNST	namaste
AAEMNTU	manteau, neumata
AAEMPST	petasma
AAEMQSU	squamae
AAEMRSS	amasser
AAEMRST	Artemas, astream, materas
AAEMRTU	amateur
AAENNNT	antenna
AAENNRV	Ravenna
AAENNST	annates, tannase
AAENNTT	tannate
AAENNTV	ventana
AAENPST	anapest, peasant
AAENPTX	antapex
AAENRRT	narrate
AAENRTT	tartane
AAENRTU	Taurean
AAENRTV	taverna
AAENRUW	unaware
AAENSSV	vanessa
AAENSSW	Swansea
AAENSTV	Avestan, savante
AAENSTW	seawant
AAENTTY	Anyetta
AAEORRT	aerator
AAEORRU	aurorae
AAEPPRT	parapet
AAEPSSW	sea wasp
AAERRRS	arrears
AAERRTT	tartare
AAERSSY	assayer
AAERTTY	tea tray
AAERTUU	taureau
AAERTXY	tax year
AAESTTT	testata
AAETTTZ	tazetta
AAFFILN	affinal
AAFFINS	saffian
AAFFINT	affiant
AAFFMRT	fat farm
AAFGHIN	afghani
AAFGLMN	flagman
AAFGNRS	farsang
AAFGORR	farrago
AAFHHIT	Fatihah
AAFHIKL	khalifa
AAFHILX	Halifax
AAFHINR	farinha
AAFHKRS	farsakh
AAFHLLP	half-lap
AAFHLPY	half pay
AAFHLWY	halfway
AAFHMNR	Farnham
AAFHRRS	farrash
AAFIILM	familia
AAFIILR	filaria
AAFILMN	fan mail
AAFILNT	fantail
AAFILQU	alfaqui
AAFIMRU	fiumara
AAFINNT	infanta
AAFINNU	infauna
AAFIPRT	parfait
AAFIRSS	safaris
AAFIRWY	fairway
AAFJLOR	alforja
AAFLLTY	fatally
AAFLMNP	fan palm
AAFLMNT	flamant
AAFLNTU	aflaunt
AAFLRSY	falsary
AAFLWYY	flyaway
AAFMOST	Mostafa
AAFNNOT	Fontana
AAFNRRT	farrant
AAFNSTT	fantast
AAFNSTY	fantasy
AAFPSUX	faux pas
AAGGHHI	hagigah
AAGGILN	ganglia
AAGGIZZ	Zagazig
AAGGLOT	Tagalog
AAGGNOY	anagogy
AAGGNST	gangsta
AAGGNTT	taggant
AAGGNWY	gangway, way-gang
AAGHILR	Aligarh, gharial
AAGHINN	anhinga
AAGHMNN	hangman
AAGHMPR	phragma
AAGHMRS	gramash
AAGHNPS	sphagna
AAGHNRY	Gharyan
AAGHNUV	Vaughan
AAGHQUU	quahaug
AAGHSTY	sagathy
AAGIJRU	guajira
AAGIKSU	Kasugai
AAGILMO	omalgia
AAGILMY	myalgia
AAGILNN	Anglian
AAGILNP	paginal
AAGILNT	Tangail
AAGILNV	vaginal
AAGILOT	otalgia
AAGILRT	ragtail
AAGILTW	wagtail
AAGIMNO	angioma
AAGIMNS	siamang
AAGIMNZ	amazing
AAGIMRU	maguari
AAGINNW	wanigan
AAGINNY	inyanga
AAGINNZ	zingana
AAGINOS	agnosia
AAGINOX	Xiaogan
AAGINPR	parangi
AAGINRR	arraign
AAGINRS	sangria, sarangi
AAGINRT	granita
AAGINRU	Guarani
AAGINST	against
AAGINSV	vaginas
AAGINSW	Saginaw
AAGINSY	gainsay
AAGINTT	agitant
AAGIOTT	agitato
AAGIPRU	piragua
AAGIRSS	sagaris
AAGIRST	Artigas
AAGIRSV	visarga
AAGIRTY	gayatri
AAGISTT	sagitta
AAGJLNO	Jalgaon
AAGKMSS	gas mask
AAGKNNY	kangany
AAGKNRS	Angarsk
AAGLLLN	lallang
AAGLLNT	gallant
AAGLMRS	salgram
AAGLNOR	granola, organal
AAGLNOY	analogy
AAGLNRU	angular, granula

AAGLNST	langsat
AAGLORT	lagarto
AAGLRST	gastral
AAGLRUU	arugula, augural
AAGLRVX	gravlax
AAGMMNS	magsman
AAGMMRR	grammar
AAGMMTU	gummata
AAGMNNR	grannam
AAGMNOS	samango, sangoma
AAGMNRT	tangram, trangam
AAGMNSW	swagman
AAGMOPY	apogamy
AAGMORS	margosa
AAGMSUY	Guaymas
AAGNNNY	Nanyang
AAGNOPR	paragon
AAGNOPT	Topanga
AAGNORZ	organza
AAGNRRY	granary
AAGNRTV	vagrant
AAGNSST	satsang
AAGNTUY	taungya
AAGOPSS	sapsago
AAGORSU	saguaro
AAGORZZ	ragazzo
AAGSTUU	Augusta
AAGTTUU	tautaug
AAHHIUU	Huaihua
AAHHNPT	naphtha
AAHHOPR	pharaoh
AAHIJLV	Jihlava
AAHIJNR	Harijan
AAHIKLS	khalasi
AAHIKRT	Katihar, kithara
AAHIKSW	Kashiwa
AAHIKTY	hikayat
AAHILMR	almirah
AAHILMT	thalami
AAHILPV	Pahlavi
AAHILTT	Talitha
AAHIMNO	mahonia
AAHIMNS	Samhain
AAHIMNT	amianth
AAHIMRT	Marathi
AAHINNU	Huainan
AAHINOP	aphonia
AAHINOR	Honiara
AAHINPR	piranha
AAHINSV	Shavian
AAHINTW	taniwha
AAHIORT	Horatia
AAHIPRT	pitarah
AAHIPST	thapsia
AAHIPTY	Hypatia
AAHISTY	sahitya
AAHJKNR	khanjar
AAHJNNO	Johanna
AAHKKSZ	Kazakhs
AAHKLMO	malkoha
AAHKLRS	lashkar
AAHKLSY	kalashy
AAHKMOR	mahorka
AAHKMSY	yashmak
AAHKNOR	korhaan
AAHKNTY	tykhana
AAHLLOO	ooh-la-la
AAHLLTT	tall hat
AAHLLWY	hallway, Whyalla
AAHLMRS	marshal
AAHLMRU	hamular
AAHLMTW	Waltham
AAHLNPX	phalanx
AAHLNRW	narwhal
AAHLNTU	Nahuatl
AAHLPRS	phrasal
AAHLPST	asphalt
AAHMNNU	hanuman
AAHMNOR	Manohar
AAHMNRW	Warnham
AAHMOPR	amphora
AAHMORR	moharra
AAHMORS	Masorah
AAHMOST	tomasha
AAHMQSU	quamash
AAHMRTU	Mathura
AAHMRUY	mauryah
AAHNNOS	hosanna
AAHNNTX	xanthan
AAHNOPR	pharaon
AAHNORT	athanor
AAHNRTX	anthrax
AAHNRTY	rhatany
AAHORSU	sahuaro
AAHPRTW	warpath
AAHPSTU	haut-pas
AAHPTWY	pathway
AAHRSST	Shastra
AAHRSTY	ashtray
AAHRTTW	athwart
AAIILMR	airmail
AAIILNR	linaria
AAIILNT	Italian
AAIILNV	Lavinia
AAIILNZ	Azilian
AAIILOS	Aloisia
AAIILPT	tilapia
AAIILSV	Visalia
AAIINNR	Iranian
AAIINRZ	Zairian
AAIINTT	titania
AAIINVV	Viviana
AAIINZZ	zizania
AAIIPRW	paiwari
AAIIRVV	vivaria
AAIJLNU	Juliana
AAIJNTU	Juanita, Tijuana
AAIKKOZ	Okazaki
AAIKLLS	alkalis
AAIKLOT	lakatoi
AAIKLPR	palikar
AAIKMNN	manakin
AAIKMSS	kamassi
AAIKMST	mastika
AAIKNRT	Katrina
AAIKNUY	Kaiyuan
AAIKOTW	Waikato
AAIKPPR	paprika
AAIKRSS	askaris
AAIKTVV	akvavit
AAILLLP	pallial
AAILLMM	mamilla
AAILLMN	laminal, manilla
AAILLMP	impalla
AAILLMR	armilla
AAILLMX	maxilla
AAILLNP	palinal
AAILLNV	vanilla
AAILLPP	applial, papilla
AAILLPV	pallavi
AAILLPX	paxilla
AAILLRX	axillar
AAILLUV	alluvia
AAILLXY	axially
AAILMMN	mailman
AAILMMO	mamaloi
AAILMMS	Lamaism, miasmal
AAILMMX	maximal
AAILMNR	laminar, railman
AAILMNT	matinal
AAILMNU	alumina
AAILMNV	Malvina
AAILMOS	Somalia
AAILMPS	malpais
AAILMRS	sail-arm
AAILMRT	marital, martial
AAILMSS	salamis
AAILMST	Lamaist
AAILNOP	pianola
AAILNOT	Laotian
AAILNOV	valonia
AAILNPT	platina
AAILNRU	Laurina, lunaria
AAILNRY	laniary
AAILNSS	Salinas
AAILNST	lanista
AAILNSV	Silvana
AAILNTV	Latvian, valiant
AAILOPP	papaloi
AAILORS	Rosalia, solaria
AAILORV	ovarial, variola
AAILOST	solatia
AAILOSY	Aloysia
AAILPRT	partial, patrial
AAILPRY	airplay
AAILPST	spatial
AAILRRV	arrival
AAILRSS	Larissa
AAILRTT	rat-tail
AAILRTV	travail

AAILRWY railway
AAILSSW wassail
AAILTTT latitat
AAIMMNO ammonia
AAIMMRS marisma
AAIMMSS miasmas
AAIMNNO omniana
AAIMNNT tannaim
AAIMNOR Romania
AAIMNOS anosmia
AAIMNRT Martian, Martina, tamarin
AAIMNST stamina
AAIMNWY minaway
AAIMRRV Armavir
AAIMRSS Marissa
AAIMRST Sitaram
AAIMRSU samurai
AAIMRVX varimax
AAIMSTV atavism
AAIMSUV mauvais
AAINNOT Antonia
AAINNRV navarin, nirvana
AAINNSX sanxian
AAINNWX Wanxian
AAINOPS anopsia, paisano
AAINORT aration
AAINORV ovarian
AAINORZ Arizona
AAINPPT Panipat
AAINPST patinas
AAINRST artisan, astrain, sanitar, tsarina
AAINRSU saurian
AAINRSV savarin
AAINRSZ sarazin
AAINRTV variant
AAINRTZ artizan, tzarina
AAINSSY sanyasi
AAINSTV vanitas
AAINTTT attaint
AAINTTU tutania
AAINTUY Taiyuan
AAIORSU saouari
AAIORTV aviator
AAIPPTT pit-a-pat
AAIPRTT partita
AAIPRTW patwari
AAIQSSU quassia
AAIQTUV aquavit
AAIRSSS sarissa
AAIRSSY Assyria
AAIRSTU Austria
AAIRTTT attrait
AAITWXY taxiway
AAJKLWY jaywalk
AAJLLLO La Jolla
AAJMNZZ jazzman
AAJMORR mojarra
AAJMORT majorat
AAJMPSY pyjamas
AAJNRUY January
AAJOPSU sapajou
AAKKLRU karakul
AAKKMOT tokamak
AAKKOPR Oak Park
AAKKSUZ zakuska
AAKLMNW Walkman
AAKLNOT lokanta
AAKLNOW Oak Lawn
AAKLOOP palooka
AAKLRSU kursaal
AAKLWWY walkway
AAKMMNR markman
AAKMOSU mousaka
AAKMRUZ mazurka
AAKMRWY waymark
AAKNNTU nunatak
AAKNOSU Anouska
AAKNSWZ kwanzas
AAKOOPP pakapoo
AAKPRWY parkway
AAKRSTU katsura
AAKRTUY autarky
AAKSTTU Katsuta
AALLLSW Walsall
AALLMPS plasmal
AALLMPU ampulla, palmula
AALLNOX alloxan
AALLNPT plantal
AALLNPU planula
AALLNSY nasally
AALLNVY navally
AALLOSS salsola
AALLOTV lavolta, vallota
AALLOWY Alloway
AALLPPY papally
AALLRST all-star
AALLRUY aurally
AALLUVV valvula
AALMMNO ammonal
AALMNOR anormal
AALMNOS Salamon
AALMNOY anomaly
AALMNPU Nampula
AALMNST last man
AALMORT alamort
AALMORY mayoral
AALMPRY palmary, palmyra
AALMPWX wax palm
AALMSSU massula
AALMTTU mulatta
AALMTUY taumaly
AALNNRU annular
AALNOOT Altoona
AALNORS also-ran
AALNORW war loan
AALNOSS Asansol
AALNOTY Anatoly
AALNPRT plantar
AALNPRU lupanar
AALNPST salt pan
AALNPUU punalua
AALNQTU quantal
AALNRTT latrant
AALNRTU natural
AALNSTT saltant
AALNSTU sultana
AALNSTY analyst
AALOORY La Oroya
AALOOTV Otavalo
AALOPRS parasol
AALOPTV Poltava
AALOPVV pavlova
AALOPZZ palazzo
AALORRU auroral
AALORSU arousal
AALORZZ lazzaro
AALOTTY talayot
AALPPRU papular
AALPPSU papulas
AALPRSU Sarapul
AALPRSW asprawl
AALPSTU spatula
AALQRTU quartal
AALRSTT stratal
AALRSTU austral
AALRSTY astylar, satyral
AALRSUZ Lazarus
AALSSTU assault
AALSTUU auslaut
AAMMMRY mammary
AAMMNNX Manxman
AAMMNPT amptman
AAMMNRY Myanmar
AAMMNTY Tammany
AAMMRST ram-stam
AAMNNOT Montana
AAMNOPP pampano
AAMNOPR panoram
AAMNORS oarsman
AAMNOTY anatomy
AAMNPRT mantrap, rampant
AAMNPSS passman
AAMNPTY tympana
AAMNQTU tanquam
AAMNRTY army ant
AAMNRUY manuary
AAMORSV samovar
AAMORTY amatory
AAMOSTT stomata
AAMOTTU automat
AAMPRRT rampart
AAMRSST matrass
AAMRSTU traumas
AAMRTWY tramway
AAMSSTU satsuma
AANNORS Rosanna
AANNORX Roxanna
AANNOTT annatto
AANNSSU Susanna
AANNSUZ Suzanna
AANOPPR panorpa
AANPRST Spartan

AANPSST passant
AANQRTU quartan
AANRRTW warrant
AANRSUV varanus
AANRUWY runaway
AANSSTT tsantsa
AANSSTW Tswanas
AANSWYY anyways
AANTUUV Vanuatu
AAOORRW woorara
AAOPPTW wappato
AAOPRRT pro rata
AAOPSST potassa
AAORRSU auroras
AAORSTV Ostrava, Saratov
AAORTTX taxator
AAPRRTT rat-trap
AAPRSTV vastrap
AAPRSTY satrapy
AAPRTWY part-way
AAPSSWY passway
AASSTUY tayassu
ABBBDEL blabbed
ABBBELR babbler, blabber, brabble
ABBBELU abubble
ABBBITT babbitt
ABBBMOY bomb bay
ABBCDER crabbed
ABBCDES scabbed
ABBCEHI babiche
ABBCELR clabber
ABBCELS scabble
ABBCEMO bombace
ABBCENO bobance
ABBCIIS bibasic
ABBCKUY buy-back
ABBCMOR car bomb
ABBCRYY cry-baby
ABBDDET bad debt
ABBDDUU dub-a-dub
ABBDEGR grabbed
ABBDELR dabbler, drabble
ABBDELS slabbed
ABBDERR drabber
ABBDERT drabbet
ABBDEST stabbed
ABBDESW swabbed
ABBDGIN big band, dabbing
ABBDGOY body bag
ABBDHIJ djibbah
ABBDILR libbard
ABBDLRU lubbard
ABBDMOR bombard
ABBDNOX bandbox
ABBEEJO bobajee
ABBEETT Babette
ABBEGIR gabbier
ABBEGLR gabbler, grabble
ABBEGMR Bamberg
ABBEGNO bogbean
ABBEGRR grabber
ABBEGRU bugbear
ABBEJRS jabbers
ABBELLR barbell
ABBELMR bramble
ABBELOR belabor
ABBELPR prabble
ABBELRU barbule
ABBEMOS bombase
ABBEMRR Bramber
ABBEMUZ bumbaze
ABBERST stabber
ABBGGIN big bang, gabbing
ABBGIJN jabbing
ABBGINN nabbing
ABBGINS sabbing
ABBGINT tabbing
ABBGOOU bugaboo
ABBGORY Babygro
ABBHISY babyish
ABBHNTU Bath bun
ABBHRRU rhubarb
ABBHTTU bathtub
ABBIIMN bambini
ABBILOT bobtail
ABBIMNO bambino
ABBIORT rabbit-o
ABBIRTY rabbity
ABBISTY babysit
ABBKNRU Burbank
ABBLLOY ballboy
ABBLMRY brambly
ABBLNOY Babylon
ABBMOOR bombora
ABBMOST bombast
ABBMOTU bumboat
ABBNRTU bran tub
ABBNRUY Banbury
ABBORRU Barbour
ABBOSTY bobstay
ABBQSUY squabby
ABCCCHI Bacchic
ABCCEER Rebecca
ABCCEHO caboche
ABCCEIR acerbic, breccia
ABCCEIS sebacic
ABCCEIT ecbatic
ABCCILU cubical
ABCCIMR cambric
ABCCIOR boracic, braccio
ABCCKMO cambock
ABCCKOW bawcock
ABCCKTU cutback
ABCCLRU club car
ABCCOOR barocco, boccaro
ABCCOOT tobacco
ABCCOOY cocobay
ABCCORU buccaro
ABCDEEL debacle
ABCDEHU debauch
ABCDEIK die-back
ABCDEIN cabined
ABCDEIP pedicab
ABCDEIR carbide
ABCDEKR red-back
ABCDEMP camp bed
ABCDEOR bar code, brocade
ABCDERU cudbear
ABCDHIO ichabod
ABCDHOR chobdar
ABCDIIS dibasic
ABCDILO cabildo
ABCDILR baldric
ABCDINS abscind
ABCDIOT cod-bait
ABCDIRS scabrid
ABCDIRT catbird
ABCDISU subacid
ABCDLNO land-boc
ABCDLOO Bacolod
ABCDNOS abscond
ABCDOOR cordoba
ABCDORR brocard
ABCEEGR begrace
ABCEEHT beteach
ABCEEMR embrace
ABCEENS absence
ABCEENU caubeen
ABCEERR cerebra
ABCEERU berceau
ABCEESU because
ABCEGIR ribcage
ABCEGOR brocage
ABCEGOS boscage
ABCEHIR Hebraic
ABCEHKO backhoe
ABCEHLN Blanche
ABCEHLU bauchle
ABCEHMR becharm, brecham, chamber
ABCEIIT abietic
ABCEIKT tie-back
ABCEILM alembic
ABCEILR Alberic, caliber, calibre
ABCEILT citable
ABCEIMO amoebic
ABCEIMR imbrace
ABCEINR carbine
ABCEINT cabinet
ABCEIOR aerobic, Arecibo
ABCEIOT ice-boat
ABCEIRS ascribe, Brescia
ABCEISS abscise, scabies
ABCEITT tabetic
ABCEKLN blacken
ABCEKNR bracken
ABCEKRT bracket
ABCEKST setback

ABCEKTU a bucket
ABCEKTW wetback
ABCELLO locable
ABCELLU bullace, cue ball
ABCELMO cembalo
ABCELMR cambrel, clamber, cramble
ABCELMS scamble
ABCELMT camblet
ABCELOP placebo
ABCELOV vocable
ABCELPY by-place
ABCELRU clauber, curable
ABCELSU bascule
ABCENOW cowbane
ABCENRU unbrace
ABCEOOS caboose
ABCEORU corbeau
ABCESSS abscess
ABCFIIT tabific
ABCFIKN fin-back
ABCFILO bifocal
ABCFLNO conflab
ABCFLNU fan club
ABCFLOX boxcalf
ABCGHKO hogback
ABCGIKN backing
ABCGKLO backlog, gablock
ABCGLOO cool bag
ABCGMSU scumbag
ABCHHII hibachi
ABCHIIT Bithica
ABCHILS Chablis
ABCHIMR brahmic
ABCHIOT cohabit
ABCHISS scabish
ABCHKTU hackbut
ABCHKUW hawbuck
ABCHNOR brochan
ABCHNRY branchy
ABCHOPU pabouch
ABCHOSX cash box
ABCHRSU curbash
ABCHRTU trabuch
ABCIILL bacilli
ABCIILS basilic
ABCIIMN minicab
ABCIIOR ciboria
ABCIIOT abiotic
ABCIJNO jacobin
ABCIKLT backlit
ABCIKSY sickbay
ABCILOU aboulic
ABCILRS scribal
ABCILTU cubital
ABCIMMU cambium
ABCIMOR Coimbra
ABCIMRU Cumbria
ABCIMST cambist
ABCINOS bocasin
ABCINOT botanic, cabotin
ABCIORR barrico
ABCIORU caribou
ABCIOUV bivouac
ABCIRTY barytic
ABCISSS absciss
ABCKLLO ballock
ABCKLLY blackly
ABCKMRU buckram
ABCKNNO bannock
ABCKOSW sowback
ABCKOTU outback
ABCKSTU sackbut
ABCKSUW sawbuck
ABCLLOX call box
ABCLLOY call-boy
ABCLMNU clubman
ABCLMOU Columba
ABCLMOY cymbalo
ABCLMUU baculum
ABCLNOY balcony
ABCLRSU buscarl
ABCMNRW Cwmbran
ABCOORS borasco
ABCOPRT crab pot
ABCORRW crowbar
ABDDEEH bedhead
ABDDEER bearded
ABDDELR bladder
ABDDENR branded
ABDDENS sand-bed
ABDDEOR roadbed
ABDDEST baddest
ABDDHIS baddish
ABDDINS disband
ABDDLLO oddball
ABDEEGR rebadge
ABDEEHS beshade
ABDEEIL Bedelia
ABDEEIR beadier, beardie
ABDEELL labeled
ABDEELM beldame
ABDEELT belated
ABDEELY dyeable
ABDEEMR embread
ABDEEMZ bemazed
ABDEERS debaser
ABDEERT debater
ABDEEST bestead
ABDEETT abetted
ABDEFOR forbade
ABDEFOS sofa bed
ABDEGGL blagged
ABDEGGR bragged
ABDEGHI big-head
ABDEGHR beghard
ABDEGII big idea
ABDEGIL big deal
ABDEGIN beading
ABDEGIR abridge, brigade
ABDEGLR belgard
ABDEGNO bondage
ABDEGNS sagbend
ABDEGOR bordage
ABDEHLR halberd
ABDEHOR Deborah
ABDEHOW bowhead
ABDEHRT breadth
ABDEHSU sub-head
ABDEIIL alibied
ABDEIIM bi-media
ABDEILN Belinda
ABDEILP bipedal, piebald
ABDEILR ridable
ABDEILS disable
ABDEILU audible
ABDEILY beadily
ABDEIMO ameboid
ABDEIMR embraid
ABDEINR bandier, inbread
ABDEIRS darbies, seabird
ABDEIRT tribade
ABDEIRW bawdier
ABDEISS biassed
ABDEIST bastide
ABDEJOU j'adoube
ABDEKRR red bark
ABDELMR marbled
ABDELOR labored
ABDELOW dowable
ABDELPU dupable
ABDELRR drabler
ABDELRU durable
ABDELRY Bradley
ABDELST blasted
ABDEMNO abdomen
ABDEMRU rumbaed
ABDENNR Brendan
ABDENOR bandore, broaden
ABDENPR penbard
ABDENRR Bernard, brander
ABDENSS badness
ABDENSW bad news
ABDEOOT tabooed
ABDEORR boarder
ABDEOST saboted
ABDEOTU boutade
ABDERSS brassed
ABDERST dabster
ABDETTU abutted
ABDFMOR bad form
ABDGGOR boggard
ABDGIIN abiding
ABDGILN badling, balding
ABDGINN banding
ABDGINO Baoding
ABDGINR brigand
ABDGINT dingbat
ABDGINW windbag
ABDGLMO gambold
ABDGLUY ladybug

ABDGNNU Bandung
ABDHIIT adhibit
ABDHILS baldish
ABDHMTU mudbath
ABDHNOO bhoodan
ABDHNSU husband
ABDIKNU baudkin
ABDIKRS disbark
ABDILLR billard
ABDILMO bimodal
ABDILNW Baldwin
ABDILOO diabolo
ABDILOR labroid
ABDILOT tabloid
ABDILRU dilruba
ABDILRY rabidly
ABDILUY audibly
ABDILWY bawdily
ABDIMOR ambroid
ABDINOR inboard
ABDINST bandits
ABDIPRU upbraid
ABDIQRU qua-bird
ABDKMNU mudbank
ABDKOOY daybook
ABDLLNY blandly
ABDLLOR bollard
ABDLMOR lombard
ABDLORY boardly, broadly
ABDLRUY durably
ABDLSUU subdual
ABDNNOR Brandon
ABDNOOR bradoon, onboard
ABDNOPR proband
ABDNOSU bausond
ABDNOSX sandbox
ABDNOSY sandboy
ABDNOYY anybody
ABDNRUY Danbury
ABDNSTY standby
ABDOORW barwood
ABDRSTU bustard
ABDRUZZ buzzard
ABEEEFT beef tea
ABEEELS seeable
ABEEERV bereave
ABEEFFL effable
ABEEFLO beefalo
ABEEFST safe bet
ABEEGHR herbage
ABEEGLL gabelle
ABEEGLR beagler
ABEEGMR embarge
ABEEGRR gerbera
ABEEGRU auberge
ABEEGRV verbage
ABEEGRW brewage
ABEEGSU eubages
ABEEHKR Rebekah
ABEEHMT embathe
ABEEHNN henbane
ABEEHNS banshee, has-been
ABEEHNT beneath
ABEEHRT breathe, herb tea
ABEEHTY eyebath
ABEEILN Abilene
ABEEILS besaiel
ABEEIMT tie-beam
ABEEINT betaine
ABEEIST beastie
ABEEITT Beattie
ABEEKNT betaken
ABEEKNV beknave
ABEEKPR barkeep
ABEEKPS bespake, bespeak
ABEEKRR breaker
ABEELLM Mabelle
ABEELLR relabel
ABEELLY eyeball
ABEELMM emblema
ABEELMW ewe lamb
ABEELMZ emblaze
ABEELNR enabler
ABEELNT Beltane, tenable
ABEELNU nebulae
ABEELOR ear lobe
ABEELQU equable
ABEELRT bleater, retable
ABEELSU useable
ABEELSV beslave
ABEELSY besayle
ABEEMRS besmear
ABEEMRT beer mat
ABEEMRV embrave
ABEENNW bawneen
ABEENRV verbena
ABEENRY beanery
ABEERRT terebra
ABEERSV beavers
ABEERTT abetter, beretta
ABEERTY bay tree
ABEESWX beeswax
ABEFFLR baffler
ABEFFOR off-bear
ABEFFOT offbeat
ABEFGLU flea-bug
ABEFGST gabfest
ABEFILN finable
ABEFILR friable
ABEFILU fibulae
ABEFILX fixable
ABEFINU beaufin
ABEFITY beatify
ABEFLLU baleful
ABEFLLY flyable
ABEFLNT fan belt
ABEFLNU baneful
ABEFLST Belfast
ABEFORR forbear
ABEGGIM big game
ABEGGIR baggier
ABEGGLR blagger
ABEGGMO gamboge
ABEGGRR bragger
ABEGGRT bragget
ABEGGRU burgage
ABEGGRY beggary
ABEGHNS shebang
ABEGHRU bear-hug
ABEGILL billage
ABEGILN Belgian, Bengali
ABEGILR Gabriel
ABEGIMN big name
ABEGIMR gambier, imbarge
ABEGINO begonia
ABEGINR bearing
ABEGINT beating
ABEGIPP bagpipe
ABEGJNO ogbanje
ABEGKOR brokage
ABEGKOS boskage
ABEGLMR gambler, gambrel
ABEGLMU Belgaum
ABEGLNR brangle
ABEGLOR albergo
ABEGLOT globate
ABEGLRR garbler
ABEGMOR Bergamo, embargo
ABEGMOY Game Boy
ABEGMRU umbrage
ABEGMTT gambett
ABEGNNT banteng
ABEGNOS nosebag
ABEGNRS grabens
ABEGOPT peatbog
ABEGOPY page-boy
ABEGORR begorra
ABEGORX gearbox
ABEGOSS bossage
ABEGOTT tote bag
ABEHIIU Huaibei
ABEHILR hirable
ABEHIMO Bohemia
ABEHIMT imbathe
ABEHINT enhabit
ABEHIRS bearish
ABEHKRU hauberk
ABEHKTU ketubah
ABEHLMS shamble
ABEHLMT Lambeth
ABEHLRT blather, halbert
ABEHNTY Bethany
ABEHOTY haybote
ABEHRRY herbary
ABEHRTY breathy
ABEIILL baillie
ABEIILR Liberia
ABEIINN biennia
ABEIINR Iberian
ABEIIOP Beipiao
ABEIJNS basenji
ABEIKLL likable

ABEIKLS skiable
ABEIKNR Bikaner, break-in, inbreak
ABEIKNT beatnik
ABEILLN linable
ABEILLO lobelia
ABEILLP pliable
ABEILLR Braille, liberal
ABEILLS Sibella
ABEILLV livable
ABEILMN minable
ABEILMO embolia
ABEILMR balmier, Mirabel, mirable
ABEILMS ableism
ABEILMT limbate, timbale
ABEILMX mixable
ABEILNP biplane
ABEILNR bar line, Linear B
ABEILNS lesbian
ABEILPT patible
ABEILRT librate, tablier, triable
ABEILRY bilayer
ABEILST astilbe, bastile, bestial, stabile
ABEILSZ sizable
ABEILTT baittle
ABEILVV bivalve
ABEIMNO abomine
ABEIMNP pembina
ABEIMNR mirbane
ABEIMNT ambient
ABEIMRR barmier
ABEINOZ Zenobia
ABEINPT bepaint
ABEINRS Serbian
ABEINRT Atebrin, rabinet
ABEINRW wine bar
ABEINRZ zebrina
ABEINST basinet, besaint, bestain
ABEINTT Bettina, tabinet, Tibetan
ABEIOTV obviate
ABEIPRT bearpit
ABEIPST baptise
ABEIPTZ baptize
ABEIRRR barrier
ABEIRRT arbiter, rarebit
ABEIRRZ bizarre, brazier
ABEIRSS brassie
ABEIRTT battier, biretta
ABEIRTV vibrate
ABEIRTX Beatrix
ABEIRUX exurbia
ABEISTT bastite, batiste
ABEISUV abusive
ABEITUX bauxite
ABEJLLR bell jar
ABEJNOR banjore
ABEJNOW jawbone
ABEJSSU bejasus
ABEKLLY bleakly
ABEKLNT blanket
ABEKMSU sambuke
ABEKNUZ banzuke
ABEKORT to-brake, to-break
ABEKPRU breakup
ABELLMN bellman
ABELLMU umbella
ABELLNT netball
ABELLOS losable
ABELLOV lovable
ABELLRU rubella
ABELLRY Bellary
ABELLSY Sybella
ABELLTU bullate
ABELMMR membral
ABELMNT beltman, lambent
ABELMNU albumen
ABELMOV movable
ABELMRR marbler, rambler
ABELMRT lambert, marblet, tramble
ABELMRY Bramley
ABELMTU mutable
ABELNNO Lebanon
ABELNOO Boolean
ABELNOT notable
ABELNOY baloney
ABELNRS bransle
ABELNRT brantle
ABELNRU nebular
ABELNRY blarney
ABELNSU bus lane, nebulas
ABELNTU tunable
ABELOOW wooable
ABELOPR lap robe, ropable
ABELOPS posable
ABELOPT potable
ABELORR laborer
ABELORS Rosabel
ABELORT bloater
ABELORU rubeola
ABELOST Lobatse
ABELOSV absolve
ABELOTU baleout
ABELOTV votable
ABELOTW towable
ABELPRU parbleu, puberal
ABELQUY equably
ABELRRW brawler, warbler
ABELRSS braless
ABELRST blaster, brastle, stabler
ABELRSU Belarus
ABELRTT battler, blatter, brattle
ABELRVY bravely
ABELSTT battels
ABELSTU abustle
ABELSTY beastly
ABELTWY beltway
ABEMNOS ambones
ABEMNST best man
ABEMNSU sunbeam
ABEMORS ambrose
ABEMORT barmote, bromate
ABEMRRT Bertram
ABEMRRU rambure
ABEMSSY embassy
ABENNOY Bayonne
ABENNRW bran-new, Branwen
ABENORT baronet
ABENORU Auberon
ABENORZ zebrano
ABENOSY soybean
ABENOTY bayonet
ABENQTU banquet
ABENRSU sun bear
ABENRUX exurban
ABENTYZ bezanty
ABEOOTV obovate
ABEOPRS saprobe
ABEOPRT probate
ABEOPTU beau-pot
ABEOQRU baroque
ABEORRS brasero
ABEORRT arboret, Roberta
ABEORST boaster, obertas
ABEORSY rosebay
ABEORTT abettor, taboret
ABEOSTU aboutes
ABEOVWW bow wave
ABEQRSU brasque
ABERRSU sabreur
ABERRTT Barrett
ABERRVY bravery
ABERSSY brassey
ABERSTY barytes
ABERSUU bureaus
ABERTTU abutter, batture
ABERTTY battery
ABERTWY bywater
ABERUUX bureaux
ABERUVY Avebury
ABFFIIL bailiff

ABFFLOO boffola
ABFFLOU buffalo
ABFGGLO golf bag
ABFGKNO fog bank
ABFHLSU bashful
ABFIILR bifilar
ABFIIMR fimbria
ABFILRU fibular
ABFILSU fibulas
ABFIMOR fibroma
ABFLOTU boatful
ABFLOTY fly-boat
ABGGGIN bagging
ABGGILY baggily
ABGGORW growbag
ABGHINT bathing
ABGHIST shitbag
ABGHLRU burghal
ABGHMOO goombah
ABGHMRU Hamburg
ABGHNOT bonaght
ABGHOTU abought
ABGIILS Galibis
ABGIINS biasing
ABGIJOO jigaboo
ABGIKNN banking
ABGIKNR Barking
ABGILMS gimbals
ABGILNR barling
ABGILNT tabling
ABGILNZ blazing
ABGILOR garboil
ABGIMST gambist
ABGINNN banning
ABGINOT boating
ABGINRR barring
ABGINTT batting
ABGINTW batwing
ABGKKNO Bangkok
ABGKLOY yolk-bag
ABGKOOR rag book
ABGKORW work-bag
ABGLMOU lumbago
ABGLNOO bologna
ABGLNOU Lubango
ABGLOOT tool bag
ABGLORT rag bolt
ABGLRRU burglar
ABGMNOY bogyman
ABGMORW bagworm
ABGNNRU barngun
ABGNOPR probang
ABGNOTU gunboat
ABGNOWY bowyang
ABGOORT botargo
ABGOORV Gabrovo
ABGOPST postbag
ABGOTTU tugboat
ABHHIPT hip bath
ABHHKTU khutbah
ABHHOOP Pooh-Bah
ABHHSUY hushaby
ABHIIMR Ibrahim
ABHIINT inhabit
ABHIINW Bhiwani

ABHIKLS bashlik
ABHIKTW hawkbit
ABHILNO hobnail
ABHILOS abolish
ABHILTU halibut
ABHIMNR brahmin
ABHIMRX Brixham
ABHINOS Siobhan
ABHINST absinth
ABHISTU habitus
ABHITUZ haubitz
ABHKRSU kurbash
ABHLMYZ Zhambyl
ABHLOUX box-haul
ABHLRSY brashly
ABHLRTU hurlbat
ABHMNSU bushman
ABHNSTU sun-bath
ABHORRU harbour
ABHOTUY hautboy
ABHRSTU tarbush
ABHSTUW washtub
ABIIIKR Bairiki
ABIIINR biriani
ABIIKKT kibitka
ABIILLS Sibilla
ABIILMM malimbi
ABIILMU bulimia
ABIILNS aiblins
ABIILOV Bolivia
ABIILRY biliary
ABIILTY ability
ABIIMNR minibar
ABIINOR Nairobi, robinia
ABIINRY biryani
ABIJLNR brinjal
ABIJNPU Punjabi
ABIJOSW Ojibwas
ABIJPRU Bijapur
ABIKLLM Kimball
ABIKLMN lambkin
ABIKLMR milk bar
ABIKMNR barmkin
ABIKRTZ britzka
ABILLMU ballium
ABILLMY balmily
ABILLNP pinball
ABILLPY pliably
ABILLST ballist
ABILLSW sawbill
ABILLSY Sibylla, Sybilla, syllabi
ABILLWX waxbill
ABILLWY waybill
ABILMNU albumin
ABILMOX mailbox
ABILMRY barmily
ABILNNO bonnail
ABILOPR bipolar, parboil
ABILORT orbital
ABILORV bolivar

ABILOTU bailout, obitual
ABILPSY bias-ply
ABILRRY library
ABILRSS brassil
ABILRTU tribual
ABILTTY battily
ABIMNRU Umbrian
ABIMOSS biomass
ABIMOTT tamboti
ABIMPST baptism
ABIMTTU tambuti
ABINOOR boronia
ABINORT taborin
ABINORW rainbow
ABINOST bastion
ABINOSU abusion
ABINRTV vibrant
ABINSTU bustian
ABIORRT orbitar
ABIORTV vibrato
ABIORUX Roubaix
ABIPRTT bit part
ABIPSTT baptist
ABISSST bassist
ABJKMOS sjambok
ABKLLNY blankly
ABKLRUW bulwark
ABKMNOO bookman
ABKNRSY Bryansk
ABLLLOW lowball
ABLLLUY lullaby
ABLLNOO balloon
ABLLNTU bull ant
ABLLORR roll bar
ABLLORU lobular
ABLLOTY tallboy
ABLLOVY lovably
ABLLPSU balls-up
ABLLRUY bullary
ABLMMOU bummalo
ABLMNOU umbonal
ABLMOOT tombola
ABLMOSY lamboys
ABLMOVY movably
ABLMPUU pabulum
ABLNORW barn owl
ABLNOTY notably
ABLOPYY playboy
ABLORST Borstal
ABLORTW blawort
ABLRRUY barruly
ABLRTUU tubular
ABMNRSU Burmans
ABMOORR bar room
ABMORTU tambour
ABNOORZ Borazon
ABNOOSS bassoon
ABNOPRU pronuba
ABNORTU a-burton
ABNORTY baryton
ABNOSSU bonasus
ABNOTUY buoyant
ABNOTUZ zabuton
ABNOTWY Baytown

ABOOPSX soapbox
ABOORTW rowboat
ABOPRST absorpt
ABORSSU sub rosa
ABORSTU abortus, robusta
ABRRSUY bursary
ABRRTUY turbary
ABRRUXY buxarry
ABRSTUU arbutus
ABSSSUY abyssus
ABSUWZZ buzz-saw
ACCCILY acyclic
ACCDDEI caddice, decadic
ACCDEEN cadence
ACCDEHR decarch
ACCDEHT catched
ACCDEII accidie
ACCDEIN Candice
ACCDEIU caducei
ACCDEKO cockade
ACCDEKR cracked
ACCDENY cadency
ACCDERU accrued, cardecu
ACCDFIL flaccid
ACCDHIL chalcid
ACCDHMU cumdach
ACCDKOR cockard
ACCDLOY cacodyl
ACCDORR crocard
ACCEELN cenacle
ACCEENR creance
ACCEERT accrete
ACCEFIT factice
ACCEFLU felucca
ACCEGIN accinge
ACCEGOS soccage
ACCEHHI chechia
ACCEHIL caliche, chalice
ACCEHIN chicane
ACCEHLN chancel
ACCEHLO cochlea
ACCEHNO conchae
ACCEHNR chancre
ACCEHNS chances
ACCEHOR caroche, coacher
ACCEHPU capuche
ACCEHRT catcher
ACCEHTU catechu
ACCEHXY cachexy
ACCEIIL Cecilia
ACCEIKP ice pack, pack ice
ACCEILL calicle
ACCEILN calcine
ACCEILO coeliac
ACCEILR Clarice
ACCEILT calcite
ACCEIMR ceramic, racemic
ACCEINO cocaine, oceanic
ACCEINV vaccine
ACCEIPR caprice
ACCEIPV peccavi
ACCEIQU cacique
ACCEIRS carices
ACCEIST ascetic
ACCEKLR clacker, crackle
ACCEKLT clacket
ACCEKMO meacock
ACCEKOP peacock
ACCEKOS seacock
ACCEKPU cupcake
ACCEKRR cracker
ACCEKRT cracket
ACCELLU calcule
ACCELLY calycle
ACCELNO conceal
ACCELOR coracle
ACCELSU saccule
ACCELSY calyces
ACCENOR conacre, crocean
ACCENOV concave
ACCENPT peccant
ACCEOPY cacoepy
ACCEOSS cocasse
ACCEOST cot-case
ACCEPRY peccary
ACCERRU accurre
ACCERSU accrues, accurse, accuser
ACCESTY ecstacy
ACCFIIP pacific
ACCFILY calcify
ACCGHIO Chicago
ACCHIMS chasmic
ACCHINO chicano
ACCHIOT chaotic
ACCHIOU acouchi
ACCHIRS scraich
ACCHKOY haycock
ACCHLRU culrach
ACCHLTU claucht
ACCHNRS scranch
ACCHNRU craunch
ACCHNUY Chauncy
ACCHOPU capouch, pachuco
ACCHOSW cash cow
ACCHOTW Choctaw
ACCHPTU catchup
ACCHRRU currach
ACCHRST scratch
ACCIILN aclinic
ACCIINT actinic
ACCIIST sciatic
ACCIKLT catlick
ACCIKRS carsick
ACCILLU calculi
ACCILMO comical
ACCILMU calcium
ACCILNO conical, laconic
ACCILNY cyclian, cynical
ACCILOR caloric
ACCILOV vocalic
ACCILRU crucial
ACCILRY acrylic
ACCILSS classic
ACCILST clastic
ACCINNO canonic
ACCINOT Occitan
ACCINRU crucian
ACCIOPR caproic
ACCIORT carotic
ACCIOTV octavic
ACCIPRT practic
ACCIRTU cruciat
ACCISTT tactics
ACCISTU caustic
ACCJKOR cro'jack
ACCKLLO cockall
ACCKLRY crackly
ACCKMMO cammock
ACCKMOY maycock
ACCKOPR cap rock
ACCKORR corrack
ACCKOSS cassock, Cossack
ACCKOST castock
ACCKPRU crack-up
ACCMOOY cocoyam
ACCMOPT accompt, compact
ACCMRUU curcuma
ACCNNOO coon-can
ACCNOOP cocopan
ACCNOOR carcoon, raccoon
ACCNOOS saccoon
ACCNOTT contact
ACCNOTU account
ACCOORT tarocco
ACCOPTY copycat
ACCOQSU squacco
ACCORSS corcass
ACCORTU accourt
ACCRSTU accurst
ACDDDEI caddied
ACDDDEL cladded
ACDDDEO dodecad
ACDDEHI didache
ACDDEHR Cheddar
ACDDEIN candied
ACDDEIS caddies
ACDDEIU decidua
ACDDELO cladode
ACDDELS scaddle, scalded
ACDDELU addulce
ACDDEOP decapod
ACDDERR red card
ACDDHIS caddish
ACDDHKO haddock
ACDDHRU chuddar

ACDDIIR acridid
ACDDIRS discard
ACDDITY catydid
ACDDKMO maddock
ACDDKOP paddock
ACDEEES decease
ACDEEFR defacer
ACDEEFT faceted
ACDEEHL Chaldee
ACDEELP deplace
ACDEELR cedrela, creedal, declare
ACDEELS descale
ACDEELV cleaved
ACDEEMV medevac
ACDEENV devance, vendace
ACDEERT decreta
ACDEETU educate
ACDEFGO dogface
ACDEFOP po-faced
ACDEFOT de facto
ACDEFRS scarfed
ACDEFRT fracted
ACDEGGR cragged
ACDEGHN Changde
ACDEGKO dockage
ACDEGNO congaed, decagon
ACDEGOR cordage
ACDEHIN chained, echidna
ACDEHIP edaphic
ACDEHKR dekarch
ACDEHLR chalder
ACDEHMR charmed, demarch
ACDEHNR endarch
ACDEHOP pochade
ACDEHOT cathode
ACDEHPP chapped
ACDEHPR parched
ACDEHRR charred
ACDEHTT chatted
ACDEIIL elaidic
ACDEIIS acidise
ACDEIIV avicide
ACDEIIZ acidize
ACDEILL cedilla
ACDEILM decimal, declaim, medical
ACDEILN decalin, Iceland
ACDEILR decrial, radicel, radicle
ACDEILT citadel, deltaic, dialect, edictal
ACDEILV caviled
ACDEIMV medivac
ACDEIMY mediacy
ACDEINO Oceanid
ACDEINY cyanide
ACDEIPR epacrid
ACDEIRS radices, sidecar
ACDEIST die-cast
ACDEITT dictate
ACDEKLT tackled, talcked
ACDEKST stacked
ACDELMM clammed
ACDELNO celadon
ACDELNR candler
ACDELNS calends
ACDELOP placode
ACDELOR caroled
ACDELPP clapped
ACDELRS scalder
ACDELSS declass
ACDELST castled
ACDELWW dewclaw
ACDEMMR crammed
ACDEMMS scammed
ACDEMNU decuman
ACDEMOR comrade
ACDENNS scanned
ACDENNT candent
ACDENNU nuanced
ACDENOR dracone
ACDENOT tacnode
ACDENPT pandect
ACDENRT cantred, Tancred
ACDENRU durance
ACDENRY ardency
ACDENST descant
ACDEOPS peascod
ACDEORR corrade
ACDEORS sarcode
ACDEORT art deco, cordate, redcoat
ACDEORU Ecuador
ACDEOTT codetta
ACDEOUV couvade
ACDEPPR crapped
ACDERRS scarred
ACDERSU crusade
ACDERTT detract
ACDERTU Decatur, educrat, traduce
ACDESTT scatted
ACDFFIR Cardiff
ACDFIIT fatidic
ACDFIIY acidify
ACDFIOT factoid
ACDFNOO fondaco
ACDGHLO Clodagh
ACDGINN dancing
ACDGNOT cant-dog
ACDGORT dog cart
ACDHIIL chiliad
ACDHIIS Hasidic
ACDHIMR madrich
ACDHIRR Richard
ACDHIRY diarchy
ACDHLOR chordal, dorlach
ACDHNOT dontcha
ACDHOPR pochard
ACDHORR orchard
ACDHRUY duarchy
ACDHRYY dyarchy
ACDIIIN indicia
ACDIINN indican
ACDIINO conidia
ACDIIRS cidaris
ACDIIRT triacid, triadic
ACDIITY acidity
ACDIKLS skaldic
ACDIKPR pickard
ACDILLO codilla
ACDILMO domical
ACDILMS cladism
ACDILNO nodical
ACDILNU dulcian, lucanid, Lucinda
ACDILOP placoid, podalic, podical
ACDILOR cordial
ACDILOT co-tidal
ACDILRT triclad
ACDILRY acridly
ACDILTW wildcat
ACDIMMU cadmium
ACDIMNO monacid, monadic, nomadic
ACDIMNY dynamic
ACDIMOO camoodi
ACDINRU candiru, iracund
ACDINRY Indycar
ACDINST discant
ACDIOPR parodic, picador
ACDIOPS sciapod
ACDIORR corrida
ACDIORS sarcoid, scaroid
ACDIORT carotid
ACDIORU courida
ACDIOTT tactoid
ACDIOXY oxyacid
ACDIQRU quadric
ACDIRST drastic
ACDISTX tax disc
ACDITUV viaduct
ACDJNTU adjunct
ACDKLOP padlock
ACDKLRY drackly
ACDKLSY sky-clad
ACDKMOO mockado
ACDKMPU mud pack
ACDKOTT dattock
ACDLLOR collard
ACDLNOR caldron

ACDLORW cold war
ACDMMNO command
ACDMNOP compand
ACDMOOW camwood
ACDMORW cad-worm
ACDNOOR cardoon
ACDNORT cordant
ACDNORU candour
ACDNORY dacryon
ACDOORT cat door
ACDORST costard
ACDORSU crusado
ACDORUZ cruzado
ACDORWY cowardy
ACDRSTU custard
ACDRSUU carduus
ACDRTTU traduct
ACEEEPS escapee
ACEEEUV evacuee
ACEEFHN enchafe
ACEEFIN faience
ACEEFNY fayence
ACEEFPR preface
ACEEGHL galeche
ACEEGHR chargee
ACEEGHV chevage
ACEEGIL elegiac
ACEEGNR engrace
ACEEGOT ecotage
ACEEGSU escuage
ACEEHHT cheetah
ACEEHIP cheapie
ACEEHIV achieve
ACEEHKO hoecake
ACEEHLS Chelsea, clashee
ACEEHLT cheetal, chelate
ACEEHMP empeach
ACEEHMR machree
ACEEHMT machete
ACEEHNN enhance
ACEEHNP cheapen
ACEEHNR erenach
ACEEHNS enchase
ACEEHRT cheater, hectare, reteach, teacher
ACEEHST escheat
ACEEHTT thecate
ACEEILP calipee
ACEEIPS a-pieces
ACEEJKN jackeen
ACEEKNP kneecap
ACEELLN nacelle
ACEELNR Carleen, Carlene, cleaner
ACEELNS cleanse, scalene
ACEELNT tenacle
ACEELNV enclave, valence
ACEELPR percale, replace
ACEELRR clearer
ACEELRT treacle
ACEELRV cleaver
ACEELST celesta
ACEELSU euclase
ACEELVX exclave
ACEEMNR menacer
ACEEMNY Mycenae
ACEEMRR creamer
ACEEMRT cremate
ACEENNP penance
ACEENNT canteen
ACEENNY cayenne
ACEENOT acetone
ACEENRT crenate, re-enact
ACEENTU cuneate
ACEEORS acerose
ACEEORT ocreate
ACEEOTV evocate
ACEEPRR caperer
ACEEPRS escaper, percase
ACEEPST pectase
ACEEPTT pectate
ACEERRT caterer, retrace, terrace
ACEERST secreta
ACEERTX exacter, excreta
ACEESTU Eustace
ACEESTY cat's-eye
ACEFFFO face-off
ACEFFHI affiche
ACEFFHR chaffer
ACEFFOR afforce
ACEFHMR chamfer
ACEFHRY chafery
ACEFIIL Felicia
ACEFILL icefall
ACEFILM malefic
ACEFILR filacer
ACEFINN finance
ACEFINR fancier, Francie
ACEFINS fascine
ACEFINT facient
ACEFITV factive
ACEFITY acetify
ACEFKLR flacker
ACEFKLT flacket
ACEFLRU careful
ACEFNRS Frances
ACEFNRU furnace
ACEFOPR proface
ACEFOTU outface
ACEFRRT refract
ACEFRRU farceur
ACEFRSU surface
ACEFRTU facture, furcate
ACEFUVY vacuefy
ACEGHLO lochage
ACEGHMN Macheng
ACEGHNR changer
ACEGHOU gouache
ACEGHOW cowhage
ACEGHRR charger
ACEGHRT creaght, gertcha
ACEGIIR craigie
ACEGIKP pickage
ACEGILL ellagic, gallice
ACEGILN angelic, anglice, galenic, Legnica
ACEGILP pelagic
ACEGILR glacier, gracile
ACEGIMR grimace
ACEGIMT gametic
ACEGINO coinage
ACEGINR Grecian, ingrace
ACEGIRT cigaret
ACEGIST cagiest
ACEGJKL jackleg
ACEGKLO lockage
ACEGKLR grackle
ACEGKOR corkage
ACEGLLO collage
ACEGLNO congeal
ACEGLNR clanger
ACEGLOU cagoule
ACEGNOR cornage
ACEGNOT cognate
ACEGORS corsage
ACEGORU courage
ACEGOTT cottage
ACEGSTU scutage
ACEHHLR Harlech
ACEHHLT hatchel
ACEHHMS Chesham
ACEHHRU hachure
ACEHHTT hatchet
ACEHILL helical
ACEHILM lechaim, Michael
ACEHILN Chilean
ACEHILR charlie
ACEHILT ethical
ACEHIMN machine
ACEHIMP impeach
ACEHIMR chimera
ACEHIMT hematic
ACEHINN enchain, inhance
ACEHINT teach-in
ACEHIOT achiote
ACEHIPP chappie
ACEHIPR charpie
ACEHIPT aphetic, hepatic
ACEHIRR charier, hire car
ACEHIRS cashier

ACEHIRT	theriac
ACEHIRV	archive
ACEHITT	Chattie
ACEHITY	yachtie
ACEHKLS	shackle
ACEHKLT	hacklet
ACEHKNY	hackney
ACEHKOR	choaker
ACEHKRW	whacker
ACEHKRY	hackery
ACEHLLS	shellac
ACEHLLT	hell-cat
ACEHLMT	chamlet
ACEHLMY	alchemy
ACEHLNN	channel
ACEHLNO	chalone
ACEHLNP	planche
ACEHLNR	charnel, larchen
ACEHLOP	epochal
ACEHLOR	cholera, chorale
ACEHLOS	sea loch
ACEHLOT	cholate
ACEHLPT	chaplet
ACEHLPY	cheaply
ACEHLRS	Charles, clasher, raschel
ACEHLRT	chartel, clethra, trachle
ACEHLRY	Charley
ACEHLST	satchel, schalet
ACEHLTT	chattel, latchet
ACEHMNR	encharm
ACEHMNT	manchet
ACEHMOT	thecoma
ACEHMRR	charmer, marcher
ACEHMRS	mesarch, schmear
ACEHMRT	rematch
ACEHMSS	schemas
ACEHMTT	matchet
ACEHMTY	ecthyma
ACEHMTZ	chametz
ACEHNNR	channer
ACEHNNT	enchant
ACEHNRR	rancher
ACEHNRT	chanter, tranche
ACEHNST	chasten
ACEHNTT	etchant
ACEHNTU	unteach
ACEHNTY	chantey
ACEHOOT	ootheca
ACEHOPR	poacher
ACEHOTY	chayote
ACEHPPS	schappe
ACEHPRT	chapter, patcher
ACEHPRY	eparchy, preachy
ACEHQUU	Quechua
ACEHQUY	queachy
ACEHRRT	charter
ACEHRRX	xerarch
ACEHRRY	archery
ACEHRSU	archeus
ACEHRSY	hyraces
ACEHRTT	chatter, ratchet
ACEHRTW	watcher
ACEHTTU	teuchat
ACEHTTW	watchet
ACEHUVX	chevaux
ACEIILM	cimelia
ACEIILS	laicise
ACEIILT	ciliate, Leticia
ACEIILZ	laicize
ACEIJKS	jacksie
ACEIJSS	Jessica
ACEIKLO	oilcake
ACEIKLT	catlike
ACEIKPX	pickaxe
ACEIKRT	tackier
ACEIKSS	seasick
ACEILLL	allelic
ACEILLM	Camille
ACEILLR	cerilla
ACEILLX	lexical
ACEILMN	cnemial, melanic
ACEILMR	claimer, miracle, reclaim
ACEILMS	limaces
ACEILMT	climate, metical
ACEILMX	exclaim
ACEILMY	mycelia
ACEILNP	capelin, panicle, pelican
ACEILNR	carline, clarine
ACEILNS	celsian, sanicle, scaleni
ACEILNU	cauline
ACEILNV	inclave
ACEILOR	calorie, cariole, Coralie
ACEILOS	celosia, coalise
ACEILOZ	coalize
ACEILPR	caliper, picarel, replica
ACEILPS	special
ACEILPT	plicate
ACEILRR	Clarrie
ACEILRS	scalier
ACEILRT	article, recital
ACEILRU	auricle
ACEILRV	caliver, clavier, valeric
ACEILSS	salices
ACEILST	elastic, laciest, latices, salicet
ACEILSV	vesical
ACEILTT	lattice, tactile
ACEILVW	wavicle
ACEIMNO	encomia
ACEIMNR	carmine
ACEIMNS	amnesic
ACEIMNT	nematic
ACEIMNX	Mexican
ACEIMPR	campier
ACEIMPY	pyaemic
ACEIMRT	matrice
ACEIMRU	Maurice, uraemic
ACEIMST	sematic
ACEIMSU	caesium
ACEIMSY	cymaise
ACEIMTY	emacity
ACEINNP	pinnace
ACEINNR	cannier
ACEINNT	ancient
ACEINNY	cyanine
ACEINOP	paeonic
ACEINOS	icosane
ACEINOT	aconite, anoetic, antoeci
ACEINPR	caprine
ACEINPS	inscape, pinaces, Piscean
ACEINRS	arsenic
ACEINRT	certain, nacrite
ACEINST	Anstice, cineast, insecta
ACEINTT	nictate, tetanic
ACEINTU	tunicae
ACEINTV	venatic
ACEINTX	inexact
ACEINTY	cyanite
ACEINVZ	Vicenza
ACEIOPT	ectopia
ACEIORS	scoriae
ACEIORT	erotica
ACEIOTX	exotica
ACEIPPR	crappie, epicarp
ACEIPRS	epacris, scrapie, spacier
ACEIPRT	paretic, picrate, tapicer
ACEIPST	aseptic, paciest, spicate

ACEIPSU auspice
ACEIPSZ capsize
ACEIPTV captive
ACEIQRU acquire
ACEIRRR carrier
ACEIRRS scarier
ACEIRRT erratic
ACEIRRW aircrew
ACEIRRZ crazier
ACEIRST cristae, raciest, stearic
ACEIRSU saucier
ACEIRSV ascrive, varices, viscera
ACEIRTT cattier, citrate
ACEIRTU curiate
ACEISSS ascesis
ACEISST ascites, ectasis
ACEISTT statice
ACEITTX extatic
ACEJLNO El Cajon
ACEJNOT jaconet
ACEJNOY joyance, Joycean
ACEJPTU cajeput
ACEJQSU Jacques
ACEJRTT traject
ACEKKNR knacker
ACEKLLP pellack
ACEKLNR crankle
ACEKLNS slacken
ACEKLOR colrake
ACEKLPT placket
ACEKLQU quackle
ACEKLRS slacker
ACEKLRT tackler
ACEKLRU caulker
ACEKMNP packmen
ACEKMRS smacker
ACEKOPT pocketa
ACEKORR croaker
ACEKPPR prepack
ACEKPTW wet pack
ACEKRRT tracker
ACEKRST stacker
ACEKRTT rackett
ACEKRTY rackety
ACELLMO calomel
ACELLNU nucleal
ACELLNY cleanly
ACELLOR corella, ocellar
ACELLOS callose
ACELLOT collate
ACELLPS scalpel
ACELLPY clypeal
ACELLRS scleral
ACELLRU cure-all
ACELLRY clearly
ACELLST scallet
ACELMMR clammer, crammle
ACELMOU leucoma
ACELMPR clamper
ACELMRY camelry
ACELMTU calumet
ACELNNU unclean
ACELNNY lyncean
ACELNOP noplace
ACELNOR corneal
ACELNOT lactone
ACELNOW lowance
ACELNPS enclasp
ACELNPU clean-up
ACELNRT central
ACELNRU lucarne, nuclear, unclear
ACELNRY larceny
ACELNST asclent, scantle
ACELNSU censual
ACELNTY latency
ACELNVY levancy, valency
ACELOPR polacre
ACELOPT polecat
ACELOQU coequal
ACELORR caroler
ACELORT crotale
ACELORY caloyer
ACELOST coastel, lactose, talcose
ACELOTT calotte
ACELOTU oculate
ACELOTY acolyte
ACELOUV vacuole
ACELPPR clapper
ACELPPS scapple
ACELPRS clasper, scalper
ACELPRT plectra
ACELPRU clear-up
ACELPRY prelacy
ACELPSU capsule, scale-up, specula, upscale
ACELPSY cypsela
ACELQRU lacquer
ACELQUY lacquey
ACELRRW crawler
ACELRST scarlet
ACELRSU secular
ACELRTT clatter
ACELRTU cuartel
ACELRTY treacly
ACELRWY Crawley
ACELSSS classes
ACELSTT castlet
ACELSTU sulcate
ACELSTY scytale
ACELSUX excusal
ACELSXY calyxes
ACELTTU Lucetta
ACELTUY acutely
ACELTXY exactly
ACEMMRR crammer
ACEMMRS scammer
ACEMNOR Cameron, cremona, romance
ACEMNRW crewman
ACEMOPR compare, compear
ACEMORT octamer
ACEMORU morceau
ACEMOSU mucosae
ACEMOUV vacuome
ACEMPRS scamper
ACEMPRT crampet
ACEMRSY screamy
ACENNOS ancones
ACENNOT connate
ACENNOY noyance
ACENNOZ canzone
ACENNRS scanner
ACENNRY cannery
ACENNST nascent
ACENNTY tenancy
ACENOOR coronae
ACENOPT patonce
ACENOPU ponceau
ACENORS carnose, coarsen
ACENORT enactor, orcanet
ACENORV carvone
ACENOSS cassone
ACENOST costean
ACENOSZ Cosenza
ACENOTV centavo
ACENOUZ canezou
ACENPRR prancer
ACENPRT carpent
ACENPTY patency
ACENRRY errancy
ACENRSS ancress
ACENRSY scenary
ACENRTT tranect
ACENRTU centaur
ACENRTY nectary
ACENSTT cast net
ACENSTU nutcase
ACEOOPP apocope
ACEOPRT coperta, pectora
ACEOPTU outpace
ACEOQSU cosaque
ACEORRT creator, reactor
ACEORSS carosse
ACEORST coaster
ACEORSU carouse
ACEORTV overact
ACEORTX exactor
ACEOSSU caseous
ACEOSTT costate
ACEOSTU acetous
ACEOSTY tea cosy
ACEOTTV cavetto

ACEOTUU autocue, couteau
ACEPPRR crapper
ACEPQTU pacquet
ACEPRRS scarper, scraper
ACEPRRY precary
ACEPRST precast, spectra
ACEPRSU scauper
ACEPRTU capture
ACEPRUV carve-up
ACEPSTU cuspate
ACEQRTU racquet
ACEQSTU acquest, casquet
ACERRTT retract
ACERRTY terracy, tracery
ACERRUV verruca
ACERRVY carvery
ACERSST actress
ACERSSV scarves
ACERSTT scatter
ACERSTY sectary
ACERSUY eucrasy, saucery
ACERTTU curtate, cut-rate
ACERTTX extract
ACERTTY cattery
ACERTUX curtaxe
ACERTUY cautery
ACESSTY ecstasy
ACESTTT Test Act
ACESTTU acutest, scutate
ACESTTY testacy
ACESTXY exstacy
ACFFHPU huff-cap
ACFFIIT caitiff
ACFFIKM maffick
ACFFILT afflict
ACFFIRT traffic
ACFFOST cast-off, offcast
ACFGHIN chafing
ACFHILS calfish
ACFHIST catfish
ACFHISU fuchsia
ACFHLNU flaunch
ACFHLTU flaucht, half-cut
ACFHNNO fanchon
ACFIILN finical
ACFIINO oficina
ACFIKNN finnack
ACFIKNU funckia
ACFILNO folacin
ACFILNY fancily
ACFILRY clarify
ACFIMOR formica
ACFIMRU fumaric
ACFIMSS Fascism
ACFINNY infancy
ACFINOT faction
ACFINRS Francis
ACFINRT frantic, infarct, infract
ACFINRY carnify
ACFIOPY opacify
ACFIPUY paucify
ACFIRSY scarify
ACFISST fascist
ACFKLSU sackful
ACFLRTU cartful
ACFLRUU furcula
ACFLTTU tactful
ACFLTUY faculty
ACFMSTU factums
ACFNRTU fructan
ACFORRU carfour
ACFORTY factory
ACGGRSY scraggy
ACGHHIR chiragh
ACGHIJN Changji
ACGHINR chagrin
ACGHINT gnathic
ACGHINW chinwag
ACGHINX Xichang
ACGHINY Yichang
ACGHIPR graphic
ACGHLTU claught
ACGHNRU graunch
ACGHNUX Xuchang
ACGHRRU curragh
ACGHRSU scraugh
ACGIILN alginic
ACGIKLN lacking
ACGIKNP packing
ACGIKNR carking
ACGIKNS sacking
ACGIKNT tacking
ACGIKRR Garrick
ACGILLN calling
ACGILLO logical
ACGILMY myalgic
ACGILNP placing
ACGILNR carling
ACGILNS scaling
ACGILNT catling, talcing
ACGILNU cingula, glucina
ACGIMNO coaming
ACGIMNP camping
ACGINNN canning
ACGINOR organic
ACGINOT coating, cognita, cotinga
ACGINPP capping
ACGINPS spacing
ACGINRS sacring
ACGINRT tracing
ACGINRV carving, craving
ACGINST casting
ACGINTT catting
ACGIRST gastric
ACGLNOR clangor
ACGLSUU glaucus
ACGMNOP campong
ACGNNOR crannog
ACGNOOT octagon
ACGORUU couguar
ACHHIIT Hitachi
ACHHPPU chuppah
ACHHRTT thratch
ACHHSTU tchaush
ACHIILS ischial
ACHIIMT Hamitic
ACHIINT Chianti
ACHIIPS pachisi
ACHIJMO Joachim
ACHIJNT jacinth
ACHIKLN kanchil, Nalchik
ACHIKNS Achinsk
ACHIKOP pak-choi
ACHIKRS ricksha
ACHIKRY hayrick
ACHILLO lochial
ACHILLP phallic
ACHILLS challis
ACHILLT thallic
ACHILLV Villach
ACHILMO malicho
ACHILMR Richmal
ACHILNO Nichola
ACHILOS scholia
ACHILPP chappli
ACHILRY charily
ACHILSV calvish
ACHILSY clayish
ACHIMNO Mohican
ACHIMOS chamiso, chamois
ACHIMRS charism
ACHIMSS schisma
ACHIMST tachism
ACHINNT inchant
ACHINNU unchain
ACHINOT Antioch
ACHINOY onychia
ACHINPS spinach
ACHINRZ zarnich
ACHINTX xanthic
ACHINTY Cynthia
ACHIOPS isopach
ACHIOPT aphotic, picotah
ACHIORT chariot, haricot
ACHIOSY choisya
ACHIPPS Sapphic
ACHIPST spathic
ACHIQRU charqui
ACHIQUU Quichua
ACHIRRT triarch
ACHIRRU Raichur
ACHIRST Christa
ACHIRTU haircut
ACHIRTY charity
ACHISSS chassis

ACHISTT cattish, tachist
ACHKLLO hallock
ACHKLOT tolkach
ACHKMMO hammock
ACHKOPS hopsack
ACHKOSS hassock
ACHKOTT hattock
ACHLLOO alcohol
ACHLLOR chloral
ACHLLOU Cholula
ACHLMPU plumach
ACHLMSY chlamys
ACHLNOR chronal
ACHLNOY halcyon
ACHLNTU unlatch
ACHLOPR raploch
ACHLORS scholar
ACHLORT trochal
ACHLOST cloaths
ACHLOSW salchow
ACHLPSY psychal
ACHMNOR monarch, nomarch
ACHMOPR camphor
ACHMOST stomach
ACHMRSW schwarm
ACHMSUW cumshaw
ACHNNOS chanson
ACHNOTW Chawton
ACHNOTY tachyon
ACHNOVY anchovy
ACHNPUY paunchy
ACHNRTY chantry
ACHNRUY raunchy
ACHNSTU canthus, staunch
ACHNSTY snatchy
ACHOOST cahoots
ACHOPPW chappow
ACHOPRT toparch
ACHOPRY charpoy
ACHORSU aurochs
ACHPTUY pauchty
ACHQSTU quatsch
ACHRSTY starchy
ACHSTUY cyathus
ACIIKRS airsick
ACIILLN allicin
ACIILMS Islamic, laicism
ACIILNS incisal, salicin
ACIILNT Caitlin
ACIILNV vicinal
ACIILOV viliaco
ACIILPU apiculi
ACIILRY ciliary
ACIILSS liassic
ACIILSU iliacus
ACIILTY laicity
ACIIMMS miasmic
ACIIMOT comitia
ACIIMST itacism
ACIINNO anionic
ACIINOS Nicosia
ACIINOT nicotia
ACIINPS piscina
ACIINTT titanic
ACIIOST isatoic
ACIIPPR priapic
ACIIPRT piratic
ACIIRSS cassiri
ACIIRST satiric
ACIIRTT triatic
ACIJNOP japonic
ACIJUZZ jacuzzi
ACIKKSS kick-ass
ACIKLNW Alnwick
ACIKLOR airlock
ACIKLTY tackily
ACIKLWY wackily
ACIKMPR rampick
ACIKNOR Koranic
ACIKNPY panicky
ACIKNTT tin-tack
ACIKOPR koi carp
ACIKPRT Patrick, tripack
ACIKPSX six-pack
ACIKPSY sick pay
ACIKRWW Warwick
ACIKUWZ Zwickau
ACILLLO illocal
ACILLMO Comilla
ACILLMS miscall
ACILLRY lyrical
ACILLSY salicyl
ACILLUU luculia
ACILMNO malonic
ACILMOT comital
ACILMPS plasmic, psalmic
ACILMPY campily
ACILMSU musical
ACILNNY cannily
ACILNOO Colonia
ACILNOP pinacol
ACILNOR clarion
ACILNOS Nicolas
ACILNOT tonical
ACILNOU inocula
ACILNPS inclasp
ACILNPY pliancy
ACILNTU lunatic
ACILNUV vincula
ACILOPT Capitol, optical, topical
ACILORR racloir
ACILORV co-rival
ACILOST stoical
ACILOTT coal tit
ACILOTV volatic, voltaic
ACILPST plastic
ACILPTY typical
ACILRSY scarily
ACILRTU curtail, trucial
ACILRTY clarity
ACILRYZ crazily
ACILSSS classis
ACILSUY saucily
ACILTTY cattily, tacitly, tactily
ACILTUV victual
ACILTVY calvity
ACIMMPS psammic
ACIMMRU muramic
ACIMNOP campion
ACIMNOR Romanic
ACIMNOS anosmic, masonic
ACIMNOU manicou
ACIMNPU panicum
ACIMNRS narcism
ACIMNRT mantric
ACIMNRU cranium
ACIMNTT catmint
ACIMNTW twin-cam
ACIMOPT potamic, tampico
ACIMOST somatic
ACIMPRT ptarmic
ACIMPRY primacy
ACIMRSU muscari
ACIMSST miscast
ACINNOR Corinna
ACINNOS canions
ACINNOT contain
ACINNST stannic
ACINNTU annicut
ACINOPP popinac
ACINOPR procain
ACINOPT caption, paction, pantoic, Pontiac
ACINOQU coquina
ACINORR carrion
ACINORT carotin, cortina
ACINORV corvina
ACINOSS caisson, cassino
ACINOSY syconia
ACINOTT taction
ACINOTU auction, caution
ACINPRS priscan
ACINPRT cantrip
ACINPRU Puranic
ACINPRY Cyprian
ACINQTU quantic
ACINRSS narciss
ACINRSV scrivan
ACINRTT tantric
ACINRTU curtain, turacin
ACIOPRS prosaic
ACIOPRT apricot, aprotic, parotic, patrico
ACIOPST postica
ACIOPTY opacity

ACIORRS	corsair
ACIORSU	acrious, carious, curiosa
ACIORTT	ricotta
ACIORZZ	carozzi
ACIPRSY	piscary
ACIPRVY	privacy
ACIPSST	spastic
ACIPTUY	paucity
ACIQRTU	quartic
ACIQSTU	acquist
ACIRSST	sacrist
ACIRSSU	cuirass
ACIRSTT	astrict, tricast
ACIRSTY	satyric
ACIRTUY	raucity
ACISSTT	statics
ACISSTU	casuist
ACISSTV	sits vac
ACISTTU	catsuit
ACISTUV	vacuist
ACITUVY	vacuity
ACJKKSY	skyjack
ACJKLOW	lockjaw
ACJKNNO	jannock
ACJKNOS	Jackson
ACJKOPT	jackpot
ACJLORU	jocular
ACJMNTU	muntjac
ACJPTUU	cajuput
ACKKLMU	Kalmuck
ACKKOOR	cork oak
ACKLLOP	pollack
ACKLLOY	laylock
ACKLLSY	slackly
ACKLMNO	lockman
ACKLMOR	armlock, lockram
ACKLMOT	Matlock
ACKLNOU	uncloak
ACKLNUW	wanluck
ACKLOOR	oarlock
ACKLORW	warlock
ACKLOSS	lassock
ACKLOSY	yolk-sac
ACKMMMO	mammock
ACKMNOO	moonack
ACKMNRU	crankum
ACKMOTT	mattock
ACKNORY	Conakry
ACKNPUU	puckaun
ACKOPRR	parrock
ACKORRT	tarrock
ACKOWZZ	wazzock
ACLLLOY	locally
ACLLMMO	Malcolm
ACLLMOS	scallom
ACLLOOR	corolla
ACLLOPS	scallop
ACLLORU	locular
ACLLOST	scallot
ACLLOSU	callous
ACLLOTU	call-out
ACLLOVY	vocally

ACLMNOU	columna
ACLMNUY	calumny
ACLMORU	clamour
ACLMSUY	masculy
ACLNOOR	coronal
ACLNOOT	coolant, octonal
ACLNOOV	volcano
ACLNORT	Carlton
ACLNORW	crownal
ACLNORY	Carolyn
ACLNOTU	cola nut
ACLNOTY	Clayton
ACLNOUV	vulcano
ACLNPSU	unclasp
ACLNPTU	punctal
ACLNRTU	truncal
ACLNSTY	scantly
ACLOORT	locator
ACLOORZ	Corozal
ACLOPRT	caltrop
ACLOPRU	copular
ACLOPSU	copulas, scopula
ACLOPSY	calypso
ACLORST	scrotal
ACLORSU	Carolus, oscular
ACLOSTU	locusta, talcous
ACLRSSY	crassly
ACLRSTU	crustal
ACLRSTY	crystal
ACLRSWY	scrawly
ACLSSTU	cutlass
ACMNOPR	crampon
ACMNOPY	company
ACMNORY	acronym
ACMNSTU	sanctum
ACMOOST	moscato, scotoma
ACMOPRT	compart
ACMOPSS	compass
ACMQTUU	cumquat
ACMRSSU	sacrums
ACMRSTU	castrum
ACMSUUV	vacuums
ACNNNUY	uncanny
ACNNORS	consarn
ACNNORY	canonry
ACNNOSY	sonancy
ACNNRSY	scranny
ACNOORR	carroon
ACNOORT	cartoon, coranto
ACNOPSW	snowcap
ACNORRU	rancour
ACNORRY	carry-on
ACNORST	contras
ACNORSU	carnous, nacrous
ACNORTU	courant
ACNOSTU	conatus
ACNPRSY	syncarp
ACNPRTU	turn-cap

ACNRRTU	currant
ACNRSWY	scrawny
ACNRTUV	curvant
ACNRTUY	truancy
ACNSSTU	sanctus
ACOOPRR	corpora, parroco
ACOOPSU	opacous
ACOOPTT	topcoat
ACOORTU	touraco
ACOPPRR	procarp
ACOPRRT	carport
ACORRTT	tractor
ACORRTU	curator
ACORRTY	carroty
ACORSSU	sarcous
ACORSTU	surcoat
ACORSUU	raucous
ACORTTY	cottary
ACOSTTU	outcast
ACOSUUV	vacuous
ACPPRSY	scrappy
ACRSTTU	tractus
ADDDDOR	doddard
ADDDEEN	dead end
ADDDEER	dreaded
ADDDEGL	gladded
ADDDENO	deodand
ADDDGOR	goddard
ADDEEEY	deadeye
ADDEEFM	defamed
ADDEEGR	degrade
ADDEEHR	redhead
ADDEELP	pedaled, pleaded
ADDEELR	Eldreda, red lead
ADDEELY	delayed
ADDEEMN	dead men
ADDEEMR	dreamed
ADDEEST	dead set
ADDEETU	due date
ADDEFIR	faddier
ADDEFRU	defraud
ADDEGGR	dragged
ADDEGHO	godhead
ADDEGIL	gladdie
ADDEGJU	adjudge
ADDEGLN	gladden
ADDEGLR	gladder
ADDEGRU	guarded
ADDEHIR	diehard
ADDEHLN	handled
ADDEIIM	diamide
ADDEILL	dialled
ADDEILP	plaided
ADDEIMN	aminded
ADDEINO	adenoid
ADDEINR	dandier
ADDEINU	unaided, unidea'd
ADDEINV	videnda
ADDEIOT	iodated
ADDEIPV	dive-dap
ADDEISV	advised

ADDEISY dayside
ADDEITU audited
ADDEJLY jadedly
ADDELLU dualled
ADDELOR old dear
ADDELPP dappled
ADDELPR paddler
ADDELRS saddler
ADDELRW dawdler, waddler
ADDELRY dreadly
ADDELST staddle
ADDELSW swaddle
ADDELTW twaddle
ADDELYZ dazedly
ADDEMST maddest
ADDENPU pudenda
ADDENSU asudden
ADDENTU undated
ADDEPST stepdad
ADDERSS address
ADDERSW swarded
ADDERTT dratted
ADDESST saddest
ADDFHIS faddish
ADDFILY faddily
ADDFIMS faddism
ADDFINY dandify
ADDFIST faddist
ADDGGIN gadding
ADDGIIR diagrid
ADDGILR gildard
ADDGIMN madding
ADDGINP padding
ADDGINW wadding
ADDGLNO gladdon
ADDGORW godward
ADDGOST dodgast
ADDGOSY dog days
ADDHIKS Kaddish
ADDHILS laddish
ADDHISS saddish
ADDHITY hydatid
ADDHLNO old hand
ADDHPRU dhrupad
ADDIIMR Diarmid
ADDIINS disdain
ADDIIPS diapsid
ADDIKST tsaddik
ADDIKTY katydid
ADDILMN midland
ADDILMO old maid
ADDIMNO diamond
ADDIMOR mordida
ADDIMRW midward
ADDINOR android, Dorinda
ADDIRZZ dizzard
ADDKLNU Dundalk
ADDLLOY old lady
ADDLLRU dullard
ADDLNRY dry land
ADDNNOR donnard
ADDORTT dottard
ADDQSUY squaddy

ADEEEFS defease
ADEEEPS deep sea
ADEEESW seaweed
ADEEFLR Elfreda, federal
ADEEFLT deflate
ADEEFMR defamer, deframe
ADEEFRT draftee
ADEEFRW wafered
ADEEGGH egghead
ADEEGGN engaged
ADEEGLL alleged
ADEEGLU leagued
ADEEGLV gaveled
ADEEGLY glad eye
ADEEGLZ deglaze
ADEEGMN endgame
ADEEGNN dennage
ADEEGNR derange, grandee, grenade
ADEEGOT dogeate
ADEEGRR regrade
ADEEGRU guardee
ADEEGRW ragweed
ADEEHIR headier
ADEEHKS sedekah
ADEEHLZ hazeled
ADEEHNN hennaed
ADEEHNS dasheen
ADEEHPR ephedra, pre-head
ADEEHRR reheard
ADEEHRS sheared
ADEEHRT hearted, red heat
ADEEHRX exhedra
ADEEHST headset
ADEEHSY hayseed
ADEEIJT jadeite
ADEEILM limeade
ADEEILN Adeline, delaine
ADEEIMT mediate
ADEEINN adenine
ADEEINP penaeid
ADEEINS aniseed
ADEEIRR readier
ADEEISS disease, seaside
ADEEITV deviate
ADEEKMR merdeka
ADEEKNR kneader
ADEEKNS sneaked
ADEEKWY weekday
ADEELLS allseed
ADEELMM melamed
ADEELMP emplead
ADEELMR emerald
ADEELMS measled
ADEELMT metaled
ADEELMZ Demelza
ADEELNP deplane, paneled

ADEELNR Darlene, Leander, learned
ADEELNS sand eel
ADEELNT al dente
ADEELNW Aledwen, new deal, Wealden
ADEELPR pearled, pedaler, pleader
ADEELPS delapse, pleased
ADEELPT depetal
ADEELQU equaled
ADEELRT related, treadle
ADEELRV raveled
ADEELRW leeward
ADEELRY delayer, layered
ADEELTV valeted
ADEELUV devalue
ADEEMNR amender, meander
ADEEMNS seedman
ADEEMOP apodeme
ADEEMRR dreamer
ADEEMRT determa, red meat
ADEEMSU medusae
ADEEMSW mawseed
ADEEMWY mayweed
ADEENOT donatee
ADEENRV Evander
ADEENRY deanery, year-end
ADEENST East End, standee
ADEENTT Danette, dentate
ADEEORW oarweed
ADEEOVW advowee
ADEEPRT predate, red tape
ADEEPRV deprave, pervade
ADEERRT retread, treader
ADEERRV averred, Everard
ADEERST dearest, estrade
ADEERSV adverse
ADEERTW dewater, watered
ADEESTT estated
ADEESTW sweated
ADEETUX exudate
ADEFFIN affined
ADEFFIR daffier
ADEFFLO lead-off
ADEFFST staffed
ADEFGGL flagged
ADEFGLO foldage

ADEFGLR	red flag
ADEFGOT	fagoted
ADEFGOU	fougade
ADEFIIL	Fidelia
ADEFILR	Elfrida
ADEFIMS	disfame
ADEFINT	defiant
ADEFIPR	dapifer
ADEFLLW	dewfall
ADEFLNN	fenland
ADEFLOR	fordeal
ADEFLPP	flapped
ADEFLRU	dareful
ADEFLTT	flatted
ADEFLTU	default
ADEFMNR	Manfred
ADEFNUZ	unfazed
ADEFOOS	seafood
ADEFORY	feodary
ADEFOTU	fade-out
ADEFPPR	frapped
ADEFRRT	drafter, redraft
ADEFRUY	feudary
ADEGGHS	shagged
ADEGGIR	daggier
ADEGGLR	draggle
ADEGGLS	slagged
ADEGGNS	snagged
ADEGGOP	pedagog
ADEGGRY	raggedy
ADEGGST	stagged
ADEGGSW	swagged
ADEGGTT	daggett
ADEGGTY	gadgety
ADEGHIN	heading
ADEGHIR	hag-ride
ADEGILN	dealing, leading
ADEGILT	lidgate
ADEGILY	lygaeid
ADEGINR	deraign, gradine, grained, reading
ADEGINW	windage
ADEGIOT	godetia
ADEGIOV	voidage
ADEGIRU	gaudier
ADEGIRV	Rig-Veda
ADEGISV	visaged
ADEGIUV	viduage
ADEGLLO	allodge
ADEGLMM	glammed
ADEGLMO	Gaeldom
ADEGLNO	Donegal
ADEGLNR	dangler, glander, gnarled, rangled
ADEGLNS	glandes
ADEGLNU	langued
ADEGLOP	galoped
ADEGLPU	plagued
ADEGLRU	raguled
ADEGLRY	gradely
ADEGMNN	mendang
ADEGMNU	agendum
ADEGMOP	megapod
ADEGNNU	dunnage
ADEGNOP	pondage
ADEGNOR	grenado
ADEGNPU	unpaged
ADEGNRT	dragnet
ADEGNUW	unwaged
ADEGORS	dog's-ear
ADEGORV	gravedo
ADEGORW	dowager, wordage
ADEGORZ	Gorazde
ADEGOTT	togated
ADEGPRU	upgrade
ADEGRRR	Gerrard
ADEGRTY	tragedy
ADEGRUY	gaudery
ADEGSSU	degauss
ADEHHOP	hophead
ADEHHOT	hothead
ADEHILL	Delilah
ADEHILP	helipad
ADEHILS	leadish
ADEHILY	headily
ADEHINP	pinhead
ADEHINR	handier
ADEHINY	hyaenid
ADEHIPR	raphide
ADEHIPS	aphides
ADEHIPT	pithead
ADEHIRR	hardier
ADEHIRS	shadier
ADEHIRW	rawhide
ADEHJMS	Jamshed
ADEHKNS	shanked
ADEHKOT	kathode
ADEHLLM	Aldhelm
ADEHLLO	hollaed
ADEHLNR	handler
ADEHLNS	handsel
ADEHLOP	Adolphe
ADEHLRY	heraldy
ADEHLSS	slashed
ADEHLSW	shawled
ADEHLTY	deathly
ADEHMMS	shammed
ADEHMMW	whammed
ADEHMNR	herdman
ADEHMOP	mophead
ADEHMOR	hadrome
ADEHNRU	unheard
ADEHNSS	sandesh
ADEHNST	handset
ADEHOPT	pothead
ADEHOPX	hexapod
ADEHORR	hard roe, hoarder
ADEHOTT	to death
ADEHOTW	tow-head
ADEHRSY	hydrase
ADEHRTY	hydrate, thready
ADEIILP	plaidie
ADEIILS	sedilia
ADEIIMN	amidine, diamine
ADEIINR	denarii
ADEIINT	inedita
ADEIINZ	diazine
ADEIIPR	peridia
ADEIIRR	Airdrie
ADEIIRS	airside, diarise
ADEIIRZ	diarize
ADEIJUZ	Judaize
ADEIKLN	dekalin, knaidel
ADEIKLR	Kildare
ADEIKLY	kaylied
ADEILLO	Deolali
ADEILLR	dialler
ADEILLS	disleal
ADEILLY	ideally
ADEILMM	dilemma
ADEILMN	Melinda
ADEILMO	melodia
ADEILMP	implead
ADEILMS	misdeal, mislead
ADEILNN	annelid, lindane
ADEILNR	Ireland
ADEILNT	land-tie, tail-end
ADEILNU	aliunde, unideal
ADEILNW	new-laid
ADEILOP	Oedipal
ADEILOR	dariole, radiole
ADEILPP	applied
ADEILPR	lip-read, predial
ADEILPS	palsied
ADEILPT	plaited
ADEILRT	dilater, trialed
ADEILRV	derival, rivaled
ADEILRY	readily
ADEILSU	dualise
ADEILSY	dialyse
ADEILUZ	dualize
ADEILYZ	dialyze
ADEIMMR	mermaid
ADEIMNO	domaine
ADEIMNR	Amerind, marined
ADEIMNT	mediant
ADEIMRR	admirer, married
ADEIMRS	misread
ADEIMRT	readmit
ADEIMST	diastem, Mideast, misdate
ADEIMTY	daytime
ADEINOR	aneroid

ADEINOX dioxane
ADEINOZ anodize
ADEINPR indrape
ADEINPS pansied
ADEINPT depaint, inadept, painted
ADEINRR darrein, drainer, randier
ADEINRS sandier, sardine
ADEINRT detrain, trade-in, trained
ADEINRV invader, ravined, viander
ADEINST destain, instead, sainted, satined
ADEINTT tainted
ADEINTU audient
ADEINTV deviant
ADEIOPS adipose
ADEIORV avoider
ADEIORX exordia
ADEIOSX oxidase
ADEIOTX oxidate
ADEIOVV vaivode
ADEIPPR drappie, prepaid
ADEIPRR rapider
ADEIPRS despair
ADEIPRT Perdita
ADEIPSS apsides, aspides
ADEIQRU querida
ADEIRRS irrased
ADEIRRT tardier
ADEIRST astride, diaster, disrate
ADEIRSU residua
ADEIRSV adviser
ADEIRTV tardive
ADEIRTW wardite
ADEIRTY dietary
ADEISTV vistaed
ADEISTW waisted
ADEISTY Tayside
ADEISWY wayside
ADEITUV viduate
ADEITUZ deutzia
ADEITWY tideway
ADEJOPR jeopard
ADEKLLN Kendall
ADEKLNS kalends
ADEKLNY nakedly
ADEKLOP polkaed
ADEKLST stalked
ADEKMNR Denmark
ADEKNPP knapped
ADEKNSU unasked
ADEKNVY vandyke

ADELLMU medulla
ADELLNW ell-wand
ADELLNY Leyland
ADELLPW lap-weld
ADELLRR Darrell
ADELMMS slammed
ADELMNN landmen
ADELMNO lodeman
ADELMNR mandrel
ADELMNT mantled
ADELMOR earldom, moraled
ADELMOS damosel
ADELMPY pelamyd
ADELNNP planned
ADELNNU unladen
ADELNOR ladrone, Leonard
ADELNOT taloned
ADELNPY end-play
ADELNRS slander
ADELNRU Arundel, launder
ADELNST Stendal
ADELNTW wetland
ADELNTZ Zetland
ADELNUU Ulan Ude
ADELOPR leopard
ADELOPS deposal
ADELOPT tadpole
ADELORS Sea Lord
ADELORT delator, leotard
ADELORU roulade
ADELORY old year
ADELOTT toadlet, totaled
ADELOTU lead-out
ADELPPS slapped
ADELPRY pedlary
ADELPTT platted
ADELPTY adeptly
ADELRRU ruderal
ADELRRW drawler
ADELRSS aldress
ADELRTU adulter
ADELRTX dextral
ADELRZZ dazzler
ADELSSY dayless
ADELSTT slatted
ADELTTW wattled
ADELTUV vaulted
ADEMNNU mundane, unnamed
ADEMNOR mandore, omander
ADEMNOS monades, nomades
ADEMNOZ Mendoza
ADEMNPR predamn
ADEMNRU duramen, maunder, unarmed
ADEMNSS desmans, madness

ADEMNSU medusan
ADEMNTU untamed
ADEMOSY Samoyed, someday
ADEMOWY meadowy
ADEMRRU eardrum
ADEMSSU medusas
ADENNOY anodyne
ADENNPS spanned
ADENNPT pendant
ADENNRT dannert
ADENNSW swanned
ADENNTT tendant
ADENOOT odonate
ADENOPR aproned, operand, padrone, pandore
ADENOPS dapsone, espadon
ADENOPT notepad, tonepad
ADENOPY open day
ADENORR red roan
ADENORU rondeau
ADENORV Andover
ADENOST onstead
ADENPPS snapped
ADENPRR pardner
ADENPSX Spandex
ADENPSY dyspnea
ADENPUV unpaved
ADENRRS Randers
ADENRRW redrawn
ADENRRY Reynard
ADENRSS sanders
ADENRST stander
ADENRSU asunder, danseur
ADENRTU durante, natured
ADENRTV ventrad, verdant
ADENRTX dextran
ADENRTY dentary
ADENRUY unready
ADENSSS sadness
ADENSUV unsaved
ADENSWY endways
ADENTUX untaxed
ADEOORT odorate
ADEOPRR pedraro
ADEOPRT readopt
ADEOPRW podware
ADEORRS drosera
ADEORST estrado, torsade
ADEORTU outdare, read-out
ADEORYZ zedoary
ADEOWWY waywode
ADEPPRT trapped
ADEPPRW wrapped
ADEPPSW swapped
ADEPRRS sparred

ADEPRRY drapery
ADEPSTT spatted
ADERRST Red Star, starred
ADERSSU assured
ADERSTW steward
ADERSTY rest day
ADERSUY dasyure
ADERSVW dwarves
ADESTTU statued
ADESTTW swatted
ADESTUY Tuesday
ADFFHNO hand-off, offhand
ADFFILY daffily
ADFFIST distaff
ADFFLOO offload
ADFFOOR off-road
ADFFORW offward
ADFGILO fidalgo
ADFGLLO dog-fall
ADFGLLU gladful
ADFHLNU handful
ADFHOOS shadoof
ADFHORS Ashford
ADFIIMT Fatimid
ADFILLU fluidal
ADFILNN Finland
ADFILOR Florida
ADFIMNY damnify
ADFINRT indraft
ADFIORS frisado
ADFIORZ frizado
ADFIOTU fatuoid
ADFJORU foujdar
ADFLMOO damfool
ADFLMPU mudflap
ADFLMTU mudflat
ADFLNOP plafond
ADFLNSY sandfly
ADFLORS Salford
ADFLORU foulard
ADFNNOR Farndon
ADFNNOT fondant
ADFOOPT footpad
ADFOORS forsado
ADFORRW forward, froward
ADFORTW dowfart, Watford
ADFPRTU updraft
ADGGGIN dagging
ADGGHNO hangdog
ADGGILN gadling
ADGGINR niggard
ADGGLRU luggard
ADGGLRY draggly
ADGHHIY high day
ADGHILO hidalgo
ADGHINS dashing, shading
ADGHIPR digraph
ADGHIRS dishrag
ADGHNNU handgun
ADGHNOS sandhog
ADGHNOV Godhavn
ADGHOOR road hog
ADGHRTU draught
ADGIILN dialing, gliadin
ADGIILT digital
ADGIINU guiniad
ADGILNN landing
ADGILNO digonal, loading
ADGILNR darling
ADGILNU languid
ADGILNW gladwin
ADGILOR goliard
ADGILOT dog-tail
ADGILRY day-girl
ADGILSU gladius
ADGILUY gaudily
ADGIMMN damming
ADGINNR darning, randing
ADGINNW dawning
ADGINOR adoring
ADGINPP dapping
ADGINPW wind gap
ADGINRT trading
ADGINRW drawing, warding
ADGINWY gwyniad
ADGIPRU pagurid
ADGIRRS grisard
ADGIRSU guisard
ADGIRZZ gizzard
ADGLLOR rag doll
ADGLMNO mangold
ADGLNOO dongola, gondola
ADGLNOR goldarn
ADGLNOY day-long, long-day
ADGLNRY grandly
ADGLOOV Vologda
ADGLORY Gaylord
ADGLOSU Douglas
ADGLSWY Gwladys
ADGMNOO goodman, Mogadon
ADGNOOR dragoon, gadroon
ADGNORS dragons
ADGNORU aground
ADGNORY organdy
ADGNRRU drungar, gurnard
ADGNRUU unguard
ADGORST dog-star
ADGORZZ gozzard
ADHHIRS hardish
ADHHIRT hard hit
ADHHMOS shahdom
ADHHNOT hand-hot
ADHIIKS dashiki
ADHIIMS Hasidim, maidish
ADHIKRS darkish
ADHILMO halidom
ADHILNY handily
ADHILOP haploid
ADHILOY holiday, hyaloid
ADHILRY hardily
ADHILSY shadily
ADHIMMS Mahdism
ADHIMMU mahmudi
ADHIMPS dampish, phasmid
ADHIMRS Midrash
ADHIMST Mahdist
ADHINNP daphnin
ADHINPS shin-pad
ADHINPU dauphin
ADHIOST doatish, toadish
ADHIRSW drawish
ADHLLLO holdall
ADHLLNO holland
ADHLMPY lymphad
ADHLOYY holy day
ADHMMNO Hammond
ADHMNOO hoodman, manhood
ADHMNPY Dymphna
ADHMNWY Wyndham
ADHNNUY unhandy
ADHNOTU handout
ADHNOVZ Zhdanov
ADHNRTU hard nut
ADHNRTY hydrant
ADHOORR rhodora
ADHOPRT hard-top
ADHOPST dashpot
ADHOSWY shadowy
ADIIILR iridial
ADIIINR iridian
ADIILMS dismail, misdial
ADIILNU iulidan
ADIILNV invalid
ADIILST dialist
ADIILUV diluvia
ADIIMPV impavid
ADIIMSS missaid
ADIINOS Sidonia
ADIINPR pridian
ADIINST distain
ADIINSU indusia
ADIIORT otariid
ADIIPRS dispair
ADIIPTU tupaiid
ADIIPXY pyxidia
ADIIRST diarist
ADIIRTY aridity
ADIITVY avidity
ADIJKOR koradji
ADIJMSU Judaism
ADIJNNO Andijon
ADIJNOT adjoint
ADIJSTU Judaist
ADIKLPS klipdas
ADIKMNN mankind

ADIKMRS dismark
ADIKMSS dismask
ADIKNPS skid-pan
ADIKNRS disrank
ADIKNRU udarnik
ADIKPRS dispark
ADIKQRU diquark
ADILLLY diallyl
ADILLMM mill-dam
ADILLOY lloydia
ADILLPY lily pad
ADILLRW Willard
ADILLTY tidally
ADILLVY validly
ADILLYY day lily
ADILMNO doliman, mondial
ADILMNU maudlin
ADILMOP diploma
ADILMOY amyloid
ADILMPS plasmid
ADILMRU Mildura
ADILMSU dualism
ADILNOR laidron, Lorinda, ordinal
ADILNOS oil-sand
ADILNRT darlint
ADILNRU diurnal
ADILNRY randily
ADILNSS Islands
ADILNSU sundial
ADILNSY Lindsay
ADILOOZ zooidal
ADILOPR dipolar
ADILORT dilator
ADILOSU diaulos
ADILOTU outlaid, touladi
ADILOTW wild oat
ADILPRY pyralid, rapidly
ADILPST plastid
ADILPSY display
ADILPTU plaudit
ADILPVY vapidly
ADILQSU squalid
ADILRTY tardily
ADILSTU dualist
ADILSTY staidly
ADILTUY duality
ADIMNNO mondain
ADIMNOR morinda
ADIMNOS Madison
ADIMNOZ Nazidom
ADIMOOR maroodi
ADIMORR mirador
ADIMOST mastoid
ADIMOTT mattoid
ADIMPRT drip-mat
ADIMPRY pyramid
ADIMRSW misdraw
ADIMRSY diasyrm
ADIMSST dismast
ADIMSTU stadium
ADINNOP dipnoan
ADINNOR andiron
ADINNRS innards
ADINNRW indrawn
ADINNST stand-in
ADINOOP poinado
ADINOOR in-a-door
ADINOPP oppidan
ADINOPR poniard
ADINOPT pintado
ADINORR ordinar, randori
ADINORS sad-iron
ADINOSV Novi Sad
ADINOTX oxidant
ADINPST sandpit
ADINRSW inwards
ADINRTU triduan
ADINSTT distant
ADINTTY dittany
ADIOOSW woodsia
ADIOPRR airdrop
ADIOPRT parotid
ADIOPRV privado
ADIORST astroid
ADIORSU radious, sauroid
ADIORTU auditor
ADIOSUV Vaudois
ADIOSVW disavow
ADIPRST dispart
ADIPRSU Dispura, Saidpur
ADIPRTY day trip, pay dirt
ADIPRUU Udaipur
ADIRSSU sardius
ADIRSTU dasturi
ADIRSTY satyrid
ADIRSUY dysuria
ADIRTTY tardity
ADISTTY saditty
ADJNNOU Don Juan
ADJNORU adjourn
ADJORTU adjutor
ADKLMRU mudlark
ADKORWY daywork, workday
ADKRSWY skyward
ADLLLOR Lollard
ADLLMOY modally
ADLLNOW lowland
ADLLOPR pollard
ADLLORW Law Lord
ADLLOST old salt
ADLLRWY drywall
ADLLTUY adultly
ADLMOOV Moldova
ADLMORU modular
ADLNNOR norland
ADLNOOR lardoon, Orlando
ADLNOOS sandolo
ADLNOPU poundal
ADLNORT troland
ADLNORU nodular
ADLNORW Rowland
ADLNOST sandlot
ADLNOSY synodal
ADLNOTU outland
ADLNRTU Rutland
ADLNRUY laundry
ADLNTWY Tynwald
ADLOOTW talwood
ADLOPRU poulard
ADLOPVY poldavy
ADLORRW warlord
ADLORUY Our Lady
ADLOSSW Sod's Law
ADLRSTY dry-salt
ADMNOOR doorman
ADMNOOW woodman
ADMNOQU quondam
ADMNORT dormant, mordant
ADMNORY Raymond
ADMNOSU osmunda
ADMNRUY Raymund
ADMNSTU dustman
ADMOOPP popadom
ADMOORT doormat
ADMOORY day room
ADMOPST post-dam, Potsdam
ADMORST stardom, tsardom
ADMORTW madwort
ADMRSTU durmast, mustard
ADNNOOV Donovan
ADNNOOY noonday
ADNNRTU dunnart
ADNNSTU Dunstan
ADNOOPR pandoor
ADNOORT donator, odorant, tandoor, tornado
ADNOOSS so-and-so
ADNOPRU pandour
ADNOPRV provand
ADNORRW norward
ADNORSW onwards
ADNORTU rotunda, tandour
ADNORTY tardyon
ADNORWY nayword
ADNOSTT stand-to
ADNOSTU astound
ADNOTWY Wyandot
ADNPSTU dustpan, stand-up
ADNRSUW sunward
ADNSTYY dynasty
ADOOPSU apodous
ADOOPSW sapwood
ADOORTU outroad
ADOORTW wood rat
ADOORWY doorway
ADOOWWX woodwax

ADORSTW towards
ADORSTY stay-rod
ADORSUU arduous
ADORTUW outward
ADPRSUW upwards
ADSSTUW sawdust
AEEEGGN engagee
AEEEGLT legatee
AEEEGNT teenage
AEEEGPR peerage
AEEEGPS seepage
AEEEGRT etagere
AEEEKMN eke-name
AEEELNR Raelene
AEEELRS release
AEEELTV elevate
AEEENVW enweave
AEEERTT tea-tree
AEEFFLL felafel
AEEFFMR fee-farm
AEEFGRS serfage
AEEFHMS mafeesh
AEEFHRT feather
AEEFILR filaree, leafier
AEEFILW alewife
AEEFIRS freesia
AEEFLLN Fenella
AEEFLLT fellate, leaflet
AEEFLMN enflame
AEEFLRT reflate
AEEFLRW welfare
AEEFLRY leafery
AEEFLRZ alferez
AEEFLSU easeful
AEEFLTX telefax
AEEFMNR enframe, freeman
AEEFNRS safener
AEEFORS Faroese
AEEFOTV foveate
AEEFRRT ferrate
AEEFRST feaster
AEEFRTU feature
AEEFRTX tax-free
AEEFRWY freeway
AEEFSSX safe sex
AEEGGLR gregale
AEEGGLT gateleg
AEEGGNT taggeen
AEEGHNN Gehenna
AEEGHNW whangee
AEEGHSU euhages
AEEGILL galilee
AEEGILM mileage
AEEGILN lineage
AEEGILP epigeal
AEEGILW weigela
AEEGINP epigean
AEEGINU eugenia
AEEGIRT Reigate
AEEGISS assiege
AEEGLLN leangle
AEEGLLZ gazelle
AEEGLNR enlarge, general, gleaner
AEEGLNS Senegal
AEEGLNT angelet, elegant
AEEGLNU euglena
AEEGLNV evangel
AEEGLNY galeeny
AEEGLRU glue ear, leaguer
AEEGLRY eagerly
AEEGLRZ reglaze
AEEGLSS ageless, sea legs
AEEGLSU leagues
AEEGLSV selvage
AEEGLTT galette
AEEGLTV gavelet, vegetal
AEEGMMT gemmate, tagmeme
AEEGMNR germane
AEEGMSS message
AEEGNNP pangene, pennage
AEEGNNR enrange
AEEGNOP peonage
AEEGNPP genappe
AEEGNRS gesnera
AEEGNRT grantee, greaten, negater, reagent
AEEGNRV avenger, engrave, Genevra, vernage
AEEGNTT tentage
AEEGNTV ventage
AEEGORV overage
AEEGPRS asperge, presage
AEEGPSS pegasse
AEEGRRS greaser
AEEGRRT greater, terrage
AEEGRST restage
AEEGRSV Gervase, greaves
AEEGRTU treague
AEEGRUZ guereza
AEEGSTT gestate, tagetes
AEEGTTZ gazette
AEEHHNT heathen
AEEHHOV heave-ho
AEEHHRT heather
AEEHHST sheathe
AEEHIMT hiemate
AEEHINR herniae
AEEHIRV heavier
AEEHIST atheise
AEEHITZ atheize
AEEHJKN khanjee
AEEHKNR hearken
AEEHKNT thankee
AEEHLMS maleesh
AEEHLNT Lethean
AEEHLOR earhole
AEEHLPT heeltap
AEEHLRT haltere, leather
AEEHLSY eyelash
AEEHLTT athlete
AEEHMNT methane
AEEHMRS mahseer
AEEHMRT thermae
AEEHMST the same
AEEHMSV Evesham
AEEHMTY hyemate
AEEHNPT heptane
AEEHNRT earthen, hearten
AEEHNSV heavens
AEEHNTW wheaten
AEEHPRS reshape
AEEHPRT preheat
AEEHPUV upheave
AEEHRRS shearer
AEEHRST Theresa
AEEHRSW whereas
AEEHRTT teather, theater, theatre, thereat
AEEHRTV threave
AEEHRTW weather, whate'er, whereat, wreathe
AEEHSST assethe
AEEHSSV sheaves
AEEHSWY eyewash
AEEIJNN Jeannie
AEEIKLR leakier
AEEIKLS sealike
AEEIKPR peakier
AEEILLU Eulalie
AEEILMN Melanie
AEEILMP pimelea
AEEILMR mealier
AEEILMS sea mile
AEEILNP alepine
AEEILNT lineate
AEEILNV Aveline, Evelina
AEEILPR Pearlie
AEEILPT epilate, pileate
AEEILRR earlier
AEEILRT atelier
AEEILRV Valerie
AEEILRZ realize
AEEILTT ailette
AEEILTV elative
AEEILTX elixate
AEEIMNS nemesia
AEEIMNT etamine, matinee
AEEIMNX examine

AEEIMPR epimera
AEEIMRS seamier, seriema
AEEIMRT emirate, meatier
AEEIMSS misease, Siamese
AEEIMTT teatime
AEEINPT peineta
AEEINRT arenite, retinae, trainee
AEEINST Etesian
AEEINTT taenite
AEEINTV Venetia
AEEINVW inweave
AEEIORT etaerio
AEEIPRR Pereira
AEEIPTX expiate
AEEIRRT Eritrea
AEEIRRW wearier
AEEIRST seriate
AEEIRTT iterate
AEEIRTV evirate
AEEISST easiest
AEEISTT aetites
AEEISTV aestive
AEEISVV evasive
AEEITTV evitate
AEEIUVX exuviae
AEEJLNY Jayleen
AEEJNTT Janette
AEEJRSW Jew's ear
AEEJTTU jetteau
AEEKKNO kokanee
AEEKLLT lakelet
AEEKLNT kantele
AEEKMRT meerkat
AEEKMSY eye mask
AEEKNNN nankeen
AEEKNNP knee-pan
AEEKNRS sneaker
AEEKNRT keertan, retaken
AEEKPRS speaker
AEEKRRW wreaker
AEEKRTU kuteera
AEELLLV velella
AEELLMM mamelle
AEELLST Estella
AEELLTV tavelle
AEELLWY wall-eye
AEELMNP empanel, emplane
AEELMNR Marlene
AEELMNT manteel
AEELMNU Emanuel
AEELMNV velamen
AEELMPR empearl
AEELMPX example, exempla
AEELMSS measles
AEELMST Maltese
AEELMTU aumelet, emulate
AEELNNP enplane
AEELNOR Eleanor
AEELNRR learner, relearn
AEELNRT enteral, eternal, teneral
AEELNRU Laureen
AEELNRV Laverne, veneral
AEELNRW renewal
AEELNSV enslave
AEELNTT latteen
AEELNUZ azulene
AEELOPR parolee
AEELOPX poleaxe
AEELORU aureole
AEELPRR pearler
AEELPRS relapse
AEELPRT prelate
AEELPRU pleurae
AEELPTT palette, peltate
AEELPTU epaulet
AEELQSU sequela
AEELRRT relater
AEELRRX relaxer
AEELRSS earless
AEELRST stealer
AEELRSV several
AEELRSY sealery
AEELRUV revalue
AEELSTT Seattle, tsatlee
AEELSTX latexes
AEELTTY layette
AEELTVW wavelet
AEEMMMR maremme
AEEMMPY empyema
AEEMMRT ammeter, metamer
AEEMNNO anemone
AEEMNNP pen-name
AEEMNPT pet name
AEEMNRU Maureen
AEEMNSS en masse
AEEMORT erotema
AEEMOSW awesome
AEEMPRT tempera
AEEMPTU amputee
AEEMQRU marquee
AEEMRRS smearer
AEEMRST steamer
AEEMRSU measure
AEEMRTX extrema
AEEMSTW Mae West
AEENNOT neonate
AEENNPT pennate, pentane
AEENNRS ensnare
AEENNRT traneen
AEENNTT Annette, Nanette
AEENNTU uneaten
AEENOPS open sea
AEENORS arenose
AEENORT onerate
AEENPRT terpane
AEENPST penates
AEENPSX expanse
AEENRRT terrane
AEENRRV ravener
AEENRRY yearner
AEENRST earnest, eastern
AEENRTT entreat, ratteen, ternate
AEENRTV nervate, veteran
AEENRVY Yerevan
AEENRWY new year
AEENSST entases, sensate
AEENSTT enstate
AEENTTV navette, vanette
AEENVWW new wave
AEEOPRT operate
AEEORST roseate, tea rose
AEEORSV oversea
AEEORTV overate, overeat
AEEORVW overawe
AEEPPRR paperer, prepare, repaper
AEEPRRT taperer
AEEPRSS asperse, pareses, praeses
AEEPRSW seerpaw
AEEPRTU epurate
AEEPRTZ trapeze
AEEPSTT septate
AEEPTTT tapette
AEERRST serrate
AEERRSU erasure
AEERRSW swearer
AEERRTT retreat, treater
AEERRTW waterer
AEERRVW waverer
AEERSST erastes, tessera
AEERSSV assever
AEERSTT estreat, restate
AEERSTU austere
AEERSTV eve-star
AEERSTW sweater
AEERTTX extreat
AEERTWX wax-tree
AEESTTT testate
AEFFGIL fig leaf
AEFFGIR giraffe
AEFFGNR engraff
AEFFIPR piaffer
AEFFKOP off-peak

AEFFKOR	rake-off	**AEFILOT**	foliate	**AEFLSST**	fatless
AEFFKOT	offtake, take-off	**AEFILPT**	fleapit	**AEFLSTU**	festual, sulfate
AEFFLLY	flyleaf	**AEFILRU**	failure	**AEFLSUV**	vaseful
AEFFLMW	flamfew	**AEFILSS**	falsies	**AEFMNOR**	foramen, foreman
AEFFLNS	snaffle	**AEFILST**	festial	**AEFMNRU**	fraenum
AEFFLOS	off-sale	**AEFILTT**	flattie	**AEFMORR**	forearm
AEFFLRU	fearful	**AEFIMNR**	fireman, inframe	**AEFMORT**	formate
AEFFLRW	waffler	**AEFIMOR**	foamier	**AEFMPRU**	frame-up
AEFFLTU	fateful	**AEFIMRR**	firearm	**AEFMRRY**	farmery
AEFFMRU	earmuff, feu-farm	**AEFIMRS**	misfare	**AEFNOPR**	profane
AEFFMTU	effatum	**AEFINNR**	Frannie	**AEFNORR**	ferroan, foreran
AEFFORR	forfare	**AEFINNT**	infante	**AEFNORT**	Torfaen
AEFFORT	tear-off	**AEFINNZ**	fanzine	**AEFNOSS**	fossane
AEFFQRU	quaffer	**AEFINRR**	ferrian, refrain	**AEFNSST**	fatness
AEFFRST	staffer	**AEFINTX**	antefix	**AEFOPRW**	forepaw
AEFGGGO	foggage	**AEFIOTY**	foyaite	**AEFORRW**	forwear
AEFGGLR	flagger	**AEFIQRU**	aquifer	**AEFORRY**	forayer
AEFGIKN	Kaifeng	**AEFIRRR**	farrier	**AEFORSW**	foresaw
AEFGILN	finagle	**AEFIRRS**	Frasier	**AEFORSY**	foresay
AEFGILO	foliage	**AEFIRST**	set fair	**AEFRRTY**	fratery
AEFGILR	fragile	**AEFIRSX**	fair sex	**AEFRSTW**	Far West, fretsaw
AEFGIRS	gas fire	**AEFIRTT**	fattier	**AEFRTUW**	wafture
AEFGIRT	frigate	**AEFKLNR**	flanker	**AEFSTTT**	fattest
AEFGIRU	figurae, refugia	**AEFKLRT**	fartlek	**AEGGGLU**	luggage
AEFGITU	fatigue	**AEFKLST**	flasket	**AEGGHLR**	haggler
AEFGLLU	fullage	**AEFKLUW**	wakeful	**AEGGHRS**	shagger
AEFGLMU	gameful	**AEFKNPR**	krapfen	**AEGGIJR**	jaggier
AEFGLOT	flotage	**AEFKNRR**	franker	**AEGGINR**	gearing
AEFGNOR	far gone	**AEFKORS**	forsake	**AEGGINS**	signage
AEFGNRR	granfer	**AEFLLNN**	fannell, flannel	**AEGGIOR**	Georgia
AEFGNRT	engraft	**AEFLLOT**	floatel	**AEGGIOS**	isagoge
AEFGNRU	furnage	**AEFLLSY**	falsely	**AEGGIRU**	garigue
AEFGNTU	fungate	**AEFLLTT**	flatlet	**AEGGJRY**	jaggery
AEFGOOR	roofage	**AEFLMOR**	femoral	**AEGGLNO**	age-long
AEFGOOT	footage	**AEFLMTY**	meat-fly	**AEGGLNR**	gangrel
AEFGORR	forager	**AEFLNNN**	flannen	**AEGGLRY**	greylag
AEFGORV	forgave	**AEFLNOV**	flavone	**AEGGNRR**	granger
AEFGRRT	grafter	**AEFLNQU**	flanque	**AEGGNTU**	Gauteng
AEFGRSU	Feargus	**AEFLNRU**	earnful, funeral	**AEGGRSS**	aggress
AEFHILP	half-pie	**AEFLNTT**	flatten	**AEGGRST**	gagster, stagger
AEFHIRW	wharfie	**AEFLNUU**	faunule	**AEGGRSW**	swagger
AEFHISS	sea-fish	**AEFLOOV**	foveola	**AEGGRWY**	waggery
AEFHLOO	ale-hoof	**AEFLOPW**	peafowl	**AEGHHIS**	high sea
AEFHLOR	fahlore	**AEFLORS**	safrole	**AEGHHIT**	a-height, high tea
AEFHLRS	flasher	**AEFLORT**	floater, floreat, refloat	**AEGHHLS**	Shelagh
AEFHLRZ	fahlerz	**AEFLORW**	aflower	**AEGHILR**	Raleigh
AEFHLTU	hateful	**AEFLORY**	forelay	**AEGHINR**	hearing
AEFHRRT	farther	**AEFLPPR**	flapper	**AEGHINS**	gaishen
AEFIILT	filiate	**AEFLPPT**	flappet	**AEGHINT**	gahnite, heating
AEFIJLO	jeofail	**AEFLPRR**	frapler	**AEGHINZ**	genizah
AEFIKLN	fanlike	**AEFLPRS**	felspar	**AEGHISS**	geishas
AEFIKLR	flakier	**AEFLPRU**	flare-up	**AEGHLNO**	halogen
AEFIKNR	Frankie	**AEFLPRY**	palfrey	**AEGHLNT**	alength
AEFILLM	famille, ill fame	**AEFLQSU**	flasque	**AEGHLRU**	laugher
AEFILLR	illfare	**AEFLRSU**	fur seal, refusal	**AEGHLTW**	thalweg
AEFILMN	feminal, inflame	**AEFLRTT**	flatter	**AEGHMOR**	homager
AEFILMR	fermail	**AEFLRTU**	faulter, refutal, tearful	**AEGHMRS**	Gresham
AEFILNT	inflate	**AEFLRZZ**	frazzle	**AEGHMSU**	meshuga
AEFILNU	infulae				
AEFILNV	flavine				

AEGHNOX hexagon
AEGHNRU ahunger
AEGHNYZ Zhangye
AEGHOPY hypogea
AEGHOST hostage
AEGIIMN imagine
AEGIINN ingenia
AEGIINR Nigeria
AEGIKLN linkage
AEGIKNO Koganei
AEGIKNP peaking
AEGIKNS kisaeng, sinkage
AEGIKNV Kavieng
AEGIKPP kippage
AEGIKPR garpike
AEGIKRW gawkier
AEGILLL illegal
AEGILLN Gillean, liangle, nigella
AEGILLP pillage
AEGILLT tillage
AEGILLV village
AEGILLY agilely
AEGILMN geminal
AEGILMR gremial
AEGILMT time lag
AEGILNN angelin, leaning
AEGILNP leaping
AEGILNR engrail, inlarge, realign
AEGILNS sealing
AEGILNT atingle, gelatin, genital, langite
AEGILNV leaving
AEGILOU eulogia
AEGILRS Algiers
AEGILRZ glazier
AEGILSS glassie
AEGILTT lettiga
AEGILTU glutaei
AEGILTY egality
AEGIMMR gammier
AEGIMNN meaning
AEGIMNR mangier, mearing
AEGIMNT mintage, tegmina
AEGIMPR epigram
AEGIMPT pig meat
AEGIMRR armiger
AEGIMRS gisarme
AEGIMRT migrate, ragtime
AEGIMRY imagery
AEGIMST gamiest, sigmate
AEGINNR earning, engrain, Grainne, grannie
AEGINNT antigen, gentian
AEGINNU anguine, guanine
AEGINNV Angevin
AEGINOR Iron Age
AEGINOS agonise, asinego
AEGINOZ agonize
AEGINPP genipap
AEGINRR angrier, earring, grainer, rangier
AEGINRS Seraing, seringa
AEGINRT Geraint, granite, ingrate, tangier, tearing, Tigrean
AEGINRV Ginevra, ingrave, vinegar
AEGINRW wearing
AEGINST easting, genista, ingesta, seating
AEGINTT gattine
AEGINTV vintage
AEGINTZ tzigane
AEGIOSV Segovia
AEGIPRS prisage
AEGIPRU Perugia
AEGIRRZ grazier
AEGIRSS gassier
AEGIRST agister, sea-girt, stagier
AEGIRSU gerusia
AEGIRSV Gervais
AEGIRSW sagwire
AEGIRTV virgate
AEGIRUZ gauzier
AEGISTY gaseity
AEGJLNO galjoen
AEGKKNO angekok
AEGKLOU kagoule
AEGKMRY kerygma
AEGKNOS Kaesong
AEGLLLY legally
AEGLLNO allonge, galleon
AEGLLNY langley
AEGLLOR allegro
AEGLLOT tollage
AEGLLRY allergy, gallery, largely, regally
AEGLLSU seagull, sullage
AEGLLTU gluteal
AEGLMNR mangler
AEGLMOR glomera
AEGLMOU moulage
AEGLMPU plumage
AEGLNOT angelot, tangelo
AEGLNOZ onglaze
AEGLNPR grapnel
AEGLNPS spangle
AEGLNRT trangle
AEGLNRU granule
AEGLNRW wangler, wrangle
AEGLNRY glarney
AEGLNSS glassen
AEGLNSU angelus
AEGLNTT gantlet
AEGLNTU languet
AEGLNTW twangle
AEGLNUU ungulae
AEGLNUW gunwale
AEGLOPP loppage
AEGLOPR pergola
AEGLORT gloater, legator
AEGLORV vorlage
AEGLORW low gear
AEGLOTT lagetto
AEGLOTV voltage
AEGLPPR grapple
AEGLPRT leg trap
AEGLPRU earplug, graupel
AEGLPSU plagues
AEGLPUY plaguey
AEGLRRU regular
AEGLRSS largess
AEGLRSV verglas
AEGLRTY greatly
AEGLRVY gravely
AEGLSSU sea slug
AEGLSTT gestalt
AEGLTUV vulgate
AEGLUUY guayule
AEGLUVY vaguely
AEGMMOP pommage
AEGMMRU rummage
AEGMMRY gemmary
AEGMNNO agnomen
AEGMNOR Marengo, megaron
AEGMNOT magneto, megaton, montage
AEGMNPY pygmean
AEGMNRT garment, margent
AEGMNRY Germany
AEGMNTU augment, mutagen
AEGMOOR moorage
AEGMOSY gaysome
AEGMOXY exogamy
AEGMRRU murager

AEGNNOT negaton, tonnage
AEGNNRT regnant
AEGNNRU gunnera, nanguer
AEGNNTT tangent
AEGNNTU genuant, tunnage
AEGNOOR oregano
AEGNOPT pontage
AEGNORR groaner
AEGNORS nose-rag
AEGNORT negator, tronage
AEGNORW wagoner
AEGNOST on-stage
AEGNOSY nosegay
AEGNOTX taxogen
AEGNPRS engrasp
AEGNPRT trepang
AEGNRRT granter
AEGNRST strange
AEGNRTT gnatter
AEGNSSY gayness
AEGNTTU tutenag
AEGNUYY Yueyang
AEGOORT rootage
AEGOPRT portage, potager, top gear
AEGOPST Gestapo, postage
AEGOPTT pottage
AEGORRT garrote
AEGORST storage
AEGORTT garotte
AEGORTU outrage
AEGORVY voyager
AEGOSSU gaseous
AEGOSTW stowage
AEGOTTU outgate
AEGOTTV gavotte
AEGPRRS grasper, sparger
AEGPRSY grapeys
AEGPSTU upstage
AEGRRUV gravure, verruga
AEGRSUY ragusye
AEGSSSU gausses
AEGSTUU auguste
AEGSTUV Gustave
AEGTTTU guttate
AEHHILS Sheilah
AEHHJOV Jehovah
AEHHJPT Japheth
AEHHLTY healthy
AEHHNRS harshen
AEHHSST sheaths
AEHIINT inhiate
AEHIIQT Qitaihe
AEHIIRR hairier
AEHIKLL kehilla
AEHIKPS peakish
AEHIKRS shakier
AEHIKSW weakish
AEHIKSY Yakeshi
AEHILLR hallier
AEHILMO hemiola
AEHILNO Heinola
AEHILNR hernial, inhaler
AEHILNY hyaline
AEHILOP Ophelia
AEHILPR harelip
AEHILRU haulier
AEHILST lateish
AEHILTY hyalite
AEHILUV vihuela
AEHILVY heavily
AEHIMMR hammier
AEHIMNR harmine
AEHIMNT hematin
AEHIMNY hymenia
AEHIMPR Ephraim
AEHIMRS mishear
AEHIMRZ zemirah
AEHIMSS Messiah
AEHIMST atheism
AEHINPR heparin
AEHINPS in-phase, Phineas
AEHINRS hernias, nearish
AEHINRT hairnet, inearth, therian
AEHINSS hessian
AEHINSV evanish
AEHINTW tawhine
AEHIORR hoarier
AEHIOTT tao-tieh
AEHIPPR happier
AEHIPPT epitaph
AEHIPSS aphesis
AEHIRRR harrier
AEHIRRT Harriet
AEHIRST hastier
AEHIRSV ashiver
AEHIRSW wareshi, washier, wearish
AEHIRWY haywire
AEHISTT atheist, staithe
AEHISTV hastive
AEHISTZ haziest
AEHISVY yeshiva
AEHITTW thwaite
AEHJLOW jaw-hole
AEHJOPS Josepha
AEHKNOS Kenosha
AEHKPSU shake-up
AEHKRTU Keturah
AEHLLRS hersall
AEHLLUV helluva
AEHLLYZ hazelly
AEHLMNO manhole
AEHLMNY hyemnal, hymenal
AEHLMOR armhole
AEHLMRT thermal
AEHLMRU humeral, malheur
AEHLNOT Athlone, ethanol
AEHLNPY hypnale
AEHLNRT enthral
AEHLNSU unleash
AEHLORT loather, rat-hole
AEHLOSS asshole
AEHLPRS spheral
AEHLPSS hapless
AEHLPSY shapely
AEHLRSS slasher
AEHLRST harslet, slather
AEHLRTY earthly, Hartley, lathery
AEHLSST Hasselt, hatless
AEHLSTT stealth
AEHLTWY wealthy
AEHMMRS shammer
AEHMNNR Hermann
AEHMNOR menorah
AEHMNOY haemony
AEHMNPY nymphae, nymphea
AEHMNRT mathern
AEHMNTY maythen
AEHMOPT apothem
AEHMPTY empathy
AEHMRSS smasher
AEHMRST hamster
AEHMRTU mauther
AEHMRTW mawther
AEHMRWX Wrexham
AEHMSTY maythes
AEHMTTW Matthew
AEHMUZZ mezuzah
AEHNNPY ha'penny
AEHNNWY anywhen
AEHNOPR Orphean
AEHNOPT phaeton, phonate
AEHNOPW wanhope
AEHNORS hoarsen, senhora
AEHNORT another
AEHNOSX hexosan
AEHNOTV have-not
AEHNOTW Wheaton
AEHNPPY enhappy
AEHNPRS sharpen
AEHNPRT panther
AEHNPTY phytane
AEHNRSS harness
AEHNRST hanster
AEHNRTU haunter, unearth
AEHNRTX narthex
AEHNTTW whatten

AEHOORT toheroa
AEHOPRT phorate
AEHOPST teashop
AEHORST asthore, earshot
AEHORUW warehou
AEHOSTT hot seat
AEHOSTU atheous
AEHPPRS perhaps
AEHPRRS sharper
AEHPRSS seraphs, Sherpas
AEHPRSW pre-wash
AEHPRTY therapy
AEHPSTY phytase
AEHPTUY eupathy
AEHRRTU urethra
AEHRSTT rathest, shatter
AEHRSTV harvest
AEHRSTW wreaths
AEHRSVW wharves
AEHRSWY washery
AEHRTTY hattery
AEHRTUU hauteur
AEHRTWY wreathy
AEHSSTW swathes
AEHSSTY assythe
AEHSTUX exhaust
AEIIKNT kainite
AEIIKSS Isesaki
AEIILLT taillie
AEIILMP lipemia
AEIILMR air mile
AEIILNN aniline
AEIILNR airline
AEIILNS Ainslie
AEIILNX exilian
AEIILOP epiloia
AEIILRS Israeli
AEIILSW lewisia
AEIILTT Letitia
AEIILTV ilvaite
AEIILTX exitial
AEIIMNT miniate
AEIIMNX Mei Xian
AEIIMPR Imperia
AEIIMRT airtime
AEIIMRV viremia
AEIIMTT imitate
AEIINNR Aneirin
AEIINNS asinine, insanie
AEIINRR rainier
AEIINRS senarii
AEIINRT inertia, itinera
AEIINTX axinite
AEIIPRR prairie
AEIIRRV riviera
AEIIRST airiest
AEIIRSV vriesia
AEIISTV Sivaite
AEIITTV vitiate
AEIJLNV javelin
AEIJLNW jawline
AEIJMMR jammier
AEIJMNS jasmine
AEIJNRT nartjie
AEIJRZZ jazzier
AEIKLLW lawlike
AEIKLMN manlike
AEIKLMT metalik
AEIKLNO eikonal
AEIKLNP panlike
AEIKLNR lankier
AEIKLNS lekanis
AEIKLNU unalike
AEIKLNV valenki
AEIKLOT keitloa
AEIKLOV live oak
AEIKLRW warlike
AEIKLSW sawlike, walkies
AEIKLUZ Zuleika
AEIKMNP pikeman
AEIKMNR mankier, ramekin
AEIKMPR rampike
AEIKMST mistake
AEIKNNT neatnik
AEIKNPS inspeak, sea pink
AEIKNRR narkier
AEIKNRS kerasin
AEIKNRT Katrine, keratin
AEIKNRU Ukraine
AEIKNSY kyanise
AEIKNTY kyanite
AEIKNYZ kyanize
AEIKPRR parkier
AEIKPRW pawkier
AEIKPSS seaskip
AEIKQRU quakier
AEIKRRS sarkier
AEIKRTT artetik
AEILLLR lirella
AEILLMN manille
AEILLMO oil-meal
AEILLMT all-time, mitella
AEILLNO linaloe
AEILLNR ralline
AEILLNT tellina
AEILLNV vanille
AEILLOV alveoli
AEILLPR pallier, perilla
AEILLPS illapse
AEILLPY epyllia
AEILLRR rallier
AEILLRT literal, tallier
AEILLSY sea lily
AEILLUV eluvial
AEILLVX vexilla
AEILLVY Viyella
AEILMMS melisma
AEILMNN lineman, melanin
AEILMNP impanel, maniple
AEILMNR manlier, marline, mineral
AEILMNS salmine, seminal
AEILMNT ailment, aliment
AEILMNV Melvina
AEILMNY El Minya
AEILMOR Meliora, Morelia
AEILMPR impearl, lempira, palmier
AEILMPT palmiet, palmite
AEILMRS mislear, realism
AEILMRT latimer, maltier, marlite
AEILMSS aimless, melissa, seismal
AEILMTY meatily
AEILNNY inanely
AEILNNZ Lizanne
AEILNOP opaline
AEILNOR aileron, alerion, Loraine
AEILNOS sea lion
AEILNOT elation, toenail
AEILNPR praline
AEILNPS Nepalis, spaniel
AEILNPT pantile, pentail
AEILNPU Pauline
AEILNPX explain
AEILNQU equinal, inequal
AEILNRS Linares
AEILNRT entrail, larnite, latrine, ratline, reliant, retinal, trainel, trenail
AEILNRV elinvar, ravelin
AEILNRY inlayer, nailery
AEILNST elastin, nail set, salient, saltine, staniel
AEILNSU inulase
AEILNSV inslave
AEILNSY Ainsley, Elysian
AEILNTU alunite
AEILNTV ventail

AEILNUV unalive
AEILNUW lauwine
AEILNUZ azuline
AEILNVY naively
AEILOPR peloria, rape-oil
AEILOPS opalise
AEILOPT opalite
AEILOPZ opalize
AEILORS Rosalie
AEILORV variole
AEILOST isolate
AEILOTV violate
AEILPPR apperil, applier, aripple
AEILPRT partile
AEILPRV prevail
AEILPST talipes
AEILPSY Paisley
AEILQTU liquate, tequila
AEILRRT retiral, retrial, trailer
AEILRSS airless
AEILRST realist, saltier, saltire
AEILRSV revisal
AEILRTT tertial
AEILRTY irately, reality
AEILRVV revival
AEILRVY virelay
AEILRWY wearily
AEILSTV estival
AEILSTZ laziest
AEILTVV Tel Aviv
AEILTVY vilayet
AEILUVX exuvial
AEIMMNS misname
AEIMMPP pip emma
AEIMMRS rammies
AEIMMRT marmite
AEIMMST mismate
AEIMMZZ mizmaze
AEIMNNT mannite
AEIMNOR moraine, romaine
AEIMNOT amniote
AEIMNOU eunomia
AEIMNPR permain, Permian
AEIMNRR mariner
AEIMNRS remains, seminar
AEIMNRT Martine, meranti, minaret, raiment
AEIMNRV Minerva, vermian
AEIMNRW wireman
AEIMNSS samisen
AEIMNST estamin, maniest, Samnite
AEIMNSW wise man
AEIMNSZ man-size
AEIMNTV Vietnam
AEIMNTY amenity, anytime
AEIMNZZ mezzani
AEIMOOP ipomoea
AEIMOPR emporia
AEIMORR armoire
AEIMOST amosite, atomise, osmiate
AEIMOTX toxemia
AEIMOTZ atomize
AEIMPRR rampier, rampire
AEIMPRS impresa, primase
AEIMPRT primate
AEIMPRV vampire
AEIMPSS impasse
AEIMPST impaste, pastime, Septima
AEIMRRR marrier
AEIMRSS merissa
AEIMRST maestri
AEIMRTU muriate
AEIMRTW wartime
AEIMSST asteism, samiest
AEIMSSV massive
AEIMSTT etatism, matlest
AEIMSTZ maziest, mestiza
AEIMSUV amusive
AEINNOT Antoine, enation, Etonian
AEINNOZ neo-Nazi
AEINNPR pannier
AEINNPT pantine, penatin, piannet, pinnate
AEINNRT entrain, trannie
AEINNRU aneurin
AEINNST ensaint
AEINOPR open air
AEINORT torenia
AEINOSS anoesis
AEINOST Estonia
AEINOSV evasion
AEINOXZ oxazine
AEINPPP pan-pipe
AEINPRS Persian, prasine
AEINPRT painter, pertain, Petrina, repaint
AEINPST panties, sapient
AEINPSU punaise
AEINPTT patient
AEINPTU petunia
AEINPTY paneity
AEINPYZ paynize
AEINQTU antique, quinate
AEINRRT retrain, terrain, trainer
AEINRRV raviner
AEINRSS Nerissa
AEINRST nastier, retinas, retsina, stainer, stearin
AEINRTT intreat, iterant, nattier, nitrate, tartine, tertian
AEINRTU taurine, urinate
AEINRTV vitrean
AEINRTW tawnier, tinware
AEINRTZ terzina
AEINRUV vaurien
AEINRUZ azurine
AEINRVV vervain
AEINSST entasis, sestina, Staines
AEINSTT instate, satinet
AEINSTU sinuate
AEINSTZ zaniest
AEINSWY anywise
AEINTVY naivety
AEINTXY anxiety
AEIOPRS soapier
AEIOPTT atiptoe
AEIOQSU sequoia
AEIORRR arriero
AEIORST osteria
AEIORTV evirato
AEIOSTT toastie
AEIPPRS apprise, sappier
AEIPPRT periapt
AEIPPRZ apprize, zappier
AEIPRRS praiser
AEIPRRT partier
AEIPRSS paresis
AEIPRST pastier, piaster, piastre, traipse
AEIPRSU upraise
AEIPRSV parvise
AEIPRTT partite
AEIPRTV private
AEIPRTY pyritae

AEIPRXY pyrexia
AEIPSSS asepsis
AEIPSSV passive
AEIPTXY epitaxy
AEIQRUV aquiver
AEIQTTU quattie
AEIRRRT tarrier
AEIRRST tarsier
AEIRRTT rattier, tartier
AEIRRTU Etruria
AEIRRVV viverra
AEIRSSS sassier
AEIRSTT artiste, striate, tastier
AEIRSTW wariest
AEIRSVV savvier
AEIRTTT attrite, tattier, titrate
AEIRTUY aureity
AEIRTUZ azurite
AEIRTVY variety
AEISSUV suasive
AEISSUX auxesis
AEISSWW wise saw
AEISTTU situate
AEISTTY satiety
AEISTVW waviest
AEISTWX waxiest
AEITTTV vittate
AEJJLNU jejunal
AEJKNRS jankers
AEJLLOV Vallejo
AEJLNUV juvenal
AEJLOSU jalouse, jealous
AEJLOTV javelot
AEJLOUZ azulejo
AEJLRSS jarless
AEJLSSW jawless
AEJMSSY jessamy
AEJMSTY majesty
AEJNOSS San Jose
AEJNSST jessant
AEKLNPR prankle
AEKLNST asklent
AEKLOVZ zelkova
AEKLPPR klapper
AEKLPPT pep talk
AEKLPRS sparkle
AEKLRST stalker
AEKNOOR Roanoke
AEKNOPS Spokane
AEKNPPR knapper
AEKNPRR pranker
AEKNPRS spanker
AEKNRVY knavery
AEKORTU outrake
AEKOTTU out-take, take-out
AEKPSSY pass-key
AEKQSUY squeaky
AEKRSTY streaky
AEKSSTT tsatske
AEKSVWY sky wave
AELLLOU Louella
AELLMOR morella
AELLMOW mallowe
AELLMSU malleus
AELLMTY metally
AELLMWX maxwell
AELLNOR llanero
AELLNOV novella
AELLNOY alonely
AELLNPY penally
AELLNUU lunulae
AELLNVY venally
AELLORS rosella
AELLORT reallot
AELLORV all-over, overall
AELLPRU pleural
AELLPTY playlet
AELLPTZ platzel
AELLQUY equally
AELLRST stellar
AELLRTY alertly
AELLRUW wall rue
AELLSSW lawless, wassell
AELLSTY stalely
AELLSWY say-well
AELLTUU ululate
AELLUVV valvule
AELMMNO mamelon
AELMMOY myeloma
AELMMRS slammer
AELMMRT trammel
AELMMSY malmsey
AELMNNS lensman
AELMNOR almoner, nemoral
AELMNOT lamento, omental, telamon
AELMNPR lampern
AELMNRU numeral
AELMNSS manless
AELMNSU mensual
AELMNTT mantlet
AELMNTU almuten
AELMNTY menalty
AELMOPR leproma, pleroma
AELMOPU ampoule
AELMOPY maypole
AELMORS marloes, molares
AELMORT mole rat
AELMORU morulae
AELMORV removal
AELMOSS molasse
AELMOST maltose
AELMOTT matelot
AELMPRS lampers, sampler
AELMPRT templar, trample
AELMPRY lamprey
AELMPSS mapless
AELMPST amplest
AELMPTU plumate
AELMPUU plumeau
AELMRSS armless
AELMRTT martlet
AELMRTW law term
AELMRWW lew-warm
AELMSST matless
AELMSTY malty se
AELNNPR planner
AELNNRS ensnarl
AELNNRT lantern
AELNNRU unlearn
AELNNTU annulet
AELNOOR Leonora
AELNOPS nespola
AELNOPT nepotal, polenta
AELNOPU apolune
AELNOPY lay open
AELNORU aleuron
AELNORV veronal
AELNORZ zeranol
AELNOSY Sloaney
AELNOTV volante
AELNPPR pre-plan
AELNPPY playpen
AELNPRT pantler, planter, replant
AELNPRY plenary
AELNPSS napless
AELNPTT platten
AELNPTX explant
AELNPTY aplenty, penalty
AELNPUV peulvan
AELNQUU unequal
AELNRRS snarler
AELNRST saltern, sternal
AELNRTT trental
AELNRTU neutral
AELNRTV ventral
AELNRUU neurula
AELNRUV unravel
AELNSSU sensual
AELNSSX laxness
AELNSTY Stanley
AELNSVV snavvle
AELOORS aerosol, roseola
AELOOXZ oxazole
AELOPPR propale
AELOPPX apoplex
AELOPRR peroral
AELOPRS lop-ears, reposal
AELOPRT prolate
AELOPRV overlap
AELOPST apostle
AELOPTT paletot
AELORRT realtor, relator
AELORSS lassoer, oarless

AELORST oestral
AELORSX oral sex
AELORTT Loretta
AELORTU torulae
AELORTV levator
AELORTZ zelator
AELORUU rouleau
AELORVY layover, overlay
AELOSTV solvate
AELOSUZ zealous
AELOSVY saveloy
AELOTUV ovulate
AELPPPR plapper
AELPPRS slapper
AELPPRY reapply
AELPPSS sapples
AELPPSU appulse
AELPRST persalt, plaster, psalter, stapler
AELPRSU perusal, serpula
AELPRSY parsley, sparely
AELPRTT partlet, platter, prattle
AELPRTY peytral, pteryla
AELPRUY epulary
AELPSSS sapless
AELPSST let-pass, tapless
AELPSSU pas seul
AELPSSY Plassey
AELPSTT peltast
AELPSTU pulsate
AELQRRU quarrel
AELQTUZ quetzal
AELRRSU surreal
AELRRTT rattler
AELRRTW trawler
AELRSST artless
AELRSSW wrassle
AELRSSY rayless
AELRSTT starlet, startle
AELRSTU saluter
AELRSTV vestral
AELRSTW wastrel, wrastle
AELRSTY saltery
AELRSVY slavery
AELRTTT tartlet, tattler
AELRTTU tutelar
AELRTUV vaulter
AELRTUY ultreya
AELRTWZ waltzer
AELSSTT stalest
AELSSTU taluses
AELSSTX taxless
AELSTTY stately
AELSUVY suavely
AELTTTW twattle
AELTTUX textual
AEMMNOT momenta
AEMMNPT pamment
AEMMNTU amentum
AEMMORW wommera
AEMMRST stammer
AEMMSUU musaeum
AEMNNOS mannose
AEMNNOT maneton, montane
AEMNNOU noumena
AEMNNOZ menazon
AEMNNRT remnant
AEMNNSU mean sun
AEMNNSW newsman
AEMNNTU unmeant
AEMNOOS mooneas
AEMNORT montera, tone arm
AEMNORU enamour, neuroma
AEMNORV mavrone, overman
AEMNORY anymore, romneya
AEMNOSX mesaxon
AEMNOTT tomenta
AEMNPST enstamp
AEMNPTU putamen
AEMNPTY payment
AEMNRST sarment, smarten
AEMNRSU surname
AEMNRTV varment
AEMNSTY amnesty
AEMNTWY wayment
AEMOOPT apotome
AEMOORS sea room
AEMOORT tearoom
AEMOORW woomera
AEMOOST osteoma
AEMOOSV vamoose
AEMOPPR pampero
AEMOPRT pteroma
AEMOPST apostem
AEMORRR armorer
AEMORRV overarm
AEMORST maestro
AEMORTT marotte
AEMORTU Euratom
AEMORTW worm-eat
AEMOSSS some ass
AEMOTTZ mozetta
AEMPRRT tramper
AEMPRST ampster, stamper
AEMPRTU tempura
AEMPRVY vampyre
AEMPTTT attempt
AEMPTTU tapetum
AEMQRSU masquer
AEMRRRY remarry
AEMRRST armrest
AEMRRTT martret
AEMRRTU erratum, maturer
AEMRSSU Erasmus, masseur, masures
AEMRSTT smatter
AEMRSTU Artemus, strumae
AEMRSTY mastery
AEMRTUU trumeau
AEMRUUV vaumure
AEMTTUU mutuate
AENNNOS non-sane
AENNNPT pennant
AENNORS Rosanne, Roseann
AENNORX Roxanne
AENNORY annoyer
AENNOTU tonneau
AENNPRS spanner
AENNRTT entrant
AENNRTV vernant
AENNRTY tannery
AENNSSU Susanne
AENNSSW wanness
AENNSTU ensuant
AENNSTW wannest
AENNSUZ Suzanne
AENOOSZ osazone
AENOPPR propane
AENOPRS persona
AENOPRT operant, pronate, protean, tropane
AENOPSU posaune
AENOPSW snow pea
AENOPTZ Potenza
AENORRV overran
AENORST santero, senator, treason
AENORTV venator
AENORWZ war zone
AENOSTU soutane
AENOSTW Sowetan
AENOSVW waveson
AENOUUV nouveau
AENPPRS snapper
AENPRRT partner
AENPRST pastern
AENPRSW spawner
AENPRTT pattern
AENPRUV parvenu
AENPSST aptness, patness
AENPSSY synapse
AENQRTU quatern
AENQUWY Newquay
AENRRTT tranter
AENRRTY ternary
AENRSSW rawness
AENRSTU saunter
AENRSTV servant, versant
AENRSTW new star, wanrest

AENRTTU taunter
AENRTTV vertant
AENRTUV vaunter, Ventura
AENRUWY unweary
AENSTTU tetanus
AENSTTX sextant
AEOOPPS papoose
AEOPPPS pappose
AEOPPRV approve
AEOPPSU pea-soup
AEOPQRU opaquer
AEOPRRT praetor, prorate
AEOPRRV vaporer
AEOPRST esparto, seaport
AEOPRTT portate
AEOPRTW war poet
AEOPRVY overpay
AEOPRWY ropeway
AEOPSST pastose
AEOPSTT poetast
AEOQRTU equator, quorate
AEOQRUV vaquero
AEOQSUU aqueous
AEORRST roaster
AEORRSU arrouse
AEORSTT Rosetta, toaster
AEORSTZ zostera
AEORSVW oversaw
AEORTTU torteau
AEORTUW outwear
AEORTVX overtax
AEOSSUX saxeous
AEPPPRU prepupa
AEPPRRT trapper
AEPPRRW wrapper
AEPPRSS appress
AEPPRSW swapper
AEPPSTT pap test
AEPPSTU paste-up
AEPQRTU parquet
AEPRRSY respray, sprayer
AEPRRTU rapture
AEPRRTY petrary
AEPRSSY pessary
AEPRSTT spatter, tapster
AEPRSTU pasture
AEPRSUX aruspex
AEPRSYY sprayey
AEPRTXY apteryx
AEPSSTU petasus
AEPSTTU upstate
AEQRRSU squarer
AEQRRTU quarter
AEQRSTU T-square
AEQRTTU quartet
AEQRUVY quavery
AERRSSU assurer
AERRSTT restart, starter
AERRSTV travers
AERRSTY strayer
AERSTTU stature
AERSTTW Stewart, swatter
AERSTUY estuary
AERSTWY wastery
AERTTTY tattery
AERTTUV vettura
AERTTUX textura
AESSTUY eustasy
AESTTTU statute
AFFFLLO fall-off
AFFGHIR ghaffir
AFFGINR ingraff
AFFHIRS raffish
AFFHLLY fly-half
AFFILOS sail-off
AFFILOT tail-off
AFFILOX Filofax
AFFILSY falsify
AFFIMST mastiff
AFFINRU funfair, ruffian
AFFINTY tiffany
AFFLOPY play-off
AFFMOPR off-ramp
AFFNORS saffron
AFFNORT affront
AFFNOSW sawn-off
AFGGGIN fagging
AFGGOTY faggoty
AFGHHIS hagfish
AFGHIRS garfish
AFGHLSU gashful
AFGHLTU flaught
AFGHOST gasthof
AFGHRTU fraught
AFGIILN failing
AFGIINR fairing
AFGILLN falling
AFGILMN flaming
AFGILNT fatling
AFGILNU gainful
AFGILRU figural
AFGIMNR farming, fingram, framing
AFGIMNY magnify
AFGINNN fanning
AFGINNW fawning
AFGINRT ingraft
AFGINST fasting
AFGINTT fatting
AFGIRTY gratify
AFGLLUY fall guy, fugally
AFGLMOP fog lamp
AFGLSTU gastful
AFGMNOR frogman
AFGNORT Grafton
AFGNOTU outfang
AFGOOTT fagotto
AFHIIRS fairish
AFHIISW waifish
AFHILTW halfwit
AFHIMNU hafnium
AFHINOS fashion
AFHIORS oarfish
AFHIPPY happify
AFHISSW sawfish
AFHISTT fattish
AFHLMRU harmful
AFHLOTY hayloft
AFIILOR airfoil
AFIILRT airlift
AFIIMOS Mafiosi
AFIINRS Frisian
AFIJYZZ jazzify
AFIKKLR Falkirk
AFIKLLY flakily
AFILLMS misfall
AFILLNY finally
AFILLOV fovilla
AFILLPT pitfall
AFILLPU pailful
AFILLRY frailly
AFILLUV fluvial
AFILLUW wailful
AFILMOR aliform
AFILMPY amplify
AFILMSS falsism
AFILNOR Florian
AFILNPU painful
AFILNTU falutin
AFILNTY faintly
AFILORW airflow
AFILOTX foxtail
AFILPSY palsify
AFILQUY qualify
AFILRRY friarly
AFILRTY frailty
AFILSSY salsify
AFILSTU fistula
AFILSTY falsity
AFIMOOS Mafioso
AFIMSSY massify
AFIMSTT fattism
AFIMSUV fauvism
AFINNOR franion
AFINNOS sanfoin
AFINORS insofar
AFINRTU furiant
AFINSTU faunist, fustian, infaust
AFIORTU faitour
AFIPRST pristaf
AFIPRTY partify
AFISSTY satisfy
AFISTTT fattist
AFISTUV fauvist
AFITTUY fatuity
AFKLNOO flookan
AFKLNRY frankly
AFKLNTU tankful
AFKRRTU Fraktur
AFLLMPU palmful
AFLLOOY aloofly
AFLLORU florula

AFLLOTU fallout, outfall
AFLLPUY playful
AFLLUWY awfully
AFLMNNO non-flam
AFLMNOU moanful
AFLMORU formula
AFLMORW wolfram
AFLMOST flotsam
AFLMSUU famulus
AFLNOOS Alfonso
AFLNORT frontal
AFLNOTT flotant
AFLNOTU no-fault
AFLNTUY flaunty
AFLOOTW wool-fat
AFLOPTT flat-top
AFLORUV flavour
AFLOSSU fossula
AFLPRTY flytrap
AFLPSTY fly-past
AFLRTUU futural
AFLRTUY trayful
AFMNOOT footman
AFMNORT formant
AFMNRTU turfman
AFMNWYY Myfanwy
AFMORRT art form
AFMORST farmost
AFMORTU foumart
AFNORRT Fortran
AFNORRW forwarn
AFNSSTU sunfast
AFOOPPR approof
AFOOTWY footway
AFOPRSS forpass
AFORRSY forsary
AFORSUV vafrous
AFOSTUU fatuous
AGGGGIN gagging
AGGGIJN jagging
AGGGILN lagging
AGGGINN nagging
AGGGINR ragging
AGGGINS sagging
AGGGINT tagging
AGGGINW wagging
AGGGINZ zagging
AGGHHIS haggish
AGGHIIL ghilgai
AGGHIMN gingham
AGGHINN hanging
AGGHISW waggish
AGGIIJJ jig-a-jig
AGGIINN gaining
AGGILLN gingall
AGGILNR glaring
AGGILNT Gatling
AGGILNZ glazing
AGGINRS gas ring
AGGINRT grating
AGGINRU arguing
AGGINRV graving
AGGINRZ grazing
AGGINSS gassing
AGGINST staging
AGGLNOO long-ago
AGGLOSW Glasgow
AGGMORR grogram
AGGMOTY maggoty
AGGNNUY gunyang
AGGNOOR gongora
AGGNOTU outgang
AGGOPRU aggroup
AGHHHIT high hat
AGHHIPS hagship
AGHHIWY highway
AGHHMNU Hamhung
AGHHOSW hogwash
AGHHTTU thaught
AGHHTUY haughty
AGHIINN Haining
AGHIINT Tighina
AGHIKSW gawkish
AGHILLN halling
AGHILNS lashing
AGHILNT halting, lathing
AGHILNU laugh-in
AGHILNW whaling
AGHILRS largish
AGHILRT alright
AGHILSU Gaulish
AGHIMMN hamming
AGHIMOS Shimoga
AGHINNT tanghin
AGHINOS gashion
AGHINPP happing
AGHINPR harping
AGHINPS phasing
AGHINRS garnish, rashing
AGHINST hasting
AGHINSU anguish
AGHINSV shaving
AGHINSW washing
AGHINTT hatting
AGHIOST goatish
AGHIPSW pigwash
AGHIRSU guarish
AGHISUV vaguish
AGHJMNO mah-jong
AGHKOSW goshawk
AGHLMPU galumph
AGHLNUY nylghau
AGHLOOS gasohol
AGHLOSU goulash
AGHLOUY Youghal
AGHLSTY ghastly
AGHMORY hygroma
AGHMOSS moss-hag
AGHMRTU Murtagh
AGHNNOU houngan
AGHNORT athrong
AGHNOTU hang-out, tohunga, Tonghua
AGHNRUY Hungary
AGHNTUY naughty
AGHORTU toughra
AGHORTW warthog
AGHPTUY paughty
AGHRSTY gytrash
AGIIJMU ujigami
AGIIJNX Jiaxing
AGIIJOT jigotai
AGIIKLT glaikit
AGIILLN Gillian
AGIILMN mailing
AGIILMT mitigal
AGIILNR railing
AGIILNS Aisling, sailing
AGIILNT iligant, tailing
AGIILNW wailing
AGIILPT pigtail
AGIILTY agility
AGIIMMS imagism
AGIIMOR origami
AGIIMST imagist
AGIINNR ingrain
AGIINOV vigonia
AGIINPR pairing
AGIINPT Taiping
AGIINRS raising
AGIINRZ Zingari
AGIINSV visaing
AGIINTW waiting
AGIINTX taxiing, Xingtai
AGIINVV vivaing
AGIJLLN jingall
AGIJMMN jamming
AGIJNNU Jungian
AGIJNRR jarring
AGIJORU guajiro
AGIKKNY yakking
AGIKLNO oakling
AGIKLNT talking
AGIKLNW walking
AGIKLWY gawkily
AGIKMNR marking
AGIKNNR ranking
AGIKNOS soaking
AGIKNPR parking
AGIKNQU quaking
AGIKNRS sarking
AGILLLN lalling
AGILLMU gallium
AGILLNP palling
AGILLNU lingual, lingula
AGILLNW walling
AGILLOR gorilla
AGILLOT galliot
AGILLSU lugsail
AGILMMN lamming
AGILMNN manling
AGILMNO almoign
AGILMNP lamping
AGILMNT malting
AGILMNY mangily
AGILMOR Milagro
AGILMPS magslip
AGILMPU plagium
AGILNNO loaning

AGILNNP	planing
AGILNNS	Lansing, linsang
AGILNNT	tanling
AGILNOP	galopin
AGILNOR	orignal, rangoli
AGILNOT	antilog, langoti
AGILNPP	lapping
AGILNPS	sapling
AGILNPT	palting, plating
AGILNPW	lapwing
AGILNPY	playing
AGILNRT	ratling
AGILNRU	rail gun
AGILNRW	warling
AGILNRY	angrily
AGILNST	Anglist, lasting, salting, slating
AGILNTW	lawting
AGILNUV	valuing
AGILNVV	valving
AGILOPR	poligar
AGILOPT	galipot
AGILORS	Argolis, girasol
AGILORW	airglow, Gwalior
AGILOST	saligot
AGILRST	garlits
AGILRUV	virgula
AGILSTY	stagily
AGILUYZ	gauzily
AGIMMNO	Maoming
AGIMMNR	ramming
AGIMNNN	manning
AGIMNNO	moaning
AGIMNNS	Sanming
AGIMNNU	muninga
AGIMNNW	wingman
AGIMNOR	moringa
AGIMNOS	agonism
AGIMNPP	mapping
AGIMNPT	tamping
AGIMNRR	marring
AGIMNRT	migrant
AGIMNST	masting
AGIMNSU	amusing
AGIMNTT	matting
AGIMORS	isogram
AGIMORT	marigot
AGIMORU	gourami
AGIMOSY	isogamy
AGIMRRT	trigram
AGIMRTY	trigamy
AGIMSST	stigmas
AGINNNP	Nanping, panning
AGINNNT	tanning
AGINNOV	Avignon
AGINNPP	napping

AGINNRW	warning
AGINNTU	tanguin
AGINNTW	wanting
AGINNTY	Yingtan
AGINNWY	yawning
AGINNXY	Xinyang
AGINORR	roaring
AGINORS	signora
AGINORV	Virgoan
AGINORZ	Zingaro
AGINOSS	ganosis
AGINOST	agonist
AGINPPR	rapping
AGINPPS	sapping
AGINPPT	tapping
AGINPPW	wapping
AGINPPY	yapping
AGINPPZ	zapping
AGINPRS	sparing
AGINPRT	parting, prating
AGINPRW	warping
AGINPRY	praying
AGINPSS	passing
AGINPST	pasting
AGINPTT	patting
AGINRRT	tarring
AGINRRW	warring
AGINRST	gastrin
AGINRSY	signary, syringa
AGINRTT	ratting
AGINRUU	inaugur
AGINSTT	tasting
AGINSTY	Stygian
AGINTTT	tatting
AGINTTV	vatting
AGINTXY	taxying
AGINWWX	waxwing
AGIORST	agistor, orgiast
AGIOUUY	ouguiya
AGIRTVY	gravity
AGISTUV	vagitus
AGJLRUU	jugular
AGJNOOR	jargoon
AGKMNOP	kampong
AGKMNPU	kampung
AGKNOPT	paktong
AGLLNOO	galloon
AGLLNTU	gallnut, nutgall
AGLLOPU	plugola
AGLLOSS	glossal
AGLLOSU	gallous
AGLLOSW	gallows
AGLLOTT	glottal
AGLLOXY	glyoxal
AGLLPTY	glyptal
AGLMOOT	logatom
AGLMORU	glamour
AGLNNOY	Longyan
AGLNOOW	own goal
AGLNOOY	naology
AGLNORU	languor

AGLNOST	alongst
AGLNPSY	spangly
AGLNPUY	gunplay
AGLNTUY	gauntly
AGLOOPY	apology
AGLRUUV	vugular
AGMMNSU	magnums
AGMNNOR	grannom
AGMNNRU	grannum
AGMNOOS	samogon
AGMNORU	organum
AGMNOST	amongst
AGMNOTU	Montagu
AGMNSTU	mustang
AGMNSTY	gymnast
AGMNSYY	syngamy
AGMOPRR	program
AGMORRW	ragworm
AGMPRSU	grampus
AGMRSSU	grassum
AGNNNOO	nonagon
AGNNOOR	organon, Rangoon
AGNNRUY	Nyungar
AGNOPRV	provang
AGNORRT	grantor
AGNORST	snot-rag
AGNORTT	torgant
AGNORTU	outrang
AGNOSTW	town gas
AGNPRRU	Rangpur
AGNPRSU	pur sang
AGNRTUY	gauntry
AGOPPST	stopgap
AGORRTW	ragwort
AGORRTY	gyrator
AGOSUYZ	azygous
AGRUUUY	Uruguay
AHHHISS	hashish
AHHIKSW	hawkish
AHHIMNS	Mishnah
AHHIMNU	hahnium
AHHKSTY	Shakhty
AHHLRSY	harshly
AHHOPRT	ha'p'orth
AHIIKSY	yashiki
AHIILNT	lithian
AHIILRY	hairily
AHIILSW	Swahili
AHIIMMS	Mishima
AHIIMNT	thiamin
AHIIMSS	sashimi
AHIINPR	hairpin
AHIINRT	thin air
AHIINTU	huitain
AHIINUY	Huaiyin
AHIIPRS	airship
AHIIRTW	tawhiri
AHIJLPS	Japlish
AHIJMOR	mohajir
AHIKLST	silk hat, tashlik
AHIKLSY	shakily
AHIKMNS	khamsin
AHIKMSW	mawkish

AHIKNSV	knavish
AHIKNTW	whatkin
AHILLMN	hillman
AHILLNO	hallion
AHILLNP	phallin
AHILLNT	anthill
AHILLOP	phalloi
AHILLRT	athrill
AHILLRY	Hillary
AHILLST	tallish
AHILLTT	tallith
AHILNOT	Lothian
AHILNPS	planish
AHILORY	hoarily
AHILPPS	Lappish, shiplap
AHILPPY	happily
AHILPSY	apishly
AHILSST	saltish
AHILSSV	slavish
AHILSTU	halitus
AHILSTY	hastily
AHILSWY	washily
AHIMMRS	rammish
AHIMMSW	mawmish
AHIMNNS	mannish
AHIMNNU	inhuman
AHIMNOT	manihot
AHIMNPS	manship
AHIMOPR	morphia
AHIMPSV	vampish
AHIMRST	thrimsa
AHIMRSW	warmish
AHIMRTU	thiuram
AHIMSUV	mauvish
AHIMSWY	wishmay
AHIMTUZ	azimuth
AHIMTVZ	mitzvah
AHINNST	tannish
AHINNTX	xanthin
AHINOOR	Honoria
AHINORT	orthian, thorian
AHINOST	Onitsha
AHINOTZ	hoatzin
AHINPSS	Spanish
AHINPTY	Pythian
AHINRST	tarnish
AHINRSV	varnish
AHINRSW	warnish
AHINSTU	inhaust
AHINTUU	tauhinu
AHIOORT	Horatio
AHIOOST	atishoo
AHIOPXY	hypoxia
AHIORSW	air show
AHIORUV	haviour
AHIPRSS	phrasis
AHIPRST	harpist, trapish
AHIPRSW	warship
AHIPRTT	tritaph
AHIPSSW	waspish
AHIPSWW	whipsaw
AHIPSWY	shipway
AHIRSTT	athirst, rattish
AHIRSTW	trishaw
AHIRSVY	yravish
AHISSTU	shiatsu
AHISTVY	Yahvist
AHISTWY	Yahwist
AHJMNOO	moonjah
AHKMORR	markhor
AHKMOSW	Mohawks
AHKMRTU	mukhtar
AHKNRTY	Kathryn
AHLLOOS	halloos
AHLLOPS	phallos
AHLLOST	shallot
AHLLOSW	shallow
AHLLOTY	loathly, tally-ho
AHLLPSU	phallus
AHLLSTU	thallus
AHLMMSU	mashlum
AHLMNPY	nymphal
AHLMNUY	humanly
AHLMORU	humoral
AHLMOSW	Ohm's law
AHLMPSU	plumash
AHLMSUU	hamulus
AHLNOPT	haplont
AHLNORT	althorn
AHLNOTU	Ulanhot
AHLORWY	holy war
AHLOTUU	outhaul
AHLPRSY	sharply
AHLPSSY	splashy
AHMMMOT	mammoth
AHMNNTU	manhunt
AHMNNUU	unhuman
AHMNOPS	shopman
AHMNOPT	Hampton, phantom
AHMNORS	Romansh
AHMNORU	man-hour
AHMNORY	harmony
AHMNOSW	showman
AHMNRSU	Rumansh
AHMNRYY	hymnary
AHMOOPS	shampoo
AHMOOSS	samshoo
AHMOPPR	propham
AHMORST	harmost
AHMOTTZ	matzoth
AHMOTWX	wax moth
AHMPSSU	smash-up
AHMRSTU	mushrat
AHMRSTY	thrymsa
AHNNNOS	Shannon
AHNNOTY	Anthony
AHNOOPR	harpoon
AHNOOSS	sashoon
AHNOPSU	ponhaus
AHNORRS	Sharron
AHNORSX	saxhorn
AHNOTTW	whatnot
AHNPPUU	pupunha
AHNPPUY	unhappy
AHNPRSU	unsharp
AHNPRXY	pharynx
AHOOPPS	papoosh
AHOPRTY	atrophy
AHOPTTW	towpath
AHORRWW	wharrow
AHORTTY	throaty
AHOSTUV	Shavuot
AHOSTUW	outwash, washout
AHPRRTY	phratry
AHPRSUU	purusha
AHPSXYY	asphyxy
AHQSSUY	squashy
AHRSTWY	swarthy
AHRTUWY	thruway
AIIILMS	Ismaili
AIIILMT	militia
AIIILNT	initial
AIIILVX	lixivia
AIIIMRS	saimiri
AIIJLLN	Jillian
AIIJMNS	Jainism
AIIJMSU	Jiamusi
AIIJNRU	injuria
AIIJNST	Jainist
AIIKLLN	killian
AIIKMMS	skimmia
AIIKMNN	manikin
AIIKNNR	narikin
AIIKNUW	Iwakuni
AIIKRRU	rauriki
AIIKSTU	Kutaisi
AIILLLN	Lillian
AIILLLP	lapilli
AIILLLS	Lillias
AIILLMN	liminal
AIILLMW	William
AIILLNV	villain
AIILMMN	minimal
AIILMNO	monilia
AIILMNT	intimal
AIILMRS	similar
AIILMRY	miliary
AIILMST	tailism
AIILNNS	Aislinn
AIILNOS	liaison
AIILNOU	niaouli
AIILNOV	Livonia
AIILNPT	pintail
AIILNPU	nauplii
AIILNRT	intrail
AIILNRY	rainily
AIILNTU	nautili
AIILNTY	anility
AIILOPP	papilio
AIILOPZ	polizia
AIILORV	ravioli
AIILOSS	loiasis
AIILOST	isolati
AIILOTT	Italiot, Ottilia
AIILPZZ	Lipizza
AIILQSU	siliqua
AIILRST	liatris
AIILRTV	trivial
AIIMMNS	animism

AIIMMNX maximin, minimax
AIIMNNZ Manzini
AIIMNPS pianism
AIIMNPT impaint, timpani
AIIMNRT Martini
AIIMNST animist
AIIMNSZ Naziism
AIIMNTU minutia
AIIMNTV vitamin
AIIMPRT mi-parti
AIIMRSS airmiss
AIIMSSV Sivaism
AIIMSSY myiasis
AIINNOP pianino
AIINNTY inanity
AIINOTT notitia
AIINPQU Inupiaq
AIINPRS aspirin
AIINPST pianist, pisatin
AIINPTU Inupiat
AIINRSY raisiny
AIINRTV vitrain
AIINSTU Tunisia
AIIOPRR a priori
AIIOPRW waipiro
AIIPRSS parisis
AIIPSTW wapitis
AIIPTTU pituita
AIJJMMS jim-jams
AIJLTTU Julitta
AIJLYZZ jazzily
AIJMORR Morarji
AIJNNOT joinant
AIJNORT janitor
AIJNQUU Jiuquan
AIJNSTU Justina
AIJOOUZ Jiaozou
AIKKMNR kirkman
AIKKMOT komatik
AIKKNOU koniaku
AIKKOOW kokowai
AIKLLNY lankily
AIKLMMN milkman
AIKLMNN linkman
AIKLNOO Kolonia
AIKLNSY snakily
AIKLOST Sialkot
AIKLOTW kotwali
AIKLOUZ Zoulika
AIKLPSU pulaski
AIKLPWY pawkily
AIKLRSY sarkily
AIKLRTT titlark
AIKLSSU salukis
AIKLSSY skysail
AIKMNNS kinsman
AIKNRTV Travnik
AIKOORW korowai
AIKOSSS Sikasso
AIKPRRT Prakrit
AIKRSTU kasturi
AILLLOY illoyal
AILLMNU luminal
AILLMOP oil lamp, oil-palm, palm oil
AILLMOT maillot, Motilal
AILLMPT lamplit
AILLMPU pallium
AILLMSW sawmill
AILLMSY misally
AILLNNO lanolin
AILLNNT Tallinn
AILLNOP pallion
AILLNOS Allison
AILLNPY plainly
AILLNST install
AILLNVY villany
AILLORZ zorilla
AILLPPU pupilla
AILLPRU pilular
AILLPUV pluvial
AILLRVY virally
AILLTVY vitally
AILLTWW witwall
AILMMOR immoral
AILMMSY myalism
AILMNNO nominal
AILMNNU numinal
AILMNOP lampion
AILMNOR marlion
AILMNOS malison, Osmanli
AILMNOY alimony
AILMNPS plasmin
AILMNPT implant
AILMNRY Marilyn
AILMOPT optimal, palmito
AILMOPY Olympia
AILMORS oralism
AILMOSS Somalis
AILMPRS prismal
AILMPRU primula
AILMPST palmist
AILMPSY impalsy, misplay
AILMRST mistral
AILMSSV Slavism
AILNNOT ant-lion
AILNNRS insnarl
AILNOOT olation
AILNOPY polynia
AILNPSX salpinx
AILNPTU nuptial
AILNPTY inaptly, ptyalin
AILNQTU quintal
AILNRSU insular
AILNSSU San Luis
AILNSTY nastily, saintly
AILNTTY nattily
AILOOST isolato
AILOPRR parloir
AILOPRS Polaris
AILOPRT portail
AILOPST apostil, topsail
AILOPSY soapily
AILOPTT talipot
AILOPTV pivotal
AILOQTU aliquot
AILORST oralist
AILORTY orality
AILORUW wourali
AILORUX uxorial
AILORVY olivary
AILOSTU outsail
AILOTVY ovality
AILPPRU pupilar
AILPPSY payslip, sappily
AILPQSU pasquil
AILPSTY pastily
AILPSWY slipway
AILQRTU Tarquil
AILQTTU quittal
AILQTUY quality
AILRRVY rivalry
AILRSTT starlit
AILRSTY trysail
AILRTTU titular
AILRTTY rattily, tartily
AILRTUV virtual
AILSSSY sassily
AILSSTU tissual
AILSTTY tastily
AILSTUW lawsuit
AILTTTY tattily
AIMMMUX maximum
AIMMNOS nomisma
AIMMNOT ommatin
AIMMNTU manumit
AIMMOST atomism
AIMMRSX Marxism
AIMNNOR iron man
AIMNNOS mansion, onanism
AIMNOOR amorino
AIMNOOT amotion
AIMNOPR rampion
AIMNOPT maintop, tampion
AIMNORT tormina
AIMNORU inamour, mainour
AIMNORW wormian
AIMNOTU manitou, tinamou
AIMNPRT mint par
AIMNPST instamp, pitmans
AIMNPTY tympani
AIMNRRU murrain
AIMNRTU natrium
AIMNRTV varmint
AIMNRUU uranium
AIMNSTT mattins
AIMNSTU tsunami
AIMOPST impasto

AIMORRU orarium
AIMORST amorist
AIMORTT tritoma
AIMORUV ovarium
AIMOSTT atomist
AIMPPRU air pump
AIMPRRY primary
AIMPRSY pyramis
AIMQRSU marquis
AIMRSST tsarism
AIMRSTT matrist
AIMRSTU atriums, matsuri
AIMRSTX Marxist
AIMRSTY maistry
AIMRTUV vitarum
AIMSSTT statism
AIMSSTY misstay
AINNNOW wannion
AINNOOT Antonio
AINNOOX Oxonian
AINNOPS saponin
AINNOST onanist
AINNOTT notatin
AINNQTU quinnat, quintan
AINNRTT intrant
AINNSTT instant
AINNTUY annuity
AINOOPR pronaoi
AINOORR orarion
AINOORT Ontario, oration
AINOOTV ovation
AINOOVV Ivanovo
AINOPPS pinsapo
AINOPPT appoint
AINOPRS parison
AINOPSS passion
AINOPTU opuntia, Utopian
AINORST astrion
AINORTU rainout
AINORTW waitron
AINORTX trioxan
AINOSSU sanious; suasion
AINOSTT station
AINOSUX anxious
AINPPRS parsnip
AINPPRY papyrin
AINPQTU piquant
AINPRST spirant, spraint
AINPRTU puritan
AINPSST pissant
AINQRTU quatrin, Tarquin
AINQRUY quinary
AINQSTU asquint
AINRRTY trinary
AINRRUY urinary
AINRSSU Russian
AINRSTT transit, Tristan
AINRTTT titrant
AINRTUY unitary
AINSSTU issuant, sustain
AINTTVY tantivy
AINTTWW want-wit
AIOPPRR propria
AIOPRRT airport, paritor
AIOPRST parotis
AIOPRSV proavis
AIOPRTT patriot
AIOPRTY topiary
AIOPRUV paviour
AIOPSSZ zopissa
AIORRRW warrior
AIORRTT traitor
AIORRTX oratrix
AIORSTU sautoir
AIORSTV travois
AIORSTY ostiary
AIORSUV saviour, various
AIPRRTT tripart
AIPRSSU prasius
AIPRSTT patrist
AIPRSTU upstair
AIPRTVY pravity
AIPZZZZ pizzazz
AIRSSTT tsarist
AIRSTTT attrist
AIRSTTU turista
AIRSTUV Rustavi
AIRSTVY varsity
AISSTTT statist
AISTTVY vastity
AISTUVY suavity
AJJKOTU Akjoujt
AJKMNTU muntjak
AJLNORU journal
AJMNRUY juryman
AJOOPRT Rajpoot
AJORRTU jurator
AKKLMSY Kalmyks
AKKLOSS koklass
AKKLRSY skylark
AKKLSWY skywalk
AKLLNOW know-all
AKLLOXY alkoxyl
AKLMNOO Kolomna
AKLNOOV novolak
AKLNORW Norwalk
AKLOOUV Kouvola
AKLOTTU out-talk
AKLOTUW outwalk, walkout
AKLPRSY sparkly
AKLRSTY starkly
AKLUUWZ KwaZulu
AKMNORW workman
AKMNRTU trankum
AKMORST Ostmark
AKMOSTU Komatsu
AKMQTUU kumquat
AKMRSTU muskrat
AKNOOPS poonask
AKNOPTT tank top
AKNORTU outrank
AKOOPRT partook
AKORRTW artwork
AKORTUV Vorkuta
AKORWWX waxwork
AKOSTTU kotatsu
ALLLOYY loyally
ALLMNPU Pullman
ALLMOOS osmolal
ALLMORY Mallory, morally
ALLMOSW mallows
ALLMPUU plumula
ALLNOOW Walloon
ALLNOTY tonally
ALLNRUU lunular
ALLNTUU ululant
ALLOOST latosol
ALLOOTX axolotl
ALLOPRY payroll, polarly
ALLOPTX poll tax
ALLORYY royally
ALLOSWW swallow
ALLOSWY sallowy
ALLOTTY totally
ALLOTUW outwall
ALLOTWY tallowy
ALLOTYY loyalty
ALLQSUY squally
ALLRRUY rurally
ALLRSTU lustral
ALLSUUY usually
ALMNNUY unmanly
ALMNOOP lampoon
ALMNOOW woolman
ALMNOPS plasmon
ALMNOPW plowman
ALMNORU unmoral
ALMNORY almonry
ALMNOSS salmons
ALMNOSY salmony
ALMNOWY womanly
ALMNPSU sunlamp
ALMNSUU alumnus
ALMOOPS ooplasm
ALMOOPY polyoma
ALMOORS osmolar
ALMOPPT palmtop
ALMOPRT marplot
ALMOSSU samolus
ALMOSSW low Mass
ALMOTTU mulatto
ALMRSTY smartly
ALMRSUU ramulus
ALMRTUU tumular
ALMSSUY alyssum
ALNNOPT planont
ALNNOPU nonupla
ALNNRSU unsnarl
ALNNSUU annulus
ALNOOPR polaron
ALNOOPT platoon

ALNOORT ortolan
ALNOPPY panoply
ALNOPRY nopalry
ALNOPTY pantoyl
ALNOPYY polynya
ALNORSY Rosalyn
ALNORUY unroyal
ALNPRSU snarl-up
ALNPSTU pulsant
ALNPTUY unaptly
ALNPTXY planxty
ALNRUWY wanruly
ALNSUUU unusual
ALOOPPS opposal
ALOOPRW poor law
ALOPPRU popular
ALOPPRY propyla
ALOPRRU parlour
ALOPRSU parlous, prosula
ALOPSSU spousal
ALOPTUY outplay
ALOQRRU rorqual
ALOQRSU squalor
ALORRST rostral
ALORTYY royalty
ALOSTTU outlast
ALOSTWX lost wax
ALQSTUY squatly
ALRSTUU sutural
AMMNRUY nummary
AMMOORR maormor, mormaor
AMMOPTU pomatum
AMMORWW mawworm
AMMOSXY myxomas
AMMRSUY summary
AMNNOSW snowman
AMNNOTT montant
AMNNOTY antonym
AMNOOPP pompano
AMNOOPR poor man
AMNOOTT ottoman
AMNOPRT portman
AMNOPRY paronym
AMNOPSS Sampson
AMNOPST postman
AMNOPTU pantoum
AMNOPUU pounamu
AMNORSS ramsons
AMNORST transom
AMNORSY masonry
AMNOTUY autonym
AMNPTYY tympany
AMNQTUU quantum
AMNRTTU tantrum
AMOOORS amoroso
AMOOPRS prosoma
AMOOPRT protoma, taproom
AMOORSU amorous
AMOORTT moratto
AMOPSTT topmast
AMORRTY mortary
AMORRUY armoury
AMORRWY marrowy
AMORSST matross
AMORTTU mutator
AMPSSTU assumpt
AMQSUUW musquaw
AMRRTYY martyry
AMRSTTU stratum
AMRTUUY mutuary
ANNOOTT annotto
ANNORST transon
ANNOTTU Taunton
ANNOTTY tantony
ANNRTYY tyranny
ANOOPRS pronaos, soprano
ANOOPRT patroon
ANOORST santoor
ANOORTT arnotto, notator
ANOORTV novator
ANOPRRS sporran
ANOPRST pastron
ANOPRTU paturon
ANOPRTV provant
ANOPSTU outspan
ANORRTW war-torn
ANORRWW war-worn
ANORSTU santour
ANORWWY way-worn
ANPRSTU suntrap, unstrap
ANPRTYY prytany
ANRSSTU sunstar
ANRSSUY sunrays
ANSSTUU nasutus
AOOPPRS apropos, Sapporo
AOOPRTT potator, tap root
AOORRTT rotator
AOORRTU outroar, Rotorua
AOORRTY oratory
AOOSTTT tattoos
AOPPRRT rapport
AOPRRSW sparrow
AOPRRTY portray, tropary
AOPRSTW postwar
AOPRTTU outpart
AOPRUVY vapoury
AOPSSTU outpass, pass-out
AOPSTTX post-tax
AOPSTUY autopsy
AOQRTUY Torquay
AORSSUY ossuary
AORSTWW saw-wort
AORSUVY savoury
AORTTUY out-tray
AOSTTUY outstay
APPRRUU purpura
APPRSTY strappy
APPRSUY papyrus
APRSSSU surpass
APRSTTU start-up, upstart
APRTUWY putwary
ARSSTTU stratus
BBBDELU blubbed
BBBELOR blobber
BBBELRU blubber
BBBEORY bobbery
BBBGIIN bibbing
BBBGINO bobbing
BBBHIOS bobbish
BBCCIKO bib-cock
BBCDEIR cribbed
BBCDELU clubbed
BBCEHIN nebbich
BBCEILR cribble
BBCEIRR cribber
BBCEKKU kebbuck
BBCELOR clobber, cobbler
BBCELRU clubber
BBCGINU cubbing
BBCHISU cubbish
BBCINOU bubonic
BBCKLOU Lubbock
BBCRSUY scrubby
BBDDERU drubbed
BBDEEEL bebleed
BBDEELP pebbled
BBDEFLU flubbed
BBDEGRU grubbed
BBDEILO bilobed
BBDEILR dribble
BBDEINS snibbed
BBDEKNO knobbed
BBDEKNU bunk bed
BBDELOO beblood
BBDELOS bobsled
BBDELSU slubbed
BBDENSU snubbed
BBDESTU stubbed
BBDFLUU flubdub
BBDGIIN dibbing
BBDGINO dobbing
BBDGINU dubbing
BBDILRY dribbly
BBDKSUY dybbuks
BBEEENT Entebbe
BBEEERU bebeeru
BBEEGIL libbege
BBEEILL belibel
BBEELSS bebless
BBEESYY bye-byes
BBEFILR fribble
BBEGILR glibber, gribble
BBEGINW webbing
BBEGIOS gibbose
BBEGLOR gobbler
BBEGLRU grubble
BBEGRRU grubber
BBEHINS nebbish
BBEHKRU khubber
BBEHLOR hobbler
BBEHMTU bethumb

BBEIIMR imbiber
BBEILNR nibbler
BBEILOS bilboes
BBEILOT bibelot
BBEILPR pribble
BBEILQU quibble
BBEINOR biberon
BBEIOOT bobotie
BBEIORW bob-wire
BBEIRRY bribery
BBEIRTU tubbier
BBEJORY jobbery
BBEKLNO knobble
BBEKLNU knubble
BBEKLOS blesbok
BBEKNOR knobber
BBELLOY bellboy
BBELMOU bumbelo
BBELMRU bumbler
BBELNOR nobbler
BBELORS slobber
BBELORW wobbler
BBELORY lobbyer
BBELOUX blue box
BBELRRU burbler
BBELSTU stubble
BBENRSU snubber
BBEORRY robbery
BBEOSTY best boy
BBERRUY rubbery
BBESTUY best buy
BBFGIIN fibbing
BBFGINO fobbing
BBGGINO gobbing
BBGIIJN jibbing
BBGIINN nibbing
BBGIINR ribbing
BBGIJNO jobbing
BBGILNO lobbing
BBGIMNO mobbing
BBGINOR robbing
BBGINOS sobbing
BBGINPU pubbing
BBGINRU rubbing
BBGINSU gubbins, subbing
BBGINTU tubbing
BBGIOSU gibbous
BBHIMOS mobbish
BBHIOSY yobbish
BBHIRSU rubbish
BBHRSUY shrubby
BBIIILM bilimbi
BBIJMOO jib-boom
BBIKTUZ kibbutz
BBINNOS nobbins
BBJLOOW blow job
BBKLNOY knobbly
BBKLNUY knubbly
BBKLUUY bulk-buy
BBKNOOT bontbok
BBKOOOO boobook
BBLOSUU bulbous
BBLSTUY stubbly
BBMOOOX boom box
BBNOORU bourbon
BBOOOTY bootboy
BCCEEIU ice cube
BCCEILO ecbolic
BCCEILU cubicle
BCCEILY bicycle
BCCEMOR crombec
BCCILOU bucolic
BCCINOO obconic
BCCISUU succubi
BCCKLOO lobcock
BCCMOOX coxcomb
BCCMSUU succumb
BCCNOOR corn cob
BCDEEIL decibel
BCDEHOU debouch
BCDEIIO biocide
BCDEIKS sickbed
BCDEILO docible
BCDEKOR bedrock, brocked, rock-bed
BCDEKOS bedsock
BCDELOU becloud
BCDHIOR Dobrich
BCDHIRU bruchid
BCDHOOU cubhood
BCDIORW cowbird
BCDKORU burdock
BCDSTUU subduct
BCEEEHS beseech
BCEEFIN benefic
BCEEGIR iceberg
BCEEHIP ephebic
BCEEHLR belcher
BCEEHLU chebule
BCEEHNR bencher
BCEEHRT betcher
BCEEILR Liberec
BCEEILU ice blue
BCEEINR Bernice
BCEEIRS escribe
BCEEIRT terebic
BCEEKNU buckeen
BCEEKPS bespeck
BCEEKUY buckeye
BCEENOS obscene
BCEENRU crubeen
BCEHINR birchen
BCEHINT benthic
BCEHIOR brioche
BCEHIOT biotech
BCEHIRR bircher
BCEHISW Wisbech
BCEHITW bewitch
BCEHLMU chumble
BCEHLRU blucher
BCEHNRU buncher
BCEHORT botcher
BCEHRTU butcher
BCEIIKR brickie
BCEIKLM limbeck
BCEIKLR brickle
BCEIKRW Berwick
BCEIKST bestick
BCEILLU lucible
BCEILMO embolic
BCEILMR climber, crimble
BCEILNO binocle
BCEILOR bricole, corbeil, orbicle
BCEILOU ciboule
BCEIMNO combine
BCEIMOR microbe
BCEINOZ benzoic
BCEINRU brucine
BCEIRRS scriber
BCEIRSU suberic
BCEIRTU brucite
BCEJSTU subject
BCEKLOR blocker
BCEKLRU bruckle, buckler
BCEKORT brocket
BCEKORU roebuck
BCEKOTY bycoket
BCEKSTU bestuck
BCELLOW cowbell
BCELMRU crumble
BCELMSU scumble
BCELNOZ Coblenz
BCELORU coluber
BCEMNTU cumbent
BCEMORS scomber
BCEMRSU scumber
BCENOOY coenoby
BCENORU bouncer
BCENORW becrown
BCEOORT October
BCEORSS becross
BCEORSU obscure
BCFLOUW wolf cub
BCFSSUU subfusc
BCGIKNO bocking
BCGIMNO combing
BCHIIOT cohibit
BCHIKOU chibouk
BCHILNU bulchin
BCHIMOR rhombic
BCHINOR bronchi
BCHIOPR pibroch
BCHLOTY blotchy
BCHNOOR broncho
BCHORST borstch, bortsch
BCIIKLN niblick
BCIILMR limbric
BCIILMU bulimic
BCIILOR colibri
BCIINOS bionics
BCIISTU biscuit
BCIITUY ubicity
BCIKORT brockit
BCIKOTT bittock
BCILMPU plumbic
BCILOOR brocoli
BCINOOR con brio
BCINOOX coin box

BCINOPR pibcorn
BCINORU Rubicon
BCINORY Byronic
BCINSUU incubus
BCIOORT robotic
BCIRTUY butyric
BCISTUU cubitus
BCJKMUU jumbuck
BCKLLOO bollock
BCKLLOU bullock
BCKLNOU unblock
BCKOORU bourock
BCKOTTU buttock
BCLMOOO Colombo
BCLMOOU coulomb
BCLMRUY crumbly
BCLOOOX cool box
BCLOOSU colobus
BCLORTU clot-bur
BCMOSTU combust
BCOOTTY boycott
BCOSTTU Cottbus
BDDEEER reed-bed
BDDEEES seedbed
BDDEEIS bedside
BDDEEIT debited
BDDEEOX deed-box
BDDEFOR Bedford
BDDEGIN bedding
BDDEIIR birdied
BDDEINR brinded
BDDEIRY biddery
BDDELOO blooded
BDDENOU bounded
BDDESUU subdued
BDDGIIN bidding
BDDGINU budding
BDDILOR old bird
BDDINRU dun-bird
BDEEELN Ndebele
BDEEELR bleeder
BDEEELV beveled
BDEEERR breeder
BDEEFIR debrief
BDEEGUY bug-eyed
BDEEILL bellied, delible, libeled
BDEEILR deliber
BDEEILV bedevil
BDEEIMT bedtime
BDEEINR bendier, inbreed
BDEEINZ bedizen
BDEEIOS deboise
BDEEIRR berried
BDEEISS besides
BDEEIST side-bet
BDEELNR blender
BDEELOV beloved
BDEELRT Delbert
BDEELSS blessed
BDEEMOW embowed
BDEEMSU embused
BDEENPR prebend
BDEENRT Derbent
BDEENTT tent-bed
BDEEORS bedsore
BDEERST bedrest
BDEERSU deburse
BDEESTT test bed
BDEFLOU bodeful
BDEFOOT footbed
BDEGHIN Denbigh
BDEGHIT bedight
BDEGINO Bendigo
BDEGIOO boogied
BDEGIOT bigoted
BDEGIRS bridges
BDEGIRT Bridget
BDEGLRU bludger
BDEGOOY goodbye
BDEHITW whitbed
BDEHMTU thumbed
BDEHORY herd-boy
BDEIIRS birdies
BDEILLR ill-bred
BDEILNR blinder, brindle
BDEILPP blipped
BDEILRT driblet
BDEILRU builder, rebuild
BDEIMMR brimmed
BDEIMOR bromide
BDEIMRU imbrued
BDEINOR broiden
BDEINOU Bedouin
BDEINRY bindery
BDEINTW twin bed
BDEIORR broider
BDEIORS disrobe
BDEIORT debitor, de-orbit, orbited
BDEIORV overbid
BDEIORZ zebroid
BDEIOSY disobey
BDEIOWY wide boy
BDEIRVY drive-by
BDEISSU subside
BDEISTU sub-edit
BDEITUY dubiety
BDEKNOO bookend
BDELLMU dumbell
BDELLOR bedroll
BDELMOO bloomed
BDELMRU drumble
BDELNOW Blodwen
BDELNRU blunder, bundler
BDELORU boulder, doubler
BDELORW bowlder
BDELOTT blotted, bottled
BDELOTU doublet
BDELOUW would-be
BDELRRU blurred
BDEMNOU embound
BDEMOOR bedroom, boredom
BDEMOOS bosomed
BDENNOU bounden
BDENORU bounder, rebound
BDENORW browden
BDENORY bone dry
BDENOUW unbowed
BDENSTU subtend
BDENSUY sebundy
BDENTTU butt-end
BDEOORR brooder
BDEOPST bedpost
BDEORRU bordure
BDEORSU rosebud
BDEORTU doubter, obtrude, redoubt
BDEORUV overdub
BDEQUUU Dubuque
BDESSUU subdues
BDFIIOR fibroid
BDFIISU fidibus
BDGHIIR Brighid
BDGIINN binding
BDGIINR birding
BDGIIOO gobioid
BDGILOO globoid
BDGJOOO good job
BDGLLOU bulldog
BDGLOOT dogbolt
BDGOOSY goodbys
BDHIMRU hum-bird
BDHINOP hop-bind
BDHIOSU bushido
BDHOOOY boyhood
BDIIKNO bodikin
BDIILNU in-build
BDIILOR oil-bird
BDIIMSU midibus
BDIJOOR jib-door
BDIKNOR brodkin
BDILLLO Old Bill
BDILLNU Billund
BDILLNY blindly
BDILNUU unbuild
BDILPUU build-up
BDILRUY buirdly, ludibry
BDIMNOU imbound
BDINNOU inbound
BDINOOR bridoon
BDINRSU sunbird
BDINRUU Burundi
BDINSTU dustbin
BDIOORU boudoir
BDIOSUU dubious
BDIRSTU disturb
BDISSUY subsidy
BDKNOOU bundook
BDLOOOP lobopod
BDLORWY blow-dry
BDNNOUU unbound
BDNOORU bourdon

BDNORUU burdoun
BDNORUW rub-down
BDOOOWX boxwood
BDRSUUY Sudbury
BEEEERY eye-bree
BEEEFIR beefier, freebie
BEEEFLR feebler
BEEEGIS besiege
BEEEGKL geelbek
BEEEGKR keg beer
BEEEHIV beehive
BEEEHNS shebeen
BEEEILL libelee
BEEEILN beeline
BEEEILV believe
BEEEIRR beerier
BEEEJLW bejewel
BEEEJLZ Jezebel
BEEELPR bleeper
BEEELPS Peebles
BEEENNZ benzene
BEEENTW between
BEEEORV veeboer
BEEFGIN beefing
BEEFGIT Bigfeet
BEEFILL flebile
BEEFILR febrile
BEEFILY beefily
BEEFINT benefit
BEEFIRS frisbee
BEEGGNU geebung
BEEGILL legible
BEEGILO obligee
BEEGILU beguile
BEEGIMR begrime
BEEGINR bigener
BEEGINT beignet
BEEGINU beguine
BEEGIRT big tree
BEEGLNO englobe
BEEGMNO gombeen
BEEGRTU beer gut
BEEHINS beshine
BEEHIRR herbier
BEEHLRT blether, herblet
BEEHMRY berhyme
BEEHNNO hebenon
BEEHOOV behoove
BEEHORS herbose
BEEHORW bewhore
BEEHRRT Herbert
BEEHRST sherbet
BEEHRSW beshrew
BEEHRTY thereby
BEEHRWY whereby
BEEHSTY bheesty
BEEIJLU jubilee
BEEIKKR brekkie
BEEILLV bi-level
BEEILNP penible
BEEILNY bye-line
BEEILOS obelise
BEEILOZ obelize

BEEILRY beerily
BEEILTT betitle
BEEIMST betimes
BEEINNZ benzine
BEEINOT ebonite
BEEINRZ zebrine
BEEIQUZ bezique
BEEIRRV brevier
BEEIRTY ebriety
BEEJSSU bejesus
BEEKKRR brekker
BEEKMOS besmoke
BEEKNOT betoken
BEEKOPS bespoke
BEEKRRS berserk
BEEKRRU rebuker
BEELLPS bespell
BEELMOW embowel
BEELMRT tremble
BEELMSU meubles
BEELNNO ennoble
BEELNOZ benzole
BEELNTY Bentley
BEELNUX Benelux
BEELOTY eye bolt
BEELRTZ bretzel
BEELRUZ zebrule
BEELRVY Beverly
BEEMNRU E-number
BEEMORW embower
BEEMRSU Burmese
BEENNTT Bennett
BEENOST boneset
BEEORRS soberer
BEEORSV observe, obverse, verbose
BEEORWY eyebrow
BEEPRRV preverb
BEEQSTU bequest
BEERRWY brewery
BEERSSU rebuses
BEERSTW bestrew, webster
BEERTTU burette
BEETTUV buvette
BEFFLRU bluffer
BEFFOOR off-bore
BEFGIIL filibeg
BEFGIRU firebug
BEFILRT filbert
BEFILRY briefly
BEFILSU fusible
BEFINOR bonfire
BEFIORS fibrose
BEFIORX firebox
BEFIRST fibster
BEFIRSU fubsier
BEFIRVY verbify
BEFITUX tubifex
BEFLMRU fumbler
BEFLORT Belfort
BEFLRTU Fulbert
BEFMNRU f-number
BEFOORR forbore

BEFOSUX fuse box
BEFRRUY furbery
BEGGGIN begging
BEGGIOR boggier
BEGGIRU buggier
BEGGIST biggest
BEGGLOR broggle
BEGGORR brogger
BEGGRUY buggery
BEGHHIT behight
BEGHIMT might-be
BEGHINT benight
BEGHRRU burgher
BEGIIJN Beijing
BEGIINN in-being
BEGILLY legibly
BEGILMT gimblet
BEGILMU Belgium
BEGILNO Gobelin, ignoble
BEGILNT belting
BEGILNU blueing
BEGILNY belying
BEGILOR obliger
BEGILRT gilbert
BEGILST giblets
BEGINRR bringer
BEGINSS bigness
BEGINTT betting
BEGIOOS boogies
BEGJNUU June bug
BEGKMOS gemsbok
BEGLLOU globule
BEGLMOO begloom
BEGLMRU grumble
BEGLMUU bluegum
BEGLNRU bungler
BEGLOOS globose
BEGLOOT bootleg
BEGLOSU glebous
BEGLOSW bow-legs
BEGLRTY bergylt
BEGNORU burgeon
BEGNOTT bettong
BEGRSSU burgess
BEHHRSU Bushehr
BEHIITX exhibit
BEHIKKS Bishkek
BEHIKNT bethink
BEHILMS blemish
BEHILMT thimble
BEHILOS Bolshie
BEHILRT blither
BEHILST Lisbeth
BEHILSU blueish
BEHILSW blewish
BEHILTZ Lizbeth
BEHIMOY yohimbe
BEHINOP hip bone, hop-bine
BEHIOTW howbeit
BEHIRRT rebirth
BEHIRSU bushier
BEHLMRU humbler
BEHLORT brothel

BEHLRSU blusher
BEHMOOY homeboy
BEHMPTU bethump
BEHMRTU Humbert
BEHNORT benorth
BEHNOST benthos
BEHNRTU burthen
BEHOORT theorbo
BEHOOSX shoebox
BEHOPRT pot-herb
BEHORRT brother
BEHORSU herbous
BEHORTT betroth
BEHOSTU besouth
BEIILRS risible
BEIILSV visible
BEIIMST bismite
BEIIOTT biotite
BEIIRTT bittier
BEIJNNO benjoin
BEIKLNR blinker
BEIKLOS obelisk
BEIKLOX boxlike
BEIKLRU bulkier
BEIKNRS brisken
BEIKOTX box kite
BEIKRST brisket
BEILLST bestill
BEILLVY bevilly
BEILMNR nimbler
BEILMOR embroil
BEILMOW imbowel
BEILMRT timbrel
BEILMRW wimbrel
BEILMSS embliss
BEILMSU blueism, sublime
BEILNNO innoble
BEILNOO obelion
BEILNOW bowline
BEILNTU betulin
BEILNTZ blintze
BEILOPY epiboly
BEILOQU oblique
BEILORR broiler
BEILORW blowier
BEILORY boilery
BEILQTU quiblet
BEILRRU burlier
BEILRSS ribless
BEILRST blister, bristle
BEILRSU buriels
BEILRTT blitter, brittle, triblet
BEILRTU rebuilt
BEILRTW Wilbert
BEILRTY liberty
BEILRUZ brulzie
BEILSTW blewits
BEILTTU blue tit
BEIMMRR brimmer
BEIMMRU Brummie
BEIMNOR bromine
BEIMNTU bitumen
BEIMORW imbower
BEIMPRU bumpier
BEIMRSU imbrues, imburse
BEIMRTU imbrute, terbium
BEINNOR bonnier
BEINNOS benison
BEINNOZ benzoin
BEINOOS besonio, boonies
BEINORT bornite
BEINORW brownie
BEINOST boniest
BEINOTT bottine
BEINOWX wine box
BEINRTT bittern
BEINRTU tribune, turbine
BEINSSY byssine
BEIOORZ boozier
BEIORRT orbiter
BEIORSS bossier
BEIORSU ebrious
BEIORTV Viterbo
BEIOSTX boxiest
BEIOSTY obesity
BEIPRST bestrip
BEIQRTU briquet
BEIRRSU brisure, bruiser
BEIRRTU true rib
BEIRSTU bustier
BEIRTTU tribute
BEIRTVY brevity
BEISSTU busiest
BEITTWX betwixt
BEJKOUX jukebox
BEJLOOW Joe Blow
BEJLOSS jobless
BEKLMOS melkbos
BEKLNTU blunket
BEKLOOT booklet
BEKLSUY sky blue
BEKMORS kombers
BEKNORS bonkers
BEKOOPR pre-book
BEKORWW webwork
BELLLMU blellum
BELLLOW lowbell
BELLOSU soluble
BELLOSW bellows
BELLOTW bowtell
BELLOUV voluble
BELMMOO embloom
BELMMRU mumbler
BELMNOU nelumbo
BELMNOY benomyl
BELMNSU numbles
BELMOOR bloomer
BELMOOT boomlet
BELMOPR problem
BELMORT temblor
BELMORU mob rule, morbleu
BELMORY Bromley
BELMOSU embolus
BELMOTU molebut
BELMPRU plumber
BELMPTU plumbet
BELMRRU rumbler
BELMRSU slumber
BELMRTU tumbler, tumbrel
BELMRTY trembly
BELMSTU stumble
BELNOOR borneol
BELNOOY boloney
BELNOST noblest
BELNOYZ benzoyl
BELNRUY Burnley
BELNSTU sunbelt, unblest
BELOOPR blooper
BELOOVV obvolve
BELORST bolster, lobster
BELORSY soberly
BELORTT blotter, bottler
BELORTU boulter, trouble
BELOSSU boluses
BELOSTU boletus
BELRSTU bluster, brustle, subtler
BEMMOOS embosom
BEMMRUY bummery
BEMNORW embrown
BEMNORY embryon
BEMNOSU umbones
BEMNTTU butment
BEMOORS morbose
BEMORST bestorm, mobster
BEMORWW webworm
BEMSSUU subsume
BENNORW Bronwen, newborn
BENOORS Osborne
BENORRT Norbert
BENORTY rent boy
BENORWY bywoner
BENOSTX nest box
BENOSWY newsboy
BENRUWY Newbury
BEOOPUZ booze-up
BEOORST booster
BEOORVW overbow
BEOOTTX tote box
BEOPRRV proverb
BEOPRST besport
BEOPSTU bespout
BEOQSTU bosquet
BEOQSUY obsequy
BEOQTUU bouquet
BEORRSW browser
BEORSUU uberous
BEORSUZ sub-zero
BEORUVY overbuy

BEPRRTU perturb
BEPRTUY puberty
BEQRSUU brusque
BERRSTU burster
BERRUVV bruvver
BERSTTU betrust, tubster
BERSTTY Bettrys
BERSTUV subvert
BERTTUY buttery
BESTTUX subtext
BFFLLUY bluffly
BFFNOOU buffoon
BFGIOOT Bigfoot
BFGIORT frogbit
BFHILOS lobfish
BFHIRSU furbish
BFIINOR fibroin
BFILMRU brimful
BFILRUY lubrify
BFINORT bifront
BFIORSU fibrous
BFIRTUY brutify
BFLLOUW bowlful
BFLLOWY blowfly, fly-blow
BFMORSU subform
BFOUXZZ fuzzbox
BGGGINO bogging
BGGGINU bugging
BGGHIIS biggish
BGGIINN binging
BGGINOY bygoing
BGHHIOY highboy
BGHILTY Blighty
BGHINOR bighorn
BGHINSU bushing
BGHINTY by-thing
BGHIOST big shot
BGHLRUU burghul
BGHMORU Homburg
BGHOOOS Oshogbo
BGHOORU borough
BGHORTU brought
BGIILNO boiling
BGIILNR birling
BGIILNS sibling
BGIIMNO imbongi
BGIIMNU imbuing
BGIINNN binning
BGIINNR inbring
BGIINRU gunibri
BGIKNOO booking
BGIKNOR broking
BGIKNSU busking
BGILMOU gumboil
BGILNOO o'goblin
BGILNOT biltong, botling
BGILNOW blowing, bowling
BGILNOY ignobly
BGILOOR obligor
BGILOOY biology
BGILRTU Tilburg

BGIMMNU bumming
BGINNRU burning
BGINNTU bunting
BGINOPP bopping
BGINSSU bussing
BGIORTY bigotry
BGJOTUY toby jug
BGKLOOO logbook
BGKORSY grysbok
BGLMRUY grumbly
BGLNOOW longbow
BGLNOUW blowgun
BGLOOSU globous
BGLOSSU bugloss
BGLOSUY bogusly
BGMOOSS bog moss
BGMOOTU gumboot
BGNPRUU burp gun
BHHIKKU bhikkhu
BHHIKSU bhikshu
BHIIINN inhibin
BHIIINT inhibit
BHIIMMU muhimbi
BHIIOOR Obihiro
BHIIPSS sibship
BHIIRST British
BHIKOOS bookish
BHILLSU bullish
BHILPSU publish
BHILSUY bushily
BHIMORT thrombi
BHIMSTU bismuth
BHINOUZ Binzhou
BHINRSU burnish
BHIOORS boorish
BHIOSWZ showbiz
BHIRSTU brutish
BHIRTTU turbith
BHJNOTU job-hunt
BHLOOPR phorbol
BHLOOPT Botolph
BHLRSUU bulrush
BHMORSU rhombus
BHOOOOS boohoos
BHOOPSY shop boy
BHOOSTW bowshot
BHPRSUU brush-up
BIIILST Tbilisi
BIIKLNS isblink
BIILLNO billion
BIILLOU bouilli
BIILLTW twibill
BIILMOR imbroil
BIILMRU Librium
BIILNTU built-in, inbuilt
BIILOSU bilious
BIILRSY risibly
BIILSVY visibly
BIILTTY bittily
BIIMNOT intombi
BIIMNOU niobium
BIIMNSU minibus
BIIMPRS biprism
BIIMPRU pribumi

BIINORV vibrion
BIIORSV vibrios
BIIOSUV bivious
BIJNOSU subjoin
BIKKLOP klipbok
BIKLLUY bulkily
BIKLRSY briskly
BIKMNPU bumpkin
BIKNRSY Rybinsk
BILLNOU bullion
BILLOPX pillbox
BILLOWY billowy
BILLPTU pit bull
BILLTWY twybill
BILMNOR nombril
BILMNRU Milburn
BILMPUY bumpily
BILMRTU tumbril
BILNNOY bonnily
BILNRSU Lisburn
BILNTUU tubulin, unbuilt
BILOORT triobol
BILOOSS olisbos
BILOOYZ boozily
BILORST Bristol
BILOSSU subsoil
BILOSSY bossily
BILPTUU built-up
BILRSTY bristly
BILRTUY tilbury
BIMMOOS imbosom
BIMMORS bromism
BIMNORS misborn
BIMNOSU omnibus
BIMRSTU brutism
BIMRSUX bruxism
BINOOSU niobous
BINORTU tiburon
BINRSTU inburst
BINSTUU subunit
BIOOORS rooibos
BIOOSUV obvious
BIOPRTY probity
BIORRTU burrito
BIORRTW ribwort
BIORSTT bistort
BISSSTU subsist
BJKOORW jobwork
BJNOORU bonjour
BJORUXY jury box
BKOOORV voorbok
BKOORWX workbox
BLLNTUY bluntly
BLLOSUU bullous, lobulus
BLLOUVY volubly
BLMOOOT tombolo
BLMOORW lobworm
BLMOOSS blossom
BLNNOUW unblown
BLNOORW low-born
BLNOOSU blouson
BLOOOTX toolbox
BLOOQUY obloquy

BLOORWW	lowbrow
BLOOTUW	blow-out
BLOPSTU	sub-plot
BLSTUUU	tubulus
BMNOOSU	unbosom
BMOOORX	boxroom
BMOORSU	morbous
BMORSUU	brumous
BNNORWY	Bronwyn
BNNOUUY	nun-buoy
BNNRSUU	sunburn
BNNRTUU	unburnt
BNOOOPR	pro bono
BNOOTTY	bottony
BNORSUU	burnous
BNORTUU	burn-out
BNOSTTU	buttons
BNOTTUY	buttony
BNRSUUY	Sunbury
BOOOPRX	poor box
BOOOPTT	top-boot
BOOPRTT	Bottrop
BOOPSTX	postbox
BOPSSTU	bus stop
BORSTTU	to-burst, turbots
BORSTXY	bostryx
CCCDIOO	coccoid
CCCEHIO	choc ice
CCCNOOT	concoct
CCCOORU	co-occur
CCDEEEN	decence
CCDEEHK	checked
CCDEEIO	ecocide
CCDEENO	concede
CCDEENY	decency
CCDEESU	succeed
CCDEHIL	cliched
CCDEHRY	Cedrych
CCDEIIT	deictic
CCDEILO	ice-cold
CCDEIMO	comedic
CCDEIOS	codices
CCDEKOR	crocked
CCDELOU	occlude
CCDENOU	conduce
CCDHIIL	cichlid
CCDIILO	codicil
CCDIIOR	cricoid
CCDILOY	cycloid
CCDJKOU	judcock
CCDKLOU	cuckold
CCDNOOR	concord
CCDNOTU	conduct
CCEEHHN	Chechen
CCEEHIV	ceviche
CCEEHKR	checker, recheck
CCEEHOU	couchee
CCEEHRS	screech
CCEEIIL	Cecilie
CCEEILN	licence
CCEEINR	eccrine
CCEEINS	science
CCEEIRV	crevice
CCEEKOY	cock-eye
CCEELNU	lucence
CCEELRU	Lucrece
CCEELRY	recycle
CCEENRY	recency
CCEEOPR	precoce
CCEERSY	secrecy
CCEFNOT	confect
CCEGNOY	cogency
CCEHIKN	check-in, chicken
CCEHIKU	chuckie
CCEHILU	culchie
CCEHINO	conchie
CCEHINT	technic
CCEHINZ	zecchin
CCEHIOV	vecchio
CCEHIST	chic-est
CCEHKLU	chuckle
CCEHKMS	schmeck
CCEHKOR	chocker
CCEHKPU	check-up
CCEHKRU	chucker
CCEHLOR	clocher
CCEHLRU	cleruch
CCEHNOS	conches
CCEHORT	crochet
CCEHORU	coucher
CCEIIKP	ice pick
CCEIIRT	icteric
CCEIIST	cecitis
CCEIKLR	clicker
CCEIKLT	clicket
CCEIKOR	cockier
CCEIKRT	cricket
CCEIKRY	crickey
CCEILNO	concile
CCEILNU	nucleic
CCEILNY	cliency
CCEILOT	coctile
CCEILRT	circlet, lectric
CCEILSY	cyclise, cylices
CCEILTU	cuticle
CCEILYZ	cyclize
CCEIMST	smectic
CCEINOR	cornice
CCEINOS	concise
CCEINOT	conceit
CCEINRT	centric
CCEIOPP	coppice
CCEIOPT	ectopic
CCEIORT	cerotic, orectic
CCEIOTT	cottice
CCEIPST	sceptic
CCEJNOT	conject
CCEKNOY	cockney
CCEKOPT	pet-cock
CCEKORR	crocker
CCEKORT	crocket
CCELLOT	collect
CCELNOY	cyclone
CCELNUY	lucency
CCELORU	corcule
CCELOSU	occluse
CCEMNOO	Comecon
CCENNOR	concern
CCENNOT	concent, connect
CCENOPT	concept
CCENORT	concert
CCENORW	concrew
CCENOTV	convect
CCEOOTT	cocotte
CCEOPRT	percoct
CCEORRT	correct
CCEORRU	reoccur
CCERTUW	crew-cut
CCESSSU	success
CCFIIIL	filicic
CCFIILU	lucific
CCFIRUY	crucify
CCFLOSU	floccus
CCGHINO	gnocchi
CCGKOOR	gorcock
CCHHILS	schlich
CCHHINY	chinchy
CCHHRUY	churchy
CCHILOR	chloric
CCHIMOR	chromic
CCHINOR	chronic
CCHINRS	scrinch
CCHIORY	chicory
CCHIOTW	cowitch
CCHIPSY	psychic
CCHIPUY	hiccupy
CCHIRST	scritch
CCHKLOS	schlock
CCHKMSU	schmuck
CCHKOSY	cockshy
CCHKPUU	upchuck
CCHNORS	scronch
CCHNRSU	scrunch
CCHNRUY	crunchy
CCHOORS	scrooch
CCHOSTU	Succoth
CCIIILS	silicic
CCIILNO	colicin
CCIILPR	circlip
CCIIRTU	circuit
CCIKLOW	cow-lick
CCIKLOY	cockily, colicky
CCIKOPT	cockpit
CCILNOO	colonic
CCILNOU	council
CCILOOP	piccolo
CCILSTY	cyclist
CCIMOTY	mycotic
CCINOOT	coction, oncotic
CCINORY	cryonic
CCINOTV	convict
CCIOORS	sirocco
CCIOPST	scoptic
CCIOPTU	occiput
CCIPRTY	cryptic
CCIRUUU	curucui
CCKOSTU	custock

CCLOPSY cyclops
CCMOOOR morocco
CCNOOPU puccoon
CCNOOTU coconut
CCNOPUY concupy
CCNOSSU concuss
CCORSUU succour
CCORSUY succory
CCSSSUU succuss
CDDDEEI decided
CDDDERU crudded
CDDDESU scudded
CDDEEER decreed
CDDEEII deicide
CDDEEIR decider
CDDEENS descend
CDDEEOR decoder
CDDEEUW cudweed
CDDEHIN chidden
CDDEHOR chorded
CDDEIIS discide
CDDEILM middle C
CDDEINU induced
CDDELOR clodder, coddler
CDDELOY dodecyl
CDDELRU cruddle
CDDELSU scuddle
CDDGINO codding
CDDGINU cudding
CDDIIIO didicoi
CDDIIKN niddick
CDDIILU dilucid
CDDIIOS discoid
CDDIIRU Druidic
CDDIKOP piddock
CDDIORS discord
CDDKOPU puddock
CDDKORU ruddock
CDDKORY dry dock
CDEEEFL fleeced
CDEEEFN defence
CDEEEIV deceive
CDEEENR decener
CDEEEPR precede
CDEEERS decrees, seceder
CDEEERT decreet
CDEEFII edifice
CDEEFLT deflect
CDEEFOR deforce
CDEEGHN Chengde
CDEEHIP cepheid
CDEEHIS dehisce
CDEEHOR chordee
CDEEHPR perched
CDEEHQU chequed
CDEEHTT tetched
CDEEIIT eidetic
CDEEILN decline
CDEEILP pedicel, pedicle
CDEEILU edicule
CDEEILV declive
CDEEIMN endemic
CDEEIMS demi-sec
CDEEINO codeine
CDEEINR deciner
CDEEIOS diocese
CDEEIOV devoice
CDEEIPR pierced
CDEEIRR decrier
CDEEIRT tierced
CDEEITX excited
CDEEKNR redneck
CDEELLR red cell
CDEELMU demulce
CDEELPU cupeled, decuple
CDEELRU ulcered
CDEELSU seclude
CDEELUX exclude
CDEEMNY demency
CDEENOR encoder
CDEENOS seconde
CDEENRT centred, red cent
CDEENST descent, scented
CDEEOPR proceed
CDEEORV covered
CDEEOST cestode, tedesco
CDEEOSX codexes
CDEEOTV coveted
CDEEPST despect
CDEERRU reducer
CDEERST crested
CDEERSU rescued, seducer
CDEERSW screwed
CDEERUV decurve
CDEFFHU chuffed
CDEFFIO coiffed
CDEFHIT fitched
CDEFIIT deficit
CDEFILN Clifden
CDEFINO confide
CDEFIRR Fredric
CDEFKOR defrock
CDEFNTU defunct
CDEFOSU defocus, focused
CDEFRTU fructed
CDEGGHU chugged
CDEGGLO clogged
CDEGHIU cudeigh
CDEGHNU Chengdu
CDEGIKN decking
CDEGIOR ergodic
CDEGKNU gun-deck
CDEHHNU hunched
CDEHIIL ceilidh
CDEHILO cheloid
CDEHILP Delphic
CDEHINO hedonic
CDEHINP pinched
CDEHIOW cowhide
CDEHIPP chipped
CDEHIPT pitched
CDEHIRT ditcher
CDEHKUY heyduck
CDEHLOT clothed
CDEHNOR doncher
CDEHNOT notched
CDEHNPU punched
CDEHNRU chunder
CDEHOPP chopped
CDEHOPR porched
CDEHOPU pouched
CDEHORW chowder, cowherd
CDEHOSU hocused
CDEHOSW cowshed
CDEHOTU touched
CDEHSSU duchess
CDEHSTY scythed
CDEIIKR dickier
CDEIIMR dimeric
CDEIINR incider
CDEIINS indices
CDEIINT identic
CDEIIOR ericoid
CDEIIOV ovicide
CDEIIST deistic, diciest
CDEIISU suicide
CDEIJST disject
CDEIKNS dickens
CDEIKPR pricked
CDEIKRR derrick
CDEILLO codille, collide
CDEILMO melodic
CDEILNU include, nuclide
CDEILPP clipped
CDEILTU ductile, dulcite
CDEIMNO demonic
CDEIMOR dormice
CDEIMOT demotic
CDEINOS secondi
CDEINOT condite, ctenoid, deontic, D-notice
CDEINOZ zincode
CDEINPT depinct
CDEINRS discern, rescind
CDEINRU inducer
CDEINRY cindery
CDEINSU incudes
CDEINSX exscind
CDEIOPR percoid
CDEIOPZ zip code
CDEIORT cordite
CDEIORV divorce
CDEIORW crowdie
CDEIOST cestoid
CDEIPPY cydippe
CDEIPRS discerp
CDEIPRT predict
CDEIPST discept
CDEIRTV verdict

CDEISST dissect
CDEISSY ecdysis
CDEKKLO kedlock
CDEKLOW wedlock
CDEKLPU plucked
CDEKNRU drucken
CDEKNSU sun deck
CDEKOOR crooked
CDEKOST destock
CDEKOTW wet dock
CDELLOU collude
CDELLRU crulled
CDELLRY dry cell
CDELMSU muscled
CDELNOO condole
CDELNOU encloud
CDELNOY condyle
CDELNWY Cledwyn
CDELOOR colored, croodle, decolor
CDELOPP clopped
CDELOPU coupled
CDELORS scolder
CDELOTT clotted
CDELOTU clouted
CDELPUU clued-up
CDELRRU curdler
CDELRUY crudely
CDELTUU ductule
CDEMMNO commend
CDEMMOO commode
CDEMMSU scummed
CDEMNNO condemn
CDEMNOP compend
CDEMORU decorum
CDENNOO condone
CDENNOT contend
CDENOOS secondo
CDENOPU pounced
CDENORS corsned
CDENORU crunode
CDENORW crowned, decrown
CDENPUY pudency
CDENRUU uncured
CDEOOPP copepod
CDEOOPT octoped
CDEOORR corrode
CDEOORV vocoder
CDEOOTV dovecot
CDEOPPR cropped
CDEOPRU produce
CDEORRW crowder
CDEORSW scowder
CDEORUU douceur
CDEOSTU custode
CDEPRTY decrypt
CDERRUY dry cure
CDERSTU crusted
CDERTUU ducture
CDFHIOS codfish
CDFIILU fluidic
CDFIISU fusidic
CDFILUY dulcify
CDFIRUY crudify
CDGHILO glochid
CDGIKNU ducking
CDGILNO codling
CDGINNO condign
CDGINOR cording
CDGINTU ducting
CDGOOOW cog-wood
CDHIINT Chindit
CDHIIST distich
CDHILOS coldish
CDHINOT dotchin
CDHINSU duncish
CDHINUW Dunwich
CDHIOOR choroid, ochroid
CDHIPTY diptych
CDHIRSY chrysid
CDHMORU Murdoch
CDHNRSU schrund
CDIIIOT idiotic
CDIIJRU juridic
CDIILLY idyllic
CDIILMO domicil
CDIILNO clinoid
CDIIMNO Dominic
CDIIMOS disomic
CDIINOR crinoid
CDIINOT diction
CDIINOV vidicon
CDIIORS cirsoid
CDIIOSS cissoid
CDIIOSV viscoid
CDIKLNO Old Nick
CDIKNOR dornick
CDILLOO colloid
CDILLUY lucidly
CDILNOU incloud, nucloid
CDILOTZ Colditz
CDILOUV Ludovic
CDILPSU disculp
CDIMMOU modicum
CDIMNOO monodic
CDIMSTU dictums
CDINOOT contoid
CDINOSY synodic
CDINOTU conduit, noctuid
CDINSSU sun-disc
CDIOPRR ripcord
CDIORTX doctrix
CDIOSSU discous
CDIOSTU custodi
CDIOSTY cystoid
CDIOTUV oviduct
CDIRTUY crudity
CDISSSU discuss
CDKNNOU dunnock
CDKNOOR dornock
CDLNOTU couldn't
CDLOOPY lycopod
CDMNOOS mod cons
CDMOORW cod-worm
CDNNOTU contund
CDNOORY Croydon
CDNOTUW cut-down
CDOOOPT octopod
CDOOPST postdoc
CDOORRY corrody
CDOOTUW woodcut
CDOPRTU product
CDORTUW cudwort
CDOSTUY custody
CEEEFIL fleecie
CEEEGLM eclegme
CEEEHLL echelle
CEEEHLV leveche
CEEEHNR encheer
CEEEINP epicene
CEEEIPR creepie
CEEEIRV receive
CEEELLU ecuelle
CEEELRT re-elect
CEEELST celeste
CEEENNS encense
CEEENPX expence
CEEENRT Terence
CEEENSS essence, senesce
CEEEPRR creeper
CEEERRT re-erect
CEEERST secrete
CEEERSV screeve
CEEERTX excrete
CEEETUX execute
CEEFFNO offence
CEEFFOR efforce
CEEFHRT fetcher
CEEFILL ficelle
CEEFILO ice floe
CEEFILU lucifee
CEEFINV venefic
CEEFIRR fiercer
CEEFKLR freckle
CEEFLNU fluence
CEEFLRT reflect
CEEFNOR enforce
CEEFNOX ox-fence
CEEFPRT perfect, prefect
CEEGINR energic, generic
CEEGINT genetic
CEEGINU eugenic
CEEGIRZ Grecize
CEEGLLO college
CEEGLNT neglect
CEEGLOU eclogue
CEEGNOR congree
CEEGNRY regency
CEEGQRU grecque
CEEHHLT hetchel
CEEHILM Michele
CEEHILN elenchi
CEEHILS helices
CEEHILV vehicle
CEEHIMR chimere
CEEHIMS chemise
CEEHINR incheer

CEEHINS Chinese
CEEHIOR cheerio
CEEHIRT etheric, heretic
CEEHIRW chewier
CEEHIST echites
CEEHKLR heckler
CEEHKNP henpeck
CEEHKRR kercher
CEEHLLS Chelles
CEEHLNO echelon
CEEHLNW wenchel
CEEHLOW cow-heel
CEEHLRY cheerly, lechery
CEEHLSS chessel
CEEHMRS schemer, schmeer
CEEHMRT merchet
CEEHNPS schepen
CEEHNPU penuche
CEEHNRW wencher
CEEHNST chesten
CEEHNYY cheyney
CEEHOPR pre-echo
CEEHOPT topchee
CEEHORT trochee
CEEHOUV vouchee
CEEHPRR percher
CEEHPRS perches
CEEHQRU chequer
CEEHRST chester
CEEIINR eirenic
CEEIIPR epeiric
CEEIJNT Cetinje
CEEIJOR rejoice
CEEIKKS kecksie
CEEIKNT necktie
CEEIKPR pickeer
CEEILLM micelle
CEEILNO cineole
CEEILNR recline
CEEILNS license, selenic, silence
CEEILNT centile
CEEILNU leucine
CEEILPS eclipse
CEEILRT reticle, tiercel
CEEILSS cessile
CEEILST sectile
CEEILSV vesicle
CEEILTT Lettice
CEEILTU leucite
CEEILUV lucivee
CEEIMNO Miocene
CEEIMNT centime
CEEIMRX excimer
CEEINNS incense
CEEINNW Ceinwen
CEEINOP open ice
CEEINOS senecio
CEEINPR crepine
CEEINPT pentice
CEEINRS ceresin, sincere
CEEINRT enteric, enticer
CEEINRV cervine
CEEINST scenite
CEEIOPT picotee
CEEIORT coterie
CEEIPPR precipe
CEEIPRR piercer, reprice
CEEIPRS precise
CEEIPRT receipt
CEEIPRU epicure
CEEIPSS species
CEEIPTZ pectize
CEEIQSU quiesce
CEEIRRT reciter
CEEIRSV scrieve, service
CEEIRTT tiercet
CEEIRTU eucrite
CEEIRTX exciter
CEEIRTZ cretize
CEEISTV sective
CEEITTZ zetetic
CEEJORT ejector
CEEKLNT necklet
CEEKLPS speckle
CEEKOSY sockeye
CEEKRRW wrecker
CEELLLU cellule
CEELLNO colleen
CEELLNT Cellnet
CEELLPU pucelle
CEELMNT clement, Tlemcen
CEELMOW welcome
CEELNOS enclose
CEELNRT lectern
CEELNRU lucerne
CEELNSU encluse
CEELOPR opercle
CEELORT elector, electro
CEELOTT Colette
CEELPRT plectre, prelect
CEELRRU crueler
CEELRSU recluse
CEELRSW crewels
CEELRTU lecture
CEELRTY erectly
CEELSSU secluse
CEELTTU lettuce, Lucette
CEEMNRU cerumen
CEEMNRY myrcene
CEEMNST centesm
CEEMOPR compeer
CEEMOPT compete
CEEMPRS permsec
CEEMRRY mercery
CEEMSTU tumesce
CEENNOU enounce
CEENNOV convene
CEENNRT centner
CEENOPT potence
CEENORS necrose
CEENORV encover
CEENOSU conusee
CEENPRS spencer
CEENPRT percent, precent
CEENPST pectens
CEENRSU censure
CEENRSY scenery
CEENTTU cunette
CEEOPST pectose
CEEOPTY ecotype
CEEORRT erector
CEEORRV recover
CEEORSU cereous
CEEORTW cow-tree
CEEOTTT octette
CEEPPRT percept, precept
CEEPPRU prepuce
CEEPRRU precure
CEEPRSS precess
CEEPRST respect, scepter, sceptre, specter, spectre
CEEPRTX excerpt
CEERRSU rescuer
CEERRSW screwer
CEERRUV recurve
CEERSST cresset
CEERSSU rescues
CEERSUX excurse
CEERTTU curette
CEETTUV cuvette
CEFFIOR officer
CEFFISU suffice
CEFFLSU scuffle
CEFFMOO offcome
CEFFORS scoffer
CEFFORT coffret
CEFFRSU scuffer
CEFGHIN Chifeng
CEFGINN fencing
CEFHIIS ice fish
CEFHILR filcher
CEFHILY chiefly
CEFHITT fitchet
CEFHITW fitchew
CEFHLTU futchel
CEFIILS filices
CEFIILT fictile
CEFIIOR orifice
CEFIITV fictive
CEFIKLR flicker
CEFILNT inflect
CEFILNU funicle
CEFILOR Leofric
CEFILRU Lucifer
CEFIMOR comfier
CEFIMRY mercify

CEFINNO confine
CEFINOR conifer, fir cone, inforce
CEFINRT frentic
CEFIPSY specify
CEFIRTY certify, rectify
CEFKLLO elf-lock
CEFKLOT fetlock
CEFKLRY freckly
CEFLNOU flounce
CEFLNUY fluency
CEFMORY comfrey
CEFNORU frounce
CEFNOSS confess
CEFNOSU confuse
CEFNOTU confute
CEFOPRS forceps
CEFORRT crofter
CEFORSU focuser, refocus
CEFOSSU focuses
CEGGHIR chigger
CEGGINR grecing
CEGGIOR georgic
CEGGORS scogger
CEGHINT etching
CEGHIRS screigh
CEGHITU guichet
CEGHORY choregy
CEGIILN ceiling, cieling
CEGIKNN necking
CEGIKNP pecking
CEGILNR clinger, cringle
CEGILNU clueing
CEGILNY glycine
CEGILOU eulogic
CEGIMRS Grecism
CEGINOY coignye
CEGINOZ cognize
CEGINRR cringer
CEGINRS scringe
CEGKLOR grockle
CEGLNOO cologne
CEGLOOY ecology
CEGLOSU glucose
CEGNORU congrue
CEGNORY cryogen
CEGNOST congest
CEGNRUW gun crew
CEGNRUY urgency
CEGOORS Scrooge
CEGORRY grocery
CEGORSU scourge, scrouge
CEHHIIK chi-hike
CEHHIRS cherish
CEHHIRT hitcher
CEHHORU hocheur
CEHIIKT thickie
CEHIILS chilies
CEHIINR hircine
CEHIINS niceish
CEHIINT nitchie
CEHIIPP chippie
CEHIIRT itchier
CEHIJOR Jericho
CEHIKNT chetnik, kitchen, thicken
CEHIKNW chewink
CEHIKOO chookie
CEHIKOR chokier
CEHIKPS peckish
CEHIKRS shicker
CEHIKRW whicker
CEHIKTT thicket
CEHILLR chiller
CEHILMN Mechlin
CEHILMT mitchel
CEHILNO choline, helicon
CEHILNT tinchel
CEHILPR pilcher
CEHILRV chervil, chilver
CEHILSU culshie
CEHILTY lecythi
CEHIMMS chemism
CEHIMNN minchen
CEHIMNU munchie
CEHIMNY chimney
CEHIMOR Homeric, moriche
CEHIMOS echoism
CEHIMRT thermic
CEHIMST chemist
CEHIMTU thecium
CEHINOP chopine
CEHINOR chorine
CEHINOX choenix
CEHINPR nephric, phrenic
CEHINQU chequin
CEHINRT cithern
CEHINRW wincher
CEHINST sthenic
CEHINSU echinus
CEHINTW witchen
CEHIOPS hospice
CEHIOPT heptoic, potiche
CEHIORT theoric
CEHIOST toisech
CEHIOSW ice show
CEHIOTV Cheviot
CEHIPPR chipper
CEHIPRR chirper
CEHIPRS spheric
CEHIPRT pitcher
CEHIRST estrich
CEHIRSU cushier
CEHIRSZ scherzi
CEHIRTT chitter
CEHIRTW wichert
CEHKKRU chukker
CEHKLMO hemlock
CEHKLRU kleruch
CEHKORS shocker
CEHKPTU ketchup
CEHKRSU shucker
CEHKSTY sketchy
CEHLMNO Chelmno
CEHLMSZ schmelz
CEHLMWY wych elm
CEHLNNU Chunnel
CEHLNOT cholent
CEHLNRU luncher
CEHLNRY lyncher
CEHLNTY lynchet
CEHLORT chortle
CEHLORY Chorley
CEHLOST clothes
CEHLPPS schlepp
CEHLQSU squelch
CEHLRRU lurcher
CEHMOOR moocher
CEHMORU moucher
CEHMOTZ chometz
CEHNNRU chunner
CEHNOOP hen-coop
CEHNOOR coehorn
CEHNORT chorten, notcher
CEHNORV chevron
CEHNPRU puncher
CEHNPST pschent
CEHNRTU chunter
CEHNSTU chesnut
CEHNTUY chutney
CEHOORS chooser
CEHOORT cheroot
CEHOPPR chopper
CEHOPRT potcher
CEHOPRU puchero
CEHORSZ scherzo
CEHORTU retouch, toucher
CEHORTW wotcher
CEHORUV voucher
CEHPRTU putcher
CEHQSTU quetsch
CEHRRSU crusher
CEHRSTT stretch
CEHRTTU chutter, Utrecht
CEIIJRU juicier
CEIIKLM ice milk
CEIIKNR ice rink
CEIIKNS kinesic
CEIIKNT kinetic
CEIIKPR pickier
CEIIKQU quickie
CEIILMP pimelic
CEIILNN incline
CEIILNT lenitic
CEIILPP clippie
CEIILPT tie-clip
CEIIMMT mimetic
CEIIMNR crimine
CEIIMNS menisci
CEIIMOT meiotic
CEIIMPR empiric
CEIIMPS epicism

CEIIMRT	micrite
CEIIMSS	seismic
CEIIMST	Semitic
CEIIMTT	titmice
CEIINNO	coniine
CEIINNR	encrini, erinnic
CEIINOR	oneiric
CEIINOV	invoice
CEIINPS	piscine
CEIINRS	irenics
CEIINRT	citrine, crinite, inciter, neritic
CEIINSS	iciness
CEIINSU	cuisine
CEIINTZ	citizen, zincite
CEIIOPT	poietic
CEIIPPR	piperic
CEIIPRR	pricier
CEIIPRS	spicier
CEIIPRT	picrite
CEIIRST	eristic
CEIIRSU	cruisie
CEIJSTU	justice
CEIKKNR	Kenrick, knicker
CEIKKSW	Keswick
CEIKLNR	clinker, crinkle
CEIKLPR	pickler, prickle
CEIKLRS	slicker
CEIKLRT	tickler, trickle
CEIKLRU	luckier
CEIKLRW	Lerwick
CEIKLTY	lickety
CEIKMRU	muckier
CEIKMRY	mickery
CEIKNOT	kenotic, ketonic
CEIKNPY	pickney
CEIKNQU	quicken
CEIKNRS	snicker
CEIKNRW	wickner
CEIKORR	corkier, rockier
CEIKOTT	ketotic
CEIKPRR	pricker
CEIKPRT	pricket
CEIKPRY	pickery
CEIKPST	skeptic
CEIKRRT	tricker
CEIKRST	rickets, sticker
CEIKRTU	truckie
CEIKRTY	rickety
CEILLLU	Lucille
CEILLNO	lioncel
CEILLOR	collier
CEILLRY	cillery
CEILLST	cellist
CEILMNS	lemnisc
CEILMOP	compile, polemic
CEILMPR	crimple

CEILNNU	nuclein
CEILNOS	close-in, inclose
CEILNOT	lection
CEILNOX	lexicon
CEILNPS	splenic
CEILNST	stencil
CEILNSU	incluse
CEILNTU	cut-line, tunicle
CEILOPT	toe clip
CEILORT	cortile
CEILOSS	ossicle
CEILOTT	cole tit
CEILOTZ	zelotic
CEILPPR	clipper, cripple
CEILPRS	scriple, splicer
CEILPRU	pleuric
CEILPSU	spicule
CEILPTU	piculet
CEILQUY	cliquey
CEILRRU	curlier
CEILRSV	clivers
CEILRSY	clerisy
CEILRTT	clitter
CEILRTU	utricle
CEILRZZ	crizzle
CEILSSS	scissel
CEILSSU	Celsius
CEILTTU	cuittle
CEIMMRR	crimmer
CEIMMRU	crummie
CEIMNNO	meconin
CEIMNOR	incomer
CEIMNOS	mesonic
CEIMNOT	tonemic
CEIMNOU	eunomic
CEIMNPU	pneumic
CEIMNRU	numeric
CEIMNYZ	enzymic
CEIMOPT	metopic
CEIMORR	morrice
CEIMORT	mortice
CEIMOST	comites
CEIMOSU	eucomis
CEIMOTT	totemic
CEIMOTV	vicomte
CEIMPRR	crimper
CEIMRRS	scrimer
CEIMRSU	murices
CEINNOR	Corinne
CEINNOV	connive
CEINNTV	Vincent
CEINNTY	nitency
CEINOOT	coontie
CEINOPR	porcine
CEINOPS	scopine
CEINOPT	nepotic
CEINORR	cornier
CEINORU	nourice
CEINORV	corvine, incover
CEINORY	oriency

CEINOSS	cession, oscines
CEINOST	section
CEINOSW	snow-ice
CEINOTT	tonetic
CEINOTX	exciton
CEINOVV	convive
CEINPRS	pincers
CEINPST	inspect
CEINRST	cistern
CEINRSV	scriven
CEINRTT	cittern
CEINRTU	nutrice
CEINRUV	incurve
CEINSTY	cystine
CEINSWY	winceys
CEINTTX	extinct
CEINVVY	vivency
CEIOPPR	croppie
CEIOPRS	persico
CEIOPRT	pteroic
CEIOPST	poetics
CEIOPSU	piceous
CEIORRS	cirrose, crosier
CEIORRU	courier
CEIORRZ	crozier
CEIORSS	croises
CEIORTT	cottier
CEIORTV	evictor
CEIORTW	co-write
CEIORTX	excitor
CEIORVY	viceroy
CEIOSST	cosiest
CEIOSSV	viscose
CEIOSTT	cottise, Scottie
CEIOSTV	costive
CEIOSTX	coexist
CEIOSTY	society
CEIPQTU	picquet
CEIPRRS	crisper
CEIPRST	escript, triceps
CEIPRTU	cuprite, picture
CEIPRTY	pyretic
CEIPRXY	pyrexic
CEIPSSS	scepsis
CEIPSST	cesspit
CEIRRRU	currier
CEIRRSU	cruiser
CEIRRTT	critter
CEIRRTU	recruit
CEIRRTX	rectrix
CEIRRUV	curvier
CEIRSTT	trisect
CEIRSTU	icterus
CEIRSUV	cursive
CEIRTTX	tectrix
CEISSTU	ictuses
CEJLNOY	Jocelyn
CEJNOOS	cojones
CEJNORU	conjure
CEJNSTU	sejunct

CEJOPRT project
CEKKLNU knuckle
CEKKNOR knocker
CEKLLOP pellock
CEKLLRY clerkly
CEKLNOR nockerl
CEKLNRU clunker, crunkle
CEKLORT rocklet
CEKLPRU plucker
CEKLRSU suckler
CEKLRTU truckle
CEKMORY mockery
CEKNOOR crooken
CEKNOOV convoke
CEKNRWY wryneck
CEKNTTU tuck-net
CEKOOPR pre-cook
CEKOOPW cowpoke
CEKOORY cookery
CEKOPTY pockety
CEKORRY rockery
CEKORST restock, stocker
CEKOSTV vestock
CEKPRUY puckery
CEKRRTU trucker
CELLMNO Clonmel
CELLMOU columel
CELLNOO colonel
CELLNOV convell
CELLORS escroll
CELLOSU ocellus
CELLOSY closely
CELLRRU cruller
CELLRSU sculler
CELLRUY cruelly
CELLTUW well-cut
CELMNOO monocle
CELMOPX complex
CELMPRU clumper, crumple
CELMSUU muscule
CELMTUU cumulet
CELNNOU nucleon
CELNOOR coronel
CELNOOS console
CELNOPU plounce
CELNOSU counsel, unclose
CELNOTU noctule
CELNSUU nucleus
CELOOPR pre-cool
CELOOPS copsole
CELOORR recolor
CELOORS creosol
CELOOSS colosse
CELOPRU coupler
CELOPSU close-up, culpose
CELOPTU couplet, octuple
CELORST corslet, costrel
CELORSU closure
CELORSW scowler
CELORSY scroyle
CELORTT clotter, crottle
CELORTU cloture, coulter
CELORUU couleur
CELOSUU leucous
CELOTTU culotte
CELPRSU scruple
CELPSUX exsculp
CELPSUY clypeus
CELRSTU cluster, custrel
CELRSTY clyster
CELRSUW curlews
CELRTTU clutter
CELRTUU culture
CELRTUV culvert
CELRTUY cruelty, cutlery
CELSTTU scuttle
CEMMNOT comment
CEMMNOU commune
CEMMOOV commove
CEMMOTU commute
CEMMRSU scummer
CEMNNOO non-come
CEMNNOT contemn
CEMNOOP compone
CEMNOOY economy
CEMNOSU consume
CEMNRTU centrum
CEMOOPS compose
CEMOOPT compote
CEMOORS Moresco
CEMOOTU outcome
CEMOPRT compter
CEMOPTU compute
CEMOSSU muscose
CEMOSTU costume
CEMPRTU crumpet
CEMRRUY mercury
CEMRSTU rectums
CENNOOT connote
CENNORW encrown
CENNOST consent
CENNOTT content
CENNOTV convent
CENNRSU scunner
CENOORR coroner, crooner
CENOORT coronet
CENOORW co-owner
CENOPRU pouncer
CENOPSY syncope
CENOPTU pouncet
CENOPTY potency
CENOQRU conquer
CENORRS scorner
CENORRW crowner
CENORSS cresson
CENORTT cornett
CENORTU cornute, counter, recount, trounce
CENORTV convert
CENORTW crownet
CENORUV uncover
CENOSSY coyness
CENOSTT contest
CENOSTU contuse
CENOTTX context
CENPRTY encrypt
CENPTUX expunct
CENRRTU current
CENRSTU encrust
CENRSUW unscrew
CENRTUY century
CEOOPRS scooper
CEOOPRY coopery
CEOORST scooter
CEOORTW co-wrote
CEOOSTY coyotes
CEOPPRR cropper
CEOPPRY coppery
CEOPRRS scorper
CEOPRRT porrect
CEOPRRU procure
CEOPRSS process
CEOPRTT protect
CEOPRTV provect
CEOPRUU coupure
CEOPRUV cover-up
CEOPSTU pectous
CEOQRTU croquet
CEORRSS recross
CEORRSU courser, scourer
CEORRSY sorcery
CEORRTY rectory
CEORRUU coureur
CEORSST scoters
CEORSSU Croesus, Scouser, sucrose
CEORSTU rose-cut, scouter
CEORTTY cottery
CEORTUU couture
CEORTUV couvert, cut-over, overcut
CEPPRRU crupper
CEPPRSU scupper
CEPPSTU scuppet
CEPRRSU sprucer
CEPRSSU percuss
CEPRSSY cypress
CEPRSUW screw-up
CEPRSUY cyperus
CEPSSTU suspect
CEPSTTU step-cut
CERSTTU scutter
CERSTUY curtesy, curtsey
CERTTUX extruct
CFFHINO chiffon
CFFIKKO kick-off
CFFIKOP pick-off

CFFIKPU	puffick
CFFMOSU	offscum
CFFNOOR	off-corn
CFFORSU	scruffo
CFFRSUY	scruffy
CFGIINO	coifing
CFGINOR	forcing
CFHHIOW	of which
CFHIOSW	cowfish
CFHORTU	futhorc
CFIIIMR	mirific
CFIIIVV	vivific
CFIIKNY	finicky
CFIILNT	inflict
CFIIMNO	omnific
CFIIMRY	micrify
CFIINOT	fiction
CFIIOSS	ossific
CFIKNOS	confisk
CFIKOSS	fossick
CFILMOY	comfily
CFILNOT	Clifton
CFILORU	fluoric
CFIMNOR	confirm
CFINORY	cornify
CFIORSY	scorify
CFKNORU	unfrock
CFKOSSU	fussock
CFKOTTU	futtock
CFLMRUU	fulcrum
CFLNOOW	conflow
CFLNOUX	conflux
CFLNOUY	flouncy
CFMNOOR	conform
CFMOORT	comfort
CFNORTU	functor
CFOSSUU	fuscous
CGHIINT	itching
CGHILPY	glyphic
CGHINNO	chignon
CGHINRU	ruching
CGHIOSY	goyisch
CGHLNOS	schlong
CGHOORT	torgoch
CGHORUY	grouchy
CGIIKKN	kicking
CGIIKLN	licking
CGIIKMM	gimmick
CGIIKNN	nicking
CGIIKNP	picking
CGIIKNT	ticking
CGIIKNW	wicking
CGIILLO	illogic
CGIINNO	coining
CGIINOV	voicing
CGIKLNO	locking
CGIKNOO	cooking
CGIKNOR	corking
CGIKNPU	kingcup
CGIKNSU	sucking
CGIKNTU	tucking
CGILLNU	culling
CGILMNY	cymling
CGILNOO	cooling
CGILNOS	closing
CGILNOW	cowling
CGILNRU	curling
CGILNTU	cutling
CGILORW	cowgirl
CGILOSS	glossic
CGILOTT	glottic
CGILPTY	glyptic
CGINNNO	conning
CGINNNU	cunning
CGINNOS	consign
CGINOPP	copping
CGINORS	scoring
CGINOST	costing, gnostic
CGINOSU	congius
CGINOTT	cotting
CGINPPU	cupping
CGINTTU	cutting
CGIOOOS	giocoso
CGIOTYZ	zygotic
CGKLNOU	gunlock
CGKOORU	Gourock
CGNOOOT	octogon
CGNRSUY	scrungy
CGOORRW	gorcrow
CHHIINT	Hitchin
CHHIKOR	chikhor
CHHINTU	unhitch
CHHOUUZ	Chuzhou
CHHRTTU	thrutch
CHIIKNN	kinchin
CHIIKSS	sickish
CHIIMSU	ischium
CHIINOT	thionic
CHIIPST	Pictish
CHIIPSW	Ipswich
CHIIRRS	scirrhi
CHIKLLO	hillock
CHIKLTY	thickly
CHIKNOO	chinook
CHIKORY	hickory
CHIKPSU	puckish
CHIKSTY	kitschy
CHILLMU	chillum
CHILNSY	lychnis
CHILOOS	coolish
CHILOSS	closish
CHILOST	coltish
CHILSTU	cultish
CHIMMOS	commish
CHIMNOO	moochin
CHIMOPR	morphic
CHIMORS	chrisom
CHIMRRY	myrrhic
CHIMSTY	chymist, mischty, tychism
CHINNOP	phinnoc
CHINOOR	chorion
CHINOPS	phonics
CHINORS	cornish
CHINORT	Corinth
CHINORW	Norwich
CHINOSU	cushion
CHINQSU	squinch
CHINTYZ	chintzy
CHIOOPR	pochoir
CHIOORZ	chorizo
CHIOPRT	trophic
CHIOPXY	hypoxic
CHIORST	chorist, ostrich
CHIPRRU	chirrup
CHIPRRY	pyrrhic
CHIPSSY	physics
CHIQSTU	squitch
CHIRRSU	cirrhus, currish
CHIRSSY	Chrissy
CHIRSTY	Christy
CHISTTU	chutist
CHISTYZ	schitzy
CHISYZZ	schizzy
CHITTWY	twitchy
CHKLLOU	hullock
CHKLOOO	hoolock
CHKLOOT	klootch
CHKLOSY	Shylock
CHKLRUU	kulchur
CHKMMOU	hummock
CHKNOOS	schnook
CHKNOOY	honyock
CHKOOST	schtook
CHLMORY	chromyl
CHLMPSU	schlump
CHLOOSY	schooly
CHLOPST	splotch
CHLOSSS	schloss
CHLOSUY	chylous, slouchy
CHMOORU	morucho
CHMOOST	schtoom
CHMOOSY	smoochy
CHMOSUY	chymous
CHMSTUZ	schmutz
CHNNOSU	nonsuch
CHNOORT	torchon
CHNOPSY	psychon
CHNORTU	cothurn
CHNOSZZ	schnozz
CHNOTUU	uncouth
CHNPPUU	punch-up
CHOOPPS	cop shop
CHOORSU	ochrous
CHOORUV	vouchor
CHOPTUU	touch-up
CHORSTU	trochus
CHPSSUY	scyphus
CHRRSUU	churrus
CIIILLT	illicit
CIIILNV	incivil
CIIINPT	incipit
CIIJLUY	juicily
CIIKKLL	killick
CIIKKMS	miskick
CIIKNOV	kinovic
CIIKNPT	nitpick
CIIKNTU	cutikin
CIIKPUW	wickiup
CIIKSTY	tisicky

CIILLTY licitly
CIILLVY civilly
CIILNOP cipolin
CIILNOS silicon
CIILNOT Nilotic
CIILNST scintil
CIILNUV uncivil
CIILOOT oolitic
CIILOPT politic
CIILOST colitis, solicit
CIILPSY spicily
CIILRTT lit crit
CIIMMRY mimicry
CIIMNOS iconism
CIIMNRY criminy, myricin
CIIMOST mistico, somitic
CIIMOTT mitotic
CIIMOTV motivic
CIINNOT nicotin
CIINNTU tunicin
CIINOOT coition
CIINOPS psionic
CIINORS incisor
CIINPRS Crispin
CIINQTU quintic
CIIOSUV vicious
CIIPRTY pyritic
CIIRTVX victrix
CIJKNNO jonnick
CIJMORW Jim Crow
CIJNNOO conjoin
CIJNNTU injunct
CIKKLLO killock
CIKLLOP pillock
CIKLLOR rollick
CIKLLOW willock
CIKLLSY slickly
CIKLLUY luckily
CIKLMOS Miskolc
CIKLNOP pinlock
CIKLNRY crinkly
CIKLORY rockily
CIKLOWW Wicklow
CIKLPRY prickly
CIKLQUY quickly
CIKLRTY trickly
CIKLSTU lustick
CIKMNRU crinkum
CIKNNOP pinnock
CIKNNOW winnock
CIKNPTU pin-tuck
CIKNSTU unstick
CIKOTUW outwick
CIKPSTU stick-up
CIKPUWY wickyup
CIKRSTY tricksy
CILLNNO Lincoln
CILLNOS Collins
CILLNOU cullion
CILLOOR criollo
CILMOPY Olympic
CILMRYY myricyl
CILMSTU cultism

CILNNOT Clinton
CILNOOR orcinol
CILNOOS cloison, scolion
CILNOPR pilcorn
CILNOPY lycopin
CILNORY cornily
CILNOTU linocut
CILNPSU insculp, sculpin
CILNPSY lip-sync
CILNSTU linctus
CILOOPT copilot
CILOORU couloir
CILOOSS colossi
CILOPRW pilcrow
CILOPRY pyloric
CILOPSW cowslip
CILOSTU oculist
CILPRSY crisply
CILPRTU culprit
CILRSUY crusily
CILSTTU cultist
CIMMOSS cosmism
CIMMRSY scrimmy
CIMNOOR moronic, omicron
CIMNORS crimson
CIMNORY myronic
CIMNPUY pycnium
CIMOORS Morisco
CIMOORT motoric
CIMOOST osmotic
CIMOPSY miscopy
CIMOSSY mycosis
CIMOSTU moustic
CIMOTYZ zymotic
CIMPRSY scrimpy
CIMRSSU crissum
CINNNOU inconnu
CINNORU unicorn
CINNOTU unction
CINNSUU nuncius
CINOOPS opsonic, pocosin
CINOORS coronis
CINORRT tricorn
CINORST cistron, cornist
CINORTU ruction
CINOSST consist
CINOSTU suction
CINOTXY oxyntic
CINRSTU incrust
CIOOPRS Scorpio
CIOOPRT portico
CIOOPRZ prozoic
CIOOPSU copious
CIOOQTU coquito
CIOORSU curioso
CIOPRTY Cypriot, pyrotic
CIOPSTY copyist
CIOQRSU croquis
CIORRSU cirrous

CIORSSS scissor
CIORSTU citrous
CIORSUU curious
CIORTVY victory
CIOSSSY sycosis
CIOSSUV viscous
CIPRSSU prussic
CIPRTTY tryptic
CIPRUVY pyruvic
CIPSTTY styptic
CIRTUVY curvity
CISSTUY cytisus
CJNORUY conjury
CKKLNUY knuckly
CKKNNOO knock-on
CKKNOPU knock-up
CKLLMOO mollock
CKLLMOU mullock
CKLLOOP pollock
CKLNOTU locknut
CKLNOUW Lucknow
CKLNUUY unlucky
CKLOORW rowlock
CKLOOTU lockout
CKLOPTU potluck, putlock
CKMNOSU mock sun
CKMSSUU mussuck
CKNSTUU unstuck
CKOOOTU cookout
CKOOTTU tucktoo
CKOPTTU puttock
CKORTUW cutwork
CKOSSTU tussock
CKPSTUU stuck-up
CLLMOSU mollusc
CLLOOPS scollop
CLLOSUU colulus, loculus
CLMOOOU Olomouc
CLMOOPT complot
CLMOPUU poculum
CLMOSUU osculum
CLMPRUY crumply
CLMSUUU cumulus
CLNOORT control
CLNOOSS consols
CLNOSTU consult
CLOOPSS scolops
CLOORTU locutor
CLOORUY coloury
CLORSSY crossly
CLORSUU lucrous
CLORTUY courtly
CMMNOOS commons
CMMRSUY scrummy
CMNNOOT Moncton
CMNOOOT con moto, monocot
CMNOOPY compony
CMNPTUU punctum
CMOOORS Comoros
CMOOPRT comport
CMOOPST compost
CMOOSTY scotomy

CMORSTU	scrotum
CMORTUW	cutworm
CMOSSUU	muscous
CMOSUVY	Muscovy
CMPRSUY	scrumpy
CNNORRU	Runcorn
CNNORTU	nocturn
CNNORUW	uncrown
CNOOOOR	oronoco
CNOOOTU	Cotonou
CNOOPPR	popcorn
CNOOPRU	croupon
CNOORRW	corn-row
CNOORST	consort
CNOORTT	contort
CNOORTU	contour,
	cornuto,
	crouton
CNOOSUU	nocuous
CNOOTTY	cottony
CNORSSU	uncross
CNORSTU	custron
CNORTUY	country
CNPSTUU	punctus
CNRSTUU	truncus
CNRSTUY	scrunty
COOPPTY	top copy
COOPRRT	proctor
COOPRTU	outcrop
COOPSTU	octopus
COOSSTU	tocusso
COPRRTU	corrupt
COPRSUU	cuprous
CORRSUY	cursory
CORSSSY	cyssors
CORSUUV	curvous
CRSTTUY	scrutty
DDDEEHS	shedded
DDDEEKS	skedded
DDDEELS	sledded
DDDEEMO	demoded
DDDEERU	uddered
DDDEGIR	gridded
DDDEHTU	thudded
DDDEIIV	divided
DDDEIKS	skidded
DDDEILR	diddler,
	driddle
DDDEIMU	muddied
DDDELOP	plodded
DDDELPU	puddled
DDDEOPR	prodded
DDDEORY	doddery
DDDEPSU	spudded
DDDESTU	studded
DDDIMSU	diddums
DDEEEOY	doe-eyed
DDEEEPS	speeded
DDEEERR	red deer
DDEEFIL	fielded
DDEEFIR	Freddie
DDEEGRR	dredger
DDEEHNU	dudheen
DDEEHRS	shedder
DDEEILR	dreidel
DDEEILV	deviled
DDEEIMS	misdeed
DDEEINX	de-index
DDEEIPS	depside,
	dispeed
DDEEIRR	Deirdre,
	derider
DDEEIRT	red tide
DDEELLU	duelled
DDEELLW	dwelled
DDEELMO	modeled
DDEELMR	meddler
DDEELOW	doweled
DDEELOY	yodeled
DDEELPR	peddler
DDEELRT	treddle
DDEELRU	deluder
DDEENOZ	dozened
DDEENRS	Dresden
DDEEORR	ordered
DDEEOTV	devoted
DDEERST	reddest
DDEERTU	detrude
DDEERYY	dry-eyed
DDEETTU	duetted
DDEFFII	diffide
DDEFILR	fiddler
DDEFILY	fiddley
DDEFIOX	fixed-do
DDEFLNO	Flodden
DDEFNOR	fronded
DDEGGRU	drugged
DDEGIIR	giddier
DDEGILR	glidder,
	griddle
DDEGIMO	demigod
DDEGINR	Redding
DDEGINT	tedding
DDEGINW	wedding
DDEGIOR	dodgier
DDEGLOS	dog sled
DDEGNOO	good-den
DDEGNOS	godsend
DDEGNOU	dudgeon
DDEGNWY	Gwynedd
DDEGORS	Gorsedd
DDEGORY	dodgery
DDEGOSS	goddess
DDEGRRU	drudger
DDEHILW	whiddle
DDEHIRS	reddish
DDEHIRY	hydride
DDEHNRU	hundred
DDEHRSU	shudder
DDEIIKR	kiddier
DDEIIOX	dioxide
DDEIIRV	divider
DDEIKNR	kindred
DDEILMR	middler,
	Mildred
DDEILNW	dwindle
DDEILOT	deltoid
DDEILPR	piddler
DDEILQU	quiddle
DDEILRR	riddler
DDEILRT	tiddler
DDEILTU	Luddite
DDEILTW	twiddle
DDEILTY	lyddite,
	tiddley
DDEIMOR	dermoid
DDEIMOS	desmoid
DDEIMRU	muddier
DDEIMST	middest
DDEIMSU	dedimus
DDEINNU	Dunedin
DDEINOT	tendido
DDEINPS	dispend
DDEINST	distend
DDEIOOR	do-or-die
DDEIOPR	Proddie
DDEIOPV	dive-dop
DDEIORV	overdid
DDEIORW	dowdier
DDEIPPR	dripped
DDEIRRU	ruddier
DDEKMOU	dukedom
DDELMOU	moulded
DDELMRU	muddler
DDELOOR	doodler
DDELOPR	plodder
DDELORT	toddler
DDELPRU	puddler
DDEMMRU	drummed
DDEMNOS	Desmond
DDEMNOT	oddment
DDENNOR	dendron
DDENNOW	Downend
DDENOPS	despond
DDENOPW	dew-pond
DDENORT	trodden
DDENORU	redound
DDENOSS	oddness
DDENOUW	wounded
DDEOORW	redwood
DDEOPPR	dropped
DDEOPRR	prodder
DDEOPRW	dewdrop
DDFGIIY	giddify
DDFIMUY	muddify
DDGGINO	dodging
DDGHOOO	godhood
DDGIIKN	kidding
DDGIILY	giddily
DDGIINR	ridding
DDGILNO	oddling
DDGINNO	nodding
DDGINOP	podding
DDGINOS	sodding
DDGINPU	pudding
DDGIPUY	giddy-up
DDGLLOO	old gold
DDGOOOW	dogwood
DDHIIRV	vriddhi
DDHIISY	Yiddish
DDHIKSU	kiddush
DDHIOPS	poddish
DDHIORY	hydroid
DDHORSY	dry-shod
DDIIIKN	dinki-di

DDIIKLS skid-lid
DDIILOP diploid
DDIIMRW widdrim
DDIIMSY didymis
DDIINNS din-dins
DDIKOOS skiddoo
DDILMSU Luddism
DDILMUY muddily
DDILOWY dowdily
DDILRUY ruddily
DDILTWY twiddly
DDIORTU turdoid
DDIPRRY drip-dry
DDLMORU doldrum
DDMNOOR dromond
DDORSTY drostdy
DEEEEHT tee-heed
DEEEFNS defense
DEEEGLP pledgee
DEEEGMR demerge
DEEEGRT deterge
DEEEHLW wheedle, wheeled
DEEEILS lee side
DEEEINR needier
DEEEINT edenite
DEEEIPY pie-eyed
DEEEIRR reedier
DEEEIRS Desiree, seedier
DEEEIRW weedier
DEEEISV devisee
DEEEJLW jeweled
DEEEJNU dejeune
DEEEKLN kneeled
DEEEKNW weekend
DEEELLV leveled
DEEELNO eledone
DEEELNR needler
DEEELPT deplete
DEEELRV reveled
DEEELSV sleeved
DEEELTW tweedle
DEEEMNS demesne
DEEEMRS demerse, emersed
DEEENTT detente
DEEEORR roe-deer
DEEEORW oreweed
DEEEOTV devotee
DEEEPRS speeder
DEEEPST deepest
DEEERSV deserve
DEEETTV vedette
DEEFFIN effendi
DEEFGIN feeding
DEEFGOR foredge
DEEFHLS fleshed
DEEFHLU heedful
DEEFILN Enfield, fielden
DEEFILR defiler, fielder
DEEFINR definer, refined
DEEFINW finewed
DEEFKLR Krefeld
DEEFLLU fuelled
DEEFLLW well-fed
DEEFLNU needful
DEEFLRY deer fly
DEEFMOR freedom
DEEFNOR fore-end
DEEFPRY deep-fry
DEEFRTT fretted
DEEGGOR degorge
DEEGHNO Hengoed
DEEGHOW hogweed
DEEGILN deleing
DEEGILS leg side
DEEGINN engined
DEEGINP deeping
DEEGINR dreeing, energid, reeding
DEEGINW weeding
DEEGIOR Geordie
DEEGIPW pigweed
DEEGIRV diverge, grieved
DEEGIST edgiest
DEEGLPR pledger
DEEGLPT pledget
DEEGLRW wergeld
DEEGLTU deglute
DEEGNNO endogen
DEEGOSY geodesy
DEEHIKV Khedive
DEEHIMT methide
DEEHIRT diether
DEEHKLW whelked
DEEHLLS shelled
DEEHNOY honeyed
DEEHNPR prehend
DEEHOPT heptode
DEEHTTW whetted
DEEIINT dietine
DEEIIRW weirdie
DEEIJLL jellied
DEEIKLN kneidel
DEEIKMW midweek
DEEIKNN in-kneed
DEEIKOV dovekie
DEEILMO Melodie
DEEILNS linseed
DEEILNU Eiluned
DEEILNY dye-line
DEEILOS oilseed
DEEILPR periled
DEEILPS seed-lip
DEEILRV deliver
DEEILRW wielder
DEEILRY yielder
DEEILSS idlesse
DEEILSY seedily
DEEIMMS misdeem
DEEIMNO dominee
DEEIMNR ermined, Meriden
DEEIMPR demirep, epiderm, per diem
DEEIMPY epidemy
DEEIMRT demerit, dimeter, merited, mitered
DEEIMTT emitted
DEEIMTY mediety
DEEINNT dentine
DEEINNW enwiden
DEEINNZ denizen
DEEINOR ordinee
DEEINRR dernier
DEEINRS resined
DEEINRW widener, wine red
DEEINRX indexer
DEEINST destine, edestin
DEEINSW endwise
DEEINSX indexes
DEEINTT dinette
DEEINTU detinue
DEEINTV evident
DEEINVW vinewed
DEEINWZ wizened
DEEIOPS episode
DEEIOPT epidote
DEEIOPX epoxide
DEEIPPT peptide
DEEIPRS preside
DEEIPRT pre-edit
DEEIPRV deprive
DEEIPSS despise
DEEIPST despite
DEEIRRS serried
DEEIRRT retired
DEEIRRV rivered
DEEIRSU residue
DEEIRSV deviser, diverse
DEEIRTU erudite
DEEIRTV riveted, verdite
DEEISSU diseuse
DEEISTW dewiest
DEEITTV vidette
DEEKKRT trekked
DEELLMS smelled
DEELLNW Wendell
DEELLPS spelled
DEELLRU dueller
DEELLRW dweller
DEELLRY elderly
DEELLSW swelled
DEELMNO lodemen
DEELMOR modeler, remodel
DEELMOT domelet
DEELMPU deplume
DEELMTT mettled
DEELNPU pendule
DEELNRS slender
DEELNRT trendle

DEELNSS endless
DEELNSY densely
DEELOPR deplore
DEELOPS lopseed
DEELOPV develop
DEELOPX explode
DEELORU urodele
DEELORW roweled
DEELOSU delouse
DEELOTW toweled
DEELOVV devolve
DEELOVW voweled
DEELPRU prelude
DEELRSS eldress
DEELVXY vexedly
DEEMMST stemmed
DEEMNOR moderne
DEEMNOU eudemon
DEEMNOV venomed
DEEMNOY moneyed
DEEMORS emerods
DEEMORX exoderm
DEEMPSU despume
DEEMRRU demurer
DEENNOT endnote
DEENNOY doyenne
DEENNOZ end zone
DEENNPT pendent
DEENNTT tendent
DEENNTZ tendenz
DEENOPS spondee
DEENOPT pentode
DEENORS endorse
DEENORV over-end
DEENORW endower
DEENORZ dozener
DEENPPR perpend, prepend
DEENPRR prender
DEENPRS spender
DEENPRT pretend
DEENRSS redness
DEENRST sterned
DEENRSU end-user
DEENRTU denture, entrude, tenured
DEENSTW West End
DEENSUX unsexed
DEEOPPY pop-eyed
DEEOPRR pedrero
DEEOPRW powered
DEEORRR reorder
DEEORRS red rose, reredos, rose red
DEEORRT orterde
DEEORST oersted
DEEORSU orsedue
DEEORTT Dorette, tetrode
DEEORTW towered
DEEORUV overdue
DEEPPPR prepped
DEEPPST stepped
DEEPPSU speed-up
DEEPRRU perdure
DEEPRSS depress
DEERRSS dresser, redress
DEERRUV verdure
DEERSST dessert, tressed
DEERSTW strewed
DEERSTY dyester
DEERTUX extrude
DEESTTT stetted
DEFFIMO fiefdom
DEFFIOR ride-off
DEFFIOS offside
DEFFISU diffuse
DEFFNOR forfend
DEFFNOS send-off
DEFGGIR frigged
DEFGGLO flogged
DEFGGOR frogged
DEFGIOR firedog
DEFGIRU figured
DEFGITY fidgety
DEFGORY Godfrey
DEFHIRS redfish
DEFIILM mid-life
DEFIILN infidel, infield
DEFIIMS fideism
DEFIIMW midwife
DEFIINN finnied
DEFIIST fideist
DEFILLR frilled
DEFILNR flinder
DEFILPP flipped
DEFILPU upfield
DEFILRU direful
DEFILRW Wilfred
DEFILSU sulfide
DEFILTT flitted
DEFILTU tideful
DEFILTY fetidly
DEFILXY fixedly
DEFIMOR deiform
DEFINOT fodient
DEFINRW Winfred
DEFINSY densify
DEFINUX unfixed
DEFIPRY perfidy
DEFIRRT drifter
DEFIRTT fritted
DEFIRTU fruited
DEFISTU feudist
DEFLLOU doleful
DEFLMOR Melford
DEFLNOO onefold
DEFLNOR fondler
DEFLNOT tenfold
DEFLOPP flopped
DEFLORT Telford
DEFLORU fuel rod
DEFLPRU purfled
DEFMORS serfdom
DEFNORU founder
DEFORST defrost
DEFORWX Wexford
DEGGGLO goggled
DEGGHIN hedging
DEGGILN gelding
DEGGINS snigged
DEGGINW wedging
DEGGIRT trigged
DEGGIRU druggie
DEGGISW swigged
DEGGITW twigged
DEGGLOP poggled
DEGGLOR doggrel
DEGGLOS slogged
DEGGLPU plugged, puggled
DEGGLSU slugged
DEGGNOO doggone
DEGGNOS snogged
DEGGNOU gudgeon
DEGGORY doggery
DEGGOSS doggess
DEGGRRU drugger, grudger
DEGGRTU drugget
DEGHILT delight, lighted
DEGHIST desight, sighted
DEGHORR drogher
DEGIINR dingier
DEGIINT dieting, editing
DEGIKLO doglike, godlike
DEGILNN lending
DEGILNO glenoid, on-glide
DEGILNR grindle
DEGILNU dueling, indulge
DEGILNW welding
DEGILOV go-devil
DEGILRR girdler
DEGILRU guilder
DEGILUV divulge
DEGIMNN mending
DEGIMNR midgern
DEGIMNS smidgen
DEGINNN denning
DEGINNP pending
DEGINNR grinned
DEGINOO goondie
DEGINOR groined, Negroid
DEGINOW wendigo, widgeon
DEGINPX ped-xing
DEGINRR grinder
DEGINRW redwing
DEGIOOS goodies
DEGIOPR podgier
DEGIORT goitred
DEGIPPR gripped
DEGIPRU pudgier
DEGIRSS digress

DEGIRTT gritted
DEGJLNU jungled
DEGJSSU judgess
DEGLMMO glommed
DEGLNNO endlong
DEGLOPR pledgor
DEGLOPS splodge
DEGLOSS dogless, godless
DEGLTTU glutted
DEGMNNO mendong
DEGMNNU mendung
DEGMOOS smoodge
DEGNNOU dungeon
DEGNOPR pronged
DEGNORU guerdon, undergo
DEGNOSU segundo
DEGNOTU tongued
DEGNRTU trudgen
DEGOORS dog rose
DEGOORV grooved, overdog
DEGORRU droguer
DEGRRTU trudger
DEHIIRS dishier
DEHILMS dishelm
DEHILNP delphin
DEHILNW whindle
DEHILRW whirled
DEHILTY diethyl
DEHIMMS shimmed
DEHIMOR heirdom
DEHIMOT ethmoid
DEHINNS shinned
DEHINNT thinned
DEHINOR hodiern
DEHINPS endship
DEHINPT in-depth
DEHINSW Wendish
DEHIORT theroid
DEHIOSU hideous
DEHIOTU hideout
DEHIPPS shipped
DEHIPPW whipped
DEHIRRU dhurrie, hurried
DEHIRRW whirred
DEHIRST shirted
DEHIRSV dervish
DEHIRTV thrived
DEHIRTY dithery
DEHISSW Swedish
DEHISTT shitted
DEHIWZZ whizzed
DEHJNOO John Doe
DEHLMNO Denholm
DEHLNOS Sheldon
DEHLOOP polhode
DEHLOOT toehold
DEHLORW whorled
DEHLOSS sloshed
DEHLRRU hurdler
DEHMORU humored
DEHMOTU mouthed

DEHNNSU shunned
DEHNOOW hoedown
DEHNOPU unhoped
DEHNOTZ dozenth
DEHNRTU thunder
DEHOOTT toothed
DEHOPPS shopped
DEHOPPW whopped
DEHORTW throwed
DEHRRTU druther
DEIIKLS dislike
DEIIKNR dinkier, drinkie
DEIIKNW kwedini
DEIILMN midline
DEIILMP implied
DEIILMT delimit, limited
DEIILNV lived-in
DEIILOS idolise
DEIILOZ idolize
DEIIMNO dominie
DEIIMNU diminue
DEIIMRT timider
DEIIMVW midwive
DEIINNV vinnied
DEIINOS dionise
DEIINOT edition
DEIINRS insider
DEIINRT nitride
DEIINRV diviner, drive-in
DEIINRW windier
DEIINSV invised
DEIIORS Isidore
DEIIORT diorite
DEIIORV ivoride, ivoried
DEIIOXZ oxidize
DEIIPPR dippier
DEIIPRT rip tide, tide-rip
DEIIPRV viperid
DEIIRRT dirtier
DEIIRZZ dizzier
DEIISTT dietist, tidiest
DEIISTV visited
DEIJNOR joinder
DEIJNOT jointed
DEIJNRU injured
DEIJNSU disjune
DEIJORY joyride
DEIJOST joisted
DEIKLLS deskill, skilled
DEIKLNR kindler
DEIKLOR rodlike
DEIKMMS skimmed
DEIKNNS skinned
DEIKNOS doeskin
DEIKNRR drinker
DEIKNRS redskin
DEIKNTT knitted
DEIKOTW witdoek
DEIKPPS skipped
DEIKQRU quirked

DEIKRST skirted
DEIKRSU duskier
DEIKSVY skydive
DEILLNW indwell
DEILLOR dollier
DEILLPS spilled
DEILLQU quilled
DEILLRR driller
DEILLSS lidless
DEILLTW twilled
DEILMMS slimmed
DEILMOP implode
DEILMOT old-time
DEILMOY myeloid
DEILMPP pimpled
DEILMWY mildewy
DEILNNU unlined
DEILNOO eidolon
DEILNOS indoles, lensoid
DEILNOT lentoid
DEILNOU unoiled
DEILNOW down-lie, lie-down
DEILNPS spindle
DEILNRT tendril, trindle
DEILNSW swindle
DEILNSY Lindsey, snidely
DEILNTU diluent
DEILNTW indwelt, twindle
DEILOPS despoil, soliped, spoiled
DEILOPT piloted
DEILOPU euploid
DEILORS soldier, solider
DEILOSV dislove
DEILOTW low tide
DEILPPR dripple
DEILPPS slipped
DEILPTY tepidly
DEILRRV L-driver
DEILRTU diluter
DEILRTY tiredly
DEILRVY devilry
DEILRWY weirdly
DEILRZZ drizzle
DEILSTT slitted, stilted
DEILSTU duelist
DEILSTY distyle
DEIMMMU mummied
DEIMMNN nemmind
DEIMMPR primmed
DEIMMRT trimmed
DEIMMST dimmest
DEIMMSU mediums
DEIMMTU tummied
DEIMNNU minuend
DEIMNOS dinsome
DEIMNOU mon Dieu
DEIMNSS dimness
DEIMNST mindset

DEIMNSW miswend
DEIMNUX unmixed
DEIMOOR moidore, moodier
DEIMOST modiste
DEIMOSW wisedom
DEIMOTT omitted
DEIMOTV vomited
DEIMOUX exodium
DEIMPRT dirempt
DEIMPRU dumpier
DEIMPSY dimpsey
DEIMPUX mixed-up
DEIMSTW Midwest
DEIMSTY stymied
DEINNNU nundine
DEINNOS Denison
DEINNTW twinned
DEINOOZ ozonide
DEINOPS dispone
DEINOPT pointed
DEINORS indorse, rosined
DEINORU dourine, neuroid
DEINORV drive-on, on-drive
DEINORW downier, windore
DEINOSY yonside
DEINPPS snipped
DEINPRT printed
DEINPST stipend
DEINRSU insured
DEINRTT trident
DEINRTU intrude, turdine, untried
DEINRTX dextrin
DEINRTY tindery
DEINSST dissent
DEINSSU niduses
DEINSTT dentist, distent
DEINSTY density, destiny
DEINSUZ unsized
DEIOORS odorise
DEIOORW woodier
DEIOORZ odorize
DEIOOSS isodose
DEIOOST osteoid
DEIOOVV voivode
DEIOPPP poppied
DEIOPRT diopter, dioptre, peridot, proteid, protide
DEIOPRV provide
DEIOPSS dispose
DEIOPST deposit, dopiest, posited, topside

DEIOPSU opus Dei
DEIOPSV vespoid
DEIOPTT diptote, tiptoed
DEIOPTV pivoted
DEIORRW rowdier, wordier, worried
DEIORSS dossier
DEIORST sortied, steroid, storied
DEIORSV devisor, visored
DEIORTT Detroit, dottier
DEIORTU ioduret, outride
DEIORVZ vizored
DEIORWW widower
DEIOSTU outside, tedious
DEIOSTZ doziest
DEIOSUV devious
DEIPPQU quipped
DEIPPRT tripped
DEIPRST striped
DEIPRSY spidery
DEIPSSU upsides
DEIPSTT spitted
DEIPSTU dispute
DEIPSXY pyxides
DEIQTTU quitted
DEIQUZZ qulzzed
DEIRRST stirred, strider
DEIRSST dissert
DEIRSTU dustier
DEIRSTV strived
DEIRSTW wristed
DEISTTW twisted
DEITTTW twitted
DEKKOOP kopdoek
DEKLLSU skulled
DEKLNRU knurled
DEKLOOY kyoodle
DEKNNOS non-sked
DEKNNRU drunken
DEKNOST Donetsk
DEKNOTT knotted
DEKNRTU trunked
DEKOPST desktop
DEKORWY keyword
DELLMOO modello
DELLOOP Leopold
DELLOOW woolled
DELLOPR redpoll
DELLOVW lowveld
DELMMSU slummed
DELMORS smolder
DELMORU moulder, remould
DELMOSU dulsome
DELMOTT mottled
DELMOUV volumed
DELMUZZ muzzled

DELNORU lounder, roundel
DELNORY Reynold
DELNOSS oldness
DELNOTW let-down
DELNOUV unloved
DELNPRU plunder
DELNRTU trundle
DELNRUU unruled
DELNSSU dulness
DELOOPP pleopod
DELOOPR old rope
DELOORS Dolores
DELOOSS dolosse
DELOOST destool
DELOPPP plopped
DELOPPS slopped
DELOPRS pre-sold
DELOPRT droplet
DELOPTT plotted
DELORRY orderly
DELORSS rodless
DELORST oldster
DELORSU Lourdes
DELORTT dottrel
DELORUV louvred
DELORUW woulder
DELOSSW dowless
DELOSTT slotted
DELOSZZ sozzled
DELOTUV voluted
DELPPRU purpled
DELRRSU slurred
DELRSTU lustred, strudel
DEMMRRU drummer
DEMMSTU stummed
DEMNOOP monoped
DEMNOPU empound
DEMNORT mordent
DEMNOST endmost
DEMNOTU demount, mounted
DEMNOUV unmoved
DEMOOPP popedom
DEMOOPR predoom
DEMOOST Modesto
DEMOOTU outmode
DEMOSTY modesty
DEMRRTU dertrum
DEMSTTU smutted
DENNORT tendron
DENNORU enround
DENNOUW enwound, unowned
DENNSTU stunned
DENNTUU untuned
DENOORT tendoor
DENOOTU duotone
DENOPPR propend
DENOPRS respond
DENOPRT portend, protend
DENOPRU pounder
DENOPRV provend

DENOPSU	unposed	**DFIMNUY**	mundify	**DGINNUY**	undying
DENOPUX	expound	**DFIMORS**	disform	**DGINOOW**	wooding
DENORRU	rounder	**DFINOTU**	Tindouf	**DGINORV**	droving
DENORSU	resound, sounder	**DFLMOUW**	mudflow	**DGINORW**	wording
		DFLOOTU	fold-out	**DGINOSW**	disgown
DENORSW	wonders	**DFLOOTW**	twofold	**DGINOTT**	dotting
DENORUW	rewound	**DFLOTWY**	twyfold	**DGINSTU**	dusting
DENOSTU	snouted	**DFNORUY**	foundry	**DGIOORR**	Rodrigo
DENPRTU	prudent	**DFNORWY**	Wynford	**DGIOPRY**	prodigy
DENPSSU	suspend	**DGGGIIN**	digging	**DGIQSUY**	squidgy
DENRSSU	undress	**DGGGINO**	dogging	**DGISSTU**	disgust
DENRSSY	dryness	**DGGHIOS**	doggish	**DGLNOUY**	ungodly
DENRSTU	dunster	**DGGIILN**	gilding, gliding	**DGLNOWY**	Goldwyn
DENSTTU	student			**DGLOOOW**	logwood
DEOOPPS	opposed	**DGGIINU**	guiding	**DGLOPSY**	splodgy
DEOOPRT	torpedo	**DGGIJNU**	judging	**DGMOPRU**	gumdrop
DEOORTU	outrode	**DGGILNO**	dogling, godling, lodging	**DGOORTT**	dogtrot
DEOORWY	woodyer			**DGOPRRU**	prodrug
DEOPPPR	propped			**DHIIKWZ**	whiz-kid
DEOPPRR	dropper	**DGGINOO**	gooding	**DHIILMS**	mildish
DEOPPST	stopped	**DGGIORY**	Diggory	**DHIILOT**	lithoid
DEOPRWY	powdery	**DGGNOSU**	dugongs	**DHIILSW**	wildish
DEOPSTT	spotted	**DGHIILN**	hilding	**DHIIMMS**	dimmish
DEOQRTU	torqued	**DGHIINS**	shindig	**DHIIMNO**	hominid
DEORRUV	verdour	**DGHILNO**	holding	**DHIIMPS**	midship
DEORRVY	overdry	**DGHILPY**	diglyph	**DHIINOU**	Houdini
DEORSTU	destour	**DGHINOO**	hooding	**DHIINRU**	hirudin
DEORSTW	strowed, worsted	**DGHIOOS**	goodish	**DHIIOPX**	xiphoid
		DGHIOPS	godship	**DHIIORZ**	rhizoid
DEORSTY	destroy	**DGHIOPU**	phugoid	**DHIIOST**	histoid
DEORTTT	trotted	**DGHORTU**	drought	**DHIIPST**	dipshit
DEOSSSU	dessous	**DGHOTUY**	doughty	**DHIKRSU**	Kurdish
DEOSSYY	odyssey	**DGIILLN**	dilling	**DHIKSSU**	duskish
DEOSTTU	testudo	**DGIILNT**	tidling	**DHILLSU**	dullish
DEOSTTW	swotted	**DGIILNW**	wilding	**DHILMUY**	humidly
DEOSTUU	duteous	**DGIILNY**	dingily	**DHILNOP**	dolphin
DEPRRSU	spurred	**DGIILRY**	rigidly	**DHILOOT**	tholoid
DEPRRUY	prudery	**DGIIMMN**	dimming	**DHILOST**	doltish
DEPRSUU	pursued	**DGIIMNS**	smidgin	**DHILOSU**	loudish
DERRSTY	dryster	**DGIIMOS**	sigmoid	**DHILRTY**	thirdly
DERSTUU	sutured	**DGIINNN**	dinning	**DHIMORU**	humidor, rhodium
DERSTUY	restudy	**DGIINNW**	winding		
DFFIIMR	midriff	**DGIINOW**	windigo	**DHIMPSU**	dumpish
DFFIIRT	triffid	**DGIINOX**	digoxin	**DHINNOS**	donnish
DFFILOR	Lifford	**DGIINPP**	dipping	**DHINOPS**	donship
DFFIMOR	difform	**DGIINPU**	pinguid	**DHINOPY**	hypnoid
DFFOOPR	drop-off	**DGIINRV**	driving	**DHINORS**	dronish
DFGHIOS	dogfish	**DGIINRY**	gyrinid	**DHINORY**	hydrion
DFGIINN	finding	**DGIINSS**	dissing	**DHINOSW**	downish
DFGIINY	dignify	**DGIINST**	tidings	**DHINSTU**	tundish
DFGILNO	folding	**DGIINTY**	dignity	**DHIOOSW**	woodish
DFGINOU	fungoid	**DGIIORT**	tigroid	**DHIOPTY**	typhoid
DFGLNUY	dung-fly	**DGIKMNO**	kingdom	**DHIORTY**	thyroid
DFGLOOW	dog-wolf	**DGIKNOS**	dogskin	**DHIPRSU**	prudish
DFHILSU	dishful	**DGILLOR**	old girl	**DHIPRSY**	syrphid
DFHIMSU	mudfish	**DGILMNO**	molding	**DHKORSY**	droshky
DFIILRW	Wilfrid	**DGILNOR**	lording	**DHLMOOU**	hoodlum
DFIINRW	Winfrid	**DGILNOW**	Goldwin	**DHLOOPR**	Rodolph
DFILLUY	fluidly	**DGILPUY**	pudgily	**DHLOOTU**	holdout
DFILMNU	mindful	**DGIMNSU**	Sigmund	**DHLOPRU**	Rudolph
DFILNOP	pinfold	**DGIMOPY**	pygmoid	**DHMMRUU**	humdrum
DFILORT	trifold	**DGIMORU**	Gordium	**DHMNOYY**	hymnody
DFILOSX	sixfold	**DGINNNO**	donning	**DHNNOOU**	nunhood
DFILOTW	twifold	**DGINNNU**	dunning	**DHNOOOW**	ownhood
DFILTUU	dutiful	**DGINNOU**	undoing	**DHOOOOS**	hoodoos

DHOORTY	Dorothy	**DIMOPSU**	podiums	**EEEEFRR**	referee
DHOPRSU	pushrod	**DIMORSW**	misword	**EEEEGTX**	exegete
DHOPRSY	hydrops	**DIMPRSU**	disrump	**EEEEHST**	tee-hees
DHORSUY	hydrous	**DIMRTUU**	triduum	**EEEFFFO**	feoffee
DIIIMRU	iridium	**DIMRUUV**	duumvir	**EEEFGRU**	refugee
DIIIMSU	isidium	**DINNOOT**	tondino	**EEEFHRS**	shereef
DIIINPS	insipid	**DINNOPW**	pin-down	**EEEFNRV**	enfever
DIIINRV	viridin	**DINNOSW**	Swindon	**EEEFORS**	foresee
DIIJNOS	disjoin	**DINOORS**	indoors,	**EEEFRRZ**	freezer
DIIKKNS	kidskin		Sondrio,	**EEEGILZ**	elegize
DIIKNOT	doitkin		sordino	**EEEGINP**	epigene
DIILLNW	ill wind	**DINOORT**	tordion	**EEEGINR**	greenie
DIILLST	distill	**DINOPPU**	duppion	**EEEGINU**	Eugenie
DIILLVY	lividly	**DINORSW**	Windsor	**EEEGIPR**	perigee
DIILMNS	dislimn	**DINORWW**	windrow	**EEEGLNT**	genteel
DIILMOS	idolism	**DINOSTW**	sit-down	**EEEGLRY**	Greeley
DIILMTY	timidly	**DINPRSY**	spin-dry	**EEEGNPR**	epergne
DIILNWY	windily	**DIOORST**	disroot	**EEEGNRR**	greener,
DIILRTY	dirtily	**DIOPRST**	disport		reneger
DIILVVY	vividly	**DIOPRTY**	tripody	**EEEGNRU**	renegue
DIILYZZ	dizzily	**DIOPSST**	dispost	**EEEGNRV**	genever,
DIIMNOR	midiron	**DIORSTT**	distort		revenge
DIIMSSS	dismiss	**DIPRSTU**	disrupt	**EEEGNRY**	greeney
DIIMSUV	vidimus	**DKLOOPS**	Podolsk	**EEEGNTT**	genette
DIINOQU	quinoid	**DLLORWY**	worldly	**EEEGRRT**	greeter
DIINORS	sordini	**DLMNOOO**	old moon	**EEEGRUX**	exergue
DIIORSV	divisor	**DLMNOOY**	mylodon	**EEEHILW**	wheelie
DIITUVY	viduity	**DLMOSUU**	modulus	**EEEHLLN**	Hellene
DIJOSTU	judoist	**DLNOOOX**	loxodon	**EEEHLNR**	Heerlen
DIKLMRY	dry milk	**DLNOOWW**	low-down	**EEEHLNW**	enwheel
DIKLNRY	kiln-dry	**DLNOOWY**	Lynwood	**EEEHLOY**	eyehole
DIKLSUY	duskily	**DLNORUY**	roundly	**EEEHLPW**	wheeple
DIKMRTU	drum kit	**DLNOSUU**	nodulus	**EEEHLRW**	wheeler
DIKNNOS	non-skid	**DLNOSUY**	soundly	**EEEHLTW**	wheetle
DIKORSW	skid row	**DLNOTUW**	wouldn't	**EEEHMMP**	phememe
DILLOSY	solidly	**DLNOUWY**	woundly	**EEEHMNT**	methene
DILLPSY	psyllid	**DLOOPPY**	polypod	**EEEHNRW**	whene'er
DILLRUY	luridly	**DLOOPRY**	polyrod	**EEEHRRW**	where'er
DILMNOR	lindorm	**DLOOPTY**	tylopod	**EEEHRWZ**	wheezer
DILMNRU	drumlin	**DLOOPUY**	duopoly	**EEEHSTT**	esthete
DILMOOR	milordo	**DLOOPWY**	plywood	**EEEIKLL**	eel-like
DILMOOY	moodily	**DLOORRU**	Our Lord	**EEEIKLZ**	Ezekiel
DILMORU	oil drum	**DLOOSTU**	outsold	**EEEIKNS**	kneesie
DILMPUY	dumpily	**DLOPRUY**	proudly	**EEEILMN**	Emeline
DILMTUY	tumidly	**DLOSTUW**	wouldst	**EEEILNV**	Eveline
DILNOPT	diplont	**DMNNOOO**	monodon	**EEEILRR**	leerier
DILNOPY	dipylon	**DMNOOOP**	monopod	**EEEILRV**	relieve
DILNOTU	indulto	**DMNOOUU**	Moundou	**EEEILVY**	evil eye
DILNOWY	downily	**DMOOOQU**	quomodo	**EEEIMNT**	emetine
DILNOXY	indoxyl	**DNNOORW**	non-word	**EEEIMPR**	epimere,
DILNPSY	spindly	**DNNORUW**	rundown		preemie
DILORWY	rowdily,	**DNNOSUU**	unsound	**EEEIMRT**	eremite
	wordily	**DNNOSUW**	sundown	**EEEINQU**	queenie
DILOSSU	dulosis,	**DNNOUUW**	unwound	**EEEINRS**	eserine
	solidus	**DNOOPTW**	top-down	**EEEINRT**	teenier
DILOSTY	styloid	**DNOORTU**	orotund	**EEEINRW**	weenier
DILOTTY	dottily	**DNOPRUU**	round-up	**EEEIPRW**	weepier
DILRYZZ	drizzly	**DNOPTUW**	put-down	**EEEIRRV**	reverie
DILSTUY	dustily	**DOOOOSV**	voodoos	**EEEIRST**	eeriest
DIMMOOY	omomyid	**DOOORSU**	odorous	**EEEISTW**	sweetie
DIMMOST	midmost	**DOOORTU**	outdoor	**EEEJLNW**	enjewel
DIMNNOO	midnoon	**DOOORWW**	Woodrow	**EEEJLRW**	jeweler
DIMNNOT	dinmont	**DOOPRSY**	prosody	**EEEJNPY**	jeepney
DIMNOPU	impound	**DOOPRTU**	drop-out	**EEEJNRV**	jenever
DIMNOTW	midtown	**DOORSTU**	dustoor	**EEEJPRS**	jeepers

EEEKLLU ukelele
EEEKLNR kneeler
EEEKLNX Kleenex
EEEKNPT keepnet
EEEKRST keester, skeeter, teskere
EEEKRTZ tezkere
EEELLNO lee-lone
EEELLRV leveler
EEELLST Estelle
EEELMNT element
EEELMOS leesome
EEELMPR plereme
EEELNNO Noeleen
EEELOTX exolete
EEELPRS espeler, sleeper
EEELPRT peletre, replete
EEELPSS esplees
EEELPST steeple
EEELRTV leveret
EEELSSY eyeless
EEELTTW tweetle
EEELTTX teletex
EEEMMSS meseems
EEEMNOS no-see-em
EEEMNSS nemeses
EEEMOSY eyesome
EEEMRTT metrete
EEEMRTX extreme
EEENNPT pentene
EEENNSS ensense
EEENNTT entente, tenente
EEENPRR preener
EEENPRT pre-teen, terpene
EEENPRV pervene, prevene
EEENPST ensteep, steepen
EEENPSX expense
EEENRRS serener, sneerer
EEENRRT re-enter, terrene
EEENRRV venerer
EEENRRW renewer
EEENRSZ sneezer
EEENRTV eventer
EEENRTX externe
EEENRUV revenue, unreeve
EEENSTV evenest
EEENSTW sweeten
EEENSTX extense
EEENSWY Sweeney
EEEOPPT peep-toe
EEEORSV oversee
EEEORSY eyesore
EEEPRSS peeress
EEEPRSW sweeper
EEEQSUZ squeeze
EEERRST steerer
EEERRSV reserve, reverse
EEERTTW tweeter
EEERTWZ tweezer
EEFFFNO enfeoff
EEFFFOR feoffer
EEFFGLU effulge
EEFFINR fen-fire
EEFFINT fifteen
EEFFJRY Jeffery, Jeffrey
EEFFLOP peel-off
EEFFNOS offense
EEFFORR offerer
EEFFOST toffees
EEFGILN feeling
EEFGLLU gleeful
EEFGLOR foreleg
EEFGORR reforge
EEFHIRT heftier
EEFHLNS enflesh
EEFHLRS flesher, herself
EEFHLTY feelthy
EEFHNRS freshen
EEFHORT thereof
EEFHORW whereof
EEFHRRS fresher, refresh
EEFHRRU fuehrer
EEFHRST freshet
EEFIIMN feminie
EEFIIRR fierier
EEFIJNR Jenifer
EEFIKPT keep-fit
EEFILLX flexile
EEFILNO olefine
EEFILRT fertile
EEFILST felsite
EEFILSX sex life
EEFILVX flexive
EEFINRR refiner
EEFINSS finesse
EEFINST festine
EEFIRRR ferrier
EEFIRRT ferrite, fir tree
EEFIRTZ fretize
EEFISTV festive
EEFLLTY fleetly
EEFLNNO enfelon
EEFLNOS oneself
EEFLNRS fresnel
EEFLNTU teenful
EEFLORS forlese
EEFLRRU ferrule
EEFLRTT fettler
EEFLRTU fleuret
EEFLRUX flexure
EEFMNOR foremen
EEFMNRT ferment
EEFMOTT mofette
EEFMPRU perfume
EEFMRRY fermery
EEFMTTU fumette
EEFNORT oftener
EEFNRRW Renfrew
EEFNRRY fernery
EEFNRST fenster
EEFNRTV fervent
EEFNSSY feyness
EEFORRV forever
EEFORRZ refroze
EEFORST foreset
EEFORTT feretto
EEFPRSU perfuse
EEFRRRY ferryer
EEFRRSU refuser
EEFRRTU refuter
EEFRRTY ferrety
EEGGHTU thuggee
EEGGILR leggier
EEGGIOR Georgie
EEGGIST eggiest
EEGGLOR leggero
EEGGLOU eglogue
EEGGLSS eggless
EEGGNOR engorge
EEGGNOY geogeny
EEGGNST nest egg
EEGGORR regorge
EEGGPRU puggree
EEGHINV enveigh
EEGHINY hygiene
EEGHIRU heurige
EEGHIRW reweigh, weigher
EEGHIWZ gee whiz
EEGHLNO Hengelo
EEGHMNO hegemon
EEGHMNU hegumen
EEGHNOX hexogen
EEGHNRT greenth
EEGHNRY greyhen
EEGHOPY hypogee
EEGIIKR kriegie
EEGIKLM gemlike
EEGIKLN keeling
EEGIKNN kneeing
EEGIKNP keeping
EEGIKNS seeking
EEGIKNT kitenge
EEGILLS Giselle
EEGILNP peeling
EEGILNT gentile
EEGILRV veliger
EEGILST elegist
EEGIMMR gremmie, immerge
EEGIMNR mereing, regimen
EEGIMNS seeming
EEGIMNT meeting
EEGIMRS remiges
EEGINNU genuine
EEGINNV evening
EEGINOP epigone
EEGINOR E-region
EEGINPP peeping
EEGINPW weeping

EEGINPY epigyne
EEGINRS greisen
EEGINRT integer
EEGINSS genesis
EEGINTT Ginette
EEGINTV vitenge
EEGINTX exigent
EEGIOST egotise
EEGIOTZ egotize
EEGIRRV griever
EEGIRTT tergite
EEGISTV vestige
EEGKNOR kerogen
EEGKNRU gerenuk
EEGLLSS legless
EEGLMMU gemmule
EEGLMNU legumen
EEGLMOR gomerel
EEGLNOR erelong
EEGLNOT telogen
EEGLNOU eugenol
EEGLNOZ lozenge
EEGLNRT gentler
EEGLNRY greenly
EEGLRST leg-rest
EEGMMRY gemmery
EEGMNST segment
EEGMRTU gum tree
EEGNNRU ungreen
EEGNPTT tent peg
EEGNPUX expunge
EEGNRSS Negress
EEGNSTU guesten
EEGORTV overget
EEGPPRR prepreg
EEGPRUX expurge
EEGRRSS regress
EEGRSSU guesser
EEGRSTU gesture
EEGRSUX exsurge
EEHHORU houhere
EEHHRTW whether
EEHILLR hellier
EEHILLT hellite
EEHILMN hemline
EEHILNX helxine
EEHILPS ephelis
EEHILPV Pehlevi
EEHILRW whilere
EEHILST sheltie
EEHIMPT epithem
EEHIMTU heumite
EEHINNV Nineveh
EEHINOR heroine
EEHINRR errhine
EEHINRT enherit, neither, therein
EEHINRW wherein
EEHIORV overhie
EEHIORZ heroize
EEHIPRT prithee
EEHIPSV peevish
EEHIPTT epithet
EEHIRSS heiress

EEHISST hessite
EEHISTV thieves
EEHKLOY keyhole
EEHKNNT Kenneth
EEHLLMP phellem
EEHLLNS enshell
EEHLLSY Shelley
EEHLMMW whemmel
EEHLMTY thymele
EEHLNUW Heulwen
EEHLOSY Holy See
EEHLPRT telpher
EEHLPST Elspeth
EEHLRST shelter
EEHLRSV shelver
EEHLRSW welsher
EEHLRSY sheerly
EEHLSSU hueless
EEHLSSV shelves
EEHMNOP phoneme
EEHMNRU enrheum
EEHMNRY mynheer
EEHMOPR proheme
EEHMORT theorem
EEHNOOR honoree
EEHNOPT potheen
EEHNORT thereon
EEHNORW nowhere, whereon
EEHNPST Stephen
EEHNRST hestern
EEHNRSW hernsew
EEHNRTW wrethen
EEHNSTU enthuse
EEHNSTV seventh
EEHOOPW whoopee
EEHOPST heptose
EEHORRV hoverer
EEHORST threose
EEHORSU rehouse
EEHORSW whereso
EEHORTT thereto
EEHORTW whereto
EEHORVW however, whoever
EEHOSTY eyeshot
EEHPPST heppest
EEHPSSU Ephesus
EEHRRST three Rs
EEHRRTW wherret
EEHRTTU the true
EEHRTTW whetter
EEHSTUY shut-eye
EEIIJMT mietjie
EEIIKTW kiewiet
EEIILNT tie line
EEIIMTZ itemize
EEIINPR pierine
EEIINRV veinier
EEIINST inesite
EEIINTV invitee
EEIISTT teistie
EEIJKRR jerkier
EEIJLNW injewel
EEIKKRR krieker

EEIKKRT trekkie
EEIKLPT pikelet
EEIKNNP pinkeen
EEIKNPP kippeen
EEIKNPY pink-eye
EEIKNRT kernite
EEIKPRR perkier
EEIKPRS peskier
EEIKRST keister
EEIKTTT tektite
EEILLMT mellite
EEILLNO Leoline
EEILLNV Neville
EEILLPS ellipse
EEILMMT meltemi
EEILMNR ermelin
EEILMPR emperil
EEILMRV vermeil, vermile
EEILNNO leonine, Noeline
EEILNNT lenient
EEILNNV enliven
EEILNOP pleione
EEILNPS penisle, pensile
EEILNRV vernile
EEILNST lisente, tensile
EEILNTT entitle, Linette
EEILNTV veinlet
EEILNUV veinule
EEILOPT petiole
EEILORV overlie, relievo
EEILOST estoile
EEILOTZ zeolite
EEILPRR replier
EEILPRS spieler
EEILPRT perlite, reptile
EEILPRU puerile
EEILPSS pelisse
EEILPST epistle
EEILPWY weepily
EEILRRV reviler
EEILRST leister, sterile
EEILRSU leisure
EEILRSV leervis, servile
EEILRTT retitle
EEILRTV viertel
EEILSSS sessile
EEILSST telesis, tieless
EEILSSV lessive
EEILSTT Lisette
EEILSTV velites
EEILSUV elusive
EEILTTX textile
EEILTUX ulexite
EEILVWY weevily
EEIMMNS immense
EEIMMPR emprime
EEIMMRS immerse
EEIMMSS misseem

EEIMNNO nominee
EEIMNNT eminent
EEIMNOT one-time
EEIMNRS ermines
EEIMNRT termine
EEIMNRU erineum
EEIMNRV minever
EEIMNSS Meissen, nemesis, siemens
EEIMNSW misween
EEIMNTT minette
EEIMOPS episome
EEIMOPT epitome
EEIMOSS meioses
EEIMOTV emotive
EEIMPRR premier
EEIMPRS emprise, imprese, premise
EEIMPRT emptier
EEIMPST septime
EEIMQRU requiem
EEIMRRR merrier
EEIMRRT trireme
EEIMRRX remixer
EEIMRSS messier, messire
EEIMRST triseme
EEIMRTT emitter, termite
EEINNNP pennine
EEINNPR enripen
EEINNPS pennies
EEINNRT interne, nitrene
EEINNRU neurine
EEINNRV innerve, nervine
EEINNSS insense
EEINNST enseint, ensient, intense, tennies
EEINNSW ensinew
EEINNTT Ninette
EEINNTW entwine
EEINOPR pereion, pioneer
EEINOPU eupione
EEINORS erinose
EEINPRS enspire, erepsin
EEINPSS penises
EEINPST insteep
EEINPSV pensive, vespine
EEINQRU enquire
EEINQTU quieten
EEINRRT reinter, rentier, terrine
EEINRRV nervier, vernier
EEINRSV inverse, versine
EEINRSW newsier
EEINRSY Erinyes
EEINRTU neurite, retinue, reunite, uterine
EEINSTU en suite
EEINSTV tensive
EEINSTX sixteen
EEINSTY syenite
EEINTTV tentive
EEIOPST poetise
EEIOPTZ poetize
EEIORST erotise
EEIORSV erosive
EEIORTZ erotize
EEIORZZ zeroize
EEIPPPR peppier, preppie
EEIPPTT pipette
EEIPPTZ peptize
EEIPQRU perique, re-equip, repique
EEIPRRR perrier
EEIPRRS prisere, reprise, respire
EEIPRSS pressie
EEIPRST respite
EEIPRSV previse
EEIPRTT pettier
EEIPRTY yperite
EEIPRVW preview
EEIPRZZ prezzie
EEIQRRU require
EEIQRSU esquire
EEIQRTU quieter, requite
EEIRRRT retirer, terrier
EEIRRSV reviser
EEIRRTV riveter
EEIRRTW rewrite
EEIRRVV reviver
EEIRSSU reissue
EEIRSTT testier, Trieste
EEIRSTV restive, sievert, veriest
EEIRSTZ zestier
EEIRSUZ seizure
EEIRTVV vetiver
EEISSTX sexiest
EEJLLMU jumelle
EEJLLWY jewelly
EEJLRWY jewelry
EEJMNTU munjeet
EEJNORY enjoyer
EEJORSS Jessore
EEJOSTT Josette
EEJPRRU perjure
EEKKRRT trekker
EEKLLSY sleekly
EEKLLUU ukulele
EEKLMNU klumene
EEKLMRZ klezmer
EEKLNOS keelson
EEKLOOS look-see
EEKLOWW Low Week
EEKLRST kestrel
EEKLSSY keyless
EEKNOTY keynote
EEKNPSU knees-up
EEKNQRU querken
EEKNRUV verneuk
EEKNSST Knesset
EEKNSTU netsuke
EEKORRV revoker
EEKOSTV voetsek
EEKRSTY keyster
EEKSTWY Key West
EELLLVY levelly
EELLMOS Moselle
EELLMRS smeller
EELLNOR Nellore
EELLORV Vellore
EELLPRS pre-sell, respell, speller
EELLQRU queller
EELLQSU quelles
EELMMPU emplume
EELMNOO oenomel
EELMNPY pelmeny
EELMOPR plerome
EELMOPT leptome
EELMOPY employe
EELMORS Melrose
EELMORT telomer
EELMORW eelworm
EELMPST stemple
EELMPTT templet
EELMRST smelter
EELMRTU lumeter
EELMSTT stemlet
EELNOPR Peronel
EELNOPV envelop
EELNOSV Slovene
EELNOTT notelet
EELNOTU toluene
EELNOVV envolve
EELNPSY spleeny
EELNQUY queenly
EELNSTY enstyle, tensely
EELNTTU lunette
EELNTTY Lynette
EELNTWY newelty
EELOPPZ zeppole
EELOPRS leprose
EELOPRX explore
EELOPSU pelouse
EELOPTU eelpout
EELORSV resolve
EELORTT Lorette
EELORVV revolve

EELOSST osselet, toeless
EELOSTT teleost
EELOTUV evolute
EELPPRX perplex
EELPQRU prequel
EELPRSS plesser, pressel
EELPRST Prestel, respelt, spelter
EELPRSU repulse
EELPRTZ pretzel
EELPRUX plexure
EELPRVY replevy
EELPSSW pewless
EELPSTY steeply
EELPSUX expulse
EELQRUY queerly
EELRRVY revelry
EELRSST tressel
EELRSTT settler, sterlet, trestle
EELRSTW swelter, wrestle
EELRSTY restyle, tersely
EELRSTZ seltzer
EELSSST lessest
EELSSSU useless
EELSSSX sexless
EELSTUY eustyle
EELSTWY sweetly
EELTVVY velvety
EEMMNOT memento
EEMMOST mestome
EEMNNOT onement
EEMNNOV envenom
EEMNOOS someone
EEMNOOY moon-eye
EEMNORV overmen
EEMNORY moneyer
EEMNOST temenos
EEMNOSU no-see-um
EEMNPTU umpteen
EEMNSTU set menu
EEMOPRR emperor
EEMOPRV emprove, premove
EEMOPRW empower
EEMORRS remorse
EEMORRT remoter
EEMORRV remover
EEMORWY eye-worm
EEMPPRT pre-empt
EEMPRRT preterm
EEMPRSS empress
EEMPRSU presume, supreme
EEMPRTT tempter
EEMPRTU permute
EEMPSTT tempest
EEMRSUX murexes
EEMSTTU musette
EENNOPT ponente
EENNORT enteron, tenoner
EENNORU neurone
EENNOSS oneness
EENNOTY neoteny
EENNPTU Neptune
EENNRUV unnerve
EENNSSW newness
EENOPPR prepone, propene
EENOPPT peptone
EENOPRT pretone
EENOPRV provene
EENOPST one-step, pentose, posteen
EENOPTY neotype
EENORRT terreno
EENORSV nervose
EENORTU en route, tournee
EENORWY wyerone
EENOSTV ventose
EENOTTT tonette
EENPRST penster, present, serpent
EENPRTV prevent
EENQRTU querent
EENQSTU enquest, sequent
EENRRTY re-entry, ternery
EENRRUV nervure
EENRSTT testern
EENRSTW western
EENRSTY styrene, yestern
EENRTTU nut tree
EENRTUV venture
EENSSTW wetness
EENSSUV Venuses
EENSSUX nexuses
EENSTVY seventy
EEOOPRS operose
EEOPPRS prepose
EEOPRRV reprove
EEOPRSX exposer
EEOPRTT proette, treetop
EEOPRTU outpeer
EEOPSST poetess
EEOPSSU espouse, poseuse
EEOPSTY eyespot
EEORRST restore
EEORRTU re-route
EEORRTV evertor
EEORRTW rewrote
EEORSTT rosette, tetrose
EEORSTV overset
EEORSUV overuse
EEORSVW oversew
EEPPPRR prepper
EEPPPRY peppery
EEPPRSX perspex
EEPRRSS repress
EEPRRST prester
EEPRRSU peruser
EEPRRTV pervert
EEPRSSX express
EEPRSTT pretest
EEPRTTX pretext
EEPSTTY typeset
EEQRRUY equerry
EEQRSTU quester, request
EEQSUYZ squeezy
EERRSTW strewer
EERRSVW swerver
EERRSVY servery
EERRTTU utterer
EERSSTT tersest
EERSTTU trustee
EERSTUV versute, vesture
EERTTUX texture
EESSTTU suttees
EESTTTW wettest
EESTTUZ Suzette
EFFFINO infeoff
EFFFOOR feoffor
EFFHILW whiffle
EFFHIRS sheriff
EFFHIRU huffier
EFFHITW whiffet
EFFHLSU shuffle
EFFIINR niffier
EFFIIST iffiest
EFFIKLS skiffle
EFFILLU lifeful
EFFILNO offline
EFFILNS sniffle
EFFILPR piffler
EFFILRY firefly
EFFIMOT off-time, time off
EFFINRS sniffer
EFFINST stiffen
EFFIOPR piffero
EFFIORT forfeit
EFFIOST toffies
EFFIPRU puffier
EFFITTU tuffite
EFFLLOS sell-off
EFFLLOW well-off
EFFLMRU muffler
EFFLNSU snuffle
EFFLOSU souffle
EFFLRTU fretful, truffle
EFFNRSU snuffer
EFFOORR offeror
EFFOPRR proffer
EFFPRUY puffery
EFFRSTU stuffer
EFFSSUU suffuse
EFGGILP egg-flip
EFGGILR friggle
EFGGIOR foggier

EFGGIRR frigger
EFGGLOR flogger
EFGHIRT fighter, freight
EFGILMN Fleming
EFGILNR ferling, flinger
EFGILNT felting
EFGILNU fueling
EFGIMNT figment
EFGINNP pfennig
EFGINOR foreign
EFGINRU gunfire
EFGINTU fungite
EFGIOOR goofier
EFGIORV forgive
EFGIRRT grifter
EFGLNTU fulgent
EFGNOOR forgone
EFGOORR forgoer
EFGORRY forgery
EFGORTT forgett
EFHIINS fineish
EFHIIRS fishier
EFHIJSW jewfish
EFHIKUY kufiyeh
EFHILMS flemish, himself
EFHILSS his-self, selfish
EFHILST leftish
EFHILTY heftily
EFHINNS fennish
EFHINST fishnet
EFHIRST fretish, shifter
EFHIRSY fishery
EFHISUW huswife
EFHLLPU helpful
EFHLLSY fleshly
EFHLOOW whoofle
EFHLOOX foxhole
EFHLOPU hopeful
EFHLRSU flusher
EFHLRSY freshly
EFHLSTY thyself
EFHLTTW twelfth
EFHOPRS profesh
EFHRRTU further
EFIILMR filmier
EFIILRY fierily
EFIILSS fissile
EFIIMRS misfire
EFIINPR pin-fire
EFIINRT niftier
EFIINRU unifier
EFIIORT fiorite
EFIIRZZ fizzier
EFIISSV fissive
EFIISTW swiftie
EFIJLLY jellify
EFIJLOT jetfoil
EFIKLOR folkier
EFIKLOX foxlike
EFIKLRU flukier
EFIKNRU funkier
EFIKRRS frisker
EFIKRST frisket
EFILLMS misfell
EFILLOO foliole
EFILLOU fuel oil
EFILLOW low life
EFILLUX fluxile
EFILMMR flimmer
EFILMNU fulmine
EFILMOT filemot
EFILMST filmset, leftism
EFILMTU timeful
EFILNOX flexion
EFILNSS finless
EFILOOS foliose
EFILOOZ floozie
EFILOPR profile, pro-life
EFILORT loftier, trefoil
EFILOSS Flossie
EFILOSX sexfoil
EFILPPR flipper
EFILPPU pipeful
EFILPRY pilfery
EFILPTT felt tip
EFILQUY liquefy
EFILRRT trifler
EFILRST stifler
EFILRTT flitter
EFILRVV flivver
EFILRZZ frizzle
EFILSTT leftist
EFILSTU sulfite
EFILUVX fluxive
EFIMMRT fremmit
EFIMMRU fermium
EFIMNOR fermion
EFIMNTT fitment
EFIMOST fomites
EFIMOTT oft-time
EFIMRTY metrify
EFINNOR inferno
EFINNPY fipenny
EFINNRU funnier
EFINOPR forpine
EFINOST festino
EFINRST snifter
EFINRSU infuser
EFINRUY reunify
EFINSST fitness
EFIOOST footsie
EFIORRT rotifer
EFIORTV overfit
EFIOSSU foussie
EFIOSTX foxiest
EFIPPRR fripper
EFIPPRT frippet
EFIPRTY petrify
EFIRRRU furrier
EFIRRSU friseur, frisure
EFIRRTT fritter
EFIRRTU fruiter, turfier
EFIRRTY terrify
EFIRSSU fissure, fussier
EFIRSTT fitters
EFIRSTU fustier, surfeit
EFIRSVY versify
EFIRTUV furtive
EFIRTUX fixture
EFIRUZZ fuzzier
EFISTTT fittest
EFISTTY testify
EFKLMNO menfolk
EFKLNUY flunkey
EFKLRSU flusker
EFLLOUV loveful
EFLMMRU flummer
EFLMORU formule
EFLMOSU fulsome
EFLMPRU frumple
EFLMSUU museful
EFLNORT florent
EFLNORU fleuron
EFLNORY felonry
EFLNOSU sulfone
EFLNOSW ownself
EFLNOTT fletton
EFLNSSU fulness
EFLNSSY flyness
EFLNSTU nestful
EFLNTTY tent-fly
EFLNTUU tuneful
EFLOORY foolery
EFLORSU ourself
EFLORTT fortlet
EFLORTW felwort
EFLORVY flyover, overfly
EFLORWW werwolf
EFLORWY flowery
EFLRSSU furless
EFLRSTU fluster, restful
EFLRTTU flutter
EFLSTTY test-fly
EFLSTUZ zestful
EFMNORT Fremont
EFMOORS formose
EFMOPRR perform, preform
EFMOPRT pomfret
EFMPRUY perfumy
EFMRTUY furmety
EFNNORT fornent
EFNOORW woonerf
EFNOOST festoon
EFNORRU forerun
EFNORRW frowner
EFNORTU fortune
EFNORTW forwent
EFNORUZ unfroze
EFNRSTU funster
EFOOPRR reproof
EFOOPRS spoofer
EFOOPRT foretop, poofter
EFOORRW forwore
EFOORST soft roe
EFOORTW woofter
EFOPPRY foppery

EFOPRRT profert
EFOPRSS profess
EFOPRSU profuse
EFOPRTY torpefy
EFORRRU ferrour
EFORRSU ferrous
EFORRTY torrefy
EFORRUV fervour
EFORSTY foresty
EFPRTUY putrefy
EFPSTUY stupefy
EGGGILN legging
EGGGILR giggler, griggle
EGGGINP pegging
EGGHILR higgler
EGGHORY hoggery
EGGHRUY huggery
EGGIIPR piggier
EGGIIPS piggies
EGGIKNR greking
EGGILLN gelling
EGGILNS sniggle
EGGILNU glueing
EGGILRW wiggler, wriggle
EGGIMMN gemming
EGGIMRU muggier
EGGINNN genning
EGGINNS ginseng
EGGINOR ingorge
EGGINOV vigogne
EGGINRS snigger
EGGINRY gingery
EGGINSU seguing
EGGINTT getting
EGGIORS soggier
EGGIPRY piggery
EGGIRRT trigger
EGGIRST gigster
EGGIRSW swigger
EGGIRWY wiggery
EGGJLRU juggler
EGGLLNO long leg
EGGLMSU smuggle
EGGLNSU snuggle
EGGLOOY geology
EGGLORS slogger
EGGLPRU plugger
EGGLRSU slugger
EGGMRSU smugger
EGGNOOY geogony
EGGNORS snogger
EGGNRSU snugger
EGGORRY gregory
EGGORTY toggery
EGGSSTU suggest
EGHHHIO heigh-ho
EGHHHIT heighth
EGHHIKY high-key
EGHIILL ghillie
EGHIINT nightie
EGHIINV inveigh
EGHIINW weigh-in
EGHIKLO hoglike
EGHIKNR gherkin
EGHILNP helping
EGHILNR herling
EGHILNS English, shingle
EGHILNT enlight, lighten
EGHILPT pightle
EGHILRT lighter, relight
EGHILST sleight
EGHIMMN hemming
EGHIMPT empight
EGHINNR Herning
EGHINNU unhinge
EGHINOS shoeing
EGHINRR herring
EGHINRT nighter, righten
EGHINRW whinger
EGHINTT tighten
EGHIORS ogreish
EGHIORU roughie
EGHIOTU toughie
EGHIRRT righter
EGHIRST sighter
EGHIRSU grushie, gushier
EGHIRSY greyish
EGHITWY weighty
EGHLLOU lughole
EGHLMPY phlegmy
EGHLNOR leghorn
EGHLNTY lengthy
EGHLOOT theolog
EGHLOSW leg-show
EGHMORS Gershom
EGHMOSU gumshoe, hugsome
EGHNORU enrough, roughen
EGHNOTU toughen
EGHNRTU Gunther
EGHNTWY Gwyneth
EGHOOPR goopher
EGHORST hogster
EGHOSUU hugeous
EGHRTUY theurgy
EGIIKLP piglike
EGIILLT illegit
EGIILMT legitim
EGIILNR glirine
EGIILNT lignite, Tieling
EGIILNV veiling
EGIILPZ Leipzig
EGIIMNP impinge
EGIIMNR mingier
EGIIMRR grimier
EGIIMSV misgive
EGIINNO ingenio
EGIINNS insigne
EGIINNT ingenit
EGIINNV veining
EGIINOP epigoni
EGIINRT igniter, tigrine
EGIINRZ zingier
EGIINSZ seizing
EGIINTX exiting
EGIINVW viewing
EGIIOTW witogie
EGIIPRS gipsire
EGIIPRW periwig
EGIIPSS gipsies
EGIIRUV viguier
EGIJLNR jingler
EGIJMNN Jingmen
EGIJNTT jetting
EGIKLLM milk-leg
EGIKLNR erl-king
EGIKLNT kinglet
EGIKNNN kenning
EGIKNNT kenting
EGIKNRU keruing
EGIKNRY keyring
EGILLMU guillem
EGILLNO log-line
EGILLNT gill-net, telling
EGILLPS leg slip
EGILLRR griller
EGILLRY gillery
EGILMMN lemming
EGILMMR glimmer
EGILMNR gremlin
EGILMNT melting
EGILMNU legumin
EGILMOS Limoges
EGILMOU elogium
EGILMPS glimpse
EGILNOR leg-iron
EGILNOS lignose, sloe gin
EGILNOT lentigo
EGILNPR pringle
EGILNPS leg spin, spignel
EGILNPT pelting
EGILNRS slinger
EGILNRT ringlet, tringle
EGILNST glisten, singlet
EGILNSW swingle
EGILNTT letting
EGILNTW twingle, winglet
EGILNTY yetling
EGILOPS Golspie
EGILORU orgueil
EGILOST logiest
EGILPPR gripple
EGILRST glister, gristle
EGILRTT glitter
EGILRUV virgule
EGILRUY guilery
EGILRZZ Grizzel, grizzle
EGILSSW wigless
EGILSTU gluiest, ugliest
EGIMMRR grimmer

EGIMMRU gummier
EGIMMTU gummite
EGIMNOT mitogen
EGIMNPR grimpen, impregn
EGIMNPT empting, pigment
EGIMNTU mugient
EGIMOST egotism
EGINNNP penning
EGINNNY yenning
EGINNOO ionogen
EGINNOP opening
EGINNOR negroni
EGINNPU penguin
EGINNRR grinner
EGINNST nesting
EGINNSU ensuing
EGINNTT netting, tenting
EGINOPR pongier
EGINORR ignorer
EGINORT genitor, Negrito, toering, trigone
EGINOST gestion
EGINOSU igneous
EGINOTT tentigo
EGINPPP pepping
EGINPPR repping
EGINPRS springe
EGINPSY pigsney
EGINPTT petting
EGINQUU queuing
EGINRRW wringer
EGINRSS ingress
EGINRST stinger
EGINRSU insurge
EGINRSV serving
EGINRSW swinger
EGINRSY syringe
EGINRTT gittern, retting
EGINRTU trueing
EGINRTY retying
EGINRVV revving
EGINSTT setting, testing
EGINSTU gun-site
EGINSTW westing
EGINTTV vetting
EGINTTW wetting
EGIOOPR goopier
EGIOOST gooiest
EGIOPRT ego trip
EGIOPRU groupie, pirogue
EGIORST goriest
EGIORTV vertigo
EGIOSTT egotist
EGIPPRR gripper
EGIPRUU guipure
EGIRRTT gritter
EGIRSST tigress
EGIRSSU Sergius
EGIRSTU gustier, gutsier
EGISUWY wise guy
EGJLNOU juglone
EGJOSTT gjetost
EGKLORW legwork
EGLLLPU leg-pull
EGLLMUW mew gull
EGLLOUY yule log
EGLLRUY gullery
EGLMMRU glummer, grummel
EGLMNNO Longmen
EGLMNOR mongrel
EGLMOOR legroom
EGLMOSU glumose
EGLNOOP pongelo
EGLNOOY enology, neology
EGLNOPP gloppen
EGLNORU lounger
EGLNOST longest
EGLNOYZ lozengy
EGLNPRU plunger
EGLNRTU gruntle
EGLNSSU gunless
EGLOOYY gooeyly
EGLOPTU glue-pot
EGLORRW growler
EGLORSS glosser
EGLPRSU splurge
EGLRSUU regulus
EGLRUZZ guzzler
EGLSSTU gutless
EGLSTUU gluteus, Telugus
EGMMORT grommet
EGMMRTU grummet
EGMNOYZ zymogen
EGMNRUY gymnure
EGMORSU grumose
EGMORTU gourmet
EGNNPTU pungent
EGNNRUY gunnery
EGNNSTU Sten gun
EGNNTUU unguent
EGNOORY orogeny
EGNOOTU outgone
EGNOPRS sponger
EGNOPRY progeny, pyrogen
EGNOPSU pug-nose
EGNORRW wronger
EGNORSS engross
EGNORSU surgeon
EGNORUY younger
EGNOSTU tongues
EGNOTUY tonguey
EGNRRTU grunter
EGNRSYY synergy
EGNRTTU turgent
EGOORSY goosery
EGOORTU outgoer
EGOORTV overgot
EGOPRRU grouper, regroup
EGORRSU grouser
EGORRTU grouter
EGORRUY roguery
EGORTUW outgrew
EGPRSUU upsurge
EGRRSUY surgery
EGRTTUY guttery
EHHIISZ Shihezi
EHHILLS hellish
EHHIMOS homeish
EHHINRS Rhenish
EHHIPRS hership
EHHIRTT thither
EHHIRTW whither
EHHOOST hot shoe
EHIIIKT hei-tiki
EHIILLR hillier
EHIINRS shinier
EHIINRT inherit
EHIINRW whinier
EHIIPRT pithier
EHIITTT Hittite
EHIJNNO Johnnie
EHIKKOS kokeshi
EHIKLTU hut-like
EHIKNRT rethink, thinker
EHIKNRU hunkier
EHIKNST Kentish
EHIKOST hokiest
EHIKRRS shirker
EHIKRSU huskier
EHIKRSW whisker
EHIKSWY whiskey
EHILLNO hellion
EHILLNS inshell
EHILLRT thiller
EHILLTY lithely
EHILNOP pinhole
EHILNOT hotline
EHILNPS plenish
EHILOPT hoplite
EHILOST holiest, hostile
EHILOTX hexitol
EHILPRT philter, philtre
EHILPSS hipless
EHILRRW whirler
EHILRST slither
EHILRSV shrivel
EHILRSY Shirley
EHILRTU luthier
EHILSTT Lettish, thistle
EHILSTW whistle
EHILTTU thulite
EHILTTW whittle
EHILTWY whitely
EHIMMPS Memphis
EHIMMRS shimmer
EHIMNRU rhenium
EHIMNTY thymine
EHIMORS heirmos,

heroism, moreish
EHIMORT moither, mothier
EHIMORZ rhizome
EHIMOST homiest
EHIMPPS pemphis
EHIMPPX pemphix
EHIMPRU humpier
EHIMPRW whimper
EHIMPTY epimyth
EHIMRSU heurism, mushier
EHIMRTT thermit
EHIMSWY whimsey
EHINNOP phone-in
EHINNRT thinner, thrinne
EHINNRW whinner
EHINOPR phonier
EHINOPX phoenix
EHINORR hornier
EHINORS inshore
EHINORT threnoi
EHINOST histone
EHINOSU heinous, in-house
EHINPSS hipness
EHINRSV shriven, vernish
EHINRTV thriven
EHINRTW writhen
EHINSSU Hussein
EHINTTU huntite
EHINTTW whitten
EHIOPRS rose-hip
EHIORRS horsier
EHIORRT heritor
EHIORST hoister, shortie
EHIORSW showier
EHIORSY hosiery
EHIORTT orthite, thorite
EHIORTW hot-wire
EHIOSST theosis
EHIOSTY isohyet
EHIPPRS shipper
EHIPPRW whipper
EHIPPST hippest
EHIPPTW whippet
EHIPRST hipster
EHIPRSU pushier
EHIPRSW whisper
EHIPSTT pettish
EHIRRRU hurrier
EHIRSTU hirsute, trueish
EHIRSTW swither, whister, withers
EHIRSVY shivery
EHIRTTW whitret, whitter
EHIRTWY withery
EHISSTU Hussite
EHISSUV hussive
EHISTTW wettish
EHJLOOY holy Joe
EHKLNOS lokshen
EHKLOOT hooklet
EHKMOOS smoke-ho
EHKNORS honkers
EHKNPST p-skhent
EHKNRSU hunkers
EHLLNOY hellyon
EHLLNSU unshell
EHLLOTW hot well
EHLLOWY wholely
EHLMMOW whommel
EHLMMUW whummel
EHLMNOT menthol
EHLMNOY homelyn
EHLNRTU luthern
EHLNTTY tenthly
EHLNTYY ethynyl
EHLOOPT pothole, top-hole
EHLOOST Lesotho
EHLOPSY spyhole
EHLORST holster, hostler
EHLORTW whortle
EHLORTY helotry, Thorley
EHLOTXY ethoxyl
EHLRSTU hustler
EHLSTTU shuttle
EHMNOOR hormone, moorhen
EHMNORU home run
EHMNPTY nymphet
EHMNTTU hutment
EHMOOST smoothe
EHMOOSW somehow
EHMOPRT Morpeth
EHMOPRW morphew
EHMORST smother, thermos
EHMORTU mouther
EHMORTY mothery
EHMOTUX Exmouth
EHMPRTU thumper
EHMRRTU murther
EHMRSUU humerus
EHMTTUY humetty
EHNNOPR nephron
EHNNORT northen, thornen
EHNNORW Rhonwen
EHNOOPR no-hoper
EHNOORR honorer, hornero
EHNOORS onshore
EHNOOWY owney-oh
EHNOPRY hyperon
EHNOPUY euphony
EHNOPXY phenoxy
EHNORRT horrent, norther
EHNORRY heronry
EHNORST shorten
EHNORSU unhorse
EHNORSY noshery
EHNORTU nouther
EHNORTW nowther
EHNOSST hotness
EHNOSTY honesty
EHNOSUU unhouse
EHNOTUY youthen
EHNOUWZ Wenzhou
EHNPRYZ phrenzy
EHNRSTU shunter
EHNSSSY shyness
EHOOPRW whooper
EHOORST shooter, soother
EHOOSSW whoseso
EHOPPRS shopper
EHOPPRT prophet
EHOPPRW whopper
EHOPPTY hoppety
EHOPRRY orphrey
EHOPRST strophe
EHOPRSY phoresy
EHOPRTW Epworth
EHORRTW thrower
EHORSTU shouter, souther
EHORSWY showery
EHOSSST hostess
EHOSTTT hottest
EHOSTUW outshew
EHPRTTU turpeth
EHRSSTY shyster
EHRSTTU shutter
EHRSTTW strewth
EHRTTTU thutter
EIIILST ileitis
EIIINPR ripieni
EIIJLOT ijolite
EIIKKNR kinkier
EIIKLLP liplike
EIIKLMR milkier
EIIKLMS mislike
EIIKLRS silkier
EIIKNNT kinetin
EIIKNSS kinesis
EIIKNST inkiest
EIIKPRS spikier
EIIKRRS riskier
EIILLMM millime
EIILLNV villein
EIILLRS sillier
EIILLSW willies
EIILLTT littlie, tillite
EIILLTV vitelli
EIILMPR imperil
EIILMPT limepit
EIILMRS milreis, slimier
EIILMRT Leitrim, limiter
EIILMSS missile
EIILMST elitism,

	limiest, limites
EIILMSU	milieus
EIILMUX	milieux
EIILNNV	inliven
EIILNOS	elision
EIILNOV	olivine, violine
EIILNOZ	lionize
EIILNPS	splenii
EIILNRT	nitrile
EIILNST	liniest
EIILNTT	intitle
EIILNTU	inutile
EIILOPZ	polizei
EIILORV	Olivier, rilievo
EIILOST	oiliest
EIILOTT	Ottilie
EIILPPR	lippier
EIILQSU	silique
EIILSTT	elitist
EIILSTW	wiliest
EIILTUZ	utilize
EIILTXY	exility
EIIMMPR	imprime
EIIMMRT	immerit
EIIMMSS	mimesis
EIIMMST	mistime
EIIMNOR	Meirion
EIIMNPR	primine
EIIMNRT	interim, mintier, termini
EIIMNRV	miniver
EIIMNTV	minivet
EIIMNTY	nimiety
EIIMOSS	meiosis
EIIMPRS	pismire
EIIMPST	pietism
EIIMPTY	impiety
EIIMRSS	merisis
EIIMRST	mistier, rimiest
EIIMSSV	missive
EIINNNP	ninepin
EIINNOS	inosine
EIINNQU	quinine
EIINNRT	tinnier
EIINNSW	insinew
EIINNTW	intwine
EIINOPR	ripieno
EIINORS	ironise, noisier
EIINORV	ivorine
EIINORZ	ionizer, ironize
EIINOST	inosite
EIINOTX	exition
EIINPPR	nippier
EIINPRS	inspire, spinier
EIINQRU	inquire
EIINQTU	inquiet
EIINRTT	nitrite
EIINRTV	inviter, vitrine
EIINRTW	write-in
EIINSST	Sistine
EIINSTT	tiniest
EIINSTW	winiest
EIINSTX	inexist, Sixtine
EIINSTY	inseity
EIINTUV	unitive
EIIOPSS	poiesis
EIIOSTZ	zoisite
EIIPPRZ	zippier
EIIPRST	tipsier
EIIPRSW	wispier
EIIPSTT	pietist
EIIPSTY	ipseity
EIIPTTT	pittite
EIIQUVV	qui vive
EIIRRTZ	ritzier
EIIRSSS	sissier
EIIRSST	Trissie
EIIRSTV	revisit
EIIRSTW	wiriest
EIIRTTW	wittier
EIIRTZZ	trizzie
EIJKKSU	jukskei
EIJKLRY	jerkily
EIJLLOR	jollier
EIJMPRU	jumpier
EIJNORT	jointer
EIJNORY	joinery
EIJNPRU	juniper
EIJNRRU	injurer
EIJNSTU	Justine
EIJPRTU	Jupiter
EIJRTTY	jittery
EIJSSUV	jussive
EIKKLNO	klonkie
EIKKLRS	Selkirk
EIKKLSY	kylikes
EIKKOOR	kookier
EIKLLMN	mill-ken
EIKLLNW	inkwell
EIKLLOW	owl-like
EIKLLRS	reskill
EIKLLST	skillet
EIKLMNR	kremlin
EIKLMOP	klompie
EIKLNNU	nunlike
EIKLNRT	tinkler, trinkle
EIKLNRW	winkler, wrinkle
EIKLNSS	kinless
EIKLNST	lentisk
EIKLNSU	sunlike
EIKLNSY	skyline
EIKLNTT	knittle
EIKLNTU	nutlike
EIKLNTW	twinkle
EIKLOPS	ski pole
EIKLOTY	toylike
EIKLPRY	perkily
EIKLPSY	peskily
EIKLRST	klister
EIKLRSU	sulkier
EIKLSTT	kittles, skittle
EIKMMRR	krimmer
EIKMMRS	skimmer
EIKMNOR	moniker
EIKMORS	irksome, smokier
EIKMOSY	misyoke
EIKMRRS	smirker
EIKMRSS	kirmess
EIKMRSU	musiker, muskier
EIKMSST	mess kit
EIKNNOR	einkorn
EIKNNRS	skinner
EIKNOOR	rooinek
EIKNOPS	inspoke
EIKNORV	invoker
EIKNORW	wonkier
EIKNOSS	kenosis
EIKNPRS	pinkers
EIKNRST	Kirsten, Kristen, stinker
EIKNRTT	knitter, trinket
EIKNTUZ	kunzite
EIKOPPR	pork pie
EIKOPRR	porkier
EIKOPRS	porkies
EIKOPST	pokiest
EIKOSST	ketosis
EIKPPRS	skipper
EIKPPST	skippet
EIKRRST	skirret, striker
EIKRSTT	skitter
EILLLOW	oil well
EILLLPU	pillule
EILLLTU	tilleul
EILLMNU	mullein
EILLMOR	morille
EILLMOT	melilot
EILLMRR	merrill
EILLMST	mistell
EILLMTU	mullite
EILLNNP	pennill
EILLNOU	nouille
EILLNSS	illness
EILLORT	lorilet
EILLORV	Orville
EILLORW	lowlier
EILLORZ	zorille
EILLOSS	oilless
EILLOSV	villose
EILLPPP	pep pill
EILLPRS	spiller
EILLPSS	lipless
EILLQTU	quillet
EILLRST	trellis
EILLRSW	swiller
EILLRTT	littler
EILMMNO	molimen
EILMMPU	implume
EILMMRS	slimmer
EILMNOT	ton-mile
EILMNRY	Merilyn
EILMOOV	moolvie
EILMOPR	implore

EILMORR lorimer
EILMORS Lismore
EILMORT motlier
EILMOSS lissome
EILMOSW wilsome
EILMPRS simpler
EILMPRU lumpier, plumier
EILMPSU impulse
EILMPSX simplex
EILMPTY emptily
EILMRRY merrily
EILMRSS rimless
EILMRSU misrule
EILMRSY miserly
EILMRVY vermily
EILMSSY messily
EILMSTU Miletus
EILMSTY mesityl
EILMSUY Elysium
EILMUUV eluvium
EILNNPU pinnule
EILNNRT lintern
EILNNRY innerly
EILNOOR loonier
EILNOOV violone
EILNOPP plenipo
EILNOPR plerion, proline
EILNOPS epsilon
EILNOPT pointel, pontile, top-line
EILNOPV invelop
EILNORR loriner
EILNORT retinol
EILNOSS lioness
EILNOST tonsile
EILNOSU elusion
EILNOTU elution, line-out, outline
EILNOTV violent
EILNOTW towline
EILNOVV involve
EILNPRS Pilsner
EILNPST plenist
EILNPSU spinule
EILNPTY ineptly
EILNPUV vulpine
EILNRSV silvern
EILNRTU lutrine
EILNRTY inertly, nitryle
EILNRVY nervily
EILNSSS sinless
EILNSSU insulse, silenus
EILNSSW winless
EILNSTU utensil
EILNSTW westlin
EILNSTY instyle
EILNTTY yettlin
EILNVXY vixenly
EILOOPR loopier
EILOORT troolie
EILOOST ostiole, stoolie, toolies
EILOPRS spoiler
EILOPRT petroil, ploiter, poitrel, politer
EILOPST pistole
EILOPSV plosive
EILOPTT plottie
EILOPTX exploit
EILORSS rissole
EILORST Estoril
EILORSU lousier
EILORSW low-rise
EILORTT tortile, triolet
EILORTU outlier
EILOSTT litotes
EILOSTZ zloties
EILOTUV outlive, ovulite
EILPPRS slipper
EILPPRT ripplet, tippler, tripple
EILPPSS pipless
EILPPST stipple
EILPPSW swipple
EILPRRT tripler
EILPRSU pluries
EILPRTT triplet
EILPRTX triplex
EILPRUU purlieu
EILPSST tipless
EILPSTT spittle
EILPSTU stipule
EILPSUV pulsive
EILPTTY pettily
EILQRTU quilter
EILQRUU liqueur
EILQRUY quirley
EILQTUY quietly
EILRRSU surlier
EILRRTW twirler
EILRSTT litster, slitter, testril
EILRSTU lustier
EILRSVY silvery
EILRSZZ sizzler
EILRTTY littery, tritely
EILRTUV rivulet
EILSSTW witless
EILSTTW twistle
EILSTTY stylite, testily
EILSTYZ stylize
EILSWZZ swizzle
EILTTTW twittle
EILTWZZ twizzle
EIMMNOS misnome
EIMMOSV mismove
EIMMPRR primmer
EIMMPRU premium
EIMMRRT trimmer
EIMMRSW swimmer
EIMMRUY yummier
EIMMSST tsimmes
EIMMSTZ tzimmes
EIMNNOT mention
EIMNNOV invenom
EIMNOOR ionomer, moonier
EIMNOOS noisome
EIMNOOT emotion
EIMNOPS pi-meson
EIMNOPT emption, pimento
EIMNOQU Monique
EIMNORR Merrion
EIMNORS mersion
EIMNOST moisten
EIMNOSW winsome
EIMNOTU Mountie
EIMNOTY omneity
EIMNPRT emprint
EIMNPTU pinetum
EIMNQSU mesquin
EIMNRST entrism, minster
EIMNSST mess tin
EIMNSTT smitten
EIMNSTU mistune, mustine
EIMNSTW miswent
EIMNUZZ muezzin
EIMOORR roomier
EIMOPPR pompier
EIMOPRR primero, rompier
EIMOPRS promise, semi-pro
EIMOPRV improve
EIMOPRW impower
EIMOPST mopiest, poetism
EIMOPTY epitomy
EIMORRT mortier
EIMORRW wormier
EIMORSS mossier
EIMORST erotism, mortise
EIMORSU mousier
EIMORSV verismo
EIMORTV vomiter
EIMOSTU timeous
EIMOSTX exotism
EIMOSTZ mestizo
EIMOSYZ isozyme
EIMOTTU time-out
EIMOTTW two-time
EIMPRRU primeur
EIMPRSS impress, premiss
EIMPRST imprest
EIMPSST misstep
EIMPSTU impetus
EIMPSTY mistype
EIMQSTU mesquit
EIMRSSU misuser, surmise
EIMRSTT metrist
EIMRSTU mustier
EIMRSTY mistery

EIMRTUX	mixture	**EINQTUU**	unquiet	**EIPRSTT**	spitter, tipster
EIMRUZZ	muzzier	**EINRRSU**	insurer	**EIPRSTU**	peritus, pisteur
EIMSSTY	stymies	**EINRRTU**	irruent	**EIPRSTY**	pyrites
EINNOPS	pension	**EINRSSU**	sunrise	**EIPRSUU**	euripus
EINNOPT	pontine	**EINRSTT**	entrist	**EIPRSUV**	pursive
EINNOQU	quinone	**EINRSTU**	intruse	**EIPRTUW**	write-up
EINNORT	intoner, ternion	**EINRSTV**	striven	**EIPRUVW**	purview
EINNORU	reunion	**EINRTTU**	nuttier, trutine	**EIPSSVY**	vipseys
EINNORV	environ	**EINRTTW**	twinter, written	**EIQRSTU**	querist
EINNOST	tension	**EINRTUV**	unrivet, venturi	**EIQRSUY**	esquiry
EINNOSV	venison	**EINRTWY**	wintery	**EIQRTTU**	quitter
EINNOTT	tontine	**EINSSTW**	witness	**EIQRUVY**	quivery
EINNPRS	spinner	**EINSTTW**	entwist, twinset	**EIQRUZZ**	quizzer
EINNPRT	enprint	**EINSTTY**	tensity	**EIQSTUU**	quietus
EINNPSY	spinney	**EINSUVV**	vesuvin	**EIQSUZZ**	quizzes
EINNPTU	pine nut	**EINTTTW**	twitten	**EIRRRST**	stirrer
EINNQTU	Quentin	**EINTTUY**	tenuity	**EIRRSTU**	rustier
EINNRRU	runnier	**EIOOPPS**	poopsie	**EIRRSTV**	striver
EINNRSU	sunnier, unrisen	**EIOOPRT**	troopie	**EIRRSTW**	wrister
EINNRTV	vintner	**EIOOPST**	isotope	**EIRRTTU**	triture
EINNRTY	tinnery	**EIOORST**	sootier	**EIRRTTW**	writter
EINNSTZ	Zennist	**EIOORTV**	Orvieto	**EIRSTTU**	tertius, trustie
EINNTTU	intuent	**EIOORWZ**	woozier	**EIRSTTW**	twister
EINNTUW	untwine	**EIOOSTT**	tootsie	**EIRSUVV**	survive
EINOOPZ	epizoon	**EIOPPRS**	soppier	**EIRTTTW**	twitter
EINOORS	erosion	**EIOPRRS**	prosier	**EIRTTTY**	tittery
EINOOSZ	ozonise	**EIOPRRT**	pierrot	**EISSTUV**	tussive
EINOOZZ	ozonize	**EIOPRSS**	perosis, prossie	**EISSWZZ**	swizzes
EINOPPR	propine	**EIOPRST**	periost, prostie, riposte, ropiest	**EISTTUW**	wetsuit
EINOPRT	pointer, protein, pterion, repoint, tropine	**EIOPRSU**	soupier	**EJJMNUU**	jejunum
EINOPSS	spinose	**EIOPRTT**	pottier	**EJJMPTU**	jump jet
EINOQUX	equinox	**EIOPSTT**	tiptoes	**EJKORUY**	joukery
EINORSS	sonsier	**EIOPSTU**	piteous, poustie	**EJLLORY**	jollyer
EINORST	instore, nitrose, oestrin, stonier	**EIOPSTX**	exposit, poxiest	**EJLOSSY**	joyless
EINORSV	version	**EIOPSTY**	isotype	**EJNORUY**	journey
EINORSW	snowier	**EIOPTUW**	wipe-out	**EJNOSUU**	Joensuu
EINORTT	tritone	**EIORRRS**	sorrier	**EJOORVY**	overjoy
EINORTU	routine	**EIORRRT**	rortier	**EJOPPRT**	prop-jet
EINORTW	tew-iron	**EIORRRW**	worrier	**EJORSTU**	jouster
EINOSSS	session	**EIORRST**	roister	**EJPRRUY**	perjury
EINOSST	nosiest	**EIORRUV**	ouvrier	**EKKLRSU**	skulker
EINOSTT	toniest	**EIORSST**	rosiest, sorties	**EKLNOOW**	new look
EINOSUV	envious, niveous, veinous	**EIORSSU**	serious	**EKLNOPR**	plonker
EINOTTT	totient	**EIORSSX**	xerosis	**EKLNORS**	snorkel
EINPPST	snippet	**EIORTTV**	tortive	**EKLNPTU**	plunket
EINPRRT	printer, reprint	**EIORTUV**	outrive, voiture	**EKLOOTW**	wet look
EINPRRZ	Prizren	**EIOSTUZ**	outsize	**EKLSSSY**	skyless
EINPRSU	uprisen	**EIPPRRT**	tripper	**EKMMOTU**	temmoku
EINPSTU	puniest	**EIPPRTT**	trippet	**EKMNORY**	monkery
EINPTTY	tin-type	**EIPQRUU**	piqueur	**EKMNOSY**	monkey's
EINQRUY	enquiry	**EIPRRUV**	upriver	**EKMNOTU**	tenmoku
EINQSTU	inquest	**EIPRSST**	persist, stirpes	**EKMNPTU**	unkempt
EINQTTU	quintet			**EKMNRTU**	Turkmen
				EKNOORS	snooker
				EKNOPPR	knopper
				EKNORSY	Yonkers
				EKNORTT	knotter
				EKNORTW	network
				EKNORUY	younker
				EKNORWY	New York, ywroken
				EKNRRTU	trunker
				EKNRTUY	turnkey
				EKOOPRV	provoke

EKOORRY rookery
EKOORSZ zookers
EKOPRRY porkery
EKOPRUY kouprey
EKORTTW trek-tow
EKPPSUU seppuku
EKPRSTY psykter
ELLMNOO moellon
ELLMOOR morello
ELLMORW Morwell
ELLMPUU plumule
ELLNOOW woollen
ELLNOSW swollen
ELLNOTT tollent
ELLNOVY novelly
ELLNTUU lunulet
ELLOOSY loosely
ELLOPTU pollute
ELLORRT troller
ELLORTY trolley
ELLORVY loverly
ELLOSTU outsell, sell-out
ELLOVWY vowelly
ELLOWYY yellowy
ELLRSSU Russell
ELMMOPU pummelo
ELMMORT trommel
ELMMPTU plummet
ELMMRTU tummler
ELMNOOT moonlet
ELMNOTT lotment
ELMNOUV volumen
ELMOORT tremolo
ELMOORY loomery
ELMOPRY polymer
ELMOPSU plumose
ELMORRT mortrel
ELMORRY lormery
ELMORTU moulter
ELMOSUU emulous
ELMPPRU plumper
ELMPRSU lumpers
ELMPRUY plumery
ELMRTUU multure
ELMRUZZ muzzler
ELNNRTU trunnel
ELNOOPT peloton
ELNOORZ Lorenzo
ELNOOST enstool
ELNOOSU unloose
ELNOPRU pleuron
ELNOPRY pronely
ELNOPST leptons
ELNOPTU opulent
ELNOQTU loquent
ELNORSY Roselyn
ELNORTY elytron
ELNOSSS sonless
ELNOSSW lowness
ELNOSTV solvent
ELNOTTW townlet
ELNOTVY novelty
ELNPRTY pentryl
ELNRSTY sternly
ELNSSSU sunless
ELNSSSY slyness
ELOOPST Spoleto
ELOORTT rootlet
ELOORVW woolver
ELOPPST stopple
ELOPPXY poplexy
ELOPRRW prowler
ELOPRRY pyrrole
ELOPRSS plessor
ELOPRSU leprous, pelorus, sporule
ELOPRSY leprosy
ELOPRTT plotter, portlet
ELOPRTU plouter, poulter
ELOPRTY protyle
ELOPSST topless
ELORSTT settlor
ELORSUV velours
ELORSUY elusory
ELORTTY lottery
ELORTUY outerly
ELORTVY overtly
ELOSSTY systole
ELOSTUU luteous
ELPPRSU suppler
ELPRUZZ puzzler
ELPSSUY pussley
ELPSTUU pluteus, pustule
ELRRSTU rustler
ELRRTTU turtler
ELRTTUY utterly
ELRTUUV vulture
ELSSSUY Ulysses
EMMMRUY mummery
EMMNOOR monomer
EMMNOSU mu-meson
EMMNOTU omentum
EMMNOTY metonym
EMMOOTY myotome
EMMOPRR prommer
EMMPSTU stepmum
EMMRSTU rummest
EMMRSUY summery
EMNNOOR moneron
EMNNOOW new moon
EMNOOPR pomeron
EMNOORT montero
EMNOOST moonset
EMNOOSW ownsome
EMNOOTY enomoty
EMNOPST postmen
EMNOPYY eponymy
EMNORRU mourner
EMNORST monster
EMNORTT torment
EMNORTU monture, mounter, remount
EMNORTV Vermont
EMNRSSU rumness
EMNRSTU Munster, sternum
EMOOPRT promote, protome
EMOOPRV promove
EMOOPRY pomeroy
EMOOSTW twosome
EMOOSTY myosote
EMOPPTU up-tempo
EMOPRST stomper
EMOPRSU supremo
EMORRSU morsure
EMORSTU oestrum
EMORSUY mousery, Seymour
EMORSUZ zero-sum
EMOSSTT mostest
EMOSTVZ zemstvo
EMPRSTU stumper, sumpter
EMPRTTU trumpet
EMQSTUU musquet
EMRSTYY mystery
ENNNRUY nunnery
ENNORSU non-user
ENNORTT Trenton
ENNORTU neutron
ENNOSSW nowness, ownness
ENNOSTU neuston
ENNOTWW new town
ENNOUVW unwoven
ENNPSTU unspent
ENNRSTU stunner
ENOOPPR propone
ENOOPPT open-top
ENOOPRS snooper, spooner
ENOOPRZ prozone
ENOORSU onerous
ENOORSZ snoozer
ENOORTW tone-row
ENOOTTW two-tone
ENOOTXY oxytone
ENOPPRY propyne
ENOPRSS press-on
ENOPRST postern, Preston
ENOPRTT portent, torpent
ENOPRTW Newport
ENOPRTY entropy
ENOPSST stepson
ENOQSTU Quonset
ENOQTUU unquote
ENORRST snorter
ENORRTT torrent
ENORRUV overrun
ENORSSY sensory
ENORSTT Stentor
ENORSTU tonsure
ENORSTW nor'-west
ENORSUV nervous
ENORTUY tourney
ENOSSTT stetson

ENOSSTU	outness	**EORRTTU**	torture	**FGGGINU**	fugging
ENOSSTW	twoness	**EORSSTU**	estrous,	**FGGHIIS**	fishgig
ENOSTUU	tenuous		oestrus,	**FGGINUU**	fuguing
ENOTTUW	outwent		toruses,	**FGHHIOS**	hog-fish
ENPRRSU	spurner		tussore	**FGHIINS**	fishing
ENPRSTU	punster	**EORSSTV**	votress	**FGHIINT**	infight
ENPSTUW	unswept	**EORSSTW**	worsest	**FGHILTY**	flighty
ENRRSUY	nursery	**EORSTTT**	stretto	**FGHNOOR**	foghorn
ENRRTUU	nurture	**EORSTTU**	tetrous	**FGHORUY**	froughy
ENRRTUY	turnery	**EORTTTY**	tottery	**FGHOTUY**	foughty
ENRSSWY	wryness	**EORTTUY**	tutoyer	**FGIILLN**	filling
ENRSTTU	entrust,	**EPPRRTU**	prerupt	**FGIILNO**	foiling
	trusten	**EPPRRUU**	purpure	**FGIILNR**	rifling
ENRTTUY	nuttery	**EPPRSSU**	press-up	**FGIILNT**	fliting, lifting
EOOPPRS	opposer,	**EPPSTUW**	swept-up,	**FGIILNY**	lignify
	propose		upswept	**FGIINNN**	finning
EOOPPRV	popover	**EPRRSUU**	pursuer,	**FGIINRY**	nigrify
EOOPRRS	spoorer		usurper	**FGIINSY**	signify
EOOPRRT	potrero,	**EPRRSUY**	spurrey	**FGIINTT**	fitting
	trooper	**EPRRTUU**	rupture	**FGILNOT**	lofting
EOOPRTV	overtop	**EPRSSTY**	spryest	**FGILNOW**	flowing,
EOOPRTW	tow rope	**EPRSSUU**	pursues		fowling,
EOORRST	rooster	**EPRSTTU**	sputter		wolfing
EOORSSS	soroses	**ERRSSTU**	trusser	**FGILNTU**	fluting
EOORSVW	oversow	**ERRSSUY**	surreys	**FGILOOY**	goofily
EOORTTU	tore-out	**ERRSTTU**	truster	**FGILORY**	glorify
EOORTUV	out-over	**ERRSTTY**	tryster	**FGIMNOR**	forming
EOORTUW	outwore	**ERSSTUY**	russety	**FGINOOR**	roofing
EOOSSSU	osseous	**ERSTTTU**	stutter	**FGINOOT**	footing
EOOSTTY	tootsey	**FFFILOT**	lift-off	**FGINRRU**	furring
EOOTTUV	outvote	**FFFLOOR**	forloff	**FGINRSU**	surfing
EOPPRRS	prosper	**FFGIINR**	griffin	**FGINTTU**	tufting
EOPPRSS	oppress	**FFGINOR**	griffon	**FGIORTW**	figwort
EOPPRST	popster,	**FFGINOS**	sign-off	**FGIOTUY**	goutify
	stopper	**FFGLNOO**	long off	**FGISTUU**	fuguist
EOPPRSU	peropus,	**FFGLRUY**	gruffly	**FGLLNUU**	lungful
	purpose	**FFGNNOO**	gonnoff	**FGLNORU**	furlong
EOPPSSU	suppose	**FFHHISU**	huffish	**FGLOOUY**	ufology
EOPRRSS	pressor	**FFHIISY**	fishify	**FGLSTUU**	gustful
EOPRRST	sporter	**FFHIKNU**	huffkin	**FGNOOOY**	foo yong
EOPRRTU	porteur,	**FFHILSY**	fly-fish	**FGNOORU**	fourgon
	trouper	**FFHILTY**	fifthly	**FGNORWY**	Gwynfor
EOPRRTY	tropery	**FFHILUY**	huffily	**FGNOSUU**	fungous
EOPRSST	portess	**FFHOOSW**	show-off	**FHIILSY**	fishily
EOPRSSW	prowess	**FFHOSTU**	shut-off	**FHIILTY**	lithify
EOPRSTT	protest,	**FFIKOPS**	offskip	**FHIINNS**	Finnish
	spotter	**FFIKOSS**	kiss-off	**FHIKLOS**	folkish
EOPRSTU	petrous,	**FFILLLU**	fulfill	**FHILOOS**	foolish
	posture,	**FFILNSY**	sniffly	**FHILOSW**	wolfish
	Proteus,	**FFILPUY**	puffily	**FHILSUW**	wishful
	spouter	**FFILRTY**	frit-fly	**FHIMTYY**	mythify
EOPRSTV	prevost	**FFILSTU**	fistful	**FHINORY**	hornify
EOPRTTX	protext	**FFILSTY**	stiffly	**FHINRSU**	furnish
EOPRTTY	pottery	**FFINOPS**	spin-off	**FHINSSU**	sunfish
EOPRTVY	poverty	**FFINOPT**	pontiff	**FHIOOPR**	hip roof
EOPSSSS	possess	**FFIORTY**	fortify	**FHIOOST**	ooftish
EOPSSST	possest	**FFIQSUY**	squiffy	**FHIOPPS**	foppish
EOPSTTU	outstep	**FFJMOPU**	jump-off	**FHIOPST**	fishpot
EOPSTTW	stewpot, two-	**FFKLOSU**	Suffolk	**FHIORRY**	horrify
	step	**FFLLOPU**	pull-off	**FHIOSST**	softish
EOQRSTU	questor,	**FFLNSUY**	snuffly	**FHIPSTU**	upshift
	torques	**FFNORTU**	turn-off	**FHIRTTY**	thrifty
EOQRTUY	torquey	**FFOOPST**	stopoff	**FHIRTUY**	thurify
EORRSTU	trouser	**FGGGIIN**	figging	**FHISSTU**	shuftis
EORRTTT	trotter	**FGGGINO**	fogging	**FHLPSUU**	pushful

FHLRTUU	hurtful	**FIOPRSY**	prosify	**GGHIIPZ**	phizgig
FHMOOPW	whoompf	**FIOPSTX**	postfix	**GGHIIWZ**	whizgig
FHNOOTU	tunhoof	**FIORSUU**	furious	**GGHILNO**	hogling
FHNOTUX	fox-hunt	**FIORTYZ**	Fitzroy	**GGHIMSU**	muggish
FHOOOTT	hotfoot	**FIPPUYY**	yuppify	**GGHINSU**	gushing
FIIIKNN	finikin	**FIRRSTY**	stir-fry	**GGHIPSU**	puggish
FIIKLST	ski lift	**FIRSSUY**	Russify	**GGIIILN**	gingili
FIILLMO	milfoil	**FKLNOOR**	Norfolk	**GGIILNP**	pigling
FIILLMY	filmily	**FKLORUW**	workful	**GGIINNN**	ginning
FIILLSU	fusilli	**FKMOOOR**	komfoor	**GGIINNO**	ingoing
FIILNOO	infolio	**FKOOORS**	forsook	**GGIINNR**	ringing
FIILNOT	tinfoil	**FLLOOPU**	loopful	**GGIINNS**	signing
FIILNTY	niftily	**FLLOSUU**	soulful	**GGIINNT**	tinging
FIILOST	foilist	**FLLOTUU**	full out	**GGIJNSU**	juggins
FIILPTU	pitiful	**FLLSTUU**	lustful	**GGILNNO**	longing
FIILQUY	liquify	**FLMMOUX**	flummox	**GGILNOS**	gosling
FIILYZZ	fizzily	**FLMNOOU**	mouflon	**GGILOSY**	soggily
FIIMMNU	infimum	**FLMOOOT**	tomfool	**GGILRWY**	wriggly
FIIMRTY	firmity	**FLMOORU**	roomful	**GGIMMNU**	gumming
FIINOSS	fission	**FLNOORR**	forlorn	**GGIMNSU**	muggins
FIINRTY	nitrify	**FLOORSW**	forslow	**GGINNNU**	gunning
FIIRTVY	vitrify	**FLOOTUW**	outflow	**GGINNOO**	ongoing
FIJLLOY	jollify	**FLOPSTY**	fly-post	**GGINNOT**	tonging
FIJSTUY	justify	**FLOSUUV**	fulvous	**GGINNRU**	gurning
FIKKLNO	kinfolk	**FLOTUUX**	outflux	**GGINORW**	growing
FIKLLSU	skilful	**FMRSTUU**	frustum	**GGINPPY**	gypping
FIKLLUY	flukily	**FNNNUUY**	unfunny	**GGINPRU**	purging
FIKLNSU	skinful	**FNNOORT**	fronton	**GGINRST**	G-string
FIKLNUY	funkily	**FNOORRW**	forworn	**GGINTTU**	gutting
FIKNNOS	finnsko	**FNOORSU**	sunroof	**GGIPRSY**	spriggy
FILLLUW	willful	**FNOPRTU**	upfront	**GHHIINP**	pin-high
FILLMOY	mollify	**FNORSTY**	Y-fronts	**GHHIKSY**	sky-high
FILLNUY	nullify	**FNSSUUY**	unfussy	**GHHORTU**	through
FILLOTY	loftily	**FOOOPRT**	rooftop	**GHHOTTU**	thought
FILLSTU	listful	**FOOORTT**	foot-rot	**GHIIKRZ**	Kirghiz
FILLSUY	fusilly	**FOOPSTT**	soft-top	**GHIILNT**	inlight
FILNNUY	funnily	**FOORSST**	of sorts	**GHIILRS**	girlish
FILNOUW	uniflow	**FOORTTX**	foxtrot	**GHIIMPT**	impight
FILNOUX	fluxion	**FOPSSTU**	fusspot	**GHIINNT**	nithing
FILNTUY	unfitly	**FORRUWY**	furrowy	**GHIINST**	insight
FILOORS	isoflor	**FORSTUY**	frousty	**GHIINSW**	wishing
FILOOTW	witloof	**FORSTWY**	frowsty	**GHIINTT**	hitting, tithing
FILORST	florist	**GGGGIIN**	gigging	**GHIINTW**	whiting
FILORTU	floruit	**GGGHINO**	hogging	**GHIKLNU**	hulking
FILPPUY	pulpify	**GGGHINU**	hugging	**GHIKNSU**	husking
FILRSTY	firstly	**GGGIIJN**	jigging	**GHILLSU**	gullish
FILRYZZ	frizzly	**GGGIILN**	ligging	**GHILLTY**	lightly
FILSSUY	fussily	**GGGIINP**	pigging	**GHILNOS**	longish
FILSTTU	flutist	**GGGIINR**	rigging	**GHILNOU**	Holguin
FILSTUW	wistful	**GGGIINW**	wigging	**GHILNOW**	howling
FILSTUY	fustily	**GGGIINZ**	zigging	**GHILNRU**	hurling
FILSTWY	swiftly	**GGGIJNO**	jogging	**GHILNSY**	shingly
FILUYZZ	fuzzily	**GGGIJNU**	jugging	**GHILNTY**	nightly
FIMMMUY	mummify	**GGGILNO**	logging	**GHILRTY**	rightly
FIMNORU	uniform	**GGGILNU**	lugging	**GHILSTY**	sightly
FIMOORV	oviform	**GGGIMNU**	mugging	**GHILSUY**	gushily
FIMORRT	triform	**GGGINNO**	nogging	**GHILTTY**	tightly
FIMORTY	mortify	**GGGINOT**	togging	**GHIMMNU**	humming
FIMSTYY	mystify	**GGGINPU**	pugging	**GHIMNOS**	gnomish
FINOOYZ	ozonify	**GGGINSU**	sugging	**GHIMNTT**	mightn't
FINORSS	frisson	**GGGINTU**	tugging	**GHIMNTU**	thingum
FINORSU	furison	**GGHHIOS**	hoggish	**GHIMRRT**	Mr Right
FINRTUY	nutrify	**GGHIIJS**	jiggish	**GHINNOT**	nothing
FIOORSU	furioso	**GGHIINN**	hinging	**GHINNTU**	hunting
FIOOSTW	woofits	**GGHIIPS**	piggish	**GHINOOP**	hooping

GHINOPP hopping
GHINORS shoring
GHINORT right-on
GHINOST hosting, onsight
GHINOSU housing
GHINOSW showing
GHINOTT hotting, tonight
GHINOTU houting
GHINPSU gunship, pushing
GHINSTU husting
GHINTTU hutting
GHIOOSS goosish
GHIOPSY physiog
GHIORRT orright
GHIORSU roguish
GHIOSTU goutish
GHIOSUV voguish
GHIPRTU upright
GHIPTTU uptight
GHKOOOR Korhogo
GHLMOOO homolog
GHLMOOT gloomth
GHLNOOP long hop
GHLORUY roughly
GHLOSTY ghostly
GHLOSUY sloughy
GHLOTUY toughly
GHMORSU sorghum
GHMOSTU mugshot
GHNOPRY gryphon
GHNOSTU gunshot, shotgun, uht-song
GHNOTTU oughtn't
GHNOTUY noughty
GHNOUWZ Wuzhong
GHORTUW wrought
GHORTUY yoghurt
GIIKLLN killing
GIIKLMN milking
GIIKLNN inkling, linking
GIIKLNT kitling
GIIKNNP kingpin, pink gin, pinking
GIIKNNW winking
GIIKNPP kipping
GIIKNPS pigskin
GIIKNRS griskin
GIIKNSS kissing
GIIKNTT kitting
GIILLMN milling
GIILLNO gillion
GIILLNW willing
GIILMNN limning
GIILMNP impling
GIILMNY mingily
GIILMPR pilgrim
GIILMRY grimily
GIILNNQ Linqing
GIILNNY inlying
GIILNOR ligroin
GIILNPP lipping
GIILNPS lisping
GIILNST listing
GIILNTT titling
GIILNTW witling
GIILOSS gliosis
GIILOST oligist
GIILRST strigil
GIIMMNR rimming
GIIMNPP pimping
GIIMNPR priming
GIIMNSS missing
GIINNNP pinning
GIINNNS innings, sinning
GIINNNT tinning
GIINNNW winning
GIINNOR ironing
GIINNPP nipping
GIINNPU pinguin
GIINOPR pig-iron
GIINORS signori
GIINORT ignitor
GIINORV invigor
GIINPPP pipping
GIINPPR ripping
GIINPPS sipping
GIINPPT tipping
GIINPPY yipping
GIINPPZ zipping
GIINPQU piquing
GIINPSS pissing
GIINPTT pitting
GIINPTW wing-tip
GIINPTY pitying
GIINRTW writing
GIINSSU issuing
GIINSTT sitting
GIINSTU suiting
GIINSTW swing it
GIINTTW witting
GIJMNPU jumping
GIJMPPU pig-jump
GIJNOTT jotting
GIJNSTU justing
GIJNTTU jutting
GIKLNOO looking
GIKMNNU Kunming
GIKNNOO kongoni
GIKNNOS Noginsk
GIKNNOW knowing
GIKNORW working
GIKNSSY sky-sign
GILLMPU pug-mill
GILLNNU nulling
GILLNOP polling
GILLNYY lyingly
GILMMUY gummily
GILMNOO looming
GILMNOR morling
GILMNPU lumping
GILMPSY gymslip
GILNNSU unsling
GILNOOT tooling
GILNOPP lopping
GILNORU louring
GILNOSU lignous
GILNOTT lotting
GILNOTU tung oil
GILOOST ologist
GILORTT triglot
GILORTY trilogy
GILOSTT glottis
GILRSTY gristly
GILRTUV virgult
GILRTUY liturgy
GILRYZZ grizzly
GILSTUY gustily, gutsily
GIMMMNU mumming
GIMMNOT tomming
GIMMNSU summing
GIMNNOR morning
GIMNOOR mooring
GIMNOPP mopping
GIMNOST gnomist
GIMNOWY Wyoming
GINNNOO nooning
GINNNOW wonning
GINNNPU punning
GINNNRU running
GINNNSU sunning
GINNNTU tunning
GINNORU grunion
GINNORW ingrown
GINNPRU pruning
GINNRSU nursing
GINNRTU turning
GINNTTU nutting
GINNTUW wing nut
GINNTUY untying
GINOOTT tooting
GINOPPP popping
GINOPPS sopping
GINOPPT topping
GINOPRT porting
GINOPRU in-group, pouring
GINOPST posting
GINOPTT potting
GINOPTU pouting
GINORSS ingross
GINORST sorting, torgsin
GINORSU nigrous, rousing
GINORSY signory
GINORTT rotting
GINORTU outring, routing
GINOSTT sotting
GINOTTT totting
GINOTWW Wigtown
GINPPPU pupping
GINPPSU supping
GINPPTU tupping
GINPRSY springy
GINPSUW upswing
GINPTTU putting
GINRSTY stringy

GINRTTU rutting
GINRTUV turving
GINSSSU sussing
GIOOPRR porrigo
GIOPRRU prurigo
GIOPSSY gossipy
GIOSSYZ zygosis
GISWWYY wysiwyg
GJKNOUY Kyongju
GJLMUUU jugulum
GJNOOSU goujons
GJOORTT jogtrot
GLLLOOR logroll
GLMNOOO monolog
GLMNORY lyngorm
GLMOOYY myology
GLMORUW lugworm
GLNNOOR lorgnon
GLNNOOT long ton
GLNNSUU unslung
GLNOOOY noology
GLNOOPR prolong
GLNOOPY polygon
GLNORWY wrongly
GLNOTTU glutton
GLOOORY orology
GLOOOTY otology
GLOOOYZ zoology
GLOORUY urology
GLORSSY grossly
GMMOSUU gummous
GMMPUUW mugwump
GMNNORU murnong
GMNOORU gunroom
GMNOORW morwong
GMORSUU grumous
GMORTUW mugwort
GMRUYYZ zymurgy
GNNORUW wrong'un
GNNORYY gyronny
GNNOUUY young 'un
GNNSTUU stun gun
GNOOOSS gossoon
GNOPPRU propugn
GNOPRUW grown-up
GNORTUU outrung
GNORYYZ Groznyy
GNPRSUY ysprung
GOOPRST Gosport
GOORTUW outgrow
GOPSSUY gypsous
HHIIPPS hippish
HHIISTV thivish
HHIISTW whitish
HHIMPTU Thimphu
HHINNSU Hunnish
HHINOSU hushion
HHIORSW whorish
HHIOSSU Shishou
HHIOSTT hottish
HHIOUUZ Huizhou
HHISTUZ shih-tzu
HHKOOSS Oshkosh
HHOOSTT hotshot
HHOOSWW who's who
HHOUUZZ Zhuzhou
HIIKMSS Sikhism
HIIKNPS kinship, pinkish
HIILLPP Phillip
HIILLPS Phillis
HIILMPS limpish
HIILMTU lithium
HIILNOT lithion
HIILNSY shinily
HIILPTY pithily
HIILRTT trilith
HIILSTT hit list
HIIMNSX minxish
HIIMPSW wimpish
HIIMSSS missish
HIIMSUZ Shimizu
HIINPPW whippin
HIINSSW swinish
HIINSTW Swithin
HIIORST histrio
HIJNOUZ Jinzhou
HIKLSSU luskish
HIKLSUY huskily
HIKMNOS monkish
HIKNNOR inkhorn
HIKNOOU hokonui
HIKNPSU punkish
HIKRSTU Turkish
HIKSUUZ kuzushi
HILLOPT hilltop
HILLPSY Phyllis
HILLRSY shrilly
HILMMOU holmium
HILMOPS phlomis
HILMOSW wholism
HILMPSU lumpish
HILMSUY mushily
HILMTUU thulium
HILNNTY ninthly
HILNOPY phonily
HILOOSS loosish
HILOOTT otolith
HILOPST lithops
HILORSY horsily
HILOSSW slowish
HILOSTU loutish
HILOSVW wolvish
HILOSWY showily
HILOTWW whitlow
HILOTXY oxylith
HILPSUY pushily
HILSSTY stylish
HILSTTY thistly
HILSTWY whistly
HILSTXY sixthly
HIMMOST Thomism
HIMMPSU mumpish
HIMOORS moorish
HIMOPRS Orphism
HIMOPSS sophism
HIMOPST photism
HIMORTU thorium
HIMOSTT Thomist
HIMOTTY timothy
HIMPRSS shrimps
HIMPRTU triumph
HIMRSTY rhymist
HIMSSTU isthmus
HIMSTTY mythist
HIMSTUW wismuth
HINNNSU nunnish
HINNORT tinhorn
HINNOST tonnish
HINNRWY whrinny
HINOOPT photino
HINOORT hornito
HINOORZ horizon
HINOOSS soonish
HINOOST inshoot
HINOPPR porphin
HINOPSS sonship
HINOQUZ Qinzhou
HINORST hornist
HINORSU nourish
HINORTW throw-in
HINOSTW townish
HINOUXZ Xinzhou
HINSTUW Whitsun
HIOPPPS poppish
HIOPPST toppish
HIOPPTY hoppity
HIOPRSW worship
HIOPSST sophist
HIORSSU sourish
HIORSTY history
HIOSSTT sottish
HIOSUUZ Suizhou
HIOTTUW outwith, without
HIQSSUY squishy
HIRSTTU ruttish
HIRSTTY thirsty
HKKLOOZ kolkhoz
HKNOOWW know-how
HKOOOPT pot-hook
HKOOUUZ Zhoukou
HKORSWY work-shy
HLLPSUY plushly
HLMNOTY monthly
HLORSTY shortly
HLOTUYY youthly
HLPRSUU sulphur
HMMNOOY homonym
HMMOOSU hoummos
HMMRTUY thrummy
HMNNOPY nymphon
HMNOOPR morphon
HMNOPYY hyponym
HNNORSU unshorn
HNOOPTY typhoon
HNPRSUU prushun
HNPSTUU hunt's-up
HNRTTUU untruth
HOOOPPT photo op
HOOPPPS pop-shop
HOOPSTT hot spot, pot-shot
HOOPSTY toyshop
HOOSTTU outshot

HOOSTUW outshow
HOPRSTU hotspur
HOPRTUW upthrow
HOPSTTU shot-put
HOPSTUU shout-up
HOPSTUY typhous
HORSTUU outrush
HORTTUU thruout
HOSTTUU outshut, shutout
HPRRUUY hurry-up
HRSSTUY thyrsus
IIIKMNN minikin
IIILTTV titivil
IIINNOT inition
IIISTTW wistiti
IIJLLNO jillion
IIJMNOS misjoin
IIJNNOT injoint
IIJNSUU Sinuiju
IIKKLNY kinkily
IIKLLSY silkily
IIKLMNP limpkin
IIKLNOS oilskin
IIKLPSY spikily
IIKLRSY riskily
IIKNRST Kristin
IILLLLW ill will
IILLLSY sillily
IILLMNO million
IILLMSY slimily
IILLNOP pillion
IILLNOV villino
IILLNOZ zillion
IILLNST instill
IILMSTU stimuli
IILMSTY mistily
IILNNOT nitinol
IILNNSU insulin
IILNNTY tinnily
IILNORS sirloin
IILNOSY noisily
IILNPPY nippily
IILNPUV pulvini
IILNSUV Vilnius
IILOPRT tripoli
IILOPST pilotis
IILORSS lissoir
IILORTV vitriol
IILOSTV violist
IILPPYZ zippily
IILPRVY privily
IILPSTY tipsily
IILPSWY wispily
IILRTYZ ritzily
IILTTUY utility
IILTTWY wittily
IIMMMNU minimum
IIMMNSU minimus
IIMNOSS mission
IIMNOSU nimious
IIMNOSZ Zionism
IIMNOTX mixtion
IIMNPRT imprint
IIMOPSU impious
IIMOSST mitosis
IIMOSTT Titoism
IIMPTUX mix it up
IIMRTTU tritium
IIMRTUV trivium
IINNOOP opinion
IINNOPS pinions
IINNOQU quinion
IINNORV inviron
IINNQTU Quintin
IINOPSS isospin
IINORST ironist
IINORTT introit
IINOSTZ Zionist
IINOSUV invious
IINOTTU tuition
IINQRUY inquiry
IINRTTY trinity
IINSTTW intwist
IIOPRSS pissoir
IIOPSTY piosity
IIORSSV virosis
IIORSTV visitor
IIOSTTU oustiti
IIOSTUV vitious
IIPRTVY privity
IJJSTUU ju-jitsu
IJKLLOY killjoy
IJKMPSU ski jump
IJLLLOY jollily
IJLLOTY jollity
IJLMPUY jumpily
IJLNOQU jonquil
IJLNOTY jointly
IJNNOTU unjoint
IJNOSSU jussion
IKKLOOY kookily
IKKSUUY Kikuyus
IKLLSUY sulkily
IKLMNRU milk run
IKLMOPS milksop
IKLMOSY smokily
IKLMRUY murkily
IKLNOOP Nikopol
IKLNOOT kiloton
IKLNORS Norilsk
IKLNOWY wonkily
IKLNRWY wrinkly
IKLNTWY twinkly
IKLOOTT tool kit
IKLOSSU souslik
IKMNOOO okimono
IKMNOOS monoski
IKMNOSW misknow
IKMNPPU pumpkin
IKMNRTU trinkum
IKMOOST mistook
IKMOSSU koumiss
IKNORSS Kinross
IKNPSTU sputnik
IKORSTY Yorkist
IKRSSSU Russkis
IKRSTUU tsukuri
ILLLOWY lowlily
ILLMNOU luminol, mullion
ILLMOOR morillo
ILLMOOT timolol
ILLMPUY lumpily
ILLMSUU limulus
ILLNOOV novillo
ILLNOQU quillon
ILLNPUU lupulin
ILLNTUY nullity
ILLOOOW wool-oil
ILLOPRY pillory
ILLOPWY pillowy
ILLORSU illusor
ILLOSUV villous
ILLOSUY lousily
ILLOTXY xylitol
ILLOWWY willowy
ILLRSUY surlily
ILLSTUY lustily
ILMMSUU mimulus
ILMNOOT moonlit
ILMOORY roomily
ILMOOSS molossi
ILMORTU turmoil
ILMOSTY moistly
ILMOSUY mousily
ILMPRTU triplum
ILMSTUY mustily
ILMUYZZ muzzily
ILNNOPS non-slip
ILNNORU linuron
ILNNOXY linoxyn
ILNNSUY sunnily
ILNOOOP poon oil
ILNOOPS plosion
ILNOPRU purloin
ILNOPSU pulsion, upsilon
ILNOPUV pulvino
ILNORST nostril
ILNOSTT Stilton
ILNOSTY stonily, tylosin
ILNOSWY snowily
ILNOTUV volutin
ILNPSTU unspilt
ILOOORS rosolio
ILOOPST topsoil
ILOORTY olitory
ILOOSST soloist
ILOOSTY sootily
ILOOWYZ woozily
ILOPPSY soppily
ILOPRSY prosily
ILOPSUY piously, soupily
ILORRSY sorrily
ILOSSTY tylosis
ILPRSUY plurisy
ILPSTTY spittly
ILRSTUY rustily
ILSSTTY stylist
ILSTTUU titulus
IMMNNOU nummion

IMMNOSU	musimon
IMMNOUU	muonium
IMMOPTU	optimum
IMNNNOU	munnion
IMNNOOR	norimon
IMNOOPP	pompion
IMNOOPR	morpion
IMNOOPT	tompion
IMNOORT	monitor, tromino
IMNOOSU	ominous
IMNOOSY	isonomy
IMNOOUX	oxonium
IMNOPPU	pumpion
IMNOPRW	pinworm
IMNOPSU	spumoni
IMNORSY	myrosin
IMNOSVY	visnomy
IMOOPRX	proximo
IMOOSSS	osmosis
IMOOSSU	osmious
IMOPRST	tropism
IMOPRTU	protium
IMORSST	missort
IMORSTU	tourism, turismo
IMORSTY	Toryism, trisomy
IMORSUV	visorum
IMOSSTU	miss-out
IMOSSYZ	zymosis
IMOSTUV	vomitus
IMQRSUY	squirmy
IMRSSTU	sistrum, trismus
IMRTTUY	yttrium
INNNOOR	non-iron
INNOOPS	opsonin
INNOPRY	pyronin
INNOPSS	pinsons
INNOQTU	quinton
INNOSTU	nonsuit
INNOSTW	Winston
INNSTUU	nuntius
INOOPRT	portion
INOOPST	positon
INOORRZ	zorrino
INOORST	isotron, torsion
INOOSUX	noxious
INOPPST	topspin
INOPPTT	pint pot
INOPPTY	pit pony
INOPRTT	tripton
INOPSSU	poussin, spinous
INOPSTU	sit-upon
INORSTU	nitrous, trusion
INORSUU	ruinous, urinous
INOSSUU	sinuous
INPRSTY	trypsin
INPRTUY	turnipy
INQSTUU	quintus
INQSTUY	squinty
INRSTTU	intrust
INSSTUU	sunsuit
INSTTUW	untwist
IOOPPST	opposit
IOOPRSU	pour-soi
IOOPRSV	proviso
IOOPSTY	isotopy
IOORSSS	sorosis
IOORSTT	risotto
IOORSTU	riotous
IOPPPRT	pit prop
IOPPRST	ripstop
IOPPSST	pisspot
IOPPSTT	pit stop
IOPRSSY	pyrosis
IOPRSTT	protist
IOQRTTU	quittor
IOQTTUY	quotity
IORRTTX	tortrix
IORSTTU	tourist
IORSTTW	twistor
IORSTUV	vitrous
IORSUXY	oxyuris
IPRRSTU	stirrup
IPRSTUU	pursuit
IPTTTUY	tittupy
JJSTUUU	ju-jutsu
JMOPTUU	outjump
JNNORUY	non-jury
JNOORSU	sojourn
KLLMOSU	mollusk
KLNOOSZ	Szolnok
KLOOOTU	lookout, outlook
KNNNOUW	unknown
KNOOPTT	topknot
KNOOSSS	Knossos
KNOPRTY	krypton
KNORRTY	krytron
KOOOTTU	out-took
KOOPRSW	Worksop
KOOPRTW	worktop
KOORTUW	outwork, workout
LLLMMUU	mulmull
LLMOOPR	rollmop
LLMPPUY	plumply
LLOOPRT	trollop
LLOORTU	roll-out
LLOPTUU	pull-out
LMMPSUU	lump sum
LMNOOOS	Solomon
LMOOSTW	lowmost
LMOPSUU	plumous
LMRSTUU	lustrum
LMSTUUU	tumulus
LNNOPSU	nonplus
LNOOPRS	nol-pros
LNOOPSU	unspool
LNOOSWW	snow owl
LNOSTYZ	Olsztyn
LNRTUUY	untruly
LOOOORS	oloroso
LOOOPSZ	Sozopol
LOPPSUU	pulpous
LOPPSUY	polypus
LOPRSUY	pylorus
LOPRTUY	poultry
LOPTUVY	volupty
LOSTTUY	stoutly
LPRSSUU	surplus
LSTTUUU	tutulus
MMNNOOY	mononym
MMNOSSU	summons
MMOOTYY	myotomy
MMOPSTY	symptom
MNNOOOS	monsoon
MNNOOTU	montuno
MNNOSYY	synonym
MNOOOPP	pompoon
MNOOOYZ	zoonomy
MNOOPTY	toponym
MNOORSU	sunroom
MNOOSUY	onymous
MNOPRTU	no trump
MNORSTU	nostrum
MNOTTUY	muttony
MOOOPPS	pomposo
MOOOTYZ	zootomy
MOOPPSU	pompous
MOOPSSU	opossum
MOOPSTT	topmost
MOOSTTU	outmost
MOPSSUU	spumous
MORRSTU	rostrum
MPSSSUU	pussums
NNNNOOY	nonny-no
NNOOOPT	pontoon
NNOOPRS	non-pros
NNOOPRU	pronoun
NNOOPSS	sponson
NNOOPST	non-stop
NNORSUW	unsworn
NOOORTT	Toronto
NOOPRSS	sponsor
NOORSTY	Royston
NOORTUW	outworn, worn out
NOOTTWY	toytown
NOPSSTU	sunspot
NOPTTUY	puttony
NORTTUU	out-turn, turnout
NRSSTUU	untruss
OOOOPRT	potoroo
OOORTTU	outroot
OOPRSSU	soursop
OOPRSTV	provost
OOPRTTU	outport
OOPRTUU	outpour
OOPSSTT	tosspot
OOPSTTU	outpost
OORSTTU	sort-out
OPPRRTU	purport
OPPRSTU	support
OPPRSTY	stroppy
ORSTTUU	surtout
SSTUXYY	xystus y

EIGHT LETTERS

AAAABCLL	alcabala
AAAABCLZ	calabaza
AAAACCRR	caracara
AAAACGNR	caragana
AAAACJRR	jararaca
AAAACLLV	alcavala
AAAACNRS	anasarca
AAAADMTV	amadavat
AAAADTVV	avadavat
AAAAFMOS	faa-Samoa
AAAAGGRR	agar-agar
AAAAGLMR	ragamala
AAAAGMMT	magatama
AAAAGMTY	Yamagata
AAAAHILV	vaalhaai
AAAAHJMR	maharaja
AAAAHMNR	maharana
AAAAHMNY	Mahayana
AAAAIMPR	arapaima
AAAAINPY	Ayia Napa
AAAAIRTX	ataraxia
AAAAKKNT	katakana
AAAAKKWW	kawakawa
AAAAKLRZ	kala-azar
AAAAKNWZ	Kanazawa
AAAALLVV	lava-lava
AAAALMRS	rasamala
AAAAMMRR	ramarama
AAAAMMTT	matamata
AAAANNST	Santa Ana
AAABBHKL	Kabbalah
AAABBILT	abbatial
AAABBIST	sabbatia
AAABBNRS	Barnabas
AAABCCLM	calambac
AAABCCRT	baccarat
AAABCHLS	calabash
AAABCINT	anabatic
AAABCITT	ciabatta
AAABCNRR	barracan, barranca
AAABCNRU	carnauba
AAABCPRY	capybara
AAABDEST	database
AAABDFIZ	Faizabad
AAABDKNT	data bank
AAABDNNN	bandanna
AAABDNRS	saraband
AAABDRST	bastarda
AAABEHNR	habanera
AAABEHRT	barathea
AAABELLR	Arabella
AAABEMPR	parabema
AAABENSS	anabases
AAABGHRS	ragabash
AAABGHST	Ashgabat
AAABGILY	galabiya
AAABGNRR	barragan
AAABGNRT	tarbagan
AAABGNRZ	Braganza
AAABGRTU	rutabaga
AAABHIMN	Bahamian
AAABHLMR	Alhambra
AAABHNOR	Barahona
AAABHPRT	Bhatpara
AAABILNN	Albanian
AAABILTT	battalia
AAABIMMR	imambara
AAABINRV	Bavarian
AAABINSS	anabasis
AAABKLSU	sakabula
AAABKPSS	baasskap
AAABLOPR	parabola
AAABNSTW	Batswana
AAABRRTT	barratta
AAACCDIN	Accadian
AAACCELN	calcanea
AAACCEPR	carapace
AAACCIMM	caimacam
AAACCRTT	cataract
AAACCTTU	tac-au-tac
AAACDEIM	academia
AAACDEMN	adamance
AAACDENR	dracaena
AAACDERZ	azedarac
AAACDFIR	faradaic
AAACDINN	Canadian
AAACDINR	arcadian
AAACDKLY	lackaday
AAACDLNR	calandra
AAACDNNO	anaconda
AAACDNPR	panda car
AAACDNRS	sandarac
AAACDNYZ	Anzac Day
AAACDOTV	advocaat
AAACDRVY	cavayard
AAACEHLZ	chalazae
AAACEHNR	Archaean
AAACEKPT	pat-a-cake
AAACELNT	analecta
AAACELST	catalase
AAACEMRT	Macerata
AAACENNP	panacean
AAACENVV	vena cava
AAACFINR	Africana
AAACGHRU	guaracha
AAACGILN	canaglia
AAACGINT	caatinga
AAACGLNT	galactan
AAACGLSW	scalawag
AAACGMNP	campagna
AAACGNRU	Rancagua
AAACHMNP	panchama
AAACIJRT	jacitara
AAACILMN	maniacal
AAACILMR	calamari
AAACILNN	Lacanian
AAACILRV	calvaria
AAACIMNP	campania
AAACINPT	capitana
AAACINTV	cavatina
AAACIPSU	sapucaia
AAACIRRS	sacraria
AAACIRTX	ataraxic
AAACKLMN	almanack
AAACKMRT	tamarack
AAACKPWY	packaway
AAACLMRY	calamary
AAACLRST	alcatras
AAACMRSS	Macassar
AAACMRSU	amaracus
AAACNOSV	Casanova
AAACSTWY	castaway
AAADDEGR	dageraad
AAADDHIL	alhidada
AAADELMS	Adam's ale
AAADEMNN	Mandaean
AAADEMNP	empanada
AAADENTV	vanadate
AAADGGHH	Haggadah
AAADGHNR	Angharad
AAADGILU	Igualada
AAADGLMY	amygdala
AAADGNRT	adragant
AAADHHSS	Hadassah
AAADHMNR	Ramadhan
AAADHMRS	madrasah
AAADIKKN	Akkadian
AAADILLP	palladia
AAADILMP	diapalma
AAADILRS	Alasdair
AAADILRU	adularia
AAADIMNY	Adiyaman
AAADJKRT	Djakarta
AAADJNNS	Sanandaj
AAADKNOR	Anadarko
AAADKRRV	aardvark
AAADMNPR	pandaram
AAADMNTU	tamandua

AAADNSTZ Zaanstad
AAADNTTU anudatta
AAADPRRU rapadura
AAADRWWY awayward
AAAEGNPP appanage
AAAEGRST gastraea
AAAEHIPT apatheia
AAAEHKNT tanekaha
AAAEHLNP phalaena
AAAEHLPR Raphaela
AAAEHMNT anathema
AAAEHNPS anaphase
AAAEKTWY takeaway
AAAELLST all at sea
AAAELMMN analemma
AAAELMTX malaxate
AAAELNPT panatela
AAAELRTV lavatera
AAAENPRV paravane
AAAENPST anapaest
AAAERTWY tearaway
AAAFFNRS saffraan
AAAFHLSS Falashas
AAAFINST fantasia
AAAFINUV avifauna
AAAFLLWY fall-away
AAAGGLLN galangal
AAAGHINN Ghanaian
AAAGHINR hiragana
AAAGHIPR agraphia
AAAGHNNT agnathan
AAAGHNTY yataghan
AAAGIKNS Nagasaki, saganaki
AAAGILMM mamaliga
AAAGILPP papalagi
AAAGINRR agrarian
AAAGINRT Itanagar
AAAGJMNR Jamnagar
AAAGJORY raja yoga
AAAGKKOW Kakogawa
AAAGKMUY Kumagaya
AAAGLLNU La Laguna
AAAGLMSY Malagasy
AAAGLNRW Warangal
AAAGLRRW warragal
AAAGLRST astragal
AAAGMNNN Namangan
AAAGNNOT onnagata
AAAGNPRS parasang
AAAGNRTU Tauranga
AAAGPRUY Paraguay
AAAHHPRS parashah
AAAHIINW Hawaiian
AAAHIKRT Hirakata
AAAHIMNR maharani
AAAHIMRT hamartia, Mata Hari
AAAHINNY Hinayana
AAAHINRT ratanhia
AAAHIPTY pitahaya
AAAHJKPW pakhawaj
AAAHJNPR paranjah
AAAHKMNS khansama
AAAHKRSS rakshasa
AAAHLLLV Valhalla
AAAHLPRY alpha ray
AAAHMMPR Parma ham
AAAHMNNS Ma'anshan, manna-ash
AAAHMNRT amaranth
AAAHMNST Samantha
AAAHMRTT Mahratta
AAAHNNSV savannah
AAAHNOPR anaphora
AAAHNPRW parwanah
AAAHSWWY washaway
AAAHTTWY thataway
AAAIINPR apiarian
AAAIKKMM kaimakam
AAAIKKST Takasaki
AAAIKKSW Kawasaki
AAAIKNRT Taranaki
AAAILLMR malarial
AAAILLPT palatial
AAAILMNR malarian
AAAILMRT Altamira
AAAILMSV malvasia
AAAILMSY Malaysia
AAAILNNR ranalian
AAAILNNS Annalisa
AAAILNPT palatian
AAAILNRS salarian
AAAILNRU aularian
AAAILNST Alsatian
AAAILPRS parasail
AAAILPRV paravail
AAAILPRX paraxial
AAAILRST Alastair, salariat
AAAIMMQQ qaimaqam
AAAIMMST miasmata
AAAIMNRR marinara
AAAIMNRT Araminta
AAAIMNST Tasmania
AAAIMRTV Amravati
AAAINNRR ranarian
AAAINNRV varanian
AAAINNTZ Tanzania
AAAINOPR paranoia
AAAINQRU Aquarian
AAAIPSSV piassava
AAAKKMRU Kamakura
AAAKMNRS namaskar
AAAKMRSS samskara
AAAKNRSS Arkansas
AAAKOSWY soakaway
AAALLNTT atlantal
AAALLPRX parallax
AAALMRTU Altamura
AAALNNPT platanna
AAALNPRT rataplan
AAALNRTT tarlatan
AAAMNOPR panorama
AAAMNRRY yarraman
AAAMNTTY manyatta
AAAMOTTU automata
AAAMPRTT pattamar
AAANOPRZ parazoan
AAANORSY sayonara
AAANPRTV paravant
AAANQSSU sasanqua
AAANQTUU aquanaut
AAANRRTW awarrant
AAAORSST Sarasota
AAAPQRTU paraquat
AABBCDOS scabbado
AABBCDRS scabbard
AABBCEFY baby face
AABBCEKR bareback
AABBCEKT backbeat
AABBCINR barbican
AABBCIRR barbaric
AABBCORS barbasco
AABBDEKR bad break
AABBDHIU Abu Dhabi
AABBDORS Barbados
AABBEELR bearable
AABBEELT beatable
AABBEILL bailable
AABBEKLN bankable
AABBELLM blamable
AABBELLS baseball
AABBELRR barrable
AABBELRY bearably
AABBHHLL blah-blah
AABBHKSU babushka
AABBHNSS habs-nabs
AABBHOOY Babahoyo
AABBIILL bilabial
AABBILRT barbital
AABBIMOR Riobamba
AABBIRSU babirusa
AABBKLTY baby talk
AABBLMOU bamboula
AABBNOOR bona-roba
AABCCEHK backache
AABCCELR cable car
AABCCELS cascabel
AABCCHIS biscacha
AABCCHIZ bizcacha
AABCCHKT backchat
AABCCHNT bacchant
AABCCIMR carbamic
AABCCKKP backpack
AABCCKLP blackcap
AABCCKLW clawback
AABCCKST scatback
AABCCMOT catacomb
AABCDEIN abidance
AABCDEIT abdicate
AABCDEKT backdate
AABCDHKN backhand
AABCDHKR hardback
AABCDIKL laid-back
AABCDIMO Cambodia
AABCDIOR radio cab
AABCDIRS Bacardis
AABCDKMS smack-dab
AABCDKNR bank card
AABCDKRW backward, drawback
AABCDKRY backyard
AABCDLNR land crab
AABCDLNS scabland

AABCDLRS Carlsbad
AABCDNRS bad scran
AABCEELT acetable, Albacete
AABCEENR bearance
AABCEENY abeyance
AABCEERS scarabee
AABCEERT acerbate
AABCEERV cave bear
AABCEGLY Glace Bay
AABCEGOT cabotage
AABCEHLS cashable
AABCEILM amicable
AABCEIMN ambiance
AABCEINR carabine
AABCEIRT bacteria
AABCEJNO Jacobean
AABCEKLP packable
AABCEKLS sackable
AABCEKLT black tea
AABCEKST back seat
AABCELLP placable
AABCELLR ball-race, Clarabel
AABCELLS scalable
AABCELNR balancer, barnacle
AABCELOR albacore
AABCELRT bracteal
AABCELSU causable
AABCELWY cableway
AABCEMPS base camp
AABCEMRT crabmeat
AABCEMRV vambrace
AABCENRR Canberra
AABCEORT boat race
AABCEPRS space bar
AABCESSU abacuses
AABCFHKL half-back
AABCFIIL bifacial
AABCFKLL backfall, fall-back
AABCFKST fastback
AABCHHIR Bahraich
AABCHILR brachial
AABCHINR branchia
AABCHKLS backlash
AABCHKRS shabrack
AABCHKSW backwash
AABCHLOO coolabah
AABCHMRY chambray
AABCHRRT bar chart
AABCHRTU chabutra
AABCIILR bi-racial
AABCIILS basilica
AABCIINR cibarian
AABCIJNO Jacobina
AABCIKLT tailback
AABCILMS balsamic
AABCILMY amicably
AABCILNN cannibal
AABCILNO anabolic
AABCILST basaltic
AABCIMNR Cambrian
AABCINNO Baconian
AABCINNR cinnabar
AABCINNS cannabis
AABCINRT Bactrian
AABCINSU banausic
AABCIRSS brassica
AABCISSS abscissa
AABCKKLT back talk, talkback
AABCKLPY playback
AABCKLRT black art
AABCKNRS snack bar
AABCKPRT brat pack
AABCKPSS passback
AABCKSTY backstay
AABCKSWY sway-back
AABCLLPY placably
AABCLNTY blatancy
AABCOORS Sorocaba
AABCRSTT abstract
AABDDEET deadbeat
AABDDEHL baldhead
AABDDEHN headband
AABDDENR brandade
AABDDINZ zindabad
AABDDLNS badlands
AABDEEHS basehead
AABDEELL leadable
AABDEELR readable
AABDEELT dealbate
AABDEELV evadable
AABDEELW wadeable
AABDEERR Aberdare
AABDEERT tea-bread
AABDEGIN badinage
AABDEGIR bigarade
AABDEGMS gambades
AABDEGOR abordage
AABDEJLL djellaba
AABDEKPR brake pad
AABDEKRY Baker day, daybreak
AABDELLS Sabadell
AABDELLU laudable
AABDELMN damnable
AABDELOR adorable
AABDELOS baseload
AABDELRS baselard
AABDELRT tradable
AABDELRW drawable
AABDELRY readably
AABDEMNS beadsman
AABDENTU unabated
AABDENUX bandeaux
AABDENVW waveband
AABDEORS seaboard
AABDEORT tea-board
AABDERTV vartabed
AABDERWY waybread
AABDFHIT bad faith
AABDGHOY Bodhgaya
AABDGNOV vagabond
AABDGORR garboard
AABDGOTU gadabout
AABDHINT Bhatinda
AABDHLLN handball
AABDHLLR hardball
AABDHLLU Abdullah
AABDHNST sand-bath
AABDILNO balanoid
AABDIRSS bassarid
AABDKLNN landbank
AABDKNNS sandbank
AABDLLRY balladry
AABDLLUY laudably
AABDLMNO aandblom
AABDLMNU labdanum
AABDLMNY damnably
AABDLNPT platband
AABDLOOT boatload
AABDLORR Labrador, larboard
AABDLORY adorably
AABDMNNS bandsman
AABDNNTU abundant
AABDNPSS bandpass, passband
AABDNRRY barnyard
AABDORRY Arbor Day
AABDORSX saxboard
AABDORWY broadway
AABDRRSS brassard
AABDRSTY bastardy
AABEEFLN fleabane
AABEEGKR breakage
AABEEGNT abnegate
AABEEHLL healable
AABEEHLR hearable
AABEEHLT hateable
AABEEKLM makeable
AABEEKLT takeable
AABEEKMT makebate
AABEEKRT tea break
AABEELLS leasable, saleable, sealable
AABEELMN amenable, nameable
AABEELMT tameable
AABEELPT tapeable
AABEELRS erasable
AABEELRT rateable, tearable
AABEELRW wearable
AABEELSV saveable
AABEELTT tea-table
AABEEMNO amoebean
AABEEMRS sea bream
AABEENOR anaerobe
AABEERRS bear's ear
AABEERRT aberrate
AABEERST base rate
AABEERTT trabeate
AABEFHKL half-beak
AABEFLMR farmable, framable
AABEFLMU flambeau
AABEFLTU fabulate
AABEGHNR berghaan
AABEGILN gainable
AABEGLLL glabella

AABEGLLM ball game
AABEGLRT glabrate
AABEGLRU arguable
AABEGLRZ grazable
AABEGMNY mangabey
AABEGNOR baronage
AABEGORT abrogate
AABEGOST sabotage
AABEGRSS brassage
AABEGRTW water-bag
AABEHIRR herbaria
AABEHITT habitate
AABEHKLS shakable
AABEHLOT oathable
AABEHLPS shapable
AABEHLPT alphabet
AABEHLRS sharable
AABEHLSW washable
AABEIKLS kielbasa
AABEIKRR air brake
AABEILLL alliable
AABEILLM mailable
AABEILLS Isabella, sailable
AABEILMN lima bean, maniable
AABEILNP plebania
AABEILNR inarable
AABEILPP papabile
AABEILRS raisable
AABEILRV variable
AABEILST satiable
AABEILTV ablative
AABEINPR pea-brain
AABEINRT Atabrine
AABEINST basanite
AABEIRSV abrasive
AABEIRTU aubretia
AABEISST abatises
AABEKKSU Kasukabe
AABEKLLW walkable
AABEKMNR brakeman
AABEKNRS Nebraska
AABEKNRV brakevan
AABEKPRR parbrake, parbreak
AABEKRRS baresark
AABEKRTX tax break
AABELLMR Marbella
AABELLMT meatball
AABELLNO loanable
AABELLPP palpable
AABELLPY playable
AABELLSV salvable
AABELLUV valuable
AABELMNY amenably
AABELMPP mappable
AABELMST blastema, lambaste
AABELMTT table mat
AABELMTU ambulate
AABELNNT tannable
AABELNPT pantable
AABELNRY balneary
AABELNSU lunabase
AABELORR arboreal
AABELPPR palpebra
AABELPPT tappable
AABELPRS sparable
AABELPSS passable
AABELPTT pattable
AABELRST arbalest
AABELRTY betrayal, rateably
AABELSTT statable, tastable
AABELSTW wastable
AABELTTU tabulate
AABELTUX tableaux
AABEMRRS embarras
AABENNPS snap bean
AABENNVY navy bean
AABENPRT pantarbe
AABENQUV va banque
AABENRRT aberrant
AABENRST ratsbane, Strabane
AABEORRT arboreta
AABERSSW sabre saw
AABESTTY Bay State
AABFGLOT flag-boat
AABFILUX fabliaux
AABFLMNT flambant
AABFLOTT faltboat, flat boat
AABGGGNN gang-bang
AABGGLRU Gulbarga
AABGGRRT braggart
AABGHPRR bar graph
AABGILNT bangtail
AABGILRR grab rail
AABGILRU Bulgaria
AABGIMNS sambaing
AABGLLLO goalball
AABGLLRY ballyrag
AABGLMNS slambang
AABGLMNU galbanum
AABGLNOW bangalow
AABGLNPS slap bang
AABGLRUW Walburga
AABGLRUY arguably
AABGNORR barragon
AABGNORZ garbanzo
AABGNRRU bungarra
AABHHORU brouhaha
AABHIIMP amphibia
AABHIINU bauhinia
AABHIKLS bashalik
AABHILNN Hannibal
AABHILTU habitual
AABHINPR Parbhani
AABHINTT habitant
AABHLLOO ballahoo
AABHLLOU ballahou
AABHLSUW Bhusawal
AABHMMOT Mmabatho
AABHNOTU autobahn
AABHOTTY thataboy
AABHRSST brass hat
AABIIJLT jailbait
AABIILRS Brasilia
AABIITTW wait-a-bit
AABILLLY labially
AABILLST ballista
AABILMNS bailsman
AABILMNU bimanual
AABILMOT mailboat
AABILNNU biannual
AABILNOR baronial
AABILNOT ablation
AABILNRU binaural
AABILNTY banality
AABILOST sailboat
AABILRRT arbitral
AABILRVY variably
AABIMNOT Manitoba
AABIMORS ambrosia
AABINNPR brainpan
AABINORS abrasion
AABINRTZ bartizan
AABIORTT abattoir
AABIOSSY bioassay
AABIOSTV Boa Vista
AABISTUZ zaibatsu
AABJLMNO jambolan
AABJLPRU Jabalpur
AABKLLPR ballpark
AABKLNOO kabloona
AABKLOOV Balakovo
AABKMNOP Bonampak
AABKMORS kombaars
AABKOPRS soapbark
AABKOSSU kabassou
AABLLMOR balmoral
AABLLPPY palpably
AABLLPRT trap-ball
AABLLSTU blastula
AABLLUVY valuably
AABLMMSU balsamum
AABLMNOR abnormal
AABLMNTU ambulant
AABLNTTT blattant
AABLORTY altar boy
AABLOTUY layabout
AABLOUWY Bulawayo
AABLPSSY passably
AABLRTUY tabulary
AABMMOSU abomasum
AABMNOTW batwoman
AABMNRTU rambutan
AABMORTU marabout, marabuto, tamboura
AABNNORR Ann Arbor
AABNNOST absonant
AABNOSTW Botswana
AABORRRT barrator
AABRRRTY barratry
AACCCDIS saccadic
AACCCFIO focaccia
AACCCHHU cachucha
AACCCHOR accroach, cacaroch
AACCCLOO Coca-Cola
AACCCRUY accuracy

AACCDEFR	face card
AACCDEHH	cha-chaed
AACCDEIM	academic
AACCDELO	accolade
AACCDERR	racecard
AACCDHRS	cash card
AACCDIOR	accaroid
AACCDOVY	advocacy
AACCEEFH	face-ache
AACCEENT	cetacean
AACCEFKP	face pack
AACCEFLO	coalface
AACCEGRU	carucage
AACCEHIX	cachexia
AACCEILN	calcanei
AACCEIMR	aceramic
AACCEIRR	cercaria
AACCEJNT	jactance
AACCEKRS	sack race
AACCELOR	caracole
AACCELPT	placcate
AACCELRR	carceral
AACCEMNU	cumacean
AACCENRT	carcanet
AACCENTU	acutance
AACCERTU	accurate, carucate
AACCFHHR	charchaf
AACCFILN	fancical
AACCFILR	farcical
AACCGILT	galactic
AACCHHIL	Halachic
AACCHHMU	muchacha
AACCHHNN	Chan Chan
AACCHILP	pachalic
AACCHINR	anarchic, characin
AACCHIRR	chair-car
AACCHISV	viscacha
AACCHIVZ	vizcacha
AACCHKOZ	kazachoc
AACCHLLT	catch-all
AACCHLOR	charcoal
AACCHLOT	cachalot
AACCHMNO	coachman
AACCHOUY	Ayacucho
AACCIINV	vaccinia
AACCIIST	sciatica
AACCILMT	malactic
AACCILNV	vaccinal
AACCILRU	acicular
AACCILTT	tactical
AACCIORT	acroatic
AACCIPTY	capacity
AACCJKRW	crack-jaw
AACCJORU	carcajou
AACCKLOS	coal-sack
AACCKMOR	maracock
AACCLNOO	Caloocan
AACCLOPU	Acapulco
AACCLPRS	calcspar
AACCLRSU	saccular
AACCLTTU	Calcutta
AACCNSTU	accusant
AACCOSTT	staccato
AACCRRWW	craw-craw
AACDDEHI	acid head
AACDDENV	advanced
AACDDERY	decadary
AACDDETY	tea caddy
AACDDHPU	Cuddapah
AACDDINR	radicand
AACDDMOR	drama-doc
AACDEEGL	decalage
AACDEEHH	headache
AACDEEHS	head case
AACDEELS	escalade
AACDEEMR	camerade
AACDEENT	decanate, tea dance
AACDEEPS	escapade
AACDEEST	estacade
AACDEETU	ecaudate
AACDEFLT	falcated
AACDEFNN	fan dance
AACDEGMR	card game
AACDEGRR	drag race
AACDEHHY	headachy
AACDEHIN	hacienda
AACDEHIR	arachide
AACDEHLN	Chaldean
AACDEHMR	drachmae
AACDEHPT	death cap
AACDEHRT	cathedra
AACDEILS	sidalcea
AACDEIMN	maenadic
AACDEINR	radiance
AACDEIRT	radicate
AACDEJNT	adjacent
AACDELNR	calander, calendar, landrace
AACDELNV	valanced
AACDELOS	caseload
AACDENOT	anecdota, cane toad
AACDENPT	tap-dance
AACDENRV	advancer
AACDENRW	war dance
AACDENSV	canvased
AACDEOPR	capeador
AACDEOST	estocada
AACDEOTV	advocate
AACDEPTU	catadupe
AACDEQUY	adequacy
AACDERST	cadastre
AACDFLNR	flancard
AACDGGHI	Haggadic
AACDGINR	arcading, carangid, cardigan
AACDGORR	cargador
AACDHHRS	hard cash
AACDHILR	diarchal
AACDHINP	handicap
AACDHINR	arachnid
AACDHKRT	hard tack
AACDHLNP	handclap
AACDHLOR	hard coal
AACDHLOT	cathodal
AACDHLRY	charlady
AACDHMRS	drachmas
AACDHNRS	schradan
AACDHNRT	handcart
AACDHPRS	crash pad
AACDIINR	acid rain
AACDIINS	ascidian
AACDIIRU	aciduria
AACDIIRV	vicariad
AACDILLP	palladic
AACDILLR	calliard
AACDILMT	dalmatic
AACDILMU	caladium
AACDILNO	calanoid, diaconal
AACDILNR	cardinal, Clarinda
AACDILNU	dulciana
AACDILNV	vandalic
AACDILOZ	zodiacal
AACDILRR	railcard
AACDIMOS	camisado
AACDIMRT	dramatic
AACDINOR	Orcadian
AACDINRT	tridacna
AACDINRY	radiancy
AACDIORR	radio car
AACDIRTY	caryatid
AACDITUY	audacity
AACDJKRY	jackyard
AACDJQRU	jacquard
AACDKLLN	lackland
AACDKLNU	Auckland
AACDLLUY	caudally
AACDLORT	cartload
AACDLOSV	calvados
AACDLSTT	scattald
AACDMMOR	cardamom
AACDMMRU	cardamum
AACDMNNO	mancando
AACDMSSU	Damascus
AACDQRSU	squad car
AACDRVYY	cavy-yard
AACEEFIT	facetiae
AACEEFLP	paleface
AACEEFNS	feasance
AACEEGIR	agacerie
AACEEGLV	cleavage
AACEEGPS	space age
AACEEHRT	tracheae
AACEEIMT	emaciate
AACEEINN	encaenia
AACEEKLN	leakance
AACEEKPR	rape-cake
AACEELRT	lacerate
AACEELST	escalate
AACEELTU	aculeate
AACEEMNN	amenance
AACEEMNS	Maecenas
AACEEMRT	camerate, cream tea, macerate, racemate
AACEEMST	casemate

AACEENRS	Canarese, Cesarean	**AACEILRV**	cavalier, variceal	**AACENSTT**	castanet
				AACENTUV	evacuant
AACEENTT	catenate	**AACEIMNR**	amacrine, American, in camera	**AACEPTUU**	aucupate
AACEEPSS	seascape			**AACERSSS**	rascasse
AACEETUV	evacuate			**AACERSSU**	caesuras
AACEETVX	excavate	**AACEIMNS**	amnesiac	**AACERSTT**	castrate
AACEFFIN	affiance	**AACEIMRS**	mesaraic	**AACERTTT**	tractate
AACEFHLP	half-pace	**AACEIMTT**	catamite	**AACESUWY**	causeway
AACEFIST	fasciate	**AACEINNO**	Oceanian	**AACFHHRS**	charshaf
AACEFKMS	face mask	**AACEINRS**	Cesarian	**AACFHLRT**	flat arch
AACEFLRT	flat race	**AACEINRT**	carinate, craniate	**AACFHMST**	camshaft
AACEFRRU	furcraea			**AACFILLY**	facially
AACEFRTT	artefact	**AACEINRV**	variance	**AACFILOS**	fasciola
AACEGHNT	chantage	**AACEINST**	estancia	**AACFIRRT**	aircraft
AACEGHRT	Carthage	**AACEIPRS**	airspace	**AACFIRST**	frascati
AACEGHRU	guarache	**AACEIPRT**	apricate	**AACFIRTT**	artifact
AACEGILN	angelica	**AACEIPTT**	capitate	**AACFJKLP**	flapjack
AACEGILT	glaciate	**AACEIRSU**	eucrasia	**AACFKLPT**	flat-pack
AACEGIRR	carriage	**AACEISTU**	Eustacia	**AACFLOPR**	parfocal
AACEGIRV	vicarage	**AACEITTV**	activate	**AACFMNNY**	fancy man
AACEGKPR	packager	**AACEJLTU**	jaculate	**AACFRRTW**	warcraft
AACEGKRT	trackage	**AACEKKLW**	cakewalk	**AACGGHHI**	chagigah
AACEGLMR	malgrace	**AACEKRTT**	attacker	**AACGHILT**	taiglach
AACEGLNY	lancegay	**AACELLLR**	all-clear	**AACGHNOY**	Chaoyang
AACEGMPR	crap game	**AACELLMR**	marcella	**AACGHOPS**	gaspacho
AACEGNRW	wangrace	**AACELLNN**	cannella	**AACGHOPZ**	gazpacho
AACEGRSV	scavager	**AACELLOT**	allocate	**AACGHORR**	garrocha
AACEGRTU	curatage	**AACELLTY**	alley cat	**AACGHORU**	guacharo
AACEHHRU	huarache	**AACELMNP**	placeman	**AACGIILR**	Cagliari
AACEHILL	achillea, heliacal	**AACELMOS**	coal-seam	**AACGIIMN**	magician
		AACELMOT	camalote	**AACGIINR**	garcinia
AACEHILM	Michaela	**AACELMPT**	place mat	**AACGILLO**	alogical
AACEHILP	phacelia	**AACELMTU**	maculate	**AACGILLU**	alguacil
AACEHIMR	chimaera	**AACELNNU**	cannulae	**AACGILNN**	Anglican
AACEHIMT	haematic	**AACELNOR**	Carolean	**AACGILNO**	analogic
AACEHINT	China tea	**AACELNPR**	parlance	**AACGILNV**	galvanic
AACEHIPT	hepatica	**AACELNPS**	scale-pan	**AACGILOU**	guaiacol
AACEHIRR	haircare	**AACELNPT**	placenta	**AACGILRT**	tragical
AACEHIRS	archaise	**AACELNPY**	anyplace	**AACGIMMT**	magmatic
AACEHIRZ	archaize	**AACELNRY**	arcanely	**AACGIMNN**	manganic
AACEHKMP	chempaka	**AACELNST**	analects	**AACGIMNP**	campaign
AACEHLMR	marechal	**AACELNTU**	tenacula	**AACGIMRR**	margaric
AACEHLRT	tracheal	**AACELORT**	coraleta	**AACGIMRS**	sciagram
AACEHLST	alcahest	**AACELPRV**	precaval	**AACGIMUU**	guaiacum
AACEHMRS	marchesa	**AACELPSU**	scapulae	**AACGINNR**	garancin
AACEHMST	schemata	**AACELRSU**	caesural	**AACGINTY**	Naga City
AACEHPUX	chapeaux	**AACELRTY**	acrylate	**AACGISTY**	sagacity
AACEHRST	tracheas	**AACELRWY**	clearway	**AACGLMOU**	glaucoma
AACEHRTT	reattach	**AACELSTY**	catalyse	**AACGLORR**	coral rag
AACEIINT	actiniae	**AACELTTY**	cattleya	**AACGLORS**	Calor gas
AACEIKMT	kamacite	**AACELTYZ**	catalyze	**AACGLOST**	catalogs
AACEILLM	camellia	**AACEMNPS**	spaceman	**AACGMNRS**	cragsman
AACEILLN	alliance, canaille	**AACEMPRT**	metacarp	**AACGNORS**	cargason
		AACEMRRS	arms race	**AACGNRVY**	vagrancy
AACEILMN	analcime, calamine	**AACEMRSS**	massacre	**AACHHIIR**	Ichihara
		AACEMRST	mascaret	**AACHHLLS**	challahs
AACEILMP	impalace	**AACENPRS**	pancreas	**AACHHORT**	horchata
AACEILMT	calamite	**AACENPST**	pastance	**AACHHTWY**	hatchway
AACEILNT	laitance	**AACENPSU**	saucepan	**AACHIIKW**	Ichikawa
AACEILNV	Valencia, valiance	**AACENPTT**	pancetta	**AACHIIMR**	mariachi
		AACENRST	canaster	**AACHIJNT**	Jacintha
AACEILNZ	canalize	**AACENRTT**	reactant	**AACHIKNR**	chinkara
AACEILOP	alopecia	**AACENRTU**	areca nut	**AACHIKRR**	Charikar
AACEILOT	aleatico	**AACENRTY**	catenary	**AACHILLR**	rachilla
AACEILRT	tail-race	**AACENRVZ**	czarevna	**AACHILMN**	machinal

AACHILMS masalchi
AACHILMT thalamic
AACHILNP chaplain
AACHILPS calipash, pashalic
AACHILRV archival
AACHIMNN Chinaman
AACHIMNP champain, champian
AACHIMNR chairman, Charmian
AACHIMNS shamanic
AACHIMNT matachin
AACHIMRR armchair
AACHIMRS archaism, charisma
AACHIMTU uchimata
AACHINNW wananchi
AACHINSW chainsaw
AACHIPTT chapatti
AACHIRRR hircarra
AACHIRSS Charissa
AACHIRTX taxiarch
AACHIRTY chirayta
AACHJKSY jackshay
AACHKMOS Machakos
AACHKMRS ramshack
AACHKPSS schapska
AACHKSTY haystack
AACHLLLU hallucal
AACHLMNO monachal
AACHLMOS chloasma
AACHLMSU macushla
AACHLORT thoracal
AACHLSTU calathus
AACHMNRU murchana
AACHMNTW watchman
AACHMORT achromat, trachoma
AACHMPRY pharmacy
AACHNOUY Huancayo
AACHNPRS sarpanch
AACHNPRT panchart
AACHNPRY panarchy
AACHNPWY panchway
AACHNRST trash can
AACHNRVY navarchy
AACHNSTU acanthus
AACHOPPR approach
AACHORTU achatour
AACHPPRY paparchy
AACHRTUY autarchy
AACIILMO maiolica
AACIILRV vicarial
AACIILTV viatical
AACIINRV vicarian
AACIIPRT Patricia
AACIIPST pistacia
AACIJLMO majolica
AACIJNOP japonica
AACIKRTU autarkic
AACILLLY laically
AACILLMR lacrimal
AACILLRR ralli car
AACILLRY racially
AACILLSW Salic law
AACILMNT calamint, claimant
AACILMPY pay claim
AACILMRS mariscal
AACILMRT mail cart, matrical
AACILMTY calamity
AACILNNO Laconian
AACILNOR Carniola, Carolina
AACILNRT cantrail
AACILNRV carnival
AACILNTT Atlantic, tantalic
AACILNTU nautical
AACILNTY analytic
AACILNUV navicula
AACILNVY valiancy
AACILOTT coat-tail, La Ciotat, tailcoat
AACILPRU piacular
AACILPST aplastic
AACILPSZ capsizal
AACILPTU capitula
AACILPTY atypical
AACILRSS Clarissa
AACILRTY alacrity
AACILRUU auricula
AACILRVY lay vicar
AACILSTT cat's-tail, statical
AACILSTY salacity
AACIMMNO ammoniac
AACIMMRS marasmic
AACIMNOR armoniac, macaroni, marocain
AACIMNPS Campinas
AACIMNRT marantic
AACIMORT aromatic
AACIMRSS samsaric
AACINOPR paranoic
AACINOPT capitano, pacation
AACINORT Catriona, Croatian, raincoat
AACINOST tacsonia
AACINOTV octavian, vacation
AACINQTU acquaint
AACINSTZ stanzaic
AACIPRST aspartic
AACIPRSU cusparia
AACIPRTY rapacity
AACIRRTT tartaric
AACIRSTT castrati
AACIRSTZ czaritsa
AACIRTVY cavitary
AACJKLPS slapjack
AACJKOOR jackaroo
AACJMNOR Majorcan
AACKKNPS knapsack
AACKLORV Karlovac
AACKMNRT trackman
AACKMNST tacksman
AACKRTWY trackway
AACLLLOO callaloo
AACLLLOS callosal
AACLLMRY lacrymal
AACLLNRY carnally
AACLLPPU Pucallpa
AACLLRRY carry-all
AACLLRSY rascally
AACLLSUU clausula
AACLLSUY casually, causally
AACLLTUY actually
AACLMNNS clansman
AACLNNOT cantonal
AACLNNOW canon law
AACLNNSU cannulas
AACLNOPR coplanar
AACLNRUY lacunary
AACLNTVY vacantly
AACLOPRU opacular
AACLOPTU tapaculo
AACLORRU oracular
AACLORSU carousal
AACLORTT Carlotta
AACLORUV vacuolar
AACLPPRT claptrap
AACLPRSU capsular, scapular
AACLPRTY calyptra
AACLPSSU scapulas
AACLPTTU catapult
AACLRSSU crassula
AACLRSSW class war
AACLRSUV vascular
AACLSTTY catalyst
AACLSTUY casualty
AACMNOOR macaroon
AACMNORS mascaron
AACMNPRY rampancy
AACMORSS sarcomas
AACMOTUY automacy
AACMPSTT Stamp Act
AACNOOPT patacoon
AACNORTT cantator
AACNPSTU pascuant
AACNRRUY naucrary
AACNRSTT transact
AACOORTX toxocara
AACORRTV varactor
AACORSTT castrato
AACORTTU actuator, autocrat
AADDDEEH deadhead
AADDDEHN dead hand
AADDDGNR granddad
AADDEEHT dead heat
AADDEEIL Adelaide
AADDEEMR adreamed
AADDEFLL deadfall
AADDEHHR hardhead
AADDEHLN headland
AADDEHMN handmade

AADDEHRW headward
AADDEIJL El Jadida
AADDEIRT radiated
AADDEIRW Diredawa
AADDEISV devadasi
AADDELNS sandaled
AADDEMOR made road
AADDEMRY daydream
AADDENPR red panda
AADDFFRU duffadar
AADDGHLN glad hand
AADDGNRU graduand
AADDHIMN handmaid
AADDHKKO kadkhoda
AADDINUY uddiyana
AADDKMMO mokaddam
AADDLLNY landlady
AADDLNRW landward
AADDLNRY yardland
AADDMRST Darmstad
AADDNRST standard
AADDOTYY day-to-day
AADEEERT de-aerate
AADEEGHR headgear
AADEEGLT galeated
AADEEGMN endamage
AADEEGNR Gadarene
AADEEHMR heemraad
AADEEILR Airedale
AADEEKNP naked ape
AADEELRW Delaware
AADEEMNR maeander
AADEEMRR demerara
AADEENNS Ensenada
AADEENTT antedate
AADEEPRT date rape
AADEEQTU adequate
AADEERTU deaurate
AADEFFRY affrayed
AADEFHLT flat-head
AADEFIJO feijoada
AADEFILM mala fide
AADEFILR fairlead
AADEFLLR falderal
AADEFLNS sand flea
AADEFLRY defrayal
AADEFLTT faldetta
AADEFSTY feast day
AADEGHMN Dagenham
AADEGHNS nag's-head
AADEGILL diallage, legal aid
AADEGILS ideal gas
AADEGILT gladiate
AADEGIMZ magadize
AADEGINR drainage, gardenia
AADEGINT indagate
AADEGIRR gerardia
AADEGITV divagate
AADEGJTU adjutage
AADEGKRS Dark Ages
AADEGLMN magdalen
AADEGLMY amygdale
AADEGLNS seladang
AADEGLOP galopade
AADEGMNR grandame
AADEGORT adrogate
AADEGPRT trade gap
AADEGRRT rag trade
AADEGRTU graduate
AADEHILN nail head
AADEHILR head-rail, railhead
AADEHILS headsail
AADEHILW Dehiwala
AADEHINP diaphane
AADEHIRR diarrhea
AADEHIWY hideaway
AADEHLLL halalled
AADEHLMP headlamp
AADEHLNR anhedral
AADEHLPS slaphead
AADEHMNS headsman
AADEHMST masthead
AADEHNNR near hand
AADEHNRV verandah
AADEHRRW hardware
AADEHTTX death tax
AADEIKLL alkalide
AADEILLN Daniella
AADEILMN Madelina
AADEILMR Armidale
AADEILMV maladive
AADEILNR Adlerian
AADEILNS saladine
AADEILNT danalite, dentalia
AADEILPR praedial
AADEILPS palisade
AADEILPT lapidate
AADEILRS salaried
AADEILRT Araldite
AADEILTT dilatate
AADEILTV validate
AADEIMNN amandine
AADEIMNR Madeiran, marinade
AADEIMNT animated
AADEIMPZ diazepam
AADEIMRV maravedi
AADEIMST diastema
AADEINNR Adrianne
AADEINRT dentaria
AADEIPRS paradise
AADEIPSU diapause
AADEIPSV pavisade
AADEIPTV adaptive
AADEISST diastase
AADEITVW viewdata
AADEJMNN N'Djamena
AADEJNNP japanned
AADEKLLN Lakeland
AADEKLNR kalendar
AADEKLOP peak load
AADEKLRY kaleyard
AADEKMNR mandrake
AADELLMP Palmdale
AADELLPP appalled
AADELLWY welladay
AADELMNR alderman
AADELMNS dalesman, leadsman
AADELNPR palander
AADELNPT peatland
AADELNST eastland
AADELORS saladero
AADELRTV larvated
AADELRTW lateward
AADEMNOS adenomas
AADEMNUZ unamazed
AADEMRRU marauder
AADENNTT denatant
AADENOTT denotata
AADENSTY asyndeta
AADENSTZ stanzaed
AADEOPRT tapadero
AADEOPST adespota
AADEORRV Varadero
AADEPPRT preadapt
AADEPRTV vardapet
AADEQRTU quadrate
AADERRRW rearward
AADERRST rat-arsed
AADERSSW seawards
AADERSTW eastward, radwaste
AADERUVY ayurveda
AADFGNNO fandango
AADFHMNR farmhand
AADFHNST handfast
AADFIINT intifada
AADFIMRS faradism
AADFINRU unafraid
AADFLLLN landfall
AADFLORW aardwolf
AADFLOTX toadflax
AADFLOWY foldaway
AADFMRRY farmyard
AADGGINR Dangriga
AADGGLNN gangland
AADGGLRS glad rags
AADGGNSY gang-days
AADGHIPR diagraph
AADGHORS Sargodha
AADGIINS gainsaid
AADGILLR galliard
AADGILMR madrigal
AADGILNO diagonal
AADGILOP podalgia
AADGIMMR gammarid
AADGIMNR main drag
AADGIMPR paradigm
AADGIMRT gradatim
AADGINRT grant aid
AADGINRU guardian
AADGIQRU quadriga
AADGLMNR grand mal
AADGLOPR podagral
AADGMNOR dragoman
AADGMNRS dragsman
AADGNORU gandoura
AADGNRTU guardant
AADGNRUV vanguard
AADGRRUW gurdwara

AADHHNSW wash-hand
AADHIKRT thikadar
AADHILNR handrail
AADHILNT Thailand
AADHILNU Ludhiana
AADHILRV havildar
AADHIMOR radio ham
AADHINRR harridan
AADHIPRS parishad
AADHLLNS all hands
AADHLNSW washland
AADHLPSS slapdash
AADHLRUY haulyard
AADHMMMU Muhammad
AADHMNNY handyman
AADHMNOS Mohandas
AADHMNOU omadhaun
AADHMNRU Damanhur, Mandurah
AADHNPSS handpass
AADHNSTT hatstand
AADHRRTW thraward
AADHRRYZ hazardry
AADIIINR aniridia
AADIILSV disavail
AADIIMNN Indiaman
AADIIMRT Diarmait
AADIISSV Adivasis
AADIKLLO alkaloid
AADIKLLR killadar
AADIKLRY kailyard
AADIKSSU Kusadasi
AADILLLO allodial
AADILLMU mudalali
AADILLNR landrail
AADILLPR palliard
AADILLRY radially
AADILMNN mainland
AADILMNO domanial
AADILMNT Maitland
AADILMVY Limavady
AADILNPR prandial
AADILNPU paludina
AADILNRU Laurinda
AADILNTT dilatant
AADILOPS palisado
AADILORR railroad
AADILPRY lapidary
AADILPSS passalid
AADILTUU auditual
AADIMMNX maximand
AADIMNNR mandarin
AADIMNRT tamarind
AADIMNRY dairyman, main yard
AADIMNRZ zamindar
AADIMNUV vanadium
AADIMSTZ samizdat
AADINOPR paranoid
AADINOPS diapason
AADINPRS Spaniard
AADINPSV pavisand
AADINRYY rainy day
AADINSSS Sassanid
AADIOPRS Diaspora
AADIORRT radiator
AADIRRSY disarray
AADJNTTU adjutant
AADJNTUV adjuvant
AADKLMNR landmark
AADKLNPR parkland
AADKLRST Karlstad
AADKLRTU talukdar
AADKMNRS darkmans
AADKORWY workaday
AADKRRST dark star
AADLLMRS mallards
AADLMNNS landsman
AADLMNOR mandorla
AADLMNRY Maryland
AADLMNSS land mass
AADLMNSY lady's man
AADLMNUU laudanum
AADLNOPR parlando
AADLOPRV Pavlodar
AADLORST loadstar
AADLORSV Salvador
AADLORSY solar day
AADLORTU adulator, laudator
AADLPPRW waldrapp
AADMMNOW madwoman
AADMMNSU mandamus
AADMNNSW wandsman
AADMNORT mandator
AADMOOSS sado-maso
AADMOPPP poppadam
AADMORRT tram road
AADNNNPY pandanny
AADNNPSU pandanus
AADNOPSS sandsoap
AADNORTY donatary
AADNOSUV vanadous
AADNOSWY nowadays
AADNQRTU quadrant
AADNQRUY quandary
AADNRTVW vantward
AADNRVYY navy yard
AADOPRRS paradors
AADOPRXY paradoxy
AADOPSUY paduasoy
AADORSVY Savoyard
AADRSTUY Saturday
AAEEEGLS sea eagle
AAEEEHRT hetaerae
AAEEFMST meat safe
AAEEFRRS seafarer
AAEEFSST safe seat
AAEEGGNR age range
AAEEGHWZ ghawazee
AAEEGILN alienage
AAEEGKMM make-game
AAEEGLLN enallage
AAEEGLLT allegate
AAEEGLNS sea-angel
AAEEGLRY eagle ray
AAEEGMPR amperage
AAEEGMST steam age
AAEEGNRS sangaree
AAEEGPRT great ape
AAEEGRRY grey area
AAEEGRTW waterage
AAEEHIMR haere mai
AAEEHLMN heelaman
AAEEHPRR perahera
AAEEHRTW aweather, wheatear
AAEEHTVW heatwave
AAEEILNT alienate
AAEEJNPS Japanese
AAEEJNSV Javanese
AAEEKLTW late-wake
AAEEKMNS namesake
AAEEKNRS Kanarese
AAEEKNRW reawaken
AAEEKNSS sea snake
AAEEKPRT parakeet
AAEEKQSU seaquake
AAEELLLM lamellae
AAEELLMT malleate
AAEELLPT patellae
AAEELMNU Emanuela
AAEELMRS Aalsmeer
AAEELNNR annealer
AAEELNOR Eleanora
AAEELNPS seaplane
AAEELNRS La Serena
AAEELNST elastane
AAEELORV aloe vera
AAEELPPR appealer
AAEELPRY leap year
AAEELQUV equaeval
AAEELRTU laureate
AAEELSST elastase
AAEELTUV evaluate
AAEELVWY way-leave
AAEEMMTT team-mate
AAEEMNPT name-tape
AAEEMNRT man-eater
AAEEMPRS paramese
AAEEMSSS Assamese
AAEENNNT antennae
AAEENNRZ Nazarene
AAEENOPR pareoean
AAEENPRT paranete
AAEENRRT narratee
AAEENRST arsenate, Near East, serenata
AAEENRTT anteater
AAEENSTU nauseate
AAEEPPRR rapparee, reappear
AAEEPPRS appeaser
AAEEPRSS passaree
AAEEPRST asperate, separate
AAEERRWW rewarewa
AAEERSTT stearate
AAEERSTW sea water
AAEFFGST staffage
AAEFFILS fail-safe
AAEFFLPR paraffle
AAEFGHRW wharfage
AAEFGIMR fair game

AAEFGITT fatigate
AAEFGLLL flagella
AAEFGLOT floatage
AAEFGNRU naufrage
AAEFHHLR half-hear
AAEFIILR filariae
AAEFILTY fayalite
AAEFIMRR airframe
AAEFINPU epifauna
AAEFLMOT meat loaf
AAEFLMTT flatmate
AAEFLNST fast lane
AAEFLRTT flat rate
AAEFLRTU featural
AAEFLRTW flatware
AAEFMRST fermatas
AAEFMRSW frame-saw, saw frame
AAEFRRWY wayfarer
AAEGGINR grainage
AAEGGIOT agiotage
AAEGGLNR langrage
AAEGGLNU language
AAEGGNOW wagonage
AAEGGNPR gang rape
AAEGGNRY garganey
AAEGGOPR paragoge
AAEGGRTT grattage
AAEGHLNP phalange
AAEGHLPS slag heap
AAEGHMRX hexagram
AAEGHNRU harangue
AAEGHPRT hag-taper
AAEGILLM Gamaliel
AAEGILLN Galilean
AAEGILLR galleria
AAEGILLT taillage, talliage
AAEGILNN Angelina
AAEGILNP pelagian
AAEGILNR geranial
AAEGILNT alginate
AAEGILTT tailgate
AAEGIMNO egomania
AAEGIMNS magnesia
AAEGIMNZ magazine
AAEGIMRR marriage
AAEGIMRT gematria
AAEGINPT paginate
AAEGINPZ paganize
AAEGINRS arginase
AAEGINST saginate
AAEGINTV navigate, vaginate
AAEGIPRU periagua
AAEGIRTX ex gratia
AAEGIVWY giveaway
AAEGKLLN lang-kale
AAEGKNUW Waukegan
AAEGKRTU great auk
AAEGLLMW wall game
AAEGLLPR pellagra
AAEGLLST stallage
AAEGLMNO Malegaon
AAEGLMNP game plan

AAEGLMOP megalopa
AAEGLMST almagest
AAEGLNOU analogue
AAEGLNPT plantage
AAEGLNTW law agent
AAEGLOSV aasvogel
AAEGLRST agrestal, gasteral
AAEGLRSV salvager
AAEGLRTY legatary
AAEGLSSV Las Vegas
AAEGLSVY savagely
AAEGLTUV vaultage
AAEGMMNS gamesman
AAEGMMRT metagram
AAEGMNPY pygmaean
AAEGMNRS Semarang
AAEGMNRU manurage
AAEGMNRV gravamen
AAEGMNRY managery
AAEGMORR aerogram
AAEGMORS sagamore
AAEGMPRR rampager
AAEGMRRT Margaret
AAEGMRRV margrave
AAEGMRRY gramarye
AAEGMRSS massager
AAEGMRST megastar, Ramsgate
AAEGMRTU ageratum
AAEGMTTW megawatt
AAEGNNPR pangeran
AAEGNOOR no-go area
AAEGNOPR paragone
AAEGNOTW tea wagon
AAEGNRRR arranger
AAEGNSTT stagnate
AAEGNSTV vagantes
AAEGORRT arrogate
AAEGORTT aegrotat
AAEGPPRR rag paper
AAEGPPRW wrappage
AAEGPRSU sugar pea
AAEGRRTW Great War
AAEGRRVW war grave
AAEGRSTZ stargaze
AAEGRSVY savagery
AAEHHMPY hyphaema
AAEHIIRT hetairai
AAEHILMN hielaman
AAEHILMT hate mail
AAEHILNT anthelia
AAEHILPR parhelia
AAEHIMNT anthemia, haematin
AAEHINNT Athenian
AAEHINPT aphanite
AAEHINST asthenia
AAEHKKMW make-hawk
AAEHKLST alkahest
AAEHKMRY haymaker
AAEHKSUW Waukesha
AAEHLMNT methanal
AAEHLMPT heat lamp
AAEHLMSY Sealyham

AAEHLNRT antheral
AAEHLPRS harp seal, pearl ash
AAEHLPUV upheaval
AAEHLRTT theatral
AAEHMMMT Hammamet
AAEHMMOT hematoma
AAEHMMRS Amersham
AAEHMNPY nymphaea
AAEHMOPR amphorae
AAEHMORT atheroma
AAEHNPST pheasant
AAEHNRST hanaster
AAEHNRTZ Nazareth
AAEHNTTX xanthate
AAEHNTVX tax haven
AAEHOPRT opera hat
AAEHRRSS harasser
AAEIIKNS akinesia
AAEIILMP lipaemia
AAEIILTT Laetitia
AAEIIMRV viraemia
AAEIJNRT naartjie
AAEIJNTV javanite
AAEIKKMZ kamikaze
AAEIKLLN alkaline
AAEIKLLZ alkalize
AAEIKMRR krameria
AAEILLLU alleluia
AAEILLMX maxillae
AAEILLNT allanite
AAEILLPP papillae
AAEILLPT palliate
AAEILLRT arillate, tiarella
AAEILLRV Vila Real
AAEILLRY aerially
AAEILLTT talliate
AAEILLTV allative
AAEILMNR manerial
AAEILMNT laminate
AAEILMNV velamina
AAEILMPR palmeira
AAEILMRT material
AAEILNNN Linnaean
AAEILNPR airplane
AAEILNPT palatine
AAEILNRR Larraine
AAEILNRT latanier
AAEILNRU aurelian, Lauraine
AAEILNRV valerian
AAEILNSS Salesian, sea snail
AAEILNSV vesalian
AAEILNSZ nasalize
AAEILNTT Latinate
AAEILNTV aventail, valentia
AAEILPPS papalise
AAEILPPZ papalize
AAEILPRT parietal
AAEILPRZ paralize
AAEILPST stapelia
AAEILPTV palative

AAEILQTU	aquatile
AAEILRRT	arterial
AAEILRTV	varietal
AAEILSTV	aestival, salivate
AAEILSTX	saxatile
AAEILTVX	laxative
AAEIMMNR	Mariamne
AAEIMNNR	Armenian, Marianne
AAEIMNOT	metanoia
AAEIMNPR	pearmain
AAEIMNPT	impanate
AAEIMNRT	marinate
AAEIMNRU	auramine
AAEIMNRZ	armazine, mazarine
AAEIMNST	Tamasine
AAEIMOPR	paroemia
AAEIMOTX	toxaemia
AAEIMOTZ	azotemia
AAEIMPRS	aspermia
AAEIMPRT	pia mater
AAEIMRST	maestria
AAEIMRTT	amaretti, Marietta
AAEINORT	aeration
AAEINORX	anorexia
AAEINPPT	antipape
AAEINPTT	patinate
AAEINPTX	anti-apex
AAEINRRW	rainwear
AAEINRST	antisera, artesian, Erastian, santeria
AAEINRSU	Eurasian
AAEINRTT	reattain
AAEINRTU	traineau
AAEINRTZ	Nazarite
AAEINSTT	astatine, sanitate
AAEINSTV	sanative
AAEINSTZ	Satanize
AAEINTTT	titanate
AAEIPPRS	appraise
AAEIPQRU	Arequipa
AAEIPRST	aspirate, parasite
AAEIPRSV	saperavi
AAEIPRTT	patriate
AAEIPRTZ	trapezia
AAEIPRXY	apyrexia
AAEIQRTU	taqueria
AAEIRRRT	terraria
AAEIRSVW	airwaves
AAEJNRTZ	jazerant
AAEJNRUZ	Aranjuez
AAEJORSV	Sarajevo
AAEKLLST	salt lake
AAEKLLTY	alkylate
AAEKLMRW	lawmaker
AAEKLMRY	malarkey
AAEKLOPP	oak-apple
AAEKLPRS	asparkle
AAEKMMPR	map-maker
AAEKNPRT	partaken
AAEKPRRT	partaker
AAEKRRUU	raurekau
AAELLLMR	lamellar
AAELLLPR	parallel
AAELLLUY	alleluya
AAELLMPU	ampullae
AAELLNSS	nassella
AAELLORV	alveolar
AAELLPRT	patellar
AAELLSWY	Wallasey
AAELLTTV	Valletta
AAELLWWY	wellaway
AAELLWYY	alleyway
AAELMMNO	melanoma
AAELMMTU	malamute
AAELMNRT	maternal
AAELMNSS	salesman
AAELMNST	last name, talesman
AAELMNSY	seamanly
AAELMNTV	lavament
AAELMOSU	mausolea
AAELMPPY	mayapple
AAELMPRR	rear lamp
AAELMPRT	malapert
AAELMPRX	examplar
AAELMPTV	vamplate
AAELMPTY	playmate
AAELMRSY	lamasery
AAELMRTT	maltreat
AAELNNNT	antennal
AAELNNOT	neonatal
AAELNNSU	Lausanne
AAELNNTU	annulate
AAELNOSS	seasonal
AAELNPRS	prenasal
AAELNPRT	parental, paternal, prenatal
AAELNPRW	warplane
AAELNPST	pleasant
AAELNPSW	panel saw
AAELNPTT	tea plant
AAELNRSY	analyser
AAELNRTX	relaxant
AAELNSSV	envassal
AAELNSSY	analyses
AAELNSTT	atlantes
AAELNSTV	Svetlana
AAELORTY	aleatory
AAELPPSU	applause
AAELPRST	palestra
AAELPRSY	paralyse
AAELPRYZ	paralyze
AAELPSTU	plateaus
AAELPSTV	palstave
AAELPSWY	paleways
AAELPTUV	vapulate
AAELPTUX	plateaux
AAELRSTZ	lazarets
AAELRTTU	Lauretta
AAELRUZZ	zarzuela
AAELRWYY	waylayer
AAELSSTX	sales tax
AAEMMNRT	armament
AAEMMOST	metasoma
AAEMMSTT	stemmata
AAEMNOST	San Mateo
AAEMNOTZ	metazoan
AAEMNPRS	Parmesan, spearman
AAEMNPRT	name part, parament
AAEMNPTT	tetampan
AAEMNRSW	manswear
AAEMNRTT	atrament
AAEMNRTW	waterman
AAEMNSSS	Manasses
AAEMOPXZ	oxazepam
AAEMORTT	amaretto, teratoma
AAEMOTTU	automate
AAEMPTTU	amputate
AAEMQRSU	marquesa
AAEMQSTU	squamate
AAEMRRTT	tarmaret
AAEMRRTU	armature
AAEMRSTU	maturase, Satu Mare
AAEMRTTU	maturate
AAENNNST	antennas
AAENNORS	Roseanna
AAENNOTT	annotate
AAENNPSY	paysanne
AAENNSTU	nauseant
AAENORSU	araneous
AAENORTU	aeronaut
AAENOSST	assonate
AAENPPRT	apparent, trappean
AAENPSTT	antepast
AAENPSTY	peasanty
AAENRRRT	narrater
AAENRSTV	tsarevna
AAENRSUW	unawares
AAENRSYY	naysayer
AAENSSTW	Setswana
AAENTTTT	attentat
AAEOPSTT	apostate
AAEORSTT	aerostat
AAEORTTV	rotavate
AAEPPRRT	art paper
AAEPPRTY	paratype, parypate
AAEPPRWX	wax paper
AAEPRTTW	tap water
AAEPRTTY	tea party
AAEPRTXY	taxpayer
AAERRTTT	tartaret, tartrate
AAERRTTW	water rat
AAERRWWY	war-weary
AAERSTTU	saturate
AAERSTUY	aestuary
AAERTTTW	terawatt
AAERTWWY	waterway
AAFFHIMS	affamish
AAFFILRT	taffrail

AAFFINPR	paraffin
AAFFLSTU	afflatus
AAFFNNOR	fanfaron
AAFGGLNN	Langfang
AAFGHINS	afghanis
AAFGHNRU	fraughan
AAFGINNX	Xiangfan
AAFGKLNR	flag-rank
AAFGLLNU	langlauf
AAFGLNRT	flagrant
AAFGNRRT	fragrant
AAFHLMST	half mast
AAFHLSTY	layshaft
AAFHQRRU	Farquhar
AAFHRSUU	hausfrau
AAFIILLM	familial
AAFIILLR	filarial
AAFIILMR	familiar
AAFIJSUW	Fujisawa
AAFILLNR	rainfall
AAFILMST	fatalism
AAFILNNU	infaunal
AAFILPRY	fair play
AAFILSTT	fatalist
AAFILTTY	fatality
AAFIMNOR	foramina
AAFIMNST	fanatism
AAFINNOV	favonian
AAFINNRS	safranin
AAFINRRW	warfarin
AAFINSTU	Faustina
AAFIRTTT	frittata
AAFKLSTT	fast-talk
AAFLLPRT	pratfall
AAFLMMNT	flammant
AAFMNORW	man-of-war
AAFMNRST	raftsman
AAFNPPRT	frappant
AAFORRTW	art of war
AAGGGGNN	gang-gang
AAGGILNR	gangliar
AAGGIMNN	managing
AAGGIRST	garagist
AAGGLLLY	lallygag
AAGGMNNS	gangsman
AAGGNNOY	yanggona
AAGHHINS	shanghai
AAGHIJNR	Jahangir
AAGHILNN	hangnail
AAGHINPS	paganish
AAGHKMNY	gymkhana
AAGHLNPY	anaglyph
AAGHMNNO	Monaghan
AAGHMNOY	hogmanay, mahogany
AAGHMNRT	Grantham
AAGHMOST	gomashta
AAGHMRSS	marsh gas
AAGHNNST	Tangshan
AAGHNOPR	agraphon
AAGHNORS	Shangrao
AAGHNOSU	Shaoguan
AAGHNOSY	Shaoyang
AAGHOPPR	apograph
AAGHSSTU	gasthaus

AAGIILMN	imaginal
AAGIILNT	intaglia
AAGIINTW	Waitangi
AAGIJRTU	Gujarati
AAGIKKNY	kayaking
AAGIKLNO	kaoliang
AAGIKMOS	sagakomi
AAGILLSS	galliass
AAGILLTV	gallivat
AAGILLUZ	alguazil
AAGILMMR	mailgram
AAGILMNO	magnolia
AAGILMNP	panglima
AAGILMNR	alarming, marginal
AAGILNOT	notalgia
AAGILNOY	Liaoyang
AAGILNRR	larrigan
AAGILNRS	sangrail
AAGILNUV	vaginula
AAGILOOP	apologia
AAGILORT	gratiola
AAGILPRY	plagiary
AAGILRRW	warrigal
AAGILSTT	sagittal
AAGIMNNN	manganin
AAGIMNNY	Mianyang
AAGIMNOS	isangoma
AAGIMNPR	Grampian
AAGIMNPS	paganism
AAGIMNRR	margarin
AAGIMNSY	gymnasia
AAGIMPTU	patagium
AAGIMSSV	savagism
AAGIMSTT	stigmata
AAGINNNY	nannygai
AAGINNOT	agnation
AAGINNTV	vaginant
AAGINNTW	awanting
AAGINNTX	Xiangtan
AAGINNXY	Xianyang
AAGINORR	rangiora
AAGINOST	Gastonia, Santiago
AAGINOTV	vagation
AAGINPRY	paginary
AAGINRSS	sarangis
AAGINRTU	au gratin
AAGINRTY	Tigrayan
AAGINSST	assignat
AAGIORTT	agitator
AAGIRSTV	gravitas
AAGKLLNS	knallgas
AAGKNOOR	kangaroo
AAGKPPRS	spark-gap
AAGLLMOY	allogamy
AAGLLNOO	lagoonal
AAGLLNRY	laryngal
AAGLLOPY	polygala
AAGLLOWY	galloway
AAGLLPSW	gall wasp
AAGLLRSU	rasgulla
AAGLNNOO	analogon
AAGLNOST	langosta
AAGLNPST	gas plant

AAGLNQUU	aqualung
AAGLNRRU	granular
AAGLPSSS	passglas
AAGLRSTU	gastrula
AAGMNOPZ	zampogna
AAGMNORT	martagon
AAGMNSTY	syntagma
AAGMORTU	tamarugo
AAGMOTUY	autogamy
AAGMOTYZ	zygomata
AAGNNOST	anagnost
AAGNNQUY	Yangquan
AAGNNSTT	stagnant
AAGNOPRT	tragopan
AAGNORRT	arrogant, tarragon
AAGNRSST	grassant
AAGNRTUY	guaranty
AAGNSTUU	Augustan
AAGOORTT	tarogato
AAGORSSS	sargasso
AAGORSST	oat-grass
AAGRSSSW	sawgrass
AAGRSSTU	sastruga
AAGRSSTW	twa-grass
AAGRSTUZ	zastruga
AAHHKKNU	Hanukkah
AAHHKSWW	hawkshaw
AAHHLLUU	hula-hula
AAHHNOSS	Shaoshan
AAHHNSSU	Shushana
AAHIIKRR	hara-kiri
AAHIIKRT	tarakihi
AAHIINPT	Panihati
AAHIINTT	Tahitian
AAHIKLSS	khalasis, khalassi
AAHIKNSS	Kinshasa
AAHIKRST	tarkashi
AAHILMRY	Hail Mary
AAHILNNT	inhalant
AAHILNOT	halation
AAHILPRS	phalaris
AAHILPXY	hypaxial
AAHIMRTT	Mahratti
AAHIMSTT	Matthias
AAHINRSW	rain-wash
AAHIPSXY	asphyxia
AAHISTWY	thisaway
AAHJNNOT	Jonathan
AAHKLLMR	hallmark
AAHKLMOO	Oklahoma
AAHKMOTW	tomahawk
AAHKNNOR	knorhaan
AAHKNORS	Noah's ark
AAHKNSUW	huskanaw
AAHLLLTU	Tallulah
AAHLLMRS	Marshall
AAHLLOPT	allopath
AAHLMSTU	thalamus
AAHLNPST	ashplant
AAHMNORT	marathon
AAHMNOTX	xanthoma
AAHMNPST	phantasm
AAHMOPRS	amphoras

AAHMORSS Massorah
AAHNNSSU Susannah
AAHNPRSU raphanus
AAHNPRUW purwanah
AAHNPSTT phantast
AAHNPSTY phantasy
AAHNTUWY huntaway
AAHOPRTU autoharp
AAHSSTTU Hattusas
AAIIILMR miliaria
AAIIILSU Siauliai
AAIIJJPP jipijapa
AAIIKKKR kakariki
AAIIKMNR marikina
AAIIKPRV rapakivi
AAIILMNS mainsail
AAIILMNT Tamilian
AAIILNRZ alizarin
AAIILNSV salvinia
AAIILNUX uniaxial
AAIILOSS loaiasis
AAIILRST Alistair
AAIILRTT attirail
AAIILRTX triaxial
AAIIMNNR Arminian
AAIIMNNT maintain
AAIIMNPX panmixia
AAIIMNRS Arianism
AAIIMNTV vitamin A
AAIINNTT titanian
AAIINOTV aviation
AAIINPRR riparian
AAIINPRS Parisian
AAIINRST intarsia
AAIIOPRT topiaria
AAIIORRT air-to-air
AAIIPRST apiarist
AAIIRSTW wistaria
AAIIRTVX aviatrix
AAIJLLQU quillaja
AAIJNRST satranji
AAIJNRYZ janizary
AAIKKLRS Karaklis
AAIKLNRS Sri Lanka
AAIKLNST nastalik
AAIKLOSV Slovakia
AAIKMNOT manitoka
AAIKMORY Koriyama
AAIKMRST tamarisk
AAIKNNTT anti-tank
AAIKNORU Kairouan
AAIKNPST Pakistan
AAIKNRTX taxi rank
AAIKRSUZ Kisarazu
AAIKSSTW swastika
AAILLLUV alluvial
AAILLMMM mammilla
AAILLMMR mamillar
AAILLMNT mantilla
AAILLMOR Amarillo
AAILLMPT tail lamp
AAILLNTX axillant
AAILLPSY pasilaly
AAILLRXY axillary
AAILMMRS alarmism
AAILMNNT lamantin
AAILMNOR manorial, morainal
AAILMNOS Somalian
AAILMNOX monaxial
AAILMNRU manurial
AAILMNRY laminary
AAILMNST talisman
AAILMORR armorial
AAILMRRU lararium
AAILMRST alarmist
AAILMTTU ultimata
AAILNNOT national
AAILNNPP panplain
AAILNNPT plantain
AAILNNRU lunarian
AAILNNST annalist, santalin
AAILNOPP Appolina
AAILNOPS Salopian
AAILNOPT talapoin
AAILNORS orinasal
AAILNORT notarial, rational
AAILNOST alstonia
AAILNOTV lavation
AAILNOTX laxation
AAILNOUY Liaoyuan
AAILNPPT appliant
AAILNPRT air plant
AAILNSSY analysis
AAILNSTY nasality
AAILNTTT latitant
AAILNTTY natality
AAILORRV variolar
AAILPPTY papality
AAILPSSV passival
AAILRSTT rat's-tail, rat's tail
AAILRSVY salivary
AAILSSTY staysail
AAIMMNST mainmast
AAIMMRSU samarium
AAIMNNOR Romanian
AAIMNNOS mansonia
AAIMNNOT manation, nominata
AAIMNNRT trainman
AAIMNNRU Rumanian
AAIMNORT animator, tamanoir
AAIMNORV Moravian
AAIMNORW airwoman
AAIMNOTY myatonia
AAIMNPQU pamaquin
AAIMNPRZ marzipan
AAIMNPST mainpast
AAIMNRRT trimaran
AAIMNRTY martynia
AAIMNSST mantissa, Satanism
AAIMNSTU amiantus
AAIMNSTY mainstay
AAIMOPRS mariposa, parosmia
AAIMPRST pastrami
AAIMQRUU aquarium
AAIMRRST Amritsar
AAINNNOT Antonina, Antonnia
AAINNOPV pavonian
AAINNOST sonatina
AAINNOTT natation
AAINNRTU Turanian
AAINNSST naissant
AAINNSSY sannyasi
AAINORRS rosarian
AAINORRT Rotarian, tornaria
AAINOSST assation
AAINOSTW watsonia
AAINOTTX taxation
AAINPRST aspirant, partisan, spartina
AAINPRTW warpaint
AAINPRTZ partizan
AAINQRRU quarrian
AAINQRTU quatrain
AAINQTTU aquatint
AAINRRSZ sarrazin
AAINRRTT tartarin
AAINRSSS sarassin
AAINRSSY Assyrian
AAINRSTU Austrian
AAINRSTY sanitary
AAINSSSS assassin
AAINSSTT Satanist
AAIOPPRS papirosa
AAIOPRSU Parousia
AAIOPRTU Irapuato
AAIORRTV variator
AAIORTUZ azoturia
AAIPRRTY partiary
AAIPRSSX sparaxis
AAIPRSTT partitas
AAIQRSTU aquarist
AAIQRSUU Aquarius
AAIRSSTT tsaritsa
AAIRSTWY stairway
AAJLMPRU Jamalpur
AAJMMORR marjoram
AAKKKNRU kurakkan
AAKKMMOO makomako
AAKKRRWW kraw-kraw
AAKLMNNS Klansman
AAKLMRUY yarmulka
AAKLOORY royal oak
AAKMMNRS marksman
AAKMOSSU moussaka
AAKMPRSS pass-mark
AAKNRRUY naukrary
AAKOPRSV Kaposvar
AALLLLMP pall-mall
AALLLSTY laystall
AALLMNTY tallyman
AALLMNUY manually
AALLMORW moral law
AALLNNUY annually
AALLNPTU plantula

AALLOOPT	Palo Alto	**AANRRTWY**	warranty	**ABBEERTT**	barbette
AALLOORW	wallaroo	**AANRSTTU**	saturant	**ABBEFILR**	flabbier
AALLORWY	rollaway	**AAOPPRSY**	papyrosa	**ABBEGIST**	gabbiest
AALLPRST	plastral	**AAOPSSTY**	apostasy	**ABBEHIRS**	shabbier
AALLPRTY	all-party	**AAORSUVV**	vavasour	**ABBEHORT**	bathrobe
AALLRUVV	valvular	**AAORSVVY**	vavasory	**ABBEILLL**	billable
AALMMOPS	plasmoma	**AAOSTWWY**	stowaway	**ABBEILNU**	bubaline
AALMNOPP	Pamplona	**AARRSSTW**	Star Wars	**ABBEILOT**	bilobate
AALMNORT	matronal	**AARRSTTU**	Tartarus	**ABBEILRU**	buriable
AALMNORU	monaural	**AARSSTTW**	at straws	**ABBEILST**	bistable
AALMNORW	Roman law	**AARSTTUY**	statuary	**ABBEIMWZ**	Zimbabwe
AALMNOWY	laywoman	**ABBBDEEL**	bedabble	**ABBEINRS**	Brisbane
AALMNPTY	tympanal	**ABBBEILR**	bribable	**ABBEIRRS**	barbiers
AALMNTTU	tantalum	**ABBBELTU**	tubbable	**ABBEIRRW**	barbwire
AALMNTUU	autumnal	**ABBBELUY**	baby blue,	**ABBEKLOO**	bookable
AALMOOSS	massoola		blue baby	**ABBELOPR**	probable
AALMOPPR	malaprop	**ABBBGILN**	blabbing	**ABBELORU**	belabour
AALMOSTT	stomatal	**ABBBHSUY**	bushbaby	**ABBELQSU**	squabble
AALMPPSU	paspalum	**ABBBMOOY**	baby boom	**ABBELRSS**	barbless
AALMPSTY	platysma	**ABBCCELN**	blancbec	**ABBEORRS**	absorber,
AALNNOPT	pantonal	**ABBCCKMO**	backcomb		reabsorb
AALNNTUZ	Zalantun	**ABBCEEHO**	bobachee	**ABBEORTW**	browbeat
AALNOORS	oronasal	**ABBCEERU**	barbecue	**ABBERRRY**	barberry
AALNOPRT	patronal	**ABBCEGIR**	cribbage	**ABBERRYY**	bayberry
AALNPSTU	platanus	**ABBCEHOU**	babouche	**ABBFILLY**	flabbily
AALNRRTY	arrantly	**ABBCEHTU**	bath cube	**ABBGGINR**	grabbing
AALNRSTU	saturnal	**ABBCEIKT**	backbite	**ABBGHMRU**	Bamburgh
AALNSTTU	tantalus	**ABBCEILR**	barbicel	**ABBGILNS**	slabbing
AALNTUVY	vauntlay	**ABBCEIRR**	crabbier	**ABBGINST**	stabbing
AALOPPRV	approval	**ABBCEIRS**	scabbier	**ABBGINSW**	swabbing
AALOPRST	pastoral	**ABBCEKNO**	backbone	**ABBGNORW**	brown bag
AALORSTV	salvator	**ABBCEKNU**	buckbean	**ABBHIIMS**	bimbashi
AALORTTW	total war	**ABBCELRS**	scrabble	**ABBHILSY**	shabbily
AALORTUV	valuator	**ABBCGINR**	crabbing	**ABBIKLLN**	bank bill
AALORTVY	lavatory	**ABBCGINS**	scabbing	**ABBILLMO**	bombilla
AALPSSSW	pass laws	**ABBCGIOR**	gabbroic	**ABBILLSU**	sillabub
AALRSSVY	vassalry	**ABBCIILL**	biblical	**ABBINORT**	barbiton
AALRSTTW	stalwart	**ABBCIINR**	rabbinic	**ABBINORX**	brainbox
AALRSTUY	salutary	**ABBCIKRT**	brickbat	**ABBINORZ**	Barbizon
AAMMMOPS	psammoma	**ABBCILRY**	crabbily	**ABBIORST**	barbitos
AAMMMRSY	ram-sammy	**ABBCINOY**	cabin boy	**ABBIRSUU**	suburbia
AAMMNNOO	mano mano	**ABBCKLOX**	black box	**ABBKKNOO**	bank book
AAMMNPRS	rampsman	**ABBCKLOY**	blackboy	**ABBLLLOW**	blow-ball
AAMMOTXY	myxomata	**ABBDDEEL**	beddable	**ABBLLSUY**	syllabub
AAMMRSSU	marasmus	**ABBDDEIL**	ad libbed,	**ABBLOPRY**	probably
AAMNNORU	anomuran		biddable	**ABBMMOOT**	atom bomb
AAMNOSTT	manostat	**ABBDDLOO**	bad blood	**ABBNRSUU**	suburban
AAMNQSUW	squaw-man	**ABBDEEER**	bee-bread	**ABCCDEHO**	caboched
AAMNRSTU	Sumatran	**ABBDEELN**	bendable	**ABCCDHIK**	dabchick
AAMNRTTU	maturant	**ABBDEELT**	bedtable	**ABCCEEHN**	bechance
AAMOPRRU	paramour	**ABBDEERT**	rabbeted	**ABCCEELP**	peccable
AAMOPRTU	Tupamaro	**ABBDEINR**	bearbind,	**ABCCEEOR**	caboceer
AAMORSSU	mosasaur		bread bin	**ABCCEIKL**	black ice
AAMORSTT	stromata	**ABBDEIRT**	rabbited	**ABCCEILY**	celibacy
AAMRSSST	smart-ass	**ABBDELRR**	drabbler	**ABCCEKMO**	comeback
AANNNORY	non-Aryan	**ABBDEMOR**	bombarde	**ABCCEKOR**	abrecock
AANNOSST	assonant	**ABBDEORS**	absorbed	**ABCCEMRU**	accumber
AANNRSTY	stannary	**ABBDERST**	drabbest	**ABCCHISU**	bacchius
AANOOPPX	opopanax	**ABBDGIOR**	Big Board,	**ABCCHKUW**	chawbuck
AANOPRTT	patronat		gabbroid	**ABCCHNOO**	cabochon
AANORRRT	narrator	**ABBDHIRT**	bird bath	**ABCCIISS**	abscisic
AANORSTY	sanatory	**ABBDHOOY**	babyhood	**ABCCIKKK**	kickback
AANORTTY	natatory	**ABBDKOOS**	bad books	**ABCCILOR**	carbolic
AANPPTTY	pattypan	**ABBEEJRS**	bejabers	**ABCCILOT**	cobaltic
AANQRTUY	quaranty	**ABBEELVW**	Ebbw Vale	**ABCCINOO**	bocconia

ABCCINOR carbonic
ABCCIORS ascorbic
ABCCKLLO ballcock
ABCCKOOT cockboat
ABCCMOOY maccoboy
ABCDDEIN biddance
ABCDEEEN bee dance
ABCDEEFK feedback
ABCDEEHR berdache
ABCDEELU educable
ABCDEGIR birdcage, cage bird
ABCDEHIR chair-bed
ABCDEHNR branched
ABCDEHOS caboshed
ABCDEIIT diabetic
ABCDEIKS backside
ABCDEILR calibred
ABCDEISY basic dye
ABCDEKLO blockade
ABCDEKLV backveld
ABCDEKNN neckband
ABCDEKNU unbacked
ABCDEKRT trackbed
ABCDELOO caboodle
ABCDELRU Bar-le-Duc
ABCDEMOT combated
ABCDENRU bean curd
ABCDENSU abducens
ABCDENTU abducent
ABCDFRUY farcy bud
ABCDHKLO holdback
ABCDIILO diabolic
ABCDILLR bird call
ABCDILOU cuboidal
ABCDINOR braconid
ABCDKLOR Black Rod
ABCDKNOW backdown
ABCDKOOR back door
ABCDKOPR backdrop
ABCDLLNU clubland
ABCDLOSU club soda
ABCDOORR brocardo
ABCDOPRU cupboard
ABCDORTU abductor
ABCDORUY obduracy
ABCEEEFK beefcake
ABCEEFNT benefact
ABCEEHLR bleacher
ABCEEHLW chewable
ABCEEILP peacible
ABCEEILT celibate
ABCEEIMN ambience
ABCEEIRT Beatrice
ABCEEKLY black eye, eyeblack
ABCEELLO eco-label
ABCEELOV evocable
ABCEELPT place-bet
ABCEELRR cerebral
ABCEELRT bracelet
ABCEEMRR embracer
ABCEENRT Cabernet
ABCEFIIT beatific
ABCEFIKR backfire, fireback
ABCEFINO Boniface
ABCEFKLT left-back
ABCEFLSS bass clef
ABCEGHIN Baicheng
ABCEGIKV giveback
ABCEGKLL blackleg
ABCEGKLO blockage
ABCEGKMU megabuck
ABCEGLSU scale-bug
ABCEGNOR bongrace
ABCEGNST scent-bag
ABCEHITT bathetic
ABCEHKTW bethwack
ABCEHLMR chambrel
ABCEHLMT chamblet
ABCEHLOR bachelor
ABCEHLSU chasuble
ABCEHMOT hecatomb
ABCEHNRR brancher
ABCEHNSW sawbench
ABCEHOOT cohobate
ABCEHORU barouche
ABCEHPRU pubarche
ABCEHRTT bratchet
ABCEIJOT Jacobite
ABCEIKKL kickable
ABCEIKLP pickable
ABCEIKLR crablike
ABCEIKLS scablike
ABCEIKLT black tie
ABCEIKWZ zwieback
ABCEILLR Claribel
ABCEILLT balletic
ABCEILNN binnacle
ABCEILNU baculine
ABCEILOP copiable
ABCEILOR cabriole
ABCEILOS sociable
ABCEILTT bittacle
ABCEINST bascinet
ABCEINTU incubate
ABCEIORS aerobics
ABCEIORT boracite
ABCEIRSW crabwise
ABCEIRTT brattice
ABCEIRTY acerbity
ABCEJKLT jet black
ABCEJLTY abjectly
ABCEKKSW skewback
ABCEKLLO lockable
ABCEKLMO mockable
ABCEKLOO cookable
ABCEKLSS backless
ABCEKOOS bookcase, casebook
ABCEKRST backrest
ABCELLMP Campbell
ABCELLOS closable
ABCELLPU culpable
ABCELLSU bucellas
ABCELMNY lambency
ABCELMRS scramble
ABCELMTU clubmate
ABCELNOT bel canto
ABCELNUU nubecula
ABCELOOT bootlace
ABCELOPY copyable
ABCELORS Barcelos
ABCELOST obstacle
ABCELRSU arbuscle
ABCELRSW bescrawl
ABCELTTU cuttable
ABCEMNOR Camborne
ABCEMNRU cream bun
ABCEMOOS camboose
ABCERRTU carburet
ABCERSTU sabre-cut
ABCERTUU cubature
ABCESTUU subacute
ABCFIKLL backfill
ABCFIKLP backflip
ABCFKLLU full-back
ABCFKLLY blackfly
ABCFKSTU fast buck
ABCGHKOS hog's back
ABCGHNPU punchbag
ABCGIINN cabining
ABCGIKLN blacking
ABCGIKNR king crab
ABCGILLO globical
ABCGILNO log cabin
ABCHIIPS biphasic
ABCHIKLS blackish
ABCHIKRS brackish
ABCHILMO choliamb
ABCHILOO coolibah
ABCHIMOR choriamb
ABCHIMRU brachium
ABCHINOR bronchia
ABCHIOOR borachio
ABCHIOTT bathotic
ABCHIRRT tribrach
ABCHIRTU tub chair
ABCHKMPU humpback
ABCHKOOP chapbook
ABCHKOOS cash book
ABCHMOTX matchbox
ABCHORSU courbash
ABCHRRSU crush bar
ABCIIKRR airbrick
ABCIINOT cibation
ABCIIORS isobaric
ABCIIRST tribasic
ABCIIRTU Curitiba
ABCIISTY basicity
ABCIITUX bauxitic
ABCIKKLL kickball
ABCIKLST backlist
ABCIKMRS Bismarck
ABCIKNPS backspin
ABCILLNY billycan
ABCILLSU bacillus
ABCILLSY syllabic
ABCILMMO cimbalom
ABCILMOO Colombia
ABCILMOU Columbia
ABCILNOR carbinol
ABCILNPU publican

ABCILOSY	sociably
ABCILRRU	rubrical
ABCIMMSU	cambiums
ABCIMNRU	Cumbrian
ABCINORY	baryonic
ABCINRVY	vibrancy
ABCIOPRS	saprobic
ABCIOSSU	scabious
ABCIOSTU	Subotica
ABCJKOOT	bootjack, jackboot
ABCKLLOR	roll-back
ABCKLLOS	ballocks
ABCKLLPU	pull-back
ABCKLNNO	non-black
ABCKLOPT	blacktop
ABCKLOTU	blackout
ABCKMOOR	back room
ABCKMOSS	moss-back
ABCKMOST	backmost
ABCKNRTU	turnback
ABCKOORU	buckaroo
ABCKOPST	backstop
ABCLLNOR	corn-ball
ABCLLOSU	local bus
ABCLLPUY	culpably
ABCLMOOO	coloboma
ABCLMRSY	scrambly
ABCLMSUY	scybalum
ABCLNORY	carbonyl
ABCLORXY	carboxyl
ABCLPRUW	pub crawl
ABCLSSSU	subclass
ABCNOUYY	buoyancy
ABCOOSST	octobass
ABCORRSS	crossbar
ABCORSSU	scabrous
ABCOSTTU	cottabus
ABCRSTTU	subtract
ABDDDEET	addebted
ABDDDGIY	Big Daddy
ABDDEEGG	debagged
ABDDEEHT	deathbed
ABDDEERR	debarred
ABDDEEST	bedstead
ABDDEHMO	hebdomad
ABDDEHMU	dumbhead
ABDDEILS	disabled
ABDDEILU	buddleia
ABDDEINS	side band
ABDDELOR	lade-bord
ABDDELOT	deadbolt
ABDDERYY	Derby Day
ABDDFORR	Bradford
ABDDIILR	dial-bird
ABDDILMO	lambdoid
ABDDILRY	ladybird
ABDDINNW	wind band
ABDDIORS	disboard
ABDDIRRY	yardbird
ABDDLNOR	bord-land
ABDEEEKR	Baedeker
ABDEEENP	beneaped
ABDEEENR	Aberdeen
ABDEEERV	beavered, bereaved
ABDEEGIT	debitage
ABDEEGLR	Belgrade
ABDEEGRU	bedeguar
ABDEEHNO	bonehead
ABDEEILN	deniable
ABDEEILR	rideable
ABDEEILV	deviable
ABDEEIST	beadiest, diabetes
ABDEEKMR	bedmaker
ABDEEKNR	bedarken
ABDEELLL	labelled
ABDEELLN	lendable
ABDEELLW	weldable
ABDEELMN	mendable
ABDEELNS	sendable
ABDEELNT	bandelet
ABDEELNV	vendable
ABDEELOR	lee-board
ABDEELPT	bedplate
ABDEELPU	dupeable
ABDEELRR	barreled
ABDEELRV	deverbal
ABDEELZZ	bedazzle
ABDEEMNS	bedesman
ABDEENNR	bannered
ABDEENRS	Bearsden
ABDEEPRS	bespread
ABDEERST	breasted
ABDEERTT	battered
ABDEERTW	waterbed
ABDEFILN	findable
ABDEFINO	bona fide
ABDEFLLO	foldable
ABDEFLOR	fordable
ABDEFNRU	faburden
ABDEGILL	gildable
ABDEGILU	guidable
ABDEGIMR	game bird
ABDEGIMX	mixed bag
ABDEGINO	badigeon
ABDEGIRR	abridger
ABDEGLMO	gamboled
ABDEGLSU	slugabed
ABDEGOPR	pegboard
ABDEGORU	bourgade
ABDEHILL	billhead
ABDEHITU	habitude
ABDEHKLU	bulkhead
ABDEHLLN	handbell
ABDEHLLO	holdable
ABDEHLLU	bullhead
ABDEHLOT	Theobald
ABDEHMNU	habendum
ABDEHNRR	Bernhard
ABDEHNSU	Dushanbe
ABDEHORR	abhorred
ABDEHOSW	beshadow
ABDEHTTU	head-butt
ABDEIIRT	diatribe
ABDEIKNU	baudekin
ABDEILLS	sabellid, slidable
ABDEILLU	laudible
ABDEILLW	wide ball
ABDEILMN	mandible
ABDEILNP	pedal bin
ABDEILNR	bilander
ABDEILNT	bidental
ABDEILOV	voidable
ABDEILOX	oxidable
ABDEILRV	drivable
ABDEILTU	dutiable
ABDEIMOO	amoeboid
ABDEIMOR	amberoid
ABDEIMRU	Drambuie
ABDEINOR	debonair, diborane
ABDEINPP	pipe band
ABDEINRS	brandise
ABDEINST	bandiest
ABDEINSU	unbiased
ABDEIPRT	biparted
ABDEIPSS	pissabed
ABDEIRRR	rare bird
ABDEIRRW	war bride
ABDEISSU	disabuse
ABDEISTW	bawdiest
ABDEITTU	dubitate
ABDEKLNP	plank bed
ABDEKLSW	skewbald
ABDEKNSU	sun-baked
ABDEKOOT	datebook
ABDEKORW	beadwork
ABDEKORY	keyboard
ABDELLOT	balloted
ABDELNOR	banderol
ABDELNOZ	deblazon
ABDELNRY	bylander
ABDELNSS	baldness
ABDELORU	laboured
ABDELOSW	Bode's law
ABDEMRSU	Bermudas
ABDEMRTU	drumbeat
ABDENNNU	unbanned
ABDENNOS	noseband
ABDENNRW	brand new
ABDENORR	Bernardo, dearborn
ABDENORW	downbear, raw-boned
ABDENOTW	downbeat
ABDENRRT	Bertrand
ABDENRRU	unbarred
ABDENRSS	drabness
ABDENRTU	turbaned
ABDENTTU	debutant
ABDEOPRR	preboard
ABDEORRU	arboured
ABDEORRW	wardrobe
ABDEORSW	sowbread
ABDEORTU	obdurate
ABDEORUX	Bordeaux
ABDEOVWY	body wave
ABDEPSTU	Budapest
ABDERSTW	bedstraw
ABDESTTU	taste bud
ABDFFNOR	off-brand

ABDFNORU funboard
ABDGGGOY doggy bag
ABDGHINR hangbird
ABDGIINR braiding
ABDGIIRS grid bias
ABDGILLY dillybag
ABDGILOR gaolbird
ABDGINNO Abingdon
ABDGINST dingbats
ABDGITTY ditty bag
ABDHIINW Bhiwandi
ABDHIIST dishabit
ABDHILLN handbill
ABDHILNS blandish
ABDHINRS brandish
ABDHIRTY birthday
ABDHKNOO handbook
ABDHLMOO lambhood
ABDHLNOS ash blond
ABDHLORW blowhard
ABDHMOTU bad mouth
ABDHNOSW showband
ABDHSTTU dust-bath
ABDIIJLR jailbird
ABDIIMNR midbrain
ABDIIMSU basidium
ABDIINOS obsidian
ABDIINRR rainbird
ABDIINTT banditti
ABDIIORT oribatid
ABDIIRTY rabidity
ABDIKLNR blinkard
ABDILLRY bridally
ABDILLSY slidably
ABDILNOS Basildon
ABDILORW wild boar
ABDILOST blastoid
ABDILRRY ribaldry
ABDILRZZ blizzard
ABDINOTY antibody
ABDINRTY banditry
ABDINTTU dubitant
ABDIORTY abditory
ABDKLNOO bookland
ABDLRSUU subdural
ABDLRSUY absurdly
ABDLSTUU subadult
ABDMNNOS bondsman
ABDMRSUU absurdum
ABDNNORU Bundoran
ABDNNORW own brand
ABDNORSU baudrons
ABDNORUY boundary
ABDOORTU outboard
ABDOOSSW basswood
ABDOPRWY body wrap
ABEEEERT bee-eater
ABEEEFRS freebase
ABEEEGLR Abergele
ABEEEGRR beeregar
ABEEEGRS begrease
ABEEEGRV beverage
ABEEEHTT hebetate
ABEEEKLP keepable
ABEEELLP peelable
ABEEELNS Lebanese
ABEEELPS Bel Paese
ABEEENRT Tenebrae
ABEEENST absentee
ABEEENTZ bezantee
ABEEFILN fineable
ABEEFILR afebrile
ABEEFILS feasible
ABEEFILT flea bite
ABEEFLLN befallen
ABEEFORR forebear
ABEEGILV giveable
ABEEGINR bergenia
ABEEGIRV verbiage
ABEEGKLR leg-break
ABEEGLTT gettable
ABEEGMTY megabyte
ABEEGNNR brennage
ABEEGRRT bargeret
ABEEGRST absterge
ABEEGTTU baguette
ABEEHILR hireable
ABEEHINT thebaine
ABEEHIRZ Hebraize
ABEEHLLL heelball
ABEEHLLR beer hall, harebell
ABEEHNPP behappen
ABEEHQTU bequeath
ABEEHRRT breather
ABEEIKLL likeable
ABEEIKLT Bakelite
ABEEIKRT tie-break
ABEEILLN lineable
ABEEILLR reliable
ABEEILLS Isabelle
ABEEILLV leviable, liveable
ABEEILMN mineable
ABEEILNN biennale
ABEEILNP plebeian
ABEEILNS Balinese, baseline, sabeline
ABEEILNV enviable
ABEEILPW wipeable
ABEEILPX expiable
ABEEILRR blearier
ABEEILRS abseiler
ABEEILRT liberate
ABEEILRW bewailer
ABEEILSV evasible
ABEEILSZ seizable, sizeable
ABEEILTV evitable
ABEEILUU Beaulieu
ABEEILVW viewable
ABEEIMNT ambiente
ABEEIPRS bepraise
ABEEIRTT batterie
ABEEIRTV breviate
ABEEISSV abessive
ABEEITUX beauxite
ABEEJMOR jamboree
ABEEKLLW Bakewell
ABEEKLOT keelboat
ABEEKMRR re-embark
ABEEKOOP peekaboo
ABEEKRST bestreak
ABEELLLR labeller
ABEELLLS sellable
ABEELLLT tellable
ABEELLMT meltable
ABEELLOS loseable
ABEELLOV loveable
ABEELLTT lettable
ABEELLTU ebullate
ABEELLVY levyable
ABEELMMR embalmer, emmarble
ABEELMNO bonemeal
ABEELMNR enmarble
ABEELMOS mesolabe
ABEELMOV moveable
ABEELMPR peramble, preamble
ABEELMRT atremble
ABEELMSS assemble
ABEELMTT embattle
ABEELNOP beanpole, openable
ABEELNRT rentable
ABEELNTU nebulate, tuneable
ABEELOPR operable, ropeable
ABEELOPS poseable
ABEELORX exorable
ABEELPTT pettable
ABEELRST balester
ABEELRSU reusable
ABEELRSV beslaver
ABEELRTT berattle
ABEELRTU bateleur
ABEELSSS baseless
ABEELSSU sub-lease
ABEELSTT seat belt, testable
ABEELSUX saxe blue
ABEELTTT tablette
ABEELTTW wettable
ABEEMMNR membrane
ABEEMMRU bummaree
ABEEMNRR embarren
ABEEMNST basement
ABEEMNTT abetment, batement
ABEEMQRU embarque
ABEEMRTT ambrette
ABEENNRT banneret
ABEENNRU eburnean
ABEENNTU unbeaten
ABEENORS seaborne
ABEENRRR barrener
ABEENRRT banterer
ABEENRSS bareness
ABEENSSS baseness
ABEEORRV overbear
ABEERRRT barterer

ABEERRTT	barrette, batterer	**ABEGNRRS**	Arnsberg	**ABEILMNT**	bailment, libament
ABEERRTV	vertebra	**ABEGNRST**	bangster	**ABEILMOR**	bromelia
ABEERRTY	betrayer	**ABEGNSTU**	subagent	**ABEILMSS**	missable
ABEERSTT	beatster	**ABEGOORS**	bar-goose	**ABEILMST**	balmiest
ABEESSTT	bassette	**ABEGOORT**	obrogate	**ABEILNNW**	winnable
ABEESTTT	beta test	**ABEGRRUV**	burgrave	**ABEILNPT**	pin-table
ABEESTWY	sweet bay	**ABEHHIPZ**	Hepzibah	**ABEILNST**	instable
ABEFFKOR	break-off, off-break	**ABEHHSUY**	hushabye	**ABEILNTU**	nubilate
ABEFHLLU	half-blue	**ABEHIILN**	inhabile	**ABEILNTV**	bivalent
ABEFILLL	fallible	**ABEHILNR**	hibernal	**ABEILNUV**	unviable
ABEFILLR	fireball	**ABEHILTT**	tithable	**ABEILNVY**	enviably
ABEFILLT	liftable	**ABEHIMMS**	memsahib	**ABEILORT**	Laborite, orbitale
ABEFILOT	lifeboat	**ABEHIMNO**	Bohemian	**ABEILPRT**	partible
ABEFILRS	false rib	**ABEHIMRS**	Hebraism	**ABEILPRZ**	prizable
ABEFILSY	feasibly	**ABEHINRT**	inbreath	**ABEILPSS**	passible
ABEFILUZ	fabulize	**ABEHIORV**	behavior	**ABEILPST**	epiblast
ABEFITUY	beautify	**ABEHIRST**	Hebraist	**ABEILRRU**	reburial
ABEFKLNT	left bank	**ABEHIRSU**	bierhaus	**ABEILRST**	balister
ABEFLLMU	blameful, full beam	**ABEHJORS**	job-share	**ABEILRTW**	writable
ABEFLLRU	furlable	**ABEHLLRT**	bethrall	**ABEILRYY**	biyearly
ABEFLLTU	tableful	**ABEHLMMU**	hummable	**ABEILSSU**	issuable
ABEFLMOR	formable	**ABEHLMSS**	shambles	**ABEILSTU**	suitable
ABEFMRSU	sub-frame	**ABEHMNOR**	hornbeam	**ABEILSUX**	bisexual
ABEFOORT	barefoot	**ABEHMOOR**	rehoboam	**ABEILSYZ**	sizeably
ABEFRRUY	February	**ABEHNSTU**	sunbathe	**ABEIMQRU**	imbarque
ABEGGGIN	a-begging	**ABEHORRR**	abhorrer	**ABEIMRST**	barmiest
ABEGGHLU	huggable	**ABEHRTUY**	Bayreuth	**ABEIMRTV**	ambivert, verbatim
ABEGGIST	baggiest	**ABEIILLZ**	labilize	**ABEIMSSU**	iambuses
ABEGGLRY	beggarly	**ABEIILMT**	imitable	**ABEINNOZ**	bezonian
ABEGHILP	philabeg	**ABEIILNN**	biennial	**ABEINNRR**	inner bar
ABEGHINR	harbinge	**ABEIILNR**	bilinear	**ABEINNRU**	inurbane
ABEGHRRY	hagberry	**ABEIILNV**	inviable	**ABEINORR**	airborne
ABEGHRST	barghest	**ABEIILPT**	pitiable	**ABEINORT**	baritone, obtainer
ABEGHTTU	betaught	**ABEIILST**	sibilate	**ABEINOST**	botanise, obeisant
ABEGIJTU	bijugate	**ABEIILTT**	albitite	**ABEINOTZ**	botanize
ABEGIKNR	breaking	**ABEIILTV**	live bait	**ABEINQSU**	basquine
ABEGILLN	labeling	**ABEIINRR**	brainier	**ABEINRRW**	brawnier
ABEGILLO	Bellagio	**ABEIINRS**	Siberian	**ABEINRST**	banister
ABEGILLW	wage bill	**ABEIIRST**	Tiberias	**ABEINRTU**	braunite, urbanite
ABEGILNR	balinger	**ABEIJLNO**	joinable	**ABEINRUZ**	urbanize
ABEGILNS	Bengalis, signable, singable	**ABEIJLNU**	jubilean	**ABEINSST**	bassinet
ABEGILNT	tangible	**ABEIJLTU**	jubilate	**ABEINSTU**	base unit
ABEGILOT	obligate	**ABEIJMNN**	benjamin	**ABEINSTW**	waste bin
ABEGILPP	Big Apple	**ABEIJNSS**	basenjis	**ABEINTTU**	intubate
ABEGILRT	Gilberta	**ABEIKLLM**	lamblike	**ABEIORTV**	abortive
ABEGINTT	abetting	**ABEIKLLY**	likeably	**ABEIPQSU**	squab pie
ABEGINTW	wing-beat	**ABEIKLNS**	sinkable	**ABEIPRRS**	spare rib
ABEGIPPR	bagpiper	**ABEIKLSS**	kissable	**ABEIRRRT**	arbitrer
ABEGJLLY	jelly bag	**ABEIKMRR**	rim-brake	**ABEIRRSS**	brassier
ABEGKMOO	gamebook	**ABEIKNOR**	beak-iron	**ABEIRRTT**	birretta
ABEGKORS	grosbeak	**ABEIKNRS**	bearskin	**ABEIRRVY**	breviary
ABEGLMUY	mealy bug	**ABEILLLM**	millable	**ABEIRRYZ**	braziery
ABEGLNOS	noble gas	**ABEILLLT**	tillable	**ABEIRSTY**	bestiary, sybarite
ABEGLORW	growable	**ABEILLLW**	willable	**ABEISTTT**	battiest
ABEGLRUU	blagueur	**ABEILLMM**	limb-meal	**ABEITTTU**	titubate
ABEGLSTU	gustable	**ABEILLNO**	bonallie	**ABEJKLOU**	kabeljou
ABEGMNOS	gambeson	**ABEILLOS**	isolable	**ABEJLMPU**	jumpable
ABEGMNOY	bogeyman	**ABEILLOV**	violable	**ABEJMOOR**	jeroboam
ABEGMORT	bergamot	**ABEILLQU**	liquable		
ABEGNOOR	Gaborone	**ABEILLRY**	Bareilly, blearily, reliably		
		ABEILLST	bastille, listable		
		ABEILMMR	immarble		

ABEJMPSU base jump
ABEKKMOO make book
ABEKLMOS smokable
ABEKLNOW knowable
ABEKLNTY blankety
ABEKLORW workable
ABEKNNOT banknote
ABEKNSTW West Bank
ABEKOORY yearbook
ABEKORTU breakout, outbreak
ABEKRSTY basketry
ABELLLMU labellum
ABELLLOR rollable
ABELLLSY syllable
ABELLMRU umbellar, umbrella
ABELLMRW Bramwell
ABELLNOT ballonet
ABELLOOT loo table
ABELLOSV solvable
ABELLOTU lobulate
ABELLRVY verbally
ABELMNNO nobleman
ABELMNOP Belmopan
ABELMNOZ emblazon
ABELMNPU plumbane, plumbean
ABELMNTU Nembutal
ABELMNUU Blumenau
ABELMORU belamour
ABELMOTY metaboly
ABELMPTU plumbate
ABELMSSY assembly
ABELNNOR bannerol
ABELNNPU punnable
ABELNNRU lean-burn, runnable
ABELNORU blue roan
ABELNORW brown ale
ABELNOYZ bone lazy
ABELNRRY barrenly
ABELNRSY Barnsley
ABELNRTY Blantyre
ABELNRUY urbanely
ABELNRYZ brazenly
ABELNSTU unstable
ABELNSTY absently
ABELNSUU unusable
ABELOPRT portable
ABELOPRU pourable
ABELOPRV provable
ABELOPSY polybase
ABELOPTT tabletop
ABELOPTX box pleat
ABELOQTU quotable
ABELORRU labourer
ABELORST sortable, storable
ABELORSU rousable
ABELOSTU absolute
ABELOSTW bestowal
ABELOTUZ outblaze
ABELPRTU pubertal
ABELRRTU barrulet
ABELRSTU baluster
ABELRTTU burletta, rebuttal
ABELSSTT stablest
ABELSTUU subulate
ABELSTUX stub-axle
ABELTTUU tubulate
ABEMMNOO moonbeam
ABEMNOTU umbonate
ABEMNPRU penumbra
ABEMNTTU abutment
ABEMOORZ rambooze
ABEMORTZ barometz
ABEMRRUW raw umber
ABEMRSUY Amesbury
ABENNNOR Narbonne
ABENNRRY nanberry
ABENOPSU subpoena
ABENORSS baroness
ABENORTT betatron
ABENORTV bevatron
ABENORTY barytone
ABENOSSW sawbones
ABENRTTU Brunetta
ABEOPPRY paper boy
ABEORRTU outer Bar
ABEORSTU saboteur
ABEORTTU obturate, tabouret
ABEORTUV outbrave
ABEOSSST asbestos
ABEOSSTT bassetto
ABEPRSSY by-passer, passer-by
ABEQRSUU arquebus
ABERRTYY tayberry
ABERRWXY waxberry
ABERSSTU abstruse
ABERSTUW water bus
ABERTTUY butyrate
ABERTUXY X-ray tube
ABFFGIJY Jiffy bag
ABFFGILN baffling
ABFFLLPU puffball
ABFFLOST blast-off
ABFFNOTU bouffant
ABFGLLLO golf ball
ABFGORUU faubourg
ABFHLOOT half-boot
ABFHOOTT footbath
ABFIILLR fibrilla
ABFILLLY fallibly
ABFILNSU basinful
ABFILSTU fabulist
ABFIMORS fibromas
ABFIRRTU fruit bar
ABFIRTTU fruitbat
ABFJORSU frabjous
ABFKLLOR korfball
ABFLLOOT football
ABFLLOST softball
ABFLLUZZ fuzz-ball
ABFLMRSY lamb's fry
ABFLOSTU boastful
ABFLOSUU fabulous
ABFNORTU turbofan
ABFNORTW brown fat
ABGGGILN blagging
ABGGGINR bragging
ABGGIJNN jingbang
ABGGILNS sling-bag
ABGGNOOT toboggan
ABGGRSUU Augsburg
ABGHHILL highball
ABGHINWZ whiz-bang
ABGHMORU brougham
ABGIIILN alibiing
ABGIIMST bigamist
ABGIINNO bignonia
ABGIINSS biassing
ABGIIRTT Birgitta, Brigitta
ABGIKNRR ringbark
ABGILLLR ballgirl
ABGILMNO ambligon
ABGILMNR marbling, rambling
ABGILNNT bantling
ABGILNOT obligant
ABGILNRW warbling
ABGILNST stabling
ABGILNTY tangibly
ABGILOOT obligato
ABGILORW brigalow
ABGIMNRU rumbaing
ABGIMOSU bigamous
ABGINNOR aborning
ABGINNRX banxring
ABGINOST bostangi
ABGINTTU abutting
ABGLLLOY globally
ABGLLORU globular
ABGLLRUY bullyrag
ABGLMNOY amblygon
ABGLMOPU plumbago
ABGLNOOT longboat
ABGLNOUW bungalow
ABGLOOOO boogaloo
ABGLORSU glabrous
ABGLRRUY burglary
ABGMNOOR gambroon
ABGNOORY boongary
ABGNORSU osnaburg
ABGNRRUY Grayburn
ABGORSSX grass box
ABHIIKNO Habikino
ABHIILTY hability
ABHIKLOR kohlrabi
ABHILNOT biathlon
ABHILOPS basophil
ABHILRTW whirlbat
ABHILSST stablish
ABHIMNRY brahminy
ABHIRRSU airbrush
ABHIRSTT brattish
ABHISTTZ sitz-bath
ABHISUYZ yuzbashi
ABHKOOOT boat-hook
ABHKORSU kourbash
ABHLLMOT mothball

ABHLLOOY ballyhoo
ABHLORTW whorlbat
ABHLOSTT hot blast
ABHLPSUY subphyla
ABHLSSTU saltbush
ABHMNSUU subhuman
ABHMOORT bathroom
ABHMORST trombash
ABHNORTY North Bay
ABHOORST tarboosh
ABHOOSTW showboat
ABHOSTWY both ways
ABHRSTTU Bathurst
ABIIIKRT Kiribati
ABIIIMMM mimiambi
ABIIKLSS basilisk
ABIILLMR millibar
ABIILLOV oblivial
ABIILLTY lability
ABIILMNO binomial
ABIILMNS albinism
ABIILNOT libation
ABIILNRY brainily
ABIILNRZ brazilin
ABIILNST sibilant
ABIILPTY pitiably
ABIIMNOT ambition
ABIIRSSV vibrissa
ABIJLNNO banjolin
ABIJLNTU jubilant
ABIJNOOT jobation
ABIJNOST banjoist
ABIJNPSU Punjabis
ABIKLMNS lambskin
ABIKMOTU tambouki
ABIKNOOT bootakin
ABIKNORR ironbark
ABIKNORU Baikonur
ABILLLPY playbill
ABILLNRT brillant
ABILLPST spitball
ABILLRTY tribally
ABILMMOZ zimbalom
ABILMNOR binormal
ABILMNOU olibanum
ABILMNPU plumbian
ABILMNTU tablinum
ABILMORS laborism
ABILNOOT lobation, oblation
ABILNOTU ablution, abutilon
ABILNRTU tribunal, turbinal
ABILNSTU Istanbul
ABILORST strobila
ABILORTY libatory
ABILOSSV bass viol
ABILOTTT tilt-boat
ABILPRSU Bilaspur
ABILRSSY brassily
ABILRTUY ruby-tail
ABILSTUY suitably
ABIMNOSU bimanous
ABIMNPRS snap-brim
ABIMNRSU urbanism
ABIMORSU biramous
ABIMORSV bovarism
ABINOORT abortion, orbation
ABINOOST Botosani
ABINOPTX paintbox
ABINORST Ratisbon
ABINORTY bonitary
ABINOSTT botanist
ABINOSTV bonavist
ABINRSTU urbanist
ABINRTUY urbanity
ABINTTTU titubant
ABIOPRSU biparous
ABIOPSTU subtopia
ABIORRRT arbitror
ABIORRST arborist
ABIORRTV vibrator
ABIORTUY obituary
ABKKMOOR bookmark
ABKLLNOR bankroll
ABKLORWY workably
ABKNOPST stopbank
ABKNPRTU bankrupt
ABKOOPSS passbook
ABKOORTW workboat
ABKOORTY york boat
ABKORUWZ zubrowka
ABLLMOOR ballroom
ABLLMOPW blowlamp
ABLLMSTU smut-ball
ABLLNOSW snowball
ABLLRTUY brutally
ABLLSSUY syllabus
ABLMNRUU alburnum, laburnum
ABLNOPST snap-bolt
ABLNORYZ blazonry
ABLNSTUY unstably
ABLOORST bar stool
ABLOORSU laborous
ABLOORTY oblatory
ABLOPRTY portably
ABLOPRVY provably
ABLOSSUU sabulous
ABLOSTTU subtotal
ABLPRTUY abruptly
ABMMORTY tommy bar
ABMNOPRT Brampton
ABMOPRTU probatum
ABNOORRT roborant
ABNOORYZ bryozoan
ABNORTUU runabout
ABOORRSU arborous
ABOPRSST top brass
ABOPRSUY spar-buoy
ABORSSSU borassus
ACCCCHIS scacchic
ACCCDIIO coccidia
ACCCDILY Cycladic
ACCCEEGO coccagee
ACCCEERS accresce
ACCCENPY peccancy
ACCCFIIL calcific
ACCCILLY cyclical
ACCDDEEN cadenced
ACCDDEKO cockaded
ACCDDIIT didactic
ACCDEELN canceled
ACCDEENS accensed
ACCDEHRY decarchy
ACCDEIIT diacetic
ACCDEILU caudicle
ACCDEILY delicacy
ACCDEINT accident
ACCDEIRT accredit
ACCDELLO accolled
ACCDELSU cul-de-sac
ACCDERSU accursed
ACCDESUU caduceus, caucused
ACCDHIIR diarchic
ACCDHIOT cathodic
ACCDHLOR clochard
ACCDHPTU Dutch cap
ACCDIIOT acidotic
ACCDIIRU uric acid
ACCDIITY dicacity
ACCDILTU caliduct
ACCDILTY dactylic
ACCDINOR cancroid, draconic
ACCDIOOR coracoid
ACCDIORR Riccardo
ACCDITUY caducity
ACCDKORR crockard
ACCDOSUU caducous
ACCEEETX excecate
ACCEEFFI efficace
ACCEEGLR cerclage
ACCEEHLO cochleae
ACCEEHRT ceterach
ACCEEHST seecatch
ACCEEILR celeriac
ACCEEILS ecclesia
ACCEEIMR ice cream
ACCEEINV vaccinee
ACCEEKLN necklace
ACCEELNR clarence
ACCEELOS coalesce
ACCEELRT calcrete
ACCEENNS nascence
ACCEENST acescent
ACCEEORT croceate
ACCEEPRT accepter, reaccept
ACCEFFIY efficacy
ACCEFILS fascicle
ACCEFKOR rock face
ACCEGILR circlage
ACCEGKMO gamecock
ACCEHIJT hic jacet
ACCEHIKP chickpea, pea-chick
ACCEHILM alchemic, chemical
ACCEHILP cephalic
ACCEHIMN mechanic
ACCEHINO anechoic

ACCEHINR	chancier	**ACCFHLTY**	catchfly	**ACCILRRU**	circular
ACCEHINT	catechin, technica	**ACCFIIOP**	pacifico	**ACCILTUU**	cuticula
		ACCFINRS	francisc	**ACCIMNOS**	moccasin
ACCEHIRT	catchier	**ACCFLNOO**	confocal	**ACCIMPSU**	capsicum
ACCEHLOR	cochlear	**ACCFOORT**	cofactor	**ACCINOOS**	occasion
ACCEHLOT	catechol	**ACCGHINT**	catching	**ACCINORS**	Corsican
ACCEHNNO	chaconne	**ACCGIKMR**	gimcrack	**ACCINORT**	narcotic
ACCEHNNY	cynanche	**ACCGIKNR**	cracking	**ACCINOTY**	cyanotic
ACCEHNOR	charneco, encroach	**ACCGILRU**	glucaric	**ACCIOPST**	spiccato
		ACCGINRU	accruing	**ACCIORST**	acrostic, Socratic
ACCEHNRY	chancery	**ACCGLOOY**	cacology		
ACCEHNUY	Chauncey	**ACCHHITT**	chit-chat	**ACCIORSY**	isocracy
ACCEHOPT	cache-pot	**ACCHHMOU**	muchacho	**ACCIOSTU**	acoustic
ACCEIIST	caecitis	**ACCHIIRT**	rachitic	**ACCIRRTT**	tric-trac
ACCEILLN	cancelli	**ACCHIIST**	chiastic	**ACCIRSTY**	scarcity
ACCEILLR	clerical	**ACCHIKTT**	chittack	**ACCKKRSU**	rucksack
ACCEILLU	caulicle	**ACCHILMY**	chymical	**ACCKOOOT**	cockatoo
ACCEILLV	clavicle	**ACCHILNY**	chancily	**ACCKOPRT**	crackpot
ACCEILNS	scenical	**ACCHILOR**	orichalc	**ACCKORST**	stock car
ACCEILNT	canticle	**ACCHILOT**	catholic	**ACCLLOSU**	occlusal
ACCEILNV	clavecin	**ACCHILOY**	Chiclayo	**ACCLLSUU**	calculus
ACCEILNY	calycine	**ACCHILTY**	catchily	**ACCLSSUU**	sacculus
ACCEILRV	cervical	**ACCHIMOR**	achromic	**ACCMNOOR**	Moroccan
ACCEILTU	euctical	**ACCHINNO**	cinchona	**ACCMOSTU**	accustom
ACCEIMRS	ceramics	**ACCHINOR**	incroach	**ACCNOOTU**	cocoanut
ACCEINNR	cancrine	**ACCHINPU**	capuchin	**ACCNOPRW**	crown cap
ACCEINNY	anciency	**ACCHINUV**	vinchuca	**ACCNOPTU**	occupant
ACCEINOR	coracine	**ACCHIORT**	thoracic, trochaic	**ACCNORTT**	contract
ACCEINRT	acentric, nearctic			**ACCOPRTU**	coup-cart
		ACCHIRRT	carritch	**ACCORRTY**	carrycot
ACCEIOPR	cecropia	**ACCHKLOR**	charlock	**ACDDDEIT**	addicted
ACCEIOTV	coactive	**ACCHKORT**	hock-cart	**ACDDDEKU**	dead duck
ACCEIPRT	practice	**ACCHLOPT**	cloth-cap	**ACDDDEOU**	duodecad
ACCEIPSV	peccavis	**ACCHNNOT**	Connacht	**ACDDEEES**	deceased
ACCEIRRR	ricercar	**ACCHNOOR**	coronach	**ACDDEEFR**	red-faced
ACCEIRTU	cicurate, cruciate, eucratic	**ACCHNOOS**	sancocho	**ACDDEEHT**	detached
		ACCHNOTU	couchant	**ACDDEEIT**	dedicate
		ACCHNRSU	scraunch	**ACDDEENO**	dodecane
ACCEISTT	ecstatic	**ACCHOPRS**	cash crop	**ACDDEENR**	credenda
ACCEKKOR	rock cake	**ACCHORTY**	octarchy	**ACDDEENT**	decadent
ACCEKLNR	cracknel	**ACCHOSTW**	Choctaws	**ACDDEERR**	red cedar
ACCEKRRS	crackers	**ACCHRSTY**	scratchy	**ACDDEERT**	dead cert
ACCELMNY	cyclamen	**ACCIIIOT**	oiticica	**ACDDEESU**	Sadducee
ACCELNOV	conclave	**ACCIILLN**	clinical	**ACDDEETU**	educated
ACCELNRU	caruncle	**ACCIILMT**	climatic	**ACDDEHIK**	dickhead
ACCELNTU	clean-cut	**ACCIILRT**	critical	**ACDDEHKN**	deckhand
ACCELOPU	accouple	**ACCIIMNN**	cinnamic	**ACDDEIIM**	Medicaid
ACCELRSY	scarcely	**ACCIINNO**	aniconic	**ACDDEINR**	riddance
ACCELRTU	clear-cut	**ACCIINOT**	cationic, itaconic	**ACDDEINT**	dedicant
ACCELWYY	cycleway			**ACDDEKLO**	deadlock
ACCENNSY	nascency	**ACCIIRTX**	cicatrix	**ACDDENTU**	adducent
ACCENOPT	Concepta	**ACCIKKNN**	nick-nack	**ACDDGILN**	cladding
ACCENORT	accentor	**ACCIKKRR**	rickrack	**ACDDGINY**	caddying
ACCENOST	cosecant	**ACCIKKTT**	tick-tack	**ACDDGLOR**	gold card
ACCENOSU	concause	**ACCIKLLS**	sick call	**ACDDHIMR**	didrachm
ACCENOTT	Concetta	**ACCIKLOT**	cocktail	**ACDDHIRY**	hydracid
ACCENRRU	currance	**ACCIKNST**	canstick	**ACDDHKOS**	shaddock
ACCEOPRT	acceptor	**ACCILMOS**	cosmical	**ACDDIIOR**	cardioid
ACCEOPTU	occupate	**ACCILMUU**	aciculum	**ACDDILNY**	candidly
ACCEORTU	accouter, accoutre	**ACCILNOT**	lactonic	**ACDDILRW**	wild card
		ACCILNOV	volcanic	**ACDDILTY**	didactyl
ACCEPRSW	screw cap	**ACCILNUV**	vulcanic	**ACDDINNU**	uncandid
ACCESSTU	cactuses	**ACCILOPY**	cyclopia	**ACDDIOPR**	acid drop
ACCESSUU	caucuses	**ACCILORT**	cortical	**ACDDKLNO**	dockland
ACCFFILL	flicflac	**ACCILPRY**	caprylic	**ACDDKORY**	dockyard

ACDDORRW drawcord
ACDDORTU adductor
ACDEEEFT defecate
ACDEEEKS seed cake
ACDEEEMR reed mace
ACDEEENT antecede
ACDEEERS decrease
ACDEEFFT affected
ACDEEFIN defiance
ACDEEFRS frescade
ACDEEFRY federacy
ACDEEGLY delegacy
ACDEEGOR coradgee
ACDEEIIP epicedia
ACDEEILT delicate
ACDEEILU aedicule
ACDEEIMN Medicean, nemacide
ACDEEIMR Medicare
ACDEEIMT decimate, medicate
ACDEEINN decennia
ACDEEINU audience
ACDEEINV deviance
ACDEEITZ decatize
ACDEEJKT jacketed
ACDEEKPT tape deck
ACDEEKRT racketed
ACDEELLT cellated
ACDEELNR calender
ACDEELNT lanceted
ACDEELPR parceled
ACDEELRR declarer
ACDEELRT decretal
ACDEEMNO code name
ACDEENNT tendance
ACDEENOT anecdote
ACDEENRS ascender, reascend
ACDEENRT crenated, decanter
ACDEENRY decenary
ACDEENRZ credenza
ACDEENTT dancette
ACDEEOPS peasecod
ACDEEORT decorate
ACDEEOST seed-coat
ACDEEPPR recapped
ACDEEPRT carpeted
ACDEERRT terraced
ACDEFHKL half-deck
ACDEFIRR Fredrica
ACDEFOTW two-faced
ACDEFRSU surfaced
ACDEGGRS scragged
ACDEGIIL algicide
ACDEGIKM magicked
ACDEGIMR decigram
ACDEGINU guidance
ACDEGIRS disgrace
ACDEGNRS scrag-end
ACDEGORS God's Acre
ACDEHILL Helladic
ACDEHILR heraldic
ACDEHIMR chedarim
ACDEHIRS rachides
ACDEHIRT tracheid
ACDEHKLO headlock
ACDEHKOV havocked
ACDEHKRU archduke
ACDEHKSS cash desk
ACDEHLNR chandler
ACDEHLOR Rochdale
ACDEHMPS campshed
ACDEHNSU uncashed
ACDEHORR hard core
ACDEHORT chordate
ACDEHOTT cot death
ACDEHPST despatch
ACDEIILP lapicide
ACDEIILR liar dice
ACDEIILT ciliated
ACDEIIMU aecidium
ACDEIINR acridine
ACDEIINS sciaenid
ACDEIINT actinide, indicate
ACDEIIRT raticide
ACDEIJNU jaundice
ACDEIKMN main deck
ACDEIKNP panicked
ACDEILLM medallic
ACDEILLV cavilled
ACDEILMN mandelic
ACDEILMT maledict
ACDEILNP panicled
ACDEILNU Claudine, dulcinea
ACDEILNY adenylic, lycaenid
ACDEILOR Cordelia, loi-cadre
ACDEILPS displace
ACDEILPT plicated
ACDEILRT lacertid
ACDEILRU radicule
ACDEILTT latticed
ACDEIMNO comedian, daemonic, demoniac
ACDEIMNP pandemic
ACDEIMNT dictamen
ACDEIMOR Mordecai
ACDEIMOU camoudie, codiaeum
ACDEIMPT impacted
ACDEINNR crannied
ACDEINOS diocesan, Oceanids
ACDEINOV voidance
ACDEINPT pedantic
ACDEINRS cardines
ACDEINRT dicentra
ACDEINSS acidness
ACDEINST disenact, distance
ACDEINTV ci-devant, Vedantic
ACDEINVY deviancy
ACDEIOPS diascope
ACDEIORS croisade, idocrase
ACDEIOSU edacious
ACDEIPPR capriped
ACDEIPRR pericard
ACDEIPSS spadices
ACDEIPST spicated
ACDEIQRU acquired
ACDEIRSS Cressida
ACDEIRTU acritude
ACDEISTT acid test
ACDEKLMU lame duck
ACDEKOST stockade
ACDEKPRS spar-deck
ACDELLNU uncalled
ACDELLOR carolled, collared
ACDELLOS so-called
ACDELMSU muscadel
ACDELMTU talcumed
ACDELNOO canoodle
ACDELNOR colander
ACDELNPU unplaced
ACDELNRS sclander
ACDELNRY dry-clean
ACDELOOW lacewood
ACDELOPU cupolaed
ACDELORR red coral
ACDELORT Certaldo
ACDELORV overclad
ACDELOVW cold wave
ACDELRSY sacredly
ACDEMMNO commenda
ACDEMMRS scrammed
ACDEMNOU manucode
ACDEMOPR compadre
ACDEMORT democrat, Tremadoc
ACDEMORY moderacy
ACDEMSTU Muscadet
ACDENNOR ordnance
ACDENNST scandent
ACDENNSU sun-dance
ACDENOPR endocarp
ACDENORT don't-care
ACDENORY deaconry
ACDENOTU outdance
ACDENPPU uncapped
ACDENRTU underact, untraced
ACDENRVY verdancy
ACDEOORS doorcase
ACDEOPRU croupade
ACDEOPRY copyread
ACDEOPTT capotted
ACDEORRT redactor
ACDEORTU educator
ACDEORTV card vote
ACDEPPRS scrapped
ACDEQTUU aqueduct
ACDERRSU crusader
ACDERRTU traducer
ACDERSTT test card
ACDERSTU crustade
ACDERTTU tear duct

ACDERTUV curvated
ACDFFHNU handcuff
ACDFFILR Radcliff
ACDFFIRT diffract
ACDFFLOS scaffold
ACDFIILU fiducial
ACDGHHIR high card
ACDGHOTW dogwatch, watchdog
ACDGIILO dialogic
ACDGILNR cradling
ACDGILNS scalding
ACDGIMOT dogmatic
ACDGIOPR podagric
ACDGLNOO Golconda
ACDHHRRY hydrarch
ACDHIINT tachinid
ACDHIIPS diphasic
ACDHIKNP hand-pick
ACDHIKOR chokidar
ACDHILNR Richland
ACDHILPR pilchard
ACDHIMRS discharm
ACDHINOO choanoid
ACDHINOR hadronic
ACDHINSW sandwich
ACDHIOPP phacopid
ACDHIOPS scaphoid
ACDHIPST dispatch
ACDHKKUW duck-hawk
ACDHKLRU hard luck
ACDHKORR hard rock
ACDHLNOR chaldron
ACDHLORS scholard
ACDHLORU dourlach
ACDHLOST scald-hot
ACDHMNTU Dutchman
ACDHMORU mouchard
ACDHNORW chawdron
ACDHNOSW cash down
ACDHOOTW woodchat
ACDHOPRS pochards
ACDHOPRY hard copy
ACDHORSS sash cord
ACDHORSW showcard
ACDIIILN indicial
ACDIIJLU judicial
ACDIILMS disclaim
ACDIILSU suicidal
ACDIILTY dialytic
ACDIIMNO daimonic, Dominica
ACDIIMOR dioramic
ACDIIMOT diatomic
ACDIINNT indicant
ACDIINOP pinacoid
ACDIINOR radionic
ACDIINOT actinoid, diatonic
ACDIIOSS acidosis
ACDIIRST carditis
ACDIIRTY acridity
ACDIISST sadistic
ACDIKLNR clinkard
ACDILLOT Clotilda
ACDILLOU caudillo
ACDILLPY placidly
ACDILMTU Talmudic
ACDILMUU diaculum
ACDILNOO conoidal
ACDILNOR ironclad
ACDILNOS scaldino
ACDILNSY syndical
ACDILOPY polyacid, polyadic
ACDILOUV oviducal
ACDILPSU cuspidal
ACDILSUU Claudius
ACDIMNOO codomain, monoacid
ACDIMNSU muscadin, scandium
ACDIMNSY dynamics
ACDIMOSY docimasy
ACDINOPS spondaic
ACDINORS sardonic
ACDINORT tornadic
ACDINORW cordwain
ACDINSTY distancy, dynastic
ACDIOPRS sporadic
ACDIORTT dictator
ACDIOSTY dystocia
ACDIPRST adscript
ACDIRSTT adstrict, distract
ACDIRTWY cityward
ACDKLMUY Lady Muck
ACDKMMOR drammock
ACDKSSSU duck's ass
ACDLLOPY polyclad
ACDLLORS collards
ACDLLOSW coldslaw
ACDLNOPS cold snap
ACDLNORU cauldron
ACDLNORY condylar
ACDLOOOR Colorado
ACDLOORT doctoral
ACDLORUW war cloud
ACDLORWY cowardly
ACDLOSTU coal dust
ACDMMNOO commando
ACDMNORY dormancy, mordancy
ACDMOOPR macropod
ACDNOORV cordovan
ACDNOOTU ducatoon
ACDNOSTW downcast
ACDNPRTY cryptand
ACDOOPPR podocarp
ACDOORST ostracod
ACDOPRST postcard
ACDOPRSU curd soap
ACDRSSYY dyscrasy
ACDRSTTU dustcart
ACEEEFRR carefree
ACEEEGLN elegance
ACEEEIPR earpiece
ACEEELMR cameleer
ACEEENRS encrease
ACEEENSV evanesce
ACEEERRT recreate
ACEEERST secretae
ACEEERTT etcetera
ACEEERTX execrate
ACEEFFIN caffeine
ACEEFHSU eschaufe
ACEEFILM malefice
ACEEFLPU peaceful
ACEEFLRT tree calf
ACEEFLSS faceless
ACEEFMOR forecame
ACEEFORV overface
ACEEFPRT perfecta, praefect
ACEEFPTY typeface
ACEEGHNR encharge
ACEEGHNX exchange
ACEEGHOR ogee arch
ACEEGHRR recharge
ACEEGILN ligeance
ACEEGIMY magic eye
ACEEGIRZ Graecize
ACEEGKRW wreckage
ACEEGLNY elegancy
ACEEGLPU pucelage
ACEEGNOZ cozenage
ACEEGNRY reagency
ACEEGNSV scavenge
ACEEGORR racegoer
ACEEGORV coverage
ACEEHHNR herenach
ACEEHHRU heuchera
ACEEHIMN Manichee
ACEEHINS Eisenach
ACEEHINT echinate
ACEEHIPR peachier
ACEEHIPT petechia
ACEEHIRV achiever
ACEEHKLO cake-hole
ACEEHKTT hackette
ACEEHLLL HeLa cell
ACEEHLLN Chellean
ACEEHLMP empleach
ACEEHLNR Charlene
ACEEHLNT Cathleen
ACEEHLOS shoelace
ACEEHLSW eschewal
ACEEHLTT chatelet
ACEEHLTV chevalet
ACEEHMNR menarche
ACEEHMRS cashmere, marchese
ACEEHNNR enhancer
ACEEHNRS ensearch
ACEEHORT ochreate
ACEEHPRR preacher
ACEEHPTY eyepatch
ACEEHRRS research, searcher
ACEEHRRT treacher
ACEEHRTT catheter
ACEEHRTY Cytherea
ACEEHSST sea-chest
ACEEHSTT tea chest

ACEEHSTX	cathexes
ACEEIIST	sacietie
ACEEIKLV	cavelike
ACEEIKNP	peacenik
ACEEIKRR	creakier
ACEEIKST	ice-skate
ACEEILMN	cameline
ACEEILNP	capeline
ACEEILNR	reliance
ACEEILNS	escaline,
	salience
ACEEILPS	especial
ACEEILRT	ericetal
ACEEIMRR	creamier
ACEEIMRS	meseraic
ACEEIMRZ	racemize
ACEEINNR	narceine
ACEEINNV	venencia
ACEEINOS	eicosane
ACEEINOT	oceanite
ACEEINPS	sapience
ACEEINPT	patience
ACEEINRS	increase
ACEEINRT	creatine,
	increate
ACEEINST	cineaste
ACEEINTV	enactive
ACEEIPPR	praecipe
ACEEIPST	speciate
ACEEIRSU	causerie
ACEEIRSW	wiseacre
ACEEIRTT	ceratite
ACEEIRTV	creative,
	reactive
ACEEIRTW	ice water,
	water ice
ACEEISTV	vesicate
ACEEITTX	excitate
ACEEKLMR	mackerel
ACEEKLOR	colerake
ACEEKMPT	empacket
ACEEKNRW	neckwear
ACEEKRRT	racketer
ACEELLMR	Marcelle
ACEELLNT	lancelet
ACEELLNY	cyanelle
ACEELLOT	ocellate
ACEELLRR	cellarer
ACEELLRS	sarcelle
ACEELLRT	cellaret,
	electral
ACEELMNO	cameleon
ACEELMOT	camelote
ACEELMRS	sclerema
ACEELNNT	Le Cannet
ACEELNPT	pentacle
ACEELNRR	larcener
ACEELNRS	cleanser
ACEELNRT	centrale
ACEELNRU	cerulean,
	Laurence
ACEELNRW	Lawrence
ACEELNSU	nuclease
ACEELNTT	tentacle
ACEELNTU	nucleate
ACEELOPS	escalope,
	opalesce
ACEELORS	escarole
ACEELORT	relocate
ACEELOSV	vocalese
ACEELPRR	replacer
ACEELPRV	Perceval
ACEELPSY	cypselae
ACEELPTU	peculate
ACEELPTY	clypeate
ACEELRSS	careless
ACEELRSV	cleavers
ACEELRTT	raclette
ACEELRTU	celature,
	ulcerate
ACEELRTV	cervelat
ACEELSTT	castelet,
	telecast
ACEEMNST	casement
ACEEMOPT	copemate
ACEEMORS	racemose
ACEEMORV	overcame
ACEEMRRS	screamer
ACEEMRRY	creamery
ACEENNPZ	Penzance
ACEENNRT	entrance
ACEENNRV	encavern
ACEENNST	enascent
ACEENOPR	operance
ACEENORT	carotene
ACEENOST	notecase
ACEENPRR	parcener
ACEENPRT	perceant
ACEENPTU	penacute
ACEENRRT	recanter,
	recreant
ACEENRST	sarcenet,
	tresance
ACEENRTT	entr'acte
ACEENRTU	uncreate
ACEENTTU	cuttanee
ACEEOQTU	coequate
ACEEORRV	overcare
ACEEPPRT	percepta
ACEEPRST	esparcet
ACEEPRTU	peracute
ACEEPSTT	spectate
ACEERRTU	creature
ACEERRUV	verrucae
ACEERSST	cateress,
	cerastes
ACEERSSU	surcease
ACEERSSV	crevasse
ACEERSTT	rascette
ACEERSTU	secateur
ACEERTTU	eructate
ACEESSTT	cassette, test
	case
ACEESSUU	causeuse
ACEFFFLU	cafuffle
ACEFFHRU	chauffer
ACEFFILT	facelift
ACEFFLLU	full face
ACEFFOPS	offscape
ACEFGLNO	long face
ACEFGLRU	graceful
ACEFHIKS	fish cake
ACEFHNNR	enfranch
ACEFHORU	farouche
ACEFHSTT	the facts
ACEFIIPR	pacifier
ACEFIIRT	artifice
ACEFIKLL	calflike
ACEFILLY	facilely
ACEFILOZ	focalize
ACEFILRT	fractile
ACEFILRY	fireclay
ACEFIMPR	campfire
ACEFINNR	Francine
ACEFINRS	francise
ACEFINRX	carnifex
ACEFINRZ	francize
ACEFINST	fanciest
ACEFIORR	air force
ACEFIRRT	craftier
ACEFIRTT	trifecta
ACEFIRTY	feracity
ACEFLLOT	alto clef
ACEFLLOV	calf love
ACEFLMNO	flamenco
ACEFLNOR	falconer
ACEFLNOT	conflate,
	falconet
ACEFLNRY	crane-fly
ACEFLORS	alfresco
ACEFLRTU	crateful,
	fulcrate
ACEFNORV	conferva
ACEFORST	forecast
ACEFRRSU	surfacer
ACEFRRTU	fracture
ACEGGIRR	craggier
ACEGHHIN	Haicheng
ACEGHHNN	Hancheng
ACEGHILT	lich-gate,
	teiglach
ACEGHINT	teaching
ACEGHLTY	lych-gate
ACEGHLUY	gauchely
ACEGHMMU	chummage
ACEGHMOR	echogram
ACEGHORV	gavroche
ACEGIIMP	epigamic
ACEGIINV	vicinage
ACEGIKMT	tickameg
ACEGILLR	allergic
ACEGILMU	mucilage
ACEGILNR	clearing
ACEGILNW	lacewing
ACEGILOR	agricole
ACEGILRV	claviger
ACEGILRY	glyceria
ACEGILST	gelastic
ACEGILTV	vectigal
ACEGIMMT	tagmemic
ACEGIMNR	germanic
ACEGIMNS	magnesic
ACEGIMNT	magnetic
ACEGIMRR	grimacer
ACEGIMRS	Graecism

ACEGINNO canoeing
ACEGINRT argentic, catering
ACEGINSS caginess
ACEGINSW wing-case
ACEGINTX exacting
ACEGIOTT cogitate
ACEGIPRT price tag
ACEGIPTY city page
ACEGIRST agrestic, ergastic
ACEGIRTT tiger-cat
ACEGJLOT joctaleg
ACEGKLOV gavelock
ACEGKRTU truckage
ACEGLLNO collagen
ACEGLNOT octangle
ACEGLNOY aglycone
ACEGLOSU glaucose
ACEGMMOS megacosm
ACEGMNOT coagment
ACEGMNOY geomancy
ACEGMOPS compages
ACEGMRRY gramercy
ACEGNNOY cyanogen
ACEGNNTY tangency
ACEGNOTT cagnotte
ACEGNRTU truncage
ACEGOORS cargoose
ACEGORST escargot
ACEGORTT cottager
ACEGORTY category
ACEGOTTY cottagey
ACEHHIPS cheapish
ACEHHIRR hierarch
ACEHHMNN henchman
ACEHHNRT ethnarch
ACEHHPRT heptarch
ACEHHRSU hachures
ACEHHRTT thatcher
ACEHHRTY hatchery, thearchy
ACEHHTTY hatchety
ACEHIIMS ischemia
ACEHIINT ethician
ACEHIIRT hieratic
ACEHIJKR hijacker
ACEHIKLR chalkier
ACEHIKRT thick ear
ACEHILLT hellicat
ACEHILMN inchmeal
ACEHILMP impleach
ACEHILMY lechayim
ACEHILNP cephalin
ACEHILNS cleanish
ACEHILNT chatline, ethnical
ACEHILNV valinche
ACEHILOR heroical
ACEHILPR parhelic
ACEHILRX exilarch
ACEHILTT athletic
ACEHIMMR arch-mime
ACEHIMPT empathic, emphatic
ACEHIMRS marchesi
ACEHIMST misteach, tachisme
ACEHIMTT thematic
ACEHINNT enanthic
ACEHINOT ethanoic, inchoate
ACEHINRR irenarch
ACEHINRS insearch
ACEHINRV vacherin
ACEHINST asthenic
ACEHIPRS aspheric, seraphic
ACEHIPRT chapiter, patchier, phreatic, pie chart, trapiche
ACEHIPST pastiche
ACEHIPTT pathetic
ACEHIPTW whitecap
ACEHIRST chariest, trash-ice
ACEHIRSU eucharis
ACEHIRTT chattier, chiretta, theatric
ACEHISST chastise
ACEHISTX cathexis
ACEHISTZ chastize
ACEHKLOV havelock
ACEHKLPR kreplach
ACEHKLTY latchkey
ACEHKOTU tuckahoe
ACEHKRSW skew arch
ACEHLLMO mallecho
ACEHLLOO coal-hole
ACEHLLOR orchella
ACEHLLSU halluces
ACEHLNOP cephalon
ACEHLNOU eulachon
ACEHLNPR plancher
ACEHLNPT planchet
ACEHLNRU launcher, relaunch
ACEHLOOT toloache, toolache
ACEHLOPU chaloupe
ACEHLORT chlorate, trochlea
ACEHLOST eschalot
ACEHLOTT tea cloth
ACEHLPRY chapelry
ACEHLRTU archlute, trauchle
ACEHLSSS cashless
ACEHLSTY chastely
ACEHLTTW twatchel
ACEHMNRT merchant
ACEHMNSS chessman
ACEHMORT chromate
ACEHMPRS champers
ACEHMRUY hyraceum
ACEHMSTT schmatte
ACEHMSTU mustache
ACEHNNOP pancheon
ACEHNNPT penchant
ACEHNOPR car phone, chaperon
ACEHNOPT cenotaph
ACEHNORR ranchero
ACEHNORT anchoret
ACEHNOST eschaton
ACEHNOSY honey sac
ACEHNPRT pentarch
ACEHNQUU Quechuan
ACEHNRSS archness
ACEHNRST snatcher
ACEHNRTT tranchet
ACEHNRTU chaunter
ACEHNSTU unchaste
ACEHOPRR reproach
ACEHOPRT parochet
ACEHORRV overarch
ACEHORST thoraces
ACEHORTT theocrat
ACEHORTU outreach
ACEHORTW cow-heart
ACEHOSST case-shot
ACEHOSSW showcase
ACEHOSTU soutache
ACEHOTWW cow-wheat
ACEHPRSU purchase
ACEHPRTY petchary
ACEHPSTY scyphate
ACEHQSUU Quechuas
ACEHRRST Chartres, starcher
ACEHRRTT tetrarch
ACEHRSSU chasseur
ACEHRSTW war chest
ACEHRTTY chattery, trachyte
ACEHSSSU chausses
ACEHSTTU cathetus
ACEIIINP epinicia
ACEIIKLN kalicine
ACEIILMN limacine
ACEIILNR irenical
ACEIILNS ensialic, salicine
ACEIILST silicate
ACEIIMSS aseismic
ACEIIMTU maieutic
ACEIINPS piscinae
ACEIINST canities
ACEIINTV inactive
ACEIIRRT criteria
ACEIIRTV caritive
ACEIJKLN jack-line
ACEIJMST majestic
ACEIJNRR jerrican
ACEIKKLS sacklike
ACEIKLLY claylike
ACEIKLRY creakily
ACEIKMNN nickname
ACEIKMRV maverick
ACEIKNPS capeskin
ACEIKNRR crankier
ACEIKNRS skincare

ACEIKORR	croakier
ACEIKOTW	Katowice
ACEIKPPR	pipe-rack
ACEIKSTT	tackiest
ACEILLMR	mill-race
ACEILLMT	metallic
ACEILLMY	mycelial
ACEILLOP	calliope
ACEILLOR	rocaille
ACEILLOT	teocalli
ACEILLOZ	alcolize, localize
ACEILLPR	calliper
ACEILLPS	allspice
ACEILLPY	epically
ACEILLRS	Carlisle
ACEILLRV	caviller
ACEILMMO	camomile
ACEILMMR	clammier
ACEILMNN	clinamen
ACEILMNO	coal mine
ACEILMNP	manciple
ACEILMNS	meniscal, mescalin
ACEILMNT	macilent
ACEILMOS	camisole
ACEILMPS	misplace
ACEILMRT	metrical
ACEILMRY	creamily
ACEILMST	clematis
ACEILMSU	musicale
ACEILNNP	pannicle, pinnacle
ACEILNNR	encrinal
ACEILNOR	acrolein, Caroline, Cornelia, lonicera
ACEILNPR	plancier
ACEILNPT	ice plant, planetic
ACEILNPU	pecunial
ACEILNRT	clarinet
ACEILNSS	laciness
ACEILNSY	saliency
ACEILOPR	capriole
ACEILOPT	poetical
ACEILORR	carriole
ACEILORS	scariole
ACEILORT	loricate
ACEILOST	societal
ACEILOSV	vocalise
ACEILOTV	locative
ACEILOTZ	zealotic
ACEILOVZ	vocalize
ACEILPPY	pipeclay
ACEILPRS	spiracle
ACEILPRT	particle, prelatic
ACEILPRU	peculiar
ACEILPRV	Percival
ACEILPSS	slip case
ACEILRSS	classier
ACEILRSV	versical, visceral

ACEILRTT	tetrical, tractile
ACEILRTU	Lucretia, reticula
ACEILRTV	vertical
ACEILRTY	literacy
ACEILRUZ	Lucrezia
ACEILSST	scaliest
ACEILSUV	vesicula
ACEILTVY	actively
ACEIMMNP	pemmican
ACEIMMST	metacism
ACEIMNOT	noematic
ACEIMNRU	manicure
ACEIMNST	semantic
ACEIMNSY	sycamine
ACEIMNTU	neumatic
ACEIMOST	osmicate
ACEIMOTX	toxaemic
ACEIMPRR	mericarp
ACEIMPSS	escapism
ACEIMPST	campiest, campsite
ACEIMRRW	war crime
ACEIMRST	matrices
ACEIMRTU	muricate
ACEIMSST	casteism
ACEINNOP	pinacone
ACEINNOT	enaction
ACEINNOZ	canonize
ACEINNRT	intrance
ACEINNST	canniest, instance
ACEINNSU	nuisance
ACEINNTU	nunciate, uncinate
ACEINNTY	ancienty
ACEINOPR	apocrine, caponier, procaine
ACEINOPZ	caponize
ACEINORS	scenario
ACEINORT	ceration, creation, reaction
ACEINORV	veronica
ACEINORX	anorexic
ACEINOST	canoeist
ACEINOTT	taconite
ACEINOTV	conative, invocate
ACEINOTX	exaction
ACEINPRS	scarpine
ACEINPRU	pecuniar
ACEINPTT	pittance
ACEINPTY	patiency
ACEINPUY	picayune
ACEINRRY	cinerary
ACEINRSS	raciness
ACEINRST	canister, cisterna, scantier
ACEINRTT	interact
ACEINRTV	navicert
ACEINRVY	vicenary

ACEINSSU	issuance
ACEINSTV	cistvaen, vesicant
ACEINTTU	tunicate
ACEINTTX	excitant
ACEINTTY	tenacity
ACEIOPRT	aporetic, operatic
ACEIORRT	race riot
ACEIORSV	varicose
ACEIOSSU	caesious
ACEIOTVV	vocative
ACEIOVVV	viva voce
ACEIPPRR	crappier, pericarp
ACEIPRRW	price war
ACEIPRST	crispate, patrices, practise
ACEIPRTY	apyretic
ACEIPSST	escapist, spaciest
ACEIQRRU	acquirer
ACEIRRSW	airscrew
ACEIRRTV	veratric
ACEIRSST	Castries, scariest
ACEIRSSV	vicaress
ACEIRSTT	cristate, scattier
ACEIRSTU	suricate
ACEIRSTZ	craziest
ACEIRTTU	urticate
ACEIRTTV	tractive
ACEIRTUV	curative
ACEIRTVY	veracity
ACEISSST	ecstasis
ACEISSSU	saucisse
ACEISSTU	sauciest, suitcase
ACEISSTV	cessavit
ACEISTTT	cattiest
ACEISTTU	eustatic
ACEISTTX	exstatic
ACEJKOOR	jackeroo
ACEJLORY	cajolery
ACEJMRST	scramjet
ACEJNRRY	jerrycan
ACEKKMRU	muckrake
ACEKKNRY	knackery
ACEKLLOY	Yale lock
ACEKLMPU	plum cake
ACEKLORV	laverock
ACEKLORW	lacework
ACEKLSSS	sackless
ACEKNNSW	swan-neck
ACEKNPRU	unpacker
ACEKNRRT	rack-rent
ACEKOORW	cookware
ACEKORSW	casework
ACEKPSSY	skyscape
ACEKQRUY	quackery
ACEKRSUV	Krusevac
ACEKSSUW	waesucks
ACELLLLW	cell wall

ACELLLRU cellular
ACELLMOU molecula
ACELLMST mast cell
ACELLMSU sacellum
ACELLNOT Lancelot
ACELLNRU lucernal
ACELLOPS collapse, escallop
ACELLORR caroller
ACELLORS sclareol
ACELLORV call-over, coverall, overcall
ACELLOSW coleslaw
ACELLOVY coevally
ACELLPSU pucellas
ACELLRSY sarcelly
ACELLRTY rectally
ACELLSSW clawless
ACELLSTU scutella
ACELMNOR amelcorn
ACELMNSS calmness
ACELMNSU scalenum, Uncle Sam
ACELMOPT compleat
ACELMORS scleroma
ACELMORY claymore
ACELMOSU maculose
ACELMSTU muscatel
ACELMTUU cumulate
ACELNNNO cannelon
ACELNNRS scrannel
ACELNNTU nucleant
ACELNORT Carleton
ACELNORV novercal
ACELNOSU lacunose
ACELNOTT Toltecan
ACELNOTU clean-out
ACELNOTV covalent
ACELNRVY cravenly
ACELNSSU scalenus
ACELOOPT octapole
ACELOOSS Colossae
ACELOPPU populace
ACELOPRS parclose
ACELOPRT pectoral
ACELOPRU opercula
ACELOPSU scopulae
ACELOPTU copulate, outplace
ACELOPTY calotype
ACELORSS lacrosse
ACELORST sectoral
ACELORSU carousel
ACELORSY coarsely
ACELORTU clear-out, colature
ACELOSTT cotsetla
ACELOSTU lacteous, osculate
ACELPPRS scrapple
ACELPRST spectral
ACELPRSU specular
ACELPTUY eucalypt
ACELQRUU claqueur

ACELRSSS scarless
ACELRSTT Scarlett, scrattle
ACELRSTU clauster, claustre
ACELRSTY castelry
ACELRSUU clausure
ACELRTTU cultrate
ACELSSTT tactless
ACEMMOTY mycetoma
ACEMNNTU nucament
ACEMNOOR Cameroon
ACEMNORR romancer
ACEMNORU cumarone
ACEMNOST camstone
ACEMNRSU sun cream
ACEMNRUY numeracy
ACEMOOST comatose
ACEMORRT cremator
ACEMORSY sycamore
ACEMORTY cometary
ACEMPSSU campuses
ACENNNOU announce
ACENNOSS canoness
ACENNOTV covenant
ACENNOTZ canzonet
ACENNPRY pernancy
ACENNSUY sea-cunny
ACENOOPT octopean
ACENOORT coronate
ACENOPRT portance
ACENOPST capstone, opencast
ACENOPTW Cape Town
ACENOQTU cotquean
ACENORRT Torrance
ACENORRW careworn
ACENORST ancestor, carstone
ACENORSU carneous, nacreous
ACENORTT contrate
ACENORTU courante, outrance
ACENOSST contessa
ACENOSSV cavesson
ACENOSTT constate
ACENOSUY cyaneous
ACENOTTT tent coat
ACENPTTU punctate
ACENRSTT transect
ACENRSTU Etruscan, recusant
ACENRSTY ancestry
ACENRTTU truncate
ACENRTUY centaury
ACENSSTW newscast
ACEOOPTT co-optate
ACEOORTV evocator, overcoat
ACEOPPRS copperas
ACEOPRTT attercop
ACEORRSU carouser
ACEORRTT retroact
ACEORRTU Eurocrat

ACEORSTT sectator
ACEORSTV overcast
ACEORTXY oxycrate
ACEOSSTU Sea Scout
ACEOSSUY soy sauce
ACEOSTTU outcaste
ACEPPRRS scrapper
ACEPPRTU per caput
ACEPRRTU capturer
ACEPRSTW screw-tap
ACEPRTTY cryptate
ACEPSTTY typecast
ACERRSUV verrucas
ACERSSUY Syracuse
ACERSTTU crustate
ACERSTTY cytaster
ACERTTUW cutwater
ACFFHNOR chaffron
ACFFIILO official
ACFFILNU fanciful
ACFFLOSW scofflaw
ACFGIIMN magnific
ACFGIIRV gravific
ACFGIKLS sick flag
ACFGITUY fugacity
ACFGLORT golf cart
ACFHHILN half-inch
ACFHHINW hawfinch
ACFHIJKS jackfish
ACFHILNO falchion
ACFHILOS coalfish
ACFHINOU fauchion
ACFHIRSW crawfish
ACFHIRSY crayfish
ACFHLOSW cash flow
ACFHLTUW watchful
ACFIILST fistical
ACFIILSV salvific
ACFIILTY facility
ACFIIMPS pacifism
ACFIIPST pacifist
ACFIISST fascitis
ACFIKLNS calfskin
ACFILLSY fiscally
ACFILMSU sulfamic
ACFILNOR florican
ACFILNPU Cup Final
ACFILORT trifocal
ACFILRTY craftily
ACFILSSY classify
ACFIMNRU francium
ACFINORT fraction
ACFINORU furicano
ACFINPRS scarf pin
ACFINSTY sanctify
ACFIOSTU factious
ACFKLLOR rockfall
ACFKLOPW wolf pack
ACFKLORS forslack
ACFKLOST lockfast
ACFKLRUW wrackful
ACFKOORR roof-rack
ACFKOSTT fatstock, soft tack
ACFLLMRU cram-full

ACFLMNOO mooncalf
ACFLNORY falconry
ACFLOOPS foolscap
ACFLOOST soft coal
ACFLORSU scrofula
ACFLOSUU faculous
ACFLRRUU furcular
ACFMOTTU factotum
ACFOOSTT cat's-foot
ACGGIINT gigantic
ACGGIIOS isagogic
ACGGILRY craggily
ACGGINNO congaing
ACGGIOOR coraggio
ACGGLNOU glucagon
ACGGLRSY scraggly
ACGHHIMP high camp
ACGHHINT hatching
ACGHHINZ Changzhi
ACGHHNSU Changshu
ACGHIIMN Michigan
ACGHIJNN Jinchang
ACGHIKNW whacking
ACGHILNO ichoglan
ACGHILNT latching
ACGHILNY achingly
ACGHILOR oligarch
ACGHILRT arc light
ACGHIMNR charming, marching
ACGHINPP chapping
ACGHINPT nightcap
ACGHINRR charring
ACGHINRS crashing
ACGHINRU churinga
ACGHINST scathing
ACGHINTT chatting
ACGHINTU Taichung
ACGHINTY yachting
ACGHIPRS graphics
ACGHLLOR gralloch
ACGHNNNO Nanchong
ACGHNOUZ Cangzhou
ACGHNRYY gynarchy
ACGHNTUU uncaught
ACGHORSU choragus
ACGIILNO logician
ACGIILNV caviling
ACGIILRS gracilis
ACGIINRT granitic
ACGIIORT cigarito
ACGIJNOR jargonic
ACGIKKLO goal kick
ACGIKLNT tackling, talcking
ACGIKLRY garlicky
ACGIKLST glastick
ACGIKNRT tracking
ACGILLLR call-girl
ACGILLNS call sign
ACGILMMN clamming
ACGILMTU glutamic
ACGILNOR caroling
ACGILNOU coagulin
ACGILNPP clapping
ACGILNST castling
ACGILNUY guanylic
ACGILRSU surgical
ACGILRTU glutaric
ACGIMMNR cramming
ACGIMMNS scamming
ACGIMORS orgasmic
ACGINNNS scanning
ACGINNRU uncaring
ACGINORY congiary
ACGINOST agnostic
ACGINPPR crapping
ACGINPRS scarping, scraping
ACGINPRU panurgic
ACGINRRS scarring
ACGINRRY carrying
ACGINSTT scatting
ACGINTUY nugacity
ACGIOORS gracioso
ACGIORST orgastic
ACGIORSU gracious
ACGJKLPU jack plug
ACGJLNOU conjugal
ACGLMOUU coagulum
ACGLNORU clangour
ACGLNOSU glucosan
ACGLOORY arcology
ACGLOSUU glaucous
ACGLSSTU cut glass
ACGNNOOT contango
ACGNORST congrats
ACHHIIJO Hachioji
ACHHILPT phthalic
ACHHINTW whinchat
ACHHINTY hyacinth
ACHHIPPR hipparch
ACHHLPRY phylarch
ACHHNTTU nuthatch
ACHHOSTW chat show
ACHHPTUZ chutzpah
ACHIILMS chiliasm
ACHIILST chiliast
ACHIIMNS Mishnaic
ACHIIMRT Mithraic
ACHIINPS Hispanic
ACHIINRT trichina
ACHIINST Chiantis
ACHIIRST rachitis
ACHIIRSU ischuria
ACHIJKPW whip-jack
ACHIKKSW kickshaw
ACHIKLLW hickwall
ACHIKLPT chalk pit
ACHIKNOP pachinko
ACHIKQSU quackish
ACHIKRSW rickshaw
ACHIKRTT hat-trick
ACHILLOR orchilla
ACHILLTT tlachtli
ACHILLTY city hall
ACHILMTY mythical
ACHILNNS clannish
ACHILNOO oolichan
ACHILNOS lichanos, Nicholas
ACHILNPS clanship
ACHILPSY physical
ACHILPTY patchily
ACHILRVY chivalry
ACHILTTY chattily
ACHIMMOS machismo
ACHIMMST mismatch
ACHIMNOP champion
ACHIMNOR choirman, harmonic
ACHIMNOX Chamonix
ACHIMNSU humanics, inasmuch
ACHIMPSS scampish
ACHIMRST Chartism
ACHIMRTY timarchy
ACHIMSSU chiasmus
ACHIMTUY cyathium
ACHINOPR parochin, prochain
ACHINORT anorthic, ranchito
ACHINOTZ hoactzin
ACHINPSY spinachy
ACHINSTY Scythian
ACHIORSS coarsish
ACHIORTV tovarich
ACHIPTTU chupatti
ACHIRRSY schryari
ACHIRRTY triarchy
ACHIRSTT Chartist
ACHISTTY chastity
ACHKMORS shamrock
ACHKNNUU nunchaku
ACHKNOOS can-hooks
ACHKNOOT cant-hook
ACHKSSUW aw-shucks
ACHKSTWY skywatch
ACHLLNWY lynch law
ACHLLOPT clapholt
ACHLLORY chorally
ACHLMOST samcloth
ACHLMSTZ schmaltz
ACHLNORT Charlton
ACHLOPRY polyarch
ACHLOPTT potlatch
ACHLOTWX waxcloth
ACHLRSTY chrystal
ACHMNORY monarchy, nomarchy
ACHMNRTU truchman
ACHMOOST samtchoo
ACHMOTTU outmatch
ACHNOPRU up-anchor
ACHNPPSS schnapps
ACHOOPRT parochot
ACHOORTU co-author
ACHOTTUW outwatch
ACHPRSTU pushcart
ACHPTTUY chupatty
ACIIILMN inimical
ACIIILNS Sicilian
ACIIILNV civilian

ACIIINST Sinaitic
ACIIKLNO kaolinic
ACIIKNNN cannikin
ACIIKNTY kyanitic
ACIILLTV villatic
ACIILLVW civil law
ACIILMNR criminal
ACIILMOT comitial
ACIILMPT palmitic
ACIILNOR ironical
ACIILNPT platinic
ACIILNRS Sinclair
ACIILRVW civil war
ACIIMNOR morainic
ACIIMNOS simoniac
ACIIMNOT amniotic
ACIIMNST actinism
ACIIMNSU musician
ACIIMNTU actinium
ACIIMNTV vitamin C
ACIIMNTY intimacy, minacity
ACIIMOST iotacism
ACIIMOTT amitotic
ACIIMPRT primatic
ACIIMPRV vampiric
ACIIMPTT pitmatic
ACIIMRST scimitar
ACIIMRSV vicarism
ACIIMRTU muriatic
ACIIMSTT atticism
ACIIMSTV activism
ACIIMTUV viaticum
ACIINNOT inaction, nicotian, nicotina
ACIINOPT optician
ACIINORZ zirconia
ACIINOSS assinico
ACIINOSV avionics
ACIINOTT citation
ACIINPRS Crispian
ACIINPSS piscinas
ACIINRSS narcissi
ACIIORST aoristic
ACIIORTV victoria
ACIIOSTT Taoistic
ACIIOTWY Iowa City
ACIIPPST papistic
ACIIPRST pirastic
ACIIRSST Triassic
ACIIRSTT artistic
ACIISTTU autistic
ACIISTTV activist
ACIITTTW Attic wit
ACIITTVY activity
ACIITVVY vivacity
ACIJKKPS skipjack
ACIJRSSU Jurassic
ACIJSUZZ jacuzzis
ACIKLLST Catskill, salt lick
ACIKLNOT anti-lock
ACIKLNPT planktic
ACIKLNRY crankily
ACIKLORY croakily
ACIKNNPR crankpin
ACIKNOTY cantikoy
ACILLLOP pollical
ACILLMMY clammily
ACILLMOS localism
ACILLMSU Camillus
ACILLNOO colonial
ACILLNOR carillon
ACILLNOS scallion
ACILLORT clitoral
ACILLORY collyria
ACILLOST localist
ACILLOSY socially
ACILLOTY locality
ACILLSSY classily
ACILMNNO non-claim
ACILMNOO cooliman
ACILMNOP complain
ACILMNOS laconism
ACILMOPR picloram, proclaim
ACILMOPT compital
ACILMOSV vocalism
ACILMPTU placitum
ACILMSSS classism
ACILMSTU salictum
ACILMSTY mystical
ACILMTUY ultimacy
ACILNOOT colation, location
ACILNOOV vocalion
ACILNOPS salpicon
ACILNOPT Platonic
ACILNORT contrail
ACILNOSU unsocial
ACILNOSV Slavonic
ACILNOUV univocal
ACILNOVV convival
ACILNRSU cislunar
ACILNRUY culinary
ACILNSTY scantily
ACILOPRT tropical
ACILOPRV valproic
ACILOPST postical
ACILORRV corrival
ACILORTV vortical
ACILORUV ovicular
ACILORYZ zircaloy
ACILOSSU ossicula
ACILOSTV vocalist
ACILOTVY vocality
ACILPRRU pluriarc
ACILPRSU spicular
ACILPSUU apiculus
ACILRTUV cultivar
ACILSSST classist
ACILSTTY scattily
ACIMMNOR cimmaron
ACIMMOSS acosmism
ACIMMTUY cymatium
ACIMNNNO cinnamon
ACIMNNOR Minorcan
ACIMNOOR acromion
ACIMNOPR maincrop
ACIMNORR cimarron
ACIMNORT romantic
ACIMNORU conarium, coumarin
ACIMNORY acrimony
ACIMNOST monastic
ACIMNOTT comitant
ACIMNOTU aconitum
ACIMNOTY onymatic
ACIMNPTY tympanic
ACIMNRSU craniums
ACIMOPRT impactor
ACIMOPTY optimacy
ACIMORSY cramoisy
ACIMOSST massicot
ACIMRRSY miscarry
ACIMRSTU Strumica
ACINNOOT conation, intonaco
ACINNOSS scansion
ACINNOST canonist, sanction
ACINNOTU continua
ACINNOTV invocant
ACINNRTY tyrannic
ACINNSTY instancy
ACINOOPR picaroon
ACINOOPT octopian
ACINOOTV vocation
ACINOPPT panoptic
ACINOPRS scoparin, Scorpian
ACINOPRT rapontic
ACINOQUV coq au vin
ACINORRT contrair
ACINORSS narcosis
ACINORST cantoris, cast iron
ACINORTT orticant, traction
ACINORTU curation, nocturia
ACINOSSY cyanosis
ACINOSTT oscitant
ACINOSTW wainscot
ACINOSWX coxswain
ACINOTTX toxicant
ACINPQUY piquancy
ACINPSTY synaptic
ACINRSTU saturnic
ACINRTTU taciturn
ACINRTUY tunicary
ACINSTTY sanctity
ACINSTYY syncytia
ACIOOPSU opacious
ACIOORRT oratoric
ACIOPRST piscator
ACIOPRTT protatic
ACIOPSST potassic
ACIOPSSU spacious
ACIOPSTU captious
ACIORRZZ carrozzi
ACIORSSU scarious
ACIORTTY atrocity, citatory

ACIORTVY voracity
ACIOSTUU cautious
ACIOSTUV Octavius
ACIRRTTX tractrix
ACIRRTUX curatrix
ACIRSSTY sacristy
ACKKLMSU Kalmucks
ACKKMOPR pockmark
ACKLLPSU skullcap
ACKLMNOS locksman
ACKLNOPS snap-lock
ACKLOOPW woolpack
ACKLOOSW woolsack
ACKLORST rock salt
ACKLPUUY puckauly
ACKMNOST stockman
ACKMOORT tack room
ACKMOPRW work camp
ACKOPRRT trap-rock
ACKOPRTT port tack
ACKPRSTU Turk's cap
ACLLLLOR roll-call
ACLLLNUU Lucullan
ACLLLOWY callowly
ACLLMNOU columnal
ACLLMORU corallum
ACLLMOSU mollusca
ACLLNORW Cornwall
ACLLOORT collator
ACLLOOSS colossal
ACLLORUY ocularly
ACLLOSSW low-class
ACLLRTUU cultural
ACLMMNOU communal
ACLMNOOO coolamon
ACLMNOOV Monclova
ACLMNORU columnar
ACLMNORY normalcy
ACLMORTU crotalum
ACLMORUU oraculum
ACLMOSTU customal
ACLMOTUU comutual
ACLMPRSU scalprum
ACLMRSUU muscular
ACLMSTUU custumal
ACLMSUUV vasculum
ACLNOORT colorant
ACLNOPSY syncopal
ACLNORSU consular
ACLNOSTU consulta, osculant
ACLNOSTY Clayton's
ACLNPSTU planctus
ACLNPTUU punctual, punctula
ACLOOPRR corporal
ACLOOPRT Coalport
ACLOORWY colorway
ACLOPPUY populacy
ACLOPRRU procural
ACLOPRRW prowl car
ACLOPRTU portulac
ACLOPRXY xylocarp
ACLOPSUU opuscula
ACLORRTU torcular
ACLORTUW law court
ACLOSSTU outclass
ACMMMOOY myocomma
ACMMNOSY scammony
ACMNNOOY onomancy
ACMNOOPR crampoon
ACMNOORT monocrat
ACMNOOTZ comozant
ACMNOOYZ zoomancy
ACMNORTU Turcoman
ACMNOSST Scotsman
ACMNSSTU sanctums
ACMOOORT coatroom
ACMOOPRS coprosma
ACMOORRT motor car
ACMOOSST scotomas
ACMORSTW worm-cast
ACMORSTY costmary
ACNNORST Scranton
ACNNOSTT constant
ACNNOSTU conusant
ACNOOORT octaroon
ACNOORRY coronary
ACNOORST ostracon
ACNOORSU canorous
ACNOORTY cartoony, octonary
ACNORRTY contrary
ACNORSTT contrast
ACNORSWW crown saw
ACNORTTU turncoat
ACNORTUY noctuary
ACNPRSUY sprauncy
ACOOPRRS corporas
ACOPRRTT protract
ACORRTTY tractory
ACORRTUY carry-out, curatory
ACORRTUZ razor cut
ACORSSTU tau cross
ACORSSUW curassow
ACORSSWY crossway
ACORSTTY cryostat
ACPSSTUY pussy cat
ADDDEEGR degraded
ADDDEELR laddered
ADDDEMNU addendum
ADDDEOOW dead wood
ADDDEOPR drop-dead
ADDDEORS addorsed
ADDEEEHS seed-head
ADDEEENR deadener
ADDEEFIL defilade
ADDEEFTT defatted
ADDEEGLN Danegeld
ADDEEGOR dog-eared
ADDEEGRR degrader
ADDEEGSS degassed
ADDEEGSW saw-edged
ADDEEHLY aldehyde
ADDEEHNR adherend
ADDEEHRT threaded
ADDEEILN deadline
ADDEEILP deep-laid
ADDEEILR deadlier, redialed
ADDEEIMT dead time
ADDEEISS diseased
ADDEELLM medalled
ADDEELLP pedalled
ADDEELNU unleaded
ADDEELUV devalued
ADDEEMNR demander
ADDEENPX expanded
ADDEENSS deadness
ADDEENTU denudate
ADDEEPRT departed
ADDEERRT retarded
ADDEFILT dead lift
ADDEFILY field day
ADDEFIST faddiest
ADDEFLRU dreadful
ADDEFORW word-deaf
ADDEFRRW red dwarf
ADDEGIRS disgrade
ADDEGLNO long-dead
ADDEGLST gladdest
ADDEGRRU Red Guard
ADDEHHLN hand-held
ADDEHHNS shedhand
ADDEHIIJ Jedidiah
ADDEHILN hideland
ADDEHILR dihedral
ADDEHIMS made dish
ADDEHINW headwind
ADDEHMRU drumhead
ADDEHNRU Dehra Dun
ADDEHNSU unshaded
ADDEHOOR door head
ADDEHOPR drophead
ADDEHORR hard doer
ADDEHORW headword
ADDEHOST dead shot
ADDEHRTY hydrated
ADDEHSTU Thaddeus
ADDEIITV additive
ADDEIKNP kidnaped
ADDEILNS landside
ADDEILNT tideland
ADDEIMNR mind-read
ADDEIMST midstead
ADDEIMTT admitted
ADDEINOS adenoids
ADDEINST dandiest
ADDEIORS roadside, side road
ADDEIPPR didapper
ADDEIPRS dispread
ADDEIQSU squaddie
ADDEIRSU radiused
ADDEIRSW sideward
ADDEISSU dissuade
ADDELMOS dolmades
ADDELNNS Land's End
ADDELNOU duodenal
ADDELNPU pudendal
ADDELNRS Redlands
ADDELNSU unsaddle
ADDELNSV sandveld

ADDELOOR eldorado
ADDELOSS dead loss
ADDELPRS spraddle
ADDELRST straddle
ADDELRSY saddlery
ADDELRTW twaddler
ADDEMOSY Domesday
ADDENNSU sand dune
ADDENPRU undraped
ADDEOTTU outdated
ADDEPRSU superadd
ADDFFILO daffodil
ADDFFNRU dandruff
ADDFNORU road fund
ADDFORRT Dartford
ADDGGILN gladding
ADDGLORU old guard
ADDGMRUU mudguard
ADDGOQSU God squad
ADDGORSW godwards
ADDHHLNO handhold
ADDHIKRS hard disk
ADDHINSY dandyish
ADDHLOOY ladyhood
ADDHOORW hardwood
ADDIILUV dividual
ADDIIMRU Diarmuid
ADDIINOT addition
ADDIINTV dividant
ADDIJMNY jim-dandy
ADDIKORS skid road
ADDILLNY dandilly
ADDILMOP diploma'd
ADDILNNW land-wind
ADDIMNSY dandyism
ADDINNOR ordinand
ADDINQUY quiddany
ADDINRWW windward
ADDIORTY additory
ADDIPTUY duty-paid
ADDKNRRU drunkard
ADDLLNOR landlord
ADDLNNOW downland
ADDLNOOW download, woodland
ADDLORSY Lord's Day
ADDMOOSY doomsday
ADDNOPWY pandowdy
ADDNORWW downward, drawdown
ADDOORRY dooryard
ADDOORWW woodward
ADDOORWY woodyard
ADEEEFLR lead-free
ADEEEFLS seed-leaf
ADEEEFNY fedayeen
ADEEEFRT federate
ADEEEGLT delegate
ADEEEGNR renegade
ADEEEGNT teenaged
ADEEEGPS gape-seed
ADEEEGRS degrease
ADEEEHSY eye-shade
ADEEEINT detainee
ADEEEIUV eau-de-vie
ADEEEKNY naked eye
ADEEELMN enameled
ADEEELSW weaseled
ADEEELTV elevated
ADEEEMNT emendate
ADEEEMRU emeraude
ADEEENRS serenade
ADEEENTT attendee, edentate
ADEEEPRS rapeseed
ADEEFHNR freehand
ADEEFHOR forehead
ADEEFILN enfilade
ADEEFIRR rarefied
ADEEFLMS self-made
ADEEFLOR freeload
ADEEFLPR pedalfer
ADEEFLRR deferral
ADEEFLSS fadeless
ADEEFLSX flaxseed
ADEEFMNR freedman
ADEEFMTU deaf mute
ADEEFNOT tone-deaf
ADEEFNSS deafness
ADEEFRRT raftered
ADEEFRTU featured
ADEEGILO ego-ideal
ADEEGINN digenean
ADEEGIRS disagree
ADEEGIRT gaitered
ADEEGLLN Glendale
ADEEGLLV gavelled
ADEEGLNT delegant
ADEEGLPR pedregal
ADEEGLRV graveled
ADEEGMNR gendarme
ADEEGMOP megapode
ADEEGNNR endanger
ADEEGNNV vendange
ADEEGNOR renegado
ADEEGNRR gardener
ADEEGNRU dungaree, under age
ADEEGORT derogate
ADEEGORV overaged
ADEEGPRT pargeted
ADEEGRRT gartered
ADEEGRSS dressage
ADEEGRTT targeted
ADEEGSWY edgeways
ADEEHIKZ Zedekiah
ADEEHILN headline
ADEEHIPR pier-head
ADEEHIST headiest
ADEEHISV adhesive
ADEEHKNR daker-hen
ADEEHKRT thekedar
ADEEHKWW hawkweed
ADEEHKWY hawk-eyed
ADEEHLLW well-head
ADEEHLNO dane-hole
ADEEHLNR rehandle
ADEEHLNU unhealed
ADEEHLRT haltered, threadle
ADEEHLSS headless
ADEEHLTY heatedly
ADEEHMMO home-made
ADEEHMNN menhaden
ADEEHNNR enharden
ADEEHNOT headnote
ADEEHNRR hardener
ADEEHNRT adherent
ADEEHNTU unheated
ADEEHORS sorehead
ADEEHORV overhead
ADEEHRRT threader
ADEEHRRW Hereward
ADEEHRST headrest
ADEEIILS idealise
ADEEIILZ idealize
ADEEIJMR jeremiad
ADEEIKKS kiskadee
ADEEIKLS lakeside
ADEEILLN Danielle
ADEEILLO oeillade
ADEEILMN endemial, Madeline
ADEEILMR remedial
ADEEILMT lead time
ADEEILMV medieval
ADEEILMZ medalize
ADEEILNT date line
ADEEILNU eau-de-Nil
ADEEILPR pedalier
ADEEILPS Pleiades
ADEEILPT depilate, pileated
ADEEILRS sidereal
ADEEIMNT dementia
ADEEIMRR dreamier
ADEEIMRT diameter, diatreme
ADEEIMST Tameside
ADEEIMTT meditate
ADEEINNR Adrienne
ADEEINNS andesine
ADEEINPT diapente, neap tide
ADEEINRS arsedine, arsenide, nearside
ADEEINRT detainer
ADEEINST andesite
ADEEINTZ denizate
ADEEIPPR piperade
ADEEIPRS air speed
ADEEIRRR drearier
ADEEIRST readiest, steadier
ADEEIRTV derivate
ADEEISST set-aside, side seat
ADEEISSV adessive
ADEEISTV sedative
ADEEITVW tidewave
ADEEKKRR Kerkrade
ADEEKMRT marketed
ADEEKNNR endarken
ADEEKNNY kennedya

ADEEKNPW knapweed
ADEEKNRR darkener
ADEEKRWY werkeday
ADEELLLP lapelled
ADEELLMT metalled
ADEELLMW well-made
ADEELLNP panelled
ADEELLNY leadenly
ADEELLPR pedaller, predella
ADEELLPT petalled
ADEELLQU equalled
ADEELLRS sardelle
ADEELLRU laureled
ADEELLRV ravelled
ADEELLRW well-read
ADEELLSS leadless
ADEELLTY elatedly
ADEELLWY wall-eyed
ADEELMNO lemonade
ADEELMNT lamented
ADEELMRS demersal
ADEELMRV marveled
ADEELNNU unaneled
ADEELNOR oleander
ADEELNRT antlered
ADEELNRV lavender
ADEELNSU unsealed
ADEELNTT talented
ADEELOPR lop-eared
ADEELORV overlade
ADEELOST desolate
ADEELPPT lappeted
ADEELPST pedestal
ADEELRRR larderer
ADEELRRY readerly
ADEELRTV traveled
ADEELRUV revalued
ADEELSST dateless, detassel, tasseled
ADEELSTY sedately
ADEELSUV devalues
ADEEMMSS Mesdames
ADEEMMXY myxedema
ADEEMNNR mannered, remanned
ADEEMNOR demeanor
ADEEMNOT nematode
ADEEMNOU eudaemon
ADEEMNPR dampener
ADEEMNPY ependyma
ADEEMNSS seedsman
ADEEMNTW metewand
ADEEMNTY metadyne
ADEEMORT moderate
ADEEMPST stampede
ADEEMRSU measured
ADEEMRTW wet dream
ADEENNPT pennated
ADEENNRU unearned
ADEENNST tenendas
ADEENNUW unweaned
ADEENOPW weaponed
ADEENORV endeavor
ADEENOTT detonate
ADEENPPR endpaper
ADEENPPW wappened
ADEENPRX expander
ADEENRRW wanderer
ADEENRSS dearness
ADEENRSU undersea
ADEENRTT attender
ADEENRTU denature
ADEENSSU danseuse, Sudanese
ADEENTTV vendetta
ADEEORTT tree toad
ADEEPPRW wappered
ADEEPRRS spreader
ADEEPRRT departer
ADEEPRST pederast
ADEEPRSU persuade
ADEEPRTU depurate
ADEEPSWY speedway
ADEERRRT retarder
ADEERRRW warderer
ADEERRTW redwater
ADEERTTT tattered
ADEERVYY everyday
ADEFFIST daffiest
ADEFFORT trade-off
ADEFFOSW sawed-off
ADEFGGOT faggoted
ADEFGILR Garfield
ADEFGILS gas field
ADEFGIRS gas-fired
ADEFGIRT driftage
ADEFGITU fatigued
ADEFGLLO gold leaf
ADEFGLOT gatefold
ADEFGLRU feldgrau
ADEFGNOR frondage
ADEFGNRR grandfer
ADEFHILT Hatfield
ADEFHILY hayfield
ADEFHLNT left hand
ADEFHLTU deathful
ADEFHNOR forehand
ADEFIILR airfield
ADEFIKRR Fredrika
ADEFILLT ill-fated
ADEFILNR filander
ADEFILOR forelaid
ADEFILOT foliated
ADEFILRW Wilfreda
ADEFIMPR firedamp
ADEFINRR infrared
ADEFINRU Freudian
ADEFINRW fine-draw
ADEFINYZ denazify
ADEFIORS foresaid
ADEFLLLU ladleful
ADEFLLRY alder fly
ADEFLLUY feudally
ADEFLMRU dreamful
ADEFLNOR foreland
ADEFLNRY lady-fern
ADEFLOPR drop-leaf
ADEFLORT deflator
ADEFLORY forelady
ADEFLPRS feldspar
ADEFLPSU spadeful
ADEFLRTW leftward
ADEFMNRU unframed
ADEFMOSU defamous
ADEFNNOR Fernando
ADEFNOOV Vodafone
ADEFORRR forrader
ADEFORRY foreyard, orfrayed
ADEFORUV favoured
ADEGGIRR draggier
ADEGGIST daggiest
ADEGGJLY jaggedly
ADEGGLRY raggedly
ADEGGMOY demagogy
ADEGGOPY pedagogy
ADEGGRTY gadgetry
ADEGHHOS hogshead
ADEGHILT alighted
ADEGHINS sheading
ADEGHIRT third age
ADEGHLNO headlong
ADEGHORT goatherd
ADEGHRTU daughter
ADEGIILP diplegia
ADEGIINN indigena
ADEGIITT digitate
ADEGIKOR Oak Ridge
ADEGILLR grillade
ADEGILNP pedaling, pleading
ADEGILNR dearling, dragline, Reginald
ADEGILNS dealings, signaled
ADEGILOU dialogue
ADEGILRS Griselda
ADEGILSS glissade
ADEGILSV disgavel
ADEGIMNR margined, mid-range
ADEGIMOR ideogram
ADEGINNR indanger
ADEGINOR organdie
ADEGINOS diagnose, San Diego
ADEGINRS disrange
ADEGINRT gradient, red giant
ADEGINST steading
ADEGINSU Agnus Dei
ADEGIORR drageoir
ADEGIRWY ridgeway
ADEGISSU disusage
ADEGISTU gaudiest
ADEGIUWY guideway
ADEGLLNU glandule
ADEGLLOP galloped
ADEGLLSS gladless
ADEGLMOS gladsome
ADEGLMPU plumaged
ADEGLNOS dal segno

ADEGLNRS glanders
ADEGLNSS gladness
ADEGLNUZ unglazed
ADEGLORW low-grade
ADEGMNOR dragomen
ADEGMNOY endogamy
ADEGMORW word game
ADEGMOST dog's meat
ADEGNNOR androgen
ADEGNNRY gynander
ADEGNOPU poundage
ADEGNORT dragonet
ADEGNORU arguendo
ADEGNRRU grandeur
ADEGNRUZ gazunder
ADEGOORY goodyear, goodyera
ADEGOPRR prograde
ADEGORTW water-dog
ADEGRRST dragster
ADEHHIPS headship
ADEHHIST shithead
ADEHHNTU headhunt
ADEHIILP hepialid
ADEHIKLT Dalkeith
ADEHIKLV Khedival
ADEHIKNS skinhead
ADEHILNP Delphian
ADEHILNR hard line
ADEHIMNR hired man
ADEHIMRY hydremia
ADEHINOP diaphone
ADEHINOS adhesion
ADEHINOY hyoidean
ADEHINRS Sheridan
ADEHINST handiest
ADEHINTT dainteth
ADEHIPRS Sephardi
ADEHIRRT trihedra
ADEHIRST disheart, hardiest
ADEHISST shadiest
ADEHJLOT jolt-head
ADEHJNOR Dear John
ADEHKLNU lunkhead
ADEHKNRS redshank
ADEHKNSU skean-dhu
ADEHKORW headwork
ADEHLLOO hallooed
ADEHLLRS hard sell
ADEHLLRW hellward
ADEHLMNO homeland
ADEHLNNO lone hand
ADEHLNSS handless
ADEHLOPS asphodel
ADEHLOST lead shot
ADEHLRRY heraldry
ADEHMMMO Mohammed
ADEHMMSU meshumad
ADEHMNOS handsome
ADEHMNOT thanedom
ADEHMNRS herdsman
ADEHMNRU unharmed
ADEHMOOR headroom
ADEHMORW homeward
ADEHMOST headmost
ADEHMOSU madhouse
ADEHNORV handover, overhand
ADEHNOSS sand-shoe
ADEHNOSW enshadow
ADEHNPRS sharp end
ADEHNRSS hardness
ADEHNRSU unshared
ADEHNRTU unthread
ADEHNSSU sunshade
ADEHNSUV unshaved
ADEHNSUW unwashed
ADEHOORT Dorothea, Theodora
ADEHOORW harewood
ADEHOPRS rhapsode
ADEHOPXY hexapody
ADEHORSW shadower
ADEHORTT throated
ADEHORTW death row
ADEHPSUW washed up
ADEIIKOT Ado-Ekiti
ADEIILMS idealism
ADEIILPT piliated
ADEIILST idealist
ADEIILTY ideality
ADEIIMNN indamine
ADEIIMNR meridian
ADEIIMNV vendimia
ADEIIMPR impaired
ADEIINNS sanidine
ADEIINOT ideation, inodiate, iodinate, taenioid
ADEIINRT daintier
ADEIINRV invaried
ADEIINST adenitis
ADEIITTV tidivate
ADEIITUV auditive
ADEIKLLY ladylike
ADEIKLNS sandlike
ADEIKLOX alkoxide
ADEIKLSW sidewalk
ADEIKMRT tidemark
ADEILLMO melodial
ADEILLMY medially
ADEILLNN landline
ADEILLNO load line
ADEILLNU unallied
ADEILLNV Danville
ADEILLOV live load
ADEILLPR pillared
ADEILLPS spadille
ADEILLPW well-paid
ADEILLRT trialled
ADEILLRV rivalled
ADEILMNN landmine
ADEILMNO melanoid
ADEILMNY maidenly, medianly
ADEILMOR modeliar
ADEILMOS modalise, soda lime
ADEILMOZ modalize
ADEILMPP palmiped
ADEILMPS sidelamp
ADEILMRY dreamily
ADEILMST medalist
ADEILMSV Maldives
ADEILNNR inlander
ADEILNNT dentinal
ADEILNNV Vineland
ADEILNOP palinode
ADEILNOT delation, dial tone
ADEILNOZ indazole
ADEILNPT pantiled
ADEILNRR lardiner
ADEILNRS islander
ADEILNST destinal
ADEILNTV divalent
ADEILNUV invalued
ADEILOPS elasipod
ADEILOPT petaloid
ADEILORT idolater, tailored
ADEILORV overlaid
ADEILORX exordial
ADEILOST diastole, isolated
ADEILOTT datolite
ADEILOTV dovetail
ADEILPPP pedipalp
ADEILPRS spiraled
ADEILPRT dipteral, tripedal
ADEILPRU epidural, preludia
ADEILPRV deprival
ADEILPTU plaudite
ADEILRRT triedral
ADEILRRY drearily
ADEILRSU residual
ADEILRTT detrital
ADEILRTY dielytra
ADEILRVY devil ray, variedly
ADEILSSY dialyses
ADEILSTY diastyle, steadily
ADEILSUV disvalue
ADEILSWY slideway
ADEILSXY dyslexia
ADEILTTU altitude, latitude
ADEIMMNO monamide
ADEIMMST mismated
ADEIMNNO demonian
ADEIMNOP dopamine
ADEIMNOT dominate, nematoid
ADEIMNOZ nomadize
ADEIMNRZ zemindar
ADEIMNSS sidesman
ADEIMNSY dynamise
ADEIMNSZ man-sized
ADEIMNTY dynamite
ADEIMNYZ dynamize

ADEIMORT mediator
ADEIMOSS sesamoid
ADEIMRRS disarmer
ADEIMRSS side arms
ADEIMRST distream
ADEIMRTW midwater
ADEIMRXY ready-mix
ADEINNOT antinode
ADEINNOV Devonian
ADEINNPT pinnated
ADEINNRZ rendzina
ADEINNSX disannex
ADEINNTU inundate
ADEINOPT antipode
ADEINORR ordainer
ADEINORT deration, ordinate
ADEINORZ anodizer
ADEINOST astonied, sedation
ADEINOTT antidote, tetanoid
ADEINOTV donative
ADEINOUZ douzaine
ADEINPPX appendix
ADEINPRT dipteran
ADEINPRU unpaired
ADEINPSV spavined
ADEINQTU antiqued
ADEINRRS serranid
ADEINRSS aridness
ADEINRST randiest, strained
ADEINRSU denarius
ADEINRSV sandiver
ADEINRTT nitrated
ADEINRTU indurate
ADEINRUV unvaried
ADEINRVY vineyard
ADEINRWW wanweird
ADEINSST sandiest
ADEINSSV vanessid
ADEINSTY desyatin
ADEINSVW swan-dive
ADEIOPRS diaspore
ADEIOPRV overpaid, poivrade
ADEIOPST dioptase
ADEIOPTV adoptive
ADEIORST asteroid
ADEIORTT teratoid
ADEIORTV deviator
ADEIPRST rapidest
ADEIPRTU eupatrid
ADEIPTTU aptitude
ADEIQSUY quayside
ADEIRRTW tawdrier
ADEIRRWW wiredraw
ADEIRSST disaster
ADEIRSSU radiuses
ADEIRSTT striated, tardiest
ADEIRTUV durative
ADEIRVWY driveway
ADEISSTT distaste
ADEISSWY sideways
ADEITTTU attitude
ADEJLMPU jump lead
ADEJMNTU adjument
ADEJOPRY jeopardy
ADEJRSTU adjuster, readjust
ADEKLMRY markedly
ADEKLNOP pelandok
ADEKLOOW Lakewood
ADEKLORW leadwork
ADEKMNRU unmarked
ADEKMORS darksome
ADEKNNSS dankness
ADEKNRSS darkness
ADEKORSY dyer's oak
ADELLMOR moralled
ADELLMRU medullar, muralled
ADELLNNU annulled
ADELLNOZ donzella
ADELLNSS landless
ADELLNSW Sandwell, Wallsend
ADELLNUW unwalled
ADELLOOW lead wool
ADELLOPW walloped
ADELLOSV lad's love
ADELLOTT allotted, totalled
ADELLOVY lady-love
ADELLRWW draw-well
ADELMMOP melampod
ADELMNNS landsmen
ADELMNOS lodesman
ADELMOOS loadsome
ADELMOST salt dome
ADELMOTU modulate
ADELMRRU demurral
ADELNOPR ponderal
ADELNORU unloader
ADELNORV overland, rondavel
ADELNOTU nodulate
ADELNPRS spandrel
ADELNPRU pendular
ADELNRSY lysarden
ADELNRTY ardently
ADELNRUY underlay
ADELNRVY lavendry
ADELNSTU unsalted
ADELNSTW westland
ADELNTUU undulate
ADELNUUV unvalued
ADELOOPV levodopa
ADELOORV overload
ADELOPRU palourde
ADELOPRW poleward
ADELOPTY petalody
ADELORSS roadless
ADELORST lodestar
ADELORTW leadwort
ADELOVWY avowedly
ADELPPRY dapperly
ADELPQUX quadplex
ADELPRRU larruped
ADELPRTY dry plate
ADELPSTT splatted
ADELRTUY adultery
ADEMMNOR memorand
ADEMMOTY ammodyte
ADEMNNNU unmanned
ADEMNOPR name-drop, pardon me, pomander
ADEMNOPT tamponed
ADEMNORT moderant
ADEMNORY Raymonde
ADEMNOUY you and me
ADEMNPPU unmapped
ADEMNPSS dampness
ADEMNRRU underarm
ADEMNRTU undreamt
ADEMNRUW unwarmed
ADEMNSUU unamused
ADEMOORT moderato
ADEMORRU armoured
ADEMORTW meadwort
ADEMPRUW warmed-up
ADENNNTU untanned
ADENNORS Anderson
ADENNOTU unatoned
ADENNRUW unwarned
ADENNTUW unwanted
ADENNTUX exundant
ADENOORW wanderoo
ADENOPRR pardoner
ADENOPSY dyspnoea
ADENORTW downrate
ADENORUX rondeaux
ADENOSSY Odyssean
ADENOUVW unavowed
ADENPPTU untapped
ADENPRTY pedantry
ADENPRUY underpay
ADENQRSU squander
ADENRSSU saunders
ADENRSTU transude
ADENSTTU unstated, untasted
ADENSTUY unsteady
ADENSUWY unswayed
ADEOOPSS apodoses
ADEOORRT toreador
ADEOOSTW Eastwood
ADEOOTTT tattooed
ADEOPPRR pear drop
ADEOPRRS ear drops
ADEOPRRT parroted, predator, teardrop
ADEOPRRY rope-yard
ADEOPRTT tetrapod
ADEOPSTT postdate
ADEOPTTU up to date
ADEORRST roadster
ADEORRVW overdraw
ADEORSST assorted
ADEORSTT road test
ADEORSTX extrados

ADEPPRST	strapped
ADEPRSTT	spratted
ADEQSTTU	squatted
ADERRSSW	wardress
ADERRSTT	redstart
ADERSTTU	statured
ADERSTWW	westward
ADFFILLO	affodill
ADFFNOST	stand-off
ADFFOOST	fast food
ADFFORRT	Trafford
ADFFORST	Stafford
ADFGIINR	infra dig
ADFGINNU	unfading
ADFGLOUW	God-awful
ADFGLRUU	guardful
ADFGMNOO	man of God
ADFHIOST	toadfish
ADFHIRSW	dwarfish
ADFHLLNU	full hand
ADFHLOST	holdfast
ADFHORRT	Hartford
ADFIILPY	lapidify
ADFIILRW	Wilfrida
ADFIINTY	daintify
ADFIIORX	radio fix
ADFIIRST	first aid
ADFILLLN	landfill
ADFILLNW	windfall
ADFILMNO	manifold
ADFILMRU	fluidram
ADFILNOS	flindosa
ADFILNTU	latifund
ADFIMNRW	wind farm
ADFIMRSW	dwarfism
ADFINSTW	fast-wind
ADFIORSV	disfavor
ADFLLNOW	downfall
ADFLMNOO	damn-fool
ADFLMNOR	landform
ADFLMNOY	manyfold
ADFLMOPR	frampold
ADFLNOST	soft-land
ADFMORRW	fromward
ADFMORST	Stamford
ADFMRSTU	stud farm
ADFNOORZ	forzando
ADFNOPRU	profunda
ADFNORST	forstand, Stanford
ADFORRSW	forwards
ADGGGINR	dragging
ADGGILNU	gaulding
ADGGLRSU	sluggard
ADGGNORR	grognard
ADGHHILN	highland
ADGHHIOR	high road
ADGHILTY	daylight
ADGHINOR	hoarding
ADGHINPR	handgrip
ADGHITTW	tightwad
ADGHLNNO	longhand
ADGHNNUU	Dunhuang
ADGHNOOZ	Zhaodong
ADGHRTUY	draughty
ADGIIIRT	tigridia
ADGIILLN	dialling
ADGIILLO	gladioli
ADGIIMNR	admiring
ADGIINRY	dairying
ADGIINTU	auditing
ADGIKLNR	darkling
ADGILLNR	land girl
ADGILLNU	dualling
ADGILLNW	Dingwall
ADGILMOR	marigold
ADGILNNS	sandling
ADGILNRY	daringly
ADGILNZZ	dazzling
ADGILOPR	prodigal
ADGILOST	dog's-tail
ADGILRTU	tragulid
ADGIMNNU	maunding
ADGINNST	standing
ADGINNTU	daunting
ADGINOOP	poignado
ADGINOOR	organoid, rigadoon
ADGINORR	ring road
ADGINORS	road sign
ADGINRTT	dratting
ADGINRTY	grandity
ADGIOPRS	grapsoid
ADGKOOSZ	gadzooks
ADGLOOPR	drop goal
ADGLOORY	gardyloo
ADGMNORU	gourmand
ADGMOOOO	moodooga
ADGNNOQU	quandong
ADGNNORS	grandson
ADGNOORU	go-around
ADGOPRST	postgrad
ADGOPRSU	podargus
ADGPRRUU	Durgapur
ADHHINPW	whip hand
ADHHIPRS	hardship
ADHHNORU	hour hand
ADHHNRTY	hydranth
ADHIILLP	Phillida
ADHIIMPS	amidship
ADHIINOP	ophidian
ADHIINTT	daintith
ADHIJMTU	mujtahid
ADHILLMN	millhand
ADHILLNS	sandhill
ADHILLOP	phalloid
ADHILLOT	thalloid
ADHILLPY	Phyllida
ADHILNST	handlist
ADHILOPS	shipload
ADHILPSY	ladyship
ADHIMNOS	admonish
ADHIMNOU	humanoid
ADHIMNRT	third man
ADHIMOPP	amphipod
ADHINNOR	iron hand
ADHINOPY	diaphony
ADHINRUZ	druzhina
ADHINRWY	whinyard
ADHINSSY	sandyish
ADHINSTU	dianthus
ADHIOSTY	toadyish
ADHIPRSW	wardship
ADHIPRSY	shipyard
ADHIRTWW	withdraw
ADHKNORW	handwork
ADHLLNOS	Hollands
ADHLLNOY	Holy Land
ADHLMORT	thraldom
ADHLNOOT	hand tool
ADHLNOPR	Randolph
ADHLNORW	waldhorn
ADHLNSTU	Landshut
ADHLOPSU	Adolphus
ADHMNPPU	handpump
ADHMOPRU	road hump
ADHNNOOR	honorand
ADHNORSU	Honduras
ADHNOSTU	thousand
ADHNOSWW	washdown
ADHOOPRS	hospodar
ADHOORSW	roadshow
ADHOPRSY	rhapsody
ADHORRTY	hydrator
ADHORSTY	short-day
ADHPSTYY	dyspathy
ADHRSTUY	Thursday
ADIIIKNN	India ink
ADIIILNR	idrialin
ADIIINNT	initiand
ADIIINRV	viridian
ADIIIQRU	daiquiri
ADIIKLLN	kallidin
ADIIKLMM	milkmaid
ADIIKLST	tail-skid
ADIIKNOP	pinakoid
ADIILLMR	milliard
ADIILLST	diallist
ADIILLUV	diluvial
ADIILMNO	dominial
ADIILNOT	dilation
ADIILNSU	indusial
ADIILNSW	wind-sail
ADIILNTW	tailwind
ADIILNTY	daintily
ADIILNUV	diluvian
ADIILOPP	diplopia
ADIILPST	lapidist
ADIILSSY	dialysis
ADIILTVY	validity
ADIIMNOT	intimado
ADIIMNTV	vitamin D
ADIINNOT	nidation
ADIINNOZ	diazinon
ADIINOSY	Dionysia
ADIINOTU	audition
ADIINPST	dispaint
ADIINRST	distrain
ADIIOPRT	tapiroid
ADIIOPSX	apodixis
ADIIORST	tarsioid
ADIIOSUV	avidious
ADIIPRTY	rapidity
ADIIPSTY	sapidity
ADIIPTVY	vapidity

ADIIRSTT	distrait	**ADIMOSTY**	toadyism	**ADLORSTW**	last word
ADIJKORS	koradjis	**ADIMOTUX**	taxodium	**ADLORTWY**	towardly
ADIJNPRU	Dinajpur	**ADIMRRSY**	dismarry	**ADLPRUWY**	upwardly
ADIKLLOR	road kill	**ADIMRSUU**	sudarium	**ADMMNOOS**	doomsman
ADIKLNPS	landskip	**ADIMSSTU**	stadiums	**ADMMNORU**	Omdurman
ADIKNNNU	dunnakin	**ADINNNTU**	inundant	**ADMNNORY**	monandry
ADIKNNST	inkstand	**ADINNOOT**	donation	**ADMNNOTU**	notandum
ADIKNOPY	pyinkado	**ADINNORT**	ordinant	**ADMNOORS**	Rosamond
ADIKNORY	dikaryon	**ADINOOPT**	adoption	**ADMNOOST**	mastodon
ADILLLPY	pallidly	**ADINOORT**	tandoori	**ADMNOOSW**	woodsman
ADILLMNR	mandrill	**ADINOOTT**	dotation	**ADMNOOSX**	Saxondom
ADILLMOU	allodium	**ADINOPRR**	raindrop	**ADMNORRU**	round-arm
ADILLMRW	millward	**ADINORRY**	ordinary	**ADMNORSU**	Rosamund
ADILLMSY	dismally	**ADINORST**	intrados	**ADMOOPPP**	poppadom
ADILLNPS	landslip	**ADINORSU**	dinosaur	**ADMOOPRR**	prodroma
ADILLOOP	poloidal	**ADINORTU**	duration	**ADMOORRW**	wardroom
ADILLOSW	disallow	**ADINORTX**	donatrix	**ADNNORTY**	dynatron
ADILLOSY	disloyal	**ADINOSTY**	dystonia	**ADNOOPPT**	pantopod
ADILLSTY	distally	**ADIOOPRS**	prosodia	**ADNOOQRU**	quadroon
ADILMMOS	modalism	**ADIOOPRT**	parotoid	**ADNOORTY**	donatory
ADILMNNO	mandolin	**ADIOOPSS**	apodosis	**ADNOOSSS**	so-and-sos
ADILMNOS	salmonid	**ADIOPPRT**	trappoid	**ADNOOSVW**	advowson
ADILMOPR	mail drop	**ADIOPPST**	post-paid	**ADNOPRWW**	downwarp
ADILMOPS	plasmoid	**ADIOPRST**	parodist	**ADNOQRSU**	squadron
ADILMOPT	diplomat	**ADIOPRTY**	podiatry	**ADNORSTW**	sandwort
ADILMOPY	Olympiad	**ADIOPSTY**	dystopia	**ADNORSXY**	sardonyx
ADILMOTY	modality	**ADIORRST**	stair-rod	**ADNORTUW**	drawn-out, untoward
ADILMPRY	lampyrid	**ADIORRTT**	traditor		
ADILMPSU	paludism	**ADIORSVY**	advisory	**ADNORTWW**	townward
ADILMRUW	wild arum	**ADIORTUY**	auditory	**ADNORWWY**	wanwordy
ADILNNNU	nundinal	**ADIORWWW**	war widow	**ADNOSTTU**	outstand, standout
ADILNNOR	Londrina	**ADIPRSUV**	Supadriv		
ADILNNSU	disannul	**ADIRRWYZ**	wizardry	**ADNRSSUW**	sunwards
ADILNNTU	nidulant	**ADJKNRUY**	junkyard	**ADOOPPRU**	pauropod
ADILNOOR	doornail	**ADKLMNSU**	slamdunk	**ADOOPRRT**	trapdoor
ADILNOOV	vindaloo	**ADKLOOPT**	polka dot	**ADOOPRSU**	sauropod
ADILNOPY	palinody	**ADKLOORW**	woodlark, workload	**ADOOPSWW**	woodwasp
ADILNORS	Rosalind			**ADOPPPYY**	Poppy Day
ADILNOTY	nodality	**ADKMNORW**	markdown	**ADOPRRWW**	word wrap
ADILNPST	displant	**ADKMOORR**	darkroom	**ADOPRSSW**	password
ADILNRWY	inwardly	**ADKOORRW**	roadwork	**ADOPSSSU**	soapsuds
ADILNSSW	windlass	**ADKORWYY**	workyday	**ADORRSUU**	ardurous
ADILOOPR	Polaroid	**ADKRSSWY**	skywards	**ADORSTUW**	outwards
ADILOORT	toroidal	**ADLLLOOY**	doolally	**ADORSTUY**	sudatory
ADILOPRS	slip road	**ADLLLORY**	Lollardy	**ADPRRSYY**	spray-dry
ADILOPRT	tripodal	**ADLLNOPW**	plowland	**ADPRSTTU**	dust-trap
ADILOPSS	disposal	**ADLLNORU**	all-round	**ADRSSTTU**	stardust
ADILORTY	adroitly, dilatory, idolatry	**ADLLOORT**	tollroad	**AEEEEGLY**	eagle eye
		ADLLOOTW	tallwood	**AEEEELRS**	releasee
		ADLLOOWW	woodwall	**AEEEFGLR**	freelage
ADILOSTW	wild oats	**ADLLORSY**	dorsally	**AEEEFORS**	Faeroese
ADILOSTY	sodality	**ADLMNOOR**	moorland	**AEEEGLLN**	leeangle
ADILRTTY	tilt-yard	**ADLMNOOW**	old woman	**AEEEGLLS**	legalese
ADILRTWY	tawdrily	**ADLMNORY**	randomly	**AEEEGLNU**	enleague
ADILRWYZ	wizardly	**ADLMOORU**	malodour	**AEEEGLRT**	eglatere, regelate, relegate
ADIMMNOS	monadism, nomadism	**ADLMOPSY**	psalmody		
		ADLNNTUU	undulant		
ADIMMNSY	dynamism	**ADLNOORW**	loanword	**AEEEGLRV**	leverage
ADIMNNOT	dominant	**ADLNOPRU**	pauldron	**AEEEGMRT**	metreage
ADIMNOST	saintdom	**ADLNOPWY**	downplay, play-down	**AEEEGNPR**	pea green
ADIMNRSY	misandry			**AEEEGNRS**	sea green
ADIMNSTY	dynamist	**ADLOORWW**	woolward	**AEEEGNRT**	generate, green tea, teenager
ADIMOPRX	proximad	**ADLOPRWY**	wordplay		
ADIMOPRY	myriapod	**ADLOQSUW**	old squaw		
ADIMOPSY	sympodia	**ADLORRWW**	world war	**AEEEGRST**	steerage

AEEEGRSW sewerage
AEEEGTTV vegetate
AEEEHLRT ethereal
AEEEHMPR ephemera
AEEEHNNV enheaven
AEEEHNRS enhearse
AEEEHNRT etherean
AEEEHRRS rehearse
AEEEHRRT reheater
AEEEHSTT aesthete
AEEEIMNX examinee
AEEEIPRT pie-eater
AEEEJNTT Jeanette
AEEEKKPS keepsake
AEEEKNRW weakener
AEEELLPP appellee
AEEELLSV sea level
AEEELNPS Nepalese
AEEELNRV venereal
AEEELNST selenate
AEEELQSU sequelae
AEEELRRS releaser
AEEELRRV revealer
AEEELRTX axle-tree
AEEEMMRT metamere
AEEEMNST easement
AEEEMPRS permease
AEEEMPRT permeate
AEEENPTT patentee
AEEENRTV enervate, venerate
AEEEPRRT repartee, repeater
AEEEPSTW sweet pea
AEEERSST tesserae
AEEFFKNR frank-fee
AEEFFLLR free fall
AEEFFLRT tafferel
AEEFFNRT afferent
AEEFGILN Fine Gael
AEEFGILR filagree
AEEFGIRR ferriage
AEEFGLSU fuselage
AEEFGNRT green fat
AEEFGRRY ferryage
AEEFHLLS self-heal
AEEFHLST self-hate
AEEFHRTY feathery
AEEFHRVY hay fever
AEEFIKLL leaflike
AEEFIKRR freakier
AEEFIKRW wakerife
AEEFILLR real life
AEEFILST leafiest
AEEFINST Stefanie
AEEFIPSW spaewife
AEEFKMNT fakement
AEEFKOPR forepeak
AEEFLLRW farewell
AEEFLLSS leafless
AEEFLMNR male fern
AEEFLMSS selfsame
AEEFLMST selfmate
AEEFLNOS nose leaf
AEEFLNRU funereal
AEEFLORS rose leaf
AEEFLORV overleaf
AEEFLPRT perflate
AEEFLRRR referral
AEEFLRRT falterer
AEEFLRSS fearless
AEEFMNOR forename
AEEFMORS fearsome
AEEFNRRY fernyear
AEEFNRST fastener, fenestra
AEEFNSSS safeness
AEEFPRSS free pass
AEEFRRTU fauterer
AEEGGINR agreeing
AEEGGIRV aggrieve
AEEGGNNR gangrene
AEEGGNST gestagen
AEEGGPRU puggaree
AEEGHHLS Sheelagh
AEEGHILN Hegelian
AEEGHIRT heritage
AEEGHLNP phenagle
AEEGHMMT mathemeg
AEEGHMPR grapheme
AEEGHNOT Goethean
AEEGHNRS shagreen
AEEGHORT heretoga
AEEGHRRT gatherer, regather
AEEGIINR aegirine
AEEGILLS legalise
AEEGILLZ legalize
AEEGILMN liegeman
AEEGILNN Angeline
AEEGILNS ensilage
AEEGILNT gelatine, legatine
AEEGILNU inleague
AEEGILNV evangile
AEEGILRS gaselier
AEEGILRT litreage
AEEGILST elegiast
AEEGILTU augelite
AEEGILTV legative, levigate
AEEGIMNR germaine
AEEGIMNT geminate
AEEGIMRT emigrate
AEEGINPR perigean
AEEGINRT enargite
AEEGINSS agenesis, assignee
AEEGINSV envisage
AEEGINTV negative
AEEGINTX exigeant
AEEGIPQU equipage
AEEGIRRS greasier
AEEGIRTT aigrette
AEEGIRTV ergative
AEEGJSTU sejugate
AEEGKLNW kelewang
AEEGKRSW skew gear
AEEGLLNR allergen
AEEGLLOW eagle owl
AEEGLLRV gaveller
AEEGLMOV love game
AEEGLMRT telegram
AEEGLMRY meagrely
AEEGLMSS gameless
AEEGLNNO Angeleno
AEEGLNNR Erlangen
AEEGLNNT entangle
AEEGLNOS gasolene
AEEGLNOT elongate
AEEGLNRR enlarger
AEEGLNSY Anglesey
AEEGLORS glareose
AEEGLORT alter ego
AEEGLOST segolate
AEEGLRRY Earl Grey
AEEGLRSS eelgrass, largesse
AEEGLRSY grey seal
AEEGLRTU regulate
AEEGLSSY eyeglass, glass eye
AEEGLTTU tutelage
AEEGLTUV evulgate
AEEGMMNS gamesmen
AEEGMMOS gamesome
AEEGMNNR green man
AEEGMNSS gameness
AEEGMRRS Grasmere
AEEGMRST gamester, gas meter
AEEGMSSU messuage
AEEGNNNO enneagon
AEEGNNPR pregnane
AEEGNNRT generant
AEEGNNRV engraven
AEEGNOST Stone Age
AEEGNPRS sap green
AEEGNPRY panegyre
AEEGNRRV engraver
AEEGNRST estrange, segreant, sergeant
AEEGNRSV nerve gas
AEEGNRTW great wen
AEEGNSSS sageness
AEEGNTTV vegetant
AEEGOOPS pea-goose
AEEGORTT great toe
AEEGORVV overgave
AEEGPRRS presager
AEEGPRSS asperges
AEEHHIKZ Hezekiah
AEEHHIMN Nehemiah
AEEHHNST ensheath
AEEHHOOP pahoehoe
AEEHHRTY heathery
AEEHIJMR Jeremiah
AEEHILRS shiralee
AEEHILRT etherial
AEEHILSW sei whale
AEEHIMPU Euphemia
AEEHIMTT hematite
AEEHINNV inheaven
AEEHINRS inhearse

AEEHINRT atherine
AEEHIPRS Hesperia, Pharisee
AEEHIRRT earthier, heartier
AEEHIRST Theresia
AEEHIRSV shivaree
AEEHIRTU hauerite
AEEHISTT hesitate
AEEHISTV heaviest
AEEHITTZ athetize
AEEHKLLR rakehell
AEEHKLLU keelhaul
AEEHKLNT Kathleen
AEEHKNRR hankerer
AEEHKRTT katheter
AEEHLLSS seashell
AEEHLMNW wheelman
AEEHLMNY hymeneal
AEEHLMOS halesome, healsome
AEEHLMPT helpmate
AEEHLNOT anethole
AEEHLNPT elephant
AEEHLNRT leathern
AEEHLNSS haleness
AEEHLNVY heavenly
AEEHLORS arsehole
AEEHLORV overhale
AEEHLOSU alehouse
AEEHLPTT telepath
AEEHLRST halteres
AEEHLRTY leathery
AEEHLSSV haveless
AEEHLSTT the least
AEEHMNNO omanhene
AEEHMNNY hymenean
AEEHMNTU atheneum
AEEHMPSS emphases
AEEHMRTY erythema
AEEHMTUX exhumate
AEEHNNRT thraneen
AEEHNNTX xanthene
AEEHNOPR earphone
AEEHNRTT threaten
AEEHNRTU urethane
AEEHNRTW wreathen
AEEHNRWY anywhere
AEEHNSTW enswathe
AEEHOPRT ephorate
AEEHORRV overhear
AEEHORSS sea horse, seashore
AEEHORTV overheat
AEEHPRRS rephrase
AEEHRRTU urethrae
AEEHRTVW whatever
AEEHRTWY three-way
AEEIJMNR Jermaine
AEEIJMRS Jeremias
AEEIJNNN Jeannine
AEEIKLMU leukemia
AEEIKLRT tearlike
AEEIKLRW weaklier
AEEIKLST leakiest
AEEIKLVW wavelike
AEEIKMNT ketamine
AEEIKNRS sneakier
AEEIKNRT ankerite
AEEIKNTZ ketazine
AEEIKPST peakiest
AEEILLNT tenaille
AEEILLRV real live
AEEILMMN melamine
AEEILMMT mealtime
AEEILMNS Milanese
AEEILMNT melanite
AEEILMPR emperial
AEEILMRS measlier
AEEILMRT real time
AEEILMST mealiest
AEEILMTZ metalize
AEEILNNS selenian
AEEILNPR perineal
AEEILNPS penalise
AEEILNPT petaline
AEEILNPZ penalize
AEEILNRT treenail
AEEILNSV Vaseline
AEEILORT aerolite
AEEILOTT etiolate
AEEILPPP apple-pie
AEEILPRR pearlier
AEEILPRS espalier
AEEILPRT pearlite
AEEILPSW palewise
AEEILPTT petalite
AEEILPTX pixelate
AEEILQSU equalise
AEEILQTU eliquate
AEEILQUX exequial
AEEILQUZ equalize
AEEILRRT irrelate, retailer
AEEILRRZ realizer
AEEILRST earliest, tresaiel
AEEILRSV velarise
AEEILRSZ sleazier
AEEILRTT laterite, literate
AEEILRTV levirate, relative
AEEILRVW liveware, reviewal
AEEILRVZ velarize
AEEILSVW alewives
AEEILTTV levitate
AEEILTUV eluviate
AEEIMMNT meantime
AEEIMNNO neomenia
AEEIMNRX examiner
AEEIMNUV mauveine
AEEIMORV Aviemore
AEEIMPRT imperate, premiate
AEEIMRST steamier
AEEIMRTT Mariette
AEEIMRZZ mezzeria
AEEIMSST seamiest
AEEIMSTT estimate, meatiest
AEEINNRR inner ear
AEEINNRS anserine
AEEINNRU aneurine
AEEINNTV Venetian
AEEINPRT aperient
AEEINPTT pianette
AEEINRRT Eritrean, retainer
AEEINRST arsenite, resinate, Teresina
AEEINRSU uneasier
AEEINSSS easiness
AEEINSTT anisette
AEEINSVW sine wave
AEEINTTZ tetanize
AEEIOOPP epopoeia
AEEIPPST appetise
AEEIPPSU eupepsia
AEEIPPTT appetite
AEEIPPTZ appetize
AEEIPRRR repairer
AEEIPRST parietes
AEEIQSTU equiseta
AEEIRSTT treatise
AEEIRSTW sweatier, weariest
AEEIRSTY yeastier
AEEIRSVV aversive
AEEIRTTT tertiate
AEEISSTT assiette
AEEISTTT steatite
AEEISTTV estivate
AEEITUVX exuviate
AEEJNRST serjeant
AEEJOPRT pejorate
AEEKKLWY lyke wake
AEEKLLNY Allen key
AEEKLLSS lakeless
AEEKLLST skeletal
AEEKLMMU Mameluke
AEEKLMRS alkermes
AEEKLMRT telemark
AEEKLMSS makeless
AEEKLSTY eye-stalk
AEEKMORV make-over
AEEKMRRT marketer
AEEKNPRS praskeen
AEEKNPSW Newspeak
AEEKNSSW weakness
AEEKNSTT stake-net
AEEKNTTT tankette
AEEKOOPP peekapoo
AEEKORST keratose
AEEKORTV overtake, takeover
AEEKQRSU squeaker
AEEKRRST streaker
AEELLLTT tell-tale
AEELLMRT tremella
AEELLNRW well-near
AEELLOTT allottee
AEELLPST plasteel

AEELLPTT	platelet	**AEELPRRS**	relapser	**AEENNSSS**	saneness
AEELLRRT	terrella	**AEELPRRT**	palterer	**AEENNSST**	neatness
AEELLSST	tessella	**AEELPRSU**	pleasure, serpulae	**AEENNSTT**	se-tenant
AEELLSTT	stellate			**AEENOPRS**	personae
AEELLSWY	weaselly	**AEELPRSV**	vesperal	**AEENOPRU**	European
AEELMMNO	melomane	**AEELPTTU**	Paulette	**AEENORRS**	reasoner
AEELMMNT	Emmental	**AEELQRSU**	squealer	**AEENORSS**	one's ears
AEELMMNU	Emmanuel	**AEELRRSV**	reversal	**AEENORST**	oestrane, resonate
AEELMMRV	emmarvel	**AEELRRTU**	ureteral		
AEELMMTU	malemute	**AEELRRTV**	traveler	**AEENORTV**	renovate
AEELMNNP	empannel	**AEELRSST**	tearless, tesseral	**AEENORVW**	ovenware
AEELMNOS	melanose			**AEENPPRT**	Peter Pan
AEELMNPS	ensample	**AEELRSSW**	wareless	**AEENPPTT**	appetent
AEELMNRT	lamenter	**AEELRSTY**	easterly, tresayle	**AEENPRRT**	panterer
AEELMNRV	enmarvel			**AEENPRUV**	parvenue
AEELMNSS	lameness, maleness, maneless, nameless	**AEELRSUV**	revalues	**AEENRRRW**	warrener
		AEELRTTU	Laurette	**AEENRRSS**	rareness
		AEELSSST	sateless, seatless	**AEENRRTT**	natterer
				AEENRRTV	taverner
AEELMNTT	mantelet	**AEELSSVW**	waveless	**AEENRSST**	assenter, sarsenet
AEELMNTV	lavement	**AEELSTTT**	statelet		
AEELMOTT	matelote	**AEEMMNTZ**	mazement	**AEENRSSW**	wareness
AEELMPRX	exemplar	**AEEMMORT**	memorate	**AEENRTTV**	antevert
AEELMPRY	empyreal	**AEEMMRRY**	yammerer	**AEENRTTX**	externat
AEELMPTT	palmette, template	**AEEMMSST**	messmate	**AEENRTTY**	entreaty
		AEEMNNRT	remanent	**AEENRTUV**	aventure
AEELMRSV	malverse	**AEEMNNSS**	meanness	**AEEOPRRT**	paterero, perorate
AEELMRTX	extremal	**AEEMNNTT**	tentamen		
AEELMSSS	melasses, seamless	**AEEMNORZ**	armozeen	**AEEOPRST**	protease
		AEEMNPRT	permeant, peterman	**AEEOPRTT**	operetta
AEELMSST	mateless, meatless, tameless			**AEEORRTV**	overrate
		AEEMNPRY	empyrean	**AEEORRTZ**	zero-rate
		AEEMNPTV	pavement	**AEEORSSV**	overseas
AEELMSTT	test meal	**AEEMNQUY**	May queen	**AEEORSTT**	sea otter
AEELNNNU	annulene	**AEEMNRSW**	menswear	**AEEORSVY**	overeasy
AEELNNRT	lanneret	**AEEMNRTU**	numerate	**AEEORTUZ**	Zouerate
AEELNNSS	leanness	**AEEMNRTV**	averment	**AEEOSSTX**	exossate
AEELNOOR	Eleonora	**AEEMNRUV**	maneuver	**AEEPPRRR**	preparer
AEELNOPR	peroneal	**AEEMNRVY**	Everyman	**AEEPPRTU**	Perpetua
AEELNOPT	antelope	**AEEMNSSS**	sameness	**AEEPRRRT**	parterre
AEELNORS	Rosaleen	**AEEMNSST**	tameness	**AEEPRRTT**	pretreat
AEELNORU	aleurone	**AEEMNSTU**	mansuete	**AEEPRRTU**	aperture
AEELNPPS	spalpeen	**AEEMOPST**	aposteme	**AEEPRSSU**	sea purse
AEELNPQU	Palenque	**AEEMORST**	Masorete	**AEEQRTTU**	raquette
AEELNPRT	penetral	**AEEMOSSU**	sea mouse	**AEERRRST**	arrester, rearrest
AEELNPRY	parylene	**AEEMPRRT**	tamperer		
AEELNPSS	paleness, paneless	**AEEMPRTT**	attemper	**AEERRSST**	asserter, reassert, terrasse
		AEEMPSTW	swap meet		
AEELNRRT	relearnt	**AEEMQTTU**	maquette		
AEELNRSS	realness	**AEEMRRST**	remaster, streamer	**AEERRSSU**	reassure
AEELNRSV	enslaver			**AEERRSTU**	austerer, treasure
AEELNRTV	levanter, relevant	**AEEMRRSU**	measurer		
		AEEMRSST	masseter, seamster	**AEERRSTV**	traverse
AEELNRTX	external			**AEERRSTW**	sewer rat
AEELNSST	lateness	**AEEMRSSU**	reassume	**AEERSSSS**	reassess
AEELNSWY	Wesleyan	**AEEMRSTT**	teamster	**AEERVWYY**	everyway
AEELNTUV	eventual	**AEEMRSTW**	stemware	**AEFFGIIL**	effigial
AEELOPRV	overleap	**AEEMRTWY**	yawmeter	**AEFFGINR**	fire-fang
AEELORRS	releasor	**AEEMSSSU**	masseuse	**AEFFGIRS**	giraffes
AEELORST	oleaster	**AEEMSSTU**	meatuses	**AEFFGOST**	off-stage
AEELORTT	tolerate	**AEEMSTTU**	amusette	**AEFFGRSU**	suffrage
AEELORTV	elevator	**AEENNORS**	Roseanne	**AEFFHIKY**	kaffiyeh
AEELOSTV	love seat	**AEENNRSS**	nearness	**AEFFHILL**	half-life
AEELOTTT	teetotal	**AEENNRTU**	enaunter	**AEFFIILR**	fife-rail
AEELOTTW	tea towel	**AEENNRTV**	revenant	**AEFFILRT**	life-raft

AEFFILUV	effluvia
AEFFIMRR	affirmer, reaffirm
AEFFLNTU	affluent
AEFFLSTU	feastful
AEFFORST	afforest
AEFGHIMS	game fish
AEFGHTTU	fughetta
AEFGIKMN	Mafikeng
AEFGILLO	foillage
AEFGILNR	finagler
AEFGIMTU	fumigate
AEFGINTU	fantigue
AEFGIORS	foie gras
AEFGIRTU	figurate, fruitage
AEFGIRTW	giftware
AEFGISTU	fatigues
AEFGITTU	fugitate
AEFGLLOP	flagpole
AEFGLLPU	full page
AEFGLMNU	flame gun, fugleman
AEFGLMOP	megaflop
AEFGLMOW	gamefowl
AEFGLNSS	fangless
AEFGLOPR	leapfrog
AEFGLORW	garefowl
AEFGLRTU	grateful
AEFGMNRT	fragment
AEFGNNOT	fontange
AEFGNORT	frontage
AEFGORTT	frottage
AEFGOSSU	fougasse
AEFHHLOS	half-hose
AEFHIKRS	freakish
AEFHIKSW	weakfish
AEFHILLN	fellahin
AEFHILMS	fishmeal
AEFHILMT	half-time
AEFHILNW	fin whale
AEFHILRS	flashier
AEFHLLLS	all flesh
AEFHLLOS	half-sole
AEFHLMRT	half-term
AEFHLMSU	shameful
AEFHLNOT	half note, half-tone
AEFHLNSS	halfness
AEFHLPST	half-step
AEFHLRTY	fatherly
AEFHMMOR	home farm
AEFHMNRS	freshman
AEFHOPRS	forshape
AEFHRSTT	farthest
AEFIILLN	nail file
AEFIILNS	finalise
AEFIILNZ	finalize
AEFIILRR	air rifle
AEFIILRS	Fair Isle
AEFIIMNZ	infamize
AEFIIMTT	Fatimite
AEFIINRS	Friesian
AEFIIPRT	aperitif
AEFIIRRT	ratifier
AEFIITVX	fixative
AEFIKLOS	Lefkosia
AEFIKLRY	freakily
AEFIKLST	flakiest
AEFIKNNO	kafenion
AEFILLOT	fellatio
AEFILLPP	fall-pipe
AEFILMNR	inflamer, rifleman
AEFILMNS	flamines
AEFILMNT	filament
AEFILNNR	infernal
AEFILNOT	olefiant
AEFILNPS	lifespan
AEFILNRT	inflater
AEFILOOR	aerofoil
AEFILOPR	fire-opal
AEFILORS	foresail
AEFILORT	floriate, foralite
AEFILRTT	filtrate
AEFILRTU	faultier, filature
AEFILRUW	weariful
AEFILRVV	valvifer
AEFILSTU	fistulae
AEFILSTV	festival
AEFILSTW	flatwise
AEFILTUU	fauteuil
AEFIMNST	manifest
AEFIMORR	aeriform
AEFIMORT	formiate
AEFIMOST	foamiest
AEFIMRRW	firmware
AEFINOPR	pinafore
AEFINORS	farinose
AEFINOTT	fetation
AEFINRRT	fair rent
AEFINRSS	fairness, sanserif
AEFINRST	fine arts
AEFINRTX	fraxetin
AEFIORTV	favorite
AEFIPRRT	fire trap
AEFIRRRY	farriery
AEFIRSTV	five-star
AEFIRSTW	wastrife
AEFIRTUX	fixature
AEFISTTT	fattiest
AEFKLLOT	folk tale
AEFKLSTT	talkfest
AEFKNORS	forsaken
AEFKOPRS	forspeak
AEFKORRS	forsaker
AEFKORRW	workfare
AEFKORTU	freak-out
AEFLLNRW	wall fern
AEFLLORT	fellator
AEFLLORV	overfall
AEFLLPTU	plateful
AEFLLRUX	flexural
AEFLLSSW	flawless
AEFLLSTY	festally
AEFLMORU	formulae, fumarole
AEFLMOSS	foamless
AEFLMOTU	flameout
AEFLNNOT	fontanel
AEFLNOPT	pantofle
AEFLNORS	farnesol
AEFLNRTU	flaunter
AEFLNRUY	yearnful
AEFLNSST	flatness
AEFLNSUY	unsafely
AEFLOPRT	teraflop
AEFLOPRY	foreplay
AEFLORST	forestal
AEFLORSU	fusarole
AEFLORTT	Floretta
AEFLORTW	fleawort
AEFLOSTT	falsetto
AEFLPPRY	fly-paper
AEFLRSTT	fattrels
AEFLRTTU	aflutter
AEFLRTTY	flattery
AEFLSTTT	flattest
AEFLSTTU	tasteful
AEFLSTUW	wasteful
AEFMNORW	men-of-war
AEFMNRRY	ferryman
AEFMORRT	reformat
AEFMORST	foremast
AEFMORVW	waveform
AEFNNSTU	unfasten
AEFNOPRR	profaner
AEFNOPRT	panforte
AEFNORRW	forewarn
AEFNORST	seafront
AEFNRRST	transfer
AEFNRRUY	funerary
AEFNSSST	fastness
AEFOORTW	footwear
AEFOPRRT	forepart
AEFOPTUU	pot-au-feu
AEFORRSW	forswear
AEFORRUU	fourreau
AEFORRUV	favourer
AEFORRWY	forweary
AEFORSTW	forwaste, software
AEFORSTY	forestay
AEGGGINN	engaging
AEGGHHIR	high gear
AEGGHILT	lightage
AEGGHIRS	shaggier
AEGGHNNY	Hengyang
AEGGHOPY	geophagy
AEGGHORU	roughage
AEGGIJST	jaggiest
AEGGILLR	grillage
AEGGILNR	ganglier
AEGGILNU	leaguing
AEGGILNV	gaveling
AEGGILRS	slaggier
AEGGIMNW	wing-game
AEGGINOR	Georgian, Georgina
AEGGINOS	seagoing
AEGGINRT	iggerant

AEGGIOPR	arpeggio, geropiga
AEGGIRRU	garrigue
AEGGLNPT	eggplant
AEGGLORY	gargoyle
AEGGLRST	straggle
AEGGMORT	mortgage
AEGGNORV	overgang
AEGGNORW	waggoner
AEGGNRST	gangster
AEGGNSST	ant's eggs
AEGGOPRU	age group, groupage
AEGGRSST	staggers
AEGHHISS	high seas
AEGHILLS	shigella
AEGHILMT	megalith
AEGHILNR	narghile
AEGHILNS	shealing
AEGHILNT	alighten, atheling
AEGHILRT	litharge, thirlage
AEGHINNN	hennaing
AEGHINOT	Goethian
AEGHINRT	ingather
AEGHINRV	Havering
AEGHINRY	Haringey
AEGHIPPR	epigraph
AEGHIPRT	earth-pig, graphite
AEGHIPSS	sageship
AEGHLOPY	hypogeal
AEGHLRTU	laughter
AEGHLRTY	lethargy
AEGHMNNT	hangment
AEGHMNOP	phenogam
AEGHMOPT	apothegm
AEGHMORT	ethogram
AEGHMOSW	game show
AEGHNNOR	hanger-on, onhanger
AEGHNNST	hang-nest
AEGHNOPT	heptagon, pathogen
AEGHNOPY	hypogean
AEGHNORV	hangover, overhang
AEGHNOST	on the gas
AEGHNRSS	gnashers
AEGHOPPR	prophage
AEGHOPPY	apophyge
AEGHORST	shortage
AEGHRTTU	retaught
AEGHSTTU	thus-gate
AEGIILLN	gillenia
AEGIILLU	aiguille
AEGIILMO	oligemia
AEGIILTT	litigate
AEGIIMNN	Geminian
AEGIIMNR	imaginer, migraine
AEGIIMNS	imagines
AEGIIMTT	mitigate
AEGIINNR	arginine
AEGIINRR	grainier
AEGIIRRT	irrigate
AEGIJMNN	Jiangmen
AEGIJPRU	jerupiga
AEGIJRTU	Gujerati
AEGIKLLN	langleik
AEGIKLNW	weakling
AEGIKMNS	skin game
AEGIKNPS	speaking
AEGIKSTW	gawkiest
AEGILLMS	legalism
AEGILLMU	Gulielma
AEGILLNO	goal line
AEGILLNY	genially
AEGILLPR	pillager
AEGILLPS	spillage
AEGILLRU	guerilla
AEGILLRV	villager
AEGILLST	legalist, stillage
AEGILLTU	ligulate
AEGILLTY	legality
AEGILLVY	villagey
AEGILMMR	aglimmer
AEGILMNN	malengin
AEGILMNR	germinal, maligner, malinger
AEGILMNT	ligament, metaling
AEGILMNU	legumina
AEGILMRS	regalism
AEGILMRX	lexigram
AEGILNNP	paneling
AEGILNNR	learning
AEGILNNT	gantline, intangle
AEGILNNU	ungenial
AEGILNNW	weanling
AEGILNNY	yeanling
AEGILNOR	geraniol, regional
AEGILNOS	gasoline
AEGILNOT	gelation, legation
AEGILNPR	pearling
AEGILNPS	pleasing
AEGILNQU	equaling
AEGILNRS	resignal, sale ring, sanglier, seal ring, slangier
AEGILNRT	integral, tanglier, teraglin, triangle
AEGILNRV	raveling
AEGILNRX	relaxing
AEGILNRY	layering, yearling
AEGILNSS	glassine
AEGILNST	aglisten
AEGILNSV	leavings, Svengali
AEGILNTT	Tintagel
AEGILNTV	valeting
AEGILNTZ	tin-glaze
AEGILOPS	spoilage
AEGILOPT	pilotage
AEGILORS	gasolier, girasole, seraglio
AEGILPPS	slippage
AEGILPPU	pupilage
AEGILRSS	glassier
AEGILRSY	greasily
AEGILRTT	aglitter
AEGILRTU	ligature
AEGILRTY	regality
AEGILRVW	lawgiver
AEGILRYZ	glaziery
AEGIMMST	gammiest
AEGIMNRT	emigrant, mantiger
AEGIMNRU	geranium
AEGIMNSS	gaminess
AEGIMNST	mangiest
AEGIMPRU	umpirage
AEGIMQRU	quagmire
AEGIMRST	magister
AEGIMSSU	misusage
AEGIMUUV	guimauve
AEGINNOT	negation
AEGINNRS	earnings
AEGINNRV	ingraven
AEGINNRY	yearning
AEGINNSU	sanguine
AEGINORZ	organize
AEGINPTY	Egyptian
AEGINRRV	averring, ingraver
AEGINRSS	assigner, reassign
AEGINRST	angriest, astringe, ganister, inert gas, rangiest
AEGINRTT	treating
AEGINRTV	vintager
AEGINRTW	watering
AEGINRVW	wavering
AEGINRVY	vinegary
AEGINSST	giantess
AEGINSTT	tangiest
AEGIOPRR	progeria
AEGIORRT	riot gear
AEGIORTV	ravigote
AEGIOSTX	geotaxis
AEGIPPRR	grappier
AEGIPPRT	trippage
AEGIRRSS	grassier
AEGIRRYZ	graziery
AEGIRTTT	great tit
AEGISSST	gassiest
AEGISSTT	stagiest
AEGISTUZ	gauziest
AEGJLTUU	jugulate
AEGJRTUW	water jug
AEGKLNWY	kleywang

AEGKMNRU gunmaker
AEGKNORT kratogen
AEGLLNOU ullagone
AEGLLNOV longeval
AEGLLOPR galloper
AEGLLORY allegory
AEGLLOSS goalless
AEGLLOTT toll gate
AEGLLRVY gravelly
AEGLLSSU galluses
AEGLMNNO mangonel
AEGLMNTU gunmetal
AEGLMOPS megalops
AEGLMOTV megavolt
AEGLMSSU gaumless
AEGLNNOR Algernon
AEGLNNOU alunogen
AEGLNNPT plangent
AEGLNNSY lang syne
AEGLNNTU untangle
AEGLNOPT gantlope
AEGLNORY year-long
AEGLNOVW long wave
AEGLNRRW wrangler
AEGLNRST strangle
AEGLNRSY larynges
AEGLNTTU gauntlet
AEGLNTUU ungulate
AEGLOOPU apologue
AEGLOORV vergaloo
AEGLOORY aerology
AEGLOPRY playgoer, pylagore
AEGLORSU glareous
AEGLORTW waterlog
AEGLPPRR grappler
AEGLRSTU gestural
AEGLSTUU glutaeus
AEGMMRRU rummager
AEGMNNOT magneton
AEGMNORV mangrove
AEGMNOST togemans
AEGMNOTU Montague
AEGMNOXY xenogamy
AEGMNRTU argument
AEGMOPRW gapeworm
AEGMORRW worm-gear
AEGMORSS gossamer
AEGMPRUZ gazumper
AEGMSTTU steam tug
AEGNNOPT pentagon
AEGNNORT negatron
AEGNNOSU non-usage
AEGNNPRT pregnant
AEGNNRTY gannetry
AEGNOPRR parergon
AEGNORRY orangery
AEGNORST ragstone
AEGNORTT tetragon
AEGNORTU outrange
AEGNORTY negatory
AEGNPRSU speargun
AEGNPRYY panegyry
AEGNRRST stranger
AEGNRSUU saugrenu

AEGNSSST gastness
AEGOORST rat-goose
AEGOOSWY waygoose
AEGOPPST stoppage
AEGOPRTU portague
AEGOPSTT gatepost
AEGORRTT garrotte
AEGORTTU tutorage
AEGORUVY voyageur
AEGOSSTU outgases
AEGPRRSU spur-gear
AEGRRSSY ryegrass
AEGRRTTY targetry
AEGRSTTY strategy
AEHHINPS Phinehas
AEHHISVY heavyish
AEHHORST haroseth
AEHHRRST thrasher
AEHIIKLR hairlike
AEHIIKRT terakihi
AEHIIKST shiitake
AEHIILMT lithemia
AEHIILNR hairline
AEHIIMNT thiamine
AEHIIMPT epithima
AEHIIOPT Ethiopia
AEHIIPTX pixie hat
AEHIIRST hairiest
AEHIKKLW hawklike
AEHIKLMR haremlik
AEHIKLNT nakhlite
AEHIKLTW what-like
AEHIKMNS Kineshma
AEHIKNST hanksite, heat sink
AEHIKOPT tophaike
AEHIKSST shakiest
AEHILLNT thalline
AEHILLOS oil-shale, shale oil
AEHILLOW whale oil
AEHILMNY hymenial
AEHILMSW Lewisham, limewash
AEHILNNT inhalent
AEHILNOP aphelion
AEHILNOT Iolanthe
AEHILNTX anthelix
AEHILNTZ zenithal
AEHILRSS hairless
AEHILRSV shrieval
AEHILRTY earthily, heartily
AEHIMMRS ashimmer
AEHIMMST hammiest
AEHIMNNU inhumane
AEHIMNSU humanise
AEHIMNTU inhumate
AEHIMNUZ humanize
AEHIMORT mahoitre
AEHIMOTT Timothea
AEHIMPRS samphire, seraphim
AEHIMPRT teraphim

AEHIMPSS emphasis, misshape
AEHIMPST mateship, shipmate
AEHIMRRS marshier
AEHIMSST mathesis
AEHINNSS san-hsien
AEHINNTX xanthine
AEHINOPS isophane
AEHINOPU euphonia
AEHINORT anti-hero
AEHINPPY epiphany
AEHINPRT perianth, triphane
AEHINPST thespian
AEHINRSV enravish, haversin
AEHINRTT thranite
AEHINRTU haurient
AEHINRTW tarwhine
AEHINSST anthesis
AEHINSSZ haziness
AEHINSTT hesitant
AEHINTTT antithet
AEHINTTW white ant
AEHIOPPR epiphora
AEHIOPRS aphorise
AEHIOPRU euphoria
AEHIOPRZ aphorize
AEHIORST hoariest
AEHIORTU thiourea
AEHIPPRS sapphire
AEHIPPST happiest
AEHIRRST trashier
AEHIRRSV ravisher
AEHIRRSY Ayrshire
AEHIRSTU thesauri
AEHIRSTW waterish
AEHIRSTY hysteria
AEHIRTYZ yahrzeit
AEHISSTT hastiest
AEHISSTU hiatuses
AEHISSTW washiest
AEHJNNOS Johannes
AEHJPRSW jew's harp
AEHKLOOU Laohekou
AEHKMOPR hamerkop
AEHKNNSU unshaken
AEHKNSTT Tashkent
AEHKOPRU peak hour
AEHKOSTU shake-out
AEHLLLTY lethally
AEHLLMOT hallmote
AEHLLMSS mess hall
AEHLLMTY methylal
AEHLLNRT enthrall
AEHLLOST thallose
AEHLLOSY sea holly
AEHLLSSS lashless
AEHLMMNS helmsman
AEHLMNOO home loan
AEHLMNOT methanol
AEHLMNOY Holy Name
AEHLMNRT tarnhelm
AEHLMNSW Welshman

AEHLMNUY	humanely
AEHLMOTT	hot metal
AEHLMPPT	pamphlet
AEHLMPTY	lymphate
AEHLMRSS	harmless
AEHLNOPS	Alphonse
AEHLNPRS	shrapnel
AEHLNPTY	enthalpy
AEHLNRTU	Lutheran
AEHLNSST	nathless
AEHLNTUZ	hazelnut
AEHLOPRT	plethora
AEHLOPTT	hotplate
AEHLORSY	hoarsely
AEHLORUV	overhaul
AEHLORYY	Holy Year
AEHLPPRT	thrapple
AEHLPSST	pathless
AEHLPSTU	sulphate
AEHLRRTU	urethral
AEHLRTTW	thwartle
AEHLSSTW	thawless
AEHLSTTY	stealthy
AEHMNNPY	nymphean
AEHMNORS	horseman
AEHMNORT	other man
AEHMNOSU	houseman
AEHMNPRU	prehuman
AEHMNPTU	pantheum
AEHMNSTW	new maths
AEHMOOPR	morphoea
AEHMOPRT	metaphor
AEHMOSTW	somewhat
AEHMPPTU	heat pump
AEHMRRTY	rat-rhyme
AEHMRTTU	theatrum
AEHMSTTY	amethyst
AEHNNOPT	pantheon
AEHNNOTX	xanthone
AEHNNPRU	nenuphar
AEHNNSUV	unshaven
AEHNOOPT	hanepoot
AEHNOPPR	prophane
AEHNOPPS	happen-so
AEHNOPPY	payphone
AEHNOPRT	hapteron
AEHNOPST	stanhope
AEHNOQTU	haqueton
AEHNORST	Sheraton
AEHNPRTY	hen-party, Tryphena
AEHNRSSS	rashness
AEHNRTTU	earth-nut
AEHNSTUW	unswathe
AEHOOPRX	exophora
AEHOPPRS	prophase
AEHOPRRY	pyorrhea
AEHOPSST	spathose
AEHOPTVY	top-heavy
AEHORRRW	harrower
AEHORRSW	warhorse
AEHORSSW	sawhorse
AEHORSTT	rheostat
AEHORSTU	share-out
AEHORSTX	thoraxes
AEHORSTY	Rothesay
AEHORSVW	overwash
AEHORTTW	hot water
AEHOSSTU	South Sea
AEHPRSST	sharp-set
AEHPRSUW	washer-up
AEHPRSUX	haruspex
AEHPRSUY	euphrasy
AEHQSSSU	squashes
AEHRRSTU	urethras
AEIIINTT	initiate
AEIIIRRT	retiarii
AEIIKRTY	teriyaki
AEIILLMR	ramillie
AEIILLTV	illative
AEIILMNN	mainline
AEIILMNS	alienism
AEIILMPR	imperial
AEIILMSZ	Islamize
AEIILMTT	limitate, militate
AEIILNPR	plein-air
AEIILNQU	aquiline, quiniela
AEIILNRR	airliner
AEIILNRT	inertial, linarite
AEIILNST	alienist, Taliesin
AEIILNTZ	Latinize
AEIILPPT	tailpipe
AEIILQSU	siliquae
AEIILRSS	Israelis
AEIILRST	listeria
AEIILRTT	literati
AEIILSTV	vitalise
AEIILTVZ	vitalize
AEIIMMRT	maritime
AEIIMMXZ	maximize
AEIIMNNT	maintien
AEIIMNRS	marinise
AEIIMNRZ	marinize
AEIIMNTT	intimate
AEIIMNTV	vitamin E
AEIIMRST	seriatim
AEIINNRS	sirenian
AEIINNRT	triennia
AEIINNTV	invinate
AEIINPRT	paintier, parietin
AEIINPST	pisanite
AEIINRSS	airiness
AEIINRST	rainiest
AEIINRSY	yersinia
AEIINRTZ	Nazirite, triazine
AEIINSTZ	sanitize
AEIINSVV	invasive
AEIINTTT	titanite
AEIINTTU	uintaite
AEIIPRSW	pairwise
AEIIPRTZ	trapezii
AEIIPRZZ	pizzeria
AEIIPSST	epitasis
AEIIRRTT	irritate
AEIIRSST	satirise
AEIIRSTW	wisteria
AEIIRSTZ	satirize
AEIIRTTT	tritiate
AEIISTVX	exit visa
AEIITTTV	titivate
AEIJLNNU	Julianne
AEIJLOSU	jalousie
AEIJMMST	jammiest
AEIJMNSS	jessamin
AEIJMORR	Marjorie
AEIJNRTU	jauntier
AEIJORST	jarosite
AEIJSTZZ	jazziest
AEIKKMRT	Kitemark
AEIKKPPR	pipkrake
AEIKLLMS	selamlik
AEIKLLOV	Oakville
AEIKLNOS	snake oil
AEIKLNPR	laperkin
AEIKLNPS	ski-plane
AEIKLNSS	sealskin
AEIKLNST	lankiest
AEIKLNSW	swanlike
AEIKLNSY	sneakily
AEIKLPRT	traplike
AEIKLPSW	wasplike
AEIKLRST	starlike
AEIKLRVY	Valkyrie
AEIKLSWY	likeways
AEIKMNST	mankiest, mistaken
AEIKMPSS	misspeak
AEIKNNTW	Winnetka
AEIKNPST	snake-pit
AEIKNRST	narkiest
AEIKNRSW	swankier
AEIKNRTW	knitwear
AEIKNSTV	kistvaen
AEIKPRST	parkiest
AEIKPSST	piss-take
AEIKPSTW	pawkiest
AEIKQSTU	quakiest
AEIKRSST	asterisk, sarkiest
AEIKRSTW	water-ski
AEILLLLN	Llanelli
AEILLLMO	malleoli
AEILLLNY	lineally
AEILLMNY	menially
AEILLMSY	mesially
AEILLNNO	all-in-one
AEILLNOR	allerion
AEILLNPS	splenial
AEILLNQU	quinella
AEILLNRY	linearly
AEILLNSS	nailless
AEILLNVY	venially
AEILLOSS	loessial
AEILLOTV	volatile
AEILLPRS	pis aller
AEILLPRT	pillaret
AEILLPST	palliest, pastille
AEILLPSV	lipsalve

AEILLRRU railleur
AEILLRRY raillery
AEILLRSS railless
AEILLRST Allister
AEILLRSY serially
AEILLRTT ill-treat
AEILLRTU tailleur
AEILLRTV trevalli
AEILLSSS sailless
AEILLSST tailless
AEILLSUV allusive
AEILLSYZ sleazily
AEILLTUZ lazulite
AEILMMNS melanism
AEILMMNT immantle
AEILMMOR memorial
AEILMMOT immolate
AEILMMRT trilemma
AEILMMSS melismas
AEILMNNO minneola
AEILMNNS linesman
AEILMNOS laminose, semolina
AEILMNPW palm wine
AEILMNQU liquamen
AEILMNRT terminal, tramline
AEILMNRU lemurian
AEILMNRV minerval
AEILMNSS islesman
AEILMNST manliest, salt mine
AEILMNTU luminate
AEILMOOV movicola
AEILMOPR proemial
AEILMORS moralise
AEILMORZ moralize
AEILMOSW wailsome
AEILMPRS premisal
AEILMPRU plumeria
AEILMPRV primeval
AEILMPSS pessimal
AEILMPST palmiest, petalism, septimal
AEILMPTT petit mal
AEILMPTY playtime
AEILMRTT remittal
AEILMRUV velarium
AEILMSTT maltiest, metalist
AEILMSTU simulate
AEILMSTY steamily
AEILMTTU mutilate, ultimate
AEILNNOP nopaline
AEILNNPP panel pin
AEILNNRT internal
AEILNNSY insanely
AEILNNTY innately
AEILNOPR parelion, parolein
AEILNOPU poulaine
AEILNORR Lorraine
AEILNORS rosaline, rose nail
AEILNORT oriental, relation, taileron
AEILNORU aureolin
AEILNORV overlain
AEILNOST insolate
AEILNOSV Slovenia
AEILNOTT tonalite
AEILNPRT interlap, triplane
AEILNPSS painless
AEILNPST panelist
AEILNPTT tin plate
AEILNPTY penality
AEILNQTU quantile
AEILNRRS snarlier
AEILNRSS rainless
AEILNRST entrails
AEILNRTT trail-net
AEILNRTU lunarite, tenurial
AEILNRTV interval
AEILNRTY interlay
AEILNSSZ laziness
AEILNSTT Intelsat
AEILNSTU insulate
AEILNSUY uneasily
AEILNTVY natively, venality
AEILNUVV univalve
AEILOORV ovariole
AEILOPPR oil-paper
AEILOPPT oppilate
AEILOPRS polarise
AEILOPRT petiolar
AEILOPRZ polarize
AEILORSV oversail
AEILORSZ solarize
AEILORTT literato
AEILORTZ triazole
AEILORVZ valorize
AEILOTTV violetta, volitate
AEILOTTZ totalize
AEILOTVZ volatize
AEILPPRU pulperia
AEILPPST split pea
AEILPRRS reprisal, sarplier
AEILPRRT paltrier, pretrial
AEILPRST pilaster, plaister
AEILPRSW slipware
AEILPRXY pyrexial
AEILPSUV plausive
AEILQRTU quartile, requital
AEILQSUY queasily
AEILQTUY equality
AEILRRTY literary
AEILRRUZ ruralize
AEILRTTU tertulia
AEILRTTY alterity
AEILRTUZ lazurite
AEILSSTT saltiest
AEILSTWY sweatily
AEILSTYY yeastily
AEIMMNNO monamine
AEIMMNNT immanent
AEIMMNOT ammonite
AEIMMNSU manumise
AEIMMNUZ manumize
AEIMMPST psammite
AEIMMRRS smarmier
AEIMMRTU immature
AEIMNNNR inner man
AEIMNNOT nominate
AEIMNOPR pomarine
AEIMNOPT ptomaine
AEIMNORT Maronite, minorate
AEIMNORZ romanize
AEIMNOSW womanise
AEIMNOTT tomatine
AEIMNOTZ monazite
AEIMNOUX exonumia
AEIMNOWZ womanize
AEIMNPRS prismane
AEIMNPRZ prizeman
AEIMNPST time span
AEIMNRSS near miss
AEIMNRST minestra, misanter
AEIMNRSU aneurism, Sumerian, Suriname
AEIMNRSY seminary
AEIMNRTT martinet
AEIMNRTU ruminate
AEIMNRTW wariment
AEIMNRTY tyramine
AEIMNSST mantises, matiness
AEIMNTTU matutine
AEIMNTVZ vizament
AEIMOPPS pome-apis
AEIMOPSX apomixes
AEIMOPTT optimate
AEIMORST amortise
AEIMORTZ amortize, atomizer
AEIMOTTV motivate
AEIMPRSW swampier
AEIMPRTT part-time
AEIMPRTW time warp
AEIMPRTX mixer tap
AEIMQRSU marquise
AEIMQSUU Esquimau
AEIMRRTU irrumate
AEIMRSST asterism
AEIMRSSY emissary
AEIMRSTT mistreat
AEIMRSTX matrixes
AEIMRSWW swimwear
AEIMRTTU Temirtau
AEIMSSTT misstate
AEIMTTUV mutative

AEINNNOT Antonine
AEINNNOX annexion
AEINNOOS sea onion
AEINNOPV pavonine
AEINNORT anointer, inornate
AEINNOST Estonian
AEINNOSZ neo-Nazis
AEINNOTT intonate
AEINNOTV innovate, venation
AEINNRRT inerrant
AEINNRTU inaunter
AEINNRTV inventar
AEINNSSV vainness
AEINNSSZ zaniness
AEINNSUV Venusian
AEINNTTW Tewantin
AEINOPPT antipope
AEINOPRT atropine
AEINOPST saponite
AEINOQTU equation
AEINORRT anterior
AEINORRW ironware
AEINORSS sensoria
AEINORST asterion, rationes
AEINORSV aversion
AEINORTZ notarize
AEINOSST assiento
AEINOSXZ Saxonize
AEINOTTV notative
AEINOTVX vexation
AEINPPPS pan pipes
AEINPPRS snappier
AEINPPTX Xantippe
AEINPRRT terrapin
AEINPRST pinaster, pristane
AEINPRTT triptane
AEINPRTU painture
AEINPRUV Peruvian
AEINPRYZ pyrazine
AEINPSTU supinate
AEINPSTY epinasty
AEINPTTY antitype
AEINQSTU antiques, quantise
AEINQSUV vasquine
AEINQTTU equitant
AEINQTUZ quantize
AEINRRST restrain, strainer, transire
AEINRRTW inter-war
AEINRSST artiness
AEINRSSU senarius
AEINRSSW wariness
AEINRSTT straiten
AEINRSTU naturise
AEINRSUX neuraxis
AEINRSUZ suzerain
AEINRSZZ snazzier
AEINRTTU tainture
AEINRTTY intreaty

AEINRTUZ naturize
AEINSSTT nastiest
AEINSSVW waviness
AEINSSWX waxiness
AEINSTTT nattiest
AEINSTTV tastevin
AEINSTTW tawniest
AEINTTUU autunite
AEIOOPTT patootie
AEIOPPST apposite
AEIOPRRT Pretoria, priorate
AEIOPRRW air power
AEIOPRST pastorie
AEIOPRSV vaporise
AEIOPRTX expiator
AEIOPRVZ vaporize
AEIOPSST soapiest
AEIOPSTX exposita
AEIOPTTV optative
AEIORRRT irrorate
AEIORRUV au revoir
AEIORSTT astroite
AEIORTTV rotative
AEIPPSST sappiest
AEIPPSTZ zappiest
AEIPQRTU pratique
AEIPRSST tapisser
AEIPRSTY asperity
AEIPRSVY vespiary
AEIPSSTT pastiest
AEIPTTUV putative
AEIQRRRU quarrier
AEIQRRTU quartier
AEIQRUVV quaviver
AEIRRRST starrier
AEIRRSTT tarriest
AEIRRTTU traiteur
AEIRRTTY tertiary
AEIRSSST assister
AEIRSSTW waitress
AEIRSTTT rattiest, tartiest
AEIRSTTZ tristeza
AEIRSTVY vestiary
AEIRSWWY way-wiser
AEIRTTTW atwitter
AEISSSST sassiest
AEISSSTY essayist
AEISSTTT tastiest
AEISSTVV savviest
AEISTTTT tattiest
AEJKLORV Kraljevo
AEJLOSUY jealousy
AEJMNRTU jurament
AEJMNSSY Jessamyn
AEJMOOSW Moose Jaw
AEJMPSTU jump seat
AEKKLNOT katonkel
AEKKMNOO kakemono
AEKKMORW make-work
AEKLLSTT stalklet
AEKLMRSS markless
AEKLMRUW lukewarm
AEKLMRUY yarmulke

AEKLNNSS lankness
AEKLNOSY ankylose
AEKLNOTW wale-knot
AEKLNPRT plankter
AEKLNSST tankless
AEKLOPRW rope-walk
AEKLORVW walkover
AEKLPRRS sparkler
AEKMNRSU unmasker
AEKMORTW teamwork, workmate
AEKMORTY toymaker
AEKMPRTU upmarket
AEKNNRSS rankness
AEKNOTTU out-taken
AEKOPSTU outspeak
AEKOPSTW weak spot
AEKORRTW work rate
AEKORRWW workwear
AEKORSTV overtask
AEKOSTTU stake-out
AEKQRSUW squawker
AEKRRSST starkers
AELLLOSV volsella
AELLLSSW wall-less
AELLLSTW salt well
AELLLSUV vulsella
AELLMNOO allomone
AELLMNOZ manzello
AELLMNTY mentally
AELLMORT Martello
AELLMOTT maletolt
AELLMOTY tomalley
AELLMPSS lampless
AELLMPTY plymetal
AELLMRSY mersalyl
AELLNOOT atenolol
AELLNOPV volplane
AELLNOSV novellas
AELLNPRU prunella
AELLNPSU napellus
AELLNPTT plantlet
AELLNPTU plantule
AELLNRUY neurally, unreally
AELLNRVY vernally
AELLNSST tallness
AELLNTTY latently
AELLNTUU lunulate
AELLOOPY alley-oop
AELLOPPR appellor
AELLOPRW walloper
AELLOPRY role-play
AELLOPTY allotype
AELLORSW sallower
AELLORWW wallower
AELLOSUV alveolus
AELLPRTY palterly
AELLRTTY latterly
AELLRTVY trevally
AELLRWYY lawyerly
AELLSSST saltless
AELLSUXY sexually
AELMMNOT momental
AELMMORW mealworm

AELMMOSY	myelomas
AELMNNOT	non-metal
AELMNNOU	noumenal
AELMNNOY	name only
AELMNNRY	mannerly
AELMNOPS	neoplasm, pleonasm
AELMNOSU	melanous
AELMNOYY	yeomanly
AELMNRSU	mensural
AELMNSTY	mesnalty
AELMOOPT	omoplate
AELMOORS	saleroom
AELMOPRR	premolar
AELMOPRT	temporal
AELMOPST	plastome
AELMOPSX	exoplasm
AELMOPSY	playsome
AELMOPTT	palmetto, pot-metal
AELMORTU	emulator
AELMOSSS	molasses
AELMOSTT	latemost
AELMOSTU	soulmate
AELMOTVZ	mazel tov
AELMPRRT	trampler
AELMPSUX	amplexus
AELMQSUU	squamule
AELMRSTT	maltster
AELMRSTY	masterly
AELMRTUY	maturely
AELMSSSS	massless
AELMTTUU	tumulate
AELNNOOP	napoleon
AELNNOOX	naloxone
AELNNOPP	open-plan
AELNNORU	enaluron, neuronal
AELNNOSU	annulose
AELNNRTU	unlearnt
AELNOPPT	Appleton
AELNOPRS	personal, psoralen
AELNOPRY	nopalery
AELNOPST	lapstone
AELNOPSU	saponule
AELNOPTW	towplane
AELNORST	Earlston
AELNORTT	tolerant
AELNORTU	outlearn
AELNORTY	ornately, Tyrolean
AELNOSSV	ovalness
AELNOTVV	evolvant
AELNPRSU	purslane, supernal
AELNPRTY	plenarty
AELNPSST	pantless
AELNPSSU	spansule
AELNPTTU	petulant
AELNPTTY	patently
AELNRSTT	slattern
AELNSSST	saltness
AELNSSTW	wantless
AELNTTUX	exultant
AELOORRS	roseolar
AELOORTW	Waterloo
AELOPPRS	prolapse, sapropel
AELOPPSU	papulose
AELOPPTU	populate
AELOPPXY	apoplexy
AELOPQUY	opaquely
AELOPRST	petrosal, polestar, portales
AELOPRVY	overplay
AELOPRYZ	pyrazole
AELOPSSS	soapless
AELOPSSU	espousal
AELORSUU	rouleaus
AELORTUY	layer-out
AELORTWW	low water
AELORTYZ	zealotry
AELORUUX	rouleaux
AELOSSTY	asystole
AELOTUUV	outvalue
AELPRRTT	prattler
AELPRSST	partless
AELPRSSY	sparsely
AELPRSTT	splatter
AELPRSTU	aplustre
AELPRSTY	plastery, psaltery
AELPSSSS	passless
AELPSSST	pastless
AELQRSUY	squarely
AELRRSTT	startler
AELRRTVY	varletry
AELRSSST	starless
AELRSSTU	tessular
AELRSTTT	trattles
AELRSTTU	lustrate
AELRTTUX	textural
AELRTTUY	tutelary
AELSTTUY	astutely
AEMMMOTU	ommateum
AEMMNORW	merwoman
AEMMNRTU	ramentum
AEMMOORT	roommate
AEMMORST	marmoset
AEMNNORS	Norseman
AEMNNORT	ornament
AEMNNORW	Morwenna
AEMNNPRU	per annum
AEMNOORT	ante-room
AEMNOORY	aeronomy
AEMNOOSZ	mesozoan
AEMNOOWY	yeowoman
AEMNOPRT	empatron
AEMNOPRW	manpower
AEMNORST	monaster, monstera, nearmost, on-stream, storeman
AEMNORSU	neuromas
AEMNORTU	outer man, route man
AEMNORTY	monetary
AEMNORVY	over-many
AEMNORYY	yeomanry
AEMNOTTY	metatony
AEMNPRSS	pressman
AEMNPRSU	superman
AEMNPSTU	spumante
AEMNPSUX	expansum
AEMNRRUY	numerary
AEMNRSSW	warmness
AEMNRSTU	menstrua, transmue, transume
AEMNRSTW	transmew
AEMNRSUY	aneurysm
AEMNSTUW	mute swan
AEMOORTT	amoretto
AEMOOSST	maestoso
AEMOOSTU	autosome
AEMOOTTY	tomatoey
AEMOPRTW	tapeworm
AEMOPSST	peatmoss
AEMOPSTU	apostume
AEMOQSSU	squamose
AEMORRRU	armourer
AEMORRST	rearmost
AEMORRSY	rosemary
AEMORSSY	mayoress
AEMORTTU	tautomer
AEMOTTZZ	mozzetta
AEMPRSTU	upstream
AEMQRSSU	marquess
AEMRRTUV	veratrum
AEMRSSST	rest mass
AEMRSSTT	mattress
AEMRSSTY	seamstry
AEMRSSUU	Sarum use
AEMRSTTU	maturest, testamur
AEMRTUUX	trumeaux
AEMSTTTU	testatum
AENNNOTU	Nuneaton
AENNNTUY	ennuyant
AENNOPRT	patronne
AENNOPST	pentosan
AENNORST	resonant
AENNORSU	unreason
AENNORVY	novenary
AENNOSTW	tenon saw
AENNPSTT	spent tan
AENNRSWY	swannery
AENNRTTY	tenantry
AENOOPST	teaspoon
AENOPRRY	rope-yarn
AENOPRSS	personas
AENOPRST	Paterson
AENOPRSV	overspan
AENOPRTT	patentor
AENOPRWY	weaponry
AENOPSTT	ante-post, postnate
AENORRRW	narrower
AENORRST	antrorse
AENORRTU	ornature
AENORSST	assentor
AENORSTU	turanose

AENORSUV	ravenous	**AEQRSTUU**	questura	**AFGORTUW**	tug-of-war
AENORTTY	attorney	**AERRSTUY**	treasury	**AFHHIKSW**	fish-hawk
AENOSSUU	nauseous	**AERSTTVY**	travesty	**AFHHLORU**	half-hour
AENOUUVX	nouveaux	**AERSTUVY**	vestuary	**AFHHLOST**	hot flash
AENPRRST	partners	**AERTTUXY**	textuary	**AFHIILSS**	sailfish
AENPRSST	partness, raptness	**AFFFFGGI**	giff-gaff	**AFHIILST**	fishtail
		AFFFFINN	niff-naff	**AFHIKLPS**	hip flask
AENPRSTT	transept	**AFFFFIPP**	piff-paff	**AFHIKNRS**	Frankish
AENPRSTU	pautners	**AFFFFIRR**	riff-raff	**AFHILLSY**	flashily
AENPSSST	pastness	**AFFGHILT**	afflight	**AFHILOSY**	oafishly
AENPSSSY	synapses	**AFFGHIRT**	affright	**AFHILSST**	salt fish
AENQRRTU	quartern	**AFFGIIRT**	graffiti	**AFHILSTT**	flattish
AENRRRTY	errantry	**AFFGINRU**	griffaun	**AFHILTWW**	whitflaw
AENRSSTT	tartness	**AFFGIORT**	graffito	**AFHIMNUY**	humanify
AENRSSTU	anestrus	**AFFGLNRU**	far-flung	**AFHIOSSU**	fashious
AENRSTWY	sternway	**AFFHILLS**	fallfish	**AFHIRSST**	starfish
AENRTUVY	vauntery	**AFFHILST**	flatfish	**AFHKLNTU**	thankful
AENSSSTV	vastness	**AFFHILTU**	faithful	**AFHLLOTU**	loathful
AENSSTTU	tautness	**AFFHIMRS**	fish farm	**AFHLMNOO**	half-moon
AEOOPRRT	operator, poor rate	**AFFIINTY**	affinity	**AFHLMOTU**	Falmouth
		AFFILLMM	flimflam	**AFHLRTUW**	wrathful
AEOOPRSV	vaporose	**AFFILLPP**	flip-flap	**AFHOOPTT**	footpath
AEOORTTT	tattooer	**AFFINTUU**	Funafuti	**AFIIILNP**	Filipina
AEOPPRRV	approver	**AFFIPSTT**	tipstaff	**AFIILLLY**	filially
AEOPQRTU	paroquet	**AFFLLOOT**	footfall	**AFIILLNU**	unfilial
AEOPQSTU	opaquest	**AFFLOOTT**	flatfoot	**AFIILMNS**	finalism
AEOPRRUV	vapourer	**AFFLORTU**	flat-four	**AFIILNST**	finalist
AEOPRRVW	wrap-over	**AFFLRRUU**	furfural	**AFIILNTY**	finality
AEOPRSST	protases	**AFFNORSY**	saffrony	**AFIINNOS**	sainfoin, sinfonia
AEOPRSSU	asperous	**AFFNORTY**	affronty		
AEOPRSSV	overpass, Passover	**AFFNRRUU**	furfuran	**AFIINNSY**	insanify
		AFGGGILN	flagging	**AFIINORT**	friation
AEOPRSTT	prostate	**AFGGILOP**	gigaflop	**AFIINOTX**	fixation
AEOPRSTU	apterous, partouse	**AFGGINOT**	fagoting	**AFIINRTY**	finitary
		AFGHILNS	flashing	**AFIIORRT**	triforia
AEOPRTUY	eupatory	**AFGHILNT**	fanlight	**AFIKLLMO**	milk-loaf
AEOPSSTT	potestas	**AFGHILNW**	wing-half	**AFIKLNNR**	franklin
AEOPTTUY	autotype	**AFGHILPS**	flagship	**AFIKLNOR**	florikan
AEOQRSTU	quaestor	**AFGHINRT**	farthing	**AFILLLOT**	flotilla
AEOQRTTU	torquate	**AFGHINST**	shafting	**AFILLLXY**	flax-lily
AEOQRTUZ	quatorze	**AFGHLLUU**	laughful	**AFILLNPU**	plainful
AEORRRST	arrestor	**AFGHLNSU**	flashgun	**AFILLTUY**	faultily
AEORRSST	assertor, oratress	**AFGHLSTU**	ghastful	**AFILMNOR**	formalin, informal
		AFGIKORT	koftgari		
AEORRSTT	rostrate	**AFGILLNT**	flatling	**AFILMRST**	film star
AEORRSTV	traverso	**AFGILLST**	flag-list	**AFILNORT**	flat iron, inflator
AEORRTZZ	terrazzo	**AFGILMNO**	flamingo		
AEORSSSS	assessor	**AFGILMRU**	fluigram	**AFILNORU**	fluorian
AEORSSTU	ossature	**AFGILNOT**	floating	**AFILNOSU**	fusional
AEORSSTV	votaress	**AFGILNPP**	flapping	**AFILNOTU**	flautino
AEORSTTT	attestor, testator	**AFGILNTT**	flatting	**AFILNPPT**	flippant
		AFGILORW	gairfowl	**AFILNPST**	flat spin
AEORSTTU	outstare, sea trout	**AFGILSSY**	glassify	**AFILNRUY**	unfairly
		AFGIMNTU	fumigant	**AFILOORT**	foliator
AEORSTVY	overstay	**AFGIMORS**	gasiform	**AFILOTTY**	fatty oil
AEORSVWY	oversway	**AFGINPPR**	frapping	**AFILPSTY**	plastify
AEOSTTTU	outstate	**AFGINRTU**	figurant	**AFILRSSU**	fissural
AEPPRRST	strapper	**AFGIPRTW**	gift-wrap	**AFILRSTU**	fistular
AEPRSSST	trespass	**AFGLLNOT**	flatlong	**AFILSSTU**	fistulas
AEPRSSTT	pattress	**AFGLLRUU**	fulgural	**AFILSTTU**	flautist
AEPRSTTU	upstater	**AFGLLRUY**	frugally	**AFIMMNOR**	maniform
AEPRSTTY	tapestry	**AFGLLSSU**	glassful	**AFIMNOPR**	napiform
AEPRSTUX	supertax	**AFGLNNOO**	gonfalon	**AFIMNORR**	raniform
AEPRTUVY	pyruvate	**AFGLORTU**	gut flora	**AFIMNORS**	nasiform
AEQRSTTU	squatter	**AFGNNNOO**	gonfanon	**AFIMNORT**	natiform

AFIMNORV naviform
AFIMNOSU infamous
AFIMORRV variform
AFIMORSV vasiform
AFIMRSUU fusarium
AFINNOTU fountain
AFINNRTY infantry
AFINOPSY saponify
AFINQTUY quantify
AFINRSTX transfix
AFIOSSTT tosafist
AFIRSTTY stratify
AFKLNOTU outflank
AFKLOSWY folkways
AFKMOORT footmark
AFLLLORY florally
AFLLLUWY lawfully
AFLLMNUY manfully
AFLLMORY formally
AFLLMRSY small fry
AFLLNOSW snowfall
AFLLNUUW unlawful
AFLLOPUY foul play
AFLLRTUY artfully
AFLMNOPR planform
AFLMNOST loftsman
AFLMOPRT platform
AFLMORRU formular
AFLMORSU formulas
AFLMORTU foulmart
AFLMORTW flatworm
AFLMORUY fumaroyl
AFLMOSUY famously
AFLNOPRU apronful
AFLNTUUV vauntful
AFLOORTT frottola
AFLOSTUU flatuous
AFLRSTUU frustula
AFMNNNUY funny man
AFMNNORT frontman
AFMOOPRR pro forma
AFNOOPRS span roof
AFOOPSST soft soap
AFOORSTZ sforzato
AFOSSTUU fastuous
AFPPPTUY puppy fat
AGGGHINS shagging
AGGGILNN gangling
AGGGILNR raggling
AGGGILNS slagging
AGGGINNS snagging
AGGGINOR grinagog
AGGGINST stagging
AGGGINSW swagging
AGGGIYZZ zigzaggy
AGGHILNU laughing
AGGHILST gaslight
AGGHILSY shaggily
AGGHISTT gas-tight
AGGHJMNO mah-jongg
AGGHLMNO holmgang
AGGHLOOT golgotha
AGGHNOSW gang show
AGGIILNV gingival
AGGIILST glaistig
AGGIINNR graining
AGGIINNS gainings
AGGILMMN glamming
AGGILMNO gloaming
AGGILNNO ganglion
AGGILNNT gnatling
AGGILNOP galoping
AGGILNPU plaguing
AGGILNPY gapingly
AGGILNRY grayling
AGGINNTT ting-tang
AGGINOOR gorgonia
AGGINOWY way-going
AGGINPRS grasping
AGGIRTUZ ziggurat
AGGKNNOT tongkang
AGGLLLOY lollygag
AGGLLOOY algology
AGGLMOOR logogram
AGGLOORY agrology
AGGLRSTY straggly
AGGMRSUU sugar-gum
AGGNUWZZ zugzwang
AGHHIILT hightail
AGHHIMSS High Mass
AGHHINSS hash sign
AGHHINSU Huangshi
AGHHLOTU although
AGHHNNOZ Hanzhong
AGHIILOS Laoighis
AGHIILRT light air
AGHIIPRR hairgrip
AGHIIRTT airtight
AGHIJLNS Janglish
AGHIJNNU Hunjiang
AGHIJNRT nightjar
AGHILLNO hollaing
AGHILLNT all-night
AGHILLRT all right
AGHILLTY laylight
AGHILMTY almighty
AGHILNOO hooligan
AGHILNOR longhair
AGHILNOT loathing
AGHILNRS ringhals
AGHILNSS lashings, slashing
AGHILNSU languish
AGHILPSU ispaghul
AGHILRSY garishly
AGHILTWX wax-light
AGHIMMNS shamming
AGHIMMNW whamming
AGHIMNSS smashing
AGHIMNTY thingamy
AGHIMRRT right arm
AGHINNOT gnathion
AGHINNTU haunting
AGHINNTY anything
AGHINOSX Shaoxing
AGHINPRS phrasing
AGHINPRY Phrygian
AGHINQSU Shangqiu
AGHINRTW thrawing
AGHINSST Hastings
AGHIOPRS isograph
AGHIPRRT trigraph
AGHIPSSW pig's wash
AGHIRSTT straight
AGHLLNOU long haul
AGHLLNUW wall-hung
AGHLMOOR hologram
AGHMMOOY homogamy
AGHMNPSU sphagnum
AGHMOOPZ gazoomph
AGHMOORR Gomorrah
AGHMOOTT goat moth
AGHNNSTU shantung
AGHNOOTZ Zhaotong
AGHNORST stag-horn
AGHNTTUU untaught
AGHOPRSS grasshop
AGHOPRXY xography
AGIIINNS insignia
AGIIINRV Virginia
AGIIJJNU Jiujiang
AGIIKNNT intaking
AGIILLNT illigant
AGIILLNU uliginal
AGIILMNS misalign
AGIILNNU inguinal
AGIILNOR original
AGIILNOT intaglio, ligation, taglioni
AGIILNOX gloxinia
AGIILNPT pig Latin
AGIILNRT ringtail, trailing, trialing
AGIILNRV rivaling, virginal
AGIILNTT litigant
AGIILNTV vigilant
AGIIMNNR ring main
AGIIMNSS amissing
AGIIMNST giantism
AGIIMNTT mitigant
AGIINNNR naringin
AGIINNNX Xianning
AGIINNOR Agrinion
AGIINNOT agnition
AGIINNPT painting
AGIINNRT training
AGIINNRW waringin
AGIINNST satining
AGIINNXX Xinxiang
AGIINORT trigonia
AGIINRSS arisings
AGIINSTU Ignatius
AGIJNNTT tjanting
AGIKLMOR kilogram
AGIKLNNP planking
AGIKLNOP polkaing
AGIKLNTY takingly
AGIKMNNS kingsman
AGIKMRUU kauri gum
AGIKNNPP knapping
AGIKNNPS spanking
AGIKNORR korrigan

AGIKNOST goatskin
AGIKRSSS grass ski
AGILLMNU mulligan
AGILLMNY malignly
AGILLMRY graymill
AGILLMSU Gaullism
AGILLNOT long-tail
AGILLNSY signally, slangily
AGILLOOR gillaroo
AGILLOPT gallipot
AGILLOPY palilogy
AGILLPRY playgirl
AGILLPUY plaguily
AGILLSSY glassily
AGILLSTU Gaullist
AGILMMNS slamming
AGILMNNT mantling
AGILMNOO Mongolia
AGILMNPS sampling
AGILMOPR lipogram
AGILMORS algorism
AGILNNNP planning
AGILNNOP pangolin
AGILNNUY ungainly
AGILNOOS isogonal
AGILNOOT Tongliao
AGILNORT trigonal
AGILNOTT totaling
AGILNOTW wagon-lit
AGILNOTY antilogy
AGILNPPS slapping
AGILNPRS laspring, sparling
AGILNPTT platting
AGILNPTU pugilant
AGILNRST starling
AGILNRSU langsuir, singular
AGILNRTT rattling
AGILNSST glissant
AGILNTUV vaulting
AGILOOXY axiology
AGILRRUV virgular
AGIMMOSY misogamy
AGIMNOOR ionogram
AGIMNORS organism
AGIMNORU origanum
AGIMNORY agrimony
AGIMNOSV Masvingo
AGIMNRRY marrying
AGIMNSSU assuming
AGIMORRT migrator
AGIMTTTU guttatim
AGINNNPS spanning
AGINNNSW swanning
AGINNOPT Paignton, poignant
AGINNORT Ignorant
AGINNOTU nugation
AGINNPPS snapping
AGINNPSW wingspan
AGINOORT rogation
AGINOPST pinto gas
AGINORRS garrison
AGINORSS assignor
AGINORST organist, roasting
AGINORTV graviton
AGINORTY gyration, organity
AGINPPRT trapping
AGINPPRW wrapping
AGINPPSW swapping
AGINPRRS sparring
AGINPSTT spatting
AGINRRST starring
AGINRSTY stingray
AGINSTTW swatting
AGINSTUU Augustin
AGIOORSU oragious
AGIOORSZ grazioso
AGIOORTU autogiro
AGIOPPRT agitprop
AGIORRTT grattoir
AGIRSSTU sastrugi
AGIRTTUY gratuity
AGJLOSUV Jugoslav
AGJNRTUU tjurunga
AGKLOORV Gorlovka
AGKMMORY kymogram
AGKORSSW gasworks
AGLLNOST long last
AGLLOOSW slag-wool
AGLLPRUW Rawlplug
AGLLRUVY vulgarly
AGLMOPRY polygram
AGLMOPYY polygamy
AGLMORUY glamoury
AGLNOOTY langooty
AGLNOSST glasnost
AGLNOSTY long-stay
AGLNOSUU angulous
AGLNOSWY longways
AGLOOPST goalpost
AGLOORSV voorslag
AGLOPRTU Portugal
AGLORSSY glossary
AGLOSUVY Yugoslav
AGLPSSSY spyglass
AGLRTTUU guttural
AGLSTUUY augustly
AGMMNOOR monogram, nomogram
AGMMNOOY monogamy
AGMMOORT tomogram
AGMNNOUY young man
AGMNOORS sonogram
AGMNOORY agronomy
AGMNORST angstrom
AGMOOOSU oogamous
AGMOOPRY porogamy
AGMOOTVY vagotomy
AGNNOOPT poontang
AGNNOSSW swansong
AGNOPRST part-song
AGNORTUY nugatory
AGNPRSUY spray-gun
AGOORTUY autogyro
AGOPRRTU purgator
AGORRSST tor-grass
AGORRTYY gyratory
AGORSSSZ zos-grass
AGSSTUUU Augustus
AGSSTUUV Gustavus
AHHHOOST hooshtah
AHHIIPSS pishashi
AHHIKLSS shashlik
AHHILPSW whiplash
AHHIMMSS mishmash
AHHIMMWW whim-wham
AHHIPPSS pish-pash
AHHIPRSS sharpish
AHHISSWW wish-wash
AHHKMOTW hawkmoth
AHHLNOPT naphthol
AHHLNPTY naphthyl
AHHLOOPU hula hoop
AHHMPRRU harrumph
AHHNORTW hawthorn
AHHOSTUV Shavuoth
AHIIILMN malihini
AHIIKMRS Kashmiri
AHIIKORS Hirosaki
AHIILLPP Phillipa
AHIILOST haliotis
AHIILPPP Philippa
AHIILPTW whiptail
AHIILRTY hilarity
AHIIMNOT himation
AHIIMNRS Irishman
AHIIMNST isthmian
AHIIMNTV vitamin H
AHIINOTX oxathiin
AHIINSTU Tianshui
AHIIOPST hospitia
AHIIOTTY titihoya
AHIKLNRS rinkhals
AHIKLPRU phulkari
AHIKLRSY rakishly
AHIKNNRS Krishnan
AHIKNPRS prankish
AHIKPRSS sparkish
AHILLMPS phallism
AHILLMPT limphalt
AHILLMSS smallish
AHILLMTU thallium
AHILLNRT inthrall
AHILLPST tall ship
AHILLSVY lavishly
AHILMNOT Hamilton
AHILMNST lithsman
AHILMOOP omphaloi
AHILMOST mailshot
AHILMOUY Mahilyou
AHILMQSU qualmish
AHILMTTY tithymal
AHILMTUZ halutzim
AHILNOOR honorial
AHILNOPS siphonal
AHILNOPT oliphant
AHILOORT Lothario
AHILOPST hospital
AHILPSSY physalis
AHILPTUY philauty

AHILRSTY trashily
AHIMMNSU humanism
AHIMMOSV moshavim
AHIMNNTU humantin
AHIMNOSW womanish
AHIMNOTW hit woman
AHIMNSTU humanist
AHIMNSTX xanthism
AHIMNTUY humanity
AHIMOPRS aphorism
AHIMOPST histomap, opsimath
AHIMPPSS sapphism
AHIMPRST trampish
AHIMRSST smartish
AHIMRSTT marsh tit
AHINNNOR Rhiannon
AHINNOPT antiphon
AHINOPRU ophiuran
AHINORRS Harrison
AHINORST trahison
AHINOSST astonish
AHINPPSS snappish
AHINPRST tranship
AHINQSUV vanquish
AHIOPRST aphorist
AHIOPRSV vaporish
AHIORSTV tovarish
AHIPRSST starship
AHIQRSSU squarish
AHKLLOOY holly oak
AHKLOPRU Kolhapur
AHKLOPST shop talk
AHKLOSTU Sukhotal
AHKLOSTW talk show
AHKMORTU Khartoum
AHKNOOPS snap-hook
AHKNOTUY thank-you
AHLLLOOP pool hall
AHLLNOTW town hall
AHLLOSTU thallous
AHLLPRYY phyllary
AHLMMOPY lymphoma
AHLMMOST mast-holm
AHLMNOOR hormonal
AHLMNOTU luna moth
AHLMOOPS omphalos
AHLMOPTY polymath
AHLNNORT lanthorn
AHLNOOPS Alphonso
AHLNORTU hortulan
AHLOOSST sash tool
AHLORRTY harlotry
AHLRSTUY lathyrus
AHMMRTTU thummart
AHMNNNOU non-human
AHMNNORT Northman
AHMNNSTU huntsman
AHMNOOTY Maynooth
AHMOOPSS shampoos
AHMOORSW washroom
AHMOPSTU posthuma
AHMORRST short-arm
AHMORSSU sour mash
AHMORTTW Tamworth
AHMORTUW warmouth
AHMPSTYY sympathy
AHMQSSUU musquash
AHMRSTUU haustrum
AHNOOPPY apophony
AHNOORRY honorary
AHNOPPSW pawnshop
AHNOPPSY pansophy
AHNOPSST snapshot
AHNOPSTT hot pants
AHNOQUUZ Quanzhou
AHNORTWW wanworth
AHNOSTUX xanthous
AHNRSTTU Thurstan
AHOOSTTW sawtooth
AHOPSTUW southpaw
AHORRTTW hartwort
AHORTTUW watt-hour
AIIILLVX lixivial
AIIILMSS Ismailis
AIIJKMOT komitaji
AIIKKSUY sukiyaki
AIIKLNRR larrikin
AIIKMNNN mannikin
AIIKMNTV vitamin K
AIIKNNNP pannikin
AIIKNNOO koinonia
AIIKNRST Kristina
AIIKORTY yakitori
AIIKPRRT prakriti
AIIKSTUW Iwatsuki
AIIKTTZZ tzatziki
AIILLLUV illuvial
AIILLMMP milliamp
AIILLMRY milliary
AIILLNNV vanillin
AIILLNOP pollinia
AIILLNOS allision
AIILLNOT illation
AIILLNRY Illyrian
AIILLNVY villainy
AIILLPRS spirilla
AIILLWWW williwaw
AIILMMSS Islamism
AIILMNOR limnoria
AIILMNOT limation, miltonia
AIILMNPT palmitin
AIILMNRY liminary
AIILMNST Latinism
AIILMNTT militant
AIILMNTU minutial
AIILMPST Milpitas
AIILMRST mistrial, trialism
AIILMRTY limitary, military
AIILMSST Islamist
AIILMSTV vitalism
AIILNOPT oil paint, politian
AIILNOPV pavilion
AIILNORT train-oil
AIILNOSV visional
AIILNOTV novitial
AIILNPST Alpinist, tailspin
AIILNRSU Silurian
AIILNSTT Latinist
AIILNSTY salinity
AIILRSST Silistra
AIILRSTT trialist
AIILRTTY triality
AIILSTTV vitalist
AIILTTVY vitality
AIIMMMST mammitis
AIIMMNNY minyanim
AIIMMNTV vitamin M
AIIMNNOS insomnia
AIIMNOSS amission
AIIMNSTV nativism
AIIMNTTU titanium
AIIMOPSX apomixis
AIIMORTT imitator, timariot
AIIMOSST amitosis
AIIMPPRS priapism
AIIMPRTY imparity
AIIMRSST satirism
AIIMRSTU tiramisu
AIIMRUVV vivarium
AIIMSSTT mastitis
AIINNOSV invasion
AIINNOTV nivation
AIINNQTU quintain
AIINNSTY insanity
AIINOSTT ostinati
AIINPRSS aspirins
AIINPRTX paintrix
AIINRRTT irritant
AIINRRTY nitriary
AIINSTTV nativist, visitant
AIINTTVY nativity
AIIORSTV ovaritis
AIIORTTV vitiator
AIIPRRST airstrip
AIIPRSST sapristi
AIIRSSTT satirist, sitarist, tarsitis
AIJKKNOU kinkajou
AIJKLMNU junk mail
AIJLLOOR jillaroo
AIJLLOVY jovially
AIJLNOPT lap joint
AIJLNTUY jauntily
AIJMORTY majority
AIJNOPPY popinjay
AIKKLLRW Kirkwall
AIKKMOOR korimako
AIKKNOTY kantikoy
AIKKRTUZ zikkurat
AIKLMRST tram silk
AIKLMWYY Milky Way
AIKLNNPS snap-link
AIKLNORS rasolnik
AIKLNOSZ Koszalin
AIKLNPST lantskip
AIKLNSWY swankily

AIKLOSUV souvlaki
AIKLOTTW kilowatt
AIKMMNOO makimono
AIKMMNRT mint mark
AIKMMOSS akosmism
AIKNNOOS nainsook
AIKNORTY karyotin
AIKNRSST Sanskrit
AIKOPPRS propiska
AILLLNOO linalool
AILLLOOP pillaloo
AILLLPSU lapillus
AILLMOSS Limassol
AILLMOST maillots
AILLMOSY loyalism
AILLMOTY molality
AILLMPRY primally
AILLMPSU palliums
AILLMRTY Myrtilla
AILLMRUY arum lily
AILLMUUV alluvium
AILLNNOV vanillon
AILLNOPP papillon
AILLNOPV pavillon
AILLNOST stallion
AILLNOSU allusion
AILLNOTW Low Latin
AILLNOUV alluvion
AILLNPSY spinally
AILLNPTU puntilla
AILLNPTY pliantly
AILLOQTU toquilla
AILLORSY sailorly
AILLORTT littoral, tortilla
AILLOSTY loyalist
AILLOTTV villotta
AILLPPRU pupillar
AILLPRSY spirally
AILLPSTY playlist
AILLPSWY spillway
AILLRTUY ritually
AILLRTWY willyart
AILLSUVY visually
AILMMNOO monomial
AILMMNUU aluminum
AILMMORS moralism
AILMMORT immortal
AILMMRSY smarmily
AILMNNOT mannitol
AILMNNTU luminant
AILMNOOP palomino
AILMNOOR monorail
AILMNOOT motional
AILMNOPY Olympian, palimony
AILMNORY molinary
AILMNOSS Osmanlis
AILMNOST tonalism
AILMNOSU laminous
AILMNOUV volumina
AILMNPTU platinum
AILMNRUU lunarium
AILMNRUY luminary
AILMOORT motorial
AILMOPRX proximal
AILMORST moralist
AILMORSU solarium
AILMORSY royalism
AILMORTY molarity, morality
AILMOSTU solatium
AILMOSTV voltaism
AILMPPSY misapply
AILMPSST psalmist
AILMPSTY ptyalism
AILMRRSU ruralism
AILMRSTU altruism, muralist, traulism, ultraism
AILMRSTY Army List
AILMTUWY multi-way
AILNNOOT notional
AILNNOSW son-in-law
AILNNOTU lunation
AILNNPRU pinnular
AILNOOPT optional
AILNOOTV volation
AILNOPRU unipolar
AILNOPTY ponytail
AILNORTZ trizonal
AILNOSTT tonalist
AILNOSUV avulsion
AILNOSVY synovial
AILNOTTV volitant
AILNOTTY tonality
AILNOTUX luxation
AILNPPSY snappily
AILNPRUV pulvinar
AILNPSUU nauplius
AILNQRTU tranquil
AILNQTUY quaintly
AILNRRTU trial run
AILNRUWY unwarily
AILNSSTU stunsail
AILNSSUV Silvanus
AILNSTTU lutanist
AILNSTUU nautilus
AILNSTVY Navy List
AILNSYZZ snazzily
AILOOPPY polyopia
AILOOPRT troopial
AILOOPST sola topi
AILOOPTT paliotto
AILOORST isolator
AILOORTV violator
AILOPRST Tiraspol
AILOPRSU pliosaur
AILOPRTU troupial
AILOPRTY polarity
AILOPRUY polyuria
AILORSTY royalist, solitary
AILORTTU tutorial
AILORTUV outrival
AILOSSUY Aloysius
AILOTTTY totality
AILPPRUY pupilary
AILPRSTU stipular
AILPSTUY playsuit
AILRRSTU ruralist
AILRRSTY starrily
AILRRTUY rurality
AILRSSTU tissular
AILRSTTU altruist, ultraist
AILRSTTY straitly
AILRSUVV survival
AILRTTUY titulary
AIMMMNOU ammonium
AIMMMSUX maximums
AIMMNORS Romanism
AIMMNORT marmiton, mortmain
AIMMNOSW womanism
AIMMRRTT trim-tram
AIMMRSUU masurium
AIMNNOTU mountain
AIMNNOTY antimony, antinomy
AIMNNRTU ruminant
AIMNOORT moration
AIMNOORV Monrovia
AIMNOOTY myotonia
AIMNOQRU maroquin
AIMNORRW rain-worm
AIMNORST Monastir, Romanist
AIMNORSU marsouin
AIMNORTU Minotaur
AIMNORTY minatory
AIMNOSSX Saxonism
AIMNOSTU Mount Isa
AIMNOSTW womanist
AIMNOTTU mutation
AIMNOTXY taxinomy
AIMNPSTU putanism
AIMNRSTT tantrism, transmit
AIMNRSTU naturism
AIMNSSTU tsunamis
AIMOPRSS prosaism
AIMOPSSY symposia
AIMORRSU rosarium
AIMORRUV variorum
AIMPPRUU puparium
AIMPRRUZ Mirzapur
AIMRRSTT Tristram
AIMRTTUY maturity
AIMSSSTY miss-stay
AINNNOST Anniston, santonin
AINNNOTU nunation
AINNOORT ornation
AINNOOTT notation
AINNOOTV novation
AINNOOTZ zonation
AINNOOXY oxyanion
AINNORST santorin
AINNOSTV vinsanto
AINNOTTU nutation
AINNPRSU prunasin
AINNRSTU insurant
AINNRSTY tyrannis

AINNSTTY nystatin
AINOOPTT optation, potation
AINOORST Oristano
AINOORTT rotation
AINOOSTT ostinato
AINOOTTV votation
AINOPPTU pupation
AINOPRSZ prazosin
AINOPRTV proviant
AINOPTWY waypoint
AINOQRRU quarrion
AINORSST arsonist
AINORSTT strontia
AINORSTY satyrion
AINORTVY vanitory
AINOSSTX Saxonist
AINOSTTU titanous
AINOSTUV vanitous
AINPPRTT trippant
AINPRSSU Prussian
AINPRSTY prytanis
AINPSSSY synapsis
AINPSSTU puissant
AINPSTTU pant suit
AINQTTUY quantity
AINRSTTT tantrist
AINRSTTU naturist
AIOOORRT oratorio
AIOPRRTT portrait
AIOPRSST prosaist, protasis
AIOQSTUY aquosity
AIORRSTV varistor
AIORSTTV votarist
AIORSTUV virtuosa
AIOSSSTY isostasy
AIPPRSTT trappist
AIPPRSTY papistry
AIPRSSTU upstairs
AIPRSSTY sparsity
AIRRRRWW wirrwarr
AIRRSTTY artistry
AJNOPSXY jasponyx
AJORRTUY juratory
AKKOOPPT pok-ta-pok
AKLLNOTW wall-knot
AKLNNOPT plankton
AKLPRRSU larkspur
AKMNOOOT tokonoma
AKMNOOPU mokopuna
AKMNORTU Turkoman
AKMOORST Kostroma
AKMOPRST postmark
AKMORRWW warm work
AKNOOUYZ yokozuna
AKNOPSTW swankpot
AKOPRRTW part-work
ALLLPRUY plurally
ALLMNORY normally
ALLMNPSU Pullmans
ALLMOPSX smallpox
ALLMORTY mortally
ALLMOUWY mulloway
ALLMPRUU plumular
ALLMTUUY mutually
ALLNOOPS planosol
ALLOPSTY postally
ALLORTWW wallwort
ALMMNRUU nummular
ALMNNOOR non-moral
ALMNORTY matronly
ALMOOPRY playroom
ALMOPPRS proplasm
ALMOPPST lamp-post, spotlamp, stop lamp
ALMOSTTU sum total
ALMRRTYY martyrly
ALMRTUUY tumulary
ALNNOTWY wantonly
ALNOOPPR propanol
ALNOOPRT portolan
ALNOOPYZ polyzoan
ALNOORTY onolatry
ALNOPPTT pot plant
ALNOPRST plastron
ALNOPRTU portunal
ALNORRWY narrowly
ALNOTWWY tawny owl
ALNPPSTU supplant
ALNPSTUU pustulan
ALNRTTUY truantly
ALNSSUVY Sylvanus
ALOOOORT tooraloo
ALOOPPRS proposal
ALOORSUV valorous
ALOORTUV ovulator
ALOORTYZ zoolatry
ALOPPRYY polypary
ALOPPSUU papulous
ALOPRRSU sporular
ALOPRSTT port-last
ALOPRSTU postural, protalus, pulsator
ALOPSSTT last post
ALOPSTUU patulous
ALORSTTW saltwort
ALORSUVY savourly
ALORTUWY outlawry
ALOSTTUZ Zlatoust
ALPPSTUY platypus
ALPRSTUU pustular
AMMNOORT motorman
AMMNPTUY tympanum
AMMORRWY army worm
AMNNOSSU mass noun
AMNNOSTW townsman
AMNNOTTU mountant
AMNNSTTU stuntman
AMNOOOPT onomatop
AMNOOSTT ottomans
AMNOOTUY autonomy
AMNOOTXY taxonomy
AMNOPRST portsman
AMNOPRSW span-worm
AMOOPRSY pyrosoma
AMOORRTY moratory
AMOORTWY motorway
AMOOTTUY autotomy
AMOPRSXY paroxysm
AMOQSSUU squamous
AMORRTUY mortuary
AMORSTTU outsmart
ANNOPRTY non-party
ANNOSSTU stannous
ANNPRSUY spun yarn
ANOOPRRT pronator
ANOPRTTU trapunto
ANOQRRSU quarrons
ANORSUVY unsavory
ANPRSTUU pursuant
ANRRSTTU star turn
ANRRTTUY truantry
AOOOPRTZ protozoa
AOOPPRSY apospory
AOOPRSSU saporous
AOOPRSTT pot roast
AOOPRSTU atropous
AOOPRSTW soapwort
AOOPRSUV vaporous
AOOPRTTY potatory
AOOPTTXY topotaxy
AOORRTTY rotatory
AOORSSUV savorous
AOPPRSST passport
AOPRRTUY portuary
AORRSTTW starwort
AORSTTTU outstart
APPRRTUY purparty
BBBCEOWY cobwebby
BBBEILRU bubblier
BBBEINOT bobbinet
BBBELRUY blubbery
BBBEOOTU boob tube
BBBGILNU blubbing
BBBINOPY bobby pin
BBCDERSU scrubbed
BBCEEILU blue bice
BBCEHIRU chubbier
BBCEILRS scribble
BBCEILRU clubbier
BBCEIRST scribbet
BBCEKLSU blesbuck
BBCELRSU scrubble
BBCEMNOU buncombe
BBCERRSU scrubber
BBCGIINR cribbing
BBCGILNU clubbing
BBCHILUY chubbily
BBCHKOOS boschbok
BBCHKSUU bushbuck
BBCILRSY scribbly
BBCKLOOU book club
BBDDDIIY biddy-bid
BBDDEEMO demobbed
BBDDEINU dubbined
BBDDIIII bidibidi
BBDDMMUU dumb-dumb
BBDEEGIT gibbeted
BBDEERSU sub-breed
BBDEHORT throbbed
BBDEILLR bellbird
BBDEILRR dribbler

BBDEILRT	dribblet	**BBILOSUU**	bibulous	**BCEEERSU**	berceuse
BBDEILRU	bluebird	**BBILSTUY**	stubbily	**BCEEFFTY**	by-effect
BBDEIMOV	dive-bomb	**BBLLNNUU**	buln-buln	**BCEEFILN**	fencible
BBDEINOR	ribboned	**BBLLOUYY**	bully boy	**BCEEGLLU**	glee club
BBDEIOSY	bobsy-die	**BBNORSTU**	stubborn	**BCEEHILN**	liebchen
BBDEIQSU	squibbed	**BCCCIILY**	bicyclic	**BCEEHKSU**	buckshee
BBDELLMU	dumb-bell	**BCCDHIKO**	dobchick	**BCEEHLOT**	beclothe
BBDELSTU	stubbled	**BCCEHIRU**	cherubic	**BCEEIILM**	imbecile
BBDGINRU	drubbing	**BCCEIILO**	libeccio	**BCEEIKRR**	bickerer
BBDIKMUY	dybbukim	**BCCEIIOS**	cicisbeo	**BCEEILLR**	belleric
BBDLOOWY	body blow	**BCCEIKLO**	iceblock	**BCEEINOT**	cenobite
BBDOSUYY	busybody	**BCCEILRU**	crucible	**BCEEIRST**	Bicester
BBEEIIRR	beriberi	**BCCEILRY**	bicycler	**BCEEIRSX**	exscribe
BBEEIRRS	berberis	**BCCEMRUU**	cucumber	**BCEELOOR**	borecole
BBEELLLU	bluebell	**BCCIIMOR**	microbic	**BCEELRTU**	tubercle
BBEELMTU	betumble	**BCCIKLLO**	cock-bill	**BCEEMNRU**	encumber
BBEEOPPR	bebopper	**BCCILMOU**	columbic	**BCEEMRRU**	cerebrum
BBEERRRY	berberry	**BCCILOOR**	broccoli	**BCEERSTU**	suberect
BBEFIMOR	firebomb	**BCCIMNUU**	buccinum	**BCEFFIIR**	febrific
BBEGIIST	gibbsite	**BCCIRTUU**	cucurbit	**BCEFGHII**	Big Chief
BBEGILRY	glibbery	**BCCLOOOO**	cocobolo	**BCEFILOR**	forcible
BBEGILST	glibbest	**BCCOSTUU**	Cub Scout	**BCEGIINO**	biogenic
BBEGIRRU	grubbier	**BCCSSUUU**	succubus	**BCEGIMNO**	becoming
BBEGMORR	Bromberg	**BCDDEHIL**	childbed	**BCEGLNOO**	conglobe
BBEGRRUY	grubbery	**BCDEEEMR**	December	**BCEHIIRT**	bitchier
BBEHILRT	thribble	**BCDEEENR**	Debrecen	**BCEHILPU**	blue-chip
BBEHIOTW	bobwhite	**BCDEEGLU**	becudgel	**BCEHILRT**	britchel
BBEIITXY	bixbyite	**BCDEEHNR**	bedrench	**BCEHIMRS**	besmirch
BBEILNNO	bonnibel	**BCDEEIKN**	Benedick	**BCEHIMRU**	cherubim
BBEILORW	wobblier	**BCDEEILR**	credible	**BCEHLRSU**	bluchers
BBEILQRU	quibbler	**BCDEEILU**	educible	**BCEHMSTU**	besmutch
BBEILRRY	bilberry	**BCDEEINT**	Benedict	**BCEHORRU**	brochure
BBEIMMOT	time bomb	**BCDEEIRS**	describe	**BCEHRTTU**	Cuthbert
BBEIMOST	bomb-site	**BCDEEKRU**	reedbuck	**BCEHRTUY**	butchery
BBEINORS	snobbier	**BCDEEKTU**	bucketed	**BCEIIKLN**	iceblink
BBEIRSTU	stubbier	**BCDEELOR**	corbeled	**BCEIILMS**	miscible
BBEISTTU	tubbiest	**BCDEEORV**	bedcover	**BCEIILNV**	vincible
BBEKLNOR	knobbler	**BCDEEOTT**	obtected	**BCEIIMRS**	imbrices
BBEKLOOU	blue book	**BCDEHINS**	disbench	**BCEIINOT**	ibotenic
BBEKNOOT	bontebok	**BCDEIKRR**	brick red,	**BCEIINRS**	inscribe
BBELLOUY	bell-buoy		red-brick	**BCEILLLU**	cullible
BBELLRUY	lubberly	**BCDEILRY**	credibly	**BCEILNOO**	colobine
BBELORSY	slobbery	**BCDEILTU**	bile duct,	**BCEILORU**	orbicule
BBELRRUY	bulberry		ductible	**BCEILORW**	rice-bowl
BBENORSY	snobbery	**BCDEIMNO**	combined	**BCEILPRU**	republic
BBERRRUY	Burberry	**BCDEINOU**	ice-bound	**BCEIMNRU**	incumber
BBFGILNU	flubbing	**BCDEKOOO**	code book	**BCEIMRRU**	crumbier
BBGGINRU	grubbing	**BCDEMNOU**	uncombed	**BCEINORU**	bouncier
BBGIILMN	blimbing	**BCDENRUU**	uncurbed	**BCEINOVX**	biconvex
BBGIINNS	snibbing	**BCDGLLOO**	gold bloc	**BCEIOOPS**	bioscope
BBGIKNNO	knobbing	**BCDIIKRT**	tick-bird	**BCEIOOVX**	voice box
BBGILNSU	slubbing	**BCDIIPSU**	bicuspid	**BCEIORRS**	cribrose
BBGILRUY	grubbily	**BCDIKLLU**	duckbill	**BCEIORST**	bisector
BBGINNSU	snubbing	**BCDIKMRU**	mudbrick	**BCEIPRTU**	B-picture
BBGINSTU	stubbing	**BCDILMOY**	molybdic	**BCEIRRTY**	crebrity
BBGLOOWY	lobby-gow	**BCDILORU**	colubrid	**BCEJOORT**	objector
BBHILOSS	slobbish	**BCDIMORS**	scombrid	**BCEKLNUU**	unbuckle
BBHINOSS	snobbish	**BCDINRUU**	rubicund	**BCEKLORU**	blue rock
BBHIORTY	hobbitry	**BCDKNOOO**	boondock	**BCEKLSUY**	Buckley's
BBHIOSTY	hobbyist	**BCEEEFIN**	benefice	**BCELMRSU**	scrumble
BBHIRSUY	rubbishy	**BCEEEHRS**	breeches	**BCELOOTV**	bloc vote
BBHRSSUU	subshrub	**BCEEEINR**	Berenice	**BCEMOORS**	rose comb
BBIIINOT	bibition	**BCEEELRT**	celebret	**BCENNOOU**	obnounce
BBIKLNOO	bobolink	**BCEEENRS**	bescreen	**BCENORRY**	by-corner
BBILOSTY	lobbyist	**BCEEEQRU**	Quebecer	**BCEOORTU**	cube root

BCEORRWY	cowberry
BCFGLLOU	golf club
BCFHILNU	bulfinch
BCFIIMOR	morbific
BCFIIORT	fibrotic
BCFILORY	forcibly
BCFIMORU	cubiform
BCFLOOTU	club foot
BCFOORRU	curb roof
BCGIIKST	big stick
BCGIKLNU	buckling
BCGINNOU	bouncing
BCHIILTY	bitchily
BCHIISSU	hibiscus
BCHIKLOS	blockish
BCHILOOS	clobiosh
BCHIOORY	choirboy
BCHKNORU	buck-horn
BCHKOSTU	buckshot
BCHLNOUX	lunch box
BCHNORSU	bronchus
BCIIILMU	umbilici
BCIIMNOO	bionomic
BCIIMORU	ciborium
BCIINORV	vibronic
BCIINOST	biscotin
BCIISTUY	biscuity
BCIKKNSU	buckskin
BCIKLNOT	block tin
BCIKLOST	lobstick
BCIKORRW	cribwork
BCILLPUY	publicly
BCILMOOU	colobium
BCILMOSY	symbollc
BCILNOUY	bouncily
BCILOORU	bicolour
BCIMOSUX	music box
BCINOSSU	subsonic
BCINOSTU	subtonic
BCINOSUU	incubous
BCIOORST	robotics
BCKKOOOO	cookbook
BCKLLOOS	bollocks
BCKLLOUY	bullocky
BCKLNOSU	sunblock
BCKNOORT	Brockton
BCKOOOPY	copybook
BCLMNOOO	monobloc
BCLMOSSU	clubmoss
BCLMOSUU	Columbus
BCLOORTU	clubroot
BCMORSUU	cumbrous
BCOORSSW	crossbow
BCOOSTUY	Boy Scout
BCORSTTU	obstruct
BDDDEIRY	red biddy
BDDEEENT	endebted
BDDEEFLU	befuddle
BDDEEGGU	debugged
BDDEEGTU	budgeted
BDDEEHOS	deboshed
BDDEEIMM	bedimmed
BDDEEINT	indebted
BDDEEINW	bindweed
BDDEEIRS	birdseed

BDDEESSU	debussed
BDDEFIOR	Bideford
BDDEGINR	Bridgend
BDDEHIIN	hidebind
BDDEILLO	bdelloid
BDDEILNR	brindled
BDDEINNU	unbidden
BDDEINRU	underbid
BDDELOOR	blood red
BDDEOTYY	teddy boy
BDDGOOSY	dogsbody
BDDHIIRY	dihybrid
BDDHIMSU	Buddhism
BDDHISTU	Buddhist
BDDINOOW	woodbind
BDDINOSU	disbound
BDDINPUU	pudibund
BDEEEGRU	budgeree
BDEEEHTU	hebetude
BDEEEKNN	knee-bend
BDEEELLR	rebelled
BDEEELLV	bevelled
BDEEELNS	Ndebeles
BDEEEMMR	demember, membered
BDEEERTV	breveted
BDEEFFTU	buffeted
BDEEFGGO	befogged
BDEEFINR	befriend
BDEEFITT	befitted
BDEEFOOR	forebode
BDEEFOOW	beefwood
BDEEGGIW	bewigged
BDEEGGRU	begrudge, debugger
BDEEGILN	bleeding
BDEEGILR	begirdle
BDEEGINR	breeding
BDEEHLNO	beholden
BDEEHLOR	beholder
BDEEIILN	inedible
BDEEIINY	bindi-eye
BDEEIKRS	kerbside
BDEEILLL	libelled
BDEEILLT	billeted
BDEEILLU	eludible
BDEEILNN	bedlinen
BDEEILNO	bone idle
BDEEILNV	vendible
BDEEILOR	erodible
BDEEILRW	bewilder
BDEEIMRT	timbered
BDEEINOS	side-bone
BDEEINOT	obedient
BDEEINRT	interbed
BDEEINST	bendiest
BDEEIORS	osier bed
BDEEIRST	bestride
BDEEIRSU	debruise
BDEEIRSY	bird's-eye
BDEEKNRU	debunker
BDEELLMU	umbelled
BDEELLRW	well-bred
BDEELMNO	embolden
BDEELMPU	beplumed

BDEELNNO	dennebol
BDEELORU	redouble
BDEELORX	box elder
BDEEMORR	emborder
BDEEMOSS	embossed
BDEEMSSU	embussed
BDEENNOT	bonneted
BDEENORV	overbend
BDEEOPRW	bepowder
BDEEORRR	borderer, broderer
BDEEORST	bestrode
BDEEORTU	outbreed
BDEEOSSY	boss-eyed
BDEEOSTT	besotted
BDEEPRRU	pure-bred
BDEERRTU	true-bred
BDEERRWY	dewberry
BDEERTTU	rebutted
BDEFIKOR	biforked
BDEGHJRU	Jedburgh
BDEGIINT	debiting
BDEGINRW	berg wind
BDEGIORX	Oxbridge
BDEGLNOU	bludgeon
BDEGLOOR	Belgorod
BDEGOOSY	goodbyes
BDEGORRY	dogberry
BDEGORUW	budgerow
BDEHIMOR	home-bird
BDEHKOOR	herd book
BDEHLORT	Berthold
BDEHLSUV	bushveld
BDEHMOOY	homebody
BDEHOOOO	boohooed
BDEHORTW	Bedworth
BDEIIKRT	dirt bike
BDEIILMR	birdlime
BDEIILNN	blenniid
BDEIILRT	trilbied
BDEIILTY	debility
BDEIKLLU	bull-dike
BDEIKNOR	brodekin
BDEIKNSU	buskined
BDEIKRST	bedskirt
BDEILLMU	bdellium
BDEILMNO	imbolden
BDEILMOS	semi-bold
BDEILNNO	blondine
BDEILNRU	unbridle
BDEILOOR	bloodier
BDEILOQU	obliqued
BDEILORV	lovebird
BDEILORW	wildbore
BDEILOSS	bodiless
BDEILOSW	disbowel
BDEILRRY	lyre-bird
BDEIMNSU	nimbused
BDEIMORR	imborder
BDEIMORY	embryoid
BDEINOOW	woodbine
BDEINORV	ovenbird
BDEINRSU	burnside, sideburn
BDEINRUU	unburied

BDEIOORR broodier
BDEIOSUX suboxide
BDEIOTUX butoxide
BDEIRSSU disburse
BDEJORRU Borujerd
BDELLOOR bordello, doorbell
BDELLOUZ bulldoze
BDELMOSY symboled
BDELNNUU unbundle
BDELNOSS boldness
BDELNOTU unbolted
BDELOORV overbold
BDELORTU troubled
BDELORUU doublure
BDELORUY bouldery
BDELTTUW butt weld
BDEMNSSU dumbness
BDEMOOSY somebody
BDEMOOTT bottomed
BDENNOTU Dubonnet
BDENNRUU unburden, unburned
BDENOORU Eurobond
BDENOOTW bentwood
BDENOSSU sub-nosed
BDENOTTU buttoned
BDEOORVY overbody
BDEORRSU suborder
BDEORRTU obtruder
BDEORSUU duberous
BDERSUWY Dewsbury
BDFGNOOU fogbound
BDFILLLO billfold
BDFINRUU furibund
BDFLOTUU doubtful
BDGHOOUY doughboy
BDGIIKNR kingbird
BDGIILNN blinding
BDGIILNU building
BDGIINRY birdying
BDGILNOU doubling
BDGILNTU blind gut
BDGINORS birdsong, songbird
BDGINOTU doubting
BDGINSUU subduing
BDGKOOOO good Book
BDGKOOOS God's book
BDGNRUUY burgundy
BDHIIPRW whipbird
BDHILNOS blondish
BDHIMOOR rhomboid
BDHMOSUW dumbshow
BDHNOOTY hybodont
BDHOOPSY body shop
BDIIJOTU Djibouti
BDIIMRUU rubidium
BDILLOOY bloodily
BDILMORY morbidly
BDILNNSU sunblind
BDILNPRU purblind
BDILOORY broodily
BDILORTU brotulid
BDILRTUY turbidly
BDIMNORU dumb-iron, moribund
BDIMOSTU misdoubt
BDINNORR Dornbirn
BDINNRUW windburn
BDINOOOR Borodino
BDIOSTUY bodysuit
BDIOTTXY ditty box
BDJKNNOU junk bond
BDKNOOOR doorknob
BDKOOORW wordbook
BDKOORWY bodywork
BDKOOSTU stud book
BDLNOOOU doubloon
BDLOSTUW dust bowl
BDNNOOTU bunodont
BDNOOPTU pot-bound
BDNOOSUX soundbox
BDNOOTUU outbound
BDORUWZZ buzzword
BEEEEFLN enfeeble
BEEEENQU queen bee
BEEEENRT terebene
BEEEENRZ Ebenezer
BEEEFIST beefiest
BEEEFLSS feebless
BEEEFLST feeblest
BEEEGIRS besieger
BEEEGNRR Berenger
BEEEGRTT begetter
BEEEHLWW web-wheel
BEEEHMPU ephebeum
BEEEHNOR bohereen
BEEEHNOY honey bee
BEEEILLL libellee
BEEEILLT billetee
BEEEILRV believer
BEEEIRRZ breezier
BEEEIRST beeriest
BEEEKLRY Berkeley
BEEELLRT bretelle
BEEELLUV Bellevue
BEEELMNS ensemble
BEEELMRS resemble
BEEELMZZ embezzle
BEEELRVY Beverley
BEEEMMRR remember
BEEEMRTT embetter
BEEENRST tenebres
BEEENSST sebesten
BEEERRTV vertebre
BEEERSTT beetster
BEEFGINR befringe
BEEFGIRR Freiberg
BEEFHILS feeblish
BEEFILLT lifebelt
BEEFILLX flexible
BEEFILNU unbelief
BEEFINOR bonefire
BEEFLORW beflower
BEEFNORR freeborn
BEEFNRRY fen-berry
BEEFOORT freeboot
BEEFOTUU boutefeu
BEEGHILW big wheel
BEEGHRRY hegberry
BEEGIILL eligible
BEEGIILX exigible
BEEGILNV beveling
BEEGILRU beguiler
BEEGIMST misbeget
BEEGINNR beginner
BEEGINSW beeswing
BEEGMRSU submerge
BEEGNOTT begotten
BEEHHIRT behither
BEEHHMOT behemoth
BEEHIKLR herblike
BEEHILMN Blenheim
BEEHIMOT boehmite
BEEHINTW bethwine
BEEHIRST herbiest
BEEHJOST jobsheet
BEEHLLNT hell-bent
BEEHLOOR borehole
BEEHLRSS herbless
BEEHMORW home-brew
BEEHNRRT brethren
BEEIILNZ zibeline
BEEIIORS boiserie
BEEIISTZ bite-size
BEEIJSTU bejesuit
BEEIKLTU tubelike
BEEIKLWY biweekly
BEEILLLR libeller
BEEILLNU belluine, blue line
BEEILLRT billeter
BEEILLTT belittle
BEEILLTU tullibee
BEEILMOZ embolize
BEEILMPR periblem
BEEILNRR Berliner
BEEILNSS sensible
BEEILNST stilbene, tensible
BEEILNSU nebulise
BEEILNUZ nebulize
BEEILOTV lovebite
BEEILRRT terrible
BEEILRSV besilver
BEEILRYZ breezily
BEEIMMMR immember
BEEIMRTT embitter, imbetter
BEEINORT tenebrio
BEEINOTW bowenite
BEEIORTV overbite
BEEISSST tsessebi
BEEKNOPS bespoken
BEEKNOST steenbok
BEELLMTU umbellet
BEELLNTT bell tent
BEELLOSS lobeless
BEELLSUY bull's-eye
BEELMMOP bepommel
BEELMRRT trembler
BEELMRRU lumberer
BEELNORS Selborne

BEELNOSS boneless, noblesse
BEELNOSU nebulose
BEELNSSU blueness
BEELNTTU betel-nut
BEELOOST obsolete
BEELOQRU breloque
BEELPUZZ bepuzzle
BEELRTUU true-blue
BEELSSTU tubeless
BEEMNORV November
BEEMNRRU renumber
BEEMOPRT obtemper
BEEMORSS embosser
BEEMPPRU beer pump
BEEMRSSU submerse
BEEMRSTU bum steer
BEEMRTUZ zerumbet
BEENNOSS bonsense
BEENORTV verboten
BEENPRST besprent
BEENRSTW bestrewn
BEENRTTU brunette
BEENSTTX next-best
BEEOORRT root beer
BEEOORRV overbore
BEEOORTT beetroot
BEEORRSV observer
BEEORRTU bourtree
BEEORSST soberest
BEEORSSU suberose
BEEORSTU tuberose
BEEPPRSU prepubes
BEERRSTW brewster
BEERRTTU rebutter
BEERSSTY bretessy
BEERSSUV subserve
BEERSTTY by-street
BEESTTTU test tube
BEFGIINR briefing
BEFGILNU fungible
BEFHILSU bluefish
BEFHINOS bonefish
BEFHIRSU bushfire
BEFILLUX fluxible
BEFILLXY flexibly
BEFILMOR forelimb
BEFILOUY lifebuoy
BEFINOTU bufonite
BEFIOORT fire-boot
BEFISSTU fubsiest
BEFKLNUU blue funk
BEFLLLUY bellyful
BEFLNORS self-born
BEFLORUW furbelow
BEFNOORR forborne
BEFORRUY fourbery
BEGGIINN bingeing
BEGGINOR Ingeborg
BEGGINOT biggonet
BEGGIOST boggiest
BEGGISTU buggiest
BEGHILRT blighter, therblig
BEGHINOR neighbor
BEGHINRT brighten
BEGHIOSU big house
BEGHLNOU bung-hole
BEGHNOTU boughten
BEGHOSTU besought
BEGHOSUU bughouse
BEGIILLN libeling, liebling
BEGIILLY eligibly
BEGIIMRT big-timer
BEGIINOS big noise
BEGIINRZ zingiber
BEGIIRTT Brigitte
BEGIKMOS big smoke
BEGILLLU gullible
BEGILLNU bullgine
BEGILNNY benignly
BEGILNOR ignobler
BEGILNOV vignoble
BEGILNSS blessing, glibness
BEGIMNOY big money
BEGIMNSU embusing
BEGINOOS besognio
BEGINORS Gisborne
BEGLLORY gorbelly
BEGLMRRU grumbler
BEGLOOVX glovebox
BEGNORRU Orenburg
BEGNORTU burgonet
BEGNSSUU subgenus
BEHIIINN inhibine
BEHIILNN hinnible
BEHIKPSU push-bike
BEHILLOS shoebill
BEHILLST shell-bit
BEHILLTY blithely
BEHILMRT thrimble
BEHILMRW whimbrel
BEHILNPY biphenyl
BEHILORR horrible
BEHILRTU thurible
BEHIMNOO bonhomie
BEHINNOS shin bone
BEHINOSW wishbone
BEHINRTW new birth
BEHIRSTU brushite
BEHISSTU bushiest
BEHJLNOU Blue John
BEHLLOOT bolt-hole
BEHLLOOW blowhole
BEHLLPSU bell push
BEHLMRTU thrumble
BEHLMSTU humblest
BEHMMNOO bonhomme
BEHMNSTU bushment
BEHMOOOX homeobox
BEHNNOUY honeybun
BEHOORSX horsebox
BEHOOSUY houseboy
BEHORSSU rose bush
BEIIJLUZ jubilize
BEIIKLLN billiken
BEIIKRTZ kibitzer
BEIILMMO immobile
BEIILMNT biliment
BEIILMOZ mobilize
BEIILNNR bin liner
BEIILRSX ex-libris
BEIILRTT libretti
BEIILRUZ bruilzie
BEIIMNNU biennium
BEIINOPT epibiont
BEIINQUU biunique
BEIISTTT bittiest
BEIJMOUZ jumboize
BEIKKLNO knoblike
BEIKLMOW womb-like
BEIKLMRY Kimberly
BEIKLOTY kilobyte
BEIKLSTU bulkiest
BEIKOORT brookite
BEILLMSS limbless
BEILLMSU ebullism
BEILLNTU bulletin
BEILLOSU libelous
BEILLRTU true bill
BEILMMOS embolism
BEILMMOU embolium
BEILMNOR bromelin
BEILMNOU nobelium
BEILMNRU unlimber
BEILMNST nimblest
BEILMNUU nebulium
BEILMPTU plumbite
BEILMRSS brlmless
BEILMRSU sublimer
BEILNNTU buntline
BEILNOPS bonspiel
BEILNOST Nobelist
BEILNOVY bovinely
BEILNSSY sensibly
BEILNSTU nebulist
BEILOPPW blowpipe
BEILOPSS possible
BEILOQSU obliques
BEILORST strobile
BEILORTT libretto
BEILORWZ blowzier
BEILOSTW blowiest
BEILRRRU blurrier
BEILRRTU turrible
BEILRRTY terribly
BEILRSTU burliest
BEILRTTY bitterly
BEILSTTU subtitle
BEIMNSSU nimbuses
BEIMOORS ribosome
BEIMOOTT tombotie
BEIMORRV overbrim
BEIMORTX mitre box
BEIMORTY biometry
BEIMPSTU bumpiest
BEIMRSTU resubmit
BEINNOSS boniness
BEINNOST bonniest
BEINORTZ bronzite
BEINRSTU turbines
BEINSSSU business
BEIOORTZ robotize

BEIOOSTZ booziest
BEIOQTUU boutique
BEIORSTY sobriety
BEIOSSST bossiest
BEIPPRSU prepubis
BEIRSTTU butteris
BEISSTTU bustiest
BEJORTTU turbojet
BEKLNORY brokenly
BEKLOORT brooklet
BEKMOORU keurboom
BEKMOOSX smoke box
BEKNNORU unbroken
BEKNOOOP open book
BEKNOOOT notebook
BEKOOORV overbook
BEKOORST book-rest
BEKOORTU outbroke
BEKOOTTX textbook
BELLLLPU bell pull
BELLMRUY lumberly
BELLNORW well-born
BELLNOSU bull-nose
BELLOORT boteroll
BELLOPTY pot belly
BELLOSWX swell-box
BELMOORS bloomers
BELMOORY bloomery
BELMORRT tremblor
BELMORSY sombrely
BELMPRUY plumbery
BELMRRUY mulberry
BELMRSTU stumbler
BELNOORT noble rot
BELNOSUU nebulous
BELNSTUU unsubtle
BELOOOSX loose box
BELOORSV Bolsover
BELOORSW rosebowl
BELOORTT tetrobol
BELOORVW overblow
BELOOSST bootless
BELOOTUV obvolute
BELORRTU troubler
BELOSTUU tubulose
BELOSTUY obtusely
BELPRSUY superbly
BELRSSSU Brussels
BELRSTTU rust belt
BELRSTUY blustery
BELRTUUU tubulure
BELSSTTU subtlest
BELSTTUY subtlety
BEMNNSSU numbness
BEMNOORT trombone
BEMNOORW new broom
BEMNOOXY money box
BEMNSTUU nembutsu
BEMOORRS sombrero
BEMORTUW tube worm
BENNNOTU unbonnet
BENNOSSU snub nose
BENOORSU burnoose
BENORRSU suborner
BENORRTU true-born
BENORRUV overburn
BENSSSUY busyness
BEOOORTV overboot
BEOORRRW borrower
BEOORRSY oso-berry
BEOPRSSX press box
BEORRRUW burrower
BEORRSTU robuster
BEORRSTW browster
BEORSSTU obstruse
BEORSTUU tuberous
BEORSUVY overbusy
BEOSSTUU busteous
BERSSTTU buttress
BESSSSUY byssuses
BFFFLMUU bum fluff
BFFHORSU brush-off
BFFNOSUX snuffbox
BFFOSSTU sob-stuff
BFGHINTU bun fight
BFGLLORU bullfrog
BFHILOST fish-bolt
BFHILOSW blowfish, fishbowl
BFHIMNSU numb-fish
BFIILMOU bifolium
BFIIORSS fibrosis
BFILLMRU brim-full
BFILLSSU blissful
BFILORTU flibutor
BFIMNOOR boniform
BFIMORTU tubiform
BFLLNOWY flyblown
BFLOORSU subfloor
BGGIILNO obliging
BGGLOOUY bugology
BGHHINOR high-born
BGHHIORW highbrow
BGHIINRT birthing
BGHILRTY brightly
BGHINORT Brighton
BGHLRSUU lushburg
BGHORRUX Roxburgh
BGIIIMNO iimbongi
BGIIKLNN blinking
BGIILLNS Billings
BGIILNPP blipping
BGIILNRS brisling
BGIILNTY bitingly
BGIIMMNR brimming
BGIIMNRU imbruing
BGIINNSW swingbin
BGIINORT orbiting
BGIKLNOT kingbolt
BGILLLUY gullibly
BGILLNOU globulin
BGILLNRU bullring
BGILMNOO blooming
BGILMNPU plumbing
BGILMNTU tumbling
BGILMOTU gumbotil
BGILNORT ringbolt
BGILNORY boringly
BGILNOTT blotting
BGILNRRU blurring
BGINNORW browning
BGINORST strobing
BGKNOOOS songbook
BGLOORXY glory-box
BGLOORYY bryology
BGMNOOOR gombroon
BGOPRSUU subgroup
BHHOOTUU tohu-bohu
BHIILMPS blimpish
BHIIMRST misbirth
BHIIOORS oshibori
BHIIOPRT prohibit
BHIKLLOO billhook
BHILLNOR hornbill
BHILLSTU bullshit
BHILORRY horribly
BHILOSYY boyishly
BHIMNORT thrombin
BHIMOOPR biomorph
BHINORSW brownish
BHINOTTU bountith
BHIORRST short rib
BHIRSTTU tristubh
BHJLLNOU John Bull
BHKMNOOY hymn book
BHKNOOOR hornbook
BHKOOOPS bookshop
BHLLNORU bullhorn
BHLLRSUU bullrush
BHLOOOTT tolbooth
BHMMOTTU Tom Thumb
BHMNTTUU thumb nut
BHMORSTU thrombus
BHMRSSUU bum's rush
BHNOOOST bosthoon
BHOOSSST boss-shot
BIIKMRSS Simbirsk
BIIKNOOT bootikin
BIILLMOR morbilli
BIILLNOS billions
BIILMMOS mobilism
BIILMOTY mobility
BIILNOOV oblivion
BIILNOTY nobility
BIILNTUY nubility
BIILORST strobili
BIILSTTW witblits
BIIQTUUY ubiquity
BIIRSSTU bursitis
BIJNOSTU subjoint
BIKLOOPT piblokto
BIKOOUUZ bouzouki
BILLNOOU bouillon
BILLOWYZ blowzily
BILMMPSU plumbism
BILMOOQU quilombo
BILMOSTU botulism
BILNNOOY loony-bin
BILNOSUU nubilous
BILOORST sorbitol
BILOPSSY possibly
BILORSST bristols
BIMNOSTY symbiont
BIMNRUUV viburnum
BIOOPSTT post-obit

BIOOSSTU	boistous
BIOPRSTW	bowsprit
BIORSTTY	botrytis
BIORSTUY	bistoury
BIOSSTUU	bustious
BIOSTTUY	obtusity
BKKOOORW	bookwork, workbook
BKMOOORW	bookworm
BKNOOPST	stop-knob
BLLLLOOY	loblolly
BLMOOOTY	lobotomy
BLMOOSSY	blossomy
BLMOPSUU	plumbous
BLNOORWW	brown owl
BLNSTUUY	unsubtly
BLOOSSTY	slyboots
BLORSTUY	robustly
BLOSTUUU	tubulous
BMNOOOOT	moon boot
BMNOOOTW	boom town
BMNOOSST	bons mots
BMOOPTTU	bottom-up
BMOORTTY	bottomry
BNNORTUW	nut brown
BNNOTTUU	unbutton
BNOOOSTW	snow boot
BNOOOSUY	sonobuoy
BNOOSTWY	Boys Town
BNORTTUU	burnt-out
BNRSSTUU	sunburst
BOOPPRRY	opprobry
BOORSSTY	sob story
BORSTTUU	outburst
BORSTUUY	butyrous
BOSSTUUU	bustuous
CCCEEILT	eclectic
CCCEGOSY	coccyges
CCCEILNY	encyclic
CCCEOSXY	coccyxes
CCCIILNO	niccolic
CCCILNOY	cyclonic
CCCINSTU	succinct
CCCIOORS	scirocco
CCCKOORW	cockcrow
CCDDIKSU	scuddick
CCDEEENR	credence
CCDEEINS	scienced
CCDEEIOP	codpiece
CCDEEKOY	cock-eyed
CCDEENOR	conceder
CCDEHIPU	hiccuped
CCDEHLTU	declutch
CCDEHORU	crouched
CCDEHRTU	crutched
CCDEIILO	cleidoic
CCDEIIMU	cecidium
CCDEIINO	coincide
CCDEINOR	corniced
CCDEINOT	Occident
CCDEIOPP	coppiced
CCDELNOU	conclude
CCDEORRU	occurred
CCDHIIOR	dichroic
CCDHIIOT	dichotic
CCDHIKOP	dopchick
CCDHINOO	conchoid
CCDIILNU	nuclidic
CCDIINOS	scincoid
CCDIINST	discinct
CCDIIORT	dicrotic
CCDINOTU	conducti
CCDKOOOW	woodcock
CCDLOSTU	cold cuts
CCEEEEHH	chee-chee
CCEEELMN	Clemence
CCEEERSX	excresce
CCEEFHHL	Ech Chlef
CCEEGINR	recceing
CCEEHIOP	Chicopee
CCEEHIPT	ephectic
CCEEHMOO	Ecce Homo
CCEEHRSY	screechy
CCEEILNR	encircle
CCEEILNT	elenctic
CCEEILPY	epicycle
CCEEILRT	electric, lectrice
CCEEINOR	cicerone
CCEEINOV	conceive
CCEEIORV	coercive
CCEEIRSV	cervices, crescive
CCEEITTU	eutectic
CCEEKLOR	cockerel
CCEEKNRW	crew neck
CCEELMNY	clemency
CCEELORV	covercle
CCEELOSS	scoleces
CCEELRRY	recycler
CCEEMMNO	commence
CCEEMMOR	commerce
CCEEMOPS	compesce
CCEENNOS	ensconce
CCEENORT	concrete
CCEENRRU	currence
CCEENRST	crescent
CCEFIIPS	specific
CCEFIRRU	crucifer
CCEFLLOU	floccule
CCEFLOOS	floccose
CCEGILRY	glyceric
CCEGNOOS	cognosce
CCEHIIMR	chimeric
CCEHIIOT	teichoic
CCEHILNR	clincher
CCEHILOR	choleric
CCEHILOT	cochlite
CCEHILOY	choicely
CCEHINOR	corniche
CCEHINOT	conchite
CCEHIORT	ricochet
CCEHKLRU	chuckler
CCEHKMSU	check sum
CCEHKOTU	checkout
CCEHLMOR	cromlech
CCEHLNNU	unclench
CCEHORRS	scorcher
CCEHORTT	crotchet
CCEHRSTU	scutcher
CCEIIKLN	nickelic
CCEIILNR	incircle
CCEIILNT	enclitic
CCEIILNU	culicine
CCEIILOR	licorice
CCEIILPT	ecliptic
CCEIILST	scilicet
CCEIINOR	ciceroni
CCEIIRRT	circiter
CCEIKOST	cockiest
CCEILMOP	complice
CCEILNOR	cornicle
CCEILNUY	unicycle
CCEILOSS	scolices
CCEILPUU	picucule
CCEILRRU	curricle
CCEILRTY	tricycle
CCEILRUU	curlicue
CCEIMNOO	economic
CCEIMOST	cosmetic
CCEIMRRU	mercuric
CCEINNOS	insconce
CCEINNOV	convince
CCEINOOR	coercion
CCEINOOZ	Cenozoic
CCEINORT	concerti, necrotic
CCEINOTT	tectonic
CCEINPRT	precinct
CCEINRTU	cincture
CCEIOORT	cocorite, crocoite
CCEIOPRU	occupier
CCEIORST	cortices
CCEIPRTU	cut-price
CCEIRSSU	circuses
CCEKLNOW	cowl neck
CCEKNOSS	Cessnock
CCEKORRY	crockery
CCEKORSU	cocksure
CCELMOPT	complect
CCELOPSY	cyclopes
CCELRUUY	curlycue
CCENOORT	concerto
CCENOOTT	concetto
CCENORTY	cornetcy
CCENRRUY	currency
CCEOPRUY	reoccupy
CCEORSSU	crocuses
CCFIIRUX	crucifix
CCFILLOU	flocculi
CCFILNOT	conflict
CCFKLOOT	cock-loft
CCFLOOOO	locofoco
CCGHHIOU	hiccough
CCGHIILN	cichling
CCGILLOY	glycolic
CCGILNOU	gluconic
CCHHIINN	chin-chin
CCHHIITY	ichthyic
CCHHINOT	chthonic
CCHHNRUU	unchurch
CCHHOOOO	choo-choo
CCHHOOPP	chop-chop
CCHHOOWW	chow-chow

CCHHSSUU	cush-cush
CCHIINUZ	zucchini
CCHIISTU	Cushitic
CCHILMOW	milch cow
CCHILNNU	unclinch
CCHKOPTU	putchock
CCHNRSUY	scrunchy
CCIIKKPW	pickwick
CCIIKKTT	tick-tick
CCIIKNPY	picnicky
CCIILLRY	Cyrillic
CCIILSTY	cyclitis
CCIIMNSY	cynicism
CCIIRTUY	circuity
CCIKKLOP	picklock
CCIKKOTT	tick-tock
CCIKNOPR	princock
CCIKNORT	con-trick
CCILLOPP	clip-clop
CCILORUU	curculio
CCILOSSY	cyclosis
CCINOPRT	procinct
CCINORSY	cryonics
CCIOOTXY	oxytocic
CCJNNOTU	conjunct
CCKKLMUU	muckluck
CCKMOOOR	moorcock
CCKNORTU	turncock
CCKOOPST	stopcock
CCKOPRSU	cockspur
CCLLOTUY	occultly
CCLMOOPU	coco-plum
CCLOORSU	occlusor
CCMMOOOO	moco-moco
CCOOOORR	corocoro
CCOOSSUU	couscous
CCOOTTUU	tuco-tuco
CCORSSTU	cross-cut
CCTTUUUU	tucutucu
CDDDIIOY	diddicoy
CDDEEEJT	dejected
CDDEEENT	decedent
CDDEEGLU	cudgeled
CDDEEIRT	credited
CDDEEKOT	docketed
CDDEEKUW	duckweed
CDDEELMO	co-meddle
CDDEELUY	deucedly
CDDEERUV	decurved
CDDEHIRT	Redditch
CDDEIIKU	cuddikie
CDDEIKOS	dockside
CDDEILNU	included
CDDEILRU	cuddlier
CDDEIRRU	cruddier
CDDGHILO	godchild
CDDGILOS	gold disc
CDDGINSU	scudding
CDDHIIRY	dihydric
CDDHILOS	cloddish
CDDIISTY	dytiscid
CDDOOORW	cordwood
CDEEEHNS	Enschede
CDEEEHOR	decohere
CDEEEINV	evidence
CDEEEIRV	deceiver
CDEEEITX	de-excite
CDEEELLX	excelled
CDEEELOS	coleseed
CDEEELST	deselect
CDEEEMRS	Mercedes
CDEEENNT	tendence
CDEEENOS	secondee
CDEEENRT	decenter, decentre
CDEEENTX	excedent
CDEEERTT	detecter
CDEEFFOR	coffered
CDEEFIIL	felicide, ice field
CDEEFIIM	femicide
CDEEFIIT	feticide
CDEEFIRR	Frederic
CDEEFKLL	fleckled
CDEEFKOR	foredeck
CDEEFLOT	cold feet
CDEEFNNU	unfenced
CDEEFNOR	confeder
CDEEFORS	frescoed
CDEEFORT	defector
CDEEGIIR	regicide
CDEEGINO	genocide
CDEEGIOS	geodesic
CDEEGIOT	geodetic
CDEEGIRU	cudgerie
CDEEHILN	lichened
CDEEHILP	cheliped
CDEEHILS	chiseled
CDEEHIOR	dichoree
CDEEHIPR	decipher
CDEEHLSU	schedule
CDEEHNNR	endrench
CDEEHPRY	decypher
CDEEHRTW	wretched
CDEEHSSU	duchesse
CDEEIILT	elicited
CDEEIIMN	medicine
CDEEIIMP	epidemic
CDEEIINT	indictee
CDEEIIPS	dispiece
CDEEIISV	decisive
CDEEIITT	dietetic
CDEEIKLN	nickeled
CDEEIKLR	deer-lick
CDEEIKNV	invecked
CDEEIKPT	picketed
CDEEIKRR	dickerer
CDEEIKRW	wickeder
CDEEIKTT	ticketed
CDEEILNP	depencil, penciled, pendicle
CDEEILNR	decliner
CDEEILNS	licensed
CDEEILNT	denticle
CDEEILRS	sclereid
CDEEILRT	derelict
CDEEIMNR	endermic
CDEEIMOR	mediocre
CDEEIMRV	decemvir
CDEEINNS	incensed
CDEEINNT	indecent
CDEEINPT	depeinct
CDEEINRW	Ceridwen
CDEEINTU	inductee
CDEEINTV	invected
CDEEINVY	evidency
CDEEIORV	divorcee
CDEEIPRT	decrepit, depicter
CDEEIPRU	pedicure
CDEEIRRS	descrier
CDEEIRRT	redirect
CDEEIRST	discreet, discrete
CDEEIRSV	descrive
CDEEIRTU	deuteric
CDEEISTT	discette
CDEEITUV	eductive
CDEEKLLW	well deck
CDEEKOPT	pocketed
CDEEKORT	rocketed
CDEEKORV	overdeck
CDEEKOST	socketed
CDEELLOR	cordelle
CDEELLPU	cupelled
CDEELLRU	cruelled
CDEELNPU	peduncle
CDEELNTY	decently
CDEELOOW	loco-weed
CDEELOPU	decouple
CDEELORV	Velcroed
CDEELOST	closeted
CDEELPRU	preclude
CDEELRUX	excluder
CDEELSTU	delectus
CDEEMORT	ectoderm
CDEEMRTU	decretum
CDEENNOS	condense
CDEENNOU	denounce
CDEENNPY	pendency
CDEENNTY	tendency
CDEENORR	cornered
CDEENORS	seconder, seedcorn
CDEENORT	centrode
CDEENOTX	coextend
CDEENPRU	prudence
CDEENRUV	verecund
CDEEOOTV	dovecote
CDEEOPRS	proceeds
CDEEORRR	recorder, re-record
CDEEORST	corseted, sectored
CDEEORSU	escudero
CDEEORSV	co-versed
CDEEORTT	detector
CDEEORTV	vectored
CDEEOSST	cosseted
CDEEOSTU	custodee
CDEEPRST	sceptred
CDEERRRU	recurred
CDEERTUV	curveted
CDEFFINO	coffined

CDEFHIMO chiefdom
CDEFIIIL filicide
CDEFIIIT citified
CDEFIIOR codifier
CDEFIIRT drift-ice
CDEFIITY cityfied
CDEFIKRR Fredrick
CDEFINNU infecund
CDEFNORU unforced
CDEFOSSU focussed
CDEGIILO Goidelic
CDEGINSY dysgenic
CDEHHOTU Dutch hoe
CDEHIIKR Diekirch
CDEHIILO helicoid
CDEHIIMO homicide
CDEHIINO echinoid
CDEHIKOT Hocktide
CDEHIKOY dohickey
CDEHIKRW Herdwick
CDEHILNR children
CDEHILOR chloride
CDEHILRT eldritch
CDEHIMOT methodic
CDEHINNR indrench
CDEHIOTY theodicy
CDEHKLSU shelduck
CDEHNNOS non-sched
CDEHORSU chorused
CDEHOSSU hocussed
CDEHSSTU dutchess
CDEIIKKS sidekick
CDEIIKMM mimicked
CDEIIKRS dricksie
CDEIIKST dickiest
CDEIILMO domicile
CDEIILNN inclined
CDEIILNO indocile
CDEIILOT idiolect
CDEIILPS disciple
CDEIILRU ridicule
CDEIILRW wild rice
CDEIINNT incident
CDEIINOS decision
CDEIINRT indicter, indirect
CDEIINTY cytidine
CDEIINUV inducive
CDEIIOPR periodic
CDEIIOPS episodic
CDEIIOSU diecious
CDEIIPRR cirriped
CDEIIRTU diuretic
CDEIKLOR cordlike
CDEIKLRU luderick
CDEIKLWY wickedly
CDEIKNPU unpicked
CDEIKORR Roderick
CDEIKSTY city desk
CDEILLOR collider
CDEILLOU lodicule
CDEILLOY docilely
CDEILLPU pellucid
CDEILMRU dulcimer
CDEILNOS closed-in
CDEILNOU nucleoid
CDEILNOY celidony
CDEILNRY cylinder
CDEILNSU unsliced
CDEILOPU clupeoid
CDEILORS scleroid
CDEILORU cloudier
CDEILOSS disclose
CDEILRTY directly
CDEILSXY dyslexic
CDEIMOST comedist, domestic
CDEINNOW wind-cone
CDEINOPU cupidone
CDEINORR cordiner
CDEINORS consider
CDEINORT centroid, doctrine
CDEINORU decurion
CDEINOTU eduction
CDEINOUV unvoiced
CDEINPRS prescind
CDEINPRU unpriced
CDEINRRU incurred
CDEINSTY syndetic
CDEIOPRT depictor
CDEIOPST despotic
CDEIOPTY copy-edit
CDEIORRT creditor, director
CDEIORRV co-driver
CDEIORSV discover
CDEIPRST descript, scripted
CDEIPRSY cyprides
CDEIPRTU pictured
CDEIPSSU cuspides
CDEIRSUV scurvied
CDEISSSU discuses
CDEKLMOR clerkdom
CDEKLNOU unlocked
CDEKNOOU uncooked
CDEKOOPP poop deck
CDEKOORV rock-dove
CDEKOPSY copydesk
CDELLNOU Culloden
CDELLNUU unculled
CDELLORS scrolled
CDELLORU colluder
CDELLOTU cloudlet
CDELMNOO monocled
CDELMNOU columned
CDELNOSS coldness
CDELNOSY secondly
CDELNSUY secundly
CDELOORS cold sore
CDELOORU coloured, decolour
CDELOORV overcold
CDELORSS cordless
CDELRSUY cursedly
CDELRTUU cultured
CDELSSTU ductless
CDELSSUY cussedly
CDELSTTU scuttled
CDEMNOOW comedown, downcome
CDEMNOSU consumed
CDEMNOTU document
CDEMNSUU secundum
CDENNOOR condoner
CDENOORT creodont
CDENOOST secodont
CDENORTU cornuted
CDENRTUU undercut
CDENSSUU secundus
CDEOOPST postcode
CDEOORSU decorous
CDEOPRRU producer
CDEORRSS Red Cross
CDEORSST doctress
CDEORSTU seductor
CDEOSSTU custodes
CDERSTTU destruct
CDFFILOR Clifford
CDFIILSU fluidics
CDFIIMOR formicid
CDFIKORS disfrock
CDFKOORR Rockford
CDFNNOOU confound
CDGHINOR chording
CDGHORUY dry cough
CDGIKLNU duckling
CDGIKLOR gridlock
CDGILNOS scolding
CDGKLOOU good luck
CDGLOOOY codology
CDHHIILS childish
CDHIIORT hidrotic
CDHIIOSZ schizoid
CDHILOOP chilopod
CDHILOOS dolichos
CDHIMNOR Richmond
CDHIMOSU dochmius
CDHINNOR chondrin
CDHIOOPW woodchip
CDHIOORT trochoid
CDHIOPRW whipcord
CDHIOPRY hydropic
CDHIOPSY psychoid
CDHIORRT trichord
CDHIORTY hydrotic
CDHLOOOT colthood
CDHLOOPY copyhold
CDIIIMNU indicium
CDIIINSV inviscid
CDIIIORT dioritic
CDIIKMNO Dominick
CDIIKPST dipstick
CDIILOTY docility
CDIILTUY lucidity
CDIIMNOO co-domini
CDIIMNOU conidium, oncidium
CDIIMOST modistic
CDIIMOTY modicity
CDIINSTT distinct
CDIIOPRT dioptric
CDIIORSU sciuroid

CDIIPTUY cupidity, pudicity
CDIIRSTT district
CDIJNSTU disjunct
CDIKKNOW kick-down
CDIKKOPR drop kick
CDIKLPUY lucky dip
CDIKNOSW windsock
CDILLOTU dulcitol
CDILLOUY cloudily
CDILOORS discolor
CDILOORT lordotic
CDILOOTY cotyloid
CDILOSTY scolytid
CDIMOORT microdot
CDIMORSU scordium
CDINNQUU quidnunc
CDINOOOR coronoid
CDINORSW discrown
CDINORTU inductor
CDINOSTU discount
CDINPSTU dispunct
CDIOOOPT octopoid
CDIOOPRS prosodic
CDIOORRR corridor
CDIOPRSU cuspidor
CDISSTUY dytiscus
CDJLNOUY jocundly
CDKKMSUU musk duck
CDKOOOPW pockwood
CDKOOORW corkwood
CDKOPSUU duck soup
CDLLLOOP clodpoll
CDLOORTY doctorly
CDLOPRUW World Cup
CDMNOOPU compound
CDMNORUU corundum
CDNNOOOT conodont
CDNNOOSU consound
CDNNOOTY cynodont
CDOORRUY corduroy
CDORSSUW cuss word
CEEEEIPY eyepiece
CEEEELST selectee
CEEEFFIR effierce
CEEEFILR fleecier
CEEEFNOR conferee
CEEEGINX exigence
CEEEGITX exegetic
CEEEGMNR mergence
CEEEGNRV vergence
CEEEHIKR cheekier
CEEEHINS echeneis
CEEEHIRR cheerier
CEEEHIRS cheesier
CEEEHIST ice sheet
CEEEHKOR Cherokee
CEEEHLLR Cherelle
CEEEHLRV cheverel
CEEEHNNY Cheyenne
CEEEHNQU chequeen
CEEEIJTV ejective
CEEEILNN lenience
CEEEILNS licensee
CEEEILNT telecine
CEEEILRT erectile
CEEEILTV cleveite, elective
CEEEIMNN eminence
CEEEIMPR empierce
CEEEINNT enceinte
CEEEINOP one-piece
CEEEIPRR creepier
CEEEIPRV perceive
CEEEIPST set piece
CEEEIRRV receiver
CEEEIRSX exercise
CEEELLNR crenelle
CEEELPRT pre-elect
CEEELRRV cleverer
CEEELRST reselect
CEEELRTT electret
CEEEMNOU oecumene
CEEEMNRT cementer, cerement
CEEEMRTY cemetery
CEEEMSUX excuse-me
CEEENNRT encentre
CEEENNST sentence
CEEENPRS presence
CEEENPRT pretence
CEEENQSU sequence
CEEENRRS screener
CEEENRRT Terrence
CEEENRTX exercent
CEEERRTX excreter
CEEERSST sesterce
CEEERSWY screw eye
CEEFFIOS officese
CEEFFORR cofferer
CEEFFORT cofferet, effector
CEEFHIKR kerchief
CEEFHILS ice shelf
CEEFHLRT fletcher
CEEFHLRU cheerful
CEEFHNNO fenchone
CEEFHPRT prefetch
CEEFIKKR free-kick
CEEFILLY fleecily
CEEFILRY fiercely
CEEFINPP fippence
CEEFINRT frenetic, reinfect
CEEFIRST fiercest
CEEFKLSS feckless
CEEFLLLU fuel cell
CEEFLNOR Florence
CEEFLNTU feculent
CEEFLRUU flue-cure
CEEFMOOR forecome
CEEFNORR enforcer
CEEFNOTU outfence
CEEFNRVY fervency
CEEFOPRR perforce
CEEFOPRT perfecto
CEEFORST scot-free
CEEGHLOW cogwheel
CEEGHLRT gletcher
CEEGHNRT Gretchen
CEEGILOT eclogite
CEEGIMNN gennemic
CEEGINNO ecgonine
CEEGINOO cooeeing
CEEGINOR erogenic
CEEGINOX exogenic
CEEGINOZ cognizee
CEEGINPR creeping
CEEGINRT gentrice
CEEGINST genetics
CEEGINSU eugenics
CEEGINXY exigency
CEEGKNOR Greenock
CEEGLLMR germ cell
CEEGLRSS clergess
CEEGNNOO oncogene
CEEGNNOR congener
CEEGNORT congreet
CEEGNORV converge
CEEGNRVY vergency
CEEHHIRS Cheshire
CEEHIINT echinite
CEEHIIST ethicise
CEEHIITZ ethicize
CEEHIKLY cheekily
CEEHIKNW cheewink
CEEHILLM Michelle
CEEHILLN chenille, Hellenic
CEEHILLV cheville
CEEHILMT thelemic
CEEHILRS schliere
CEEHILRW clerihew
CEEHILRY cheerily
CEEHIMRT hermetic
CEEHINPR encipher
CEEHINPT phenetic
CEEHIOSU ice house
CEEHIOSV cohesive
CEEHIPRT herpetic
CEEHIRST chestier, estriche
CEEHIRTU heuretic
CEEHISTT esthetic
CEEHISTW chewiest
CEEHKRST sketcher
CEEHLLOR Rochelle
CEEHLMNU muncheel
CEEHLMOO hemocoel
CEEHLNOO Holocene
CEEHLNOT enclothe
CEEHLNSU elenchus
CEEHLORT reclothe
CEEHLOSS echoless
CEEHLRSU Hercules
CEEHNNOW nowhence
CEEHNNRT entrench
CEEHNOOO oenochoe
CEEHNORT coherent
CEEHNPRY encypher
CEEHNQRU quencher
CEEHNRRT retrench, trencher
CEEHNRSY chrysene
CEEHOPTT pochette

CEEHORST the score
CEEHOTTU chouette
CEEHRTTU teuchter
CEEHSSST chess set
CEEIIKLV vice-like
CEEIIMNP mince pie
CEEIIMPR epimeric, impierce
CEEIIMRT eremitic
CEEIINRT icterine
CEEIINVV evincive
CEEIIOPR perioeci
CEEIITVX excitive
CEEIJNOT ejection
CEEIJORR rejoicer
CEEIJRUV verjuice
CEEIKLLL cell-like
CEEIKLNN neckline
CEEIKLPR pickerel
CEEIKNNT kennetic
CEEIKNRS sickener
CEEIKPRT picketer
CEEILLLP pellicle
CEEILLNT lenticel, lenticle
CEEILLRV Vercelli
CEEILMNT Melicent
CEEILMOR comelier
CEEILMRV vermicle
CEEILNNT centinel
CEEILNNY leniency
CEEILNOP Pliocene
CEEILNOT election
CEEILNOV violence
CEEILNRR recliner
CEEILNRS licenser, silencer
CEEILNRV vernicle
CEEILORZ creolize
CEEILPRY creepily
CEEILPXX exciplex
CEEILQSU liquesce
CEEILRST sclerite
CEEILRSV versicle
CEEILRTU reticule
CEEILRTY celerity
CEEILSSV viceless
CEEILSTT telestic, testicle
CEEIMMRS mesmeric
CEEIMNNY eminency
CEEIMNPS specimen
CEEIMORT core time, meteoric
CEEINNOP pine cone
CEEINNOT neotenic
CEEINNPZ pince-nez
CEEINNRS incenser
CEEINNRT incenter, incentre
CEEINNSS niceness
CEEINNST nescient
CEEINORR encierro
CEEINORT erection, neoteric
CEEINORV overnice
CEEINORX exocrine
CEEINOST seicento
CEEINOTV evection
CEEINPRT prentice
CEEINPST pectines
CEEINPSX sixpence
CEEINPTT pincette
CEEINQRU quercine
CEEINRRS sincerer
CEEINRST scienter, secretin
CEEINRSU insecure, sinecure
CEEINRTT reticent
CEEINRTU ceinture, enuretic
CEEINSTY cysteine
CEEIOPPR pericope
CEEIOPPS episcope
CEEIOPST to pieces
CEEIOPTW two-piece
CEEIORST esoteric
CEEIORSX exorcise
CEEIORTX exoteric
CEEIORXZ exorcize
CEEIOSTV covetise
CEEIPPRU Curepipe
CEEIPPSS cesspipe
CEEIPPTU eupeptic
CEEIRRSW screwier
CEEIRRTU ureteric
CEEIRSTV vertices
CEEJKOTT jockette
CEEJORRT rejector
CEEKKNPS kenspeck
CEEKLNSS neckless
CEEKLRSS clerkess, reckless
CEEKMOPT empocket
CEEKNORR reckoner
CEEKOPRX ox-pecker
CEELLMOU molecule
CEELLMST stem cell
CEELLORT coterell
CEELLRRU crueller
CEELLRVY cleverly
CEELLSSU clueless
CEELMOPT complete
CEELMORW welcomer
CEELMOST telecoms
CEELMRTU electrum
CEELNOPU opulence
CEELNOPY lycopene
CEELNORT El Centro, electron
CEELNPTU centuple
CEELNRTY recently
CEELNSTU esculent, unselect
CEELOPRS preclose
CEELORSS sclerose
CEELORST corselet, selector
CEELORTT cotterel
CEELORTV coverlet
CEELOSST close-set
CEELOSSU leucoses
CEELRRTU lecturer
CEELRSTU cruelest
CEELRSTY secretly
CEELRSUY securely
CEEMMNTU cementum
CEEMMOTY mycetome
CEEMNORW newcomer
CEEMNORY ceremony
CEEMNOYZ coenzyme
CEEMNSST cessment
CEEMOORV overcome
CEEMOOTY oomycete
CEEMOSST comtesse
CEEMRSTU secretum
CEENNOOS nose-cone
CEENNORS on-screen
CEENNORT cretonne
CEENNORU renounce
CEENNORV convener
CEENNPPU nuppence
CEENOORV once-over
CEENOPRS scorpene
CEENOPTW twopence
CEENORSV conserve, converse
CEENORTT trecento
CEENORVY conveyer
CEENPPTU tuppence
CEENSSSU censuses
CEENSSTU cuteness
CEEOORST creosote
CEEOPRRT receptor
CEEOPRTX exceptor
CEEOQTTU coquette
CEEORRRS sorcerer
CEEORRST secretor
CEEORRSU recourse, resource
CEEORRUV overcure
CEEORRVY recovery
CEEORTTV corvette
CEEORTUX executor
CEEPRRSU precurse
CEERRSTU rest-cure
CEERSSTW set screw
CEERTUXY executry
CEFFFLUU cufuffle
CEFFINNO encoffin
CEFFIOPR off-price
CEFFIORU coiffeur, coiffure
CEFFLORU forceful
CEFFORSY scoffery
CEFGHINT fetching
CEFHIIMS mischief
CEFHILNR flincher
CEFHILRT flichter
CEFHINSU fuchsine
CEFHISTU fuchsite
CEFHKOOR forehock
CEFIILTY felicity
CEFIIOPR opificer

CEFIIPRT petrific
CEFIIRRT ferritic, terrific
CEFIKLOR firelock
CEFILLLO follicle
CEFILLPT cleft lip
CEFILMRU merciful
CEFILNOT flection
CEFILOUV voiceful
CEFIMNTU infectum
CEFIMOST comfiest
CEFINNOR confiner
CEFINORS forensic, forinsec
CEFINORT infector
CEFINOTT confetti
CEFIORTY ferocity
CEFIRSTU frutices
CEFKLOOR forelock
CEFKLRUW wreckful
CEFLLOSU floscule
CEFLNRUU furuncle
CEFOORST soft-core
CEFOPRSU prefocus
CEFORSTU fructose
CEGGILOO geologic
CEGGILOR cloggier
CEGGILRS scriggle
CEGGLNOU glucogen
CEGGLNOY glycogen
CEGHHHIT high-tech
CEGHIINY hygienic
CEGHIJNN Jincheng
CEGHIMNS scheming
CEGHIRTU theurgic
CEGHMRUY chemurgy
CEGHNNUY Yuncheng
CEGHNORS groschen
CEGHORSU choregus
CEGIILNR clingier
CEGIILNT gentilic
CEGIILOS logicise
CEGIILOZ logicize
CEGIINNT enticing
CEGIINOS isogenic
CEGIINPR piercing
CEGIINRT trigenic
CEGIINRV vice ring
CEGIINSS gneissic
CEGIINTX exciting
CEGIIOST egoistic
CEGIKNNR ring-neck
CEGIKNRW wrecking
CEGILMNO comeling, comingle
CEGILNOO neologic
CEGILNPU cupeling
CEGILNRY glycerin
CEGILNTU cultigen
CEGILRSY lysergic
CEGIMNOR grincome
CEGIMNOY myogenic
CEGINNOP pnicogen
CEGINNOS consigne
CEGINNRT centring
CEGINNSY ensigncy
CEGINOOP geoponic
CEGINOOR orogenic
CEGINORT gerontic
CEGINORV covering
CEGINOTV coveting
CEGINOXY oxygenic
CEGINRSU rescuing, scungier
CEGINRSW screwing
CEGINRSY synergic
CEGLLOOU collogue
CEGLLORY glycerol
CEGLLRYY glyceryl
CEGLNOTY cogently
CEGLOOTY cetology
CEGMNNOO cognomen
CEGMOORU comrogue
CEGMOORY gerocomy
CEGNNORY conynger
CEGNNPUY pungency
CEGNORSS congress
CEGNORSU scrounge
CEGORRSU scourger
CEHHIIMS heimisch
CEHHIORS ochreish
CEHHNORU hurcheon
CEHHOPTY hypothec
CEHHPSSU peshcush
CEHIILLR chillier
CEHIILLS chillies
CEHIILNT lecithin
CEHIILOT eolithic
CEHIILTY helicity
CEHIIMOS isocheim
CEHIIMPT mephitic
CEHIIMRT hermitic
CEHIIMTT itch mite
CEHIINOT ethionic
CEHIINPR incipher
CEHIIOPT Ethiopic
CEHIIPRR chirpier
CEHIIPRT pitchier
CEHIIRSS Chrissie
CEHIIRST Christie
CEHIIRTT titchier, trichite
CEHIISTT ethicist, itchiest, theistic
CEHIKLRS clerkish
CEHIKLSU suchlike
CEHIKMOS homesick
CEHIKNNS schinken
CEHIKNRU chunkier
CEHIKNST tschinke
CEHIKOST chokiest
CEHIKSTT thickset
CEHILLMT Mitchell
CEHILLNV vellinch
CEHILLOV helvolic
CEHILLRS schiller
CEHILMMS schimmel
CEHILMTW witch elm
CEHILMTY methylic
CEHILNOP phenolic, pinochle
CEHILNOR chlorine
CEHILNSS chinless
CEHILOOS schoolie
CEHILORT chlorite, clothier
CEHILPTY phyletic
CEHILSTY chestily
CEHILTTW twitchel
CEHILTTY tetchily
CEHIMMRU chummier
CEHIMNOP phonemic
CEHIMNOR choirmen, Nichrome
CEHIMNOW chow mein
CEHIMNTZ Chemnitz
CEHIMORT chromite, trichome
CEHIMOSS chemosis
CEHIMSST schemist
CEHINNRT intrench
CEHINOOO oinochoe
CEHINOOS cohesion
CEHINOPT phonetic
CEHINOPU euphonic
CEHINORT notchier
CEHINORU unheroic
CEHINOSY hyoscine
CEHINOTV nitchevo
CEHINPRS pinscher
CEHINPRU punchier
CEHINRSS richness
CEHINRST christen
CEHINRSW Schwerin
CEHIOORS choosier
CEHIOPPR choppier
CEHIOPRT phoretic
CEHIOPRU euphoric
CEHIOPST postiche
CEHIORRT rhetoric
CEHIORTU touchier
CEHIRSTT stitcher
CEHIRSTW switcher
CEHIRSTY hysteric
CEHIRTTW twitcher
CEHIRTWY witchery
CEHISSTU cushiest
CEHITTUW cutwithe
CEHKLOTY hockelty, hocklety
CEHKNPUY keypunch
CEHKRSTU huckster
CEHLLMOY mecholyl
CEHLNNOU luncheon
CEHLNOTU unclothe
CEHLOORS schooler
CEHLQSUY squelchy
CEHLSTUY lecythus
CEHMMRUY chummery
CEHMNOOR chromone
CEHMNSSU muchness
CEHMOORS smoocher
CEHMOOSZ schmooze
CEHMORUV overmuch

CEHNNNOU	nuncheon
CEHNNOPU	puncheon
CEHNNOSU	nonesuch, unchosen
CEHNOORS	schooner
CEHNSTTU	chestnut
CEHOORSU	ochreous
CEHOOSUW	cow-house
CEHOPPRY	prophecy
CEHOPSSY	scyphose
CEHOPSUY	chopsuey
CEHORSSU	choruses
CEHOSTTU	tetchous
CEHRSTTY	stretchy
CEIIILSV	civilise
CEIIILVZ	civilize
CEIIINSV	incisive
CEIIINTV	incitive
CEIIJSTU	juiciest
CEIIKKSS	kicksies
CEIIKLMR	limerick
CEIIKLRS	sicklier
CEIIKMMR	mimicker
CEIIKNSS	kinesics
CEIIKNST	kinetics
CEIIKPST	pickiest
CEIIKRRT	trickier
CEIIKRST	stickier
CEIIKSST	ekistics
CEIILLMO	limicole
CEIILLMT	mellitic
CEIILLNO	linoleic
CEIILLPT	elliptic
CEIILMNT	limnetic
CEIILMSS	melissic
CEIILNNR	incliner
CEIILNOP	picoline
CEIILNOS	isocline, silicone
CEIILNSS	enclisis
CEIILOPP	epiploic
CEIILOPR	policier
CEIILORT	elicitor
CEIILOTZ	zeolitic
CEIILPRT	triplice
CEIILPSS	eclipsis
CEIILPTX	explicit
CEIILQRU	cliquier
CEIILRSY	lyricise
CEIILRTV	verticil
CEIILRYZ	lyricize
CEIILSSS	scissile
CEIIMNOT	emiction
CEIIMORS	isomeric
CEIIMOST	semiotic
CEIIMPTU	pumicite
CEIIMRRT	trimeric
CEIIMRST	meristic
CEIINNOP	nepionic
CEIINNOR	irenicon
CEIINNOS	oscinine
CEIINNOT	nicotine
CEIINNST	inscient
CEIINOSX	excision
CEIINOTV	eviction
CEIINPPR	principe
CEIINRSU	incisure, sciurine
CEIINRTU	neuritic
CEIINSTY	cytisine, syenitic
CEIIPPRT	precipit
CEIIPRRS	crispier
CEIIPRST	priciest
CEIIPSST	spiciest
CEIIQRTU	critique
CEIIRSTV	veristic
CEIISTVV	vivisect
CEIJLNOS	Joscelin
CEIJNNOO	coonjine
CEIJNORT	injector
CEIJNOUV	cunjevoi
CEIJRSTU	justicer
CEIKKLOR	corklike, rocklike
CEIKKLPU	pucklike
CEIKKNRS	knickers
CEIKKRRS	skerrick
CEIKKSSY	kickseys
CEIKLMOT	time lock
CEIKLNRU	clunkier
CEIKLOSV	lovesick
CEIKLPRU	pluckier
CEIKLRST	stickler, strickle
CEIKLSSW	wickless
CEIKLSTU	luckiest
CEIKMNOR	monicker
CEIKMOPS	picksome
CEIKMOPT	impocket
CEIKMPPU	pick-me-up
CEIKMRSU	musicker
CEIKMSTU	muckiest
CEIKNOQU	quick one
CEIKNRST	stricken
CEIKNSSS	sickness
CEIKORST	corkiest, rockiest, stockier
CEIKQSTU	quickset
CEIKRRTY	trickery
CEILLLOY	ice lolly
CEILLNOU	nucleoli
CEILLNTU	unit cell
CEILLOPS	pollices
CEILLORY	colliery
CEILLRTU	telluric
CEILMMUY	mycelium
CEILMNOP	compline
CEILMNOT	monticle
CEILMOPR	compiler, complier
CEILMOSS	solecism
CEILMOSU	coliseum
CEILMPRU	clumpier
CEILMPUU	peculium
CEILMRSU	clumsier
CEILMTUU	lutecium
CEILNNOT	contline, non-licet
CEILNNSY	syncline
CEILNOOS	eclosion
CEILNOOZ	colonize
CEILNOPR	procline
CEILNORS	licensor
CEILNOSU	leucosin
CEILNPRY	princely
CEILNRTU	lincture
CEILNRUV	culverin
CEILOPPS	Popsicle
CEILOPRT	petrolic
CEILOPRV	proclive
CEILOPSU	pulicose
CEILOPTU	epulotic, poultice
CEILOPTY	epicotyl
CEILORST	cloister, coistrel, costlier
CEILORTY	cryolite
CEILOSST	solecist, solstice
CEILOSSU	coulisse, leucosis
CEILOTVY	velocity
CEILPPRR	crippler
CEILPRSU	surplice
CEILRRSU	scurrile
CEILRSTU	curliest
CEIMMNNO	mnemonic
CEIMMNOU	encomium, meconium
CEIMMORT	recommit
CEIMMRRU	crummier
CEIMMRSU	scummier
CEIMMRSY	merycism
CEIMNNOY	neomycin
CEIMNOOO	oeconomi
CEIMNORT	intercom
CEIMNRST	centrism
CEIMNSSU	meniscus
CEIMOOSZ	Mesozoic
CEIMOPRS	comprise
CEIMOPRX	proxemic
CEIMORST	ice storm
CEIMORSX	exorcism
CEIMRRTU	turmeric
CEIMRTUU	teucrium
CEIMSSTY	systemic
CEINNNOT	innocent
CEINNOOS	oncosine
CEINNOOT	no notice
CEINNORT	incentor
CEINNORU	neuronic
CEINNORV	conniver
CEINNOTU	continue
CEINNPTU	neptunic
CEINNRSU	encrinus
CEINOOPR	pecorino
CEINOOPT	octopine
CEINOOTZ	enzootic
CEINOPRS	conspire
CEINOPRT	entropic, inceptor
CEINOPRV	province

CEINOPTT	entoptic
CEINOPTU	unpoetic
CEINORRS	resorcin
CEINORRT	tricorne
CEINORSS	necrosis
CEINORST	corniest
CEINORSU	incourse
CEINORSV	conversi
CEINORTT	contrite, cornetti
CEINORTU	neurotic
CEINORTV	contrive
CEINORTX	excitron
CEINOSSS	cosiness
CEINOSTT	stenotic
CEINOSTY	cytosine
CEINOTTU	Teutonic
CEINPPRS	princeps
CEINPRSS	princess
CEINRSTT	centrist
CEINRSVV	crivvens
CEINRTTU	intercut, tincture
CEIOOPTV	co-optive
CEIOPRRU	croupier
CEIOPRSU	precious
CEIOPRTT	pterotic
CEIOPRTY	Cypriote
CEIOPSSU	specious
CEIORRSV	corviser
CEIORRTU	courtier, outcrier
CEIORRTW	co-writer
CEIORRUZ	cruzeiro
CEIORSTV	vortices
CEIORSTX	exorcist
CEIORTTU	toreutic
CEIORTXY	excitory
CEIPRRST	rescript, scripter
CEIPRSTU	crepitus, piecrust
CEIRRRSU	scurrier
CEIRRSTT	restrict
CEIRRSTU	crustier
CEIRRSUV	scurvier
CEIRSSSU	scissure
CEIRSSTU	citruses
CEIRSSTV	victress
CEIRSTUV	curviest
CEIRSTUY	security
CEJLOOSY	jocosely
CEJNORRU	conjurer
CEJNRTUU	juncture
CEKKNTUY	Kentucky
CEKLLNOR	roll-neck
CEKLLOOV	lovelock
CEKLLOSS	lockless
CEKLLSSU	luckless
CEKLNOOP	polo neck
CEKLOPST	lock step
CEKLORSS	rockless
CEKLRRTU	truckler
CEKNOPST	penstock
CEKOOORV	overcook
CEKOOPRU	puckeroo
CEKOORRS	rock rose
CEKOORRW	co-worker
CEKOORRY	crookery
CEKOPRST	sprocket
CEKOPRUW	puckerow
CEKORRTY	rocketry
CELLLOSU	locellus
CELLLOVY	Clovelly
CELLNORS	enscroll
CELLNSUU	nucellus
CELLNTUU	luculent
CELLOOPR	procello
CELLOOQU	colloque
CELLORRS	scroller
CELLRSUY	scullery
CELMNOTU	Uncle Tom
CELMNOUY	uncomely
CELMNTUU	muculent
CELMOOOT	locomote
CELMOPSU	compulse
CELMPRSU	scrumple
CELMPRTU	plectrum
CELMPSUU	speculum
CELNOORS	consoler
CELNOORU	encolour
CELNOOSS	coolness
CELNOOVV	convolve
CELNOPUU	uncouple
CELNOQUY	loquency
CELNORSU	close-run
CELNORWY	clownery
CELNOSUV	convulse
CELNOSVY	solvency
CELNOVXY	convexly
CELNPTUU	punctule
CELOOOPT	octopole
CELOOPSS	cesspool
CELOOPTU	octupole
CELOOPTY	polocyte
CELOOPXY	colopexy
CELOORRU	recolour
CELOPSUU	opuscule
CELORSST	crosslet
CELORSSU	sclerous
CELORSTT	crottels
CELORSUU	ulcerous
CELORTVY	covertly
CELOSTTU	culottes
CELPRSUU	scrupule
CELPRSUY	sprucely
CEMMNOOR	commoner
CEMMORTU	commuter
CEMNOOPU	compoune
CEMNOORR	cromorne
CEMNOOTY	monocyte
CEMNOPTT	contempt
CEMNORSU	consumer, mucrones
CEMOOPRS	composer
CEMOORSY	sycomore
CEMOPRSS	compress
CEMOPRTU	computer
CEMORSTU	costumer, customer
CEMPRSTU	spectrum
CEMRSSTU	set scrum
CENNOORV	convenor
CENNORTU	nocturne
CENOOPST	scoop-net
CENOORSU	corneous
CENOORTT	cornetto
CENOORVY	conveyor
CENOPRSY	necropsy
CENOQSTU	conquest
CENORRTU	trouncer
CENORSTU	construe
CENORSUU	cernuous, coenurus
CENORSUY	cynosure
CENORTUY	Courtney
CENORTVY	Coventry
CENOSSTU	countess
CENPRTUU	puncture
CENRSSTU	curtness
CEOOOPST	otoscope
CEOOPRRV	crop-over, overcrop
CEOOPRTY	porocyte
CEOOPRXY	xerocopy
CEOOSTUV	covetous
CEOPPRST	prospect
CEOPRRRU	procurer
CEOPRSSU	corpuses
CEOPRSTT	Prescott
CEOPRSTU	postcure
CEOPRSTW	crow step, screw top
CEOPRSUU	cupreous
CEOPRTUW	power cut
CEOPRTUY	courtepy
CEOQRTUY	coquetry
CEORRSTY	corsetry
CEORSSTU	crustose
CEORSTUY	courtesy
CEORTUUV	outcurve
CEPPRTUU	uppercut
CEPRSTUU	cutpurse
CERSSUUX	excursus
CERSTTUX	exstruct
CFFGIINO	coiffing
CFFGINSU	scuffing
CFFHIILS	schiffli
CFFIINNO	incoffin
CFFIKLNU	cuff link
CFFIRTUY	fructify
CFFKKNOO	knock-off
CFGINOSU	focusing
CFHIIORR	horrific
CFHIKORS	rockfish
CFHIMOSS	scomfish
CFIIILSY	silicify
CFIIIMNS	finicism
CFIIKQUX	quick fix
CFIILLMP	film clip
CFIILMNU	fulminic
CFIILNOQ	cinqfoil
CFIILOPR	prolific
CFIILPSU	pulsific
CFIIMOPR	piciform

CFIIMORT mortific
CFIINORT friction
CFIIOSTU fictious
CFIKKOPR pickfork
CFILMORU luciform
CFILRSUU sulfuric
CFIMNOOR coniform
CFIMNORU cuniform, unciform
CFINNOTU function
CFIORSST Scots fir
CFKKLOOR folk rock
CFKLLLOU full lock
CFLLOORU colorful
CFLLOPRU crop-full
CFLMRSUU fulcrums
CFLMRUUU furculum
CFLNORSU scornful
CFLOOPSU scoopful
CFNNOORT confront
CFOOORTW crowfoot
CFRSTUUU usufruct
CGGGHINU chugging
CGGGILNO clogging
CGGIINNO coigning
CGGIINNR cringing
CGGINORS scroggin
CGHHIIKK high kick
CGHIINPP chipping
CGHIINPT pitching
CGHIINTW witching
CGHIKNOS shocking
CGHILNNY lynching
CGHILNOT clothing
CGHINNOT notching
CGHINNPU punching
CGHINOPP chopping
CGHINOSU hocusing
CGHINOTU touching
CGHINOUX Chuxiong
CGHINRSU crushing
CGHNOOSU souchong
CGIIILNT lignitic
CGIIKLNT tickling
CGIIKMMY gimmicky
CGIIKNPR pricking
CGIIKNPS pickings
CGIILMOS logicism
CGIILNPP clipping
CGIILOST logicist, logistic
CGIILRTU liturgic
CGIIMNNO incoming
CGIINOOS isogonic
CGIKKNNO knocking
CGIKLNOR rockling
CGIKLNSU suckling
CGIKMNOS smocking
CGIKNOST stocking
CGIKNRTU trucking
CGIKPSTU stuck pig
CGILMNUU cingulum, glucinum
CGILNOOR coloring
CGILNOPP clopping
CGILNOPU coupling
CGILNOTT clotting
CGILNSTU cutlings
CGILOORU urologic
CGIMMNSU scumming
CGIMNNOO gnomonic, oncoming
CGIMNOPT compting
CGIMNOPU upcoming
CGIMNOTU cognitum
CGIMRRUY micrurgy
CGINNORW crowning
CGINNOTU counting
CGINOORZ cognizor
CGINOOTV cognovit
CGINOPPR cropping
CGINORSS crossing
CGINORSU scouring
CGINOSTU scouting
CGINSTTU tungstic
CGKNOSTU gunstock
CGLLOSYY glycosyl
CGLMOOYY mycology
CGLNOOOY oncology
CGLOOTYY cytology
CHHIIKST thickish
CHHIINPT pinch-hit
CHHIIPST phthisic
CHHILRSU churlish
CHHIMRTY rhythmic
CHHIOPST chip shot
CHHOOPTT hotchpot
CHIIKLST ticklish
CHIIKRST trickish
CHIILNNP linchpin
CHIILORT trochili
CHIILOST holistic
CHIILPRY chirpily
CHIILQSU cliquish
CHIIMNOO Onomichi
CHIIMOPT phimotic
CHIIMPRU pichurim
CHIIMRSS scrimish
CHIINOPS siphonic
CHIINORT ornithic
CHIIORST historic, orchitis
CHIIPPRU hippuric
CHIIRSTT tristich
CHIKLLOY hillocky
CHIKMNPU chipmunk
CHIKMNTU mutchkin
CHIKNOOS Chinooks
CHIKOPTY kyphotic
CHIKORST trochisk
CHIKPSYY physicky
CHILLOOT oilcloth
CHILMMUY chummily
CHILMOPS complish
CHILMOSU scholium
CHILNNPY lynchpin
CHILNOOP ocnophil
CHILNOOS scholion
CHILNOSW clownish
CHILNPUY punchily
CHILOOSY choosily
CHILOPPY choppily
CHILORTT torchlit
CHILOTUY touchily
CHILOTYY Holy City
CHILRSTY Christly
CHIMMORU chromium
CHIMNOOU homuncio
CHIMNORS chrismon
CHIMNORW inchworm
CHIMNOSU insomuch
CHIMOOPS pochismo
CHIMOORU mouchoir
CHIMPSSY psychism
CHINNPRU pinch-run
CHINOORS isochron
CHINOORT orthicon
CHINOPSY syphonic
CHINOPTY hypnotic, pythonic, typhonic
CHINOSTZ schizont
CHINOSUY cushiony
CHINSTTU unstitch
CHIOOPPT photopic
CHIOOPSS cophosis
CHIOORSU ichorous
CHIOORTT orthotic
CHIOPRST strophic
CHIOPSSY cyphosis
CHIOSSTT Scottish
CHIPRRUY chirrupy
CHIPRTTY triptych
CHIPSTTU stitch-up
CHIRRSSU scirrhus
CHKLOSTY sky cloth
CHKMMOUY hummocky
CHKOPSTU tuck shop
CHKORRTU thurrock
CHLNOOOP colophon
CHLOORSU chlorous
CHLOPSTY splotchy
CHLORTUY choultry
CHMNORRU crumhorn
CHMOORSU chromous
CHNOOPTT top-notch
CHOOPSTU octopush
CHOOSTUU touchous
CHOPSSTU cost push
CHOPSTUY outpsych
CHORSTTU short cut
CIIILMPT implicit
CIIILTVY civility
CIIIMNSV incivism, vicinism
CIIINNOS incision, inosinic
CIIINOOS isoionic
CIIINOTY ionicity
CIIINPPR principi
CIIINTVY vicinity
CIIJRSTU juristic
CIIKKSST ski stick
CIIKLLOS oil slick
CIIKLOPT politick

CIIKLPST lipstick
CIIKLRTY trickily
CIIKLSST sick list
CIIKLSTY stickily
CIIKNPPR pinprick
CIIKNPST stickpin
CIILLMTU tillicum
CIILLNOP pollinic
CIILMOPY impolicy
CIILMOSS sciolism
CIILMPRY crimpily
CIILMRSY lyricism
CIILOOPT politico
CIILOPST politics
CIILORST clitoris
CIILOSST sciolist
CIILRSTY lyricist
CIIMNOST monistic
CIIMNOTU mucoitin
CIIMNOVY viomycin
CIIMNPUY municipy
CIIMORRT trimoric
CIIMORST trisomic
CIIMOSST Stoicism
CIIMRSTY myristic
CIINNOOT intonico
CIINNSTT instinct
CIINOOST isotonic
CIINOPSU opinicus
CIINOQUV quinovic
CIINORST crostini
CIINORTV victorin
CIINORTY incitory
CIINOSSS scission
CIINOTTY tonicity
CIINPRST inscript
CIINPSTU sinciput
CIIOOPST isotopic
CIIOOSTY ociosity
CIIOPSTY isotypic
CIIOQTUX quixotic
CIIOTTXY toxicity
CIIPRRTU pruritic
CIIPRSTU puristic
CIIRSTTU truistic
CIISSTTY cystitis
CIJKOSTY joystick
CIJNNOOT conjoint
CIJNNOTU junction
CIJOOSTY jocosity
CIKKLNOT lock-knit
CIKKNRTU kick-turn
CIKLLOPR killcrop
CIKLLPUY pluckily
CIKLNOST linstock
CIKLOPST lockspit, lopstick
CIKLOSTY stockily
CIKLRSSU kiss-curl
CIKMOORS sickroom
CIKNNOOS coonskin
CIKNNOST non-stick
CIKNRSTU turnsick
CIKOPSTT potstick
CIKOSSTT stockist
CILLMSUY clumsily
CILLNORS inscroll
CILLNOSU scullion
CILLOOOT ocotillo
CILLORSU cursillo
CILMMOSU muscimol
CILMMRUY crummily
CILMNOOU monoculi
CILMNOPU pulmonic
CILMNOUU inoculum
CILMNUUV vinculum
CILMOPTY polymict
CILNOOOS isocolon
CILNOOST colonist
CILNOOTU locution
CILNOPTU plutonic
CILNORYZ zirconyl
CILNOSUY cousinly
CILOORRT tricolor
CILOORST colorist, cortisol
CILOOSSU sciolous
CILOSSTY systolic
CILOSSUU luscious
CILRSTTY strictly
CILRSTUY crustily
CILRSUVY scurvily
CIMNOOPT monoptic
CIMNOORU coronium
CIMNOOTY myotonic
CIMNOPTU ponticum
CIMNOSTU miscount
CIMNOSUU mucinous
CIMNOSUY syconium
CIMOOPRT comptoir
CIMOPPSU pop music
CIMOPSTU posticum
CIMOSTUU muticous
CIMOSTUY mucosity
CINNOORT contorni
CINNOOSS scoinson
CINNOOTU continuo
CINNOOTX non-toxic
CINNOPTU punction
CINNQUUX quincunx
CINOOOPT co-option
CINOOPRS scorpion
CINOOPRT protonic
CINOOTXY oxytocin, oxytonic
CINOPSSY pycnosis
CINOPSTY synoptic
CINORSTT contrist
CINOSTTU unit cost
CINOSTUV viscount
CINRSTTU instruct
CINRSTUY scrutiny
CIOORRWW worricow
CIOORSSU scorious
CIOPRRST scriptor
CIOPRSSU Scorpius
CIOPRSTU porticus
CIORRSTU cursitor
CIORRUUY ouricury
CIORSSSS scissors
CIOSSUUV viscuous
CIPPRRUU purpuric
CJNOORRU conjuror
CKKNOOTU knockout
CKLOOOPR rock pool
CKLOOORW rock-wool
CKMMNOOO mock moon
CKNOOOTW Cooktown
CKNOOSTT Stockton
CKOOPSTT stockpot
CKOOSTTU stockout
CKOSSTUY tussocky
CLLOOQUY colloquy
CLMMNOOY commonly
CLMNOUUY lucumony
CLMOOOTY colotomy
CLMOOPRT comptrol
CLMOSUUU cumulous
CLMSTUUU scutulum
CLNOORTU controul
CLNOOSTU consulto
CLOOOPRT protocol
CLOORTUY locutory
CLOOSSSU colossus
CLOPRSSY cross-ply
CLOPRSTU sculptor
CLOPSSTU cost-plus
CMMNNOOU uncommon
CMMNOOTY commonty
CMNOOSTY monocyst
CMNOPSTU consumpt
CMOOPRTU computor
CMOOPSTU compotus
CMOPPRUY cryopump
CMOPSTUU computus
CMORSSTU scrotums
CNNOOORT contorno
CNOOOORT octoroon
CNOORRSW cornrows
CNOORTUU countour
CNOSTUUU unctuous
COOPRSUY uroscopy
COORSSTU outcross
DDDDEEOR doddered
DDDEEHRS shredded
DDDEELOR dodderel
DDDEEMNU dedendum
DDDEENUW unwedded
DDDEEORR dodderer
DDDEIINV dividend
DDDEIMOS dismoded
DDDEINOR dendroid
DDDEIQSU squidded
DDEEEERS deseeder
DDEEEFLX deflexed
DDEEEFNR defender
DDEEEFRR deferred
DDEEEGNR gendered
DDEEEHNU unheeded
DDEEEIWY wide-eyed
DDEEEMNT demented
DDEEENNU unneeded
DDEEENRZ Enzedder
DDEEENSU unseeded
DDEEENTT de-netted

DDEEENTX extended
DDEEENUW unweeded
DDEEERRT deterred
DDEEERSV deserved
DDEEEWYY dewy-eyed
DDEEFGIT fidgeted
DDEEFINR friended
DDEEFIPR drip-feed
DDEEFMOR deformed
DDEEFNRU underfed
DDEEGGIR de-rigged
DDEEGHNU unhedged
DDEEGINR enridged
DDEEGINS designed
DDEEGOPS Godspeed
DDEEGOTW two-edged
DDEEHRRS shredder
DDEEIIJM medjidie
DDEEIIKR diederik
DDEEIINT inedited
DDEEIIRV redivide
DDEEILLV devilled
DDEEILRV driveled
DDEEIMTT demitted
DDEEINNT indented, intended
DDEEINNU undenied
DDEEINOS one-sided
DDEEINRT dendrite
DDEEINTU unedited
DDEEIPRT deperdit
DDEEIRTT detrited
DDEELLMO modelled
DDEELLOP deed poll
DDEELLOW dowelled
DDEELLOY yodelled
DDEELNOT dedolent
DDEEMNOR endoderm
DDEEMORV verdomde
DDEEMRRU demurred, murdered
DDEENNTU undented, untended
DDEENOPW pondweed
DDEEORTT dottered
DDEERRUV verdured
DDEFHIOX fixed-doh
DDEFIILM midfield
DDEFIILR fiddlier
DDEFIISY disedify
DDEFILNO infolded
DDEFNNUU unfunded
DDEGGIOU guide dog
DDEGGLOY doggedly
DDEGGNOO dog-goned
DDEGHINS shedding
DDEGIIST giddiest
DDEGIKNS skedding
DDEGILNS sledding
DDEGILNU deluding, indulged
DDEGILOS dislodge
DDEGINOR der-doing
DDEGINUU unguided
DDEGIORT dog-tired
DDEGIOST dodgiest
DDEGNORU grounded, underdog
DDEGOOOR do-gooder
DDEGOOWW Wedgwood
DDEGRRUY drudgery
DDEHIISS side dish
DDEHIORS shoddier
DDEHNRSU hundreds
DDEHOOOO hoodooed
DDEHOOSW woodshed
DDEHOOWY how-d'ye-do
DDEHRSUY shuddery
DDEIIKNY dinky-die
DDEIILNR dieldrin
DDEIILRT tiddlier
DDEIINOT dedition
DDEIINSW side wind
DDEIINTV divident
DDEIIOPS diopside
DDEIIOXZ oxidized
DDEILNPS splendid
DDEILNRU unriddle
DDEILOPS displode, lopsided
DDEILRTW twiddler
DDEIMOSU medusoid
DDEIMRSU side drum
DDEIMSTU muddiest
DDEINNRU unridden
DDEINORT trendoid
DDEINOSW disendow, downside
DDEINOWW windowed
DDEINRST stridden
DDEINRSU sun-dried
DDEINRTU intruded
DDEINRUV dun-diver
DDEIOORS side door
DDEIOOSW woodside
DDEIOPRS dropsied
DDEIOPRV provided
DDEIOPSS disposed
DDEIORRS disorder
DDEIOSTW dowdiest, two-sided
DDEIRSSU Druidess
DDEIRSTU ruddiest, sturdied
DDEKMOPU dumpoked
DDELLOOP dolloped
DDELNOSY soddenly
DDELNSUY suddenly
DDEMNOUU duodenum
DDEMNPUU pudendum
DDEMOOTU outmoded
DDENOOUW unwooded
DDEOOOOV voodooed
DDEPRSTY pryddest
DDFGIILN fiddling
DDFIILUW widdiful
DDFLNOOW downfold
DDFMNOUU dumfound
DDGGIIUU guidguid
DDGGINNO ding-dong
DDGHINTU thudding
DDGIIINO indigoid
DDGIIKNS skidding
DDGIILMN middling
DDGIILNR riddling
DDGIILNU Dindigul
DDGILNOP plodding
DDGINOPR prodding
DDGINPSU spudding
DDGINPUY puddingy
DDGINSTU studding
DDGIORTY dirty dog
DDGLOOOR good Lord
DDGLOSTU gold dust
DDGOOORW good word
DDGOORSY dry goods
DDHILOSY shoddily
DDHLNOOW hold-down
DDIIIIVV divi-divi
DDIILOPY diploidy
DDIIMMUY didymium
DDIIMRSU Druidism
DDIIQTUY quiddity
DDILOOWW wildwood
DDILORSY sordidly
DDIMOSUY didymous
DDINNOWW downwind, wind-down
DDINOOOT odontoid
DDINOOWW woodwind
DDIOPPRR drip-drop
DDIOQTUY quoddity
DDLLOORW Old World
DDLMORSU doldrums
DDMNORTU Dortmund
DEEEEFRR refereed
DEEEEFRZ defreeze
DEEEEGKR kedgeree
DEEEEKNP knee-deep
DEEEELTY eyeleted
DEEEEMRR redeemer
DEEEFGOR fore-edge
DEEEFILN linefeed
DEEEFINR redefine
DEEEFIRW fireweed
DEEEFKST keftedes
DEEEFLRU refueled
DEEEFLSS self-seed
DEEEFNRT deferent
DEEEFORV overfeed
DEEEFRRR deferrer, referred
DEEEFRRT ferreted
DEEEGHLR heregeld
DEEEGIPR pedigree
DEEEGIRR greedier
DEEEGISW edgewise
DEEEGLMP empledge
DEEEGLSS edgeless
DEEEGLSV selvedge
DEEEGMRR demerger
DEEEGNNR engender
DEEEHLMT helmeted
DEEEHLNO dene-hole
DEEEHLRT Ethelred

DEEEHLRW wheedler
DEEEHLSS heedless
DEEEIKKS keskidee
DEEEILNS selenide
DEEEILRV relieved
DEEEIMRT emerited
DEEEIMST seed-time
DEEEINNZ endenize
DEEEINRR reindeer
DEEEINST neediest
DEEEINTV eventide
DEEEIPPR reed pipe
DEEEIPRS speedier
DEEEIPTX expedite
DEEEIRST reediest
DEEEIRTW tweedier
DEEEISST seediest
DEEEISTW weediest
DEEEJLLW jewelled
DEEEKLNN kenneled
DEEEKOPW pokeweed
DEEELLLV levelled
DEEELLNT dentelle
DEEELLPR repelled
DEEELLPT pelleted
DEEELLPX expelled
DEEELLRV revelled
DEEELMRU mule deer
DEEELNPU unpeeled
DEEELNSS needless, seldseen
DEEELOPP depeople
DEEELOSY sloe-eyed
DEEELPST steepled
DEEELRTT lettered
DEEELSSS seedless
DEEELSSW weedless
DEEELTVV velveted
DEEEMNNT needment
DEEEMOPS deepsome
DEEEMPRT tempered
DEEEMRST deemster
DEEENNRT entender
DEEENOPY open-eyed
DEEENORS endorsee
DEEENPRT repetend
DEEENPSS deepness
DEEENRRR renderer
DEEENRRT tenderer
DEEENRRV reverend
DEEENRTV Deventer
DEEENRTX extender
DEEENSUV vendeuse
DEEEOPPT peep-toed
DEEEOPRT deportee
DEEEORTV dove tree
DEEEPPPR peppered
DEEERRRV verderer
DEEERRST deserter
DEEERRSV reserved
DEEERSTT detester, streeted
DEEERTTV revetted
DEEFFINS effendis
DEEFFIRS seriffed
DEEFFNOR forefend, offender, reoffend
DEEFFNRT treffend
DEEFGINR fingered
DEEFGLOO feel-good
DEEFGLUW gulfweed
DEEFHISS seed-fish
DEEFHLOR freehold
DEEFHLRS feldsher
DEEFHORR Hereford
DEEFIINT definite
DEEFIIRS fireside
DEEFILLT filleted
DEEFILNX inflexed
DEEFILWX flixweed
DEEFINRR inferred
DEEFINRW Winefred
DEEFIRTT refitted
DEEFLNNU funneled
DEEFLNTU defluent
DEEFLORW deflower, flowered
DEEFMPRU perfumed
DEEFNORS defensor
DEEFNSST deftness
DEEFORST deforest
DEEFRTUY duty-free
DEEGGHHO hedgehog
DEEGGIJR rejigged
DEEGGLOR doggerel
DEEGGNPU unpegged
DEEGHHOP hedge-hop
DEEGHNRU hungered
DEEGHOPS sheepdog
DEEGHORW hedgerow
DEEGIIMM megimide
DEEGIINN indigene
DEEGIINT digenite
DEEGIISS diegesis
DEEGILMP impledge
DEEGILNO legioned
DEEGILNP pinledge
DEEGILNR engirdle, reedling
DEEGILNS seedling
DEEGILRY greedily
DEEGIMRU demiurge
DEEGINNR ingender
DEEGINRS designer, redesign, resigned
DEEGINRT digerent
DEEGINSS edginess
DEEGIRST digester, estridge
DEEGJPRU prejudge
DEEGLMNT ledgment
DEEGLNNO engolden
DEEGLNOU engouled
DEEGLNOZ lozenged
DEEGLNRY legendry
DEEGLOOT edge-tool
DEEGLORV groveled
DEEGNNOY endogeny
DEEGNOOV good-even
DEEGORVY dove grey
DEEGRRTU Gertrude
DEEGRTTU guttered
DEEGSSTU gusseted
DEEHHPRS shepherd
DEEHILNP Delphine
DEEHILNS enshield
DEEHILNW New Delhi
DEEHILSV dishevel, she-devil
DEEHIMOP hemipode
DEEHIMRT Meredith
DEEHINRS drisheen
DEEHIOTX ethoxide
DEEHIPPS sheep-dip
DEEHIPRS hesperid
DEEHIRRT ditherer
DEEHIRTY heredity, third eye
DEEHKNOS keeshond
DEEHLMSW weldmesh
DEEHLOSV shoveled
DEEHMORT mothered, thermode
DEEHNORT dethrone, threnode
DEEHNOWY honeydew
DEEHOORT Theodore
DEEIILNS lineside, sideline
DEEIILNT tideline
DEEIILRV liveried
DEEIILRW wieldier
DEEIIMPT impedite
DEEIIMRZ dimerize
DEEIINOZ deionize
DEEIIPRU prie-dieu
DEEIIRSS dieresis
DEEIIRST siderite
DEEIIRSV derisive
DEEIISSS disseise
DEEIISSW sidewise
DEEIISSZ disseize
DEEIISVW side view
DEEIKLLR killdeer
DEEIKLMO domelike
DEEIKLMW milkweed
DEEIKLNN enkindle
DEEIKLNR rekindle
DEEIKLOV dovelike
DEEIKNOT diketone
DEEIKNPS skin-deep
DEEIKNRS deerskin
DEEIKPSS deep kiss
DEEIKSTT diskette
DEEILLMP impelled
DEEILLNO nielloed
DEEILLNT linteled
DEEILLPR perilled
DEEILMNU demilune
DEEILMOS melodise
DEEILMOZ melodize
DEEILNOP pedelion
DEEILNOT deletion

DEEILNRU underlie
DEEILNSS idleness
DEEILNST tinseled
DEEILNSV sniveled
DEEILOPT lepidote
DEEILORT dolerite
DEEILORV evildoer
DEEILOTT toileted
DEEILPSY speedily
DEEILRRV driveler
DEEILRSU leisured
DEEILRSV desilver
DEEILRVY delivery
DEEILSSS sideless
DEEILSST tideless
DEEILSTY slit-eyed
DEEILSUV delusive
DEEILSVW swiveled
DEEILTWY tweedily
DEEIMMNS endemism
DEEIMMOR memoried
DEEIMMOS semi-dome
DEEIMMRS immersed
DEEIMNOR domineer
DEEIMNOS demonise
DEEIMNOZ demonize
DEEIMNPT pediment
DEEIMNRR reminder
DEEIMNST sediment
DEEIMNTT ditement, mittened
DEEIMNTU minueted
DEEIMPRR periderm
DEEIMRST demister
DEEIMRTT remitted
DEEIMRTV vermetid
DEEIMRUX murexide
DEEINNQU quindene
DEEINNRT indenter, intender
DEEINNST tendines
DEEINNUV unenvied
DEEINOPS open-side
DEEINOPW wide open
DEEINOST side note
DEEINOSV nosedive
DEEINOTZ detonize
DEEINPSS dispense
DEEINQSU sequined
DEEINRRT interred, trendier
DEEINRRW rewinder
DEEINRSS direness
DEEINRST indesert, resident
DEEINRTT entredit
DEEINRTV inverted
DEEINSSW dewiness, wideness
DEEINSTT insetted
DEEIOPRX peroxide
DEEIORRV override
DEEIORSV overside
DEEIOTVX videotex
DEEIPPQU equipped
DEEIPPRZ zippered
DEEIPQRU repiqued
DEEIPRSS despiser, disperse
DEEIPSST sidestep
DEEIPTUZ deputize
DEEIQRUV quivered
DEEIQSTU quesited
DEEIQTUU quietude
DEEIRRSS dressier
DEEIRRST destrier
DEEIRRTV verditer
DEEIRSSU reissued
DEEIRSSV disserve, dissever
DEEISSTW West Side
DEEJKNTU junketed
DEEJLLOP jelloped
DEEJPRRU perjured
DEEKKOOY okey-doke
DEEKMRSU musk deer
DEEKNOPW knopweed
DEEKNOTW knotweed
DEELLMOP pomelled
DEELLMOR modeller
DEELLNOR enrolled
DEELLNOT dentello
DEELLNOW well done
DEELLORW rowelled
DEELLORY yodeller
DEELLOTW towelled
DEELLOTX extolled
DEELLOVW vowelled
DEELLSUW well-used
DEELLSUX duxelles
DEELMMOP pommeled
DEELMMPU pummeled
DEELMNOO melodeon
DEELMNTU unmelted
DEELMOOS dolesome
DEELMOPR empolder
DEELMRUY demurely
DEELNNTU tunneled
DEELNORT redolent
DEELNOVY velodyne
DEELNRTU underlet
DEELNRTY tenderly
DEELNSSW lewdness
DEELNWWY newly-wed
DEELNXYY lynx-eyed
DEELOPRX exploder
DEELOPRY redeploy
DEELOPST seed-plot
DEELORRS solderer
DEELORSV resolved
DEELORTT dotterel
DEELORTW troweled
DEELOTUV devolute
DEELPRTU drupelet
DEELRSTU deluster, delustre, lustered
DEEMMNNT mendment
DEEMMORS mesoderm
DEEMMRRU dummerer
DEEMNNTU tenendum
DEEMNOOY moon-eyed
DEEMNOQU queendom
DEEMNORR moderner
DEEMNOUY eudemony
DEEMOORT odometer
DEEMORSU dormeuse
DEEMORSW wormseed
DEEMORTU udometer
DEEMPRST dempster
DEEMRRRU demurrer, murderer
DEEMRSTU demurest
DEENNNOP pennoned
DEENNOPT deponent
DEENNOPU unopened
DEENNORW renowned
DEENNOST sonneted
DEENNOVW evendown
DEENOORV overdone
DEENOPRS rope's end
DEENOPRW pre-owned
DEENORRS endorser
DEENORRW wonderer
DEENORTU deuteron
DEENRSSU rudeness
DEENRSTU sederunt, underset, unrested
DEENRSUU underuse
DEENRSUV unversed
DEENSSSY syndeses
DEENSTTU untested
DEENTTUW unwetted
DEEOORRV overrode
DEEOORSV overdose
DEEOPPST estopped
DEEOPRST reed-stop
DEEOPRTT repotted
DEEOPRUZ douzeper
DEEOQRTU roqueted
DEEORRUV devourer
DEEORRVW overdrew
DEEORSST dosseret
DEEORSTT rosetted
DEEORSTX dextrose
DEERRRUV verdurer
DEERRTTU turreted
DEERTTUX textured
DEFFGILO off-glide
DEFFHILW whiffled
DEFFIINT tiffined
DEFFILOV fivefold
DEFFIORS offsider
DEFFIORV off-drive
DEFFIQSU squiffed
DEFFIRSU diffuser
DEFFSTUY dyestuff
DEFGHILT flighted
DEFGIINY edifying
DEFGIIST digestif
DEFGILOS dog's life
DEFGILRU dirgeful
DEFGILTY giftedly
DEFGINTU ungifted

DEFGIOOW goodwife
DEFGJORU forjudge
DEFGMOOY fogeydom
DEFHIINS fiendish, finished
DEFHIOOW wifehood
DEFHIRST red shift
DEFHLOOS selfhood
DEFHMOOU fume hood
DEFHOORS serfhood
DEFHORRT Hertford
DEFHORTT Thetford
DEFIILLO oilfield
DEFIILLP filliped
DEFIILLW wildlife
DEFIILMS misfield
DEFIILOR oil-fired
DEFIILOX fixed oil
DEFIILPS flip side
DEFIILRW wildfire
DEFIILSU fluidise
DEFIILTY fidelity
DEFIILUZ fluidize
DEFIIMNO feminoid
DEFIIMOR modifier
DEFIINRW Winifred
DEFIINTU finitude
DEFIINTY identify
DEFIIOTV videofit
DEFIIPSS fissiped
DEFILLNU unfilled
DEFILNNO ninefold
DEFILNOP pond life
DEFILNRS flinders
DEFILNRY friendly
DEFILORU fluoride
DEFILORV frivoled
DEFILORY foryield
DEFILOTU outfield
DEFILPRU prideful
DEFILRVY fervidly, fly-drive
DEFIMNOR informed
DEFIMORY remodify
DEFIMRRU drumfire
DEFIMRSU Dumfries
DEFINNOW finnowed
DEFINOSU defusion
DEFINRTT drift-net
DEFINRTY trendify
DEFINTTU unfitted
DEFIOORR fire door
DEFIOORW firewood
DEFIOPRT profited
DEFIOTXY detoxify
DEFLLOOR folderol
DEFLNORU flounder
DEFLOORT foretold
DEFLOORV overfold
DEFLORSS fordless
DEFMNOOR formedon
DEFMNORU unformed
DEFMOOOR foredoom
DEFNNORT frondent
DEFNNOSS fondness
DEFNOORS frondose
DEFNOORU unroofed
DEFNOORV overfond
DEFNOPRS forspend
DEFNORRU frondeur
DEFNORTU fortuned
DEFNORUY foundery
DEFNRRUU underfur
DEFOORRW foreword
DEGGHRSU shrugged
DEGGILNO doegling
DEGGILNS sledging
DEGGINOV God-given
DEGGINRU unrigged
DEGGIORS disgorge
DEGGIPRS sprigged
DEGGLRUY ruggedly
DEGGRRUY druggery
DEGHHIIT high tide
DEGHHILV highveld
DEGHIILN hideling
DEGHILRT red light
DEGHINTT tight end
DEGHIORU doughier
DEGHIPST despight
DEGHLORY hydrogel
DEGHNORY hydrogen
DEGHOOPT hodgepot
DEGHOORS dogshore
DEGHOOSU doghouse, house dog
DEGIIITZ digitize
DEGIILNR gridelin
DEGIILNT diligent
DEGIILNV deviling
DEGIILNY yielding
DEGIIMSU misguide
DEGIINNR nidering
DEGIINNT indigent
DEGIINRS ringside
DEGIINRT dirigent
DEGIINST dingiest, indigest
DEGIISSU disguise
DEGIJMSU misjudge
DEGIKLOO goodlike
DEGIKLOV kid-glove
DEGILLNU duelling
DEGILLNW dwelling
DEGILMNO gold mine, modeling
DEGILNNO Leonding
DEGILNOS sidelong
DEGILNOW doweling
DEGILNOY yodeling
DEGILNRU indulger
DEGILOOR goodlier
DEGILOOY ideology
DEGILORV overgild
DEGILOUV vuilgoed
DEGILRZZ grizzled
DEGIMNOS smidgeon
DEGIMOOT good-time
DEGIMRSU smudgier
DEGINNNU unending
DEGINNSU unsigned
DEGINNTU untinged
DEGINOPS disponge
DEGINORV ring-dove
DEGINPSU dispunge
DEGINRRY grindery
DEGINRSS dressing
DEGINRST Ringsted, stringed
DEGINTTU duetting
DEGIOPRR porridge
DEGIOPSS gossiped
DEGIOPST podgiest
DEGIORST stodgier
DEGIPSTU pudgiest
DEGJMNTU judgment
DEGLLNOY goldenly
DEGLLOOP golloped
DEGLMNOT lodgment
DEGLNOUV ungloved
DEGLOOPY pedology
DEGLOOUU duologue
DEGNOOSS goodness
DEGNOPSU pug-nosed
DEGNORRU grounder
DEGOORTT grottoed, otter-dog
DEGRRSTU drugster
DEHHILOY hidy-hole
DEHIILLS hillside, sidehill
DEHIILSV devilish
DEHIIMRU mudirieh
DEHIIMST ditheism
DEHIIMTU ethidium
DEHIINUZ Hinduize
DEHIIRST disherit
DEHIISST dishiest
DEHIISTT ditheist
DEHIJMNO demijohn
DEHIKLOO hoodlike
DEHIKNOW Windhoek
DEHILMOS demolish
DEHILMTY dimethyl
DEHILNOO heliodon
DEHILNPY diphenyl
DEHILOOR heliodor
DEHILOPS depolish
DEHILPSU sulphide
DEHILRTW writhled
DEHIMNOS hedonism
DEHINOPR nephroid
DEHINOPS sphenoid
DEHINOST hedonist
DEHINSUW unwished
DEHIOPRS spheroid
DEHIOPRT trophied
DEHIOSSU dishouse
DEHIOSSW sideshow
DEHIPSSU pseudish
DEHIRTWW withdrew
DEHKLNOU elk-hound
DEHLLOPY phyllode
DEHLMORY hydromel
DEHLNOOW downhole

DEHLOORV hold-over
DEHLOOSS hoodless
DEHLOOST tool shed
DEHLOOSW woolshed
DEHLOPRU upholder
DEHLORSU shoulder
DEHLRSWY shrewdly
DEHMMRTU thrummed
DEHMNOOW down-home
DEHMNRUY unrhymed
DEHMOORW whoredom
DEHMORUU humoured
DEHNORSU enshroud
DEHNORTY threnody
DEHNRTUY thundery
DEHOOOPP popehood
DEHOOPRT theropod
DEHOORTU out-Herod
DEHOPRST potsherd
DEHRRTUY hydruret
DEIIINRV viridine
DEIIINSV divinise
DEIIINVZ divinize
DEIIISVV divisive
DEIIKLNN inkindle
DEIIKLNR kindlier
DEIIKLNS disliken
DEIIKNST dinkiest
DEIILLMT ill-timed, tide mill
DEIILLYZ idyllize
DEIILMRU delirium
DEIILNNU induline
DEIILNOT tolidine
DEIILNPV vilipend
DEIILNTT intilted
DEIILNTU lutidine
DEIILNVY divinely
DEIILNXY xylidine
DEIILORZ idolizer
DEIILPSS side-slip
DEIIMNRT diriment
DEIIMNTU diminute
DEIIMNUV venidium
DEIIMPRU peridium
DEIIMSTT timidest
DEIIMSVW midwives
DEIINNPP pinniped
DEIINORS derision, resinoid
DEIINOST desition, sedition
DEIINPPW windpipe
DEIINPRT intrepid
DEIINPRY pyridine
DEIINPSS side spin
DEIINPTU unpitied
DEIINQSU quinsied
DEIINRST disinter
DEIINRTU untidier
DEIINSST tidiness
DEIINSTU disunite
DEIINSTV divinest
DEIINSTW windiest
DEIINTTY identity
DEIIOOPT idiotope
DEIIOPRS presidio
DEIIOPRT piedroit
DEIIOPTY idiotype
DEIIORTX trioxide
DEIIORTY iodyrite
DEIIORXZ oxidizer
DEIIPPRR drippier
DEIIPPST dippiest
DEIIPRST side trip, spirited
DEIIPRSZ disprize
DEIIPTTY tepidity
DEIIQSTU disquiet
DEIIRRVV viverrid
DEIIRSSU diuresis
DEIIRSTT dirtiest
DEIISTZZ dizziest
DEIJNNOU unjoined
DEIJORRY joyrider
DEIKKLNO Klondike
DEIKLLOR lordlike
DEIKLNRW wrinkled
DEIKLNSS kindless
DEIKLSSS diskless
DEIKMNOO kimonoed
DEIKNNNU dunniken
DEIKNNSS kindness
DEIKNRRY drinkery
DEIKRSVY skydiver
DEIKSSTU duskiest
DEILLNOR inrolled
DEILLNTU untilled
DEILLORR lordlier
DEILLOST dolliest
DEILLOSV Eidsvoll
DEILLOTT do-little
DEILLSTU duellist
DEILMMOU melodium
DEILMNOO melodion
DEILMNSS mildness, mindless
DEILMNSU muslined
DEILMOOT dolomite
DEILMOPR impolder
DEILMORT old-timer
DEILMORU lemuroid
DEILMOST melodist, modelist
DEILMOSU emulsoid
DEILMPPU plumiped
DEILMPTU multiped
DEILMSTU mustelid
DEILNNOT indolent
DEILNOOS eidolons, solenoid
DEILNOPS splenoid
DEILNOSU delusion, unsoiled
DEILNOUZ nodulize
DEILNOVV involved
DEILNPRU underlip
DEILNPST split end
DEILNRSS rindless
DEILNRSW swindler
DEILNRTY trendily
DEILNSSW wildness, windless
DEILNSTU unlisted
DEILNTTU untitled
DEILNTUY unitedly
DEILNUWY unwieldy
DEILOOPS poolside
DEILOOPW woodpile
DEILOPPY polypide
DEILOPRU preludio
DEILOPST pistoled
DEILOPSU depilous
DEILOPSV disvelop
DEILORSU delirous
DEILORSY soldiery
DEILOSST solidest
DEILOSSV dissolve
DEILOSTU solitude
DEILPTWY wild type
DEILRTVY deviltry
DEILRWZZ wrizzled
DEILSSTU dutiless
DEILSTUY sedulity
DEILSTWW Wild West
DEIMMNOS demonism
DEIMMNSU medimnus
DEIMMORX mordexim
DEIMMOST immodest
DEIMNNTU indument
DEIMNOOT demotion
DEIMNOOX monoxide
DEIMNOPT piedmont
DEIMNOPU opium den
DEIMNORT dormient
DEIMNOTU omnitude
DEIMNOTW down time
DEIMNPRU unprimed
DEIMNPSS misspend
DEIMNPTU impudent
DEIMNRTU rudiment
DEIMOOST moodiest, sodomite
DEIMOOSZ sodomize
DEIMOPTU podetium
DEIMORRS misorder
DEIMORSU dimerous
DEIMORUX exordium
DEIMPRSY dispermy
DEIMPSTU dumpiest
DEIMRSTU diestrum
DEIMRSUU residuum
DEINNNOU innuendo
DEINNNPU unpinned
DEINNOOT noontide
DEINNOPT end point
DEINNORT indentor
DEINNORU unironed
DEINNPRU underpin
DEINOOPP doppione
DEINOOPV povidone
DEINOOPW pinewood
DEINOOSU idoneous
DEINOOTV devotion
DEINOPPW downpipe

DEINOPRS	prisoned
DEINOPRY	pyrenoid
DEINOPSS	dopiness
DEINOPTW	dew point
DEINORSW	disowner, wind-rose
DEINORTT	intorted
DEINORVW	overwind
DEINOSSV	voidness
DEINOSSZ	doziness
DEINOSTW	downiest
DEINOSWZ	downsize
DEINOTTU	duettino
DEINOTUV	indevout
DEINPPRU	unripped
DEINPPUZ	unzipped
DEINPTTU	inputted
DEINRRTU	intruder
DEINRSTT	strident
DEINSSSY	syndesis
DEINSSUU	unissued
DEINSTUU	unsuited
DEIOOPRR	droopier
DEIOOSTW	woodiest
DEIOPRRV	provider
DEIOPRSS	disposer
DEIOPRSV	disprove
DEIOPSTT	post-edit
DEIORRSW	drowsier
DEIORRSY	derisory
DEIORRTU	outrider
DEIORRTW	worrited
DEIORSSU	desirous
DEIORSTU	outsider
DEIORSTW	rowdiest, wordiest
DEIOSTTT	dottiest
DEIPPRST	stripped
DEIPRSSU	dispurse
DEIPRSTU	disputer, stupider
DEIPTTTU	tittuped
DEIRRSTU	sturdier
DEIRRTTU	turrited
DEIRSSST	distress
DEIRSSTU	diestrus
DEIRSTTU	detritus
DEISSTTU	dustiest
DEISTTTU	duettist
DEJMPPUU	jumped-up
DEKMNOSU	unsmoked
DEKNORUW	unworked
DELLLOOP	lolloped
DELLNOPU	unpolled
DELLNOWW	downwell
DELLNSSU	dullness
DELLOORT	tol-de-rol
DELLOOTW	well-to-do
DELLOPTU	polluted
DELLORRY	drollery
DELLORSS	lordless
DELLOSTY	Old Style
DELMNORY	modernly
DELMNOTW	meltdown
DELMNPUU	pendulum
DELMORSU	smoulder
DELMOSTY	modestly
DELNNOOR	Londoner
DELNOORS	Old Norse
DELNOOSU	nodulose
DELNOOWY	woodenly
DELNOPRS	splendor
DELNOPUW	unplowed
DELNORSU	unsolder
DELNORWW	New World
DELNOSSU	loudness
DELNOSUV	unsolved
DELOOOOT	toodle-oo
DELOORRV	overlord
DELOORSV	oversold
DELOOSSW	woodless
DELOPRSY	dry slope
DELOPSTU	postlude
DELOPSTW	spot weld
DELORSSW	wordless
DELORSUY	delusory
DELOSSUU	sedulous
DELOSTUW	wouldest
DELOTUVY	devoutly
DELPRTUU	pultrude
DELSSSTU	dustless
DEMMRSTU	strummed
DEMNNOOT	Edmonton
DEMNOOOT	odontome
DEMNORSY	syndrome
DEMNOSTU	mudstone
DEMOOPRR	prodrome
DEMOORST	doomster
DEMOORSU	dormouse
DEMOORTY	odometry
DEMPRSTU	dumpster
DENNOSTU	dunstone
DENNOTUW	unwonted
DENNRTUU	unturned
DENNRTUY	untrendy
DENOOOPR	open door
DENOOOTW	woodnote
DENOOPRZ	drop zone
DENOORTT	tetrodon
DENOORTX	next door
DENOPRUV	unproved
DENOPSTU	outspend
DENOQTUU	unquoted
DENORSSU	dourness
DENORSTU	unsorted
DENORSTY	drystone
DENORSUU	unsoured
DENORSUW	undersow
DENORTUW	undertow
DENRRSUY	dry-nurse
DENRSSSU	sundress
DEOOORSW	rosewood
DEOOOSWW	woodwose
DEOOPPRT	pteropod
DEOOPRST	doorstep
DEOPPRST	stropped
DEOPRRTU	protrude
DEOPRSST	top dress
DEOPRSTT	drop test
DEORRSTU	detrusor
DEORSTUX	dextrous
DERSTTTU	strutted
DFFFFHUU	huff-duff
DFFIILUY	fluidify
DFFIORSU	diffusor
DFFLMPUU	plum duff
DFFLOORU	fourfold
DFFOORUW	woodruff
DFGGHIOT	dogfight
DFGGIOST	God's gift
DFGHILOS	goldfish
DFGIIIRY	rigidify
DFGIILRY	frigidly
DFGILLOO	gold foil
DFGILNNO	fondling
DFGILORU	fulgorid
DFGINNOU	founding
DFGLNOOR	Longford
DFGLORUU	gourdful
DFGMOOOR	good form
DFHIIMUY	humidify
DFHIMRSU	drum fish
DFHINNOR	findhorn
DFHINOPS	fish pond
DFHLOOOT	foothold
DFHNOOUX	foxhound
DFIIINVY	divinify
DFIIITXY	fixidity
DFIILMSU	fluidism
DFIILMTU	multifid
DFIILOSY	solidify
DFIILTUY	fluidity
DFIKNOOS	skin-food
DFILLOOT	floodlit
DFILLORY	floridly
DFILLOWW	wildfowl
DFILORTU	old fruit
DFIMOOOR	iodoform
DFIMOOPR	podiform
DFINOPRU	profundi
DFINOPST	find-spot
DFINRSUW	windsurf
DFIOOPRS	disproof
DFJKNOOU	junk food
DFKMMOPU	dummkopf
DFLOOORT	rood-loft
DFLOOOSU	soul food
DFMNOORU	morfound
DFNOOPRU	profound
DFNOORSU	frondous
DFOOORST	forstood
DFOOOSTW	softwood
DGGGIINS	diggings
DGGGINRU	drugging, grudging
DGGIINNR	grinding
DGGIINNW	wingding
DGGINNOY	Dongying
DGGIRSTU	druggist
DGGNTUUY	gundy-gut
DGHIILNS	hidlings
DGHIIMNT	midnight
DGHIINPS	sphingid
DGHIINTY	dithying
DGHIKNOO	kinghood

DGHILLNU dunghill
DGHILOOR girlhood
DGHINNOU hounding
DGHLORSU gold rush
DGHNOOTU do-nought
DGHNOTUU doughnut
DGHOOOTT dog-tooth
DGHORRUY rough-dry
DGHORTUY droughty
DGIIIRTY rigidity
DGIIKLNN kindling
DGIIKNNR drinking
DGIILLNR drilling
DGIILLNW wildling
DGIILNNW windling
DGIILNOS disloign
DGIIMNOS misdoing
DGIIMNOU gonidium
DGIIMPUY pygidium
DGIINNOR non-rigid
DGIINORR gridiron
DGIINPPR dripping
DGIKLOOY kidology
DGILLNOR lordling
DGILLOOW goodwill
DGILMNOU moulding
DGILMNPU dumpling
DGILMSUY smudgily
DGILNOOW woolding
DGILNOOY Indology
DGILNOPR dropling
DGILNOTY dotingly
DGILNOUW woulding
DGILOOTW giltwood
DGILOSTY stodgily
DGILRTUY turgidly
DGIMMNRU drumming
DGINNOSU sounding
DGINNOUW wounding
DGINOPPR dropping
DGIOPRRY porridgy
DGIORSSS disgross
DGIOSUYZ dizygous
DGLLOORY Old Glory
DGLOOOXY doxology
DGMNNOOO mondongo
DGMNORUW dung-worm
DGNOOORV Novgorod
DGNOORTU to ground
DHHIKRSU Khurshid
DHHILOTW withhold
DHIIIMNS diminish
DHIIIOST histioid
DHIIKWZZ whizz-kid
DHIILOOP lophioid
DHIIMNOO hominoid
DHIIMNSU Hinduism
DHIIMPSS midships
DHIIMTUY humidity
DHIINTWW withwind
DHIIORSS hidrosis
DHIKNOOW hoodwink
DHILLNOW downhill
DHILLOPY phylloid
DHILMOPY lymphoid

DHILMOSY modishly
DHILOPRS lordship
DHILOPSS slipshod
DHILORRY horridly
DHIMNOST hindmost
DHIMNOSU muishond
DHIMOPPY hippydom
DHINOOPR phoronid
DHINOORS dishonor
DHINORSU roundish
DHINOTUW whodunit
DHIOOOPR iodophor
DHIOOPRZ rhizopod
DHIORSTY thyrsoid
DHJNOORY John Dory
DHJOPRSU jodhpurs
DHLLOPYY phyllody
DHLNOSTU shouldn't
DHLOORSY hydrosol
DHLORXYY hydroxyl
DHNOOSWW showdown
DHNORSUW downrush
DHNOSTUW shutdown
DHOOOPRT orthopod
DHOOORTX orthodox
DHOOPRST drop shot
DHOOPRTY hydropot
DHOORSUW woodrush
DHOPRSYY hydropsy
DHOSSTTU dust-shot
DIIILLQU illiquid
DIIILMPU pilidium
DIIILTVY lividity
DIIIMOST idiotism
DIIIMTTY timidity
DIIINOSV division
DIIINTVY divinity
DIIIORSU iridious
DIIIPRST dispirit
DIIIRTVY viridity
DIIJNOST disjoint
DIIKLLNY kindlily
DIIKLLSW wild silk
DIILLMNW windmill
DIILLMPY limpidly
DIILLMTU mutillid
DIILLQUY liquidly
DIILLSTY idyllist
DIILMOPP pompilid
DIILMUUV diluvium
DIILNOTU dilution
DIILNTUY untidily
DIILOPRT triploid
DIILOSTY solidity
DIILPPRY drippily
DIILQSUU liquidus
DIIMMNOU dominium
DIIMNNOO dominion
DIIMNNOR morindin
DIIMNOXY myxinoid
DIIMNSUU indusium
DIIMOPRS prismoid
DIIMPUXY pyxidium
DIIMTTUY tumidity
DIINNOSU disunion

DIINOSSU sinusoid
DIINSTUY disunity
DIIOPRVZ Pozidriv
DIIORSVY divisory
DIKLNNUY unkindly
DILLMNOP millpond
DILLOSTY stolidly
DILMNOOR iron-mold
DILMNORW lindworm
DILMOOSS molossid
DILMOOSU modiolus
DILNOPSU lispound
DILNOPTW Piltdown
DILNOUWY woundily
DILOOPPY polypoid
DILOOPRY droopily
DILOORSS lordosis
DILOOSUY odiously
DILOPRTY torpidly
DILORRTY torridly
DILORSWY drowsily
DILPRTUY putridly
DILPSTUY stupidly
DILRSTUY sturdily
DIMMNORY myrmidon
DIMMORRY mormyrid
DIMNOOST monodist
DIMNOSSU missound
DIMNOSTU dismount
DIMNOSUW unwisdom
DIMORSWY rowdyism
DIMOSTUY dumosity
DINOOPPU douppion
DINOORSU nidorous
DINOORTU tourdion
DINOOSTY nodosity
DINOPRTY dry-point
DINPRTUY punditry
DINRSTUY industry
DIOOPRRT proditor
DIOSSTUU studious
DIRSSTTU distrust
DKLNOOOW look-down
DKMOOSUW muskwood
DKNNOOTW don't-know
DKOOORWW woodwork
DLLNOPUW pull-down
DLLOOPTY dotypoll
DLNOOPRU pouldron
DLNOOSUU nodulous
DLNOOSWW slowdown
DLNORTUY rotundly
DLOOOORS doloroso
DLOOOOWW wood wool
DLOOORSU dolorous
DLOOPPUW pulpwood, wood pulp
DLOOPPYY polypody
DMMNRUUY dummy run
DMMOOORT motordom
DMNNOOOT monodont
DMNOOOPY monopody
DMNOOSTW downmost
DMOOORWW woodworm, wormwood

DMPPPUUY mud puppy
DNNOOPRU pundonor
DNNOOTWW downtown
DNNORTUW downturn, turndown
DNOOPPRU propound
DNOOPRSW snowdrop
DNOOPRUW downpour
DNOORSUW wondrous
DNORRSUU surround
DOOOPRST doorpost, doorstop
DOOORSTU outdoors
DOOOSTTU outstood
DOOPRRTW dropwort
EEEEFGNR green fee
EEEEFPRR preferee
EEEEFRRS referees
EEEEFRRZ refreeze
EEEEGGRR greegree
EEEEGMRR re-emerge
EEEEGQSU squeegee
EEEEGSSX exegeses
EEEEHSTT theetsee
EEEELLPX expellee
EEEELLVY eye level
EEEELPRT Peterlee
EEEEMNRT ne temere
EEEEPPSW peesweep
EEEEPTTW peetweet
EEEETTWW weet-weet
EEEFFLOR forefeel
EEEFFMTU muffetee
EEEFFNOR Freefone
EEEFFNRT efferent
EEEFFRVW feverfew
EEEFILPR life peer
EEEFLLMR femerell
EEEFLMOS feme sole
EEEFLORV free love
EEEFLSST feetless
EEEFNRRT referent, rent-free, tree fern
EEEFNRSS freeness
EEEFNRST fenester
EEEFNRTT enfetter
EEEFNRUZ unfreeze
EEEFORRS foreseer
EEEFORTV free vote
EEEFPRUZ freeze-up
EEEFRRRR referrer
EEEFRRRT ferreter
EEEFRRTW fewterer
EEEGGILN negligee
EEEGHINT eighteen
EEEGILNV enveigle
EEEGILPS espiegle
EEEGINNR engineer
EEEGINRZ energize
EEEGIRTY tiger-eye
EEEGISSX exegesis
EEEGITVV vegetive
EEEGLMOS gleesome
EEEGLNRT greenlet
EEEGMNRT emergent
EEEGMNRU merengue
EEEGMORT geometer
EEEGNRRU reneguer
EEEGNRRV revenger
EEEGNRRY greenery
EEEHILRW erewhile
EEEHILSW Helewise
EEEHIMRT heremite
EEEHIRST etherise
EEEHIRTZ etherize
EEEHITWY white-eye
EEEHKLNO kneehole
EEEHLLSS heelless
EEEHLMPT helpmeet
EEEHLNTV eleventh
EEEHLNTY ethylene
EEEHLOPP peephole
EEEHLORS lee shore
EEEHMNTV vehement
EEEHMRYY eye-rhyme
EEEHNNPT nepenthe
EEEHNNQU henequen
EEEHNORW onewhere
EEEHNPRS ensphere
EEEHNRTT Ethernet
EEEHNRVW whenever
EEEHORST shoe-tree
EEEHRRVW wherever
EEEIKLRT treelike
EEEIKNPS Pekinese
EEEILLOT eleolite
EEEILLRV reveille
EEEILMMN Emmeline
EEEILMRS seemlier
EEEILNPR pelerine
EEEILNPS snipe eel
EEEILNRT tree line
EEEILNRY eyeliner
EEEILNST selenite
EEEILNSU eleusine
EEEILPRS sleepier
EEEILRRV reliever
EEEILRST leeriest, steelier
EEEILSSW elsewise
EEEILSTV televise
EEEIMNTY Yemenite
EEEIMPRR premiere
EEEIMRRS miserere
EEEIMRTT remittee
EEEINNNT nineteen
EEEINNRT internee
EEEINNST seine-net
EEEINNSV Viennese
EEEINNTT teniente
EEEINOSS essoinee
EEEINPRT perentie
EEEINRSS eeriness
EEEINRST eternise, teensier
EEEINRTZ eternize
EEEINSTT teeniest
EEEINSTW weeniest
EEEINTUX euxenite
EEEIPPRT peperite
EEEIPRRV reprieve
EEEIPSTW weepiest
EEEIQSUX exequies
EEEIRRTV retrieve
EEEIRRVW reviewer
EEEIRSVV eversive
EEEISSTX essexite
EEEJKKNR knee-jerk
EEEJLLRW jeweller
EEEJNSSU jeunesse
EEEKLLSS keelless
EEEKLNNN enkennel
EEEKMNSS meekness
EEEKMRSS kermesse
EEEKNNSS keenness
EEEKNORS kerosene
EEELLLRV leveller
EEELLNOR enrollee
EEELLNQU quenelle
EEELLPRR repeller
EEELLPRT pelleter
EEELLPRX expeller
EEELLRRS reseller
EEELLRRV reveller
EEELMNPT entemple
EEELMOPP empeople
EEELMOPY employee
EEELMOTT omelette
EEELMRTU muleteer
EEELMRTY meeterly
EEELMSSS seemless
EEELNOPP Penelope
EEELNOPR open-reel
EEELNOPV envelope
EEELNOSV novelese
EEELNPRY perylene
EEELNRSW newsreel
EEELNRSY serenely
EEELNRTV nervelet
EEELNRTY Terylene
EEELOPPR repeople
EEELPRSS espelers, peerless
EEELPTTY teletype
EEELRSST treeless
EEELRSTT resettle
EEELRSTV verselet
EEELRSVY Eversley, severely
EEELRTTT letteret
EEELRTVV velveret
EEELSSTW weetless
EEELTTTX teletext
EEEMNNTT tenement
EEEMNORZ mezereon
EEEMNRTT entremet
EEEMNSST meetness
EEEMORRV evermore
EEEMPRRT temperer
EEEMQSTU mesteque
EEEMRSST semester
EEENNOPR neoprene
EEENNOSV venenose
EEENNSSV evenness

EEENORVW	overween	**EEFIIMNN**	feminine	**EEFMORRT**	formeret
EEENORVY	everyone	**EEFIIMNS**	feminise	**EEFMPRRU**	perfumer
EEENPPRS	prepense	**EEFIIMNZ**	feminize	**EEFMRRTU**	feretrum
EEENPRRT	repenter	**EEFIIRRV**	verifier	**EEFNNRYZ**	enfrenzy
EEENPRST	pretense	**EEFIIRST**	feistier,	**EEFNORRZ**	refrozen
EEENRRTU	returnee		fieriest	**EEFNORST**	softener
EEENRRTV	reverent	**EEFIJNNR**	Jennifer	**EEFNORTU**	fourteen
EEENRSST	serenest	**EEFIKNNP**	penknife	**EEFNORTW**	forewent,
EEENRSTY	yestreen	**EEFILLMT**	telefilm		Freetown
EEENSSTW	tweeness	**EEFILLOV**	love life	**EEFNOSTT**	oftenest
EEEOPPSY	pope's eye	**EEFILLRT**	filleter	**EEFNQRTU**	frequent
EEEOPRRT	peterero	**EEFILLRW**	free will	**EEFNRTTU**	unfetter
EEEOPRTT	operette	**EEFILLSS**	lifeless	**EEFOORRT**	roof-tree
EEEORRST	rose tree	**EEFILLTT**	fillette	**EEFOPRRT**	free port
EEEORRSV	overseer	**EEFILLTU**	feuillet	**EEFOPRST**	Freepost,
EEEPPPRR	pepperer	**EEFILMOS**	lifesome		post-free
EEEPRRST	pesterer	**EEFILMST**	fistmele	**EEFOPRTT**	prefetto
EEEPRRSV	persever,	**EEFILMTX**	flextime	**EEFORRST**	forester,
	perverse,	**EEFILNSS**	fineless		fosterer,
	preserve	**EEFILNUV**	nieveful		reforest
EEEPRRTW	pewterer	**EEFILPPU**	flue pipe	**EEFORRSU**	ferreous
EEEPSTTT	septette	**EEFILPRR**	pilferer	**EEFORRTY**	feretory
EEEQRSUZ	squeezer	**EEFILRSS**	fireless	**EEFORSUV**	feverous
EEERRRSV	reserver,	**EEFILRSU**	fusileer	**EEFORSUY**	four-eyes
	reverser	**EEFILSSW**	wifeless	**EEFOSSTT**	fossette
EEERRRTV	reverter	**EEFIMSTU**	time-fuse	**EEGGGOOS**	goose egg
EEERSTTT	tresette	**EEFINNSS**	fineness	**EEGGHITW**	egg white
EEERSTVX	vertexes	**EEFINNTU**	fine-tune	**EEGGHLLS**	eggshell,
EEERSTWZ	tweezers	**EEFINORV**	overfine		shell egg
EEESTTTX	sextette	**EEFINRRY**	refinery	**EEGGHLOR**	hoggerel
EEFFGIRR	greffier	**EEFINRSS**	rifeness	**EEGGILOR**	leggiero
EEFFGORY	Geoffrey	**EEFIPRST**	fire-step	**EEGGILST**	leggiest
EEFFHIKY	keffiyeh	**EEFIPRSU**	perifuse	**EEGGIMRT**	egg-timer
EEFFISUV	effusive	**EEFIRRSU**	sure-fire	**EEGGINNR**	greening
EEFFLMNU	enmuffle	**EEFIRRTW**	wertfrei	**EEGGINRT**	greeting
EEFFLNTU	effluent	**EEFIRSTT**	frisette	**EEGGINSU**	siege gun
EEFFMORR	free-form	**EEFIRSTY**	esterify	**EEGGNOST**	gestogen
EEFFRRSU	sufferer	**EEFIRSUW**	fuse wire	**EEGGORRT**	gorgeret
EEFFTTUU	teuf-teuf	**EEFKNORT**	reef knot	**EEGGORTT**	go-getter
EEFGIILR	filigree	**EEFLLLNU**	fluellen	**EEGGPRRS**	preggers
EEFGILNT	fleeting	**EEFLLORT**	foretell	**EEGHHIKN**	knee-high
EEFGINRZ	freezing	**EEFLLORV**	overfell	**EEGHHINT**	heighten
EEFGLNRY	greenfly	**EEFLLOSV**	self-love	**EEGHINPT**	phengite
EEFGLNUV	vengeful	**EEFLLRSU**	self-rule	**EEGHINRS**	greenish
EEFGNOOR	foregone	**EEFLLRXY**	reflexly	**EEGHINST**	sheeting
EEFGOORR	foregoer	**EEFLLSSS**	selfless	**EEGHINTT**	teething
EEFGORRT	tree frog	**EEFLMORU**	fumerole	**EEGHIOTT**	goethite
EEFHILLR	hellfire	**EEFLMSSU**	fumeless	**EEGHISST**	sightsee
EEFHILRS	fleshier	**EEFLNORU**	fluorene	**EEGHISTY**	eyesight
EEFHIORS	fire hose	**EEFLNORW**	enflower	**EEGHLNNT**	lengthen
EEFHIRSV	feverish	**EEFLNOST**	felstone	**EEGHLOTU**	geelhout
EEFHIRTY	etherify	**EEFLNPSU**	penseful	**EEGHMNOO**	homogene
EEFHISTT	heftiest	**EEFLNRTU**	refluent	**EEGHMNOY**	hegemony
EEFHLLPS	self-help	**EEFLNSSS**	selfness	**EEGHNOPS**	phosgene
EEFHLLWY	flywheel	**EEFLNTUV**	eventful	**EEGHNOPY**	hypogene
EEFHLMST	themself	**EEFLORRW**	flowerer	**EEGHNSSU**	hugeness
EEFHLNOS	one flesh	**EEFLORTV**	leftover	**EEGHORTT**	together
EEFHLSTY	flysheet	**EEFLORTW**	floweret	**EEGIILMT**	legitime
EEFHORRT	therefor	**EEFLORVW**	overflew	**EEGIILNR**	lingerie
EEFHORSW	foreshew	**EEFLORWW**	werewolf	**EEGIILNV**	inveigle
EEFIIKLL	lifelike	**EEFLPRUW**	purflewe	**EEGIINNR**	ingineer
EEFIIKLW	wifelike	**EEFLRSST**	fretless	**EEGIINNS**	inseeing
EEFIILLN	lifeline	**EEFLSSSU**	fuseless	**EEGIINRT**	reignite
EEFIILMT	lifetime	**EEFMNORT**	fomenter	**EEGIINTV**	genitive
EEFIILSZ	life-size	**EEFMORRR**	reformer	**EEGIJLNW**	jeweling

EEGIJMNN Nijmegen
EEGIJOPR jerepigo
EEGIKLLU glue-like
EEGILLNV leveling
EEGILMNR germ line
EEGILNPS peelings, sleeping
EEGILNRR lingerer
EEGILNRU reguline
EEGILNRV reveling
EEGILNSV sleeving
EEGILOPU epilogue
EEGILOSU eulogise
EEGILOUZ eulogize
EEGILRTV verligte
EEGILRTY legerity
EEGIMNNS meninges
EEGIMNPT pimgenet
EEGIMNRT regiment
EEGIMNRU meringue
EEGIMNST gisement
EEGINNOZ Gneizeno
EEGINNQU queening
EEGINNRS sneering
EEGINNRT entering
EEGINNRY enginery
EEGINNSU unseeing
EEGINNSV evenings
EEGINNTV eventing
EEGINOPS epigones
EEGINORR erigeron
EEGINOST egestion
EEGINPSW sweeping
EEGINQUU queueing
EEGINRRS resigner
EEGINRRT tree ring
EEGINRST steering
EEGINRSU seigneur
EEGINRTT ringette
EEGINRTU geniture
EEGINRTX genetrix
EEGINSSU geniuses
EEGINSTU eugenist
EEGINSTW sweeting
EEGINTTV vignette
EEGINTUX teguexin
EEGIOPSU epigeous
EEGIORVV overgive
EEGIOSTV vogesite
EEGIPRRY periergy
EEGIPRST prestige
EEGIRRST register
EEGIRSTT grisette
EEGKLNOW week-long
EEGKNSSS Skegness
EEGLMNPU emplunge
EEGLMNTU emulgent
EEGLMOSS glosseme
EEGLNNTU ungentle
EEGLNOOP gene pool
EEGLNOPY polygene
EEGLNOTY telegony
EEGLNSTT gentlest
EEGLOOST Togolese
EEGLOPRS gospeler
EEGMMOSU gemmeous
EEGMNOST gemstone
EEGMNRRU murenger
EEGMNTTU tegument
EEGMORSU gruesome
EEGMORTY geometry
EEGNNORT roentgen
EEGNNOSV evensong
EEGNOORV engroove
EEGNOPPT peptogen
EEGNOPTY genotype
EEGNORST estrogen
EEGNORSU generous
EEGNOTYZ zygotene
EEGNPRUX expunger
EEGNRSSY greyness
EEGNRSUY Guernsey
EEGOPRSU superego
EEGORRST ostreger
EEGORRVW overgrew
EEHHIPSS sheepish
EEHHIRTW herewith
EEHHKKOO kohekohe
EEHHLLLO hell-hole
EEHHLMOP home help
EEHHLRST threshel
EEHHNNSZ Shenzhen
EEHHNOSU hen house
EEHHRRST thresher
EEHHTTUU huet-huet
EEHIILTW white lie
EEHIITTW white tie
EEHIJMNR mijnheer
EEHIKLLL hell-like
EEHIKLMO homelike
EEHIKRRS shrieker
EEHILLNP helpline
EEHILMNU helenium
EEHILMOR homelier
EEHILMOT homilete
EEHILNPW pinwheel
EEHILORT hotelier
EEHILPRT herptile
EEHILRSS heirless
EEHILRTW wehrlite
EEHILWYZ wheezily
EEHIMNOR Hermione
EEHIMNRT theremin
EEHIMPTY epithyme
EEHIMRST erethism, etherism
EEHIMRTT thermite
EEHINNRS enshrine
EEHINNRT inherent
EEHINOPS isophene
EEHINPRS insphere
EEHINPRT nephrite, prehnite, trephine
EEHINRTT thirteen
EEHINRTW whitener
EEHIOPPS hosepipe
EEHIORST isothere, theorise
EEHIORTZ theorize
EEHIPPST psephite
EEHIPPTY epiphyte
EEHIPRRS perisher
EEHIPRTT perthite, tephrite
EEHIPSST steepish
EEHIQRSU queerish
EEHIRRSV shiverer
EEHIRSTT tee shirt
EEHIRTVY thievery
EEHISSST esthesis
EEHISSTW sweetish
EEHKLOOR look here
EEHKLOWY Holy Week
EEHLLORV hoveller
EEHLLPSS helpless
EEHLMORU home rule
EEHLMOSS homeless
EEHLNOTT telethon
EEHLNOTV vent-hole
EEHLOPSS hopeless
EEHLORST hosteler
EEHLORSV shoveler
EEHLOSSS shoeless
EEHLPRSU spherule
EEHLPRTY three-ply
EEHLSSTW thewless
EEHMMOPR home perm, morpheme
EEHMMORT ohmmeter
EEHMNNOT menthone
EEHMNOOS moonshee
EEHMNOSW somewhen
EEHMORST homester, rest home
EEHMORTX exotherm
EEHMORVW whomever
EEHNNORT enthrone
EEHNOORS one-horse
EEHNOPRU hereupon
EEHNOPST poshteen, potsheen
EEHNOPTY neophyte
EEHNORST Hortense
EEHNORTU hereunto
EEHNORTV overhent
EEHNPRSU sheep-run
EEHNRRTY Tyrrhene
EEHNRTTU untether
EEHOORSV overshoe
EEHOORSW howsoe'er
EEHOOTTY eye-tooth
EEHOPPSW peep-show
EEHORRTX exhorter
EEHORSVW whosever
EEHORTTU thereout
EEHORVWY everyhow
EEHPPRRY hyperper
EEHPRSST the press
EEHPRSSU Hesperus
EEHPRSTU superhet
EEHPRSTY physeter
EEIIKLLR likelier
EEIIKLNV veinlike

EEIIKLSW	likewise, wiselike
EEIIKMNT	ketimine
EEIILLMT	melilite
EEIILLRV	livelier
EEIILMNT	ilmenite, melinite
EEIILMRT	timelier
EEIILMSS	emissile
EEIILNNT	Leninite
EEIILNPP	pipeline
EEIILNRW	wireline
EEIILNTV	lenitive
EEIILNTX	exilient
EEIILRVW	live wire
EEIILSTW	lewisite
EEIIMMTT	mimetite
EEIIMPRT	imperite
EEIIMRTZ	itemizer
EEIIMSSV	emissive
EEIIMSTW	timewise
EEIIMSTZ	Semitize
EEIINNVV	Vivienne
EEIINPPR	piperine
EEIINPRV	viperine
EEIINRRV	riverine
EEIINRTT	intertie
EEIINSSV	inessive
EEIINSTV	veiniest
EEIIPRTT	epitrite
EEIIPTTV	petitive
EEIIRRTV	tirrivee
EEIJKRST	jerkiest
EEIJLNNU	julienne
EEIJLNUV	juvenile
EEIJLOTT	Joliette
EEIJLTTU	Juliette
EEIKKLRS	Kirklees
EEIKKNRS	Kirkenes
EEIKLLRY	kyrielle
EEIKLMOR	more like
EEIKLMOS	likesome
EEIKLMST	stemlike
EEIKLNSS	likeness
EEIKLNST	nestlike
EEIKLORS	roselike
EEIKLORT	lorikeet
EEIKLPST	spikelet, steplike
EEIKNOOT	ookinete
EEIKNORS	kerosine
EEIKNRRT	tinkerer
EEIKOQUV	equivoke
EEIKPRST	perkiest
EEIKPSST	peskiest
EEILLLMV	Melville
EEILLMPR	impeller, per mille
EEILLMRS	smellier
EEILLMSS	limeless
EEILLMSY	seemlily
EEILLNOR	lonelier
EEILLNSS	lineless
EEILLNVV	venville
EEILLORT	oreillet
EEILLORV	lovelier
EEILLPSS	ellipses, pileless
EEILLPSY	sleepily
EEILLSSV	veilless
EEILLTVY	velleity
EEILMNNO	limonene
EEILMNNU	enlumine
EEILMNOP	pemoline
EEILMNOT	molinete
EEILMNST	Melisent
EEILMNSU	melusine, selenium
EEILMOPP	impeople
EEILMOPS	polemise
EEILMOPZ	polemize
EEILMOST	melitose
EEILMSST	timeless
EEILMSUV	emulsive
EEILNNOR	one-liner
EEILNNST	sentinel
EEILNOPR	leporine
EEILNORS	Roseline
EEILNOSV	novelise
EEILNOVZ	novelize
EEILNPPZ	Zeppelin
EEILNPRS	Pilsener
EEILNPRT	interpel
EEILNPRU	perilune
EEILNPRV	replevin
EEILNRSS	reinless
EEILNRST	enlister, Leinster, listener, re-enlist
EEILNRTT	lettrine
EEILNRTY	entirely, lientery
EEILNSSV	evilness, veinless, vileness
EEILNSSW	wineless
EEILNTTU	entitule
EEILNTUV	veinulet
EEILORRT	loiterer
EEILORST	literose
EEILORTZ	tolerize
EEILOSST	isoteles
EEILOTTT	toilette
EEILOTTV	olivette, violette, voilette
EEILOVWZ	vowelize
EEILPPSS	pipeless
EEILPPSY	epilepsy
EEILPRST	epistler
EEILPRTU	pleurite
EEILPSSV	pelvises
EEILPSTY	epistyle
EEILRSST	riteless, tireless
EEILRSSW	wireless
EEILSSVW	viewless
EEIMMNSS	nemesism
EEIMMORS	memorise
EEIMMORZ	memorize
EEIMMOST	sometime
EEIMMRST	meristem, mimester
EEIMMRTT	term-time
EEIMNNOT	intoneme
EEIMNOPR	epimeron
EEIMNORS	emersion
EEIMNORT	timoneer
EEIMNOST	monetise, semitone
EEIMNOTT	monetite
EEIMNOTX	xenotime
EEIMNOTZ	monetize, time zone
EEIMNPRT	periment
EEIMNPRU	perineum
EEIMNRRT	terminer
EEIMNRTU	mutineer
EEIMNRTV	virement
EEIMNSSS	missense
EEIMNSTV	visement
EEIMOPRS	promisee, reimpose
EEIMOPRT	importee
EEIMOPST	epsomite
EEIMORST	Timorese, tiresome
EEIMORTT	moirette
EEIMORTV	overtime
EEIMORTX	oximeter
EEIMPPST	pipe-stem
EEIMPSTT	emptiest
EEIMQSTU	mesquite
EEIMRRST	merriest
EEIMRRTT	remitter, trimeter
EEIMRRTX	meretrix
EEIMRSTU	emeritus
EEIMRTTY	temerity
EEIMSSST	messiest
EEINNOPR	ponerine
EEINNOPS	pensione
EEINNPTT	penitent
EEINNRST	intenser
EEINNRTT	Internet
EEINNRTV	inventer, reinvent
EEINNSTT	sentient
EEINOPPR	peperino, peperoni
EEINOPPS	nosepipe
EEINOPRS	isoprene, pensiero
EEINOPRT	ereption
EEINORRT	reorient
EEINORSS	essoiner
EEINORST	serotine
EEINORSV	eversion
EEINORTT	tenorite
EEINORTX	exertion
EEINOSST	essonite
EEINOSTT	noisette, teosinte
EEINPRSS	ripeness

EEINPRTX	inexpert
EEINQRRU	enquirer
EEINQRSU	squireen
EEINRRRT	interrer
EEINRRST	inserter, reinsert
EEINRRSU	reinsure
EEINRRTV	inverter
EEINRRTW	winterer
EEINRRTX	interrex
EEINRSST	interess
EEINRSSU	enuresis
EEINRSTT	insetter, interest
EEINRSTU	esurient
EEINRSTV	nerviest, reinvest
EEINRSTX	intersex
EEINRSTY	serenity
EEINRSUV	universe
EEINRSUX	unsexier
EEINRTTX	intertex
EEINRTTY	entierty, entirety, eternity
EEINSSSX	sexiness
EEINSSTW	newsiest
EEINSTTX	existent
EEIOPPRS	presepio
EEIOPPRT	epitrope
EEIOPRRV	overripe
EEIOPRRW	wire rope
EEIOPTTT	pettitoe
EEIORRTV	overtire
EEIORRTX	exterior
EEIORSST	erotesis, isostere
EEIORSVZ	oversize
EEIORVVW	overview
EEIPPPRR	preppier
EEIPPPST	peppiest
EEIPPQRU	equipper
EEIPPRRS	perspire
EEIPPRRT	peripter
EEIPQRSU	repiques
EEIPRRTT	preterit, prettier
EEIPRSSV	pressive
EEIPRSTX	pre-exist
EEIPRSTY	perseity
EEIPRTUV	eruptive
EEIPSSTW	stepwise
EEIPSTTT	pettiest
EEIPSTTY	type site
EEIPSTXX	extispex
EEIPSTYZ	type size
EEIQRRRU	requirer
EEIQSSSU	esquisse
EEIQSTTU	quietest
EEIRRSST	resister
EEIRRSVV	Verviers
EEIRRTTT	titterer
EEIRRTTY	terreity
EEIRSSSU	reissues
EEIRSTVY	severity
EEIRTTTZ	terzetti
EEISSTTT	testiest
EEISSTTZ	zestiest
EEJJLNUY	jejunely
EEJKORST	jokester
EEJPRRRU	perjurer
EEKKOOTT	tekoteko
EEKLLPTW	well-kept
EEKLMRTT	melktert
EEKLNOST	skeleton
EEKLORTW	telework
EEKMNOYY	key money
EEKMOORV	Kemerovo
EEKMRSTU	musk tree
EEKNOSTY	keystone
EEKNSSSW	skewness
EEKNSSTU	netsukes
EEKRRTUZ	kreutzer
EELLLLMP	pell-mell
EELLLNWY	Llewelyn
EELLLOVV	volvelle
EELLLOVW	low-level
EELLMNOY	Melloney
EELLMOSU	melleous
EELLNNOT	tonnelle
EELLNOUV	nouvelle
EELLNPRU	prunelle
EELLNSSS	lensless
EELLNSSW	wellness
EELLNSTU	entellus
EELLOPTV	top-level
EELLORSV	oversell
EELLORTU	tourelle
EELLORTX	extoller
EELLORVY	volleyer
EELLOSSV	loveless
EELLOSUV	levulose
EELLRSSU	ruleless
EELMMPUX	exemplum
EELMNOOS	lonesome
EELMNRTT	Lent term
EELMNRTU	lurement
EELMNSUY	unseemly
EELMNTTU	temulent
EELMOOSV	lovesome
EELMOPRY	employer, re-employ
EELMORST	molester
EELMORTY	remotely
EELMOSST	moteless
EELMOSSV	moveless
EELMOTVW	twelvemo
EELMPPRU	empurple
EELMRRTU	murrelet
EELMRSST	termless
EELMRSTY	smeltery
EELMSSST	stemless
EELMSSSU	museless
EELNNTTY	Lynnette
EELNNUVY	unevenly
EELNOOPS	polonese
EELNOORS	loosener
EELNOPPU	unpeople
EELNOPRT	petronel
EELNOPTY	polytene
EELNOQTU	eloquent
EELNORST	entresol
EELNOSSS	noseless
EELNOSST	noteless, toneless
EELNOSTV	love nest
EELNOTVV	evolvent
EELNSSSS	lessness
EELNSSSW	newsless
EELNSSTU	tuneless
EELNSSTV	ventless
EELNSTTU	unsettle
EELNSTWY	New Style
EELOPPSS	popeless
EELOPPST	estoppel
EELOPRRX	explorer
EELOPRTT	teleport
EELOPSTU	sleep-out
EELOPTTU	poulette
EELORRSV	resolver
EELORRUV	overrule
EELORRVV	revolver
EELORSSS	roseless
EELORSTU	resolute
EELORSTY	Tyrolese
EELORTTU	roulette
EELORTUV	revolute, true love
EELOSSTV	voteless
EELPPSTU	septuple
EELPRTXY	expertly
EELPSSUX	plexuses
EELPSTUX	sextuple
EELRRSTW	wrestler
EELRSSST	restless
EELRSTWY	westerly
EELSSTTX	textless
EEMMNOTV	movement
EEMMOOSS	mesosome
EEMMPRUY	empyreum
EEMMRTUX	extremum
EEMNNRSU	mensuren
EEMNOOPT	tone poem
EEMNOORS	eromenos
EEMNOPRU	noumpere
EEMNORSS	moreness
EEMNORSU	mounseer
EEMNORTY	Monterey
EEMNPRTU	erumpent
EEMNSSTU	muteness, tenesmus
EEMNSTTV	vestment
EEMOORRV	moreover
EEMOORTT	roomette
EEMOPRRS	premorse
EEMOQRSU	Moresque
EEMOQTTU	moquette
EEMORSST	Somerset
EEMORSTT	remotest
EEMORSTU	temerous
EEMORTXY	oxymeter
EEMOTTTU	teetotum
EEMRRSTU	musterer
EEMRRSUU	eremurus
EEMRRTTU	mutterer

EENNNOSS nonsense
EENNNOTV non-event
EENNOOOT one-to-one
EENNOORT rotenone
EENNOPSS openness
EENNOPTX exponent
EENNORTT Ronnette
EENOORST oestrone, roe-stone
EENOORTV overtone
EENOOSTV one's vote
EENOPPRS propense
EENOPRSS response
EENOPRST protense
EENOPRSU peroneus
EENOPRXY pyroxene
EENORRTT rottener
EENORSSS soreness
EENORSSU neuroses
EENORSTT onsetter, on-street
EENORSTX extensor
EENORSUV enervous, venerous
EENORTVW overwent
EENOSTUV ventouse
EENPPRSU purpense
EENPRSST pertness
EENPRSSU pureness
EENPSSSU suspense
EENPSTTU petuntse
EENRRRTU returner
EENRRTUV venturer
EENRSSSU sureness
EENRSSTU trueness
EENRSTUW wet-nurse
EEOOPRST proteose
EEOOPRTZ zoetrope
EEOPRRRT reporter
EEOPRRRV reprover
EEOPRRTT potterer
EEOPRRTX exporter, re-export
EEOPRSSS espresso
EEOPRSST poetress
EEOPRSSU espouser
EEOPRSSX expresso
EEOPRSTV overstep
EEOPRSUX exposure
EEOPSSTW sweetsop
EEOQRSTU questore
EEORRRST resorter, restorer, retrorse
EEORRRSW worserer
EEORRSTU terreous
EEORRSTX extrorse
EEORRTTT totterer
EEORRTTU teru-tero
EEORRTTX extorter
EEORRTUV overture
EEORSSTV estovers
EEORSTVX vortexes
EEORSUUV ouvreuse
EEORTTTZ terzetto
EEPRRSSU pressure
EEPRSTTU upsetter
EERRSSTU tressure
EERRSUVY resurvey
EFFFILRU fluffier
EFFGINOR offering
EFFHIILS filefish
EFFHIIRW whiffier
EFFHIISW fishwife
EFFHIITT fiftieth
EFFHILRW whiffler
EFFHIOTW off-white
EFFHISTU huffiest
EFFHLLSU shelfful
EFFHLLSY flesh-fly
EFFHLRSU shuffler
EFFHMORY off-rhyme
EFFHOORS offshore
EFFIINRS sniffier
EFFIINST niffiest
EFFIIPRS spiffier
EFFIKLRU rufflike
EFFILMOR life form
EFFILNRS sniffler
EFFILRTW twiffler
EFFINOSU effusion
EFFINRSU snuffier
EFFIOPST off-piste
EFFIORTW write-off
EFFIPSTU puffiest
EFFIRSTU stuffier
EFFLMNUU unmuffle
EFFLNRSU snuffler
EFFOOORT forefoot
EFFORRUV overruff
EFGGILOS solfeggi
EFGGIOST foggiest
EFGHHIIL high life
EFGHHIIV high-five
EFGHILNS fleshing
EFGHILRT flighter
EFGHILSU fish-glue
EFGHINRT frighten
EFGHINSU feng-shui
EFGHIOSY fogeyish
EFGHNOTU foughten
EFGIILNU figuline
EFGIIMNS misfeign
EFGIINNR infringe
EFGIINRU figurine
EFGIITUV fugitive
EFGILLNO lifelong, long-life
EFGILLNU fuelling
EFGILLUU guileful
EFGILMOR film-goer
EFGILNOR florigen
EFGILNTW left wing
EFGILPRU fireplug
EFGIMRUU refugium
EFGINORV forgiven
EFGINORW forewing
EFGINPUY pinguefy
EFGINRTT fretting
EFGINRTY gentrify
EFGIOOST goofiest
EFGIOPTT pettifog
EFGIORRV forgiver
EFGLOOVX foxglove
EFGNSSUU funguses
EFHIIKLS fishlike
EFHIILRT filthier
EFHIINRS finisher, refinish
EFHIIPPS pipefish
EFHIIPRS fireship
EFHIIRST shiftier
EFHIISST fishiest
EFHILTWY whitefly
EFHIOPRS foreship
EFHIORRT frothier
EFHIORSS rose-fish
EFHIORSV overfish
EFHIORTT fortieth
EFHIRRTU thurifer
EFHIRSTT frettish
EFHLNORS hornfels
EFHLORSY horsefly
EFHLORVY hoverfly
EFHLOSUU houseful
EFHLOSUY housefly
EFHOORST foreshot
EFHOORSW foreshow
EFHRSTTU furthest
EFIIILRV vilifier
EFIIINNT infinite
EFIIINST finitise
EFIIINTZ finitize
EFIIKRRS friskier
EFIILLNT tefillin
EFIILLRR frillier
EFIILMRS flimsier
EFIILMST filmiest
EFIILNRT flintier, infilter
EFIILNTY felinity, finitely
EFIILRRT flirtier
EFIILRSU fusilier
EFIILSTY feistily
EFIIMMNS feminism
EFIIMNST feminist
EFIIMNTY feminity
EFIIMRSS miss-fire
EFIINNNS Sinn Fein
EFIINORR fire-iron, inferior
EFIINPSX spinifex
EFIINRRT ferritin
EFIINSTT niftiest
EFIIPRRU purifier
EFIIPRST spitfire
EFIIPRTY typifier
EFIIPRXX prix fixe
EFIIRRTU fruitier
EFIIRRZZ frizzier
EFIIRTUV fruitive
EFIIRVVY revivify
EFIISTZZ fizziest
EFIJLORS frijoles

EFIKLLOW wolflike
EFIKLMOR foremilk
EFIKLORS folksier
EFIKLOST folkiest
EFIKLSTU flukiest
EFIKNNOS finnesko
EFIKNORS foreskin
EFIKNSTU funkiest
EFIKORRW firework
EFILLLSW self-will
EFILLMTU full time
EFILLORV overfill
EFILLOSU fusel oil
EFILLRRY frillery
EFILLTUY futilely
EFILMRSS firmless
EFILMSUY emulsify
EFILNNTU influent
EFILNORU fluorine
EFILNPSU pensiful
EFILNPTY plentify
EFILNRTT flittern
EFILOORV folivore
EFILOPPR floppier
EFILOPRR profiler
EFILOPST septfoil
EFILORRU flourier
EFILORSS flossier
EFILORTU fluorite
EFILOSTT loftiest
EFILPRTU uplifter
EFILPSTU spiteful
EFILPSTY self-pity
EFILRSST riftless
EFILRSTT flitters
EFILRSTW fewtrils
EFILRTTU fruitlet
EFILSTTW swiftlet
EFIMNORR informer, reniform
EFIMNORS ensiform
EFIMNRSS firmness
EFIMORRT retiform
EFIMOSTT oft-times
EFIMPRRU frumpier
EFIMRSTU fremitus
EFINNPPY fippenny
EFINNPSU fine-spun
EFINNSTU funniest
EFINOOSS oofiness
EFINOPRR perforin
EFINOPTX pontifex
EFINORRT frontier
EFINOSSX foxiness
EFIOPRRS forprise
EFIOPRRT portfire, profiter
EFIORRRU fourrier
EFIORRST frostier
EFIORRTT retrofit
EFIPPRRY frippery
EFIPRRUY repurify
EFIPRTTY prettify
EFIRRRUY furriery
EFIRRSTU furriest
EFIRRTUY fruitery
EFIRSTTU turfiest
EFISSSTU fussiest
EFISSTTU fustiest
EFISTUZZ fuzziest
EFKLLOOR folklore
EFKLOOOR forelook
EFKMNOYY monkeyfy
EFKNOORW foreknow
EFKNRSTU funkster
EFKOOPRS forspoke
EFKORRTW fretwork
EFLLLOOW wool-fell
EFLLLOWY fellowly
EFLLMRTU full term
EFLLNOOW lone wolf
EFLLNSSU fullness
EFLLNTUY fluently
EFLLOORW follower
EFLLOOTW footwell
EFLLORUV overfull
EFLLOSST soft sell
EFLLOUWY woefully
EFLLRUUY ruefully
EFLLSUUY usefully
EFLMMRUY flummery
EFLMNRUU frenulum
EFLMORRY formerly
EFLMORSS formless
EFLMOSTT leftmost
EFLNOOSU felonous
EFLNORTT frontlet
EFLNORYZ frozenly
EFLNOSSU foulness
EFLNOSSW self-sown
EFLNOSTY stonefly
EFLNRTTU left turn
EFLOORSS roofless
EFLOORSW foreslow
EFLOORTU foot-rule
EFLOORVW overflow
EFLOOSST footless
EFLOPRUW powerful
EFLOPSTW fowl pest
EFLORSUY yourself
EFLOSUUX flexuous
EFLRSTUU frustule
EFLRTTUY fluttery
EFMNRTUY frumenty
EFMOOORR foreroom
EFMOORST foremost
EFMOORSU foursome
EFNNOOOR forenoon
EFNNORUZ unfrozen
EFNOOOTT footnote
EFNOOPRT pent roof
EFNOOSST eftsoons
EFNOSSST softness
EFOOORST footsore
EFOOPRSY spoofery
EFOOPSTT footstep
EFOORRSW forswore
EFOORSTT footrest
EFORRSST fortress
EFORRSTW frowster
EFORRSTY forestry
EFORSSST fostress
EGGGIILR gigglier
EGGGIORR groggier
EGGGOOOS goosegog
EGGHIINN hingeing
EGGHIINW weighing
EGGHINNT ghenting
EGGHIRWY Whiggery
EGGHOOTT egg-tooth
EGGHRTUY thuggery
EGGIILRW wigglier
EGGIINNS singeing
EGGIINNT tingeing
EGGIIPST piggiest
EGGILNNU lungeing
EGGILNRU grueling
EGGILNRY gingerly
EGGILQSU squiggle
EGGILRRW wriggler
EGGIMORS smoggier
EGGIMSTU muggiest
EGGINNST gestning
EGGINORR gorgerin
EGGINRSY sniggery
EGGIOSST soggiest
EGGIPRRY priggery
EGGJLRUY jugglery
EGGLMRSU smuggler
EGGLRSTU struggle
EGGMSSTU smuggest
EGGNOOPS egg-spoon
EGGNOOST geognost
EGGNOOSY geognosy
EGGNORSU gurgeons
EGGNRSUY snuggery
EGGNSSTU snuggest
EGGOORSU gorgeous
EGGOPTTY peggotty
EGHHHILO high-hole
EGHHIIMT high time
EGHHIIRS high-rise
EGHHIIRW high wire
EGHHILNO high-lone
EGHHILTY eighthly
EGHHINSS highness
EGHHINSU Hengshui
EGHHIPRU higher-up
EGHHORUW rough-hew
EGHIILNR hireling
EGHIILNS shieling
EGHIIMRT mightier
EGHIIPRT griphite
EGHIIRST tigerish
EGHILLNW well-nigh
EGHILMNO homeling
EGHILNOT leighton
EGHILNPT light-pen, penlight
EGHILNSS shingles
EGHILNSV shelving
EGHILORT regolith
EGHIMSTT mightest
EGHINNST sennight
EGHINOOP poonghie

EGHINOST histogen
EGHINRRU hungrier
EGHINTTW whetting
EGHINTUW unweight
EGHIOPSU pishogue
EGHIOSST thegosis
EGHIOTUW outweigh
EGHIPRTY gryphite
EGHIRRUY hierurgy
EGHISSTU gushiest
EGHITTUW tugwithe
EGHKLNOU gunk-hole
EGHLLNUW well-hung
EGHLLOPU plughole
EGHLMNOP phlegmon
EGHLNPUU penghulu
EGHLNRUY hungerly
EGHLOOOR horologe
EGHLOORY rheology
EGHLOOTY ethology, theology
EGHLOPRU plougher
EGHLOPRY hypergol
EGHMNOOY homogeny
EGHMNOPU gumpheon
EGHMNORS gemshorn
EGHMOPUY hypogeum
EGHNNTWY Gwynneth
EGHNOOPT photogen
EGHNOOTY theogony
EGHNORUV hung-over, overhung
EGHNOTUU Huguenot
EGHNRSTT strength
EGHOOOSW hoosegow
EGHORRTW regrowth
EGIIKKLN kinglike
EGIIKLLO killogie
EGIIKLNW winglike
EGIIKNSZ king-size
EGIILMMN immingle
EGIILMNU glunimie
EGIILNNU linguine
EGIILNOR religion
EGIILNPR periling
EGIILNRS Riesling
EGIILNRT girtline, tinglier, tireling
EGIILNRV reviling
EGIILRRS grislier
EGIILRTU guiltier
EGIILRTZ glitzier
EGIIMNNU ingenium
EGIIMNPR impinger
EGIIMNRT meriting
EGIIMNST mingiest
EGIIMNTT emitting
EGIIMOPT impetigo
EGIIMORR grimoire
EGIIMRST grimiest
EGIINNPW Winnipeg
EGIINNRS resining
EGIINOPR peignoir
EGIINORS seignior
EGIINRRT retiring
EGIINRST stingier
EGIINRSW swingier
EGIINRTU intrigue
EGIINRTV riveting
EGIINSTZ zingiest
EGIIRRTT grittier
EGIITUXY exiguity
EGIKKNRT trekking
EGIKLNSS kingless
EGIKLNSY Kingsley
EGIKNNOT tokening
EGILLNOR Negrillo
EGILLNOV livelong, loveling
EGILLNOW Lilongwe
EGILLNPS spelling
EGILLNSW swelling
EGILLOOR gloriole
EGILMNOT long-time, moteling
EGILMNPU implunge
EGILMOOR gloomier, oligomer
EGILMOUU eulogium
EGILNNOS noseling, Solingen
EGILNNST nestling
EGILNNTU glutenin
EGILNOOV viologen
EGILNORV overling
EGILNORW roweling
EGILNOSU ligneous
EGILNOSW longwise
EGILNOTW toweling
EGILNOVW Longview
EGILNRSS ringless
EGILNRST sterling
EGILNRSW newsgirl
EGILNRTY ringlety
EGILNSSU ugliness
EGILNSSW wingless
EGILNSUW Lewis gun
EGILNVXY vexingly
EGILOOSU isologue
EGILOOTY etiology
EGILORSS glossier
EGILOSTU eulogist
EGILRRZZ grizzler
EGILRTTY glittery
EGIMMNST stemming
EGIMMRST grimmest
EGIMMSTU gummiest
EGIMNNNO mignonne
EGIMNOOR Geronimo
EGIMNOSU geminous
EGIMNPTT tempting
EGIMNPTY emptying
EGIMNPUY epigynum
EGIMNRRU muringer
EGIMNRSS grimness
EGIMNRSU gum resin
EGIMNRUY eryngium
EGIMNSTT gistment
EGIMORST ergotism
EGIMOSTW wegotism
EGIMPRRU grumpier
EGIMTTTY tittymeg
EGINNORS nosering
EGINNORT nitrogen
EGINNORV vigneron
EGINNRRU unerring
EGINOORV ingroove
EGINOOSS gooiness
EGINOPRS spongier
EGINOPRY pigeonry
EGINOPST pongiest
EGINORRY iron-grey
EGINORSS goriness
EGINORSY seignory
EGINORTU routeing
EGINORTW towering
EGINORTY genitory
EGINORUV envigour
EGINPPPR prepping
EGINPPST stepping
EGINPRRS springer
EGINPRSS pressing
EGINRRST restring, ringster, stringer
EGINRSSY syringes
EGINSTTT stetting
EGIOOPST goopiest
EGIOORRV groovier
EGIOPRSS gossiper
EGIORRTT grottier
EGIORSST strigose
EGIORSSU griseous
EGIORSUV grievous
EGIOSUUX exiguous
EGIRRSTY registry
EGISSTTU gustiest, gutsiest
EGJLNORU jongleur
EGJLNORY jonglery
EGJLNOTU jelutong
EGLLMORW gromwell
EGLLNSSU lungless
EGLMMSTU glummest
EGLMNOOS longsome
EGLMNOOY menology
EGLMNORT long-term
EGLMNSSU glumness
EGLMOPRU promulge
EGLMORSS gormless
EGLMPSTU leg stump
EGLNNOOR longeron
EGLNNOPU plungeon
EGLNNOSS longness
EGLNNTUY ungently
EGLNOOOY oenology
EGLNOOPR prolonge
EGLNOOPY penology
EGLNOORV overlong
EGLNOPYY polygeny
EGLNORUU longueur
EGLNOSSS songless
EGLNOSUU lungeous
EGLNRSSU rungless

EGLNRTUY urgently
EGLOOORY oreology
EGLOOPRU prologue
EGLOOPTY logotype
EGLOORSY serology
EGLOOSXY sexology
EGLORRWY growlery
EGLORSUY rugosely
EGMNNOOY monogeny
EGMNOOOS mongoose
EGMNOOSU mungoose
EGMNSSSU smugness
EGMOORRW Growmore
EGNNOOTY ontogeny
EGNNSSSU snugness
EGNNSTTU tungsten
EGNOOPRS prognose
EGNOORRV governor
EGNOOTUX ox-tongue
EGNOPPRU oppugner
EGNOPRUW gunpower
EGNORRST stronger
EGNORSST songster
EGNORSTU sturgeon
EGNORSTY sentry-go
EGNOSTUY youngest
EGNRRSTU restrung
EGOOPRRU prorogue
EGOORRVW overgrow
EGOPRRSS progress
EGOPSSUY gypseous
EGOSSTUU outguess
EHHIIPRS heirship
EHHIISTV thievish
EHHILMNT helminth
EHHIORTT hitherto
EHHIOTTW white-hot
EHHIPSST phthises
EHHIRSSW shrewish
EHHMOOSW show home
EHHMPRUY Humphrey
EHHNOORS shoehorn
EHHOOPST theosoph
EHHOOSTU hothouse
EHIIKLNS Helsinki
EHIIKLPW whip-like
EHIILLST hilliest
EHIILMOS homilise
EHIILMOT homilite
EHIILMOZ homilize
EHIILRSV liverish
EHIIMNNO hominine
EHIIMPST mephitis
EHIINNOS inhesion
EHIINNRS inshrine
EHIINSST shiniest
EHIINSTW whiniest
EHIINSVX vixenish
EHIIPRSV viperish
EHIIPSTT pithiest
EHIIRRST shirtier
EHIIRSTT shittier
EHIIRTTW Whittier
EHIISSTW thiswise
EHIISTTX sixtieth
EHIJLSWY Jewishly
EHIJOSTV Jehovist
EHIKKLOO hooklike
EHIKLNOR hornlike
EHIKLRSU rushlike
EHIKMNST methinks
EHIKNORS shonkier
EHIKNOSS hokiness
EHIKNRRS shrinker
EHIKNSTU hunkiest
EHIKOPRS pokerish
EHIKRSWY whiskery
EHIKSSTU huskiest
EHILLLMO molehill
EHILLMOP Philomel
EHILLOPY lyophile
EHILLPTY phyllite
EHILLRRT thriller
EHILLSSW swellish
EHILMNOP Philemon
EHILMOOR heirloom
EHILMOST helotism
EHILNOPX phloxine
EHILNORU unholier
EHILNOSS holiness
EHILNOST Holstein
EHILNOTX xenolith
EHILOOPZ zoophile
EHILOPRS polisher, repolish
EHILOPRT heliport
EHILOPST isopleth
EHILORSS sloshier
EHILORTT threitol
EHILORTY rhyolite
EHILPPRT thripple
EHILPRSU plushier
EHILPSSS shipless
EHILPSST pithless
EHILPSSW whipless
EHILPSTU sulphite
EHILRSSU slushier
EHILRSTW whistler
EHILRSTY slithery
EHILRTTY triethyl
EHILSSST shitless
EHILTTTW thwittle
EHIMMNUY hymenium
EHIMMRSY shimmery
EHIMNOPR morphine
EHIMNORT thermion
EHIMNOSS hominess
EHIMNOSW womenish
EHIMNOTT monteith
EHIMNOTU home unit
EHIMNOTW hit women
EHIMNPST shipment
EHIMNRRU murrhine
EHIMOOST smoothie
EHIMORST isotherm, theorism
EHIMORSU humorise
EHIMORTU mouthier
EHIMORUZ humorize
EHIMOSTT mothiest
EHIMPPSS psephism
EHIMPRRS shrimper
EHIMPSTU humpiest
EHIMPSUU euphuism
EHIMRSST smithers
EHIMRSTY smithery
EHIMSSTU mushiest
EHINNORT inthrone
EHINNOTW non-white
EHINNSST thinness
EHINNSSU sunshine
EHINNSTT thinnest
EHINOOPS isophone
EHINOPPR hornpipe
EHINOPST phoniest
EHINORRT thornier
EHINORSS herisson
EHINORST horniest
EHINORTT no-hitter
EHINOSTU outshine
EHINPRSU punisher
EHINRRTT thrinter
EHINSSTW withness
EHIOOPST isophote
EHIOOPSW whoopsie
EHIOORTT toothier
EHIOPRSS phoresis
EHIOPRSV poverish
EHIORRTW Iorwerth, worthier
EHIORSST horsiest, orthesis
EHIORSTT theorist
EHIORTVW over with
EHIORTWZ howitzer
EHIOSSTU house-sit
EHIOSSTW showiest
EHIOTTUW white-out
EHIPQSUY physique
EHIPRSTW whipster
EHIPSSTU pushiest
EHIPSTUU euphuist
EHIRSTTW whitster
EHKLNOOT knot-hole
EHKLOOSS hookless
EHKLOSTY lekythos
EHKMNSTY Shymkent
EHKMOORW homework
EHKNNRSU shrunken
EHKNOOOS hook-nose
EHLLMOPY phyllome
EHLLNSTU nutshell
EHLLOOOP loophole
EHLLOOTW whole lot
EHLLOPST top-shell
EHLLOSTU shell-out
EHLMNOUU humulone
EHLMOORW wormhole
EHLMORTY motherly
EHLMOTXY methoxyl
EHLMPSSU humpless
EHLNOPRT plethron
EHLNOPST Helpston
EHLNOPSU sulphone
EHLNORSS hornless

EHLNOSTY honestly
EHLNPRTU plunther
EHLNSSSU lushness
EHLOOPRT porthole, potholer
EHLOOPTY holotype
EHLOPPRT thropple
EHLOPRTY plethory
EHLOPSSS shopless
EHLORRTY erythrol
EHLORSTT throstle
EHLORSTY hostelry
EHLORTTT throttle
EHLOSSTW thowless
EHLRSSTU hurtless, ruthless
EHMMNPUY nympheum
EHMMRRTU thrummer
EHMNOOPR neomorph
EHMNOOTW home town
EHMNOOTY hot money
EHMNOPSU homespun
EHMNPRYY hypernym
EHMOOPRT home port
EHMOORST smoother
EHMORSTU hurtsome
EHMORSTY smothery
EHMORTUV vermouth
EHMOTUWY Weymouth
EHMOTUZZ mezuzoth
EHMRTUYY eurythmy
EHNNOOPR neophron
EHNNOOPU euphonon
EHNNOPRT penn'orth
EHNNORRT northern
EHNNORTU unthrone
EHNOOPPS open shop
EHNOOPTY honey pot
EHNOORRU honourer
EHNOORST hen-roost
EHNOORSW whoreson
EHNOORTW honewort
EHNOORVZ Voronezh
EHNOOSSW snowshoe
EHNOOSTU outshone
EHNOPPRS nephrops
EHNOPSSS poshness
EHNORSTT northest
EHNORSTU southern
EHNOSTUU nuthouse
EHNRSSTU huntress
EHOOPRRT horopter
EHOOPRTY orthoepy
EHOOPSTT photoset
EHOOPSTU housetop
EHOOPTYZ zoophyte
EHOORSTV overshot
EHOORSUW row house
EHOOSTUU outhouse
EHOPPRSY prophesy
EHOPRSST hot-press
EHOPRSUV pushover
EHOPRTUY eutrophy
EHORRSTY herstory
EHORRTTW hertwort
EHORSTTW the worst
EHPRSUYZ zephyrus
EHRRSTTU thruster
EIIILPPR liripipe
EIIMMNS minimise
EIIMMNZ minimize
EIIKKLLS silklike
EIIKKLNS skinlike
EIIKKNST kinkiest
EIIKLLMN limekiln
EIIKLLNO lion-like
EIIKLMST milkiest
EIIKLNOR iron-like
EIIKLNRS slinkier
EIIKLNRW wrinklie
EIIKLSST silkiest
EIIKMPRS skimpier
EIIKNNRS skinnier
EIIKNNSS inkiness
EIIKNNSW wineskin
EIIKNRST Kristine, stinkier
EIIKPSST spikiest
EIIKQRRU quirkier
EIIKRSST riskiest
EIILLLVY livelily
EIILLMNR milliner
EIILLMNS slimline
EIILLMNU illumine
EIILLNTV vitellin
EIILLOOV olive oil
EIILLPRV pilliver
EIILLPSS ellipsis
EIILLSST silliest
EIILLSUV illusive
EIILMMOT immotile
EIILMNNS Leninism
EIILMNNT liniment
EIILMNOT limonite
EIILMNSS liminess, melissin
EIILMNSU luminise
EIILMNTT melittin
EIILMNUZ luminize
EIILMOPT impolite
EIILMPRT prelimit
EIILMSST slimiest
EIILMSTT mistitle
EIILMSTY myelitis
EIILNNOT lenition
EIILNNST Leninist
EIILNORZ lionizer
EIILNOSS oiliness
EIILNOTT toilinet
EIILNQTU quintile
EIILNSSW wiliness
EIILNSTW wine list
EIILNSTY senility
EIILNTTU intitule
EIILNTUV vituline
EIILOPPS soil pipe
EIILOPSS peliosis
EIILOPST pisolite
EIILORTT troilite
EIILOTVV volitive
EIILPPRS slippier
EIILPPST lippiest
EIILPSST pitiless
EIILPSTY pyelitis
EIILQSSU siliques
EIILRSTT slittier
EIILRTUZ utilizer
EIIMMMST mimetism
EIIMMNNT imminent
EIIMMNSU immunise
EIIMMNUZ immunize
EIIMMOTV immotive
EIIMMPRS empirism
EIIMMPRU imperium
EIIMMSST Semitism
EIIMNOPT pimiento
EIIMNORS erminois
EIIMNOSS emission
EIIMNRST minister
EIIMNRTT intermit
EIIMNRTW winterim
EIIMNRTX intermix
EIIMNSTT mintiest
EIIMNTUZ mutinize
EIIMOPRX mirepoix
EIIMOPST optimise
EIIMOPTZ optimize
EIIMOSSV omissive
EIIMOSUX eximious
EIIMOTVV vomitive
EIIMPRSZ misprize
EIIMQSTU quietism
EIIMRSTT metritis
EIIMRSTW miswrite
EIIMSSTT mistiest, Semitist
EIINNNTT tinnient
EIINNOPS pensioni
EIINNORT inertion
EIINNOSV envision
EIINNOUZ unionize
EIINNRST intrinse
EIINNRTW inwinter
EIINNSST tininess
EIINNSTT tinniest
EIINOPRT pointier
EIINOPTT petition
EIINORRT interior
EIINORSV revision
EIINOSST noisiest
EIINPPRS snippier
EIINPPST nippiest
EIINPRRS inspirer
EIINPRST pristine
EIINPSST spiniest
EIINPTUV punitive
EIINQRRU inquirer
EIINQTUY inequity
EIINRRTW wintrier
EIINRSST sinister
EIINRSSW wiriness
EIINRSTU neuritis
EIIOPRST Poitiers
EIIOPSTV positive
EIIOSSTT osteitis

EIIOSTUX	exitious
EIIPPRRT	trippier
EIIPPRTV	pit viper
EIIPPSTZ	zippiest
EIIPRRSS	prissier
EIIPRRST	stripier
EIIPRRTW	tripwire
EIIPRTYZ	pyritize
EIIPSSTT	stipites, tipsiest
EIIPSSTW	wispiest
EIIQSTTU	quietist
EIIRSTTU	it is true, uteritis
EIIRSTTW	twistier
EIIRSTTZ	ritziest
EIISSSST	sissiest
EIISTTTW	wittiest
EIJKNOSS	jokiness
EIJKORRS	ski-jorer
EIJLLOST	jolliest
EIJMOPRS	pejorism
EIJMPSTU	jumpiest
EIJNORTU	jointure
EIJNOSTT	jettison
EIKKLNNY	Kilkenny
EIKKOOST	kookiest
EIKLLNTW	well-knit
EIKLLNUY	unlikely
EIKLLOOW	wool-like
EIKLLORV	overkill
EIKLMNOS	moleskin
EIKLMORW	wormlike
EIKLMOSS	mosslike
EIKLMOST	most like
EIKLNOOR	inlooker
EIKLNOSU	leukosin
EIKLNOSW	snowlike
EIKLNPRS	sprinkle
EIKLNRTT	trinklet
EIKLNRTW	twinkler
EIKLNSSS	skinless
EIKLOORT	rootlike
EIKLOSSU	leukosis
EIKLSSTU	sulkiest
EIKMNNOR	monniker
EIKMNOST	tokenism
EIKMOPSS	misspoke
EIKMOSST	smokiest
EIKMSSTU	muskiest
EIKNNPSS	pinkness
EIKNOPRS	rose pink
EIKNOPSS	pokiness
EIKNOPSZ	skip zone
EIKNORST	in-stroke
EIKNORTT	knottier
EIKNOSTW	wonkiest
EIKNPRST	Pinkster
EIKNPRSU	spunkier
EIKNPRTU	turnpike
EIKNSSTT	skin test
EIKOOPRS	spookier
EIKOPPRS	skip-rope
EIKOPPRW	pipework
EIKOPPRY	porky-pie
EIKOPRST	porkiest
EIKORRWW	wirework
EIKORSTW	worksite
EIKPRRSU	spruiker
EIKRSTTY	skittery
EILLLNOY	lonelily
EILLLNTY	Lent lily
EILLLOPV	poll-evil
EILLLOVY	lovelily
EILLLSSW	will-less
EILLMMSU	musellim
EILLMNNO	monellin
EILLMNOT	mollient
EILLMNOU	linoleum
EILLMOPS	plimsole
EILLMOSW	willsome
EILLMPSS	misspell, psellism
EILLMPTU	multiple
EILLMSSY	melissyl
EILLMUVX	vexillum
EILLNNOP	pollenin
EILLNOPR	leprolin
EILLNOPY	epyllion
EILLNPSW	pinswell
EILLNSTY	silently, tinselly
EILLOORW	woollier
EILLOPPR	pipe roll
EILLOPTX	exit poll
EILLOPTY	politely
EILLORST	tresillo
EILLORTT	tortelli
EILLOSSS	soil-less
EILLOSTW	lowliest
EILLOSVW	low-lives
EILLSSST	listless
EILLSTTT	littlest
EILLSTUV	vitellus
EILMMPRU	plummier
EILMMRSU	slummier
EILMMRTU	multimer
EILMMSST	slimmest
EILMNOPR	lepromin
EILMNOPU	pinoleum
EILMNOSU	emulsion
EILMNOSV	novelism
EILMNOTU	moulinet
EILMNOTY	mylonite
EILMNPSS	limpness
EILMNPTU	pilentum, tump-line
EILMNRRY	Merrilyn
EILMNRST	minstrel
EILMNSSS	slimness
EILMNTUY	minutely, untimely
EILMOOPS	liposome
EILMOOST	toilsome
EILMOPRS	sperm oil
EILMOPST	milepost, polemist
EILMOSTT	motliest
EILMOSTY	molysite
EILMPPRU	impurple
EILMPRUY	impurely
EILMPSST	simplest
EILMPSSU	mespilus
EILMPSTU	lumpiest, plumetis, plumiest
EILMRSSY	remissly
EILMRSTT	lettrism
EILMTTUU	lutetium
EILMTTUY	multeity
EILNNOSS	onliness
EILNNOST	insolent
EILNNOSW	snowline
EILNNOTV	Ventolin, vinolent
EILNNTTY	intently
EILNOOPP	epiploon
EILNOOST	looniest, oilstone
EILNOPRT	Interpol, pointrel
EILNOPRU	neuropil
EILNOPSY	lysopine
EILNOPTT	pentitol, pointlet
EILNOPTY	Linotype
EILNOQTU	quintole
EILNORSS	ironless
EILNOSTV	novelist
EILNOSUV	evulsion
EILNOTUV	involute
EILNOTXY	Xylonite
EILNPRST	splinter
EILNPSSU	splenius
EILNPSUY	supinely
EILNQUUY	uniquely
EILNRRUU	unrulier
EILNRSTU	insulter
EILNRSUU	Ursuline
EILNRTUV	virulent
EILNRTWY	winterly
EILNSTTU	lutenist
EILNSUWY	unwisely
EILOOPST	loopiest
EILOOPTZ	zopilote
EILOORST	oestriol
EILOORWW	wire wool
EILOOSTY	otiosely
EILOPPRS	slip-rope, sloppier
EILOPPRY	polypier
EILOPPTY	polypite
EILOPRRT	portlier
EILOPRSS	oil-press
EILOPRSU	perilous
EILOPRSV	overslip, slipover
EILOPRTU	politure
EILOPRTW	pilewort
EILOPSTT	pistolet, politest
EILORRTU	ulterior
EILORTTW	Rottweil
EILORTTY	toiletry
EILOSSTU	lousiest

EILOSTTT stiletto
EILPPRST stippler
EILPPRSU periplus, supplier
EILPPRSY slippery
EILPRSTT splitter
EILPRSTY priestly, spritely
EILPRSUU purlieus
EILPRSUY pleurisy
EILPRTTY prettily
EILQRRSU squirrel
EILQRSUY squirely
EILRRSTU sultrier
EILRRTWY writerly
EILRSSST stirless
EILRSSTU surliest
EILRSSTY sisterly
EILRSTTU surtitle
EILRSTTW wristlet
EILSSSTW wistless
EILSSTTU lustiest
EIMMMNOT immoment
EIMMNNTU muniment
EIMMNORS misnomer
EIMMOPRU emporium, pomerium
EIMMORRT Mortimer
EIMMORST memorist
EIMMOSTT totemism
EIMMPRST primmest
EIMMPRSU premiums
EIMMPSSU pessimum
EIMMRRST strimmer
EIMMRSTT trimmest
EIMMSTUY yummiest
EIMNNNOS monensin
EIMNNOOT noontime
EIMNNOPT imponent
EIMNNOPY pin money
EIMNNOTT ointment
EIMNOOPS empoison
EIMNOORS moonrise
EIMNOORV omnivore
EIMNOOST mooniest
EIMNOPRS emprison
EIMNOPRT orpiment
EIMNOPSS mopiness
EIMNOPST nepotism
EIMNOPTT impotent
EIMNORSU Monsieur
EIMNORTW time-worn
EIMNORTY enormity
EIMNOTTU minuetto
EIMNPRSS primness
EIMNPSST misspent
EIMNRSST trimness
EIMNRSTU numerist, terminus
EIMNRSTY entryism
EIMNSTTU minutest
EIMOORST motorise, roomiest
EIMOORTZ motorize
EIMOPPRR improper
EIMOPRRS primrose, promiser
EIMOPRRT importer, reimport
EIMOPRRV improver
EIMOPRST imposter, rompiest, tripsome
EIMOPRSU imposure
EIMOPRUU europium
EIMOQSTU misquote
EIMORRST stormier
EIMORRWW wireworm
EIMORSTU moisture
EIMORSTW wormiest
EIMORSTY isometry
EIMORTTW two-timer
EIMOSSST mossiest
EIMOSSTU mousiest
EIMOSTTT totemist
EIMOSTTU titmouse
EIMPRSTU stumpier
EIMPRTTU Permutit
EIMPSSTU Septimus
EIMQRRSU squirmer
EIMQSTUY mystique
EIMRSSST mistress
EIMRSTTU smuttier
EIMSSTTU mustiest
EIMSTUZZ muzziest
EINNOORT tenorino
EINNORSV environs
EINNORTU neutrino
EINNORTV inventor
EINNORWW winnower
EINNORYZ oryzenin
EINNOSSS nosiness
EINNOSTT tinstone, tonstein
EINNPSSU puniness
EINNPSXY sixpenny
EINNRSTU runniest
EINNRTTU nutrient
EINNSSTU sunniest
EINOOPRS poisoner, spoonier
EINOORST snootier
EINOORSZ snoozier
EINOORZZ ozonizer
EINOOTXX exotoxin
EINOPRRS prisoner
EINOPRSS pression, ropiness
EINOPRSU pruinose
EINOPRSV overspin
EINOPRTU eruption
EINOPRTW port wine
EINOPSTT nepotist, set point, stone-pit
EINOQRTU quiteron
EINOQSTU question
EINOQTTU quotient
EINORRST introrse
EINORRSV inversor
EINORRTV invertor
EINORSSS rosiness
EINORSSU neurosis, resinous
EINORSTT ortstein, snottier, tenorist
EINORSTV investor
EINORSTY tyrosine
EINORSUV souvenir
EINORTTU ritenuto
EINOSSST sonsiest, stenosis
EINOSSTT stoniest, tot siens
EINOSSTW snowiest
EINOSTUU tenuious
EINOSTUX exustion
EINOSTVY venosity
EINPPRRT preprint
EINPPSTY snippety
EINPRRST sprinter
EINPRRTU prurient
EINPRRTY printery
EINPRSST spinster
EINPRSTW wrest-pin
EINPRTTU inputter
EINQRSTU squinter
EINRSSST instress
EINRSSXY syrinxes
EINRSTTY entryist
EINRSTUV venturis
EINSTTTU nuttiest
EIOOPPRS porpoise
EIOOPPST opposite
EIOOPPSV opposive
EIOOPRST portoise
EIOORSTT tortoise
EIOOSSTT sootiest
EIOOSTWZ wooziest
EIOPPSST soppiest
EIOPPSTU poupiets
EIOPPTTY tippy-toe
EIOPQSTU postique
EIOPRRSS prioress
EIOPRRST sportier
EIOPRRSU superior
EIOPRSST prosiest
EIOPRSTT spottier
EIOPRSTU positure
EIOPRSTV sportive
EIOPRSUV pervious, previous, viperous
EIOPRTTT triptote
EIOPRTTY petitory
EIOPSSTU soupiest
EIOPSTTT pottiest
EIORRSST resistor, sorriest
EIORRSTT rortiest
EIORRSTV servitor
EIORRSVY revisory
EIORSSTY serosity
EIORSTUV vitreous

EIPPRRST stripper
EIPQRSTU quipster
EIPRRRSU spurrier
EIPRRSSU surprise
EIPRRSTZ spritzer
EIQRRSTU squirter
EIRRSTTU trustier
EIRSSTTU rustiest
EIRTTTUY tityre-tu
EIRTTTWY twittery
EIRTTUWZ wurtzite
EISTTTUX textuist
EJMNOSTU monte-jus
EJMOPPRU jump rope
EJNSSSTU justness
EKKMORSY kromesky
EKLLOSSY yolkless
EKLMNOSS Smolensk
EKLNOOOR looker-on, onlooker
EKLNOSST knotless
EKLNOSWY Knowsley
EKLOOORV look-over, overlook
EKLOOPSW slowpoke
EKLORSSW workless
EKMNRSTU Turkmens
EKMOOPRR morepork
EKMOORSW worksome
EKMORSSU musk-rose
EKMRSTUY musketry
EKNNOPSU unspoken
EKNOOPRW openwork
EKOOORTV overtook
EKOOPRRV provoker
EKOORRVW overwork
EKOPPRST prospekt
EKOPRSTU upstroke
EKORRUVY kurveyor
ELLLMOWY mellowly
ELLLNSUY sullenly
ELLLOWYY yellowly
ELLMNOOT molleton
ELLMNOSY solemnly
ELLMPSSU lumpless
ELLNOORV lovelorn
ELLNOPRU prunello
ELLNOPUU lupulone
ELLNORRT rent roll
ELLNORWW well-worn
ELLNOSVY slovenly
ELLNOUVY unlovely
ELLNTTUU lutulent
ELLOORRV roll-over
ELLOPRST pollster
ELLOPRTU polluter
ELLOPRUV pullover
ELLOPSST plotless
ELLORRST stroller
ELLOSSSS lossless
ELLOSSSU soulless
ELLOSUXY xylulose
ELLPPSUY supplely
ELLRSSTU trussell
ELLSSSTU lustless
ELMMNOTU lomentum
ELMMNOTY momently
ELMMRSUY summerly
ELMNOOOP monopole
ELMNOOSS moonless
ELMNOOSZ zoom lens
ELMNUUZZ unmuzzle
ELMOOPSY polysome
ELMOORST tremolos
ELMOORSY morosely
ELMOOSSY lysosome
ELMOPRYY polymery
ELMOPSYY polysemy
ELMOSYYZ lysozyme
ELMPRSSU rumpless
ELMPTTUY plumetty
ELNNOOSU unloosen
ELNNOPTU nonuplet
ELNOPTTU potulent
ELNOPTTY potently
ELNORSTU turnsole
ELNORTTY rottenly
ELNOSSSW slowness, snowless
ELNOSSTW townless, wontless
ELNOSUVY venously
ELNPRTUU purulent
ELNRSUUY unsurely
ELOOPPRY polypore
ELOOPPSY polypose
ELOOPPTY polytope
ELOOPRSV overslop
ELOORSST rootless
ELOORSTU torulose
ELOORSUV oversoul
ELOOSTUU Toulouse
ELOPPRRY properly
ELOPPRSS propless
ELOPPRSU propulse
ELOPPTYY polytype
ELOPRSTY prostyle
ELOPRSUV overplus
ELOPRSYY pyrolyse
ELOPRYYZ pyrolyze
ELOPSSST spotless, stopless
ELORSTTT trottles
ELORTTTU troutlet
ELPPRSUY resupply
ELPPSSTU supplest
ELPRSSSU spurless
ELPRSTTU splutter
ELPSTUXY sextuply
ELRSSSTU rustless
EMMMNOTU momentum
EMMNNOTU monument
EMMNOOOS monosome
EMMNOOSY monosemy
EMMNORSU summoner
EMMNOTTU tomentum
EMMNOTYY metonymy
EMMOPTTY pommetty
EMMRRRUU murmurer
EMMRRSTU strummer
EMMRSTYY symmetry
EMNNNOOU noumenon
EMNNOOOT monotone
EMNOOOSZ mesozoon
EMNOOPTY monotype
EMNOORST mesotron
EMNOORSU enormous
EMNOORSW newsroom
EMNOORUY munyeroo
EMNOOSUV venomous
EMNOOTTY tenotomy
EMNOPSUY eponymus
EMNORSUU numerous
EMNORTUU mounture
EMNORTUX Montreux
EMNOSUUY euonymus
EMNRSSTU sternums
EMNRSTTU stem turn
EMOOPRRT promoter, protomer
EMOOPRTT portmote
EMOORRRT tomorrer
EMOORRST restroom
EMOOTTTT mottetto
EMOPPPRU mopper-up
EMOPPRRT prompter
EMOPRSTT post-term
EMORSSTU strumose
EMOSSUUX mousseux
EMPRRTUY trumpery
EMPRSSUU rumpuses
EMPRSTTU strumpet
ENNOOORT tenoroon
ENNOOPPS opponens
ENNOOPPT opponent
ENNOORTV non-voter
ENNOPRSU unperson
ENNOPRUV unproven
ENNOPTWY twopenny
ENNOSSTU sunstone
ENNPPTUY tuppenny
ENNPRRUU runner-up
ENOOPPST postpone
ENOOPRSS poorness
ENOOPSTT potstone
ENOORRST Sorrento
ENOPRSUV overspun
ENOPRSUX proxenus
ENOPRTUW uptowner
ENOPSSSY synopses
ENORRTUU tournure
ENORRTUV overturn, turnover
ENORSSSU sourness
ENORTTTW tentwort
ENOSSSUU sensuous
ENPRSSSY spryness
ENRRRTUU nurturer
EOOOPRSZ zoospore
EOOORRST rose-root
EOOPPRRS proposer
EOOPPSST postpose
EOOPRRTU uprooter
EOOPRSTU porteous
EOOPRSTV stopover

EOORRRSW sorrower
EOORSSTU oestrous
EOORSTTU tortuose
EOPPRRTY property
EOPRRSST portress
EOPRRSTU posturer
EOPRRUVY purveyor
EORRRTTU torturer
EORRSSTU trousers
EORRSUVY surveyor
EORRTTTU trotteur
EORSSTTU tutoress
EPPPRTUY puppetry
EPPRSSSU suppress
ERRSTTTU strutter
FFFFPPUU puff-puff
FFFFTTUU tuff-tuff
FFFILLUY fluffily
FFGHIIRT Griffith
FFGHIORS frogfish
FFGIILNP piffling
FFGIINPS spiffing
FFGILMNU muffling
FFGILNOY off-lying
FFGINSTU stuffing
FFHIISST stiffish
FFHILOSW wolf-fish
FFHILOSY offishly
FFHOOOST offshoot
FFHOORTW throw-off
FFHOSTTU hot stuff
FFIILMOR filiform
FFIILNSY sniffily
FFIILPSY spiffily
FFILLLOU folliful
FFILLNNO Flin Flon
FFILLOPP flip-flop
FFILLTUY fitfully
FFILRTUU fruitful
FFILRTUY fruit fly
FFILSTUY stuffily
FFIMNOOS moonsiff
FFIMNORU funiform
FFIMORSU fusiform
FFINOPRT offprint
FFLMNOOU moufflon
FFLORRUU furfurol
FFLRRUUY furfuryl
FFNSTUUY unstuffy
FFOORRUU frou-frou
FFORUUWY yuffrouw
FGGGIINR frigging
FGGGILNO flogging
FGGGINOR frogging
FGGHIINT fighting
FGGHILOT foglight
FGGHINTU gunfight
FGGHLPUU guglhupf
FGGIINNR fringing
FGGIINOR fingrigo
FGHIIKNS kingfish
FGHIILNT inflight
FGHILLTU lightful
FGHILNSU lungfish
FGHILOTT to-flight
FGHILRTU rightful
FGHIOTTU outfight
FGHLORUU furlough
FGIILLNR frilling
FGIILMNO minigolf
FGIILNPP flipping
FGIILNRT trifling
FGIILNST stifling
FGIILNTT flitting
FGIINRTT fritting
FGIIRSTU figurist
FGILMNUY fumingly
FGILNOOR flooring
FGILNOOT footling
FGILNOPP flopping
FGILNPRU purfling
FGIMORRU gruiform
FGINORST frosting
FGKLNOOS folk song
FGLNORUW wrongful
FGLNOTUU outflung
FGLOOOST footslog
FHHIKOOS fish-hook
FHHLOSTU hot flush
FHHOORST shofroth
FHIIKLPS klipfish
FHIILLTY filthily
FHIILSTY shiftily
FHIKMNOS monkfish
FHIKNORT forthink
FHILLOOT foothill
FHILLORT hill fort
FHILMPSU lumpfish
FHILMRTU mirthful
FHILOPST shoplift
FHILORSU flourish
FHILORTY frothily
FHIMNOOS moonfish
FHIMPRSU frumpish
FHIMSUUY humusify
FHIOOPTT photofit
FHIOPPRS froppish
FHIOTUYY youthify
FHLLOSTU slothful
FHLMOTUU mouthful
FHLORTUW worthful, wrothful
FHLORTUY fourthly
FHLOTUUY youthful
FHLRTTUU truthful
FHOOORST forsooth
FIIILNOP Filipino
FIIIMNST finitism
FIIINNTY infinity
FIIINSTT finitist
FIIKLRSY friskily
FIILLMSY flimsily
FIILLNTY flintily
FIILMNRY infirmly
FIILMOPR piliform
FIILMPSY simplify
FIILNOPR profilin
FIILRTUY fruitily
FIILTTUY futility
FIIMOPRR piriform
FIIMOPRS pisiform
FIIMPRUY impurify
FIINNOSU infusion
FIINORTU fruition
FIIPRTYY pyritify
FIIRSTTU fruitist
FIISTTWY twistify
FIKKLNOS kinsfolk
FIKLLLSU skillful
FIKLLOSW silk-fowl
FIKLNOSW wolfskin
FILLLTTU full tilt
FILLLUWY wilfully
FILLNORS no-frills
FILLNSUY sinfully
FILLOPPY floppily
FILMOORT lotiform
FILMOPRS slip form
FILMORRY lyriform
FILMOSSU mofussil
FILMPRUY frumpily
FILNOPTU pointful
FILORSTY frostily
FILOSTUU futilous
FILRSTTU tristful
FILSTTUY stultify
FIMMNOOR omniform
FIMMOORR moriform
FIMMORRU muriform
FIMOPPRU pupiform
FIMOPRRU puriform
FIMOPRRY pyriform
FIMORSUU frumious
FIMORTUY fumitory
FIMOSTUY fumosity
FIMRSTUU futurism
FINORSUY infusory
FIOPRTTU top fruit
FIORTTUY fortuity
FIRSTTUU futurist
FIRTTUUY futurity
FJLLOUYY joyfully
FKLNRTUU trunkful
FKMOORRW formwork
FKOOORTW footwork
FLLMNOOU full moon
FLLNOOOW follow-on
FLLOOPUW follow-up
FLLOPSTU full stop
FLLOSSTU full toss
FLMNORUU mournful
FLMOOORW moorfowl
FLNOOPSU spoonful
FLOOOPPR propofol
FLOOOPTT polt-foot
FLOOPTTY toplofty
FLRSTTUU trustful
FMRRSTUU frustrum
FMRSSTUU frustums
FNOOPRRU Unprofor
FNOORRSW forsworn
FNOORTTU out-front
GGGGNNOO gong-gong
GGGIILNN niggling
GGGIINNS snigging

GGGIINRT	trigging
GGGIINSW	swigging
GGGIINTW	twigging
GGGILNOS	slogging
GGGILNPU	plugging
GGGILNSU	slugging
GGGILORY	groggily
GGGINNOS	snogging
GGHHIINS	high sign
GGHHIISW	Whiggish
GGHHISTU	thuggish
GGHIILNT	lighting
GGHIIMSW	Whiggism
GGHIIPRS	priggish
GGHILNTU	light-gun
GGHILSSU	sluggish
GGHIMSTU	thuggism
GGHINOST	ghosting
GGHINSTU	gunsight
GGHOTUUY	tough guy
GGIILLNR	grilling
GGIILMNY	ginglymi
GGIINNNR	grinning
GGIINNOR	groining
GGIINNPW	ping-wing
GGIINNRW	wringing
GGIINNSW	swinging
GGIINNTT	ting-ting
GGIINNTW	twinging
GGIINPPR	gripping
GGIINRTT	gritting
GGIIRRSS	gris-gris
GGILLOOW	golliwog
GGILMMNO	glomming
GGILNNOT	Tongling
GGILNTTU	glutting
GGILQSUY	squiggly
GGINNNNO	ning-nong
GGINNOOS	goings-on
GGINNOPP	ping-pong
GGINNOPS	sponging
GGINNOSS	sing-song
GGINNOTU	tonguing
GGINOOTU	outgoing
GGINOPRU	grouping
GGLLOOOY	logology
GGLLPUUY	plug-ugly
GGLOOYYZ	zygology
GGOOOORR	groo-groo
GHHIIKRS	high-risk
GHHIILST	lightish
GHHIIRST	rightish
GHHIJMPU	high jump
GHHILOSU	ghoulish
GHHILOSW	high-lows
GHHIMOST	highmost, Most High
GHHIOPST	high spot
GHHIORSU	roughish
GHHIORTY	righty-ho
GHHIOSTU	toughish
GHHOORTU	thorough
GHIIKNNT	thinking
GHIIKNPS	kingship
GHIILLNS	shilling
GHIILMTY	mightily
GHIILNRW	whirling
GHIILNTW	whitling
GHIILTTW	twilight
GHIIMMNS	shimming
GHIIMRST	rightism
GHIINNNS	shinning
GHIINNNT	thinning
GHIINPPS	shipping
GHIINPPW	whipping
GHIINRRS	shirring
GHIINRRW	whirring
GHIINRST	shirting
GHIINRTT	trithing
GHIINSTT	shitting
GHIINTTW	twi-night
GHIINWZZ	whizzing
GHIIORSV	vigorish
GHIIOSTV	Visigoth
GHIIRSTT	rightist
GHIKLNTY	knightly
GHIKLSTY	skylight
GHILLOTW	lowlight, owl-light
GHILLSTY	slightly
GHILNOPS	long ship
GHILNOTW	night owl
GHILNRUY	hungrily
GHILNSTU	sunlight
GHILOPRS	shop girl
GHILORSW	showgirl
GHILPRTY	triglyph
GHIMNOPR	morphing
GHIMNPTU	thumping
GHIMNSTU	gunsmith
GHIMPRSU	grumpish
GHINNNSU	shunning
GHINNORT	northing
GHINOOPW	whooping
GHINOOST	shooting, soothing
GHINOOTT	toothing
GHINOPPS	shopping
GHINOPPW	whopping
GHINORTW	ingrowth, throwing, worthing
GHINOSTU	southing
GHINOSUY	youngish
GHINSSTU	hustings
GHINSTTU	shutting
GHIOOTWZ	howgozit
GHIORTTU	outright
GHIOSTTU	outsight
GHIPSSYY	gypsyish
GHLMOOOY	homology
GHLNNOOR	longhorn
GHLNOORU	hour-long
GHLNOOST	long shot
GHLOOORY	horology
GHLORTUU	turlough
GHNOOUYZ	Yongzhou
GHNOSTUU	unsought
GHOPRTUW	upgrowth
GHORRTUW	throw rug
GIIILMNT	limiting
GIIILOTV	vitiligo
GIIINNOT	ignition
GIIINNSS	insignis
GIIINNTV	inviting
GIIINSTV	visiting
GIIJMNOS	jingoism
GIIJNNOT	jointing
GIIJNOST	jingoist
GIIKKLNP	kingklip
GIIKMMNS	skimming
GIIKNNNS	skinning
GIIKNNST	stinking
GIIKNNTT	knitting
GIIKNPPS	skipping
GIIKNRST	skirting, striking
GIILLNQU	quilling
GIILLNRT	trilling
GIILLNTT	littling
GIILLPSW	pigswill
GIILLTUY	guiltily
GIILLTYZ	glitzily
GIILMMNS	slimming
GIILMPSU	pugilism
GIILNOPT	piloting
GIILNPPS	slipping
GIILNPRS	slip ring
GIILNQSU	quisling
GIILNQTU	quilting
GIILNRST	Stirling
GIILNSTT	slitting
GIILNSTU	linguist
GIILNSTY	stingily
GIILNSZZ	sizzling
GIILPSTU	pugilist
GIILRTTY	grittily
GIIMMNPR	primming
GIIMMNRT	trimming
GIIMMNSW	swimming
GIIMNNOY	ignominy
GIIMNOPS	imposing
GIIMNOTT	omitting
GIIMNOTV	vomiting
GIINNNPS	spinning
GIINNNTW	twinning
GIINNOPT	pointing
GIINNOQU	quoining
GIINNORS	rosining
GIINNORT	ignitron
GIINNPPS	snipping
GIINNPRT	printing
GIINNRTU	untiring
GIINOPST	positing
GIINOPTV	pivoting
GIINORSS	grissino
GIINORUV	invigour
GIINPPQU	quipping
GIINPPRT	tripping
GIINPRSU	uprising
GIINPSTT	spitting
GIINQTTU	quitting
GIINQUZZ	quizzing
GIINRRST	stirring
GIINTTTW	twitting

GIIORSTV vigorist
GIJKLNOY jokingly
GIKLNOPR porkling
GIKMORRU korrigum
GIKNNOST kingston, stonking
GIKNNOTT knotting
GIKNNRTU trunking
GIKNOPST king post
GILLMOOY gloomily
GILLNOVY lovingly
GILLNOWY low-lying
GILLNPRU ring-pull
GILLNRUY luringly
GILLOOPW polliwog
GILLOSSY glossily
GILMMNSU slumming
GILMNORW lingworm, wormling
GILMNOVY movingly
GILMNSUY musingly
GILMPRUY grumpily
GILNNORU iron lung
GILNNOUV unloving
GILNNRSU nursling
GILNOOSY sinology
GILNOOWY wooingly
GILNOPPP plopping
GILNOPPS slopping
GILNOPSY spongily
GILNOPTT plotting
GILNOSTT slotting
GILNOSTU long suit
GILNOTUY outlying
GILNPRYY pryingly
GILNPSSU plus sign
GILNRRSU slurring
GILNRSTU lustring
GILNRTYY tryingly
GILOOORS rosoglio
GILOOOST oologist
GILOORSU glorious
GILOORTY triology
GILOORVY groovily, virology
GILOOSSS isogloss
GILOSTUY gulosity
GIMMNRUY gin rummy
GIMMNSTU stumming
GIMMOSSU gummosis
GIMNNOOS monosign
GIMNNORS mornings
GIMNNORU mourning
GIMNNOTU mounting
GIMNNOUV unmoving
GIMNOOOU oogonium
GIMNOORT motoring
GIMNOPTU gumption
GIMNORRW ringworm
GIMNORST storming
GIMNORTU trigonum
GIMNOSYY misogyny
GIMNSTTU smutting
GIMNSTYY stymying
GIMOPRSU groupism
GINNNSTU stunning
GINNOOOP pogonion
GINNOORT trigonon
GINNOPTU gunpoint
GINNRSTU unstring
GINOOPPS opposing
GINOORST root sign
GINOPPPR propping
GINOPPST stopping
GINOPRST sporting
GINOPRSY posy ring
GINOPSST signpost
GINOPSTT spotting
GINORTTT trotting
GINORTTU trouting
GINOSTTW swotting
GINPRRSU spurring
GINPRSUU pursuing
GINRSTTU trusting
GIOORRSU rigorous
GIOORSTU goitrous
GIOORSUV vigorous
GIOPRSSY gossipry
GIORSTUY rugosity
GIOSTYYZ zygosity
GJLMNOPU long jump
GLLNOOST long-lost
GLLOOPTY polyglot
GLLOOPWY pollywog
GLLOOPYY polylogy
GLMNNOOT Longmont
GLMNOOOT monoglot
GLMNOOOY nomology
GLMNORUW lungworm
GLMOOOPY pomology
GLMOOORY morology
GLMOORWW glow-worm
GLMOOYYZ zymology
GLNOOOSY nosology
GLNOOOTY ontology
GLNOOPST longstop
GLNOOPYY polygony
GLNOORTW longwort
GLNOPRSU longspur
GLNOPYYY polygyny
GLNORSTY strongly
GLNORTUW lungwort
GLNOTTUY gluttony
GLOOOPSY posology
GLOOOPTY topology
GLOOOTXY toxology
GLOOPRYY pyrology
GLOOPSSY gossypol
GLOOPTYY typology
GLOORSUU orgulous
GMMNOTUY tommy-gun
GMNNOOYY monogyny
GMNNORRU murrnong
GMNNORYY myrnyong
GMNOSTUY gymnotus
GMOOOORR Morogoro
GNNPRSUU unsprung
GNNRSTUU unstrung
GNOORSST gross ton
GNOORSUW wrongous
GNOORTUW outgrown
GOOPRTUU out-group
HHHHSSUU hush-hush
HHIIMPSW whimpish
HHIINNST thinnish
HHIIPSST phthisis
HHIORSST shortish
HHKKSSUU khus-khus
HHMOOOOO mohoohoo
HHOOOOPP pooh-pooh
HHOOOORS hooroosh
HHOOPPRS phosphor
HHOORRSU hurroosh
HHOORSTT hot-short
HHORRSUU rush hour
HHPPTTUU phut-phut
HIIILMNS nihilism
HIIILNST nihilist
HIIILNTY nihility
HIIINRST rhinitis
HIIJNOPT hip joint
HIIKMNST misthink
HIIKMRSS skirmish
HIIKOPRS piroshki
HIIKOPRZ pirozhki
HIIKQRSU quirkish
HIIKSSTT skittish
HIILLPPS Phillips
HIILLSTT littlish
HIILMOST homilist
HIILMPSY impishly
HIILMTUY humility
HIILNOTX Xilinhot
HIILOPST pisolith
HIILPSSY syphilis
HIILRSTY shirtily
HIILSSTW wish-list
HIIMNSTT tinsmith
HIIMOPSS phimosis
HIIMSTTY thymitis
HIINORST histrion
HIIPSSVV spivvish
HIISSSSY sissyish
HIISSTTT tsitsith
HIISTTTW twittish
HIKKNOST kinkhost
HIKLMOST silk moth
HIKLNOOP oknophil
HIKLOOPS slip-hook
HIKNOOOR koh-i-noor
HIKNOTTU out-think
HIKOPSSY kyphosis
HILLLOSU Solihull
HILLMSUY mulishly
HILLOOPT lopolith
HILLOSWY owlishly
HILMNOOT monolith
HILMPPSU plumpish
HILMPRTU philtrum
HILNORTY thornily
HILOOTTY toothily
HILOPPSY popishly
HILORTWY Holy Writ, worthily
HILPPRSU purplish

HILPPSUY	uppishly	**HOOOPSTT**	pot-shoot	**IILPRSSY**	prissily
HILSSTTU	sluttish	**HOOOSTTU**	outshoot, shoot-out	**IILSTUVV**	vulvitis
HIMMOPRS	morphism	**HOOOSTTW**	two hoots	**IIMMMNSU**	minimums
HIMMOPRU	phormium	**HOOPRSUZ**	zophorus	**IIMMNOTU**	Timimoun
HIMMORSU	humorism	**HOORTTUW**	out-throw	**IIMMNTUY**	immunity
HIMNOPRX	phorminx	**HOPPRRYY**	porphyry	**IIMMOPST**	optimism
HIMOOPRS	isomorph	**HPRSTTUU**	upthrust	**IIMMSTTU**	mittimus
HIMOPRSW	shipworm	**IIIILLWW**	wiliwili	**IIMNNOOT**	monition
HIMORSTU	humorist	**IIIIPPRR**	piripiri	**IIMNNOSU**	unionism
HIMOTTVZ	mitzvoth	**IIIKMNSS**	missikin	**IIMNNOTU**	munition
HINNSSUY	sunshiny	**IIILLMNP**	minipill	**IIMNOOPS**	impoison
HINOOOPR	hoop-iron	**IIILLMNU**	illinium	**IIMNOOSS**	omission
HINOPRTW	Winthrop	**IIILLNOS**	Illinois	**IIMNOOTV**	vomition
HINOPSSY	hypnosis	**IIILMRSV**	virilism	**IIMNOPRS**	imprison
HINOPSTW	township	**IIILMUVX**	lixivium	**IIMNORTT**	intromit
HINRSTTU	inthrust	**IIILNOPP**	Pilipino	**IIMNORTY**	minority
HIOOPRTT	poortith	**IIILRTVY**	virility	**IIMNPRST**	misprint
HIOORSST	orthosis	**IIIMMMNS**	minimism	**IIMNPTUY**	impunity
HIOORSUV	voorhuis	**IIIMMNST**	intimism	**IIMNRSTY**	ministry
HIOQSUWZ	quiz show	**IIIMMPRS**	imprimis	**IIMOPSTT**	optimist
HIOSSTTU	stoutish	**IIIMNSTT**	intimist	**IIMOPTTY**	optimity
HIPPPSUY	puppyish	**IIIMNTTY**	intimity	**IIMORSSU**	Missouri
HIPSUYZZ	zizyphus	**IIINNOST**	insition	**IIMOSSTY**	myositis
HJKNOPSU	junk shop	**IIINORRS**	irrision	**IIMOTTVY**	motivity
HJMOPSUW	showjump	**IIINPRST**	inspirit	**IIMPRSTU**	impurist
HJNNOOST	Johnston	**IIINQTUY**	iniquity	**IIMPRTUY**	impurity
HKMOOORW	hookworm	**IIIOSTTU**	ouistiti	**IIMRRTUV**	triumvir
HKNOOSWW	knows how	**IIJJSTUU**	jiu-jitsu	**IIMSSTUW**	swimsuit
HKOOPRSW	workshop	**IIKKLMMS**	skim milk	**IINNOPPT**	pinpoint
HLLLOOWY	hollowly	**IIKKMMOO**	moki-moki	**IINNOPTU**	punition
HLLMNOOU	monohull	**IIKLLNSY**	slinkily	**IINNOSTU**	inustion, unionist
HLLNOOUU	Honolulu	**IIKLMPSY**	skimpily	**IINNPSST**	tinsnips
HLLOPPRY	prophyll	**IIKLMRSY**	smirkily	**IINNSTTU**	tinnitus
HLLPPSUU	push-pull	**IIKLNPPS**	pink slip	**IINOOPST**	position
HLMOOSTY	smoothly	**IIKLOSTT**	kittisol	**IINOQSUU**	iniquous
HLMOPSUY	lymphous	**IIKLQRUY**	quirkily	**IINORSTT**	institor
HLMOPTUY	Plymouth	**IIKMNNOO**	monokini	**IINORTVY**	invitory
HLNOOSUW	Hounslow	**IILLLPTU**	lilliput	**IINOSTVY**	vinosity
HLPRSUUY	sulphury	**IILLMMOO**	lomi-lomi	**IINPRSTW**	wrist-pin
HMMNOOYY	homonymy	**IILLMNOS**	millions	**IINRTTUY**	triunity
HMMOOPRY	myomorph	**IILLMRTU**	trillium	**IIOOPPUU**	piou-piou
HMMOORSU	mushroom	**IILLNOOR**	orillion	**IIOOPSTV**	oviposit
HMMPRSUU	mushrump	**IILLNORT**	trillion	**IIOOQRSU**	Iroquois
HMMRSTUU	humstrum	**IILLNOSU**	illusion	**IIOOSTTY**	otiosity
HMNNOOOO	mohonono	**IILLOPUV**	pulvilio	**IIOPRRTY**	priority
HMNOOOST	moonshot	**IILMMNOU**	limonium	**IIORSTUV**	virtuosi
HMNOPSYY	symphony	**IILMMNSU**	luminism	**IITTTTWW**	twit-twit
HMNOPYYY	hyponymy	**IILMMPSS**	simplism	**IJLLORTY**	jollitry
HMOOOPRS	morosoph	**IILMNORT**	mirliton	**IJMPSTUU**	jumpsuit
HMOOOPRZ	zoomorph	**IILMNPTU**	ptilinum	**IJNNSTUU**	ninjutsu
HMOOOPTY	homotopy	**IILMORST**	troilism	**IKKLNOSY**	kolinsky
HMOOORSW	showroom	**IILMOTTY**	motility	**IKKLOPSU**	klipkous
HMOORSUU	humorous	**IILMTTUY**	ultimity	**IKKMOOOR**	koromiko
HMOPSSTU	puss moth	**IILNNOOT**	nolition	**IKKNOSTV**	Votkinsk
HMORTUWY	wry-mouth	**IILNOOST**	inositol	**IKLLLNNU**	null link
HNNOORTT	Thornton	**IILNOOTV**	volition	**IKLLOOTV**	kilovolt
HNOOOOPR	oophoron	**IILNPPST**	split pin	**IKLMORSW**	silkworm
HNOOPPYY	hypopyon	**IILNPPSY**	snippily	**IKLMORTW**	milkwort
HNOOPRST	post-horn	**IILNRTWY**	wintrily	**IKLNOOSW**	wool-skin
HNOOPRSW	shopworn	**IILOOPSS**	poliosis	**IKLNOPST**	slip-knot
HNOOPTYY	hypotony	**IILOPSSS**	psilosis	**IKLNOTTY**	knottily
HNOORRTW	hornwort	**IILOPSST**	ptilosis	**IKLNPSSU**	spun silk
HNOORSTT	short ton	**IILOPSTY**	pilosity	**IKLNPSUY**	spunkily
HNORSTTU	Thurston	**IILPPSTU**	pulpitis	**IKLOOPSY**	spookily
HNORTUWY	unworthy				

IKLOPSTY	sky pilot	**IMNNOOTT**	monotint	**KKMMOOOO**	moko-moko
IKNOORRW	ironwork	**IMNNOSUU**	numinous	**KKNOORTW**	knotwork
IKNOPSSY	pyknosis	**IMNOOPTU**	toponium	**KKOOSSUU**	kouskous
IKNOPSTT	stinkpot	**IMNOORTY**	monitory	**KKTTUUUU**	tukutuku
IKORSSTU	kurtosis	**IMNOSTUU**	mutinous	**KLLMNSUU**	numskull
IKORSTTU	outskirt	**IMNRTTUU**	nutritum	**KLLOPPSU**	popskull
ILLLMOOP	mill-pool	**IMOOPRRS**	promisor	**KLMMOOOS**	Komsomol
ILLLMOPS	plimsoll	**IMOOPRST**	impostor	**KLNORSTY**	klystron
ILLLOOPP	lollipop	**IMOOPRSU**	imporous	**KLNRTUUY**	kulturny
ILLMMSTU	smut-mill	**IMOOQSTU**	mosquito	**KMOOORRW**	workroom
ILLMNOOR	morillon	**IMOORRTT**	trimotor	**KNOORTWY**	Yorktown
ILLMOORR	morrillo	**IMOORSTT**	motorist	**LLLOOPPY**	poplolly
ILLMOPST	post-mill	**IMOORSTU**	timorous	**LLNOPTUY**	plutonyl
ILLMOSSY	lissomly	**IMOORTVY**	vomitory	**LLOOPRYY**	roly-poly
ILLMPSUY	psyllium	**IMOOSSTY**	myosotis	**LLOOSSTU**	lost soul
ILLMPTUY	multiply	**IMOOSTUV**	vomitous	**LLOSUUVV**	volvulus
ILLNOORT	tornillo	**IMOPPRRU**	proprium	**LMNOOOPY**	monopoly
ILLNOSST	Stillson	**IMRSSTTU**	mistrust	**LMOOOOPR**	pool room
ILLOOPRW	poor-will	**IMRSSTTY**	mistryst	**LMOOPRTU**	pulmotor
ILLOORTT	rototill	**INNNNOOU**	non-union	**LMOORSWW**	slow-worm
ILLOPPPP	plip-plop	**INNNORTU**	trunnion	**LMOOSSSU**	molossus
ILLOPPSY	sloppily	**INNOOPSS**	sponsion	**LMOPPRTY**	promptly
ILLOPRTW	pillwort	**INNOORST**	notornis	**LMOSTUUU**	tumulous
ILLOPRXY	prolixly	**INNOTTWW**	twin town	**LMRSSTUU**	lustrums
ILLOPSUU	pilulous	**INOOOSSZ**	zoonosis	**LNOOOPRT**	poltroon
ILLORSTU	trollius	**INOOPQSU**	poquosin	**LNOOPPRY**	propylon
ILLORSUY	illusory	**INOOPRST**	positron,	**LNOOPSWW**	snowplow
ILLORTTY	tortilly		sorption	**LNOOSWWY**	snowy owl
ILLRSTUY	sultrily	**INOOPSTT**	spittoon	**LOOOPSST**	solo stop
ILMNOOPU	polonium	**INOOPTTU**	outpoint	**LOOPPSUU**	populous
ILMNOSUU	luminous	**INOORSTY**	sonority	**LOOPPSUY**	polypous
ILMOPPSU	populism	**INOPRTTU**	printout	**LOOPRSUY**	porously
ILMOPRSU	impulsor	**INOPRTUY**	punitory	**LORSSTUU**	lustrous
ILMORSTY	stormily	**INOPSSSY**	synopsis	**MMOOPPRU**	pump room
ILMOSTUU	mutilous	**INORSSUV**	sun visor	**MMOORTTY**	tommyrot
ILMPPTUU	pulpitum	**INORTUVY**	ivory-nut	**MMPPTTUU**	tump-tump
ILMPSTUY	stumpily	**INPPRRUU**	purpurin	**MMRRUUUU**	murumuru
ILMSSTUU	stimulus	**INPRSTTU**	turnspit	**MNNOOOTY**	monotony
ILMSTTUY	smuttily	**IOOPRRSV**	provisor	**MNNOSYYY**	synonymy
ILNOOPRT	pliotron	**IOOPRSTU**	tsipouro	**MNOOORXY**	oxymoron
ILNOOPSS	polisson	**IOOPRSTY**	isotropy,	**MNOOPTYY**	toponymy
ILNOOPSY	spoonily		porosity	**MNOPRSTU**	no trumps
ILNOORTW	toil-worn	**IOORRSTY**	sorority	**MNORSTUU**	surmount
ILNOOSTU	solution	**IOORRTTT**	trottoir	**MOOOPRRT**	promotor
ILNOOSTY	snootily	**IOORSSUV**	voussoir	**MOOOPRST**	post room
ILNOOTUV	volution	**IOORSTTU**	tortious	**MOOOPRTU**	moor-pout
ILNOPSSW	snow-slip	**IOORSTUV**	virtuoso	**MOOORRTW**	tomorrow
ILNOPSTU	unspoilt	**IOORSUUX**	uxorious	**MOORSTUU**	tumorous
ILNORSTY	nitrosyl	**IOOSTTUZ**	zoot suit	**MORRSSTU**	rostrums
ILNORTXY	nitroxyl	**IOPRRSUV**	provirus	**MORSSTUU**	strumous
ILNOSTTY	snottily	**IOPRSSUU**	spurious	**MSSTTUUU**	tsutsumu
ILNPSUUV	pulvinus	**IOPRSTTU**	outstrip	**NOOOPPRS**	prosopon
ILOOPPRS	propolis	**IOPRSTUY**	pyritous	**NOOORSSU**	sonorous
ILOPPSTU	populist	**IOQRTUXY**	quixotry	**NOOPPRTY**	protypon
ILOPRSTY	sportily	**IORRSUVV**	survivor	**NOOPSTTW**	post town
ILOPSTTY	spottily	**IORRTTTT**	trit-trot	**OOOOPPRR**	poroporo
ILOPSUUV	pluvious	**IORSSUUU**	usurious	**OOOOPPWW**	woop woop
ILOQRTUU	loquitur	**IORSTTUY**	touristy	**OOPPRRUX**	propoxur
ILRSTTUY	trustily	**IORSTUUV**	virtuous	**OORRRTYY**	tory-rory
ILRSTUUX	luxurist	**IPPRRTUU**	Tiruppur	**OORSTTUU**	tortuous
IMMNNOOO	monomino	**IPRRSTUU**	pruritus	**OPPTUUUY**	put-you-up
IMMOORST	motorism	**JLNSTUUY**	unjustly	**OPRSSSUU**	sourpuss
IMMOORTU	motorium	**JLOOSUYY**	joyously	**PPTTTTUU**	putt-putt
IMMOPPRT	imprompt	**JNNOORRU**	nonjuror	**RRSSSUUU**	susurrus
IMMOPSTU	optimums	**JOORSTUU**	toujours		

NINE LETTERS

AAAABCLLV	balaclava
AAAABDDHM	Ahmadabad
AAAABDHLL	Allahabad
AAAABDJLL	Jalalabad
AAAABIKLL	balalaika
AAAABJLMY	jambalaya
AAAACCHMT	tacamahac
AAAACCJMR	Cajamarca
AAAACDIMM	macadamia
AAAACDJNR	jacaranda
AAAACDKLY	alack-a-day
AAAACIRRU	araucaria
AAAACLMNS	Salamanca
AAAACMNRT	catamaran
AAAADILLM	Dalai Lama
AAAADIPRZ	Adapazari
AAAAGIKMS	Amagasaki
AAAAGLPRT	alpargata
AAAAHHJMR	maharajah
AAAAHIKSW	Asahikawa
AAAAIMRTV	Amaravati
AAAAINSST	Anastasia
AAAALLMMY	Malayalam
AAAAMPRTT	paramatta
AAABBCDJO	Jacobabad
AAABBDINR	Barbadian
AAABBINRR	barbarian
AAABCCEMN	Maccabean
AAABCCHLN	bacchanal
AAABCCHNR	charabanc
AAABCDIIT	adiabatic
AAABCDLOR	Baracaldo
AAABCDRRU	barracuda
AAABCELTU	acetabula
AAABCELTV	vacatable
AAABCEMRT	carbamate
AAABCHNNR	anabranch
AAABCIKTT	katabatic
AAABCISTT	ciabattas
AAABCLMOR	carambola
AAABCLNOT	canal boat
AAABDDFIR	Faridabad
AAABDDMOR	Moradabad
AAABDELPT	adaptable
AAABDGHIZ	Ghaziabad
AAABDGHNR	Darbhanga
AAABDGIJN	Baagandji
AAABDILLS	sabadilla
AAABDILMS	Islamabad
AAABDIMNZ	Nizamabad
AAABDLPTY	adaptably
AAABEILLV	available
AAABEKRRS	Skara Brae
AAABEKRWY	breakaway
AAABELLNN	Annabella
AAABELLPT	palatable
AAABELOPR	parabolae
AAABELRST	alabaster
AAABGJNNW	Nawabganj
AAABHHNSW	Nawabshah
AAABHIKNZ	Abkhazian
AAABHLRST	Balthasar
AAABHLRTZ	Balthazar
AAABILLVY	availably
AAABILQRU	Aqua Libra
AAABJKLNU	Banja Luka
AAABLLPTY	palatably
AAABLOPRS	parabolas
AAABMRSTU	Matsubara
AAABNNOPT	top banana
AAACCCHHH	cha-cha-cha
AAACCCIIR	Cariacica
AAACCDELV	cavalcade
AAACCINSU	Caucasian
AAACCIRTT	ataractic
AAACCLMNO	calamanco
AAACCLMST	cataclasm
AAACDHIKT	kadaitcha
AAACDHNRS	sandarach
AAACDLRST	cadastral
AAACDNRSS	Cassandra
AAACEENRS	Caesarean
AAACEHLNV	avalanche
AAACEIMNR	Americana
AAACEINNT	Canaanite
AAACEINOR	oceanaria
AAACEINRS	Caesarian
AAACELLPP	a cappella
AAACEMMNR	cameraman
AAACFILNT	fanatical
AAACGINRU	Nicaragua
AAACGLLSW	scallawag
AAACGLNTU	Latacunga
AAACGMOUY	Comayagua
AAACHHIRZ	Zachariah
AAACHILNW	Walachian
AAACHIMST	chiasmata
AAACHIRSZ	Zacharias
AAACHLNRT	charlatan
AAACHLPRR	chaparral
AAACHLPTU	Tapachula
AAACHLRRT	catarrhal
AAACHMNRY	Charmanay
AAACHNPTY	panchayat
AAACILLMR	camarilla
AAACILNPT	aplanatic
AAACILRTU	actuarial
AAACINOPR	paranoiac
AAACINOTT	catatonia
AAACINRSU	casuarina
AAACLMNPU	campanula
AAACMORST	sarcomata
AAACMRTUX	taraxacum
AAACNORTZ	Catanzaro
AAADDHMRY	hamadryad
AAADDLSSY	salad days
AAADEFIST	asafetida
AAADEGLMN	Magdalena
AAADEGMRW	war damage
AAADEGNTV	advantage
AAADEHRTV	Theravada
AAADELMMR	marmalade
AAADELNRX	Alexandra
AAADEMNOT	adenomata
AAADEMNSU	ad nauseam
AAADEOPTZ	zapateado
AAADFHILW	Wadi Halfa
AAADGLRVX	gravadlax
AAADGMMNR	grandmama
AAADGNPPR	grandpapa
AAADHHPRZ	haphazard
AAADHMRSY	hamadryas
AAADHPRYZ	hazard pay
AAADILLNP	Palladian
AAADILMNT	Dalmatian
AAADILPRS	paradisal
AAADLLRTY	Lady altar
AAADLMNTY	adamantly
AAADLNNSY	analysand
AAADMNRTY	mandatary
AAADPRRRT	radar trap
AAAEEGRRR	arrearage
AAAEEHMNR	maharanee
AAAEGGHNR	hangarage
AAAEGGRTV	aggravate
AAAEGILNS	analgesia
AAAEGIQRU	aqua regia
AAAEGLLPR	paralegal
AAAEGLMTU	Guatemala
AAAEGLSSV	vassalage
AAAEGMNNT	manganate
AAAEGMRRT	Margareta
AAAEHLMPY	Mahalapye
AAAEHLNNT	Nathanael
AAAEHMMOT	haematoma
AAAEHMNST	anathemas
AAAEIMNRS	Amerasian
AAAEIQTUV	aqua vitae
AAAELLNPT	panatella

AAAELMMRT alma mater
AAAELNNTT antenatal, Atlantean
AAAELNPQU aquaplane
AAAELPRST palaestra
AAAEMPRST aspartame
AAAEMRRRT terramara
AAAENRRTT Tartarean
AAAFGMSTU Famagusta
AAAFIKNRS Afrikaans
AAAFILNUV avifaunal
AAAFLORST solfatara
AAAFRSSSS sassafras
AAAGHHOTY hatha yoga
AAAGHPPRR paragraph
AAAGILRST astragali
AAAGIMNOT angiomata
AAAGIMNRV gravamina
AAAGIMRRT Margarita
AAAGINRRT rangatira
AAAGINRTT Gattinara
AAAGLNPTY Anaglypta
AAAGMMRSY gamma rays
AAAGPRSSU asparagus
AAAHHIKRS Kashihara
AAAHILMNY Himalayan
AAAHILMST Tashi Lama
AAAHIMNRT Aramintha
AAAHIMNRU marihuana
AAAHINSVV Vaishnava
AAAHKNRST astrakhan
AAAHLLOTY ayatollah
AAAHLNNTU Nahuatlan
AAAHMMSTU Hamamatsu
AAAHMNNTT manhattan
AAAHMNRTT harmattan
AAAHTTUYY Ayutthaya
AAAIINRST sanitaria
AAAIJMNRU marijuana
AAAILMMMN mammalian
AAAILMNSY Malaysian
AAAILNNPR planarian
AAAILNORT arational
AAAILNSST assailant
AAAILPPRS appraisal
AAAILRSTU Australia
AAAIMNNOZ Amazonian
AAAIMNNST Tasmanian
AAAIMNNTZ manzanita
AAAIMNORT inamorata
AAAIMNRST Samaritan
AAAINNSSS Sassanian
AAAINORST sanatoria
AAAINRRTT Tartarian
AAAIPPRZZ paparazzi
AAAIPRSTX parataxis
AAAKLMOOZ Kalamazoo
AAAKMRSTU Kama Sutra
AAALLLPTY palatally
AAALMNRSY salaryman
AAALNRTTU tarantula
AAALOOPPS Appaloosa
AAAMMNRST man-at-arms
AAAMMSTUY Matsuyama
AAAMNNOTZ amazon ant
AAANNPRTU Anantapur
AAANORSST Santa Rosa
AAANRSSTT tarantass
AAAOPPRZZ paparazzo
AAAPPRSTU apparatus
AAARTTTTT rat-tat-tat
AABBCCIRR bricabrac, bric-a-brac
AABBCDEFY baby-faced
AABBCDKOR backboard
AABBCEHLL beach ball
AABBCEINR Caribbean
AABBCEKLN black bean
AABBCEOOT babacoote
AABBCILMS cabbalism
AABBCILST cabbalist
AABBCKLLL blackball
AABBCKLSS black bass
AABBCKMRR barmbrack
AABBCKNRR barnbrack
AABBDDNOR broadband
AABBDEELT debatable
AABBDEHRT bad breath
AABBDELTY debatably
AABBDENOR broad bean
AABBDEORS baseboard
AABBDGNRY baby grand
AABBDNRSS brass band
AABBEEKLR breakable
AABBEELLM blameable
AABBEELRT rebatable
AABBEHHST Bathsheba
AABBEHILT habitable
AABBEINRT rabbinate
AABBEIRRZ barbarize
AABBIKLMS Kabbalism
AABBIKLST Kabbalist
AABBIMRRS barbarism
AABBIRRTY barbarity
AABBORRSU barbarous
AABCCEEMS Maccabees
AABCCEFKL blackface
AABCCEHLT catchable
AABCCEHNT bacchante
AABCCEKPS backspace
AABCCENOO cocoa bean
AABCCHHKT hatchback
AABCCHHSW Schwabach
AABCCHKKU huckaback
AABCCHNST bacchants
AABCCIKKP pickaback
AABCCILOT catabolic
AABCCIORT acrobatic
AABCCJKKL blackjack
AABCCKKRT backtrack
AABCCKLLO coal black
AABCCKLRW back-crawl
AABCDDENN dance band
AABCDDORR cardboard
AABCDEEFR barefaced
AABCDEEHH beachhead
AABCDEELN danceable
AABCDEETY beta decay
AABCDEHKL blackhead
AABCDEILL cable-laid
AABCDEIRR barricade
AABCDEKLL blacklead
AABCDEKLP back-pedal
AABCDELNR barnacled
AABCDELRT card table
AABCDEMSU ambuscade
AABCDENNR barn dance
AABCDENNU abundance
AABCDHILN baldachin
AABCDHILR Archibald
AABCDHNTW watchband
AABCDIMNO Cambodian
AABCDIORT abdicator
AABCDKRSW backwards
AABCDLOPR clapboard
AABCDLSUU subcaudal
AABCDNOOR carbonado
AABCDORST broadcast
AABCEEELP peaceable
AABCEEHLR reachable
AABCEEHLT teachable
AABCEEHRW beachwear
AABCEEKLS leaseback
AABCEEKNR cane-brake
AABCEELLN cleanable
AABCEELLR care label, clearable, lacerable
AABCEELLV cleavable
AABCEELNT enactable
AABCEELPS escapable
AABCEELPY peaceably
AABCEELRS calabrese
AABCEELRT creatable, traceable
AABCEELTX exactable
AABCEENRR aberrance
AABCEERTT bracteate
AABCEFILN fanciable
AABCEFIRT fabricate
AABCEFOTU about-face
AABCEGILR algebraic
AABCEGISW basic wage
AABCEGKLM black game
AABCEGKST backstage
AABCEGLMR cablegram
AABCEGPRT carpet-bag
AABCEHINR branchiae
AABCEHIRT brachiate
AABCEHKLW whaleback
AABCEHLMP Palm Beach
AABCEHLMT matchable
AABCEHLTW watchable
AABCEILLM claimable
AABCEILMN imbalance
AABCEILMR bicameral
AABCEILNP incapable
AABCEILNT cantabile
AABCEILRT bacterial, calibrate
AABCEIMNR main brace
AABCEINOR anaerobic
AABCEISSS abscissae
AABCEJKMR amberjack
AABCEKLST stackable

AABCEKPPR	paperback
AABCEKRTW	backwater
AABCELLLO	allocable
AABCELLOR	caballero
AABCELLOT	locatable
AABCELMNU	ambulance
AABCELNNS	scannable
AABCELNNU	unbalance
AABCELNOR	Barcelona
AABCELOOS	calaboose
AABCELORR	barcarole
AABCELRST	Castlebar
AABCELRTT	tractable
AABCELRTU	trabecula
AABCEMORX	box camera
AABCENORT	carbonate
AABCENRRY	aberrancy
AABCEOSTU	sauce-boat
AABCFGKLL	black flag
AABCFHKLS	flashback
AABCGILSS	basic slag
AABCGIMRU	gum arabic
AABCGKLNS	back slang
AABCGNOUW	cowabunga
AABCGRRSS	crabgrass
AABCHHIRT	bath chair
AABCHILNR	branchial
AABCHIMNR	Brahmanic
AABCHKLSS	backslash
AABCIILNS	basilican
AABCIINOT	anabiotic
AABCIKLLM	blackmail
AABCIKRST	backstair
AABCILLRY	bacillary
AABCILLSY	basically
AABCILNOT	botanical
AABCILNPY	incapably
AABCILOPR	parabolic
AABCILRUV	vibracula
AABCISSSS	abscissas
AABCKKLMR	black mark
AABCKLLLS	All Blacks
AABCKLLMP	lampblack
AABCKLLRT	trackball
AABCKLMSS	black mass
AABCKLNSW	black swan
AABCKORRZ	razorback
AABCLRTTY	tractably
AABCMNOTT	combatant
AABCNOORT	Boca Raton
AABCNORTX	carbon tax
AABCORSXZ	Cox's Bazar
AABDDEGLS	saddlebag
AABDDEHOR	headboard
AABDDEHRY	Hyderabad
AABDDEINR	brain-dead
AABDDENNO	abandoned
AABDDEORS	soda bread
AABDDHORR	hardboard
AABDDHORS	dashboard
AABDDNNST	bandstand
AABDDORRT	dartboard
AABDEEGLL	bald eagle
AABDEEKLN	kneadable
AABDEELLP	pleadable
AABDEELLR	balladeer
AABDEELMN	amendable
AABDEELRT	tradeable
AABDEFHKL	half-baked
AABDEFLOR	broadleaf
AABDEGINR	gabardine
AABDEGMOR	board game
AABDEGRRY	graybeard
AABDEHJLL	djellabah
AABDEHKNR	handbrake
AABDEHLNR	handlebar
AABDEHNSU	unabashed
AABDEILLT	dilatable
AABDEILMR	admirable
AABDEILOV	avoidable
AABDEILRV	adverbial
AABDEILSV	advisable
AABDEINNR	Bernadina
AABDELLNT	tableland
AABDELLST	stable lad
AABDELTWY	twayblade
AABDEMNNR	brand name
AABDEMORT	dreamboat
AABDEMRTU	adumbrate
AABDENSTW	sweatband
AABDEORST	adsorbate
AABDFHLOR	half board
AABDFIORZ	Firozabad
AABDGGNOR	gangboard
AABDGIILR	garibaldi
AABDGNNOW	bandwagon
AABDHINNS	handbasin
AABDHIORZ	biohazard
AABDHORSW	washboard
AABDIJNOR	jaborandi
AABDILMNO	abdominal
AABDILMRY	admirably
AABDILNQU	baldaquin
AABDILORS	sailboard
AABDILORT	broadtail, tailboard
AABDILOVY	avoidably
AABDILSVY	advisably
AABDINNRT	trainband
AABDINOST	bastinado
AABDINSTW	waistband
AABDKLORW	boardwalk
AABDLLORW	wallboard
AABDLNSST	sandblast
AABDLOOSW	balsa wood
AABDLORUY	Labour Day
AABDNOPRR	Porbandar
AABDORRST	starboard
AABDORSWY	broadways
AABEEEGLR	agreeable
AABEEFNST	beanfeast
AABEEGGLU	gaugeable
AABEEGILM	imageable
AABEEGLLL	glabellae
AABEEGLLT	bagatelle
AABEEGLRY	agreeably
AABEEGLST	stageable
AABEEGLSZ	sleazebag
AABEEGLTT	get-at-able
AABEEGRRT	Great Bear
AABEEHKLS	shakeable
AABEEHLLX	exhalable
AABEEHLPS	shapeable
AABEEHLRS	shareable
AABEEHRRS	earbasher
AABEEHRTT	heartbeat
AABEEILLN	alienable
AABEEKLPS	speakable
AABEELLLM	malleable
AABEELLNN	Annabelle
AABEELLNR	learnable
AABEELLRS	resalable
AABEELLRT	alterable, relatable
AABEELLRV	alla breve
AABEELNTU	uneatable
AABEELORT	elaborate
AABEELPRR	reparable
AABEELPRS	separable
AABEELPRY	repayable
AABEELQTU	equatable
AABEELRTT	treatable
AABEELRTV	avertable
AABEELRTW	tableware
AABEELSTT	tasteable
AABEELTTX	battleaxe
AABEEMNST	abasement
AABEEMNTT	abatement
AABEENORR	Aberaeron
AABEEQRSU	arabesque
AABEERRTW	water bear
AABEESTVW	beta waves
AABEFFLQU	quaffable
AABEFGILT	fatigable
AABEFILRU	Albufeira
AABEFIMRS	frambesia
AABEFKLNR	frankable
AABEFKRST	breakfast
AABEFLLMM	flammable
AABEFLLOT	floatable
AABEFLMSU	flambeaus
AABEFLMUX	flambeaux
AABEFLORV	favorable
AABEGGINO	gabionage
AABEGHLLU	laughable
AABEGHORR	harborage
AABEGILLR	Gabriella
AABEGILNV	navigable
AABEGINRR	bargainer
AABEGIRRT	arbitrage
AABEGKLOR	gaolbreak
AABEGLLLR	glabellar
AABEGLMNP	Palembang
AABEGLMPS	sample bag
AABEGLNOR	Bangalore
AABEGLNRT	grantable
AABEGLPRS	graspable
AABEGNORT	abnegator
AABEHITTU	habituate
AABEHKSWY	Hawkes Bay
AABEHLOTW	whaleboat
AABEHMNST	abashment
AABEHMSTT	steam bath
AABEHRTTW	bathwater
AABEIILLZ	labialize

AABEIIMNR bain-marie
AABEIIMSS amebiasis
AABEIIRTU aubrietia
AABEIJKLR jailbreak
AABEIKLNZ Balkanize
AABEIKNRR karabiner
AABEILLMR Mirabella
AABEILLNR ballerina
AABEILLRT bilateral
AABEILLST ballistae
AABEILMNR lamebrain
AABEILMNU unamiable
AABEILNPT paintable
AABEILNRT Albertina, trainable
AABEILNST stainable
AABEILPST basipetal
AABEIMNOT abominate
AABEIMRSU Beaumaris
AABEINRST abstainer, Antsirabe
AABEINRVW brainwave
AABEINSST Sebastian
AABEIRRTT arbitrate
AABEISSTT abattises
AABEKLLTT table talk
AABEKLNST beanstalk
AABEKMNRS brakesman
AABEKNNOT tonka bean
AABEKNPRU Buena Park
AABEKOSTT stake-boat
AABELLLMY malleably
AABELLLOW allowable
AABELLLVV ball valve
AABELLMNY Ballymena
AABELLMPT table lamp
AABELLNPT plantable
AABELLNSU unsalable
AABELLORS Rosabella
AABELLPPR palpebral
AABELLRUY bay laurel
AABELLSTT table salt
AABELLSTU blastulae
AABELMNST stableman
AABELMNTU untamable
AABELMRSS lamb's ears
AABELMSSU assumable
AABELNPPS snappable
AABELNSUY unsayable
AABELOPRR polar bear
AABELOPRV vaporable
AABELORST astrolabe
AABELORSU arousable
AABELORTT rotatable
AABELPRSY separably, sprayable
AABELRSTU saturable
AABELRTTU tablature
AABEMOSTT steamboat
AABEMRRSS embarrass
AABEOPPRT approbate
AABFIIMNS Fabianism
AABFIINST Fabianist
AABFIKNRS Fairbanks
AABFILMRS balsam fir
AABFIMORT fibromata
AABFMOSSU Bafoussam
AABGGRRYY argy-bargy
AABGHLLUY laughably
AABGHLPRU Bhagalpur
AABGHOPRR barograph
AABGILNRU Bulgarian
AABGINNOR born-again
AABGINTVY vanity bag
AABGNRRUW burrawang
AABGOORRT abrogator
AABGORTVY gravy boat
AABHIILRZ bilharzia
AABHIIMNP amphibian
AABHINRSW brainwash
AABHINSSW washbasin
AABHLSSTT bath salts
AABHPRRTU Bharatpur
AABIILNRR librarian
AABIINNRT Britannia
AABIINOSS anabiosis
AABILLNPT paintball
AABILMNOS anabolism
AABILMOPY amblyopia
AABILMORS ambrosial
AABILMPST baptismal
AABILNOTT battalion
AABILRRSU bursarial
AABIMNORS ambrosian
AABINORTT boat-train
AABINOSTW boatswain
AABIRRRTY arbitrary
AABJJLLNU Ljubljana
AABKLOTUW walkabout
AABLLLOWY allowably
AABLLMSYY abysmally
AABLLNTTY blatantly
AABLLRSYY syllabary
AABLLRTUY tabularly
AABLLSSTU blastulas
AABLMNORY myrobalan
AABLMPRSU Sambalpur
AABLNOPSS Bolan Pass
AABLNORTU Ulan Bator
AABLORSST albatross
AABLORTTU tabulator
AABLRSSTU subastral
AABNNSTTU Bantustan
AABNOOSSV bossa nova
AABRSSTTU substrata
AACCCFIOS focaccias
AACCCIOPR carpaccio
AACCDDEIR caddie car
AACCDDINY candidacy
AACCDEIIR acaricide
AACCDEIRV cadaveric
AACCDEJNY adjacency
AACCDELPR place card
AACCDHLOO coachload
AACCDHLRU archducal
AACCDIILM malic acid
AACCDIINR circadian
AACCDIOSU Caucasoid
AACCDKNRS sand-crack
AACCDNORT accordant
AACCEEFMR face cream
AACCEEKMR cream cake
AACCEELNR clearance
AACCEENRT reactance
AACCEFNRS Francesca
AACCEHINR cane chair
AACCEHJKP cheapjack
AACCEHRRT character
AACCEHSTW watch-case
AACCEIILN caecilian
AACCEILMT acclimate
AACCEINNR Cancerian
AACCEINRS Saracenic
AACCEINTV vaccinate
AACCEJKLN lance-jack
AACCEJKRR carjacker
AACCEKNRS crankcase
AACCEKRRT racetrack
AACCELLTU calculate
AACCELMNU calcaneum
AACCELMTY cyclamate
AACCELNSU calcaneus
AACCELNTU accentual
AACCELOPR Cape Coral
AACCENPTT acceptant
AACCEORTT coarctate
AACCERSSY accessary
AACCFINRS Francisca
AACCGHHIN cha-chaing
AACCGINRR racing car
AACCHILMO mail coach
AACCHILNY china clay
AACCHIMSY sciamachy
AACCHINRS saccharin
AACCHIRTT cathartic
AACCHIRTU autarchic
AACCIINTT tactician
AACCILLSS classical
AACCILMNU cacuminal
AACCILNNO canonical
AACCILPRT practical
AACCILSTT stalactic
AACCILTTY catalytic
AACCIMNOR carcinoma, macaronic
AACCINOTT catatonic
AACCINPTY captaincy
AACCINRTT Antarctic
AACCIOPRT capacitor
AACCIOPSU capacious
AACCIORST Costa Rica
AACCIRSST sarcastic
AACCKMNRS cracksman
AACCKRRTT cart track
AACCLMORY cyclorama
AACCLMSTY cataclysm
AACCMNOPY accompany
AACCORTUY autocracy
AACDDEEHR decahedra
AACDDEHMR dead march
AACDDEINT candidate
AACDDENOP decapodan
AACDDENSU Sadducean
AACDDGNOT cat-and-dog
AACDDIIST Dadaistic

AACDDMORU docudrama
AACDEEFLT defalcate
AACDEEIRT eradicate
AACDEEMNS damascene
AACDEEMRT demarcate
AACDEENOT deaconate
AACDEFHRS headscarf
AACDEFIST fasciated
AACDEGILT glaciated
AACDEGLNO decagonal
AACDEGLOT cataloged
AACDEHILN enchilada
AACDEHLLN dance hall
AACDEHLRT cathedral
AACDEHMNR hand cream
AACDEHMPT death camp
AACDEHORT octahedra
AACDEHPST pas de chat
AACDEHRSU hard sauce
AACDEILLN dalliance
AACDEILLT dialectal
AACDEILNO Laodicean
AACDEILNT cadential
AACDEILTU acidulate
AACDEIMMS academism
AACDEIMNO Macedonia
AACDEIMNY cyanamide
AACDEIMPR paramedic
AACDEINOR androecia
AACDEINOT diaconate
AACDEINOV avoidance
AACDEJKMP jam-packed
AACDEKLRY lardy-cake
AACDEKMRT tarmacked
AACDELLNU calendula
AACDELLWY weald-clay
AACDELMNS Candlemas
AACDELNOT anecdotal
AACDELNPS landscape
AACDELNRT declarant
AACDEMNTU manducate
AACDEMORS cream soda
AACDENNNO cannonade
AACDENNST ascendant
AACDENORW oceanward
AACDENPRS parascend
AACDENPRT tap-dancer
AACDENSSV canvassed
AACDERTTV cravatted
AACDFHLRS flashcard
AACDFHNRT handcraft
AACDFITTY fatty acid
AACDGLMOR cladogram
AACDHIILR rachidial
AACDHIKNR Chandrika
AACDHILMY chlamydia
AACDHILRY chairlady
AACDHINOR arachnoid
AACDHLNPU launch pad
AACDHLNRS crash-land
AACDHLNTY land yacht
AACDHNSTY sand yacht
AACDHPRRS card-sharp
AACDIIIMR miracidia
AACDIIMNO amino acid
AACDIINRR Ricardian
AACDIISST diastasic
AACDIISTT diastatic
AACDILLRY radically
AACDILMNY dynamical
AACDILNPR plain card
AACDILRRU radicular
AACDIMORY myocardia
AACDIMRST dramatics
AACDINNOR draconian
AACDIOSUU audacious
AACDIQRTU quadratic
AACDIRSTY caryatids
AACDJNTUY adjutancy
AACDKRSTY stack-yard
AACDLNORS corn salad
AACDLNOST coastland
AACDMRRST smart card
AACDNOSTT coat-stand
AACDPRRSY scrapyard
AACEEEGNR careenage
AACEEFIRT cafeteria
AACEEFLLS scale-leaf
AACEEFLPT faceplate
AACEEFLUV face value
AACEEFRRT aftercare
AACEEFRSV face-saver
AACEEGHNS sea change
AACEEGHRT hectarage
AACEEGKLN angel cake
AACEEGKPR repackage
AACEEGLLR cellarage
AACEEGNRR carrageen
AACEEHHRT heartache
AACEEHLNU Acheulean
AACEEHRTT tracheate
AACEEHRTX exarchate
AACEEILRU Eau Claire
AACEEJKPT pea-jacket
AACEEJKRS seajacker
AACEEJLTU ejaculate
AACEEKLMR lacemaker
AACEEKLRY layer cake
AACEEKMPR pacemaker
AACEEKRRT caretaker
AACEELMNP place name
AACEELNPS pleasance
AACEELNPT placentae
AACEELPRT Paraclete
AACEELRRY relay race
AACEELRTT altercate
AACEEMNNY Mycenaean
AACEEMRRW creamware
AACEENNRT nectarean
AACEEOPRS aerospace
AACEERSTT estate car
AACEFFIRT affricate
AACEFGNRR fragrance
AACEFGOPR forage cap
AACEFGORT factorage
AACEFHLST half-caste
AACEFIKRY fairy cake
AACEFINPT face paint
AACEFINST fascinate
AACEGHINR chain gear
AACEGHLNR archangel
AACEGHLTT Gaeltacht
AACEGHMNP champagne
AACEGHNOR anchorage
AACEGHRST gatecrash
AACEGILLN angelical, galenical
AACEGILMW wage claim
AACEGILNS analgesic
AACEGILRS Algeciras
AACEGILRT cartilage
AACEGIMNO egomaniac
AACEGISTT castigate
AACEGKRWY graywacke
AACEGLLSS lace-glass
AACEGLMOU guacamole
AACEGLORT cataloger
AACEGLOST galactose
AACEGLOTU catalogue, coagulate
AACEGLSSS glass case
AACEGNORR arrogance
AACEGNRSU cane sugar, sugar cane
AACEGOPST scapegoat
AACEGORTT greatcoat
AACEHHIRZ Zechariah
AACEHHMRR March hare
AACEHIIMS ischaemia
AACEHILLO echolalia
AACEHILMR camel-hair
AACEHILMT malachite
AACEHILNS selachian
AACEHILNU Acheulian
AACEHILNW chain-wale
AACEHILPT caliphate
AACEHIMNN Manichean
AACEHIMNR Charmaine
AACEHIMNT machinate
AACEHIMTT athematic
AACEHINRT Catharine
AACEHINST Hanseatic
AACEHIOST Taoiseach
AACEHIPRR crape hair
AACEHIPTT apathetic
AACEHIRSY easy chair
AACEHKLNO kalanchoe
AACEHKRSV haversack
AACEHLRSU Archelaus
AACEHLRTT clathrate
AACEHMNPR marchpane
AACEHNORS sea anchor
AACEHNOTV anchoveta
AACEHNRST cane-trash
AACEHNRSV Avranches
AACEHNSSS Sassenach
AACEHPPRS scrap heap
AACEHPRTU parachute
AACEHRSST catharses
AACEIILNT laciniate
AACEIINRR cineraria
AACEIIRTV vicariate
AACEIKLNS Aleksinac
AACEILLRV varicella
AACEILLTV vacillate

AACEILLVV Vacaville
AACEILMNP campanile
AACEILMPS eclampsia
AACEILMRT Carmelita
AACEILMST mica-slate
AACEILMTV calmative
AACEILNNR carnelian
AACEILNNT cantilena
AACEILNPP appliance
AACEILNPT analeptic
AACEILNRS arsenical
AACEILNRT lacertian
AACEILNRU Laurencia
AACEILNRZ carnalize
AACEILORT aleatoric
AACEILTUZ actualize
AACEIMNSX sex maniac
AACEIMNTU acuminate
AACEIMPRT metacarpi
AACEIMRST marcasite
AACEIMSTT masticate
AACEINNRT incarnate
AACEINPRT Patna rice
AACEINRST ascertain, Cartesian, sectarian
AACEIOSST associate
AACEIPPRT per capita
AACEIPTTV captivate
AACEIRSST staircase
AACEISTUV causative
AACEJKLNP jack plane
AACEJKLPP applejack
AACEJQTTU Jacquetta
AACEKLPRT plate rack
AACEKLPSW space walk
AACEKMRST caste mark
AACEKNRRS ransacker
AACEKPPTY pay packet
AACELLLRU acellular
AACELLLUV vallecula
AACELLMNR cellarman
AACELLNOW allowance
AACELLNPT placental
AACELLNST castellan
AACELLPSW wall space
AACELMNTT cattleman
AACELMRST smart alec
AACELMSST classmate
AACELNNTU cannulate
AACELNPST placentas
AACELNRST ancestral, Lancaster
AACELOPRT acropetal, Cleopatra
AACELORST escalator
AACELOTUV autoclave
AACELPSTU aspectual, capsulate
AACELPSTY catalepsy
AACELPTXY cataplexy
AACELRSTY catalyser
AACELRTUW caterwaul
AACELSSTY catalyses
AACEMNOVW cavewoman
AACEMNPRT mercaptan
AACEMNPRU Capernaum
AACEMNRST sacrament
AACEMORRT macerator
AACEMOSST Costa Mesa
AACENNNOY annoyance
AACENNOSS assonance
AACENRSSU anacruses, assurance
AACENRSSV canvasser
AACEORTUV evacuator
AACEORTVX excavator
AACEOSSUY soya sauce
AACFFJKST jackstaff
AACFGILRY fly agaric
AACFGLNRY flagrancy
AACFGNRRY fragrancy
AACFHKLRT half-track
AACFIILNN financial
AACFILNOT factional
AACFILORT factorial
AACFILORV varifocal
AACFINSTT fantastic
AACFIRSST frascatis
AACFKNNPY fanny pack
AACFKRSTT fast track
AACFLLTUY factually
AACFMNRST craftsman
AACGGHINN chain gang
AACGGIKNP packaging
AACGGIOPR paragogic
AACGHIIKS Chigasaki
AACGHIIMN Chiangmai
AACGHILPR graphical
AACGHIMNP champaign
AACGHIMUY Yamaguchi
AACGHIPRS sciagraph
AACGILLLY glacially
AACGILLMY magically
AACGILLOS scagliola
AACGIMPRT pragmatic
AACGINNSV canvasing
AACGINORV Craigavon
AACGIOSSU sagacious
AACGLLSWY scallywag
AACGLNOOT octagonal
AACGLNOTU coagulant
AACGLOORY acarology
AACGMORRT cartogram
AACGNNSTY stagnancy
AACHHHIUU chihuahua
AACHHINTY Hyacintha
AACHHKKNU Chanukkah
AACHHLRST crash-halt
AACHIILMN chain mail
AACHIILPT aliphatic
AACHIIPRS Pharisaic
AACHIIRRV charivari
AACHIKMSY skiamachy
AACHILLNS Callanish
AACHILNPS ship canal
AACHILOPR parochial
AACHILOPT chipolata
AACHILORS Charolais
AACHILPST asphaltic
AACHILSST thalassic
AACHIMNOR harmonica
AACHIMNRS anarchism
AACHIMRRT matriarch
AACHIMRST Catharism
AACHIMSTT asthmatic
AACHINOPR anaphoric, Pharaonic
AACHINORT Tocharian
AACHINRST anarchist
AACHIOPPT happi-coat
AACHIPRRT patriarch
AACHIRSST catharsis
AACHIRSTT Catharist
AACHLLMRY lachrymal
AACHLLRTW wallchart
AACHLMNOR monarchal
AACHLMPTY matchplay
AACHMNNOR anchorman
AACHMNORW charwoman
AACHMNSTY yachtsman
AACHMPRST march past
AACHOPPRY Apocrypha
AACHQSSTU Sasquatch
AACIIILNS siciliana
AACIILLRT altricial
AACIILMRS racialism
AACIILNST Castilian
AACIILNTV vaticinal
AACIILPRT piratical
AACIILRST racialist, satirical
AACIIMMST miasmatic
AACIIMOTX axiomatic
AACIINNOP poinciana
AACIINNOT nicotiana
AACIINPRT patrician
AACIIPRST parasitic
AACIIRRTU urticaria
AACIISTTV atavistic
AACILLMNY manically
AACILLMOR Camarillo
AACILLNOT allantoic
AACILLNRY ancillary
AACILLOXY coaxially
AACILLPRY capillary
AACILLPTY capitally
AACILLRRT ralli cart
AACILMOSW Mosaic Law
AACILMPST plasmatic
AACILMRSU simulacra
AACILNNOR non-racial
AACILNOPT placation
AACILNORT cantorial
AACILNOTT lactation
AACILNPPT applicant
AACILNRTY carnality
AACILNRUV navicular
AACILORSW social war
AACILOSSU salacious
AACILPRSU spiracula
AACILPRTU capitular
AACILPRTY paralytic
AACILQTTU acquittal
AACILRRTU articular

AACILRRUU auricular
AACILRSTY rascality
AACILSSTY catalysis
AACILSTTT Attic salt
AACILSTUY causality
AACILTTUY actuality
AACIMNNNU Mancunian
AACIMNOPR panoramic
AACIMORTU amaurotic
AACIMOTTU automatic
AACIMRRSU sacrarium
AACIMRTTU traumatic
AACINNORT carnation
AACINNOST santonica
AACINOOTV avocation
AACINOPRS caparison
AACINOSST cassation
AACINOSTU causation
AACINOTTU actuation
AACINRSST sacristan
AACINRSSU anacrusis
AACIOPRSU rapacious
AACIORTTV activator
AACIOSTTW waistcoat
AACJKRSTW jackstraw
AACKORSTT toastrack
AACLLMNTY clamantly
AACLLOORT allocator
AACLLOPRS collapsar
AACLLRSTU claustral
AACLNOORT root canal
AACLNOPTU cantaloup
AACLNRUUV avuncular
AACLOPRRT patrol car
AACLOPRTY placatory, play-actor
AACLPRSUY scapulary
AACMNOTTU catamount
AACMOOSTT scotomata
AACNNOSTZ Constanza
AACNORTUU au courant
AACNOSTTY at any cost
AACNRSTUY sanctuary
AACOOPSTT capo tasto
AACORRSTT castrator
AACORRTTT attractor
AACORSSWY cassowary
AADDEEFHT fat-headed
AADDEEMRY ready-made
AADDEGIMR diagramed
AADDEGMNU undamaged
AADDEHHMN ham-handed
AADDEHHRS hardheads
AADDEILNO adenoidal
AADDEILSS side salad
AADDEINRW Edwardian
AADDELLNS sandalled
AADDELLUV Uddevalla
AADDELMNR dreamland
AADDELRST astraddle
AADDENPTU unadapted
AADDEORST roadstead
AADDHNNST handstand
AADDIIMRY dairymaid
AADDIINRV Dravidian
AADDILMSY lady's maid
AADDILNNR land drain
AADDLNRSW landwards
AADDLRSTY dastardly
AADEEGHMT megadeath
AADEEGHST Gateshead
AADEEGLMN Magdalene
AADEEGLRT great deal
AADEEGNOR orangeade
AADEEGNPP appendage
AADEEGNRT Great Dane, tea garden
AADEEGNRV Davangere
AADEEHHRX hexahedra
AADEEHHTT heat death
AADEEHPRS spearhead
AADEEHRTT death rate
AADEEHRTW headwater
AADEEIKWW wideawake
AADEEILMV mediaeval
AADEELLMN allemande
AADEELMRS Esmeralda
AADEELNPS esplanade
AADEELNRX Alexander
AADEELPPR appareled
AADEELPTU plateaued
AADEELRRY lay reader
AADEEMNRT trade name
AADEEMPRR map-reader
AADEEMRSU admeasure
AADEEORTT toad-eater
AADEEPPRT parapeted
AADEEPRST paederast
AADEERRTT retardate
AADEERSTY Easter Day
AADEESTTV devastate
AADEFGLNN fandangle
AADEFGRSU safeguard
AADEFHHLR half-heard
AADEFILNT fantailed
AADEFLNOR farandole
AADEFLNSW false dawn
AADEFLORY yard of ale
AADEFMPRT afterdamp
AADEFMRST farmstead
AADEFRRTW afterward
AADEFSSTT steadfast
AADEGHNRY hydrangea
AADEGHNST stagehand
AADEGILPR paraglide
AADEGINRT tragedian
AADEGIPRS disparage
AADEGLNNT land agent
AADEGLNRV landgrave
AADEGMNNR danger man
AADEGMNNU unmanaged
AADEGMOSV savagedom
AADEGNRRT regardant
AADEGRRRU rearguard
AADEGRRVY graveyard
AADEHHKNS handshake
AADEHHLNT heathland
AADEHHRTW hard wheat
AADEHIORR diarrhoea
AADEHIPRT apartheid, hit parade
AADEHIRST stairhead
AADEHKMST death mask
AADEHLLST headstall
AADEHLMNN manhandle
AADEHLMPS lampshade
AADEHLMRS marshaled
AADEHLMSY ashamedly
AADEHLNNP panhandle
AADEHLNRT heartland
AADEHMNSU unashamed
AADEHORRW arrowhead
AADEHPRST hard-paste
AADEHPRTT death trap
AADEHRRTW earthward
AADEHRSTT head start
AADEIIRRT irradiate
AADEIIRTV radiative
AADEILMNN almandine
AADEILMNS ladies' man
AADEILMRT diametral
AADEILNNN annelidan
AADEILNNR adrenalin
AADEILNVZ vandalize
AADEILPPR laid paper
AADEILRTY radiately
AADEILTUV laudative
AADEILTVW tidal wave
AADEIMMSS mass media
AADEIMNNR mandarine
AADEIMRRR ram-raider
AADEIMRTZ dramatize
AADEINPTT patinated
AADEINRST steradian
AADEINRTT attainder
AADEIOPTU audiotape
AADEIPPRS disappear
AADEIPRST disparate
AADEKMMNR marked man
AADEKMMRU Marmaduke
AADEKMRRT trademark
AADEKMRTY market day
AADELLMPY medal play
AADELLNPR Laplander
AADELLNTU landaulet
AADELLSSY saleslady
AADELMMOR melodrama
AADELMNRS malanders
AADELMORT road metal
AADELNRRU rural dean
AADELNSTW wasteland
AADELOPRT pardalote
AADELRSTT trade-last
AADELRSTY delta rays
AADELRSYY early days
AADELRTTY latter-day
AADEMMNOR memoranda
AADEMMRST Amsterdam
AADEMNOPT tamponade
AADEMNPRS ampersand
AADEMNRST tradesman
AADEMPSTT date stamp
AADEMRRTU dura mater
AADENNPPT appendant

AADENNTTT attendant
AADENPPRS sandpaper
AADENRRTT retardant
AADENRSTY Satyendra
AADEOPRRS paradores
AADEORSTW soda water
AADERRRSW rearwards
AADERRSVY adversary
AADERSSTW eastwards
AADFFIITV affidavit
AADFHHLRY half-hardy
AADFIINNR infradian
AADFILNRY fairyland
AADFIMNRY man Friday
AADFMNRST draftsman
AADGGHLRY haggardly
AADGGLLRY laggardly
AADGHIMPR diaphragm
AADGHIOPR pariah dog
AADGHIRRU guard hair
AADGHLNSS handglass
AADGILNNS sandaling
AADGILORT gladiator
AADGILRRU guard rail
AADGIMORR radiogram
AADGIMRRS Mardi Gras
AADGINORT gradation
AADGLLNRU glandular
AADGLLOPR dollar gap
AADGLLRUY gradually
AADGLMNRS grand slam
AADGLNOOW wagonload
AADGLNRSS grassland
AADGLNSSS sand-glass
AADGLOPRV Pavlograd
AADGMNORS dragomans
AADGMNRSU guardsman
AADGNNRTU grand-aunt
AADGNRSUV guard's van
AADGORRTU graduator
AADHIMNUZ Zhumadian
AADHINNOT danthonia
AADHINPSU Upanishad
AADHIPSSY dysphasia
AADHKMNTU Kathmandu
AADHLLNST hallstand
AADHLMNRS marshland
AADHNSSTW washstand
AADHORRSU hadrosaur
AADHORSUZ hazardous
AADIILSUV visual aid
AADIIMMOT ommatidia
AADIINNRS Sardinian
AADIINNRW Darwinian
AADIINORT radiation
AADIINRRT irradiant
AADIIORTU auditoria
AADIJNNOR Jordanian
AADILLMOR armadillo
AADILLMPS Aldis lamp
AADILLMPU palladium
AADILLOPS sapodilla
AADILMNNO adnominal
AADILMNSV vandalism
AADILMOPS plasmodia
AADILMORT maladroit
AADILMORV Almoravid
AADILMPRY pyramidal
AADILMRTY Admiralty
AADILNOPT antipodal
AADILNORS Rosalinda
AADILNORT trainload
AADILNOTT antidotal
AADILNOTU adulation, laudation
AADILNRTU ultradian
AADILNRTY radiantly
AADILNSWZ Swaziland
AADILOSVW disavowal
AADILPSSY dysplasia
AADIMNNOT damnation
AADIMNUVZ avizandum
AADIMRSTT dramatist
AADINNNOT andantino
AADINNORY Indo-Aryan
AADINOORT adoration
AADINORRT road train
AADINSSTY saint's day
AADINSTTX taxi stand
AADIORSTU sudatoria
AADIPSSUY ups-a-daisy
AADKLRWWY awkwardly
AADLLNORU all-around
AADLMNPSW swampland
AADLORTUY adulatory, laudatory
AADLRWWYY waywardly
AADMMNOOR monodrama
AADMNORTY damnatory, mandatory
AADNNORSU anandrous
AADNOOPSW sapanwood
AADNOORRS Aaron's rod
AADNORTTU Taroudant
AADOPPRST strappado
AAEEEGRTT tree agate
AAEEFGRST fare stage
AAEEFHNRT fan heater
AAEEFLLMP maple leaf
AAEEFLRSW self-aware
AAEEFLRTW water flea
AAEEFLTTY Lafayette
AAEEGGGRT aggregate
AAEEGINTV evaginate
AAEEGIRTV variegate
AAEEGLMNP panel game
AAEEGLMNT mental age
AAEEGLRST Great Seal
AAEEGLRVY averagely
AAEEGLSVW wage slave
AAEEGLTVV gate valve
AAEEGMNNS manganese
AAEEGMNST stage name
AAEEGNPRT parentage
AAEEGNRRR rearrange
AAEEGNRTU guarantee
AAEEGRTTW watergate
AAEEHIMTT haematite
AAEEHLMTW wheatmeal
AAEEHLRRS rehearsal
AAEEHMNNT enanthema
AAEEHMNTU athenaeum
AAEEHMNTX exanthema
AAEEHMPST metaphase
AAEEHMSTT steam-heat
AAEEHNOTT ethanoate
AAEEHRRRT rare earth
AAEEHRRSW shareware
AAEEHRTTT heat-treat
AAEEIKLMU leukaemia
AAEEILLTV alleviate
AAEEILRTT retaliate
AAEEIMNRT reanimate
AAEEIMNTV emanative
AAEEIPPRS appraisee
AAEEIPTTX expatiate
AAEEISTTV aestivate
AAEEKLNNP palankeen
AAEEKNPTW wapentake
AAEEKPSSY speakeasy
AAEELLLMT lamellate
AAEELLOTV alveolate
AAEELLPPT appellate
AAEELLPTT patellate
AAEELLQRU aquarelle
AAEELLRST all-seater
AAEELLRWW well aware
AAEELMMNU Emmanuela
AAEELMNPT nameplate
AAEELMSTT stalemate
AAEELNOPR aeroplane
AAEELNRSY lean years
AAEELNRTT alternate
AAEELPPSX sex appeal
AAEELPRRW pearlware
AAEELPRST lapse rate
AAEEMMNTZ amazement
AAEEMNNSS anamneses
AAEEMPRRT parameter
AAEEMRRRT terramare
AAEENQRTU Antequera
AAEENRRTW warrantee
AAEENRSSW awareness
AAEENTTTU attenuate
AAEEOPRTV evaporate
AAEEPPPRT paper tape
AAEEPRRTY ratepayer
AAEEPSSYY easy-peasy
AAEERRTTW water rate
AAEFFIILT affiliate
AAEFFINRT raffinate
AAEFGHMNR Fermanagh
AAEFGINRS seafaring
AAEFGIRSX saxifrage
AAEFGLLLR flagellar
AAEFGLRVW flag-waver
AAEFHLLPT half-plate
AAEFHLPRT flare-path
AAEFHMRTT aftermath
AAEFIKNRR Afrikaner
AAEFILMRR fire alarm
AAEFILNPU epifaunal
AAEFILRTY fairy tale
AAEFIMMNR mainframe
AAEFINNRS safranine

AAEFINSTZ	fantasize	**AAEHILMMS**	hamamelis	**AAEINRRTV**	narrative
AAEFINTTU	infatuate	**AAEHILNNT**	Nathaniel	**AAEINRRTW**	rainwater
AAEFIRRTW	fairwater	**AAEHILNTV**	leviathan	**AAEINRTVW**	wave train
AAEFKLLST	leaf-stalk	**AAEHILRTW**	heir-at-law	**AAEIORSSU**	Essaouira
AAEFLLRTW	waterfall	**AAEHIMRTU**	hematuria	**AAEIPPRRS**	appraiser
AAEFLNRRT	fraternal	**AAEHINPRS**	Seraphina	**AAEIPSSTV**	passivate
AAEGGILLN	galingale	**AAEHINPRT**	Parthenia	**AAEIRRTTZ**	tartarize
AAEGGINOR	Georgiana	**AAEHLNPSX**	phalanxes	**AAEIRTTWX**	water taxi
AAEGGINRU	rain gauge	**AAEHLNSTT**	Athelstan	**AAEJKLRWY**	jaywalker
AAEGGLLNO	gallonage	**AAEHLOPPR**	phalarope	**AAEKKPRST**	skatepark
AAEGGLPUY	gay plague	**AAEHLPSTT**	alpha test	**AAEKLLSST**	sales talk
AAEGHLLPY	hypallage	**AAEHLTTWX**	wealth tax	**AAEKLMPRY**	playmaker
AAEGHLNOX	hexagonal	**AAEHMRSTU**	shamateur	**AAEKLPRST**	lap-strake
AAEGHLNPR	phalanger	**AAEHNSSTY**	sea shanty	**AAEKMRRTW**	watermark
AAEGHLNPS	phalanges	**AAEHRRSTT**	earthstar	**AAEKMRRWY**	waymarker
AAEGHNOPR	orphanage	**AAEIILMNZ**	animalize	**AAELLLPTW**	wall-plate
AAEGHNRRU	haranguer	**AAEIILPTX**	epitaxial	**AAELLLRTY**	laterally
AAEGIILNT	genitalia	**AAEIILRST**	aerialist	**AAELLNPPT**	appellant
AAEGIILQU	aquilegia	**AAEIILRTY**	aeriality	**AAELLPPRW**	wallpaper
AAEGILNNT	galantine	**AAEIIMNNT**	inanimate	**AAELLQRSU**	all square
AAEGILNOZ	analogize	**AAEIIMRST**	artemisia	**AAELLSUXY**	asexually
AAEGILNPP	appealing	**AAEIINSTT**	insatiate	**AAELMMORR**	marmoreal
AAEGILNRU	neuralgia	**AAEIKLMRS**	sailmaker	**AAELMMOTY**	myelomata
AAEGILNVZ	galvanize	**AAEIKLTTV**	talkative	**AAELMNORU**	anomalure
AAEGILRTT	tailgater	**AAEIKMNRR**	rainmaker	**AAELMNRSU**	El Mansura
AAEGIMMNS	mismanage	**AAEILLMMT**	mamillate	**AAELMNRSY**	salarymen
AAEGIMNNS	magnesian	**AAEILLMNT**	alimental	**AAELNPRTY**	planetary
AAEGIMNRR	margarine	**AAEILLNPS**	sailplane	**AAELNPSTT**	pantalets
AAEGIMNRT	marginate	**AAEILLNPT**	tailplane	**AAELNRRUY**	lunar year
AAEGINNRT	Argentina	**AAEILLNTT**	Late Latin	**AAELNRSTT**	translate
AAEGINNRW	Wagnerian	**AAEILLPPT**	papillate	**AAELNRTUU**	au naturel
AAEGINRSY	gainsayer	**AAEILLPSS**	paillasse, palliasse	**AAELNSTTU**	sultanate
AAEGIRTTV	gravitate			**AAELOPPRY**	propylaea
AAEGISTTT	sagittate	**AAEILLRTV**	relatival	**AAELOPRST**	pastorale
AAEGLLNRY	laryngeal	**AAEILMMST**	melismata	**AAELOPSTU**	apetalous
AAEGLLSTZ	salt-glaze	**AAEILMNNP**	mainplane	**AAELORRSY**	solar year
AAEGLMTTU	glutamate	**AAEILMNSZ**	Manizales	**AAELORSTV**	Salvatore
AAEGLNNOS	San Angelo	**AAEILMPRV**	primaeval	**AAELORTTZ**	lazaretto
AAEGLNRTU	granulate	**AAEILMPTT**	palmitate	**AAELORTUV**	evaluator
AAEGLPRSV	palsgrave	**AAEILMRST**	mare's tail	**AAELPPRST**	star-apple
AAEGLPSTY	stage play	**AAEILMRTU**	tularemia	**AAELPRSSY**	paralyses
AAEGLRSSW	glassware	**AAEILNNTV**	Valentina	**AAELPSTTU**	spatulate
AAEGLRSTU	gastrulae	**AAEILNORT**	alienator, rationale	**AAELRRSTV**	traversal
AAEGMNNOR	Orangeman			**AAELRSSTU**	assaulter, saleratus
AAEGMNOPT	tamponage	**AAEILNPRT**	perinatal		
AAEGMNPRT	pentagram	**AAEILNRTU**	Laurentia	**AAELRSTTW**	salt water
AAEGMNRSV	gravamens	**AAEILNTTT**	tantalite	**AAELSSTWY**	leastways
AAEGMNRTT	termagant	**AAEILNTTZ**	tantalize	**AAEMMNRST**	men-at-arms
AAEGMOSST	moss agate	**AAEILPPTT**	palpitate	**AAEMNORTU**	neuromata
AAEGMRRTT	tetragram	**AAEILRRTW**	water rail	**AAEMNPRTT**	apartment
AAEGMRSTT	stratagem	**AAEILRSSW**	wassailer	**AAEMNSSTT**	statesman
AAEGNOPRS	parsonage	**AAEIMNNOT**	emanation	**AAEMOORRT**	motor area
AAEGNOPRT	patronage	**AAEIMNNSS**	anamnesis	**AAEMPRRTY**	prayer mat
AAEGNPRTY	pageantry	**AAEIMNOTZ**	anatomize	**AAEMPRSTY**	paymaster
AAEGNRSTV	Stavanger	**AAEIMNPRR**	repairman	**AAEMRRSST**	smart-arse
AAEGNRTTU	great-aunt	**AAEIMNRTU**	animateur	**AAENNNRTY**	antennary
AAEGOPPRT	propagate	**AAEIMNRTW**	water main	**AAENNPSST**	en passant
AAEGPRSTU	pasturage	**AAEIMNSTT**	staminate	**AAENPRSST**	apartness
AAEGRRSTZ	stargazer	**AAEIMORTZ**	aromatize	**AAENPRSTY**	peasantry
AAEHHINPZ	Zephaniah	**AAEIMPRRV**	primavera	**AAENRRRST**	Stranraer
AAEHHLNOT	halothane	**AAEIMRRST**	airstream	**AAENRRRTW**	warranter
AAEHHLPTT	phthalate	**AAEIMRSTT**	metatarsi	**AAEOOPPRS**	soap opera
AAEHIKNRT	Katharine	**AAEINNRSW**	raw sienna	**AAEOPRRST**	separator
AAEHIKNSZ	Ashkenazi	**AAEINORRT**	aerotrain	**AAEOPRSTT**	pastorate
AAEHILLVV	Vila Velha	**AAEINPPRT**	appertain	**AAEPPRRST**	spare part

AAFFFGLST flagstaff
AAFFGNRSU suffragan
AAFGILMNS Falangism
AAFGILNRS franglais
AAFGILNST Falangist
AAFGINRWY wayfaring
AAFGLLORT allograft
AAFGLORSU loaf sugar, sugar loaf
AAFGORTTU autograft
AAFHHNNUY funny-ha-ha
AAFHLLMPS flash lamp
AAFIIRRYY airy-fairy
AAFILMMNY family man
AAFILNNOU Fionnuala
AAFILNOTX aflatoxin
AAFINSSTT fantasist
AAFKLNOUU Nuku'alofa
AAFLORSWW laws of war
AAFMORRTW marrowfat
AAFRRTTYY arty-farty
AAGGIMNOR angiogram
AAGGIMNRW war gaming
AAGGINOWY going away
AAGGKLNNP gangplank
AAGGLLLSS glass-gall
AAGGLMNOR Glamorgan
AAGGLNOSY synagogal
AAGHHILRT high altar
AAGHHINSS shanghais
AAGHHNNSU Huangshan
AAGHIKMNY haymaking
AAGHIKMOS Kagoshima
AAGHIKOSY Koshigaya
AAGHILLLN halalling
AAGHILNRS ashlaring, Shangri-La
AAGHINNRU Hungarian
AAGHIRRSS hair-grass
AAGHKPRRU Kharagpur
AAGHLNPRY pharyngal
AAGHNPRST strap-hang
AAGHOPRTU autograph
AAGIIJJNO Jiaojiang
AAGIIKNNS Kisangani
AAGIIMMNS magianism
AAGIIMNRY imaginary
AAGIINOTT agitation
AAGIJNNNP japanning
AAGIJNUUY Jiayuguan
AAGIJRSTU Gujaratis
AAGIKLMNW law-making
AAGIKLNNO Algonkian
AAGIKMMNP map-making
AAGIKMRSS Kissagram
AAGILLNPP appalling
AAGILLNTV gallivant
AAGILLORT alligator
AAGILLPSW galliwasp
AAGILMNNS signalman
AAGILMNNT malignant
AAGILMNSV galvanism
AAGILMNSY gymnasial
AAGILMNYZ amazingly
AAGILMRST magistral
AAGILNOST nostalgia
AAGILNRUU inaugural
AAGILNRUV vulgarian
AAGILNSTV galvanist
AAGILQUUY Guayaquil
AAGIMNPRT ptarmigan
AAGIMNRST Gram stain
AAGINOPRS sporangia
AAGINORTV navigator
AAGINSTTU sitatunga
AAGINSTUU Augustina
AAGIORSUV vagarious
AAGIPSSTY paysagist
AAGLLLNTY gallantly
AAGLLNNTU ungallant
AAGLLNRTY gallantry
AAGLLNRUY angularly
AAGLLOPSS opal glass
AAGLMMMOY mammalogy
AAGLNOOSU analogous
AAGLNORRT Traralgon
AAGLNOSTY last agony
AAGLNRTVY vagrantly
AAGLORSTY royal stag
AAGLRSSST salt grass
AAGMMMMOR mammogram
AAGMNNOSU manganous
AAGMNSSTY syntagmas
AAGMRSSSU sargassum
AAGNNORTU orangutan
AAGNNOTUY agony aunt
AAGNOOPSY Soyapango
AAGNORRTU guarantor
AAGNORSTU angostura
AAGNPRSSU sugar snap
AAGOPRSSU sugar soap
AAGPRSTTY stag-party
AAHHIIMRS maharishi
AAHHILLNS inshallah
AAHHKMRSW marsh hawk
AAHHNNSSU Shushanna
AAHIIKNSW Kawanishi
AAHIILNTU Lithuania
AAHIKLSTY Khaylitsa
AAHIKRSTU Hiratsuka
AAHIKRSTY Kshatriya
AAHILMNOT malathion
AAHILMTUZ azimuthal
AAHILNSTU ailanthus
AAHILORST sailor hat
AAHILORTU authorial
AAHILPSXY asphyxial
AAHIMMNSS shamanism
AAHIMNOPY hypomania
AAHIMNOST Thomasina
AAHIMNSST shamanist
AAHIMNSTU amianthus
AAHINOORR honoraria
AAHINOPRT parathion, phanariot
AAHINPTTY antipathy
AAHINRRTU Arthurian
AAHIPRRSY hairspray
AAHKLNORS loan shark
AAHKLNOTT talkathon
AAHKLNOTW walkathon
AAHKNOSTV Stakhanov
AAHLLOPTY allopathy
AAHLLSTTT Hallstatt
AAHLMNNTU lanthanum
AAHLMRSST salt marsh
AAHLPPPSY slap-happy
AAHMNOSTX xanthomas
AAHNNOOTZ anthozoan
AAHNPPRSY nappy rash
AAHORTWWY throwaway
AAIIILMRT militaria
AAIIKLMOR Kamilaroi
AAIIKNNRU Ukrainian
AAIIKNPST Pakistani
AAIILLMNS snail mail
AAIILLRST Allistair
AAIILMMNS animalism
AAIILMNRT mail train
AAIILMNTY animality
AAIILMPRT impartial, primatial
AAIILNOSU Louisiana
AAIILNRTV antiviral
AAIILRUXY auxiliary
AAIIMNNOT animation
AAIIMPPRR primipara
AAIINNRTU Unitarian
AAIINNRTV invariant
AAIINOPRT topiarian
AAIINORTV variation
AAIINOSTT satiation
AAIINPSTT antipasti
AAIJMORSX major axis
AAIJNRSSY janissary
AAIJRSSTW Swarajist
AAIKKSTTU Takatsuki
AAIKLLOSS alkalosis
AAIKLNNRS Sri Lankan
AAIKLOSUV souvlakia
AAIKRSTTU autarkist
AAILLLNOT lallation
AAILLMMRY mamillary
AAILLMMXY maximally
AAILLMOPP papilloma
AAILLMORT tamarillo
AAILLMRSY amaryllis
AAILLMRTY maritally, martially
AAILLMRXY maxillary
AAILLNOOP Apollonia
AAILLNOST allantois
AAILLNPRU nullipara
AAILLNTVY valiantly
AAILLOPRT palliator
AAILLORSY royal sail
AAILLPPRY papillary
AAILLPRTY partially
AAILLPSTY spatially
AAILMMORS amoralism
AAILMNNPS plainsman
AAILMNORT laminator
AAILMNSST talismans

AAILMNTTU matutinal
AAILMORST amoralist
AAILMORSU malarious
AAILMORTY amorality
AAILMPRSU marsupial
AAILNNOPS Annapolis
AAILNNOST santolina
AAILNNPQU palanquin
AAILNNPRU uniplanar
AAILNOOTV ovational
AAILNOPPT palpation
AAILNOPSS passional
AAILNOPUW paulownia
AAILNOPVV Pavlovian
AAILNOSTT saltation
AAILNOSTV salvation
AAILNOTTY atonality
AAILNOTUV valuation
AAILNPPTT palpitant
AAILNPRTU tarpaulin
AAILOORRT oratorial
AAILOPRRT raptorial
AAILOPRRY pair royal
AAILOPRST pastorali
AAILORRST sartorial
AAILOSSTU Sausalito
AAILPRSSY paralysis
AAILRSUVY visual ray
AAIMMNNOO monomania
AAIMMNRST Martinmas
AAIMNNORS San Marino
AAIMNNORU Roumanian
AAIMNOORT inamorato
AAIMNOPRY pyromania
AAIMNOSTT anatomist
AAIMNRSTT tarantism
AAIMOORRT moratoria
AAIMORSSU amaurosis
AAIMQRSUU aquariums
AAINNNTTU annuitant
AAINNORRT narration
AAINNRSTU Saturnian
AAINOORRT oratorian
AAINOPSTT antipasto
AAINPRSST satin spar
AAINPSTXY anaptyxis
AAINQRTUY antiquary
AAINSSSTT assistant
AAIOPRRST aspirator
AAIOPSTTU autopista
AAIORRTTT trattoria
AAIPSSTWW wasp-waist
AAJMOPRRT major part
AAJMORRSU Ursa Major
AAKKMORRU Karakorum
AAKLLLMST small talk
AAKLNSSVY Slavyansk
AAKNOOSST Saskatoon
AALLLMMSS small slam
AALLMMRSS small arms
AALLMOOSS Los Alamos
AALLNNOPY Pollyanna
AALLNNRUY annularly
AALLNQTUY quantally
AALLNRTUY naturally
AALLNSTUY Aunt Sally
AALLPRTWY party wall
AALMNNPST plantsman
AALMNOOSU anomalous
AALMNOPRT patrolman
AALMNPRTY rampantly
AALMORSTY royal mast
AALMORTYY mayoralty
AALNNOOPT pantaloon
AALNNOTUV anovulant
AALNNRTUU unnatural
AALNOOPZZ pozzolana
AALNOPSTT post-natal
AALNOPUZZ puzzolana
AALNORVYY Royal Navy
AALOPRRST polar star
AALOPRRTY portrayal
AALORSTTY saltatory
AALRSSTTW last straw
AAMMNNOWX Manxwoman
AAMMOORST Matamoros
AAMNNPRTY pantryman
AAMNOORSW oarswoman
AAMNOOTTU automaton
AAMNOPRTU paramount
AAMNQRRUY quarryman
AAMOPRTTU amputator
AANNOORTT annotator
AANORRRTW warrantor
AANORRTWY Norway rat
AANORSTTU astronaut
AANORSTWY Stornaway
AAOOPPRRT paratroop
AAOORRTTV Rotavator
ABBBCELLU clubbable
ABBBCELRU bubble car
ABBBEEJRS bejabbers
ABBBGGUYY baby buggy
ABBBIRTTY Babbittry
ABBCCEHKN backbench
ABBCCKKLU blackbuck
ABBCDEERU barbecued
ABBCDEFNO confabbed
ABBCDELRY crabbedly
ABBCDIKLR blackbird
ABBCDKLOY black body
ABBCDKORU buckboard
ABBCEERSU barbecues
ABBCEIKLL black bile
ABBCEIKRT backbiter
ABBCEILLM climbable
ABBCEIRST crabbiest
ABBCEISST scabbiest
ABBCEKLLT black belt
ABBCEKLLU blue-black
ABBCELRRS Scrabbler
ABBCHIKRR birch-bark
ABBCHNRSU sub-branch
ABBCILPRU public bar
ABBCIMOST bombastic
ABBCKLNRU Blackburn
ABBCKLOOT bootblack
ABBDEELRU Bluebeard
ABBDEGINR Banbridge
ABBDEGNRU Bundaberg
ABBDEILRT bird table
ABBDELLNY bellyband
ABBDELOTU doubtable
ABBDELSUU subduable
ABBDGIILN ad libbing
ABBDHLOOT bloodbath
ABBDIINRR birdbrain
ABBDILLOR billboard
ABBDKLNOO blood bank
ABBDMNOOR bombardon
ABBDMOQSU bomb squad
ABBEEEHRS Beersheba
ABBEEILLV Abbeville
ABBEELLMS semblable
ABBEELOPR probeable
ABBEELRRY blaeberry
ABBEENRRY baneberry
ABBEERRRY bearberry
ABBEFILST flabbiest
ABBEGINRT rabbeting
ABBEHILOT Bible oath
ABBEHISST shabbiest
ABBEHLOTU tabbouleh
ABBEILMSU Abu Simbel
ABBEIMNOS bombasine
ABBEIMNOZ bombazine
ABBEINORT barbitone
ABBEIQRSU squabbier
ABBEJLLYY jelly baby
ABBELLPRU pearl bulb
ABBELMOOZ bamboozle
ABBELOSTY stable boy
ABBELQRSU squabbler
ABBELSTTU battlebus
ABBENORRW brown bear
ABBENORST absorbent
ABBFHLLSU flashbulb
ABBGIINRT rabbiting
ABBGILLNO billabong
ABBGILMNR brambling
ABBGILOOT obbligato
ABBGINORS absorbing
ABBHHISSY shabbyish
ABBHILSSU bush basil
ABBHILSYY babyishly
ABBHIOPST abbotship
ABBJMRUUU Bujumbura
ABBLLOOTX ballot box
ABBOOPRTY booby trap
ABBOORRWY barrow boy
ABCCCKKLO blackcock
ABCCDIIOR boric acid
ABCCDIKLS black disc
ABCCEEHKL checkable
ABCCEEIRT brecciate
ABCCEENRU buccaneer
ABCCEINOV biconcave
ABCCEINRW cabin crew
ABCCELNRU carbuncle
ABCCGHLTU clutch bag
ABCCHHKNU hunchback
ABCCHKLOT backcloth
ABCCHKOTU touchback
ABCCHLTUY yacht club

ABCCIIJNO Jacobinic
ABCCILLUY cubically
ABCCILNOO obconical
ABCCILPTU public act
ABCCIRSTU subarctic
ABCCKKKNO knock-back
ABCCKKOOR crookback
ABCCKNOTU countback
ABCCKORSS back cross
ABCCLLSSU club class
ABCCMOORY mobocracy
ABCDDEEIL decidable
ABCDDEELO decodable
ABCDDEILU adducible
ABCDDEIRT debit card
ABCDDKORU duckboard
ABCDEEEHU debauchee
ABCDEEHIS beachside
ABCDEEHMR chambered
ABCDEEHRU debaucher
ABCDEEILM medicable
ABCDEEIMR Barmecide
ABCDEEJKT bedjacket
ABCDEEKRT bracketed
ABCDEESSS abscessed
ABCDEFIKL backfield
ABCDEGIMR Cambridge
ABCDEHIOT cohabited
ABCDEHKLO blockhead
ABCDEIKLS backslide
ABCDEIKRS brake disc, disc brake
ABCDEIKRU rudbeckia
ABCDEILNO balconied
ABCDEIRRV cab driver
ABCDEISUV scuba-dive
ABCDEKLOR blockader
ABCDELLOT cold table
ABCDELOSU cloud base
ABCDELOTU double act
ABCDENORR cornbread
ABCDENORS absconder
ABCDENOSU case-bound, subdeacon
ABCDEOORT obcordate
ABCDHIOPR chipboard
ABCDHIRSY Charybdis
ABCDHNRTU Dutch barn
ABCDIKRRY brickyard
ABCDILLNO blind coal
ABCDILMOR Lombardic
ABCDILOPR clipboard
ABCDINOOT bandicoot
ABCDINOTU abduction
ABCDIOOSU bodacious
ABCDKLOOR roadblock
ABCDKOOSW backwoods
ABCDLNRSU scrubland
ABCDNOOXX Box and Cox
ABCEEELLR cerebella
ABCEEELLT electable
ABCEEELRT celebrate, erectable
ABCEEELRX execrable
ABCEEERRT cerebrate
ABCEEFFOR coffee bar
ABCEEFIRS briefcase
ABCEEFLOR forceable
ABCEEGKNR greenback
ABCEEHIOT cohabitee
ABCEEHKLW wheel-back
ABCEEHKMN Beckenham
ABCEEHLLY bellyache
ABCEEHLNU Cuban heel
ABCEEHMST beechmast
ABCEEILLS sliceable
ABCEEILTX excitable
ABCEEINOS obeisance
ABCEEKKNR breakneck
ABCEEKPSW sweepback
ABCEELMNS semblance
ABCEELMRY Camberley
ABCEELNRT celebrant
ABCEELNST albescent
ABCEELORV coverable, revocable
ABCEELOTV covetable
ABCEELRSU rescuable, securable
ABCEELRSW screwable
ABCEELRXY execrably
ABCEELSUX excusable
ABCEEMMOR Morecambe
ABCEEMMRT Camembert
ABCEENRTY cybernate
ABCEEOSSU sebaceous
ABCEEPRRU cupbearer
ABCEFFRTU buffet car
ABCEFHLSU flash-cube
ABCEFIRTU bifurcate
ABCEFOSTU obfuscate
ABCEGHLNO Long Beach
ABCEGIINO abiogenic
ABCEGILOT cogitable
ABCEGKRTU tucker-bag
ABCEGNSUY subagency
ABCEHINNO bone china
ABCEHINOT aitchbone
ABCEHIORT cohabiter
ABCEHKLLO black hole
ABCEHKLLS shellback
ABCEHKLOS shockable, shoeblack
ABCEHKMNR benchmark
ABCEHKORS horseback
ABCEHKRRY hackberry
ABCEHKTUW buckwheat
ABCEHLMPU beach plum
ABCEHLNRT branchlet
ABCEHLOPW peach-blow
ABCEHLOTU touchable
ABCEHLRSU crushable
ABCEHRSTU Bucharest
ABCEIILNS sibilance
ABCEIILRS irascible
ABCEIIMRT imbricate
ABCEIJLNU jubilance
ABCEIJNOT abjection
ABCEILLPP clippable
ABCEILMOT metabolic
ABCEILMST cembalist
ABCEILNNU incunable
ABCEILNOV invocable
ABCEILNRU incurable
ABCEILNVY bivalency
ABCEILORT cabriolet
ABCEILRTU lubricate
ABCEILTXY excitably
ABCEIMOTV combative
ABCEIMRTU bacterium
ABCEINORZ carbonize
ABCEINRTY cabinetry
ABCEIRRTU rubricate
ABCEIRRUZ carburize
ABCEJNSTU subjacent
ABCEKLLNR Bracknell
ABCEKLNSS blackness
ABCEKLPRU parbuckle
ABCEKOPRR break crop
ABCEKORTU outbacker
ABCEKPSTW swept-back
ABCEKRTUW water-buck
ABCELLOOR colorable
ABCELLRSW screwball
ABCELMOOR rocambole
ABCELMRRS scrambler
ABCELNOST constable
ABCELNOTU countable
ABCELORSU crab louse
ABCELRTTY battle-cry
ABCELRTUU lucubrate
ABCELSSUU sub-clause
ABCELSUXY excusably
ABCEMPRRU bumper car
ABCEMRSUV verbascum
ABCENORTY baronetcy
ABCENORYZ crazy bone
ABCENRRRY cranberry
ABCENSSTU substance
ABCFGHIKT fightback
ABCFHIKLS blackfish
ABCFKLOOT Blackfoot
ABCGGIKPY piggyback
ABCGHIKLT backlight
ABCGHIKRT right-back
ABCGHIKST backsight
ABCGIKLNS sling-back
ABCGIKNOR king cobra
ABCGILNRY bracingly
ABCGIMNOT combating
ABCGINNOS sonic bang
ABCHHKSUW bushwhack
ABCHIILLN chilblain
ABCHIIMOR choriambi
ABCHILMOS shambolic
ABCHILNOR bronchial
ABCHILORR charbroil
ABCHKMTTU thumbtack
ABCHKNORT thornback
ABCHKORTW throwback
ABCHLLNPU punchball
ABCHNORRS cornbrash
ABCIIIKLW bailiwick
ABCIILLMU umbilical
ABCIILLST ballistic

ABCIILMOR microbial
ABCIILNOT albinotic
ABCIILNSY sibilancy
ABCIILRSY irascibly
ABCIINNRT Britannic
ABCIIRSTY sybaritic
ABCIKLLST blacklist
ABCILLPUW public law
ABCILMNOU Columbina
ABCILMOPY amblyopic
ABCILMSTY cymbalist
ABCILNNOU connubial
ABCILNORU binocular
ABCILNRTU lubricant
ABCILNRUY incurably
ABCILORRU orbicular
ABCIMNOOS monobasic
ABCIMOSTU subatomic
ABCINOORR Rio Branco
ABCINORTU incubator
ABCINOSTY obstinacy
ABCKKLMNO Black Monk
ABCKLOPST black spot
ABCKOOPRS scrapbook
ABCLLORRS scroll bar
ABCLNOORW brown coal
ABCLNOWYY Colwyn Bay
ABCLOORRU colour bar
ABCLOOSTU cobaltous
ABCLORSUU subocular
ABCLOSSTU subcostal
ABCNORSTU obscurant
ABDDEEEYY beady-eyed
ABDDEEGHI big-headed
ABDDEEPRS bedspread
ABDDEFILN deaf-blind
ABDDEHIIT adhibited
ABDDEILNT blind date
ABDDEIORS broadside, sideboard
ABDDEIRRS disbarred
ABDDELOSW saddle bow
ABDDENNRU unbranded
ABDDGORUY bodyguard
ABDDHINTW bandwidth
ABDDJMNOO odd-job man
ABDEEEGLL delegable
ABDEEELLR relabeled
ABDEEFHLR half-breed
ABDEEFILN definable
ABDEEFORR freeboard
ABDEEGGLR bedraggle
ABDEEGINR gaberdine
ABDEEGRRY greybeard
ABDEEGRSY sage Derby
ABDEEHINR Hebridean
ABDEEHRSW shewbread
ABDEEIILR diablerie
ABDEEILMS Ambleside
ABDEEILNR breadline
ABDEEILRS desirable
ABDEEILRV derivable, driveable
ABDEEILST side table
ABDEEILSV devisable
ABDEEILTT tide table
ABDEEINSS beadiness
ABDEEINTU butadiene
ABDEEITTU beatitude
ABDEEKLNT blanketed
ABDEELLNU unlabeled
ABDEELLPS speedball
ABDEELLRR barrelled
ABDEELLRV verballed
ABDEELLTY belatedly
ABDEELNOR banderole, bandoleer
ABDEELNPR prebendal
ABDEELNPS spendable
ABDEELNRU endurable
ABDEELNST steel band
ABDEELOUX double axe
ABDEELRSS beardless
ABDEEMNOU beau monde
ABDEEMNRT debarment
ABDEEMRSY Ember days
ABDEENOTY bayoneted
ABDEENQTU banqueted
ABDEENRRT bartender
ABDEENTTU debutante
ABDEEOPST speedboat
ABDEERRST redbreast
ABDEESTUY use-by date
ABDEFFGLU duffel bag
ABDEFINOS bona fides
ABDEFINRR firebrand
ABDEFORRT fretboard
ABDEGGGIN debagging
ABDEGGMRU Magdeburg
ABDEGHLRU Aldeburgh
ABDEGIIRR air bridge, brigadier
ABDEGILLM gimballed
ABDEGINRR debarring
ABDEGLLMO gambolled
ABDEGNSTU Bundestag
ABDEGRTUY budgetary
ABDEHIINT inhabited
ABDEHILNO hobnailed
ABDEHLNOS ash blonde
ABDEHLOOT blood-heat
ABDEHLOTW death blow
ABDEHNRSU husbander
ABDEIILNU inaudible
ABDEIILOZ diabolize
ABDEIKLNR drinkable
ABDEIKMRS disembark
ABDEIKNRS snake bird
ABDEIKNRW windbreak
ABDEILLOY Old Bailey
ABDEILMOR bromeliad
ABDEILNOR bandolier
ABDEILNRU unridable
ABDEILORT tidal bore
ABDEILORV olive drab
ABDEILRRY early bird
ABDEILRSY desirably
ABDEILRWY bridleway
ABDEINRSS rabidness
ABDEINSSU unbiassed
ABDEINSSW bawdiness
ABDEIORSW broadwise
ABDEIRRTW waterbird
ABDEJORTT objet d'art
ABDEKMRRU brake drum, drum brake
ABDEKNORW breakdown
ABDEKNOSY naked boys
ABDEKOORT trade book
ABDEKOSTY stake-body
ABDELLLSY syllabled
ABDELLMOU mouldable
ABDELMNOY baldmoney
ABDELNNSS blandness
ABDELNORU unlabored
ABDELOOPS paso doble
ABDELORUV boulevard
ABDEMNNOR Dobermann
ABDENOPPR bond paper
ABDENOPRR Paderborn
ABDENOPSU subpoena'd
ABDENORSS broadness
ABDENORST adsorbent
ABDENOSTU eastbound
ABDENRSTU Bundesrat
ABDENRSTY bystander
ABDEOORRV overboard
ABDFGLMOO Lamb of God
ABDFHLLOO half-blood
ABDFLLORU full board
ABDFNORRT Brantford
ABDFOOORT footboard
ABDFORRSU surfboard
ABDGIILNY abidingly
ABDGILNNR brandling
ABDGILOOX dialog box
ABDGINORS signboard
ABDGINOXY Boxing Day
ABDGINRRY brigandry
ABDGIRRSS grass bird
ABDGLNOOR longboard
ABDHIINNR hindbrain
ABDHIMRTY dithyramb
ABDHIOPRS shipboard
ABDHLNSUY husbandly
ABDHNRSUY husbandry
ABDIIILLN libidinal
ABDIILLRS billiards
ABDIILMOS diabolism
ABDIILNUY inaudibly
ABDIILOST diabolist
ABDIILSST disablist
ABDIIMRST tribadism
ABDILLMOR millboard
ABDILNNOT not a blind
ABDILNOOR Bardolino
ABDILRSSU disbursal
ABDIMNNOT badminton
ABDIMNOPU dumb piano
ABDIMPQSU damp squib
ABDIMRSSU absurdism
ABDINOWWY bay window
ABDINRSTW wristband
ABDIRSSTU absurdist
ABDIRSTUY absurdity

ABDKLNORW World Bank
ABDLMOOOR broadloom
ABDLOOPRY polar body
ABDMMNOSU ombudsman
ABDMNORTU Dumbarton
ABDMOOORR boardroom
ABDNOORSW snowboard
ABEEEEFRT beefeater
ABEEEERSZ sea breeze
ABEEEFKST beefsteak
ABEEEFLRR referable
ABEEEFLRZ freezable
ABEEEGGRT egg-beater
ABEEEGLLR relegable
ABEEEGLNR generable
ABEEEGLRU beleaguer
ABEEEGLRV bevel gear
ABEEEGLTV vegetable
ABEEEHLMT Mehetabel
ABEEEHLSW wheelbase
ABEEEKNRV even break
ABEEEKPRR barkeeper
ABEEELMPR permeable
ABEEELNRV venerable
ABEEELNRW renewable
ABEEELNSU unseeable
ABEEELRST steerable
ABEEELRSV severable
ABEEEMRST bee-master
ABEEERRTV vertebrae
ABEEERTUX exuberate
ABEEFFILN ineffable
ABEEFGLOR forgeable
ABEEFIKRR firebreak
ABEEFILNR inferable, refinable
ABEEFILRS bas-relief
ABEEFLORY Aberfoyle
ABEEFLRTU refutable
ABEEFLSSU self-abuse
ABEEGGILU big league
ABEEGHILW weighable
ABEEGHNOR habergeon
ABEEGILLR Gabrielle
ABEEGINRU aubergine
ABEEGKORR brokerage
ABEEGLLRU regulable
ABEEGLNPR pregnable
ABEEGLNPS bespangle
ABEEGLOPR bargepole, porbeagle
ABEEGLSSU guessable
ABEEGNOOS bean goose
ABEEGNORZ Bronze Age
ABEEGNRSU subgenera
ABEEGRSTU beet sugar, sugar beet
ABEEHHKSS baksheesh
ABEEHILMT Mehitabel
ABEEHILRT heritable
ABEEHILST Elisabeth
ABEEHILTT biathlete
ABEEHILTZ Elizabeth
ABEEHIMSV misbehave
ABEEHIMTW whitebeam
ABEEHINRT hibernate, inbreathe
ABEEHIRRT breathier
ABEEHKORS brake shoe
ABEEHKOSU bakehouse
ABEEHLLUW blue whale
ABEEHLMPS blaspheme
ABEEHLNOW whalebone
ABEEHLTTW wheat belt
ABEEHNORS horsebean
ABEEHORRS seborrhea
ABEEHORTU hereabout
ABEEHRVYY Hervey Bay
ABEEIINRT inebriate
ABEEIKLNR break-line
ABEEILLMR mirabelle
ABEEILMRS miserable
ABEEILMST estimable
ABEEILMTT timetable
ABEEILNQU inequable
ABEEILNRT Albertine
ABEEILNTW table wine
ABEEILQTU equitable
ABEEILRRW rewirable
ABEEILRST beastlier, bleariest
ABEEILRSV revisable
ABEEILRTV avertible, veritable
ABEEILRVV revivable
ABEEILRVZ verbalize
ABEEINRRT Braintree
ABEEINSST asbestine
ABEEIRRSS brasserie, brassiere
ABEEJLLNY jelly bean
ABEEJLNOY enjoyable
ABEEKLMOS smokeable
ABEEKLNNO ankle-bone
ABEEKLNSS bleakness
ABEELLLMS smellable
ABEELLLMT bell metal
ABEELLLPS spellable
ABEELLMRS small beer
ABEELLMSS blameless
ABEELLMTU blue metal, umbellate
ABEELLORS Rosabelle
ABEELLORT tolerable
ABEELLOVV evolvable
ABEELLSTU slate blue
ABEELMMOR memorable
ABEELMNRU numerable
ABEELMORV removable
ABEELMPTT temptable
ABEELMRSS assembler
ABEELMRSU resumable
ABEELMSSY Les Abymes
ABEELNNTU untenable
ABEELNRVY venerably
ABEELPRSU superable
ABEELPRTU reputable
ABEELRRTV vertebral
ABEELRTTU utterable
ABEELRTUW blue water
ABEEMMNTY embayment
ABEEMNPRU penumbrae
ABEEMORRT barometer
ABEEMRRSU embrasure
ABEENORTV Beaverton
ABEENORWY an eyebrow
ABEENQRTU banqueter
ABEENQTTU banquette
ABEENRRST barrenest
ABEENRRSY naseberry
ABEENRSSV braveness
ABEENRTUX exuberant
ABEEOPRRT reprobate
ABEEOPRSW power base
ABEEOSTUU beauteous
ABEEPRSTT bespatter
ABEFFILNY ineffably
ABEFGILNR frangible
ABEFHILST shiftable
ABEFIIMRT fimbriate
ABEFILLRT filtrable
ABEFILNSU infusable
ABEFILSTU bisulfate
ABEFILTUU beautiful
ABEFINORR forebrain
ABEFKLSTU basketful
ABEFKOORT footbrake
ABEFLLLUY balefully
ABEFLLNUY banefully
ABEFLLRWY warble fly
ABEFLLSTU stableful
ABEFLNOSW wolfsbane
ABEFOORST bear's foot
ABEFRTTTU butterfat
ABEGGINSS bagginess
ABEGGNOPS sponge bag
ABEGHHILT high table
ABEGHILRT rightable
ABEGHINRR harbinger
ABEGHINRT breathing
ABEGHMRRU hamburger
ABEGHRSSU sagebrush
ABEGIILLT litigable
ABEGIILMT mitigable
ABEGIILNT ignitable
ABEGIILRR irrigable
ABEGIINOR aborigine
ABEGILLLN labelling
ABEGILLOZ globalize
ABEGILNOR ignorable
ABEGILNRR barreling
ABEGILOTT toilet bag
ABEGIMRRS ambergris
ABEGINNNT benignant
ABEGINRSW sabrewing
ABEGJORTU objurgate
ABEGJSTUU subjugate
ABEGKRSTU grubstake
ABEGLLLSS bell-glass
ABEGLNORU lounge bar
ABEGLNRTU Altenburg
ABEGLRSSU bluegrass
ABEGMMMRU Brummagem
ABEGMNOOR boomerang
ABEGMNOSY moneybags

ABEGNOOTY geobotany
ABEGNOOVY bon voyage
ABEGORSTU subrogate
ABEHHOSTU bathhouse
ABEHIINNR Hibernian
ABEHIITTW whitebait
ABEHIKLNT thinkable
ABEHILMOP amphibole
ABEHILMRS herbalism
ABEHILORS abolisher
ABEHILPPS shippable
ABEHILRST herbalist
ABEHILRTY breathily, heritably
ABEHILSST establish
ABEHIMRRU herbarium
ABEHINOOP neophobia
ABEHINRTT tithe barn
ABEHIOPRU euphorbia
ABEHIORUV behaviour
ABEHIPRRS herb Paris
ABEHIRRTT birth rate
ABEHLLOST blast-hole
ABEHLMPSY blasphemy
ABEHLNOOR honorable
ABEHLOOST shootable
ABEHLOPRY hyperbola
ABEHLORST sloth bear
ABEHLORTT betrothal
ABEHLORTW bowler-hat, throwable
ABEHNORRT abhorrent
ABEHNRRTU heartburn
ABEHNRSSS brashness
ABEHNRSTU sunbather
ABEHNRSUY Neyshabur
ABEHOOSTU boathouse, houseboat
ABEHQRSUU harquebus
ABEIIKLRT trail bike
ABEIILLLR illiberal
ABEIILLMT limitable
ABEIILMOR airmobile
ABEIILNOZ ionizable
ABEIILRRT irritable
ABEIILRTV vibratile
ABEIILSTV visitable
ABEIILSTZ stabilize
ABEIINNPT bipinnate
ABEIINRST brainiest
ABEIIPRTT bipartite
ABEIIRSSV vibrissae
ABEIIRTVV vibrative
ABEIKLLNU unlikable
ABEIKLRST strikable
ABEIKNNRT interbank
ABEIKNORW wake-robin
ABEIKSTUZ Ekibastuz
ABEILLLRY liberally
ABEILLNUV unlivable
ABEILLPSU plausible
ABEILLSSU subsellia
ABEILLSTY bestially
ABEILLSYZ syllabize
ABEILMMOV immovable
ABEILMMSW swimmable
ABEILMMTU immutable
ABEILMNSS balminess
ABEILMORT Baltimore
ABEILMPTU imputable
ABEILMRSV verbalism
ABEILMRSY miserably
ABEILMSTU sublimate
ABEILMSTY estimably
ABEILNPRT printable
ABEILNPSU subalpine
ABEILNRSS brainless
ABEILNRSU insurable
ABEILOPTV pivotable
ABEILOQSU obsequial
ABEILORRT liberator
ABEILORTU Labourite
ABEILQTUY equitably
ABEILRRYZ bizarrely
ABEILRSTV verbalist
ABEILRTUZ brutalize
ABEILRTVY veritably
ABEILSTTW twistable
ABEILSUVY abusively
ABEIMMNRT timberman
ABEIMNRSS barminess
ABEIMNRST brainstem, tribesman
ABEIMNRSU submarine
ABEINNRST bannister
ABEINNSTT abstinent
ABEINNTYZ Byzantine
ABEINOSTT obstinate
ABEINPRST breast-pin
ABEINRSTW brawniest
ABEINRTTU tribunate, tube train, turbinate
ABEINSSTT battiness
ABEIOPRTV probative
ABEIORRTV riverboat
ABEIRRRST barrister
ABEIRRSST arbitress
ABEIRSSST brassiest
ABEIRTTTU attribute
ABEJLNOYY enjoyably
ABEJORSST Job's tears
ABEKKMOOR bookmaker
ABEKKNRSU skunk-bear
ABEKLLMOS smoke-ball
ABEKLNNSS blankness
ABEKLOOPT bookplate
ABEKLOOUV book value
ABEKLORTW work table
ABEKMNPRS sperm bank
ABEKMOORT bootmaker
ABEKMPPRU pump-brake
ABELLMMNO lemon balm
ABELLMNTY lambently
ABELLMORS small-bore
ABELLMOTY Ballymote
ABELLNOUV unlovable
ABELLORTY tolerably
ABELLORUY royal blue
ABELLOSWY Boyle's law
ABELMMNRU lumberman
ABELMMORY memorably
ABELMNORY embryonal
ABELMNOTU mountable
ABELMNOUV unmovable
ABELMNPRU penumbral
ABELMNRUY numerably
ABELMNSTU submental
ABELMOORT motorable
ABELMORWY barleymow
ABELMOSST mesoblast
ABELNNORV non-verbal
ABELNNTUU untunable
ABELNNTUY untenably
ABELNORSV slave-born
ABELNOSUX Saxon blue
ABELNOSYZ lazybones
ABELNRSTU subaltern, unstabler
ABELNRTTU turntable
ABELOOPPS opposable
ABELOORTT Attleboro
ABELOPPST stoppable
ABELORTTX rattlebox
ABELOSTTY stylobate
ABELPRSUU pursuable
ABELPRTUY reputably
ABELRSTTU trustable
ABELRSUYY Aylesbury
ABEMNORSW Sam Browne
ABEMNPRSU penumbras
ABEMOOPRR broomrape
ABEMORRTU arboretum
ABEMORRTY barometry
ABEMRSSTU submaster
ABENNSTTU subtenant
ABENOPRRS bar person
ABENORSTV observant
ABEOOPRTW powerboat
ABEOORRSU arboreous
ABEOPRRSY soapberry
ABEPRRRSY raspberry
ABEPRSSSY passers-by
ABERRTUWY Waterbury
ABERSSTTU substrate
ABERTTTUW water-butt
ABFGGHILT flight bag
ABFHLLSUY bashfully
ABFHLNRSU flash burn
ABFIILLRR fibrillar
ABFILLSYY syllabify
ABFILMSUY subfamily
ABGGIKNPY piggy bank
ABGGILMNO gamboling
ABGGLOORY garbology
ABGGNTTUY butty-gang
ABGHIKNRT right bank
ABGHIKORU Khouribga
ABGHINORR abhorring
ABGHINWZZ whizz-bang
ABGHIOPRY biography
ABGHQSSUU squash bug
ABGIILLNU bilingual
ABGIIMTUY ambiguity
ABGILLNOT balloting

ABGILLNYZ blazingly
ABGILLOTY billy goat
ABGILNOSX signal box
ABGILOORT obligator
ABGIMOSUU ambiguous
ABGINNNNU unbanning
ABGINNRRU unbarring
ABGINOPSV bog spavin
ABGINOSTW swingboat
ABGLMNOOS boomslang
ABGLRSSUY ruby glass
ABHHILOTT batholith
ABHHIRRSU hairbrush
ABHIKLLSW hawksbill
ABHIKMRRT birthmark
ABHILMNTU thumbnail
ABHILNRSU nail brush
ABHILNRTY labyrinth
ABHIOPSST ship's boat
ABHLOPSTY hypoblast
ABHLOSSTT shot-blast
ABHMNRTUY urban myth
ABHNORRUU unharbour
ABIIILLTY liability
ABIIILNTY inability
ABIIILTVY viability
ABIILLNRT brilliant
ABIILMNNO binominal
ABIILMRST tribalism
ABIILNOOT abolition
ABIILNOOV boliviano
ABIILNORT libration
ABIILNORY nobiliary
ABIILRRTY irritably
ABIILRSTT tribalist
ABIILSTTY stability
ABIILSTUY suability, usability
ABIIMOSTU ambitious
ABIINOOTV obviation
ABIINORTV vibration
ABIKLOSTY Bialystok
ABILLNOPT ballpoint
ABILLOPRX pillar box
ABILLORRZ razorbill
ABILLPSUY plausibly
ABILMMOVY immovably
ABILMMTUY immutably
ABILMOORS ribosomal
ABILMORSU labourism
ABILMRSTU brutalism
ABILNOPSS slop basin
ABILNRTVY vibrantly
ABILOORSU laborious
ABILRSSUY Salisbury
ABILRSTTU brutalist
ABILRSTUY salubrity
ABILRTTUY brutality
ABIMNORTU tambourin
ABIMNTUYZ Byzantium
ABIMPRTUU bumiputra
ABINNOTVV bon vivant
ABINOOPRT probation
ABINOPSTU subtopian
ABIORRSUV arbovirus
ABIORRTVY vibratory
ABIPRSTTY baptistry
ABIRRTTUY tributary
ABKLLOOST bookstall
ABKLMOOPS psalm-book
ABKOQSUWX squawk-box
ABLLLOOST stoolball
ABLLMOOSW lambswool
ABLMNORSU subnormal
ABLNOTUYY buoyantly
ABLNRSUUY sublunary
ABLNRTUUW bur walnut
ABMNORRST barnstorm
ABMOOORTT motor boat
ABMPRSTTU bump-start
ABNORTTUU about-turn, turnabout
ABOOPRSTT bootstrap
ABORSSSTW straw boss
ABRRSSTTU starburst
ABRRSTTUW bratwurst
ACCCCEHIT cachectic
ACCCDEEIN accidence
ACCCDILOY cacodylic
ACCCEGLOY coccygeal
ACCCEHITT cathectic
ACCCEHKOT coat check
ACCCEIIRT cicatrice
ACCCEILLO calcicole
ACCCEIOPT copacetic
ACCCHKOOR cockroach
ACCCHOPRT catch crop
ACCCHOPST Scotch cap
ACCCIILLY alicyclic
ACCCIILMT climactic
ACCCIIOPR capriccio
ACCCNOPUY occupancy
ACCDDEEEN decadence
ACCDDEILS discalced
ACCDDIORS disaccord
ACCDEEHIK chickadee
ACCDEEIST desiccate
ACCDEELLN cancelled
ACCDEFILS fascicled
ACCDEFILY decalcify
ACCDEGLNO clog dance
ACCDEHIKR deckchair
ACCDEHILR childcare
ACCDEHKOT cocked hat
ACCDEHLNO Chalcedon
ACCDEHPTU Cape Dutch
ACCDEIILN Icelandic
ACCDEIILO oleic acid
ACCDEIILT dialectic
ACCDEILNR calendric
ACCDEINOT anecdotic
ACCDEINST desiccant
ACCDEIORW cowardice
ACCDEKOSS cassocked
ACCDELMOR cold cream
ACCDELSSU culs-de-sac
ACCDEMNOO cacodemon
ACCDEMORR camcorder
ACCDEMORY democracy
ACCDENPSU dunce's cap
ACCDEORRS scorecard
ACCDEORSW sacred cow
ACCDFIILO folic acid
ACCDFILLY flaccidly
ACCDGINOR according
ACCDHHRUY archduchy
ACCDHIIOR radicchio
ACCDHINOR chancroid
ACCDHNPRU punchcard
ACCDHOOOW coachwood
ACCDHOPRT patch cord
ACCDHORTW catchword
ACCDIIIRT diacritic
ACCDIILST cladistic
ACCDIIOPT apodictic
ACCDIKNOR draincock
ACCDILLOY cycloidal
ACCDINOOR accordion
ACCDKNORW crackdown
ACCDKNORY rock candy
ACCDNOORT concordat
ACCDORRTU court card
ACCEEHITY haecceity
ACCEEHITZ catechize
ACCEEHKMT checkmate
ACCEEHNPR perchance
ACCEEHOST cacoethes
ACCEEILLS ecclesial
ACCEEIQSU acquiesce
ACCEEIRRR ricercare
ACCEEIRTV accretive
ACCEEKLOT cockateel
ACCEELLNR canceller
ACCEELLOR clearcole
ACCEELNOR concealer
ACCEELNOV covalence
ACCEELPST spectacle
ACCEENRRY recreancy
ACCEENRSU recusance
ACCEEOSTU cetaceous
ACCEFFHNO off chance
ACCEFGILU calcifuge
ACCEFHLOT facecloth
ACCEFIIRS sacrifice
ACCEFILSU fascicule
ACCEFNORS Francesco
ACCEGILNN canceling
ACCEGIORT categoric
ACCEHIIMS ischaemic
ACCEHIKNR rain check
ACCEHILNO cochineal
ACCEHILNT catchline, technical
ACCEHILOR choleraic
ACCEHIMNS mechanics, mischance
ACCEHIMST catechism, schematic
ACCEHINRY chicanery
ACCEHINST chanciest
ACCEHIRTT architect
ACCEHIRVZ czarevich
ACCEHISTT catchiest, catechist
ACCEHLNOR chloracne

ACCEHLOOT	chocolate
ACCEHMNTT	catchment
ACCEHORRT	torch race
ACCEHORTU	cartouche
ACCEHORTY	theocracy
ACCEHRRST	scratcher
ACCEIILNO	coecilian
ACCEIIMNT	cinematic
ACCEIINRT	circinate
ACCEIIPRT	accipiter
ACCEIIRTZ	cicatrize
ACCEIISTV	siccative
ACCEIKKLP	place-kick
ACCEIKLOT	cockatiel
ACCEIKRSW	wisecrack
ACCEILMPT	eclamptic
ACCEILNRT	centrical
ACCEILNST	lac insect
ACCEILNTU	inculcate
ACCEILOPR	precocial
ACCEILPST	sceptical
ACCEILRTU	circulate
ACCEIMOSU	micaceous
ACCEINORT	accretion, anorectic
ACCEINOSS	accession
ACCEINSTU	encaustic, succinate
ACCEIORTT	corticate
ACCEIPSTY	cityscape
ACCEJKOPY	jockey cap
ACCEJKRSW	screw-jack
ACCEKNORR	corncrake
ACCELLOOT	collocate
ACCELMNSY	cyclamens
ACCELNOPY	Cyclopean
ACCELNOVY	concavely, covalency
ACCELRSSU	Las Cruces
ACCENNOSS	non-access
ACCENNOST	Constance
ACCENORSU	cancerous
ACCENRSUY	recusancy
ACCEORRSW	scarecrow
ACCEORSSY	accessory
ACCEORSTU	coruscate
ACCFFHHIN	chaffinch
ACCFIILOR	calorific
ACCFIISST	fascistic
ACCFIMORS	sacciform
ACCFINNOU	Confucian
ACCFINORS	Francisco
ACCFKOORT	frock coat
ACCGHHNNU	Changchun
ACCGHLNOO	cacholong
ACCGIKLNR	crackling
ACCGIKMRY	gimcracky
ACCGINSUU	caucusing
ACCGLORTU	cargo cult
ACCHHMNRU	churchman
ACCHIILRV	chivalric
ACCHILLOO	alcoholic
ACCHILLOT	laccolith
ACCHILOPS	slip-coach
ACCHILORT	Holarctic
ACCHILPSY	psychical
ACCHIMNOR	monarchic
ACCHIMOPR	camphoric
ACCHIMORT	chromatic
ACCHIMOST	stomachic
ACCHIRTTY	trachytic
ACCHKLMOT	matchlock
ACCHKLOST	sackcloth
ACCHKOOOP	cock-a-hoop
ACCHKOORW	coachwork
ACCHLOORT	ochlocrat
ACCHLOOSW	slowcoach
ACCHLOOTY	chocolaty
ACCHMNOST	Scotchman
ACCHNOOPY	cacophony
ACCHORRSU	churrasco
ACCHOSSTU	succotash
ACCIIILNN	clinician
ACCIILLVY	civically
ACCIILNOR	conciliar
ACCIILOPT	occipital
ACCIILTVY	acclivity
ACCIIMOPT	apomictic
ACCIINOOZ	Cainozoic
ACCIINRTY	intricacy
ACCIIOPST	pasticcio
ACCIISSTU	casuistic
ACCILLMOY	comically
ACCILLNOY	conically
ACCILLNYY	cynically
ACCILLRUY	crucially
ACCILNOPY	Cyclopian
ACCILORVY	acyclovir
ACCILRRUU	curricula
ACCILRTUU	cuticular
ACCIMORTY	timocracy
ACCINOPRR	Capricorn
ACCINOTVY	concavity
ACCINSTTY	syntactic
ACCIOPRTT	catoptric
ACCLLOSUU	calculous
ACCLMOPTY	compactly
ACCLRSSUU	succursal
ACCMMOORS	macrocosm
ACCMNOORY	monocracy
ACCMNOTUY	contumacy
ACCMOOPRT	compactor
ACCNNOOTU	no-account
ACCNNOSTY	constancy
ACDDEEEIT	dedicatee
ACDDEEMNO	code-named
ACDDEGNOO	dodecagon
ACDDEHILY	aldehydic
ACDDEHNRU	dude ranch
ACDDEIITV	addictive
ACDDEINRX	card index
ACDDEIORT	dedicator
ACDDEKOST	deadstock
ACDDEOORW	cedarwood
ACDDFILSY	caddis-fly
ACDDHHNSU	dachshund
ACDDHILSY	caddishly
ACDDIILRU	Druidical
ACDDIINOT	addiction
ACDDIIORT	idiot card
ACDDINOTU	adduction
ACDDLLNOU	cloud-land
ACDDLNOSU	sand cloud
ACDDNOORR	donor card
ACDDNORSU	sound card
ACDEEEHIP	headpiece
ACDEEEHNR	adherence
ACDEEEMRT	decameter, decametre
ACDEEEPPS	deep space
ACDEEEPRT	deprecate
ACDEEERST	desecrate
ACDEEERTU	re-educate
ACDEEFFLS	self-faced
ACDEEFHWY	whey-faced
ACDEEFIRR	Frederica
ACDEEFNOP	open-faced
ACDEEFNTU	fecundate
ACDEEGLOU	Decalogue
ACDEEGNRR	green card
ACDEEHIOV	head voice
ACDEEHIPS	Cheapside
ACDEEHKNY	hackneyed
ACDEEHLLT	death cell
ACDEEHLNN	channeled
ACDEEHLPT	chapleted
ACDEEHNRU	unreached
ACDEEHPSY	speech day
ACDEEHRRT	chartered
ACDEEHRTT	ratcheted
ACDEEIINP	epicedian
ACDEEIJTV	adjective
ACDEEILMR	declaimer
ACDEEILNN	celandine, decennial
ACDEEILNR	Icelander
ACDEEILNU	Euclidean
ACDEEILRT	decaliter, decalitre
ACDEEILTU	elucidate
ACDEEILTY	acetylide
ACDEEIMNP	impedance
ACDEEINOS	Oceanides, Oceanside
ACDEEIOPR	adipocere
ACDEEIPRT	predicate
ACDEEIRRT	traceried
ACDEEITUV	educative
ACDEEITVV	advective
ACDEELLMR	marcelled
ACDEELLNV	Cleveland
ACDEELLOT	decollate, ocellated
ACDEELLPR	parcelled
ACDEELLST	steel-clad
ACDEELNRU	uncleared
ACDEELNTT	tentacled
ACDEELSTY	decastyle
ACDEELTTU	Claudette
ACDEEMMUV	vade-mecum
ACDEENNRU	endurance
ACDEENOSS	deaconess
ACDEENRTU	uncreated
ACDEENRTY	day centre
ACDEEOPRR	crop-eared

ACDEEPRRT red carpet
ACDEESSTU decussate
ACDEFFMOR coffer-dam
ACDEFGLNO long-faced
ACDEFILLO coalfield
ACDEFILOR coal-fired
ACDEFINNU unfancied
ACDEFKLNO folk dance
ACDEFLMOR cold frame
ACDEFLNOR force-land, land force
ACDEFMNOO moon-faced
ACDEFORSS cross-fade
ACDEGGIMO demagogic
ACDEGGIOP pedagogic
ACDEGHIRS discharge
ACDEGHNNU unchanged
ACDEGHNRU uncharged
ACDEGIILR regicidal
ACDEGILNO genocidal
ACDEGIRRT cartridge
ACDEGLLRU guard cell
ACDEGLOOS gas-cooled
ACDEGNNOU undecagon
ACDEHHIKT thickhead
ACDEHHNTU unhatched
ACDEHHORX hexachord
ACDEHIINS side chain
ACDEHILMN name-child
ACDEHINNR hindrance
ACDEHINRT theandric
ACDEHIOSU acid house
ACDEHIPRS Sephardic
ACDEHIPRT dirt cheap
ACDEHIPST cadetship
ACDEHIRSV crash-dive
ACDEHKMOP choke-damp
ACDEHKOST headstock
ACDEHKPST sketch pad
ACDEHLNOT decathlon
ACDEHLNRY chandlery
ACDEHLOOR choral ode
ACDEHLRSU schedular
ACDEHMNTU unmatched
ACDEHMPRY pachyderm
ACDEHNOPR cardphone, phonecard
ACDEHNOTU headcount
ACDEHNRTU uncharted
ACDEHNRUY hue and cry
ACDEHNSTU unscathed
ACDEHNTUW unwatched
ACDEHORRV hardcover
ACDEHORSS cross-head
ACDEIIINT dietician
ACDEIILMN adminicle, medicinal
ACDEIILNO lidocaine
ACDEIILNT identical
ACDEIILNX indexical
ACDEIILRV larvicide, veridical
ACDEIILST deistical
ACDEIIMMY immediacy
ACDEIIMNO Nicomedia
ACDEIIMRT diametric, matricide
ACDEIINTV vindicate
ACDEIIOPR aperiodic
ACDEIIPRR parricide
ACDEIIPRT patricide
ACDEIKMOS mosaicked
ACDEIKRST sidetrack
ACDEIKTTY ticket-day
ACDEILLMY decimally, medically
ACDEILLNT candlelit
ACDEILMNU unclaimed
ACDEILOOR air-cooled
ACDEILOST dislocate
ACDEILPRU pedicular
ACDEILPTU duplicate
ACDEILRSS laserdisc
ACDEILTUV victualed
ACDEIMNNO dominance
ACDEIMNNT mendicant
ACDEIMNOP compendia
ACDEIMNSU muscadine
ACDEIMNTY mendacity
ACDEIMORT decimator
ACDEIMOSY Samoyedic
ACDEINNOR ordinance
ACDEINORR coriander
ACDEINORT redaction
ACDEINOTU education
ACDEINOTV advection
ACDEINPRT predicant
ACDEINSTY asyndetic, syndicate
ACDEIPRSW swipe card
ACDEIPRTY predacity
ACDEIQSUV vice squad
ACDEIQTTU acquitted
ACDEIRTTX direct tax
ACDEIRUVY ayurvedic
ACDEKNOPU pound cake
ACDEKNRTU untracked
ACDEKOPTU packed out
ACDEKRSSU duck's arse
ACDELLOPS scalloped
ACDELLORR corralled
ACDELLOSU calloused
ACDELMORY comradely
ACDELNNOO colonnade
ACDELNOOW lancewood
ACDELNOSW downscale
ACDELNRUY underclay
ACDELOSTW cold sweat
ACDELPRSY clepsydra
ACDEMMNOR commander
ACDEMOORT motorcade
ACDEMOPRS compadres
ACDENNRST transcend
ACDENORST Doncaster, transcode
ACDENORSY secondary
ACDENORTU undercoat
ACDENRRSU unscarred
ACDENRRTU undercart
ACDENRSTU transduce
ACDEOORRT decorator
ACDEOORTT doctorate
ACDEORRST store card
ACDEORRSW score draw
ACDEORRTT detractor
ACDEORSST coat dress, dress coat
ACDEORSUU rudaceous
ACDESSTUY case study
ACDFHINOO food chain
ACDFIIRUY fiduciary
ACDFINNOT confidant
ACDFNTTUY candytuft
ACDFOORTW woodcraft
ACDGHIIPR digraphic
ACDGHNNOU Dongchuan
ACDGIINNR dining car
ACDGIIRST digastric
ACDGIMOST dogmatics
ACDGIOOPR Podgorica
ACDGKLOSS dock-glass
ACDGLLOOR dog collar
ACDGMNORU conga drum
ACDHIILMO homicidal
ACDHIKORW chowkidar
ACDHIKPRT pitch-dark
ACDHILRSY chrysalid
ACDHILRUY hydraulic
ACDHILSTT last ditch
ACDHIMORT chromatid
ACDHINORY diachrony
ACDHIOPRS rhapsodic
ACDHIPSSY dysphasic
ACDHLOOSY day school
ACDHMOOTW doomwatch, matchwood
ACDHORTWW watchword
ACDIIIMOT idiomatic
ACDIIIRST diaristic
ACDIIJLRU juridical
ACDIIJMOT comitadji
ACDIIJRUY judiciary
ACDIILMNO dominical
ACDIILNOR crinoidal
ACDIILOST diastolic
ACDIILPTY placidity
ACDIILSTU dualistic
ACDIIMNNO Dominican
ACDIIMPRY pyramidic
ACDIINORS radionics
ACDIINORT indicator
ACDIINOSY Dionysiac
ACDIINOTT dictation
ACDIINRTY rancidity
ACDIIPRTY Rapid City
ACDIKKLRY Kirkcaldy
ACDIKKNST kickstand
ACDIKLLPR pack drill
ACDIKNQSU quicksand
ACDIKRRTT dirt track
ACDIKRSTY yardstick
ACDILLLOO colloidal
ACDILLOOR coralloid
ACDILLORY cordially
ACDILMOPS psalmodic

ACDILMOPY diplomacy
ACDILNORT doctrinal
ACDILNORU rain cloud
ACDILNOSY synodical
ACDILOORT doctorial
ACDILOPRS dropsical
ACDILOSTU custodial
ACDILOSUU acidulous
ACDILOTUV oviductal
ACDILRTTY tridactyl
ACDIMOPSS spasmodic
ACDINNOOT anticodon
ACDINOSTU custodian
ACDIRSTWY citywards
ACDJOORTU coadjutor
ACDKLORTU truckload
ACDKMNNOO monadnock
ACDKNOSST sandstock
ACDKORSTY stockyard
ACDLMNOPW clampdown
ACDLNSTYY syndactyl
ACDLORSTT cold start
ACDMMNORU communard
ACDMOOPRR comprador
ACDMOOSUV muscovado
ACDMPRRTU trump card
ACDOORRSS crossroad
ACDOORSTW saw-doctor
ACDORRTUY courtyard
ACEEEFIRS ceasefire
ACEEEFLNR freelance
ACEEEGNNV vengeance
ACEEEHIPT petechiae
ACEEEHIRV echeveria
ACEEEILMP piecemeal
ACEEEIMPT peacetime
ACEEEIPPP peace pipe
ACEEEIPRT piece-rate
ACEEEKNQU queen cake
ACEEEKRRT racketeer
ACEEELNOP Paleocene
ACEEELNRT crenelate
ACEEELNRV relevance
ACEEELNTU enucleate
ACEEELNTY acetylene
ACEEELPSV cap sleeve
ACEEELSSS ceaseless
ACEEEMNNR remanence
ACEEEMNPR permeance
ACEEENPPT appetence
ACEEENRSV severance
ACEEFFHRR chafferer
ACEEFFITV affective
ACEEFFLNU affluence
ACEEFFLTU effectual
ACEEFFNRY fancy-free
ACEEFHITW whiteface
ACEEFHSTT fact sheet
ACEEFIKNS case knife
ACEEFILNR rail fence
ACEEFILPR fireplace
ACEEFINNR refinance
ACEEFINRT interface
ACEEFIRSS fricassee
ACEEFKOPR poker-face

ACEEFLNRS scale-fern
ACEEFLORR coral reef
ACEEFLOTV volte-face
ACEEFLRRX reflex arc
ACEEFMORT forcemeat
ACEEFNPRR crape fern
ACEEFRRSU resurface
ACEEGHIOR heroic age
ACEEGHIRU gaucherie
ACEEGHLLN challenge
ACEEGHNRX exchanger
ACEEGHNSX sex change
ACEEGHRRR recharger
ACEEGILNS Cingalese
ACEEGILNV evangelic
ACEEGILRS sacrilege
ACEEGILRV viceregal
ACEEGINRV grievance
ACEEGIRRV caregiver
ACEEGIRTT cigarette
ACEEGKRWY greywacke
ACEEGLLOU colleague
ACEEGLNRT rectangle
ACEEGLRSS graceless
ACEEGMNUY gynaeceum
ACEEGNORT grace note
ACEEGNORU encourage
ACEEGNRSV scavenger
ACEEGNRSY sergeancy
ACEEGNSSY cageyness
ACEEGOOPR cooperage
ACEEGRRSW screw gear
ACEEGRTTU curettage
ACEEHHORT each other
ACEEHHTUX Hexateuch
ACEEHIIPR hairpiece
ACEEHILMZ alchemize
ACEEHILPT petechial
ACEEHILRT heretical
ACEEHILRV chevalier
ACEEHIMNZ mechanize
ACEEHINRT Catherine
ACEEHINST hesitance
ACEEHIPRR preachier
ACEEHIPST peachiest
ACEEHISTT aesthetic
ACEEHKLRW rack-wheel
ACEEHLMNO chameleon
ACEEHLMOO haemocoel
ACEEHLNRU Herculean
ACEEHLNSS seneschal
ACEEHLORT trochleae
ACEEHLRTW cartwheel
ACEEHLRTY teacherly
ACEEHMMRT Machmeter
ACEEHMNRY arch-enemy
ACEEHMRSU charmeuse
ACEEHNNRT enchanter
ACEEHNOPR chaperone
ACEEHNPSS cheapness
ACEEHNPTY pachytene
ACEEHNRST chastener
ACEEHNRTT entrechat
ACEEHNSTU chanteuse

ACEEHORRS horse race, racehorse
ACEEHORRV overreach
ACEEHPRTY archetype
ACEEHRRRT charterer
ACEEHRRTT chatterer
ACEEHRRTY treachery
ACEEIILPT tailpiece
ACEEIKLMU leukaemic
ACEEIKLSV sick leave
ACEEIKRST creakiest, ice-skater
ACEEILLNR cleanlier
ACEEILLST celestial
ACEEILMNS mescaline
ACEEILMNT Clementia
ACEEILMRR reclaimer
ACEEILMRT Carmelite
ACEEILMST timescale
ACEEILNOR Coleraine
ACEEILNRT interlace, lacertine, reclinate
ACEEILNST Celestina
ACEEILPRS periclase
ACEEILPRT replicate
ACEEILPTX explicate
ACEEILRTZ cartelize
ACEEIMMNN immanence
ACEEIMMNT mincemeat
ACEEIMMRT metameric
ACEEIMNPR mepacrine
ACEEIMNSX exciseman
ACEEIMPST space-time
ACEEIMRRS careerism
ACEEIMRST creamiest
ACEEIMRTT metricate
ACEEIMRVW crime wave
ACEEINNRT nectarine
ACEEINNTU enunciate
ACEEINPRU Epicurean
ACEEINPTT pectinate
ACEEIORTX excoriate
ACEEIOTVV evocative
ACEEIPPRR rice-paper
ACEEIPRTT crepitate
ACEEIPRTV precative
ACEEIQRRU reacquire
ACEEIRRST careerist
ACEEIRSVV vice versa
ACEEIRTTX extricate
ACEEIRTUZ cauterize
ACEEISSTZ ecstasize
ACEEKLMRS mackerels
ACEEKORST East Coker
ACEELLLTU cellulate
ACEELLORT electoral
ACEELLPSS placeless
ACEELLSSS scaleless
ACEELMNPT placement
ACEELMOOT coelomate
ACEELMOPS someplace
ACEELMORT latecomer
ACEELNNRU cannelure
ACEELNNSS cleanness

ACEELNORT tolerance
ACEELNPTU petulance
ACEELNRSS clearness
ACEELNRTU calenture
ACEELNRTW law centre
ACEELNRVY relevancy
ACEELOOSU oleaceous
ACEELOPRT percolate
ACEELORRT correlate
ACEELORSS casserole
ACEELORSW lower case
ACEELORTU urceolate
ACEELPSTU speculate
ACEELPTUX exculpate
ACEELQRRU lacquerer
ACEELRSST traceless
ACEELRTUY electuary
ACEELSSSU causeless, sauceless
ACEEMNNTT enactment
ACEEMNOYZ coenzyme A
ACEEMNRRY mercenary
ACEEMOVZZ mezza voce
ACEENNOPR can-opener
ACEENNORS resonance
ACEENNOST Cantonese
ACEENNRST renascent
ACEENNRTY centenary
ACEENPPTY appetency
ACEENPRRT carpenter
ACEENPTTX expectant
ACEENRRTU crenature
ACEENRSSY necessary
ACEENRTTU utterance
ACEENSSTU acuteness
ACEENSSTX exactness
ACEENTTUX executant
ACEEOOPRT cooperate
ACEEOPRRT procreate
ACEEORRTT rectorate
ACEEORRTV overreact
ACEEORTUY eucaryote
ACEEOSSTU setaceous
ACEEPPRSU upper case
ACEEPRRTU recapture
ACEERRSTT scatterer, streetcar
ACEERRSTY secretary
ACEERRTUV recurvate
ACEERRTUW water cure
ACEERSSTU secateurs
ACEFFGINT affecting
ACEFFHRUU chauffeur
ACEFFIIOT officiate
ACEFFINOT affection
ACEFFIORW War Office
ACEFFMPRU cream puff
ACEFFNNUY funny-face
ACEFFOSTU suffocate
ACEFGHLNU changeful
ACEFGLNOR gerfalcon
ACEFHIINT chieftain
ACEFHINRS franchise
ACEFHIPRY preachify
ACEFHIRTW watchfire
ACEFHMNNR Frenchman
ACEFHOSUV vouchsafe
ACEFIILMS facsimile
ACEFIILRR clarifier
ACEFIINNR financier
ACEFIIOPR opacifier
ACEFIIRRS scarifier
ACEFIIRRT artificer
ACEFIIRTV fricative
ACEFIITTV factitive
ACEFIJKKN jackknife
ACEFIKRTU fruit cake
ACEFILLPR filler cap
ACEFILOTV olfactive
ACEFINNSS fanciness
ACEFINORT fornicate
ACEFINTTV ventifact
ACEFIORTZ factorize
ACEFIOSTU facetious
ACEFIRSTT craftiest
ACEFKLNOR cornflake
ACEFKORST task force
ACEFLLLSU full-scale
ACEFLLMRU full-cream
ACEFLLRUY carefully
ACEFLNORR conferral
ACEFLPTUU teacupful
ACEFLRSUU saucerful
ACEFLTTUU fluctuate
ACEFOOPRS roofscape
ACEFORRRT refractor
ACEFOSTUU tufaceous
ACEGGIRRS scraggier
ACEGGIRST craggiest
ACEGHHOPR echograph
ACEGHILNO halogenic, Liaocheng
ACEGHILRT lethargic
ACEGHIMPR graphemic
ACEGHIRST Reichstag
ACEGHLOOS school age
ACEGHMNOS cheongsam
ACEGHMORT hectogram
ACEGHOPTY phagocyte
ACEGHRRSU surcharge
ACEGIILLS silica gel
ACEGIILLZ Gallicize
ACEGIILNV vigilance
ACEGIILNZ Anglicize
ACEGIIMNT enigmatic
ACEGIINNT antigenic
ACEGIIRRT geriatric
ACEGIJKNT jacketing
ACEGIKNRT racketing
ACEGIKPRR ragpicker
ACEGIKRST gearstick
ACEGILLLO collegial
ACEGILLNO collegian
ACEGILLOR allegoric
ACEGILLOT colligate
ACEGILNNO congenial
ACEGILNOR Cerignola, Nagercoil
ACEGILNPR parceling
ACEGILNRU neuralgic
ACEGILNRW clearwing
ACEGILNSS cassingle
ACEGILRTU curtilage, graticule
ACEGIMMRS scrimmage
ACEGIMMST smegmatic
ACEGIMNOT geomantic
ACEGIMNRT centigram
ACEGIMNTU mutagenic
ACEGIMTUZ zeugmatic
ACEGINNOP poignance
ACEGINNOR ignorance
ACEGINNSU unceasing
ACEGINPPR recapping
ACEGINPRT carpeting
ACEGINPRY panegyric
ACEGIOPRR paregoric
ACEGIRSTT strategic
ACEGJNOTU conjugate
ACEGLMNRY clergyman
ACEGLNNPY plangency
ACEGLNOTY cognately
ACEGMMNOO commonage
ACEGMMRSU scrummage
ACEGNNOTT cotangent
ACEGNNPRY pregnancy
ACEGORRTU corrugate
ACEHHHINO Hachinohe
ACEHHIRRY hierarchy
ACEHHLWYZ wych hazel
ACEHHMNTT hatchment
ACEHHMOTY theomachy
ACEHHOOTT toothache
ACEHHPRTY heptarchy
ACEHIILTU halieutic
ACEHIINPP epiphanic
ACEHIINRT trichinae
ACEHIISTT atheistic
ACEHIKLST chalkiest
ACEHIKORT artichoke
ACEHIKRST heartsick
ACEHILLLY helically
ACEHILLTY ethically
ACEHILMMO chamomile
ACEHILMST alchemist
ACEHILNNO chelonian
ACEHILNOT chelation
ACEHILNTU unethical
ACEHILNTY thylacine
ACEHILOOT coolie hat
ACEHILORR Charleroi
ACEHILOTW white coal
ACEHILPRS spherical
ACEHILRUV vehicular
ACEHILSTT athletics
ACEHIMMNS mechanism
ACEHIMNRY machinery
ACEHIMNST mechanist
ACEHIMRTU rheumatic
ACEHINNRY Hercynian
ACEHINORT anchorite
ACEHINPRU paunchier
ACEHINPRW whip-crane
ACEHINRRU hurricane, raunchier

ACEHINRSU sea urchin
ACEHINSST Caithness
ACEHINSTY hesitancy
ACEHINTTU authentic
ACEHIPPSS spaceship
ACEHIPSTT patchiest
ACEHIRRST starchier
ACEHIRSST chastiser
ACEHIRSTU Eucharist
ACEHIRSTV tsarevich
ACEHISTTT chattiest
ACEHKLNSU unshackle
ACEHKMPST sketch map
ACEHKOPRS packhorse
ACEHKORST shortcake, track shoe
ACEHKOSVW shock wave
ACEHKRSSY Cherkassy
ACEHLLLMS clamshell
ACEHLLLOR chlorella
ACEHLLOPY holy place
ACEHLMOST moschatel
ACEHLMOTV love match
ACEHLMRSS charmless
ACEHLMSST matchless
ACEHLNOSY anchylose
ACEHLOOSU coalhouse
ACEHLOPSW showplace
ACEHLORRT trochlear
ACEHLORSU housecarl
ACEHLORTT charlotte
ACEHMNPRT parchment
ACEHMNTTU humectant
ACEHMORST stomacher
ACEHMORTV overmatch
ACEHMOSTU moustache
ACEHMPRTY champerty
ACEHMSTTT test match
ACEHNNRTT trenchant
ACEHNORSS anchoress
ACEHNOSTT stonechat
ACEHNOSTU ceanothus
ACEHNPPTU punch tape
ACEHNRSUZ schnauzer
ACEHOOSTU housecoat
ACEHOPRRS sharecrop
ACEHORRST carthorse, orchestra
ACEHORSTY theocrasy
ACEHOSTUY easy touch
ACEHPRRSU purchaser
ACEHPSTTT patch test
ACEHPSTTY petty cash
ACEHRRTTY tetrarchy
ACEIIILTZ italicize
ACEIIKMNT kinematic
ACEIILLTV Levitical
ACEIILMPR empirical
ACEIILMPT implicate
ACEIILMSS seismical
ACEIILNNT anticline
ACEIILNNV vicennial
ACEIILNPS cisalpine
ACEIILNST inelastic, sciential
ACEIILOST socialite
ACEIILOSZ socialize
ACEIILRRT criterial
ACEIILRST realistic
ACEIILRTT lateritic
ACEIILRTV leviratic
ACEIILRVY civil year
ACEIIMMRU americium
ACEIIMNSS Messianic
ACEIIMRST armistice
ACEIINNOT aconitine
ACEIINNST Encinitas
ACEIINOTV noviciate
ACEIINPRS precisian
ACEIINRTT intricate
ACEIINRTY itineracy
ACEIINTTT nictitate
ACEIISTTT steatitic
ACEIJKNPS jack snipe
ACEIJLPTU Juliet cap
ACEIJMNOS Mejicanos
ACEIKKLPT kick-pleat
ACEIKLLMS slack lime
ACEIKLLTT all-ticket
ACEIKLNNS cleanskin
ACEIKLPST skeptical
ACEIKNRST crankiest
ACEIKNSST tackiness
ACEIKNSSW wackiness
ACEIKOPRT air pocket
ACEIKORST croakiest
ACEIKPSTY tipsy-cake
ACEILLLXY lexically
ACEILLMOP polemical
ACEILLMOT collimate, local time
ACEILLNOR collinear, coralline
ACEILLNPS spellican
ACEILLORT corallite
ACEILLOST oscillate, teocallis, Tesla coil
ACEILLPSY specially
ACEILMMST clammiest
ACEILMNNU luminance
ACEILMNOP policeman
ACEILMNOR coal miner
ACEILMNOT melanotic
ACEILMNRU numerical
ACEILMNSU masculine
ACEILMNTU culminate
ACEILMOPT Ptolemaic
ACEILMOSS coseismal
ACEILMRRU mercurial
ACEILNNOR cornelian
ACEILNNOT octennial
ACEILNNTY anciently
ACEILNOPR porcelain
ACEILNOPT point lace
ACEILNORS censorial
ACEILNOST coastline, sectional
ACEILNOTU inoculate
ACEILNPTU inculpate
ACEILNRST larcenist
ACEILNRTY certainly
ACEILNSSS scaliness
ACEILNSTU Escuintla
ACEILNTUV vulcanite
ACEILNTXY inexactly
ACEILNUVZ vulcanize
ACEILOOPZ Paleozoic
ACEILOPPS episcopal, Pepsi-Cola
ACEILOPRT pre-coital
ACEILOQUV equivocal
ACEILORRT rectorial
ACEILORST sectorial
ACEILORTT tectorial
ACEILORTV vectorial
ACEILORVY viceroyal
ACEILORVZ vocalizer
ACEILOTTU autotelic
ACEILOTVY coevality
ACEILPPPR paper clip
ACEILPRSS spiracles
ACEILPRXY pyrexical
ACEILPSTU spiculate
ACEILPSTY specialty
ACEILPSUZ capsulize
ACEILPTUY eucalypti
ACEILRRTU reticular
ACEILRSUV vesicular
ACEILRTUV lucrative, victualer
ACEILSSST classiest
ACEILSUWY sluice-way
ACEILTTUV cultivate
ACEIMMNNY immanency
ACEIMNORT cremation
ACEIMNOST encomiast
ACEIMNOTX income tax
ACEIMNPSS campiness
ACEIMNPTU pneumatic
ACEIMNRST miscreant
ACEIMNRSU muscarine
ACEIMNSST semantics
ACEIMNSTU mint sauce
ACEIMNTYZ enzymatic
ACEIMOPRT preatomic
ACEIMORST Masoretic
ACEIMORVW microwave
ACEIMPRST spermatic
ACEIMRSTU cerastium
ACEINNNRU uncannier
ACEINNNSS canniness
ACEINNOOV novocaine
ACEINNORT container, crenation
ACEINNOSS ascension
ACEINNRRY inerrancy
ACEINNRSU insurance
ACEINNRTU runcinate, uncertain
ACEINNSST incessant
ACEINOOTV evocation
ACEINOPRS proscenia
ACEINORRV carnivore
ACEINORTU Cointreau

ACEINORTZ narcotize
ACEINOSST cessation
ACEINOSTU tenacious
ACEINOSUV vinaceous
ACEINPRTT crepitant
ACEINPRUY pecuniary
ACEINPSSU puissance
ACEINQTTU quittance
ACEINRRSW scrawnier
ACEINRSSS scariness
ACEINRSST scenarist
ACEINRSSZ craziness
ACEINRSTY insectary
ACEINRTTY certainty
ACEINSSSU sauciness
ACEINSSTT cattiness, scantiest
ACEINSTTY intestacy
ACEIOPRST operatics
ACEIOPRTV proactive
ACEIOPTTT petticoat
ACEIORSTZ ostracize
ACEIORSUV veracious
ACEIOSSTW coastwise
ACEIPPRRS scrappier
ACEIPPRST crappiest
ACEIPRRST practiser
ACEIPSSTU spacesuit
ACEIQSTUY sequacity
ACEIRSTTU rusticate
ACEISSTTT scattiest
ACEISTTTY city state
ACEJJKNOS Jack Jones
ACEJKKRSY skyjacker
ACEJKNOST jackstone
ACEJLMSUU majuscule
ACEJLNQUY Jacquelyn
ACEKKLNOS ankle sock
ACEKKMRRU muckraker
ACEKKOSTT stocktake
ACEKLLMMU mallemuck
ACEKLLRUY curly kale
ACEKLNSSS slackness
ACEKLOPRW workplace
ACEKLORSW scale work
ACEKLRSST trackless
ACEKMSTUW muck sweat
ACEKNORSU cankerous
ACEKOPPRW power pack
ACEKOPRSW workspace
ACEKOSSTW sweat sock
ACEKPRSSU sapsucker
ACEKPTTUW Pawtucket
ACEKRSTUW awestruck
ACELLLORS solar cell
ACELLMORS all comers
ACELLMORU molecular
ACELLMRSU Marcellus
ACELLNNUY uncleanly
ACELLNORU nucleolar
ACELLNOSS localness
ACELLNOTU Launcelot
ACELLNRTY centrally
ACELLNRUY unclearly
ACELLOOTV local veto
ACELLOPRS scalloper
ACELLOQUY co-equally
ACELLPSSS scalpless
ACELLRSSW wall cress
ACELLRSUY secularly
ACELLSSSS classless
ACELMMNOS commensal
ACELMMNSU muscle-man
ACELMNTUU tenaculum
ACELMOOSU coalmouse
ACELMOPST ectoplasm
ACELMOSSS scale-moss
ACELNNOOR olecranon
ACELNOOST stone-coal
ACELNORSU larcenous
ACELNOSTU consulate
ACELNPRTU crapulent
ACELNRTTU reluctant
ACELNTUXY exultancy
ACELOOPRR corporeal
ACELOOSTT coelostat
ACELOPRRU opercular, preocular
ACELOPRST precostal
ACELOPRTU peculator
ACELORRTU true coral
ACELOSSTU cassoulet, lost cause
ACELOSTTY octastyle
ACELPSTUY eucalypts
ACEMMNOOR Common Era
ACEMMOTTU commutate
ACEMNOOPS moonscape
ACEMNOORU coumarone
ACEMNOPSS encompass
ACEMNORTU mucronate
ACEMORRSU sour cream
ACEMORRTY crematory
ACEMOSTVY vasectomy
ACEMPRSUY supremacy
ACENNNORU announcer
ACENNPTUU nuncupate
ACENNSSST scantness
ACENOOPRT cooperant
ACENOPRRT co-partner, per contra, procreant
ACENOPSSW snowscape
ACENOPSTW townscape
ACENOPSTY syncopate
ACENORRTU raconteur
ACENORSTU courtesan, nectarous
ACENORSUV cavernous
ACENORTUY Courtenay
ACENORUVV Vancouver
ACENOSTUU cutaneous
ACENPRRTY carpentry
ACENPRSUU pursuance
ACENPTTUU punctuate
ACENRSSSS crassness
ACEOOPRRT corporate
ACEOORSSU rosaceous
ACEOPRSSY caryopses
ACEOPRSTT spectator
ACEORRRTT retractor
ACEORRRVY carry-over
ACEORRSTU craterous
ACEORRTTX extractor
ACEOSSTTW West Coast
ACERRTUUV curvature
ACFFIILNO officinal
ACFFIINOT officiant
ACFFILMOR falciform
ACFGHILNN flanching
ACFGHMORR frogmarch
ACFGIIMNO magnifico
ACFGIKNRT kingcraft
ACFGINRRS scarf ring
ACFGIOSUU fugacious
ACFGLNORY gyrfalcon
ACFHHHILT half hitch
ACFHIILRT chairlift
ACFHILPRT flip chart
ACFHKORST rock-shaft
ACFHLMRSU scrum-half
ACFHLNORW half-crown
ACFHLORTW flow chart
ACFIIISST fasciitis
ACFIILLNY finically
ACFIILNOT fictional
ACFIILRSU surficial
ACFIILSTY fiscality
ACFIINSTU faunistic
ACFIIOPRV vaporific
ACFIJKRTU jackfruit
ACFIKNRSS scarf-skin
ACFILLOPT floptical
ACFILMORU formulaic, fumarolic
ACFILMORV claviform
ACFILNNOR francolin
ACFILNOOT olfaction
ACFILNPPY flippancy
ACFILNRTY franticly
ACFILNRUU funicular
ACFINORRT infractor
ACFINORTU furcation
ACFIORSTU fractious
ACFJKORST Jack Frost
ACFKNORWY fancy-work
ACFKORRTW craftwork
ACFLLORSU floscular
ACFLLTTUY tactfully
ACFLMNOOR conformal
ACFLMORSS form class
ACFLOORTY olfactory
ACFMOSTTU factotums
ACFOOSTUU autofocus
ACGGGINRS scragging
ACGGIIKMN magicking
ACGGIIOSS isagogics
ACGGILRSY scraggily
ACGHHHIIR high chair
ACGHHILNT hatchling
ACGHHILSS high-class
ACGHHNOUZ Changzhou
ACGHIINRW wing chair
ACGHIIPRT graphitic
ACGHIKNOV havocking

ACGHILNNO	long-chain	**ACHIILRTY**	chirality	**ACIILLNOY**	ionically
ACGHILORY	oligarchy	**ACHIIMNST**	machinist	**ACIILLNST**	scintilla
ACGHINRSU	churingas	**ACHIINPSY**	physician	**ACIILLOPT**	political
ACGHLMOOY	logomachy	**ACHIINRST**	Christian, Christina	**ACIILLPRS**	Priscilla
ACGHNNOTU	Tongchuan	**ACHIIOPST**	pistachio	**ACIILMNPU**	municipal
ACGHOORTU	rough coat	**ACHIIPRSV**	vicarship	**ACIILMNSV**	Calvinism
ACGHORSTU	roughcast	**ACHIIRRTT**	arthritic	**ACIILMNTY**	militancy
ACGIIIMST	imagistic	**ACHIIRSTV**	archivist	**ACIILMOSS**	socialism
ACGIIKNNP	panicking	**ACHIKLMST**	mahlstick	**ACIILMOSU**	malicious
ACGIILLLO	illogical	**ACHIKMNOS**	Chomskian	**ACIILNOOT**	coalition
ACGIILLMS	Gallicism	**ACHILLMSU**	music hall	**ACIILNOPT**	plication
ACGIILLNV	cavilling	**ACHILLNTY**	Chantilly	**ACIILNOVV**	convivial
ACGIILLOR	cigarillo	**ACHILLOST**	sailcloth	**ACIILNOVY**	inviolacy
ACGIILMNS	Anglicism	**ACHILMPTY**	lymphatic	**ACIILNPPR**	principal
ACGIILNTT	latticing	**ACHILNNPU**	nail punch	**ACIILNSTV**	Calvinist
ACGIILRTY	gracility	**ACHILNRUY**	raunchily	**ACIILOPRT**	pictorial
ACGIIMSTT	stigmatic	**ACHILNSTU**	clianthus	**ACIILOSST**	socialist
ACGIINNOR	inorganic	**ACHILOPTU**	patchouli	**ACIILOSTY**	sociality
ACGIINOST	agonistic	**ACHILORTV**	archivolt	**ACIILQUZZ**	quizzical
ACGIIORST	orgiastic	**ACHILOSST**	scholiast	**ACIILTTTY**	tactility
ACGILLLOY	logically	**ACHILRSSY**	chrysalis	**ACIIMNNOS**	insomniac
ACGILLNOR	carolling	**ACHILRSTY**	starchily	**ACIIMNNOT**	antimonic
ACGILLOOO	oological	**ACHILSTTY**	cattishly	**ACIIMNOPT**	impaction
ACGILLOST	collagist	**ACHIMMOSS**	masochism	**ACIIMNORT**	mortician
ACGILMNTU	talcuming	**ACHIMNOPY**	hypomanic	**ACIIMOPST**	simpatico
ACGILMOPY	polygamic	**ACHIMNORT**	chromatin	**ACIIMORTT**	triatomic
ACGILNNST	scantling	**ACHIMNOST**	macintosh	**ACIIMOSST**	mosaicist
ACGILNOST	nostalgic	**ACHIMOSST**	masochist	**ACIIMOSTT**	atomistic
ACGILNOXY	coaxingly	**ACHIMOSTU**	mustachio	**ACIIMOTTY**	atomicity
ACGIMMNRS	scramming	**ACHIMRSST**	Christmas	**ACIIMPRST**	prismatic
ACGIMMORR	microgram	**ACHIMRSSW**	scrimshaw	**ACIINNOST**	onanistic
ACGIMNOOR	agronomic	**ACHINNOST**	stanchion	**ACIINNOTU**	incaution
ACGIMNORR	cairngorm	**ACHINNOTW**	Chinatown	**ACIINORTV**	Victorian
ACGIMNSTY	gymnastic, nystagmic, syntagmic	**ACHINOPST**	cashpoint	**ACIINOTTX**	antitoxic
		ACHINPRST	chinstrap	**ACIINRRTY**	irritancy
ACGIMOPRT	pictogram	**ACHIOPPRS**	hippocras	**ACIIOPRST**	psoriatic
ACGIMOTYZ	zygomatic	**ACHIOPRRZ**	rhizocarp	**ACIIOPRTT**	patriotic
ACGINNOOT	contagion	**ACHIORRSS**	cross-hair	**ACIIOPSTX**	optic axis
ACGINNOPY	poignancy	**ACHKMORTU**	touch-mark	**ACIIOPTZZ**	pizzicato
ACGINNOST	cognisant	**ACHKOPRTW**	patchwork	**ACIIORSUV**	vicarious
ACGINNOTZ	cognizant	**ACHLLOOPT**	photocall	**ACIIOSSTT**	isostatic
ACGINNPPU	uncapping	**ACHLLORSY**	scholarly	**ACIIOSUVV**	vivacious
ACGINOPSW	coping saw	**ACHLMMOOS**	school-ma'm	**ACIIPRSTT**	patristic
ACGINOPTT	capotting	**ACHLMNOOS**	schoolman	**ACIIPTTVY**	captivity
ACGINORTU	Agincourt	**ACHLMORSW**	slow march	**ACIISSTTT**	statistic
ACGINPPRS	scrapping	**ACHLMOSTW**	slow match	**ACIJKNNOU**	Union Jack
ACGINPTUY	pugnacity	**ACHLMSTYZ**	schmaltzy	**ACIKKNNOT**	antiknock
ACGIOORTT	cogitator	**ACHLNSTUY**	staunchly	**ACIKKRSTT**	kick-start
ACGJNORRU	currajong	**ACHLOOSTU**	holocaust	**ACIKLMSTU**	maulstick
ACGLOOPRY	carpology	**ACHLPRTUY**	plutarchy	**ACIKLNOOP**	plain cook
ACGLOOSTY	scatology	**ACHNOPSTY**	sycophant	**ACIKLNOTY**	ankylotic
ACGMNNOOR	Cro-Magnon	**ACHOPRSST**	crash-stop	**ACIKLOSTT**	tailstock
ACGMOPRTY	cryptogam	**ACHOPRTTW**	port watch	**ACIKLPSST**	slapstick
ACGNORRUW	currawong	**ACHOPSTTW**	stopwatch	**ACIKLPSTY**	plasticky
ACGORRSUY	surrogacy	**ACHOPSTUY**	hypocaust	**ACIKLSSTU**	slack suit
ACHHILORT	haircloth	**ACHORTTTU**	cut-throat	**ACIKRSTTU**	tracksuit
ACHHINNOT	chthonian	**ACIIILNOS**	siciliano	**ACILLLRYY**	lyrically
ACHHINOST	chain-shot	**ACIIILNOT**	ciliation	**ACILLMOSY**	osmically
ACHHIPRSU	pushchair	**ACIIILNRT**	triclinia	**ACILLMSUY**	musically
ACHHLOSTU	slouch hat	**ACIIIMNST**	animistic	**ACILLNNSY**	synclinal
ACHHNRSTY	chrysanth	**ACIIINPST**	pianistic	**ACILLNOOT**	collation
ACHIIKKOY	Yokkaichi	**ACIIIPTZZ**	pizzicati	**ACILLNOSY**	sonically
ACHIIKLNN	chain link	**ACIIKNRST**	trainsick	**ACILLNOTY**	tonically
ACHIILMSW	whimsical	**ACIILLNOS**	isoclinal	**ACILLOOQU**	colloquia

ACILLOPTY optically, topically
ACILLORST cloistral
ACILLOSTY callosity, stoically
ACILLOTXY toxically
ACILLPTYY typically
ACILLSSST class-list
ACILMMOTT committal
ACILMNNTU culminant
ACILMNOPT complaint, compliant
ACILMNOSV volcanism
ACILMNSUU unmusical
ACILMNSUV vulcanism
ACILMPTUU capitulum
ACILMSSTU masculist, simulcast
ACILNNNUY uncannily
ACILNNOTU continual
ACILNNRUU ranunculi
ACILNOPRT prolactin
ACILNPTUY untypical
ACILNSTYY syncytial
ACILOOPRS acropolis
ACILOOPST apostolic
ACILOORST castor oil
ACILOQTUY loquacity
ACILORRSU cursorial
ACILORSTU ocularist, suctorial
ACILOTTUY autolytic
ACILPPRSY scrappily
ACILRRTUU utricular
ACILSSTTY systaltic
ACIMMNOOT monatomic
ACIMMORSS commissar
ACIMNNOOP companion
ACIMNOOST onomastic
ACIMNOOTU autonomic
ACIMNOOTX taxonomic
ACIMNOPRR cramp-iron
ACIMNORST narcotism
ACIMNOUVX nux vomica
ACIMORSST ostracism
ACIMORSTT stromatic
ACIMPRSTY sympatric
ACINNORST constrain, transonic
ACINOOPRT proaction
ACINOORRS corrasion
ACINOORST consortia
ACINOPSUU usucapion
ACINORSST croissant
ACINORSTU suctorian
ACINRSSSU narcissus
ACIOOPPTT apoptotic
ACIOORRTU Rio Cuarto
ACIOORSTU atrocious
ACIOORSUV voracious
ACIOOTTUX autotoxic
ACIOPRSSY caryopsis
ACIOPRSTT prostatic
ACIOPRSTY piscatory
ACIRRSTYZ stir-crazy
ACIRSSTUY casuistry
ACJKOPRST jockstrap
ACJLLORUY jocularly
ACKLLNRTU trunk call
ACKLMOOOR cloakroom
ACKLNOPRT rock plant
ACKLORSST crosstalk
ACKLORSSW crosswalk
ACKLORSTW slow track
ACKMOORST stack-room
ACLLLOSUY callously
ACLLMNOSU molluscan
ACLLOORRY corollary
ACLLORSSW scroll saw
ACLMMNOOW common law
ACLMNOORU monocular
ACLMOORSS classroom
ACLMOORSU clamorous
ACLMOPSTY cytoplasm
ACLNNORTU nocturnal
ACLNOORTT contralto
ACLNOORTU colourant
ACLNORSTU construal
ACLOOORRT coral-root
ACLOORUWY colourway
ACLOPRSTY pyroclast
ACLOPRSUU crapulous
ACLOPRTTU plutocrat
ACLORSUUY raucously
ACLOSUUVY vacuously
ACMNOORRT cormorant
ACMNOORRW acorn worm
ACMNOOSTU cosmonaut
ACMORSTUY customary
ACNNNOOST consonant
ACNOOPRST corposant
ACNOORRSU rancorous
ACNORSTTY contrasty
ACOORSSTU autocross
ACOPRRSST sports car
ACORSSSWY crossways
ADDDEEEHR red-headed
ADDDEEELR Elder Edda
ADDDEEHNR red-handed
ADDDEEKLS skedaddle
ADDDEELMN demand-led
ADDDEGLOP dog-paddle
ADDDEGMNO goddamned
ADDEEERRT retreaded
ADDEEERSS addressee
ADDEEFIIX fixed idea
ADDEEFNNT defendant
ADDEEFRRU defrauder
ADDEEGHIP pig-headed
ADDEEGILM middle age
ADDEEGIRS disagreed
ADDEEGLNR glandered
ADDEEHHOT hot-headed
ADDEEHINP pinheaded
ADDEEHLNR elder hand
ADDEEHLNS handseled
ADDEEHOTW tow-headed
ADDEEHRSS headdress
ADDEEHRTY dehydrate
ADDEEILLR redialled
ADDEEILMR middle ear
ADDEEILRV daredevil
ADDEEILST deadliest
ADDEEJNSS jadedness
ADDEEMNOS Desdemona
ADDEEMNRU undreamed
ADDEENNPT dependant
ADDEENOST stone-dead
ADDEENPRW deep-drawn
ADDEENRRU under-read
ADDEENSWY Wednesday
ADDEEOPRS desperado, Prose Edda
ADDEEPSUX pas de deux
ADDEERRSS addresser, readdress
ADDEFFHNO offhanded
ADDEFFPRU puff-adder
ADDEFINNR Ferdinand
ADDEFINSS faddiness
ADDEGGINR degrading
ADDEGGOOT dog-eat-dog
ADDEGHILR Hildegard
ADDEGHILT deadlight
ADDEGHINR hag-ridden
ADDEGIMNN maddening
ADDEGIRRS disregard
ADDEGKNRU grand duke
ADDEGLLMO gold medal
ADDEGLNOT long-dated
ADDEGLRUY guardedly
ADDEGNOOR gadrooned
ADDEGNORW downgrade
ADDEGNRRU undergrad
ADDEGNRUU unguarded
ADDEHINRY anhydride
ADDEHINSY hendiadys
ADDEHIRRW hard-wired
ADDEHNNRU underhand
ADDEHNORS hard-nosed
ADDEHNORU Roundhead
ADDEHNOTW two-handed
ADDEHTTUY death duty
ADDEIILNV invalided
ADDEIILNX Dixieland
ADDEIINNR Red Indian
ADDEIKNPP kidnapped
ADDEILLNS landslide
ADDEILMMN middleman
ADDEILMNR Midlander
ADDEILMOP diplomaed
ADDEILMWY middle way
ADDEILNNO dandelion
ADDEILNSY deadly sin
ADDEILSVY advisedly
ADDEIMNOT demantoid
ADDEIMNSY many-sided
ADDEINNRU undrained
ADDEINPRU underpaid
ADDEINRTW trade wind
ADDEINSUV unadvised
ADDEINTUU unaudited
ADDEIRSSU dissuader
ADDEIRSSW sidewards
ADDELMNOO doom-laden

ADDELNOTU nodulated
ADDELRRST straddler
ADDEMORRY dromedary
ADDENNORU end-around, unadorned
ADDENNRTU redundant
ADDENNTUU undaunted
ADDENOORT deodorant
ADDENOPTU unadopted
ADDENORUY duodenary
ADDEOORRV drove road
ADDEPQRUU quadruped
ADDFHILSY faddishly
ADDFIIQRU quadrifid
ADDGHNORU drag-hound
ADDGQRSUU drug squad
ADDHHIOOR hardihood
ADDHLOOTU adulthood
ADDINORSU diandrous
ADDLLNNOU Llandudno
ADDLLNORY dandy roll
ADDMNOOTU odd man out
ADDNORSWW downwards
ADDOPRRTU Proddatur
ADEEEEGLY eagle-eyed
ADEEEELNR leaderene
ADEEEERST seed-eater
ADEEEFHRT feathered
ADEEEFLLT leafleted
ADEEEFNRR referenda
ADEEEFRRT free trade
ADEEEGGRT gadgeteer
ADEEEGHNR greenhead
ADEEEGRRS degreaser
ADEEEHLST steelhead
ADEEEILMN madeleine
ADEEEILNT delineate
ADEEEKKNW weak-kneed
ADEEELLMN enamelled
ADEEELLNS Lend-Lease
ADEEELLSW weaselled
ADEEELNRR relearned
ADEEELPRS seedpearl
ADEEENRRS serenader
ADEEENRST East Ender
ADEEEPRST desperate
ADEEERTTU deuterate
ADEEERTWW waterweed
ADEEFFILR fieldfare
ADEEFGGLR reflagged
ADEEFIISV five-a-side
ADEEFIKLW Wakefield
ADEEFIKRR fire-drake, Frederika
ADEEFILOT defoliate
ADEEFILUZ feudalize
ADEEFIMST defeatism
ADEEFISTT defeatist
ADEEFLLNN flanneled
ADEEFLLRY federally
ADEEFLLST stall-feed
ADEEFLRTU defaulter
ADEEFLRTW delftware
ADEEFNOST stone-deaf
ADEEGGINS disengage
ADEEGGIRV aggrieved
ADEEGGIRW earwigged
ADEEGGJLT jet-lagged
ADEEGGLNO golden age
ADEEGGMOU demagogue
ADEEGGNNU unengaged
ADEEGGOPU pedagogue
ADEEGILLR galleried
ADEEGILNR Geraldine
ADEEGILNW wide-angle
ADEEGIMOV video game
ADEEGINNR endearing, grenadine
ADEEGINRR grenadier
ADEEGINRT denigrate
ADEEGINST designate
ADEEGIRSS disagrees
ADEEGIRSV graveside
ADEEGIUVW waveguide
ADEEGLLLY allegedly
ADEEGLLRV gravelled
ADEEGLNOT elongated
ADEEGLNRY legendary
ADEEGLORT delegator
ADEEGMNRR germander
ADEEGMRRU demurrage
ADEEGNNRS greensand
ADEEGNORR reed-organ
ADEEGNQRU drag queen
ADEEGNRRY greenyard
ADEEGNRST estranged
ADEEGNRSV Gravesend
ADEEGORRZ razor edge
ADEEGRSSU degausser
ADEEGRSUY Argus-eyed
ADEEGRTTT targetted
ADEEHHITW whitehead
ADEEHHNOP headphone
ADEEHIKLT deathlike
ADEEHILNR headliner
ADEEHILNT Ethelinda
ADEEHILRT deathlier
ADEEHILTW white lead
ADEEHINRT herniated
ADEEHINSS headiness
ADEEHIRRT threadier
ADEEHKLRS sheldrake
ADEEHLLOS leasehold
ADEEHLOSU head louse
ADEEHLSSS shadeless
ADEEHLSST deathless
ADEEHMNOT methadone
ADEEHMORT home trade
ADEEHMOST homestead
ADEEHNOST headstone
ADEEHNPPR apprehend
ADEEHOSWY eyeshadow
ADEEHRRTY rehydrate
ADEEHRSTW draw-sheet, watershed
ADEEIILRZ idealizer
ADEEIIMMT immediate
ADEEIIRSS diaeresis
ADEEIKLMR dreamlike
ADEEILLNY delay line
ADEEILLUV Deauville
ADEEILMNN Mendelian
ADEEILMPP palmipede
ADEEILMPR epidermal
ADEEILMRS misleader
ADEEILMTY mediately
ADEEILNRT tail-ender
ADEEILNTZ dentalize
ADEEILPRR lip-reader
ADEEILPRZ pearlized
ADEEILPSS displease
ADEEILPST side plate
ADEEILSVV side valve
ADEEIMMRT dreamtime
ADEEIMNRR remainder
ADEEIMNRT minareted
ADEEIMPPR pipe dream
ADEEIMPRY Empire Day
ADEEIMRST dreamiest
ADEEIMSST demitasse
ADEEINNOS adenosine
ADEEINPTZ pedantize
ADEEINRSS readiness
ADEEINRUW unwearied
ADEEIOPRT periodate
ADEEIOPTV videotape
ADEEIPPSS passepied
ADEEIPRSS spear side
ADEEIPRTU repudiate
ADEEIPSTW waist-deep
ADEEIRRST dreariest
ADEEIRRTW read-write
ADEEIRSTV advertise
ADEEIRSTW waterside
ADEEIRTTW tidewater
ADEEIRTTX extradite
ADEEISSTT stateside, steadiest
ADEEISTTW statewide
ADEEITUVX exudative
ADEEJLNRY Leyden jar
ADEEJRSTU Judas tree
ADEEKLSTY stalk-eyed
ADEEKNNSS nakedness
ADEEKNRTU undertake
ADEELLLRU laurelled
ADEELLMRV marvelled
ADEELLNOV old leaven
ADEELLNRY learnedly
ADEELLORV overalled
ADEELLPPR rappelled
ADEELLRTV travelled
ADEELLRWY leewardly
ADEELLRXY relaxedly
ADEELLSST tasselled
ADEELLSTT stellated
ADEELLTXY exaltedly
ADEELMMRT trammeled
ADEELMNOP pademelon
ADEELMRSS dreamless
ADEELNNPR replanned
ADEELNNRU unlearned
ADEELNORV overladen
ADEELNQUU unequaled
ADEELNRRS slanderer

ADEELNRRU launderer
ADEELNRSU underseal
ADEELNRTU unaltered, unrelated
ADEELNRUV unraveled
ADEELNRUX unrelaxed
ADEELNSSW Waldenses
ADEELNSTY slant-eyed
ADEELOPRV paloverde
ADEELQRRU quarreled
ADEELRRSS redressal
ADEELRRTT red rattle
ADEELRRTU adulterer
ADEELRSTY steelyard
ADEELRSVY adversely
ADEEMMNNT amendment
ADEEMMOXY myxoedema
ADEEMNOPR open-armed, promenade
ADEEMNORT emendator
ADEEMNORU demeanour
ADEEMOORR aerodrome
ADEEMOPRR madrepore
ADEEMORRX xeroderma
ADEEMORTT trematode
ADEEMORUW meadow rue
ADEEMPRST stampeder
ADEENNORR non-reader
ADEENNPRT trepanned
ADEENNTTY Yattenden
ADEENORSS road sense
ADEENORUV endeavour
ADEENORVY oven-ready
ADEENPPRT entrapped
ADEENPSST adeptness
ADEENQSTU Dantesque
ADEENRRTU underrate
ADEENRRUW underwear
ADEENRSTY sedentary
ADEENRTTU untreated
ADEENRTUV adventure
ADEENRTUW unwatered
ADEEOPRSV eavesdrop
ADEEPPRRW rewrapped
ADEEPQRTU parqueted
ADEEPRRSU persuader
ADEEPRRTU departure
ADEEPRSTU depasture
ADEEPRSTY pederasty
ADEERRSTT desert rat
ADEERSTYY yesterday
ADEFFIILR Fairfield
ADEFFINSS daffiness
ADEFFOORR off-roader
ADEFGHORT godfather
ADEFGILLO field goal
ADEFGILOT lag of tide
ADEFGILRU lifeguard
ADEFGINTT defatting
ADEFGIRRU fireguard
ADEFGLOOT floodgate
ADEFGLRRU regardful
ADEFHIMST ham-fisted
ADEFHINRT threadfin
ADEFHIRST head first
ADEFHLNOZ half-dozen
ADEFHLOOS falsehood
ADEFIIPRR rapid-fire
ADEFIKLNR field rank
ADEFILLSU fusillade
ADEFILMNS fieldsman
ADEFILMSU feudalism
ADEFILNOT deflation, defoliant
ADEFILNTY defiantly
ADEFILSTU feudalist
ADEFILTUY feudality
ADEFINNRW fine-drawn
ADEFIRSTX fixed star
ADEFLLMOU leaf mould
ADEFLLMSY damselfly
ADEFLMMOR malformed
ADEFLOOUV food value
ADEFLOPST soft pedal
ADEFLORSY Aylesford
ADEFLRRUW drawerful
ADEFLRSTW leftwards
ADEFMNNTU fundament
ADEFMOORR door frame
ADEFMORTT formatted
ADEFOOPRR proof-read
ADEFOOPST spade foot
ADEFOOTTU out of date
ADEFORRRW forwarder
ADEFORRTV overdraft
ADEFORRTW afterword, Waterford
ADEFORTUY feudatory
ADEFRRSTU fraudster
ADEGGGIWW wigwagged
ADEGGGIZZ zigzagged
ADEGGHHIR high-grade
ADEGGHILN hang-glide
ADEGGINNR gardening
ADEGGINRR regarding
ADEGGINSS degassing
ADEGGINUW wind-gauge
ADEGGIRST draggiest
ADEGGNORU groundage
ADEGHHILT headlight
ADEGHILPT glide path
ADEGHINNR hardening
ADEGHINSU anguished
ADEGHIOPR ideograph
ADEGHIRRT third gear
ADEGHIRST sight-read
ADEGHLORS gasholder
ADEGHLORU rough deal
ADEGHMORU Home Guard
ADEGIILNR redialing
ADEGIILPT pigtailed
ADEGIINRS grain side
ADEGILLNP pedalling
ADEGILLNS signalled
ADEGILNNU unaligned
ADEGILNOR girandole
ADEGILNOS alongside
ADEGILNTW delta wing
ADEGILNUV devaluing
ADEGIMNTU magnitude
ADEGIMOTZ dogmatize
ADEGINNRT integrand
ADEGINNRW wandering
ADEGINORS grandiose
ADEGINOSS diagnoses
ADEGINRRS grandsire
ADEGINRRW rewarding
ADEGINSSU gaudiness
ADEGIPRRT partridge
ADEGIRTTU gratitude
ADEGLLLOU Dolgellau
ADEGLLOPT gold plate
ADEGLNSTU angel dust
ADEGLORST old stager
ADEGNNOPR pendragon
ADEGNNORY androgyne
ADEGNNRSS grandness
ADEGNOORS goosander
ADEGNOPRT godparent
ADEGNORSU dangerous
ADEGNOSTW downstage
ADEGNRSUU unsugared
ADEGOORST stage door
ADEGOSSTU outgassed
ADEHHISTW death wish
ADEHHLLRS hardshell
ADEHHORST short head
ADEHIIKLV Khedivial
ADEHIILRS hairslide
ADEHIIMNS maidenish
ADEHIIRRR hairdrier
ADEHIISST diathesis
ADEHIJMNU mujahedin
ADEHIKNPS handspike
ADEHILMNS mishandle
ADEHILMOT ethmoidal
ADEHILNOR hodiernal
ADEHILNPR philander
ADEHILNRR hardliner
ADEHILNRS hard lines
ADEHILRRT trihedral
ADEHILRST heraldist
ADEHIMNOR rhodamine
ADEHIMNRS Sanhedrim
ADEHIMOSU housemaid
ADEHIMPRS Sephardim
ADEHIMRTY diathermy
ADEHINNRS Sanhedrin
ADEHINNSS handiness
ADEHINPRT printhead
ADEHINRSS hardiness
ADEHINRST train-shed
ADEHINRSW wind shear
ADEHINRTY anhydrite
ADEHINRYZ hydrazine
ADEHINSSS shadiness
ADEHIOOST Theodosia
ADEHIPRST therapsid
ADEHIRRRY hairdryer
ADEHIRRTT third-rate
ADEHIRSTW dishwater
ADEHKNNTU unthanked
ADEHKNOSW hawk-nosed, shakedown
ADEHKORRS dark horse

ADEHKRSTU Turk's head
ADEHLLNOR Hollander
ADEHLLORT death roll
ADEHLLOTT death toll
ADEHLOPRY polyhedra
ADEHLORST Aldershot
ADEHLORSY hydrolase
ADEHMNORS handsomer
ADEHMOOPS shampooed
ADEHMORSW homewards
ADEHNPPRU upper hand
ADEHOORSU roadhouse
ADEHOORTW heartwood
ADEHOOSTT statehood
ADEHOPPPY poppy-head
ADEHORRRR hard error
ADEHORRSW shoreward
ADEHORRSY dray horse
ADEHORSTT short date
ADEHOSTUW washed out
ADEHTUVYY heavy-duty
ADEIIILNT initialed
ADEIIINTT dietitian
ADEIILNST disentail
ADEIILORT editorial
ADEIILPTX pixilated
ADEIILQTU liquidate
ADEIIMNOT mediation
ADEIIMOTT diatomite
ADEIINNOS Indonesia
ADEIINOTV deviation
ADEIINPPR drainpipe
ADEIINSTT daintiest
ADEIINSTZ satinized
ADEIIOTVX oxidative
ADEIIPRRS disrepair
ADEIIPRSS dispraise
ADEIIPSST dissipate
ADEIIRSTT distraite
ADEIKLLNW Aldwinkle
ADEIKNNNP pen and ink
ADEIKNPPR kidnapper
ADEIKNPRS spikenard
ADEILLMNO medallion
ADEILLMOT metalloid
ADEILLMRT treadmill
ADEILLMST medallist
ADEILLNST installed
ADEILLPRS spiralled
ADEILLPRU preludial
ADEILLQRU quadrille
ADEILLRTW dill-water
ADEILMNNO mandoline
ADEILMNST dismantle
ADEILMNTU dentalium
ADEILMOPT diplomate
ADEILMOPY polyamide
ADEILMORR mail order
ADEILMPTU amplitude
ADEILNOPP panoplied
ADEILNOPT planetoid
ADEILNORT rodential
ADEILNPPU unapplied
ADEILNRRT interlard
ADEILNRTU Uitlander
ADEILNRUV unrivaled
ADEILNRUY unreadily
ADEILOQSU odalisque
ADEILORST steroidal
ADEILPPRY reply-paid
ADEILPRSS dispersal
ADEILPRSY displayer
ADEILPTTU platitude
ADEILSSTU lassitude
ADEIMMRST midstream
ADEIMNNTU indumenta
ADEIMNORZ randomize
ADEIMNOST Maidstone
ADEIMNPRR reprimand
ADEIMNPRS spiderman
ADEIMNRRU unmarried
ADEIMNRSU nursemaid
ADEIMNRTY dynamiter
ADEIMNSTV Adventism
ADEIMORTT meditator
ADEIMORTY mediatory
ADEIMPRST spermatid
ADEIMRTUX admixture
ADEIMRTXY taxidermy
ADEINNNPS inspanned
ADEINNNTT intendant
ADEINNPTU unpainted
ADEINNRSS randiness
ADEINNRTU untrained
ADEINNSSS sandiness
ADEINNSTU unstained
ADEINNTTU untainted
ADEINOPRR preordain
ADEINOPRT predation
ADEINOPST antipodes
ADEINOTUX exudation
ADEINPPRS sandpiper
ADEINPPST standpipe
ADEINPRSS rapidness
ADEINPSSV vapidness
ADEINRSST tardiness
ADEINRSTT transited
ADEINSSST staidness
ADEINSTTV Adventist, Vedantist
ADEIOPRTZ trapezoid
ADEIORSTT storiated
ADEIORTVY deviatory
ADEIPPSSY dyspepsia
ADEIPRSUU Epidaurus
ADEIPRTVY depravity
ADEIRRSUY residuary
ADEIRSTTW tawdriest
ADEIRSTVY adversity
ADEIRTTTT attritted
ADEJNOSVY Davy Jones
ADEKLORUY royal duke
ADEKNOOTW tae kwon do
ADEKOPRSW spadework
ADELLLOWY allowedly
ADELLMRUY medullary
ADELLNOPR landloper
ADELLNORW lowlander
ADELLNOUY unalloyed
ADELLOORW low-loader
ADELLOPRT patrolled
ADELLORRT tall order
ADELLRTXY dextrally
ADELMNNUY mundanely
ADELMNOPS endoplasm
ADELMORST old master
ADELMSSUY assumedly
ADELNNNPU unplanned
ADELNNORU lunar node
ADELNNORW landowner
ADELNNPTU unplanted
ADELNOOPR Apeldoorn
ADELNOOST loadstone
ADELNORTU outlander
ADELNORUY roundelay
ADELNPRUY underplay
ADELNRSSU laundress
ADELNRTVY verdantly
ADELNSSTU dauntless
ADELOOPRT door plate
ADELOORST desolator
ADELOPRRS predorsal
ADELOPRSW polewards
ADELORSTY lead story
ADELPQRUU quadruple
ADELRRSTY dry-salter
ADELRSSUY assuredly
ADEMMORST masterdom
ADEMNNORT adornment
ADEMNORST transomed
ADEMNPSTU unstamped
ADEMNRRST Dr Martens
ADEMNRTUU unmatured
ADEMOORRT moderator
ADEMOORST astrodome
ADEMOORSY doomsayer
ADEMOPPRU pauperdom
ADEMORRTT Rotterdam
ADENNOSST sandstone
ADENNOSTY asyndeton
ADENNPPSU unsnapped
ADENNSSTW news-stand
ADENOOPRS ponderosa
ADENOORTT detonator
ADENOOSTT toadstone
ADENOPRTV Davenport
ADENOPRUV up-and-over
ADENORRUY year-round
ADENOSTTW downstate
ADENOSUVW sound wave
ADENOTTWY Wyandotte
ADENPPRUW unwrapped
ADENPRRTU underpart
ADENPRSSU underpass
ADENPRSUY unsprayed
ADENRRSTW sternward
ADENRRTUY day return
ADEOPRRTU depurator
ADEOPRRTW top drawer
ADEOPRRTY predatory
ADEOPRSTU outspread
ADEORRSTT rostrated
ADEORRSWW swear word
ADERSSTWW westwards
ADFFHRSTU hard stuff

ADFFIIMRS disaffirm
ADFGHIOOT good faith
ADFGINORS sang-froid
ADFGLNORY dragonfly
ADFGOORSW dogs of war
ADFHINRST first-hand
ADFHLOORY foolhardy
ADFILLOTW tidal flow
ADFILORRW world fair
ADFILRSTY First Lady
ADFINORSZ sforzandi
ADFIORSUV disfavour
ADFLLOOST faldstool
ADFLORRWY forwardly, frowardly
ADFMOOPPR damp-proof
ADFNOORSZ sforzando
ADFNORRTW frontward
ADGGGNNOU Dongguang
ADGGIILNN ding-a-ling
ADGGILMNO Godalming
ADGGILNRY niggardly
ADGGILRSY Yggdrasil
ADGGINRRU guard ring
ADGGLOORV Volgograd
ADGGMNORU gum dragon
ADGHHINRT right hand
ADGHHOOPR hodograph
ADGHILLLU guildhall
ADGHILNSY dashingly
ADGHIMOSU Mogadishu
ADGHINORS dragonish, hoardings
ADGHINOTY dying oath
ADGHINRSU shin-guard
ADGHINRTU indraught
ADGHIRRTW rightward
ADGHNORSU ground ash
ADGHNOSTU staghound
ADGHNSSUW swung dash
ADGHPRTUU updraught
ADGIIILNT digitalin
ADGIIILST digitalis
ADGIIKNNP kidnaping
ADGIILLTY digitally
ADGIILNPS Pig Island
ADGIILNSS glissandi
ADGIILOST dialogist
ADGIIMNRS disarming
ADGIIMNTT admitting
ADGIIMRUU Maiduguri
ADGIINNNT indignant
ADGIINORT granitoid
ADGIINOSS diagnosis
ADGIINRSU radiusing
ADGIINRTY dignitary
ADGIKLLNS silk-gland
ADGILLNUY languidly
ADGILLOSU gladiolus
ADGILMNNY damningly
ADGILMNSU guildsman
ADGILNORY adoringly
ADGILNOSS glissando
ADGILOORY radiology
ADGILOOUY audiology
ADGILORST dog trials
ADGIMMOST dogmatism
ADGIMOSTT dogmatist
ADGINNOOU iguanodon
ADGINOORW wood-grain
ADGINPRRX Grand Prix
ADGJNRRUY grand jury
ADGLNNORW long-drawn
ADGLNOUYY young lady
ADGMOORRU guardroom
ADGNNNNOU Dungannon
ADGNNORYY androgyny
ADGNORRTU grand tour
ADGOOPRST gastropod
ADGOOPRSU podagrous
ADHHNOORU hoarhound
ADHHNORST shorthand
ADHHOSUWZ Dashhowuz
ADHIIJMNU mujahidin
ADHIILNNS inlandish
ADHIILPRS lairdship
ADHIIMMRS Midrashim
ADHIIMPSS amidships
ADHIIOPTY idiopathy
ADHIIRRUW Wiradhuri
ADHIKMNNU humankind
ADHIKNORW handiwork
ADHIKOORV Kirovohad
ADHILMNPY nymphalid
ADHILMSTY Ladysmith
ADHILNNUY unhandily
ADHILNOPS island-hop
ADHILOPTY typhoidal
ADHILPSSY Ladyships
ADHINOOST sainthood
ADHINORTY hydration
ADHINRTWW withdrawn
ADHINSTTW withstand
ADHIOPRSY dysphoria
ADHISTWWY widthways
ADHLLMORT thralldom
ADHLNNORT Northland
ADHLNOSTU Southland
ADHMNOOOW womanhood
ADHMORTTU Dartmouth
ADHNOORYZ hydrozoan
ADHNORRTW northward
ADHNORSUY anhydrous
ADHNOSSTU thousands
ADHOOPRRT arthropod
ADHORSTUW southward
ADIIIKNNN Indian ink
ADIIIQRSU daiquiris
ADIIJKMOT komitadji
ADIILLNVY invalidly
ADIILLPTY pallidity
ADIILMSSS dismissal
ADIILNOPT platinoid
ADIILOORV varioloid
ADIIMNOSS admission
ADIIMNRSW Darwinism
ADIIMOPRR primordia
ADIIMRSSY mydriasis
ADIINNOSY Dionysian
ADIINOOTX oxidation
ADIINOQTU quotidian
ADIINORTT tradition
ADIINRSTT distraint
ADIINRSTU saturniid
ADIINRSTW Darwinist
ADIIOPSTY adiposity
ADIIOSTUY you said it
ADIIPRSTY disparity
ADIISSTUY assiduity
ADIKLLNRT tall drink
ADIKMNNOW womankind
ADILLMNOO almond oil
ADILLNRUY diurnally
ADILLQSUY squalidly
ADILMNOOS salmonoid
ADILMNOST daltonism
ADILMNRUU Duralumin
ADILMOPSY olympiads, sympodial
ADILMSTTU Talmudist
ADILNNOPS pond snail
ADILNORSW solar wind
ADILNSTTY distantly
ADILORSTW swordtail
ADIMNNTUY mundanity
ADIMNOORT dominator
ADIMNORSZ smorzandi
ADIMORTTX dot matrix
ADINNOSST dissonant
ADINNPRTU tip-and-run
ADINOOSTW satinwood, wood stain
ADINOPSTY dystopian
ADINORSTW downstair
ADINOTWWX window tax
ADINPSTTU disputant
ADIORRSTT traditors
ADIOSSSUU assiduous
ADIPSSUYY upsy-daisy
ADJMMOOOR major-domo
ADJMMORRU drum major
ADKNORRTU trunk road
ADKNORRWW drawn work
ADLLNOSTU lotus-land
ADLLNSSUV Sundsvall
ADLMNORTY mordantly
ADLMOOPRR prodromal
ADLMOORRY Lord Mayor
ADLMOORTU modulator
ADLNOPRYY polyandry
ADLNOSUWY Low Sunday
ADLNRSSTU Stralsund
ADLOOOSTT toadstool
ADLOPRSWY swordplay
ADLORSUUY arduously
ADLORTUWY outwardly
ADLPQRUUY quadruply
ADMMORRTY martyrdom
ADMNNORSU roundsman
ADMNOORSZ smorzando
ADMNORSST sandstorm
ADMNORSSW swordsman
ADMOOPPRU pompadour
ADMPSTTUY stamp duty
ADNNOPTYY Tonypandy

ADNNORRUU run-around
ADNNOSSWW swansdown
ADNOOTTUU out and out
ADNOOTTWW two and two
ADNORSTWW townwards
AEEEEHMPR ephemerae
AEEEELRRS re-release
AEEEFGLNR leaf green
AEEEFGNRR free-range
AEEEFGNRT free agent
AEEEFHRRT hereafter
AEEEFIRRT fire-eater
AEEEFLMRT flame tree
AEEEFNRST fenestrae
AEEEFRSTT Free State
AEEEGGGNR greengage
AEEEGGNPR pre-engage
AEEEGGNRS sage green
AEEEGGRST Easter egg, segregate
AEEEGHLRW gearwheel
AEEEGIMNR menagerie
AEEEGLRRV gear lever
AEEEGLSTW sweet gale
AEEEGMNNP empennage
AEEEGMNRT agreement
AEEEGNRSS eagerness
AEEEGNSTV Stevenage
AEEEGORRV overeager
AEEEGRTTZ gazetteer
AEEEHHRTT tree heath
AEEEHLLMN mallee hen
AEEEHLMPR ephemeral
AEEEHMPRS ephemeras
AEEEHMRTX hexameter
AEEEHNRTW enwreathe
AEEEHRRRS rehearser
AEEEHRSTT tear sheet
AEEEILNNS Anneliese
AEEEIMNRX re-examine
AEEEIRRTT reiterate
AEEEJNNTT Jeannette
AEEEKMRRT marketeer
AEEEKRSWX weaker sex
AEEELLMNR enameller
AEEELLMNT elemental
AEEELLSST telesales
AEEELMSTW sweetmeal
AEEELNUVZ Venezuela
AEEELPTTU epaulette
AEEEMMNST semanteme
AEEEMNNRT nemertean
AEEEMNRTU enumerate
AEEEMPRTT temperate
AEEEMRRSU remeasure
AEEEMSTTW sweetmeat
AEEENNNQU Queen-Anne
AEEENORTX exonerate
AEEENPRTT penetrate
AEEENPSTT septenate
AEEENRRST easterner
AEEENSSSV seven seas
AEEENTTUV eventuate
AEEENTTUX extenuate
AEEFFILRT afterlife
AEEFGHILS fish eagle
AEEFGILMS self-image
AEEFGILPR pilferage
AEEFGINRS far-seeing
AEEFGLLOT flageolet
AEEFGLSTT stage left
AEEFGLSTW sweet flag
AEEFGORST fosterage
AEEFHLRTT heartfelt
AEEFHOSSU safe house
AEEFIKLLM flamelike
AEEFIKRST freakiest
AEEFILMNR leaf miner
AEEFILMPR relief map
AEEFILNRT interleaf
AEEFILNSS leafiness
AEEFILOTX exfoliate
AEEFILRSV life-saver
AEEFIMMRT time frame
AEEFIRRTW firewater
AEEFKLOVW folkweave
AEEFKORST far to seek
AEEFLLMSS flameless
AEEFLLOOS loose-leaf
AEEFLMOSV false move
AEEFLMRSS frameless
AEEFLNRTT flattener
AEEFLNSSS falseness
AEEFLOSTV love feast
AEEFLPSST false step
AEEFLRRTT flatterer
AEEFMNORS Freemason
AEEFNSTTY safety net
AEEFOPRRT perforate
AEEFORSTT foretaste
AEEGGILNR ginger ale
AEEGGIMRT gigametre
AEEGGIRUW wire gauge
AEEGGLNOY genealogy
AEEGGMORT mortgagee
AEEGGNRSU grease gun
AEEGGRRST staggerer
AEEGGRRSW swaggerer
AEEGGRTUY tyre gauge
AEEGHHIMN high enema
AEEGHIMRT hermitage
AEEGHINRS garnishee
AEEGHLLMS shell game
AEEGHLPRT telegraph
AEEGHMNOP megaphone
AEEGHMRTW wheatgerm
AEEGHMRTZ megahertz
AEEGHOSTU gatehouse
AEEGILLST legislate
AEEGILMNN enameling, meningeal
AEEGILMNR greenmail
AEEGILMSS imageless
AEEGILNNT eglantine, inelegant
AEEGILNQU Angelique
AEEGILNSW weaseling
AEEGILPTT title-page
AEEGILRSV silver age
AEEGILRTU gauleiter
AEEGILUVY Ivy League
AEEGIMNNV given name
AEEGIMNRT germinate
AEEGIMNRZ Germanize
AEEGIMNST magnesite
AEEGIMNTT magnetite
AEEGIMNTZ magnetize
AEEGIMPTT pegmatite
AEEGINNRT argentine, tangerine
AEEGINOPS espionage
AEEGINOTT negotiate
AEEGINPRV grapevine
AEEGINRST stingaree
AEEGINRTT integrate
AEEGIRSST greasiest
AEEGIRUWZ wire gauze
AEEGLLNOR organelle
AEEGLLNRY generally
AEEGLLNTY elegantly
AEEGLMNNT gentleman
AEEGLMNRY germanely
AEEGLMNST segmental
AEEGLMORT glomerate
AEEGLMRRW leg warmer
AEEGLMRRY germ layer
AEEGLNNPT pentangle
AEEGLNRSS largeness
AEEGLORRV over-large
AEEGLORST alter egos
AEEGLORVZ overglaze
AEEGLQRSU square leg
AEEGLRSTY slate grey
AEEGMNNOT megatonne
AEEGMNOTY gate money
AEEGMNRRS merganser
AEEGMNRTU augmenter
AEEGMOPRS megaspore
AEEGMORST gasometer, megastore
AEEGNNSTW newsagent
AEEGNOPRS personage
AEEGNORRT generator
AEEGNORTT teratogen
AEEGNORTU entourage
AEEGNOTTW wagonette
AEEGNOTXY oxygenate
AEEGNPRSS passenger
AEEGNRSST greatness
AEEGNRSSV graveness
AEEGNSSUV vagueness
AEEGOPPST estoppage
AEEGOPRRT porterage, reportage
AEEGORRVZ overgraze
AEEGPRTUX expurgate
AEEGRRSST grass tree
AEEHHILRT healthier
AEEHHITTW white heat
AEEHHLLPS shell-heap
AEEHHLOSW hawse-hole
AEEHHNNPT naphthene
AEEHHNPTY hyphenate
AEEHHNSTU unsheathe
AEEHHOOVY yo-heave-ho

AEEHIILPR perihelia
AEEHIILPT epithelia
AEEHIKNRT Katherine
AEEHILLSV Asheville
AEEHILLTW tailwheel
AEEHILMNW meanwhile
AEEHILNSS Sinhalese
AEEHILNTV Helvetian
AEEHILPRS shapelier
AEEHILRTW wealthier
AEEHILSTW white sale
AEEHIMNST mainsheet
AEEHIMNTW mean white
AEEHIMPRY hyperemia
AEEHIMPSZ emphasize
AEEHIMPTZ empathize
AEEHIMRST hetaerism, timeshare
AEEHIMTTW white meat
AEEHINPRS Hesperian
AEEHINPST Stephanie
AEEHINRSV haversine
AEEHINRTT Henrietta
AEEHINRTU eutherian
AEEHINRTW inwreathe
AEEHINSSV heaviness
AEEHIPPSW hawse-pipe
AEEHIPRRT rathe-ripe
AEEHIRRTT Harriette
AEEHIRSTT earthiest, heartiest, hesitater
AEEHKLPSW sheepwalk
AEEHKMMOR homemaker
AEEHKMORS shoemaker
AEEHKMPRT theme park
AEEHKRSSS Shakeress
AEEHLLMOW wholemeal
AEEHLLNOW Hallowe'en
AEEHLLOSW wholesale
AEEHLMMNT Emmenthal
AEEHLMNSW wheelsman
AEEHLMOPT home plate
AEEHLMRTY erythemal
AEEHLMSSS shameless
AEEHLMTTY methylate
AEEHLNOPS anopheles
AEEHLNOSW Halesowen
AEEHLNPST elephants
AEEHLNSST natheless
AEEHLOPST telophase
AEEHLORTW waterhole
AEEHLPRSU phase rule
AEEHLPSSS shapeless
AEEHLPTTY telepathy
AEEHLRSST heartless
AEEHLRTWY weatherly
AEEHLSTXY hexastyle
AEEHMMORT hammer-toe
AEEHMMPSY emphysema
AEEHMNNOP phenomena
AEEHMNOTT moth-eaten
AEEHMOPRS semaphore
AEEHMORSU mouse hare
AEEHMPRST petersham
AEEHMRSTW Westerham
AEEHMSTTW Westmeath
AEEHNPRRS sharpener
AEEHNRRSS harnesser
AEEHNRTTT tenth-rate
AEEHORRST heartsore
AEEHORRSW raree-show
AEEHORRTT to the rear
AEEHORSTV overhaste
AEEHORSTW whatsoe'er
AEEHORSUW warehouse
AEEHPRSST set phrase
AEEHPRSTU superheat
AEEHRRSTT shatterer
AEEHRRSTV harvester
AEEHRSTUX exhauster
AEEIILMNT eliminate
AEEIILNRZ linearize
AEEIILRST Israelite
AEEIILRSZ serialize
AEEIINNTV Vientiane
AEEIINRTT itinerate
AEEIIRTTV iterative
AEEIIRTVZ vizierate
AEEIJMNSS jessamine
AEEIKKLNS snakelike
AEEIKLLPT petal-like
AEEIKLNPR Keplerian
AEEIKLNSS leakiness
AEEIKLSTW weakliest
AEEIKLSTY yeastlike
AEEIKMNRW winemaker
AEEIKNNSY Keynesian
AEEIKNPSS peakiness
AEEIKNSST sneakiest
AEEIKQRSU squeakier
AEEIKRRSS seraskier
AEEIKRRST streakier
AEEILLMTZ metallize
AEEILLPTT paillette
AEEILLPTZ palletize
AEEILLSTT satellite
AEEILMMST semi-metal
AEEILMNNT lineament
AEEILMNPZ Pelmanize
AEEILMNRY minelayer
AEEILMNSS mealiness
AEEILMORT meliorate
AEEILMPST time-lapse
AEEILMRTT altimeter
AEEILMRTW lime water
AEEILMSST measliest
AEEILMTUV emulative
AEEILNNPP peneplain
AEEILNNPR perennial
AEEILNNSS alienness
AEEILNNSX sexennial
AEEILNNTV Levantine, valentine
AEEILNOTV elevation
AEEILNPPP pineapple
AEEILNPRX explainer
AEEILNPSX expansile
AEEILNRSS earliness
AEEILNRTW waterline
AEEILNRVZ vernalize
AEEILNSST essential
AEEILNSSV aliveness
AEEILNTTV ventilate
AEEILOPTT petiolate
AEEILORRT arteriole
AEEILPRST pearliest
AEEILQRUZ equalizer
AEEILRRTT air letter
AEEILRRTV retrieval
AEEILRSSW weariless
AEEILRSTT statelier
AEEILRSTV versatile
AEEILRTTU elutriate
AEEILSSTW leastwise
AEEILSSTZ sleaziest
AEEILSVVY evasively
AEEIMNNZZ mezzanine
AEEIMNRTT terminate
AEEIMNRTV verminate
AEEIMNSSS seaminess
AEEIMNSST meatiness
AEEIMORRS Rosemarie
AEEIMORSW wearisome
AEEIMPRRT prime rate
AEEIMPRSS Parseeism
AEEIMPRST spare time
AEEIMRTTX extra time, taximeter
AEEIMSSTT steamiest
AEEINNNSS inaneness
AEEINNPST septennia
AEEINNRTT entertain
AEEINNRTV innervate
AEEINNSST insensate
AEEINNSSV naiveness
AEEINOPPT appointee
AEEINOPRT peritonea
AEEINORTT orientate
AEEINPRSS passerine
AEEINPSVX expansive
AEEINRRTV veratrine
AEEINRSST irateness
AEEINRSSW weariness
AEEINRSTT reinstate
AEEINRSTU estuarine
AEEINRSTV invertase
AEEINRSTY eye strain
AEEINSSTU uneasiest
AEEINSTTT intestate, satinette
AEEINTTTV attentive, tentative
AEEIOPRST periostea
AEEIOPRTV evaporite, operative
AEEIPPRTW water pipe
AEEIPPRTZ appetizer
AEEIPPRUZ pauperize
AEEIPPSTW waste pipe
AEEIPRRST respirate
AEEIPRRTV privateer
AEEIPRSVV pervasive
AEEIPRTTX extirpate
AEEIRRSTZ rasterize

AEEIRSSTV assertive
AEEISSTTW sweatiest
AEEISSTTY yeastiest
AEEJLMRSU Jerusalem
AEEJMORTT majorette
AEEJMRSTT jet stream
AEEKLLNTW well-taken
AEEKLLPSW sleepwalk
AEEKLOPST Lake Poets
AEEKLSTTW sweet talk
AEEKMNRTW Newmarket
AEEKMRSTY master key
AEEKNOSSV Sevenoaks
AEEKORTUY eukaryote
AEELLLMOS lamellose
AEELLMNTW well-meant
AEELLMRRV marveller
AEELLNRTY eternally
AEELLOPPV love-apple
AEELLOPST Sellotape, sole-plate
AEELLOSUV laevulose
AEELLPSST last sleep, plateless
AEELLRRTV traveller
AEELLRSVY severally
AEELLRTTU tellurate
AEELLSSUV valueless
AEELLSSVV valveless
AEELMMNRT entrammel
AEELMNORY real money
AEELMNOST telamones
AEELMNPSS ampleness
AEELMORST elastomer
AEELMOSWY awesomely
AEELMPRXY exemplary
AEELMPTTY type metal
AEELMRSTT streamlet
AEELMRTTW melt water
AEELNNOSS aloneness
AEELNNRTU neural net
AEELNOPST antelopes
AEELNPRTV prevalent
AEELNRSST alertness
AEELNRSTY earnestly
AEELNRTTV tervalent
AEELNRTTY ternately
AEELNSSST staleness
AEELNSTVX sexvalent
AEELNTTVV velvet ant
AEELOPPRS rose-apple
AEELORTVW water vole
AEELORTVY elevatory
AEELORUVV overvalue
AEELPPRRU puerperal
AEELPPRSS paperless
AEELPPRTU perpetual
AEELPQTTU plaquette
AEELPRRST plasterer
AEELPRRTU prelature
AEELPRSTT saltpeter, saltpetre
AEELRRSTU serrulate
AEELRSSTW waterless
AEELRSTUY austerely
AEELRSTVY severalty
AEELSSSTT stateless, tasteless
AEELSSSTW wasteless
AEELSSSTY yeastless
AEEMMNORT manometer
AEEMMNSTU amusement
AEEMMRRST stammerer
AEEMNNOPR praenomen
AEEMNNORT nanometer, nanometre
AEEMNNOTT atonement
AEEMNNPRT permanent
AEEMNOPSU menopause
AEEMNORTW worm-eaten
AEEMNORUV manoeuvre
AEEMNOSYY easy money
AEEMNPRTY repayment
AEEMNRSST mare's nest, steersman
AEEMNRTTT treatment
AEEMNSSSY sameyness
AEEMNSSTT means test
AEEMNSSTY mateyness
AEEMNSTTT Amstetten, statement, testament
AEEMOPRRT permeator
AEEMOPSSU mesopause
AEEMORSST Massorete
AEEMPPRRT term paper
AEEMPRRTU premature
AEEMPRTTT reattempt
AEEMPRTTU permutate
AEEMRRSTT smatterer
AEEMRSSTT smear test
AEEMRSSTY easy terms
AEEMRTTTW wattmeter
AEENNPRTT penetrant, repentant
AEENNRRTT re-entrant
AEENOPPRT notepaper
AEENOPRSS pre-season
AEENOPRST Esperanto, personate
AEENOPTTT potentate
AEENORRTV venerator
AEENORSTW stoneware
AEENPPRSW newspaper
AEENPRRTU enrapture
AEENPRSSS spareness
AEENPRSTY septenary
AEENRRSTU saunterer
AEENRSSTU Sauternes
AEENSSSUV suaveness
AEEOOPRTZ azeotrope
AEEOPPRSU pea-souper
AEEOPRSTT poetaster
AEEORRSTW rose water
AEEORRTUW outerwear
AEEORRTVW overwater
AEEORSTTV overstate
AEEORSTTW two-seater
AEEPPRSTT test paper
AEEPRRSTY spare tyre
AEEQRSSTU sequestra, set square
AEEQRTTTU quartette
AEERRRSTU treasurer
AEERRRSTV traverser
AEERRTTVX extravert
AEERSSTTU austerest
AEESTTTTU statuette
AEFFIKPST pikestaff
AEFFLLRUY fearfully
AEFFLLTUY fatefully
AEFFLORSW safflower
AEFFNOOSS off-season
AEFFNRSTU rune-staff
AEFFORSTV overstaff
AEFFORSTY for safety
AEFGHILNS angelfish
AEFGHILST safe light
AEFGHILTW white flag
AEFGHINST night safe
AEFGHIRST gear shift
AEFGHLOSU house-flag
AEFGHORRT forgather
AEFGIIMNR magnifier
AEFGIIRRT gratifier
AEFGILLNN Llangefni
AEFGILLRY fragilely
AEFGILRUY lay figure
AEFGINNST fastening
AEFGINNTT fattening
AEFGIRRRY Grey Friar
AEFGIRRST first gear
AEFGLLLMU flagellum
AEFGLNOST flagstone
AEFGLORTW afterglow
AEFGNOPRT front page
AEFGNORRT frontager
AEFGNORTX xenograft
AEFHHLLTU healthful
AEFHHLORT other half
AEFHIKMST makeshift
AEFHILLRT half-litre
AEFHILLTT half-title
AEFHILPST fish-plate
AEFHILSST faithless, flashiest
AEFHIMNRS fisherman
AEFHIMNST mine shaft
AEFHINORS fashioner, refashion
AEFHINRTW wafer-thin
AEFHKLMRS shelf mark
AEFHKORSW freak show
AEFHLLTUY hatefully
AEFHLNNPY halfpenny
AEFHLNSSW newsflash
AEFHLORSV flash-over
AEFHMORSU farmhouse
AEFHOOPRT heatproof
AEFHOORST hare's-foot
AEFHORRTU Our Father
AEFIIKLRY fairy-like
AEFIILMNS semi-final
AEFIILMPR amplifier
AEFIILNNT infantile

AEFIILQRU qualifier
AEFIIMNNS Fenianism
AEFIINRTU infuriate
AEFIKLLSU sail-fluke
AEFIKLMMR film-maker
AEFIKLNSS flakiness
AEFILLNOX flexional
AEFILLRRV Fall River
AEFILMMOR oriflamme
AEFILMNTU fulminate
AEFILMORZ formalize
AEFILMRSW welfarism
AEFILNNUZ influenza
AEFILNORT reflation
AEFILNRSS frailness
AEFILPRSU praiseful
AEFILRSTW welfarist
AEFILSTTU faultiest
AEFIMMNRT firmament
AEFIMNOST manifesto
AEFIMNOTX tamoxifen
AEFIMNOTY fiat money
AEFIMNRST first name
AEFIMORTV formative
AEFIMRSTT first mate
AEFINNSST faintness
AEFINOPRR poriferan
AEFINORSU nefarious
AEFINOSTY Sainte-Foy
AEFINPSTY safety pin
AEFINRSSS sans serif
AEFINSSTT fattiness
AEFIORTUV favourite
AEFIRRSTT first-rate
AEFKLLUWY wakefully
AEFKLNOSW snowflake
AEFKLORSW falsework
AEFKMORRW framework
AEFKNNRSS frankness
AEFLLNTTU flatulent
AEFLLORST forestall
AEFLLRTUY tearfully
AEFLLSSTU faultless
AEFLMNRUU fraenulum
AEFLMOOST fool's mate
AEFLMORTU formulate
AEFLMORWY mayflower
AEFLMRSTU masterful
AEFLNOOSS aloofness
AEFLNOPRY profanely
AEFLNORRY royal fern
AEFLNSSUW awfulness
AEFLOOPTT footplate
AEFLORTWW waterfowl
AEFLPRRUY prayerful
AEFLRSTUU sulfurate
AEFMNOORW forewoman
AEFMORRRT terraform
AEFMORSTT aftermost
AEFNNOORT afternoon
AEFNORTTU fortunate
AEFNORTVW wavefront
AEFNORTWY Fort Wayne
AEFNRSSTU transfuse
AEFOPRRTY prefatory
AEFOPSSTT soft-paste
AEFRRSTTU frustrate
AEGGHIKNT knightage
AEGGHINRT gathering
AEGGHISST shaggiest
AEGGHOPRY geography
AEGGIINPU guinea pig
AEGGILLNV gavelling
AEGGILNNS gleanings
AEGGILNRV graveling
AEGGILNST gangliest
AEGGILSST slaggiest
AEGGINNRV engraving
AEGGINOSY easygoing
AEGGINPRT pargeting
AEGGINRTT targeting
AEGGLNNOR long-range
AEGGLNRRY glengarry
AEGGLRRST straggler
AEGGMORRT mortgager
AEGGNOSUY synagogue
AEGGNPRSS press-gang
AEGGORRSS aggressor
AEGHHINST sheathing
AEGHHIRTU haughtier
AEGHHIRTW high water
AEGHHRRTU hearthrug
AEGHIILNS Ghislaine
AEGHIKNNR hankering
AEGHIKNRS shrinkage
AEGHILMOR heliogram
AEGHILNRS shearling
AEGHILNRT earthling
AEGHILNSV shaveling
AEGHILRRT rear light
AEGHILRST ghastlier
AEGHILRTY light year
AEGHIMMNR hammering
AEGHIMNRT nightmare
AEGHIMORR hierogram
AEGHINNPP happening
AEGHINNRT near thing
AEGHINRST near sight
AEGHINRTU naughtier
AEGHINRTW nightwear
AEGHIOOPS oesophagi
AEGHIPPRY epigraphy
AEGHIPRRS serigraph
AEGHIPRVW viewgraph
AEGHIPSTT spaghetti
AEGHIRRST rear sight
AEGHLMNNT lengthman
AEGHLOOPR oleograph
AEGHLOORR logorrhea
AEGHLORTT larghetto
AEGHLRSTU slaughter
AEGHMORST short game
AEGHMPRYY hypergamy
AEGHNNORS hangers-on
AEGHNNPRU pergunnah
AEGHNOORR gonorrhea
AEGHNOPSY syphonage
AEGHNOPTY pathogeny
AEGHNOSTU shogunate
AEGHNPRSY pharynges
AEGHOPRRX xerograph
AEGHOPRST grapeshot
AEGHOPSSU esophagus
AEGIIKLNT giant-like
AEGIILLRS grisaille
AEGIILLST sigillate
AEGIILMSV vigesimal
AEGIILNSZ signalize
AEGIILNTV genitival, vigilante
AEGIILNTY geniality
AEGIILSTV vestigial
AEGIIMMRT immigrate
AEGIINORT originate
AEGIINRST grainiest
AEGIINSTT instigate
AEGIJNORZ jargonize
AEGIKKMNR kingmaker
AEGIKLLSS glasslike
AEGIKLRSS grasslike
AEGIKMNRT marketing
AEGIKNRST streaking
AEGIKNSSW gawkiness
AEGILLLLY illegally
AEGILLLNU gallinule
AEGILLMNT metalling
AEGILLMNY geminally
AEGILLNNP panelling
AEGILLNNW Gwenllian
AEGILLNQU equalling
AEGILLNRS signaller
AEGILLNRU laureling
AEGILLNRV Granville, ravelling
AEGILLPPU pupillage
AEGILLPSX plexiglas
AEGILLRRU guerrilla
AEGILLRSS salesgirl
AEGILLRST allergist
AEGILMNNT alignment
AEGILMNNY meaningly
AEGILMNPT pigmental
AEGILMNRV marveling
AEGILMNRY Mayerling
AEGILMNSU San Miguel
AEGILMNTU glutamine
AEGILMORR rigmarole
AEGILMORZ glamorize
AEGILNNOR angle-iron
AEGILNORU neuroglia
AEGILNORY legionary
AEGILNQSU equal sign
AEGILNRSS grainless
AEGILNRSY syringeal
AEGILNRTV traveling
AEGILNRUV revaluing
AEGILNRWY wearingly
AEGILNSST slangiest, tasseling
AEGILNSSV Svengalis
AEGILNSSW wineglass
AEGILNSTT tangliest
AEGILNSTY teasingly
AEGILOOPZ apologize
AEGILOOTY aetiology

AEGILPPRR paper girl
AEGILPRSS pier glass
AEGILPRST split gear
AEGILRRRU irregular
AEGILRUVZ vulgarize
AEGILSSST glassiest
AEGIMMNOT gemmation
AEGIMMNRU germanium
AEGIMMNST magnetism
AEGIMMNSU magnesium
AEGIMNNNR remanning
AEGIMNNNU unmeaning
AEGIMNNSS manginess
AEGIMNOPT game point
AEGIMNORS Orangeism
AEGIMNRST Germanist
AEGIMNSTT agistment
AEGINNORS reasoning
AEGINNORW Norwegian
AEGINNORZ organzine
AEGINNOSS seasoning
AEGINNOTT negotiant
AEGINNPPR Perpignan
AEGINNPRT parenting
AEGINNRTT integrant
AEGINNSST tanginess
AEGINOPPR organ pipe, pipe organ
AEGINOPRS Singapore
AEGINORRV granivore
AEGINORRZ organizer
AEGINOSTT gestation
AEGINRRTU garniture
AEGINRSTU signature
AEGINSSSS gassiness
AEGINSSST staginess
AEGINSSUZ gauziness
AEGINSTUU Augustine
AEGIPRTUV purgative
AEGIRRRST registrar
AEGIRRSSW wire grass
AEGIRSSST grassiest
AEGISTTUV gustative
AEGKNRSTU surge tank
AEGLLNOST gallstone
AEGLLORTU lager lout
AEGLLRRUY regularly
AEGLLSSSS glassless
AEGLMMPRS germ plasm
AEGLMNORW Low German
AEGLNNOOT Long Eaton
AEGLNOPRY gyroplane
AEGLNOSTU langouste
AEGLNOSTV Galveston
AEGLNPSTU staple gun
AEGLNRRST strangler
AEGLNRSST strangles
AEGLNRSTY strangely
AEGLORRTU regulator
AEGLORTTY tetralogy
AEGLRSSSS grassless
AEGLRSSSU sugarless
AEGMMOPRR programme
AEGMNNORT magnetron
AEGMNORRW warmonger
AEGMNORSU germanous
AEGMNOTTU mangetout
AEGMOOSUX exogamous
AEGMOPRRR reprogram
AEGMORSSY gossamery
AEGMPRSSU grampuses
AEGNNNOTU agent noun
AEGNNPRTU repugnant
AEGNNSSTU gauntness
AEGNSTTTU tungstate
AEGOOSWYZ wayzgoose
AEGOPRRTY party-goer
AEGOPRRUW groupware
AEGORRSTU surrogate
AEGORSSTU stegosaur
AEHHILLLT ill health
AEHHILLRV Haverhill
AEHHILLTW Whitehall
AEHHILLTY healthily
AEHHILOPT Theophila
AEHHIMPRS Hampshire
AEHHIORRS horsehair
AEHHIPPSS shipshape
AEHHISTWW whitewash
AEHHLNTUY unhealthy
AEHHLOPTY halophyte
AEHHLOSTV shovel hat
AEHHLPRSW Welsh harp
AEHHLPRTY hypethral
AEHHMOOPT homeopath
AEHHMORRT Rotherham
AEHHNOPTY theophany
AEHHNORTW Hawthorne
AEHHNRSSS harshness
AEHHOPPST phosphate
AEHHOSSUW wash-house
AEHIILMTU humiliate
AEHIIMNST histamine
AEHIIMRST hetairism
AEHIINOPT Ethiopian
AEHIINRSS hairiness
AEHIIPSTT hepatitis
AEHIJLOSU jailhouse
AEHIKKLMS milk shake
AEHIKMRSS Shakerism
AEHIKNPSW whip snake
AEHIKNSSS shakiness
AEHIKQRSU Quakerish
AEHILLMOP Philomela
AEHILLNSV Nashville
AEHILLPTY philately
AEHILLTTY lethality
AEHILLTWY wealthily
AEHILMNOP Philomena
AEHILNNOT anthelion
AEHILNOPR parhelion
AEHILNORT lion-heart
AEHILNOST hailstone
AEHILNPRS planisher
AEHILNQRU harlequin
AEHILORST horsetail
AEHILOSTT heliostat
AEHILPPTY epiphytal
AEHILPRSS splashier
AEHILPSSV slave ship
AEHILRSTY hairstyle
AEHIMNNOT anthemion
AEHIMNORZ harmonize
AEHIMNOST Thomasine
AEHIMNPSS misshapen
AEHIMNPST pantheism
AEHIMOPXY hypoxemia
AEHIMPSST steamship
AEHIMPSTT empathist
AEHIMQSSU squeamish
AEHIMRSST marshiest
AEHINOPRZ orphanize
AEHINOPST pantihose
AEHINORSS hoariness
AEHINORST hortensia, senhorita
AEHINPPRT paper-thin
AEHINPPRU unhappier
AEHINPPSS happiness
AEHINPPTX Xanthippe
AEHINPSSS apishness
AEHINPSSY Sisyphean
AEHINPSTT pantheist
AEHINRRSV revarnish, varnisher
AEHINSSST hastiness
AEHINSSSW washiness
AEHIOPPRY hyperopia
AEHIORRTT throatier
AEHIORTTV hortative
AEHIORTUZ authorize
AEHIPRSTT therapist
AEHIQRSSU squashier
AEHIRRSTW swarthier
AEHIRSSTT trashiest
AEHKLNSST thankless
AEHKLOOSW Hooke's law
AEHKLRRSU Karlsruhe
AEHKORRTW earthwork
AEHLLLMPS lamp shell
AEHLLLOSY sally-hole
AEHLLMRTY thermally
AEHLLNOOP allophone
AEHLLPSSU phalluses
AEHLLPSSY haplessly
AEHLLRSST star shell
AEHLMOOST loathsome
AEHLMOSSU almshouse
AEHLMOSTU malthouse
AEHLNNOPR alpenhorn
AEHLNOPTT Pentothal
AEHLNOQSU Ashquelon
AEHLNPSUY unshapely
AEHLNRTUY unearthly
AEHLOPPSY polyphase
AEHLOPRSW plowshare
AEHLOPRSY horseplay
AEHLOPSUY playhouse
AEHLORSST salt horse
AEHLORTWY holy water
AEHLPRRSU spherular
AEHMNNSSU humanness
AEHMNRRWY wherryman
AEHMOPPRT top-hamper
AEHMORRTW earthworm

AEHNNRSSU	unharness	**AEIIMNRTU**	miniature	**AEILLNRST**	installer
AEHNOOPRR	harpooner	**AEIIMPSSV**	impassive	**AEILLNRTU**	ill nature,
AEHNOOPSX	saxophone	**AEIINNNTV**	antivenin		tellurian
AEHNOORST	hoarstone	**AEIINNPTT**	in-patient	**AEILLNSTY**	saliently
AEHNOPRTU	neuropath	**AEIINNRSS**	raininess	**AEILLOPPS**	papillose
AEHNOPSTY	pantyhose	**AEIINNRTT**	itinerant	**AEILLOPPT**	popliteal
AEHNORSTT	north-east	**AEIINNSTU**	insinuate	**AEILLORTW**	towel rail
AEHNPRSSS	sharpness	**AEIINOPTX**	expiation	**AEILLPRUZ**	pluralize
AEHOOPRRY	pyorrhoea	**AEIINORST**	seriation	**AEILLPSTU**	pulsatile
AEHOOPSTT	osteopath	**AEIINORTT**	iteration	**AEILLRRTY**	artillery
AEHOOSSTU	oast house	**AEIINOTTV**	novitiate	**AEILLRSTW**	stairwell
AEHOPSSTT	post-haste	**AEIINPSTT**	paintiest	**AEILLRTWY**	water lily
AEHOPSSTW	sweatshop	**AEIINRRTY**	itinerary	**AEILMMNPS**	Pelmanism
AEHORSSTU	authoress	**AEIINRSTZ**	sanitizer	**AEILMMNST**	mentalism
AEHORSTVW	short wave	**AEIIPRTTV**	partitive	**AEILMNNSS**	manliness
AEHORSTVY	overhasty	**AEIIPRTVV**	privative	**AEILMNOOT**	emotional
AEHORSTWY	seaworthy	**AEIIPRTVZ**	privatize	**AEILMNORZ**	normalize
AEHOSSTTU	south-east	**AEIIPSSTX**	epistaxis	**AEILMNOSS**	loaminess,
AEHPRSSUW	washers-up	**AEIIPSTTT**	stipitate		melanosis
AEHRSSTUU	thesaurus	**AEIIRRSTT**	arteritis	**AEILMNOTU**	emulation
AEIIILMNP	epilimnia	**AEIIRRSTU**	retiarius	**AEILMNRSU**	semi-lunar,
AEIIILRVZ	vizierial	**AEIIRRSTV**	arriviste		unrealism
AEIIILTVX	lixiviate	**AEIIRSTTV**	varietist	**AEILMNRVY**	liveryman
AEIIIMTTV	imitative	**AEIITTTTV**	tittivate	**AEILMNSST**	maltiness
AEIIJLNUV	juvenilia	**AEIJKKRVY**	Reykjavik	**AEILMNSTT**	mentalist
AEIIKKTTW	kittiwake	**AEIJKLNSU**	Seljukian	**AEILMNTTY**	mentality
AEIIKLLNS	snail-like	**AEIJMOPPR**	pipe major	**AEILMORRZ**	moralizer
AEIIKLNOZ	kaolinize	**AEIJNNNRZ**	Zrenjanin	**AEILMOSTZ**	solmizate
AEIIKLNST	saintlike	**AEIJNSSZZ**	jazziness	**AEILMSSVY**	massively
AEIIKRSTT	keratitis	**AEIJNSTTU**	jauntiest	**AEILMSTTU**	stimulate
AEIILLMNN	millennia	**AEIKKLLOO**	lookalike	**AEILNNNOR**	non-linear
AEIILLMRS	Ramillies	**AEIKKLLST**	stalklike	**AEILNNOPR**	nonpareil
AEIILLTTT	titillate	**AEIKKNNSS**	snakeskin	**AEILNNOST**	tensional
AEIILMNNR	mainliner	**AEIKLLNPT**	plantlike	**AEILNNOSV**	Slovenian
AEIILMNPT	plain time	**AEIKLLNRY**	Killarney	**AEILNNOTV**	antinovel
AEIILMNRT	train-mile	**AEIKLLTTU**	little auk	**AEILNNPSS**	plainness
AEIILMNRU	luminaire	**AEIKLMNOW**	womanlike	**AEILNNPSU**	peninsula
AEIILMNUZ	aluminize	**AEIKLNNSS**	lankiness	**AEILNNPTY**	pinnately
AEIILMOSV	malvoisie	**AEIKLNORT**	oil tanker	**AEILNNTUV**	univalent
AEIILMRSS	serialism	**AEIKLNRSS**	larkiness	**AEILNOOPS**	polonaise
AEIILMRTT	time trial	**AEIKLNRUW**	unwarlike	**AEILNOORS**	erosional
AEIILNNOT	lineation	**AEIKLQSUY**	squeakily	**AEILNOPST**	sealpoint
AEIILNNRT	triennial	**AEIKLRSTY**	streakily	**AEILNOPTT**	potential
AEIILNOPT	epilation	**AEIKMQRSU**	Quakerism	**AEILNORSS**	sensorial
AEIILNOTV	inviolate	**AEIKNNPRS**	spinnaker	**AEILNORST**	tensorial
AEIILNPRT	reptilian	**AEIKNNSSS**	snakiness	**AEILNORSV**	versional
AEIILNPTV	plaintive	**AEIKNOPTW**	weak point	**AEILNOSSS**	sessional
AEIILNPTZ	platinize	**AEIKNORTU**	ketonuria	**AEILNPRTY**	interplay,
AEIILNRRT	trilinear	**AEIKNPSSW**	pawkiness		painterly,
AEIILNRST	saintlier	**AEIKNRSSS**	sarkiness		party line
AEIILNRSU	uniserial	**AEIKNSSTW**	swankiest	**AEILNPSTY**	sapiently
AEIILNRTY	linearity	**AEIKPPQSU**	pipsqueak	**AEILNPTTX**	plain text
AEIILNRTZ	Latinizer	**AEIKPRSST**	piss-taker	**AEILNPTTY**	patiently
AEIILNSTW	waistline	**AEIKPRSTY**	strike pay	**AEILNRSST**	snarliest
AEIILNTVY	veniality	**AEILLLRTY**	literally	**AEILNRSUV**	universal
AEIILORST	solitaire	**AEILLMMST**	small-time	**AEILNRTTV**	trivalent
AEIILORTV	variolite	**AEILLMNRY**	millenary	**AEILNRTUY**	unreality
AEIILRSST	serialist	**AEILLMNSY**	seminally	**AEILNSSST**	saltiness,
AEIILRSTY	seriality	**AEILLMNTT**	little man		stainless
AEIILRTUZ	ritualize	**AEILLMPPR**	paper mill	**AEILNSSTT**	taintless
AEIILSUVZ	visualize	**AEILLMRTW**	watermill	**AEILNSSTW**	slantwise
AEIIMMRXZ	maximizer	**AEILLMSSY**	aimlessly	**AEILNSUUX**	unisexual
AEIIMNORV	Rovaniemi	**AEILLNOPT**	pollinate	**AEILOPRRZ**	polarizer
AEIIMNPST	impatiens	**AEILLNORW**	Orwellian	**AEILOPRTV**	prolative
AEIIMNPTT	impatient	**AEILLNPST**	panellist	**AEILORTTV**	levitator

AEILORTTZ totalizer
AEILPPRTU preputial
AEILPRSTT paltriest
AEILPRSVY privy seal
AEILPRTVY privately
AEILPSSTT pastelist
AEILPSSVY passively
AEILPSTTU stipulate
AEILQRRUY reliquary
AEILRSSTT last rites
AEILRSSTY lay sister
AEILRTUUX luxuriate
AEILSSSTW waistless
AEILSTUXY sexuality
AEIMMNNRS mannerism
AEIMMNNTU Minuteman
AEIMMNOPT pantomime
AEIMMRSST smarmiest
AEIMMRSUZ summarize
AEIMMSTUV summative
AEIMNNNQU mannequin
AEIMNNOPU pneumonia
AEIMNNORZ Normanize
AEIMNNOSS San Simeon
AEIMNNOST Minnesota
AEIMNNOSZ neo-Nazism
AEIMNNOTT mentation
AEIMNNOTV antivenom
AEIMNNRST mannerist
AEIMNOPRT protamine
AEIMNORST steam iron
AEIMNORTV normative
AEIMNORWZ womanizer
AEIMNPRSS Pirmasens
AEIMNPRST spearmint
AEIMNRRSU Surinamer
AEIMNRSTU antiserum
AEIMNRSTX Axminster
AEIMNRTTY maternity
AEIMOPRRT imperator
AEIMOPRTX proximate
AEIMORSTT estimator
AEIMPPRSU pauperism
AEIMPRRTT part-timer
AEIMPRTUZ trapezium
AEIMPSSTW swampiest
AEIMQSUUX Esquimaux
AEIMRRRTU terrarium
AEIMRRTTY termitary
AEIMRRTYZ martyrize
AEINNNOTW Newtonian
AEINNOPSX expansion
AEINNORST Nestorian
AEINNORTV nervation, vernation
AEINNOSST sensation
AEINNOTTT attention
AEINNRSTT instanter, transient
AEINNRSTU saturnine
AEINNRTYZ tyrannize
AEINNSSST nastiness
AEINNSSTT nattiness
AEINNSSTW tawniness
AEINOOPRT operation
AEINOPPRT appointer, reappoint
AEINOPRRT pretorian
AEINOPRSS aspersion
AEINOPRSV pervasion
AEINOPRTV overpaint
AEINOPRTZ patronize
AEINOPSSS soapiness
AEINOPSTT septation
AEINOQRTU inquorate, ortanique
AEINORRST serration
AEINORRTV overtrain
AEINORSST assertion
AEINORSSU arsenious
AEINORSTT stationer
AEINPPSSS sappiness
AEINPPSST snappiest
AEINPRRST transpire
AEINPRSTW rainswept
AEINPRTTY paternity
AEINPSSST pastiness
AEINRRSST tarriness
AEINRRSTT restraint
AEINRSSTT rattiness, resistant, tartiness
AEINRSSTU sustainer
AEINSSSSS sassiness
AEINSSSTT tastiness
AEINSSTTT tattiness
AEINSSTZZ snazziest
AEIOOPRST patio rose
AEIOPRRVZ vaporizer
AEIOPRTTV portative, vaporetti
AEIOPRTXY expiatory
AEIORRRWZ razor wire
AEIOSTUVX vexatious
AEIPPRRTY Tipperary
AEIPRSTUZ trapezius
AEIQRRTTU triquetra
AEIQRSSTU sea squirt
AEIQRTTUZ quartzite
AEIRRSSTT starriest, traitress
AEIRRTTTU triturate
AEIRSSTTU tessitura
AEIRSTTTX testatrix
AEIRSTTUY austerity
AEISSTTUW sweatsuit
AEJLLOSUY jealously
AEJLNOPSU Paul Jones
AEJMPRTUW water jump
AEJOPSTUX juxtapose
AEKLLSSST stalkless
AEKLMOORT toolmaker
AEKLMORSS loss-maker
AEKLMORTW metalwork
AEKLPRSSS sparkless
AEKMNOOQU moonquake
AEKMNOPRS pranksome
AEKMNOPSS spokesman
AEKMPRRSS pressmark
AEKMPRSTU rump steak
AEKNOORST snakeroot
AEKNPRRST prankster
AEKNRSSST starkness
AEKOPPRRW paperwork
AEKOPRTYY karyotype
AELLLMOSU malleolus
AELLLNSSW Snell's law
AELLLPTUU pullulate
AELLLRSTU stellular
AELLLSSWY lawlessly
AELLMNOTT allotment
AELLMNOWW well woman
AELLMNSSS smallness
AELLMOPRY permalloy
AELLMORST steamroll
AELLMORTU Tullamore
AELLNNOTW Allentown
AELLNOSTW stonewall
AELLNQUUY unequally
AELLNRTUY neutrally
AELLNRTVY ventrally
AELLNSSUY sensually
AELLOOPRT allotrope
AELLOPRRT patroller
AELLOPRTY prolately
AELLOPTUV pole vault
AELLORSWW swallower
AELLOSSTW sallowest
AELLOSUYZ zealously
AELLRRSUY surreally
AELLRSSTY artlessly
AELLTTUXY textually
AELMMORST maelstrom
AELMMOSUU mausoleum
AELMNNNTU annulment
AELMNNOOP monoplane
AELMNOOPR lampooner
AELMNOORY monolayer
AELMNOPTU pulmonate
AELMNORWW lawnmower
AELMNOSSW womanless
AELMNRSTU menstrual, Ulsterman
AELMOORSS salesroom
AELMORSUV marvelous
AELMRTWXY wax myrtle
AELNNOSUX non-sexual
AELNOOSSW low season
AELNOOSTT stolonate
AELNOPRSY layperson
AELNORSTU Solutrean
AELNORTVW navelwort
AELNOTUVV vol-au-vent
AELNRRUVY vulnerary
AELNRSTTU resultant
AELNSSSUU usualness
AELOOPRTW water polo
AELOORRTT tolerator
AELOPPRWY power play
AELOPPSTU soup plate
AELOPRRTW pearlwort
AELOPSTTU postulate
AELOPSTVV stop valve
AELPPRTUW Wuppertal
AELPRSSST strapless

AELPSTTUU pustulate
AELQRRTUY quarterly
AEMMNORTY momentary
AEMMRSTYY asymmetry
AEMNNOORS Roman nose
AEMNNORTT remontant
AEMNORRTU numerator
AEMNORSTY monastery
AEMNRSSST smartness
AEMNRSTTU transmute
AEMNRSTVY vestryman
AEMOORSTT stateroom
AEMOPRRTY temporary
AEMOPRSTU mousetrap
AEMOPSTTY asymptote
AEMPRSSTY spymaster
AEMQRRTUY marquetry
AENNOOPPR propanone
AENNOOSST Sonsonate
AENNPSSTU unaptness
AENOOPSST soapstone
AENOORRST resonator
AENOORRTV renovator
AENOPRSST patroness, transpose
AENOPRSUV supernova
AENORRSTW narrowest
AENQSSSTU squatness
AENRRTTUX tax return
AEOOPRTTV vaporetto
AEOORTTUU autoroute
AEOPRRRTY portrayer
AEOPRRSTT prostrate
AEOPRRSTU pterosaur
AEOPRRSTW spearwort
AEOPRSTWY top-sawyer
AEOQRRSSU squarrose
AEORRSTTU star route
AEORSSTUU trousseau
AEORSTTVW straw vote
AEPPRSTUU suppurate
AEPQRRTUY parquetry
AEPRRSSTU superstar
AEQRRSTUY try-square
AEQSSTTTU squattest
AFFGIIRST sgraffiti
AFFGIORST sgraffito
AFFHILRSY raffishly
AFFIILNPT plaintiff
AFFILNRUY ruffianly
AFFIMMNNU muffin man
AFFKNORRT Frankfort
AFFLOOTTU foot-fault
AFFMNNRUY funny farm
AFFMOORST staffroom
AFGGGINOT faggoting
AFGGIINTU fatiguing
AFGGILNOS fog signal
AFGHHILLT half-light
AFGHILLNT nightfall
AFGHILSTT lightfast
AFGHIPRTW whip-graft
AFGHMOORT homograft
AFGIILNNU unfailing
AFGIILRTY fragility
AFGIINRRY fairy ring
AFGIKNRST skin graft
AFGILLNUY gainfully
AFGILNNOU Union flag
AFGILNNWY fawningly
AFGILNORV flavoring
AFGILRTUY frugality
AFGIMNORR graniform
AFGIMORTU fumigator
AFGINNPRY frying pan
AFGLNOORT organ loft
AFGNNOOSU son of a gun
AFGNOOORW wagon-roof
AFGNOPRSW frogspawn
AFGORSSTU soft sugar
AFHHLRTTU half-truth
AFHIIKNOP kniphofia
AFHILNSTU flash unit
AFHIORRSZ razor-fish
AFHIORSTY forsythia
AFHLLMRUY harmfully
AFHLLORST shortfall
AFHLMNRUU unharmful
AFHOORRST hoar frost
AFIIILNOT filiation
AFIILNNOT inflation
AFIILNOOT foliation
AFIILRSTT stairlift
AFIIMNRRY infirmary
AFIINORSU infusoria
AFIIOORRT a fortiori
AFIIORRTU fioritura
AFIKLLMOT milk float
AFILLNPUY painfully
AFILLOOPR April Fool
AFILLRTUW wall-fruit
AFILMMORS formalism
AFILMNNTU fulminant
AFILMORST formalist
AFILMORTY formality
AFILNOOTT flotation
AFILOORSS fossorial
AFIMMMMOR mammiform
AFIMNNORT informant
AFIMNOORT formation
AFINOOPRR rainproof
AFINOPRTY profanity
AFIRRSTTU star fruit
AFKLLMRSU full marks
AFKLOOSTT footstalk
AFKOORRTW work of art
AFLLLPUYY playfully
AFLLMOOPR floor lamp
AFLLNOOPR floor plan
AFLLNORTY frontally
AFLMORRUY formulary
AFLOOPSTY splay-foot
AFLOORSUV flavorous
AFLOPRRSU fluorspar
AFLOSTUUY fatuously
AFMNORRST transform
AFMNORRTW warm front
AFMOORSTY styrofoam
AFORRSTTU AstroTurf
AGGGILNNY naggingly
AGGHILOOY hagiology
AGGHILSWY waggishly
AGGHINSTT stag-night
AGGHIRSTY gay rights
AGGIILNNS signaling
AGGIIMNNR margining
AGGIIMNST gigantism
AGGIINNPX Pingxiang
AGGILLLNY gallingly
AGGILLNOP galloping
AGGILLNRY glaringly
AGGILNNOS ganglions, singalong
AGGILNNRW wrangling
AGGILNNWY gnawingly
AGGILNRTY gratingly
AGGINNOOR gorgonian
AGGINORRS grosgrain
AGGMOORRT mortgagor
AGGNNOPYY Pyongyang
AGHHIISTW waist-high
AGHHIKNTW nighthawk
AGHHILRTU ultra-high
AGHHILTUY haughtily
AGHHINRST thrashing
AGHHLOOPR holograph
AGHHMOOPR homograph
AGHHNOUZZ Zhangzhou
AGHIILLTT tail light
AGHIINRSV ravishing
AGHIKMNOW Wokingham
AGHILLMPT lamplight
AGHILLNTY haltingly
AGHILLORY Holy Grail
AGHILLSTY ghastlily
AGHILMORT algorithm, logarithm
AGHILNPTY plaything
AGHILNSTT last thing
AGHILNTUY naughtily
AGHILRSTT starlight
AGHIMNRST hamstring
AGHIMORST histogram
AGHINNOST Ashington
AGHINORTU authoring
AGHINPSUW washing-up
AGHKMOPRY kymograph
AGHKOPRRU Gorakhpur
AGHLLOOPY haplology
AGHLMNOPU ploughman
AGHLMOOPR lagomorph
AGHLMOOTU goalmouth
AGHLNOOTY anthology
AGHLNOSTU onslaught
AGHLOOPTY pathology
AGHLOPPRY polygraph
AGHLOPRXY xylograph
AGHLORSSU hourglass
AGHMNOOPR monograph, nomograph, phonogram
AGHMNRSTU hamstrung
AGHMOOPRT photogram
AGHNOOPRS sonograph
AGHNORSST stag's horn

AGHOOPRRY orography
AGHOOPRYZ zoography
AGIIILNRV Virgilian
AGIIINNRV Virginian
AGIIINSTV vaginitis
AGIIKLMNR grimalkin
AGIILLMMR milligram
AGIILLNRT trialling
AGIILLNRV rivalling
AGIILLNWY wailingly
AGIILMNTY malignity
AGIILNNST saintling
AGIILNNWZ Zwinglian
AGIILNORS sailoring
AGIILNORT tailoring
AGIILNOST isolating
AGIILNPRS spiraling
AGIILNSSS isinglass
AGIILORTT litigator
AGIIMMNRT immigrant
AGIIMNORT migration
AGIIMORTT mitigator
AGIIMRSTT trigamist
AGIINNORS signorina
AGIINNQTU antiquing
AGIINNRTT intrigant
AGIINORST Trisagion
AGIIORRRT irrigator
AGIIRSSTT gastritis
AGIIRSTTU guitarist
AGIKLMRSU milk sugar
AGIKLNOTT talking-to
AGIKMORSS kissogram
AGIKNNPRW king prawn
AGIKNNPSW king's pawn
AGILLLNUY lingually
AGILLMNRU Mullingar
AGILLNNNU annulling
AGILLNOPW walloping
AGILLNOTT allotting, totalling
AGILLNSTY lastingly
AGILMNNOO Mongolian
AGILMNNOY moaningly
AGILMNSUY amusingly
AGILMRSUV vulgarism
AGILNNOPS plainsong
AGILNNOQU Algonquin
AGILNNORT Arlington
AGILNNPTY pantingly
AGILNNRTY rantingly
AGILNNRWY warningly
AGILNNWYY yawningly
AGILNOOTT agnolotti
AGILNORRY roaringly
AGILNORSY soaringly
AGILNORVY vainglory
AGILNOSTW long waist
AGILNPRRU larruping
AGILNPRSY raspingly, sparingly
AGILNPRTT prattling
AGILNPSSY passingly
AGILNPSTT splatting
AGILNRSTT startling
AGILNRVYY varyingly
AGILOOPST apologist
AGILRRTUY garrulity
AGILRTUVY vulgarity
AGIMMNSUY gymnasium
AGIMNNNNU unmanning
AGIMNNOPT tamponing
AGIMNORSU ignoramus
AGIMORRTY migratory
AGIMORSTU trigamous
AGINNPRSU unsparing
AGINNRUVY unvarying
AGINOOPSS poison gas
AGINOPRRT parroting
AGINOPRTU purgation
AGINOPRUV vapouring
AGINORSTY signatory
AGINOSTTU gustation
AGINPPRST strapping, trappings
AGINPRSTT spratting
AGINQSTTU squatting
AGIOPRRSY spirogyra
AGJKNORRU kurrajong
AGKLPPRSU spark plug
AGKNORSST knotgrass
AGKOPRSTU task group
AGLLNOOPY polygonal
AGLLOOSSW glass wool
AGLMOORSU glamorous
AGLMPRSUU lump sugar, sugarplum
AGLOOPRTY patrology
AGLOORSST glossator
AGLOORSTY astrology
AGLOOTTUY tautology
AGLOPPRUY playgroup
AGLORRSUU garrulous
AGLORSSTW glasswort
AGMMOSTUU gummatous
AGMNNORST strongman
AGMNORRST strong-arm
AGMNOSSUY syngamous
AGMNSSTUY nystagmus
AGNNOPPTU oppugnant
AGNOOPRST organ stop
AGNRRSTUY strangury
AGOPRRTUY purgatory
AGORSTTUY gustatory
AGRSTTTTU Stuttgart
AHHIIRRST hair shirt
AHHIORRST shorthair
AHHLORSTU short haul
AHHMOSTUW mouthwash
AHHNORRST hartshorn
AHHOPPRUY happy hour
AHIIIKLSW Kiswahili
AHIIKKRSU Kurashiki
AHIILLPPP Phillippa
AHIILMORY homiliary
AHIILORSU hilarious
AHIILOSST halitosis
AHIILRSTT shirt-tail
AHIIMMRST Mithraism
AHIIMRSTT Mithraist
AHIINORST historian
AHIINPSST Hispanist, saintship
AHIIPRSSZ sizarship
AHIIRRSTT arthritis
AHIJMOPRS majorship
AHIJNNOST Saint John
AHIKKNNTT think-tank
AHIKKNRSS sharkskin
AHIKKTTWY Kitty Hawk
AHIKLLSUU Kalulushi
AHIKLMSWY mawkishly
AHIKLNSVY knavishly
AHIKLRSTU hula skirt
AHILLOPRT prothalli
AHILLOSSW sallowish
AHILLOSTW tallowish
AHILLSSVY slavishly
AHILMNNSY mannishly
AHILMNNUY inhumanly
AHILMNOUZ Manzhouli
AHILMORST hailstorm
AHILMPRTU triumphal
AHILNORTT thorntail, triathlon
AHILNPPUY unhappily
AHILOPPTY Hippolyta
AHILORSTW show trial
AHILORTTY throatily
AHILPSSWY waspishly
AHILQSSUY squashily
AHILRSTWY swarthily
AHIMMNORU harmonium
AHIMNOOSU homousian
AHIMNORST harmonist
AHIMOPRSY mayorship
AHIMOPSTY opsimathy
AHIMOPSUX amphioxus
AHINNOOPT phonation
AHINNOPTY antiphony
AHINOOPRS Sophronia
AHINOORTT hortation
AHINOPPST paint shop
AHINORRSW narrowish
AHINPRSST trans-ship
AHIOPPRRY porphyria
AHIOPRSUV vapourish
AHIOPSTXY hypotaxis
AHIORRTWY airworthy
AHIORTTUY authority
AHJOPSSWY phossy jaw
AHKMORRST short mark
AHKORSTUW Southwark
AHLLLOSWY shallowly
AHLLMOOPR allomorph
AHLLOPSUY aphyllous
AHLMMOPSY lymphomas
AHLMOOOPR homopolar
AHLMOPTYY polymathy
AHLMORSTY solar myth
AHLNOPSSU Alphonsus
AHMNOOPTY taphonomy
AHMOOPRSU amorphous
AHMOPRTTU mouthpart
AHNNORSTT Northants

AHNOOPRTY phonatory
AHNOPSTYY hyponasty
AHNORRSTT North Star
AHOOOPTTT hot potato
AHOOPSTTT photostat
AHOORRTTY hortatory
AHPRSSTTU push-start
AIIILLNTY initially
AIIILMNST laminitis
AIIIMNOTT imitation
AIIINNNOT inanition
AIIINNSTY asininity
AIIINORTT initiator
AIIINOTTV vitiation
AIIJLOTVY joviality
AIIKLMNRT milk train
AIILLMMNY minimally
AIILLMRSY similarly
AIILLRSTT triallist
AIILLRTVY trivially
AIILMMNUU aluminium
AIILMNORT trinomial
AIILMNSST Stalinism
AIILMPRRY primarily
AIILMRSTU ritualism
AIILNOOST isolation
AIILNOOTV violation
AIILNOQTU liquation
AIILNOSTT siltation
AIILNOTTU tuitional
AIILNPSTU plain suit
AIILNRSST sinistral
AIILNRTUY unitarily
AIILNSSTT Stalinist
AIILPRSST spritsail
AIILPRSTU spiritual
AIILPRSTY spirality
AIILRSTTU ritualist
AIILSTUVY visuality
AIIMMPRSV vampirism
AIIMNNTUY unanimity
AIIMNOPRS prosimian
AIIMNOPSS impassion
AIIMNORSX minor axis
AIIMNOSTY animosity
AIIMNPSTT timpanist
AIIMOORTV vomitoria
AIIMOPRRS apriorism
AIIMRSTUU Mauritius
AIINNNOPT pinnation
AIINNORTT nitration
AIINNORTU ruination, urination
AIINNOTTX antitoxin
AIINOOPRT piano trio
AIINOOQRU Iroquoian
AIINOPRTT partition
AIINOPRTV privation
AIINORSTT striation
AIINORSVY visionary
AIINORTTT attrition, titration
AIINOSTTU situation
AIINQTTUY antiquity
AIINRTTUY unitarity
AIIOPRSSS psoriasis
AIIOPRSTT parotitis, topiarist
AIIOPRTVY oviparity
AIIORRRTT irritator
AIIPRTTUY pituitary
AIIPSSTVY passivity
AIJLRRTUY trial jury
AIJMORSTU major suit
AIKKLMOSS Solikamsk
AIKLLNOTW know-it-all
AIKLMOVYY Mykolayiv
AIKLMSTTU multitask
AIKLNOSSY ankylosis
AIKLOSSUV souvlakis
AIKMNNOSW kinswoman
AIKNOOOPS poison oak
AIKNOPRTW paintwork
AILLMMORY immorally
AILLMMPST stamp-mill
AILLMNNOY nominally
AILLMOOTT tomatillo
AILLMOPTY optimally
AILLMPRSU pluralism
AILLMSUUV alluviums
AILLNORST tonsillar
AILLNORSU lunisolar
AILLNOTUU ululation
AILLNRSUY insularly
AILLOSSTY loyalists
AILLPPRUY pupillary
AILLPRSTU pluralist
AILLPRTUY plurality
AILLRTTUY titularly
AILLRTUVY virtually
AILMMOORT immolator
AILMMRSUY summarily
AILMMSTUU mutualism
AILMMTTUU ultimatum
AILMNOPSS spoilsman
AILMNOPST Platonism
AILMNOPSY amylopsin
AILMNORST mortal sin
AILMNORTY normality
AILMNSTTU stimulant
AILMORSST storm-sail
AILMORSSU solariums
AILMORSTU simulator
AILMORTTU mutilator
AILMORTTY mortality
AILMPRSTY palmistry
AILMSTTUU mutualist
AILMTTUUY mutuality
AILNNOPTU Plutonian
AILNNOSSW sons-in-law
AILNNSTTY instantly
AILNOORST tonsorial, torsional
AILNOOSTV solvation
AILNOOTUV ovulation
AILNOPSTT Platonist
AILNOPSTU pulsation
AILNORSTU insulator, Solutrian
AILNOSUXY anxiously
AILNPPSTU suppliant
AILNPQTUY piquantly
AILNRTUUX luxuriant
AILOOPRST spoliator
AILOOPTTU autopilot
AILOORSUV variolous
AILORSUVY savourily, variously
AILOSSTUY autolysis
AIMMMMNOS Mammonism
AIMMMNOST Mammonist
AIMMNNORS Normanism
AIMMNORTY matrimony
AIMMNOSTU summation
AIMMRSSTU summarist
AIMNNOORT nominator
AIMNNOPST pointsman
AIMNNOSUU unanimous
AIMNNOTUY mountainy
AIMNNOTYY anonymity
AIMNOPRSY parsimony
AIMNOPRTT important
AIMNOPRTY patrimony
AIMNORRST rainstorm
AIMNORRSU Ursa Minor
AIMNORRTU ruminator
AIMNRSSTU saturnism
AIMOORTTV motivator
AIMOPSSTU potassium
AINNNOSTU unisonant
AINNOOPRS sopranino
AINNOOPRT pronation
AINNOORTV innovator
AINOOPPRT apportion
AINOOPRRT proration
AINOOQTTU quotation
AINOOTTUX autotoxin
AINOPRSTU supinator
AINOPRSUU uniparous
AINPSSTTU pants suit
AINRSTTTU antitrust
AIOOPPSST apoptosis
AIOOPRSUV oviparous
AIOOSTTTT tattooist
AIOPRSSTT spit-roast
AIORRSSTU sartorius
AJMMMNNOPU Panmunjom
AJMNOORTW town-major
AJMNORUWY jurywoman
AJMPRSTTU jump-start
AKLLMMOWY mollymawk
AKLORSSTW salt works
AKMNOORWW workwoman
AKOPRRSTW strap-work
ALLLNNSUY Sally Lunn
ALLLNPTUU pullulant
ALLMNOSTW small-town
ALLNOOPTY polytonal
ALLNOPTTU pollutant
ALLNSUUUY unusually
ALLOOPRTY allotropy
ALLOPPRUY popularly
ALLOPRSTW straw poll
ALLOPRSTY sally-port

ALLOPRSUY parlously
ALLORRSTY rostrally
ALMMNSSUU Mussulman
ALMNNOOOS monsoonal
ALMNNOUWY unwomanly
ALMNOPRUY pulmonary
ALMOORSUY amorously
ALMPRSTTU last trump
ALNOOOPRT portolano
ALNOOPRST portolans
ALNOOPSST salt spoon
ALNOPPRUU unpopular
ALNOPSTTU postulant
ALNORTUVY voluntary
ALOOOPRTZ protozoal
ALOOPRTUV pot-valour
ALOORTUVY ovulatory
ALOPPRSSU prolapsus
ALOPRRSUY spur royal
ALOPRSTTU Port Salut
ALOPRSTUY pulsatory
AMMNPSTUY tympanums
AMMOOSTTU Matsumoto
AMNNOOSUY anonymous
AMNOOPSTW postwoman
AMNOORSTY astronomy
AMNOORTWY town mayor
AMNOPRSST sportsman
AMOOORSTV vasomotor
AMOORRRWW arrow worm
AMORRSTWW straw-worm
AMPRSTUUY sumptuary
ANNORSTUY tyrannous
ANOOOPRTZ protozoan
ANOORSTWY Stornoway
ANOPRRSTT transport
ANORSUUVY unsavoury
AOOORRRTW arrowroot
AOOORRTTV Rotovator
AOOPPPRTY party-poop
AOPRRSTUU rapturous
AOQSSTTUU status quo
AORRRTWWY worry-wart
AORSTTTUY statutory
BBBCDEEOW cobwebbed
BBBDEHNOO hobnobbed
BBBEEELMU bumble-bee
BBBEEELUZ Beelzebub
BBBEEILLT Bible belt
BBBEELRRU blubberer
BBBEGLMUU bubblegum
BBBEIKORS ski-bobber
BBBEILSTU bubbliest
BBCEHISTU chubbiest
BBCEILRRS scribbler
BBCEILSTU clubbiest
BBCEIRSSU subscribe
BBCGILMOO logic bomb
BBCGINRSU scrubbing
BBDDEESYY beddy-byes
BBDDEJOOR odd jobber
BBDEGIMNO demobbing
BBDEHMOPT depth bomb
BBDEIORRW bowerbird
BBDELLOOU blue blood
BBDEMOOTU bombed-out
BBDGIINNU dubbining
BBEEEHLMU humble-bee
BBEEELLRY beer belly
BBEEIRRUZ rubberize
BBEELRRUY blueberry
BBEEORSTW best bower
BBEGGIINT gibbeting
BBEGGNOOW wobbegong
BBEGHIIRS gibberish
BBEGHILOS bobsleigh
BBEGINNOT Bebington
BBEGIRSTU grubbiest
BBEHLLMOS bombshell
BBEHRRSUY shrubbery
BBEILOSTW wobbliest
BBEINOSST snobbiest
BBEINSSTU tubbiness
BBEISSTTU stubbiest
BBEKMMOOS smoke bomb
BBEMNORUX box number
BBEOORVVY bovver boy
BBERRTTUU butterbur
BBFMOOOPR bombproof
BBGHILLTU light bulb
BBGHILNOO hobgoblin
BBGHIMOST bombsight
BBGHINORT throbbing
BBGIILNQU quibbling
BBGIINQSU squibbing
BBGIIOSTY gibbosity
BBGILNOSY sobbingly
BBGILOSUY gibbously
BBHILOSYY yobbishly
BBIIILNRU bilirubin
BBIIKMTUZ kibbutzim
BBIKMNOST stink bomb
BBILLMMOS Mills bomb
BCCCKMOOS cockscomb
BCCDEHKOY body-check
BCCDKLMUU dumb cluck
BCCEEIKTU ice bucket
BCCEEILOR coercible
BCCEEKOOU cuckoo bee
BCCEHIKNP pinchbeck
BCCEIIILM imbecilic
BCCEINNOU concubine
BCCEINORS conscribe
BCCEKLLLO cell block
BCCEKLORU cocklebur
BCCIILSTY bicyclist
BCCIORSTU scorbutic
BCCMOORXY coxcombry
BCCMORRUY curry-comb
BCCOOOSSU osso bucco
BCDDEEILU deducible
BCDEEEEHS beseeched
BCDEEEFIN beneficed
BCDEEEINO obedience
BCDEEHIIR herbicide
BCDEEHIOR bee orchid
BCDEEHOOW beechwood
BCDEEILRU reducible
BCDEEILSU seducible
BCDEEIRRS describer
BCDEEIRSU rescue bid
BCDEELLOR corbelled
BCDEEMNTU decumbent
BCDEFIKOR dock brief
BCDEIILNU inducible
BCDEIJSUU sub judice
BCDEIKORR Broderick
BCDEILMNU unclimbed
BCDELLLOO blood cell
BCDGIKLOR gold brick
BCDHHIIOT dhobi itch
BCDHKNOUU buck-hound
BCDIILOOS discoboli
BCDIIMMUY cymbidium
BCDILMNOW climbdown
BCDIMOORS scombroid
BCDIOPSUW Cupid's bow
BCDKLOOOW woodblock
BCDKNOORU rock-bound
BCDOPRTUY by-product
BCEEEFHNR beech-fern
BCEEEGHIS big cheese
BCEEEHKNO cheekbone
BCEEEKQRU Quebecker
BCEEELQRU becquerel
BCEEFKRUV buck fever
BCEEHNSTT bench test
BCEEHORTT brochette
BCEEHPRUY hypercube
BCEEHRTTU trebuchet
BCEEIILNV evincible
BCEEIJOTV objective
BCEEIKLOR Lockerbie
BCEEILLOS bellicose
BCEEILRTY celebrity
BCEEIMNOR recombine
BCEEINOOT coenobite
BCEEINRTT centre bit
BCEEIPRRS prescribe
BCEEJNORT jobcentre
BCEEJOSTX sex object
BCEEKRTTU trebucket
BCEELMRRY Brylcreem
BCEELNOSY obscenely
BCEEMNRTU recumbent
BCEENPSTU pubescent
BCEFFIOOX box office
BCEFFIOOY office boy
BCEFIIKRR firebrick
BCEFIJOTY objectify
BCEFKLTUU bucketful
BCEGIKNTU bucketing
BCEGILNOR corbeling
BCEGRRSUW grub-screw
BCEHIILPT phlebitic
BCEHIIOST bioethics
BCEHIISTT bitchiest
BCEHILORT blotchier
BCEHIOQUU chibouque
BCEHIPSSU spicebush
BCEHKNORW workbench
BCEHLNORY Chernobyl
BCEHLOSUU clubhouse
BCEHMNOOY honeycomb

BCEHNNRTU turn-bench
BCEIILPUZ publicize
BCEIIMORT biometric
BCEIINOST bisection
BCEIINRRS inscriber
BCEIJLOPU Joe Public
BCEIJNOOT objection
BCEIKNOST steinbock
BCEILMNOU columbine
BCEILMORY cor blimey
BCEILMOTU columbite
BCEILMRRU crumblier
BCEILNOPX pencil box
BCEILNORU colubrine
BCEILOOPT optic lobe
BCEIMNNTU incumbent
BCEIMNORY embryonic
BCEIMRSTU crumbiest
BCEINORRW brown rice
BCEINOSTU bounciest
BCEINOSTY obscenity
BCEIOPPRT copper bit
BCEIOPRRS proscribe
BCEIORSTT obstetric
BCEJLLMOY comb-jelly
BCEKLOOTV block vote
BCEKMRSUU bum-sucker
BCEKNPRUY cyberpunk
BCEKOOORS scorebook
BCEKORTUX tucker-box
BCELMOOTY lobectomy
BCELOOSSU lobscouse
BCELORSUY obscurely
BCEMOORSY corymbose
BCEMOTTUY tubectomy
BCEOOPRSS probosces
BCEORRRWY crowberry
BCEPRTTUU buttercup
BCFHILLNU bullfinch
BCFIKSUZZ Buck's Fizz
BCFIMMORY cymbiform
BCGHILNTU nightclub
BCGHLNRUY Lynchburg
BCGIKRSUV Vicksburg
BCGNOOOTT bog cotton
BCHIILLLM hill climb
BCHIIOPRS bishopric
BCHIIRSTU hubristic
BCHIKLOPS blockship
BCHILOOPY lyophobic
BCHINORTY Brythonic
BCHKNORTU buckthorn
BCHKOOTTU buck-tooth
BCHLNOPUW punchbowl
BCHLOOOSY schoolboy
BCHLOORTW blowtorch
BCHLOTUUY youth club
BCHMOOOTT toothcomb
BCIIIMRST Briticism
BCIILMSUU umbilicus
BCIILPSTU publicist
BCIILPTUY publicity
BCIILRTUY lubricity
BCIIMNOOS bionomics
BCIIMOSTY symbiotic

BCIINORTT Brittonic
BCIKKNOST knobstick
BCIKKORRW brickwork
BCIKNNRSU Innsbruck
BCIKNRSUW Brunswick
BCILLORSS crossbill
BCILMMOUU columbium
BCILORSUU lubricous
BCILPRSTU strip club
BCIMNOOOS sonic boom
BCIMOOTTU Timbuctoo
BCIOOPRSS proboscis
BCIOORSTT Octobrist
BCIORSTUY obscurity
BCIPRSSTU subscript
BCKKOOOST stock-book
BCKORRSTU rockburst
BCOOTTUUX cut-out box
BDDDDEISU disbudded
BDDDEEINR bedridden
BDDEEEILV bedeviled
BDDEEGIRR Redbridge
BDDEENRRU underbred
BDDEFINOR forbidden
BDDEFLOOU blood feud
BDDEGIINR rebidding
BDDEGLOOU doodlebug
BDDEHINOU hidebound
BDDEHLOOS bloodshed
BDDEIILNS blind side
BDDEIISUV subdivide
BDDEIMOSY disembody
BDDEINRSU disburden
BDDEKNOSU desk-bound
BDDENNOUU unbounded
BDDENORUY underbody
BDDENOTUU undoubted
BDDENSUUU unsubdued
BDDFILLNO blindfold
BDDFMNOUU dumbfound
BDDIIORWW widow-bird
BDDILLORY dolly-bird
BDDILNORW word-blind
BDDINNOUW windbound
BDDNOTUUY duty-bound
BDDOOORUY body odour
BDEEEEJLW bejeweled
BDEEEELRV belvedere
BDEEEFILL Bielefeld
BDEEEFINT benefited
BDEEEHNST sheet bend
BDEEELMOW emboweled
BDEEELNOS nosebleed
BDEEEMMNT embedment
BDEEENRTU debenture
BDEEERSTW bestrewed
BDEEERTTV brevetted
BDEEERTTW bed-wetter
BDEEFIILS disbelief
BDEEFILRT filter-bed
BDEEFLLOW bedfellow
BDEEFLORW flower bed
BDEEFOOTW web-footed
BDEEGGLOW bow-legged
BDEEGHINT benighted

BDEEHIITX exhibited
BDEEIILLN indelible
BDEEIILNX indexible
BDEEIILRS derisible
BDEEIISTZ bite-sized
BDEEILLRW bridewell
BDEEILMSS dissemble
BDEEILRRU rebuilder
BDEEILRTV belt drive
BDEEIMMRS dismember
BDEEIMORR embroider
BDEEINNOZ benzenoid
BDEEINNSS bendiness
BDEEIORSY disobeyer
BDEEIRRST bestirred
BDEEIRSTT bedsitter
BDEEKOORW brookweed
BDEELLSSY blessedly
BDEELMSUY bemusedly
BDEELNOUV unbeloved
BDEELNRRU blunderer
BDEELNSSU unblessed
BDEEMPPSU speed bump
BDEENORRU rebounder
BDEENORST desorbent
BDEEORSTY oyster bed
BDEEORVYY everybody
BDEFIILRR rifle bird
BDEFIKLOO field-book
BDEFILLOO lifeblood
BDEFILLSU self-build
BDEFINORY boyfriend
BDEFIOORW wood fibre
BDEFLOSTU self-doubt
BDEGGGINU debugging
BDEGGHMUU humbugged
BDEGGINTU budgeting
BDEGGNUUY dune buggy
BDEGHILSU shield bug
BDEGHINRU Edinburgh
BDEGIIILR dirigible
BDEGIILOS disoblige
BDEGIIMMN bedimming
BDEGIIPPR big dipper
BDEGIKOOU guidebook
BDEGINNNU unbending
BDEGINPRS spring bed
BDEGINSSU debussing
BDEGIORRX box girder
BDEGLNOOY golden boy
BDEGLNORU Oldenburg
BDEHIIINT inhibited
BDEHIIRYZ hybridize
BDEHIORRS shorebird
BDEHIRSTT third-best
BDEHNOSTU South Bend
BDEHOORTU brutehood
BDEIIILSV divisible
BDEIIILTY edibility
BDEIIJNOS inside job
BDEIILLNY indelibly
BDEIILSTV devil's bit
BDEIISSUZ subsidize
BDEIKLLRR kerb drill
BDEILLNOO bloodline

BDEILLNPS spellbind
BDEILMOOR Dormobile
BDEILNNSS blindness
BDEILOOST bloodiest
BDEILOQTU quodlibet
BDEILORUV overbuild
BDEIMNOST disentomb
BDEIMSTTU submitted
BDEINORTX tinderbox
BDEINOSTU sound bite
BDEINRSUU unbruised
BDEIOORST broodiest
BDEIORSTU sub-editor
BDEIRRSSU disburser
BDEIRRSTU disturber
BDEKOOORR order book
BDELLMOSY symbolled
BDELLMOUU blue mould
BDELLNOSU bull-nosed
BDELLOOSS bloodless
BDELLORUZ bulldozer
BDELMNPUU unplumbed
BDELMRTUY tumble-dry
BDELNNOSS blondness
BDELNNRUU unbundler
BDELNOSSU boundless
BDELOOPTU double top
BDELOORWW lowbrowed
BDELOOSTT blood test
BDELORRWY blow-dryer
BDELOSSTU doubtless
BDENOORTW Brentwood
BDENOSTUW westbound
BDFIIINOR fibrinoid
BDFIOORST bird's-foot
BDFIORTUY fruit-body
BDFLNOOSY dobsonfly
BDFLOOORU foul brood
BDGGILOOY Golgi body
BDGHIINRT nightbird
BDGMOOOTT bottom dog
BDHIIMRSY hybridism
BDHIIRTYY hybridity
BDHLOOOST bloodshot
BDHOORSUW brushwood
BDIILOPRT pilot-bird
BDIIMORTY morbidity
BDIIRTTUY turbidity
BDIKNORUV Dubrovnik
BDILLORSW swordbill
BDILMNORW blindworm
BDILNNOSW snow-blind
BDILNOPST blind spot
BDILOSUUY dubiously
BDIMORRST storm-bird
BDINNOORU iron-bound
BDINOOWWW bow window
BDINOOWWX window box
BDLLOOSTU bloodlust
BDLMOOORW bloodworm
BDLOOORTW blood-wort
BDNNOOSUW snowbound
BEEEEEKPR bee-keeper
BEEEFGLOR leg before
BEEEFINSS beefiness
BEEEGHILN Beenleigh
BEEEGIKLL bilge keel
BEEEGLNRT green belt
BEEEGNOOW woebegone
BEEEGNOTW go-between
BEEEGRSTU guest beer
BEEEHHLMT Bethlehem
BEEEHLLOR hellebore
BEEEHLRTT Ethelbert
BEEEHORSU beerhouse
BEEEIKLLR killer bee
BEEEILMNT belemnite
BEEEIMRSV semibreve
BEEEINNTW in between
BEEEINRSS beeriness
BEEEIRSTZ breeziest
BEEEKRRRS berserker
BEEELMRRS resembler
BEEELMRZZ embezzler
BEEELORRU Euro-rebel
BEEELPRTU Blue Peter
BEEELSSSU sub-lessee
BEEEMPRST September
BEEENOSSS obeseness
BEEFFGIRU febrifuge
BEEFFORTT better off
BEEFFOSTW web offset
BEEFIILMS misbelief
BEEFILRSS briefless, fibreless
BEEFINRSS briefness
BEEFINRSW newsbrief
BEEFLORTW left bower
BEEGGINTT begetting
BEEGHIRTY eyebright
BEEGIILLL illegible
BEEGIKLLO globelike
BEEGILLNR rebelling
BEEGILLNV bevelling
BEEGILLNW well-being
BEEGILNRS inselberg
BEEGINRTV breveting
BEEGINSST beestings
BEEGINSTT besetting
BEEHIKRRS Berkshire
BEEHILLMS embellish
BEEHILNWY wheely bin
BEEHINRTT terebinth
BEEHIOPRS biosphere
BEEHIORRV herbivore
BEEHIPSST sheep's-bit
BEEHIRRRT rebirther
BEEHLOPRY hyperbole
BEEHMORUY homebuyer
BEEHNOOPX xenophobe
BEEIIKNRZ Berezniki
BEEIILNRT libertine
BEEIINRTY inebriety
BEEIKLMRU berkelium
BEEIKLMRY Kimberley
BEEILLNOR rebellion
BEEILLNTU ebullient
BEEILLRTT belittler
BEEILLRTU rubellite
BEEILMRRT tremblier
BEEILMRTT embrittle
BEEILNRSU blue rinse
BEEILNRUZ nebulizer
BEEILOTTU oubliette
BEEILSTUV vestibule
BEEIMRRSU reimburse
BEEINNOTT bentonite
BEEINNRTU inner tube
BEEINRRWY wineberry
BEEINSTTT Binet test
BEEIOQSSU obsequies
BEEIORRRS brier rose
BEEIOSSSV obsessive
BEEIQRTTU briquette
BEEKLRRUY Kerry blue
BEEKNORST kerbstone
BEELLLMUU umbellule
BEELLORSU resoluble
BEELLRTUY bully tree
BEELMNORU Melbourne
BEELMOORT bolometer
BEELMRRSU slumberer
BEELNNOSS nobleness
BEELNOSTU bluestone
BEELORRST bolsterer
BEELORSVY obversely, verbosely
BEELORTTX letter box
BEELQRSUU burlesque
BEELRRSTU blusterer
BEEMMNNOR non-member
BEEMNNORU number one
BEEMNNRTU Number Ten
BEEMNRTTU rebutment
BEEMOPRRY pre-embryo
BEENOORRV overborne
BEENORRST resorbent
BEENORSTU tenebrous
BEEOPPPRX pepperbox
BEEORSSUU subereous
BEEORSTTU soubrette
BEEPRRSTY presbyter
BEERRSTUV subverter
BEFFGINTU buffeting
BEFFIILLR fibrefill
BEFFILNPU Pine Bluff
BEFFLNSSU bluffness
BEFGGGINO befogging
BEFGHILOS globe-fish
BEFGIINTT befitting
BEFGLORSW Wolfsberg
BEFHIRRSU furbisher, refurbish
BEFHKLOOS bookshelf
BEFHLLSUU bushelful
BEFIILNSU infusible
BEFIILRTY febrility
BEFILRWYY fly-by-wire
BEFINOPRU ibuprofen
BEFIORSTT frostbite
BEFLLLOPY bellyflop
BEFLRTTUY butterfly
BEFNNNOUY funny bone
BEFOORSUW subwoofer
BEGGGLOOX goggle-box

BEGGIILNU beguiling
BEGGIINNN beginning
BEGGIINOO boogieing
BEGGINOSS bogginess
BEGGJLOOS Joe Bloggs
BEGHHINOT thigh bone
BEGHHOTTU bethought
BEGHINORU neighbour
BEGHIORSU Brighouse
BEGHLNORU bugle-horn
BEGIILLLN libelling
BEGIILLLY illegibly
BEGIILLNT billeting
BEGIIMNRT timbering
BEGIINNTY benignity
BEGIJRTTU jitterbug
BEGILLNOR Bollinger
BEGILMNRU lumbering
BEGILMORY gorblimey
BEGILMRRU Limburger
BEGILNOST ignoblest
BEGILRTTU litterbug
BEGIMNSSU embussing
BEGINORSU subregion
BEGINRTTU rebutting
BEGIOORSU bourgeois
BEGLMORTY bog myrtle
BEGNOSSSU bogusness
BEHHMOOOP homophobe
BEHIILPRT Philibert
BEHIILPST phlebitis
BEHIIORTX exhibitor
BEHIIRRST Britisher
BEHIKLOSV Bolshevik
BEHIKLRSU brushlike
BEHILNNOR Heilbronn
BEHILPRSU publisher, republish
BEHINRRSU burnisher
BEHINSSSU bushiness
BEHIORSTT theorbist
BEHIRRSUW wire brush
BEHKMOSSU smoke bush
BEHKNOOOP phone book
BEHKNOSUU bunkhouse
BEHLMSSTU thumbless
BEHLORRTY brotherly
BEHLRSSSU brushless
BEHMOORST thrombose
BEHMORSSU rhombuses
BEHOPRTYY bryophyte
BEIIILNSV invisible
BEIILLNSY sibylline
BEIILMORZ mobilizer
BEIILMOSS omissible
BEIILORTT trilobite
BEIILSTUZ subtilize
BEIIMNNSU bienniums
BEIINNRSS brininess
BEIINOOVV ovibovine
BEIINORSV vibriones
BEIINSSTT bittiness
BEIKLMOOR brooklime
BEIKLNOOR Brookline
BEIKLNSSU bulkiness
BEIKMOORT motorbike
BEIKNRSSS briskness
BEIKSSTVY Vitsyebsk
BEILLLOSU libellous
BEILLLTUW well-built
BEILLMNPU plumb line
BEILLMRUY beryllium
BEILLMSUY sublimely
BEILLNOSU insoluble
BEILLOQUY obliquely
BEILLRTTY brittlely
BEILMNOSW women's lib
BEILMOSYZ symbolize
BEILMSSTU sublimest
BEILNPRTU blueprint
BEILNRSSU burliness
BEILOOPRT potboiler
BEILOSTWZ blowziest
BEILRRSTU blurriest
BEIMNORST brimstone
BEIMNPSSU bumpiness
BEIMOSSSY symbioses
BEIMRSTTU submitter
BEIMRTTUY ytterbium
BEINNNOSS bonniness
BEINNOOTT obtention
BEINOORSV obversion
BEINOOSSS obsession
BEINOOSSZ booziness
BEINORUVV bon viveur
BEINOSSSS bossiness
BEINSSSTU bustiness
BEIOPTTTU Pitot tube
BEIOQRSTU sobriquet
BEIORSSST sob sister
BEIORSTUV obtrusive
BEIORSTVY verbosity
BEKKNOOOT book token
BEKLOOOSU book-louse
BEKNNNOUW unbeknown
BEKNNOSTW best-known
BEKOOORST bookstore
BELLMPRUU plumb rule
BELLMPSSU plumbless
BELMOOORW elbow room
BELMOORTY bolometry
BELMOPSUU plumbeous
BELMOSSXY sex symbol
BELNNSSTU bluntness
BELNOORVW overblown
BELNRTTUU turbulent
BELOPRSUW Super Bowl
BELORSSSU sub-lessor
BELQRSUUY brusquely
BEMNOOSTT tombstone
BEMNORTUU outnumber
BEMNORTUW number two
BEMNOSSUX buxomness
BEMRRTTUU rum butter
BEMSSSTUY subsystem
BENNNOSTU sun-bonnet
BENNOORSW brown-nose
BENNORSSW brownness
BENOOSTUU bounteous
BENORRSWY snowberry
BENORSTTU toneburst
BENORSTXY sentry box
BENRTTTUU butternut
BEORSSTTU robustest
BFFIIMORR fibriform
BFGHILLTU bullfight
BFGLORSUW Wolfsburg
BFGNOORSU Bofors gun
BFIILMORY myofibril
BFILNOTUU bountiful
BFILORSUY fibrously
BFINORRST first-born
BFLLLNOUW full-blown
BFOORTUWY two-by-four
BGGILLNUY bulgingly
BGGILMNRU grumbling
BGHHIIRST brightish
BGHMOOOOS Ogbomosho
BGIIIKPRR Kirbigrip
BGIIKPRRY kirby grip
BGIILMOOR imbroglio
BGIILNOQU obliquing
BGIILNRSS brislings
BGIILOOST biologist
BGIKNOPRS springbok
BGILMNOOY myoglobin
BGILMNOSY symboling
BGILMNRSU rumblings
BGILNNRUY burningly
BGILNOPRY probingly
BGILOORTY tribology
BGINNORTU binturong
BGINOORRW borrowing
BGINOPRSX box spring
BGINORSTW bowstring
BGLLOOSUU globulous
BGLMOOSYY symbology
BGNOORSTX strongbox
BHHIMORTY biorhythm
BHIIINORT inhibitor
BHIILLLLY hill-billy
BHIILLNOT billionth
BHIILLPRT birth pill
BHIILLRSU Irish bull
BHIIMORUZ rhizobium
BHIKLOOSY bookishly
BHIKNNSUU shubunkin
BHIKNOOSU unbookish
BHILLLSUY bullishly
BHILLNORT thornbill
BHILMNOTY bimonthly
BHILOORSY boorishly
BHILRSTUY brutishly
BHIMOOSTY tomboyish
BHJOORSTW jobsworth
BHKORRSUW brushwork
BHLLOOOTT toll-booth
BHLMPSUUY subphylum
BHMNOOOSU bonhomous
BHNOORSTW snow-broth
BIIILNSVY invisibly
BIILLOSUY biliously
BIILMSTUY sublimity
BIILOOSUV oblivious
BIILOQTUY obliquity

BIIMOPRTY improbity
BIIMOSSSY symbiosis
BIISSTTYY itsy-bitsy
BIITTTTYY itty-bitty
BIJKKNOUU Kokubunji
BIKLNNOSW snow-blink
BILLNOOPS spoonbill
BILLNORST stillborn
BILLNOSUY insolubly
BILMMOSSY symbolism
BILMOSSTY symbolist
BILOOPRTU politburo
BILOOSUVY obviously
BILORSSTU strobilus
BIMNOPSSU mons pubis
BIMOPSTUU bumptious
BINOOOSUX obnoxious
BINOORSTU obtrusion
BIOOPRRTW borrow pit
BKLLMNSUU numbskull
BKOOORSTY story book
BKORSSTUV Rubtsovsk
BLLORTTUU bulltrout
BLMORSSUU slumbrous
BLOORSTUU troublous
BMOOPPRTX prompt box
BOOPPRRTU turboprop
CCCEEINRT eccentric
CCCEIILPY epicyclic
CCCENOORT concocter
CCCGINOOO gonococci
CCCHIINNO cinchonic
CCCHILMOU colchicum
CCCIILRTY tricyclic
CCCNOOORT concoctor
CCDEEERSU succeeder
CCDEEHIKW chickweed
CCDEEHKNU unchecked
CCDEEHORT crocheted
CCDEEIINN incidence
CCDEEIKRT cricketed
CCDEEINNY indecency
CCDEEINOT conceited
CCDEEINRS crescendi
CCDEEKNOS scene-dock
CCDEEMOOR coco-de-mer
CCDEENNOR concerned
CCDEENNOT connected
CCDEENORS crescendo
CCDEENORT concerted
CCDEIIKNP picnicked
CCDEILOOR crocodile
CCDEILSTY dyslectic
CCDEIMOOR microcode
CCDEINOOT decoction
CCDEINOUV conducive
CCDENORRU concurred
CCDEOOPRU co-produce
CCDGHLOTU dog-clutch
CCDHKOORS shock cord
CCDHKOOUW woodchuck
CCDKLORUY cuckoldry
CCDNOORTU conductor
CCDNOSTUU conductus
CCEEEFLNU feculence

CCEEEHNOR coherence
CCEEEHRRS screecher
CCEEEINNS nescience
CCEEEINRT reticence
CCEEFFOPU coffee cup
CCEEFILLY life cycle
CCEEGINOR concierge
CCEEGINOT ectogenic
CCEEHIKNR check-rein
CCEEHIKOY ice hockey
CCEEHILMY hemicycle
CCEEHKORV overcheck
CCEEHLORT cerecloth
CCEEHNORY coherency
CCEEHORRT crocheter
CCEEHOTTU couchette
CCEEIIPPR precipice
CCEEIKRRT cricketer
CCEEILNOR reconcile
CCEEINNNO innocence
CCEEINRTX excentric
CCEEIRRST rectrices
CCEEIRSTT tectrices
CCEELLORT recollect
CCEELOTUY leucocyte
CCEENNORT concenter,
concentre,
reconnect
CCEFIIRRU crucifier
CCEGGHOST Scotch egg
CCEGHIMRU chemurgic
CCEGINNOO oncogenic
CCEGINORY cryogenic
CCEGLNOSY song cycle
CCEHIKLST checklist
CCEHILNOR chronicle
CCEHILNPU cup lichen
CCEHINRRU crunchier
CCEHINRSU scrunchie
CCEHIOOPR pro-choice
CCEHKLNOT neckcloth
CCEHKMOOR checkroom
CCEHKOPST spot check
CCEHNNOSU scuncheon
CCEHNOSTU scutcheon
CCEHORTTY crotchety
CCEHOTTUZ zucchetto
CCEIIIRTZ criticize
CCEIIKNPR picnicker
CCEIILMST Celticism
CCEIIOSTZ Scoticize
CCEIIRSTV victrices
CCEIKLLOY kilocycle
CCEIKLMOT time clock
CCEIKLOSW clockwise
CCEIKNOSS cockiness
CCEILNNOU nucleonic
CCEILNOSY concisely
CCEILORST sclerotic
CCEILOSUV occlusive
CCEIMNOOS economics
CCEINNNOY innocency
CCEINNORV convincer
CCEINORRT incorrect
CCEINOSTT tectonics

CCEINRSTY syncretic
CCEIOPRST cost price
CCEIOPRTY precocity
CCEKLORST cost clerk
CCEKNOOPS scoop neck
CCEKORRSS rock cress
CCEKORRSW corkscrew
CCELLNOOY colonelcy
CCELLOORT collector
CCELMNOOY monocycle
CCELNSTUU succulent
CCELOPRSU corpuscle
CCELOPSSY Cyclopses
CCELORRTY correctly
CCENNNORU unconcern
CCENNOORT connector
CCENOORSU concourse
CCENOORTV convector
CCENOPSTU conceptus
CCENORSTU succentor
CCENSSSUU unsuccess
CCEOOPRRV cover crop
CCEOORRRT corrector
CCEOPPRUY preoccupy
CCEORSSSU successor
CCFGHIKOT cockfight
CCFGKLLOO clock golf
CCFHIORST Scotch fir
CCFHKLLOU chock-full
CCFIILOOR colorific
CCFIMORRU cruciform
CCFKOOOST cocksfoot
CCFLLOSUU flocculus
CCGHIINPU hiccuping
CCGIINNOR cornicing
CCGILLLOY glycollic
CCGINORRU occurring
CCHHILLRU Churchill
CCHHLORUW Low Church
CCHHOOPST hopscotch
CCHIILORT chloritic
CCHIIMOPR microchip
CCHIINOOR chorionic
CCHIINSUZ zucchinis
CCHIIORRT cirrhotic,
trichroic
CCHIKLLOO cook-chill
CCHIKOPST chopstick
CCHILNRUY crunchily
CCHILOORT chlorotic
CCHINRSTY strychnic
CCHIOPSTY psychotic
CCHLNOOTY colocynth
CCIIILNOS isoclinic
CCIIILNRT triclinic
CCIIILOST silicotic
CCIIIMRST criticism
CCIIINOTY iconicity
CCIILMOPT complicit
CCIILOOST scoliotic
CCIILOPRT proclitic
CCIILOSTU oculistic
CCIIMOSST Scoticism
CCIINNOOS concision
CCIIORRTT tricrotic

CCIIRRTUY circuitry
CCILMOSTU occultism
CCILNOORU councilor
CCILNOOSU occlusion
CCILOSTTU occultist
CCIMMOORS microcosm
CCIMOOPRY microcopy
CCINOOSSU conscious
CCINOPRST conscript
CCINORSTT constrict
CCIOOOPST otoscopic
CCIOOTTXY cytotoxic
CCKKLOORW clockwork
CCKMOORST storm-cock
CCKNOORRW crown cork
CCKOOPPPY poppycock
CCLNOORTY cyclotron
CCLNORRUY Cloncurry
CCNORSTTU construct
CDDDEEILY decidedly
CDDDEEINU undecided
CDDDKRUUY ruddy duck
CDDEEENRS descender
CDDEEFOSU defocused
CDDEEGLLU cudgelled
CDDEEITUV deductive
CDDEELNOS closed-end
CDDEGIOTY Dodge City
CDDEHORRT Dordrecht
CDDEIINRT dendritic
CDDEIIOSV videodisc
CDDEIIRST discredit
CDDEILSTU cuddliest
CDDEIMOOU duodecimo
CDDEINOOS Escondido
CDDEINOTU deduction
CDDEIOSUU deciduous
CDDEIRSTU cruddiest
CDDELNOUU unclouded
CDDENORUW uncrowded
CDDHHILOO childhood
CDDHLLOTU Dutch doll
CDDHOORTU Dutch door
CDDILNOOY condyloid
CDEEEEFNR deference
CDEEEEKNW ewe-necked
CDEEEFFOR force-feed
CDEEEFITV defective
CDEEEGINR decreeing
CDEEEGINX exceeding
CDEEEIMRT decimeter, decimetre
CDEEEINPT centipede
CDEEEINRS residence
CDEEEINRT intercede
CDEEEINUV undeceive
CDEEEIPTV deceptive
CDEEEITTV detective
CDEEELNOR redolence
CDEEELNTU unelected
CDEEELORT electrode
CDEEEMNRT decrement
CDEEENPRT precedent
CDEEEORRT retrocede
CDEEEPRSU supercede
CDEEFIINT deficient
CDEEFIIOT foeticide
CDEEFIKRR Frederick
CDEEFILTU deceitful
CDEEFINOT defection
CDEEFKOST feedstock
CDEEFLORT deflector
CDEEFNORR conferred
CDEEFORSU refocused
CDEEGIILN diligence
CDEEGIIMR germicide
CDEEGIINN indigence
CDEEGILRY glyceride
CDEEGINRS screeding
CDEEHIKRS shickered
CDEEHILLS chiselled
CDEEHIMRS Remscheid
CDEEHINST dehiscent
CDEEHLORY hydrocele
CDEEHLPPS schlepped
CDEEHLRSU scheduler
CDEEHRRRY cherry red
CDEEIILRT deciliter, decilitre
CDEEIILTV videlicet
CDEEIIMPR epidermic
CDEEIIMPU epicedium
CDEEIIMRV vermicide
CDEEIIPRR cirripede
CDEEIIPST pesticide
CDEEIIPTV depictive
CDEEIIRTV directive
CDEEIISTT dietetics
CDEEIJNOT dejection
CDEEIJPRU prejudice
CDEEIKLLN nickelled
CDEEIKOPR poker dice
CDEEIKSTW stickweed, wickedest
CDEEILLNP pencilled
CDEEILNNO indolence
CDEEILNST stenciled
CDEEILORR Cordelier
CDEEILTXY excitedly
CDEEIMNOU eudemonic
CDEEIMNPU impudence
CDEEINNOR endocrine
CDEEINOPT deception
CDEEINORT recondite
CDEEINOTT detection
CDEEINRRS discerner
CDEEINRSY residency
CDEEIRTTU certitude, rectitude
CDEEIRTUV reductive
CDEEISTUV seductive
CDEEKLORW lower deck
CDEEKOORR crookeder
CDEEKOPRR peck order
CDEELLMOP compelled
CDEELLOST cold steel
CDEELMNTU demulcent
CDEELNOSU counseled
CDEELOPSU pulse code
CDEELORSS sclerosed
CDEELRSTU clustered
CDEEMMNOR recommend
CDEEMNOOS comedones
CDEEMOOPS decompose
CDEENNORS condenser
CDEENNORT contender
CDEENNORU denouncer
CDEENNOTT contented
CDEENNSTU unscented
CDEENOOPS endoscope
CDEENOORT coroneted
CDEENOPRS drop scene
CDEENRSSU crudeness
CDEENRSUU unsecured
CDEEOPRRR pre-record
CDEEOPRRU procedure, reproduce
CDEEOQRTU croqueted
CDEEORSSY cross-eyed
CDEERTTUV curvetted
CDEFFIORU coiffured
CDEFGIINU fungicide
CDEFHIILL Lichfield
CDEFHIKLR Feldkirch
CDEFHITUW Dutch wife
CDEFHLNOR Old French
CDEFIIIST fideistic
CDEFIINST disinfect
CDEFIKLOR frolicked
CDEFILNOR cornfield
CDEFIMNOR confirmed
CDEFINNOT confident
CDEFINORW wind force
CDEFINTUY fecundity
CDEFNOSUU unfocused
CDEGGILNU cudgeling
CDEGGLNOU unclogged
CDEGIIMRU demiurgic
CDEGIINRT crediting
CDEGIKNOT docketing
CDEGILOOP police dog
CDEGILOSU glucoside
CDEGILOSY glycoside
CDEGINORR recording
CDEGIOOOV good voice
CDEGLLOOU collogued
CDEGLORST goldcrest
CDEHIIKLL childlike
CDEHIKOOY doohickey
CDEHIKPSY physicked
CDEHILLOV love child
CDEHILLSS childless
CDEHILPST stepchild
CDEHINORT chondrite, threnodic
CDEHIOORT Theodoric
CDEHIORTW dowitcher
CDEHIPRRU chirruped
CDEHKLSSU shelducks
CDEHLNOTU unclothed
CDEHNOTUU untouched
CDEHNOTUV Dutch oven
CDEHNRSUU uncrushed
CDEIIKMTW midwicket
CDEIILOST solicited

CDEIILOSU	delicious
CDEIILTVY	declivity
CDEIIMNOS	meniscoid
CDEIIMNTY	mendicity
CDEIIMRST	misdirect
CDEIINOPT	depiction
CDEIINORT	direction
CDEIINOXZ	zinc oxide
CDEIINRTT	interdict
CDEIINTUV	inductive
CDEIIOOSU	dioecious
CDEIIORUX	uxoricide
CDEIIQRTU	critiqued
CDEIIRRTX	directrix
CDEILLLOU	celluloid
CDEILLLOY	iced lolly
CDEILNOTU	dulcitone
CDEILNSSU	lucidness
CDEILORSS	discloser
CDEILOSTU	cloudiest
CDEILPRSU	surpliced
CDEILRTUY	credulity
CDEIMMNOO	incommode
CDEIMMOTT	committed
CDEIMNNOT	condiment
CDEIMNOPR	princedom
CDEIMNORU	indecorum
CDEIMNOSU	Nicodemus
CDEINNOTU	continued, unnoticed
CDEINOPSY	dyspnoeic
CDEINORTU	introduce, reduction
CDEINORTV	contrived
CDEINOSTU	seduction
CDEINRSTY	stridency
CDEINTTUV	ventiduct
CDEIOPRRT	predictor
CDEIORRST	recordist
CDEIORRTY	directory
CDEIORSST	dissector
CDEIORSSU	discourse
CDEIORSVY	discovery
CDEIPPSTY	dyspeptic
CDEIRRTYY	Derry City
CDEIRSSSU	discusser
CDEJKMOOY	jockeydom
CDEKLNPUU	unplucked
CDEKLOORY	crookedly
CDEKNOORU	undercook
CDEKOOSTV	stock dove
CDELLOSSU	cloudless
CDELMNORU	lemon curd
CDELMOOWY	low comedy
CDELNOORT	decontrol
CDELNOORU	uncolored
CDELNOOST	stone-cold
CDELNOOSW	close-down
CDELNOOTY	cotyledon
CDELNOPUU	uncoupled
CDELNORSU	scoundrel
CDELOORST	cold store
CDELOORUV	overcloud
CDELORSUU	credulous
CDEMMOOOR	commodore
CDEMNOORW	downcomer
CDENNOORW	nonce-word
CDENNOTUU	uncounted
CDENOOPRS	drop scone
CDENOOPSY	endoscopy
CDENOPPRU	uncropped
CDENORSTU	construed
CDEOOOPSW	copsewood
CDEOORRVW	overcrowd
CDEOORSWW	woodscrew
CDEORSTUV	dust cover
CDFFIILTU	difficult
CDFGHILNO	goldfinch
CDFIIMOST	discomfit
CDFIIORSU	sudorific
CDFILOSTU	old fustic
CDFIMMOOY	commodify
CDFLNOORT	cold front
CDGHIILNY	chidingly
CDGHOOPRU	cough drop
CDGIIINOT	indigotic
CDGIKLOST	Gold Stick
CDGILNNOY	condignly
CDGOORUYZ	Godoy Cruz
CDHHIIOTY	ichthyoid
CDHHILOST	dishcloth
CDHIILLNW	wind-chill
CDHIIMOPR	dimorphic
CDHIIMORS	dichroism
CDHIIORRS	scirrhoid
CDHIIORST	orchidist
CDHIIORTW	Droitwich
CDHIIPSTW	dip switch
CDHIIRRTY	trihydric
CDHIMOOTY	dichotomy
CDHIOOPRY	chiropody
CDHIOPRSY	dysphoric
CDHLLOOOS	old school
CDHLOORST	cold-short
CDHMNOOOR	monochord
CDHNOOORT	notochord
CDHNOOTUW	touchdown
CDHOOOTUW	touchwood
CDIIISTVY	viscidity
CDIIJOSUU	judicious
CDIILMOOT	dolomitic
CDIILPTUY	duplicity
CDIILTTUY	ductility
CDIINNOOT	condition
CDIINNOTU	induction
CDIINOPRY	cyprinoid
CDIINPSUU	unicuspid
CDIIOOPRS	scorpioid
CDIIOPRST	dioptrics
CDIIPRSTU	tricuspid
CDIJNOTUY	jocundity
CDIKLOORS	rock-solid
CDIKMRSTU	drumstick
CDILLNOOO	collodion
CDILOORSU	discolour
CDILORSUU	ludicrous
CDIMMOOTY	commodity
CDIMNOORU	doronicum
CDIMNORSY	syndromic
CDIMOOPRR	prodromic
CDINNOOPU	pound coin
CDINORSSW	crosswind
CDIRRSTUU	duricrust
CDKKNNOOW	knock-down
CDKKNOOOR	doorknock
CDKLNOOPU	pound lock
CDKMPRTUU	dump truck
CDKOOOSTW	Woodstock
CDLLNOORY	corn dolly
CDLOOORTU	Oort cloud
CDMNNORUU	conundrum
CDNNOOTUW	countdown
CDOORRSSW	crossword
CEEEEFNRR	reference
CEEEEGMNR	emergence
CEEEEHMNV	vehemence
CEEEENRRV	reverence
CEEEFFITV	effective
CEEEFFLNU	effluence
CEEEFHLSY	cheese-fly
CEEEFILST	fleeciest
CEEEFINNR	inference
CEEEFLNRU	refluence
CEEEFLNSS	fenceless
CEEEFPRRT	perfecter
CEEEGILNT	telegenic
CEEEGINRT	energetic
CEEEGMNRY	emergency
CEEEHIKST	cheekiest
CEEEHILST	scheelite
CEEEHINNR	inherence
CEEEHIRST	cheeriest
CEEEHISST	cheesiest
CEEEHLNTY	entelechy
CEEEHLRSS	cheerless
CEEEHOPRS	ecosphere
CEEEHOPST	pot cheese
CEEEHORSV	echo verse
CEEEHQRUX	exchequer
CEEEIIMPT	timepiece
CEEEIINRV	vicereine
CEEEIJRTV	rejective
CEEEILLNT	clientele
CEEEILNST	Celestine
CEEEILRST	Leicester
CEEEILSTV	selective
CEEEIMRRZ	mercerize
CEEEINNPT	penitence
CEEEINNST	sentience
CEEEINOPS	nose-piece
CEEEINPRT	epicenter, epicentre
CEEEINSTX	existence
CEEEIPRRV	perceiver
CEEEIPRST	creepiest
CEEEIPRTV	receptive
CEEEIRRSX	exerciser
CEEEIRSSV	recessive
CEEEIRSTV	secretive
CEEEIRSVX	ex-service
CEEEIRTVX	excretive
CEEEISSVX	excessive
CEEEITUVX	executive
CEEEJMNTT	ejectment
CEEEKORRT	rocketeer

CEELLNRV nerve cell
CEELLNTX excellent
CEELNOQU eloquence
CEELOPST telescope
CEELPRST pre-select
CEELRSST Electress
CEELRSTV cleverest
CEEMNRTX excrement
CEENNORV reconvene
CEENNSST senescent
CEENQRSU sequencer
CEENRSST erectness
CEEORRRV recoverer
CEEPRRST respecter
CEEPRSTU persecute
CEERSSST sesterces
CEEFFIINT efficient
CEEFFILOR life-force
CEEFFIOSU coiffeuse
CEEFFNORS off-screen
CEEFFNORT off-centre
CEEFGINNR ring-fence
CEEFGLNTU genuflect
CEEFHIPSY speechify
CEEFHLPSU speechful
CEEFIINTV infective
CEEFIIPRS specifier
CEEFIIRRT rectifier
CEEFIKRTV tick fever
CEEFILNNU influence
CEEFILRTY electrify
CEEFIMPRT imperfect
CEEFINORR reinforce
CEEFINORT refection
CEEFIRRST firecrest
CEEFKNNSU sunk fence
CEEFLNORT tenor clef
CEEFLOORS foreclose
CEEFLORRT reflector
CEEFLORSU fluoresce
CEEFLPRTY perfectly
CEEFNOPRU fourpence
CEEFNOPST fence post
CEEFNQRUY frequency
CEEFNRSTU rufescent
CEEFORRTY refectory
CEEGHIMNO hegemonic
CEEGHINRW Greenwich
CEEGIKNRS greensick
CEEGILLNX excelling
CEEGILNOO Oligocene
CEEGILNOT telegonic
CEEGILNRY glycerine
CEEGIMORT geometric
CEEGINNOS consignee
CEEGINNRS screening
CEEGINNRT centering, centreing
CEEGINORS congeries
CEEGINORZ recognize
CEEGINPTX excepting
CEEGLNOOS Congolese
CEEGLRTTU leg-cutter
CEEGNOPRR green crop
CEEGORTTU courgette
CEEHHIRVW whichever
CEEHHOPST hope chest
CEEHIILNP Chile pine, cinephile
CEEHIIPTT epithetic
CEEHIKKNT thick-knee
CEEHIKNRT Kitchener, thickener
CEEHIKPPR pikeperch
CEEHIKRST sketchier
CEEHILLMS schlemiel
CEEHILLRS chiseller
CEEHILLTW white cell
CEEHILNRS schlieren
CEEHILNTY ethylenic
CEEHINQTU technique
CEEHINSSW chewiness
CEEHIOPSW showpiece
CEEHIORTT theoretic
CEEHIPRRY cherry pie
CEEHISSTT chestiest
CEEHKLLOW wheel lock
CEEHKNORV Cherenkov
CEEHLLNOP cellphone
CEEHLORSU lecherous
CEEHLPRSU sepulcher, sepulchre
CEEHLQRSU squelcher
CEEHMNORZ chernozem
CEEHNOPRR percheron
CEEHORRST Rochester
CEEHORRTU retoucher
CEEHRRSTT stretcher
CEEIILNST insectile, selenitic
CEEIILPPT epileptic
CEEIIMMNN imminence
CEEIIMNRS reminisce
CEEIIMPRS imprecise
CEEIIMPST epistemic
CEEIIMRTZ metricize
CEEIINNOR eirenicon
CEEIINNRS insincere
CEEIINNTV incentive
CEEIINPRT recipient
CEEIINPTV inceptive
CEEIINRSV in-service
CEEIINRTZ cretinize
CEEIINTVV invective
CEEIIOPTZ poeticize
CEEIIORTZ eroticize
CEEIJLNOS Sincelejo
CEEIJLSSU juiceless
CEEIJNORT rejection
CEEIJNRTT interject
CEEIKLPRS pickerels
CEEIKNSTU tuck-seine
CEEIKOPRW piecework, workpiece
CEEILLLTU cellulite
CEEILLNPR penciller
CEEILLNTT intellect
CEEILMNNT inclement
CEEILMNPR crimplene
CEEILMOST comeliest
CEEILMRSS merciless
CEEILNNOS insolence
CEEILNORS scoreline
CEEILNORT centriole
CEEILNOST selection
CEEILNOTT Nicolette
CEEILNPST splenetic
CEEILNRSY sincerely
CEEILNRTV ventricle
CEEILNRUV virulence
CEEILORSX excelsior
CEEILOSSS isosceles
CEEILOSSV voiceless
CEEILPRSS priceless
CEEILPRSY precisely
CEEILRSUV reclusive
CEEILSSUV seclusive
CEEILSUVX exclusive
CEEIMMNSU ecumenism
CEEIMMOTT committee
CEEIMNNRT increment
CEEIMNOOZ economize
CEEIMNOPT impotence
CEEIMNOWX New Mexico
CEEIMNSTU intumesce
CEEINNORS recension
CEEINNSTY sentiency
CEEINOPRT reception
CEEINOPRZ preconize
CEEINOPTX exception
CEEINORSS recession
CEEINORST resection, secretion
CEEINORSU cinereous
CEEINORTX excretion
CEEINORTZ necrotize
CEEINOSSS secession
CEEINOTUX execution
CEEINPRRU prurience
CEEINPRST prescient
CEEINPRSW screw pine
CEEINPRTT intercept
CEEINQSTU quiescent
CEEINRRSV scrivener
CEEINRSST sincerest
CEEINRSTT intersect
CEEINRSTV virescent
CEEINRSUV sine curve
CEEINSSTY necessity
CEEIOORTZ ozocerite
CEEIOORVV voice-over
CEEIOOTVV voice vote
CEEIOPPRS periscope
CEEIOPRRV overprice
CEEIORSSU sericeous
CEEIORTVZ vectorize
CEEIRRRTU recruiter
CEEIRRSUV recursive
CEEIRSSTW screwiest
CEEIRSUVX excursive
CEEIRTUXX executrix
CEEJORRTT retroject
CEEKLOTUY leukocyte
CEEKLPSSS speckless
CEELLLOSU cellulose

CEELLMOWY welcomely
CEELLRSTU cruellest
CEELMMOST telecomms
CEELMNOUW unwelcome
CEELMOOSU colemouse
CEELNORSU enclosure
CEELNOSSS closeness
CEELNOSTU consultee
CEELNPRUU purulence
CEELNRSSU cruelness
CEELNSSST scentless
CEELORSSS scoreless
CEELORSTU Le Creusot
CEELORSUX exclosure
CEELORTTU Court leet
CEELRSSST crestless
CEELRSSTU truceless
CEEMMNORT commenter
CEEMNNORT contemner
CEEMNOPTT competent
CEEMNSTTU tumescent
CEEMOOPRS recompose
CEEMOSSTY ecosystem
CEENNORRT rencontre
CEENNORRU renouncer
CEENNORTU encounter
CEENNRSSU sunscreen
CEENOOPST copestone
CEENOORTV cover note
CEENOPRRT precentor
CEENOPSTT Pentecost
CEENOQRRU reconquer
CEENORRSV converser
CEENORRTV converter, reconvert
CEENORSTT contester
CEENORSTW sweetcorn
CEENORTUY Courteney
CEENRRRTU recurrent
CEEOPPRRT preceptor
CEEOPRRSS reprocess
CEEOPRSTT top secret
CEEOPRSTU prosecute
CEEOQRTTU croquette
CEEORRSSS sorceress
CEEORRSTW Worcester
CEEORRSTY secretory
CEEORRSUV verrucose
CEEORRTUV coverture
CEEORRTXY excretory
CEEORTUXY executory
CEERRRSTU resurrect
CEFFHINRY Frenchify
CEFFIIKLL clifflike
CEFFIIOOX ex officio
CEFFIKNST stiff neck
CEFFIRRSU scruffier
CEFGINORU configure
CEFHIILSS fish slice
CEFHKOORS foreshock
CEFIIKQRU quick-fire
CEFIILNRT inflicter
CEFIINNOT infection
CEFIINTTU fettucini
CEFIIORRS scorifier
CEFIKLORR frolicker
CEFIKORSS fossicker
CEFIMNORR reconfirm
CEFIMNORU cuneiform
CEFIMNOSS comfiness
CEFIOORSU ferocious
CEFIORRSS crossfire
CEFIORSTU fruticose
CEFKLOPTU pocketful
CEFKOORRW workforce
CEFLLORSU full score
CEFLNNOTU confluent
CEFMNOORR conformer
CEFMOORRT comforter
CEFMOPPRU force-pump
CEFNOORSS confessor
CEFOORRSU fourscore
CEFOORRTU forecourt
CEGGILOST cloggiest
CEGHIILNS chiseling
CEGHIINSY hygienics
CEGHIIOTZ Gothicize
CEGHILLOU guilloche
CEGHILNTV vetchling
CEGHINORV Chernigov
CEGHIORRU grouchier
CEGHKNORU roughneck
CEGIIILNT eliciting
CEGIIKLNN nickeling
CEGIIKNPT picketing
CEGIIKNTT ticketing
CEGIILNNP penciling
CEGIILNST clingiest
CEGIINOTV cognitive
CEGIINPRR price ring
CEGIIOSTT egotistic
CEGIKNNOR reckoning
CEGIKNOPT pocketing
CEGIKNORT rocketing
CEGIKNOST socketing
CEGILLNPU cupelling
CEGILLNRU cruelling
CEGILLORV gill cover
CEGILMMNO commingle
CEGILNOPR long price
CEGILNOST closeting
CEGILNRSU surcingle
CEGILNSTU single cut
CEGILOOST ecologist
CEGILORRV cover girl
CEGIMNOOR ergonomic
CEGIMNOUY gynoecium
CEGINNNRU cunninger
CEGINNOOT ontogenic
CEGINNORS reconsign
CEGINOPRY pyrogenic
CEGINOPTY genotypic
CEGINORST corseting
CEGINOSST cosseting
CEGINRRRU recurring
CEGINRTUV curveting
CEGINSSTU scungiest
CEGIOOPRT geotropic
CEGLLOOSU collogues
CEGLNOORY necrology
CEGNNORTU congruent
CEGNORRSU scrounger
CEGOOPRSY gyroscope
CEHHHIIKT hitch-hike
CEHHIIMST hemistich
CEHHIMSTT hemstitch
CEHHLOOTU touch-hole
CEHIIKLRS lickerish
CEHIIKLTW witchlike
CEHIIKRST kitschier
CEHIILLST chilliest
CEHIILMOT homiletic
CEHIILNOT neolithic
CEHIIMTYZ mythicize
CEHIINPPT pitch pine
CEHIINPRT nephritic
CEHIINRST Christine
CEHIINRTZ chintzier
CEHIINSST itchiness
CEHIINTTY ethnicity
CEHIIPPPT pitch-pipe
CEHIIPPTY epiphytic
CEHIIPRST chirpiest
CEHIIPSTT pitchiest
CEHIIRSTU heuristic
CEHIIRTTW twitchier
CEHIISTTT titchiest
CEHIKLMTV milk-vetch
CEHIKLPRS clerkship
CEHIKLSTY sketchily
CEHIKNSST thickness
CEHIKNSTU chunkiest
CEHIKOPPT hip pocket
CEHIKOSTW white sock
CEHIKOSTY hockeyist
CEHIKPRSW shipwreck
CEHILLMOS chillsome
CEHILLNSS chillness
CEHILMNTU lunchtime
CEHILNNPU punchline
CEHILNOSU lichenous
CEHILNOTU touchline
CEHILNSTZ schnitzel
CEHILOPRT plethoric
CEHILORTW wire cloth
CEHIMMOPR morphemic
CEHIMMORS micromesh
CEHIMMSTU chummiest
CEHIMNNOU ichneumon
CEHIMNOPS phonemics
CEHIMOORS smoochier
CEHIMPRUY hypericum
CEHIMRSTY chemistry
CEHINOPST Ctesiphon, phonetics
CEHINORTV chevrotin
CEHINOSTT notchiest
CEHINPRST sphincter
CEHINPSTU punchiest
CEHINSSSU cushiness
CEHINSTTY synthetic
CEHIOOPRT orthoepic
CEHIOOSST choosiest
CEHIOPPRT prophetic
CEHIOPPRY hyperopic

CEHIOPPST choppiest
CEHIOPRTT prothetic
CEHIOPRTU eutrophic
CEHIOPRTV overpitch
CEHIOPRTY hypocrite
CEHIORRST chorister
CEHIORSUV echovirus
CEHIOSSST schistose
CEHIOSTTU touchiest
CEHIRSTTY stitchery
CEHITTTWY witchetty
CEHKLNORS schnorkel
CEHKOOOSU cookhouse
CEHKOORSW screw hook
CEHLLOOPT photocell
CEHLMNOUU homuncule
CEHLOOPRS pre-school
CEHLOPRSS porchless
CEHMOOPRT ectomorph
CEHNNORTU truncheon
CEHNORRRS schnorrer
CEHOOOPRS horoscope
CEHOORSTU court shoe
CEHOPSSSY psychoses
CEHOPTTUY touch-type
CEIIILRVZ civilizer
CEIIIMTVZ victimize
CEIIINNPT incipient
CEIIIPSTT pietistic
CEIIJNNOT injection
CEIIJNSSU juiciness
CEIIJNSTU injustice
CEIIKKLST sticklike
CEIIKLMPS mispickel
CEIIKLMQU quicklime
CEIIKLPRR pricklier
CEIIKLSST sickliest
CEIIKMQTU quick time
CEIIKNPRT nit-picker
CEIIKNPSS pickiness
CEIIKRRST tricksier
CEIIKRSTT trickiest
CEIIKSSTT stickiest
CEIIKSSTZ size-stick
CEIILLMNT Millicent
CEIILMNSU miniscule
CEIILNNOR crinoline
CEIILNPPR principle
CEIILNSUV inclusive
CEIILOQRU liquorice
CEIILOSSU siliceous
CEIILPRST list price, price list
CEIILPRTU pleuritic
CEIILQSTU cliquiest
CEIILRSST scleritis
CEIIMNNOS sonic mine
CEIIMNRST cretinism
CEIIMNSST scientism
CEIIMORST eroticism, isometric
CEIIMOSST semiotics
CEIIMOSTX exoticism
CEIIMPRSU epicurism
CEIIMRRTT trimetric
CEIINNOPT inception
CEIINNRTY inner city
CEIINOPRS precision
CEIINOPRT proteinic
CEIINORRT criterion
CEIINORTV Victorine
CEIINPRSS priciness
CEIINPRTU unit price
CEIINPSSS spiciness
CEIINRSTX extrinsic
CEIINRSTY sincerity
CEIINRSUV incursive
CEIINRTTY intercity
CEIINRTYZ citizenry
CEIINSSTT scientist
CEIIOOPTZ epizootic
CEIIPRSST crispiest
CEIIPSTTY septicity
CEIIQRSTU critiques
CEIKLNOPV clove pink
CEIKLNORT interlock
CEIKLNOST close-knit
CEIKLNOSU nickelous
CEIKLNRUU unluckier
CEIKLNSSS slickness
CEIKLNSSU luckiness
CEIKLNSTU clunkiest
CEIKLOPST stockpile
CEIKLOSTV livestock
CEIKLPSTU pluckiest
CEIKLSSST stickless
CEIKMNSSU muckiness
CEIKNORSS rockiness
CEIKNOSTT stockinet
CEIKNQSSU quickness
CEIKNRSSU sick nurse
CEIKORRTV overtrick
CEIKOSSTT stockiest
CEIKPQSTU quickstep
CEIKRRSTT trickster
CEILLOSUV collusive
CEILLPSTY sylleptic
CEILMNNOO monocline
CEILMNOOS semicolon
CEILMNOOW low-income
CEILMNOTU monticule
CEILMNSUU minuscule
CEILMOPRY micropyle, polymeric
CEILMOPSY polysemic
CEILMPSTU clumpiest
CEILMRTUU reticulum
CEILMSSTU clumsiest
CEILNOORT intercool
CEILNOORZ colonizer
CEILNOOTU elocution
CEILNORSU Cornelius, inclosure, reclusion
CEILNORUV involucre
CEILNOSSU seclusion
CEILNOSUX exclusion
CEILNPRSY lip-syncer
CEILNRSSU curliness
CEILOOPRT coprolite
CEILOPPRT proleptic
CEILOPRSV cover slip, slip cover
CEILORRTU courtlier
CEILORSSS sclerosis
CEILOSSTT costliest
CEILOSTVY costively
CEILRSUVY cursively
CEIMMNNOS mnemonics
CEIMMNOOR monomeric
CEIMMNOSU encomiums
CEIMMNOTU comminute
CEIMMNOTY metonymic
CEIMMNOUZ communize
CEIMMOORS microsome
CEIMMOORT microtome
CEIMMORTT committer
CEIMMRSTU crummiest
CEIMMRSTY symmetric
CEIMMSSTU scummiest
CEIMNNOPU pneumonic
CEIMNNORT Comintern
CEIMNOORT microtone
CEIMNOOST economist
CEIMNOPTY impotency
CEIMNORTT metric ton
CEIMOOPST composite
CEIMOPRST prime cost
CEIMOPRSX proxemics
CEIMOPSUU pumiceous
CEIMORSTU costumier
CEIMOSTUV muscovite
CEIMOSTUZ customize
CEINNNOTT continent
CEINNOPRT Princeton
CEINNORSS corniness
CEINNORSY incensory
CEINNORTU centurion, continuer
CEINNOSTU continues
CEINOORST cortisone
CEINOOSSW Sosnowiec
CEINOPPRU porcupine
CEINOPRRT intercrop
CEINOPRST inspector
CEINOPSST Scots pine
CEINOPTYZ zincotype
CEINORRSU recursion
CEINORRTV contriver
CEINORRTW town crier
CEINORSTT cornetist
CEINORSTU cretinous
CEINORSUX excursion
CEINORTTW co-written
CEINOSSUY synecious
CEINOTVXY convexity
CEINPRRUY pruriency
CEINPRSSS crispness
CEINRSSUV curviness
CEINRSTWW twin-screw
CEIOOPRSS coreopsis
CEIOORRSV corrosive
CEIOORSTV vorticose
CEIORRSTT trisector
CEIORRTUU couturier

CEIORSSSW crosswise
CEIPPRRST prescript
CEIPRRSTU scripture
CEIRRSTTU stricture
CEIRSSTTU crustiest
CEIRSSTUV scurviest
CEJKOOTUY outjockey
CEJOOPRRT projector
CEKKNOPRU knocker-up
CEKKORSTY skyrocket
CEKLLPSSU pluckless
CEKLNORTW town clerk
CEKLOSSST stockless
CEKOORSTV overstock
CELLLOSUU cellulous
CELLMOPXY complexly
CELLMSTUU scutellum
CELLNOSUU nucleolus
CELLOOPTY collotype
CELLOORSS colorless
CELMNOTUY contumely
CELMOOPRY copolymer
CELMOOSSU colosseum
CELMOOTUY leucotomy
CELMOPRUU operculum
CELMPRSTU plectrums
CELNOORSU counselor
CELNOPRTU corpulent
CELNOSSTU countless
CELNPRUUY purulency
CELNRRTUY currently
CELNRTTUU truculent
CELNTTTUU nut cutlet
CELOOPRSU supercool
CELOPSSUU opuscules
CELORSSUU surculose
CELPRSTUU sculpture
CEMMNOOST commonest
CEMNNOOPT component
CEMNOOOQU monocoque
CEMNOORST storm cone
CEMOOPRSU composure
CEMORRSUU mercurous
CENNOOPPY opponency
CENNOOPRU pronounce
CENNOORST cornstone
CENNOSSSU consensus
CENOOPRST stonecrop
CENOOQRRU conqueror
CENOORRTV convertor
CENORSSSS crossness
CENORSSTU construes
CENORSSTW crow's-nest
CEOOPRRSS processor
CEOOPRRST prosector
CEOOPRRTT protector
CEOOPSSTU octopuses
CEOORRSSU sorcerous
CEOORRSSV crossover
CEOORSTUU courteous, outsource
CEOPRRRSU precursor
CEOPRRRTU corrupter
CEOPRRSSU procuress
CEORRRSTY try-scorer
CEORRSUUV verrucous
CERRSTTUU structure
CFFGIINNO coffining
CFFIIOOSU officious
CFFILRSUY scruffily
CFFLOOORU off colour
CFFOOSSTU soft focus
CFFORRSSU cross-ruff
CFGIIIKNN finicking
CFGIILLMN cling film
CFGINNOSU confusing
CFGINOSSU focussing
CFHIINOOR honorific
CFHIKOPRT pitchfork
CFHIKOSST stockfish
CFHILLPTU full pitch
CFHKLNORU fork lunch
CFHOOSTTU soft touch
CFIIKKLNS skin-flick
CFIILMMOR microfilm
CFIILNORT inflictor
CFIILORST floristic
CFIIOOPRS soporific
CFIKLLNOT flintlock
CFIKLLOOR folkloric
CFIKLMOSU folk music
CFILNNORT flint corn
CFIMMOORR microform
CFIMORRUV curviform
CFINNOOSU confusion
CFLLOORUU colourful
CFLNOORRU cornflour
CFLOOOSTT coltsfoot
CFOOORSTW crow's-foot
CFORSTUUU fructuous
CGGHINNOQ Chongqing
CGHHIORTU High Court
CGHIILLNS schilling
CGHIILORR choirgirl
CGHIIMOST Gothicism
CGHILNOOS schooling
CGHILOOOR horologic
CGHILORUY grouchily
CGHINORSU chorusing
CGHINOSSU hocussing
CGHIOPRTY copyright
CGHLOOPYY phycology
CGHNOORST torch song
CGHOOPRUY rough copy
CGIIIKMMN mimicking
CGIIKMMRY gimmickry
CGIILMNNY mincingly
CGIILNNWY wincingly
CGIILOSST logistics
CGIINNOOT cognition, incognito
CGIINNRRU incurring
CGIKLMNOY mockingly
CGIKOOPST pogo stick
CGILLNOYY cloyingly
CGILMNOOO monologic
CGILNNNUY cunningly
CGILNNOOR longicorn
CGILNOOOY iconology
CGILNOORU colouring
CGILNOPUV loving cup
CGILNTTUY cuttingly
CGILOOOSY sociology
CGILORSTU Girl Scout
CGINNOORS consignor
CGINNOOTT cotton gin
CGINNORTU trouncing
CGINOORTU Tourcoing
CGINORTUY congruity
CGLMOOOSY cosmology
CGLMOOSUY muscology
CGMNOOOSY cosmogony
CGNNOOTTU gun cotton
CGNOORSUU congruous
CHHINTTUW witch-hunt
CHHIOPSTT pitch shot
CHHKLLOOY hollyhock
CHHLNORUU lunch hour
CHIIILPPP philippic
CHIIILRTT trilithic
CHIILLOPY lyophilic
CHIILMORT microlith
CHIILNTYZ chintzily
CHIILOOTT otolithic
CHIILPTTY typhlitic
CHIIMMSTY mythicism
CHIIMOSTT Thomistic
CHIIMSTTY mythicist
CHIINOSTU chitinous
CHIIOPSST sophistic
CHIIORRSS cirrhosis
CHIIPSSTY physicist
CHIKLMOST locksmith
CHIKLPSUY puckishly
CHIKOOPTT toothpick
CHIKOPSTW whipstock
CHILLNOOT loincloth
CHILLOSTY coltishly
CHILMNOUU homunculi
CHILMOOSS Los Mochis
CHILNOPSU sulphonic
CHILOORSS chlorosis
CHILPRSUU sulphuric
CHILRRSUY currishly
CHIMMNOOY homonymic
CHIMNOPSY symphonic
CHINOOPST photonics
CHINOPSTU countship
CHIOOPRTT orthoptic
CHIOOPTYZ zoophytic
CHIOPRSTU courtship
CHIOPRSYY hypocrisy
CHIOPSSSY psychosis
CHIOPSTTT topstitch
CHIORRSSU scirrhous
CHKLMOOST Stockholm
CHLNOOOPY colophony
CHLNOTUUY uncouthly
CHLOOPTYY hypocotyl
CHNNORSYY synchrony
CHOOOPPTY photocopy
CHOOOPRSY horoscopy
CIIILLLTY illicitly
CIIILLSTV Civil List
CIIILMOPT impolitic

CIIILORTV vitriolic
CIIILOSSS silicosis
CIIILOSSU silicious
CIIIMSTTW witticism
CIIINNRST intrinsic
CIIJLNOPT clip joint
CIIKLRSTY tricksily
CIIKOPPRT rock pipit
CIILLNOOS collision
CIILLNOOT cotillion
CIILLNUVY uncivilly
CIILLOPTY politicly
CIILNNOSU inclusion
CIILNOOPS Nicopolis
CIILNOPTU punctilio, unpolitic
CIILOORST solicitor
CIILOOSSS scoliosis
CIILOSUVY viciously
CIILSSTTY stylistic
CIIMMSSTY mysticism
CIIMNORUZ zirconium
CIIMORSTV vorticism
CIINNORSU incursion
CIINNOSSW Wisconsin
CIINOPSSU suspicion
CIINORSUU incurious
CIINORTTU Tuticorin
CIIOOPRST isotropic
CIIORSTTU touristic
CIIORSTTV vorticist
CIIORSTUV virtuosic
CIIORSTUY curiosity
CIIORTTVY vorticity
CIIOSSTVY viscosity
CIIOSTUXY Sioux City
CIIRSTTUY rusticity
CIJKOSSST joss stick
CIJNNOTTU T-junction
CIKLLNUUY unluckily
CIKLNORSS cross-link
CIKLOOPST polo stick
CIKLOSSTT stocklist
CILLMORUY collyrium
CILLNOOSU collusion
CILLOOORU oil colour
CILMNOOOS Solomonic
CILMNOSTU columnist
CILMOSSUU soul music
CILNOOORT croton oil
CILNOORUU unicolour
CILOOPSUY copiously
CILOORRTU tricolour
CILOORSTU colourist
CILOPRTYY pyrolytic
CILORRSUY cursorily
CILORSUUY curiously
CILOSSUVY viscously
CIMMMNOSU communism
CIMMNNOOU communion
CIMMNOOOT commotion
CIMMNOSTU communist
CIMMNOTUY community
CIMNNOOOT monotonic
CIMNNOSYY synonymic
CIMNNOTUU continuum
CIMNOOPTY monotypic, toponymic
CIMNOOTXY mycotoxin
CIMNSTUYY syncytium
CINNOOPRU pro-nuncio
CINNOOSTU contusion
CINNOOSUU innocuous
CINOOORRS corrosion
CINOORRSS Iron Cross
CINOSTUVY viscounty
CIOOOPRSZ zoosporic
CIOOOPRTZ protozoic
CKLLNOORR rock 'n' roll
CKMOOORST stockroom
CKNOOOSTW Cookstown
CKOOORSTT rootstock
CKOOPRSTT Stockport
CKOPRSTTU truck stop
CLLOORRTU court roll
CLMOOOORT locomotor
CLMOOOSTY colostomy
CLMOORSTU colostrum
CLMOPSUUU opusculum
CLNOOPRSU proconsul
CLNOORTUY Lyon Court
CLNORTUUY uncourtly
CLOPRRTUY corruptly
CMMNOOORS Roscommon
CMNNOOOPS non compos
CMOOORRTU courtroom
CMOOORSST motocross
CMOOSTTYY cystotomy
CNNNOOTUU count noun
CNOOORTUZ corozo-nut
CNOPRTUUY up-country
COOOOPPPS poop scoop
COOPRSSTY sporocyst
DDDEFIOSX fixed odds
DDDEIINUV undivided
DDEEEGIPR pedigreed
DDEEEILTT title deed
DDEEEINRX Dexedrine
DDEEELMOR remodeled
DDEEELOPV developed
DDEEENNOP open-ended
DDEEENNPT dependent
DDEEESTUU desuetude
DDEEFGLNU unfledged
DDEEFILNU undefiled
DDEEFINNU undefined
DDEEGGGLO dog-legged
DDEEGGILT gilt-edged
DDEEGHILT delighted
DDEEHNORU deerhound
DDEEIILMT delimited
DDEEIIPPT dipeptide
DDEEILLPS dispelled
DDEEILLRV drivelled
DDEEIMNPU unimpeded
DDEEINORW eiderdown
DDEEINRSU underside, undesired
DDEEINSSS sidedness
DDEEIOORZ deodorize
DDEEIOPST deposited
DDEEIPRRS red spider
DDEELOTVY devotedly
DDEENNORU underdone
DDEENNOUW unendowed
DDEENORRT retrodden
DDEENRSSU undressed
DDEERRSTU red duster
DDEFFIINT diffident
DDEFGIIIN dignified
DDEFGILLO goldfield
DDEFIILST fiddliest
DDEFIILSU disulfide
DDEFILNOW downfield
DDEFILOOT flood tide
DDEFLLOOW Oddfellow
DDEFNNOUU unfounded
DDEFNNRUU underfund
DDEGGHOOT hotdogged
DDEGHINRS shredding
DDEGIINSS giddiness
DDEGIJLLU ill-judged
DDEGINNPU puddening
DDEGINORR derring-do
DDEGINRRU undergird
DDEGLNOOR golden rod
DDEGOOORY do-goodery
DDEHHNRTU hundredth
DDEHIIRSY Yiddisher
DDEHIORXY hydroxide
DDEHIOSST shoddiest
DDEHOORRT hot-rodder
DDEIIKRSV disk drive
DDEIILLST distilled
DDEIILSTT tiddliest
DDEIIMTTW dim-witted
DDEIINSST dissident
DDEILMNOW low-minded
DDEILNRRU unriddler
DDEILNTUU undiluted
DDEILORWW wide world, worldwide
DDEILSTUV dust devil
DDEILSTUY studiedly
DDEIMMRUY medium dry
DDEIMNSSU muddiness
DDEINOSSW dowdiness
DDEINRSSU ruddiness
DDEINSTUU unstudied
DDELLOPTU Tolpuddle
DDELNORSU undersold
DDELNORSW world's end
DDENNORTU untrodden
DDENNORUU unrounded
DDENNORUW down under
DDENNOSUU unsounded
DDENNOUUW unwounded
DDENOORUW underwood
DDEOOPPSU pseudopod
DDEOORRRW word order
DDFGILORU Guildford
DDFGOOORW Word of God
DDFIOORTW driftwood
DDGIIKLNY kiddingly
DDGIINQSU squidding

DDGIMOOOS do-goodism
DDHIOOOWW widowhood
DDHLMOOOU hood-mould
DDHOORSST short odds
DDIIIISVV divi-divis
DDIILMSTU Ludditism
DDIORRTWY dirty word
DEEEEFGNR greenfeed
DEEEEGNRW greenweed
DEEEEGNRY green-eyed
DEEEEGQSU squeegeed
DEEEEKNRW weekender
DEEEFGIKN knife-edge
DEEEFINSV defensive
DEEEFLLNU needleful
DEEEFLLRU refuelled
DEEEFMNRT deferment
DEEEFPRRR preferred
DEEEFRRYZ freeze-dry
DEEEGHNRT nth degree
DEEEGIKLW wedgelike
DEEEGIRRT ridge tree
DEEEGIRST greediest
DEEEGISWW wedgewise
DEEEGKLNT kentledge
DEEEGLNOY golden-eye
DEEEGNRTT detergent
DEEEGRRTT regretted
DEEEHILLW idle wheel
DEEEHINPR ephedrine
DEEEHNPRR reprehend
DEEEHNRRU hereunder
DEEEHORSW shoreweed
DEEEIILSZ dieselize
DEEEILLMP millepede
DEEEILRRV deliverer
DEEEILSSW edelweiss
DEEEIMNRT determine
DEEEIMSST disesteem
DEEEINNSS neediness
DEEEINPTX expedient
DEEEINRRS reindeers
DEEEINRSS reediness
DEEEINRTZ tenderize
DEEEINSSS seediness
DEEEINSSW weediness
DEEEIPRTX expediter
DEEEIPSST speediest
DEEEISTTW tweediest
DEEEKLLNN kennelled
DEEELLPRS respelled
DEEELLPSW speedwell
DEEELNOPV enveloped
DEEELNRRS slenderer
DEEELOPRV developer, redevelop
DEEEMNOSY seed money
DEEEMOPRT pedometer
DEEEMORST dosemeter
DEEEMORSU deer mouse, mouse deer
DEEENNRUW unrenewed
DEEENNSSS denseness
DEEENOSTW stoneweed
DEEENPRRT pretender
DEEENRRTT deterrent
DEEENRSTT tenderest
DEEEORSTV stevedore
DEEEORSVX oversexed
DEEEPPPRR red pepper
DEEEPRSSU supersede
DEEERRRSS redresser
DEEFFFSTU feedstuff
DEEFFHILS Sheffield
DEEFFILLT left field
DEEFFINRT different
DEEFFIORT forfeited
DEEFGIILR filigreed
DEEFGIIRS Siegfried
DEEFGINNU unfeigned
DEEFGINRR deferring
DEEFGJORU forejudge
DEEFHILSS flesh side
DEEFHLLUY heedfully
DEEFHLNSU unfleshed
DEEFHLNUU unheedful
DEEFHLOPS sheepfold
DEEFHLORT threefold
DEEFIIKLN fiendlike
DEEFIILMN minefield
DEEFIILNR infielder
DEEFIILSZ life-sized
DEEFILNOX deflexion
DEEFILORT trefoiled
DEEFILRSV self-drive
DEEFINNPR penfriend
DEEFINNRU unrefined
DEEFINSST fetidness
DEEFINSSX fixedness
DEEFIPRRV perfervid
DEEFIRSTU surfeited
DEEFLLNNU funnelled
DEEFLLNUY needfully
DEEFLNOSV sevenfold
DEEFLNRTU underfelt
DEEFLORRW free world
DEEFMNORU unfreedom
DEEFNOOPS spoon-feed
DEEFOPRSS professed
DEEFORRST defroster
DEEGGIRRT triggered
DEEGHHIPS high-speed
DEEGHILNW wheedling
DEEGHILRT relighted
DEEGHINNU unheeding
DEEGHINUW unweighed
DEEGHLMOP help me God
DEEGIILNU guideline
DEEGIILRT ridge tile
DEEGIISTV digestive
DEEGILNRT ringleted
DEEGILOOU ideologue
DEEGILOPR ridge pole
DEEGIMORT geometrid
DEEGINNRR rendering
DEEGINNRS red ensign
DEEGINNTT de-netting, Dettingen
DEEGINORT redingote
DEEGINRRR derringer
DEEGINRRT deterring
DEEGINRSV deserving
DEEGINRTU Negritude
DEEGINRTV divergent
DEEGINRUV gerundive
DEEGIOPRU guide rope
DEEGIOSST geodesist
DEEGIPRST predigest
DEEGIRRSS digresser
DEEGIRRUU de rigueur
DEEGJMNTU judgement
DEEGKLNOW knowledge
DEEGKOPRW powder keg
DEEGLLORV grovelled
DEEGLMNOT lodgement
DEEGLNNOU Guendolen
DEEGLNNOW Gwendolen
DEEGNOORW greenwood
DEEGNORWW weed-grown
DEEGORRSU red grouse
DEEHHILOY hidey-hole
DEEHIINPT pethidine
DEEHIINRT inherited
DEEHIKRSW whiskered
DEEHILOPP pedophile
DEEHILPRS eldership
DEEHILRSV shriveled
DEEHIMOTZ methodize
DEEHINORT dinothere
DEEHINRSW swineherd
DEEHKLORY keyholder
DEEHLLOSV shovelled
DEEHLNOPR pen holder
DEEHLPSST depthless
DEEHMOORT hodometer
DEEHMPPSU speed hump
DEEHNNORS Henderson
DEEHNOOQU queenhood
DEEHNORST threnodes
DEEHNRRTU thunderer
DEEHOORTX heterodox
DEEHOPSTU Deep South
DEEHSSTTU dust sheet
DEEIIKNRS die-sinker
DEEIILLMP millipede
DEEIILLOS diesel oil
DEEIILMPR imperiled
DEEIILMRT delimiter
DEEIILSTW wieldiest
DEEIIMNTT midinette
DEEIIMPRS epidermis
DEEIIMRTV drive-time
DEEIINORT re-edition
DEEIINORZ deionizer
DEEIIPPPR Pied Piper
DEEIIPRUX prie-dieux
DEEIIPSSW sideswipe
DEEIIRRSV riverside
DEEIIRSTV revisited
DEEIISSSU side issue
DEEIJNORR rejoinder
DEEIKLLLW well-liked
DEEIKLNSX sex-linked
DEEIKNSTW stinkweed
DEEILLLNT lintelled

DEEILLLOW well-oiled
DEEILLMNO ill-omened
DEEILLMST mild steel
DEEILLMTW well-timed
DEEILLNRW indweller
DEEILLNST tinselled
DEEILLNSV snivelled
DEEILLNTT little end
DEEILLPRS dispeller
DEEILLRRV driveller
DEEILLRST trellised
DEEILLRSU slide rule
DEEILLRTU telluride
DEEILLRTW well-tried
DEEILLSVW swivelled
DEEILMMNS Mendelism
DEEILMNOV dime novel
DEEILMNTV devilment
DEEILMORZ melodizer
DEEILMPTU duple time
DEEILNNPU penduline
DEEILNNRU underline
DEEILNOPT depletion, diplotene
DEEILNPTU plenitude
DEEILNRTU interlude
DEEILNSSX indexless
DEEILNTVY evidently
DEEILOPRS despoiler
DEEILPPRS slippered
DEEILPRSS prideless
DEEILRRSS riderless
DEEILRSVY diversely
DEEILRTUY eruditely
DEEIMNNRU undermine
DEEIMNORZ modernize
DEEIMNOSS Des Moines
DEEIMNRTT detriment
DEEIMNRTU unmerited
DEEIMNSSX mixedness
DEEIMOORT meteoroid
DEEIMORST dosimeter
DEEIMPRST distemper
DEEIMPRTT permitted
DEEIMRTUU deuterium
DEEINNORT internode
DEEINNOTT detention
DEEINNQSU sequinned
DEEINNRTU indenture
DEEINNSSS snideness
DEEINORST desertion
DEEINPRSS dispenser
DEEINPRST president
DEEINPRUX unexpired
DEEINPSST tepidness
DEEINRSST dissenter, tiredness
DEEINRSSW weirdness
DEEINRSTT trendiest
DEEINRSTY Tynesider
DEEINRSUV unrevised
DEEINRSUZ undersize
DEEINRTUV unriveted
DEEIOPRVW power-dive
DEEIORRRV overrider
DEEIORRVV overdrive
DEEIOTTVX videotext
DEEIPRRSS disperser
DEEIPRSTU disrepute
DEEIRSSST dressiest
DEEIRSTTV test drive
DEEIRSTUV divesture, servitude
DEEIRTTXY dexterity
DEEISTTTU destitute
DEEJOORVY overjoyed
DEEKKOOYY okey-dokey
DEEKLNORS snorkeled
DEEKLNOSV veldskoen
DEEKNORST stonkered
DEEKNORUV unrevoked
DEEKRRTUY Turkey red
DEELLLOVW well-loved
DEELLMMOP pommelled
DEELLMMPU pummelled
DEELLMOOR role model
DEELLMRTU red mullet
DEELLNNTU tunnelled
DEELLNRSU undersell
DEELLNRSY slenderly
DEELLNSSY endlessly
DEELLOPPR propelled
DEELLORTW trowelled
DEELMMPTU plummeted
DEELMNORS mesne lord
DEELMOORV velodrome
DEELMOSUW would seem
DEELNNPST splendent
DEELNOOST lodestone
DEELNPRRU plunderer
DEELNRSTU end result
DEELNSTTU unsettled
DEELORSSW dowerless
DEELORTTU rouletted
DEELPRTUY reputedly
DEEMNNOTW endowment
DEEMNOPRS endosperm
DEEMOORSV Smederovo
DEEMPRTTU trumpeted
DEEMRRSSU murderess
DEENNORTU undertone
DEENNRTUU untenured
DEENNRTUW underwent
DEENOOPRS endospore
DEENOPRRS responder
DEENOPRRV provender
DEENOPRSV overspend
DEENOPRUW unpowered
DEENOPRUX expounder
DEENOPSUX unexposed
DEENPRSSU suspender, unpressed
DEENRRRSU surrender
DEENRSSTT tent dress
DEENRSTUV undervest
DEENRSTYY dysentery
DEENRTTUU unuttered
DEEOPRRSS depressor
DEEORRRSS redressor
DEEORRSSV overdress
DEEORRSTU trousered
DEEORRSTX dextrorse
DEEORRSTY destroyer
DEEORSTUX dexterous
DEFFGINNO offending
DEFFIISUV diffusive
DEFFILLLU fulfilled
DEFFILSUY diffusely
DEFFLNRUU unruffled
DEFFNSTUU unstuffed
DEFGGIINT fidgeting
DEFGGILLN fledgling
DEFGHILOT eightfold
DEFGIIRSU disfigure
DEFGILLNO long field
DEFGINRRY finger-dry
DEFGOOPRR drop-forge
DEFHIILSV devilfish
DEFHINRSU furnished
DEFHLOOOW wholefood
DEFIIISSS sissified
DEFIILLRR fire drill
DEFIILMOV video film
DEFIILMSU semi-fluid
DEFIIMNNY indemnify
DEFIIMRWY midwifery
DEFIINNRW Winnifred
DEFIINRTY denitrify
DEFIINSST disinfest
DEFIIRSVY diversify
DEFIIRTVY devitrify
DEFIKLORW fieldwork
DEFILLNNO linenfold
DEFILLORV frivolled
DEFILLRUY direfully
DEFILMNRU remindful
DEFILNOSW snowfield
DEFILNSSU fluidness
DEFIMORRT triformed
DEFIMORTY deformity
DEFIMSTYY demystify
DEFIOOSTU outside of
DEFIORSST disforest
DEFIORTTU fortitude
DEFLLLOUY dolefully
DEFLLNOUW well-found
DEFLLRSSU full dress
DEFLNORUW underflow, wonderful
DEFMOORRR order form
DEFNOORTU underfoot
DEFOOOSTV dove's-foot
DEFORRSTT Stretford
DEGGGIINR de-rigging
DEGGHNNOS Dongsheng
DEGGHOORT hotdogger
DEGGIILRU Girl Guide
DEGGIINNS designing
DEGGIJOOR doojigger
DEGGINOSS dogginess
DEGGIORTU outrigged
DEGGLNPUU unplugged
DEGHHINOT high-toned
DEGHIILRR hired girl
DEGHIILST sidelight

DEGHIIRST right side
DEGHIJPSU judgeship
DEGHILMSU gumshield
DEGHILNTU unlighted
DEGHILOTW white gold
DEGHIMNRU humdinger
DEGHINSTU unsighted
DEGHIORRU rough ride
DEGHIORTU doughtier
DEGHIOSTU doughiest
DEGHMOORT godmother
DEGHNNRUU underhung
DEGHNORUY greyhound
DEGIIIMRS dirigisme, semi-rigid
DEGIIIRST dirigiste
DEGIIKNSZ king-sized
DEGIILLNV devilling
DEGIILMPR pilgrimed
DEGIILNOV evildoing
DEGIILNRV driveling
DEGIIMNNP impending
DEGIIMNTT demitting
DEGIINNSS dinginess
DEGIINOSS gneissoid
DEGIINOST digestion
DEGIINRRS ringsider
DEGIINRSS rigidness
DEGIINRTU intrigued, nigritude
DEGIIQRSU squidgier
DEGIIRRSV verdigris
DEGILLMNO modelling
DEGILLNOV long-lived
DEGILLNOW dowelling
DEGILLNOY yodelling
DEGILNNRU underling
DEGILNNTU indulgent
DEGILNOOR gondolier
DEGILNOSS godliness
DEGILNOTU longitude
DEGILOOST goodliest
DEGILOOTV dog-violet
DEGIMNRRU demurring
DEGIMOORT good-timer
DEGIMOOST good times
DEGIMSSTU smudgiest
DEGINNORW wondering
DEGINNRUW underwing
DEGINOPSS podginess
DEGINORSW wrong side
DEGINPSSU pudginess
DEGIOORTW tiger-wood
DEGIOPSTU guidepost
DEGIOSSTT stodgiest
DEGLNNOOZ long dozen
DEGLNNOWY Gwendolyn
DEGLNORSU groundsel
DEGLOOPRU prologued
DEGMNOOOY good money
DEGMOPSTU smudge pot
DEGNOORRW wrongdoer
DEGNOPRUW gunpowder
DEGOOPRRU prorogued
DEGOORUVW vogue word
DEGORRSTU drugstore
DEHHIKMOS shelkhdom
DEHHINOSY hoydenish
DEHHIOPPS phosphide
DEHHLLNOU hell-hound
DEHHLOOSU household
DEHHLORST threshold
DEHHNOORU horehound
DEHIIINST histidine
DEHIILRSS disrelish
DEHIINNRU hirundine
DEHIIOOPX pixie hood
DEHIIOSTY hideosity
DEHIIPRSS spiderish
DEHIIPRST Petri dish
DEHIISTWW widthwise
DEHILORSW wild horse
DEHILOSUY hideously
DEHILRRUY hurriedly
DEHIMMOST Methodism
DEHIMORRT thermidor
DEHIMOSTT Methodist
DEHINNOPR endorphin
DEHINORRT trihedron
DEHINORVW windhover
DEHINOSST dishonest
DEHINPPSU unshipped
DEHINPPUW unwhipped
DEHINRRUU unhurried
DEHIOOTWW whitewood
DEHIOPRSW worshiped
DEHIORRTY erythroid
DEHKLOOST stokehold
DEHKNOOOS hook-nosed
DEHLLOOSU dollhouse
DEHLMNOPY endolymph, lymph node
DEHLNOORW horned owl
DEHLNOOSU soundhole
DEHLORSYY hydrolyse
DEHLORYYZ hydrolyze
DEHMNOOPR endomorph
DEHNNOSUW news hound
DEHNOOPRS horse-pond
DEHNORSTU undershot
DEHOOPRRY doryphore
DEHOOSSSU doss-house
DEHORSSTU stud-horse
DEIIIKNTT identikit
DEIIILQUZ liquidize
DEIIKKLNR kilderkin
DEIIKLLOS oiled silk
DEIIKLNST kindliest
DEIIKNRSV skin diver
DEIIKRSST kid sister
DEIILLMPY impliedly
DEIILLNST instilled
DEIILLOPS ellipsoid
DEIILLRST distiller
DEIILLSTU ill-suited
DEIILMNTU unlimited
DEIILMOSS semi-solid
DEIILNNUV unlived-in
DEIILNPRS spindlier
DEIILNSSV lividness
DEIILORSU delirious
DEIIMMMSU mediumism
DEIIMNNOS dimension
DEIIMNNTY indemnity
DEIIMNOQU Dominique
DEIIMNOSS demission
DEIIMNRTW midwinter
DEIIMNSST timidness
DEIIMPRSU presidium
DEIIMRTTY tridymite
DEIINNNOT indention
DEIINNORT rendition
DEIINNOTT dentition
DEIINNOUZ un-ionized
DEIINNRTW interwind
DEIINNSSW windiness
DEIINNTUV uninvited
DEIINOPRT perdition
DEIINOPSS indispose
DEIINORSS Ironsides
DEIINORST disorient
DEIINORSV diversion
DEIINORTT detrition
DEIINORTU erudition
DEIINOSTU inside out
DEIINPRRS spin-drier
DEIINPSTZ pint-sized
DEIINRSST dirtiness
DEIINSSTV disinvest
DEIINSSVV vividness
DEIINSSZZ dizziness
DEIINSTTU untidiest
DEIINSTUV unvisited
DEIINTTTW nitwitted
DEIIOSSTU seditious
DEIIPPRST drippiest
DEIIRSTVY diversity
DEIIRSUVV redivivus
DEIJNNRUU uninjured
DEIKLLNSU unskilled
DEIKLORSW swordlike
DEIKMMNSU unskimmed
DEIKMNNOW womenkind
DEIKNNOUV uninvoked
DEIKNNTTU unknitted
DEIKNORRV overdrink
DEIKNSSSU duskiness, sun-kissed
DEILLMNOU mullioned
DEILLMRST drill stem
DEILLNORW world-line
DEILLNPSU unspilled
DEILLNSUU unsullied
DEILLOPST pistolled
DEILLORRW worldlier
DEILLORST lordliest
DEILLORSY soldierly
DEILLSTTY stiltedly
DEILMOOSU melodious
DEILMTTUU multitude
DEILNOPSU unspoiled
DEILNOPTY pointedly
DEILNOSSS solidness
DEILNOTUV involuted
DEILNRSSU luridness

DEILOOPZZ podzolize
DEILORRWY worriedly
DEILORVWW world-view
DEILOSSTU dissolute
DEILOSTUY tediously
DEILOSUVY deviously
DEIMMMRSU midsummer
DEIMMNORS modernism
DEIMMNOUY neodymium
DEIMMNRTU untrimmed
DEIMMOSTY immodesty
DEIMNNOOO onion dome
DEIMNOOSS moodiness
DEIMNOPRU impounder
DEIMNORST modernist
DEIMNORTY modernity
DEIMNPRTU imprudent
DEIMNPSSU dumpiness
DEIMOPPUY yuppiedom
DEIMOPSST despotism
DEIMOQRSU squiredom
DEIMORSTY dosimetry
DEIMORSUX exordiums
DEINNOOTX endotoxin
DEINNOPTU unpointed
DEINNORRV non-driver
DEINNOSSW downiness
DEINNOSTU tendinous
DEINNPRTU unprinted
DEINNRSUU uninsured
DEINNRTTU undertint
DEINNSSUY sunny side
DEINNSTTU unstinted
DEINOOSSW woodiness
DEINOPRST dripstone
DEINOPRTV provident
DEINORRUW unworried
DEINORRVW downriver
DEINORSSW rowdiness, wordiness
DEINORTWW write-down
DEINOSSTT dottiness
DEINPRRSY spin-dryer
DEINPSTWW windswept
DEINRRSTU unstirred
DEINRSTTU denturist
DEINRSTTY dentistry
DEINSSSTU dustiness
DEIOOPRST depositor, droopiest
DEIOPRSTU dipterous
DEIORSSTU dioestrus
DEIORSSTW drowsiest
DEIPPTTTU tittupped
DEIPRRSTU disrupter
DEIPRTTUU turpitude
DEIPSSTTU stupidest
DEIRSSTTU sturdiest
DEJKMNORU junkerdom
DEKLNNRUY drunkenly
DEKMOOOSW woodsmoke
DEKNNOTTU unknotted
DEKNOORTU undertook
DEKNORRUW underwork
DEKOPRSTU stud poker
DELLNORSS drollness
DELMNOOPR lemon drop
DELNOPRSU splendour
DELNOPRTU underplot
DELNOPSUU pendulous
DELNORTWX next world
DELNOSSSU soundless
DELNOSSUW woundless
DELNPRTUY prudently
DELOOOSUW woodlouse
DELOORSSU odourless
DELORSTUY desultory
DELOSTUUY duteously
DEMNNORUU unmourned
DEMNNOTUU unmounted
DEMNOPSUY pseudonym
DEMNORSTU undermost
DEMOOOSUW wood mouse
DEMORRSUU murderous
DENNORSSU roundness
DENNORSUW sundowner
DENNOSSSU soundness
DENOOPPSU unopposed
DENOOPRSU ponderous
DENOORSTU tournedos
DENOORUVW overwound
DENOPPRRU underprop
DENOPPSTU unstopped
DENOPRSSU proudness
DENOPSTTU unspotted
DENORTTUU untutored
DEOORRSTU Tudor rose
DEORRSUUV verdurous
DEORSTUVY overstudy
DEPPTTTUU put-putted
DEPRSSSTU press stud
DFFFILOTY fiftyfold
DFFOOSTU foodstuff
DFFIINOSU diffusion
DFFLLLOOU full flood
DFFLOORTY fortyfold
DFGIIIRTY frigidity
DFGILNNOU foundling
DFGLLOOOS fool's gold
DFGOOOSST soft goods
DFHILOORY hydrofoil
DFHINOSTW downshift
DFHIORSSW swordfish
DFHLNOOUW wolfhound
DFHLNSSUU slush fund
DFIILORTY floridity
DFIINPRST spindrift
DFIKNORST soft drink
DFILLMNUY mindfully
DFILLTUUY dutifully
DFILMNNUU unmindful
DFILNTUUU undutiful
DFILOSTXY sixtyfold
DFINORSTW snowdrift
DFINORSUW four winds
DFIOORTUW fruitwood
DFNOOOPTU foot-pound
DFNOOORRT front door
DFNRSTTUU trust fund
DGGHINOOT goodnight
DGGHNOORU groundhog
DGGINNORU grounding
DGHHIINST hindsight
DGHHINOPT diphthong
DGHHIORSW high words
DGHHOORSU roughshod
DGHILMOST goldsmith
DGHILOOTW lightwood
DGHILOTUY doughtily
DGHINORTW downright
DGHLOORYY hydrology
DGHOOOSTT dog's tooth
DGHOORSUU sourdough
DGHORSTTU God's truth
DGHRRTTUU truth drug
DGIIINNTY indignity
DGIIKNSVY skydiving
DGIILOORY iridology
DGIIMNSSU Sigismund
DGIINNOWW windowing
DGIINOPRV providing
DGIINORTU outriding
DGIIRTTUY turgidity
DGILLNOOP dolloping
DGILLNORW worldling
DGILMNOOO Mongoloid
DGILNNUYY undyingly
DGIMNRSUY Grundyism
DGINNOPSU pound sign
DGINNOSWW downswing
DGINOORSW swing-door
DGINOPPRS droppings
DGINORUVY ground ivy
DGKOOORSW good works
DGKOOOUUU Koudougou
DGMNRRSUY Mrs Grundy
DGNNORTUU groundnut
DHHILOPRY hydrophil
DHHLOORST shorthold
DHIILNRWW whirlwind
DHIILOPSY syphiloid
DHILLOSTY doltishly
DHILNNOSY donnishly
DHILOPRSS lordships
DHILPRSUY prudishly
DHIMNOSTY hymnodist
DHIMORSTW wordsmith
DHINNOTUW whodunnit
DHINOOPRS rhodopsin
DHINOORSU dishonour
DHINOPRUW whip-round
DHINORSTW short wind
DHINOSTUW south wind
DHKMNOOOS monkshood
DHKNORUYY hunky-dory
DHLLOOOWY Hollywood
DHLMOOTUU loudmouth
DHLNOOOPT lophodont
DHMNOOPWY wood nymph
DHNNOORTW North Down
DHNOORTWW downthrow
DHNOOSTUW Southdown
DHOOORTXY orthodoxy
DHOOPPPUY puppyhood

DHOPRSTYY	dystrophy
DIIILMPTY	limpidity
DIIILNPSY	insipidly
DIIILOPSS	lipidosis
DIIILQTUY	liquidity
DIIINOSSU	insidious
DIIINOSUV	invidious
DIIKLMNOU	dinkum oil
DIILLMNOO	modillion
DIILOPRTY	triploidy
DIILOSTTY	stolidity
DIIMORSSY	dimissory
DIINOSSUY	Dionysius
DIIOPRTTY	torpidity
DIIORRTTY	torridity
DIIPRTTUY	putridity
DIIPSTTUY	stupidity
DIISTTUVY	duty visit
DIKLMNORU	milk round
DIKLOORTY	dirty look
DIKNOOSTW	stinkwood
DIKORRTWY	dirty work
DILLOOPPY	polyploid
DILLOPRST	stop-drill
DILLORSWY	sword lily
DILMNOORU	iron-mould
DILOOPTUW	tulipwood
DIMMOPSUY	sympodium
DIMNORSTW	windstorm
DIMOOOOSV	voodooism
DIMOORRTY	dormitory
DINNNOOUW	union down
DINOOORSU	inodorous
DINOOPRST	piston rod
DINOPRRTU	round trip
DINOPTTUY	point duty
DINORTTUY	rotundity
DIOOOOSTV	voodooist
DIOOPRSST	prosodist
DIOPRRSTU	disruptor
DIOPRRSTW	wrist-drop
DKNOORSTW	sword knot
DKORSTUWY	work study
DLLNORUWY	unworldly
DLNNOSUUY	unsoundly
DLOOORSUY	odorously
DMNOORRUW	roundworm
DMOOORRST	storm-door
DMORSSTTU	dust storm
DNNORRTUU	turnround
DNOOPSSTU	sound post
DNOOPSTUW	downspout
DNOORTUWW	woundwort
EEEEFGNRS	greens fee
EEEEFHLRW	freewheel
EEEEFHRST	free sheet
EEEEFRRSV	free verse
EEEEFRRTV	fever tree
EEEEGINVV	Genevieve
EEEEGKLNR	green leek
EEEEGNRRV	evergreen
EEEEGQSSU	squeegees
EEEEHLRSW	elsewhere
EEEEKLNSX	Kleenexes
EEEELMRTT	telemeter
EEEELNSSV	elevenses
EEEELNTVV	velveteen
EEEENNSST	Tennessee
EEEENNSTV	seventeen
EEEENOPRY	eye-opener
EEEENPRST	presentee
EEEENRSTW	sweetener
EEEEPRRSV	persevere
EEEFGIKRR	Greek fire
EEEFGKNRU	fenugreek
EEEFHNOPR	Freephone
EEEFHORRT	therefore
EEEFHORRW	wherefore
EEEFHORSU	free house
EEEFHRRRS	refresher
EEEFILRRV	free-liver
EEEFILRVX	reflexive
EEEFINRRT	interfere
EEEFKMORS	smoke-free
EEEFLLNRU	fullerene
EEEFLNSST	fleetness
EEEFLRSTY	freestyle
EEEFMNRRT	fermenter
EEEFMOORS	See of Rome
EEEFNORST	freestone
EEEGGORTT	georgette
EEEGHLRSS	sheerlegs
EEEGHOPRS	geosphere
EEEGIJNNT	jet engine
EEEGIKNPS	Pekingese
EEEGILLNR	leger line
EEEGILMNR	lime green
EEEGILMTY	gimlet eye
EEEGILNTY	eyeleting
EEEGINNRV	veneering
EEEGINPRR	peregrine
EEEGINRRZ	energizer
EEEGINRUV	Guinevere
EEEGIRSTY	tiger's-eye
EEEGISTTX	exegetist
EEEGKNRSS	Greekness
EEEGLLNTY	genteelly
EEEGMNNRU	energumen
EEEGMNRSS	messenger
EEEGNNRSS	greenness
EEEHIKLPS	sheeplike, spike heel
EEEHILLNZ	Hellenize
EEEHILRWW	wire wheel
EEEHIMPRS	ephemeris
EEEHIMPUZ	euphemize
EEEHIMSTT	time sheet
EEEHINRTT	Henriette
EEEHKLOSU	houseleek
EEEHKOPSU	housekeep
EEEHLLLWW	wheel well
EEEHLLSSW	wheelless
EEEHLMNTY	methylene
EEEHLNOPT	telephone
EEEHLNOSW	nose wheel
EEEHLRRST	shelterer
EEEHMMNTY	enthymeme
EEEHMNOPR	ephemeron
EEEHMNTTU	theme tune
EEEHMORST	threesome
EEEHMORSW	somewhere
EEEHNNPST	nepenthes
EEEHNORSW	whensoe'er
EEEHNQSTU	the queen's
EEEHNRSSS	sheerness
EEEHNSSTW	news-sheet
EEEHOPRSX	exosphere
EEEHORSTU	tree house
EEEHRRSTW	tree shrew
EEEHRSTTU	usherette
EEEIIKLSV	sievelike
EEEIIMPRZ	epimerize
EEEIKLNQU	queenlike
EEEIKNNPR	innkeeper
EEEILLPTZ	pelletize
EEEILMPSY	simple eye
EEEILMSST	seemliest
EEEILNNRV	enlivener
EEEILNQRU	queenlier
EEEILNRSS	leeriness
EEEILNSTX	extensile
EEEILPSST	sleepiest
EEEILPTVX	expletive
EEEILSSTT	steeliest
EEEIMMRSZ	mesmerize
EEEIMNNRT	nemertine
EEEIMORTT	meteorite
EEEIMPRRT	perimeter
EEEIMPRTT	permittee
EEEIMRSTV	serve time
EEEIMSSTW	semi-sweet
EEEINNRST	Ernestine
EEEINNRTV	intervene
EEEINORRT	orienteer
EEEINPRRS	reserpine
EEEINPSSW	weepiness
EEEINPSVX	expensive
EEEINQSUZ	queen-size
EEEINRSTT	serinette
EEEINRTTV	retentive
EEEINSSTT	teensiest
EEEINSTVX	extensive
EEEIPRRTT	pierrette, preterite
EEEIPRSTX	expertise
EEEIPRTXZ	expertize
EEEIQTTTU	etiquette
EEEIRRRTV	retriever
EEEIRSTTV	serviette
EEEJLLRWY	jewellery
EEEJNRSWY	New Jersey
EEEJRSTTT	jet-setter
EEEKLNSSS	sleekness
EEEKMORST	smoke tree
EEEKMRSTU	musketeer
EEEKOOPRZ	zookeeper
EEELLNPRT	repellent
EEELLNPTX	expellent
EEELLNSSV	levelness
EEELLPSSS	sleepless
EEELMNOPT	elopement
EEELMOORT	oleometer
EEELMRTTY	telemetry
EEELMRTXY	extremely
EEELNOPTT	leptotene

EEELNORVW wolverene
EEELNOTTV novelette
EEELNQSSU queenless
EEELNRSSV nerveless
EEELNSSSS senseless
EEELNSSST tenseless
EEELNSSTV eventless
EEELNSTUV sleeve-nut
EEELOPRSV oversleep, sleepover
EEELRRSVY reversely
EEEMNNOVY even money
EEEMNORRV nevermore
EEEMNRSTY mesentery
EEEMNRTTV revetment
EEEMOPRTX extempore
EEENNORST sonneteer
EEENNSSST tenseness
EEENPRRST presenter, represent
EEENPRRTV preventer
EEENPRSUV supervene
EEENPSSST steepness
EEENQRSSU queerness
EEENRRSTW westerner
EEENRRSUV unreserve
EEENRSSST terseness
EEENSSSTW sweetness
EEEORRSTV oversteer
EEEORRTVX overexert
EEEPPPRTU puppeteer
EEEPRRRSS represser
EEEPRRRSV preserver
EEEPRRRTV perverter
EEEPRRSSX expresser
EEEQRRSTU requester
EEEQRSSTU sequester
EEERRTTUX retexture
EEFFFKLRU kerfuffle
EEFFFMNOT feoffment
EEFFGHIRT free fight
EEFFGLNTU effulgent
EEFFHILLS shelf-life
EEFFHINTT fifteenth
EEFFHLRSU reshuffle
EEFFINOSV offensive
EEFFINRST stiffener
EEFFIORRT forfeiter
EEFFJNORS Jefferson
EEFFORSTT off-street
EEFGHIRRT freighter
EEFGILLNY feelingly
EEFGILNNU unfeeling
EEFGILNRU refueling
EEFGIMRUV vermifuge
EEFGINORR foreigner
EEFGINRRR referring
EEFGINRRT ferreting
EEFGIPRRU prefigure
EEFGLLLUY gleefully
EEFGLNRTU refulgent
EEFGLRRTU regretful
EEFGORRTT forgetter
EEFHIISTZ fetishize
EEFHIJLSW jewel-fish
EEFHIKLLS shelf-like
EEFHILLRS fleshlier, shellfire
EEFHILSST fleshiest
EEFHINSST heftiness
EEFHIORSU firehouse
EEFHIOSUW housewife
EEFHIPRSV ship-fever
EEFHLLSSS fleshless
EEFHLOSTW flowsheet
EEFHMORRT therefrom
EEFHMORRW wherefrom
EEFHNRSSS freshness
EEFHOORRS foreshore
EEFHORRTW free throw
EEFHRRRTU furtherer
EEFIIKKLN knifelike
EEFIILMTX flexitime
EEFIILNRT infertile, interfile
EEFIILQRU liquefier
EEFIILRTZ fertilize
EEFIIMNTY femineity
EEFIINRSS fieriness
EEFIIRRRT terrifier
EEFIIRRSV versifier
EEFIIRSTT testifier
EEFIISSTT feistiest
EEFIKLLTU flutelike
EEFIKLMRV milk fever
EEFIKNRST knife rest
EEFIKNRSU refusenik
EEFILLLOS filoselle
EEFILLORW low relief
EEFILLSTY lifestyle
EEFILMPXY exemplify
EEFILNORX reflexion
EEFILORTU out-relief
EEFILSTVY festively
EEFIMNRTT refitment
EEFINOPRT reefpoint
EEFINORST fire-stone, set on fire
EEFINPRSU superfine
EEFINRSTU interfuse
EEFIOPRRT profiteer
EEFIOPRRW firepower
EEFIPRSTU stupefier
EEFIPRSUV perfusive
EEFIRRRTU fruiterer
EEFIRRTTU fruit tree
EEFKLLTTU kettleful
EEFKNOORT foretoken
EEFLLNPSU spleenful
EEFLMORTW flowmeter
EEFLNOSTU nose flute
EEFLNRSTU resentful
EEFLNRTVY fervently
EEFLOPRSU reposeful
EEFLORRTX retroflex
EEFLRRTTU flutterer
EEFMOPRRR performer
EEFMPRRUY perfumery
EEGGIILNT gelignite
EEGGILNNT negligent
EEGGILNSS legginess
EEGGILOOZ geologize
EEGGINRRS sniggerer
EEGGINRST gee-string
EEGGIORSU egregious
EEGGNOOOS gone goose
EEGGOORSY grey goose
EEGGRSSTU suggester
EEGHHHILS high heels
EEGHHIITT eightieth
EEGHHILLV high-level
EEGHIINSW hingewise
EEGHIIRTW weightier
EEGHILNNT enlighten
EEGHILNRT lengthier
EEGHILNSS hingeless
EEGHIMOST eightsome
EEGHIMRRT mere right
EEGHIOSTT ghettoise
EEGHIOTTZ ghettoize
EEGHIPPST peep-sight
EEGHIRSST sightseer
EEGHLORTY leg theory
EEGHMNOST theme song
EEGHNNORR greenhorn
EEGHNORTU toughener
EEGIILNNO oil engine
EEGIILORS religiose
EEGIILPRV privilege
EEGIINSTV ingestive
EEGIISTTZ Zeitgeist
EEGIJLLNW jewelling
EEGIJLNRY jeeringly
EEGIKLNNN kenneling
EEGIKNNRT Kentigern
EEGIKNRTT Kettering
EEGILLLNV levelling
EEGILLNPR repelling
EEGILLNPT pelleting
EEGILLNPX expelling
EEGILLNRV Grenville, revelling
EEGILLNRY leeringly
EEGILLSSU guileless
EEGILMMSU gelsemium
EEGILMNSY seemingly
EEGILNNSS Esslingen
EEGILNNUY genuinely
EEGILNOOZ neologize
EEGILNPWY weepingly
EEGILNRTT lettering
EEGILORST sortilege
EEGIMOORV movie-goer
EEGINOOSS oogenesis
EEGINORSV sovereign
EEGINORVY roving eye
EEGINOSSS gneissose
EEGINOTTU tongue-tie
EEGINOXYZ oxygenize
EEGINRSTT resetting
EEGINRSTW westering
EEGINRSUY seigneury
EEGINRTTV revetting
EEGIRRSSU regisseur
EEGLLMORU glomerule

EEGLLOOTY	teleology
EEGLLOPRS	gospeller
EEGLLORRV	groveller
EEGLLOSSV	gloveless
EEGLMNORT	long metre
EEGLNORTT	lorgnette
EEGLNSSUY	glueyness
EEGLOORVZ	gloze over
EEGLPRSUU	superglue
EEGLRSSUU	reguluses
EEGMNOORR	green room
EEGMORSTZ	Esztergom
EEGNOORST	oestrogen
EEGNOORSU	erogenous
EEGNOOSSY	gooeyness
EEGNOOSUX	exogenous
EEGNORSSV	governess
EEGNRRSTU	resurgent
EEGOOPSST	goose-step
EEGOPPRRU	peer group
EEGOPRSSU	guess-rope
EEGOPRSTU	guest-rope
EEGOQRSTU	grotesque
EEHHILNOT	in the hole
EEHHINOSS	shoeshine
EEHHIOPTW	white hope
EEHHIRTTW	therewith
EEHHIRTWW	wherewith
EEHHNOPPS	phosphene
EEHHOORSS	horseshoe
EEHIILMTW	white lime
EEHIILRTT	Hitlerite
EEHIINNTT	ninetieth
EEHIJNOPS	Josephine
EEHIKLLLS	shell-like
EEHIKLORS	horselike
EEHIKMNSV	Menshevik
EEHIKNPSS	sheepskin
EEHILLLMS	shell-lime
EEHILLLMW	mill-wheel
EEHILLMNS	Hellenism
EEHILLNST	Hellenist
EEHILMOST	homeliest, lithesome
EEHILNNOO	hole-in-one
EEHILNOOP	oenophile
EEHILNORS	shoreline
EEHILNPRS	replenish
EEHILNPSW	wheelspin
EEHILNSST	litheness
EEHILOPRX	xerophile
EEHILOPTY	heliotype
EEHILPSST	slip sheet
EEHILPSVY	peevishly
EEHILRSTW	erstwhile
EEHIMMOOV	home movie
EEHIMMPSU	euphemism
EEHIMMRST	hermetism
EEHIMNORS	Rosenheim
EEHIMNRST	intermesh
EEHIMPRRW	whimperer
EEHIMPSTU	euphemist
EEHINNORT	threonine
EEHINOPUZ	euphonize
EEHINORTT	thereinto
EEHINPQSU	queenship
EEHINSSTW	whiteness
EEHINSTTX	sixteenth
EEHINTTTW	twentieth
EEHIORRTZ	theorizer
EEHIORSST	heterosis
EEHIORSTW	otherwise, white rose
EEHIPPRRY	periphery
EEHIPPSSY	epiphyses
EEHIPRRSW	whisperer
EEHKLOOST	stokehole
EEHKNOSSY	hokeyness
EEHKORSTW	worksheet
EEHLLLSSS	shell-less
EEHLLORST	hosteller
EEHLLORSV	shoveller
EEHLMNSTU	sun-helmet
EEHLMOOSW	wholesome
EEHLMORVW	overwhelm
EEHLMORWW	worm-wheel
EEHLMOSTY	homestyle
EEHLMOSZZ	shemozzle
EEHLMRSSY	rhymeless
EEHLNOOOZ	ozone hole
EEHLNOOTW	whole note
EEHLNOPTY	polythene, telephony
EEHLNOSSW	wholeness
EEHLNSSSW	Welshness
EEHLNSTVY	seventhly
EEHLOOPTT	telephoto
EEHLORSSS	horseless, shoreless
EEHLORSTT	short leet
EEHLOSSSU	houseless
EEHLPRSUW	spur-wheel
EEHMNOOPR	pheromone
EEHMNOORW	homeowner
EEHMNOSSY	homeyness
EEHMNPTTU	umpteenth
EEHMOPSTY	mesophyte
EEHMORSTT	rest homes, thermoset
EEHMRRSTY	rhymester
EEHNOOPSU	open house
EEHNOPPTY	phenotype
EEHNOPRTU	thereupon
EEHNOPRUW	whereupon
EEHNOPSTU	penthouse
EEHNOPTTY	entophyte
EEHNORSST	otherness
EEHNORTTU	thereunto
EEHNOSTTW	whetstone
EEHNPPRSU	pen-pusher
EEHNSSSTY	syntheses
EEHOORSSV	overshoes
EEHOORSVW	howsoever, whosoever
EEHOPRRSU	superhero
EEHOPRSST	protheses
EEHOPRSTY	hey presto
EEHOPRTXY	xerophyte
EEHOPSSTU	pest-house
EEHOPSSTW	sweetshop
EEHORSSTU	rest house
EEHORSTTY	set theory
EEHPRTTXY	hypertext
EEHRSSTUW	sweet rush
EEIIKLLST	likeliest
EEIIKLPRV	viper-like
EEIIKPPRT	kipper tie
EEIILLNTV	vitelline
EEIILLSTV	liveliest
EEIILMMSS	semi-smile
EEIILMSTT	timeliest
EEIILNNRT	interline
EEIILNRST	resilient
EEIILRSTU	Tuileries
EEIILRSTZ	sterilize
EEIILRTUZ	reutilize
EEIIMMPRS	epimerism
EEIIMMPRT	prime time
EEIIMOPTZ	epitomize
EEIIMORSZ	isomerize
EEIIMRSSV	remissive
EEIINNSTT	intestine
EEIINNSTV	intensive
EEIINNTVV	inventive
EEIINRSTT	enteritis
EEIINRSVV	inversive
EEIINRTVW	interview
EEIINRTWZ	winterize
EEIINSSTV	sensitive
EEIINSSTZ	sensitize
EEIIOPQSU	equipoise
EEIIOSTVZ	Sovietize
EEIIQRSTU	requisite
EEIIQSTUX	exquisite
EEIIRSSTT	sestertii
EEIIRSSTV	resistive
EEIJKLLLY	jelly-like
EEIJKNNOT	knee joint
EEIJKNRSS	jerkiness
EEIKLLMPU	plumelike
EEIKLMORT	kilometer, kilometre
EEIKLMOSU	mouselike
EEIKLRTWY	tri-weekly
EEIKNNPSV	penknives
EEIKNPRSS	perkiness
EEIKNPSSS	peskiness
EEIKNSTTX	sex kitten
EEIKOORTZ	ozokerite
EEIKOPSSW	spokewise
EEILLMNOT	emollient
EEILLMOPR	millepore
EEILLMPRT	ill temper
EEILLMSSS	smileless
EEILLMSST	smelliest
EEILLNNTY	leniently
EEILLNOST	loneliest
EEILLNRSV	sniveller
EEILLORTT	title role
EEILLOSTV	loveliest
EEILLPRUY	puerilely
EEILLRSTY	sterilely
EEILLRSUY	leisurely
EEILLRSVY	servilely

EEILLRTTU	tellurite
EEILLSUVY	elusively
EEILMMNPT	implement
EEILMMNSY	immensely
EEILMMORS	sommelier
EEILMMORT	milometer
EEILMMPSU	semi-plume
EEILMNNTY	eminently
EEILMNOST	limestone, milestone
EEILMNOSZ	solemnize
EEILMNPPR	pimpernel
EEILMORRV	Livermore
EEILMOSTT	mistletoe
EEILMOSVW	semivowel
EEILMOTVY	emotively
EEILNNPSS	penniless
EEILNNSTY	intensely
EEILNOORS	oleoresin
EEILNOPRT	interlope, repletion
EEILNOPRW	power line
EEILNOPTT	telepoint
EEILNORVW	wolverine
EEILNOSSS	noiseless
EEILNOSSU	selenious
EEILNPSSS	spineless
EEILNPSTT	pestilent
EEILNPSVY	pensively
EEILNRSTU	unsterile
EEILNRSVY	inversely
EEILNSSSW	sinewless
EEILOPRST	pistoleer
EEILOPRTX	exploiter
EEILOPSST	politesse
EEILOPSVX	explosive
EEILOSTTT	toilet set
EEILPRSTY	peristyle
EEILPRSUV	repulsive
EEILPRTTU	tulip tree
EEILPRUVZ	pulverize
EEILPSUVX	expulsive
EEILQRSTU	squirelet
EEILRRSSV	riverless
EEILRSSTV	Silvester
EEILRSTUX	extrusile
EEILRSTVY	restively
EEILRSUVV	revulsive
EEILSSSSU	issueless
EEIMMMRSS	mesmerism
EEIMMNRRT	merriment
EEIMMORRZ	memorizer
EEIMMOSST	sometimes
EEIMMRSST	mesmerist
EEIMMRSTU	summiteer
EEIMMRSTW	swimmeret
EEIMMRSTX	extremism
EEIMNNNOT	Mennonite
EEIMNNRTT	interment
EEIMNNRTU	inurement
EEIMNNSTT	sentiment
EEIMNOPTX	exemption
EEIMNORSZ	sermonize
EEIMNOSTX	sixteenmo
EEIMNOSYZ	isoenzyme
EEIMNPQTU	equipment
EEIMNPRSS	primeness
EEIMNPSST	emptiness
EEIMNRRSS	merriness
EEIMNRTTT	remittent
EEIMNSSSS	messiness
EEIMOPRST	peristome
EEIMOPRTZ	temporize
EEIMPPRRS	perisperm
EEIMPRRTT	permitter, pretermit, tripmeter
EEIMQSTUU	equisetum
EEIMRRSTT	trimester
EEIMRSSSU	Messieurs
EEIMRSTTX	extremist
EEIMRTTXY	extremity
EEIMSSTYZ	systemize
EEINNNRSS	innerness
EEINNOPPS	Nipponese
EEINNOPRS	pensioner
EEINNOPRT	tin-opener
EEINNOPST	stone pine
EEINNORST	tensioner
EEINNORTT	retention
EEINNOSTV	veinstone
EEINNOSTX	extension
EEINNPRST	spinneret
EEINNPRTT	pertinent
EEINNPSST	ineptness
EEINNPSWY	penny wise
EEINNRSST	inertness
EEINNRSSV	Inverness, nerviness
EEINNSSTT	intensest
EEINOPPPR	pepperoni
EEINOPPST	pipe-stone
EEINOPPTZ	peptonize
EEINOPRST	interpose
EEINORRSV	reversion
EEINOSSTV	ostensive
EEINPRRRT	reprinter
EEINPRRTT	interpret
EEINPRSSW	winepress
EEINPSSTT	pettiness
EEINQSSTU	quietness
EEINQTTTU	quintette
EEINRRRSU	reinsurer
EEINRRTTW	rewritten
EEINRSSSY	syneresis
EEINRSSTT	triteness
EEINSSSTT	testiness
EEINSSTUX	unsexiest
EEIOPPSTV	stove-pipe
EEIOPRTTU	pirouette
EEIOQQUUV	equivoque
EEIORRRST	roisterer
EEIORRRSV	reservoir
EEIORRRTZ	terrorize
EEIORRTVW	overwrite
EEIORSSUV	overissue
EEIORTTVX	extortive
EEIPPPRST	preppiest
EEIPRSSST	priestess
EEIPRSSUV	supervise
EEIPRSTTT	prettiest
EEIQSSTUU	quietuses
EEIRRSSTV	reservist
EEIRRTTTW	twitterer
EEIRSTTUV	vestiture
EEIRSTUVX	extrusive
EEIRTTUXZ	texturize
EEJMNNOTY	enjoyment
EEJMPQUUU	queue-jump
EEJNNNRWY	jenny-wren
EEJNORRUY	journeyer
EEKKORSTY	keystroke
EEKLMOSSS	smokeless
EEKLNPRSU	spelunker
EEKLORSTW	steelwork
EEKNOOTTV	token vote
EEKNORRTW	networker
EEKNORRWY	New Yorker
EEKNRRTTU	tree trunk
EELLLLNWY	Llewellyn
EELLLMSSS	smell-less
EELLMNOOS	lemon sole
EELLMPSSU	plumeless
EELLNNRTU	tunneller
EELLNPSTW	well spent
EELLOOSTW	steel wool
EELLOPPRR	propeller
EELLORSSV	loverless
EELLOSSVW	vowelless
EELLPSSSU	pulseless
EELLPSSSY	syllepses
EELLSSSTY	styleless
EELLSSSUY	uselessly
EELLSSSXY	sexlessly
EELMMNOTU	emolument
EELMNNORT	enrolment
EELMNOSSS	solemness
EELMNOSSY	moneyless
EELMNOTTX	extolment
EELMOOPTT	totem pole
EELMOPRTU	petroleum
EELMORTTV	voltmeter
EELMPRSUY	supremely
EELNNNTTU	tunnel-net
EELNNOPRS	personnel
EELNOOSSS	looseness
EELNOPPRY	propylene
EELNOPSTU	plenteous
EELNORSSW	ownerless
EELNORSTV	resolvent
EELNORTUV	volunteer
EELNOSSST	stoneless
EELNPRSTY	presently
EELNQSTUY	sequently
EELOPPRSS	prolepses
EELOPRRTU	poulterer
EELOPRSSW	powerless
EELOPRSTY	polyester, proselyte
EELORRRSS	errorless
EELORSSUV	ourselves
EELPPSTTU	septuplet
EELPRSSXY	expressly
EELPRSTUU	sepulture
EELPSTTUX	sextuplet

EELRSSTVY Sylvester
EEMMNOORT metronome, monotreme
EEMMRSTUX extremums
EEMNNOPST penstemon
EEMNOORST sonometer
EEMNOORTT tonometer
EEMNOOSTT tomentose
EEMNORRTY Monterrey
EEMOOPPRS prose poem
EEMOOPRTT optometer
EEMOPPRRT pre-emptor
EEMOPRRTY pyrometer
EEMPRRTTU trumpeter
EEMPRSSTT temptress
EENNOOSTU neotenous
EENNOPRSS proneness
EENNOSTTV Steventon
EENNRSSST sternness
EENOORRSU erroneous
EENOPPRTT prepotent
EENOPQSTU queen post
EENOPSTTY stenotype
EENORRSTW nor'wester
EENORSSTV overtness
EENORSTTT rottenest
EENRSSTTU utterness
EEOOPRRVW overpower
EEOPPPPRT pepper pot
EEOPPRSSU superpose
EEOPRRRSS repressor
EEOPRRRTY repertory
EEOPRRSTT protester
EEOPRSSSS repossess
EEORRRTTV retrovert
EEORRTTVX extrovert
EEORSSTUW sou'wester
EEPRRSTTU sputterer
EERRSTTTU stutterer
EFFFILSTU fluffiest
EFFFLORTU effortful
EFFGHIIRT firefight
EFFGINRSU suffering
EFFGLORTU forgetful
EFFGNRSSU gruffness
EFFHIIKNS fish-knife
EFFHIISTW whiffiest
EFFHIKSWW skew-whiff
EFFHINSSU huffiness
EFFIINSST sniffiest
EFFIIORRT fortifier
EFFIIPSST spiffiest
EFFIIQRSU squiffier
EFFILLLRU fulfiller
EFFILMUUV effluvium
EFFILNOUX effluxion
EFFINOOSS noises off
EFFINPSSU puffiness
EFFINSSST stiffness
EFFINSSTU snuffiest
EFFIOOPRR fireproof
EFFIORTVY forty-five
EFFISSTTU stuffiest
EFFLLRTUY fretfully
EFFNOORRT forefront
EFFNOSSTU one's stuff
EFFOORRTY offertory
EFFORSTUV overstuff
EFGGIINNR fingering
EFGGILOOS solfeggio
EFGGINOOR foregoing
EFGGINOSS fogginess
EFGHHIILR high-flier
EFGHHILRY high-flyer
EFGHIILNT nightlife
EFGHIILRT firelight, flightier
EFGHIINRT infighter
EFGHILNSS fleshings
EFGHILPRT pre-flight
EFGHILTWY flyweight
EFGHIORST foresight
EFGIIINRS signifier
EFGIILLNT filleting
EFGIILORR glorifier
EFGIINNRR inferring, infringer
EFGIINPRT fingertip
EFGIINRTT refitting
EFGIKNOTT gift token
EFGILNNNU funneling
EFGILNORW flowering
EFGILRTUU fulgurite
EFGINOOSS goofiness
EFGINORST fire-tongs
EFGLOOTUV tug of love
EFGNOORTT forgotten
EFGOOOOST goosefoot
EFHHIISTW whitefish
EFHHILLSS shellfish
EFHIILSTT filthiest
EFHIIMSST fetishism
EFHIIMSTT time-shift
EFHIINPSS snipe fish
EFHIINSSS fishiness
EFHIIRRTT thriftier
EFHIISSTT fetishist, shiftiest
EFHIJLLSY jellyfish
EFHILLSSY selfishly
EFHILNSSU unselfish
EFHILORST rifle shot
EFHILSSST shiftless
EFHIMOPRZ Pforzheim
EFHINORRT firethorn
EFHINOSST stonefish
EFHINRRSU furnisher, refurnish
EFHIORRST shot-firer
EFHIORSTT frothiest
EFHLLLPUY helpfully
EFHLLNPUU unhelpful
EFHLLOPUY hopefully
EFHLLOSUU full house
EFHLLOSUV shovelful
EFHLLTTWY twelfthly
EFHLMOORS shelf room
EFHLNSSSU flushness
EFHLOOOPR hole-proof
EFHLOOPSU flophouse
EFHLOPSST fleshpots
EFHLORSTW self-worth
EFHNORTUX fox-hunter
EFHORSSTU short fuse
EFIIJRSTU justifier
EFIIKRSST friskiest
EFIILLLST still life
EFIILLMOR mollifier
EFIILLNRU nullifier
EFIILLRST fillister, frilliest
EFIILLTXY flexility
EFIILMNSS filminess
EFIILMOTT leitmotif
EFIILMSST flimsiest
EFIILNNOX inflexion
EFIILNSTT flintiest
EFIILOSSZ fossilize
EFIILPRTT filter tip
EFIILRRSV silver fir
EFIILRSTT flirtiest
EFIILRTTY fertility
EFIINNPRT fine print
EFIINNSST niftiness
EFIINNSTY intensify
EFIINOPRX prefixion
EFIINORRS fire-irons
EFIINSSZZ fizziness
EFIIORRTU fioriture
EFIIRSTTU fruitiest
EFIIRSTZZ frizziest
EFIISTTVY festivity
EFIKLNOSS folkiness
EFIKLNSSU flukiness
EFIKLORSW life's work
EFIKLOSST folksiest
EFIKNNOTX next of kin
EFIKNNSSU funkiness
EFILLMRTU full-timer
EFILLNOWY yellowfin
EFILLNPTU plentiful
EFILMOPRX plexiform
EFILMORUZ formulize
EFILNNORT front line
EFILNOORS Solferino
EFILNOOSU felonious
EFILNORTW interflow
EFILNOSST loftiness
EFILOPPST floppiest
EFILORSTU flouriest
EFILORSVX silver fox
EFILOSSST flossiest
EFILPPRTY fly-tipper
EFILQRUUV quiverful
EFILRSSTU fruitless
EFILRSUUZ sulfurize
EFILRTUVY furtively
EFIMMORRS reformism
EFIMMORRV vermiform
EFIMORRST firestorm, reformist
EFIMPRSTU frumpiest
EFINNNRUU unfunnier
EFINNNSSU funniness
EFINNSSTU unfitness

EFINOPRSU perfusion
EFINOPRSY personify
EFINOPRTT net profit
EFINOPSST fess point
EFINRRSSU furriness
EFINRRTUU furniture
EFINSSSSU fussiness
EFINSSSTU fustiness
EFINSSSTW swiftness
EFINSSUZZ fuzziness
EFIOPRTTU petit four
EFIORRSTW frowstier
EFIORSSTT frostiest
EFIORTTTU outfitter
EFKLMNOOW womenfolk
EFLLMOSUY fulsomely
EFLLNORTU Fullerton
EFLLNTUUY tunefully
EFLLOORSS floorless
EFLLRSTUY restfully
EFLLSTUYZ zestfully
EFLNNOOYZ no-fly zone
EFLNNTUUU untuneful
EFLNOOSTW flowstone
EFLNORSST frontless
EFLNORSUW sunflower
EFLNRSTUU unrestful
EFLOOOOST footloose
EFLOOPRSS proofless
EFLOOPRTW flowerpot
EFLOOSTTW Lowestoft
EFLOPRSUY profusely
EFLORSSST frostless
EFLRSSSTU stressful
EFMNORRTY entry form
EFNNOPRUY fourpenny
EFNOOOPRV ovenproof
EFOOOPRRV overproof
EFOOPRRSS professor
EFOOQRRTU Roquefort
EGGGIIJNR rejigging
EGGGIILST giggliest
EGGGINNPU unpegging
EGGGIORST groggiest
EGGHIINNW whingeing
EGGHIINTW weighting
EGGIILNNR lingering
EGGIILSTW wiggliest
EGGIINNSW swingeing
EGGIINNTW twingeing
EGGILLNRU gruelling
EGGILNORV groveling
EGGILOOST geologist
EGGIMNSSU mugginess, mugginses
EGGIMOSST smoggiest
EGGINNOPS spongeing
EGGINNPTU tuning peg
EGGINNRTU ginger nut
EGGINOORV going-over
EGGINOORZ gorgonize
EGGINOSSS sogginess
EGGINRTTU guttering
EGGIORRTU outrigger
EGGLMMOOY gemmology
EGGLRRSTU struggler
EGHHILNPT hip-length
EGHHIPRSU higher-ups
EGHHMOTTU methought
EGHHNORUW rough-hewn
EGHHORTTU rethought
EGHIILLMT limelight
EGHIILNST sight line
EGHIILPPT pipe-light
EGHIILTWY weightily
EGHIIMNTT night-time
EGHIIMSTT mightiest
EGHIINNTW whitening
EGHIINPRS perishing
EGHIINSTY hygienist
EGHIKLOST ghostlike
EGHILLNTY lengthily
EGHILLSST lightless
EGHILMOST lightsome
EGHILNNSU un-English
EGHILNOST hosteling
EGHILNOSV shoveling
EGHILNSST lightness, nightless
EGHILOORY hierology
EGHILORST ghostlier
EGHILPRTU uplighter
EGHILRSST rightless
EGHILRTVY Very light
EGHILSSST sightless
EGHIMNOST something
EGHIMORTT tiger moth
EGHIMPPSU pemphigus
EGHINORTV overnight
EGHINOSTY histogeny
EGHINRSST rightness
EGHINRSTU hungriest
EGHINSSSU gushiness
EGHINSSTT tightness
EGHIOPRTT tightrope
EGHIORSTU righteous
EGHIORSTV oversight
EGHIPSSTU guestship
EGHIRSTTU theurgist
EGHLLLOUY gully-hole
EGHLLOORY glory-hole
EGHLMOOOU homologue
EGHLNOOPY nephology
EGHLNOORS longshore
EGHLNOOSU longhouse
EGHLNOOTY ethnology
EGHLNOPYY phylogeny
EGHLOOORR horologer
EGHMNOORW home-grown
EGHNOPTYY phytogeny
EGHNORSSU roughness
EGHNOSSTU toughness
EGIIIMNRT trigemini
EGIIKLNSV king's evil
EGIILLMNP impelling
EGIILLNPR perilling
EGIILLRTY tiger lily
EGIILNNST tinseling
EGIILNNSV sniveling
EGIILNOSU uliginose
EGIILNOTT toileting
EGIILNSTT tingliest
EGIILNSVW swiveling
EGIILNTTY gentility
EGIILOPST epilogist
EGIILORSU religious
EGIILRRZZ grizzlier
EGIILRSST grisliest
EGIILSTTU guiltiest
EGIILSTTZ glitziest
EGIIMNNTU minueting
EGIIMNRSS griminess
EGIIMNRTT remitting
EGIIMNSTY stymieing
EGIINNNSS inningses
EGIINNOST ingestion
EGIINNOSU ingenious
EGIINNQRU enquiring
EGIINNRRT interring
EGIINNRSW in-swinger
EGIINNSTT insetting
EGIINNTUY ingenuity
EGIINOPTT tiptoeing
EGIINORST sortieing
EGIINORSY seigniory
EGIINPPQU equipping
EGIINPQRU repiquing
EGIINPRRS springier
EGIINPRRZ prize ring
EGIINRRST stringier
EGIINRRTU intriguer
EGIINRSSU reissuing
EGIINRSTT resitting, string tie
EGIINRSTU intrigues
EGIINRTTY integrity
EGIINSSTT stingiest
EGIINSSTW swingiest
EGIIRSTTT grittiest
EGIJKNNTU junketing
EGIKLNNOO inglenook
EGIKMNORS smoke ring
EGIKNOOSS goose-skin
EGIKNORRW reworking
EGILLLNTY tellingly
EGILLMNTY meltingly
EGILLMORU glomeruli
EGILLMOTU guillemot
EGILLNNOR enrolling
EGILLNORW rowelling
EGILLNOTT ill-gotten
EGILLNOTW towelling
EGILLNOTX extolling
EGILLOSYZ syllogize
EGILLSSTU guiltless
EGILMMNOP pommeling
EGILMMNPU pummeling
EGILMNOOS neologism
EGILMOOST gloomiest
EGILMOOSY semiology
EGILNNNTU tunneling
EGILNNOST singleton
EGILNNOTX Lexington
EGILNNRSU nurseling
EGILNOOST neologist

EGILNOOSU sinologue
EGILNORTV revolting
EGILNORTW troweling
EGILNORUZ ring ouzel
EGILNORVY overlying
EGILNOTVY longevity
EGILNPRST springlet
EGILNRSTW wrestling
EGILNSSST stingless
EGILOOPRZ prologize
EGILOSSST glossiest
EGIMMNSSU gumminess
EGIMNNTUU minute-gun
EGIMNORST Germiston
EGIMNORSV misgovern
EGIMNPRSU presuming
EGIMNRSSY synergism
EGIMPRSTU grumpiest
EGINNNOST sonneting
EGINNNRRU rerunning
EGINNNRUV unnerving
EGINNOSUU ingenuous
EGINNOTTW towing-net
EGINNRSTT stringent
EGINNRSTU insurgent, unresting
EGINOOPSS goopiness
EGINOPPST estopping
EGINOPRRR porringer
EGINOPRTT repotting
EGINOPSST spongiest
EGINOQRTU roqueting
EGINOSSTU goutiness
EGINPSTTU upsetting
EGINPSTWW swept-wing
EGINRSSTY synergist
EGINSSSTU gustiness, gutsiness
EGIOORSTV grooviest
EGIORSTTT grottiest
EGKORSSUW guesswork
EGLLLOORR logroller
EGLLSSTUY gutlessly
EGLMNOOOU monologue
EGLMOORTY metrology
EGLMOOSUY museology
EGLMOOTYY etymology
EGLNNOSUU sun lounge
EGLNNPTUY pungently
EGLNOOPRR prolonger
EGLNOORUY neurology
EGLNOPRUW lung-power
EGLOOORTY erotology
EGLOOOSTY osteology
EGLOOPRSU prologues
EGLOOPRTY petrology
EGLOOPSTY pestology
EGMNOOOSS mongooses
EGNNNRRUU gun-runner
EGNNORSSW wrongness
EGNOOOSSW snow goose
EGNOOPRSS prognoses
EGNOOSUXY oxygenous
EGNORSSSS grossness
EGNORSSTT strongest
EGNORSTUY youngster
EGOOPRRSU prorogues
EGOOPRSYZ zygospore
EHHIIRTTT thirtieth
EHHILLLSY hellishly
EHHINOPPS phosphine
EHHIOPPST phosphite
EHHIOPRSW horsewhip
EHHIOSSTU shithouse
EHHIPRSSU ushership
EHHLMMOPY hemolymph
EHHLOOPTY holophyte
EHHMNNOPP Phnom Penh
EHHMNOOOP homophone
EHHMNOSUY hush money
EHHMORTTU home truth
EHHMRTUYY eurhythmy
EHHNOSTUU house-hunt
EHHOOPSTY theosophy
EHHOOSSUW show house
EHIIKLMTW milk white
EHIIKNSTT kittenish
EHIILLNSS hilliness
EHIILLTWY lily white
EHIILMRST Hitlerism
EHIILPSYZ syphilize
EHIILRSTW Wiltshire
EHIINNSSS shininess
EHIINORRT inheritor
EHIINPPRW whipper-in
EHIINPRST nephritis
EHIINPSST pithiness
EHIINRSSS Irishness
EHIINSTUV Vishnuite
EHIIPPSSY epiphysis
EHIIQRSSU squishier
EHIIRRSTT thirstier
EHIIRSSTT shirtiest
EHIIRSSTW Irish stew
EHIIRSTTZ zitherist
EHIISSTTT shittiest
EHIKLLNPS shell pink
EHIKLLPSY sylphlike
EHIKLMNPY nymphlike
EHIKLOOTT toothlike
EHIKLORTZ kilohertz
EHIKMNOSY monkeyish
EHIKMNOTW White Monk
EHIKNOSST shonkiest
EHIKNOSTT to the skin
EHIKNSSSU huskiness
EHILLOSTY hostilely
EHILLOSWY yellowish
EHILLSSTU shell suit
EHILMOSSY hemolysis
EHILMPPRY perilymph
EHILMRSST mirthless
EHILMRSUV Hilversum
EHILNOOPT lithopone
EHILNOSTU unholiest
EHILNOSUY heinously
EHILOSSST sloshiest
EHILPRRSU rulership
EHILPSSTU plushiest
EHILPSTTY pettishly
EHILRSSST shirtless
EHILSSSTU slushiest
EHIMNNOOS moonshine
EHIMNOPSY ship money
EHIMNOPUU euphonium
EHIMNRTUU ruthenium
EHIMNSSSU mushiness
EHIMORSTT short time
EHIMORTTW mother wit
EHIMOSTTU mouthiest
EHIMRRSTY erythrism
EHIMSSSTU isthmuses
EHINNOPSS phoniness
EHINNORSS horniness
EHINNOSTW whinstone
EHINNSSTU Nissen hut
EHINOPRSW ownership, shipowner
EHINOPSTT phonetist
EHINOPSVY envoyship
EHINOPTYZ hypnotize
EHINORRSU nourisher
EHINORSSS horsiness
EHINORSTT thorniest
EHINORTXY thyroxine
EHINOSSSW showiness
EHINOSTWW snow white
EHINPRRTY pyrethrin
EHINPSSSU pushiness
EHINSSSTY synthesis
EHIOOPRTW poor white
EHIOOSTTT toothiest
EHIOPRRSW worshiper
EHIOPRSST prothesis
EHIORSTTW worthiest
EHIORSTVW short view
EHIPRSTTY prettyish
EHKLLORSW shell-work
EHKLLSSTU tusk shell
EHKNPRRSU pre-shrunk
EHKOORRSW workhorse
EHKOORSUW housework, workhouse
EHLLMOPSY mesophyll
EHLLOOPSW Welshpool
EHLLOOSTU toll-house
EHLMMOPTU plume moth
EHLMOSSTU mouthless
EHLNOOPPY polyphone
EHLNOOPRT North Pole
EHLNOOPXY xylophone
EHLNOOSTY holystone
EHLNORRTY northerly
EHLNORSST thornless
EHLNPSSSU plushness
EHLOOPSTU south pole
EHLOOPSTY photolyse
EHLOOSSTT toothless
EHLOPRSTU upholster
EHLOPSTYY hypostyle
EHLORRTTT throttler
EHLORSSTW worthless
EHLORSTUY southerly
EHLORTTUW Lower Hutt
EHMMOOORT motorhome

EHMMOOPRS mesomorph
EHMNNOOOY honeymoon
EHMOOOPRS sophomore
EHMOOORSU houseroom
EHMOOOSTT toothsome
EHMORRSTT short-term
EHMPRRTUY pyrethrum
EHMPSSSYY symphyses
EHNOOOPPT optophone
EHNOOORTT orthotone
EHNOORSSW snowshoer
EHNOOSTUW town house
EHNOOTTTT Hottentot
EHNOPRTTU pot-hunter
EHNOPSSTY pythoness
EHNORRTTU true north
EHNORSSST shortness
EHNORSTTW north-west
EHOOOPRSU poorhouse
EHOOORSTV overshoot
EHOOPRRTV hoverport
EHOORRTVW overthrow, throw-over
EHOORSTTW shot-tower
EHORRSTTW throwster
EHOSSTTUW south-west
EIIILMMTT time limit
EIIILNNQU inquiline
EIIIMMNRZ minimizer
EIIIMPRTV primitive
EIIINRSTT retinitis
EIIINTTUV intuitive
EIIJLLNOV Joinville
EIIKKNNSS kinkiness
EIIKLLORT kilolitre
EIIKLMNSS milkiness
EIIKLNNRT interlink
EIIKLNRRW wrinklier
EIIKLNSSS silkiness
EIIKLNSST slinkiest
EIIKMPSST skimpiest
EIIKNNRTT interknit
EIIKNNSST skinniest
EIIKNPSSS spikiness
EIIKNRSSS riskiness
EIIKNSSTT stinkiest
EIIKQRSTU quirkiest
EIILLMNRY millinery
EIILLMSST limitless
EIILLNSSS silliness
EIILMMORS meliorism
EIILMNORV vermilion
EIILMNOSU limousine
EIILMNSSS sliminess
EIILMOPSV implosive
EIILMORST meliorist
EIILMOTTV leitmotiv
EIILMPSUV impulsive
EIILMRSSY missilery
EIILNNOQU quinoline
EIILNPSST splenitis
EIILNSTTY tensility
EIILNTUVY unitively
EIILOQSSU siliquose
EIILPPSST slippiest
EIILPRSTU spirituel
EIILPRTUY puerility
EIILRSTTY sterility
EIILRSTVY servility
EIILSSTTT slittiest
EIIMMNORS immersion
EIIMMNRST terminism
EIIMMNRUZ immunizer
EIIMMNSTY immensity
EIIMMORSS isomerism
EIIMMORST memoirist
EIIMMPSSS pessimism
EIIMMRTUX immixture
EIIMNNRTU triennium
EIIMNORSS missioner, remission
EIIMNOSUV vimineous
EIIMNPRST strip mine
EIIMNRSTT terminist
EIIMNSSST mistiness
EIIMOPRSU imperious
EIIMOPRSV improvise
EIIMOPSTT epitomist
EIIMOTTVY emotivity
EIIMPSSST pessimist
EIIMQRRSU squirmier
EIINNNOST intension
EIINNNOTT intention
EIINNNOTV invention
EIINNNSST tinniness
EIINNORST insertion
EIINNORSV inversion
EIINNOSSS noisiness
EIINNPSSS spininess
EIINNRSTT internist
EIINNSSTT insistent
EIINNSTTY intensity
EIINOPRSV prevision
EIINOPSTT pointiest
EIINOPTVW viewpoint
EIINORSTY seniority
EIINORTUZ routinize
EIINPPRST pinstripe
EIINPPSST snippiest
EIINPPSSZ zippiness
EIINPSSST tipsiness
EIINPSSSW wispiness
EIINRSSTU siren suit
EIINRSSTZ ritziness
EIINRSTTW wintriest
EIINRSTUV intrusive
EIINRTTUV nutritive
EIINSSSSS sissiness
EIINSSTTW wittiness
EIINSTTTU institute
EIIPPRSTT trippiest
EIIPRRTUV irruptive
EIIPRSSST prissiest
EIIPRSSTT stripiest
EIISSTTTW twistiest
EIJKLLOOU kilojoule
EIJKMPRSU ski jumper
EIJLLNOSS jolliness
EIJLMNPTU mint julep
EIJLNOSST jointless
EIJMNPSSU jumpiness
EIJNORSST jointress
EIJPRTTUY petit jury
EIKKNOOSS kookiness
EIKLLLSSS skill-less
EIKLLNOVX Knoxville
EIKLMORSY irksomely
EIKLNNOOT kilotonne
EIKLNNRTU trunk line
EIKLNPRRS sprinkler
EIKLNSSSU sulkiness
EIKLRSSST skirtless
EIKMNOSSS smokiness
EIKMNRSSU murkiness
EIKMNSSSU muskiness
EIKNNOSSW wonkiness
EIKNORRTW interwork
EIKNOSTTT knottiest
EIKNPSSTU spunkiest
EIKNRRTTY trinketry
EIKOOPSST spookiest
EIKORRSTV overskirt
EIKORSTTU strike-out
EILLLOTTW little owl
EILLMNOST millstone
EILLMOOPT Melitopol
EILLMORTU multi-role
EILLMPTUX multiplex
EILLMRTUU tellurium
EILLNOPRU nullipore
EILLNOSSW lowliness
EILLNOTVY violently
EILLNSSST stillness
EILLNSSSY sinlessly
EILLOOPRV Liverpool
EILLOOSTW woolliest
EILLOPRSV overspill, spillover
EILLOPRTY pellitory
EILLOPRWW will-power
EILLOPSST pilotless
EILLPSSSY syllepsis
EILLSSTWY witlessly
EILMMNTUU nummulite
EILMMOPSY misemploy
EILMMPSTU plummiest
EILMMSSTU slummiest
EILMNOPST simpleton
EILMNORTT tormentil
EILMNOSTY solemnity
EILMNOSWY winsomely
EILMNPSSU lumpiness
EILMOOSTY ileostomy
EILMRSTUU multi-user
EILNNOOSS looniness
EILNNOSTV insolvent
EILNOOPSX explosion
EILNOOTUV evolution
EILNOPRRU purloiner
EILNOPRSU repulsion
EILNOPSST pointless
EILNOPSSU spinulose
EILNOPSTT Intelpost
EILNOPSUX expulsion
EILNORSSY sensorily

EILNORSTY storyline
EILNORSUV revulsion
EILNORTUY routinely
EILNOSSSU lousiness
EILNOSSTT siltstone
EILNOSTTU listen out
EILNOSUVY enviously
EILNOTTVW Levittown
EILNPPSSU pulpiness
EILNPQTUU quintuple
EILNPRSST printless
EILNPRSTU Nelspruit
EILNPRSTY splintery
EILNQTUUY unquietly
EILNRSSSU surliness
EILNRSTTU turnstile
EILNRSTUU unruliest
EILNRTUUV vulturine
EILNSSSTT stintless
EILNSSSTU lustiness
EILOPPRSS prolepsis
EILOPPSST sloppiest
EILOPRSTT portliest
EILOPSTTT test pilot
EILOPSTUY piteously
EILORRTVW liverwort
EILORSSSV visorless
EILORSSUY seriously
EILRSSTTU sultriest
EIMMNNOST mnemonist
EIMMNOPRS persimmon
EIMNNOPRT prominent
EIMNNORST innermost
EIMNNPTUU neptunium
EIMNNRTTU nutriment
EIMNOORSS roominess
EIMNOPRSU simon-pure
EIMNOPRTU importune
EIMNORRTW worriment
EIMNORSSU sensorium
EIMNORSSW worminess
EIMNORSUV verminous
EIMNOSSSS mossiness
EIMNOSSST moistness
EIMNOSSSU mousiness
EIMNOSTTY testimony
EIMNOTTZZ mezzotint
EIMNSSSTU mustiness
EIMNSSUZZ muzziness
EIMOOPRTV promotive
EIMOORRSW worrisome
EIMOORSSU isomerous
EIMOPRRST misreport
EIMOPRSTU imposture
EIMOPSTUU impetuous
EIMORRRST terrorism
EIMORRSTU trimerous
EIMORSSTT stormiest
EIMORSUVY voyeurism
EIMPRSTTY prettyism
EIMPSSTTU stumpiest
EIMSSTTTU smuttiest
EINNNOTTY nonentity
EINNNSSSU sunniness
EINNOORST ironstone, serotonin
EINNORTVY inventory
EINNOSSST stoniness
EINNOSSSW snowiness
EINNPRSTW newsprint
EINNRTTUW unwritten
EINNSSTTU nuttiness
EINOOPRST rose-point, sore point
EINOOPSST spooniest
EINOORRTT retortion
EINOORTTX extortion
EINOORTTY notoriety
EINOOSSST sootiness
EINOOSSTT snootiest
EINOOSSTZ snooziest
EINOOSSWZ wooziness
EINOPPSSS soppiness
EINOPRRTV overprint
EINOPRSSS prosiness
EINOPRSUU penurious
EINOPSSSU piousness, soupiness
EINOPSSTT pottiness
EINOPSSYZ synopsize
EINORRSSS sorriness
EINORRTTV introvert
EINORSSUU unserious
EINORSTUX extrusion
EINOSSTTT snottiest
EINPRRTTU interrupt
EINPRSSSU pursiness
EINRSSSTU rustiness
EIOOPRRST posterior
EIOOPRSTX expositor
EIOOSSTTV ovotestis
EIOPPRRST stroppier
EIOPPRRTY propriety
EIOPPRSUV purposive
EIOPRSSTT sportiest
EIOPRSTTY posterity
EIOPSSTTT spottiest
EIOQRSTUU turquoise
EIORRRSTT terrorist
EIORRRTTY territory
EIPQRTTUY triptyque
EIPRSSSTU pertussis
EIQRSSTTU squitters
EIRSSTTTU trustiest
EJLLLLORY jelly roll
EJLLOSSYY joylessly
EJNOORRSU sojourner
EJPRTTUYY petty jury
EKKOOPRRW pokerwork
EKLLNNOWW well-known
EKLMMNOSU musk melon
EKLMNOOWY owl monkey
EKLMNPTUY unkemptly
EKLNRSSTU trunkless
EKMMOOORS smoke-room
EKMNNOORS non-smoker
EKMNNOTUY monkey-nut
EKNOOPSTU outspoken
EKNOORSTW stonework
EKNORSSTU sunstroke
EKOORRTUW outworker
EKOORSTTW two-stroke
EKOPRRSSW presswork
ELLMOSUUY emulously
ELLMRSTUU surmullet
ELLNOPTUY opulently
ELLORSTUU tellurous
ELMNNOOST somnolent
ELMNPPSSU plumpness
ELMOORSTW lowermost
ELMORSSST stormless
ELMORSTUU tremulous
ELNOORSUY onerously
ELNORSUVY nervously
ELNOSTUUY tenuously
ELOOOPRTW power tool
ELOOORSSU roseolous
ELOORSTUW lousewort
ELOPPPUVY puppy love
ELOPPRSUY purposely
ELOPPSSUY polypuses
ELOPSSSTU spoutless
ELOQRSUUU querulous
EMMNOOSTU momentous
EMMNOSSSU summonses
EMMNRSTUU menstruum
EMNNOOOST moonstone
EMNOOPSUY eponymous
EMNOORRTT tormentor
EMNOORTUY neurotomy
EMNOORTWY moneywort
EMNOOSTTU tomentous
EMNOPRRTU no-trumper
EMNORSSTT sternmost
EMOOORRST storeroom
EMOOPRTTY optometry
EMOORSTTU outermost
EMOPPRSTU uppermost
EMOPRRTUV overtrump
EMOPRRTYY pyrometry
EMORSTTTU uttermost
ENNNOOPRS non-person
ENNOOPPRT proponent
ENNOPPSTY penny post
ENNOPRTWY pennywort
ENNORSTTU turnstone
ENNPRRSUU runners-up, runner-ups
ENOOPPRST postponer
ENOOPPRTU opportune
ENOORSSTY ostensory
ENOORSTTW stonewort
ENOOSSTTU sostenuto
ENOPPRSTU unstopper
ENOPRSSTT sternpost
ENOPRSTTY post-entry
ENORSSTUU strenuous
ENOSSSTTU stoutness
EOOPPRRSS oppressor
EOOPPRRST prepostor
EOOPPRTTY prototype
EOOPRRSTT protestor
EOOPRSSSS possessor
EOPPRRSTU supporter

EOPPRSSST	stop press
FFGHIISTT	fist fight
FFGHILRTU	frightful
FFGIIINNT	tiffining
FFGILNOXY	flying fox
FFGIMNORU	fungiform
FFGINNOTU	Uffington
FFGINOPRS	offspring
FFGNOSTUW	stuff gown
FFHLORSUU	four-flush
FFIILMOST	off-limits
FFINOSSUU	suffusion
FFIOORSTT	first-foot
FFIORSTTU	soft fruit
FFLOOOOPR	foolproof
FFMMORTUY	tommy ruff
FGGIILMNO	film-going
FGGIINORV	forgiving
FGHHILNOW	high-flown
FGHIILLTY	flightily
FGHILOORT	roof light
FGHILOPTT	top-flight
FGHINORTT	fortnight
FGHMOORTU	frogmouth
FGIIILLNN	infilling
FGIIILLNP	filliping
FGIILNNOW	inflowing
FGIILNORV	frivoling
FGIILNPTU	uplifting
FGIILNRST	firstling
FGIILNTTY	fittingly
FGIILRTUU	ugli fruit
FGIINNTTU	unfitting
FGIINOPRT	profiting
FGIKLLNOS	golf links
FGILLNOOW	following
FGILLNOWY	flowingly
FGILOOSTU	ufologist
FGLLNORUW	full-grown
FGNOOORTW	wrong-foot
FHHIORTTW	forthwith
FHIIIKLLS	killifish
FHIILOPST	pilot fish
FHIILRTTY	thriftily
FHIKORSTW	shift work
FHILLOOSY	foolishly
FHILLOSWY	wolfishly
FHILLSUWY	wishfully
FHILOPPSY	foppishly
FHIMORSTT	Fort Smith
FHIMORSTX	sixth form
FHINRTTUY	unthrifty
FHLLPSUUY	pushfully
FHLLRTUUY	hurtfully
FHLMOOTUU	foul mouth
FHLOOOPRS	shop floor
FHLOOORSW	floor show
FHMOOOPRT	mothproof
FHNOOPRST	shopfront
FHOOOPRST	shotproof
FHOORRTTW	Fort Worth
FIIIKRTUW	kiwi fruit
FIIILSSTY	fissility
FIIIMNRTY	infirmity
FIIKLNNST	skinflint
FIILLMORV	villiform
FIILLMOTU	multifoil
FIILLPTUY	pitifully
FIILMPRST	filmstrip
FIILOPRST	profilist
FIILORTVY	frivolity
FIIMMNORS	misinform
FIIMOPRST	stipiform
FIIMORRTU	triforium
FIIMORRTV	vitriform
FIKLLLSUY	skilfully
FIKLLMOSW	wolf's-milk
FIKLLNSUU	unskilful
FIKLLOSSS	floss silk
FILLNOPTU	full point
FILLSTUWY	wistfully
FILMMORSU	formulism
FILMMORTU	multiform
FILMNORUY	uniformly
FILNNNUUY	unfunnily
FILOOOPRT	portfolio
FILOORSSU	fluorosis
FILOORSUV	frivolous
FILORRSTY	floristry
FILORSUUY	furiously
FILOSSTUU	fistulous
FINNOOPRT	non-profit
FINOOPRSU	profusion
FINOOPRTT	footprint
FIOPRSSTT	first post
FKLNOOSTW	townsfolk
FKOORRSTW	frost-work
FLLLOSUUY	soulfully
FLLLSTUUY	lustfully
FLLNOORRY	forlornly
FLOOOOSTT	footstool
FLOORRSUW	sorrowful
FLOPRSSUU	plus fours
FLORSSUUU	sulfurous
FNOOOTTUW	out-of-town
FOOPRRSTU	rustproof
FOOPSSTUY	pussyfoot
GGGHINRSU	shrugging
GGGIINNRU	unrigging
GGGIINPRS	sprigging
GGGILMNSU	smuggling
GGHHHIILT	highlight
GGHHILOSY	hoggishly
GGHIIILRW	whirligig
GGHIILNNT	lightning
GGHIINRTW	right wing
GGHIINSST	sight-sing
GGHILNNOT	night-long
GGHILNOST	long sight
GGHILNSUY	gushingly
GGHINNOTW	nightgown
GGHLOORYY	hygrology
GGIIIMNNP	impinging
GGIIIMNSV	misgiving
GGIILNNRY	ringingly
GGIILNNSY	singingly
GGIILNPRY	gripingly
GGIINNORW	ingrowing
GGIINNRSY	syringing
GGIINNSWW	swing-wing
GGIINOPSS	gossiping
GGILLNNOY	longingly
GGILLNOOP	golloping
GGILLNOWY	glowingly
GGILMNSUY	ginglymus
GGILNNOUY	youngling
GGILNOPRY	gropingly
GHHIIJKNS	high jinks
GHHIILPST	lightship
GHHIILSST	slightish
GHHIINOPT	high point
GHHILOSTW	light show
GHHILRSTU	rushlight
GHHLOOSTY	Holy Ghost
GHHNOTTUU	unthought
GHIIKNSTT	skintight
GHIIKNTTT	tight-knit
GHIILLNRT	thrilling
GHIILLRSY	girlishly
GHIILNNSY	shiningly
GHIILNNWY	whiningly
GHIILNOST	night-soil
GHIINNNST	thinnings
GHIINNPSU	punishing
GHIINNRSU	inrushing
GHIINOPPT	piping hot
GHILLOOPY	philology
GHILLOOTY	lithology
GHILMNOOT	moonlight
GHILNOOPT	potholing
GHILNOSST	slingshot
GHILNRSUY	rushingly
GHILNSTUY	unsightly
GHILOOSTY	histology
GHILOPSTT	spotlight, stop light
GHILORSUY	roguishly
GHILPRSTY	sprightly
GHILPRTUY	uprightly
GHIMMNRTU	thrumming
GHIMMNTUY	thingummy
GHIMNOSST	songsmith
GHIMORSTT	rightmost
GHINOPRST	hot spring
GHINOPSTT	nightspot
GHINORSST	strongish
GHINORTUW	inwrought
GHINRRTTU	right turn
GHJLNNOOS	long johns
GHKOORRUW	rough work
GHLMNOOYY	hymnology
GHLMOOTYY	mythology
GHLNOOOPY	phonology
GHLNOOPYY	hypnology
GHLNOSSTU	slung shot
GHMNOOSUU	humongous
GHMNOSUUU	humungous
GHMOPSTYY	gypsy moth
GHNNOOPRR	pronghorn
GHNOOSTTW	ghost town
GHNORTUUW	unwrought
GHOOORSTT	Ostrogoth
GHOORTTUW	outgrowth
GIIILOSTU	litigious
GIIIMRSST	mistigris

GIIINNPRS	inspiring	**GILOORSTU**	urologist	**HIMNOPSTY**	hypnotism
GIIINPRST	spiriting	**GIMMNPSUU**	summing-up	**HIMPSSSYY**	symphysis
GIIINRTVY	virginity	**GIMMNRSTU**	strumming	**HINNOOPSU**	union shop
GIIJKNORS	ski-joring	**GIMNNOORS**	Monsignor	**HINOPPRRY**	porphyrin
GIIKLLLNY	killingly	**GIMNOORSU**	ginormous	**HINOPRSUU**	Onuphrius
GIIKNNNUW	unwinking	**GIMNOPPRT**	prompting	**HINOPSTTY**	hypnotist
GIILLLNWY	willingly	**GIMOPRUUY**	uropygium	**HIOOPPRST**	troopship
GIILLMNPY	limpingly	**GINNNOOTV**	non-voting	**HIOPRSSTY**	sophistry
GIILLMNSY	smilingly	**GINOOPRSS**	prognosis	**HIOPRSTTU**	tutorship
GIILLNNUW	unwilling	**GINOOPRST**	gros point	**HIORRSTTY**	thyristor
GIILLNPSY	lispingly	**GINOORRSW**	sorrowing	**HIORSSTTU**	short suit
GIILMNNSU	unsmiling	**GINOPPRST**	stropping	**HKKNNOOTY**	honky-tonk
GIILNNNWY	winningly	**GINOPTTTU**	totting-up	**HKMMNORRU**	krummhorn
GIILNNOST	Islington	**GINORSTUY**	trigynous	**HLNOOPPYY**	polyphony
GIILNNSTU	insulting	**GINQRSTUU**	squirt gun	**HMMOORSUY**	mushroomy
GIILNOPST	pistoling	**GINRSTTTU**	strutting	**HMOOPTTYY**	phytotomy
GIILNOSUU	uliginous	**GKNORTUUY**	Young Turk	**HOOORTTTW**	toothwort
GIILNPPRY	rippingly	**GKOOPRRUW**	group work,	**HOOPRSSTT**	shortstop
GIILNPPST	stippling		work group	**HOOPRSTTU**	Southport
GIILNPRST	split ring,	**GLMNOOPUY**	polygonum	**HORSTTTUU**	out-thrust
	stripling	**GLOOOPRTY**	tropology	**IIIIPPRRS**	piripiris
GIILNPRSY	springily	**GMNOORSSW**	moss-grown	**IIIKLLNPS**	spillikin
GIILNPSTT	splitting	**GNOOOPRSY**	sporogony	**IIIKMNRST**	miniskirt
GIILNPTYY	pityingly	**GNOSSTTUU**	tungstous	**IIILNOSTV**	violinist
GIILNRSTY	stringily	**GORRSTUWY**	worry-guts	**IIIMRRTUV**	triumviri
GIILNTTWY	wittingly	**HHILORSWY**	whorishly	**IIINNOTTU**	intuition
GIILOSSST	glossitis	**HHIMOOSST**	smoothish	**IIINSSSTU**	sinusitis
GIILRSTTU	liturgist	**HHMNOOOPY**	homophony	**IIJNORSUU**	injurious
GIIMNNSSU	minus sign	**HHNOORRST**	shorthorn	**IIJNORTUY**	juniority
GIIMNOPRS	promising	**HHPPPSUUY**	hush puppy	**IIKNNNOOS**	onion-skin
GIIMPRSTU	spirit gum	**HIILLMNOT**	millionth	**IILLLMOTV**	millivolt
GIINNNNPU	unpinning	**HIILLNOTZ**	zillionth	**IILLMPRST**	strip mill
GIINNOPRS	prisoning	**HIILLOOOP**	hoi polloi	**IILLMPRSU**	spirillum
GIINNPPRU	unripping	**HIILMPSWY**	wimpishly	**IILLNORST**	trillions
GIINNPPUZ	unzipping	**HIILNORTT**	trilithon	**IILLOSTVY**	villosity
GIINNPTTU	inputting	**HIILNSSWY**	swinishly	**IILLOTTWW**	willow tit
GIINNPTUY	unpitying	**HIILOQRSU**	liquorish	**IILMNOOPS**	implosion
GIINNTTUW	unwitting	**HIILOSTTY**	hostility	**IILMNOPSU**	impulsion
GIINOPRTT	trig point	**HIILPSTTY**	typhlitis	**IILMOPSSS**	solipsism
GIINORRTW	worriting	**HIILRSTTY**	thirstily	**IILMOPSUY**	impiously
GIINPPRST	stripping	**HIIMNOSST**	Shintoism	**IILNOOPST**	postilion
GIINPTTTU	tittuping	**HIIMNSSUV**	Vishnuism	**IILOPRTXY**	prolixity
GIJNNNORU	nonjuring	**HIIMORSSS**	Irish moss	**IILOPSSST**	solipsist
GIKKNOORS	king's rook	**HIIMRSSTU**	hirsutism	**IILOQSSUU**	siliquous
GIKLNNNSY	King's Lynn	**HIIMSSSTU**	Hussitism	**IILOSTVVZ**	slivovitz
GIKLNNOOO	onlooking	**HIINOSSTT**	Shintoist	**IIMNOPSSZ**	Spinozism
GIKLNNOWY	knowingly	**HIIOPPRRS**	priorship	**IIMNORSTU**	minor suit,
GIKNNNOUW	unknowing	**HIKLMOOTT**	milk tooth		routinism
GIKNNOSTW	Kingstown	**HIKLOSVYZ**	Volzhskiy	**IIMOPRTXY**	proximity
GILLLNOOP	lolloping	**HIKNNORST**	stinkhorn	**IIMOQSTUX**	quixotism
GILLMNOOY	limnology	**HILLLMTUU**	multihull	**IIMRRSTUV**	triumvirs
GILLMOORR	grill room	**HILLMORUU**	ill humour	**IINNORSTU**	intrusion
GILLMOSSY	syllogism	**HILLMPSUY**	lumpishly	**IINNORTTU**	nutrition
GILLNORUY	louringly	**HILLOOPRW**	whirlpool	**IINNOSTUU**	union suit
GILLOOOPY	oligopoly	**HILLOSTUY**	loutishly	**IINOOPRSV**	provision
GILMMNOOS	mongolism	**HILLSSTYY**	stylishly	**IINOOPSVY**	poison ivy
GILMRSTUU	ligustrum	**HILMOOSYZ**	hylozoism	**IINOPRRTU**	irruption
GILNNNPUY	punningly	**HILMOOTTY**	lithotomy	**IINOPSSTZ**	Spinozist
GILNOPTUY	poutingly	**HILNSSTUY**	unstylish	**IINORSTTU**	routinist
GILNORSUY	rousingly	**HILOOPRST**	polo shirt	**IINOSSTUY**	sinuosity
GILNORTTU	troutling	**HILOOPTXY**	toxophily	**IINOSSTVY**	synovitis
GILNOSTUU	glutinous	**HILOOSSTW**	solo whist	**IIOPRSSTU**	spiritous
GILOOOSTT	otologist	**HILOPSSTT**	split shot	**IKMOPPRUY**	Yom Kippur
GILOOOSTZ	zoologist	**HILORSSTT**	shortlist	**IKNOORRSW**	ironworks
GILOOPRTY	gyropilot	**HILRSTUUV**	vulturish	**IKORRSTWW**	wrist-work

IKORSSTTU	outskirts	**ILOPPRSTY**	stroppily	**IOOPPRSST**	proptosis
ILLMOORST	still room	**ILOPRSSYY**	pyrolysis	**IOOPRRSVY**	provisory
ILLNOOPTU	pollution	**ILORSSUVW**	slow virus	**LMOOPPSUY**	pompously
ILLOOQSUY	soliloquy	**ILORSUUUX**	luxurious	**LNOOOPPTY**	Pontypool
ILLOORSSW	slow loris	**IMMMNOORS**	Mormonism	**LNOOPPRSY**	propylons
ILLORSSSW	Swiss roll	**IMMOPPRTU**	impromptu	**LOOPRRSUY**	prolusory
ILMNOOSUY	ominously	**IMMOPSSUY**	symposium	**LOPSSTUUU**	pustulous
ILMNOPTUU	plutonium	**IMNOOOPRT**	promotion	**LORSTUUUV**	vulturous
ILNOOPRSU	prolusion	**IMNORSTTU**	strontium	**MMORRSUUU**	murmurous
ILNOOSUXY	noxiously	**IMOOPPSTY**	pomposity	**MNOORSSTU**	monstrous
ILNOPRXYY	pyroxylin	**IMORSUVXY**	myxovirus	**MNOORSSTW**	snowstorm
ILNOPSSUU	spinulous	**INNOOSSUU**	unisonous	**MOPSSTUUU**	sumptuous
ILNORSUUY	ruinously	**INOOOPSSU**	poisonous	**NNOOOPRSU**	non-porous
ILNOSSUUY	sinuously	**INOOORSTU**	notorious	**NOOOOPRTV**	Porto Novo
ILNPQTUUY	quintuply	**INOPSSTTY**	synoptist	**NOOOOPRTZ**	protozoon
ILOOPRSTU	Port Louis	**INRSTTTUU**	unit trust	**NOOOPPSSU**	soup spoon
ILOOPRTTU	tulip-root	**IOOORRRST**	orris root	**OOPRSSTUU**	stuporous
ILOORSTUY	riotously	**IOOPPRRTU**	pot-pourri	**OORRSTTUU**	torturous

TEN LETTERS

AAAABBDDIS Addis Ababa
AAAABCCLNS Casablanca
AAAABDFILS Faisalabad
AAAABDGNRU Aurangabad
AAAABLRSTU tabula rasa
AAAACDGMRS Madagascar
AAAACDMMRT tarmacadam
AAAACGMNRT Magna Carta
AAAACLMNRT almacantar
AAAACLNRST Santa Clara
AAAADHLMRS Dharamsala
AAAAEGLMMT amalgamate
AAAAGGGNNR Ganganagar
AAAAGHIMRS Sagamihara
AAAAGHRSTY satyagraha
AAAAGMSSSU massasauga
AAAAGNRTTW Wangaratta
AAAAHJLLRW Jawaharlal
AAAAIMNNNP Panamanian
AAAAIMNRST Santa Maria
AAAALMNRSZ salmanazar
AAAALPRSTT parastatal
AAAAMPRRTT parramatta
AAABBBDOTT Abbottabad
AAABBCILST sabbatical
AAABBEPRRY Barbary ape
AAABBGMNTT Battambang
AAABCCIIPR Piracicaba
AAABCCKNSV canvas-back
AAABCDEIRS scarabaeid
AAABCDELNR candelabra
AAABCDRRSU barracudas
AAABCEGGNR garbage can
AAABCEHLMR Beach-la-mar
AAABCEHLTT attachable
AAABCELLLR clarabella
AAABCHINRT batrachian
AAABCIKLMR Black Maria
AAABCILNRR Albarracin
AAABCILOTT Batticaloa
AAABCORRTU barracouta
AAABDHIRTV Bhadravati
AAABDMORSS ambassador
AAABEEGLMN manageable
AAABEELLPP appealable
AAABEELMNS able seaman
AAABEGLMNY manageably
AAABEIJNRZ Azerbaijan
AAABEILLMR Mariabella
AAABEILLSS assailable
AAABEILNTT attainable
AAABEKLPRT partakable
AAABELLNSY analysable
AAABELNRRT narratable
AAABHHIKLS Balashikha
AAABHLPRUW Bahawalpur
AAABHMPRRU Baharampur
AAABHNRSSU sub-Saharan
AAABIKNNNS banana skin
AAABILRSTV Bratislava
AAABIMNPST Anabaptism
AAABIMOPRR Paramaribo
AAABINPSTT Anabaptist
AAACCCRSTU Caractacus
AAACCDEILM academical
AAACCEEIRT acacia tree
AAACCEHNNT catananche
AAACCEIPTT capacitate
AAACCELSST cataclases
AAACCENRUV Cuernavaca
AAACCHILNR anarchical
AAACCILSST cataclasis
AAACCIPRTT paratactic
AAACCMOPRR macrocarpa
AAACDEHLPY alpha decay
AAACDEIMMZ macadamize
AAACDEKNPY Pancake Day
AAACDELMNR calamander
AAACDELMRS salad cream
AAACDEMNNV advance man
AAACDENNRV caravanned
AAACDHINNR arachnidan
AAACDILNOP pina colada
AAACEEENVV venae cavae
AAACEENPPR appearance
AAACEFLQTU catafalque
AAACEHIMNN Manichaean
AAACEILLMR all-America
AAACEINPST anapaestic
AAACEJKNPS jackanapes
AAACELMPRT metacarpal
AAACENNRRV caravanner
AAACGHNRTT tragacanth
AAACGILLNO analogical
AAACHILLNW Wallachian
AAACHIMRST charismata
AAACHJOPRS chaparajos
AAACHLNOTU anacolutha
AAACHNPRTY pyracantha
AAACHQTUUU chautauqua
AAACIKLMNP pack animal
AAACIKLMNR Lamarckian
AAACIKLRTU autarkical
AAACILLMNY maniacally
AAACILLNTY analytical
AAACILLRTU Ural-Altaic
AAACILMMNO ammoniacal
AAACILMNOT anatomical
AAACILNRSS carnassial
AAACILNRST scarlatina
AAACIMNPTY Panama City
AAACINRRTT Tractarian
AAACLMNRTU almucantar
AAACLMNRVY cavalryman
AAACLNSSTU Santa Claus
AAACNRTTTT attractant
AAADEFIOST asafoetida
AAADEGINRV Devanagari
AAADEGNRTV avant-garde
AAADEHLPRT hard palate
AAADEILNRX Alexandria
AAADEIMNNT adamantine
AAADELLORR dollar area
AAADELMNRS salamander
AAADELMPPS Adam's apple
AAADFMNNSY Fanny Adams
AAADGHNQRY Qaraghandy
AAADGIILLR gaillardia
AAADGILLNR granadilla
AAADGINNPT giant panda
AAADGMNORR mandragora
AAADGNOPPR propaganda
AAADHMMMNU Muhammadan
AAADILNNSU Andalusian
AAADINOPTT adaptation
AAADIORSSY radio-assay
AAADLNQRTU quadrantal
AAADORSTTU autostrada
AAAEEGGLRS garage sale
AAAEEGNRST arena stage
AAAEEKMNSS Asamankese
AAAEFLLMRS false alarm
AAAEFLMNST malfeasant
AAAEGGIMNT gametangia
AAAEGHLLNP phalangeal
AAAEGIILRY Yagi aerial
AAAEGILMNR managerial
AAAEGILNOR in-goal area
AAAEGILPPR paraplegia
AAAEGINPRS asparagine
AAAEGMNOPR magna opera
AAAEGMRRTT Margaretta
AAAEGMRRTV margravate

AAAEGPSSWY passageway
AAAEHIMRTU haematuria
AAAEHINSTU euthanasia
AAAEHLPSVW alpha waves
AAAEHMMOST haematomas
AAAEHPPRRS paraphrase
AAAEIILNTT Italianate
AAAEILLPTZ palatalize
AAAEILMPST metaplasia
AAAEILMRTU tularaemia
AAAEILNPRT planetaria
AAAEILNPTT palatinate
AAAEIMNPRS paramnesia
AAAEIMNQRU aquamarine
AAAEIMNRSW Samian ware
AAAELLNRTT tarantella
AAAELMRSTT metatarsal
AAAFIKPRRS safari park
AAAGGILLNO algolagnia
AAAGGNNRTU gargantuan
AAAGHLNRSU Ulhasnagar
AAAGHNPSTU agapanthus
AAAGIILMNR marginalia
AAAGILMNNO Anglomania
AAAGIMMNRR grammarian
AAAGIMNSTT anastigmat
AAAGLMMNPU Mpumalanga
AAAGLNRSTU natural gas
AAAGLRSSTU astragalus
AAAGMNSTTY syntagmata
AAAHILMRRS Air Marshal
AAAHKKNSTZ Kazakhstan
AAAHLMNPST phantasmal
AAAHMNOTTX xanthomata
AAAHNPRRSU Saharanpur
AAAIIMNRTU Mauritania
AAAIINNRST sanitarian
AAAILLLPTY palatially
AAAILLMNNZ manzanilla
AAAILLMRTW martial law
AAAILLORTV lavatorial
AAAILMNRWY railwayman
AAAILNORTT natatorial
AAAILNRSTU Australian, saturnalia
AAAIMORTTV ottava rima
AAAINNPRSS Parnassian
AAALLNRTUW natural law
AAALMNOPRR paranormal
AAAMNNORTT tramontana
AAAMRTZZZZ razzmatazz
AABBBELORS absorbable
AABBCCKKOT back-to-back
AABBCDEKLR black bread
AABBCDKLOR blackboard
AABBCEENRS Cerne Abbas
AABBCEILRS ascribable
AABBCENORS absorbance
AABBCIILNR rabbinical
AABBCIJKRT jackrabbit
AABBDDEENN Baden-Baden
AABBDDEORR breadboard
AABBDEEKNS baked beans
AABBDEGORR bargeboard
AABBDELORS adsorbable
AABBDEOORV above board
AABBDIILNT bail bandit
AABBDLLNRY brandy ball
AABBEEHLRT breathable
AABBEEIRTV abbreviate
AABBEELMRV beaver lamb
AABBEELNRU unbearable
AABBEELNTU unbeatable
AABBEEMMWW Wemba-wemba
AABBEGGINR garbage bin
AABBEILMNO abominable
AABBEILNOT obtainable
AABBEKLLST basketball
AABBEKLRWY baby walker
AABBELNRUY unbearably
AABBGGILNR Balbriggan
AABBILMNOY abominably
AABBILNNOY Babylonian
AABBIORSSU babiroussa
AABBMMNPYY namby-pamby
AABBNNUUYY bunya bunya
AABCCCHINT bacchantic
AABCCEELPT acceptable
AABCCEHNST bacchantes
AABCCEKKPR backpacker
AABCCELLLU calculable
AABCCELPTY acceptably
AABCCGIKLM black magic
AABCCHKLTW Black Watch
AABCCILNSS cabin class
AABCCIORST acrobatics
AABCCLLLUY calculably
AABCDDEHKN backhanded
AABCDDEKLR ladder-back
AABCDDEKLS saddleback
AABCDEEEFL defaceable
AABCDEEHLT detachable
AABCDEEILR eradicable
AABCDEELLR declarable
AABCDEELTU educatable
AABCDEERSU bread sauce
AABCDEHKLT Black Death
AABCDEHKNR backhander
AABCDEKSWY sway-backed
AABCDELNOS Alcobendas
AABCDELORS scale-board
AABCDENNOR carbonnade
AABCDERSTT abstracted
AABCDGKLRU blackguard
AABCDHKLOR chalkboard
AABCDHMORT matchboard
AABCDHOPRT patchboard
AABCDIILLO diabolical
AABCDIINOT abdication
AABCDMNOPY bad company
AABCDNNORT contraband
AABCEEEMRR mace-bearer
AABCEEERTX exacerbate
AABCEEFLNU unfaceable
AABCEEGHLN changeable
AABCEEGHLR chargeable
AABCEEHILV achievable
AABCEEHLMP peach Melba
AABCEEHLNS encashable
AABCEEHLPR preachable
AABCEEHLRS searchable
AABCEEHLTY chalybeate
AABCEEHRST sabretache
AABCEEILMR amerciable
AABCEEINRR carabineer
AABCEEIRTV abreactive
AABCEEKLMR marble cake
AABCEEKLNR clean break
AABCEEKSST basket case
AABCEELLLR recallable
AABCEELMOT come-at-able
AABCEELMSU Melba sauce
AABCEELNRT tabernacle
AABCEELRTU trabeculae
AABCEFLORT factorable
AABCEGHLNY changeably
AABCEGHMRS gas chamber
AABCEGIRRR carrier bag
AABCEGLLOU coagulable
AABCEGLMNN blancmange
AABCEHIIMM Miami Beach
AABCEHILMN machinable
AABCEHILPT alphabetic
AABCEHILRT charitable
AABCEHINRT branchiate
AABCEHKLRT black earth
AABCEIINRR carabinier
AABCEIINTU beautician
AABCEILLMP implacable
AABCEILLPP applicable
AABCEILNOT actionable
AABCEILOSS associable
AABCEILQRU acquirable
AABCEINORT abreaction
AABCEIORST aerobatics
AABCEKKMRR backmarker
AABCEKPRRT brat packer
AABCELLLRY Ballyclare
AABCELLMOR collar-beam
AABCELLNSU unscalable
AABCELLORR barcarolle
AABCELMOPR comparable
AABCELMTUU acetabulum
AABCELNOTU outbalance
AABCELRRTU trabecular
AABCENORST castor bean
AABCERRRTY bar tracery
AABCERRTUU bureaucrat
AABCFIKLRR Black Friar
AABCFIORRT fabricator
AABCGILLSU subglacial
AABCGKMMNO backgammon

AABCGLRRTU cat burglar
AABCHILNOS Choibalsan
AABCHILRTY charitably
AABCHINOTT cohabitant
AABCHIOOPR acrophobia
AABCHIORRT brachiator
AABCHKLPSS splashback
AABCIILPTY capability
AABCIILTTY actability
AABCIIOPRT parabiotic
AABCIKRSST backstairs
AABCILLMPY implacably
AABCILLPPY applicably
AABCILMOST catabolism
AABCILNNNO cannabinol
AABCILNNUU incunabula
AABCILNORR brain coral
AABCILNRSU subcranial
AABCILNSUV subclavian
AABCILORRT calibrator
AABCILRRUV vibracular
AABCIQSTUU subaquatic
AABCKLMOOR blackamoor
AABCKRSSST brass tacks
AABCLLNNNO cannon ball
AABCLMOPRU labour camp
AABCLMOPRY comparably
AABCLORUVY vocabulary
AABCLRSTTY abstractly
AABCNORSST contrabass
AABCORRSTT abstractor
AABDDEEEHR bareheaded
AABDDEEGLR degradable
AABDDEELNR bandleader
AABDDEEPRS spade beard
AABDDEHLMO hebdomadal
AABDDEHLRS balderdash
AABDDEILRR air bladder
AABDDEILRY daily bread
AABDDELOPT paddle boat
AABDDEORRT Trade Board
AABDDINORR drainboard
AABDEEELMS sealed-beam
AABDEEELRR re-readable
AABDEEFLRY defrayable
AABDEEGHNR headbanger
AABDEEGNRR beargarden
AABDEEHLLN handleable
AABDEEHRRT threadbare
AABDEEINPR pea-brained
AABDEELNPX expandable
AABDEELNRU unreadable
AABDEELPRS spreadable
AABDEELRRV laver bread
AABDEERSTW water-based
AABDEFFLOR affordable
AABDEGGINR brigandage
AABDEGGNRS sandbagger
AABDEGGORU broad gauge
AABDEGHLNR grab handle
AABDEGHLNS Bangladesh
AABDEGLPRU upgradable
AABDEGORST goat's-beard
AABDEHINRT brain death
AABDEHLRTY hydratable
AABDEILLNR banderilla
AABDEINNOR Aberdonian
AABDEINNRR Bernardina
AABDEIRSTZ bastardize
AABDEJLSTU adjustable
AABDEKLLMS masked ball
AABDEKORST skateboard
AABDELLNNO belladonna
AABDELNOPR pardonable
AABDELNRUY unreadably
AABDELNTUY unabatedly
AABDELORRZ razor blade
AABDELRSTU balustrade
AABDEMNRST bandmaster
AABDEOPRST pasteboard
AABDFHLORS flash-board
AABDFLOORT float-board
AABDGIILNW law-abiding
AABDGIILRS garibaldis
AABDGIKNOS baking soda
AABDHLORRU hard labour
AABDHMNNSU husbandman
AABDIINNRR brain drain
AABDIJNORS jaborandis
AABDILMNRU mandibular
AABDILOOPR paraboloid
AABDIMNRRU barramundi
AABDLNNTUY abundantly
AABDLNOPRY pardonably
AABDLOORRW barrowload
AABDNNPRSY brandy snap
AABDOORRRW broad arrow
AABDORRSTW strawboard
AABEEEKRRX axe-breaker
AABEEELLPR repealable
AABEEELLRS releasable, resaleable, resealable
AABEEELLRV revealable
AABEEELPRT repeatable
AABEEELRRT talebearer
AABEEGLMSS assemblage
AABEEGLOVY voyageable
AABEEGLRTT targetable
AABEEGNORT baronetage
AABEEHKRRT heartbreak
AABEEHLQTU bequeathal
AABEEILLRZ realizable
AABEEILMNX examinable
AABEEILNRT retainable
AABEEILPRR repairable
AABEEIMOSS amoebiases
AABEEINRTV native bear
AABEEJKRRW jaw-breaker
AABEEKLMRR remarkable
AABEEKLMRT marketable
AABEEKLRRW lawbreaker
AABEEKMRRT bear market
AABEEKRRTW breakwater
AABEELLLSZ sleazeball
AABEELLMNT lamentable
AABEELLNPT plane-table
AABEELLNSU unsaleable
AABEELLPRR pall-bearer
AABEELMNNU unnameable
AABEELMNTU untameable
AABEELMRSU measurable
AABEELMSTT metastable, stablemate
AABEELNNTT tenantable
AABEELNORS reasonable
AABEELNOSS seasonable
AABEELNPTT patentable
AABEELNRSW answerable
AABEELNRTU untearable
AABEELNRUW unwearable
AABEELOPRV evaporable
AABEELPPRY prepayable
AABEELRRST arrestable
AABEELRTTW water-table
AABEELSSSS assessable
AABEELSTTT attestable
AABEERRSTT street Arab
AABEFFOPRU opera buffa
AABEFGILTU fatiguable
AABEFHLMOT fathomable
AABEFIILRT ratifiable
AABEFILLNT inflatable
AABEFIMORS framboesia
AABEFLORUV favourable
AABEGHINRS earbashing
AABEGHOOPR agoraphobe
AABEGHORRU harbourage
AABEGIILMN imaginable
AABEGILNOZ zabaglione
AABEGILNRT able rating
AABEGILNRU inarguable
AABEGILNSS assignable
AABEGILRST algebraist
AABEGINNOT abnegation
AABEGIRRRT arbitrager
AABEGLNRUU unarguable
AABEHIILTT habilitate
AABEHILORV behavioral
AABEHKLNSU unshakable
AABEHRRSTW waterbrash
AABEIILLPP labial pipe
AABEIILNRV invariable
AABEIILNST insatiable
AABEIILRTT trilabiate
AABEIILSST assibilate
AABEIIMNRS bains-marie
AABEIIMOSS amoebiasis
AABEIJLOSU Beaujolais
AABEIKLMST mistakable
AABEILLMPP impalpable
AABEILLNUV invaluable
AABEILLORV labiovelar
AABEILLOST isolatable
AABEILMNTV ambivalent
AABEILMPSS impassable
AABEILNRST strainable
AABEILRTTT titratable
AABEINORRT aberration
AABEINORTT trabeation
AABEIORRTV arbor vitae
AABEKLLNSU unslakable
AABEKLMRRY remarkably
AABELLLRWY wall-barley

AABELLMNTY lamentably
AABELLNPUY unplayable
AABELMOSTT Melba toast
AABELMPRRU preambular
AABELMRRST Lambersart
AABELMRSUY measurably
AABELNORSY reasonably
AABELNOSSY seasonably
AABELNPRST Barnstaple
AABELOORRT elaborator
AABELSTTTU statutable
AABEMRSTTU masturbate
AABEQRRSTU Quatre Bras
AABFFIILTY affability
AABFLMNOTY flamboyant
AABFLORUVY favourably
AABGIILMNY imaginably
AABGIILNOR aboriginal
AABGILNRUY inarguably
AABGINNOTW angwantibo
AABGINOORT abrogation
AABGKMNNOS Nkongsamba
AABGLNRUUY unarguably
AABHIINNTT inhabitant
AABHIINOTT habitation
AABHILLTUY habitually
AABHIMMNRS Brahmanism
AABHIMRTVZ bar mitzvah
AABHLLLOOU hullabaloo
AABHLLMNOY Ballymahon
AABIIILMTY amiability
AABIILNRVY invariably
AABIILNSTY insatiably
AABIILORTU obituarial
AABIINPRST bipartisan
AABIIOPRSS parabiosis
AABIJNORTU abjuration
AABIKLMOST katabolism
AABIKLMSTY mistakably
AABIKNOPRT Portakabin
AABILLMPPY impalpably
AABILLMSST lamb's-tails
AABILLNNUY biannually
AABILLNOOT oblational
AABILLNUVY invaluably
AABILMPSSY impassably
AABILMRSST strabismal
AABILNOTTU tabulation
AABILORSTT stabilator
AABIMNOORT abominator
AABINRRSTY binary star
AABIORRRTT arbitrator
AABJLNOSTY job analyst
AABKKOORRU kookaburra
AABLLMNORY abnormally
AABLLMOSTU salbutamol
AABLLNPUYY unplayably
AABLMORTUY ambulatory
AABLOORRTY laboratory
AABLSTTTUY statutably
AABNOORRTW narrow boat
AABORRRSTU barratrous
AACCCDEIIT acetic acid
AACCCDENOR accordance
AACCCDIILT lactic acid
AACCCDIINY cyanic acid
AACCCEENPT acceptance
AACCCEILTT catalectic
AACCCEOSTU cactaceous
AACCCINRUY inaccuracy
AACCDDEHKN cack-handed
AACCDDEIRT caddie cart
AACCDEENSU succedanea
AACCDEGHRR charge card
AACCDEHIRS saccharide
AACCDEHNOR archdeacon
AACCDEIILM maleic acid
AACCDEILNT accidental
AACCDEIMNU unacademic
AACCDELLTU calculated
AACCDELRST cat's cradle
AACCDEMNOO cacodaemon
AACCDENNSY ascendancy
AACCDEORSS access road
AACCDERSTY scaredy-cat
AACCDGIILL gallic acid
AACCDHPRST scratch pad
AACCDIILOX oxalic acid
AACCDIINNT tannic acid
AACCDNOTUY account day
AACCEEELRT accelerate
AACCEEFFOT face-to-face
AACCEEGPRS scapegrace
AACCEEKLTT cattle cake
AACCEELLNT cancellate
AACCEELLOT calceolate
AACCEENTTU accentuate
AACCEFPRST spacecraft
AACCEGHOST stagecoach
AACCEHILLM alchemical
AACCEHILMN mechanical
AACCEHIMNN main chance
AACCEHINNT cachinnate
AACCEHINRS saccharine
AACCEHINRU Chaucerian
AACCEHLNOT coelacanth
AACCEHLNRT lancet arch
AACCEHORSS saccharose
AACCEHRRTT rat-catcher
AACCEIIPTV capacitive
AACCEILOPR praecocial
AACCEILPRT Palearctic
AACCEILPTT cataleptic
AACCEINNOT canonicate
AACCEINPRT pancreatic
AACCEINRTU inaccurate
AACCEIRRTU caricature
AACCEISTUV accusative
AACCELMTUU accumulate
AACCELOPPU palace coup
AACCELORSU calcareous
AACCELPRSW crawl space
AACCELRTUY accurately
AACCENRSTU crustacean
AACCFILLRY farcically
AACCFILRSU fascicular
AACCFINNRS Franciscan
AACCGHIPRY graphicacy
AACCGHOPRY cacography
AACCGIJKNR carjacking
AACCHHINTW watch-chain
AACCHIIRST archaistic
AACCHILNPY chaplaincy
AACCHIMORT achromatic
AACCHMORSU scaramouch
AACCIILLMT climatical
AACCIILORS sacroiliac
AACCIINNOT Occitanian
AACCIINPRT practician
AACCIINPTY incapacity
AACCIJNOPR Canopic jar
AACCILLRUV clavicular
AACCILLTTY tactically
AACCILMMUY immaculacy
AACCILNOOS occasional
AACCILORSU calcarious
AACCILOSTU acoustical
AACCILRTUY articulacy
AACCIMNORS carcinomas
AACCINORTV vaccinator
AACCINOSTU accusation
AACCINPTTY anaptyctic
AACCIORTTU autocratic
AACCJLNOPU Cluj-Napoca
AACCKLLMOR alarm clock
AACCLLORTU calculator
AACCLNRRUU caruncular
AACCMNOPRY company car
AACCMNORTY cartomancy
AACCNNOTTU accountant
AACCNORSST sacrosanct
AACCORSTUY accusatory
AACDDEEHLR decahedral
AACDDEEIMP aide-de-camp
AACDDEELLR Calderdale
AACDDEIJTU adjudicate
AACDDEKLPS packsaddle
AACDDIOTTU autodidact
AACDEEEFNS defeasance
AACDEEELST de-escalate
AACDEEFHMS shamefaced
AACDEEFHNS ashen-faced
AACDEEGNOT anecdotage
AACDEEHIMN Achaemenid
AACDEEHNRS case-harden
AACDEEINRT deracinate
AACDEEIPTT decapitate
AACDEEITTV deactivate
AACDEEMPRS dreamscape
AACDEENNTT attendance
AACDEEOPRS escape road
AACDEFGNRR fragranced
AACDEFINRR Africander
AACDEFINRU fricandeau
AACDEFINST fascinated
AACDEFLORT defalcator
AACDEGHHNR chargehand
AACDEGLNNY land agency
AACDEGLOTU catalogued
AACDEHHTTW death-watch
AACDEHILMY chlamydiae
AACDEHIORS icosahedra

AACDEHJKLT Jack the Lad
AACDEHKPRT packthread
AACDEHLLPY Lady chapel
AACDEHLNNS clean hands
AACDEHLORT octahedral
AACDEHNTTU unattached
AACDEHORTY cathode ray
AACDEIILNT laciniated
AACDEIILRZ radicalize
AACDEIINRR irradiance
AACDEIIPRR pericardia
AACDEIIPRT paediatric
AACDEIIRTV divaricate
AACDEIJLTV adjectival
AACDEILMNO demoniacal
AACDEILMNR aldermanic
AACDEILNNO Caledonian
AACDEILNSZ scandalize
AACDEIMNTT admittance
AACDEINQUY inadequacy
AACDEINRST discarnate
AACDEINRTX taxi dancer
AACDEIORRT eradicator
AACDEIRSTY caryatides
AACDEJNNTU unadjacent
AACDELMOPR camelopard
AACDELNPPY candy apple
AACDELNSST sandcastle
AACDELORST sacerdotal
AACDEMORRT demarcator
AACDEORSUV cadaverous
AACDFHINRT handicraft
AACDFIINOO aficionado
AACDGHHINR Chandigarh
AACDGHNORR drag-anchor
AACDGIMORR cardiogram
AACDGINNPT tap-dancing
AACDGLNOOR gondola car
AACDGNRSUY sugar-candy
AACDGORSTU coastguard
AACDHIINSY daisy chain
AACDHIKRTU kurdaitcha
AACDHMNORR orchardman
AACDHNNORY Chardonnay
AACDIILMRS radicalism
AACDIILMRT matricidal
AACDIILPRR parricidal
AACDIILPRT patricidal
AACDILLMTU Talmudical
AACDILLNRY cardinally
AACDILMORY myocardial
AACDIMMRSU music drama
AACDIMNRTU undramatic
AACDINORRT ration card
AACDLLOPST Old Pals Act
AACDLNOSSU scandalous
AACDLOPRST postal card
AACDMMNNOT commandant
AACDMOORRU Rocamadour
AACEEEHKPS Chesapeake
AACEEEKMPR peacemaker
AACEEELMNP elecampane
AACEEELMRT telecamera
AACEEELNOP Palaeocene
AACEEGGHNR gear change
AACEEGHNRR carragheen
AACEEGILLN allegiance
AACEEGKPPR pre-package
AACEEGLLRS large-scale
AACEEHILNT chatelaine
AACEEHKPST cheapskate
AACEEHLNPT antechapel
AACEEHMNRY aerenchyma
AACEEHNNRT anthracene
AACEEHPPRS paperchase
AACEEILMRZ caramelize
AACEEILPRT altarpiece
AACEEIMNPT emancipate
AACEEIPPRT appreciate
AACEEIRTTT triacetate
AACEEIRTTV reactivate
AACEEITUVV evacuative
AACEEKLNNS lance-snake
AACEELLLUV valleculae
AACEELLNOT lanceolate
AACEELLNST clean slate
AACEELLORT reallocate
AACEELMSTU emasculate
AACEELRRTW Clearwater
AACEENORSU arenaceous
AACEENRRTV veteran car
AACEERSSTV stavesacre
AACEFGINSV face-saving
AACEFGLMOU camouflage
AACEFGRSTT stagecraft
AACEFHLLNP chap-fallen
AACEFIILTT facilitate
AACEFIIMPR prima facie
AACEFIINRZ Africanize
AACEFIINTZ fanaticize
AACEFILNSU final cause
AACEFILRSY fiscal year
AACEFJKKLT flak jacket
AACEFKLLLT tackle-fall
AACEFLLLOR flea collar
AACEFLLNOP focal plane
AACEFLMORT malefactor
AACEFNNORR Caernarfon
AACEFRSTTT statecraft
AACEGGKORR garage rock
AACEGHILNR alcheringa
AACEGHINOR archegonia
AACEGHMOPR macrophage
AACEGHNORT coat-hanger
AACEGIKLMN lacemaking
AACEGIKMNP pacemaking
AACEGILLPR preglacial
AACEGILORT categorial
AACEGILPPR paraplegic
AACEGIMNPR campaigner
AACEGINRTV vintage car
AACEGJKRUV Kragujevac
AACEGLMORY acromegaly
AACEGLORTU cataloguer
AACEGLOSTU catalogues
AACEHHMNTT hatchet man
AACEHIKNSZ Ashkenazic
AACEHILMMS Michaelmas
AACEHILMRS camel's-hair
AACEHILNRS Lancashire
AACEHILRTT theatrical
AACEHINRRT catarrhine
AACEHINRST China aster
AACEHINRTT anthracite
AACEHIORST Oireachtas
AACEHIRRTV architrave
AACEHJKMMR jackhammer
AACEHKLMRS ramshackle
AACEHKMMRT matchmaker
AACEHKMNPU Kampuchean
AACEHKMRTW watchmaker
AACEHLLRSW Charles' Law
AACEHLMMRW claw hammer
AACEHLNPPT patch panel
AACEHLNPRT plane chart
AACEHLOPSU acephalous
AACEHLPRTY archetypal
AACEHLRSTT scarlet hat
AACEHMNPRY parenchyma
AACEHMNRRT Carmarthen
AACEHMNTTT attachment
AACEHMOPRT camphorate
AACEHNPRRT Petrarchan
AACEHOPRTY apothecary
AACEIILPTZ capitalize
AACEIIMNOT emaciation
AACEIINNRV invariance
AACEIINPTT anticipate
AACEIINTTV inactivate, vaticinate
AACEIIPRTT patriciate
AACEIKLRTT racket-tail
AACEILLMNU animalcule
AACEILLNOS escallonia
AACEILLNTT cantillate
AACEILLOSU alliaceous
AACEILLPRT prelatical
AACEILLRVY cavalierly
AACEILLSTY salicylate
AACEILMMTU immaculate
AACEILMNRU unicameral
AACEILMNSU main clause
AACEILMNTU calumniate
AACEILMRTU tularaemic
AACEILNORT laceration
AACEILNOST escalation
AACEILNPSS snail's pace
AACEILOOPZ Palaeozoic
AACEILPTTU capitulate
AACEILRTTU articulate
AACEILRTUU auriculate
AACEILSTTT stalactite
AACEIMMPRU paramecium
AACEIMNNRU un-American
AACEIMNORS macaronies
AACEIMNORT maceration
AACEIMNORU oceanarium
AACEIMOPST aposematic
AACEIMORRT crematoria
AACEIMPRRT parametric

AACEIMSTTT metastatic
AACEINNNTU annunciate
AACEINNOTT catenation
AACEINNPRT pancreatin
AACEINORTU aeronautic
AACEINORTV vacationer
AACEINOTUV evacuation
AACEINOTVX excavation
AACEINQRTU reacquaint
AACEINSSST assistance
AACEINSTVY vanity case
AACEIOSTVV vasoactive
AACEIRTTTV attractive
AACEJKNRTT natterjack
AACEJLORTU ejaculator
AACEKLMRST smart aleck
AACEKLNORS coral snake
AACEKLRRTY tracklayer
AACEKLRSTW slack water
AACEKMORRW camerawork
AACELLLMSS small-scale
AACELLLORT collateral
AACELLLRST salt cellar
AACELLLRUV vallecular
AACELLPRRY carpellary
AACELMOPSU palmaceous
AACELMORST scleromata
AACELMOSUV malvaceous
AACELNNOTV covenantal
AACELNOPTU cantaloupe
AACELNOTTV octavalent
AACELNRRUV vernacular
AACELNRTTU tentacular
AACELNSSSU casualness
AACELOPPSY apocalypse
AACEMNOPRS mascarpone
AACEMNOPRT ocean tramp
AACEMNOPSW spacewoman
AACEMNORST Sacramento
AACEMPRSTU metacarpus
AACENNOTTZ canzonetta
AACEORRTTT terracotta
AACFFIJMRT traffic jam
AACFGIIMNT magnificat
AACFGILNRT flat racing
AACFHKNRST crankshaft
AACFHLNORW half a crown
AACFIIILRT artificial
AACFIILNOR California
AACFIILSTT fatalistic
AACFIIMNST fanaticism
AACFIINOST fasciation
AACFILLOSU fallacious
AACFILMOOT coat of mail
AACFILNORT fractional
AACFILNRSS infraclass
AACFILTTUY factuality
AACFINORST fascinator
AACFLLMRST small craft
AACFMNNOWY fancy woman
AACFMOORST coat of arms
AACFNRSTTU surfactant
AACFRRTTYY arty-crafty

AACGGILLNO algolagnic
AACGGILNOT cataloging
AACGHHINPR chinagraph
AACGHHOPRT tachograph
AACGHILNPY anaglyphic
AACGHIOPRS sarcophagi
AACGHIPRSY sciagraphy
AACGHLSSTW watch-glass
AACGIILNOT glaciation
AACGIIMSTT astigmatic
AACGIKMNRT tarmacking
AACGILLLNS call signal
AACGILLRTY tragically
AACGILMNNY malignancy
AACGILNORS cor anglais
AACGILNORW organic law
AACGILNPTY play-acting
AACGIMNORT morganatic
AACGIMPRST pragmatics
AACGIMRSTY magistracy
AACGINNSSV canvassing
AACGIORSTT castigator
AACGKRRSSW grass-wrack
AACGLLMOOY malacology
AACGLOORTU coagulator
AACHHHIKSU shakuhachi
AACHHILNPT naphthalic
AACHHIMNNU human chain
AACHHORSTT astrohatch
AACHIINPTT antipathic
AACHIINRST Christiana
AACHILLOPT allopathic
AACHILLORS Charollais
AACHILMNOR monarchial
AACHILMNRT Altrincham
AACHILNNPT plainchant
AACHILSTUV Chula Vista
AACHIMMNRS Rachmanism
AACHIMNOPR anamorphic
AACHIMNORS maraschino
AACHIMNORT machinator
AACHIMNORW chairwoman
AACHIMNPST phantasmic
AACHIMPRST pharmacist
AACHIMRRTY matriarchy
AACHINRSTU Carthusian
AACHIPRRTY patriarchy
AACHLNNNOT nonchalant
AACHLOPPRY apocryphal
AACHMOOPRT apochromat
AACHMORTUY tauromachy
AACHPRSTTW watch strap
AACIILLNNT anticlinal
AACIILLNOS salicional
AACIILLOPT apolitical
AACIILMNOS simoniacal
AACIILMNST talismanic
AACIILMNTX anticlimax
AACIILMPST capitalism
AACIILNNST annalistic
AACIILNOST antisocial
AACIILPPST papistical
AACIILPSTT capitalist

AACIIMNRST anti-racism
AACIIMNSTV Vaticanism
AACIINOPTT capitation
AACIINORTV Victoriana
AACIINOTTV activation, cavitation
AACIINRSTT anti-racist
AACIINSTTT antistatic
AACIINSTTV Vaticanist
AACIIORSUV avaricious
AACIKLMMRS Lamarckism
AACIKLMRST smart alick
AACILLMORT matrilocal
AACILLMOTY atomically
AACILLNOOT allocation, locational
AACILLNORT local train
AACILLNTUY nautically
AACILLOPRT allopatric
AACILLORTV vacillator
AACILLPTYY atypically
AACILLSTTY statically
AACILLTVWY cavity wall
AACILMNOTU maculation
AACILMOSTU calamitous
AACILMPPRY Paralympic
AACILMPSTU capital sum
AACILMSSUW musical saw
AACILNNOPT non-capital
AACILNNRTY tyrannical
AACILNOOTV vocational
AACILNOPRS parsonical
AACILNOPTY nyctalopia
AACILNORTT tractional
AACILOORRT oratorical
AACILOPPRT applicator
AACILOPRTT optical art
AACILORRTU curatorial
AACILPRRSU spiracular
AACILPRRTU particular
AACILPRTUY capitulary
AACILPSSUW wassail-cup
AACIMMNNOO monomaniac
AACIMMOSST atomic mass
AACIMNOPRY pyromaniac
AACIMORSTT masticator
AACINNOSTT Constantia
AACINOOSTV Nova Scotia
AACINORSTT castration
AACINORTTT attraction
AACINORTUY cautionary
AACINPPRST Capri pants
AACIOOPPRT apotropaic
AACIOORSST associator
AACIORRSTT aristocrat
AACJLMRSUU majuscular
AACLLORRUY oracularly
AACLLRSUVY vascularly
AACLMMOPSY mycoplasma
AACLMNNOSW clanswoman
AACLMNOOSU monocausal
AACLMOPRSS sarcoplasm
AACLNNORTU connatural
AACLOORRTU coloratura

AACLOOSSTU Tuscaloosa
AACMOOPRRT comparator
AACMOORRTU coat armour
AACMOPSSSW compass saw
AACNNNOSTT constantan
AACNOORSST Cosa Nostra
AACNORRSTT transactor
AACNORRSTW narrowcast
AACOOPPRSU apocarpous
AACOOPSSTT capo tastos
AADDDEEHHR hard-headed
AADDDEEHRT death adder
AADDDEELUV value added
AADDDEENNP deadpanned
AADDDEILPR paradiddle
AADDDEILRT taradiddle
AADDDGRSUY sugar daddy
AADDEEGMNR grande dame
AADDEEHHOT head-to-head
AADDEEHHST death's head
AADDEEHIMN maidenhead
AADDEEHNRR hard-earned
AADDEEIRST desiderata
AADDEEMRRY daydreamer
AADDEGHLNR glad-hander
AADDEGIMMR diagrammed
AADDEGIRRT tardigrade
AADDEGMNOR Armageddon
AADDEGNNOR dragonnade
AADDEHIMNN handmaiden
AADDEHQSTU death squad
AADDEIILPT dilapidate
AADDEILMRR red admiral
AADDELMNOW meadowland
AADDGILMOY amygdaloid
AADDGILNNP landing pad
AADDGNNRST grandstand
AADDGNOPWY paddy wagon
AADDHHNNOT hand-to-hand
AADDIILNOT additional
AADDIINRRT ritardandi
AADDINORRT ritardando
AADDLLNORS sand dollar
AADDLNOOSW sandalwood
AADEEELLNS leaden seal
AADEEELRSY day release
AADEEFGLRT deflagrate
AADEEGGINR reading age
AADEEGMNRW game warden
AADEEGNRTU guaranteed
AADEEGOPRT pagoda tree
AADEEHHLRX hexahedral
AADEEHHMMR hammerhead
AADEEHHPRT heptahedra
AADEEHKNSS snake's head
AADEEHMRST headmaster
AADEEHNPRT pentahedra
AADEEHNRVW heavenward
AADEEHQRSU headsquare
AADEEHRRTT tetrahedra
AADEEILNNR adrenaline
AADEEILNST desalinate
AADEEIMMNN maiden name
AADEEINORT de-aeration
AADEEINQTU inadequate
AADEEKNNUW unawakened
AADEELLLPR paralleled
AADEELLPPR apparelled
AADEELNNWZ New Zealand
AADEELNRST sandal tree
AADEELNRSX alexanders
AADEELQRSU square deal
AADEELQTUY adequately
AADEELRSTV slave trade
AADEELRTTU adulterate
AADEELSTVW delta waves
AADEEMQRSU masquerade
AADEEMQSTU desquamate
AADEENPPSU unappeased
AADEENSTVZ Zend-Avesta
AADEENTTTU attenuated
AADEEPPRRT trade paper
AADEEPPRWX waxed paper
AADEEPRSTY paederasty
AADEFFNORT fore and aft
AADEFHHIOR head of hair
AADEFHLNOZ half a dozen
AADEFHLNRT fatherland
AADEFHRSTY Father's Day
AADEFIKNRR Afrikander
AADEFIMNOT defamation
AADEFINTTU infatuated
AADEFMORTY defamatory
AADEFNOPRR Ponferrada
AADEFRRSTW afterwards
AADEGGINRZ aggrandize
AADEGGOSSU sausage dog
AADEGHHINS shanghaied
AADEGHIINR hearing aid
AADEGHNRTT death grant
AADEGILLNR grenadilla
AADEGILMNN leading man
AADEGILPRR paraglider
AADEGILRST saltigrade
AADEGILTTY agitatedly
AADEGINRRS disarrange
AADEGLNQRU quadrangle
AADEGLNSTW sweat gland
AADEGMRRTU dramaturge
AADEGNOPRR grand opera
AADEGNSSUU unassuaged
AADEHIIMNR maidenhair
AADEHIINRT antheridia
AADEHILNNT lanthanide
AADEHILORR diarrhoeal
AADEHKMRRT thread mark
AADEHLLMRS marshalled
AADEHLNNPR panhandler
AADEHMMMNO Mohammedan
AADEHMNRST master hand
AADEHRRSTW earthwards
AADEIILNOT ideational
AADEIILNTV invalidate
AADEIIMNNR Amerindian
AADEIIMNNT diamantine
AADEIIMNST mediastina
AADEIINPPR India paper
AADEILLRRS serradilla
AADEILMNNR mainlander
AADEILMNTY animatedly
AADEILMORT tailor-made
AADEILMRTX taxidermal
AADEILNNSW Waldensian
AADEILNNUZ annualized
AADEILNRSU unsalaried
AADEILORST asteroidal
AADEIMMNOT ammoniated
AADEIMNRTV animadvert
AADEINNOPT antipodean
AADEINNQRU quadrennia
AADEINPQSU pasquinade
AADEINQTTU antiquated
AADEINRSTT antitrades
AADEIOPQRU radiopaque
AADEJNORST Oranjestad
AADEKLMORW meadowlark
AADEKMORSS damask rose
AADEKMRRTT dark matter
AADELLLNOS soldanella
AADELLMORT mortadella
AADELLNPTT platteland
AADELLORSV El Salvador
AADELLPRUV Valledupar
AADELMNORW alderwoman
AADELMOSTW salt meadow
AADELNNOST stand-alone
AADELNNSUY unanalysed
AADELNNUYZ unanalyzed
AADELNOPRS personal ad
AADELNRTTU adulterant
AADELORSVW aardwolves
AADELRSTWY eastwardly
AADENNRTTU denaturant
AADENPPSSW passed pawn
AADEORSTTV devastator
AADEQRRTUU quadrature
AADEQRRTUY quarter day
AADFILRSTU fruit salad
AADGGIIMNR diagraming
AADGGILMNY damagingly
AADGHIOPRR radiograph
AADGHIPRSY dysgraphia
AADGIIIRSS giardiasis
AADGIIMNRR ram-raiding
AADGIINNRT grant-in-aid
AADGIINOTV divagation
AADGIJMNNU Mudanjiang
AADGIJNRUU jaguarundi
AADGILLNNS sandalling
AADGILLNOY diagonally

AADGILMNSU salmagundi
AADGILMRSU gradualism
AADGILPSUV Daugavpils
AADGILRSTU gradualist
AADGINNOPR grand piano
AADGINORTU graduation
AADGLNORTT grand total
AADGMRRTUY dramaturgy
AADGMRSSTU mustard gas
AADGNNOPRS snapdragon
AADGNOPRTU Punta Gorda
AADGNPPPRY grandpappy
AADHIKPRZZ Pazardzhik
AADHILNNOT lanthanoid
AADHILRTWW withdrawal
AADHIMNORY hydromania
AADHINOPSU diaphanous
AADHINORSW rain shadow
AADIIKKKRU Karaikkudi
AADIILNOTT dilatation
AADIILNOTV validation
AADIILNPRW Rawalpindi
AADIILORTU auditorial
AADIIMNOPS dipsomania
AADIIMNORT admiration
AADIIOPRST parasitoid
AADIIPRSST aspidistra
AADIJNORTU adjuration
AADILLMOPS plasmodial
AADILNORTU durational
AADIMNNOPR prima donna
AADIMNNRST sand martin
AADIOOPSSY oops-a-daisy
AADJMNNPRU panjandrum
AADJORRTUY adjuratory
AADKLLMORR dollar mark
AADLMNNNOS no man's land
AADLMNNRUY laundryman
AADLMNORTU laundromat
AADLMNPSUY Palm Sunday
AADMNOORSU anadromous
AADNOOPPSW sappanwood
AADNOPRRUW wraparound
AAEEEGGRTX exaggerate
AAEEEGNRRW wage earner
AAEEEHRSST heartsease
AAEEELMNRW enamelware
AAEEELNPRS paraselene
AAEEELRTUV re-evaluate
AAEEEMNNOS sea anemone
AAEEEPRSTX exasperate
AAEEERSSTV asseverate
AAEEFGIMRT after-image
AAEEFGLLLT flagellate
AAEEFGMRSW sewage farm
AAEEFHRSTV aftershave
AAEEFKKQSU Kafkaesque
AAEEFKLMRT flea market
AAEEFLRSSV Lassa fever
AAEEFNRRST Far Eastern
AAEEFRSTTT aftertaste
AAEEGGMSTU steam gauge
AAEEGGRTUW water gauge
AAEEGHLPRY harpy eagle
AAEEGIKMMR mage-maker
AAEEGILNNV Evangelina
AAEEGIMRRR remarriage
AAEEGIMSSX Sexagesima
AAEEGINPRT repaginate
AAEEGINRTV vegetarian
AAEEGKLRST Great Lakes
AAEEGLNRRY regnal year
AAEEGLNTWY tawny eagle
AAEEGLRRVY early grave
AAEEGMMNNT management
AAEEGMMORR aerogramme
AAEEGMNRSS manageress
AAEEGNORST East Orange
AAEEGNPRRR pre-arrange
AAEEGNRSTU guarantees
AAEEGNSSSV savageness
AAEEGQRRTU quarterage
AAEEHILRTX exhilarate
AAEEHIMPRY hyperaemia
AAEEHINSST anesthesia
AAEEHIPRSS aphaeresis
AAEEHIRSTW washeteria
AAEEHKQRTU earthquake
AAEEHLLRTW all-weather
AAEEHLMTVY heavy metal
AAEEHLNTTT latent heat
AAEEHLNTVX hexavalent
AAEEHMNORR amenorrhea
AAEEHMNRTW weatherman
AAEEHMPRST metaphrase
AAEEHMPRTW weather map
AAEEHRRSTW shearwater
AAEEHRTVWY heavy water
AAEEIJMNST jasmine tea
AAEEIKLMNS seamanlike
AAEEILLMNN nail enamel
AAEEILLNST lateen sail
AAEEILLRTT alliterate
AAEEILMNNS Melanesian
AAEEILMORT ameliorate
AAEEILNPRT penetralia
AAEEILRTTV alterative
AAEEILTUVV evaluative
AAEEIMNRRW Weimaraner
AAEEIOPRRS opera seria
AAEEIPPRRS reappraise
AAEEIPRRTT repatriate
AAEEIPRRTV reparative
AAEEIPRSTV separative
AAEEIPRTTX expatriate
AAEEKKWWYY wakey-wakey
AAEEKLMPRT platemaker
AAEEKMPPRR papermaker
AAEELLNRTT tarantelle
AAEELLPRTY platelayer
AAEELLTTTT tattle-tale
AAEELMPRTY team player
AAEELMQRSU square meal
AAEELMRRTT maltreater
AAEELNPRRT parenteral
AAEELNPRST pleasanter
AAEELNPRTT tea planter
AAEELPRSTY separately
AAEELSSTTV Slave State
AAEEMMNRRT rearmament
AAEEMNNSSU amanuenses
AAEEMSSSTT metastases
AAEEPPRSTW waste paper
AAEEQRSUVW square wave
AAEFFHLLMO Hall of Fame
AAEFFILORV love affair
AAEFGIISTT fastigiate
AAEFGINNPR frangipane
AAEFGLLLNT flagellant
AAEFGLLRST Great Falls
AAEFGLMNRT fragmental
AAEFGLORWW wager of law
AAEFHHLMRT health farm
AAEFHINRTT faint heart
AAEFHLLRYY half-yearly
AAEFIILRSS filariases
AAEFILLNRX fraxinella
AAEFILMMNY family name
AAEFIMRRRT terra firma
AAEFINPRST afterpains
AAEFKLOPSS soap flakes
AAEFLLNSTU fustanella
AAEFLMPSTY safety lamp
AAEFLOPSTT soft palate
AAEFLOPSTZ false topaz
AAEFLRSSTT false start
AAEFORSTTW state of war
AAEGGGLNUV luggage van
AAEGGILNSW Glaswegian
AAEGGNORRT great organ
AAEGGPRRSU grape-sugar
AAEGHILLSS Galashiels
AAEGHINNNS shenanigan
AAEGHKLNRS angel-shark
AAEGHLNOPT heptagonal
AAEGHLNPRY pharyngeal
AAEGHMNOPR anemograph, phanerogam
AAEGHPPPRR graph paper
AAEGHRSSTW wheatgrass
AAEGIILPRZ plagiarize
AAEGIINNTV invaginate
AAEGIINRTT ingratiate
AAEGIIPRST epigastria
AAEGIKLMPR magpie lark
AAEGILLMNO galia melon
AAEGILLMNT ligamental
AAEGILLNOT allegation
AAEGILMNRT martingale
AAEGILMSTT stalagmite
AAEGILNNTT tangential
AAEGILNPPR appareling

AAEGILNRVZ galvanizer
AAEGILNSWX sealing wax
AAEGILOPRZ paralogize
AAEGILPPRS Paris-Plage
AAEGIMNRRV margravine
AAEGIMPRTZ pragmatize
AAEGIMRRTU Marguerita
AAEGIMRSTT magistrate
AAEGINNOTZ antagonize
AAEGINNSTU nauseating
AAEGINRTUU inaugurate
AAEGKLMRSS glassmaker
AAEGKLNORW Orange Walk
AAEGKLNSSS glass snake
AAEGKNRSSS grass snake
AAEGLLPSST plate glass
AAEGLMORSU megalosaur
AAEGLMPRSU maple sugar, sugar maple
AAEGLNNOPT pentagonal
AAEGLNORTT tetragonal
AAEGLPPRSS glasspaper
AAEGLRSSTW water-glass
AAEGMNORST steam organ
AAEGMOPRSU rampageous
AAEGNORTWW water wagon
AAEHHINOPT Theophania
AAEHHJLLLU hallelujah
AAEHHJOPST Jehosaphat
AAEHHKLRSW whale shark
AAEHHLPRTY hypaethral
AAEHIILNNT annihilate
AAEHIIMNOP hemianopia
AAEHIIPSTT hepatitis A
AAEHIKMNSZ Ashkenazim
AAEHIKRRST hairstreak
AAEHILNOTX exhalation
AAEHILNRTX exhilarant
AAEHILRSTW heirs-at-law
AAEHIMNPSS seamanship
AAEHIMNSTY myasthenia
AAEHIMOPXY hypoxaemia
AAEHIMRSTU amateurish
AAEHINNORV Hanoverian
AAEHINPSTZ phantasize
AAEHIPSTXY asphyxiate
AAEHKLRSST salt shaker
AAEHLLMRRS marshaller
AAEHLMPSTU sulphamate
AAEHLPSSTW swash-plate
AAEHMNORRT marathoner
AAEHMNRSST harassment
AAEHMNRSTV harvestman
AAEHMOSTTY stay-at-home
AAEHNOPRST anastrophe
AAEHNPRSTY pheasantry
AAEIILLPTV palliative
AAEIILMMRT immaterial
AAEIILMSST assimilate
AAEIILNNOT alienation
AAEIILNNST salientian
AAEIILNPST sapiential
AAEIILPSTZ spatialize
AAEIIMNNRS seminarian
AAEIIMNNRT maintainer
AAEIIMPPRR primiparae
AAEIIPPRSV appraisive
AAEIIPRSTZ parasitize
AAEILLLRST saltarelli
AAEILLMRTY materially
AAEILLNORT relational
AAEILLNRTU unilateral
AAEILLORTV alleviator
AAEILLRRTT trilateral
AAEILLRTVY varietally
AAEILMNNSU semi-annual
AAEILMNPRT parliament
AAEILMNPTU manipulate
AAEILMNRSU aneurismal
AAEILMNRTY alimentary
AAEILMNRWX mineral wax
AAEILMPRRT premarital
AAEILNNOPT Neapolitan
AAEILNNOTV venational
AAEILNOQTU equational
AAEILNORST senatorial
AAEILNORTT alteration
AAEILNORTX relaxation
AAEILNOTTX exaltation
AAEILNOTUV evaluation
AAEILNRRVW new arrival
AAEILNRTTZ tantalizer
AAEILNRTUZ naturalize
AAEILOPRRT praetorial
AAEILOQRTU equatorial
AAEILORRTT retaliator
AAEILPRTVW private law
AAEILQRSSU square sail
AAEILRSTTT state trial
AAEILSSTTV saliva test
AAEILSSTUV assaultive
AAEILSTUXY asexuality
AAEIMMNRST mainstream
AAEIMMRSTU amateurism
AAEIMNNOPR Pomeranian
AAEIMNNOSY mayonnaise
AAEIMNNSSU amanuensis
AAEIMNNTTT attainment
AAEIMNOORT erotomania
AAEIMNRSTT steam train
AAEIMNRTTT antimatter
AAEIMOTTUZ automatize
AAEIMPRSST separatism
AAEIMQRSTU marquisate
AAEIMRTTUV maturative
AAEIMRTTUZ traumatize
AAEIMSSSTT metastasis
AAEINNNOTX annexation
AAEINNOTTV annotative
AAEINNQRTU quarantine
AAEINOPRRT praetorian, reparation
AAEINOPRST separation
AAEINOPSST passionate
AAEINOSTVX tax evasion
AAEINPPRST satin paper
AAEINRRTTZ tartrazine
AAEIOPSTTZ apostatize
AAEIPRRTVW private war
AAEIPRSSTT separatist
AAEKMMRSST mass market
AAEKMRSSTT taskmaster
AAEKRRSTUU sauerkraut
AAELLLMNOS salmonella
AAELLLORST saltarello
AAELLMNOPS salmon-leap
AAELLMNRTY maternally
AAELLMORZZ mozzarella
AAELLMPQTU Malplaquet
AAELLNOPRS solar panel
AAELLNOSSY seasonally
AAELLNPRTY parentally, paternally, prenatally
AAELLNPSTY pleasantly
AAELLRSTTT tattersall
AAELMNNORT ornamental
AAELMNOPSU menopausal
AAELMNOSSW saleswoman
AAELMNRRTW trawlerman
AAELMNRSUY aneurysmal
AAELMRRTUX extramural
AAELNNNPRU penannular
AAELNNOPST Pleasanton
AAELNNOSSU unseasonal
AAELNNPSTU unpleasant
AAELNORRTT alternator
AAELNPPRTY apparently
AAELNPRRSU suprarenal
AAELNPRSTT transeptal
AAELNPRSTY pleasantry
AAELNRSTUX transexual
AAELOOPSTT apostolate
AAELOPRSST pastorales
AAELORSTTZ lazarettos
AAELOSTTWY lay waste to
AAELPRRSTU superaltar
AAELPRRTTT rattletrap
AAELSTTTUW statute law
AAEMNNORTT tramontane
AAEMNNRSTV manservant
AAEMNOOSST anastomose
AAEMPPPRST stamp paper
AAEMPRSSTT past master
AAEMRRSSTT star stream
AAEMRSSTTU metatarsus
AAENNPPRTU unapparent
AAENOOPPRT propanoate
AAENORRSSW narrow seas
AAENORTTTU attenuator
AAENORTUUV art nouveau
AAENPSSTTW sweatpants
AAENQRRTUY quaternary
AAENRRSTTU restaurant
AAEOOPRRTV evaporator
AAEOORTTTU autorotate
AAEOPRRSTY separatory
AAFFGIMNRU ragamuffin
AAFFIINOTX affixation
AAFGGILNVW flag-waving
AAFGIINNPR frangipani

AAFGLLNRTY flagrantly
AAFGLLOSST float glass
AAFGLNNRTY granny flat
AAFGLNRRTY fragrantly
AAFIIILRSS filariasis
AAFIILLMRY familiarly
AAFIILMNRU unfamiliar
AAFIINRRTU fruitarian
AAFIINRTVY Vanity Fair
AAFIIRSSTU safari suit
AAFILNOOTT floatation
AAFIMOORRS afrormosia
AAFIOQRSTU aqua fortis
AAFMNOORST sonata form
AAFMNORSTW man of straw
AAGGIILLNN ilang-ilang
AAGGLLNNYY ylang-ylang
AAGHHIMNWY highwayman
AAGHIKPRSY skiagraphy
AAGHILMNRS marshaling
AAGHILMNSW Walsingham
AAGHILNPST Phalangist
AAGHILORTY hagiolatry
AAGHNOPPRT pantograph
AAGHOPRTUY autography
AAGIIKLMNS sailmaking
AAGIIKMNNR rainmaking
AAGIILMPRS plagiarism
AAGIILNNUV unavailing
AAGIILPRST plagiarist
AAGIINNOPT pagination
AAGIINNOTV navigation
AAGILLMNRY alarmingly, marginally
AAGILLNNOT Anglo-Latin
AAGILLORSS glossarial
AAGILMOPRS paralogism
AAGILNNNRU annual ring
AAGILNNOQU Algonquian
AAGILNOORT rogational
AAGILNOPRS sporangial
AAGILNRRTU triangular
AAGILNRTUY angularity
AAGILOPRST paralogist
AAGILOSUVY Yugoslavia
AAGIMMPRST pragmatism
AAGIMNNOST antagonism
AAGIMNNPRW warming-pan
AAGIMNRSST Gram's stain
AAGIMPRRST stripagram
AAGIMPRSTT pragmatist
AAGINNOOPR piano organ
AAGINNORTW wagon train
AAGINNOSTT antagonist, stagnation
AAGINNRSUY sanguinary
AAGINOORRT arrogation
AAGINOSSTT gas station
AAGINRRTVY gravy train
AAGLLNOPTT topgallant
AAGLLNRRUY granularly
AAGLNNOOSX Anglo-Saxon
AAGLNNSTTY stagnantly
AAGLNOOORW angora wool
AAGLNOOSTY Satanology
AAGLNORRTU granulator
AAGLNORRTY arrogantly
AAGLNOTUVW wagon-vault
AAGMOOSTUU autogamous
AAGOOPPRRT propagator
AAGOOPSUYY pay-as-you-go
AAGORRRSSW arrow-grass
AAHHILMOPT ophthalmia
AAHHILORST aloha shirt
AAHHIMRRTY arrhythmia
AAHIILNNOT inhalation
AAHIILNNTU Lithuanian
AAHIIMPRSS Pharisaism
AAHILLOPRT prothallia
AAHILMNSTU Malthusian
AAHILMTTUZ altazimuth
AAHILNNOPS Alphonsina
AAHILNNOPT antiphonal
AAHIMMNOTY mythomania
AAHINPSTXY asphyxiant
AAHKKNNPYY hanky-panky
AAHKLOORSY Yoshkar-Ola
AAHLLLLOSW All Hallows
AAHLMMOPTY lymphomata
AAHNOPRTTU naturopath
AAHOPRRRSZ razor-sharp
AAIIILLMNW Williamina
AAIIILMMNT militiaman
AAIIILMMNX Maximillan
AAIIJKNSTT Tajikistan
AAIIJLNORT janitorial
AAIIKLLNTY alkalinity
AAIILLMTUX multiaxial
AAIILLNOPT palliation
AAIILLNUXY uniaxially
AAIILMMSTX maximalist
AAIILMNNOT antimonial, lamination
AAIILNORRT irrational
AAIILNOSTV salivation
AAIILNRSTY sanitarily
AAIILPPRSS paralipsis
AAIILPRTTY partiality, patriality
AAIILPSTTY spatiality
AAIIMNNNOT antinomian
AAIIMNNORT maintainor, marination
AAIIMNRSTU sanitarium
AAIIMPRSST parasitism
AAIINNOPTT patination
AAIINNOSTT sanitation
AAIINNRRTU Ruritanian
AAIINNRSTY insanitary
AAIINOPPRT apparition
AAIINOPRST aspiration
AAIIRSSSTY satyriasis
AAILLLOPVW pillow lava
AAILLLPSTU pulsatilla
AAILLMOPPS papillomas
AAILLNNOOP Apollonian
AAILLNNOTY nationally
AAILLNNSTT installant
AAILLNOPST spallation
AAILLNORTY notarially, rationally
AAILMNOTTU mutational
AAILMNRRTU intramural
AAILMNRSTU naturalism
AAILMORRTY Mariolatry
AAILNNNOTU annulation
AAILNNOOTT notational
AAILNNOPTT plantation
AAILNOORTT rotational
AAILNOPTTV pot-valiant
AAILNOSTTU salutation
AAILNRSTTU naturalist
AAILNSSSTU Stanislaus
AAIMMOSTTU automatism
AAIMMRSTTU traumatism
AAIMNOOTTU automation
AAIMNOPTTU amputation
AAIMNORSTU sanatorium
AAIMNORTTU maturation, natatorium
AAINNNOOST San Antonio
AAINNNOOTT annotation
AAINNRSTUY unsanitary
AAINOPSTTY pay station
AAINOQRTUZ quatorzain
AAINORSTTU saturation
AAINORSTTV starvation
AAINORSTTY stationary
AAINOSTTWY way station
AAINPPRSTY spray-paint
AAKKMORRST Kramatorsk
AAKLMNNOSW Klanswoman
AAKLNORSUY ankylosaur
AAKMMNORSS mason's mark
AALLLLNNUU nulla-nulla
AALLLLOTWW wall-to-wall
AALLMNORUY monaurally
AALLOOSTTY loyal toast
AALLOPRSTY pastorally
AALLRSTTWY stalwartly
AALMOOPPRS malapropos
AALMOOPRTY laparotomy
AALMOPRSXY paroxysmal
AALMPQRTUZ quartz lamp
AALNNNORTU non-natural
AALNNPRSTT transplant
AALNNRRSTU translunar
AALNOPRSST transposal
AALNORRSTT translator
AALNPRTTUY play truant
AALORSTTUY salutatory
AAMNNOTTTU tantamount
AAMNOOSTTU automatons
AAMORSSSUU mosasaurus
AAOOPPRRST paratroops
ABBBBEHLTU bubble bath
ABBBCEILNO bobbin lace

ABBBCEKLPU bubble pack
ABBBDENRRU rubber band
ABBBEELMNT babblement
ABBBEILNRU unbribable
ABBBELPRUW bubble wrap
ABBBEMOORY baby boomer
ABBCCKKLOS backblocks
ABBCDEEHMR bedchamber
ABBCDEMRRU breadcrumb
ABBCDKLOOR blockboard
ABBCDKMOUY Bombay duck
ABBCEELORW bower-cable
ABBCEFHIIR Chief Rabbi
ABBCEGGHUY beach buggy
ABBCEGINRU barbecuing
ABBCEIKLOR back boiler
ABBCEILMNO combinable
ABBCEINRSS crabbiness
ABBCEINSSS scabbiness
ABBCEJLLOT object-ball
ABBCEKKLOR brake block
ABBCEKLRRY blackberry
ABBCEKMNRU back number
ABBCELLOTU cobalt blue
ABBCENORSY absorbency
ABBCFGINNO confabbing
ABBCGIIKNT backbiting
ABBCHHOOTY booby-hatch
ABBCIILLLY biblically
ABBCIILLNU unbiblical
ABBCIKORRT rock rabbit
ABBCIMMOOT atomic bomb
ABBCKNOTTU button-back
ABBDDEEILO able-bodied
ABBDDEILNU unbiddable
ABBDEEGILR bridgeable
ABBDEEHLPS pebble-dash
ABBDEEIRRW barbed wire
ABBDEEKNOR doner kebab
ABBDEFIORR fiberboard, fibreboard
ABBDEILLOR Barbie doll
ABBDEILOUY Douay Bible
ABBDEIMORR bombardier
ABBDELLNRU landlubber
ABBDELORSY absorbedly
ABBDELOSSU double bass
ABBDENORSU unabsorbed
ABBDHORRSU broad-brush
ABBEEEILLV believable
ABBEEEKLRT bark beetle
ABBEEGNRTT Battenberg
ABBEEILPPR Bible paper
ABBEELORSV observable
ABBEELRTTU rebuttable
ABBEENORST breastbone
ABBEENRTTU butter-bean
ABBEEORRTW browbeater
ABBEFILNSS flabbiness
ABBEGJLSUU subjugable
ABBEGKLNOT blanket bog
ABBEHHIKSS shish kebab
ABBEHINSSS shabbiness
ABBEHOPRRS barber-shop
ABBEHRSSUY rhesus baby
ABBEILMOPR improbable
ABBEIQSSTU squabbiest
ABBEIRSTTY babysitter
ABBEKLNOTT bottle bank
ABBELLRTTU butterball
ABBELMOORZ bamboozler
ABBELMSSUU subsumable
ABBELORSVY observably
ABBFFIILMU bum-bailiff
ABBFILORST fibroblast
ABBHILMSUU Lubumbashi
ABBILMOPRY improbably
ABBILORSTU sub-orbital
ABCCDIIMOR bromic acid
ABCCEEILMP impeccable
ABCCEEILSS accessible
ABCCEEKNRT centre-back
ABCCEELLRY recyclable
ABCCEEPRSY cyberspace
ABCCEGIKRT cricket bag
ABCCEIKLPR place brick
ABCCEILMPY impeccably
ABCCEILSSY accessibly
ABCCEKNORR cornerback
ABCCHIILMO choliambic
ABCCHIIMOR choriambic
ABCCHIIRRT tribrachic
ABCCHIKLPT pitch-black
ABCCHIKQSU squab-chick
ABCCHIKSTT backstitch
ABCCHIKSTW switchback
ABCCHILOTU coach-built
ABCCHIOOPR acrophobic
ABCCILNOSU subconical
ABCCINORTU buccinator
ABCCINORTY corybantic
ABCCKLLOUY cockabully
ABCCNOOPRY carbon copy
ABCDDEFIKL fiddle-back
ABCDEEEILV deceivable
ABCDEEELLT delectable
ABCDEEELTT detectable
ABCDEEHLNU unbleached
ABCDEEHRUY debauchery
ABCDEEILLN declinable
ABCDEEILNU ineducable
ABCDEEILPR predicable
ABCDEEILPS despicable
ABCDEEILRT creditable
ABCDEEKLRV backvelder
ABCDEELLNY belly dance
ABCDEELLTY delectably
ABCDEELLUX excludable
ABCDEELMRS descramble
ABCDEELNUU uneducable
ABCDEELORR recordable
ABCDEELTTY detectably
ABCDEERRTU carbureted
ABCDEGIORT Coatbridge
ABCDEGKMOS gobsmacked
ABCDEHILSU child abuse
ABCDEHKMPU humpbacked
ABCDEHLNUW Buchenwald
ABCDEHORSS chessboard
ABCDEHORSY body search
ABCDEIILMO biomedical
ABCDEIILNT indictable
ABCDEIILNV vindicable
ABCDEIIRSS sacred ibis
ABCDEIKLRS backslider
ABCDEIKOUV bivouacked
ABCDEILLPU duplicable
ABCDEILPSY despicably
ABCDEILRTY creditably
ABCDEINORY binary code
ABCDEIPRRS crispbread, spider crab
ABCDEIRSUV scuba-diver
ABCDEJKOOT jackbooted
ABCDELLORY local derby
ABCDELMNRU Cumberland
ABCDEOORRS scoreboard
ABCDEORSTU subcordate
ABCDGKNORU background
ABCDHIILNR brainchild
ABCDHINNRU nudibranch
ABCDHIOOPR brachiopod
ABCDHLOORT broadcloth
ABCDIILLSY disyllabic
ABCDIILNNU Indian club
ABCDIISTUY subacidity
ABCDIKLOWW black widow
ABCEEEEFLL fleeceable
ABCEEEFFNO coffee bean
ABCEEEIKRR ice-breaker
ABCEEEILRV receivable
ABCEEEJLRT rejectable
ABCEEELLRR beer cellar, cerebellar
ABCEEELLST selectable
ABCEEELNRS screenable
ABCEEELPTX expectable
ABCEEELTUX executable
ABCEEENRUX exuberance
ABCEEFHNNR French bean
ABCEEFIILN beneficial
ABCEEFNORT benefactor
ABCEEHHKSS backsheesh
ABCEEHKLPS black sheep
ABCEEHLLRY bellyacher
ABCEEHLNQU quenchable
ABCEEHLNSU Chelsea bun
ABCEEHNORR abhorrence
ABCEEHORSU herbaceous
ABCEEIJLNT injectable
ABCEEIKLNR linebacker
ABCEEILLNR reclinable
ABCEEILLNS licensable
ABCEEILLPR replicable
ABCEEILLPX explicable
ABCEEILMMT emblematic
ABCEEILNOT noticeable
ABCEEILRTX extricable
ABCEEINNST abstinence

ABCEEJKLTU bluejacket
ABCEEJNSST abjectness
ABCEEKLOPT pocketable
ABCEEKRSTT backstreet
ABCEEKSTTU bucket seat
ABCEELLRRY cerebrally
ABCEELNNOV convenable
ABCEELNOVY conveyable
ABCEELNRSU censurable
ABCEELOPRU recoupable
ABCEELOPRW pace bowler
ABCEELORRT celebrator
ABCEENORSV observance
ABCEEOPPRS space probe
ABCEFHILMT flitch beam
ABCEFHINRZ zebra finch
ABCEFHNORT beachfront
ABCEFLNOSU confusable
ABCEFRSSUU subsurface
ABCEGIKNRT bracketing
ABCEGILNOZ cognizable
ABCEGINNNY benignancy
ABCEGKLOSW swage-block
ABCEHHJOTT hatchet job
ABCEHIIRST Hebraistic
ABCEHIKLNR branchlike
ABCEHILPRT birthplace
ABCEHILRST Christabel
ABCEHILSTW switchable
ABCEHIMNRT Chambertin
ABCEHIMRRT hermit crab
ABCEHINORR chair-borne
ABCEHIPRRY hyperbaric
ABCEHJKSTU bush jacket
ABCEHLLOOS schoolable
ABCEHLLOTT tablecloth
ABCEHLMOOP peach-bloom
ABCEHMMNRU Mach number
ABCEHMOPRT chamber pot
ABCEHORTTX chatterbox
ABCEIILLMT bimetallic
ABCEIILLNR brilliance
ABCEIILMTU umbilicate
ABCEIINTUV incubative
ABCEIJLOTV objectival
ABCEIKKSTY stickybeak
ABCEIKLRRY bricklayer
ABCEILLNOU inoculable
ABCEILLNRS cranesbill
ABCEILLTUV cultivable
ABCEILMOPT compatible
ABCEILNOPU uncopiable
ABCEILNOSU unsociable
ABCEILNOTY noticeably
ABCEILNPRU republican
ABCEILNRRU incurrable
ABCEILORTU orbiculate
ABCEIMOORT Coimbatore
ABCEIMORRT barometric
ABCEINRRST transcribe
ABCEJKLMRU lumberjack
ABCEKKORST backstroke
ABCEKLLOWY yellowback
ABCEKLNNPY penny black
ABCEKLOPRW black power
ABCELLLORU blue-collar
ABCELLNOOR collarbone
ABCELLNOOS consolable
ABCELLOORU colourable
ABCELMMNOO commonable
ABCELMMOTU commutable
ABCELMNOSU consumable
ABCELMNRSU unscramble
ABCELMOPTU computable
ABCELNORRY barleycorn
ABCELNRSUU sub-nuclear
ABCELOPRRU procurable
ABCELRRTUU tubercular
ABCEMTUUUV vacuum tube
ABCENNNNOO cannon-bone
ABCENNORRU Cranbourne
ABCENNSTUY subtenancy
ABCENRRTUY canterbury
ABCEOORRST Serbo-Croat
ABCEORRRTU carburetor
ABCERRSTTU subtracter
ABCFKLORST black frost
ABCGHIINOT cohabiting
ABCGHIIOPR biographic
ABCGHIKLLT black light
ABCGHIKMNU Buckingham
ABCGHLORYY brachylogy
ABCGHNRSSU bunch grass
ABCGIILLOO biological
ABCGILNOYZ cognizably
ABCHHIOPRS archbishop
ABCHIILOPS basophilic
ABCHIKLMST blacksmith
ABCHIKLRST blackshirt
ABCHIMORSU choriambus
ABCHKLNORT blackthorn
ABCIIINOTT antibiotic
ABCIIJMNOS Jacobinism
ABCIIJMOST Jacobitism
ABCIILLNOY bionically
ABCIILLNRY brilliancy
ABCIILLSST ballistics
ABCIILRTUY curability
ABCIIMNOSS ambisonics
ABCIIMRSST strabismic
ABCIINNOTU incubation
ABCIINOSSS abscission
ABCIKLLORY rockabilly
ABCIKLORVY ivory black
ABCILLMOSY symbolical
ABCILLRTUU bicultural
ABCILMOPTY compatibly
ABCILMOSUX musical box
ABCILMRUUV vibraculum
ABCILNORSU binoculars
ABCILNOSUY unsociably
ABCILORRTU lubricator
ABCINORTUY incubatory
ABCIORRRTU rubricator
ABCKKNOOTU knockabout
ABCKNPRTUY bankruptcy
ABCLLOORUY colourably
ABCLORRTUU lucubrator
ABCLORRTUY Rotary club
ABCLORSSUY scabrously
ABCMOOPSSW bow-compass
ABCORRSTTU subtractor
ABDDEEEFLN defendable
ABDDEEEHNO boneheaded
ABDDEEELNP dependable
ABDDEEGHIR bridgehead
ABDDEEHLLU bull-headed
ABDDEEIRTT bearded tit
ABDDEELNPY dependably
ABDDEGILNR land bridge
ABDDEGINRU unabridged
ABDDEGIRRW drawbridge
ABDDEHHINN behindhand
ABDDEHILOR hard-boiled
ABDDEHNORY hard-done-by
ABDDEIIMRS bridesmaid
ABDDELNORR borderland
ABDDGIINRW wading bird
ABDDHLNOOY bloody hand
ABDDHNRSUY dandy brush
ABDDIIOORT idiot board
ABDDLMOORU mould-board
ABDDNOORSU soundboard
ABDDOORRSW broadsword
ABDEEEELMR redeemable
ABDEEEFHRT feather bed
ABDEEEFILS defeasible
ABDEEEFLRR deferrable
ABDEEEFRST breastfeed
ABDEEEGLLP pledgeable
ABDEEEGNRR beer garden
ABDEEEILMR remediable
ABDEEEILRT deliberate
ABDEEELLLR relabelled
ABDEEELNPX expendable
ABDEEELNRZ land breeze
ABDEEELNTX extendable
ABDEEELRYY bleary-eyed
ABDEEELSTT detestable
ABDEEEMNST debasement
ABDEEENRTT Bernadette
ABDEEERSTW sweetbread
ABDEEFFHLU bufflehead
ABDEEFHNOR beforehand
ABDEEFILSY defeasibly
ABDEEFLMOR deformable
ABDEEFLNRU refundable
ABDEEFOORT barefooted
ABDEEGHIRT big-hearted
ABDEEGHRRR herb Gerard
ABDEEGLORT gold-beater
ABDEEHIKNR Birkenhead
ABDEEHILLV ill-behaved
ABDEEHILPS beadleship
ABDEEHILRR halberdier
ABDEEHNNOT bonnethead
ABDEEHORSS shore-based

ABDEEHORST broadsheet
ABDEEIILTT debilitate
ABDEEIKNNY kidney bean
ABDEEILLMR mallee bird
ABDEEILNNU undeniable
ABDEEILNRU unrideable
ABDEEILPRV deprivable
ABDEEIMNTY amenity bed
ABDEEKLOOS sealed book
ABDEEKLOTU double take
ABDEEKORRY keyboarder
ABDEELLLNU unlabelled
ABDEELLMRU umbrellaed
ABDEELLOPR deplorable
ABDEELLORS solderable
ABDEELLSTY sell-by date
ABDEELMRRU demurrable
ABDEELNOPR ponderable
ABDEELNORS endorsable
ABDEELNPXY expendably
ABDEELOPRT deportable
ABDEELORTT battledore
ABDEELPRRU perdurable
ABDEELSTTY detestably
ABDEEMOOOR oboe d'amore
ABDEEMORRY emery board
ABDEEMRRSU embrasured
ABDEENOPSU subpoenaed
ABDEENPRRY prebendary
ABDEFHNOOP Band of Hope
ABDEFIILMO modifiable
ABDEFIIMRT fimbriated
ABDEFIKLRU brake fluid
ABDEFIKNOR knife-board
ABDEFILMOR formidable
ABDEFIRRTU breadfruit
ABDEFLNORU unfordable
ABDEGGIRRU budgerigar
ABDEGHINSU sub-heading
ABDEGIMNRT abridgment
ABDEGIRRTW Bridgwater
ABDEGLNPTU budget plan
ABDEHIILLS dishabille
ABDEHILNSU Danish blue
ABDEHILPRT bridle path
ABDEHINRRS brandisher
ABDEHINRTT hardbitten
ABDEHIORTW whiteboard
ABDEHLMOOV movable-doh
ABDEHNORTU earthbound
ABDEHNRSTU subtrahend
ABDEHNRTUY Thunder Bay
ABDEHORRST shortbread
ABDEHOSUWY bawdy house
ABDEIIKLLS dislikable
ABDEIILMPS bipedalism
ABDEIILMSS admissible
ABDEIILOXZ oxidizable
ABDEIILPTY bipedality
ABDEIITTUV dubitative
ABDEILLLNY blind alley
ABDEILLLSY disyllable
ABDEILMNRT timberland
ABDEILNNUY undeniably
ABDEILNOPY pineal body
ABDEILNORY debonairly
ABDEILNOSU Adonis blue
ABDEILNRSV silver band
ABDEILOPSS disposable
ABDEILPSTU disputable
ABDEILRTTW wattlebird
ABDEIMNRST disbarment
ABDEIMNSTU submediant
ABDEIMORRT mitre board
ABDEIMRTUW dumb waiter
ABDEJORSTT objets d'art
ABDEKLLOTU double-talk
ABDEKLOPRU double-park
ABDELLOPRY deplorably
ABDELLOPUY double play
ABDELLOSTU double salt
ABDELMNRUU dual number
ABDELNORTU Round Table
ABDELNORUU unlaboured
ABDELOORST stable door
ABDELORSTU double star
ABDELORTUY obdurately
ABDELPRRUY perdurably
ABDEMORRWY body warmer
ABDENOOPRS spoon-bread
ABDENRSSSU absurdness
ABDENSSTUY Sunday best
ABDEOORRTT otter-board
ABDEORRSWY worry beads
ABDERRTTYY dry battery
ABDFGOORSX Oxford bags
ABDFILMORY formidably
ABDFILNORU floribunda
ABDFLOOORR floorboard
ABDGHIIINT adhibiting
ABDGIINPRU upbraiding
ABDGIINRRS disbarring
ABDGINORTU groundbait
ABDGLLNOTU bulldog ant
ABDGLOORSU blood sugar
ABDGNNNORY granny bond
ABDGNORSSU ground bass
ABDHIIINOT adhibition
ABDHILMOOR rhomboidal
ABDHINRTUY unbirthday
ABDIIILSTY disability
ABDIIILTUY audibility
ABDIILMNOU albuminoid
ABDIILORRT tailor-bird
ABDIILRTUY durability
ABDIINOTTU dubitation
ABDIIRSSUY subsidiary
ABDILNOOST bloodstain
ABDILNORSU subordinal
ABDILOORTY botryoidal
ABDILPSTUY disputably
ABDINOORST adsorbtion
ABDLLOOORY blood royal
ABDLMOORYY Bloody Mary
ABDNNOORTU baton round
ABDNOORTUU roundabout
ABDOORRSTY storyboard
ABDOORRTUU troubadour
ABEEEELLMT meal-beetle
ABEEEFIKLM make-belief
ABEEEFLPRR preferable
ABEEEGGLRS segregable
ABEEEGLSTT stag beetle
ABEEEHQRTU bequeather
ABEEEHRSTT hartebeest
ABEEEIKRRT tie-breaker
ABEEEILLRV relievable
ABEEEILRVW reviewable
ABEEELLLPX expellable
ABEEELLSTT settleable
ABEEELMNNT enablement
ABEEELMNRU enumerable
ABEEELMRSS reassemble
ABEEELNPRT penetrable
ABEEELQSUZ squeezable
ABEEELRRSV reservable
ABEEELRSTT resettable
ABEEEORSTT stereobate
ABEEERRSST Basseterre
ABEEERRTTV vertebrate
ABEEFFLMNT bafflement
ABEEFFLRSU sufferable
ABEEFGKNPR Kapfenberg
ABEEFHLRTT better half
ABEEFIILNS infeasible
ABEEFIILRV verifiable
ABEEFIIRTU beautifier
ABEEFIKLNT table knife
ABEEFILLLR refillable
ABEEFILLRT filterable
ABEEFILNOR Froebelian
ABEEFILNRR inferrable
ABEEFILNSU unfeasible
ABEEFILNTT flea-bitten
ABEEFINRRV brain fever
ABEEFKKLOR Beaker Folk
ABEEFKNRUU Kaufbeuren
ABEEFLMORR reformable
ABEEFLORRU free labour
ABEEFLORSW safe-blower
ABEEFLPRRY preferably
ABEEFLSTTY safety belt
ABEEFMOOTT beef tomato
ABEEGHLSUU bush league
ABEEGILLNR relabeling
ABEEGILNOT negotiable
ABEEGILNRT integrable
ABEEGILNSS Albigenses
ABEEGLNOPS spongeable
ABEEGLNORV governable
ABEEGLRRTT garter belt
ABEEGMMNNO gombeen man
ABEEHILLRS relishable
ABEEHILPRS perishable
ABEEHIMNTT Benthamite
ABEEHIRSTT breathiest
ABEEHKNORS boneshaker
ABEEHLMPRS blasphemer
ABEEHLOPRY hyperbolae

ABEEHLRSST breathless
ABEEHMORTT bathometer
ABEEHMRTTY bathymeter
ABEEHNORSU Oberhausen
ABEEHOORRS seborrhoea
ABEEHORSTU hereabouts
ABEEHORTTU thereabout
ABEEHPRRSY barysphere
ABEEHRSTTT breath test
ABEEHRSTTU shea-butter
ABEEIILLMN eliminable
ABEEIILLRZ liberalize
ABEEIILNPX inexpiable
ABEEIILNTV inevitable
ABEEIILSTZ bestialize
ABEEIIRRRZ bizarrerie
ABEEIKLLNU unlikeable
ABEEIKLNRT ankle-biter
ABEEIKNNRT barkentine
ABEEILLNNT table linen
ABEEILLNRU unreliable
ABEEILLNST listenable
ABEEILLRTT Little Bear
ABEEILMMOV immoveable
ABEEILMNRT terminable
ABEEILMOTT metabolite
ABEEILMOTZ metabolize
ABEEILMRTT remittable
ABEEILNNUV unenviable
ABEEILNOPR inoperable
ABEEILNORX inexorable
ABEEILNPSX expansible
ABEEILNRSS bleariness
ABEEILNRST insertable
ABEEILNSTV investable
ABEEILORTT obliterate
ABEEILPRRS respirable
ABEEILRRVZ verbalizer
ABEEILSSTT beastliest
ABEEILSSTW sweet basil
ABEEINRRTY binary tree
ABEEINRTUX exurbanite
ABEEJLLMSU jumble sale
ABEEJMMNNT enjambment
ABEEKLNRST Bernkastel
ABEEKLNRSV blank verse
ABEEKLNTTW wet blanket
ABEEKMMNNT embankment
ABEELLMNOT noble metal
ABEELLMNTU ante-bellum, Bluemantle
ABEELLMOPY employable
ABEELLNOUV unloveable
ABEELLNRUV vulnerable
ABEELLORSV resolvable
ABEELLSSSY baselessly
ABEELMMMNT embalmment
ABEELMNOUV unmoveable
ABEELMNRST resemblant
ABEELMNRSU mensurable
ABEELMNTTT battlement
ABEELMORSW seam bowler
ABEELMPRSU presumable
ABEELMRSSY reassembly
ABEELMRSTU rumble seat
ABEELNNOTU lunate bone
ABEELNOPRS personable
ABEELNQTTU blanquette
ABEELNRRTU returnable
ABEELNSTTU untestable
ABEELOOPPT boat people
ABEELOPRRT reportable
ABEELOPRRV reprovable
ABEELOPRTX exportable
ABEELORRST restorable
ABEEMNRUVW wave number
ABEENNRRSS barrenness
ABEENNRSSZ brazenness
ABEENORRTW water-borne
ABEENORSTU Eastbourne
ABEFFGILRU febrifugal
ABEFFILLOR bill of fare
ABEFGILORV forgivable
ABEFGILRSS fiberglass, fibreglass, glass fibre
ABEFHIRRTT afterbirth
ABEFHLLOTT half-bottle
ABEFIILLLN infallible
ABEFIILLRT fibrillate
ABEFIILNOT notifiable
ABEFIILNTU infibulate
ABEFIILRVY verifiably
ABEFILLLOS bill of sale
ABEFILNSUY unfeasibly
ABEFILOPRT profitable
ABEFLLLMUY blamefully
ABEFLLOORT footballer
ABEGGNOORT tobogganer
ABEGHHIRST breast-high
ABEGHILLMN Bellingham
ABEGHIMNNU human being
ABEGHIOPRR biographer
ABEGHLLLUY belly laugh
ABEGHLLOPU ploughable
ABEGHLNOOP Anglophobe
ABEGHNOPST sponge bath
ABEGHNRRSU bushranger
ABEGHQSUUU usquebaugh
ABEGIILNNT intangible
ABEGIINNRT brigantine
ABEGIKLNNT blanketing
ABEGILLNRR barrelling
ABEGILLNRV verballing
ABEGILLNTY bleatingly
ABEGILLRST stable girl
ABEGILMNPU impugnable
ABEGILNRSS singles bar
ABEGILRRUZ burglarize
ABEGILRSST blister gas
ABEGIMORSU seaborgium
ABEGINNOTY bayoneting
ABEGINNQTU banqueting
ABEGINNRST string bean
ABEGINRSTU gas turbine
ABEGKRRSTU grubstaker
ABEGLLNOOY balneology
ABEGLNORRY loganberry
ABEGMOORTT bottom gear
ABEGNOORTU Baton Rouge
ABEHHMRTTY beta rhythm
ABEHHORRTT heart-throb
ABEHIILMNT habiliment
ABEHIIPSTT hepatitis B
ABEHIKLNRS shrinkable
ABEHIKLORS kohlrabies
ABEHILLOPS polishable
ABEHILNPSU punishable
ABEHILOPST hospitable
ABEHILORTV Bath Oliver
ABEHILPSTT battleship
ABEHILPSTU bisulphate
ABEHIMMNST Benthamism
ABEHIMNNST banishment
ABEHINOOPX xenophobia
ABEHINOPRV vibraphone
ABEHINORRT hibernator
ABEHKOOPRS phrase book
ABEHLMOOST smoothable
ABEHLNOORU honourable
ABEHLOPRSY hyperbolas
ABEHLORRTY lay brother
ABEHLRSUWY bush lawyer
ABEHLRTTTU truth table
ABEHMRSSTU bushmaster
ABEHMRTTYY bathymetry
ABEHNOPRTY hyperbaton
ABEHNORSST basset-horn
ABEHORRSSS horse brass
ABEIIILMNT inimitable
ABEIIILNNZ Leibnizian
ABEIIILQRU equilibria
ABEIILLMRS liberalism
ABEIILLNNY biennially
ABEIILLNOV inviolable
ABEIILLRST liberalist
ABEIILLRTY liberality
ABEIILLTUZ utilizable
ABEIILMNSS lesbianism
ABEIILMPSS impassible
ABEIILNORT liberation
ABEIILNPXY inexpiably
ABEIILNTTU intuitable
ABEIILNTTY tenability
ABEIILNTVY inevitably
ABEIILQTUY equability
ABEIILRSTZ stabilizer
ABEIILSTTY bestiality
ABEIINNRSS braininess
ABEIINNRTW New Britain
ABEIKLLLNU unkillable
ABEIKLNNSU unsinkable
ABEIKNOPRT break point
ABEIKNSTUZ Uzbekistan
ABEILLNNST tennis ball
ABEILLNOSV insolvable
ABEILLNRUY unreliably
ABEILLPRST spitballer
ABEILMMOST metabolism

ABEILMNQRU lambrequin
ABEILMNRTY liberty man
ABEILMNSSU unmissable
ABEILMOOTU automobile
ABEILMOPRT importable
ABEILMOPRV improvable
ABEILNNNUW unwinnable
ABEILNNUVY unenviably
ABEILNOPRY inoperably
ABEILNORXY inexorably
ABEILNRRST sternal rib
ABEILNRTUW unwritable
ABEILNSTUU unsuitable
ABEILOPRRV proverbial
ABEILORTVY abortively
ABEILRRTTU triturable
ABEILRSTUV vestibular
ABEILRSUVV survivable
ABEIMMOQUZ Mozambique
ABEIMNNOTT obtainment
ABEIMNORTT montbretia
ABEIMNORTU tambourine
ABEIMNRRSU submariner
ABEIMOSSTU abstemious
ABEINNOPSV bone spavin
ABEINNOSTT abstention
ABEINNRSSW brawniness
ABEINOPRRW brainpower
ABEINORTTX exorbitant
ABEINRSSSS brassiness
ABEIOPPRSY presbyopia
ABEIOPRSTV absorptive
ABEIOSSSST asbestosis
ABEIPRSTTY baptistery
ABEKKORSTW basketwork, work-basket
ABEKLLMRTU bull market
ABEKLNNOUW unknowable
ABEKLNORUW unworkable
ABEKLOOPRV provokable
ABEKLOPRRR pork barrel
ABEKMMNORY memory bank
ABEKMNNOTU mountebank
ABEKMNORSY monkey bars
ABEKNOPRRW pawnbroker
ABEKOOPRRY prayer book
ABEKORRSTW breastwork
ABELLLLORR rollerball
ABELLLLOVY volleyball
ABELLLORRR barrel roll
ABELLLPSSY Bell's palsy
ABELLMNOYY Ballymoney
ABELLMORSW small bower
ABELLNOSUV unsolvable
ABELLNRUVY vulnerably
ABELLOORWY woolly-bear
ABELLOSTUY absolutely
ABELLSSSUY syllabuses
ABELMMNOSU summonable
ABELMMRSUY Malmesbury
ABELMNNOOW noblewoman
ABELMNNOTZ blazonment
ABELMNORXY onyx marble
ABELMOOPRT promotable
ABELMOORTW water-bloom
ABELMPRSUY presumably
ABELNNORUV verbal noun
ABELNOOPST tablespoon
ABELNOPRSY personably
ABELNOPRUV unprovable
ABELNOPTXY penalty box
ABELNOQTUU unquotable
ABELNSSTTU unstablest
ABELOPPSSU supposable
ABELORRTTU torturable
ABELPRRTUU rupturable
ABELRSSTUY abstrusely
ABELRSSUYY Aylesburys
ABEMMNORSU membranous
ABEMMNRSSU mass number
ABEMNOORRW bone marrow, marrowbone
ABEMORRSTU arboretums
ABENNOPRSX box spanner
ABENOPRSTU bean sprout
ABENPRSSTU abruptness
ABEOORSTUU rouseabout
ABEOPSTTUY beauty spot
ABEOQSSUUU subaqueous
ABERRRSTWY strawberry
ABFFGILLNY bafflingly
ABFGILNOTY flying boat
ABFGILORVY forgivably
ABFHORSTTU turboshaft
ABFIIILRTY friability
ABFIILLLNY infallibly
ABFIILLRRY fibrillary
ABFIILNORV riboflavin
ABFILOPRTY profitably
ABFILOSTUY fabulosity
ABFJLORSUY frabjously
ABFLLOSTUY boastfully
ABFLLOSUUY fabulously
ABGGGILNRY braggingly
ABGGGINORW growing bag
ABGGILLMNO gambolling
ABGHIIINNT inhabiting
ABGHIIMMNR Birmingham
ABGHIJNORS job-sharing
ABGHIMNNOT Binghamton
ABGHIORTTU right about
ABGHIRRRSU Harrisburg
ABGHLORRUY royal burgh
ABGHOORRUY yarborough
ABGIIILNNT nail-biting
ABGIILNNTY intangibly
ABGIILNOOT obligation
ABGIKKMNOO bookmaking
ABGIKLNOOS signal-book
ABGILLMNRY ramblingly
ABGILLNSUU sublingual
ABGILNOSTY boastingly
ABGILOORTY obligatory
ABGINNORRT Barrington
ABGINOORTW rowing boat
ABGINRSSST string bass
ABGJORSTUU subjugator
ABGLLLORUY globularly
ABGLMOORUY glamour boy
ABGMOPRRSU subprogram
ABGNORRSUW brown sugar
ABHHIMOOOP homophobia
ABHHNORSSW hash browns
ABHIILPRSU ship burial
ABHIIMOPSU amphibious
ABHILOPSTY hospitably
ABHINPRSTU paintbrush
ABHIPRRSSU bursarship
ABHLNOORUY honourably
ABIIILLPTY pliability
ABIIILMNTY inimitably
ABIIILNOST sibilation
ABIIINOSST antibiosis
ABIIIORSTT tibiotarsi
ABIIJLNOTU jubilation
ABIILLMNOY binomially
ABIILLMNSU subliminal
ABIILLNOVY inviolably
ABIILLOTVY lovability
ABIILMOTVY movability
ABIILMPSSY impassibly
ABIILMTTUY mutability
ABIILNOTTY notability
ABIILOPRTY bipolarity
ABIILOPTTY potability
ABIIMRSSTY sybaritism
ABIINNOTTU intubation
ABIINOTTTU titubation
ABIIORSTTU obituarist
ABIJLLNTUY jubilantly
ABIKLNNOPT point-blank
ABIKNOOORT ration book
ABILLNOOST balloonist
ABILMNOSUU albuminous
ABILMOPSTU suboptimal
ABILMOSSTU absolutism
ABILNOOSTU absolution
ABILNORRTU lunar orbit
ABILNSTUUY unsuitably
ABILORSSUU salubrious
ABILOSSTTU absolutist
ABIMNORRST brainstorm
ABIMRSSSTU strabismus
ABINNOSTVV bon vivants
ABINOOPRST absorption
ABINOORRST torsion bar
ABINOOSSST bassoonist
ABINOSSTTU bus station, sub-station
ABINRRSTTU brain trust
ABKLNORUWY unworkably
ABLLOORSTU lost labour
ABLOOPRTTT Port Talbot
ABMRSSTTUU substratum
ABNOORRSTU brontosaur

ABOORSTTUU roustabout
ACCCCIKKLL click-clack
ACCCDIIIPR picric acid
ACCCDIIIRT citric acid
ACCCEEEKLS Eccles cake
ACCCEEHITT catechetic
ACCCEFHKOR cockchafer
ACCCEHORTW cowcatcher
ACCCEIIRST cicatrices
ACCCEIKORT cockatrice
ACCCEILLNY encyclical
ACCCEILMOP accomplice
ACCCEKLRTY cycle track
ACCCGLNOOO gonococcal
ACCCHHILOO chocaholic
ACCCHKLOTW clock-watch
ACCCHKOPST spatchcock
ACCCHLOORY ochlocracy
ACCCHOOTUU caoutchouc
ACCCILLLYY cyclically
ACCCILMORY cycloramic
ACCCINOPPU cappuccino
ACCDDEEIRT accredited
ACCDDEIRRT credit card
ACCDEEHQRU cheque card
ACCDEEINNS incandesce
ACCDEELLPY pedal cycle
ACCDEELPST spectacled
ACCDEELRTY trade cycle
ACCDEENNSY ascendency
ACCDEENNTU unaccented
ACCDEGIINN ice dancing
ACCDEHLNOY chalcedony
ACCDEIILNY indelicacy
ACCDEIILST dialectics
ACCDEIIOPT apodeictic
ACCDEIKLNW candlewick
ACCDEILLOP peccadillo
ACCDEILNOT occidental
ACCDEILOPY cyclopedia
ACCDEIMNNY mendicancy
ACCDEIMORT democratic
ACCDEINNTU inductance
ACCDEINOPR endocarpic
ACCDEIORST desiccator
ACCDEIORTT corticated
ACCDELOPSU cloudscape
ACCDEMOSTU accustomed
ACCDEOOPRT Cape doctor
ACCDFIILTY flaccidity
ACCDFIIMOR formic acid
ACCDHHRRUY churchyard
ACCDHIINOR diachronic
ACCDHILNOO conchoidal
ACCDHILORV clavichord
ACCDIIINRT nitric acid
ACCDIILSST cladistics
ACCDIKLOOR clock radio
ACCDINORTT contradict
ACCDLOORSV vocal cords
ACCDNNOORT concordant
ACCEEEEHKS cheesecake
ACCEEEHNNV even chance
ACCEEELPRT receptacle
ACCEEENNRS renascence
ACCEEFHLRT leechcraft
ACCEEHILNP encephalic
ACCEEHIRTZ catechizer
ACCEEHKLVV check valve
ACCEEHKMNR checkerman
ACCEEHMNTU catechumen
ACCEEHNORR encroacher
ACCEEILLRT electrical
ACCEEILMNU ecumenical
ACCEEILMOT ecoclimate
ACCEEILNPS pencil case
ACCEEILORV varicocele
ACCEEIMSST access time
ACCEEIORSU ericaceous
ACCEEIRRSV service car
ACCEEIRTUX excruciate
ACCEELNOST coalescent
ACCEELNOSV convalesce
ACCEELNPRU crapulence
ACCEELNRTU reluctance
ACCEELNRUX Clarenceux
ACCEELNSTT lactescent
ACCEELPSST spectacles
ACCEEMNRST marcescent
ACCEENNOVY conveyance
ACCEENORST consecrate
ACCEENOTTY eye contact
ACCEENPTXY expectancy
ACCEENRSSS scarceness
ACCEEOPPRS Peace Corps
ACCEEORRSU racecourse
ACCEEORSTU cretaceous
ACCEFFIINY inefficacy
ACCEFHLRTY flycatcher
ACCEFILLOR calciferol
ACCEFILRSU flea-circus
ACCEFILRYY fairy cycle
ACCEFINOST confiscate
ACCEFLLOTU flocculate
ACCEGIINOR cariogenic
ACCEGILLNN cancelling
ACCEGILLOO ecological
ACCEGINNOR carcinogen
ACCEGINNOS cognisance
ACCEGINNOY cyanogenic
ACCEGINNOZ cognizance
ACCEHHIIRR hierarchic
ACCEHHIKNO choke chain
ACCEHHIMRS Carchemish
ACCEHHIPRT heptarchic
ACCEHHOOSU coach house
ACCEHIILMR chimerical
ACCEHIINNT technician
ACCEHILLMY chemically
ACCEHILLOY echoically
ACCEHILLTY hectically
ACCEHINNSS chanciness
ACCEHINORT anchoretic
ACCEHINSST catchiness
ACCEHIORRY hierocracy
ACCEHIORTT theocratic
ACCEHIRRST scratchier
ACCEHKLOST Scotch kale
ACCEHLLNOR chancellor
ACCEHLOOTY chocolatey
ACCEHNNPTY catchpenny
ACCEHNNRTY trenchancy
ACCEHNORTT technocrat, trench coat
ACCEHOPSTT Scotch tape
ACCEIILNOT conciliate
ACCEIILSSZ classicize
ACCEIIMRST ceramicist
ACCEIIMSST asceticism
ACCEIINNOR Ciceronian
ACCEIINRST Cistercian
ACCEILLLRY clerically
ACCEILLNSY scenically
ACCEILMMOR commercial
ACCEILMNOO economical
ACCEILMNOP compliance
ACCEILMOPT complicate
ACCEILMOST cacomistle
ACCEILNOSS neoclassic
ACCEILOPPT apoplectic
ACCEILOPRR reciprocal
ACCEIMOOPR comic opera
ACCEINNNOV connivance
ACCEINNORT concertina
ACCEINNSSY incessancy
ACCEIOORSU coriaceous
ACCEIOPPSY episcopacy
ACCEJKKOST jack socket
ACCEKKLMOR clockmaker
ACCEKLORTW water-clock
ACCEKNOOTT cotton cake
ACCEKNRRTU nutcracker
ACCELLNOSU cancellous
ACCELLNRUY lunar cycle
ACCELLSSUU calculuses
ACCELMNOPT complacent
ACCELNOPTU conceptual
ACCELOORSV vocal score
ACCEMNNORY necromancy
ACCEMORSTU reaccustom
ACCENNNOOS consonance
ACCENORTTU counteract
ACCEOORTTV covert coat
ACCEORSUUV curvaceous
ACCFFFFHHI chiffchaff
ACCFFIOPRT traffic cop
ACCFHIRTTW witchcraft
ACCFIIIMPR Pacific Rim
ACCFILSSUU fasciculus
ACCFNOORRT corn-factor
ACCGHIIIOP pichiciago
ACCGHIILOR oligarchic
ACCGHIOPTY phagocytic
ACCGHKNOUW chuckwagon
ACCGHLOPRY cyclograph
ACCGIIMORT tragicomic
ACCGILNSUY accusingly
ACCGINNOTU accounting
ACCHHIILLN chinchilla
ACCHHMRRUY Church Army
ACCHHORSST cross-hatch
ACCHIIILST chiliastic
ACCHIIMSST mica-schist, schismatic

ACCHIINORT	anchoritic
ACCHIKMQRU	quick march
ACCHIKMSTT	matchstick
ACCHILLOTY	catholicly
ACCHILMOPS	accomplish
ACCHILNNPS	splanchnic
ACCHILOSST	scholastic
ACCHILRSTY	scratchily
ACCHIMNORY	chiromancy
ACCHIOPRSZ	schizocarp
ACCHIOPTTY	hypotactic
ACCHIOSSTT	stochastic
ACCHMOOORT	motor coach
ACCHMORSST	crossmatch
ACCHNOPSST	Scotch snap
ACCHNOPSYY	sycophancy
ACCHNORRST	cornstarch
ACCHOPRSST	crosspatch
ACCIIILLLP	piccalilli
ACCIIINNNT	Cincinnati
ACCIILLLNY	clinically
ACCIILLRTY	critically
ACCIILMNOS	laconicism
ACCIILMOTY	comicality
ACCIILMSSS	classicism
ACCIILNRTU	uncritical
ACCIILRTUY	cruciality
ACCIILSSST	classicist
ACCIIMORTT	timocratic
ACCIINNNPY	piccaninny
ACCIINNOTY	canonicity
ACCIINNSST	scintiscan
ACCIIOPRSU	capricious
ACCIISTTUY	causticity
ACCIKKKKNN	knick-knack
ACCILLMOSY	cosmically
ACCILLRRUY	circularly
ACCILMNNOU	councilman
ACCILMNOOS	iconoclasm
ACCILNOOST	iconoclast
ACCILNORTU	inculcator
ACCILNOTUX	council tax
ACCILORRTU	circulator
ACCILRRRUU	curricular
ACCIMNOOPR	monocarpic
ACCIMNOOPT	compaction
ACCIMNOORT	monocratic
ACCIMORSSY	cosmic rays
ACCINOOPRU	cornucopia
ACCINOOPTU	occupation
ACCINOPRSY	conspiracy
ACCINORSTY	Carson City
ACCIOPRSTT	catoptrics
ACCKLMOORU	cockalorum
ACCKOOPSUW	cuckoo wasp
ACCLOPRTUY	plutocracy
ACCNOORRTT	contractor
ACDDDEELLP	padded cell
ACDDDGIRTU	drug addict
ACDDEEEIRT	rededicate
ACDDEEEKNU	Dundee cake
ACDDEEENRT	dead centre
ACDDEEGGIL	gilded cage
ACDDEEHLOO	cool-headed
ACDDEEHLTY	detachedly
ACDDEEHNOR	decahedron
ACDDEEIITV	dedicative
ACDDEEILOR	I do declare
ACDDEEIOPT	Poetic Edda
ACDDEELLRY	declaredly
ACDDEELLSY	Clydesdale
ACDDEELNRU	undeclared
ACDDEELNTY	decadently
ACDDEENNST	descendant
ACDDEENTUU	uneducated
ACDDEHLORR	cardholder
ACDDEHNNOS	second hand
ACDDEIILRT	direct dial
ACDDEIINOT	dedication
ACDDEIKLOT	dock-tailed
ACDDEILMOU	duodecimal
ACDDEINNSS	candidness
ACDDEIORTY	dedicatory
ACDDEKLLNO	landlocked
ACDDEKLORS	dreadlocks
ACDDELNNOO	colonnaded
ACDDENNORU	round dance
ACDDENNRUY	redundancy
ACDDENORSU	decandrous
ACDDENORSW	sword dance
ACDDFHIORU	chaud-froid
ACDDGHILNR	grandchild
ACDDGHNRUY	grand duchy
ACDDIMORSW	caddis-worm
ACDDINORST	discordant
ACDEEEEHHS	cheese-head
ACDEEEELLN	needle-lace
ACDEEEELRT	decelerate
ACDEEEEPRS	predecease
ACDEEEFLNR	fer de lance
ACDEEEFMNN	defenceman
ACDEEEFMNT	defacement
ACDEEEGNRY	degeneracy
ACDEEEHHRS	hard cheese
ACDEEEHLTT	decathlete
ACDEEEIPRT	depreciate
ACDEEENNTT	antecedent
ACDEEEORRT	redecorate
ACDEEFFHRS	fresh-faced
ACDEEFFHRT	far-fetched
ACDEEFFLTY	affectedly
ACDEEFFNTU	unaffected
ACDEEFINOT	defecation
ACDEEFIRSS	fricasseed
ACDEEFKOPR	poker-faced
ACDEEFMSST	mass defect
ACDEEFOPRW	face powder
ACDEEGHLLN	challenged
ACDEEGHNNO	hendecagon
ACDEEGILNS	side glance
ACDEEGIMMR	decigramme
ACDEEGINNR	grand-niece
ACDEEGINRT	centigrade
ACDEEGNORS	second gear
ACDEEHILNR	chandelier
ACDEEHILPS	side chapel
ACDEEHINOT	theodicean
ACDEEHKLLS	shellacked
ACDEEHLLNN	channelled
ACDEEHLORT	cloth-eared
ACDEEHMNTT	detachment
ACDEEHNRSU	unsearched
ACDEEHOPPR	copperhead
ACDEEIILMZ	decimalize
ACDEEIILNT	indelicate
ACDEEIIMTV	medicative
ACDEEILLNP	lead pencil
ACDEEILLNR	Cinderella
ACDEEILLOZ	delocalize
ACDEEILLRS	escadrille
ACDEEILLTY	delicately
ACDEEILMPR	pre-decimal, premedical
ACDEEILNRT	credential
ACDEEILRST	credit sale
ACDEEIMMNT	medicament
ACDEEIMNOU	eudaemonic
ACDEEIMSTU	miseducate
ACDEEINNTU	denunciate
ACDEEINPPS	appendices
ACDEEINPTT	pectinated
ACDEEINRRS	red arsenic
ACDEEIORTV	decorative
ACDEEIOTTX	detoxicate
ACDEEIPRRT	trade price
ACDEEIRTTV	detractive
ACDEEITTUX	exactitude
ACDEELLLPW	well placed
ACDEELLOTT	Dolcelatte
ACDEELMORT	ectodermal
ACDEELNOST	adolescent
ACDEELNRRY	dry-cleaner
ACDEELRRTT	letter-card
ACDEEMMNOR	commandeer
ACDEEMMNPT	decampment
ACDEEMNNOS	second name
ACDEEMNRRY	merry dance
ACDEENNOST	condensate
ACDEENNOTV	covenanted
ACDEENORST	second-rate
ACDEENPRTU	uncarpeted
ACDEENRRSZ	Zener cards
ACDEENRSSS	sacredness
ACDEEOPRRT	deprecator, tape-record
ACDEEOPRRY	copyreader
ACDEEOPRSU	predaceous
ACDEEORRST	desecrator
ACDEFFIKRT	trafficked
ACDEFFILNO	land office
ACDEFFLORS	scaffolder
ACDEFFLOTU	duffel coat
ACDEFGLLNO	golden calf
ACDEFIIINT	nidificate
ACDEFIILMS	facsimiled
ACDEFIILSS	classified
ACDEFIIRRT	fratricide
ACDEFILSSY	declassify
ACDEFINNOT	confidante
ACDEFKLNOR	folk dancer

ACDEFLNOOR dance floor
ACDEFLNORS land forces
ACDEFNORRU uncared for
ACDEFNRSSY fancy dress
ACDEFNRSUU unsurfaced
ACDEGGIOPS pedagogics
ACDEGGRSTU egg custard
ACDEGHIRRS discharger
ACDEGIILMR germicidal
ACDEGIINOR radiogenic
ACDEGIINST die-casting
ACDEGILNRW arc welding
ACDEGILRTT cattle grid
ACDEGINNOR androgenic
ACDEGINORR corrigenda
ACDEGINRTY garden city
ACDEGIORSU discourage
ACDEGKNORR rock garden
ACDEGLNNRU grand-uncle
ACDEGLNNST scent gland
ACDEGLNORS cradle song
ACDEGNOSUY decagynous
ACDEHHOOTT hot cathode
ACDEHIIINR enchiridia
ACDEHIIMRT diathermic
ACDEHIINRV chain drive
ACDEHIIORR diarrhoeic
ACDEHILLMT ill-matched
ACDEHILMOT methodical
ACDEHILMRS Childermas
ACDEHILRTW witch alder
ACDEHINNST disenchant
ACDEHINOPS deaconship
ACDEHINOPT Dictaphone
ACDEHINRSZ scherzandi
ACDEHIPRST dispatcher
ACDEHIRSST shit-scared
ACDEHIRTTW ditchwater
ACDEHLMOOS dame school
ACDEHLMTTU Dutch metal
ACDEHLNRSU rush candle
ACDEHLOOPP cephalopod
ACDEHMOSTU moustached
ACDEHNOORT octahedron
ACDEHNOPRT pentachord
ACDEHNORSZ scherzando
ACDEHNRSTU unstarched
ACDEHORRSW wordsearch
ACDEHORRTT tetrachord
ACDEHRTTTU Dutch treat
ACDEIIILST idealistic
ACDEIIINTV indicative
ACDEIIKNNR Kincardine
ACDEIIKNNS Dickensian
ACDEIILMRS disclaimer
ACDEIILMRT direct mail
ACDEIILNNT incidental
ACDEIILOPR periodical
ACDEIILOPS episodical
ACDEIILPST pesticidal
ACDEIIMNOT decimation, medication
ACDEIIMRTX taxidermic
ACDEIIMRTY acidimetry
ACDEIINNRY incendiary
ACDEIIORSU iridaceous
ACDEIIOSST dissociate
ACDEIIPRST pediatrics
ACDEIJNTUV adjunctive
ACDEIJRTUU judicature
ACDEILLORR cordillera
ACDEILLTUV victualled
ACDEILNPSS placidness
ACDEILOPRR precordial
ACDEILORTU elucidator
ACDEILOTTU co-latitude
ACDEIMNORU androecium
ACDEIMNOSU mendacious
ACDEIMOPRR madreporic
ACDEINNNTY intendancy
ACDEINNOSS dissonance
ACDEINNRSS rancidness
ACDEINOORT carotenoid, coordinate, decoration
ACDEINORRW cordwainer
ACDEINORTT detraction
ACDEINOSTT anecdotist
ACDEINOSTW wainscoted
ACDEINPRST discrepant
ACDEINSTTU sanctitude
ACDEIOPRSU predacious
ACDEIOPSSU spadiceous
ACDEIPQRSU quadriceps
ACDEIPRSTU custard pie
ACDEIRSSTU crassitude
ACDEITTUVY active duty
ACDEJKSTTU dust jacket
ACDEKKMOPR pock-marked
ACDEKLNOOS saloon deck
ACDELLORWY yellow card
ACDELMNOTU documental
ACDELNOOTY acotyledon
ACDELNPRUU peduncular
ACDELNRSSU underclass
ACDELOOPST postal code
ACDELOPPTU clapped out
ACDELOPRRU procedural
ACDEMMOSTU custom-made
ACDEMNOPRU up-and-comer
ACDEMNOPRW Camperdown
ACDEMNORST Doc Martens
ACDEMOOPRR compradore
ACDEMOPRSU damp course
ACDENNNOOR ordonnance
ACDENNNOOS nanosecond
ACDENOPPSW snow-capped
ACDENRRRTU redcurrant
ACDENRRSTU transducer
ACDEOORRVW woodcarver
ACDEOPPRSU pseudocarp
ACDEOPRSUU drupaceous
ACDFGIILNU fungicidal
ACDFGILRTU craft guild
ACDFGNOOSY fancy goods
ACDFIMNNOR confirmand
ACDFLLOOSV vocal folds
ACDFLNOSSY candyfloss
ACDGHILTUW wild-caught
ACDGHINORR orcharding
ACDGHIPRSY dysgraphic
ACDGHNOOTU touch-and-go
ACDGIILOOR radiologic
ACDGIINOST diagnostic
ACDGILMOOS mosaic gold
ACDGILOORY cardiology
ACDGIMMNNO commanding
ACDGLOTYYZ zygodactyl
ACDGMNOPRU campground
ACDHIIIOPT idiopathic
ACDHILLPSY child's play
ACDHILOORT trochoidal
ACDHILRSST third class
ACDHILRSUY hydraulics
ACDHIMOSTU Midas touch
ACDHINOOOX chionodoxa
ACDHINORRS Richardson
ACDHIORRST orchardist
ACDHIORRSW disc harrow
ACDHIRSSSW Swiss chard
ACDHLOOSSY schooldays
ACDHMNOTUW Dutchwoman
ACDHNORSUW dawn chorus
ACDIIIMMRU miracidium
ACDIIINNOT indication
ACDIIJLLUY judicially
ACDIILLSUY suicidally
ACDIILMOPT diplomatic
ACDIILORTY cordiality
ACDIILORUX uxoricidal
ACDIILPRSU discipular
ACDIIMNOSY isodynamic
ACDIIMNOTU coatimundi
ACDIIMNSTY dynamicist
ACDIINNNOR Indian corn
ACDIINOORV Ordovician
ACDIINORTV vindicator
ACDIINORTY dictionary, indicatory
ACDIKNNPTU nip and tuck
ACDILNOPRS spinal cord
ACDILOPRTU duplicator
ACDILPSSTY dysplastic
ACDIMMORUY myocardium
ACDIMNSSTU music stand
ACDINOOPRS Coon Rapids
ACDINSSSTU discussant
ACDIOOPRSY radioscopy
ACDIORRSTT distractor
ACDKLMOSSY lady's smock
ACDKNORSTU soundtrack
ACDLLNNOOY London clay
ACDLLOOPSW codswallop
ACDLLOPTYY polydactyl

ACDLLORSSW world-class
ACDLMNOOUV mud volcano
ACEEEEHPRS cheese-pare
ACEEEFFMNT effacement
ACEEEFFTTU effectuate
ACEEEFIPRS fire escape
ACEEEFLNRR freelancer
ACEEEGILNN inelegance
ACEEEGILTX exegetical
ACEEEGINRT great-niece
ACEEEGNPRT percentage
ACEEEHLMOT hematocele
ACEEEHLNST clean sheet
ACEEEHRRRS researcher
ACEEEHRSTT chaste tree
ACEEEIPPRV apperceive
ACEEEIRRST secretaire
ACEEEIRRTV recreative
ACEEEIRSTV eviscerate
ACEEEIRTVX execrative
ACEEELLNRT crenellate
ACEEELLRTT cellarette
ACEEELMNNT enlacement
ACEEELNPRV prevalence
ACEEELORTT electorate
ACEEELRSTT telecaster
ACEEEMMNRT amercement
ACEEEMNNPR permanence
ACEEEMNNST encasement
ACEEEMNPRT temperance
ACEEEMNPST escapement
ACEEEMNRTT metacenter, metacentre
ACEEENNPRT repentance
ACEEENNRRT re-entrance
ACEEENNSTV evanescent
ACEEEPRRTU recuperate
ACEEEPRSTT pace-setter
ACEEFFHSUU chauffeuse
ACEEFFIMNY effeminacy
ACEEFFNRSU sufferance
ACEEFHINRS franchisee
ACEEFHLNRT centre half
ACEEFHMNRS French seam
ACEEFHORRS rose-chafer
ACEEFIILTT felicitate
ACEEFIJKLT life jacket
ACEEFILMNT maleficent
ACEEFILNSS facileness
ACEEFILNST leaf insect
ACEEFIORTV vociferate
ACEEFIRRTV refractive
ACEEFIRSSS fricassees
ACEEFKORRW faceworker
ACEEFLLNTU flatulence
ACEEFLLORV cloverleaf
ACEEFLLPUY peacefully
ACEEFLNSST false scent
ACEEFLNSTV flavescent
ACEEFLORST forecastle
ACEEFLRTTU leafcutter
ACEEFORRST forecaster
ACEEGGNORT congregate
ACEEGGRSTU curate's egg
ACEEGHLLNR challenger
ACEEGHLNSS changeless
ACEEGHNNOP Copenhagen
ACEEGHNORV changeover
ACEEGHNSSU gaucheness
ACEEGHORRV overcharge
ACEEGIKNPS king's peace
ACEEGILLNR allergenic
ACEEGILLOT collegiate
ACEEGILSTU sluice-gate
ACEEGIOPTT cottage pie
ACEEGIORTZ categorize
ACEEGIOTTX excogitate
ACEEGKNOPS sponge cake
ACEEGLNORS close-range
ACEEGLNRTU great-uncle
ACEEGMOTTY gametocyte
ACEEGNNORV governance
ACEEGNNPRU repugnance
ACEEGNNSWY news agency
ACEEGNORRU encourager
ACEEGNRSVY scavengery
ACEEHHILNW chain wheel
ACEEHHILRW wheelchair
ACEEHHIPRT chip heater
ACEEHHIRRS heresiarch
ACEEHHPTTU Heptateuch
ACEEHIKNTT kitchen tea
ACEEHILMNN manchineel
ACEEHILMRT hermetical
ACEEHILNNP encephalin
ACEEHILNNZ channelize
ACEEHILPTT telepathic
ACEEHIMNPZ chimpanzee
ACEEHIMNRZ mechanizer
ACEEHIMPRY hyperaemic
ACEEHIMPTT empathetic
ACEEHIMRTX hexametric
ACEEHIMSTZ schematize
ACEEHIMTTT metathetic
ACEEHINNPT phenacetin
ACEEHINPSS peachiness
ACEEHINSTT anesthetic
ACEEHIORRT charioteer
ACEEHIPRST preachiest
ACEEHISTUW white sauce
ACEEHKLNRT halter-neck
ACEEHLLMPW wheel clamp
ACEEHLLNOP cellophane
ACEEHLNNOP encephalon
ACEEHLNPRU leprechaun
ACEEHLNPTT planchette
ACEEHLOPRT other place
ACEEHLOPTY polychaete
ACEEHLORRU leucorrhea
ACEEHLORSU housecarle
ACEEHLOSSV close shave
ACEEHLRTVW lever watch
ACEEHLSSST scatheless
ACEEHMMRSU meerschaum
ACEEHMNNST encashment
ACEEHMNPRT preachment
ACEEHMNRST Manchester
ACEEHMORTT tachometer
ACEEHMRTTY tachymeter
ACEEHNPTTU Pentateuch
ACEEHNSSST chasteness
ACEEHOPRRR reproacher
ACEEHORRST trace-horse
ACEEHPPRSY hyperspace
ACEEHPRRSU repurchase
ACEEHRRSTU chartreuse
ACEEIILMRT eremitical
ACEEIILNTT licentiate
ACEEIILPSZ specialize
ACEEIILSTZ elasticize
ACEEIIMNPT impatience
ACEEIIMPST episematic, septicemia
ACEEIINNRT incinerate
ACEEIIRTTV recitative
ACEEIITTVX excitative
ACEEIJLNQU Jacqueline
ACEEIJMOPR major piece
ACEEIKLMNS simnel cake
ACEEIKLMTT meal ticket
ACEEIKLNRT trance-like
ACEEIKLRRS arse-licker
ACEEIKNRSS creakiness
ACEEIKPRTT ticker tape
ACEEILLNRW wine cellar
ACEEILLNST cleanliest
ACEEILLORS El Escorial
ACEEILLPSY especially
ACEEILMNNT Clementina
ACEEILMNOR ceremonial
ACEEILMNRT mercantile
ACEEILMNST centesimal
ACEEILNNNT centennial
ACEEILNPRT epicentral
ACEEILNRTV cantilever
ACEEILNRTZ centralize
ACEEILRRTT retractile
ACEEILRSUZ secularize
ACEEILRTTU reticulate
ACEEILRTUV ulcerative
ACEEILRTVY creatively
ACEEILSTUV vesiculate
ACEEIMNRSS creaminess
ACEEIMNRSV serviceman
ACEEIMNRTT remittance
ACEEIMPRST spermaceti
ACEEINNPRS inner space
ACEEINNRST transience
ACEEINORRT recreation
ACEEINORTU auctioneer
ACEEINORTX execration
ACEEINPPRT apprentice
ACEEINPRST interspace
ACEEINRSST resistance
ACEEINRTUV uncreative
ACEEINRTVY inveteracy
ACEEINSSTV activeness
ACEEIOPPST episcopate
ACEEIOQTUV equivocate
ACEEIORTVV overactive
ACEEIPQRSU picaresque
ACEEIQRSTU requiescat

ACEEIRRTTV retractive
ACEEIRTTVX extractive
ACEEJKMSST mess jacket
ACEEJKNOTT Eton jacket
ACEEJLMNOT cajolement
ACEEKLLOWY yellowcake
ACEEKLLRSS sales clerk
ACEEKLNOST nose tackle
ACEEKNRRRT rack-renter
ACEEKORRSW caseworker
ACEELLNRSW Allen screw
ACEELLRSSY carelessly
ACEELLSTTU scutellate
ACEELMORTT lactometer
ACEELNOPST opalescent
ACEELNPRSY screenplay
ACEELNRRTY recreantly
ACEELOPRTU operculate
ACEELPPRTU perceptual
ACEELPRSTW screw-plate
ACEELQRRUU craquelure
ACEELRRTUY creaturely
ACEELRSSSU saucerless
ACEELRSVVW screw valve
ACEEMMNNPT encampment
ACEEMMNOTT commentate
ACEEMMORRY race memory
ACEEMNNPRY permanency
ACEEMNOPST compensate
ACEEMNPRST escarpment
ACEEMOSTUZ eczematous
ACEENNOPRV provenance
ACEENNORTV contravene, covenanter
ACEENNRSSV cravenness
ACEENNSSTU sustenance
ACEENOPRTT pernoctate
ACEENORSSS coarseness
ACEENORSTU nectareous, raconteuse
ACEENPRUVY purveyance
ACEENRRTUU nature cure
ACEENRSSST ancestress
ACEENRSSTW newscaster
ACEEOPRSTU outer space
ACEEORRTVX extra cover
ACEEORRTXY execratory
ACEEOSSTTU testaceous
ACEERRSSTW watercress
ACEFFHLNOR French loaf
ACEFFIILTV afflictive
ACEFFIIORR Air Officer
ACEFFIKRRT trafficker
ACEFFILLNU in full face
ACEFFILOOV Oval Office
ACEFFOSTUU tuffaceous
ACEFGHIRRT freight car
ACEFGHLLNT calf-length
ACEFGILNST self-acting
ACEFGLLRUY gracefully
ACEFGLNRUU ungraceful
ACEFHHIRRS archer fish
ACEFHINOTT fianchetto
ACEFHINRRS franchiser
ACEFHIORSS coarse fish
ACEFHIRTTY city father
ACEFHKORST aftershock
ACEFHORRTV hovercraft
ACEFHORSTU housecraft
ACEFIILPST spiflicate
ACEFIILRSS classifier
ACEFIINRST sanctifier
ACEFIKLNPS clasp-knife
ACEFILNOST self-action
ACEFILOOSU foliaceous
ACEFILORTV vital force
ACEFILRSSY reclassify
ACEFIMNOSS neo-fascism
ACEFIMORTT time factor
ACEFINORRT refraction
ACEFINORTV vociferant
ACEFINORUY in-your-face
ACEFINOSST neo-fascist
ACEFINRSST craftiness
ACEFIRRTTU trifurcate
ACEFIRSSTU First Cause
ACEFKLOPPR flock paper
ACEFLLNOOR once for all
ACEFLLNTUY flatulency
ACEFNNOSST confessant
ACEFNOPRTT Pontefract
ACEFORRRTY refractory
ACEGGHILNN changeling
ACEGGHIOPR geographic
ACEGGILLOO geological
ACEGGINNOO ocean-going
ACEGGINRSS cragginess
ACEGGIRSST scraggiest
ACEGGNNORT congregant
ACEGHHILPS high places
ACEGHHINOT high-octane
ACEGHHOPRT hectograph
ACEGHIILMT megalithic
ACEGHIIMTW white magic
ACEGHIIPPR epigraphic
ACEGHILMPT phlegmatic
ACEGHILNNN channeling
ACEGHILRTU theurgical
ACEGHIMNNU machine-gun
ACEGHINNNT enchanting
ACEGHINOPT pathogenic
ACEGHINRTT ratcheting
ACEGHIRSTW switchgear
ACEGHLOORY archeology
ACEGHOPRRY cerography
ACEGIIKNST ice-skating
ACEGIILLST legalistic
ACEGIILMTY legitimacy
ACEGIILNNO agonic line, lignocaine
ACEGIILOOT aetiologic
ACEGIILOST egoistical
ACEGIINORT iatrogenic
ACEGIIOTTV cogitative
ACEGIIPRST epigastric
ACEGIIRRST geriatrics
ACEGIKKLOR goal-kicker
ACEGIKLNRY creakingly
ACEGILLMNR marcelling
ACEGILLNPR parcelling
ACEGILMNNY menacingly
ACEGILNNOT congenital
ACEGILNOPT optic angle
ACEGILNOPY clay pigeon
ACEGILNTXY exactingly
ACEGILOOPT apologetic
ACEGIMMRRS scrimmager
ACEGINNNRT entrancing
ACEGINNRST transgenic
ACEGINOPRS saprogenic
ACEGIRSSTT strategics
ACEGKMNOOR mock orange
ACEGKORSTU goatsucker
ACEGLMOSUU glumaceous
ACEGLNNOUY agony uncle
ACEGLOOPSY escapology
ACEGLOORRS goalscorer
ACEGMMRRSU scrummager
ACEGNNOPPU oppugnance
ACEGNNORST scent organ
ACEGNNPRUY repugnancy
ACEGNRSTTU scatter-gun
ACEGOORSUU courageous
ACEGOPRRSU supercargo
ACEGRRSTTU scatter rug
ACEHHIKNOV Chekhovian
ACEHHILTWZ witch hazel
ACEHHINNPT naphthenic
ACEHHNOSTT stonehatch
ACEHIILLPT philatelic
ACEHIILSTT thelstical
ACEHIILTTY ethicality
ACEHIIMMNS Manicheism
ACEHIIMRTT arithmetic
ACEHIINNOP Phoenician
ACEHIINOTV inchoative
ACEHIINTTT antithetic
ACEHIKLNSS chalkiness
ACEHIKMNOS chain-smoke
ACEHILLNTY ethnically
ACEHILLORY heroically
ACEHILLOSU hellacious
ACEHILLPRY Caerphilly
ACEHILMMST misch metal
ACEHILMOTY haemolytic
ACEHILNORT chlorinate
ACEHILNOTY inchoately
ACEHILORRT rhetorical
ACEHILRSTY hysterical
ACEHIMMSST schematism
ACEHIMNNOR enharmonic
ACEHIMNNOY hemocyanin
ACEHIMNPTU unemphatic
ACEHIMNRSV revanchism
ACEHIMOPRS semaphoric
ACEHIMOPRT amphoteric, metaphoric
ACEHIMORTT hematocrit
ACEHIMPSTY metaphysic
ACEHIMRSTU rheumatics
ACEHINORST chain store

ACEHINORTV	chevrotain
ACEHINPSST	patchiness
ACEHINPSTU	paunchiest
ACEHINRSTU	raunchiest
ACEHINRSTV	revanchist
ACEHINSSTT	chattiness
ACEHIOPSST	post-chaise
ACEHIORSTT	rheostatic
ACEHIPRSSU	haruspices
ACEHIPRTTU	picture hat
ACEHIPSTTU	chupatties
ACEHIQRRSU	squirearch
ACEHIRSSTT	starchiest
ACEHIRSTTT	tetrastich
ACEHIRTVWY	Vichy water
ACEHKLMMOR	hammerlock
ACEHKLMOTY	lackey moth
ACEHKLNOST	chalk-stone
ACEHLLMNOY	melancholy
ACEHLLPRSU	sepulchral
ACEHLMOOST	schoolmate
ACEHLMORSY	lachrymose
ACEHLNORST	charleston
ACEHLNSTUY	unchastely
ACEHLOORST	orthoclase
ACEHLOORSY	school year
ACEHLORRST	orchestral
ACEHLPRTYY	phylactery
ACEHMNOTUV	avouchment
ACEHMORRTU	route march
ACEHNORRTT	trochanter
ACEHNPRSTT	stench trap
ACEHOPPRTU	touchpaper
ACEHORTTWW	watchtower
ACEIIJLSTU	Jesuitical
ACEIIKMNST	kinematics
ACEIIKNRTT	kinetic art
ACEIIKRSTT	rickettsia
ACEIILLLPT	elliptical
ACEIILLNPR	periclinal
ACEIILLOSU	liliaceous
ACEIILLRTY	illiteracy
ACEIILLSTT	satellitic
ACEIILMMST	melismatic
ACEIILMOPT	atomic pile
ACEIILMOST	semiotical
ACEIILMPSS	specialism
ACEIILMSUZ	musicalize
ACEIILNOSX	saxicoline
ACEIILNPST	plasticine
ACEIILNSTT	static line
ACEIILNTVY	inactively
ACEIILPPRT	participle
ACEIILPRTT	triplicate
ACEIILPSST	specialist
ACEIILPSTY	speciality
ACEIILPSTZ	plasticize
ACEIILRSTT	recitalist
ACEIILSTTV	civil state
ACEIILSTTY	elasticity
ACEIIMMNTT	immittance
ACEIIMNORS	Micronesia
ACEIIMNRRU	cinerarium
ACEIIMRRST	erraticism
ACEIINNQRU	quinacrine
ACEIINNRTY	itinerancy
ACEIINOPST	speciation
ACEIINORTT	recitation
ACEIINOSTT	ice station
ACEIINOSTV	vesication
ACEIINOTTX	excitation, intoxicate
ACEIINPPRT	principate
ACEIINPSTT	antiseptic, psittacine
ACEIIOPRRV	Pico Rivera
ACEIIORRRT	certiorari
ACEIIRRSSU	cuirassier
ACEIIRTTVY	creativity, reactivity
ACEIKLLRST	strike call
ACEIKLLSTY	acetyl silk
ACEIKLRSTV	travel-sick
ACEIKNNRSS	crankiness
ACEIKNORTV	native rock
ACEIKNPSTT	septic tank
ACEIKORTUY	eukaryotic
ACEILLLOPW	lace-pillow, pillow lace
ACEILLLPRU	pellicular
ACEILLMNSY	miscellany
ACEILLMRTY	metrically
ACEILLNNNO	cannelloni
ACEILLNORT	citronella
ACEILLNRTU	lenticular
ACEILLOPSW	pillowcase
ACEILLOPTY	poetically
ACEILLORTV	vorticella
ACEILLORTY	erotically
ACEILLOSTY	societally
ACEILLOTXY	exotically
ACEILLPRUY	peculiarly
ACEILLPSTY	septically
ACEILLRSVY	viscerally
ACEILLRTUV	victualler
ACEILLRTVY	vertically
ACEILMMNSS	clamminess
ACEILMNOPR	complainer
ACEILMNRST	centralism
ACEILMNRTU	unmetrical
ACEILMNRUW	lawrencium
ACEILMOPRR	proclaimer
ACEILMRRUV	vermicular
ACEILMRSSU	secularism
ACEILMRSUY	early music
ACEILMTUUV	cumulative
ACEILNNOOP	Napoleonic
ACEILNNOTU	nucleation
ACEILNOORT	corelation, relocation
ACEILNOPRT	pratincole
ACEILNOPST	neoplastic, pleonastic
ACEILNOPTU	peculation, unpoetical
ACEILNORTU	ulceration
ACEILNORTY	lectionary
ACEILNOSTU	inosculate
ACEILNRSST	inter-class
ACEILNRSTT	centralist
ACEILNRSTU	lacustrine
ACEILNRTTY	centrality
ACEILNRTVY	trivalency
ACEILNRUUX	luxuriance
ACEILNRUVZ	vulcanizer
ACEILNSSSS	classiness
ACEILOOSUV	olivaceous, violaceous
ACEILOPRRT	replicator
ACEILOPRTX	explicator
ACEILOPTUV	copulative
ACEILOQTUY	co-equality
ACEILORTTV	tail covert
ACEILPPSTU	supplicate
ACEILPRTUU	apiculture
ACEILRRSUV	versicular
ACEILRSSTU	secularist
ACEILRSTTU	testicular
ACEILRSTUY	secularity
ACEILRTUUV	aviculture
ACEIMMNORT	manometric
ACEIMMRSTY	asymmetric
ACEIMNNRUY	innumeracy
ACEIMNOPRT	importance
ACEIMNORSU	main course
ACEIMNPSTU	pneumatics
ACEIMORTTT	tetratomic
ACEIMORTTU	tautomeric
ACEIMPPRSU	music paper
ACEIMSSTTY	systematic
ACEINNNRTU	renunciant
ACEINNNSTU	uncanniest
ACEINNOPTT	pentatonic
ACEINNORTU	enunciator
ACEINNRSTY	transiency
ACEINNRTUU	nunciature
ACEINNSSST	scantiness
ACEINNSSTT	intactness
ACEINOORTV	revocation
ACEINOPRTU	precaution
ACEINOPSTT	constipate
ACEINORRTT	retraction
ACEINORSSY	cessionary
ACEINORTTU	eructation
ACEINORTTW	tonic water
ACEINORTTX	extraction
ACEINOSTVW	West Covina
ACEINPRRSU	sprauncier
ACEINRSSTW	scrawniest
ACEINSSSTT	scattiness
ACEIOOPRTZ	azeotropic
ACEIOORTTU	auto-erotic
ACEIOPRRSU	precarious
ACEIOQSSUU	sequacious
ACEIORSTVY	vesicatory
ACEIORTTXY	excitatory
ACEIPPRSST	scrappiest
ACEJKLLOWY	yellow jack
ACEJKLPPSU	supplejack
ACEJORRTTY	trajectory
ACEKKMOSST	smokestack
ACEKKORSTT	stocktaker
ACEKLLLRTY	tally clerk
ACEKLLORTW	wall rocket

ACEKLLRSTU lackluster, lacklustre
ACEKLNOPST alpenstock
ACEKLNPRTU panel truck
ACEKMNORRW cankerworm
ACEKPRRSSY skyscraper
ACELLLORSS collarless
ACELLMMRSY small mercy
ACELLNOORT Eton collar
ACELLNOSSW callowness
ACELLNOTVY covalently
ACELLOPSTY closet play
ACELLORRTY trolley-car
ACELLORSSW lower class
ACELLPRSTY spectrally
ACELLSSTTY tactlessly
ACELMMNOOS common seal
ACELMMNOOW commonweal
ACELMNNOTT malcontent
ACELMNOOSV mooncalves
ACELNNNORU non-nuclear
ACELNNOSSU consensual
ACELNNOSTU Launceston
ACELNNOTUV conventual
ACELNOPRSY narcolepsy
ACELNORRTY necrolatry
ACELNOTTUX contextual
ACELNRTTUY truncately
ACELOOPRRT percolator
ACELOORRTW watercolor
ACELOPPRST parcel post
ACELOPRRUV polar curve
ACELOPRSTU speculator
ACELOPRSWY cow-parsley
ACELOPSTTT cattle stop
ACELORRSTY clearstory
ACELPPRSSU upper class
ACELPRSSSU superclass
ACELPSTUUY eucalyptus
ACELRSSTTY crystal set
ACEMMMNNOO common name
ACEMMNOORY common year
ACEMMNORTY commentary
ACEMMNOSTU consummate
ACEMMOSTTY mastectomy
ACEMNNNOTT cantonment
ACEMNNORST monstrance
ACEMNOSTTY nematocyst
ACEMOORSTU octamerous
ACEMORSTUY myrtaceous
ACENNOORTV covenantor
ACENNORSTV conversant
ACENNOSTTT contestant
ACENOORRSZ scorzonera
ACENOSTTUY county seat
ACEOOOPRRT cooperator
ACEOOPRRRT procreator
ACEOOPRRTY procaryote
ACEOOPSSTT statoscope
ACEOORRTVY revocatory
ACEORSTUXY excusatory
ACFFGINORU Rouffignac
ACFFIILLOY officially
ACFFIILNNO coffin-nail
ACFFIILNOT affliction
ACFFIILNOU unofficial
ACFFIIOORT officiator
ACFFILLNUY fancifully
ACFGILOPRY profligacy
ACFGILRSTU gastric flu
ACFHIINPTU Punic faith
ACFHINORRS franchisor
ACFHLLTUWY watchfully
ACFHLMOSTU stomachful
ACFHLNTUUW unwatchful
ACFIIILNST finalistic
ACFIIILNTY finicality
ACFIIIORTV factor VIII
ACFIILNOPT pontifical
ACFIILNORT frictional
ACFIINNORS infrasonic
ACFIINNORT infarction, infraction
ACFIIOSTTU factitious
ACFILLLORU follicular
ACFILNNOOT conflation
ACFILNNOTU functional
ACFILNOOPT focal point
ACFILNOOST tonic sol-fa
ACFILOSTUY factiously
ACFILRSSST first class
ACFINOORRT fornicator
ACFLLOOPRT port of call
ACFLNOORTW contraflow
ACFLNRRUUU furuncular
ACFLOORSTU colour fast
ACFLOORTUW court of law
ACFMNOORSW can of worms
ACGGHINNNU unchanging
ACGGIILLOT Glagolitic
ACGGIILNNO ganglionic
ACGGIINRSU icing sugar
ACGGILLNNY glancingly
ACGGILLOOY glaciology
ACGHHINTTW watch-night
ACGHIKMNOR Rockingham
ACGHILLOTY Gothically
ACGHILMNRY charmingly
ACGHILNRTU nautch girl
ACGHILNSTY scathingly
ACGHIMOPRR micrograph
ACGHINOORR choir organ
ACGHINOPRT prognathic
ACGHINOPRZ zincograph
ACGHIOOPRR orographic
ACGHIOPPRT pictograph
ACGHIRRTTW cartwright
ACGHLLOSST glass cloth
ACGHLORSST grasscloth
ACGIIKKMNS sick-making
ACGIIKLNSS ass-licking
ACGIIKMNOS mosaicking
ACGIILLOST logistical
ACGIILLOTY logicality
ACGIILLRTU liturgical
ACGIILMNNO coal mining
ACGIILNORY royal icing
ACGIILNRTY laryngitic
ACGIILNSST Anglistics
ACGIILNTUV victualing
ACGIIMNRST scintigram
ACGIINOOTT cogitation
ACGIINQTTU acquitting
ACGIIORSTY graciosity
ACGIKKMNRU muckraking
ACGIKLLNNY clankingly
ACGILLMNOY gnomically
ACGILLNNOO non-logical
ACGILLNOPS scalloping
ACGILLNORR corralling
ACGILLNORW wing collar
ACGILLNRWY crawlingly
ACGILLOOOT otological
ACGILLOOOZ zoological
ACGILLOORU urological
ACGILLRSUY surgically
ACGILNOORY craniology
ACGILORSUY glycosuria, graciously
ACGIMNSSTY gymnastics
ACGINNNOOR non-organic
ACGINNORRY carrying-on
ACGINOOSTU contagious
ACGINOPSUU pugnacious
ACGINORRSS cross-grain
ACGINORRTU touring car
ACGINORSUU ungracious
ACGJLLNOUY conjugally
ACGLNOORSU clangorous
ACGLNORSSW crown glass
ACGMOPRRTY cryptogram
ACGNNOPPUY oppugnancy
ACGOORRRTU corrugator
ACGORRSSTU grass court
ACHHIILPST phthisical
ACHHILMOPT ophthalmic
ACHHILMRTY rhythmical
ACHHILOOPS shopaholic
ACHHINOPRS archonship
ACHHIOPPST phosphatic
ACHHNOOTTU autochthon
ACHHOPPSTY psychopath
ACHIIIMNOY Ichinomiya
ACHIIIMNST histaminic
ACHIIIRSST trichiasis
ACHIILLMPS phallicism
ACHIILORST historical
ACHIIMNNOR inharmonic
ACHIIMNSTU humanistic
ACHIIMNSUV chauvinism
ACHIIMOPPP hippocampi
ACHIINNORT Corinthian
ACHIINORSU air cushion
ACHIINRSTT Antichrist
ACHIINSTUV chauvinist
ACHIIOPRST aphoristic
ACHIKLOORW workaholic
ACHIKMNOST mackintosh
ACHIKMNRSS scrimshank

ACHILLMOOS alcoholism
ACHILLMTYY mythically
ACHILLNNSY clannishly
ACHILLNOOP allophonic
ACHILLNOPY phonically
ACHILLORST choir stall
ACHILLPSYY physically
ACHILMOPTY polymathic
ACHILNORTU ulotrichan
ACHILNOSSY anchylosis
ACHILORSUV chivalrous
ACHILOSTTW waist-cloth
ACHIMMNORS monarchism
ACHIMNNORS Cornishman
ACHIMNOOPT taphonomic
ACHIMNOPTT match point
ACHIMNORST monarchist
ACHIMORRYZ mycorrhiza
ACHINOOPSX saxophonic
ACHINOORST cartoonish
ACHINOPSTY hyponastic
ACHINSTTUY unchastity
ACHIOOPPTT potato chip
ACHIOPRSTY physiocrat
ACHIOPSTTY hypostatic
ACHIPRSTYY psychiatry
ACHIQRRSUY squirarchy
ACHIRSTTWW wristwatch
ACHKLLOSST shock stall
ACHKNOOTTU Nouakchott
ACHLLOOPSY play school
ACHLMMOORS school-marm
ACHLOORSUW colour wash
ACHMOORTTY motor yacht
ACHNOOPSYZ scyphozoan
ACIIILLMNP ampicillin
ACIIILLMNY inimically
ACIIILNOPT politician
ACIIILNPST sincipital
ACIIILORTV variolitic
ACIIILSTTV vitalistic
ACIIINNOTT incitation
ACIIINRSTT inartistic
ACIIINTTVY inactivity
ACIIJLRSTU juristical
ACIIJRSTUY justiciary
ACIIKNNNPY pickaninny
ACIIKNPSTT paintstick
ACIIKNRSST Sanskritic
ACIIKTTUWY Kuwait City
ACIILLMNRY criminally
ACIILLNNOS Scillonian
ACIILLNORY ironically
ACIILLNRUY culinarily
ACIILMNSUY musicianly
ACIILMORST moralistic
ACIILMSTUY musicality
ACIILNOPRV provincial
ACIILNORTT tinctorial
ACIILNOTXY anxiolytic
ACIILOPTTY topicality
ACIILOSSUV lascivious
ACIILPSTTY plasticity
ACIILPTTYY typicality
ACIILRSTTU altruistic
ACIIMMNOPT pantomimic
ACIIMMNSTU numismatic
ACIIMNPTTY tympanitic
ACIIMNRSSS narcissism
ACIIMNRSTU manicurist
ACIIMPSSTT psittacism
ACIINNOOTV invocation
ACIINNOSTU insouciant
ACIINNOTTX intoxicant
ACIINOOSTT oscitation
ACIINOPRST ascription
ACIINORTTU urtication
ACIINOSTUU incautious
ACIINRSSST narcissist
ACIINRSTTU unartistic
ACIIOPRRST scriptoria
ACIIOPSSUU auspicious
ACIIOPSTZZ pizzicatos
ACIIORSTVY varicosity
ACIIPRSSTT patristics
ACIIPSSTTY spasticity
ACIISSSTTT statistics
ACIJLORTUY jocularity
ACIKKLMNOR Kilmarnock
ACIKLLNOPR pink-collar
ACIKLLNOTY Clonakilty
ACIKLMRTTU multi-track
ACIKLNNOPT planktonic
ACIKLOORSW social work
ACIKOPRTYY karyotypic
ACILLLNOOY colonially
ACILLLOOQU colloquial
ACILLMNNOO monoclinal
ACILLMOORT collimator
ACILLMOPYY myopically
ACILLMOTUV multivocal
ACILLMSTYY mystically
ACILLNOOTU allocution
ACILLNOPST splint-coal
ACILLNORUU unilocular
ACILLNORUV involucral
ACILLNOSUY unsocially
ACILLNOUVY univocally
ACILLOOPRT allotropic
ACILLOORST oscillator
ACILLOPRTY tropically
ACILLORTVY vortically
ACILLRSTUY rustically
ACILMMRSUU simulacrum
ACILMNOSSU salon music
ACILMNOSUU calumnious
ACILMNOTUU cumulation
ACILMNRSUU minuscular
ACILMORSUU miraculous
ACILMPRSUU spiraculum
ACILNOOORT coloration
ACILNOOPTU copulation
ACILNOORTU inoculator
ACILNOORTY iconolatry
ACILNOOSTU osculation
ACILNOOTTT cottontail
ACILNOPSTY synoptical
ACILNORRTY contrarily
ACILNORSST Latin cross
ACILNORSTU ultrasonic
ACILNPPSTU supplicant
ACILNRTTUY taciturnly
ACILOOPRRT proctorial
ACILOOPSTT post-coital
ACILOOQSUU loquacious
ACILOOSSUX saxicolous
ACILOPSSUY spaciously
ACILOPSTUY captiously
ACILORRTUV vorticular
ACILORTTUV cultivator
ACILOSTUUY cautiously
ACILPRRSTU scriptural
ACIMMORSSY commissary
ACIMNNNOOR minor canon
ACIMNNORTU unromantic
ACIMNNOSTY sanctimony
ACIMNOOPRS comparison
ACIMNOOPSS compassion
ACIMNOORST astronomic
ACIMNOORTY craniotomy
ACIMNOOSST onomastics
ACIMNOPPRS prison camp
ACIMNOPPTU pump-action
ACIMNOPRTY patronymic
ACIMNOPSST tonic spasm
ACIMNPRSTU manuscript
ACIMOOPRTT compatriot
ACIMOPRRRR mirror carp
ACIMOPSTTY asymptotic
ACINNNOSTT inconstant
ACINNNOTTU continuant
ACINNOOORT coronation
ACINNOPTTU punctation
ACINNORSST trans-sonic
ACINNORSTT constraint
ACINNORTTU truncation
ACINOOOPTT co-optation
ACINOORSTT cartoonist
ACINOORTVY invocatory
ACINOPSTUU usucaption
ACINPRRSTT transcript
ACIOORSTVY Ivory Coast
ACKLMNOORS rock salmon
ACKOOPRSTY pastry-cook
ACKRRSSTTU star-struck
ACLLLOOSSY colossally
ACLLLRTUUY culturally
ACLLMMNOUY communally
ACLLMNNOOO monoclonal
ACLLMRSUUY muscularly
ACLLNPTUUY punctually
ACLLOOPRRY corporally
ACLLORRSSY rallycross
ACLLPRSTUU sculptural
ACLMMNOOST common salt
ACLMMNOOTY commonalty
ACLMNORRUW mural crown
ACLNNOSTTU consultant
ACLNNOSTTY constantly
ACLNNOSTUV convulsant
ACLNNPTUUU unpunctual
ACLNNRSUUU ranunculus
ACLNOORSTY stony coral

ACLOOPRTUY copulatory
ACLOORSTUY osculatory
ACLRRSTTUU structural
ACMMOORTTU commutator
ACMMPPUUUV vacuum pump
ACMNNORTUY countryman
ACMNOOPRTU contour map
ACMNOOSSTW Scotswoman
ACNOOPRSTY syncopator
ACNOORRSTW crown roast
ACNOPRSSUY syncarpous
ACOOPRRRTT protractor
ACOOPRRRTU procurator
ACOOPRSSTT sports coat
ACOPRSSSTT sportscast
ADDDEEFHIL fiddle-head
ADDDEEGILM middle-aged
ADDDEEHNRU dunderhead
ADDDEEILSS side-saddle
ADDDEGINWY wedding day
ADDEEEEPST deep-seated
ADDEEEFHNR free-handed
ADDEEEFNTU undefeated
ADDEEEHLRT Etheldreda
ADDEEEHNNV even-handed
ADDEEEIRST desiderate
ADDEEELNTT dead nettle
ADDEEELPST pedestaled
ADDEEELRST saddle tree
ADDEEELRTT dead letter
ADDEEFHLNT left-handed
ADDEEFHNOR forehanded
ADDEEFHOST soft-headed
ADDEEFHOTT fed to death
ADDEEGHILR Hildegarde
ADDEEGHITW dead weight
ADDEEGHLNO long-headed
ADDEEGILMM middle game
ADDEEGILMS Middle Ages
ADDEEGINRR dead ringer
ADDEEGNRRU unregarded
ADDEEGORRZ razor-edged
ADDEEHLLNS handselled
ADDEEHLNRU unheralded
ADDEEHLNST eldest hand
ADDEEHNNOP open-handed
ADDEEHNOOW wooden-head
ADDEEIIMMX mixed media
ADDEEIKMNW weak-minded
ADDEEILMMN middle name
ADDEEILMST Middle East
ADDEEILNSS deadliness
ADDEEIMNRR mind-reader
ADDEEIMNTU unmediated
ADDEEIMRTT readmitted
ADDEEIMRXY ready-mixed
ADDEEINTUV denudative
ADDEEIPRSW widespread
ADDEELLSSS saddleless
ADDEELMNOR endodermal
ADDEELMOTU demodulate
ADDEELOPRR rope ladder
ADDEELORSS saddle-sore
ADDEELPRST stepladder
ADDEEMNNOT demand note
ADDEEMORRS rose madder
ADDEENNTTU unattended
ADDEENRRUW unrewarded
ADDEEOPRRT depredator
ADDEFIIMNR fair-minded
ADDEFLLOOP flapdoodle
ADDEFLLRUY dreadfully
ADDEGHHHIN high-handed
ADDEGHLNOR dog handler
ADDEGHLORT gold thread
ADDEGJMNTU adjudgment
ADDEGMNORR dendrogram
ADDEHIMNOO maidenhood
ADDEHKNORW handworked
ADDEHLLNOR landholder
ADDEHLORST stadholder
ADDEHMNNOW hand-me-down
ADDEHNOORT horned toad
ADDEHORRTY dehydrator
ADDEHORSTT short-dated
ADDEIILLSV ill-advised
ADDEIIORVY video diary
ADDEILMNOY Lydian mode
ADDEILMTTY admittedly
ADDEILNNRY dinner lady
ADDEILNOYZ daily dozen
ADDEIMNOOR Dorian mode
ADDEIMNSUY undismayed
ADDEIMRSSS misaddress
ADDEINNORU unordained
ADDEINNOTU denudation
ADDEINOORS radiosonde
ADDEJNSTUU unadjusted
ADDELLMNPU demand pull
ADDELMORRW dream-world
ADDELNNORW wonderland
ADDELNNRSU Sunderland
ADDELNOORW woodlander
ADDENNPRUU up-and-under
ADDENNRSTU understand
ADDFGIOORY Good Friday
ADDFIILNSU disdainful
ADDGHHINRY high and dry
ADDGHINNOT Haddington
ADDHIILMOS old-maidish
ADDHILORSU shroud-laid
ADDIIILNUV individual
ADDILLLLYY dilly-dally
ADDILNNTUY inland duty
ADDILNORSW solid-drawn
ADDLNORWWY downwardly
ADDNNOOTUW down and out
ADEEEEGLMN needle game
ADEEEEGNRT degenerate
ADEEEFILRZ federalize
ADEEEFIRTV federative
ADEEEFLORR freeloader
ADEEEFMNNS defenseman
ADEEEGGGLT gatelegged
ADEEEGKNRR green drake
ADEEEGLRTU deregulate
ADEEEHLPSY sleepyhead
ADEEEHLRRW ward-heeler
ADEEEHLRTT letterhead
ADEEEHLRTW treadwheel
ADEEEILMNR emeraldine
ADEEEIMNTV media event
ADEEEINNTV venetianed
ADEEEIOPSU peau-de-soie
ADEEEIRSTT Eastertide
ADEEELLNRW well-earned
ADEEELLRSS leaderless
ADEEELNNSS leadenness
ADEEELNNUV unleavened
ADEEELNPRU unrepealed
ADEEELNRSU underlease, unreleased
ADEEELNRUV unrevealed
ADEEELNSST elatedness
ADEEELPRTY repeatedly
ADEEEMNNRT endearment
ADEEENRRSW newsreader
ADEEENSSST sedateness
ADEEEQRSUY square-eyed
ADEEFFILOR foliar feed
ADEEFFLNRU Frauenfeld
ADEEFGHIRU figurehead
ADEEFGLNNW newfangled
ADEEFGLNRT Grand Fleet
ADEEFGLRRS self-regard
ADEEFHLNRT left-hander
ADEEFHLORW flower head
ADEEFHLRST self-hatred
ADEEFHNRTU unfathered
ADEEFILLNS self denial
ADEEFILMNT filamented
ADEEFILMRS federalism
ADEEFILORR relief road
ADEEFILRST federalist
ADEEFINORT federation
ADEEFINRRW fire warden
ADEEFIOPRS safe period
ADEEFLLLNN flannelled
ADEEFLLORS self-loader
ADEEFLLORW fallow deer
ADEEFMNRRU underframe
ADEEFMNRTY defrayment
ADEEFNNSTU unfastened
ADEEFNOPRR free pardon
ADEEGGHLOR loggerhead
ADEEGGJNSS jaggedness

ADEEGGLNOR golden ager
ADEEGGNRSS raggedness
ADEEGHINRS garnisheed
ADEEGIINSS diagenesis
ADEEGIJLNR Darjeeling
ADEEGIKNNW weak ending
ADEEGILNOT delegation
ADEEGILNRR ringleader
ADEEGILNRS resignaled
ADEEGIMNNR meandering
ADEEGINNRS Grenadines
ADEEGINRRT intergrade
ADEEGIORTV derogative
ADEEGLMNNO golden mean
ADEEGLMOST Maltese dog
ADEEGLNNPR preen gland
ADEEGLNORT goaltender
ADEEGLNRUZ underglaze
ADEEGLPPRY dapple grey
ADEEGLRRSS regardless
ADEEGMORSS gossamered
ADEEGNORRT dragon tree
ADEEGNRRSW greensward
ADEEGOORSV overdosage
ADEEGORRRT retrograde
ADEEGORRSZ razor's edge
ADEEHHILMR hemihedral
ADEEHHILST heat shield
ADEEHHLOSV shovelhead
ADEEHHMNOT heathendom
ADEEHHNORX hexahedron
ADEEHHNRTU headhunter
ADEEHIILPS aedileship
ADEEHIIPRS hesperidia
ADEEHIIRRW wire-haired
ADEEHIJMNU mujahideen
ADEEHIKLRT threadlike
ADEEHILNOT ethanediol
ADEEHILOPP paedophile
ADEEHILPPR harelipped
ADEEHILPRS dealership, leadership
ADEEHILSTT deathliest
ADEEHILSVY adhesively
ADEEHILSWY daisy wheel
ADEEHIMNUZ dehumanize
ADEEHIMPRY hypermedia
ADEEHINRST dishearten
ADEEHINRTV thread vein
ADEEHIPRRS readership
ADEEHIRRSZ sherardize
ADEEHIRRTY hereditary
ADEEHIRSTT threadiest
ADEEHKLLNT death knell
ADEEHKLRSS sheldrakes
ADEEHKNOOY hook and eye
ADEEHLLOST lethal dose
ADEEHLLSSY headlessly
ADEEHLMPPT pamphleted
ADEEHLNOTW down at heel
ADEEHLNRST Shetlander
ADEEHMNPRU unhampered
ADEEHNNRTU underneath
ADEEHOPPPT poppet-head
ADEEIIKLMN maidenlike
ADEEIIKNSS diakineses
ADEEIILMTT delimitate
ADEEIILNNY aniline dye
ADEEIILNSZ desalinize
ADEEIILNTV evidential
ADEEIILTVZ devitalize
ADEEIIMTTV meditative
ADEEIINSST East Indies
ADEEIIRTTW tidewaiter
ADEEIIRTVV derivative
ADEEIJOPRZ jeopardize
ADEEIKLLMS slaked lime
ADEEILLMRY remedially
ADEEILLMVY medievally
ADEEILLPRS espadrille
ADEEILLRRU derailleur
ADEEILLSVV slide-valve
ADEEILLUVV vaudeville
ADEEILMNPT pedimental
ADEEILMNRT derailment
ADEEILMORZ demoralize
ADEEILNORT delineator
ADEEILNPRT interplead
ADEEILNRTU adulterine
ADEEILNRUZ unrealized
ADEEILNTTT dilettante
ADEEILOPRZ depolarize
ADEEILORTX radiotelex
ADEEILPRRV pearl-diver
ADEEILPRST pilastered
ADEEILRSTW water slide
ADEEILRSVV slave-drive
ADEEIMMORT immoderate
ADEEIMMUVW medium wave
ADEEIMNNOT denominate, emendation
ADEEIMNNTT detainment
ADEEIMNNUX unexamined
ADEEIMNORV maiden over
ADEEIMNRSS dreaminess
ADEEIMORRT radiometer
ADEEIMORTU audiometer
ADEEIMOTTV demotivate
ADEEINOTTV denotative, detonative
ADEEINPPSX appendixes
ADEEINPRST pedestrian
ADEEINRRSS dreariness
ADEEINRSTU unsteadier
ADEEINRTTT tridentate
ADEEINSSST steadiness
ADEEIOPRSX peroxidase
ADEEIPRSTT tapestried
ADEEIPRTUV depurative
ADEEIRRRWW wiredrawer
ADEEIRRSTV advertiser
ADEEKLLMRW well-marked
ADEEKMNRRU unremarked
ADEEKMNRSS markedness
ADEEKMRRSS dressmaker
ADEEKNRRTU undertaker
ADEELLMMRT trammelled
ADEELLMNRS mallenders
ADEELLMNTU unmetalled
ADEELLMORT mortadelle
ADEELLNQUU unequalled
ADEELLNRUV unravelled
ADEELLORSS loss-leader
ADEELLORTT reallotted
ADEELLOSTY desolately
ADEELLQRRU quarrelled
ADEELMMORS mesodermal
ADEELMNNTU unlamented
ADEELMNOSY almond eyes
ADEELMNPUX unexampled
ADEELMNTZZ dazzlement
ADEELMORTY moderately
ADEELMRSUY measuredly
ADEELNNPPR pre-planned
ADEELNNQSU Queensland
ADEELNNTTU untalented
ADEELNORRV overlander
ADEELNRTTU laundrette
ADEELNRTUV untraveled
ADEELNRUUV undervalue
ADEELOPPTU depopulate
ADEELOPRSS leopardess
ADEELORSWW weasel word
ADEELRRSSW rewardless
ADEELRSSTU adulteress
ADEEMNNNRU unmannered
ADEEMNOPRR promenader
ADEEMNORTY emendatory
ADEEMNORYY ready money
ADEEMNPRTT department
ADEEMNRRTT retardment
ADEEMNRSTU unstreamed
ADEEMNRSUU unmeasured
ADEEMNSSTU sense datum
ADEEMNSTUU mansuetude
ADEEMOOSTU oedematous
ADEEMORRVW warmed-over
ADEEMRRSUY dry measure
ADEENNORSU unreasoned
ADEENNOSSU unseasoned
ADEENNPTTU unpatented
ADEENNRSUW unanswered
ADEENPPRRS red snapper
ADEENPPRRU unprepared
ADEENPPRSS dapperness
ADEENPRSST depressant
ADEENPRSTY present-day
ADEENQRRSU squanderer
ADEENRRTUV adventurer
ADEENRRTUW underwater
ADEENRSTTU understate
ADEEOOPSTT seed potato
ADEEOPPRRR order paper
ADEEOPRRSV overspread
ADEEOPRRTV overparted
ADEEOQRSTU square-toed
ADEEORRRVW overdrawer
ADEERRSTTW streetward
ADEERRSTYY starry-eyed

ADEERSSSTW stewardess
ADEERSSTVX sex-starved
ADEESTTTUY estate duty
ADEFFGIIRT graffitied
ADEFFLOOTT flat-footed
ADEFGGINOR God-fearing
ADEFGHIRST far-sighted
ADEFGIINOR foreign aid
ADEFGILNRY ladyfinger
ADEFGILRSU Life Guards
ADEFGILRSW Greifswald
ADEFGLNOST flagstoned
ADEFGNOORR roof garden
ADEFHHLOOT health food
ADEFHHOORT fatherhood
ADEFHILMSS damselfish
ADEFHILTTW half-witted
ADEFHINPRT pathfinder
ADEFHIRSTV driveshaft
ADEFHIRTWW white dwarf
ADEFHLLPUX half-duplex
ADEFHLTTWY Twelfth Day
ADEFHMNOTU unfathomed
ADEFHOORSW foreshadow
ADEFIIILNN Indian file
ADEFIILMST mailed fist
ADEFIILNNZ Finlandize
ADEFIILNRV final drive
ADEFIIRRST first aider
ADEFILLNTY inflatedly
ADEFILLORV ill-favored
ADEFILMNNU uninflamed
ADEFILOORT defoliator
ADEFILORTU fluoridate
ADEFINNOTU fountained
ADEFINOORR foreordain
ADEFINORSZ Sanforized
ADEFINRRSU fund-raiser
ADEFKNORSU unasked-for
ADEFLLOSUU useful load
ADEFLNORUV unflavored
ADEFLNRTUU fraudulent
ADEFLOORTW flood water
ADEFLOPRSY self-parody
ADEGGHILNR hang-glider
ADEGGIMOPS pedagogism
ADEGGIPRSW digger wasp
ADEGHHILNR highlander
ADEGHHINST nightshade
ADEGHILNNS handseling
ADEGHINPRS headspring
ADEGHIOPRY ideography
ADEGHLRTUY daughterly
ADEGHMOPRY demography
ADEGHNORST headstrong
ADEGHOOPTT gap-toothed
ADEGHORRTU rough trade
ADEGHORSUU guardhouse
ADEGIIILTZ digitalize
ADEGIILLNR redialling
ADEGIILLSU seguidilla
ADEGIILMNS misleading
ADEGIILNOT gadolinite
ADEGIILNRT ring-tailed
ADEGIILTTY digitately
ADEGIIOPRR prairie dog
ADEGILLNOS solid angle
ADEGILLNPY pleadingly
ADEGILMNOR goalminder
ADEGILMRTU multigrade
ADEGILNNNO non-aligned
ADEGILNNNT landing net
ADEGILNNRS sanderling
ADEGILNRST danger list
ADEGIMNORZ gormandize
ADEGINNSSU unassigned
ADEGINOORT derogation
ADEGINORRT denigrator
ADEGINORST designator
ADEGINPRSW wingspread
ADEGIPRRST partridges
ADEGJLMNTU judgmental
ADEGKNNORT knot-garden
ADEGKNRRRU krugerrand
ADEGLNORSU glanderous
ADEGLNPRUW wander plug
ADEGMMOPRR programmed
ADEGMNOOSU endogamous
ADEGNOOORW orange-wood
ADEGNOORTU good nature
ADEGNOPRRS sand-groper
ADEGNORSSU sandgrouse
ADEGOOPRST gasteropod
ADEGOORRTY derogatory
ADEHHIIPRT diphtheria
ADEHHIRRTW hitherward
ADEHHIRSSW dishwasher
ADEHHLLOOR holohedral
ADEHIILOPP pedophilia
ADEHIILOPU audiophile
ADEHIIMNNP Indian hemp
ADEHILLORU loud hailer
ADEHILNNRT hinterland
ADEHILNOPS sphenoidal
ADEHILNORT threnodial
ADEHILNRST disenthral
ADEHILOPRS spheroidal
ADEHIMNNTU minute hand
ADEHIMORTU rheumatoid
ADEHINOPPY hypnopedia
ADEHINPRSW wardenship
ADEHIOPRSZ rhapsodize
ADEHLLMOPR lamp holder
ADEHLLNOOR loanholder
ADEHLLNOUW unhallowed
ADEHLLOPRY polyhedral
ADEHLMNORT motherland
ADEHLMNOSY handsomely
ADEHLMNPPU pump-handle
ADEHLNOPRY hydroplane
ADEHLNRSTU Sutherland
ADEHLOSSSW shadowless
ADEHMMOPRR drop hammer
ADEHMNNOSU unhandsome
ADEHMNOSST handsomest
ADEHMNOTTU mutton-head
ADEHMOORST masterhood
ADEHMORRTW threadworm
ADEHMORSTY Mother's Day
ADEHNNNOTW now and then
ADEHNOOPRT parenthood
ADEHNOPPRS sand-hopper
ADEHNORRSW horse-drawn
ADEHOORSVW overshadow
ADEHOOSTTW sawtoothed
ADEHORRSSW shorewards
ADEHORSTWW Westward Ho
ADEIIIKNSS diakinesis
ADEIIILLNT initialled
ADEIIIMNTT intimidate
ADEIILLPTX pixillated
ADEIILLSTT distillate
ADEIILMMTU multimedia
ADEIILMNOR meridional
ADEIILNOPT depilation
ADEIILNRTT intertidal
ADEIILNTTT dilettanti
ADEIIMNNOO Ionian mode
ADEIIMNNOR iron maiden
ADEIIMNOTT meditation
ADEIIMNPRU unimpaired
ADEIIMNRST administer
ADEIIMNSTY disamenity
ADEIIMPRSU praesidium
ADEIIMRSTT dermatitis
ADEIINNNOS Indonesian
ADEIINNORT inordinate
ADEIINNOTW nationwide
ADEIINNOTX indexation
ADEIINNSST daintiness
ADEIINNSTW West Indian
ADEIINORTV derivation
ADEIINPTTU inaptitude
ADEIINRRST distrainer
ADEIINRTUV indurative
ADEIINTTUV unvitiated
ADEIIPRSST dissipater
ADEIISSSUV dissuasive
ADEIJKKLNR Kralendijk
ADEIJMMNRW windjammer
ADEIKLLLRY ladykiller
ADEIKLLMMT malted milk
ADEIKLLNUY unladylike
ADEIKLNOSU soundalike
ADEIKOPSWW widow's peak
ADEILLNOOS solenoidal
ADEILLNOSU delusional
ADEILLNPSS pallidness
ADEILLNRTU ill-natured
ADEILLNRUV unrivalled
ADEILLRRST ill-starred
ADEILLRSUY residually
ADEILMNOPR palindrome
ADEILMNORT intermodal

ADEILMNRST dismantler
ADEILMNSSS dismalness
ADEILMOORS ladies' room
ADEILMOPSZ psalmodize
ADEILNOOST desolation
ADEILNOOTV devotional
ADEILNOTUV unviolated
ADEILNPRTU prudential
ADEILNRSSV silver sand
ADEILNSTTU testudinal
ADEILNSTUY unsteadily
ADEILOORST oestradiol
ADEILOPRTT tetraploid
ADEILOPRTU duple ratio
ADEILOPRTY depilatory
ADEILOPTVY adoptively
ADEILORSST idolatress
ADEILOSSTT solid state
ADEILRSTTU stridulate
ADEILRTTXY dextrality
ADEIMMNRST mastermind
ADEIMMNTTU manumitted
ADEIMMORST moderatism
ADEIMNNORT ordainment
ADEIMNOORT moderation
ADEIMNRYZZ mizzen yard
ADEIMORRTY radiometry
ADEIMRTUUV duumvirate
ADEINNOOTT denotation, detonation
ADEINNOPWW window pane
ADEINNORTU trade union
ADEINNRSSW inwardness
ADEINNRSTU unstrained
ADEINOOPRT readoption
ADEINOPRTU depuration
ADEINOPTTU deputation
ADEINORSST adroitness
ADEINOSTVY video nasty
ADEINOSTWW window seat
ADEINPRSST dispersant
ADEINPRSSY dispensary
ADEINRSSTW tawdriness
ADEINSSSTU unassisted
ADEIOPPRSV disapprove
ADEIOPRRTU repudiator
ADEIOPRSTV adsorptive
ADEIOPRSTY depositary
ADEIORRSTT traditores
ADEIORSSTT siderostat
ADEIPPRRTY day tripper
ADEJMNSTTU adjustment
ADEKMNORTW downmarket
ADEKNOPRST pond-skater
ADELLNORRU all-rounder
ADELLNTUUY undulately
ADELLOORRR roadroller
ADELLOORRU Eurodollar
ADELLOORST rolled oats
ADELNNPRTU underplant
ADELNORSSU slanderous
ADELNRSTUW wanderlust
ADELORRWWY world-weary
ADELORSTUU adulterous

ADELPQRTUU quadruplet
ADEMMMNORU memorandum
ADEMNNOPWY Down Ampney
ADEMNNORSS randomness
ADEMNORSTW downstream
ADENNORRRU roadrunner
ADENNORSTW Newtonards
ADENNPRSTU underpants
ADENOPPRRU paper round
ADENOPPRUV unapproved
ADENPPRSTU unstrapped
ADENRRSSTW sternwards
ADENRRSUYY day nursery
ADEOOPPRSW soap powder
ADEOQRRSUW word-square
ADFFGINOOR off-roading
ADFFHLLOOS flash flood
ADFGHILOTY light of day
ADFGHINORS dragonfish
ADFGIILRRY girl Friday
ADFGILNNUY unfadingly
ADFGILORSU Douglas fir
ADFGINORRU fairground
ADFHINNORU four-in-hand
ADFIILQSUY disqualify
ADFIIOSSTU fastidious
ADFIISSSTY dissatisfy
ADFILLMNOY manifoldly
ADFILOSTTU studio flat
ADFINNOOTU foundation
ADFINNORSU infrasound
ADFIOPRSUU pious fraud
ADFLMNTUUU mutual fund
ADFNORRSTW frontwards
ADGGINNORR ranging-rod
ADGGLLRSUY sluggardly
ADGHHILNOW high and low
ADGHIILLNN dining hall
ADGHILRTUY draughtily
ADGHIMNOPP hopping mad
ADGHINNPRS handspring
ADGHIRRSTW rightwards
ADGHIRSTTU distraught
ADGHLLMNPY lymph gland
ADGHLLNOPU ploughland
ADGIIILNNV invaliding
ADGIIINNNS Indian sign
ADGIIINOTT digitation
ADGIIKNNPP kidnapping
ADGIILMNOU gadolinium
ADGIILMNPR riding lamp
ADGIILMNRY admiringly
ADGIIMNPRS rising damp
ADGIINNPRW drawing pin
ADGIINPRTW writing pad
ADGIKNORWY working day
ADGILLNOPY polling day
ADGILLNORS dollar sign
ADGILLNYZZ dazzlingly
ADGILLOPRY prodigally

ADGILNNNOW landowning
ADGILNNORT Darlington
ADGILNNTUY dauntingly
ADGILNOSTT Ingolstadt
ADGIMNOOSY doomsaying
ADGINNOSTU astounding
ADGINNPSTU upstanding
ADGINPRRSX Grands Prix
ADGINRRSTW drawstring
ADGIORSSWW grass widow
ADGLLMOOSS smallgoods
ADGLNNOPRU ground plan
ADGLNOPRUY playground
ADGMNNORSU groundsman
ADGNNORSUY gynandrous
ADGORRSSSW sword grass
ADHHNOOOPR orphanhood
ADHHNOSTTU thousandth
ADHHOPRTYY hydropathy
ADHIILMNOT Midlothian
ADHIIMMNPS midshipman
ADHIINNSTU Hindustani
ADHILNOSTU outlandish
ADHILOOPRS drosophila
ADHIMNORSY disharmony
ADHINNOOOT nationhood
ADHINOOPRT anthropoid
ADHINOSSWW sash window
ADHINSTUWY Whit Sunday
ADHIOPRSST rhapsodist
ADHIPRRTTY third party
ADHLNOPSSW splashdown
ADHMNOOORT matronhood
ADHNOOPSSY soda syphon
ADHNORRSTW northwards
ADHNORSTWW Wandsworth
ADHOORRTWY roadworthy
ADHORSSTUW southwards
ADIIILMNSV invalidism
ADIIILMRSS dissimilar
ADIIILNOSV divisional
ADIIILNTVY invalidity
ADIIINNOOT iodination
ADIIINNOTV divination
ADIIINOOTZ iodization
ADIILLORTY dilatorily
ADIILMOPRR primordial
ADIILMOPRS prismoidal
ADIILNORRY ordinarily
ADIILNOSSU sinusoidal
ADIILNRSTU industrial
ADIILOQRTU liquidator
ADIILORSTY solidarity
ADIILQSTUY squalidity
ADIIMMMOTU ommatidium
ADIIMNNNOO Anno Domini
ADIIMNNOOT admonition, domination
ADIIMNORTX dominatrix
ADIIMORTUU auditorium
ADIIMQRUUV quadrivium

ADIINNNOTU inundation
ADIINNOORT ordination
ADIINNORTU induration
ADIINOPPST disappoint
ADIINORRST distrainor
ADIINORTVY divinatory
ADIINOSSSU dissuasion
ADIIOPRSST dissipator
ADIIOPRSTT podiatrist
ADIKMORSTT ditto marks
ADILLLMORS Lollardism
ADILLLOSYY disloyally
ADILLNSSTT standstill
ADILLOORTY toroidally
ADILLOSTYY disloyalty
ADILMMOPSU plasmodium, sodium lamp
ADILMNNOTY dominantly
ADILMNOOTU modulation
ADILMOPSST psalmodist
ADILMORTUY modularity
ADILNNOOTU nodulation
ADILNNOTUU undulation
ADILNRSTTU stridulant
ADILOORSTU idolatrous
ADIMNOORTY admonitory
ADIMORSTUU sudatorium
ADINNOPSTT standpoint
ADINNORRUY unordinary
ADINOOPRST adsorption
ADINORRSTU triandrous
ADINORSSTW downstairs
ADIORSSSTU disastrous
ADKMNOPSUW Swakopmund
ADLLMORSSW small-sword
ADLLOOPRST dollar spot
ADLMOOORSU malodorous
ADLNORSTUU ultrasound
ADLNORTUUY undulatory
ADLNORTUWY untowardly
ADMNNOORSU monandrous
ADNNORRTUU turnaround
AEEEEGKMPR gamekeeper
AEEEEGKPRT gatekeeper
AEEEEGNRRT regenerate
AEEEEGRTTV revegetate
AEEEEKRSTW Easter week
AEEEFFGLRU effleurage
AEEEFFIMNT effeminate
AEEEFHNPRT pen-feather
AEEEFHRRTT thereafter
AEEEFHRRTW whereafter
AEEEFINRTZ antifreeze
AEEEFKMRRT free market
AEEEFLLNST fenestella
AEEEFLMNSS femaleness
AEEEFLNNRT Lenten fare
AEEEFNRRST transferee
AEEEFNRSTT fenestrate
AEEEGGMNNT engagement
AEEEGHINNT heat engine
AEEEGHLPRT telpherage

AEEEGHNRRT green earth, greenheart
AEEEGILNNV Evangeline
AEEEGILNRZ generalize
AEEEGILNUV eigenvalue
AEEEGILNVZ evangelize
AEEEGINNOR aero-engine
AEEEGINRTV generative
AEEEGITTVV vegetative
AEEEGKLOPR goalkeeper
AEEEGLMNRT regalement
AEEEGLNOPR orange peel
AEEEGLRSSS greaseless
AEEEGMNNRT enragement
AEEEGMNRSS meagreness
AEEEGNPPRR Green Paper
AEEEHHPRST three-phase
AEEEHLLRTY ethereally
AEEEHLMSTT sheet metal
AEEEHLORSV shore leave
AEEEHLRTWW waterwheel
AEEEHMPRTT heptameter
AEEEHMSSTT metatheses
AEEEHNNRTT thereanent
AEEEHNNSTV heaven-sent
AEEEHNORTY honeyeater
AEEEHNRRTT threatener
AEEEHRRTTU Terre Haute
AEEEHRSTTW sweetheart
AEEEHRTTWW wet-weather
AEEEIIPPRT peripeteia
AEEEILNRTV interleave
AEEEILNRTZ eternalize
AEEEIMNSTV Vietnamese
AEEEINRTTV inveterate
AEEEINRTVW interweave
AEEEIPRTVY private eye
AEEEJKRRRT tear-jerker
AEEEJNRTUV rejuvenate
AEEEKPSSTW sweepstake
AEEELLLRTT taleteller
AEEELLNRVY venereally
AEEELLRTVW water level
AEEELLSSTT tessellate
AEEELMNNTT tenemental
AEEELMNRTY elementary
AEEELORTTT teetotaler
AEEEMMNORT anemometer
AEEEMNOPSS open sesame
AEEEMNPRTT pentameter
AEEEMNRRTU remunerate
AEEEMPPRRY emery paper
AEEEMRRTTT tetrameter
AEEEMRRTTW water meter
AEEENPRSST sea serpent
AEEENQRSUW queen's-ware
AEEENRSSSY synaereses
AEEENRTUVX revenue tax
AEEEPPRRTT perpetrate
AEEEPPRTTU perpetuate
AEEERRSTYY yesteryear
AEEERSSTTY Easy Street
AEEFFHILLR half-relief

AEEFFHORRT forefather
AEEFFLLORR free-for-all
AEEFFORRST reafforest
AEEFFSSTUY safety fuse
AEEFGGHIRT freightage
AEEFGHINRT feathering
AEEFGHORRT foregather
AEEFGILLNT leafleting
AEEFGILNRR rifle range
AEEFGILPRS persiflage
AEEFGLLNSS flangeless
AEEFGLPRSU presageful
AEEFHHINRT Fahrenheit
AEEFHIKLRT fatherlike
AEEFHIKNST sneak thief
AEEFHILRTU haut-relief
AEEFHIMRTT Father Time
AEEFHINPRT pin-feather
AEEFHLOPPR leafhopper
AEEFHLRSST fatherless
AEEFHMORSU frame house
AEEFHMORTT fathometer
AEEFHMRRSV marsh fever
AEEFHPRSTT stepfather
AEEFHRRSTW freshwater
AEEFIIRRRS fire-raiser
AEEFIKKNST steak knife
AEEFIKLNPT knife-pleat
AEEFIKLRRW fire-walker
AEEFIKNPPR paperknife
AEEFIKNRSS freakiness
AEEFILLRSV silver-leaf
AEEFILMRTY family tree
AEEFILOPRT perfoliate
AEEFILPRSS self-praise
AEEFILRTTX exfiltrate
AEEFIMNRRT freemartin
AEEFINRRTZ fraternize
AEEFKLLLRW fell walker
AEEFKLMNOY leaf monkey
AEEFLLLMOW mallee fowl
AEEFLLNNOT fontanelle
AEEFLLNNSS fallenness
AEEFLLNRUY funereally
AEEFLLRSSY fearlessly
AEEFLMORSY fearsomely
AEEFMNNOSS man of sense
AEEFNNSSSU unsafeness
AEEFNORRRW forewarner
AEEFNOSTYZ safety zone
AEEGGHILRT lighterage
AEEGGHOPRR geographer
AEEGGINORS seignorage
AEEGGIRSSV aggressive
AEEGGMORRT remortgage
AEEGGNOTTW waggonette
AEEGGORSSU sage grouse
AEEGHHMORR hemorrhage
AEEGHIILMP hemiplegia
AEEGHIKMTW makeweight
AEEGHILNSS Singhalese
AEEGHILPST legateship
AEEGHINNRT heartening
AEEGHINRSS garnishees

AEEGHINRTW	weathering
AEEGHKNNRS	greenshank
AEEGHLLLNS	Hell's Angel
AEEGHLMORT	geothermal
AEEGHLNTVW	wavelength
AEEGHLORTT	altogether
AEEGHLPRTY	telegraphy
AEEGHMNOOT	homogenate
AEEGHMORTY	game theory, heterogamy
AEEGHNOSTU	house agent
AEEGIILLNV	villeinage
AEEGIILMTT	legitimate
AEEGIILNTZ	gelatinize
AEEGIIMNNT	ingeminate
AEEGIIMNTZ	enigmatize
AEEGIINRST	siege-train
AEEGIKNNNT	tank engine
AEEGILLLNO	legionella
AEEGILLMNN	enamelling
AEEGILLNSW	weaselling
AEEGILLORZ	allegorize
AEEGILLRTY	galleryite
AEEGILMNRR	malingerer
AEEGILMNRT	regimental
AEEGILMNSV	evangelism
AEEGILNOPS	anglepoise
AEEGILNORT	regelation, relegation
AEEGILNRST	generalist
AEEGILNRTY	generality
AEEGILNSTV	evangelist
AEEGILNTVY	negatively
AEEGILRRUZ	regularize
AEEGILRTUV	regulative
AEEGIMNPRT	impregnate
AEEGIMNRRZ	Germanizer
AEEGIMNRTZ	magnetizer
AEEGIMPRRR	Grim Reaper
AEEGIMRRTU	marguerite
AEEGIMRRTV	gravimeter
AEEGIMSTTU	guestimate
AEEGINNORT	generation
AEEGINNRRT	interregna
AEEGINORRZ	reorganize
AEEGINOTTV	vegetation
AEEGINPRRS	Paris green
AEEGINPRYZ	panegyrize
AEEGINRSSS	greasiness
AEEGIPPRRT	paper tiger
AEEGIPRRTW	gripe water
AEEGJLLNOR	jargonelle
AEEGKMRRTY	grey market
AEEGLLNOSS	Los Angeles
AEEGLLORTT	allegretto
AEEGLMMOSY	gamesomely
AEEGLMNTTU	tegumental
AEEGLMOPSU	plaguesome
AEEGLNORTU	outgeneral
AEEGLNORTV	lovat green
AEEGLOPRRT	Portalegre
AEEGLOPRSY	greasy pole
AEEGLORTUV	travelogue
AEEGMNNOST	mangosteen
AEEGMNRSSY	mass energy
AEEGMNRSTY	segmentary
AEEGMRRSTU	steamer rug
AEEGMRRTTY	grey matter
AEEGNNORSS	sense organ
AEEGNORSTV	gravestone
AEEGNORSTW	West Orange
AEEGNORTTY	teratogeny
AEEGNPRSST	press agent
AEEHHILSTT	healthiest
AEEHHILTWW	white whale
AEEHHIMNST	heathenism
AEEHHINRRR	hen harrier
AEEHHINRST	earthshine
AEEHHKNPSS	sheepshank
AEEHHLMSTU	Methuselah
AEEHHLOTWW	wholewheat
AEEHHLSSST	sheathless
AEEHIILLPT	epithelial
AEEHIINPRR	prairie hen
AEEHIINPRZ	heparinize
AEEHIISTTV	hesitative
AEEHIKLNNP	enkephalin
AEEHILLRRS	hellraiser
AEEHILMRTZ	thermalize
AEEHILMTTW	white metal
AEEHILPPRR	peripheral
AEEHILPRST	sphalerite
AEEHILPSST	shapeliest
AEEHILRSTT	stealthier
AEEHILRTTT	triathlete
AEEHILSTTW	wealthiest
AEEHILSTVW	white slave
AEEHIMPRSS	re-emphasis
AEEHIMSSTT	metathesis
AEEHINPRST	interphase
AEEHINRSST	earthiness, heartiness
AEEHINSSTT	antitheses
AEEHIPPRTW	White Paper
AEEHIRTTWW	white water
AEEHISTUVX	exhaustive
AEEHJORSTU	Joshua tree
AEEHKOPSSV	spokeshave
AEEHKORSTT	heatstroke
AEEHKOSSTU	steakhouse
AEEHLLORSW	wholesaler
AEEHLLSTTY	tally sheet
AEEHLMMRSS	hammerless
AEEHLMNNOP	phenomenal
AEEHLMORTX	exothermal
AEEHLMPRSW	sperm whale
AEEHLNRSTT	nettle-rash
AEEHLRSTTX	tax shelter
AEEHMNNSSU	humaneness
AEEHMNOORR	menorrhoea
AEEHMNOPRT	Promethean
AEEHMOPRST	atmosphere
AEEHMORRTV	earth mover
AEEHMRSTVY	stave rhyme
AEEHNNOORT	one another
AEEHNNOSTV	Stonehaven
AEEHNORSSS	hoarseness
AEEHNPPTVY	happy event
AEEHOOPRRS	horse opera
AEEHOOPRST	pea-shooter
AEEHOOPRSU	opera house
AEEHOOPSST	apotheoses
AEEHORSTVW	whatsoever
AEEHORTTXY	heterotaxy
AEEHORTVWY	wave theory
AEEHOSSTTU	state house
AEEHPRRSTT	three parts
AEEIIKNRTZ	keratinize
AEEIILLRTT	illiterate
AEEIILLRTZ	literalize
AEEIILMNRZ	mineralize
AEEIILNNSU	Eleusinian
AEEIILRRTV	irrelative
AEEIILRTVZ	revitalize
AEEIIMNNST	inseminate
AEEIIMNSTT	anti-Semite
AEEIIMPRTV	imperative
AEEIIMSTTV	estimative
AEEIINPRST	septenarii
AEEIINRTWW	wine waiter
AEEIINTTTV	entitative
AEEIIPPTTV	appetitive
AEEIIPRSST	patisserie
AEEIJLLNSV	Janesville
AEEIJOPRTV	pejorative
AEEIKLNNRT	Interlaken
AEEIKLNSSW	weakliness
AEEIKLOSSS	sessile oak
AEEIKLRRWW	wire-walker
AEEIKMMORV	movie-maker
AEEIKMNORS	noise-maker
AEEIKNNSSS	sneakiness
AEEIKQSSTU	squeakiest
AEEIKRRSTT	strike rate
AEEIKRRSTW	water-skier
AEEIKRSSTT	streakiest
AEEILLLLNV	villanelle
AEEILLMNNT	Le Lamentin
AEEILLNPRV	Naperville
AEEILLNSVV	Evansville
AEEILLPSTT	stipellate
AEEILLRSSV	Versailles
AEEILLRTTY	literately
AEEILLRTVY	relatively
AEEILLSTUV	televisual
AEEILMMNPT	impalement
AEEILMNNTT	entailment
AEEILMNPRT	planimeter
AEEILMNRST	streamline
AEEILMQRSU	Square Mile
AEEILMRTTV	time travel
AEEILNNPST	septennial
AEEILNNRST	real tennis
AEEILNNSTT	sentential
AEEILNNTTU	lieutenant
AEEILNOPRT	peritoneal
AEEILNORTV	revelation
AEEILNPRSS	pearliness
AEEILNQSTU	sequential
AEEILNQTUV	equivalent

AEEILNQUUZ unequalize
AEEILNRRTV irrelevant
AEEILNRTTY eternality
AEEILNRTUZ neutralize
AEEILNSSSZ sleaziness
AEEILNSSUZ sensualize
AEEILNSTVX sexivalent
AEEILOPRST periosteal
AEEILPPRRT peripteral
AEEILPRSSY erysipelas
AEEILRRSVW silverware
AEEILRRTTU literature
AEEILSSTTT stateliest
AEEIMMMRST metamerism
AEEIMMRSSU mismeasure
AEEIMNNORT enantiomer, renominate
AEEIMNNPRT pine marten
AEEIMNNRTT retainment
AEEIMNNRTU innumerate
AEEIMNOPRT permeation
AEEIMNORTT marionette
AEEIMNOSTT maisonette
AEEIMNPRRU praemunire
AEEIMNRSSU Surinamese
AEEIMNRSTT main street, martensite
AEEIMNSSST steaminess
AEEIMOPQSU semi-opaque
AEEIMORRTV variometer
AEEIMQRSUV semiquaver
AEEIMRSTTW time-waster
AEEINNNSST innateness
AEEINNNTVY in any event
AEEINNORTV enervation, veneration
AEEINNOTTT Antoinette
AEEINNPRSS Spenserian
AEEINNRTUV aventurine
AEEINNSSSU uneasiness
AEEINNSSTT assentient
AEEINNSSTV nativeness
AEEINOPTTT potentiate
AEEINPRSTU resupinate
AEEINQRSTU equestrian
AEEINQSSSU queasiness
AEEINRRRST restrainer
AEEINRRTTV travertine
AEEINRRTVY veterinary
AEEINRSSSY synaeresis
AEEINRSSTW wateriness
AEEINRSTTT interstate
AEEINRSTTW wine taster
AEEINSSSTW sweatiness
AEEINSSSTY yeastiness
AEEIPPRRTW wire-tapper
AEEIPRSSTT striptease
AEEIPRSSUV persuasive
AEEIPRSTTX sexpartite
AEEIPRSTUZ pasteurize
AEEIPRTTUV vituperate
AEEIQRRTTU triquetrae
AEEIRRRSTZ rasterizer
AEEJLNORSU journalese
AEEKLLLSTY skeletally
AEEKLMNORW enamelwork
AEEKLMSTVY Almetyevsk
AEEKLOPRRW rope-walker
AEEKMMNORY moneymaker
AEEKMMNOTW weak moment
AEEKMMRRRY merrymaker
AEEKMNOPRT open market
AEEKMORRTU Euromarket
AEELLMNOTV malevolent
AEELLMNRTU allurement
AEELLMNSSY namelessly
AEELLMORTW tree mallow
AEELLMSSSY seamlessly
AEELLNOPRT Petronella
AEELLNRTVY relevantly
AEELLNRTXY externally
AEELLNSSTT talentless
AEELLNTUVY eventually
AEELLORTTW tallow tree
AEELLORTTY tea trolley
AEELLPPPRW wall pepper
AEELLQRRRU quarreller
AEELLRSSTY tearlessly
AEELLRSTTW Wall Street
AEELMMNORY memory lane
AEELMNNRSS mannerless
AEELMNOPRT planometer
AEELMNORSS moral sense
AEELMNORTV overmantel
AEELMNORTW watermelon
AEELMOPRSY polymerase
AEELMORTTV voltameter
AEELMPRSTT street lamp
AEELMRSSST masterless, streamless
AEELMRSUUX Les Mureaux
AEELNNORSW New Orleans
AEELNNPTTU antepenult
AEELNNQSTU lansquenet
AEELNNSSTT tenantless
AEELNOORYZ ozone layer
AEELNOPSSW weaponless
AEELNOPTTU Puente Alto
AEELNORSSS reasonless
AEELNPRTTW wentletrap
AEELOPPRST ear-stopple
AEELOPPRTU repopulate
AEELOPSSTT salopettes
AEELORRTVY revelatory
AEELORSTTU lotus-eater
AEELORTUWZ water ouzel
AEELPRRSSY prayerless
AEELQRSSTU sequestral
AEELRRSTUW lusterware, lustreware
AEELRSTTTY tetrastyle
AEEMMNORTY anemometry
AEEMNNPRTT entrapment
AEEMNOPPRR proper name
AEEMNOPPRY paper money
AEEMNOPTTT tapotement
AEEMNOQRSU Romanesque
AEEMNORRTU enumerator
AEEMNORRUV manoeuvrer
AEEMNORSST sarmentose
AEEMNORSWW womenswear
AEEMNPPRTY prepayment
AEEMNRRSTT arrestment
AEEMNRSTTU menstruate
AEEMNSSSST assessment
AEEMOORTTT tree tomato
AEEMOPRSTW steam power
AEEMORRSTV overmaster
AEEMORSTUU outmeasure
AEEMPRRTTU ear-trumpet
AEEMRSSSST seamstress
AEENNOOPSS open season
AEENNORSST ornateness
AEENNPQSUW queen's pawn
AEENOPQSSU opaqueness
AEENOPRRTT penetrator
AEENORSTUX extraneous
AEENPPRSTT step-parent
AEENPRSSSS sparseness
AEENQRSSSU squareness
AEENRRSSTV transverse
AEENSSSTTU astuteness
AEEOPPRRTU paper route
AEEOPRRTWW water-power
AEEORRTTWW water tower
AEEORSTTXY stereotaxy
AEEPPRRTUW Tupperware
AEEPRRSSST trespasser
AEEPRSSTTU superstate
AEEPRSSWXY expressway
AEEQSSTTUU statuesque
AEFFHLLOTW off the wall
AEFFIKLLOW walk of life
AEFFILMSTY safety film
AEFFILNORW waffle-iron
AEFFILNSTU insufflate
AEFFLLNTUY affluently
AEFFLMOOPR flameproof
AEFFNRSSTU staff nurse
AEFGGGILNR reflagging
AEFGHHLLNT half-length
AEFGHILNRS angler fish
AEFGHINRRW wharfinger
AEFGHLSTTU self-taught
AEFGIILLOR florilegia
AEFGIILNNR fingernail
AEFGIINSTU ignes fatui
AEFGIIRTUV figurative
AEFGIKMNRR fingermark
AEFGILLNNN flanneling
AEFGILMNNU meaningful
AEFGILMNRY ley farming

AEFGILNOUW guinea fowl
AEFGILNPRS leaf spring
AEFGILNRTT flattering
AEFGILOPRT profligate
AEFGIPRRTU grapefruit
AEFGKLNRTU Klagenfurt
AEFGLLLOWY yellow flag
AEFGLLRTUY gratefully
AEFGLMRSTU Gulf Stream
AEFGLNRSSU frugalness
AEFGLNRTUU ungrateful
AEFGORSTTT soft target
AEFHHLNRTU half-hunter
AEFHHLORTY Holy Father
AEFHIINRTT interfaith
AEFHIIRRTW White Friar
AEFHIKLRSY freakishly
AEFHILNSSS flashiness
AEFHILNSSY Hessian fly
AEFHILRSST half-sister
AEFHINOSSS oafishness
AEFHLLLOVY half-volley
AEFHLLMSUY shamefully
AEFHLLNNOS half nelson
AEFHLMNTTW twelfth man
AEFHLMOSST fathomless
AEFHLNRTUY unfatherly
AEFHORRSTU after-hours
AEFHRSTTTU at furthest
AEFIILLTUV fluviatile
AEFIILMNTY feminality
AEFIILNRTT infiltrate
AEFIILORTT trifoliate
AEFIINQRTU quantifier
AEFIKNOPRS fair-spoken
AEFILLNNRY infernally
AEFILLNNUZ influenzal
AEFILLRTVY rift valley
AEFILMNSTY manifestly
AEFILMORTW wolframite
AEFILMPSTY stepfamily
AEFILNNRTV ventral fin
AEFILNORSU laniferous
AEFILNORTU fluorinate
AEFILNSSTU faultiness
AEFILOQRTU quatrefoil
AEFILORSSU saliferous
AEFILOSSUW issue of law
AEFILPQRUY pre-qualify
AEFINNRSSU unfairness
AEFINOOPRT fortepiano, pianoforte
AEFINORRST rainforest
AEFINORTTU refutation
AEFINORTUV unfavorite
AEFINRRRTY train ferry
AEFINRRTTY fraternity
AEFIORRSUU auriferous
AEFKLOORSW sale of work
AEFKORRSTW fast worker
AEFLLLOPWY playfellow
AEFLLLORWW wallflower
AEFLLLSSWY flawlessly
AEFLLNNRTY lantern-fly
AEFLLNOSSW fallowness
AEFLLNSSUW lawfulness
AEFLLSTTUY tastefully
AEFLLSTUWY wastefully
AEFLMNNSSU manfulness
AEFLNNRRUU funeral urn
AEFLNOOPPR proof-plane
AEFLNOOSTT float-stone
AEFLNOPRRT prefrontal
AEFLNORSTW Forest Lawn
AEFLNRSSTU artfulness
AEFMNOSSSU famousness
AEFMOORRST Amersfoort
AEFMOPRRST permafrost
AEFMORRSTY oyster-farm
AEFNNPPRUY funny paper
AEFNORRRST transferor
AEFNORRTTW waterfront
AEFNORSSTW soft answer
AEFOOPRRRT perforator
AEFOOPRRTW waterproof
AEFOORRSTT tortfeasor
AEFOQRRSUU four-square
AEFRRRSTTU frustrater
AEGGGIINRW earwigging
AEGGGILNNY engagingly
AEGGGINRST staggering
AEGGHHIMNR High German
AEGGHIILRS geisha girl
AEGGHIINTW weight gain
AEGGHILNRT right angle
AEGGHINOVY heavy going
AEGGHINSSS shagginess
AEGGHIRSTT stage right
AEGGIILMPR pilgrimage
AEGGIILNVW living wage
AEGGILLMNY gleamingly
AEGGILLNRV gravelling
AEGGILOOSU sialogogue
AEGGILRRST stragglier
AEGGINNPRS ginger snap
AEGGINORSS aggression
AEGGINRTTT targetting
AEGGIORRSU gregarious
AEGGJNRTUU juggernaut
AEGGNNORSU gangrenous
AEGGOORSSS goosegrass
AEGHHILLLS shillelagh
AEGHHILOPR heliograph
AEGHHILRTW right whale
AEGHHINOSS high season
AEGHHIOPRR hierograph
AEGHHISSTW sash weight
AEGHHISTTU haughtiest
AEGHHMOPPT apophthegm
AEGHIINRSV vinegarish
AEGHIIPRTZ graphitize
AEGHIKMMNO home-making
AEGHIKMNOS shoemaking
AEGHIKNOPW pigeon-hawk
AEGHIKRRST tiger shark
AEGHILLNOP Anglophile
AEGHILMNNS Englishman
AEGHILMNOS home signal
AEGHILMNRT lighterman
AEGHILNOOT theologian
AEGHILNORW wholegrain
AEGHILNRSU languisher
AEGHILNRTY early night
AEGHILPRXY lexigraphy
AEGHILSSTT ghastliest
AEGHIMMOPR mimeograph
AEGHIMMOPT magpie moth
AEGHIMNPST stamp hinge
AEGHIMSTTT steam-tight
AEGHINPRRS rangership
AEGHINRSSS garishness
AEGHINRSTT shattering, straighten
AEGHINSTTU naughtiest
AEGHIPRRSY serigraphy
AEGHIRSTUW white sugar
AEGHIRTTTW watertight
AEGHLMOOOT homologate
AEGHLMOOTY hematology
AEGHLNNOOP anglophone
AEGHLNOORS alongshore
AEGHLNSTWY lengthways
AEGHLOOORR logorrhoea
AEGHLORSUV overslaugh
AEGHLOSSSU glasshouse
AEGHMMORRT thermogram
AEGHMNOOPR gramophone
AEGHNOOORR gonorrhoea
AEGHNORRST short-range
AEGHOOPRRY oreography
AEGHOOPSSU oesophagus
AEGHOPRRXY xerography
AEGIIILNTV invigilate
AEGIIIRRTV irrigative
AEGIIKMNNW winemaking
AEGIILLLTY illegality
AEGIILLNUZ lingualize
AEGIILMNST time signal
AEGIILNOTV levigation
AEGIILRTTT glitterati
AEGIIMNNOT gemination
AEGIIMNORT emigration
AEGIIMNSTV negativism
AEGIIMSTTZ stigmatize
AEGIINNRSS graininess
AEGIINNRTT intrigante
AEGIINOPPR pigeon pair
AEGIINORTV invigorate
AEGIINPPTZ appetizing
AEGIINSTTV negativist
AEGIINTTVY negativity
AEGIKLLOOR Kalgoorlie
AEGIKLMNOV lovemaking
AEGIKLNNSY sneakingly
AEGIKLNPRY pearly king
AEGIKMNNOS maskinonge
AEGIKNNPSU unspeaking
AEGIKNNSST takingness
AEGILLLNRU laurelling

AEGILLMNRV marvelling
AEGILLMNRY germinally
AEGILLNORY regionally
AEGILLNPPR rappelling
AEGILLNPSY pleasingly
AEGILLNRTV travelling
AEGILLNRTY integrally
AEGILLNSST tasselling
AEGILLOPTT epiglottal
AEGILLORST allegorist, legislator
AEGILMMNRT trammeling
AEGILMNORS rosemaling
AEGILMNORY mineralogy
AEGILMORUZ glamourize
AEGILMSSTT gestaltism
AEGILMSTTU multi-stage
AEGILNNNPR replanning
AEGILNNOOT elongation
AEGILNNPSU unpleasing
AEGILNNRUV unraveling
AEGILNNRYY yearningly
AEGILNNSSS slanginess
AEGILNNSUY sanguinely
AEGILNOOSU oleaginous
AEGILNORSU lanigerous
AEGILNORTU regulation, urogenital
AEGILNOSTU gelatinous
AEGILNQRRU quarreling
AEGILNQSSU equals sign
AEGILNRSTV starveling
AEGILNRVWY waveringly
AEGILNRWYY wearyingly
AEGILNSSSS glassiness
AEGILOPRTT graptolite
AEGILORRSS gressorial
AEGILRRTUY regularity
AEGILRSTTZ Salzgitter
AEGILSSTTT gestaltist
AEGIMMORSS seismogram
AEGIMNNSST assignment
AEGIMNOPRS angiosperm
AEGIMNORRT germinator
AEGIMNORSU gramineous
AEGIMNORUW Guinea worm
AEGIMNPRTY pigmentary
AEGIMNRRST ringmaster
AEGIMNRSTT smattering
AEGIMORRTY emigratory
AEGIMRRTVY gravimetry
AEGINNNNOR non-earning
AEGINNNOTV non-vintage
AEGINNNPRT trepanning
AEGINNPPRT entrapping
AEGINNRSTT astringent
AEGINNRUVW unwavering
AEGINNRUWY unwearying
AEGINOORTT negotiator
AEGINOORTW aerotowing
AEGINORRTT integrator
AEGINPPRRW rewrapping
AEGINPQRTU parqueting
AEGINPRRSU Persian rug
AEGINPRSTU supergiant
AEGINPRSTY panegyrist
AEGINPSTTU Septuagint
AEGINQRRTU quartering
AEGINRRSSU reassuring
AEGINRSSSS grassiness
AEGINRSSSU sugariness
AEGINRSTWW water wings
AEGIRRRSTY registrary
AEGIRSSTTT strategist
AEGKMNOSXY oxygen mask
AEGLLLLNNO Llangollen
AEGLLMORRU glomerular
AEGLLMRTUY metallurgy
AEGLLNNPTY plangently
AEGLLNOPRY long-player
AEGLLNORSW swell-organ
AEGLLOPRSU pellagrous
AEGLMNORSS lemon grass
AEGLMOPRTU promulgate
AEGLNNPRTY pregnantly
AEGLNSSSSU sunglasses
AEGLOORRST astrologer
AEGLOORTTY teratology
AEGLORRTUY regulatory
AEGMMOPRRR programmer
AEGMNOORST gastronome
AEGMNOOSUX xenogamous
AEGMNORSTT strong meat
AEGMOPPRRR pre-program
AEGNOORTXY oxygenator
AEGNOOSTUU autogenous
AEGNRRSSST transgress
AEGNSSSTUU augustness
AEGOORSTUU outrageous
AEGOPRRSSU sour grapes
AEGOPRRTUX expurgator
AEGPRRSSSU supergrass
AEHHIILMOP hemophilia
AEHHILNSTU helianthus
AEHHINOPRT hierophant
AEHHLMMOPY haemolymph
AEHHLNOPTT heptathlon
AEHHMOOOPT homoeopath
AEHHMOOPTY homeopathy
AEHIIKLRTW wraithlike
AEHIIKPRSS kaisership
AEHIILLMNW Wilhelmina
AEHIINOSTT hesitation
AEHIINPPRS sapphirine
AEHIINSSTT antithesis
AEHIKLLLRW hillwalker
AEHIKMSTWY Wykehamist
AEHIKNRSSS rakishness
AEHIKOPPRT pork-pie hat
AEHILLOOVW view halloo
AEHILLOPTW pilot whale
AEHILLSTTY stealthily
AEHILMMRTT tilt-hammer
AEHILMNNUY inhumanely
AEHILMORST isothermal
AEHILMOSSY haemolysis
AEHILMPSTU multiphase
AEHILMRRTY Hilary term
AEHILNORSS lion's share
AEHILNSSSV lavishness
AEHILNSTTY hesitantly
AEHILOPPRS saprophile
AEHILOPRST hospitaler
AEHILOPTVY top-heavily
AEHILORRTY hierolatry
AEHILPSSST splashiest
AEHILRSTVW silver thaw
AEHILRSTVY shrievalty
AEHIMMPRRT trip-hammer
AEHIMMRSTU rheumatism
AEHIMNNPPS penmanship
AEHIMNOTUX exhumation
AEHIMNRSSS marshiness
AEHIMNRSTV ravishment
AEHIMNSSTU enthusiasm
AEHIMOOPTY mythopoeia
AEHIMOSSST hemostasis
AEHIMPRSST mastership, shipmaster
AEHIMPSTYZ sympathize
AEHINNRRTY Tyrrhenian
AEHINOPRTU euphoriant
AEHINOPRTY hypertonia
AEHINORRTV hovertrain
AEHINORSTU house-train
AEHINOSTUX exhaustion
AEHINPPSTU unhappiest
AEHINQRSUV vanquisher
AEHINRSSST trashiness
AEHINSSTTU enthusiast
AEHIOOPSST apotheosis
AEHIORSSST air hostess
AEHIORSTTT throatiest
AEHIQSSSTU squashiest
AEHIRSSTTW swarthiest, sweatshirt
AEHKLNNSUY unshakenly
AEHKLOPRSW shopwalker
AEHKNORRST other ranks
AEHLLMRSSY harmlessly
AEHLLOOPRT Hartlepool
AEHLLOORWW hollowware
AEHLLOPRRT hall porter
AEHLLOPRXY phylloxera
AEHLLORRSZ razor-shell
AEHLMNOOPR pheromonal
AEHLMNOSWW Welshwoman
AEHLMOOSUX homosexual
AEHLMPSSYY symphyseal
AEHLNNOPTT pentathlon
AEHLNOPPRT thorn apple
AEHLNOPSTU house plant, sulphonate
AEHLNORTTT tetrathlon
AEHLORRSUY early hours
AEHLPRSTUU sulphurate
AEHMNOOPRT homopteran
AEHMNOORSU manor house

AEHMNOORSW horsewoman
AEHMNOORTW other woman
AEHMNPRSUU superhuman
AEHMNPRTWY water nymph
AEHMORSTTT thermostat
AEHNNNOOTY hootenanny
AEHNOOPSSU sousaphone
AEHNOPPRST Shepparton
AEHNOPRTUY neuropathy
AEHOOPPRST apostrophe
AEHOOPSTTT toothpaste
AEHOOPSTTY osteopathy
AEHOORRSTT sore throat
AEHOORSSTY soothsayer
AEHOPPRSTY saprophyte
AEHOPRSTUY house party
AEHOPSSSTY hypostases
AEHORRRSTW rest-harrow
AEHORSTTTU stout heart
AEHPRSSTTY strathspey
AEIIIILNTZ initialize
AEIIIINTTV initiative
AEIIILMRTZ militarize
AEIIILMTTV limitative
AEIIILRTVZ trivialize
AEIIIMNTVZ vitaminize
AEIIIRRTTV irritative
AEIIKLLNPR painkiller
AEIILLLMMS millesimal
AEIILLLMNN millennial
AEIILLLTVY illatively
AEIILLMNOR mineral oil
AEIILLMNTU illuminate
AEIILLMPRY imperially
AEIILLMRST literalism
AEIILLMSVY Simi Valley
AEIILLMTVY Amityville
AEIILLNRTU uniliteral
AEIILLOTVZ volatilize
AEIILLPSTT pistillate
AEIILLRRTT triliteral
AEIILLRRTU tirailleur
AEIILLRRTY literarily
AEIILLRSTT literalist
AEIILLRTTY literality
AEIILMMMOR immemorial
AEIILMNNOZ nominalize
AEIILMNORT eliminator
AEIILMNTTY intimately
AEIILMOSSS isoseismal
AEIILMRSTV relativism
AEIILMRSVV revivalism
AEIILMSTUV simulative
AEIILNNORS rosaniline
AEIILNNRRT liner train
AEIILNNSTT intestinal
AEIILNOOTT etiolation
AEIILNOPTX pixelation
AEIILNORTT literation
AEIILNOTTV levitation, velitation
AEIILNPPRZ Lippizaner
AEIILNPRTT interplait
AEIILNPRZZ Lipizzaner
AEIILNQTUY inequality
AEIILNSSTT saintliest
AEIILRSTTV relativist
AEIILRSTTZ strelitzia
AEIILRSTVV revivalist
AEIILRTTVY relativity
AEIIMMMNOR in memoriam
AEIIMMNPRT impairment
AEIIMMNSSS Messianism
AEIIMMRSTT mime artist
AEIIMNNNOT innominate
AEIIMNNOTV nominative
AEIIMNOSTT estimation
AEIIMNQTUY equanimity
AEIIMNRSST seminarist
AEIIMNRTUV ruminative
AEIIMOPRRS impresario
AEIIMPRRTZ Imperatriz
AEIIMPRSTT team spirit
AEIIMPTTUV imputative
AEIINNOTVV innovative
AEIINOPPST inapposite
AEIINOPPTV appointive
AEIINOPRTX expiration
AEIINOPSTT poinsettia
AEIINOQTTU equitation
AEIINOSTTV estivation
AEIINOTUVX exuviation
AEIINPSSST antisepsis, inspissate
AEIINQTTUV quantitive
AEIINRSSUZ Russianize
AEIINRSTTV transitive
AEIIOPPRTT propitiate
AEIIPRRTTT tripartite
AEIIPRRTVZ privatizer
AEIJLNORUZ journalize
AEIJMNOSSS jam session
AEIJNNSSTU jauntiness
AEIKLMNSTY mistakenly
AEIKLMPPRR ripple mark
AEIKMNNSTU unmistaken
AEIKMNPRRT printmaker
AEIKNNSSSW swankiness
AEILLLMPTY tilley lamp
AEILLLMSTT little slam
AEILLLNQSU squall line
AEILLLSUVY allusively
AEILLMMRST millstream, small-timer
AEILLMNRTY terminally
AEILLMPRVY primevally
AEILLMTTUY ultimately
AEILLMTUVV multivalve
AEILLNNRTY internally
AEILLNOPRT Petronilla
AEILLNOPTT potentilla
AEILLNORTY orientally
AEILLNPSSY painlessly
AEILLNRTUY tenurially
AEILLORSSS sailorless
AEILLPPRTY triple play
AEILLPSSTT pastellist
AEILLRSSTV liver salts
AEILLRSTTU illustrate
AEILMMRTUY immaturely
AEILMNNSTT instalment
AEILMNOPRS impersonal
AEILMNOPRT trampoline
AEILMNORRZ normalizer
AEILMNORTU tourmaline
AEILMNORTY monetarily
AEILMNPRTY planimetry
AEILMNRSTU neutralism
AEILMNSSSU sensualism
AEILMNSTTU last minute
AEILMOPPSS ampelopsis
AEILMPPSST palimpsest
AEILMPRSST slipstream
AEILMPRSSU plumassier
AEILMPRSTU psalterium
AEILMPRTUU pari-mutuel
AEILMRRSSU surrealism
AEILMRRSTT trimestral
AEILMSTTUX textualism
AEILNNNSTW lawn tennis
AEILNNOOPR pearl onion
AEILNNOPSY Polynesian
AEILNNORTT intolerant
AEILNNPRSU peninsular
AEILNOORTT toleration
AEILNOOSTT nose-to-tail
AEILNOPRTV portal vein
AEILNORRTT torrential
AEILNORRTY anteriorly
AEILNORTTV ventilator
AEILNOSTTW its own tale
AEILNOTTUX exultation
AEILNPPRTU prenuptial
AEILNPRSST paltriness
AEILNRSSUY urinalyses
AEILNRSTTU neutralist
AEILNRTTUY neutrality
AEILNSSSTU sensualist
AEILNSSTUU nautiluses
AEILNSSTUY sensuality
AEILOOPRST Portlaoise
AEILOOPSTT toilet soap
AEILOOPTTZ topazolite
AEILOPPRUZ popularize
AEILOPPSTY appositely
AEILOPRSSU plesiosaur
AEILOPRSTY epistolary
AEILOPRTVW vital power
AEILOPTTVY optatively
AEILPQSSUU Esquipulas
AEILPTTUVY putatively
AEILRRSSTU surrealist
AEILRRSTUY surreality
AEILSTTTUX textualist
AEILTTTUXY textuality
AEIMMNORST monetarism
AEIMMNOTUU autoimmune
AEIMMNRSSS smarminess
AEIMMNRSTT mint master
AEIMMNSTZZ mizzen-mast
AEIMMRRSUZ summarizer

AEIMNNNORW inner woman
AEIMNNORTU numeration
AEIMNOOPZZ mezzo piano
AEIMNOPRTT portamenti
AEIMNOPTTT temptation
AEIMNOQSUU equanimous
AEIMNORRST ironmaster
AEIMNORRTT terminator
AEIMNORSTT monetarist
AEIMNORSTU Mousterian
AEIMNPPRST pentaprism
AEIMNPSTTY tympanites
AEIMNRRRTY intermarry
AEIMNRRSTT retransmit
AEIMOOTTUV automotive
AEIMOSSTVV votive Mass
AEIMPRSTUZ trapeziums
AEIMPSSTUV assumptive
AEIMQRSTUZ quizmaster
AEIMRRRSTU terrariums
AEINNNOQSU sine qua non
AEINNOORTV renovation
AEINNOPRSW war pension
AEINNOPRSY pensionary
AEINNOPRTU piano-tuner
AEINNOQRTU quaternion
AEINNORSTT stentorian
AEINNPPSSS snappiness
AEINNQSSTU quaintness
AEINNRSSUW unwariness
AEINNSSSZZ snazziness
AEINOOPPRT propionate
AEINOOPRRT peroration
AEINOPRRTW power train
AEINOPRRTZ patronizer
AEINOPRSSU persuasion
AEINOPRSTW waitperson
AEINOPRTTU reputation
AEINOPTTTU outpatient
AEINORRSTU souterrain
AEINORRSTV overstrain
AEINORSTTY stationery
AEINPRRSTU rupestrian
AEINPRRTTU parturient
AEINRRSSST starriness
AEINRSSSTT straitness
AEINRSTUYZ suzerainty
AEIOPRRRST respirator
AEIOPRRTTX extirpator
AEIOPRRTXY expiratory
AEJLLLORYY royal jelly
AEJLLSSTUW just as well
AEJMNNORUY journeyman
AEKLLMRUWY lukewarmly
AEKLMNOPST smoke plant
AEKLNPRSTW wrest-plank
AEKLOPRSTY stroke play
AEKMNORTTW market town
AEKMOORTTY keratotomy
AEKMORRSTW masterwork
AEKNOPRRSY Nosy Parker
AEKOOPRRTY prokaryote
AEKORRSTWW waterworks

AELLMNNOPT lemon plant
AELLMOORSW rose-mallow
AELLMOPRTY temporally
AELLMOPSSY plasmolyse
AELLMOPSYZ plasmolyze
AELLMORSUV marvellous
AELLNOPPRT propellant
AELLNOPRSY personally
AELLNOPRTT Patent Roll
AELLNOPSTU plant-louse
AELLNOPTVY polyvalent
AELLNORTTY tolerantly
AELLNOSSSW sallowness
AELLNPRSUY supernally
AELLNPTTUY petulantly
AELLNRSTTY slatternly
AELLNTTUXY exultantly
AELLOPPRSU all-purpose
AELLRTTUXY texturally
AELMMNNOTU monumental
AELMMNOSSS Solemn Mass
AELMMNOSTT last moment
AELMMNTTUZ Muntz metal
AELMMOSSUU mausoleums
AELMNNNRUY unmannerly
AELMNNOOTV monovalent
AELMNOOPRY lampoonery
AELMOOPRTU tropaeolum
AELMOPPRUY propylaeum
AELMOPRTTU petrolatum
AELMOPSSST Epsom salts
AELMORRSST mortarless
AELMORRSSW marrowless
AELMORSSTU somersault
AELMPPRSUY maple syrup
AELNNOPRYY pennyroyal
AELNNORSTY resonantly
AELNOOPSTT postal note
AELNOPPRTW power plant
AELNOPRSTY personalty
AELNOPSTTT talent-spot
AELNORSUVY ravenously
AELNOSSUUY nauseously
AELNPPRSTU supplanter
AELOOPRRSW solar power
AELORSSSUV savourless
AELPPRSSTU Last Supper
AELPPSSTUY platypuses
AEMMNORSTY smart money
AEMNNNOPTY non-payment
AEMNNOOSST stonemason
AEMNNORTTU tournament
AEMNNRRSUY nurseryman
AEMNOOPRTT portamento
AEMNOORRST astronomer
AEMNOORTUW outer woman
AEMNOPRSUW superwoman
AEMNORSSTT assortment
AEMNORSSTU sarmentous

AEMNRRSTTU transmuter
AEMOOPSTTY somatotype
AEMOPRSSTT postmaster
AENNNOSSTW wantonness
AENNORRSSW narrowness
AENNORRSTT non-starter
AENOOPRRST personator
AENOOPRTXY paroxytone
AENOORSSTU treasonous
AENOPRRSST transposer
AENOPRSTTT Protestant
AENPRRSTTU transputer
AEOOPPRRST praepostor
AEOOPPRSTU tropopause
AEOOQRRSTU square root
AEOPPRRRTU rapporteur
AEOPRRSSTW sportswear
AEOPRRSTTW water sport
AEOPRRTTTY treaty port
AEOPRSTTUW waterspout
AEOQRRSTUZ rose quartz
AEORSSSTUU trousseaus
AEORSSTUUX trousseaux
AFFGIIRSTT graffitist
AFFGIMRSSU suffragism
AFFGIRSSTU suffragist
AFFGNOORST Stroganoff
AFFHILLTUY faithfully
AFFHILNTUU unfaithful
AFFIIMNRSU ruffianism
AFFLLORUUV flavourful
AFFPPRSTUY puff pastry
AFGGGILNNU unflagging
AFGGIINRTY gratifying
AFGGILMNOR gangliform
AFGHHILLST flashlight
AFGHHILPTT flight path
AFGHILLNPT flight plan
AFGHIORTWY right of way
AFGIIKLMMN film-making
AFGIILOSTU flagitious
AFGIIMNOTU fumigation
AFGIINORTU figuration
AFGIINSSTY satisfying
AFGIKMNORS King of Arms
AFGILLNOTU falling-out
AFGILLNOTY floatingly
AFGILLNSST flint glass
AFGILNORUV flavouring
AFGIMNORTT formatting
AFGIRRSTUU fruit sugar
AFHHLLORUY half-hourly
AFHILLMOYY Holy Family
AFHILNOPST flashpoint
AFHILNPSSY Spanish fly
AFHIOORTTY tooth fairy
AFHIOPRRST parrotfish
AFHKLLNTUY thankfully
AFHKLNNTUU unthankful
AFHLLORSUY royal flush
AFHLLRTUWY wrathfully
AFIIINNOTX infixation
AFIILLLNUY unfilially
AFIILLRRTY fritillary

AFIILNORTT filtration, flirtation
AFIIMORSTV favoritism
AFILLMNORY informally
AFILLNOPRU plain flour
AFILLNPPTY flippantly
AFILLNRSTU full strain
AFILLOSSUX Sioux Falls
AFILMNOSUY infamously
AFIORRSTYY fairy story
AFLLLNUUWY unlawfully
AFLMOORRTU formulator
AFNORSTTUU Fortunatus
AGGGGIINWW wigwagging
AGGGGIINZZ zigzagging
AGGHIILLMN Gillingham
AGGHIINNRS garnishing
AGGHILLNUY laughingly
AGGHILSSST sight-glass
AGGHLOOPRY graphology
AGGIIIMNNS imaginings
AGGIILLNNS signalling
AGGIILNNTU agglutinin
AGGIINNSSW singing saw
AGGILLNOTY gloatingly
AGGILLOOST algologist
AGGILMORSY gargoylism
AGGILNNORY groaningly
AGGILNPRSY graspingly
AGGINOSSTU outgassing
AGGLNOOORZ Gorgonzola
AGHHILOPRT lithograph
AGHHLOOPRY holography
AGHHNOOPPR phonograph
AGHHOOPPRT photograph
AGHHORTUWY throughway
AGHIILNORS Anglo-Irish
AGHIINNOST Antigonish
AGHIINPRRS hairspring
AGHIINRTWW wainwright
AGHILMNSSY smashingly
AGHILNNTUY hauntingly
AGHILNRSTT stringhalt
AGHILOPPRY lipography
AGHILOPPSY gypsophila
AGHILORSTT gastrolith
AGHILPRTWY playwright
AGHILRSTTY straightly
AGHIMNNOTT Nottingham
AGHINNOSTW Washington
AGHINOPTTW towing-path
AGHINORSTT ghost train
AGHIOPPRRS spirograph
AGHIPRSTTU straight-up
AGHKMMRSUY gummy shark
AGHLNOOORT orthogonal
AGHLOOSSTT tooth-glass
AGHLOPRSTY stylograph
AGHLOPRXYY xylography
AGHMMOOOSU homogamous
AGHMNOOPRY nomography
AGHMNOORTU mouth organ
AGHMOOPRTY tomography
AGHNNOOPRU harpoon gun
AGHNOOPRSY nosography
AGHOOPPRTY topography
AGHOPPRRYY pyrography
AGHOPPRTYY typography
AGIIIILNNT initialing
AGIIILNOTT litigation
AGIIIMNOTT mitigation
AGIIINORRT irrigation
AGIIINRRTT irritating
AGIIKKMNNR marking ink
AGIIKLNNTW a twinkling
AGIIKNNNPR napkin ring
AGIIKNPSST piss-taking
AGIIKNSSSS ass-kissing
AGIILLNNST installing
AGIILLNNUU unilingual
AGIILLNNUY inguinally
AGIILLNORY originally
AGIILLNPRS spiralling
AGIILLNRTU trilingual
AGIILLNRVY virginally
AGIILLNTVY vigilantly
AGIILNNORU unoriginal
AGIILNPRST springtail
AGIILNRSTY laryngitis
AGIIMMOSST misogamist
AGIIMNNPRS mainspring
AGIIMNORSU migrainous
AGIIMNSSUV vaginismus
AGIIMORTTY mitigatory
AGIIMSSTTT stigmatist
AGIINNNNPS inspanning
AGIINNRSTT transiting
AGIINOORRT originator
AGIINOPRRR rip-roaring
AGIINORSTT instigator
AGIINRTTTT attritting
AGIKLMNOOT toolmaking
AGIKLMNOSS loss-making
AGIKLNOPRT parking lot
AGIKMNNORW working man
AGIKMNNOSW snowmaking
AGIKOPRSTY Pyatigorsk
AGIKRRSSST grass skirt
AGILLNNRSY snarlingly
AGILLNOPRT patrolling
AGILLNORTY trigonally
AGILLNRSUY singularly
AGILMNRSTY smartingly
AGILMOPSTY polygamist
AGILNNNOPY non-playing
AGILNNOPTY poignantly
AGILNNORTY ignorantly
AGILNNPPSY snappingly
AGILNNTTUY tauntingly
AGILNNTUVY vauntingly
AGILNOSSTW wagons-lits
AGILORSSST glossarist
AGIMMNOOST monogamist
AGIMMNSSUY gymnasiums
AGIMNNSSUU unassuming
AGIMNOORST agronomist
AGIMNOPRSU sporangium
AGINNNPPSU unsnapping
AGINNORRTW Warrington
AGINNPPRUW unwrapping
AGINNPPSUW swan-upping
AGINORRTWY rotary-wing
AGIORSTTUU gratuitous
AGKNNNORTY granny knot
AGKNRSTYYZ Kyrgyzstan
AGLLLLOPPU Gallup poll
AGLLLOOPRY pyrogallol
AGLLNOOPYY palynology
AGLLRTTUUY gutturally
AGLMOOOPTY potamology
AGLMOOOSTY somatology
AGLMOOPSUY polygamous
AGLMORSSST storm-glass
AGLNOORSUU languorous
AGLOOPPRYY papyrology
AGMMNOOOSU monogamous
AGMMNOPSUU magnum opus
AGMNNOOUWY young woman
AGMNOORSTY gastronomy
AGOORRSSST grass roots
AHHIINSSUZ Shizuishan
AHHIOPRSTU authorship
AHHISSWWYY wishy-washy
AHIIIMMPSX amphimixis
AHIIKLNSTV Tskhinvali
AHIIKMNRSS Krishnaism
AHIILLNOPS nail polish
AHIILMNOPY hypolimnia
AHIILMORTU humiliator
AHIIMNNOTU inhumation
AHIIMNNTUY inhumanity
AHIIMNORSW Irishwoman
AHIIRSSTTW shirtwaist
AHIJNNNOOS Johnsonian
AHIKKSTUUY Kitakyushu
AHIKLMSTWY malt whisky
AHIKNPRRSW shrink-wrap
AHILMNOSWY womanishly
AHILMPSSYY symphysial
AHILNOORTZ horizontal
AHILNPPSSY snappishly
AHIMNOOOSU homoousian
AHIMNOORRU honorarium
AHIMNOORSU harmonious
AHIMNPRTTU triumphant
AHIMPPPRSU parish pump
AHIOPPRSST pastorship
AHIOPSSSTY hypostasis
AHIORSSTTW short waist
AHKLMOOSTT smooth talk
AHLLMORSSU small hours

AHLLOPRSTU prothallus
AHLLOPTXYY phyllotaxy
AHLMNNORTU lunar month
AHLMNOORST solar month
AHLMPRSUWY Murphy's Law
AHLNOPSTUY polyanthus
AHNNOSTTWY shanty town
AHNOOPTTUY tautophony
AHNOPPRTTY tryptophan
AHOPRRRTTU Port Arthur
AIIIILMNST initialism
AIIIIMNPSS pianissimi
AIIIINNOTT initiation
AIIILLMNTU illuminati
AIIILLMNTY liminality
AIIILLMRTY militarily
AIIILMMMNS minimalism
AIIILMMNST minimalist
AIIILMMRST militarism
AIIILMNOTT limitation
AIIILMRSTT militarist
AIIILMRSTY similarity
AIIILORSTV visitorial
AIIILRTTVY triviality
AIIIMNNOTT intimation
AIIIMNOPSS pianissimo
AIIINNOOTZ ionization
AIIINNOTTV invitation
AIIINORRTT irritation
AIIINORTTT tritiation
AIIINORTTY initiatory
AIIINOSTTV visitation
AIIINOTTTV titivation
AIIIPRSSTY pityriasis
AIIIPRTVVY viviparity
AIILLLNOSU illusional
AIILLMNNTU illuminant
AIILLMNTTY militantly
AIILLNOOTV volitional
AIILLNOSUV villainous
AIILLORSTY solitarily
AIILLOSSTT solstitial
AIILLOTTVY volatility
AIILLPRSTY pistillary
AIILLSTUVV valvulitis
AIILMMNNOS nominalism
AIILMMNOOT immolation
AIILMMORTY immorality
AIILMNNOST nominalist
AIILMNOORT monitorial
AIILMNOSTU simulation
AIILMNOTTU mutilation
AIILMNRSSU insularism
AIILMNRTUY unmilitary
AIILMPPRST spirit lamp
AIILMRRTUV triumviral
AIILNNOOST insolation
AIILNNOSTU insulation
AIILNOOPST positional, spoliation
AIILNRSSUY urinalysis
AIILNRSTUY insularity
AIILORSSTU sailor suit
AIILRTTUVY virtuality
AIIMMNNOTU ammunition
AIIMMPRRTU imprimatur
AIIMMRTTUY immaturity
AIIMNNNOOT nomination
AIIMNNORTU rumination
AIIMNNRSTT ministrant
AIIMNOOTTV motivation
AIIMNOPSTU Utopianism
AIIMNOPTTU imputation
AIIMNORSSY missionary
AIIMNPRSTU puritanism
AIIMNPSSTU impuissant
AIIMOPRSTT patriotism
AIIMOSSTTT stomatitis
AIINNNOOTT intonation
AIINNNOOTV innovation
AIINNOPSTU supination
AIINNORSTT transition
AIINNORSTU insinuator
AIINNTTUVY vanity unit
AIINOOPPST apposition
AIINOORSTT storiation
AIINOPRRST inspirator
AIIOPRSUVV viviparous
AIIPRSSSTT piss artist
AIJKMNOOOY Miyakonojo
AIJLMNORSU journalism
AIJLNORSTU journalist
AIJMNOQRTU quint major
AIKLLLOPTW pillow talk
AIKLMNNOPS salmon pink
AILLMMORTY immortally
AILLMNOOPY polynomial
AILLMNPRST small print
AILLMOPRTU multipolar
AILLMOPRXY proximally
AILLMOQRTU malt liquor
AILLNNOOTY notionally
AILLNOOPRT pollinator
AILLNOOPTY optionally
AILLNQRTUY tranquilly
AILLORTTUY tutorially
AILMMSTTUU ultimatums
AILMNNOOPR pronominal
AILMNOOPST lampoonist
AILMNORTUY unmorality
AILMOPPRSU popularism
AILMORSTTU stimulator
AILMPRTTUY multi-party
AILNOOPPTU population
AILNOOPRSS sponsorial
AILNORSTTU lustration
AILNPSSTUY puissantly
AILOOPRSTY spoliatory
AILOPPRTUY popularity
AILOPRSTTU stipulator
AIMMNORSTU stramonium
AIMMOORRTU moratorium
AIMNOOSTTU autonomist
AIMNOOSTTX taxonomist
AIMNOPSSTU assumption
AIMNOSTUUY Utsunomiya
AIMNRSTTUU nasturtium
AIMOOORTVY ovariotomy
AINNOOPRTT antiproton
AINNOORTVY innovatory
AINOOPRSTY anisotropy
AINOOSTTTU outstation
AINOPRSTUU usurpation
AINOPRTTTY potty-train
AINORRSSTT transistor
AINORRSTTY transitory
AINPRSTUUV pursuivant
AIOOPRRSUU uproarious
AIOORRSTTU traitorous
AIOORRSUUV Our Saviour
AIOPPPRSUU pupiparous
AIOPRRSUVV parvovirus
AIORRRTTTU triturator
AKKKLLNUUX Ku Klux Klan
ALLMNNOORY non-morally
ALLOOPPRRT poll parrot
ALMOOPPRST protoplasm
ALNOOOPRST portolanos
ALNPRSTUUY pursuantly
ALOOPPRSTT protoplast
ALOOPPRTTY prototypal
ALOOPRSTTU postulator
ALOPRTUUVY voluptuary
AMMOOSTUXY myxomatous
AMNNOOSTUY antonymous
AMNNOOSTWW townswoman
AMNOOOSTUU autonomous
AMNOOPRSUY paronymous
AMNOOPSSST Samson post
AMOPPRSTTU post-partum
ANOOOPRSTZ protozoans
BBBCJKLOUY bubbly-jock
BBBCKOOSSY bobby socks
BBBDEEINOR beribboned
BBBEEIINRW winebibber
BBBEILNORU blue ribbon
BBBEOORSXY bobby-soxer
BBBGHINNOO hobnobbing
BBBLLOOWWY blow-by-blow
BBCEEKNRRU rubberneck
BBCEHINSSU chubbiness
BBCEIKRSUU Rubik's cube
BBCEIRRSSU subscriber
BBCGIIINRT crib-biting
BBCHRRSSUU scrub-brush
BBCIIKLRTU brick-built
BBCIILLLPU public bill
BBDDEILNOU double bind
BBDDELMNOU dumb blonde
BBDDELNOOU double bond
BBDDELOOUY body double
BBDEEIMORV dive-bomber
BBDEIKNOOR bookbinder
BBDEILLLOU double bill
BBDEKLOOOU double-book
BBDELNOOOR blood-borne
BBEEEFGRRU beefburger
BBEEEHNNRT herb bennet
BBEEHORRRT herb Robert

BBEEIKLLRU lubberlike
BBEEILLNRU lubber line
BBEELLOTTU bluebottle
BBEELMORTT letter bomb
BBEGHIORRT Big Brother
BBEGINRSSU grubbiness
BBEGJNOORR Bjorneborg
BBEHHILOST shibboleth
BBEHHOORSY hobby horse
BBEIILLOOP bibliopole
BBEIKLMOOO bookmobile
BBEILNOSSW wobbliness
BBEILNOSUY boys in blue
BBEINSSSTU stubbiness
BBEIOOPRYZ booby prize
BBELLMOOTT bell-bottom
BBELMMSTUU stumblebum
BBELMOOPRT petrol bomb
BBEMNRRTUU burnt umber
BBEOOORTVV bovver boot
BBFGILMNOY flying bomb
BBFHIINORS ribbonfish
BBFIMNOOSU fusion bomb
BBGIKLNUUY bulk buying
BBGILNNSUY snubbingly
BBGIMOORRY borborygmi
BBHILNOSSY snobbishly
BBIIIIMNOT imbibition
BBIIKKNTUZ kibbutznik
BBILLOSUUY bibulously
BBIMNOORRW ribbon worm
BBJMMMOOUU mumbo-jumbo
BBLMOORSUY Bloomsbury
BBLNORSTUY stubbornly
BBOOOSSSTY bossy-boots
BCCEEENPSU pubescence
BCCEEINRTY cybernetic
BCCEEMNRUY recumbency
BCCEHNORSS cross-bench
BCCEIINOOT coenobitic
BCCEIMNNUY incumbency
BCCHIINORT bronchitic
BCDDEEILTU deductible
BCDDHIISTU Buddhistic
BCDEEEIINT benedicite
BCDEEHLOST bedclothes
BCDEEIILNR incredible
BCDEEIIPRR bride price
BCDEEILNNZ zinc blende
BCDEEINSSU subsidence
BCDEEINSTU Benedictus
BCDEEMNORU code number
BCDEENOSST second-best
BCDEEOOPRY Coober Pedy
BCDEEORRSS cross-breed
BCDEFIIKLR brick-field
BCDEFLOOTU club-footed
BCDEHILNOU double chin
BCDEHIMNUX mixed bunch
BCDEHIRRRY bird cherry
BCDEIILNRY incredibly
BCDEILOORR corrodible
BCDEILOPRU producible
BCDEKLLOOU double-lock
BCDEKLOOOS closed book
BCDELNOORU cordon bleu
BCDELORRUY cloudberry
BCDEMMNRUU cummerbund
BCDENORRWY Crown Derby
BCDENORSUU unobscured
BCDGIIOSTU dog biscuit
BCDHHIILRT childbirth
BCDHHIIOST dhobi's itch
BCDIIOPRRT tropic bird
BCDILOOSSU discobolus
BCDILORSTU locust-bird
BCDINOSTUU subduction
BCDKLOOOST bloodstock
BCDKMRSTUU dumbstruck
BCDLNOOOTU blood count
BCDLOOORUY body colour
BCDLORSTUU cloudburst
BCEEEEHLSU blue cheese
BCEEEFINNT beneficent
BCEEEFLLRT treble clef
BCEEEGHINS beseeching
BCEEEILLNU ebullience
BCEEELLMRU cerebellum
BCEEENORRS resorbence
BCEEENRSTU erubescent
BCEEEPRRSU spruce beer
BCEEFFINOS coffee nibs
BCEEGHMOOU gobemouche
BCEEGIINOT biogenetic
BCEEGINRSU subgeneric
BCEEHKLOSU shoe-buckle
BCEEHKOOQU chequebook
BCEEHKORRY chokeberry
BCEEHMORUU embouchure
BCEEIILPST plebiscite
BCEEIILTYZ Belize City
BCEEIJSTUV subjective
BCEEILLNPU blue-pencil
BCEEILLNUY ebulliency
BCEEILMOST comestible
BCEEILNOTY by-election
BCEEIOPRST corbie-step
BCEEIPRRRS prescriber
BCEEIPSSSU subspecies
BCEEIRSSUV service bus
BCEEJLOSST objectless
BCEEKLNOTT bottleneck
BCEELNOTTU cuttle-bone
BCEELNRTUU turbulence
BCEELOPPRT copper belt
BCEEMMORSU cumbersome
BCEEOOORRR corroboree
BCEFFINNOO coffin-bone
BCEFHNNORT front bench
BCEGHIINTW bewitching
BCEGHIKNNS King's Bench
BCEGIILORR corrigible
BCEGILLNOR corbelling
BCEGILMNOY becomingly
BCEGIMNNOU unbecoming
BCEHHNNOUY honeybunch
BCEHIIMOST biochemist
BCEHIINSST bitchiness
BCEHIISSSU hibiscuses
BCEHILNOOR bronchiole
BCEHILOPRY hyperbolic
BCEHILOSTT blotchiest
BCEHINOOPX xenophobic
BCEHKKOOST sketchbook
BCEHKLOORS horse-block
BCEHKLOOSU blockhouse
BCEHKOPSTU bucket shop
BCEHMRSTUW thumbscrew
BCEHNORRTU burnt ochre
BCEIIILMMS immiscible
BCEIIILMTY imbecility
BCEIIILNNV invincible
BCEIIKLLLS sickle-bill
BCEIIKLRRT rib-tickler
BCEIIMORST biometrics
BCEIINOOSS biocenosis
BCEIJNOSTU subjection
BCEIKLMORT mitre block
BCEIKLOORT bootlicker
BCEIKOOTTY tickety-boo
BCEILMOORT bolometric
BCEILMRSTU crumbliest
BCEILNRTUU tuberculin
BCEIMOSTUV combustive
BCEINNOSSU bounciness
BCEINORTTU contribute
BCEINOSSTU subsection
BCEIOPPRSY presbyopic
BCEIORSSTT obstetrics
BCEKKOOOPT pocketbook
BCEKLNRTUU turn-buckle
BCEKLOOPRW power block
BCEKLOORTW tower block
BCEKLOPSTU slop bucket
BCEKLORSTW wrest-block
BCEKOOORSU coursebook, sourcebook
BCELRSTUUU subculture
BCEMNOPRTU procumbent
BCEMNOSSUV Venus's comb
BCENOOPTUX pouncet-box
BCENOORSSS crossbones
BCFIIIORST fibrositic
BCFIIMORRR cribriform
BCGIIKKNOX kick-boxing
BCGIILORRY corrigibly
BCGIIMNORV virgin comb
BCGIKLLNOO bollocking
BCGIKMNSUU bum-sucking
BCHHIMOOOP homophobic
BCHIIMOOPR biomorphic
BCHIINORST bronchitis
BCHIIOPSSY biophysics
BCHIMOORTT thrombotic

BCHIOPRTYY bryophytic
BCIIILMMSY immiscibly
BCIIILNNVY invincibly
BCIILNOPSY psilocybin
BCIILORSUU lubricious
BCIKMOORST broomstick
BCIMNOOSTU combustion
BCIMORRSTU microburst
BCIOPRSSTU subtropics
BCKMOOORTT rock-bottom
BCLMORSUUY cumbrously
BCOORRSTTU obstructor
BDDDEEINTW twin-bedded
BDDDEELOOR red-blooded
BDDDEELOUY double-dyed
BDDDGIINSU disbudding
BDDEEEILLV bedevilled
BDDEEINRST bestridden
BDDEEIORRV overbidder
BDDEELNRTU trundle-bed
BDDEENNRUU unburdened
BDDEFILLLU bull-fiddle
BDDEFILLOU full-bodied
BDDEHLNOOR bondholder
BDDEHLOOOT hot-blooded
BDDEILMORW middlebrow
BDDEIMOUVY buddy movie
BDDFGIINOR forbidding
BDDHLNOOOU bloodhound
BDDIKLNNRU blind drunk
BDDLNOOOOR blood donor
BDEEEEJLLW bejewelled
BDEEEFILNS defensible
BDEEEFINTT benefitted
BDEEEFLOTT bottle-feed
BDEEEGHILR Heidelberg
BDEEEGLNTU dung-beetle
BDEEEHLLNR hellbender
BDEEEHMORW home-brewed
BDEEEIILSV disbelieve
BDEEEILNTX extendible
BDEEEILSTW wildebeest
BDEEEINNRZ Benzedrine
BDEEEINRRT interbreed
BDEEEKNORR broken reed
BDEEELLMOW embowelled
BDEEELMTUW tumbleweed
BDEEELRRRY elderberry
BDEEFGIINR debriefing
BDEEFIINST disbenefit
BDEEFILNRS self-binder
BDEEFILNSY defensibly
BDEEGHILRT Lethbridge
BDEEGIILNV bedeviling
BDEEGIILST digestible
BDEEGIINNR inbreeding
BDEEGIKRSW skew bridge
BDEEGIMOSU disembogue
BDEEGINRRT regent-bird
BDEEGINTTW bed-wetting
BDEEHIILNN behind line
BDEEHIMRSU Humberside
BDEEHIRRSY Derbyshire
BDEEHLNNOR hornblende
BDEEHLNNOU unbeholden
BDEEHNORTU unbothered
BDEEIILMOZ demobilize
BDEEILLOPT pot-bellied
BDEEILMOSU semi-double
BDEEILMOSW disembowel
BDEEILMOTU double time
BDEEILMRSS dissembler
BDEEILNNRT interblend
BDEEILNORR borderline
BDEEILNOTY obediently
BDEEILORWZ bowdlerize
BDEEIMMNOT embodiment
BDEEIMORRY embroidery
BDEEKNOOTY ketone body
BDEELLNRUY underbelly
BDEELMRRUU blue murder
BDEELOPRUW powder blue
BDEELQRSUU burlesqued
BDEEMNNRUU unnumbered
BDEEMNORSU burdensome
BDEENNNOTU unbonneted
BDEENORRUV overburden
BDEENORSUV unobserved
BDEENORTTU buttered on
BDEEOORSTT desert boot
BDEFFIILSU diffusible
BDEFFNOORW browned off
BDEFGINOOR foreboding
BDEFGIOORT footbridge
BDEFILOOST soft-boiled
BDEFIOPRRY bird of prey
BDEFKLLOOU blood fluke
BDEFLOORUX Oxford blue
BDEGGLNOOO boondoggle
BDEGHHIINR highbinder
BDEGHIMPRU hump bridge
BDEGHIOTWY body weight
BDEGIILLNV diving bell
BDEGIINNRR ring-binder
BDEGIKORRW bridgework
BDEGILLORR bridge roll
BDEGILLORT toll bridge
BDEGILNNOT Bedlington
BDEGIMOORR bridegroom
BDEGINORTW Bridgetown
BDEGIOPRRT Bridgeport
BDEGIORRTW Trowbridge
BDEGLNORUU blue ground
BDEHIIMOOR rhomboidei
BDEHIIOPRT prohibited
BDEHIKORRT kid brother
BDEHIMNTUX thumb index
BDEHLOOORS blood horse
BDEHNOOSUU housebound
BDEHNORTUX thunderbox
BDEHNRRSUU underbrush, undershrub
BDEIIKRRST bird-strike
BDEIILMORS disembroil
BDEIIRSSUZ subsidizer
BDEIIRSTTU distribute
BDEIKNNORW broken wind
BDEILLOSSU dissoluble
BDEILLOTUX billet-doux
BDEILMORSW bowdlerism
BDEILNOOSS bloodiness
BDEIMNORSS morbidness
BDEINOORSS broodiness
BDEINRSSTU turbidness
BDEKNNOORW broken-down
BDELLNOPSU spellbound
BDELMMNOUY molybdenum
BDELMNOOOY blood money
BDELMNOTUW tumbledown
BDELMOORSU blood serum
BDELNOOOST bloodstone
BDELNORTUU untroubled
BDELOOPSTU double stop
BDEMOORRSY dyer's broom
BDFILOORST first blood
BDFIOORSST bird's-foots
BDFLLOTUUY doubtfully
BDGIILLNNY blindingly
BDGIINRSTU disturbing
BDGIKMNOSU subkingdom
BDGILNOORY broodingly
BDGILNOTUY doubtingly
BDGLNOOOUY young blood
BDGLOOOPRU blood group
BDGNOOORSW brown goods
BDHIILRRWY whirlybird
BDHILOOPRS Lord Bishop
BDHIMNOORY monohybrid
BDHIOSTTUU shut-out bid
BDHNNOORTU northbound
BDHNOOSTUU southbound
BDIIILNOSU libidinous
BDILLOSSUY dissolubly
BDILNRSTTU blind trust
BDIMNORTTU mutton-bird
BDINNOORRU round robin
BDLOOOPRST blood sport
BDMNOORSTU stormbound
BDNNOOTTUW button-down
BEEEEFLNSS feebleness
BEEEEGIKNP bee-keeping
BEEEEGINNR beer engine
BEEEEGNRRT Green Beret
BEEEEHLLVW bevel wheel
BEEEELORTV rove beetle
BEEEEMMRRR rememberer
BEEEFILLRX reflexible
BEEEFILMMR life member
BEEEFOORRT freebooter
BEEEGGINRR ginger beer
BEEEGGRRUV Vegeburger
BEEEGIILLR re-eligible
BEEEHIILNW wheelie bin
BEEEHLLRTW bell-wether
BEEEILLLLV Belleville

BEEEILNRUV unbeliever
BEEEILNSTX extensible
BEEEILRRSV reversible
BEEEILRRTV revertible
BEEEINRSSZ breeziness
BEEEIRRSTW sweet-brier
BEEEKKOOPR bookkeeper
BEEELLRSST best-seller
BEEELMMNST emblements
BEEELMMRSS memberless
BEEELNNOTV benevolent
BEEELORTTT bottle tree
BEEEMMNSTU bemusement
BEEEMNRTTT betterment
BEEENORSTT bone-setter
BEEEOQSUXZ squeeze-box
BEEFFNORUZ buffer zone
BEEFGIINNT benefiting
BEEFGRSTUU subterfuge
BEEFIILLNX inflexible
BEEFILLMRU umbellifer
BEEFILMORS Froebelism
BEEFILNOST stifle-bone
BEEFLLLORW bellflower
BEEGGIILLN negligible
BEEGGLOORT bootlegger
BEEGHILLLS sleigh bell
BEEGHMNRTU green thumb
BEEGIIILLN ineligible
BEEGIILNRT Gilbertine
BEEGIINOSS biogenesis
BEEGILLNRR bell-ringer
BEEGILMNOW emboweling
BEEGILNNSU blue ensign
BEEGINRTTV brevetting
BEEGINRTTW Wittenberg
BEEGNNOTTU unbegotten
BEEGNOORRS Greensboro
BEEGOORRSY gooseberry
BEEGRRSTTU Grub Street
BEEHILMMOO mobile home
BEEHILMOST blithesome
BEEHILNSST blitheness
BEEHIMMPRS membership
BEEHKMNOOR broken home
BEEHKOORRS Sherbrooke
BEEHLMNSSU humbleness
BEEHLORTTU the trouble
BEEHLRSSTU bus shelter
BEEHMOORST bothersome
BEEHMOORTT mother-to-be
BEEHORSUUY housebuyer
BEEIIKLMRT kimberlite
BEEIILLLRV Libreville
BEEIILMNRT timberline
BEEIILMRSS remissible
BEEIILNNSS insensible
BEEIILNRTV invertible
BEEIILNSTV investible
BEEIILRSST resistible
BEEIKKNORR knobkerrie
BEEIKLNPRS besprinkle
BEEILLLNTU Lutine Bell
BEEILLLOVW boll-weevil
BEEILLLOWY yellow bile
BEEILLMRST belletrism
BEEILLORSU rebellious
BEEILLRSTT belletrist
BEEILMNNSS nimbleness
BEEILMNRSS limberness
BEEILMOOPP Popemobile
BEEILMRSTT trembliest
BEEILNOPRZ Nobel Prize
BEEILNOSST ostensible
BEEILNOTTW wine bottle
BEEILRRSVY reversibly
BEEIMORRTT tribometer
BEEINRSSTT bitterness
BEEIQRRSUU brusquerie
BEEIRSSUVV subversive
BEEKLLOORS bookseller
BEEKNNORSS brokenness
BEELLMNOOT Montebello
BEELLOOSTY obsoletely
BEELMMORSU lumbersome
BEELMNRSSU numberless
BEELNOOSTT bottlenose
BEELNSSSTU subtleness
BEELOORSUV overblouse
BEELORSTUV oversubtle
BEELQRRSUU burlesquer
BEELQRSSUU burlesques
BEEMMNNOTT entombment
BEEMMNOSST embossment
BEEMNORSSS sombreness
BEENOSSSTU obtuseness
BEENPRSSSU superbness
BEENQSSTUU subsequent
BEEPRRSTYY presbytery
BEFFNOORUY buffoonery
BEFGHIILRT fire blight
BEFGIINNOR fibrinogen
BEFGILNORW finger bowl
BEFHILLMTU thimbleful
BEFHIRSTTU butterfish
BEFIILLNXY inflexibly
BEFIILRSTU filibuster
BEFILMORTW timber wolf
BEFLLMRTUU tumblerful
BEGGHMRUUY humbuggery
BEGGIILLNY negligibly
BEGGILNNOS belongings
BEGGRSTTUY Gettysburg
BEGHIIINTX exhibiting
BEGHIILMRT thimblerig
BEGHIILNRT blithering
BEGHIINRRT rebirthing
BEGHILMNOO hemoglobin
BEGHILNORY neighborly
BEGHINRSST brightness
BEGHIORRTW right bower
BEGHOORTUV overbought
BEGIIILLNY ineligibly
BEGIIILLTY legibility
BEGIIIMNRT ignimbrite
BEGIIKLRTZ blitzkrieg
BEGIILNRTT bitterling
BEGIINRRST bestirring
BEGIKLNRUY rebukingly
BEGILNORSY soberingly
BEGILOOOXY exobiology
BEGINNORSS boringness
BEGINNOSTX nesting box
BEGLMOORYY embryology
BEGLMORUUX Luxembourg
BEGMOOPSSU goose bumps
BEGMOORRSV Bromsgrove
BEGOOPPRST gobstopper
BEGOORRTTT bogtrotter
BEHIIIINTV inhibitive
BEHIIINOTX exhibition
BEHIIOPRRT prohibiter
BEHIIORTXY exhibitory
BEHIKLLNOR Broken Hill
BEHIKOPRRS shipbroker
BEHILLORWW willowherb
BEHILMOSSV Bolshevism
BEHILNOSSS bolshiness
BEHILOSSTV Bolshevist
BEHINORSTT birthstone
BEHINOSSSY boyishness
BEHLMOOPTY phlebotomy
BEHLNOOTTU buttonhole
BEHMOOORST smooth-bore
BEHMOORSST thromboses
BEHMPRTTUU tub-thumper
BEHRRSSUWY Shrewsbury
BEIIIIKLNN bikini line
BEIIILMMOZ immobilize
BEIIIMNTUZ bituminize
BEIIILLOSUZ solubilize
BEIIILLPRTT bitter pill
BEIIILMOPSS impossible
BEIIILMRTUY muliebrity
BEIIILNNSSY insensibly
BEIIILORSTU boiler suit
BEIIILRSTTT librettist
BEIIILSUYZZ busy Lizzie
BEIIIMSSSUV submissive
BEIIINORSTY insobriety
BEIJLRRTUY jerry-built
BEIKLMRTTU buttermilk
BEILLMSSUU subsellium
BEILLNORUV Bournville
BEILLNRSUV Burnsville
BEILLOPRST billposter
BEILMNOOSW snowmobile
BEILMNOOTT bottom line
BEILMOOORR boiler room
BEILMOOOTZ lobotomize
BEILMOOSST obsoletism
BEILNNOPST splint-bone
BEILNOORST Orion's belt
BEILNOPRSW spin bowler
BEILNOSSTY ostensibly

BEILNOSSWZ blowziness
BEILNOSTUY nebulosity
BEILNPRSUY spinel ruby
BEIMNNOOPT embonpoint
BEIMNORSSU submersion
BEINNOSTUV subvention
BEINOPRSTU subreption
BEINORSSUV subversion
BEINORSTUU subroutine
BEINORSUVV bon viveurs
BEINOSSTWX witness box
BEINSSSTTU subsistent
BEIOOQSSUU obsequious
BEIOORSSTU boisterous
BEIOQRSTUU soubriquet
BEIORSTTUY tuberosity
BEISSTTTUU substitute
BEKLNNORUY unbrokenly
BEKMOORSTU muster-book
BEKNOORSTY stony-broke
BELLNNOOSU non-soluble
BELLNOSUUY nebulously
BELLORSTUY trolleybus
BELMMOORRU lumber-room
BELMOOSSTT bottomless
BELMORSSUU slumberous
BELNOORSWW snowblower
BELNOSSTTU buttonless
BELOOPRSTT lobster pot
BEMNOTTTUU mute button
BENNOORRSW brown-noser
BENNOORSTW brownstone
BENORSSSTU robustness
BEORRTTTUW butterwort
BFFHINOOSU buffoonish
BFGHILNTYY fly-by-night
BFGILLMNUY fumblingly
BFIIILSTUY fusibility
BFIIIORSST fibrositis
BFIIKORSTT bit of skirt
BFILLLSSUY blissfully
BFOOPRRSTU burstproof
BGGGHIMNUU humbugging
BGGIILLNOY obligingly
BGGIILNNOU unobliging
BGGIILNORS Gibson girl
BGGIINNPRU upbringing
BGHHIIRRTT birthright
BGHHOOPSTU shop-bought
BGHIIIINNT inhibiting
BGHIILNOOT boiling hot
BGHILLOUWY Willoughby
BGHILMOORU Milborough
BGHILNNSUU unblushing
BGHIPRSTTU Pittsburgh
BGIIILNOTY ignobility
BGIIKLNNNU unblinking
BGIIMNSTTU submitting
BGIINORSUU rubiginous
BGILLMMNUY mumblingly
BGILLMNOSY symbolling
BGILNNORTU Burlington
BGILOORSTY bryologist
BGILORSUUU lugubrious
BGINNORUUY Rugby Union
BHHOORSTTU toothbrush
BHIIIINNOT inhibition
BHIIIMRSST Britishism
BHIIINORTY inhibitory
BHIILLRSTT stillbirth
BHIIOOPRRT prohibitor
BHIMNPRTTU thumbprint
BHIMOORSST thrombosis
BHINORRSTW Brownshirt
BHKNOOOTTU buttonhook
BHLLOOSSUU holus-bolus
BHLLRRUUYY hurly-burly
BHNOPSTTUU push-button
BIIIILRSTY risibility
BIIIILSTVY visibility
BIIILMMOTY immobility
BIILLLLSYY silly billy
BIILLOSTUY solubility
BIILLOTUVY volubility
BIILMOPSSY impossibly
BIIMNOSSSU submission
BIIMNOSTUU bituminous
BIINOSSSSY byssinosis
BIIOQSTUUU ubiquitous
BIKLLORSST stork's-bill
BIMNOORSTT trombonist
BIMOOPPRRU opprobrium
BKMOOOPPRT prompt book
BMMOOOSTTT bottommost
BNOORRTTUW brown trout
CCCDEILOPY cyclopedic
CCCDIILOOP diplococci
CCCEEINNOS conscience
CCCEEINRST crescentic
CCCEELNSUU succulence
CCCEENORRU occurrence
CCCEHIILNO colchicine
CCCEHKORSS cross-check
CCCEIIMRSU circumcise
CCCEILNORR corn circle
CCCEILOPRR crop circle
CCCEILOTUY leucocytic
CCCEINNORT concentric
CCCEINOOTU coconut ice
CCCEKLNOOR corncockle
CCCGNOOOSU gonococcus
CCCHHILOOO chocoholic
CCCHIKOPST spitchcock
CCCILLOPYY polycyclic
CCCILNSTUY succinctly
CCCINNOOOT concoction
CCCLOORSSY cyclo-cross
CCDDEENNOS condescend
CCDEEEENPR precedence
CCDEEEHINS dehiscence
CCDEEEHRSU curd cheese
CCDEEENPRY precedency
CCDEEENRST decrescent
CCDEEERRSU recrudesce
CCDEEFIINY deficiency
CCDEEFINNO confidence
CCDEEHIORT ricocheted
CCDEEHNOSY synecdoche
CCDEEIIIPT epideictic
CCDEEIILRT dielectric
CCDEEIIRRT directrice
CCDEEIKLRV clever Dick
CCDEELNNOO condolence
CCDEEORRRU reoccurred
CCDEHILLOS cold chisel
CCDEHKNOSU soundcheck
CCDEHLNTUU Dutch uncle
CCDEIILOPY epicycloid
CCDEIINNOT coincident
CCDEIJKOSY disc jockey
CCDEIMOOOT octodecimo
CCDEINNOST disconnect
CCDEINOOPS endoscopic
CCDEINOPUU unoccupied
CCDEINORST disconcert
CCDEINOTUV conductive
CCDELOOORU colour code
CCDELOORUV cloud cover
CCDEOOPRRU co-producer
CCDGIILOSU glucosidic
CCDGIILOSY glycosidic
CCDGILOOOY codicology
CCDHIIMOOT dichotomic
CCDHNRRSUY scrunch-dry
CCDIIMOSSU disco music
CCDIMNOSTU misconduct
CCDIMOSSTU cosmic dust
CCDINNOOTU conduction
CCEEEELLNX excellence
CCEEEENNSS senescence
CCEEEFNNOR conference
CCEEEFNRSU rufescence
CCEEEGINOS geoscience
CCEEEHIRRS screechier
CCEEEINPRS prescience
CCEEEINQSU quiescence
CCEEEINRSV virescence
CCEEELLNXY Excellency
CCEEEMMNOR recommence
CCEEEMNOPT competence
CCEEEMNSTU tumescence
CCEEENRRRU recurrence
CCEEENRSTX excrescent
CCEEFFIINY efficiency
CCEEFFILNO off-licence
CCEEFHHRRU Free Church
CCEEFINTTU fettuccine
CCEEFLNNOU confluence
CCEEGINNOR congeneric
CCEEGINORT egocentric, geocentric
CCEEGNNORU congruence
CCEEHHIRST Chichester
CCEEHINOSS choiceness
CCEEHIOSTV chest voice
CCEEHKLLPS spell-check
CCEEHLORST Colchester
CCEEHLORSW screech owl
CCEEHMOSSY ecchymoses
CCEEHNOSTU escutcheon

CCEEIIINNP incipience
CCEEIILMRS semicircle
CCEEIINPRY recipiency
CCEEILLOTV collective
CCEEILMNNY inclemency
CCEEILNORR reconciler
CCEEILNORT electronic
CCEEILOPST telescopic
CCEEILORVY coercively
CCEEINNNOT continence
CCEEINNOTV connective
CCEEINOPTV conceptive
CCEEINORTZ concretize
CCEEINOSSV concessive
CCEEINOTVV convective
CCEEINQSUY quiescency
CCEEIOPRSS crosspiece
CCEEIORRTV corrective
CCEEISSSUV successive
CCEEJNORTU conjecture
CCEEKKLOYY cocky-leeky
CCEELMORTY cyclometer
CCEELNOPRU corpulence
CCEELNORTY concretely
CCEELNRTUU truculence
CCEEMNOPTY competency
CCEENOPRRT preconcert
CCEFFFHNRU French cuff
CCEFHIIMOR microfiche
CCEFIIINST scientific
CCEFIINPSU unspecific
CCEFILMRUX circumflex
CCEFIMRSUU circumfuse
CCEFINNOOT confection
CCEFLLNOTU flocculent
CCEFLSSSUU successful
CCEGGILNOY glycogenic
CCEGHHORRU churchgoer
CCEGHIIIOP pichiciego
CCEGHINORT crocheting
CCEGIIKNRT cricketing
CCEGINNNOR concerning
CCEGINORSY cryogenics
CCEGNNORUY congruency
CCEHHILOTV clove hitch
CCEHIIMOOR heroi-comic
CCEHIINNNO cinchonine
CCEHIINSTT technicist
CCEHIKMOOR mock-heroic
CCEHIKNOPT checkpoint
CCEHIKNOPX chickenpox
CCEHIKPRRY cherry-pick
CCEHILNORR chronicler
CCEHILOOPR pleochroic
CCEHIMOSSY ecchymosis
CCEHINRSTU crunchiest
CCEHKNOOST chockstone
CCEHKORTUU chucker-out
CCEHMOORTY cytochrome
CCEHNOPRUW cowpuncher
CCEIIINNPY incipiency
CCEIIRRTZ criticizer
CCEIILOSST solecistic
CCEIIMOORS serio-comic
CCEIIMOTXY Mexico City
CCEIIMPSST scepticism
CCEIINRTTY centricity
CCEIIOPPRS periscopic
CCEIIORTVY coercivity
CCEIIOSTTZ Scotticize
CCEIKKOPPT pickpocket
CCEIKLNRTU crinkle-cut
CCEIKMNOSY cockneyism
CCEILLLOSU cellulosic
CCEILLNOOT collection
CCEILNNOSU nucleonics
CCEILNOSUV conclusive
CCEIMNNOOU uneconomic
CCEIMNRTUV circumvent
CCEIMOOPRS microscope
CCEINNNOOT connection
CCEINNOOPT conception
CCEINNOORT concertino, concretion
CCEINNOOSS concession
CCEINNOOTV convection
CCEINOORRT correction
CCEINOSSSU succession
CCEINOSSUV concussive
CCEIOOPRSU precocious
CCEKKORTUY turkeycock
CCEKLOORTW clock tower
CCEKLORSUY cocksurely
CCELLOSTYY cyclostyle
CCELMOORTY motorcycle
CCELMOOSTY cyclostome
CCELNOPRUY corpulency
CCELNOSSTU occultness
CCELNRTUUY truculency
CCELOOOPPS colposcope
CCENNORRTU concurrent
CCENOOPRSY necroscopy
CCENOPSSTU conspectus
CCEOOPSSTY cystoscope
CCFKKMOORS smock-frock
CCFKLOOORU four o'clock
CCGHHHHIRU High Church
CCGHLNOOOY conchology
CCGIIIKNNP picnicking
CCGIINNNOV convincing
CCGILORSUY glycosuric
CCGIMNOOOS cosmogonic
CCGINNORRU concurring
CCGIOOPRSY gyroscopic
CCHHHOOPTT hotchpotch
CCHHIIOTTY ichthyotic
CCHIIIMOTU Chicoutimi
CCHIILMOOX Xochimilco
CCHIINORTY chronicity
CCHIIPSSTY psychicist
CCHIKLOSTT lock stitch
CCHILMNNOU column-inch
CCHIMOSSTT Scotch mist
CCHINNORSY synchronic
CCHIOOOPRS horoscopic
CCHNOOSTUY coconut shy
CCHOOPSSUU hocus-pocus
CCIIILOSST sciolistic
CCIIKKQRTU quick trick
CCIILLNOPY polyclinic
CCIILMNNOO monoclinic
CCIILMOPTY complicity
CCIILNSTUY unicyclist
CCIILRSTTY tricyclist
CCIIMOPRST comic strip
CCIIMOSSTT Scotticism
CCIINNNOTY concinnity
CCIINNOOTV conviction
CCIIORSTUU circuitous
CCIKNOOPTU cuckoo pint
CCIKOOPSTU cuckoo spit
CCILLNOORU councillor
CCILMRRUUU curriculum
CCILNNOOSU conclusion
CCIMOOPRSY microscopy
CCINNOOSSU concussion
CCINOSSSUU succussion
CCINOSTUVY viscountcy
CCIORRSSSS criss-cross
CCLLOOORTU collocutor
CCLOOOPPSY colposcopy
CCNOORRTUW Crown Court
CCOOPSSTYY cystoscopy
CDDEEEEGKL deckle edge
CDDEEEENNP dependence
CDDEEEJLTY dejectedly
CDDEEELNOR needlecord
CDDEEENNPY dependency
CDDEEENNST descendent
CDDEEENTTU undetected
CDDEEFFIIN diffidence
CDDEEFOSSU defocussed
CDDEEIINSS dissidence
CDDEEINRTU uncredited, undirected
CDDEEINTUY Dundee City
CDDEELMOSU cuddlesome
CDDEENORRU unrecorded
CDDEFKTTUU tufted duck
CDDEFNNOOU confounded
CDDEGIKLOR gridlocked
CDDEGLOORR gold record
CDDEHOOORW hooded crow
CDDEIMMOOS discommode
CDDEINNOSW second wind
CDDENOPRTU end product
CDDGIIKNUV diving duck
CDDHILLOSY cloddishly
CDDILOOPSU diplodocus
CDEEEEINPX expedience
CDEEEENRRT deterrence
CDEEEFFINR difference
CDEEEFFIST side effect
CDEEEFHIKR kerchiefed
CDEEEFILST self-deceit
CDEEEGIIPR ridge piece
CDEEEGINRV divergence
CDEEEHLRSU reschedule
CDEEEHOOSW cheesewood
CDEEEHRRTW wretcheder
CDEEEIINRS decree nisi
CDEEEILOPV velocipede
CDEEEILQSU deliquesce

CDEEEIMNNO comedienne
CDEEEINPXY expediency
CDEEEINRRT interceder
CDEEEINRSW wide-screen
CDEEEIRRST discreeter
CDEEELORRT telerecord
CDEEENNRSU unscreened
CDEEENPTUX unexpected
CDEEENTUUX unexecuted
CDEEERRSTT street cred
CDEEFFILOR force field
CDEEFIINRT dentifrice
CDEEFILNOT deflection
CDEEFINNTU uninfected
CDEEFLNORT centerfold, centrefold
CDEEFLNORY enforcedly
CDEEFLNOSS second self
CDEEFORSSU refocussed
CDEEGIINOR Ceredigion
CDEEGIKNNR ring-necked
CDEEGILNNU indulgence
CDEEGILNUV divulgence
CDEEGINOPR proceeding
CDEEGINRVY divergency
CDEEGIOOPS piece-goods
CDEEHIILOP ophicleide
CDEEHIMNOR echinoderm
CDEEHLOSTU suede-cloth
CDEEHLRTWY wretchedly
CDEEHMNOPR comprehend
CDEEHNNQUU unquenched
CDEEHORRST Dorchester
CDEEIIINSV indecisive
CDEEIILSVY decisively
CDEEIIMNTY endemicity
CDEEIIMPRS spermicide
CDEEIINRRR dernier cri
CDEEIINRST indiscreet, indiscrete, iridescent
CDEEIIORRT Directoire
CDEEIIPRTV predictive
CDEEIIRSSV disservice
CDEEIKNNST deck tennis
CDEEIKNSSW wickedness
CDEEILLNST stencilled
CDEEILNNOS declension
CDEEILNNSU unlicensed
CDEEILNNTY indecently
CDEEILNOOZ decolonize
CDEEILNOSU nucleoside
CDEEILNOTU nucleotide
CDEEILNRVY Inverclyde
CDEEILOORZ decolorize
CDEEILORST cloistered
CDEEILRSTY discreetly, discretely
CDEEIMNNTU inducement
CDEEIMNPRU imprudence
CDEEINNRSW windscreen
CDEEINOPRV providence
CDEEINORRS reconsider
CDEEINORTT credit note
CDEEINPRRU underprice
CDEEINPRSY presidency
CDEEINRSST directness
CDEEINRSTY dysenteric
CDEEIORRSV discoverer, rediscover
CDEEIORRVV cover drive
CDEEIPRRSS cider press
CDEEIPRSST disrespect
CDEEIRRSST directress
CDEEIRRSTT derestrict
CDEEKKKNNO knock-kneed
CDEEKNNORU unreckoned
CDEEKOOORV overcooked
CDEEKOOPRW woodpecker
CDEEKOORST crookedest
CDEELLNOSU counselled
CDEELNNOSU unenclosed
CDEEMNNOST secondment
CDEEMOOPRS decomposer
CDEEMOPRSS decompress
CDEENNORSU uncensored
CDEENNRSUU uncensured
CDEENOORRS rood-screen
CDEENORRSU underscore
CDEENORRUV undercover
CDEENORSTU unescorted
CDEENOSTUU consuetude
CDEENRSSSU cursedness
CDEENSSSSU cussedness
CDEEOPRRRU reproducer
CDEERSSSTU seductress
CDEFFILNRU undercliff
CDEFFIOSUX fixed focus
CDEFGHIKLT flight deck
CDEFGINOSU defocusing
CDEFGIOOOV voice of God
CDEFHIORRT third force
CDEFHLMORS Chelmsford
CDEFHNOORR French door
CDEFILNOUU fluid ounce
CDEFINNNOU unconfined
CDEFLNORUY unforcedly
CDEFLNOSUY confusedly
CDEFNORRTU undercroft
CDEFNOSSUU unfocussed
CDEGGILLNU cudgelling
CDEGHJOTUU touch judge
CDEGIINNRS discerning
CDEGIKNOST stockinged
CDEGIOOSTT Scottie dog
CDEGMNORUU curmudgeon
CDEGNORRUW ground crew
CDEHHIIPRT diphtheric
CDEHHIIRRT Third Reich
CDEHIINOST hedonistic
CDEHILOPRY polyhedric
CDEHILOPTW low-pitched
CDEHIMOPRY hypodermic
CDEHINOSTW switched-on
CDEHLNOOSU unschooled
CDEHLOOPPR clodhopper
CDEHLOOPRY copyholder
CDEHLOOPSS closed shop
CDEHOORRWY cherrywood
CDEIIILNNS disincline
CDEIIILNPS discipline
CDEIIIMRSV recidivism
CDEIIINNOS indecision
CDEIIINTVV vindictive
CDEIIIRSTV recidivist
CDEIIKLLLP dill pickle
CDEIIKLOPT politicked
CDEIILNPPR principled
CDEIILNRTY indirectly
CDEIILOSTU solicitude
CDEIIMNNTT indictment
CDEIIMORRS misericord
CDEIIMORST dosimetric
CDEIIMORTY mediocrity
CDEIIMPPSU piped music
CDEIINOPRT prediction
CDEIINORST discretion
CDEIINOSST dissection
CDEIIORTTY City editor
CDEIIRSSUV discursive
CDEIKNRRTU undertrick
CDEIKOPPRT cork-tipped
CDEIKOQSTU deck quoits
CDEILLLPUY pellucidly
CDEILMOPPR crippledom
CDEILNOSSU cloudiness
CDEILOPSUU pediculous
CDEILORSSU disclosure
CDEIMMNOPU compendium
CDEIMNOOSY diseconomy
CDEIMOOPSS discompose
CDEINNOSTT discontent
CDEINOORSU indecorous
CDEINOPRTY decryption
CDEINORRTU introducer
CDEINORSTU discounter
CDEINPRSTU unscripted
CDEIOOPRTY copy editor
CDEIOPRRST descriptor
CDEIOPRTUV productive
CDEIRRSTTU strictured
CDEKLORTUY cold turkey
CDELLNOORT controlled
CDELMOOPSY composedly
CDELNOORUU uncoloured
CDELNOOTUV convoluted
CDELNRTUUU uncultured
CDELOORSUY decorously
CDEMNNOSUU unconsumed
CDEMNOOPRU compounder
CDENNOOPRU pronounced
CDENOOPRRS correspond
CDEOORRRTU court order
CDEOORTTUW woodcutter
CDEORRSSSS cross-dress
CDEORRSSTU court dress
CDEORRSTTU destructor
CDERRSTTUU structured
CDFFIILTUY difficulty
CDFHILOOPR childproof
CDFIIMNORS disconfirm
CDFIMOORST discomfort
CDGHILOORY hydrologic

CDGIKLLOOS	goldilocks
CDHHIILLSY	childishly
CDHHIOORST	Christhood
CDHIIOSSTU	distichous
CDHILLLOSU	Clouds Hill
CDHILORTYY	hydrolytic
CDHIMNOORY	monohydric
CDHINOOOSU	cousinhood
CDHINOOPRY	hydroponic
CDHIOOPRST	doctorship
CDHIOPRSTY	dystrophic
CDHKNNPRUU	punch-drunk
CDHLMMNOOO	commonhold
CDIIILNOTY	indocility
CDIIIMPTUY	impudicity
CDIIINNSTT	indistinct
CDIIKRRTTY	dirty trick
CDIILNSTTY	distinctly
CDIILORSUU	ridiculous
CDIIMNORST	doctrinism
CDIINORSTT	doctrinist
CDIINOSSSU	discussion
CDIKORSSTW	swordstick
CDILLMOOSU	molluscoid
CDILMOOPUY	lycopodium
CDILMORSUW	world music
CDIMMOOOSU	commodious
CDINNOOORS	con sordino
CDINOOPRST	spin doctor
CDINOOPRTU	production
CDLMOORSTU	storm cloud
CDLNOOORRT	control rod
CDLNOORTUY	old country
CDNOOOOTTW	cottonwood
CDNOOPSSTU	pound Scots
CEEEEFFRSV	effervesce
CEEEEFHPRS	free speech
CEEEEFNPRR	preference
CEEEEGIPTX	epexegetic
CEEEEHIMST	cheese-mite
CEEEEHIPRT	three-piece
CEEEEHNPRT	threepence
CEEEEINPRX	experience
CEEEELLNPR	repellence
CEEEFFGLNU	effulgence
CEEEFFLORS	effloresce
CEEEFGLNRU	refulgence
CEEEFILNSS	fleeciness
CEEEFILRTV	reflective
CEEEFINRRS	fire screen
CEEEFINRSS	fierceness
CEEEFIPRTV	perfective
CEEEFMORTV	feme covert
CEEEFPRRTU	prefecture
CEEEGGILNN	negligence
CEEEGIINPT	epigenetic
CEEEGINRST	energetics
CEEEGINRTV	vicegerent
CEEEGNRRSU	resurgence
CEEEHHLORS	horseleech
CEEEHIKNSS	cheekiness
CEEEHIMRST	crime sheet
CEEEHINPTT	epenthetic

CEEEHINRSS	cheeriness
CEEEHINSSS	cheesiness
CEEEHLLSSY	Seychelles
CEEEHLPSSS	speechless
CEEEHMORTT	hectometer, hectometre
CEEEHNORSS	chersonese
CEEEHOQRUU	Eurocheque
CEEEHORRST	threescore
CEEEHORSST	score sheet
CEEEIILNRS	resilience
CEEEILLMNO	emollience
CEEEILLTVY	electively
CEEEILMNNT	clementine
CEEEILMRTT	telemetric
CEEEILNNRT	centre line
CEEEILNORT	re-election
CEEEILNPRT	percentile
CEEEILNPRY	celery pine
CEEEILNPST	pestilence
CEEEIMNNTT	enticement
CEEEIMNRST	mesenteric
CEEEIMNRTT	centimeter, centimetre
CEEEIMNTTX	excitement
CEEEINNPRT	pertinence
CEEEINORRT	re-erection
CEEEINPRSS	creepiness
CEEEINTTWY	winceyette
CEEEIORTVX	overexcite
CEEEIPPRTV	perceptive, preceptive
CEEEIPRSTV	respective
CEEEKKLNPS	kenspeckle
CEEEKKLOPR	lock-keeper
CEEEKRRSSU	seersucker
CEEELLNPRY	repellency
CEEELNRSSV	cleverness
CEEELNSSST	selectness
CEEELORSTT	corselette
CEEEMNOPRS	recompense
CEEEMNORRT	centromere
CEEEMNRSTU	securement
CEEENNRSST	recentness
CEEENOPPRT	prepotence
CEEENOPRST	open secret
CEEENRSSTT	screen test
CEEFFFIIOR	fire-office
CEEFFHIMOO	Home Office
CEEFFHOOPS	coffee shop
CEEFFIKNST	skin effect
CEEFFILLMO	coffee mill
CEEFGHINNR	greenfinch
CEEFGINOSU	Cienfuegos
CEEFGINRTU	centrifuge
CEEFGLLNTU	neglectful
CEEFHHNORT	henceforth
CEEFHIPRTV	fever pitch
CEEFHLLRUY	cheerfully
CEEFHLOORS	free school
CEEFHMNORT	from thence
CEEFHNNRSS	Frenchness
CEEFHORTTU	fourchette
CEEFIILNTV	inflective
CEEFIKLNSS	fickleness

CEEFILNNRU	influencer
CEEFILNORT	reflection
CEEFINOPRT	perfection
CEEFINORRR	reinforcer
CEEFINORRV	five-corner
CEEFKLLSSY	fecklessly
CEEFKLORTT	fetterlock
CEEFLNSTUV	fulvescent
CEEFLPPRTU	pluperfect
CEEFLPRSTU	respectful
CEEFMNNORT	conferment
CEEFNRSTTU	frutescent
CEEFORRRSS	cross-refer
CEEGHIILMP	hemiplegic
CEEGHIMOST	geochemist
CEEGHLNORT	Green Cloth
CEEGHLOPST	clothes-peg
CEEGHOSTUW	cough sweet
CEEGIINSTT	geneticist
CEEGIINSTU	eugenicist
CEEGILLOOT	teleologic
CEEGINNORU	neurogenic
CEEGINNRSS	screenings
CEEGINNRST	nigrescent
CEEGINNRSU	insurgence
CEEGINOORT	erotogenic, orogenetic
CEEGINORRZ	recognizer
CEEGINOSTV	congestive
CEEGINPRST	respecting
CEEGINRSTY	synergetic
CEEGKORRSS	Greek cross
CEEGLORSTU	Gloucester
CEEGNNORRW	crown green
CEEGNNORTV	convergent
CEEGNOOSTU	ectogenous
CEEGNRSTTU	turgescent
CEEHHIMORT	come-hither
CEEHIILNRT	Chile nitre
CEEHIKLSSW	skew chisel
CEEHIKPPRS	schipperke
CEEHIKSSTT	sketchiest
CEEHILNOPR	necrophile
CEEHILNOPT	telephonic
CEEHILOPRT	helicopter
CEEHILORTT	hectoliter, hectolitre
CEEHILOSVY	cohesively
CEEHILRSST	Silchester
CEEHIMNNRT	enrichment
CEEHIMNTTU	technetium
CEEHIMOPTU	mouthpiece
CEEHIMORTX	exothermic
CEEHIMSSTU	sheet music
CEEHINNORT	incoherent
CEEHINOPPR	Hippocrene
CEEHINRRST	christener, rechristen
CEEHINRSTW	winchester
CEEHINSSST	chestiness
CEEHINSSTT	tetchiness
CEEHIOPRST	spirochete
CEEHKKOOYY	hokey-cokey
CEEHKMOSTU	much to seek

CEEHKNORSS horse's neck
CEEHKNPRUY keypuncher
CEEHLLNOSW well-chosen
CEEHLMORTY emery cloth
CEEHLMOSZZ schemozzle
CEEHLNORTY coherently
CEEHLNORWW crown wheel
CEEHLNQSSU quenchless
CEEHNOOPRT ctenophore
CEEHOOPRRS horse-coper
CEEIIKLNPR princelike
CEEIIKLNPT picket line
CEEIILLMRV vermicelli
CEEIILMOPZ polemicize
CEEIILNOSU isoleucine
CEEIILNPRR princelier
CEEIILNRSY resiliency
CEEIILNRTT centiliter, centilitre
CEEIILPRSV lip-service
CEEIIMNNTT incitement
CEEIIMNOPR minor piece
CEEIIMNRRS reminiscer
CEEIIMORTT meteoritic
CEEIIMOSST semeiotics
CEEIIMPRRT perimetric
CEEIIMPSSS speciesism
CEEIINNSST insistence
CEEIINPPRT percipient
CEEIINRSTT interstice
CEEIINSSTT seicentist
CEEIINTTVX extinctive
CEEIIORRST escritoire
CEEIIPSSST speciesist
CEEIIRSTUZ securitize
CEEIJLOPRT projectile
CEEIJOPRTV projective
CEEIJRSTYY Jersey City
CEEIKLLLLR killer cell
CEEIKLNRSS silk screen
CEEIKLSSTT ticketless
CEEIKNPRTY pernickety
CEEILLOOPT coleoptile
CEEILMNOPT incomplete
CEEILMNORT clinometer
CEEILMNOSS comeliness
CEEILNOORZ recolonize
CEEILNQSTU liquescent
CEEILNRSUY insecurely
CEEILNRTTY reticently
CEEILORSTU reticulose
CEEILPRSUV preclusive
CEEIMMORRT micrometer, micrometre
CEEIMNNOPR prominence
CEEIMNOORZ economizer
CEEIMORSTV viscometer
CEEINNNOTV convenient
CEEINNPRTY pertinency
CEEINOPPRT perception
CEEINOPRSS precession
CEEINOPRTV optic nerve
CEEINOPRTX excerption
CEEINORRSW cornerwise
CEEINORSTV ventricose

CEEINORTVY overnicety
CEEINOSTTX coexistent
CEEINRRSTU scrutineer
CEEINRSSSW screwiness
CEEINRSTTT trecentist
CEEINRSTTV vitrescent
CEEINRSTYZ syncretize
CEEIOPRSTT stereoptic
CEEIOPRTTV protective
CEEIPPRSTU upset price
CEEIPRRSUV precursive
CEEIPRSSUV percussive
CEEIPSSTUV susceptive
CEEIRRTTUW wire-cutter
CEEJNOOSSS jocoseness
CEEKKKNNOS knock knees
CEEKLLRSSY recklessly
CEEKLNRTTU turtleneck
CEEKLOPSST pocketless
CEEKLORRWW crewel work
CEEKOPSTTV vest-pocket
CEELLLSSUY cluelessly
CEELLMOPTY completely
CEELLMSSSU muscleless
CEELMMNOPT complement
CEELMNNOOS somnolence
CEELNORSVY conversely
CEELOOORSV loose cover
CEELORRSTY clerestory
CEEMMOORRY core memory
CEEMMOTXYY myxomycete
CEEMNNSTTY encystment
CEEMNOORST centrosome
CEEMNOPRTU recoupment
CEEMNORSTT centremost
CEENNOQSTU consequent
CEENNORRTU rencounter
CEENNPRSSY penny cress
CEENOPPPRR peppercorn
CEENOPPRTY prepotency
CEENOQRSTU reconquest
CEENORRTUV rev counter
CEENORSSTV covertness
CEENPRSSSU spruceness
CEENPRSTTU putrescent
CEEOPPRRSS pre-process
CEEOPRRSTT retrospect
CEEOPRRSTU persecutor
CEEORRSSST crosstrees
CEEORRTUUV couverture
CEERSSSUUX excursuses
CEFFFFHOTU off the cuff
CEFFGIILOR office girl
CEFFHIINOR chiffonier
CEFFHILOOY Holy Office
CEFFHNOORR French roof
CEFFIIKKLN flick knife
CEFFIINSTU sufficient
CEFFIOOPST Post Office
CEFFIRSSTU scruffiest
CEFFLLORUY forcefully
CEFGHILNTY fetchingly
CEFGIIKNPR fingerpick

CEFGINNORR conferring
CEFGINORSU refocusing
CEFGLOORSU golf course
CEFHHINOSU house finch
CEFHHNNORR French horn
CEFHIIRRST First Reich
CEFHIKNRSS French kiss
CEFHILPRTU pitcherful
CEFHILPRTY fly-pitcher
CEFHILSTTU cuttlefish
CEFHLNOOOV cloven hoof
CEFHNOORTT trench foot
CEFIIILNTY infelicity
CEFIIKMNNY Mickey Finn
CEFIILNNOT inflection
CEFIILNOQU cinquefoil
CEFIILOSTU felicitous
CEFIIMNNTU munificent
CEFIINOPRT proficient
CEFIINOPST pontifices
CEFIINOSTU infectious
CEFIKOSTTW soft wicket
CEFILLMRUY mercifully
CEFILMNRUU unmerciful
CEFILMOORS frolicsome
CEFINNOOSS confession
CEFINOORSU coniferous
CEFINORSUU nuciferous
CEFIOORSUV vociferous
CEFIORRSSY fiery cross
CEFLLRSTUY cluster fly
CEFLNOOOTV cloven foot
CEFLNOORRW cornflower
CEGGHIMNUW chewing gum
CEGGLNOOYY gynecology
CEGHHIIMNO high-income
CEGHIIKNNT thickening
CEGHIILLNS chiselling
CEGHIINNUY unhygienic
CEGHIINOST histogenic
CEGHILMNSY schemingly
CEGHILNOOT ethnologic
CEGHILNOPY phylogenic
CEGHILNPPS schlepping
CEGHILOPRY hypergolic
CEGHILORSW Welsh corgi
CEGHIMMNOO homecoming
CEGHINOOPT photogenic
CEGHIOPSSY geophysics
CEGHIORSTU grouchiest
CEGHLNOOTY technology
CEGHLOOORY choreology
CEGHOOPRSY hygroscope
CEGIIIMNNT meningitic
CEGIIKLLNN nickelling
CEGIIKPRST pig-sticker
CEGIILLNNP pencilling
CEGIILNNPR princeling
CEGIILNNSS clinginess
CEGIILNNST stenciling
CEGIILNNTY enticingly
CEGIILNPRY piercingly
CEGIILNTXY excitingly

CEGIILOPTT epiglottic
CEGIILOSTU eulogistic
CEGIINNTUX unexciting
CEGIINOSTZ gnosticize
CEGIKNOOPR rock-pigeon
CEGILLMNOP compelling
CEGILLOOXY lexicology
CEGILMOORT metrologic
CEGILNNOST clingstone
CEGILNNOSU counseling
CEGILOOPRT petrologic
CEGIMNOORS ergonomics
CEGINNNOTT contingent
CEGINNNSTU cunningest
CEGINNOOST congestion
CEGINNRSTY stringency
CEGINNRSUY insurgency
CEGINOQRTU croqueting
CEGINORTVW wing covert
CEGINRTTUV curvetting
CEGLNOOSYY synecology
CEHHHIIKRT hitch-hiker
CEHHIILMNT helminthic
CEHHIMRTUY eurhythmic
CEHHIOOPRT theophoric
CEHHIOOPST theosophic
CEHHKLLOSS shell-shock
CEHHLLOOTW whole cloth
CEHHLOORST horse-cloth
CEHHLORTTW Letchworth
CEHIIKLRST Christlike
CEHIIKSSTT kitschiest
CEHIILLNSS chilliness
CEHIILMOST mesolithic
CEHIILNPST clientship
CEHIIMNORT thermionic
CEHIIMSTTW time switch
CEHIINPPRS princeship
CEHIINPRSS chirpiness
CEHIINRSTV Chernivtsi
CEHIINSTTZ chintziest
CEHIIPRSTY sphericity
CEHIIPSTUU euphuistic
CEHIISTTTW twitchiest
CEHIJKOPSY jockeyship
CEHIKNNSSU chunkiness
CEHILMOOST school time
CEHILNOPRY necrophily
CEHILNOPST clothes-pin
CEHILNRSTT slit trench
CEHILOPTTU pilot chute
CEHILORSTY chrysolite, chrysotile
CEHILSSSTT stitchless
CEHIMMNSSU chumminess
CEHIMMOPRS morphemics
CEHIMNOOPR microphone
CEHIMNOOTT nomothetic
CEHIMNOPTY chimney pot
CEHIMOOORT homoerotic
CEHIMOOPTY mythopoeic
CEHIMOOSST smoochiest
CEHIMOPRTY microphyte
CEHIMOSSUU house music
CEHIMRSTUY eurythmics
CEHIMSSTTT stem stitch
CEHINNNPPY pinchpenny
CEHINNPSSU punchiness
CEHINNRSTY strychnine
CEHINOORRS rhinoceros
CEHINOOSSS choosiness
CEHINOPPSS choppiness
CEHINOPPTY phenotypic
CEHINOPRSS censorship
CEHINOPRSY hypersonic
CEHINOPRTY hypertonic
CEHINOPSTT pitchstone
CEHINOSSTU touchiness
CEHINSTTTT tent stitch
CEHIOORRRT retrochoir
CEHIOPRRST rectorship
CEHIOPRSTT prosthetic
CEHIOQSTTU coquettish
CEHIORSTTV overstitch
CEHIORSTVW switch-over
CEHKOOPPRR rockhopper
CEHLMNOSUU homuncules
CEHLMOOPRY polychrome
CEHLMOPTYY lymphocyte
CEHLMPRRUY cherry plum
CEHLOOOPRT tocopherol
CEHLOOPPRS prep school
CEHMMNOOOR monochrome
CEHMMOOORS chromosome
CEHMNOOTTU touch-me-not
CEHMOOPRTY ectomorphy
CEHNOOPRRS corner shop
CEHNOOPRTT top-notcher
CEHNOOSTTU touchstone
CEHNOPRSTU Scunthorpe
CEHNOPRSTY phenocryst
CEHNOPRTYY pyrotechny
CEHOORRSST short score
CEHOORSTUU courthouse
CEHORSTTTU outstretch
CEIIIKNOST isokinetic
CEIIILLNNP penicillin
CEIIILNPTX inexplicit
CEIIILNSVY incisively
CEIIILOPTZ politicize
CEIIIMMPRS empiricism
CEIIIMOSSS isoseismic
CEIIIMPRST empiricist
CEIIIMRTVZ victimizer
CEIIIMSSTY seismicity
CEIIINNOTZ nicotinize
CEIIIQSTTU quietistic
CEIIJNNTUV injunctive
CEIIKLMORT kilometric
CEIIKLNSSS sickliness
CEIIKLPRST prickliest
CEIIKMPSST skepticism
CEIIKNOSTT tokenistic
CEIIKNRSST trickiness
CEIIKNSSST stickiness
CEIIKRSSTT tricksiest
CEIILLLSTU cellulitis
CEIILLPTXY explicitly
CEIILMOPST polemicist
CEIILMSSTV victimless
CEIILNOSTU licentious
CEIILNOSTV novelistic
CEIILRSTVY Silver City
CEIIMNNOST omniscient
CEIIMNPRSS crimpiness
CEIIMNRSSU sinecurism
CEIIMORSST isometrics
CEIIMOSTTT totemistic
CEIINNNOTZ non-citizen
CEIINNOPST cispontine, inspection
CEIINNOTTX extinction
CEIINNSSTY insistency
CEIINOPRST isentropic
CEIINOPRSU pernicious
CEIINOPRTV voiceprint
CEIINOPSTT nepotistic
CEIINORSSS rescission
CEIINORSTT trisection
CEIINPRSSS crispiness
CEIINRSSTU sinecurist
CEIINRSTUY insecurity
CEIINRSTUZ scrutinize
CEIIOPRSTY preciosity
CEIIOPSSTY speciosity
CEIIORSTVV vivisector
CEIIRSSTTY sister city
CEIJNOOPRT projection
CEIKKORRST kicksorter
CEIKKORRWW wickerwork
CEIKLLORTT Little Rock
CEIKLNNOST clinkstone
CEIKLNPSSU pluckiness
CEIKLNSTUU unluckiest
CEIKLOPRST stockpiler
CEIKLOPSTT slit pocket
CEIKNOSSST stockiness
CEIKOTTTTU ticket tout
CEILMMNOPT compliment
CEILMNOOPT completion
CEILMNOOPX complexion
CEILMNSSSU clumsiness
CEILMOOOTV locomotive
CEILMOPSTT completist
CEILMOPSUV compulsive
CEILMOPTXY complexity
CEILMORTUV volumetric
CEILMOSTUU meticulous
CEILNNNOTY innocently
CEILNNOSVY insolvency
CEILNOOPRS necropolis
CEILNOORRS resorcinol
CEILNOORVW olive crown
CEILNOPRSU preclusion
CEILNORTTY contritely
CEILNOSSST costliness
CEILNOSUVV convulsive
CEILOPRSUY preciously
CEILOPSSUY speciously
CEILORSTTU courtliest
CEIMMMNOTT commitment
CEIMMNOORT metronomic

CEIMMNORTY metronymic
CEIMMNRSSU crumminess
CEIMMOOPRS compromise
CEIMMOORTV overcommit
CEIMMORRTY micrometry
CEIMMORSSU commissure
CEIMMORTUX commixture
CEIMNNOPRY prominency
CEIMNOOOSU monoecious
CEIMNOPRSU proscenium
CEIMNORSUU ceruminous
CEIMNRSSTY syncretism
CEIMOOPRRS microspore
CEIMOOPRTT competitor, optometric
CEIMOORSTU ecotourism
CEIMOORSTY sociometry
CEIMOPRRTY pyrometric
CEIMORSTVY viscometry
CEINNNOOTT contention
CEINNNOOTV convention
CEINNOORSV conversion
CEINNOPRTY encryption
CEINNOPTUX expunction
CEINNOSSTT consistent
CEINOOPRSS procession
CEINOOPRTT protection
CEINOOPRTV cover point
CEINOORSSU censorious
CEINOOSSUY synoecious
CEINOPRSSU percussion, supersonic
CEINOPRSTU supertonic
CEINOQTUYZ Quezon City
CEINORRSST intercross
CEINORSTTT cornettist
CEINOSSTUU incestuous
CEINOSTTTU constitute
CEINPRRRTU rip current
CEINRSSSTT strictness
CEINRSSSTU crustiness
CEINRSSTTY syncretist
CEIOOPRRTY corporeity
CEIOORSSTT scooterist
CEIOORSTTU ecotourist
CEIOPRRTUV corruptive
CEIOPRRTUZ prize court
CEIOPRRTWY copywriter
CEIPPRSTTY typescript
CEKLLLSSUY lucklessly
CEKLMOOORR locker room
CEKLMPRSUU lumpsucker
CEKLOOORSW slow cooker
CEKOORRSUW coursework
CELLNOORRT controller
CELLNOORSU counsellor
CELLOORSSU colourless
CELMMOPTUY lumpectomy
CELMNNOOSY somnolency
CELMNOOSSY Ceylon moss
CELMOORSTY sclerotomy
CELMOORTUY coulometry
CELOOORRSU rose colour
CELOOSSSSU colossuses
CELOOSTUVY covetously
CELOPPRTUU pop culture
CELPRSSSTU sculptress
CEMMNNOOSS commonness
CEMNOPRSTU sperm count
CEMOOPRRSS compressor
CENNNNOOTT non-content
CENNOOPRRU pronouncer
CENOOPRTTU countertop
CENOORRTTV controvert
CEOOPPRRST prospector
CEOOPRRSTU prosecutor
CEOORRSTVY cover story
CEOPPRSSTU prospectus
CEOPRRRSUY precursory
CEPPRRSTUU upper crust
CFFFIISSTU fisticuffs
CFFGILNOSY scoffingly
CFGIIKLNOR frolicking
CFGIINNORU Finno-Ugric
CFGIMNOORT comforting
CFHIMNORST storm-finch
CFHKOOOPRS shockproof
CFHLLOOORT floorcloth
CFHLMOOORR chloroform
CFIIILNNOT infliction
CFIIINOSTT fictionist
CFIIIOSTTU fictitious
CFIILORSST floristics
CFIINNNOOT non-fiction
CFIIOOPRRT torporific
CFIIRSTTUU futuristic
CFIMMNOORS conformism
CFIMNOORST conformist
CFIMNOORTY conformity
CFINNOORTU Inn of Court
CFLLLOORUU full colour
CFLLNORSUY scornfully
CFLLOOSSUU flosculous
CFLOOOSSTT coltsfoots
CFLOORSSUU scrofulous
CFOOORTTUU out-of-court
CGGGILNNOU unclogging
CGGIILLNNY clingingly
CGGILLNOOU colloguing
CGHHHILOOS high school
CGHHILOORU high colour
CGHHILORTT torchlight
CGHHILOTTU light touch
CGHIIKNPSY physicking
CGHIIKNSTT nightstick
CGHIILLLNY chillingly
CGHIILMORT microlight
CGHIILPRTY triglyphic
CGHIINPRRU chirruping
CGHIKLNOSY shockingly
CGHILLOORS schoolgirl
CGHILMOOTY mythologic
CGHILNOTUY touchingly
CGHILNRSUY crushingly
CGHILOORTY trichology
CGHILORRSU chorus girl
CGHLNOOORY chronology
CGHLOOPSYY psychology
CGIIIJNOST jingoistic
CGIIIKNNPT nit-picking
CGIIILNOST soliciting
CGIIILNSTU linguistic
CGIIILPSTU pugilistic
CGIIINQRTU critiquing
CGIILMNOOV moving-coil
CGIILNNPSY lip-syncing
CGIILNOPST top-slicing
CGIIMMNOTT committing
CGIIMNOSST Gnosticism
CGIINNNOTU continuing
CGIINOTTUY contiguity
CGIKNOSSTU King's Scout
CGILLOSSYY glycolysis
CGILMOOSTY mycologist
CGILMOOSUY musicology
CGILNNOSTU consulting
CGILNOOOST oncologist
CGILOOOTXY toxicology
CGILOOSTTY cytologist
CGINNORSTU construing
CGINOOPRST prognostic
CGINOOSTUU contiguous
CGINORRSTY try-scoring
CGLOOOPRTY proctology
CGLOOPRTYY cryptology
CHHIINOPPS phosphinic
CHHIIOSSTY ichthyosis
CHHIIPSTTW whip stitch
CHHILLRSUY churlishly
CHHILOOPSS school-ship
CHHILOOPTY holophytic
CHHIMNOOOP homophonic
CHHIOOPPRS phosphoric
CHIIIILNST nihilistic
CHIIILPSTY syphilitic
CHIIINORST histrionic
CHIIKLLSTY ticklishly
CHIIKMNRSU Michurinsk
CHIILMNOOT monolithic
CHIILOSTTY histolytic
CHIILPSSTT slip stitch
CHIIMOOPRS isomorphic
CHIIMOPRRT trimorphic
CHIIMORRST trichroism
CHIIMORSTU humoristic
CHIINNOPSU pincushion
CHIINOPSSU cousinship
CHIINORSTU trichinous, unhistoric
CHIKNOQRTU quickthorn
CHILLNOSWY clownishly
CHILLOOPTT pilot-cloth
CHILNOOPPY polyphonic
CHILNOOPXY xylophonic
CHILNOPSSU consulship
CHILOOPTTY photolytic
CHIMNNOOOP monophonic
CHIMOOOPRS sophomoric
CHIMOOOPRZ zoomorphic
CHIMOORTTY trichotomy
CHIMOSSSTT moss stitch
CHIOOPPRRY pyrophoric
CHIOOPRSTT orthoptics

CHIOOPTTXY phytotoxic
CHIORSTTTW stitchwort
CHKNOOPRTY rock python
CHLMNOSUUU homunculus
CHLMOOOORS schoolroom
CHLMOOPRYY polychromy
CHLNOOTTUU out to lunch
CHMNOOPTTU mutton chop
CHMOOPRTYY mycotrophy
CHORRSSTTU shortcrust
CIIILNTVY incivility
CIIILLMPTY implicitly
CIIILMNRTU triclinium
CIIILMPSST simplistic
CIIILMPSTY simplicity
CIIILPRTTY triplicity
CIIIMNNOST nicotinism
CIIIMOPSTT optimistic
CIIINNNOTT intinction
CIIINNOSTU unionistic
CIIJMMORSW Jim Crowism
CIIJNNNOTU injunction
CIILOOSSTU solicitous
CIILOPPSTU populistic
CIILOPRTVY proclivity
CIILRRSTUY scurrility
CIILSSSTTY stylistics
CIIMMNOOSS commission
CIINNOORTT contrition
CIINNOTTUY continuity
CIIOORSTUV victorious
CIIOPSSSUU suspicious
CIJKNOOSTT joint stock
CIJLNNOOTY conjointly
CIKLLOSSTT stock-still
CIKLNOOSTT silk cotton
CILLMNOOST Tom Collins
CILLMOOQUU colloquium
CILLOPRSTU portcullis
CILLOSSUUY lusciously
CILMNOOOOT locomotion
CILMNOOPSU compulsion
CILMOOOPSS cosmopolis
CILMOOSSTU music stool
CILNNOOSUV convulsion
CILORRSSUU scurrilous
CIMNNOOOPP nincompoop
CIMNOORSTU consortium
CIMOOOPRST compositor
CINNOOORTT contortion
CINNOOSTUU continuous
CINOOPRRTU corruption
CINOORSSTY consistory
CINORRSTTU instructor
CIOOPPRTTY prototypic
CIOOPRSTTU prosciutto
CIOPPRSSTT postscript
CIOPPSTTYY copy-typist
CIPPRRSTUU stirrup cup
CJMMNOORUY common jury
CKLLOORRSW scrollwork
CKMNOORSTU moonstruck
CLLMOOSSUU molluscous
CLMMNNOOUY uncommonly
CLMOOPRSUY compulsory
CLNOOOOTTW cotton wool
CLNOOOPTTY polycotton
CLNOSTUUUY unctuously
CLOOOPRRTU prolocutor
CLOOSTTTUY cutty-stool
CLOPRSSUUU scrupulous
CMMMNOOOOR common room
CMMNNNOOOU common noun
CNNOOTTUWY county town
DDDDDFUUYY fuddy-duddy
DDDEEEFNNU undefended
DDDEEFIOST eisteddfod
DDDEEIINVX ex dividend
DDDEEIORRS disordered
DDDEGIIOOR didgeridoo
DDDEIIJOOR didjeridoo
DDEEEEMNRU unredeemed
DDEEEENRTY tender-eyed
DDEEEHILSV disheveled
DDEEEIMNPT pedimented
DDEEEIMNRT determined
DDEEEINORZ Zener diode
DDEEELLMOR remodelled
DDEEELMMOS meddlesome
DDEEELMNTY dementedly
DDEEELRSVY deservedly
DDEEENRRTU undeterred
DDEEENRSUV undeserved
DDEEENRSUX undersexed
DDEEEOOPRT deep-rooted
DDEEFFLNOY offendedly
DDEEFFNNOU unoffended
DDEEFIILLN ill-defined
DDEEFIILMR midfielder
DDEEFINNRU unfriended
DDEEGGHOOP hodgepodge
DDEEGGIRUZ ruggedized
DDEEGGNOSS doggedness
DDEEGHNORY hodden grey
DDEEGIINST indigested
DDEEGILNSY designedly
DDEEGINNSU undesigned
DDEEGINSTU undigested
DDEEGJLLUW well-judged
DDEEHILNSU unshielded
DDEEHINNRU unhindered
DDEEHINNSS hiddenness
DDEEHLORSU shouldered
DDEEIIKLMN like-minded
DDEEIIMOPR epidermoid
DDEEIINRSW sidewinder
DDEEIKMORS smoke-dried
DDEEILMMRT middle term
DDEEILMSTW Middle West
DDEEILNNTY intendedly
DDEEILNOSY one-sidedly
DDEEILNOTT dotted line
DDEEIMNNOP open-minded
DDEEINNNTU unintended
DDEEINRRUW underwired
DDEEINRSUZ undersized
DDEEIOORRZ deodorizer
DDEEIRSSST distressed
DDEELLOORW olde worlde
DDEELNOPUX unexploded
DDEELRRSSU rudderless
DDEENNOPST despondent
DDEENNOSSS soddenness
DDEENNPRSU underspend
DDEENNSSSU suddenness
DDEENOPPST end-stopped
DDEENRRSSU underdress
DDEFHIIMUY dehumidify
DDEFHLNORU fundholder
DDEFIIMNOU unmodified
DDEFILLNOU ill-founded
DDEGGGILOR gold-digger
DDEGHHIIMN high-minded
DDEGIILNRY deridingly
DDEGILNNOW long-winded
DDEGLLLOOR rolled gold
DDEGLNOORY dendrology
DDEGNNORUU ungrounded
DDEGOOPSTT spotted dog
DDEHIIIMNS diminished
DDEHIIKNSY kidney dish
DDEHIILNOP delphinoid
DDEHIILNSW windshield
DDEHIILPSU disulphide
DDEHINOSSS shoddiness
DDEHIOOOPT photodiode
DDEIIIMNNU diminuendi
DDEIIIMPSY epididymis
DDEIIMNNOU diminuendo
DDEIINOPSS indisposed
DDEIINOSTU duodenitis
DDEIINOUVZ zidovudine
DDEIKNNRUW wunderkind
DDEILLNPSY splendidly
DDEILLOORS old soldier
DDEILLOPSY lopsidedly
DDEILORRSY disorderly
DDEIMNOORT dimetrodon
DDEINOPRUV unprovided
DDEINOPSUW upside down
DDEINORSSS sordidness
DDEINPSTUU undisputed
DDELMOOTUY outmodedly
DDELNORRUW underworld
DDELOORRRW world order
DDENOORSTU understood
DDENRSTUUY understudy
DDGGOOOOYY goody-goody
DDGHILNTUY thuddingly
DDGHRRUUYY hurdy-gurdy
DDGIILLMNY middlingly
DDGIILLNRY riddlingly
DDGILLMNUY muddlingly
DDGILLNOPY ploddingly
DDGINOORSW dowsing rod
DDHIIIMSSY Yiddishism

DDHILORRTW Third World
DDHOOOOUWY how-do-you-do
DDIIKLNTWY tiddlywink
DDIILMNORU drumlinoid
DDINOPPRTY Pontypridd
DDOOOOORRT door-to-door
DEEEEEFPRZ deep-freeze
DEEEEELNSY needle's eye
DEEEEFFLRS self-feeder
DEEEEFLRSS self-seeder
DEEEEGLRSS degreeless
DEEEEGSSTW sweet sedge
DEEEEHLLLW well-heeled
DEEEEILMNT needle time
DEEEELSSSV seed vessel
DEEEEMNNPU Peenemunde
DEEEFGILNR greenfield
DEEEFHILNS needlefish
DEEEFHLORR freeholder
DEEEFILMNT defilement
DEEEFLLNOV elevenfold
DEEEFMNRRU referendum
DEEEFNRTTU unfettered
DEEEFORRST deer forest
DEEEGGGLOY goggle-eyed
DEEEGHHHIL high-heeled
DEEEGILLNR ledger line
DEEEGINRSS greediness
DEEEGIRSSV degressive
DEEEHIMNRT methedrine
DEEEHINORT deinothere
DEEEHLNORS lederhosen
DEEEHNORTY heterodyne
DEEEHNRRTU thereunder
DEEEHNRTTU untethered
DEEEIIMNPR meperidine
DEEEIKLLRW weedkiller
DEEEILLMOS demoiselle
DEEEILLRVY relievedly
DEEEILNNST sentineled
DEEEILNRSZ slenderize
DEEEILNRUV unrelieved
DEEEILNSVW wind-sleeve
DEEEILRSVW silverweed
DEEEIMNOTZ demonetize
DEEEIMNRRT determiner
DEEEIMORTU eudiometer
DEEEIMPRTV redemptive
DEEEIMRSTV time-served
DEEEINNPTV pendentive
DEEEINPRST predestine
DEEEINPSSS speediness
DEEEINQSUZ queen-sized
DEEEINRRTZ tenderizer
DEEEINRSSV versed sine
DEEEINSSTW tweediness
DEEEIPRSSV depressive
DEEEIRSSTT side street
DEEEKLNORW needlework
DEEEKOOPRR doorkeeper
DEEELLNORW ne'er-do-well
DEEELLNSSY needlessly
DEEELNRSST slenderest
DEEELNRTTU unlettered
DEEELRRSVY reservedly
DEEEMNNOTU denouement
DEEEMNOTTV devotement
DEEEMNPRTU untempered
DEEEMNRSSU demureness
DEEENNRSST tenderness
DEEENORTVX overextend
DEEENRRSTU understeer
DEEENRRSUV unreserved, unreversed
DEEFFLOOTT left-footed
DEEFGGILLN fledgeling
DEEFGINSST giftedness
DEEFGLNOOR golden orfe
DEEFHILNRS shield fern
DEEFIIINNT indefinite
DEEFIIINRT identifier
DEEFIIINTV definitive
DEEFIILNRR friendlier
DEEFIILNTY definitely
DEEFIIMSTT semi-fitted
DEEFIINRUV unverified
DEEFIINRVW viewfinder
DEEFILLLSW self-willed
DEEFILLRSU fleur-de-lis
DEEFILLTTW well fitted
DEEFILMOSU field mouse
DEEFILNOST field notes, fieldstone
DEEFILNRSS friendless
DEEFILNRTU unfiltered
DEEFILNRYZ frenziedly
DEEFILORTU outfielder
DEEFILPSTU despiteful
DEEFINRSUV under-fives
DEEFLLMORW well-formed
DEEFLLOTVW twelvefold
DEEFLLRSUY fleur-de-lys
DEEFLLSSTY self-styled
DEEFLMRRSU self-murder
DEEFLNORRU flounderer
DEEFLRSTUU sulfureted
DEEFMNORRU unreformed
DEEFMNPRUU unperfumed
DEEFNOORTT tenderfoot
DEEFOORSTU sure-footed
DEEGGGILOV goggle-dive
DEEGGGLLNO long-legged
DEEGGHLLOO dog-leg hole
DEEGGIIPRW periwigged
DEEGGNRSSU ruggedness
DEEGHINOUY honeyguide
DEEGHINRRR red herring
DEEGIIINNZ indigenize
DEEGIILPRV privileged
DEEGIINNRT ingredient
DEEGIIRSSV digressive
DEEGILMNOR remodeling
DEEGILNNOW Gwendoline
DEEGILNOPV developing
DEEGILNRSY resignedly
DEEGILNRTT ringletted
DEEGILOPSS Gospel side
DEEGINOOPT pigeon-toed
DEEGINOTTU tongue-tied
DEEGINPRSS depressing
DEEGLLNORU golden rule
DEEGLMSSSU smudgeless
DEEGLNNOSS goldenness
DEEGNNOOSU endogenous
DEEGNNOPRU green pound
DEEHHIILMS Hildesheim
DEEHIILOPV videophile
DEEHILLRSV shrivelled
DEEHILLSSS shieldless
DEEHILMORS demolisher
DEEHILOOTT theodolite
DEEHIMORTZ methodizer
DEEHINOOPV videophone
DEEHINORVV vinho verde
DEEHINRTUW unwithered
DEEHIORSTV Shrovetide
DEEHLLOOWY hollow-eyed
DEEHLMNRUW underwhelm
DEEHLMOORT mother lode
DEEHMNORTY endothermy
DEEHMORRTY hydrometer
DEEHNOSUWY Wendy house
DEEHNRSSSW shrewdness
DEEHOORSUW dower house
DEEHOORTXY heterodoxy
DEEIIINPPR piperidine
DEEIILLMPR imperilled
DEEIILLNOS linseed oil
DEEIILMPST speed limit
DEEIILNRUW unwieldier
DEEIILNSTT disentitle
DEEIILPRRV piledriver
DEEIILRSSV silverside
DEEIILRSVY derisively
DEEIIMMNPT impediment
DEEIIMNNRT dinner time
DEEIIMPRST spider mite
DEEIINNRTT Tridentine
DEEIINNSSV divineness
DEEIINOPTX expedition
DEEIINPTTU ineptitude
DEEIINQTUU inquietude
DEEIINRTTW winter-tide
DEEIINSSTW West Indies
DEEIIPRSSV dispersive
DEEIKORSST sidestroke
DEEILLMNOU linoleumed
DEEILLSUVY delusively
DEEILNNNRU underlinen
DEEILNNORT tenderloin
DEEILNNQTU delinquent
DEEILNRSSW wilderness
DEEILORSSV redissolve
DEEILQRRSU squirreled
DEEILRRSSV driverless
DEEIMMNOSU eudemonism
DEEIMNNRRU underminer
DEEIMNNRUV menu-driven
DEEIMNOOTV Montevideo

DEEIMNOPRT redemption
DEEIMNORRZ modernizer
DEEIMNOSTU eudemonist
DEEIMNRRTU Ermintrude
DEEIMNRSTW Midwestern, stem-winder
DEEIMNSTTV divestment
DEEIMOPRSW disempower
DEEIMORTUY eudiometry
DEEINNOPRS prednisone
DEEINNRSST trendiness
DEEINOPRSS depression
DEEINORSTT rose-tinted
DEEINPPQUU unequipped
DEEINPRRST rinderpest
DEEINQRTUU unrequited
DEEINQSTUY squint-eyed
DEEINRRTUW underwrite
DEEINRSSSS dressiness
DEEINRSSTU unresisted
DEEINSSTTU testudines
DEEIOPPRRT propertied
DEEIOPPRSS predispose
DEEIORTTTX text editor
DEEKLLNORS snorkelled
DEEKLMRTTU kettledrum
DEELLNORTY redolently
DEELLNRTUW well-turned
DEELLORSVY resolvedly
DEELMMNOPU nom de plume
DEELMNOPTY deployment
DEELMNOPUY unemployed
DEELMNOSTU unmolested
DEELMOPRSU supermodel
DEELMPRSUY presumedly
DEELNOPRUX unexplored
DEELNORSUV unresolved
DEELOOORRS loose order
DEELOOVVYY lovey-dovey
DEELOPRRTY reportedly
DEELOPRSTW spot-welder
DEELORTTUV turtle-dove
DEEMNNORSS modernness
DEEMNNORTW wonderment
DEEMNOORRY money order
DEEMNOPRTT deportment
DEEMNORSTU tremendous
DEEMNRRTUY Ermyntrude
DEENNOOSSW woodenness
DEENNOPRST respondent
DEENNORSVW news-vendor
DEENNRRTUU unreturned
DEENOOPPPT open-topped
DEENOOPRTT torpedo-net
DEENOORSST rootedness
DEENOPRRTU unreported
DEENOPRRUV unreproved
DEENOPRSTT tender spot
DEENOQRTUU underquote
DEENORRSTU unrestored
DEENORSUVZ rendezvous
DEENOSSTUV devoutness
DEENRSSSTU unstressed
DEEOORRSTT street door
DEEOPRRRSU superorder
DEEPPRRSUU super-duper
DEFFGINORS sniffer dog
DEFFHIMORS sheriffdom
DEFFINOSUV snuff video
DEFFOPPRUW powder puff
DEFGGHIORT dogfighter
DEFGHIILRT right field
DEFGHILLTU delightful
DEFGHILOTY eightyfold
DEFGHOOOSU house of God
DEFGIILNRR girlfriend
DEFGIILNYY edifyingly
DEFGIINNUY unedifying
DEFGIINORZ frigid zone
DEFGIINRSS frigidness
DEFGNOORRU foreground
DEFHIIIMRU humidifier
DEFHIILNSY fiendishly
DEFHIINNSU unfinished
DEFHIINPRS friendship
DEFHIOOPPR hipped roof
DEFHLNOSUW flesh wound
DEFHLNRTUY thunderfly
DEFIIILNTY infidelity
DEFIIILORS solidifier
DEFIIINNOT definition
DEFIIINNTU infinitude
DEFIILLNRY friendlily
DEFIINOPTX fixed point
DEFIINPRUU unpurified
DEFIIOPRSU perfidious
DEFILLPRUY pridefully
DEFILMNORY informedly
DEFILNNOTY ninetyfold
DEFILNNRUY unfriendly
DEFILNORSS floridness
DEFILNORWW windflower
DEFILOPRSW wolf spider
DEFILPRSUU superfluid
DEFIMNNORU uninformed
DEFINRRSUW windsurfer
DEFLMNNOTU unfoldment
DEFLNOORRU underfloor
DEFLNOORTU unforetold
DEFLNOORVY overfondly
DEFLNOTTWY twentyfold
DEFNOOPRRU profounder, underproof
DEFOORTTTX foxtrotted
DEGGHIIPRS ship-rigged
DEGGIIKNSU King's Guide
DEGGIJRRUY jury-rigged
DEGGILLNOR golden girl
DEGGINNOPU gudgeon pin
DEGGINNOSS sing-songed
DEGHIILTTW twilighted
DEGHIIMOPP pemphigoid
DEGHIKNOST hot-desking
DEGHILLNOS Old English
DEGHINNRTU thundering
DEGHINOSSU doughiness
DEGHINRSST nightdress
DEGHIOOSTW white goods
DEGHIORRRU rough-rider
DEGHIOSTTU doughtiest
DEGHLNNOOR Golden Horn
DEGHLNOPUU unploughed
DEGHPRRSUU drug pusher
DEGIIILMNT delimiting
DEGIILLMRX mixed grill
DEGIILLNNW indwelling
DEGIILLNPS dispelling
DEGIILLNRV drivelling
DEGIILLNTY diligently
DEGIILLNYY yieldingly
DEGIILNNUY unyielding
DEGIILOOST ideologist
DEGIINNOSU indigenous
DEGIINNSST dissenting
DEGIINOPST depositing
DEGIINORSS digression
DEGIINPRST springtide
DEGIIQSSTU squidgiest
DEGILLOOTY deltiology
DEGILMNRSU mud-slinger
DEGILNNNUY unendingly
DEGILNNRUY enduringly, underlying
DEGILNOOSS goodliness
DEGILOOPST pedologist
DEGIMNSSSU smudginess
DEGINNORST grindstone, stringendo
DEGINNORSU resounding
DEGINOOOPW wood pigeon
DEGINOSSST stodginess
DEGINRSSTU turgidness
DEGKLOOOOR good-looker
DEGLMNOOOY demonology
DEGLNNRSUU underslung
DEGLNOOOTY deontology
DEGLNORRUU ground rule
DEGLNORSSU groundless
DEGLOORTTY troglodyte
DEGNNORRTU ground rent
DEGNOORRUV overground
DEGNOORRUZ ground zero
DEGOOORSUW woodgrouse
DEGOORTTWY Godwottery
DEHHILOPRY hydrophile
DEHHILORTW withholder
DEHHIMOORR hemorrhoid
DEHHMOOORT motherhood
DEHHNOOPRY hydrophone
DEHHOPRTYY hydrophyte
DEHIIINRST disinherit
DEHIIKLLOO likelihood
DEHIILLOOV livelihood
DEHIILLSVY devilishly
DEHIILMNPU delphinium
DEHIIMMPSU mediumship
DEHIIOPRST editorship
DEHIIRSTVW whist drive
DEHIKNRSZZ Dzerzhinsk
DEHILLNORW downhiller

DEHILNOPSU unpolished
DEHILNORTU unitholder
DEHILOOPSS shop-soiled
DEHILORSTV short-lived
DEHIMMNORR horn-rimmed
DEHIMNOSSS modishness
DEHIMOOPPR hippodrome
DEHINNPSUU unpunished
DEHINORRSS horridness
DEHINORRST trihedrons
DEHINORSTT threnodist
DEHINOSSTY dishonesty
DEHINRRSTU undershirt
DEHIOOPRST priesthood
DEHIOOQRSU squirehood
DEHIOORSST sisterhood
DEHIOPPRSW worshipped
DEHIOPRRTY pyrethroid
DEHIPPSTUY deputyship
DEHIRRSSST dress shirt, shirt-dress
DEHLLMNOSU shell-mound
DEHLLOOSSU doll's house
DEHLNOOPRY polyhedron
DEHLOORRSY holy orders
DEHLOORRTW other world
DEHLORSSSU shroudless
DEHMNOOPRY endomorphy
DEHMORRTYY hydrometry
DEHNNOORUU unhonoured
DEHNOOOPRS personhood
DEHNOORRSU horrendous
DEHNOORSTU undershoot
DEHNOORSUU roundhouse
DEHNOORTTU otter-hound
DEHNORSTUU thunderous
DEHOOPRSUU house-proud
DEHOORRRST short order
DEIIILMQSU semi-liquid
DEIIILMSTU similitude
DEIIILQRUZ liquidizer
DEIIILSVVY divisively
DEIIIMNPRY pyrimidine
DEIIIMNTUV diminutive
DEIIIMSSSV dismissive
DEIIINNSTT tendinitis
DEIIINORSV redivision
DEIIINPRST inspirited
DEIIKLNNSS kindliness
DEIIKLNNTU unit-linked
DEIIILLNUWY unwieldily
DEIILLRSTY distillery
DEIILMNOOT demolition
DEIILMNPSS limpidness
DEIILNNRTY dirty linen
DEIILNOPTY yield point
DEIILNORST tin soldier
DEIILNPRSY inspiredly
DEIILNPRTY intrepidly
DEIILNPSST spindliest
DEIILNQSSU liquidness
DEIILPRSTY spiritedly
DEIIMMSSTY midi system
DEIIMOSTWW widow's mite
DEIIMSSTUW swimsuited
DEIINNOSSS dissension
DEIINNOSST distension
DEIINNOSTT tendonitis
DEIINNPRSU uninspired
DEIINNSSTU untidiness
DEIINOOPST deposition
DEIINOPRSS dispersion
DEIINOPRXY pyridoxine
DEIINPPRSS drippiness
DEIINPPRST pinstriped
DEIIOOPSTV oviposited
DEIIPRSTUV disruptive
DEIJNNNOOR nonjoinder
DEIKLMOPRW milk powder
DEIKLNNRUW unwrinkled
DEIKLNSTUY Kyustendil
DEIKMPPRSU mudskipper
DEIKNNNORR non-drinker
DEIKNNNSSU unkindness
DEIKNRRSTU underskirt
DEILLMMOSU slime mould
DEILLMNSSY mindlessly
DEILLNNOTY indolently
DEILLNORSS lordliness
DEILLNORST nostrilled
DEILLOPRSY prose idyll
DEILLORSTW worldliest
DEILMMOSTY immodestly
DEILMNOSSU mouldiness
DEILMNPTUY impudently
DEILNNNTUW wind tunnel
DEILNNOUVV uninvolved
DEILNOOTUV devolution
DEILNOSSST stolidness
DEILNOSSTV dissolvent
DEILNOSSWW windowless
DEILNRSTTY stridently
DEILOORSTY toy soldier
DEILPPSSUY supply-side
DEIMMNNTUU indumentum
DEIMNOPRUV unimproved
DEIMNORTYY dirty money
DEIMOPPRST prompt side
DEINOOPRSS droopiness
DEINOOPRST desorption
DEINOORRTZ torrid zone
DEINOORSWW rose window
DEINOOSSSU odiousness
DEINOPRSST torpidness
DEINORSSSW drowsiness
DEINORSSUU undesirous
DEINPRSSTU putridness
DEINRSSSTU sturdiness
DEIOOPRSTY depository
DEIOPRRSTW spiderwort
DEIOPSSSSS dispossess
DEIRRSSTTU distruster
DEKKLOPRRS Klerksdorp
DEKKNOORWY donkey work
DEKNOOPRUV unprovoked
DEKNOORSTW downstroke
DEKOOORRWW woodworker
DELLNOPTUU unpolluted
DELLOORRWW lower world
DELLORSSWY wordlessly
DELLOSSUUY sedulously
DELNNOPSSU nonplussed
DELNNOTUWY unwontedly
DELOOORRSW wood sorrel
DELOOPRRWW world power
DELOORRTUW outer world
DELOPPSSUY supposedly
DEMMNNOSUU unsummoned
DEMNOOPRST postmodern
DEMNOPPRTU unprompted
DEMOOOPRRW powder room
DENOOPPRRU propounder
DENOOPRSWW powder snow
DENOORRTUW woodturner
DENOPRRTTU protrudent
DENOPSSTUU stupendous
DENORRSTUY understory
DFGHIINORS fishing rod
DFGHILLOOT floodlight
DFGIINRRSU surf-riding
DFGILSSTUU disgustful
DFHILORTTY thirtyfold
DFHINOSSTU sound shift
DFINOPRTUY profundity
DFLNOOPRUY profoundly
DFNOOOPRSU soundproof
DFNOOOPSTU foot-pounds
DFOOOORSTU out of doors
DGGGHINOOT hotdogging
DGGGILNRUY grudgingly
DGGGINNRUU ungrudging
DGGHHINORU high ground
DGGIILNNRY grindingly
DGGIINSSTU disgusting
DGGILNNORU groundling
DGGINNOORW wrongdoing
DGHHIKNOOT knighthood
DGHHNOORUU rough hound
DGHIILLNNO Hillingdon
DGHIINOORV virginhood
DGHINNNOTU Huntingdon
DGHLNOORST stronghold
DGHMOOORUU good humour
DGHNOORSUW showground
DGIIIKNNSV skin diving
DGIIILLNST distilling
DGIIINSTUV diving suit
DGIILNOOST Indologist
DGIIMNNOOR dining room
DGIIOOPRSU prodigious
DGILNNOUWY woundingly
DGILOOPRTT proglottid
DGKLNOOOSV Volgodonsk
DGKNOORRUW groundwork
DGLNOOOOTY odontology

DGLNOOPTTY glyptodont
DGOPRSTUUY study group
DHIIMMOPRS dimorphism
DHIKNORRST short drink
DHILORSSYY hydrolysis
DHIMOOPRSU dimorphous
DHINOOOPRT ornithopod
DHINOOPSWW shop window, window-shop
DHINOOSWWW show-window
DHLOOORTXY orthodoxly
DHNOOORTUX unorthodox
DIIIINPSTY insipidity
DIIILOOPSS lipoidosis
DIIILSTTUY disutility
DIIIMNNOTU diminution
DIILLNOSWW window sill
DIIMMOPRRU primordium
DIINOORSTT distortion
DIINOPRSTU disruption
DIIOOPRSTW wood spirit
DIKKLOOSSV Kislovodsk
DILLLOSSTY Lloyd's List
DILLOOPPYY polyploidy
DILOSSTUUY studiously
DIMOPRSSUY dysprosium
DIOOPQQRUU quid pro quo
DLLOOORSUY dolorously
DLNOORSUWY wondrously
DLOOOPSTUY tylopodous
DNOOOOPRST droop-snoot
EEEEEGPSSX epexegeses
EEEEFFNSST effeteness
EEEEFKLRSS self-seeker
EEEEFLMSST self-esteem
EEEEGIPSSX epexegesis
EEEEGMNRRT re-emergent
EEEEHNPSST epentheses
EEEEHORRSW wheresoe'er
EEEEHPSSSY sheep's eyes
EEEEHRRVWY everywhere
EEEEIIPSTW sweetie-pie
EEEEIKMPRT timekeeper
EEEEILRTVW televiewer
EEEEKMRRSY kerseymere
EEEELLSSSV sleeveless
EEEELNOSTV sleeve note
EEEELORSVV oversleeve
EEEEMORRTZ Zoetermeer
EEEENNRRVV never-never
EEEENNRSSS sereneness
EEEENNTWYY teeny-weeny
EEEERRRTTV terre-verte
EEEETTTTWW tweet tweet
EEEFFILORT tree of life
EEEFGIINNR fire engine
EEEFGLNRUV revengeful
EEEFHOORRT heretofore
EEEFHORSST foresheets
EEEFILRRSV file server
EEEFIMNNRT refinement
EEEFINORRV over-refine
EEEFINRRRT interferer
EEEFINRSVW swine fever
EEEFINSSSV five senses
EEEFKNOPRS free-spoken
EEEFLLORRT foreteller
EEEFLRRSTY freestyler
EEEFMNPRRT preferment
EEEFNNORSU unforeseen
EEEFNQRRTU frequenter
EEEFORRSTT forest tree
EEEGGNOORS green goose
EEEGHHINTT eighteenth
EEEGHIMNOT eighteenmo
EEEGHKLNNT knee-length
EEEGHLNNRT lengthener
EEEGHNORSU greenhouse
EEEGIINNUW Nieuwegein
EEEGIINPSS epigenesis
EEEGILLNRV Greenville
EEEGILMNST genteelism
EEEGILNNSS engineless
EEEGILNORV olive green
EEEGILNRST singletree
EEEGINNOPY eye-opening
EEEGINNORS rose-engine
EEEGINNSTW sweetening
EEEGINOPRY epeirogeny
EEEGIRRSSV regressive
EEEGLNNSST gentleness
EEEGNNORST greenstone
EEEGNOPRST sponge tree
EEEHHIMPRS hemisphere
EEEHHLOSUW wheelhouse
EEEHHORRTW otherwhere
EEEHILMORT heliometer
EEEHILMRTW mitre wheel
EEEHILNPRS prehensile
EEEHILPSSS lesseeship
EEEHIMPRST ephemerist
EEEHINNNTT nineteenth
EEEHINPSST epenthesis
EEEHINSSWZ wheeziness
EEEHINSTTV seventieth
EEEHIOTWXY white ox-eye
EEEHKLLOTT kettle hole
EEEHKOPPRS shopkeeper
EEEHLMNPTT hemp-nettle
EEEHLMNTVY vehemently
EEEHLMSSTV themselves
EEEHLNOPRT telephoner
EEEHLNOPTY polyethene
EEEHLORTWW two-wheeler
EEEHMMNNST enmeshment
EEEHMNOPRS ephemerons
EEEHMOPRSS mesosphere
EEEHNNPRTY threepenny
EEEHNORSSS horse sense
EEEHNORSVW whensoever
EEEHNOSTWY honey-sweet
EEEHOPPRRT tree hopper
EEEIIPRTTV repetitive
EEEIKLLNSV sleeve link
EEEIKLMSWY semi-weekly
EEEILMNRSU unseemlier
EEEILMNRTV revilement
EEEILMNSSS seemliness
EEEILNPRRT terreplein
EEEILNPSSS sleepiness
EEEILNQSTU queenliest
EEEILNRRST re-enlister
EEEILNSSST steeliness
EEEIMMRRSZ mesmerizer
EEEIMNNPRT pre-eminent
EEEIMNORTZ remonetize
EEEIMNPRTX experiment
EEEIMNRRTT retirement
EEEIMNRSTT tensimeter
EEEIMOPRTZ piezometer
EEEIMPPRTV pre-emptive
EEEIMRRSTV time-server
EEEINNPRSS persiennes
EEEINNPRST serpentine
EEEINNPRTV prevenient
EEEINNRRTV intervener
EEEINPRRST enterprise
EEEINPRSSU purse seine
EEEINPRSTV vespertine
EEEINPRTVV preventive
EEEINRRRTV irreverent
EEEINRSTWZ westernize
EEEINSSTWY eyewitness
EEEIOPRRRT repertoire
EEEIPRRSSV repressive
EEEIPRRSVV perversive
EEEIPRSSVX expressive
EEEIRSSTTW streetwise
EEEJJNNSSU jejuneness
EEEKLNRSUV Leverkusen
EEEKLORRTW teleworker
EEELLNPSUV eleven-plus
EEELLNRSST relentless
EEELLORTTV love letter
EEELLRSSTT letterless
EEELMMOSTT mettlesome
EEELMNOTVV evolvement
EEELMNSTTT settlement
EEELNOPRTT open letter
EEELNOTTVW twelve-note, twelve-tone
EEELNPPRSY prepensely
EEELNRRTVY reverently
EEELNRSTTW newsletter
EEELPRRSVY perversely
EEELRSSSVW swerveless
EEEMNNRSTT resentment
EEEMNORSST remoteness
EEEMNORSTT sermonette
EEENNNSSUV unevenness
EEENORSTWZ sneezewort
EEENPRSSTX expertness
EEENRRSSTX sterner sex
EEEOOPRSVX overexpose
EEEOPRRRTX re-exporter
EEEOPRSTTY stereotype
EEEPRSTTTY typesetter
EEFFGINORR forefinger
EEFFGNRSTU greenstuff
EEFFHHILTW fifth wheel
EEFFIILNOR line of fire

EEFFILSUVY effusively
EEFFIORRTU forfeiture
EEFFLORSST effortless
EEFFNORRTY effrontery
EEFGHHIILR high relief
EEFGHHIITV five-eighth
EEFGHINRRS refreshing
EEFGHINRRT frightener
EEFGHLOOSS goose-flesh
EEFGIILLLN ill feeling
EEFGIILLNS single file
EEFGIILNRV free-living
EEFGIINRRT gentrifier
EEFGILLNRU refuelling
EEFGILLNTY fleetingly
EEFGILNRSS fingerless, fringeless
EEFGILNRTW left-winger
EEFGILRSSU figureless
EEFGINNRRT refringent
EEFGINPRRR preferring
EEFGKLLNOT gentlefolk
EEFGLLNUVY vengefully
EEFGLMNNTU engulfment
EEFHHLORSS horseflesh
EEFHIKLSTT fish kettle
EEFHILLSST fleshliest
EEFHILNSSS fleshiness
EEFHILRSVY feverishly
EEFHMOORRT foremother
EEFHNORTTU fourteenth
EEFHOOPRST proof-sheet
EEFIILMNNY femininely
EEFIILMRSU emulsifier
EEFIILNSSW wifeliness
EEFIILRRTZ fertilizer
EEFIIMNNNU unfeminine
EEFIINNNRS Sinn Feiner
EEFIINNOTV nine-to-five
EEFIINNSST finiteness
EEFIINSSST feistiness
EEFIIPRRST free spirit
EEFIIPRRTT prettifier
EEFIKLLNNU funnel-like
EEFIKLLORW flower-like
EEFIKLLRUV liver fluke
EEFILLLSSY lifelessly
EEFILLNOTU feuilleton
EEFILMRSTT filmsetter
EEFILNNORT Florentine
EEFILNPPTT felt-tip pen
EEFILNRRSV silver fern
EEFILOORSU oleiferous
EEFIMNOSTT oftentimes
EEFINNORRT interferon
EEFINNQRTU infrequent
EEFINOSSTV fivestones
EEFIORRRTX fox terrier
EEFIORSSTU setiferous
EEFLLLSSSY selflessly
EEFLLNTUVY eventfully
EEFLLORRWY lyre-flower
EEFLLORSSW flowerless
EEFLMORRSU remorseful
EEFLMORRTT form letter
EEFLNNTUUV uneventful
EEFLNOSSUW woefulness
EEFLNQRTUY frequently
EEFLNRSSUU ruefulness
EEFLNSSSUU usefulness
EEFLRSSTUU futureless
EEFMOORTZZ mezzo forte
EEFNNORRRU forerunner
EEFNOORSTY festoonery
EEFNOOTTWW own two feet
EEGGHILNRT green light
EEGGIINNRW ginger wine
EEGGINRRTT regretting
EEGGISSTUV suggestive
EEGGNOORTW Georgetown
EEGHHINOTT eighth note
EEGHHIRSTT high street
EEGHHORSTU see-through
EEGHIISTTW weightiest
EEGHIKLRSU kieselguhr
EEGHILLMNS English elm
EEGHILMRTT light meter
EEGHILNOOP pigeon-hole
EEGHILNSTT lengthiest
EEGHILNSTW lengthwise
EEGHILNSTY seethingly
EEGHILNWYZ wheezingly
EEGHILOOTZ theologize
EEGHILSSTW weightless
EEGHIMNOOZ homogenize
EEGHINRTVY everything
EEGHIORTVW overweight
EEGHIPRRSV vergership
EEGHLNORST Glenrothes
EEGHLOORTY heterology
EEGHMORRTY hygrometer
EEGHNNRSTT strengthen
EEGHNOOPRU enough rope
EEGHNOORTY heterogony
EEGHOSSTUU guest house, house guest
EEGIIILMTZ legitimize
EEGIIKLPRS kriegspiel
EEGIILLNNS single-line
EEGIILNNST lentigines
EEGIJNSTTT jet-setting
EEGIKLLNNN kennelling
EEGIKLNOPS spongelike
EEGILMNORZ mongrelize
EEGILMOOSY semeiology
EEGILNNOPV enveloping
EEGILNNPRS leg-spinner
EEGILNNPSU unsleeping
EEGILNNRSY sneeringly
EEGILNNSSS singleness
EEGILNNSUY unseeingly
EEGILNPPRX perplexing
EEGILNPSWY sweepingly
EEGILRRSVY silver grey
EEGIMNNOOR engine room
EEGIMNNOTT mignonette
EEGIMNNTTU integument
EEGIMNOORT goniometer
EEGIMNOPPT peeping Tom
EEGINNSSSY syngenesis
EEGINOORSS orogenesis
EEGINORRSS regression
EEGINORRWW wine-grower
EEGINORSTY generosity
EEGIORSSTU setigerous
EEGLLLOSWY yellowlegs
EEGLLLPSTU slug pellet
EEGLLMRTUY grey mullet
EEGLLNOOSY selenology
EEGLLOOPSY speleology
EEGLMORSUY gruesomely
EEGLNORSUY generously
EEGLNOSSTU tongueless
EEGLOORRST ergosterol
EEGMNNOORT Montenegro
EEGMNNORSW newsmonger
EEGMNNORTV government
EEGNNORSUU ungenerous
EEGNNOTTXY oxygen tent
EEGNORSSVY governessy
EEGOPRSTUU Portuguese
EEGORRRSST retrogress
EEHHILMPTT pith helmet
EEHHILPSSY sheepishly
EEHHIMNOST henotheism
EEHHINRTTT thirteenth
EEHHIORRSS shire-horse
EEHHIORSTW Whitehorse
EEHHIOSTUW White House
EEHHMMOORT homeotherm
EEHHNRRRTU Herrnhuter
EEHHOOPRST theosopher
EEHHOORSUW whorehouse
EEHHOPSSTY hypotheses
EEHIILMPTU epithelium
EEHIILNOPR perihelion
EEHIIMNNOT methionine
EEHIINOSTW white noise
EEHIIPRSVW viewership
EEHIJNSSSW Jewishness
EEHIKLMORT motherlike
EEHILLPRST tellership
EEHILLPSTW split wheel
EEHILLRSWW well-wisher
EEHILMNOSS homeliness
EEHILMOPRT thermopile
EEHILNNOOS holes-in-one
EEHILNNRTY inherently
EEHILOOPRT heliotrope
EEHILOSTTU silhouette
EEHILPRSSS perishless
EEHILPRSTU spherulite
EEHIMNNRTU mine hunter
EEHIMNPRRT permethrin
EEHIMOOSUV movie house
EEHINNNSTT nine-tenths
EEHINNOPRS prehension
EEHINNORST rhinestone
EEHINNOSST tennis shoe

EEHINOOPRS ionosphere
EEHINSSSTX sixth sense
EEHINSSTYZ synthesize
EEHINSTTYZ synthetize
EEHIOPPRRS prophesier
EEHIOPPRST epistrophe
EEHIRSSSTY hysteresis
EEHKKOOPYY hokey-pokey
EEHKMOORRW homeworker
EEHKNOORTT tenterhook
EEHLLLPSSY helplessly
EEHLLMNOSY shell-money
EEHLLMORTW Motherwell
EEHLLOPSSY hopelessly
EEHLMMNOTY lemon thyme
EEHLMNOOYZ holoenzyme
EEHLMORSST motherless
EEHLNORSST throneless
EEHLOORSTW towel-horse
EEHLOORSUW Lower House
EEHLOSSTUY house style
EEHMNNNOOP phenomenon
EEHMNOORSX sex hormone
EEHMNOORTY heteronomy
EEHMNORSTT nethermost
EEHMOOPRTT photometer
EEHMOORSVW whomsoever
EEHMOOSSUU house mouse
EEHMOPRSTT stepmother
EEHMOPRSTY hypsometer
EEHMOQRSUU humoresque
EEHMORRSTT short metre
EEHNNOPRTY entryphone
EEHNNORRRT northerner
EEHNOPSTUY hypotenuse
EEHNORRSTU southerner
EEHOOPRRSW horsepower
EEHOOPRSUW powerhouse
EEHOOPRTTV over-the-top
EEHOORRTTW two or three
EEHOORSSTU storehouse
EEHOORSTUU Outer House
EEHOOSTTTW sweet tooth
EEHOPPRSST prophetess
EEHOPPRSUU Upper House
EEHOPRRSTV Shreveport
EEHOPRSSST prostheses
EEIIIMNRSS miniseries
EEIIKKNOPR knopkierie
EEIIKLLNRU unlikelier
EEIIKLLNSS likeliness
EEIIKLNPRW periwinkle
EEIIKLPRST priestlike
EEIILLMMRT millimeter, millimetre
EEIILLNSSV liveliness
EEIILMMNPT limpet mine
EEIILMMPST simple time
EEIILMNSST timeliness
EEIILMPRTT triple time
EEIILNOSTV television
EEIILOPTVX exploitive
EEIILRRSTZ sterilizer
EEIIMNNPTT impenitent, pentimenti
EEIIMNRTTW wintertime
EEIIMNRTZZ intermezzi
EEIIMPRSSV impressive, permissive
EEIIMPRTTX exit permit
EEIINNNSTT insentient
EEIINNRTTW intertwine
EEIINOPRTT petitioner, repetition
EEIINRRTWW wine writer
EEIINRSSTZ sensitizer
EEIIOPSTVX expositive
EEIIORRSST rotisserie
EEIIPQRSTU perquisite
EEIIRRSTTU ureteritis
EEIJLLNUVY juvenilely
EEIJMNNNOT enjoinment
EEIKLNNSSU unlikeness
EEIKMNORRW mineworker
EEIKNORSTZ strike zone
EEILLLNOWY yellow line
EEILLLPSTV split-level
EEILLMMORT immortelle
EEILLMNSSS smelliness
EEILLMPPPR pepper mill
EEILLMSSTY timelessly
EEILLNNOSS loneliness
EEILLNOSSV loveliness
EEILLNOSTT little ones
EEILLNSSTT littleness
EEILLPRRUW wirepuller
EEILLRSSTY tirelessly
EEILMNNSTT enlistment
EEILMNOPRT Montpelier
EEILMNOSSU mousseline
EEILMNPSSS simpleness
EEILMOPRYZ polymerize
EEILMORSTY tiresomely
EEILMOSSTV motiveless
EEILMPRSTU pulsimeter
EEILNNPTTY penitently
EEILNNSTTY sentiently
EEILNOPRRT interloper
EEILNOPSST politeness
EEILNPRTXY inexpertly
EEILNRSSTW winterless
EEILNRSTUY esuriently
EEILOPPRSS Persepolis
EEILORRSTU irresolute
EEILORRTTW Rottweiler
EEILORRTXY exteriorly
EEILORSTUV resolutive
EEILPPRTXY perplexity
EEILPPSTUV suppletive
EEILPRRUVZ pulverizer
EEILPRSSST priestless
EEILRSSSST resistless, sisterless
EEILRSSTUV virtueless
EEIMMMNRTU immurement
EEIMMMRSTU summertime
EEIMMOPRRV prime mover
EEIMMRSTYZ symmetrize
EEIMNNNRTT internment
EEIMNNOPTT pentimento
EEIMNNORST minestrone
EEIMNNPSTU septennium
EEIMNNSSTU minuteness
EEIMNNSTTV investment
EEIMNOPPRT pre-emption
EEIMNOPRTU peritoneum
EEIMNOPRYZ prize money
EEIMNORRSZ sermonizer
EEIMNORTZZ intermezzo
EEIMNPPPRT peppermint
EEIMNPRSSU impureness
EEIMNRSSSS remissness
EEIMNRSSTU terminuses
EEIMOPRRST spirometer
EEIMOPRRTZ temporizer
EEIMOPRSTU periosteum
EEIMPRSTUV resumptive
EEIMRSSTYZ systemizer
EEINNNSSTT intentness
EEINNOPRST pretension
EEINNOPRTV prevention
EEINNORRSS orneriness
EEINNORRTV intervenor
EEINNPRSSU unripeness
EEINNPRTTU turpentine
EEINNPSSSU supineness
EEINNQSSUU uniqueness
EEINNRSSTV inventress
EEINOOSSST otioseness
EEINOPRRSS repression
EEINOPRRSV perversion
EEINOPRSSV responsive
EEINOPRSSX expression
EEINOPRSXY epoxy resin
EEINOQRSTU questioner
EEINORRSUV over-insure
EEINORRTVW overwinter
EEINPRSSTT persistent, prettiness
EEINPSSSUV suspensive
EEIOPPRSSV oppressive
EEIOPRRSTV resorptive
EEIOPRSSST stereopsis
EEIOPSSSSV possessive
EEIORRRRTZ terrorizer
EEIPPRTTUY perpetuity
EEIPRRSSUZ pressurize
EEIPRRSTVY perversity
EEIPRRTTWY typewriter
EEIPRSSSTT stepsister
EEIRSSSTTU sestertius
EEKLLNOPSW well-spoken
EEKLLNORRS snorkeller
EEKLOOORRV overlooker
EEKLOOPPRW workpeople
EEKLORSSTW steelworks

EEKMNNOOTY token money
EEKMNOOSST smoke-stone
EEKNOOQRSU queen's rook
EELLLMOOOP Molepolole
EELLLNOPSS pollenless
EELLLOSSVY lovelessly
EELLMNNORT enrollment
EELLMNOOSY lonesomely
EELLMNOSSW mellowness
EELLNNSSSU sullenness
EELLNOPPRT propellent
EELLNOQTUY eloquently
EELLNOSSTY tonelessly
EELLNOSSWY yellowness
EELLNSSTUY tunelessly
EELLORSTUY resolutely
EELLRSSSTU lusterless, lustreless, resultless
EELLRSSSTY restlessly
EELMMNOPTY employment
EELMMRSSSU summerless
EELMNPPSTU supplement
EELMNPTUZZ puzzlement
EELMSSSSTY systemless
EELNOPRSTW spleenwort
EELNPPRSSU purpleness
EELNPPSSSU suppleness
EELNRRSSTU returnless
EELORRRSTY retrorsely
EELORSSUVY yourselves
EELPPRSSSU supperless
EELPRRSTTU splutterer
EELRSSSSST stressless
EEMMOORRTT tromometer
EEMNNOPSTT pentstemon
EEMNOORRTV motor nerve
EEMNOORSSS moroseness
EEMNOORTTY enterotomy
EEMOPPRRTY peremptory
EEMPRSSSST sempstress
EEMQRSSTUU sequestrum
EENNNNOOSS no nonsense
EENNOQRSTU quern-stone
EENNORSSTT rottenness
EENNRSSSUU unsureness
EENOPPRRSS properness
EEOPPPRRTW pepperwort
EEOPPPRSSU presuppose
EEOPPRRSUW superpower
EEOPPRSSSS prepossess
EEOPRRSSTU superstore
EEOPRSTTYY stereotypy
EEORRSSSTV overstress
EFFFHIPRSU puffer fish
EFFFILNSSU fluffiness
EFFGHIINRS fish finger
EFFGIINNST stiffening
EFFGIINORT forfeiting
EFFGILLNOT telling-off
EFFHIKLORS fisherfolk
EFFHINOSSS offishness
EFFIIKLOSS kiss of life
EFFIINNSSS sniffiness
EFFIIQSSTU squiffiest
EFFILLMNTU fulfilment
EFFILLORUV overfulfil
EFFILLOSSU fossil fuel
EFFILNSSTU fitfulness
EFFIMNOSUV snuff movie
EFFINSSSTU stuffiness
EFGGHINRTU gunfighter
EFGGIIILNV life-giving
EFGGIILNNR fingerling
EFGGIINNRR ring finger
EFGGILNORU long figure
EFGGINORTT forgetting
EFGGNOOUYY young fogey
EFGHIIKNRS kingfisher
EFGHIILSTT flightiest
EFGHIIPRTZ prizefight
EFGHILLSST flightless
EFGHILORTV overflight
EFGHILSTTT flight-test, test flight
EFGHIMNORS fishmonger
EFGHINORTT freight ton
EFGHLLLNTU full-length
EFGHLLNORU flugelhorn
EFGHOOPPRR froghopper
EFGIIILNNR firing line
EFGIIKLNTY kite-flying
EFGIILNRSS self-rising
EFGIILTUVY fugitively
EFGIINNNTU fine tuning
EFGIINPRST firing-step
EFGIINRSTU surfeiting
EFGIKLNORS folk singer
EFGILLLUUY guilefully
EFGILLNNNU funnelling
EFGILLORRW flower girl
EFGILMNOSV self-moving
EFGILNORST fosterling
EFGIMNOPRR performing
EFGINNORUV unforgiven
EFGINOPRST finger-post
EFGINPSTUY stupefying
EFHIILNRST Flintshire
EFHIILNSST filthiness
EFHIILRSSV silverfish
EFHIINSSST shiftiness
EFHIIRSTTT thriftiest
EFHILLOPSW fellowship
EFHILNSSTT flesh tints
EFHILOPRST shoplifter
EFHILORRSU flourisher
EFHILRSSTT thriftless
EFHINORSST frothiness
EFHIOPRSTT shopfitter
EFHIORSTTW white frost
EFHLLOOPRS shellproof
EFIIIINNTV infinitive
EFIIILNNTY infinitely
EFIIIMNNTY femininity
EFIIKNNOPT knifepoint
EFIIKNRSSS friskiness
EFIILLLSST still lifes
EFIILLNRSS frilliness
EFIILMNSSS flimsiness
EFIILNNSST flintiness
EFIILNORRY inferiorly
EFIILRSTTU stultifier
EFIINRSSTU fruitiness
EFIINRSSZZ frizziness
EFIKLMNSUY flunkeyism
EFIKLNOSSS folksiness
EFILLMORST stelliform
EFILLNSSUW wilfulness
EFILLOOPRW low profile
EFILLPSTUY spitefully
EFILLRSSTU full sister
EFILMNOOST self-motion
EFILMOOPRS Simferopol
EFILNNSSSU sinfulness
EFILNOPPSS floppiness
EFILNORSSU flouriness
EFILOPRSST profitless
EFILOSTUXY flexuosity
EFIMNORSTU misfortune
EFIMNORTTZ frozen mitt
EFIMNPRSSU frumpiness
EFIMOOPRSU pomiferous
EFINNNSTUU unfunniest
EFINNORRTY forty-niner
EFINOOPRSS profession
EFINORSSST frostiness
EFINORSSWZ frowziness
EFINORSTTU stone fruit
EFIORSSTTW frowstiest
EFJLNOSSUY joyfulness
EFKLMMOORY folk memory
EFKNOOPSST soft-spoken
EFKOORRSTU four-stroke
EFKOPPRRSU fork supper
EFLLMORSSY formlessly
EFLLOPRUWY powerfully
EFLLOSUUXY flexuously
EFLMOOORTY tomfoolery
EFLOPPRSUU purposeful
EFLORRSSUW furrowless
EFLORSSUUU sulfureous
EFMNNNOUYY funny money
EFMOOPRRTU outperform
EFNNOORRSU non-ferrous
EFNOORRSTT storefront
EFOOPRRSTU four-poster
EGGGINORSS grogginess
EGGHIIKLLT klieg light
EGGHIILNNT lightening
EGGIILMMNR glimmering
EGGIIMNOOV movie-going
EGGIINNRST signet ring
EGGILLLNPU leg-pulling
EGGILLNORV grovelling
EGGILNNRSU gunslinger
EGGINNORSS engrossing
EGGINOORSV goings-over
EGGINOSSTU suggestion
EGGLLOOOPX googolplex
EGGLNNOOTU long tongue
EGGLNOOORZ gongoozler

EGGLOOPTYY	Egyptology
EGGLOORSUY	gorgeously
EGHHIILTTW	white light
EGHHIINTTW	white night
EGHHIIPRST	high priest
EGHHIJMPRU	high-jumper
EGHHILLORR	high roller
EGHHILLOWY	high yellow
EGHHILOPRY	hieroglyph
EGHHILOSTU	lighthouse
EGHHIOPSTT	spot height
EGHHOORSUU	rough house
EGHHOPRTYY	hygrophyte
EGHIIIKLNS	heli-skiing
EGHIIINNRT	inheriting
EGHIIKKLNT	knightlike
EGHIILNRSV	shriveling
EGHIILRSTY	tigerishly
EGHIIMNSST	mightiness
EGHIINPRSW	whispering
EGHIINSTUX	extinguish
EGHILLNOST	hostelling
EGHILLNOSV	shovelling
EGHILMOOOZ	homologize
EGHILNSSST	slightness
EGHILOORST	rheologist
EGHILOOSTT	ethologist, theologist
EGHILOSSTT	ghostliest
EGHILOSSTW	weight loss
EGHIMOPPSU	pemphigous
EGHIMORTVY	over-mighty
EGHINNORST	shortening
EGHINNPPSU	pen-pushing
EGHINNRSSU	hungriness
EGHINNRSTU	night nurse
EGHINORSST	shoestring
EGHINRSTTU	shuttering
EGHIORSTTW	ghost-write
EGHLMOORTY	mythologer
EGHLNOOPRY	phrenology
EGHLOOORTY	heortology
EGHLOOPPSY	psephology
EGHLOPPRTY	petroglyph
EGHMNOOOSU	homogenous
EGHMOOOTYZ	homozygote
EGHMORRTYY	hygrometry
EGHOORRTVW	overgrowth
EGIIILMMST	legitimism
EGIIILMNPR	imperiling
EGIIILMPRZ	pilgrimize
EGIIILMSTT	legitimist
EGIIILNORR	irreligion
EGIIIMNNST	meningitis
EGIIINRSTV	revisiting
EGIIKLNNSS	kingliness
EGIIKLNPRS	springlike
EGIIKLNRST	stringlike
EGIILLNNST	tinselling
EGIILLNNSV	snivelling
EGIILLNOTU	guillotine
EGIILLNRST	trellising
EGIILLNSVW	swivelling
EGIILLRSTV	silver gilt
EGIILNPRST	priestling
EGIILNQRSU	squireling
EGIILNRRTY	retiringly
EGIILNRSSS	grisliness
EGIILNSSTU	guiltiness
EGIILNSSTZ	glitziness
EGIILOPSTT	epiglottis
EGIILRSTZZ	grizzliest
EGIIMNPRST	springtime
EGIIMNPRTT	permitting
EGIIMNRSTU	trigeminus
EGIINNORSS	ingression
EGIINNRTUV	unriveting
EGIINNSSST	stinginess
EGIINORRST	roistering
EGIINORRTT	intertrigo
EGIINPRSST	springiest
EGIINRRSTW	signwriter
EGIINRSSTT	grittiness, stringiest
EGIINSTTTV	vignettist
EGIJMNPRUU	gum juniper
EGIKLNNORS	snorkeling
EGIKLNNPSU	spelunking
EGIKNNNOST	Kensington
EGIKNNORTW	networking
EGIKNORSTW	wing-stroke
EGILLMMNOP	pommelling
EGILLMMNPU	pummelling
EGILLNNNTU	tunnelling
EGILLNNOTW	wellington
EGILLNOPPR	propelling
EGILLNORTW	trowelling
EGILLNPRSW	wellspring
EGILLNTUXY	exultingly
EGILMMNORS	mongrelism
EGILMMNPTU	plummeting
EGILMNOOOZ	monologize
EGILMNOOSS	gloominess
EGILMNOPSY	polygenism
EGILMNOPTT	melting pot
EGILMNOSUU	leguminous
EGILMNPTTY	temptingly
EGILMOOSSY	seismology
EGILNNOSSV	lovingness
EGILNNRRUY	unerringly
EGILNOOOST	oenologist
EGILNOOPST	penologist
EGILNOPSTY	polygenist
EGILNOSSSS	glossiness
EGILNOSTUU	lounge suit
EGILNOTTUZ	gluttonize
EGILNPRSSS	springless
EGILNPRSSY	pressingly
EGILNQSTUY	questingly
EGILNRSSST	stringless
EGILNRSTTU	lutestring
EGILOOPRUZ	prologuize
EGILOORSST	serologist
EGILOOSSTX	sexologist
EGILORSSUV	vigourless
EGILORSUVY	grievously
EGILOSUUXY	exiguously
EGIMMNNPTU	impugnment
EGIMNNOORR	ironmonger
EGIMNOORST	ergonomist
EGIMNOORTY	goniometry
EGIMNPRSSU	grumpiness
EGIMNPRTTU	trumpeting
EGIMOOPRST	geotropism
EGINNOPSSS	sponginess
EGINNRSUVW	unswerving
EGINOOPRRT	progenitor
EGINOOPRTW	towing-rope
EGINOORSSV	grooviness
EGINOPPSTW	sopping wet
EGINOPRSUY	perigynous
EGINORRSTW	songwriter
EGINORRTVX	vortex ring
EGINORSSTT	grottiness
EGINORSTUW	out-swinger
EGINRSSTTV	string vest
EGINRSTTTU	Turing test
EGJLLOORRY	Jolly Roger
EGJLMNOPRU	long-jumper
EGLLMORSSY	gormlessly
EGLLMORSUU	glomerulus
EGLLNOOPSY	splenology
EGLMNOOOTY	entomology
EGLMNOORUY	numerology
EGLMNOOYYZ	enzymology
EGLNNORSUU	sunlounger
EGLOOORRWW	wool-grower
EGMMNOORTY	Montgomery
EGMMNOPRSY	gymnosperm
EGMOOORRSU	grouse moor
EGNOOPRSUY	pyrogenous
EGNORRSTUV	overstrung
EGNORSSSST	songstress
EHHIILSTVY	thievishly
EHHIIMSTTW	whitesmith
EHHILLORST	thill-horse
EHHILMOPRT	thermophil
EHHILOPSTU	Theophilus
EHHILOPTTY	lithophyte
EHHILORTWW	worthwhile
EHHILRSSWY	shrewishly
EHHINORTTW	whitethorn
EHHIOPRRSS	Shropshire
EHHIOPSSTY	hypothesis
EHHLLOOSTT	tooth shell
EHHLMRSSTY	rhythmless
EHHLOOOPPR	lophophore
EHHOPPSSYY	hypophyses
EHIIILNPPP	Philippine
EHIIILNPST	Philistine
EHIIINRRTX	inheritrix
EHIIIPRSVZ	viziership
EHIIKMRRSS	skirmisher
EHIILLNOTV	Thionville
EHIILLOPYZ	lyophilize
EHIILLRSVY	liverishly
EHIILNOOPS	eosinophil
EHIILNQRSU	relinquish
EHIILNSTTW	tin whistle
EHIIMNPSSS	impishness

EHIIMOPRSV impoverish
EHIIMPPRSU umpireship
EHIIMPRSST hipsterism
EHIINNPRST internship
EHIINPPRSW whippers-in
EHIINPPSSW whippiness
EHIINRSSST shirtiness
EHIIPQRSSU squireship
EHIIQSSSTU squishiest
EHIIRRSTTU urethritis
EHIIRSSTTT thirstiest
EHIKLNORTW Kenilworth
EHILLMNPUY phillumeny
EHILLNRSSS shrillness
EHILLNSTUV Huntsville
EHILMNSSSU mulishness
EHILMOPSTY polytheism
EHILNNOOSW Welsh onion
EHILNNOSSU unholiness
EHILNOSSSW owlishness
EHILNPSSSU plushiness
EHILNSSSSU slushiness
EHILOOPSTU pilot house
EHILOPRSSU Russophile
EHILOPSTTY polytheist
EHILORSTTT short title
EHILOSSTTW sowthistle
EHILPRSUUZ sulphurize
EHIMMNOOST monotheism
EHIMMOPRTU promethium
EHIMNNOORS moonshiner
EHIMNNPSTU punishment
EHIMNOOSTT monotheist
EHIMNORSUY Hieronymus
EHIMOPPRST prophetism
EHIMORRSTT thermistor
EHINNORSST thorniness
EHINOOPSUU euphonious
EHINORRTUW unworthier
EHINORSSTW worthiness
EHINPPSSSU uppishness
EHINRRTTUW Winterthur
EHINSSSTTY synthesist
EHIOOPRSTT orthoepist
EHIOORSSTX six-shooter
EHIOPPRRSW worshipper
EHIOPRRSTY prehistory
EHIOPRSSST prosthesis
EHIPRSSTUY suretyship
EHJMOPRSUW showjumper
EHKMOOPRSU skeuomorph
EHKMOSSTTU musket shot
EHKOOPRRSW shopworker
EHLLLOORRY holy roller
EHLLNOOSSW hollowness
EHLLRSSTUY ruthlessly
EHLMNOPPTY nympholept
EHLMNORTUY unmotherly
EHLMORSSUU humourless
EHLNOOOPTV photonovel
EHLOOPRSTU tool-pusher
EHLOORRRTY holy terror
EHLOORTVWY loveworthy
EHLOPRSTUY upholstery

EHMNOORSST mother's son
EHMNOOSSST smoothness
EHMOOPRTTY photometry
EHNNOPRTWY pennyworth
EHNOORTTWY noteworthy
EHNOOSTTTT Hottentots
EHNORSTWWY newsworthy
EHOOOPPRRS sporophore
EHOOPPRSTY sporophyte
EHOOPPRTTY protophyte
EHOPRSTTTU shot-putter
EHORRSTTUV overthrust
EIIIKMRRRU Kirriemuir
EIIILLLMRT milliliter, millilitre
EIIILLNPST pistilline
EIIILMNNOP epilimnion
EIIIMSSTVY emissivity
EIIIOPRRTZ prioritize
EIIJLNTUVY juvenility
EIIJMNRTUY injury time
EIIJMNSTTU just-in-time
EIIKLNNSSS slinkiness
EIIKLNORST triskelion
EIIKLNRSTW wrinkliest
EIIKMNPSSS skimpiness
EIIKNNNSSS skinniness
EIIKNQRSSU quirkiness
EIILLLOSUV Louisville
EIILLMMNNU millennium
EIILLMOPTY impolitely
EIILLMPRTU multiplier
EIILLNOPST septillion
EIILLNORRT ritornelli
EIILLNORTT tortellini
EIILLNOSTX sextillion
EIILLPPRSY slipperily
EIILLPSSTY pitilessly
EIILMMNNTY imminently
EIILMNNSTT instilment
EIILNORRTY interiorly
EIILNOSSSV visionless
EIILNPPSSS slippiness
EIILNPTUVY punitively
EIILNRSSTY sinisterly
EIILOPSTVY positively
EIILPRSSST spiritless
EIIMNNORTU munitioner
EIIMNNRSTU trienniums
EIIMNOPRSS impression, permission
EIIMOOPSTY episiotomy
EIIMOPRRSV improviser
EIIMOPRSUV impervious
EIIMORSTUZ moisturize
EIIMQRSSTU squirmiest
EIINNPPSSS snippiness
EIINNRSSTW wintriness
EIINOOPRST positioner, reposition
EIINOOPSTX exposition
EIINOORSUV Eurovision
EIINOPPTTT petit point
EIINORTTWZ zwitterion

EIINPRSSSS prissiness
EIINRSTTTW intertwist
EIINRSTUVY university
EIINRTTTWY nitwittery
EIIOPPSSTT petits pois
EIJLMPPRTU triple jump
EIJOOOPRTV Portoviejo
EIJOPRRSUU perjurious
EIKLLMORRW millworker
EIKLLNNNTU tunnel-kiln
EIKMNOSTUY monkey suit
EIKNNOSSTT knottiness
EIKNOOPSSS spookiness
EIKORSTTTY Trotskyite
EILLLOORTT toilet roll
EILLLSSSTY listlessly
EILLMOOSTY toilsomely
EILLNNOSTY insolently
EILLNOORRT ritornello
EILLNOOSSW woolliness
EILLNORWWW willow wren
EILLNRTUVY virulently
EILLOPPPPR pill-popper
EILLOPRSUY perilously
EILLORRTUY ulteriorly
EILLORTTTU litter lout
EILLQRRSUY squirrelly
EILMMNSSSU slumminess
EILMMOPRSY polymerism
EILMMSSSTU summitless
EILMNOOOPZ monopolize
EILMNOOSST motionless
EILMNOPTTY impotently
EILMNOSSSS lissomness
EILMNRSSTY minstrelsy
EILMOOPRST metropolis
EILMOPPRRY improperly
EILMSSTTTU litmus test
EILNNNOOTV non-violent
EILNNRSSUU unruliness
EILNOOPTVW vowel-point
EILNOORSTU resolution
EILNOORTUV revolution
EILNOPPRTW nipplewort
EILNOPPSSS sloppiness
EILNOPPSTU suppletion
EILNOPRSST portliness
EILNOSTUUV velutinous
EILNPQTTUU quintuplet
EILNPRRTUY pruriently
EILNRSSSTU sultriness
EILOOPPRTY pleiotropy
EILOOPPSTY oppositely
EILOPPRSUV propulsive
EILOPRRSTU protrusile
EILOPRRSUY superiorly
EILOPRSTVY sportively, Very pistol
EILOPRSUVY previously
EIMMNNORSW non-swimmer
EIMNNOOOTZ monotonize
EIMNNOOPTT omnipotent
EIMNNRSTTU instrument
EIMNOOPRRT premonitor

EIMNOOPRSS spoonerism
EIMNOORSST Montessori
EIMNOPRSTU resumption
EIMNORSSST storminess
EIMNORSSSU sensoriums
EIMNPSSSTU stumpiness
EIMNSSSTTU smuttiness
EIMOPRRSTU romper suit
EIMORSSTUY mysterious
EINNOOPPRS open prison
EINNOOPSSS spooniness
EINNOORTUX neurotoxin
EINNOOSSST snootiness
EINNOPSSSU suspension
EINNOSSSTT snottiness
EINOOOPRTZ zero option
EINOOPPRSS oppression
EINOOPPRTW power point
EINOOPRRST resorption
EINOOPRSTU proteinous
EINOOPSSSS possession
EINOPPRSTY propensity
EINOPRRRST ripsnorter
EINOPRSSST sportiness
EINOPSSSTT spottiness
EINOQRTTUU tourniquet
EINRSSSTTU trustiness
EIOOOPRSTZ sporozoite
EIOOPPRRRT proprietor
EIOOPRRSTY repository
EIOOPRSTXY expository
EIOORRSSTU roisterous
EIOORRTVWY ivory tower
EIOPPRRSTY prosperity
EIOPPRSSTT stroppiest
EIOPPRSTUV supportive
EIOPRRSSUV supervisor
EIOPRRSTUV protrusive
EIOPRSTTTU prostitute
EIORRRSTUV retrovirus
EIPPRRSUVY privy purse
EJNNSSSTUU unjustness
EJNOOSSSUY joyousness
EKLOORRTUW work-to-rule
EKOPPRRSUW upper works
ELLLOSSSUY soullessly
ELLMORRSTU muster-roll
ELLNPRTUUY purulently
ELLOOPSTVY stop-volley
ELLOOPSTWY yellow spot
ELLOPSSSTY spotlessly
ELMNOOPSTY splenotomy
ELMNOORSUY enormously
ELMNOOSUVY venomously
ELMNORSUUY numerously
ELMOOPRSUY polymerous
ELMOOPSSUY polysemous
ELNOSSSUUY sensuously
ELOPPRSUVY oversupply
EMMOOPRSTT post-mortem
EMNOOPPRTT prompt-note
EMNOPPRSST promptness
EMNORSSTUU menstruous
ENNOOPPRRU proper noun
ENOOPRRSSY responsory
ENOOPRSSSU porousness
ENOOPRSTTU portentous
ENOPRSSSUY suspensory
EOOPPRRSSU prosperous
EOOPRSSSSY possessory
EOORRSSTTU stertorous
EOPPRRSSSU suppressor
FFFFIITTYY fifty-fifty
FFGHIILNSY fishing-fly, flying fish
FFGHIIOPPR hippogriff
FFGHORSTUU rough stuff
FFGIILLLNU fulfilling
FFGIILNNSY sniffingly
FFGINOPTTU off-putting
FFIIRRSTTU first-fruit
FFILLRTUUY fruitfully
FFILNRTUUU unfruitful
FFILOORRST first floor
FGGHHIILNY high-flying
FGGHIIINNT infighting
FGGIILNNWY flying wing
FGHHIINSTT night shift
FGHHIORRTT forthright
FGHHLOTTUU thoughtful
FGHIILNSTU insightful
FGHIILRSTT first light
FGHIINORRY horrifying
FGHIINRSTT first night, first thing
FGHIINSSTW swing shift
FGHILLRTUY rightfully
FGHILOOPRT lightproof
FGHILOOSTT footlights
FGHINNOTUX fox-hunting
FGHLLORTUW full growth
FGIIILLNTT ill-fitting
FGIILLNORV frivolling
FGIILLNRTY triflingly
FGIILLNSTY stiflingly
FGIILMNORU linguiform
FGIILNOSUU fuliginous
FGIILNPPTY fly-tipping
FGIILNSTUY flying suit
FGIIMNORTY mortifying
FGIIMNSTYY mystifying
FGIKNNORTU tuning fork
FGILNNORWY frowningly
FGIMNOOPRS spongiform
FGLLNORUWY wrongfully
FGLOORTUUY futurology
FGNNOOSSSU sons of guns
FHHIOPRSTT thrift shop
FHIILPSSTT split shift
FHILLMRTUY mirthfully
FHILMPRSUY frumpishly
FHILOPRSUW worshipful
FHINORRSTT shirt-front
FHLLLOSTUY slothfully
FHLLOTUUYY youthfully
FHLLRTTUUY truthfully
FHLNRTTUUU untruthful
FHNOOOPRRT thornproof
FIIIMORSST fortissimi
FIILMMNOOR moniliform
FIIMNORTUY uniformity
FIIMOORSST fortissimo
FIINNOSTUY funniosity
FIKLLLNSUU unskillful
FIKLLOORST folklorist
FIKNORSTWY forty winks
FIMNNNOORU non-uniform
FIMOORRRST rostriform
FINOOOPSTT soft option
FIOORSTTUU fortuitous
FLLMNORUUY mournfully
FLLRSTTUUY trustfully
FMOOOPRRST stormproof
FUUWYYZZZZ fuzzy-wuzzy
GGGIILLNNY nigglingly
GGGILNNPUU unplugging
GGHHIIILNV high living
GGHHIILNTT night light
GGHHILSTUY thuggishly
GGHHINRSTU high-strung
GGHIILPRSY priggishly
GGHILLSSUY sluggishly
GGHINNOTUY young thing
GGHINORRTW growth ring
GGIIIINSTV gingivitis
GGIIILMNPR pilgriming
GGIIINNRTU intriguing
GGIILNNNRY grinningly
GGIILNNSTY stingingly
GGIILNNSWY swingingly
GGIILNPPRY grippingly
GGIKMNNOSU smoking gun
GGILLLNOOR logrolling
GGILLNORWY growlingly
GGILNOOPRU prologuing
GGINNNNRUU gun-running
GGINOOPRRU proroguing
GHHIIIPRST high spirit
GHHIINRSTT nightshirt
GHHIIPRSTW shipwright
GHHILLOSUY ghoulishly
GHHILNORTT north light
GHHINOPRTT triphthong
GHHIOPPPRY hippogryph
GHHIORSSTT short sight
GHHLOORTUY thoroughly
GHHNORRTUU run-through
GHHNORSSTU song thrush
GHHOORTTUU throughout
GHHOPRTTUU throughput
GHIIKNNNTU unthinking
GHIILLMRTW millwright
GHIILLNOTW Linlithgow
GHIILLNRWY whirlingly
GHIILLOPTT pilot light
GHIILPRSTT strip light
GHIINNORSU nourishing
GHIINNPPSU unshipping
GHIINOPRSW worshiping
GHIKNOPRTU groupthink
GHILMPRSUY grumpishly
GHILNOOPST phlogiston
GHILNOOSTY soothingly

GHILOOORST horologist
GHILOOPSYY physiology
GHIMMNOPTU humming-top
GHINNNOTTU Huntington
GHLMOOOOSU homologous
GHLMOOOPRY morphology
GHLNOOPSUW snowplough
GHMNOOPSYY gymnosophy
GHMOOOSUYZ homozygous
GIIIKKNNSS kissing kin
GIIILLLNVW living will
GIIILLNNST instilling
GIIILNNTVY invitingly
GIIINNNTUV uninviting
GIIJKMNPSU ski jumping
GIIKLMNRSY smirkingly
GIIKLNNPRS sprinkling
GIIKLNNSTY stinkingly
GIIKLNRSTY strikingly
GIIKNNNTTU unknitting
GIIKNRSTWY sky-writing
GIILLLNOPU louping-ill
GIILLNNOPR rolling pin
GIILLNOPST pistolling
GIILMMNSWY swimmingly
GIILMNOORV living room
GIILMNOPSY imposingly
GIILNNOSTV Livingston
GIILNNRTUY untiringly
GIILNOORSU inglorious
GIILNOOSST sinologist
GIILNRRSTY stirringly
GIILOORSTV virologist
GIILOPPRST pistol grip
GIIMNNOORS Monsignori
GIIMNNOPSU unimposing
GIIMNOSSTY misogynist
GIINNNSTTU unstinting
GIINNOPRST piston ring
GIINPPTTTU tittupping
GIINPRRSSU surprising
GIKMNNNOOS non-smoking
GIKNNNOTTU unknotting
GIKNOORTUW outworking, working-out
GILLNNOUVY unlovingly
GILLNOPRRS spring roll
GILLNPUYZZ puzzlingly
GILLOORSUY gloriously
GILMMNOOUY immunology
GILMNOOOST monologist
GILMOOOPST pomologist
GILMOOSTYZ zymologist
GILNNNSTUY stunningly
GILNOOOSTT ontologist
GILNOPRSTY sportingly
GILNORRWYY worryingly
GILNRSTTUY trustingly
GILOOOPSTT topologist
GILOOPRSTT proglottis
GILOOPSTTY typologist

GILOORRSUY rigorously
GILOORSUVY vigorously
GIMMPPTUYY gippy tummy
GIMNOOSSUY misogynous
GINNOPPSTU unstopping
GINNOPRSTU unsporting
GINNRSTTUU untrusting
GINOOPRTUU outpouring
GINORSSTTU strong suit
GINPPTTTUU put-putting
GLNOOPSUYY polygynous
GLNOOSTTUU gluttonous
GMMPPTUYYY gyppy tummy
GMNNOOOSUY monogynous
GMNOOORRST strongroom
HHILOOOPTT photolitho
HHILOOPPSY philosophy
HHIOPPSSYY hypophysis
HHIORSSTTW short whist
HHMMOOOPRY homomorphy
HHNOORSTTU north-south
HHOOOOPSTT photo shoot
HHOOORRTUU hour to hour
HHOOPPRSSU phosphorus
HIIKLSSTTY skittishly
HIILLNORTT trillionth
HIILOPPSTW pistol-whip
HIILOPRSTY Holy Spirit
HIILOSSSTY histolysis
HIIMMNOPRS morphinism
HIIOOTTTYY hoity-toity
HILNORTUWY unworthily
HILOOPRSTY polyhistor
HILOOPSSTT pistol shot
HILOOPSSTY photolysis
HILOPPSTUY Hippolytus
HIMNOPRRSY Pyrrhonism
HIMNOPSSTY symphonist
HINOOPTTXY phytotoxin
HINOPRRSTY Pyrrhonist
HIOOPRSTTT orthoptist
HIOOPRTTXY thixotropy
HIORSSTTUU struthious
HKNOOOUWWY you-know-who
HLMOORSUUY humorously
HLOPRSSUUU sulphurous
HMMNOOOSUY homonymous
HMMOOORTTU motormouth
HMOOPRSTTU Portsmouth
HMOOPSSTUU posthumous
HOORRSSTTY short story
IIIKLLNPSW pilliwinks
IIILLMMNSU illuminism
IIILLMNSTU illuminist
IIIMNOOPST imposition
IIIMNOPRSS misprision
IIIMOPSSTV positivism
IIINOQRSTU inquisitor
IIINOQSTUU iniquitous

IIIOPSSTTV positivist
IIIOPSTTVY positivity
IIKLOOPSTT Ostpolitik
IILLLLNWYY willy-nilly
IILLLLWWYY willy-willy
IILLLOPPSW pillowslip
IILLLORSUY illusorily
IILLNOOPPS poison pill
IILLNOOPST postillion
IILMNOORSU orimulsion
IILMNOPSTY postliminy
IILMNOSTUY luminosity
IILNNOOTUV involution
IILOPRSSTW low spirits
IIMMOORTUV vomitorium
IINOOOPPST opposition
IINORSTTUU nutritious
IIOOOPRSTV ovipositor
IIOOPPRSTU propitious
IIOPRSSTUU spirituous
IIORSTTUVY virtuosity
IKMORSSTTY Trotskyism
IKNOPRRSTW printworks
IKORSSTTTY Trotskyist
ILLMNOSUUY luminously
ILMNOOOPST monopolist
ILMNOOOSTW slow motion
ILMNOOSUUV voluminous
ILMNOSTUUY mutinously
ILMOORSTUY timorously
ILNOOPPRSU propulsion
ILOOPPRSST spoilsport
ILOORSTTUY tortiously
ILOORSUUXY uxoriously
ILOPRSSUUY spuriously
ILORSSUUUY usuriously
ILORSTUUVY virtuously
IMMOPPRSTU impromptus
IMMOPSSSUY symposiums
IMNNOSTYYY synonymity
IMNOOORSUV omnivorous
IMNOORRSTW Morristown
IMOOPPPPUY opium poppy
IMOOPRRSSY promissory
INOOOPPRRT proportion
INOOPRRSTU protrusion
INOOSSSSTY synostosis
INOPPRSTTU turnip-tops
IOOPPRRSTU pot-pourris
IOORSTTTUY tortuosity
LLOOPPSUUY populously
LLORSSTUUY lustrously
LMOSTTUUUU tumultuous
LNOOORSSUY sonorously
LOOPSTUUUV voluptuous
LOORSTTUUY tortuously
MMOOPRRSUU rumpus room
MNNOOOOSTU monotonous
MNNOOSSUYY synonymous
MNOOOPRRTY promontory
MOOOPRRSTT motor sport
OPRSTTUVYY topsy-turvy

ELEVEN LETTERS

AAAAABBCDRR	abracadabra	**AAABELLNPTU**	unpalatable
AAAAAGLMMRS	garam masala	**AAABELNNOTT**	annotatable
AAAAAJLMPRY	Rajapalayam	**AAABELNRRTW**	warrantable
AAAAALRUWYY	Yuwaalaraay	**AAABEMRSTTT**	Stabat Mater
AAAABBCELNR	Calabar bean	**AAABGHIOOPR**	agoraphobia
AAAABBINRST	Sabbatarian	**AAABHMPRRTU**	brahmaputra
AAAABCCHILN	Bacchanalia	**AAABIILMNOR**	labia minora
AAAABCGMNRU	Bucaramanga	**AAABILNNPST**	banana split
AAAABDEKKLS	baked Alaska	**AAABLNRRTWY**	warrantably
AAAABDIIRSU	Saudi Arabia	**AAACCCEINPT**	capacitance
AAAABIJLMOR	labia majora	**AAACCCILSTT**	cataclastic
AAAACCEFILS	false acacia	**AAACCDDIILR**	acid radical
AAAACDEFGRY	Faraday cage	**AAACCDEIIMN**	academician
AAAACDELRSS	Caesar salad	**AAACCDHIRTY**	tachycardia
AAAACDGINNU	Canandaigua	**AAACCEHINPU**	ipecacuanha
AAAACGHMNRT	Magna Charta	**AAACCEILLOR**	calceolaria
AAAACGILPSS	passacaglia	**AAACCEILPRT**	Palaearctic
AAAACKNPRRV	caravan park	**AAACCEMRSST**	carcass meat
AAAACNRRSVY	caravansary	**AAACCHILLRY**	archaically
AAAAEHMMOTT	haematomata	**AAACCHILRTU**	autarchical
AAAAFINRRST	Rastafarian	**AAACCILLPRT**	parallactic
AAAALLLOOPZ	lalapalooza	**AAACCILMNOT**	acclamation
AAAAMRTZZZZ	razzamatazz	**AAACCILRRTU**	caricatural
AAABBCEGLMP	cabbage palm	**AAACCIMNORT**	carcinomata
AAABBCEKLNN	bank balance	**AAACCLLMSTY**	cataclysmal
AAABCCFIKLR	black Africa	**AAACDDELLRW**	Cadwallader
AAABCDDIRRY	bradycardia	**AAACDEEIMRR**	camaraderie
AAABCDELNRS	candelabras	**AAACDEEMRRY**	camera-ready
AAABCEGHLNU	Laguna Beach	**AAACDEERSWY**	caraway seed
AAABCEGILLR	algebraical	**AAACDEGNOOS**	Canada goose
AAABCEGKPSS	back passage	**AAACDEILMPR**	paramedical
AAABCELRTTT	attractable	**AAACDEILNRT**	cardinalate
AAABCHILMNR	Brahmanical	**AAACDEMNRST**	stand camera
AAABCHLLMPS	paschal lamb	**AAACDEPRTTU**	data capture
AAABCILLOPR	parabolical	**AAACDFHNRST**	cardan shaft
AAABCORRSTU	barracoutas	**AAACDIILPRS**	paradisical
AAABDEGGLNU	bad language	**AAACDIIMNRS**	Arcadianism
AAABDEGGNOV	vagabondage	**AAACDILOPRX**	paradoxical
AAABDEGIMNR	brain damage	**AAACEEFLMNS**	malfeasance
AAABDELNPTU	unadaptable	**AAACEEGNNRR**	carrageenan
AAABDENORRS	Aaron's beard	**AAACEEHIMNN**	Achaemenian
AAABDFHKRRU	Farrukhabad	**AAACEEILPRS**	special area
AAABDHKMORR	Khorramabad	**AAACEENRTTV**	caravanette
AAABEEGLLSV	salvageable	**AAACEFLRTTU**	artefactual
AAABEEGLNRR	arrangeable	**AAACEGILMNO**	egomaniacal
AAABEGILNPR	plea bargain	**AAACEGIRRWY**	carriageway
AAABEGKMNNR	bank manager	**AAACEHILLPR**	parheliacal
AAABEHIMNPS	amphisbaena	**AAACEHKRTTT**	heart attack
AAABEIIJNRZ	Azerbaijani	**AAACEHLMNNP**	Panchen Lama
AAABEIILNRS	Rabelaisian	**AAACEILLMNR**	all-American
AAABEILLNUV	unavailable	**AAACEILNPSU**	Aesculapian
AAABEILNRST	alabastrine	**AAACEINRSTV**	caravan site
AAABEILPPRS	appraisable	**AAACELMNPTU**	campanulate

AAACELMNRST sacramental
AAACELMOPRT paracetamol
AAACERRSTTU tartar sauce
AAACFGILNPT flag-captain
AAACFILLNTY fanatically
AAACFILNSTT fantastical
AAACFIMNRRT aircraftman
AAACGHIPPRR paragraphic
AAACGHNOOTT Chattanooga
AAACGIILNPT capital gain
AAACGIINNRU Aurignacian
AAACGILMMRT grammatical
AAACGILMPRT pragmatical
AAACGINNNRV caravanning
AAACGNRRSSY canary grass
AAACHIILPRS Pharisaical
AAACHIKPPRT apparatchik
AAACHILMRRT matriarchal
AAACHILPRRT patriarchal
AAACHLNRRTY charlatanry
AAACIILMNNS Lacanianism
AAACIILPRST parasitical
AAACIKLRRWY rack railway
AAACILLMNRU animalcular
AAACILLNNPS spinal canal
AAACILLNSTY satanically
AAACILLRTUY actuarially
AAACILMMNOS sal ammoniac
AAACILNNRST Lancastrian
AAACILOPSTT apostatical
AAADDFHNRST hard and fast
AAADEFFNNOR fanfaronade
AAADEGILMNN Magdalenian
AAADEGMNORR road manager
AAADEHINRTT radiant heat
AAADEILMPTV maladaptive
AAADEILMRRR rear admiral
AAADEILNNRX Alexandrian, Alexandrina
AAADEILNRSS Alessandria
AAADEILRRSV adversarial
AAADEIMNNRT mandarinate
AAADELNNPRT rataplanned
AAADELNORSV Salvadorean
AAADENNSSYY yeas and nays
AAADFFHHLLN half-and-half
AAADGGHINNR Gandhinagar
AAADGGLLMMO gold amalgam
AAADGIILMNR madrigalian
AAADGILNORT gradational
AAADGILORXY radio galaxy
AAADHHLPRYZ haphazardly
AAADHISSSTY Shasta daisy
AAADHLNNRUY hardy annual
AAADIILNORR radiolarian
AAADIILNORT radiational
AAADIKKLVVZ Vladikavkaz
AAADILRRWYY railway yard
AAADLNORSSV San Salvador
AAAEEELNPRS paraselenae
AAAEEGGLORV goal average
AAAEEGGMNST stage-manage
AAAEEGMSSTU sausage meat
AAAEEHINSST anaesthesia
AAAEEHLLSST Tallahassee
AAAEELNPRTY penalty area
AAAEERSTTVX extravasate
AAAEGGINRST staging area
AAAEGIILNRT egalitarian
AAAEGILMMNO megalomania
AAAEGINNNTY Yagi antenna
AAAEGMNNOTZ Mazatenango
AAAEGNRTTVX extravagant
AAAEHIILMPT epithalamia
AAAEHILMSST thalassemia
AAAEHILNOPR aeolian harp
AAAEHIMNNRT amaranthine
AAAEHKNNSTV Savannakhet
AAAEHLLMRRS Earl Marshal
AAAEIKLLLMT alkali metal
AAAEILMRRTW raw material
AAAEILPPRRS reappraisal
AAAEINSSSST assassinate
AAAELNRRTUY natural year
AAAELPPSSTT Papal States
AAAFFFILNST Falstaffian
AAAFFINPRWX paraffin wax
AAAFGHINNST Afghanistan
AAAGGGINRTV aggravating
AAAGGHHIOPR Hagiographa
AAAGGINORTV aggravation
AAAGIILNPRS parasailing
AAAGIINRSTT Sagittarian
AAAGKNOOPRW kangaroo paw
AAAGKNOORRT kangaroo rat, rat kangaroo
AAAGMPPRSSS pampas grass
AAAHHHNORSS Rosh Hashana
AAAHHNOPRST Pharaoh's ant
AAAHILMOPRT prothalamia
AAAHILNPSXY anaphylaxis
AAAHLLMMNTY Tammany Hall
AAAIILNORTV variational
AAAIILNPSTU saintpaulia
AAAIINNQRTU antiquarian
AAAILLMOPPT papillomata
AAAILLORSTT saltatorial
AAAILMRRSTT martial arts
AAAILNNRSTU saturnalian
AAAILNRSSTU saturnalias
AAAIMNNOOST antonomasia
AAAIMNOOPRS paronomasia
AAAJOPRRSVW Java sparrow
AAAOPRSSTUU apatosaurus
AABBBEHRSTY baby's breath
AABBCCIILST cabbalistic
AABBCCKLNOR carbon black
AABBCDEINRT brace and bit
AABBCEEEGRT cabbage tree
AABBCEEELMR embraceable
AABBCEEGORS cabbage rose
AABBCEINORT bicarbonate
AABBCEINSYY Biscayne Bay
AABBCEKNRUY Banbury cake
AABBCIIKLST Kabbalistic
AABBDDDENOR bed and board
AABBDEEGILR abridgeable
AABBDEEKRST breadbasket
AABBDEEORRV beaverboard
AABBDEFFLOR baffle board

AABBDEGLNRR land-grabber
AABBEEIRRTV rebarbative
AABBEEKLNRU unbreakable
AABBEELLRST barbastelle
AABBEELNPRT rabbet plane
AABBEFGLRST flabbergast
AABBEGIINRT bear-baiting
AABBEGILLNR ball-bearing
AABBEHIILNT inhabitable
AABBEHILLOS abolishable
AABBEHKLNTT blanket bath
AABBEIILLNV Abbevillian
AABBEIILRTY bearability
AABBEIRRTTU barbiturate
AABBGHIMNOT thingamabob
AABBIIILMNO bibliomania
AABBIIKLNTY bankability
AABBLORRSUY barbarously
AABCCCDIIOR boracic acid
AABCCEHLNTU uncatchable
AABCCEILLRY acerbically
AABCCEILPRT practicable
AABCCEKRSTT backscatter
AABCCELNOTT contactable
AABCCELNOTU accountable
AABCCERRUUY bureaucracy
AABCCIIJLNO Jacobinical
AABCCIIJLOT Jacobitical
AABCCILPRTY practicably
AABCCLNOTUY accountably
AABCCLNRRUU carbuncular
AABCDDEILRS discardable
AABCDDEORST broadcasted
AABCDDIKMNO diamondback
AABCDEEFLRY barefacedly
AABCDEEFNRZ brazen-faced
AABCDEEHIRS raised beach
AABCDEELNRT tabernacled
AABCDEGGNNO egg and bacon
AABCDEHIMMR chambermaid
AABCDEILNST elastic band
AABCDEKNRRS banker's card
AABCDELMNRU candelabrum
AABCDEORRST broadcaster, rebroadcast
AABCDGGIOOR braggadocio
AABCDHMNORY rhabdomancy
AABCDINOORR radiocarbon
AABCDINOUYY buoyancy aid
AABCEEELLPR replaceable
AABCEEFNORR forbearance
AABCEEGLLNO congealable
AABCEEHILMP impeachable
AABCEEHKLRT leatherback
AABCEEHLNRU unreachable
AABCEEHLNTU unteachable
AABCEEHMNRT antechamber
AABCEEILLMR reclaimable
AABCEEILMNV ambivalence
AABCEEILNPS inescapable
AABCEEILNRS increasable
AABCEEILPPR appreciable
AABCEELLNPU unplaceable
AABCEELNORV overbalance
AABCEELNPSU unescapable
AABCEELNRTU untraceable
AABCEELRRTT retractable
AABCEELRTTU trabeculate
AABCEELRTTX extractable
AABCEFFLOPU Cape buffalo
AABCEFILNOT labefaction
AABCEFLMNOY flamboyance
AABCEFLNOTU confabulate
AABCEGILNNT enabling act
AABCEHHPSTY bathyscaphe
AABCEHIINNT inhabitance
AABCEHIKMNN bank machine
AABCEHILLRY Hebraically
AABCEHILMNR chamberlain
AABCEHLMNTU unmatchable
AABCEHLNRUY unreachably
AABCEHLNTUW unwatchable
AABCEHLPRSU purchasable
AABCEHMRRST Star Chamber
AABCEIILNNZ cannibalize
AABCEIKLLMR blackmailer
AABCEILLLOZ localizable
AABCEILMNVY ambivalency
AABCEILNNOT containable
AABCEILNPSY inescapably
AABCEILNRTT intractable
AABCEILPPRY appreciably
AABCEIMNPRR Precambrian
AABCEKKLMRT black market
AABCEKLNNRT central bank
AABCEKMRUUV vacuum brake
AABCEKQRRTU quarterback
AABCELLLSTY Ballycastle
AABCELLOORT collaborate
AABCELMOPSS compassable
AABCELNRTUY untraceably
AABCELOORST car boot sale
AABCELORTXY carboxylate
AABCEMMOPSS beam-compass
AABCENOPPRR carbon paper
AABCEOORRSU arboraceous
AABCFFJOSST Jacob's staff
AABCFIINORT fabrication
AABCFLMNOYY flamboyancy
AABCGHIOOPR agoraphobic
AABCHIINNTY inhabitancy
AABCHIINORT brachiation
AABCHLMNTUY unmatchably
AABCIIILMTY amicability
AABCIILLPTY placability
AABCIILLSTY scalability
AABCIILMNNS cannibalism
AABCIILNORT calibration
AABCIILRSTY sybaritical
AABCIJMRRRU Bajram Curri
AABCILLMNOZ Monbazillac
AABCILLNOTY botanically
AABCILNRTTY intractably
AABCINNOORT carbonation
AABCINORRTU carburation
AABCINORSTT abstraction
AABCLLLRSTY crystal ball
AABDDEELNRR brand leader
AABDDEELORR leader board
AABDDEELORV broadleaved

AABDDEELRSS addressable
AABDDEGGORR daggerboard
AABDDEGLLLR gall bladder
AABDDELRSTU balustraded
AABDDNRSSTU sub-standard
AABDEEGLPRU upgradeable
AABDEEGNNSV Geneva bands
AABDEEHHRRS haberdasher
AABDEEHINRR hare-brained
AABDEEILMNR lamebrained
AABDEELLMRT ballad metre
AABDEELPRSU persuadable
AABDEFLNNOS self-abandon
AABDEGGHINN headbanging
AABDEGGLORV Blagoevgrad
AABDEGHILNS Bangladeshi
AABDEGILNOS diagnosable
AABDEHHIRRT hairbreadth
AABDEHLNSUY unabashedly
AABDEHRSTWY breadthways
AABDEIILNSV inadvisable
AABDEIILRTY readability
AABDEIKNORT debarkation
AABDEILLNOT labiodental
AABDEILMNTU mandibulate
AABDEILNOUV unavoidable
AABDEILNSUV unadvisable
AABDEILORRS boardsailer, sailboarder
AABDEILORRT labradorite
AABDEIMRTUV adumbrative
AABDELNRSST sandblaster
AABDELORRUY day labourer
AABDEMNNNOT abandonment
AABDENNORRS San Bernardo
AABDFIIINPS spina bifida
AABDGGGHINN handbagging
AABDHIKLNOY bank holiday
AABDHIOSTTV Bodhisattva
AABDIILLTUY laudability
AABDIILMQRU liquidambar
AABDILMMNSU dumb animals
AABDILNOUVY unavoidably
AABDILOORRS boardsailor
AABDILOQRSU squail-board
AABDIMNORTU adumbration
AABDIMNRRSU barramundis
AABDMOORRRT mortarboard
AABDNOOPRSX Pandora's box
AABEEEEGRRV eager beaver
AABEEEEKLST seakale beet
AABEEEFKRRS safe-breaker
AABEEEGLLTU league table
AABEEEHLLNW baleen whale
AABEEEKSTVW basket weave
AABEEELNPRT panel beater
AABEEERRRTW Water-bearer
AABEEFFLLPT baffle plate
AABEEFKRRST breakfaster
AABEEGHILNR Belgian hare
AABEEGILNRT talebearing
AABEEGLLNSV slave-bangle
AABEEGLNOSV noble savage
AABEEGLNTTU unget-at-able
AABEEHILNTZ Elizabethan
AABEEHILPTZ alphabetize
AABEEHIRRRT heat barrier
AABEEHKLNSU unshakeable
AABEEHKLRRT halter-break
AABEEHLRSTV harvestable
AABEEHLRSTY breathalyse
AABEEIILLNN inalienable
AABEEILLNNU unalienable
AABEEILLNPX explainable
AABEEILLNRT inalterable
AABEEILMNSS amiableness
AABEEILNPRS inseparable
AABEEILORTV elaborative
AABEEILPRRR irreparable
AABEEINRRRT train-bearer
AABEEINRRST brain-teaser
AABEEKKMRST basket-maker
AABEEKLLNSU unslakeable
AABEEKLNPSU unspeakable
AABEEKSSTTW wastebasket
AABEELLLMNU unmalleable
AABEELLMNOT balletomane
AABEELLNRTU unalterable
AABEELLORTY elaborately
AABEELLPRRY pearl barley
AABEELLPRSU pleasurable
AABEELMPRTU perambulate
AABEELMPTTT attemptable
AABEELNORST treasonable
AABEELNRTTU entablature, untreatable
AABEELPRSTT breastplate
AABEELRRSTV traversable
AABEELRRTWY barley water
AABEFFIILLS falsifiable
AABEFGIILMN magnifiable
AABEFHILNOS fashionable
AABEFIILLQU qualifiable
AABEFIILSST satisfiable
AABEFILLMMN inflammable
AABEFILMNOT lifeboatman
AABEFLLNPPU unflappable
AABEFLNORUV unfavorable
AABEGGILMNT gaming table
AABEGHORTTW hot-water bag
AABEGIILNNS Albigensian
AABEGIINPRS base pairing
AABEGIKLNRW lawbreaking
AABEGILNNUV unnavigable
AABEGILNORZ organizable
AABEGIRRRTU arbitrageur
AABEGLNORRR barrel organ
AABEGLNPRSU ungraspable
AABEGLRRSUY barley sugar
AABEHILNRST tarnishable
AABEHILORUV behavioural
AABEHKLNSUY unshakeably
AABEHKORRRW brake harrow
AABEHLORRSU harbour seal
AABEHLPRRSV phrasal verb
AABEIILLMSS assimilable
AABEIILLNNY inalienably
AABEIILLSTY saleability
AABEIILMMOR memorabilia
AABEIILMNTY amenability
AABEIILMRUX bulimarexia
AABEIILMTTY tameability

AABEIILNRRT libertarian
AABEIILNSSX Aix-les-Bains
AABEIILRTTY rateability
AABEIILRTWY wearability
AABEIKLNNPT table napkin
AABEIKMNORT embarkation
AABEIKNORSS banksia rose
AABEILLLRTY bilaterally
AABEILLMNPU manipulable
AABEILLNPRT paintballer
AABEILLNRTY inalterably
AABEILLOPRZ polarizable
AABEILLPSTY basipetally
AABEILLRRST liberal arts
AABEILLRRTZ trailblazer
AABEILLRVZZ Brazzaville
AABEILMNPRS Persian lamb
AABEILNNRTU untrainable
AABEILNOORT elaboration
AABEILNPRSY inseparably
AABEILNSSTU sustainable
AABEILOPRVZ vaporizable
AABEILPRRRY irreparably
AABEILPRTYY play it by ear
AABEIMNRRTT arbitrament
AABEIOPPRTV approbative
AABEKLNPSUY unspeakably
AABELLLNOUW unallowable
AABELLLOSWW swallowable
AABELLNRTUY unalterably
AABELLOPPRT ballot paper
AABELLORSUV slave labour
AABELLORTTY battle royal
AABELLPRSUY pleasurably
AABELLRRTUV barrel vault
AABELNOOPTY paleobotany
AABELNORSTY treasonably
AABELNOSTUY beauty salon
AABELOPRRTY portrayable
AABELPRSSSU surpassable
AABFHILNOSY fashionably
AABFIKNORSU Burkina Faso
AABFILLMMNY inflammably
AABFLLNPPUY unflappably
AABGHILNOOP Anglophobia
AABGIILNOST sailing boat
AABGIKNNSSV savings bank
AABGILMNRSU submarginal
AABGINSSSSU assassin bug
AABHIILSTWY washability
AABHIINOTTU habituation
AABHILLLORT Blair Atholl
AABHIMNPSST batsmanship
AABHLLLOOSU hullabaloos
AABIIILRTVY variability
AABIILLPPTY palpability
AABIILLPTYY playability
AABIILMNRUU albuminuria
AABIILNORTV vibrational
AABIILORSTU atrabilious
AABIILRRRTY arbitrarily
AABIIMNNOOT abomination
AABIINORRTT arbitration
AABIJLNOSSY job analysis
AABILLOSSWW wassail-bowl
AABILLRSUXY subaxillary
AABILMNORTY abnormality
AABILNOOPRT probational
AABILNORTUY ablutionary
AABILNSSTTU substantial
AABILNSSTUY sustainably
AABINOOPPRT approbation
AABLMNOORRW Warrnambool
AABLNNORRTU natural-born
AABLNPRRSUW urban sprawl
AABLOPRRTUY Labour Party
AABMORRSTTU masturbator
AABOOPPRRTY approbatory
AACCCDHIILR radical chic
AACCCDIILRY acrylic acid
AACCCEENTTU acute accent
AACCCEILPTT cataplectic
AACCCEILRSS classic race
AACCCEINORT Arctic Ocean
AACCCEJKKRR crackerjack
AACCCGHIOPR cacographic
AACCCIIILRT cicatricial
AACCCILMSTY cataclysmic
AACCCNNOTUY accountancy
AACCDEEILNR accelerandi
AACCDEELLNT cancellated
AACCDEELNOR accelerando
AACCDEIILLT dialectical
AACCDEIILRV valeric acid
AACCDEIIMMS academicism
AACCDEIIPRR pericardiac
AACCDEIIRST stearic acid
AACCDEILLNR calendrical
AACCDEILOPY cyclopaedia
AACCDEMMOOT accommodate
AACCDGIIILN alginic acid
AACCDGILLNR calling card
AACCDHIINTX xanthic acid
AACCDIIILRT diacritical
AACCDIOSSTU caustic soda
AACCDMOPRSS compass card
AACCEEFILNT calefacient
AACCEEFKRRS safe-cracker
AACCEEGNRTV grave accent
AACCEEHRSST catachreses
AACCEEILPSS special case
AACCEEINRRT incarcerate
AACCEEINRTV revaccinate
AACCEELLRTU recalculate
AACCEELORRT accelerator
AACCEENNOTT concatenate
AACCEFHSTTY safety catch
AACCEFILSTU fasciculate
AACCEGHILNR archangelic
AACCEGHOPRR cacographer
AACCEGIKNPS packing case
AACCEGILMOR acromegalic
AACCEGILORT categorical
AACCEGIMPRT magic carpet
AACCEHHMOST stomach-ache
AACCEHHPRST catchphrase
AACCEHIIMNN mechanician
AACCEHILMOT machicolate
AACCEHILMST catechismal
AACCEHIRSST catachresis

AACCEHKLRST crash-tackle
AACCEHLNNNO nonchalance
AACCEIIIMRU amici curiae
AACCEIILMTZ acclimatize
AACCEIKLNSV Salk vaccine
AACCEILLSTY ascetically
AACCEILLTUV calculative
AACCEILMPRT malpractice
AACCEILNNOT cancelation
AACCEILORSS accessorial
AACCEINNORT anacreontic
AACCEINOPSV Canopic vase
AACCEINOPTT acceptation
AACCEINQTTU acquittance
AACCEKKTYYY yackety-yack
AACCEKLLNOY cycloalkane
AACCELMNUUV vacuum-clean
AACCELPRSTU spectacular
AACCELRTTUU acculturate
AACCENNORRS Saracen corn
AACCENNORSS Carcassonne
AACCFIIILRS sacrificial
AACCFIILLPY pacifically
AACCFIILRTY farcicality
AACCGHHIIMN chimichanga
AACCGHIIPRS sciagraphic
AACCGILLNTU calculating
AACCHHIINTU t'ai chi ch'uan
AACCHIIMRST charismatic
AACCHIINRST anarchistic
AACCHIINRTT anthracitic
AACCHILLOTY chaotically
AACCHILMNOR monarchical
AACCHILNOTU anacoluthic
AACCIILLSTY sciatically
AACCIILMNOT acclimation
AACCIILMPRT impractical
AACCIILNNOT calcination
AACCIILNSTT cisatlantic
AACCIILSSTU casuistical
AACCIILSTTT stalactitic
AACCIINNOTV vaccination
AACCIINOSTU acoustician
AACCIINTTVY Vatican City
AACCILLLNOY laconically
AACCILLLSSY classically
AACCILLNNOY canonically
AACCILLNOTU calculation
AACCILLNRTU curtain call
AACCILLPRTY practically
AACCILLSTUY caustically
AACCILNNNOU uncanonical
AACCILNPRTU unpractical
AACCILNSTTY syntactical
AACCILOPPTY apocalyptic
AACCILOPSUY capaciously
AACCILRRSUW circular saw
AACCIMNOPST accompanist
AACCINOORTT coarctation
AACCIORRSTY aristocracy
AACCLMORTUU accumulator
AACCLNORTTU contractual
AACCMOORRSZ Occam's razor
AACCORRSTTY stratocracy
AACDDDEEHOR dodecahedra
AACDDEEEHLR clear-headed
AACDDEEIMPS aides-de-camp
AACDDEHINPP handicapped
AACDDEINRTU candidature
AACDDEIPRRS Cedar Rapids
AACDDIJORTU adjudicator
AACDEEEFLSW weasel-faced
AACDEEEHHRT head teacher
AACDEEFILRR free radical
AACDEEHILMX hexadecimal
AACDEEHIMNR Archimedean
AACDEEHRRST Sacred Heart
AACDEEILRTV declarative
AACDEEILSTT elasticated
AACDEEIMORV video camera
AACDEEJKTWX waxed jacket
AACDEELLSTT castellated
AACDEELNRSY denary scale
AACDEEMNNTV advancement
AACDEENPRRS parascender
AACDEENQRSU square dance
AACDEFILNOT defalcation
AACDEFINRSU fricandeaus
AACDEFINRUX fricandeaux
AACDEGGILOP pedagogical
AACDEGGIORR carriage dog
AACDEGIIMNT diamagnetic
AACDEGLRTTU cattle guard
AACDEGORSTU sugar-coated
AACDEHIILNS ladies' chain
AACDEHILORS icosahedral
AACDEHINOTT anticathode
AACDEHINPPR handicapper
AACDEHINRST cantharides
AACDEHNNOTT non-attached
AACDEHPRRRS card-sharper
AACDEIILMRT diametrical
AACDEIILMRV vice admiral
AACDEIILPRR pericardial
AACDEIINNNO Indian Ocean
AACDEIINNNR incarnadine
AACDEIINORT eradication
AACDEIIORTV radioactive
AACDEIIPRST paediatrics
AACDEIIPRSU parasuicide
AACDEILMNOT declamation
AACDEILNORT declaration, redactional
AACDEILNOTU educational
AACDEILNPRS Iceland spar
AACDEILNRSS radicalness
AACDEILRSTT strait-laced
AACDEIMNORT demarcation
AACDEIMNORY aerodynamic
AACDEIOPRTT decapitator
AACDEIORTTV deactivator
AACDELMNNOR Roman candle
AACDELMORST closet drama
AACDELMORTY declamatory
AACDELNPTTY pentadactyl
AACDELORRTY declaratory
AACDELRTTTY tetradactyl
AACDEMNNOPR Ordnance map
AACDENPSTTU cut-and-paste
AACDFIILRRT fratricidal
AACDGHIOPRR cardiograph

AACDGIILNRS radical sign
AACDGILNPRY card-playing, playing card
AACDGIMRRTU dramaturgic
AACDGNNOOTY contango day
AACDHIIOPRS aphrodisiac
AACDHIKLLNO kachina doll
AACDHILMOPY holiday camp
AACDHILOPRS rhapsodical
AACDHIMNNSW sandwich-man
AACDHMOPRSY psychodrama
AACDHNQSSTU snatch squad
AACDIILLRTY triadically
AACDIILMNRU adminicular
AACDIILMPRY pyramidical
AACDIILNOTU acidulation
AACDIILNSTV vandalistic
AACDIILORTT dictatorial
AACDIIMNOPS dipsomaniac
AACDIIOPRTY radiopacity
AACDIJNNORT cardan joint
AACDILLMNOY nomadically
AACDILLMNYY dynamically
AACDILLNORS coral island
AACDILLRSTY drastically
AACDILNPSST landscapist
AACDILORTTY artiodactyl
AACDILOSSUX Caxias do Sul
AACDILOSUUY audaciously
AACDIMNNOTU manducation
AACDINNPPSS spic and span
AACDMNOORTU Cootamundra
AACDMNORTUY manducatory
AACDMOORSTU catadromous
AACEEEHLMOT haematocele
AACEEEHLRSW Chelsea ware
AACEEEIRRSV service area
AACEEENPRST Eastern Cape
AACEEFFLLNN face flannel
AACEEFFMNRT Raman effect
AACEEFGORRY year of grace
AACEEFIMNSS misfeasance
AACEEFINPRT face-painter
AACEEFIRRTV rarefactive
AACEEFIRSSW Caesar's wife
AACEEFLLPTT cleft palate
AACEEFNNNOS nonfeasance
AACEEGHLRST Castlereagh
AACEEGHNOPR chaperonage
AACEEGHRRST gatecrasher
AACEEGIKMNP peacemaking
AACEEGILLLY elegiacally
AACEEGILLNV evangelical
AACEEGOPRST scapegoater
AACEEHHMPTY chamaephyte
AACEEHIMNPT tape machine
AACEEHIMNVW wave machine
AACEEHINSTT anaesthetic
AACEEHKLLRS Lake Charles
AACEEHLNNSV clean-shaven
AACEEHLPPSW cashew apple
AACEEHRRTTT tetrarchate
AACEEIIMNRZ Americanize
AACEEIIMPST septicaemia
AACEEIKLSTT acetate silk
AACEEILLMNS miscellanea
AACEEILMMOT camomile tea
AACEEILNRTT intercalate
AACEEILRRST secretarial
AACEEIMNNNT maintenance
AACEEIMNVWX Mexican wave
AACEEINNNRT centenarian
AACEEINNRRT reincarnate
AACEEINNRSS necessarian, Renaissance
AACEEIPRRTV prevaricate
AACEEIRRRVW carrier wave
AACEEIRRSST tracasserie
AACEEIRRSTT secretariat
AACEEJKMSTT steam-jacket
AACEEKLMPRT market place
AACEELLLTUV valleculate
AACEELNPSTU encapsulate
AACEELNTTTU tentaculate
AACEELPRRTY carpet layer
AACEELPRSTV space travel
AACEELQRRUW lacquerware
AACEENRRSSU reassurance
AACEFFHINRS affranchise
AACEFFIIIRS fieri facias
AACEFFILNOT affectional
AACEFFINOTT affectation
AACEFFIOSSY assay office
AACEFGHINRR far-reaching
AACEFGLOOTT cottage loaf
AACEFHMSTTY safety match
AACEFIILNRT interfacial
AACEFIILNRV acriflavine
AACEFILLNSU final clause
AACEFILMNOT malefaction
AACEFILMRSU surface mail
AACEFILTTUV facultative
AACEFINORRT rarefaction
AACEFINORSU farinaceous
AACEFINORTT fractionate
AACEFLNPSUU saucepanful
AACEFLNSSTU factualness
AACEFMNRTUU manufacture
AACEFORRSTT fast reactor
AACEGGIKNPR repackaging
AACEGGILPTU Tegucigalpa
AACEGGINRRU gun carriage
AACEGGINRSV saving grace
AACEGGMUUUV vacuum gauge
AACEGHHNOTT chaetognath
AACEGHILOPR archipelago
AACEGHIMPRT graphematic
AACEGHLLMNS small change
AACEGHLLSSV cheval glass
AACEGHLOORY archaeology
AACEGHPRTTU gutta-percha
AACEGIILLPR periglacial
AACEGIILMNT enigmatical
AACEGIIMRRS miscarriage
AACEGILLLNY angelically
AACEGILLLOR allegorical
AACEGILLMNN name-calling
AACEGILLOOR aerological
AACEGILLOPS plagioclase
AACEGILMMNO megalomanic

AACEGILNPRY panegyrical
AACEGILOTUV coagulative
AACEGILRSTT strategical
AACEGIMMNRT engrammatic
AACEGIMNNOR cinema organ
AACEGIMNRTY city manager
AACEGIMQRSU magic square
AACEGINNRTW watering can
AACEGINPPRT rate-capping
AACEGINPSSV space-saving
AACEGKOPRTU package tour
AACEGLLLOPS plagal close
AACEGLNRRTU rectangular
AACEGMNOORR Graeco-Roman
AACEGRRSSTU caster sugar
AACEHIILMPT epithalamic
AACEHIILSTT atheistical
AACEHIIMMNS Manichaeism
AACEHILLMNO melancholia
AACEHILLNTU hallucinate
AACEHILLPTY aphetically
AACEHIMMSTT mathematics
AACEHIMNNOY haemocyanin
AACEHIMORTT haematocrit
AACEHIMOSTT haemostatic
AACEHKMRRRT Charter Mark
AACEHLLOPRY chapel royal
AACEHLLRSSW Charles's Law
AACEHLMNPRY parenchymal
AACEHLNOPRT anchor plate
AACEHLNOPTY polychaetan
AACEHLRRSST scarlet rash
AACEHMMNNRT merchantman
AACEHNNORST anthracnose
AACEHNOPRVY anchovy pear
AACEHOPRSTT catastrophe
AACEHOPSSTU spathaceous
AACEHPRRSTY search party
AACEHPRSTUX purchase tax
AACEIILLMNS misalliance
AACEIILLNRT lacertilian
AACEIILLRTV leviratical
AACEIILMRRR mail carrier
AACEIILNRRT interracial
AACEIIMMNRS Americanism
AACEIIMNNST semantician
AACEIIMNRTV carmlnatlve
AACEIIMQSTU semiaquatic
AACEIINORTT ratiocinate
AACEIIOSSTV associative
AACEIIPPRTT participate
AACEIJLNOTU ejaculation
AACEILLLSTY elastically
AACEILLMPRY miracle play
AACEILLNTTY tetanically
AACEILLPRRT caterpillar
AACEILLPTVY capital levy
AACEILLRRTY erratically
AACEILMNORT reclamation
AACEILMNOTX exclamation
AACEILMPSTT metaplastic
AACEILMRTTU matriculate
AACEILNNOSS ascensional
AACEILNNRTU anti-nuclear
AACEILNORTT altercation
AACEILNOSTU auction sale
AACEILNRRTY intercalary
AACEILOPSST Castile soap
AACEILPRTTU particulate, tau particle
AACEILRSUVZ vascularize
AACEILSTUVY causatively
AACEIMMOPRU paramoecium
AACEIMNNOTT contaminate
AACEIMNOORT erotomaniac
AACEIMNOPRT emancipator
AACEIMNORSU oceanariums
AACEIMOPRTV comparative
AACEINNORTT recantation
AACEINNRTTT interactant
AACEINORRTY reactionary
AACEINORSTU aeronautics
AACEIOPPRRT appreciator
AACEIOPRSTT aspect ratio
AACEJLORTUY ejaculatory
AACEKLMRSTY smart-alecky
AACELLLORTT total recall
AACELLOPRTY acropetally
AACELMORRSU scale armour
AACELMORSTU emasculator
AACELMORTXY exclamatory
AACELMRSSST masterclass
AACELNOOSSU solanaceous
AACELNORSTT translocate
AACELOOPPRS laparoscope
AACELPRSSTT plaster cast
AACELQRTUUU aquaculture
AACENNNORTW water-cannon
AACENOOPSSU saponaceous
AACFFIORRTT trafficator
AACFFMORRTY factory farm
AACFGIINNST fascinating
AACFHIORSTU South Africa
AACFHMORSSU forasmuch as
AACFIILLNNY financially
AACFIILNNOR Californian
AACFIILORTT facilitator
AACFIINNOST fascination
AACFILLNOTY factionally
AACFILLNRTY frantically
AACFILLORTY factorially
AACFINORRTY fractionary
AACFKLMSUUV vacuum flask
AACFMNORSTW craftswoman
AACFMNORTUY manufactory
AACGGILLLOO algological
AACGGILNOSY synagogical
AACGGILNOTU cataloguing
AACGHHPRTYY tachygraphy
AACGHIKMMNT matchmaking
AACGHIKMNTW watchmaking
AACGHILLPRY calligraphy, graphically
AACGHINPPRY Phrygian cap
AACGHIOPRTU autographic
AACGHIPRRST graphic arts
AACGHLMOORU chaulmoogra
AACGHNOOPRR coronagraph
AACGHOPRRTY cartography
AACGHOPRSSU sarcophagus
AACGIILMNNS Anglicanism
AACGIILMSTT stalagmitic

AACGIILNNOR Carolingian
AACGIINOSTT castigation
AACGIJNNRTU jaunting car
AACGIKLNRTY track-laying
AACGILLNORY organically
AACGILLNPTY placatingly
AACGILLOPST postglacial
AACGILMNOOR agronomical
AACGILNOOTU coagulation
AACGILNORSS cors anglais
AACGILOSSUY sagaciously
AACGIMNNRST canting arms
AACGIMNSTTY syntagmatic
AACGINORSST nasogastric
AACGINPRVYZ crazy paving
AACGIORSTTY castigatory
AACGLLNOOTY octagonally
AACGLMNOOPY campanology
AACGORRSSTU castor sugar
AACHHHIKSSU shakuhachis
AACHHIIMPPT amphipathic
AACHIIINRST Christiania
AACHIIMNNOT machination
AACHIIMNSST shamanistic
AACHIINPPST captainship
AACHIINRSSU saurischian
AACHILLLLPY phallically
AACHILLNNTU hallucinant
AACHILLOPRY parochially
AACHIMMNOTY mythomaniac
AACHIMMORST achromatism
AACHIMNNORS anachronism
AACHIMNORRU chain armour
AACHIPRSTTU parachutist
AACHLLLORSW shawl collar
AACHLMORRTY lachrymator
AACHLNNOOTU anacoluthon
AACHMMRRSUU harum-scarum
AACHMNNOORW anchorwoman
AACHMNOSTWY yachtswoman
AACHQRTTUWZ quartz watch
AACIIILNNOT laciniation
AACIIILNOTZ laicization
AACIIILPPRT participial
AACIIJNOTTT jactitation
AACIIKLPRST risk capital
AACIILLMMSY miasmically
AACIILLMNRW criminal law
AACIILLMRTU multiracial
AACIILLNOTV vacillation
AACIILLNTTY titanically
AACIILLPRTY capillarity, piratically
AACIILLRSTY satirically
AACIILMNORT lacrimation
AACIILMNOST anomalistic
AACIILMNRRW war criminal
AACIILMNSTT Atlanticism
AACIILNOPPT application
AACIILNPRTU puritanical
AACIILNPTTY antitypical
AACIILNSTTT Atlanticist
AACIILOPRST piscatorial
AACIILSSTTT statistical
AACIIMNNORT animatronic
AACIIMNOSTT mastication
AACIIMORTTY aromaticity
AACIINNNORT incarnation
AACIINNNOTT incantation
AACIINOOSST association
AACIINOPRTT anticipator
AACIINOPTTV captivation
AACIINORTTV vaticinator
AACIINOSTTV vacationist
AACIINPPRTT participant
AACILLLPSTY plastically
AACILLMOSTY somatically
AACILLNOPRS rapscallion
AACILLNRTUW curtain wall
AACILLOPRSY prosaically
AACILLOSSUY salaciously
AACILLPRTUU apicultural
AACILLPSSTY spastically
AACILMNNOPT complainant
AACILMNOOTX taxonomical
AACILMNOPST complaisant
AACILMNORTU calumniator
AACILMNORTY lacrymation
AACILMPPRSY Paralympics
AACILNOOTUV vacuolation
AACILNOPRTY coplanarity
AACILNORTVY clairvoyant
AACILOPRSUY rapaciously
AACILOPRTTU capitulator
AACILORRTTU articulator
AACILORRTUY oracularity
AACILPRSSTT plastic arts
AACILRSTUVY vascularity
AACIMNNNOTT contaminant
AACIMNPRSTT transit camp
AACIMORSTTY masticatory
AACINNNORTU annunciator
AACINNORSTT transaction
AACINNORTTY incantatory
AACINNRRSTU transuranic
AACLMMOPSSY mycoplasmas
AACLNNNOOST consonantal
AACLOOPPRSY laparoscopy
AACMNOPRTUY paramountcy
AACMOORSSTU sarcomatous
AACNRSSTTUW Tuscan straw
AADDDEIILPT dilapidated
AADDDEILRRT tarradiddle
AADDDENNRST end standard
AADDEEGHNNR hand grenade
AADDEEGIRTV degradative
AADDEEHHNVY heavy-handed
AADDEEHHRRT hard-hearted
AADDEEHLPRY paraldehyde
AADDEEIKLNS naked ladies
AADDEEILRSY sidereal day
AADDEEPRRSS dress parade
AADDEGILLNY leading lady
AADDEGINNNP deadpanning
AADDEGINORT degradation
AADDEHHLMNY ham-handedly
AADDEILNPTY painted lady
AADDEINRSTZ standardize
AADDEJLMSTU maladjusted
AADDELPQRUU quadrupedal
AADDFIORSTV Star of David

AADDGHILNNR hard landing
AADDGHLORTU load draught
AADDGINPRRS Grand Rapids
AADDIIINNRT Trinidadian
AADDILLOOPR olla podrida
AADDNNNORST non-standard
AADEEEFHHRT feather-head
AADEEEGLPRS spread eagle
AADEEEHMRST East Dereham
AADEEELNRSV sea lavender
AADEEFHHLRT half-hearted
AADEEFHOSTT head of state
AADEEGHLNOT halogenated
AADEEGIMRRT tree diagram
AADEEGINPSU spade guinea
AADEEGPRSTU depasturage
AADEEHHLPRT heptahedral
AADEEHLNNRT Neanderthal
AADEEHLNPRT pentahedral
AADEEHLRRTT tetrahedral
AADEEHLRTTT death rattle
AADEEHMRRTW warm-hearted
AADEEHNRSVW heavenwards
AADEEILMNOO Aeolian mode
AADEEILNNRX alexandrine
AADEEILNRRV red valerian
AADEEILNRTX alexandrite
AADEEINRSTT tear-stained
AADEEIRRTTV retardative
AADEEIRSTVV adversative
AADEELPRSTT trade plates
AADEELRRSTV slave trader
AADEEMORTWW water-meadow
AADEEMQRRSU masquerader
AADEENPRSTU unseparated
AADEENRRTTT tare and tret
AADEENRSWYY New Year's Day
AADEEORRTWY ready-to-wear
AADEESSTTTY steady state
AADEFGHNRRT grandfather
AADEFGLORRT deflagrator
AADEFGLORSU sugar of lead
AADEFIKLNNR rank and file
AADEFLMNNTU fundamental
AADEFLSSTTY steadfastly
AADEFNSSTTU unsteadfast
AADEGGGLLLY lallygagged
AADEGGHNRSS haggardness
AADEGGILNNR landing gear
AADEGGINRRZ aggrandizer
AADEGGLNRSS laggardness
AADEGHIKLNT talking head
AADEGHINRRW hard-wearing
AADEGIILNTT intagliated
AADEGIILPTW pied wagtail
AADEGIKMNRW waking dream
AADEGILLNNP pineal gland
AADEGILNNRV landgravine
AADEGILNOTW long-awaited
AADEGILNPRT plantigrade
AADEGILNPRY play-reading
AADEGIMNNRV Venn diagram
AADEGINSTTV devastating
AADEGKLRSSS dark glasses
AADEGLNRSSU gradualness
AADEGMNRRST grand master
AADEGMORSSW meadow grass
AADEGNNPRRT grandparent
AADEGNPRRTY garden party
AADEHIILOPP paedophilia
AADEHINOPPY hypnopaedia
AADEHLMNSUY unashamedly
AADEHPRSSTT spatterdash
AADEIIIRRTV irradiative
AADEIILMNST mediastinal
AADEIILNOTV deviational
AADEILLNNRT rallentandi
AADEILLNOST allantoides
AADEILLRRSS serradillas
AADEILMMORY Memorial Day
AADEILMOORV viola d'amore
AADEILMPRST spermatidal
AADEILNNQRU quadrennial
AADEILNOOPR Adrianopole
AADEILNOTUV devaluation
AADEILNPPRR pre-prandial
AADEILOPRTZ trapezoidal
AADEILORRTV advertorial
AADEILPRSTY disparately
AADEIMMNRST disarmament
AADEIMNNPRZ marzipanned
AADEIMNRSTV maidservant
AADEINOPRTV depravation
AADEINORRTT retardation
AADEINOSTTV devastation
AADEIOOPQRU radio-opaque
AADEIPSSTWW wasp-waisted
AADEKNRSSWW awkwardness
AADELLMNSTY lady's mantle
AADELLNNORT rallentando
AADELMMOPSS plasmodesma
AADELMNOPST almond paste
AADELMNORST Aldermaston
AADELNPRSTU pastureland
AADELORRTTU adulterator
AADEMNORSTW tradeswoman
AADENNRRTUW unwarranted
AADENRSSWWY waywardness
AADENRSTTUU unsaturated
AADEORRRTTY retardatory
AADFFORRSTW fast forward
AADFGHHNNOU Afghan hound
AADFGHILLNN half-landing
AADFGILMORW flow diagram
AADFGILNORR grandiflora
AADFHHILLOY half holiday
AADFLLLOOSY All Fools' Day
AADFLNOORTU natural food
AADFMNORSST stand of arms
AADGGIILNPR paragliding
AADGGIIMMNR diagramming
AADGGOOOUUU Ouagadougou
AADGHHIILMR High Admiral
AADGHHILMNN Highlandman
AADGHHILRTZ hazard light
AADGHHOPRSW shadowgraph
AADGHINOSSW washing soda
AADGHIOPRRY radiography
AADGHMNRSTU draughtsman
AADGIILMRST madrigalist

AADGIILNNNO Anglo-Indian
AADGIINNRST grants-in-aid
AADGIJKNNOU Danjiangkou
AADGIJNRSUU jaguarundis
AADGIKLLNWY walking lady
AADGILMNSSU salmagundis
AADHIILMPRS admiralship
AADHIIOPRSS Aphrodisias
AADHINNOSTT station hand
AADHIOPPRTY paratyphoid
AADHIOPRRTY parathyroid
AADHJMNRRUY Rajahmundry
AADHKNOORTT North Dakota
AADHKOOSTTU South Dakota
AADHLORSUYZ hazardously
AADHNOPQRUY quadraphony
AADIIINNNOR Indo-Iranian
AADIIINORRT irradiation
AADIIJNOTUZ Judaization
AADIILLNTTU altitudinal, latitudinal
AADIILNOOTX oxidational
AADIILNORTT traditional
AADIILNTTTU attitudinal
AADIILOSUUV audio-visual
AADIINNORSU dinosaurian
AADIINNOTTX antioxidant
AADIINOSTTV idiot savant
AADILLMNNOY madonna lily
AADILLMNOOT amontillado
AADILLMORTY maladroitly
AADILLMPRYY pyramidally
AADILMNORTY mandatorily
AADILMOPRRU parlourmaid
AADILOORSTV vasodilator
AADILOPPRSV disapproval
AADIMNNOPRS prima donnas
AADLLLOSSUY All Souls' Day
AADMNORSSTU Nostradamus
AAEEEFFLMMT femme fatale
AAEEEGGLNUY eye language
AAEEEGNSTTT estate agent
AAEEEGRSTWY steerage-way
AAEEEHLNPST sea elephant
AAEEEHLRRTW leatherwear
AAEEEHNRRTW earthenware
AAEEEHNRTVW weathervane
AAEEEHRRTTW water heater
AAEEEMNPPST appeasement
AAEEEMPRSTU tape-measure
AAEEENNRRST Near Eastern
AAEEFFGHLRT flag-feather
AAEEFFGILLO foliage leaf
AAEEFGHLMRT Magherafelt
AAEEFGMRRRW germ warfare
AAEEFHHILRT faith healer
AAEEFHILRTT tail feather
AAEEFHMRRRS share-farmer
AAEEFILMRRT Fleet Air Arm
AAEEFKMRRTT aftermarket
AAEEFLSTVVY safety valve
AAEEGGGIRTV aggregative
AAEEGGGNNRS gas gangrene
AAEEGGIMNRV graven image
AAEEGGINNRW wage-earning
AAEEGGLMORT agglomerate
AAEEGGNOORS Osage orange
AAEEGGORRTX exaggerator
AAEEGHHMORR haemorrhage
AAEEGHLOOPS oesophageal
AAEEGHNPPRR paperhanger
AAEEGIKLNTV leave-taking
AAEEGILLLTT tagliatelle
AAEEGILMNNR line manager
AAEEGILMNTT latent image
AAEEGILMSSX sexagesimal
AAEEGILNRSV Salve Regina
AAEEGILPRTT tetraplegia
AAEEGINPRST greasepaint
AAEEGINRRTW graniteware
AAEEGJLMORU major league
AAEEGKNRRST garter snake
AAEEGLLLSVY galley slave
AAEEGLMMRSU rummage sale
AAEEGLNNORV navel orange
AAEEGLNNPTT Plantagenet
AAEEGLNRTTV travel agent
AAEEGLPRSTY Pearly Gates
AAEEGMNNRRT arrangement
AAEEGMNOPRT pomegranate
AAEEGMNSSTU assuagement
AAEEGRRTVWY watery grave
AAEEHHLNNPT naphthalene
AAEEHHLRSTW wash-leather
AAEEHIMMNPT amphetamine
AAEEHIPRSST paresthesia
AAEEHKMOPTY take-home pay
AAEEHLNPTTV heptavalent
AAEEHMMMRST steam hammer
AAEEHMMRRTW water hammer
AAEEHMNOORR amenorrhoea
AAEEIILLTVV alleviative
AAEEIILMRTZ materialize
AAEEIILRRTZ arterialize
AAEEIILRTTV retaliative
AAEEIKLLMRT alkalimeter
AAEEILLLNRT lateral line
AAEEILLNOTV elevational
AAEEILLPPTV appellative
AAEEILLQRTU equilateral
AAEEILMNNPT enamel paint
AAEEILNRTTV alternative
AAEEIMPRRTZ parametrize
AAEEIMSSTTZ metastasize
AAEEINRRSTT tea-strainer
AAEEIOPRTVV evaporative
AAEEIPPRRTV preparative
AAEEKKMMRRT market maker
AAEEKLMRTUV market value
AAEEKLNRSTT rattlesnake
AAEELLLMNOS salmonellae
AAEELLNRTTY alternately
AAEELNNPTTV pentavalent
AAEELNPRTTY penalty rate
AAEELNPSSTT pleasantest
AAEELNPSTTT pantalettes
AAEELNPSTTV septavalent
AAEELNRRSTT retranslate
AAEELNRTTTV tetravalent
AAEELOPRTTX extrapolate
AAEEMQRSSTU marquessate

AAEENNRSSUW unawareness
AAEFFIIILTV affiliative
AAEFFIIMRTV affirmative
AAEFGHILNRT farthingale
AAEFGIKLLNW walking leaf
AAEFGLLLORT flagellator
AAEFGLSSSTY safety glass
AAEFGMNRRTY fragmentary
AAEFHILLNWY halfway line
AAEFHILNRTW father-in-law
AAEFHKLNNRT Frankenthal
AAEFIIILMRZ familiarize
AAEFIIORRSV savoir faire
AAEFILLNRTU natural life
AAEFILMMNRT firmamental
AAEFILMNRTY filamentary
AAEFILOPRRT prefatorial
AAEFLLNRRTY fraternally
AAEFLMORTTW matter of law
AAEFLNORTUW law of nature
AAEFLNRRRST transferral
AAEFNNRRRST transfer RNA
AAEFORRSTYZ safety razor
AAEGGGINORT aggregation
AAEGGIIMNTW waiting game
AAEGGILNNVZ navel-gazing
AAEGGILNTTU agglutinate
AAEGGIMMNTU gametangium
AAEGGINRSTU strain gauge
AAEGGLMMORU grammalogue
AAEGGNORRUW narrow gauge
AAEGHIMNORR menorrhagia
AAEGHIMNPRS managership
AAEGHLMOOTY haematology
AAEGHLMRSSW Gresham's law
AAEGHLOPPRY paleography
AAEGHMOPRRS phraseogram
AAEGHMRTTUU thaumaturge
AAEGHNOPRTY Pythagorean
AAEGHNPRRST straphanger
AAEGIIIMNTV imaginative
AAEGIILMNPS Pelagianism
AAEGIILMNRZ marginalize
AAEGIILMRST magisterial
AAEGIILPRRZ plagiarizer
AAEGIIMMRRS mismarriage
AAEGIINNNRT Argentinian
AAEGIINNOTV evagination
AAEGIINORTV variegation
AAEGIKMNPPR papermaking
AAEGIKMNPST masking tape
AAEGILLLNPR paralleling
AAEGILLNPPR apparelling
AAEGILLNPPY appealingly
AAEGILLNSUV visual angle
AAEGILMMNOS Maglemosian
AAEGILMNRTY ligamentary
AAEGILNNPPU unappealing
AAEGILNNSST East Lansing
AAEGILNOORZ Zielona Gora
AAEGILNQRUU equiangular
AAEGILNRTTU triangulate
AAEGIMNNRRT arraignment
AAEGIMNNSSZ amazingness
AAEGIOPPRTV propagative
AAEGIOPSTTY steatopygia
AAEGLLORSSU sausage roll
AAEGLMMRRSS grammarless
AAEGLMOPRRU parlour game
AAEGLNRRSSV vernal grass
AAEGLNRSTTU strangulate
AAEGMMOPRSY agamospermy
AAEHHHJOPST Jehoshaphat
AAEHHIILMOP haemophilia
AAEHHIKNRRS Hare Krishna
AAEHHOPPSST phosphatase
AAEHIIMNOPS hemianopsia
AAEHILNOSTT East Lothian
AAEHILPPRSY hyperplasia
AAEHIMOSSST haemostasis
AAEHKMNRSSS shanks's mare
AAEHLPRRSWY prayer shawl
AAEHLPRSSTW water-splash
AAEHMMORSST atom smasher
AAEHMNNRTUU human nature
AAEHMNORSTT tam-o'-shanter
AAEHMNORSWW washerwoman
AAEHMOPRTTU thaumatrope
AAEHRRSSTTU Arthur's Seat
AAEIILLMNNR millenarian
AAEIILLMNRT matrilineal
AAEIILLNOTV alleviation
AAEIILLNPRT patrilineal
AAEIILLPRST ipsilateral
AAEIILMMRST materialism
AAEIILMNNTY inanimately
AAEIILMNRRT air terminal
AAEIILMPRTV imperatival
AAEIILMRSTT materialist
AAEIILMRTTY materiality
AAEIILNNOTZ nationalize
AAEIILNNPST Palestinian
AAEIILNORTT retaliation
AAEIILNORTZ rationalize, realization
AAEIILPPRSS paraleipsis
AAEIILQTTUV qualitative
AAEIIMNNORT reanimation
AAEIIMNNOTX examination
AAEIIMNRSST Erastianism
AAEIINNSTTT instantiate
AAEIINOPTTX expatiation
AAEIINOSTTV aestivation
AAEIKLLMRTY alkalimetry
AAEIKLLTTVY talkatively
AAEIKLMNOPT kleptomania
AAEIKLMRSTT Sterlitamak
AAEIKLPRRRT trailer park
AAEILLLMPRS parallelism
AAEILLLOSTV sal volatile
AAEILLMRTVV mitral valve
AAEILLNNPTY Tin Pan Alley
AAEILLNOPPT appellation
AAEILLORTTU ratatouille
AAEILLORTVY alleviatory
AAEILMMNRST maternalism
AAEILMMORRW war memorial
AAEILMNNOTT lamentation
AAEILMNORRY Royal Marine
AAEILMNPRST paternalism
AAEILMNPRTU planetarium

AAEILMNRRTU ultramarine
AAEILMOORRT ameliorator
AAEILMOPRTV Parma violet
AAEILNNOPTX explanation
AAEILNNORTT alternation
AAEILNNOSST sensational
AAEILNNOTTT attentional
AAEILNNPRST transalpine
AAEILNNPTTU antenuptial
AAEILNOOPRT operational
AAEILNOPPRY piano player, player-piano
AAEILNOPRRT proletarian
AAEILNORTUV revaluation
AAEILNOSSTY seasonality
AAEILNPRSST partialness
AAEILNPRSTT paternalist
AAEILNRRTTU nature trail
AAEILNRRTVY narratively
AAEILOPRRTT proletariat
AAEILOQRSTU quaestorial
AAEILORRTTY retaliatory
AAEIMNNRRST transmarine
AAEIMOPPRTX approximate
AAEIMRRSSTT air mattress
AAEINNOPRTT trepanation
AAEINNOSTTT nation state
AAEINNOTTTU attenuation
AAEINNRRSVY anniversary
AAEINNSTTTU antitetanus
AAEINOOPRTV evaporation
AAEINOPPRRT preparation
AAEINOPQRSU square piano
AAEINOSTTTT attestation
AAEIOPPPRRT appropriate
AAEIOPRTTXY expatiatory
AAEIORSSTTV assortative
AAEJLMNOPRT major planet
AAEJLNNRSTW lantern jaws
AAELLMMORRY marmoreally
AAELLOPSSTT Elastoplast
AAELMNPQTUU quantum leap
AAELMNSSTTY statesmanly
AAELMOPRRTU plate armour
AAELNNORTTU natural note
AAELNNRSSTU naturalness
AAELNOPRTXY explanatory
AAELNORSSTV naval stores
AAELNORSSTY royal assent
AAELNRRSSTV transversal
AAELNRSSTUX transsexual
AAELOPPRTTU Puerto Plata
AAEMMNORSST master mason
AAEMNOOSSST anastomoses
AAEMNOPRTTU portmanteau
AAEMNOSSTTW stateswoman
AAEMOOPRSTZ spermatozoa
AAEMORSSTTT toastmaster
AAENNPPRTTU appurtenant
AAENNPRRSTT transparent
AAENNPRSTTU supernatant
AAEOOPPRRRT paratrooper
AAEOPPQRRTU quarto paper
AAEOPPRRRTY preparatory
AAEOPRSSTTU stratopause
AAFFGGIMNRU raggamuffin
AAFFIIILNOT affiliation
AAFFIIMNORT affirmation
AAFFIMORRTY affirmatory
AAFGGGGILNW flag-wagging
AAFGGINRTWX grafting wax
AAFGHILNNOU Fionnghuala
AAFGIINNPRS frangipanis
AAFGIKMNNRT tank-farming
AAFGILLMRUY gallimaufry
AAFGILLNRST falling star
AAFGILNOSTT flag-station, stagflation
AAFGINORRSU farraginous
AAFIIILMRTY familiarity
AAFIINNOTTU infatuation
AAFILLMORYY royal family
AAFILMNOORT formational
AAFIMNNNRTY infantryman
AAFINNOOPRT profanation
AAFKLPRSTYY flaky pastry
AAFRRSSTTYY artsy-fartsy
AAGGGHILNSU laughing gas
AAGGHHIINNS shanghaiing
AAGGHHIOPRY hagiography
AAGGHIIJMNT thingamajig
AAGGHILLNNW wall hanging
AAGGHINOPRY angiography
AAGGIKLMNSS glass-making
AAGGNNOORTU orang-outang
AAGHHLOPPRY haplography
AAGHIIINRRS hair-raising
AAGHILLMNRS marshalling
AAGHILNRSSY harassingly
AAGHIMNRSTT straight man
AAGHINOPSST Spanish goat
AAGHIOPRSTY hypogastria
AAGHIRSTTWY straightway
AAGHLNOOTTY thanatology
AAGHLNOPPRY planography
AAGHMMMOPRY mammography
AAGHMRTTUUY thaumaturgy
AAGHNOPRRUY uranography
AAGHNRTUUWW Wathawurung
AAGIIILMNRY imaginarily
AAGIIIMNNOT imagination
AAGIIKNNPST painstaking
AAGIILLLNWW Wailing Wall
AAGIILMNORT migrational
AAGIILMNRTY marginality
AAGIIMMNNTY magnanimity
AAGIIMMSSTT astigmatism
AAGIIMNNORT margination
AAGIIMSSSSU Mississauga
AAGIINNOSST assignation
AAGIINNPTWX wax-painting
AAGIINNSTUU Augustinian
AAGIINORTTV gravitation
AAGIINPRTUU Tupi-Guarani
AAGIINRTTVY anti-gravity
AAGIIRSSTTU Sagittarius
AAGILLLNPPY appallingly
AAGILLLOOSS glossolalia
AAGILLMNNTY malignantly
AAGILLNRTUV vulgar Latin
AAGILNNORTU granulation

AAGILNOPSTY	angioplasty
AAGILNOSUVY	Yugoslavian
AAGILNRRTUY	granularity
AAGILOPRRTU	purgatorial
AAGIMMNNOSU	magnanimous
AAGINOOPPRT	propagation
AAGINORRTUU	inaugurator
AAGLLLNNTUY	ungallantly
AAGLLMNRTUU	multangular
AAGLLNOOSUY	analogously
AAGLMNNNOOR	Anglo-Norman
AAGLNOOPRTW	patrol wagon
AAGLNOORRTY	narratology
AAGLORRTTUY	gratulatory
AAHHHLMPRTY	alpha rhythm
AAHHIKRRRST	rah-rah skirt
AAHHILMPRSS	marshalship
AAHIILNNORT	annihilator
AAHIILNNRSV	nail varnish
AAHIIMNNPSS	Spanish Main
AAHIKKLNOSV	Kalashnikov
AAHILLOPSTT	allopathist
AAHIMMNNOPY	nymphomania
AAHIMNNOSTU	mountain ash
AAHIMNOPRSS	oarsmanship
AAHINNOPRTY	antiphonary
AAHIOPRSTXY	asphyxiator
AAHIOSSTTTY	that is to say
AAHKOPRRSWW	sparrowhawk
AAHLLMMORSW	marshmallow
AAHNOPRTTUY	naturopathy
AAIIILNRTTU	utilitarian
AAIIIMMNNRS	Arminianism
AAIIIMNNNOT	inanimation
AAIIINNRRTT	Trinitarian
AAIILLLPSUZ	lapis lazuli
AAIILLMPRTY	impartially
AAIILLNOPRS	Apollinaris
AAIILMMNORT	matrimonial
AAIILMNNOST	nationalism
AAIILMNNOTV	nominatival
AAIILMNOPRT	patrimonial
AAIILMNORST	rationalism
AAIILMORSST	assimilator
AAIILNNOSTT	nationalist
AAIILNNOTTY	nationality
AAIILNOPPTT	palpitation
AAIILNORSTT	rationalist
AAIILNORTTT	attritional
AAIILNORTTY	rationality
AAIILNOSTTU	situational
AAIIMNOOTTZ	atomization
AAIIMNOPRTT	impartation
AAIIMNRSSTU	sanitariums
AAIINOPSSTV	passivation
AAIINRSSTTV	transit visa
AAILLLOSTWW	swallowtail
AAILLORRSTY	sartorially
AAILMMNOSTU	summational
AAILMMOPPRS	malapropism
AAILMNOPRTU	manipulator
AAILMNRSTTT	transmittal
AAILMOPRSST	pastoralism
AAILNNORSTT	translation
AAILNOPPSSY	passion play
AAILOORSTTT	totalisator
AAILOORTTTZ	totalizator
AAILOPRRTUV	vapour trail
AAILOPRSSTT	pastoralist
AAILOPRSTTY	pastorality
AAIMMNOPSTT	maintopmast
AAIMMNOSSUY	immunoassay
AAIMNOOSSST	anastomosis
AAIMNORSSTU	sanatoriums
AAINNNOPRST	non-partisan
AAINNOPRSTT	patron saint
AAINOORRSTZ	Zoroastrian
AAINORRSTTU	instaurator
AAKLLMPRUUU	Kuala Lumpur
AAKLORSSTYY	Staryy Oskal
AALLLOPRRUY	royal plural
AALLMNOOSUY	anomalously
AALLNNRTUUY	unnaturally
AALLNOPSTTY	post-natally
AALMNNOPSTW	plantswoman
AALMNOPRTUY	paramountly
AALNNOOPRUW	Polonnaruwa
AALORSSTTTU	altostratus
AAMNPRSSTTY	smarty-pants
AANNORRSTUY	tyrannosaur
ABBBCENORUY	baby bouncer
ABBBDELOORW	wobble-board
ABBBEEHILRS	Bible-basher
ABBBENOORRR	robber baron
ABBCCEEHKNR	backbencher
ABBCCEEHMOR	beachcomber
ABBCCEHOORT	herb tobacco
ABBCDEEFIKO	biofeedback
ABBCDEEILRS	describable
ABBCDEENRSS	crabbedness
ABBCEEEHRRS	bear's breech
ABBCEEEKLLT	black beetle
ABBCEEKLORT	beta blocker
ABBCEELLORT	corbel-table
ABBCEFINORR	carbon fibre
ABBCEIILNRS	inscribable
ABBCEIKRRTU	buck rarebit
ABBCEILLMNU	unclimbable
ABBCEJKORWY	jabberwocky
ABBCELMNORU	nuclear bomb
ABBCHINPRTU	rabbit punch
ABBCIILMNOY	bibliomancy
ABBCILMOPST	plastic bomb
ABBCKLMOOTT	black bottom
ABBCKLNORYY	black bryony
ABBCKNNNORU	Bannockburn
ABBDDEIINRR	birdbrained
ABBDDIIILTY	biddability
ABBDEELORTU	redoubtable
ABBDEIILNTU	indubitable
ABBDEIINRRU	India rubber
ABBDEILORTU	boatbuilder
ABBDELNOTUU	undoubtable
ABBDELORTUY	redoubtably
ABBDEMMNORT	bombardment
ABBDGIIINNS	bias binding
ABBDIILNTUY	indubitably
ABBDLNOTUUY	undoubtably
ABBEEFFNOOR	baron of beef
ABBEEKLOOPR	pre-bookable

ABBEELOPRRS	barber's pole
ABBEELPRRTU	perturbable
ABBEEMNSSTU	sub-basement
ABBEGGNORRW	brown-bagger
ABBEHILLPSU	publishable
ABBEHILRSTW	Welsh rabbit
ABBEHINSSSY	babyishness
ABBEIILLMOZ	mobilizable
ABBEILORTTY	liberty boat
ABBEINRSTUU	suburbanite
ABBEINRSUUZ	suburbanize
ABBELLMNPUU	unplumbable
ABBELNPRRTU	rubber plant
ABBEMPRRSTU	rubber stamp
ABBENNOOTTW	Newton Abbot
ABBGHIMNOTU	thingumabob
ABBGILMNTUY	tumbling-bay
ABBGILNORSY	absorbingly
ABBHMOOOOST	bamboo shoot
ABBIILOPRTY	probability
ABCCCELNORY	carbon cycle
ABCCCHKKLOO	chock-a-block
ABCCDEEIIRT	bactericide
ABCCDEHHKNU	hunchbacked
ABCCDEIINOZ	benzoic acid
ABCCDEIKNRR	carrick bend
ABCCDEKKOOR	crookbacked
ABCCDHHORRU	Broad Church
ABCCDIIRTUY	butyric acid
ABCCEEHHMOR	echo chamber
ABCCEEILNOV	conceivable
ABCCEEKLOPU	peacock blue
ABCCEELLLOT	collectable
ABCCEELNNOT	connectable
ABCCEELORRT	correctable
ABCCEEMNNRU	encumbrance
ABCCEEMRSUU	sea cucumber
ABCCEFILNOS	confiscable
ABCCEGINNOU	concubinage
ABCCEHIILMO	biochemical
ABCCEHILSTT	cable stitch
ABCCEIILPTY	peccability
ABCCEIINORT	brecciation
ABCCEIKKLST	stickleback
ABCCEILNOVY	conceivably
ABCCEIOOPPT	tobacco pipe
ABCCEKKLLOT	tackle-block
ABCCEOORTTU	cocoa butter
ABCCIILLNSU	subclinical
ABCCIILRSTU	subcritical
ABCCIIMOORT	macrobiotic
ABCCILLLOUY	bucolically
ABCCILORSTU	subcortical
ABCCINNORUY	concubinary
ABCCINOOSTT	tobacconist
ABCCKNORTUY	backcountry
ABCCNORSTTU	subcontract
ABCDDEEFLOU	double-faced
ABCDDEEHKLO	blockheaded
ABCDDEEILNU	undecidable
ABCDEEEERRT	decerebrate
ABCDEEEHORS	cheeseboard
ABCDEEEKORR	code-breaker
ABCDEEFHNRR	French bread
ABCDEEIILMM	immedicable
ABCDEEILNRS	rescindable
ABCDEEILPRT	predictable
ABCDEEINORZ	decarbonize
ABCDEELLNRY	belly dancer
ABCDEELMMNO	commendable
ABCDEELMNNO	condemnable
ABCDEELMORU	double cream
ABCDEELMRRS	descrambler
ABCDEELNNOS	condensable
ABCDEENORRT	centerboard, centreboard
ABCDEERRTTU	carburetted
ABCDEFIINRR	bird-fancier
ABCDEGHIINR	chain bridge
ABCDEHIILLN	chilblained
ABCDEHILSTW	switchblade
ABCDEHIRRTW	birdwatcher
ABCDEIILTUY	educability
ABCDEIIPSTU	bicuspidate
ABCDEILPRTY	predictably
ABCDEILPRUY	Republic Day
ABCDEILSSSU	discussable
ABCDEINOORT	noticeboard
ABCDEINRSTU	disturbance
ABCDELLORUY	boulder clay
ABCDELMMNOY	commendably
ABCDEMORSST	combat dress
ABCDENNORSY	body scanner
ABCDGIINSUV	scuba-diving
ABCDHIIMRTY	dithyrambic
ABCDHIOPSTX	dispatch box
ABCDHIORSTW	switchboard
ABCDHLOOORS	school board
ABCDHNOORRY	hydrocarbon
ABCDMNORRUU	carborundum
ABCEEEFFLOT	coffee table
ABCEEEFLNOR	enforceable
ABCEEEHMNRT	beech marten
ABCEEEILPRV	perceivable
ABCEEEILRSV	serviceable
ABCEEEILRSX	exercisable
ABCEEEKLRTT	Battle Creek
ABCEEELLNTU	unelectable
ABCEEELMNRS	resemblance
ABCEEELORRV	recoverable
ABCEEELPRRU	recuperable
ABCEEELPRST	respectable
ABCEEEMMNRR	remembrance
ABCEEEMMNRT	embracement
ABCEEFHMMRU	fume chamber
ABCEEFIILPS	specifiable
ABCEEFIILRT	certifiable, rectifiable
ABCEEFIINRY	beneficiary
ABCEEFINNOT	benefaction
ABCEEFLNORR	conferrable
ABCEEHIKLPU	pickelhaube
ABCEEHINPST	spinach beet
ABCEEHKLNQU	blank cheque
ABCEEHLRSTT	stretchable
ABCEEHMRTTU	butcher meat
ABCEEHORRRT	torch-bearer
ABCEEILLNTU	ineluctable
ABCEEILNORT	celebration
ABCEEILNSUX	inexcusable
ABCEEILNTUX	unexcitable

ABCEEILORRV irrevocable
ABCEEILRRSU irrecusable
ABCEEILRRTU recruitable
ABCEEILRSVY serviceably
ABCEEINNRTY bicentenary
ABCEEINORRT cerebration
ABCEEINORTX exorbitance
ABCEEJLMPRU jumper cable
ABCEEKKLNRU bare-knuckle
ABCEEKLLRTT black letter
ABCEEKLLTVV black velvet
ABCEEKLPPPR black pepper
ABCEEKLRRRW kerb-crawler
ABCEELLLMOP compellable
ABCEELNOQRU conquerable
ABCEELNORST carbon steel
ABCEELNOSTT contestable
ABCEELOPRSS processable
ABCEELORRTY celebratory
ABCEELPRSTY respectably
ABCEELRTTUU tuberculate
ABCEEMRRTTU butter-cream
ABCEENNORTU bean-counter
ABCEENORRST arborescent
ABCEERRRTTU carburetter
ABCEFIILLNT inflictable
ABCEFKLLLOW blackfellow
ABCEFLMNOOR conformable
ABCEFLMOORT comfortable
ABCEFLOORRU labour force
ABCEGGIKLNR black ginger
ABCEGHORRTU turbocharge
ABCEGILLMTU magic bullet
ABCEGILLNRS sacring bell
ABCEGINNRSS bracingness
ABCEGINRRTU carbureting
ABCEGJLOSST object-glass
ABCEGKLORSU black grouse
ABCEGORSTUY subcategory
ABCEHHKRSUW bushwhacker
ABCEHIIRTTV active birth
ABCEHIKLNSY Chelyabinsk
ABCEHILNORV olive branch
ABCEHILOPSU bicephalous
ABCEHIMRTTY bathymetric
ABCEHINOOPR necrophobia
ABCEHIOPRRS broach spire
ABCEHKLLOST shackle-bolt
ABCEHKLNOSU unshockable
ABCEHLNOTUU untouchable
ABCEHLNRSUU uncrushable
ABCEHMOSTTU stomach tube
ABCEHRRSTTU chartbuster
ABCEIIILLVZ civilizable
ABCEIIJLSTU justiciable
ABCEIILMORT biometrical
ABCEIILMRUX bulimarexic
ABCEIILRSTV verbalistic
ABCEIILRTUV lubricative
ABCEIIMNOTV combinative
ABCEIKLNRSS nickel brass
ABCEIKLPRST blister pack
ABCEIKNSSWW Bewick's swan
ABCEILLLOPS collapsible
ABCEILLNTUY ineluctably
ABCEILLRTUV carvel-built
ABCEILMMOTT committable
ABCEILMOPRS comprisable
ABCEILMOPRT problematic
ABCEILMOTVY combatively
ABCEILNNOTU continuable
ABCEILNORTV contrivable
ABCEILNRSTU inscrutable
ABCEILNSUXY inexcusably
ABCEILORRVY irrevocably
ABCEILORSTT obstetrical
ABCEIMNNORT recombinant
ABCEIMNOORT embrocation
ABCEINNORTY cybernation
ABCEINOORST obsecration
ABCEINRRRST transcriber
ABCEIRSTTUV subtractive
ABCEKLLMNOT mental block
ABCELLNSSTU sanctus bell
ABCELMNRRSU unscrambler
ABCELNNOOOR coronal bone
ABCELNNOTUU uncountable
ABCELNORSTU construable
ABCEOOORRRT corroborate
ABCEORRRTTU carburettor
ABCFHINOOST son of a bitch
ABCFIILLMOR bacilliform
ABCFIINORTU bifurcation
ABCFINOOSTU obfuscation
ABCFKNOORTT back to front
ABCFLMNOORY conformably
ABCFLMOORTY comfortably
ABCFNORTTUY farcy button
ABCFOORSTUY obfuscatory
ABCGGHINNPU punching bag
ABCGGIKMNOS gobsmacking
ABCGHIKLPTU backup light
ABCGHOORRSU Scarborough
ABCGIIKLNRY bricklaying
ABCGIIKNOUV bivouacking
ABCGIKNNNRU running back
ABCGIKNPSSU buck-passing
ABCGILLOORY bryological
ABCHIILOPSY biophysical
ABCHILNOORR bronchiolar
ABCHKLNOSUY unshockably
ABCIIILOSTY sociability
ABCIIILRSTT tribalistic
ABCIIIMNORT imbrication
ABCIILLLMUY umbilically
ABCIILLPTUY culpability
ABCIILLRSTY trisyllabic
ABCIILLSTYY syllabicity
ABCIILNOPTU publication
ABCIILNORTU lubrication
ABCIIMNNOOT combination
ABCIINORRTU rubrication
ABCIKLLMMSU black Muslim
ABCILLNNOUY connubially
ABCILLOORTY robotically
ABCILLORRUY orbicularly
ABCILMMORUU columbarium
ABCILMNNUUU incunabulum
ABCILNORTUU lucubration
ABCILNRSTUY inscrutably

ABCILOPRSTU subtropical
ABCIMNOORTY combinatory
ABCINNOORTU conurbation
ABCINNOPTTU panic button
ABCINOORSTU obscuration
ABCINORSTTU subtraction
ABCLLRSTUUU subcultural
ABCLNNOTUUY uncountably
ABCMNOORSSW crossbowman
ABCNORRSTUY subcontrary
ABDDDEIMNOR broad-minded
ABDDDIIMNOR diamond-bird
ABDDEEEMPRT bad-tempered
ABDDEEGGLNY bandy-legged
ABDDEFHLLOO half-blooded
ABDDEHILQRU Balquhidder
ABDDEILMRSW swim-bladder
ABDDEIMNNST disbandment
ABDDELMOORW warm-blooded
ABDDELORRTW bladderwort
ABDDGIINORV diving board
ABDDHHNOOSU husbandhood
ABDEEEFRRST fast breeder
ABDEEEGLLOU double eagle
ABDEEEHILRT hereditable
ABDEEEHLLVW well-behaved
ABDEEEILLRV deliverable
ABDEEEILPPP apple-pie bed
ABDEEELLOPV developable
ABDEEELMNRU denumerable
ABDEEELNSST belatedness
ABDEEELORSV sleeve board
ABDEEELRRRW reed warbler
ABDEEELRRSS redressable
ABDEEFGIIRR fire brigade
ABDEEFIILNN indefinable
ABDEEFIKLRS Bakersfield
ABDEEFILLTT battlefield
ABDEEFILNNU undefinable
ABDEEGGINRR gingerbread
ABDEEGHNORY honey badger
ABDEEGHRRTU draught beer
ABDEEGIMNRT abridgement
ABDEEGIRSSS asses' bridge
ABDEEGLNOTU double agent
ABDEEHIRSTW breadthwise
ABDEEHKMRST Berkhamsted
ABDEEIIKLLS dislikeable
ABDEEIILRTZ detribalize
ABDEEIILSTZ destabilize
ABDEEIKNRRW windbreaker
ABDEEILMNST disablement
ABDEEILMSSS disassemble
ABDEEILNPSS dispensable
ABDEEILNRSU undesirable
ABDEEILNRTU unliberated
ABDEEILNSSU audibleness
ABDEEILORRT deliberator
ABDEEILPRSS dispersable
ABDEEINNRRW breadwinner
ABDEEIRTTTU deattribute
ABDEEKLOPSU doublespeak
ABDEEKMNORY monkey bread
ABDEEKNORSZ baker's dozen
ABDEELLLORR Rollerblade
ABDEELMNORZ bronze medal
ABDEELMNOTU demountable
ABDEELMNRUY denumerably
ABDEELNNRUU unendurable
ABDEELNRSSU durableness
ABDEELORRTW world-beater
ABDEELRSSTT battledress
ABDEENORRTT Bernardotte
ABDEEORRRSW sword-bearer
ABDEFGIIRRT frigate bird
ABDEFGINORR fingerboard
ABDEFGIRSSU figured bass
ABDEFIILNNY indefinably
ABDEFILNNUY undefinably
ABDEFLLOTUU double fault
ABDEGGINORR ragged robin
ABDEGHLOOPS bog asphodel
ABDEGHLORSU shoulder bag
ABDEGIILNNT dining table
ABDEGILOOUX dialogue box
ABDEGLLLNOS golden balls
ABDEGLNOOOR blood orange
ABDEHHMOORR rhombohedra
ABDEHIINNPR hairpin bend
ABDEHIINNTU uninhabited
ABDEHLNSSSU husbandless
ABDEHLOORST heart's-blood
ABDEHLOORSV shovelboard
ABDEHMOORRT motherboard
ABDEHNORTTU Tudorbethan
ABDEIIILNTY deniability
ABDEIILLTWY weldability
ABDEIILMNOT indomitable
ABDEIKLNNRU undrinkable
ABDEIKORSTY keyboardist
ABDEILLLSSY dissyllable
ABDEILLOSSV dissolvable
ABDEILMNOPU impoundable
ABDEILMSSSY disassembly
ABDEILNRSUY undesirably
ABDEILOPRST apostle-bird
ABDEILOPRSV disprovable
ABDEINORSTU subordinate
ABDELMOORST bloodstream
ABDELNNRUUY unendurably
ABDELOORRUV louvre-board
ABDELOORRWW wood warbler
ABDEMMOORRY memory board
ABDEMNOORWW meadow brown
ABDENOORRSW snowboarder
ABDENOPRSUU superabound
ABDEOOOPRTT torpedo boat
ABDFGHIILNN half-binding
ABDGHIIINRT riding habit
ABDGHILNSTY sandy blight
ABDGHINNOSW bond-washing
ABDGHINPSSU spud-bashing
ABDGIIINRTY binary digit
ABDGINOPRRS springboard
ABDGINORRST stringboard
ABDGMOORRSS smorgasbord
ABDHHIOOPRY hydrophobia
ABDIIILLLNY libidinally
ABDIILMNOTY indomitably
ABDIINOSTUU subaudition

ABDILNOOPSV	blood spavin
ABDIMNNOSTU	subdominant
ABDINORRSUY	subordinary
ABEEEEFLORS	foreseeable
ABEEEEIKLMV	make-believe
ABEEEEMNRTV	bereavement
ABEEEERRRTV	reverberate
ABEEEFIRRRR	barrier reef
ABEEEFLMNRT	fermentable
ABEEEFLORSY	foreseeably
ABEEEFLRSTZ	blast freeze
ABEEEGLORSW	elbow grease
ABEEEGLRRTT	regrettable
ABEEEILLSTV	televisable
ABEEEILMMPR	impermeable
ABEEEILMMTZ	emblematize
ABEEEILRRTV	retrievable
ABEEEIMNSST	absenteeism
ABEEEJMMNNT	enjambement
ABEEELMNNTT	entablement
ABEEELNNRUW	unrenewable
ABEEELNNSST	tenableness
ABEEELNPRST	presentable
ABEEELNPRTV	preventable
ABEEELPRRSV	preservable
ABEEELPSTUY	beauty sleep
ABEEENQTUUY	beauty queen
ABEEENRRRTV	reverberant
ABEEFFILORT	forfeitable
ABEEFFRSTTU	buffer state
ABEEFGILNRR	refrangible
ABEEFGLORTT	forgettable
ABEEFIILLQU	liquefiable
ABEEFILNRSS	friableness
ABEEFILRRTU	irrefutable
ABEEFIMMRRT	timber-frame
ABEEFLLNSSU	balefulness
ABEEFLMOPRR	performable
ABEEFNRRRTU	afterburner
ABEEFOPRSTY	beast of prey
ABEEGGILNPS	sleeping bag
ABEEGGLRUUY	Rugby League
ABEEGHLRSUU	bush-leaguer
ABEEGIILNRT	libertinage
ABEEGIINNRR	bearing-rein
ABEEGIINOSS	abiogenesis
ABEEGIKLNNT	telebanking
ABEEGILLLNR	relabelling
ABEEGILMNPR	impregnable
ABEEGILRRST	registrable
ABEEGLNSSUU	unguessable
ABEEGLRRTTY	regrettably
ABEEGMMNRSU	numbers game
ABEEHHPRSTY	bathysphere
ABEEHIILNRT	inheritable
ABEEHIKPRRS	ship-breaker
ABEEHILRSST	establisher, re-establish
ABEEHILSTUX	exhaustible
ABEEHINRSST	breathiness
ABEEHKNORRT	heartbroken
ABEEHLORRWW	wheelbarrow
ABEEHNOPRRY	hyperborean
ABEEHORSTTU	thereabouts
ABEEHORSTUW	whereabouts
ABEEIILLRRZ	liberalizer
ABEEIILMNPS	plebeianism
ABEEIILMNST	inestimable
ABEEIILNQTU	inequitable
ABEEIILQRTU	equilibrate
ABEEIKKRRST	strike-break
ABEEIKLMORR	boilermaker
ABEEIKLNNST	linen basket
ABEEILLLRTV	Albertville
ABEEILLNORT	intolerable
ABEEILLNPSS	pliableness
ABEEILLNRSS	liberalness
ABEEILLOPTX	exploitable
ABEEILLOTTT	toilet table
ABEEILMMORZ	memorizable
ABEEILMNNOT	mentionable
ABEEILMNNRU	innumerable
ABEEILMORRV	irremovable
ABEEILMORST	steam boiler
ABEEILNNOPS	pensionable
ABEEILNNSTT	table tennis
ABEEILNPRSU	insuperable
ABEEILNSSST	beastliness
ABEEILORSTT	bitter aloes
ABEEILPPRTT	bitter-apple
ABEEILPRSSU	persuasible
ABEEILRTTTV	trivet table
ABEEINNQRTU	barquentine
ABEEINORSSU	Buenos Aires
ABEEINRRSSZ	bizarreness
ABEEINSSSUV	abusiveness
ABEEJLNNOUY	unenjoyable
ABEELLLMSSY	blamelessly
ABEELLNOSSV	lovableness
ABEELMMNORU	unmemorable
ABEELMNORUV	unremovable
ABEELMNOSSV	movableness
ABEELMNPRTU	number plate
ABEELMRRSUW	slumberwear
ABEELNPRSTY	presentably
ABEELNRTTUU	unutterable
ABEELNRTUXY	exuberantly
ABEELPPRRTU	pre-pubertal
ABEELPRRSTY	presbyteral
ABEELQQRUUU	Albuquerque
ABEEMMNORSU	membraneous
ABEFFIILORT	fortifiable
ABEFFILLLLU	fulfillable
ABEFGIILNNR	infrangible
ABEFHHLORRT	half-brother
ABEFHLNSSSU	bashfulness
ABEFIIILNRT	nitrifiable
ABEFIIILRTV	vitrifiable
ABEFIIILSTY	feasibility
ABEFIIJLSTU	justifiable
ABEFIILNORV	riboflavine
ABEFIILNOSS	fissionable
ABEFILLNOOR	fire-balloon
ABEFILLTUUY	beautifully
ABEFILNTUUU	unbeautiful
ABEFILRRTUY	irrefutably
ABEFLLNOORT	frontal lobe
ABEFLNOPTYY	Bay of Plenty
ABEGGHILLNT	Bengal light
ABEGGIILNOR	globigerina
ABEGHILMNOO	haemoglobin

ABEGIIILMMT	immitigable	**ABEILMORRVY**	irremovably
ABEGIIKLNNR	brake lining	**ABEILNNPRTU**	unprintable
ABEGIILNNPY	belaying-pin	**ABEILNNRSUU**	uninsurable
ABEGIJMMNNU	gum benjamin	**ABEILNNSTTY**	abstinently
ABEGIJMNNPU	jumping bean	**ABEILNOOSSS**	obsessional
ABEGILMNPRY	impregnably	**ABEILNORSSU**	Belorussian
ABEGILNNNTY	benignantly	**ABEILNOSTTY**	obstinately
ABEGILNORSU	subregional	**ABEILNPRRST**	splinter-bar
ABEGILOOORY	aerobiology	**ABEILNPRSUY**	insuperably
ABEGINOOSTT	geobotanist	**ABEILOORRTT**	obliterator
ABEGLLORSSW	glass-blower	**ABEILQRSTUU**	square-built
ABEGLNOORRW	organ-blower	**ABEILRRSTTT**	brittle-star
ABEGMORRSTU	burgomaster	**ABEIMNNSSSU**	businessman
ABEHIILMOPT	amphibolite	**ABEIMNORSTW**	tribeswoman
ABEHIILPRST	blepharitis	**ABEINNNRSTU**	burnt sienna
ABEHIIMMNOS	bohemianism	**ABEINOOPRRT**	probationer,
ABEHIIMORSV	behaviorism		reprobation
ABEHIINNORT	hibernation	**ABEINOORSTV**	observation
ABEHIINPSSX	Spanish ibex	**ABEINSSTTUV**	substantive
ABEHIKLNNTU	unthinkable	**ABEKMNORSSY**	brass monkey
ABEHILLLRTY	liberty hall	**ABEKNOORRRW**	Broken Arrow
ABEHILMNOST	abolishment	**ABEKOOSTTTU**	statute book
ABEHILPPRST	slipper bath	**ABELLNNORVY**	non-verbally
ABEHINOORTT	botheration	**ABELMMNORUY**	unmemorably
ABEHINOOSST	Hessian boot	**ABELNOOPPST**	postponable
ABEHINRSTTU	Saint-Hubert	**ABELNOPPSTU**	unstoppable
ABEHLMOORTW	Bartholomew	**ABELNOPRTTU**	pearl button
ABEHLMOPSSU	blasphemous	**ABELNORSTVY**	observantly
ABEHLMORTWY	blameworthy	**ABELNRTTUUY**	unutterably
ABEHLORRSSU	harbourless	**ABELOPPRSTU**	supportable
ABEHNNOOTTY	ethnobotany	**ABELOPRTTTY**	bottle party
ABEHRSTTWYY	Aberystwyth	**ABELRRTTUUY**	tubular tyre
ABEIIIKLLTY	likeability	**ABEMNORRRST**	barnstormer
ABEIIILLLMT	illimitable	**ABENNORSTUV**	unobservant
ABEIIILLNOR	billionaire	**ABENOPRRTTU**	protuberant
ABEIIILLRTY	reliability	**ABEOORRSTVY**	observatory
ABEIIILLTVY	liveability	**ABFGHNOORRU**	Farnborough
ABEIIINNORT	inebriation	**ABFGIILNNRY**	infrangibly
ABEIILLLLRY	illiberally	**ABFGIILNORT**	floating rib
ABEIILLMMST	bimetallism	**ABFIIILLLTY**	fallibility
ABEIILLMNRY	bimillenary	**ABFIIJLSTUY**	justifiably
ABEIILLMPSU	implausible	**ABFIINOOTTT**	not a bit of it
ABEIILLMSTT	bimetallist	**ABFILMNSTUU**	funambulist
ABEIILLPRTV	private bill	**ABGGGINNOOT**	tobogganing
ABEIILLRSTT	bristletail	**ABGGILOORST**	garbologist
ABEIILMNRST	ministrable	**ABGGINOOSTT**	tobogganist
ABEIILMNSTY	inestimably	**ABGHIINSTTU**	bathing suit
ABEIILNQTUY	inequitably	**ABGHIKLLNOO**	booking hall
ABEIILNRRTT	intertribal	**ABGHIKPRRST**	bright spark
ABEIILNRTTY	rentability	**ABGHILMOOPY**	amphibology
ABEIILOPRTY	operability	**ABGHLMOORRU**	Marlborough
ABEIILSTTTY	testability	**ABGIIILMMTY**	immitigably
ABEIILSTUXY	bisexuality	**ABGIIILNTTY**	tangibility
ABEIIMNORSV	ambiversion	**ABGIIMNTUUY**	unambiguity
ABEIINRRSST	bar sinister	**ABGIJNOORTU**	objurgation
ABEIIRTTTUV	attributive	**ABGIJNOSTUU**	subjugation
ABEIKLLNOOT	kite balloon	**ABGIKKLNOOT**	talking book
ABEIKNNRRSU	brank-ursine	**ABGIKNNOPRW**	pawnbroking
ABEILLLRSTY	trisyllable	**ABGIKNRRSTY**	stringy-bark
ABEILLMORTU	Rambouillet	**ABGILLORTUY**	globularity
ABEILLNORTY	intolerably	**ABGILMOSUUY**	ambiguously
ABEILLNPSUU	unplausible	**ABGILORRSUU**	burglarious
ABEILLNRTTU	bullet train	**ABGIMNOSUUU**	unambiguous
ABEILMNNRUY	innumerably	**ABGINOORSTU**	subrogation
ABEILMNRSTU	subterminal	**ABGJOORRTUY**	objurgatory

ABGLNORSTUY	Glastonbury	**ACCCIKLMOOT**	atomic clock
ABHHIKRSTTU	Turkish bath	**ACCCIMMOORS**	macrocosmic
ABHHIOOOPPT	photophobia	**ACCCIMOOPRS**	macroscopic
ABHIKLNNTUY	unthinkably	**ACCDDEHLOOT**	cold cathode
ABHILMMNOPT	phantom limb	**ACCDDEHNPRU**	punched card
ABHLOOPRSTT	trophoblast	**ACCDDEINORS**	discordance
ABIIILLLMTY	illimitably	**ACCDDIIIMST**	didacticism
ABIIILNSTTY	instability	**ACCDDINORSY**	discordancy
ABIIILNTUVY	unviability	**ACCDEEEENNT**	antecedence
ABIIILPSSTY	passibility	**ACCDEEELNOS**	adolescence
ABIIILSTTUY	suitability	**ACCDEEFIILR**	decalcifier
ABIIKLORTWY	workability	**ACCDEEFNORY**	confederacy
ABIILLLNRTY	brilliantly	**ACCDEEHHKLU**	chucklehead
ABIILLMPSUY	implausibly	**ACCDEEHIMNO**	machine code
ABIILLNOSTT	station-bill	**ACCDEEHIORS**	archdiocese
ABIILMNOSTU	sublimation	**ACCDEEHNSTY**	Schenectady
ABIILMOSTUY	ambitiously	**ACCDEEIISTV**	desiccative
ABIILNORTTU	tribulation	**ACCDEEINOSS**	deaccession
ABIILNRSTUY	insalubrity	**ACCDEEIORTT**	decorticate
ABIILOPRTTY	portability	**ACCDEELNNOU**	unconcealed
ABIILOPRTVY	provability	**ACCDEEMNSUU**	succedaneum
ABIILOQTTUY	quotability	**ACCDEENOSSU**	second cause
ABIILRRTTUY	tributarily	**ACCDEFHMORR**	forced march
ABIIMNNSTYZ	Byzantinism	**ACCDEFNOSTU**	safe conduct
ABIIMNOSTUU	unambitious	**ACCDEGIINRT**	accrediting
ABIINNORTTU	turbination	**ACCDEHHRSSU**	archduchess
ABIINNSTTYZ	Byzantinist	**ACCDEHKLNPU**	packed lunch
ABIINOORSTT	abortionist	**ACCDEIINOST**	desiccation
ABIINORTTTU	attribution	**ACCDEIIPSTU**	suicide pact
ABIIORSSTTU	tibiotarsus	**ACCDEIKLNST**	candlestick
ABILLOORSUY	laboriously	**ACCDEILLMMU**	cadmium cell
ABILLORSTTU	sublittoral	**ACCDEINNORT**	concertina'd
ABILNNOORUU	labour union	**ACCDEINOOTU**	co-education
ABILNNPRTUY	unprintably	**ACCDEINPRSY**	discrepancy
ABILNOSTUUX	subluxation	**ACCDEINPRTU**	unpracticed
ABINNOORSTU	subornation	**ACCDEIPRRTU**	picture card
ABINNOSSTVV	bons vivants	**ACCDEKORRRT**	track record
ABINOORSSTU	Russian boot	**ACCDELLOSTU**	cloud-castle
ABINRRSSTTU	brains trust	**ACCDELNOSSS**	second class
ABLNOPPSTUY	unstoppably	**ACCDENNOTUU**	unaccounted
ABLOPPRSTUY	supportably	**ACCDFHHLOOT**	catch hold of
ABMOORSSTTY	smarty-boots	**ACCDGILNORY**	accordingly
ACCCCHHOSTT	Scotch catch	**ACCDGNOOOTU**	good account
ACCCDEHILNO	chalcedonic	**ACCDHIIILOP**	acidophilic
ACCCDEIILNU	nucleic acid	**ACCDHIIMORT**	dichromatic
ACCCDENNOOR	concordance	**ACCDHILORST**	trochal disc
ACCCDENNOTU	conductance	**ACCDIILLNRY**	cylindrical
ACCCDHIILOR	chloric acid	**ACCDIILLORY**	codicillary
ACCCDHIIMOR	chromic acid	**ACCDIILNOOR**	crocodilian
ACCCDIMOPST	compact disc	**ACCDIILOPST**	optical disc
ACCCEEEFHLN	Ecclefechan	**ACCDIIOOPRS**	radioscopic
ACCCEEELNOS	coalescence	**ACCDIIPRSSU**	prussic acid
ACCCEEELNST	lactescence	**ACCDIIPRUVY**	pyruvic acid
ACCCEEEMNRS	marcescence	**ACCDNNOOTTY**	cotton candy
ACCCEEHISTT	catechetics	**ACCEEEEHMRS**	cream cheese
ACCCEEHKORT	coat checker	**ACCEEEENNSV**	evanescence
ACCCEELMNOP	complacence	**ACCEEEFILMN**	maleficence
ACCCEHNORTY	technocracy	**ACCEEEFLNRT**	reflectance
ACCCEIILMRT	climacteric	**ACCEEEHILRT**	chelicerate
ACCCEIKNRST	cancer stick	**ACCEEEIKKLO**	cock-a-leekie
ACCCEILRTTY	tetracyclic	**ACCEEELNNOS**	scalene cone
ACCCEINNOTT	tonic accent	**ACCEEELNOPS**	opalescence
ACCCELMNOPY	complacency	**ACCEEELNRST**	recalescent
ACCCHILOORT	ochlocratic	**ACCEEFIIRTT**	certificate
ACCCIIOOPRS	capriccioso	**ACCEEFIKRRR**	firecracker

ACCEEFINORV	vociferance
ACCEEGHILMO	geochemical
ACCEEGHINTY	eye-catching
ACCEEGHORRV	cover charge
ACCEEGILRRT	great circle
ACCEEHILMNO	chameleonic
ACCEEHILNRT	chanticleer
ACCEEHIRRTU	charcuterie
ACCEEHIRSTW	Cesarewitch
ACCEEHKORTW	weathercock
ACCEEHLLNRY	chancellery
ACCEEHLNOXY	cyclohexane
ACCEEIILNRT	electrician
ACCEEIIMPST	septicaemic
ACCEEIKKLPR	place-kicker
ACCEEIKNPRS	science park
ACCEEIKRRSW	wisecracker
ACCEEILLRST	electricals
ACCEEILNSST	scale insect
ACCEEILRRTU	recirculate
ACCEEILRRTY	electric ray
ACCEEIMNRTT	metacentric
ACCEEIMPRST	spermacetic
ACCEEINQSTU	acquiescent
ACCEEIOPRRT	reciprocate
ACCEEIORSSZ	accessorize
ACCEEKOPRST	space rocket
ACCEELMNNOT	concealment
ACCEEMNNORR	necromancer
ACCEEMNOPPU	come-uppance
ACCEENNNOTU	countenance
ACCEENNORSV	conversance
ACCEENNORTT	concentrate, concertante
ACCEENNORVY	conveyancer
ACCEENORRRT	cater-corner
ACCEFFHRTTU	chaff-cutter
ACCEFFIIOSU	efficacious
ACCEFHHKLNR	French chalk
ACCEFHIINTY	chieftaincy
ACCEFIIIMPT	Pacific Time
ACCEFILORSU	calciferous
ACCEFINORRT	Afrocentric
ACCEFMNNOOR	conformance
ACCEGHHITTW	catchweight
ACCEGIKMRRY	gimcrackery
ACCEHIILLSU	chilli sauce
ACCEHIILOTZ	catholicize
ACCEHIIMNST	mechanistic
ACCEHIIRSTU	Eucharistic
ACCEHILLMNO	melancholic
ACCEHILLNTY	technically
ACCEHILNNTU	untechnical
ACCEHIMNNOR	chrominance
ACCEHIRSSTT	scratchiest
ACCEHKOPPTT	patch pocket
ACCEHLLMNOY	collenchyma
ACCEHLLNORT	concert hall
ACCEIIILLNN	aclinic line
ACCEIILLMRS	clericalism
ACCEIILLNPR	preclinical
ACCEIILLRST	clericalist
ACCEIILRRUZ	circularize
ACCEIILRTUV	circulative
ACCEIIMNOST	encomiastic
ACCEIINNOSU	insouciance
ACCEIIRRSTT	criticaster
ACCEIKKOTTT	tick-tack-toe
ACCEIKNRSSS	carsickness
ACCEILLLMRS	small circle
ACCEILLMOST	somatic cell
ACCEILLNNOR	non-clerical
ACCEILLPSTY	sceptically
ACCEILMOPST	ectoplasmic
ACCEILMSSTU	multi-access
ACCEILNNOTY	anticyclone
ACCEILNOPRT	narcoleptic
ACCEILNORTT	contractile
ACCEILOPRST	ceroplastic
ACCEIMMNOTU	communicate
ACCEIMNNORT	necromantic
ACCEIMORRTY	meritocracy
ACCEINNNOTU	continuance
ACCEINNORST	concertinas
ACCEINNORTT	concertanti
ACCEINNORTV	contrivance
ACCEINORTTV	contractive
ACCEIOORSSU	scoriaceous
ACCEIOPRRST	presocratic
ACCEJLNORTU	conjectural
ACCELLOSTTU	coal scuttle
ACCELMMNOOP	commonplace
ACCELNNOSTT	contact lens
ACCELPRRSUU	crepuscular
ACCEMNOPSST	compactness
ACCENNORSVY	conservancy, conversancy
ACCENOORRST	consecrator
ACCENPRTUUU	acupuncture
ACCEORSSTUU	crustaceous
ACCFHILLORT	chill factor
ACCFIILOPRY	prolificacy
ACCFILLNOTU	conflictual
ACCFINOORST	confiscator
ACCGHINRSST	scratchings
ACCGIKKLMNO	clockmaking
ACCGIKNOPST	stocking cap
ACCGILLMOOY	mycological
ACCGILLOOTY	cytological
ACCGIMOPRTY	cryptogamic
ACCHHIINSTT	chain stitch
ACCHHILNRTU	Latin Church
ACCHHMNORUW	churchwoman
ACCHIIIMMPT	amphimictic
ACCHIILMOST	Catholicism
ACCHIILOSST	scholiastic
ACCHIILOTTY	catholicity
ACCHIIMOSST	masochistic
ACCHIIPRSTY	psychiatric
ACCHILLNORY	chronically
ACCHILLPSYY	psychically
ACCHILMOTYY	cyclothymia
ACCHILNNOOT	non-Catholic
ACCHINOPSTY	sycophantic
ACCHIOORRSU	chiaroscuro
ACCHIOPRSYY	physiocracy
ACCHMNOOSTW	Scotchwoman
ACCHNOOOPSU	cacophonous
ACCHOOOPTTU	couch potato
ACCIIIKKNPW	Pickwickian

ACCIIILLLPS piccalillis
ACCIIILNSTV Calvinistic
ACCIIILOSST socialistic
ACCIIILRTTY criticality
ACCIILNNOTU inculcation
ACCIILNNQUU quincuncial
ACCIILNOORT conciliator
ACCIILNORTU circulation
ACCIILNOTVY volcanicity
ACCIILOSTUV acclivitous
ACCIILRRTUY circularity
ACCIINORRSU Rosicrucian
ACCIJNNOTUV conjunctiva
ACCIKLLORWW crack willow
ACCIKNPRSTU panic-struck
ACCILLNOOOT collocation
ACCILLPRTYY cryptically
ACCILMNRRUU circumlunar
ACCILMOPRRU circumpolar
ACCILMOPSTY cytoplasmic
ACCILMORRSU circumsolar
ACCILNOOTTU occultation
ACCILOPRSTY pyroclastic
ACCILOPRTTU plutocratic
ACCILORRTUY circulatory
ACCIMMNNOTU communicant
ACCIMNNOOTT concomitant
ACCIMNOPTYY City Company
ACCINNNOSTY inconstancy
ACCINNOOOTV convocation
ACCINNOOPRU cornucopian
ACCINNOORTT contraction
ACCINOORRRW carrion crow
ACCINOORSTU coruscation
ACCKLOQRTUZ quartz clock
ACCKLORRSTY rock crystal
ACCKOOPRRSW cock sparrow
ACCLMNOOPTU coconut palm
ACCLNNOSTUY consultancy
ACCLOPRRSUU corpuscular
ACCORSSSTUW cross-cut saw
ACDDDEEILTY dedicatedly
ACDDDEEKLOR dreadlocked
ACDDEEFFIST disaffected
ACDDEEGIKNW wedding cake
ACDDEEHHIKT thickheaded
ACDDEEHLORT cold-hearted
ACDDEEHNORS decahedrons
ACDDEEILPTU pediculated
ACDDEEINNNR dinner dance
ACDDEENORTU undecorated
ACDDEFGINPU pudding face
ACDDEHILMTW middle watch
ACDDEHINSSS caddishness
ACDDEHLLOST saddle-cloth
ACDDEILLMSS middle class
ACDDEILNOOV Vila do Conde
ACDDEIMNORU endocardium
ACDDFHILMRU fluid drachm
ACDDIOPRTTU parotid duct
ACDEEEEHLRR cheerleader
ACDEEEFLNRS fer de lances, fers de lance
ACDEEEFLNRT needlecraft
ACDEEEFLRST self-created
ACDEEEFNORT confederate
ACDEEEHLMNT needle match
ACDEEEIKLNS linseed cake
ACDEEEILLPT pedicellate
ACDEEEILNRV deliverance
ACDEEEIPRTT decrepitate
ACDEEEIPRTV deprecative
ACDEEELLRVW cave dweller
ACDEEELORRT decelerator
ACDEEERRSTT trade secret
ACDEEFFILLT ill-affected
ACDEEFHLSTT flat-chested
ACDEEFLNRUU fraudulence
ACDEEFMORRS armed forces
ACDEEGHHPRT depth charge
ACDEEGHNRRU undercharge
ACDEEGILNSW scale-winged
ACDEEGKLNOW acknowledge
ACDEEGNRRSS garden cress
ACDEEHIIMNT Medicine Hat
ACDEEHILNPP Chippendale
ACDEEHILPSY psychedelia
ACDEEHIMNRS merchandise
ACDEEHINRTW windcheater
ACDEEHKKLNU knucklehead
ACDEEHLLMTW well-matched
ACDEEHLLOSU close-hauled
ACDEEHLNNTY enchantedly
ACDEEHMNORW reach-me-down
ACDEEHNNSTU unchastened
ACDEEHNPPTU punched tape
ACDEEHNRRTU unchartered
ACDEEIILLTY eidetically
ACDEEIILMTV maledictive
ACDEEIILTUV elucidative
ACDEEIIMMNN medicine man
ACDEEIIOPPS epidiascope
ACDEEIIPRTV predicative
ACDEEIKMRTT dream ticket
ACDEEILLLLN Daniell cell
ACDEEILLMNY endemically
ACDEEILLNNY decennially
ACDEEILMNRU unreclaimed
ACDEEILNNST clandestine
ACDEEILNOTT delectation
ACDEEILNTTU denticulate
ACDEEILPRTU reduplicate
ACDEEIMNPRT predicament
ACDEEIMNRTY determinacy
ACDEEIMORTZ democratize
ACDEEIMOSTT domesticate
ACDEEINOPRT deprecation
ACDEEINORST considerate, desecration
ACDEEINORTU re-education
ACDEEIOPTTT petticoated
ACDEEIORRSV service road
ACDEEIORRTT directorate
ACDEEKNORSW Dawson Creek
ACDEEKQRRTU quarterdeck
ACDEELMORRS scleroderma
ACDEELNOPRW candlepower
ACDEELNPTUU pedunculate
ACDEELOORTW water-cooled
ACDEELRSSTY seed crystal

ACDEEMNRTTU	traducement
ACDEENORRST	second rater
ACDEEOPRRTY	deprecatory
ACDEERRTUUV	decurvature
ACDEFFIIRTV	diffractive
ACDEFGILRSU	disgraceful
ACDEFHILPST	feldspathic
ACDEFHMOOST	smooth-faced
ACDEFIIINNT	infanticide
ACDEFIIINOT	deification, edification
ACDEFIILSTU	feudalistic
ACDEFINNOTU	fecundation
ACDEFLMMNOS	self-command
ACDEGHHIOWY	Highway Code
ACDEGHIILNP	hiding place
ACDEGHIIOPR	ideographic
ACDEGHILLNT	candlelight
ACDEGHILNNO	golden chain
ACDEGHIMOPR	demographic
ACDEGHLOORS	grade school
ACDEGIILLOO	ideological
ACDEGIIMNSU	misguidance
ACDEGILLOOP	pedological
ACDEGILMRRU	miracle drug
ACDEGILNPPT	peptic gland
ACDEGIMORTY	tragicomedy
ACDEGINOORT	Ticonderoga
ACDEGLOORST	cold storage
ACDEGOPRRSU	producer gas
ACDEHIIMNNW	wind machine
ACDEHIIOPRT	diaphoretic
ACDEHIKKLTY	latchkey kid
ACDEHILRSSY	chrysalides
ACDEHIMMNRU	drum machine
ACDEHIMOPRS	comradeship
ACDEHIMOSTU	mustachioed
ACDEHINOORS	icosahedron
ACDEHIOOPRT	orthopaedic
ACDEHKMRSTU	Deutschmark
ACDEHLNPRTU	thunderclap
ACDEHLRSTTY	Strathclyde
ACDEHMOORTW	doomwatcher
ACDEHNOORST	octahedrons
ACDEHOORRTU	urochordate
ACDEIIINTVV	vindicative
ACDEIIJLPRU	prejudicial
ACDEIIKNRST	inside track
ACDEIILLMNY	medicinally
ACDEIILLNOT	co-tidal line
ACDEIILLNTY	identically
ACDEIILLRVY	veridically
ACDEIILMNOT	malediction
ACDEIILMPRS	spermicidal
ACDEIILNNOT	declination
ACDEIILNORT	directional
ACDEIILNOTU	elucidation
ACDEIILNOTV	valediction
ACDEIILORRT	directorial
ACDEIILRTUV	diverticula
ACDEIIMORRT	radiometric
ACDEIIMPRRU	pericardium
ACDEIINNRTY	tyrannicide
ACDEIINOPRT	predication
ACDEIINORRT	doctrinaire
ACDEIINRTTX	indirect tax
ACDEIKRRRTT	dirt-tracker
ACDEILLLMOY	melodically
ACDEILLNOOT	decollation
ACDEILMNOSS	Iceland moss
ACDEILMORTY	maledictory
ACDEILNOOST	consolidate
ACDEILNORSY	secondarily
ACDEILNRSWY	cylinder saw
ACDEILNRTUU	uncurtailed
ACDEILOORRS	social order
ACDEILOORRV	varicolored
ACDEILORTUY	elucidatory
ACDEILORTVY	valedictory
ACDEIMNOOPT	Capo di Monte
ACDEIMNORRS	morris dance
ACDEINNORTU	denunciator
ACDEINNRTUU	uncurtained
ACDEINOSSTU	decussation
ACDEINOSTTU	outdistance
ACDEINOSTTW	wainscotted
ACDEINPRSTU	unpractised
ACDEINPRSTY	candy stripe, predynastic
ACDEIRSTTUY	daisy-cutter
ACDELLOPTTY	leptodactyl
ACDELOPRTTY	pterodactyl
ACDEMMMNNOT	commandment
ACDEMNNORTU	countermand
ACDEMNORTUY	documentary
ACDEMOPRSSU	mass-produce
ACDENNNNOUU	unannounced
ACDENOORRSW	no-score draw
ACDEORRSSST	star-crossed
ACDFFGILNOS	scaffolding
ACDFFIILMOO	officialdom
ACDFFIINORT	diffraction
ACDFGHHIINS	chafing dish
ACDFGIKLNNO	folk dancing
ACDFKLOORRW	lock forward
ACDFOORRTUW	ward of court
ACDGGIILNNR	dancing girl
ACDGGIKNORV	graving dock
ACDGHHIMMNO	high command
ACDGHIOPRSY	discography
ACDGIINOPRR	road-pricing
ACDGIINOSST	diagnostics
ACDGILLOOOX	doxological
ACDGILNOORW	carding wool
ACDGIMNNOPU	up-and-coming
ACDGINOORVW	woodcarving
ACDGINOPRSU	scouring pad
ACDGINORSST	cross-dating
ACDGMNOOOPY	good company
ACDHHIOPRRS	harpsichord
ACDHHIOPRTY	hydropathic
ACDHIIIMRTT	mithridatic
ACDHIILOPSU	acidophilus
ACDHIIMNORS	diachronism
ACDHIINOOPR	radiophonic
ACDHIMNOORT	trichomonad
ACDHINOORSU	diachronous
ACDHIORSTTY	hydrostatic
ACDHLLOOOOW	wood alcohol
ACDIIILLNPS	disciplinal
ACDIIILLOTY	idiotically

ACDIIILMORY	domiciliary	**ACEEEJORSTT**	ejector seat
ACDIIINNOTV	vindication	**ACEEEKLORTW**	electroweak
ACDIIJLLRUY	juridically	**ACEEELLMNOV**	malevolence
ACDIILLLLYY	idyllically	**ACEEELLSSSY**	ceaselessly
ACDIILLORST	clostridial	**ACEEELMMNPT**	emplacement
ACDIILMNOPR	palindromic	**ACEEELMNPRT**	replacement
ACDIILMNSSY	syndicalism	**ACEEELMNRTX**	excremental
ACDIILNNOOT	conditional	**ACEEELNPRST**	pearlescent
ACDIILNOOST	dislocation	**ACEEELQRRTU**	lacquer tree
ACDIILNOPTU	duplication	**ACEEEMNNRTT**	re-enactment
ACDIILNSSTY	syndicalist	**ACEEEMNORTY**	tea ceremony
ACDIIMNORSS	sardonicism	**ACEEENPPRTU**	perpetuance
ACDIIMNOSTU	coatimundis	**ACEEENPRSTW**	Western Cape
ACDIIMORSTY	myocarditis	**ACEEENRRSSV**	screen saver
ACDIINNOSTY	syndication	**ACEEEOPRTTX**	expectorate
ACDIINORSTT	distraction	**ACEEFFIILOS**	officialese
ACDIINORSTU	nitrous acid	**ACEEFFILNTU**	ineffectual
ACDIINORTVY	vindicatory	**ACEEFFKRSTT**	Stark effect
ACDIIOORRRR	air corridor	**ACEEFFLLTUY**	effectually
ACDIKNOPRTW	Downpatrick	**ACEEFHINNRS**	enfranchise
ACDILLNORTY	doctrinally	**ACEEFHIRRTW**	fire-watcher
ACDILLORSTY	crystalloid	**ACEEFHLLOOR**	alcohol-free
ACDILOOPSTW	plastic wood	**ACEEFHNRRTU**	furtherance
ACDIMNOOSTT	mastodontic	**ACEEFIKOPSS**	kiss of peace
ACDINNNOOOT	condonation	**ACEEFILRSTV**	service flat
ACDINOOORRT	coordinator	**ACEEFIMNTTU**	tumefacient
ACDINOPRRTU	drop curtain	**ACEEFKMOPRT**	pomfret-cake
ACDKLLNOORR	rock and roll	**ACEEFLLNRST**	crestfallen
ACDLLNOORTU	dual control	**ACEEFLLNRUU**	nuclear fuel
ACDLNOOORTY	condolatory	**ACEEFLNRSSU**	carefulness
ACDMMNOOPST	command post	**ACEEFLOPRRT**	prefectoral
ACDNNOOPRSS	pros and cons	**ACEEFLORRUV**	overcareful
ACEEEEEKPPR	peacekeeper	**ACEEFLPRRTU**	prefectural
ACEEEEHKMRS	cheesemaker	**ACEEFMNOPRR**	performance
ACEEEEHLPSW	escape wheel	**ACEEFPPRSTT**	past perfect
ACEEEFFFRTT	after-effect	**ACEEGGIMNOT**	geomagnetic
ACEEEFFGSTT	stage effect	**ACEEGHILOOT**	oligochaete
ACEEEFFKMOR	coffee-maker	**ACEEGHILPRT**	telegraphic
ACEEEFHILNS	Chinese leaf	**ACEEGHINNOX**	ion exchange
ACEEEFHLNRV	French leave	**ACEEGHINNRT**	interchange
ACEEEFLNRRU	nuclear-free	**ACEEGHLNOOS**	loose change
ACEEEGHHRST	charge sheet	**ACEEGHMMORT**	hectogramme
ACEEEGIMNRT	race meeting	**ACEEGHNRRSU**	charge nurse
ACEEEGIMNTT	metagenetic	**ACEEGHPRRSU**	supercharge
ACEEEGIMRSV	service game	**ACEEGIINPRR**	ear-piercing
ACEEEGLOTTT	telecottage	**ACEEGIKNNPP**	kneecapping
ACEEEGNRSTT	centre stage, secret agent	**ACEEGILLNRS**	selling race
		ACEEGILLNRY	generically
ACEEEHIMNTV	achievement	**ACEEGILLNTY**	genetically
ACEEEHIORVV	overachieve	**ACEEGILLNUY**	eugenically
ACEEEHIRTTZ	catheterize	**ACEEGILLRVY**	viceregally
ACEEEHKLNRT	leatherneck	**ACEEGILMNRS**	single cream
ACEEEHKPRTW	watchkeeper	**ACEEGILMORT**	geometrical
ACEEEHLLNRT	chanterelle	**ACEEGILNPRS**	sleeping car
ACEEEHLLRSV	Sacheverell	**ACEEGILPRTT**	tetraplegic
ACEEEHLNPST	cheese plant	**ACEEGILSTTU**	gesticulate
ACEEEHMNNNT	enhancement	**ACEEGIMMNRT**	centigramme
ACEEEHRSSTW	cheese straw	**ACEEGIMNSUW**	New Age music
ACEEEILMNPT	mantelpiece	**ACEEGINNORS**	Grecian nose
ACEEEILNPPR	pipe-cleaner	**ACEEGINORTT**	teratogenic
ACEEEILNQUV	equivalence	**ACEEGINPSTT**	pace-setting
ACEEEILNRRV	irrelevance	**ACEEGLLORST**	storage cell
ACEEEIMPRST	masterpiece	**ACEEGLLRSSY**	gracelessly
ACEEEINSSTT	necessitate	**ACEEGLMNNOT**	congealment
ACEEEJKLPST	steeplejack	**ACEEGMNORRS**	scaremonger

ACEEGNNORRS organ-screen
ACEEGNNOSST cognateness
ACEEHHIIRRZ hierarchize
ACEEHHLMRST crash helmet
ACEEHHNORST sheet anchor
ACEEHHOPTTY hypothecate
ACEEHIILPTT epithetical
ACEEHIINNRT inheritance
ACEEHIINSTT esthetician
ACEEHIKNRTW kitchenware
ACEEHILLRTY heretically
ACEEHILNRTT chain letter
ACEEHILORTT theoretical
ACEEHIMMNPT impeachment
ACEEHIMNNNT enchainment
ACEEHIMORTT theorematic
ACEEHIMRTTY erythematic
ACEEHINPRSS preachiness
ACEEHINPRTT parenthetic
ACEEHINSTTU unaesthetic
ACEEHIOPRST spirochaete
ACEEHIPRTTU therapeutic
ACEEHIPRTVY hyperactive
ACEEHJKLLST shell-jacket
ACEEHLMNRUU Herculaneum
ACEEHLOORRU leucorrhoea
ACEEHLOPRRT perchlorate
ACEEHLORSTT earth closet
ACEEHMNNNTT enchantment
ACEEHMNNRRT trencherman
ACEEHNNRSST enchantress
ACEEHORRSTT orchestrate
ACEEHORRSTU treacherous
ACEEHPQRRSU square perch
ACEEIILLNPT penicillate
ACEEIILLNRT rectilineal
ACEEIILNRRT rectilinear
ACEEIILPRTV replicative
ACEEIILPTVX explicative
ACEEIILRTVZ verticalize
ACEEIIMNRRT recriminate
ACEEIINNTUV enunciative
ACEEIINRSST insectaries
ACEEIINRTTV interactive
ACEEIIPPRTT peripatetic, precipitate
ACEEIIRSSTT cassiterite
ACEEIKLLNSV Kelvin scale
ACEEIKMPRRT market price
ACEEIKNRSTW awestricken
ACEEIKNSSSS seasickness
ACEEILLLSTY celestially
ACEEILLNNSS cleanliness
ACEEILLNOST selectional
ACEEILLNPST slate-pencil
ACEEILLSUVV sluice-valve
ACEEILMNNRT incremental
ACEEILMNRTT Central Time
ACEEILMORRT calorimeter
ACEEILMORST elastomeric
ACEEILMPSTU time capsule
ACEEILMRTUV vermiculate
ACEEILNNORT intolerance
ACEEILNNOTU enucleation
ACEEILNNRST intercensal
ACEEILNNTUU uninucleate
ACEEILNNTUY lieutenancy
ACEEILNOPTX exceptional
ACEEILNORSS recessional
ACEEILNORST resectional
ACEEILNOSSS secessional
ACEEILNPRTT centripetal
ACEEILNPSSS specialness
ACEEILNQUVY equivalency
ACEEILNRRVY irrelevancy
ACEEILNRSSY necessarily
ACEEILNRTTY Eternal City
ACEEILOPSTT police state
ACEEILORRTV correlative
ACEEILORTUX executorial
ACEEILOTVVY evocatively
ACEEILPSTUV speculative
ACEEILSTTTU testiculate
ACEEIMMNORT anemometric
ACEEIMMORST commiserate
ACEEIMNNOTT cementation
ACEEIMNORTT actinometer
ACEEIMNQRTU acquirement
ACEEIMOSTVZ vasectomize
ACEEINNNSST ancientness
ACEEINNORSS reascension
ACEEINNRRSU reinsurance
ACEEINNSSTX inexactness
ACEEINOPTTX expectation
ACEEINPRRST transpierce
ACEEINRRSTV transceiver
ACEEIOOPRTV cooperative
ACEEIOPRRTV procreative
ACEEIORRTTV retroactive
ACEEIORSTTX stereotaxic
ACEEIRSSTTU resuscitate
ACEEJNPRSTU superjacent
ACEEKKLMRSY mackerel sky
ACEEKLMNRTT tracklement
ACEEKLNRTUW Walnut Creek
ACEEKMRRSTW wreck-master
ACEEKNRSTTV track events
ACEELLLORTY electorally
ACEELLNOPVY polyvalence
ACEELLNOSTT constellate
ACEELMNOPTT contemplate
ACEELNNNSSU uncleanness
ACEELNNRSSU unclearness
ACEELNOOPRT coleopteran
ACEELNOOSSS close season
ACEELNOPSTT Pentecostal
ACEELNPTTXY expectantly
ACEELOORRTW water-cooler
ACEELOPPPRT copperplate
ACEELORSTTU locust-eater
ACEELORSTTW water closet
ACEEMMMOORT commemorate
ACEEMOPRTTU computerate
ACEENNOPRTU counterpane
ACEENNORRTV contravener
ACEENNORSTT consternate
ACEENNRSSUY unnecessary
ACEENOORSTT cotoneaster
ACEENOPRTTX expectorant
ACEEOPRRRTU recuperator
ACEEORRSTUW watercourse

ACEEPRRSSUU acupressure
ACEERRRTUUV recurvature
ACEFFFGILOR flag-officer
ACEFFFILOST facts of life
ACEFFGHILNR cliffhanger
ACEFFGILNTY affectingly
ACEFFGLORTU flag of truce
ACEFFIILPST spifflicate
ACEFFIITTVY affectivity
ACEFFILOSST last offices
ACEFFILRSST trafficless
ACEFFIMOPST stamp office
ACEFFIOSSTU issue of fact
ACEFGHHIINN high finance
ACEFGHILPST space flight
ACEFGHIORTT factor eight
ACEFGHLLNOT focal length
ACEFGHLNNOR Anglo-French
ACEFGIIMNNT magnificent
ACEFGIINNRT interfacing
ACEFGILNRTU centrifugal
ACEFHILMNOR line of march
ACEFHILNOPR Francophile
ACEFHLLOORW fowl cholera
ACEFHLNRTUY half-century
ACEFHLOORST after-school
ACEFHLOPRRU reproachful
ACEFHMNNORW Frenchwoman
ACEFHMORRTT mothercraft
ACEFHNNOOPR francophone
ACEFHNORSTT French toast
ACEFIIINORT reification
ACEFIILMNOR infomercial
ACEFIILNNSS finicalness
ACEFIILNRTV vertical fin
ACEFIILPRSU superficial
ACEFIINOPTT pontificate
ACEFIINORTZ fractionize
ACEFIINRRTU curtain fire
ACEFIIORRTY reificatory
ACEFILLLOTU folliculate
ACEFILLORUW cauliflower
ACEFILORSST trace fossil
ACEFILORSTU lactiferous
ACEFILOSTUY facetiously
ACEFILSSTUU suitcaseful
ACEFIMNOPRY fire company
ACEFIMNOTTU tumefaction
ACEFINNRSST franticness
ACEFIOORRTV vociferator
ACEFIPRRSTT priestcraft
ACEFKORRRTW craftworker
ACEFKORRSUW work surface
ACEFLLOORSU false colour
ACEFLNOOPRS soprano clef
ACEFLNSSTTU tactfulness
ACEGGINNORU encouraging
ACEGGINRSSS scragginess
ACEGGLNOOYY gynaecology
ACEGHHILRST searchlight
ACEGHHMNRRU hunger march
ACEGHHNORST short change
ACEGHHOOPRR choreograph
ACEGHIKLLNS shellacking
ACEGHIKMNOP epoch-making
ACEGHILLNNN channelling
ACEGHILLNTT lancet light
ACEGHILLOOR rheological
ACEGHILLOOT ethological, theological
ACEGHILNRSY searchingly
ACEGHILOPSY geophysical
ACEGHIMMOOT homogametic
ACEGHIMNORU archegonium
ACEGHINORRS horse racing
ACEGHINORRV overarching
ACEGHINPRSS graphicness
ACEGHIOPRRX xerographic
ACEGHIOPTYZ phagocytize
ACEGHLOOSTY eschatology
ACEGHNOPRSY scenography
ACEGHOOPSTY phagocytose
ACEGIIKLNRS arse-licking
ACEGIIKNPRS asking price
ACEGIILLNNV clean-living
ACEGIILOSTT egotistical
ACEGIIMRRTV gravimetric
ACEGIKNORST orange stick
ACEGILLMRTU metallurgic
ACEGILLNNOR non-allergic
ACEGILLNNOY congenially
ACEGILLNOOO oenological
ACEGILLNOOP penological
ACEGILLOORS serological
ACEGILLOOSX sexological
ACEGILMNRSY screamingly
ACEGILNNNOU uncongenial
ACEGILNNOOT congelation
ACEGILNNPRS spring-clean
ACEGILNNSUY unceasingly
ACEGILNORRS carol-singer
ACEGILNRSSY caressingly
ACEGILNTUUU unguiculate
ACEGILRRTUU agriculture
ACEGIMNNNOT non-magnetic
ACEGIMNNOPR panicmonger
ACEGIMNOOST somatogenic
ACEGINNORST recognisant
ACEGINNORTZ recognizant
ACEGINNRSTY astringency
ACEGINOSTTV casting vote
ACEGKRSSTTU stage-struck
ACEGLMNORWY clergywoman
ACEGLNORTUY granulocyte
ACEGLRSSTTU glass cutter
ACEGMNNORSS congressman
ACEGMOPRRST spectrogram
ACEGMORSTTY gastrectomy
ACEGNOORRTT gerontocrat
ACEGOOPRSST gastroscope
ACEHHIILMOP haemophilic, hemophiliac
ACEHHIIMRRS hierarchism
ACEHHIINNTY hyacinthine
ACEHHIMRSTT Thatcherism
ACEHHOORSTY chaos theory
ACEHHOPRTYY hypothecary
ACEHIIINPSZ Hispanicize
ACEHIILLOPT paleolithic
ACEHIILMSTT athleticism
ACEHIILNOPR necrophilia

ACEHIILOSTT	heliostatic
ACEHIILRSVW	swivel chair
ACEHIINNOPT	phonetician
ACEHIINNTTU	inauthentic
ACEHIINORRT	rhetorician
ACEHIINPSTT	pantheistic
ACEHIKLLRWY	illywhacker
ACEHIKLPRRS	parish clerk
ACEHIKLPRST	chalk-stripe
ACEHIKLPRTY	prickly heat
ACEHIKMNORS	chain-smoker
ACEHIKMRTUY	rheumaticky
ACEHIKRSSTW	cat's whisker
ACEHILLNTUY	unethically
ACEHILLORTW	white-collar
ACEHILLPRSY	spherically
ACEHILMMNPY	lamp-chimney
ACEHILMNOOT	machine tool
ACEHILMNOST	slot machine
ACEHILMRSTZ	schmaltzier
ACEHILNPRST	sphincteral
ACEHILNSTTY	synthetical
ACEHILOPPRT	prophetical
ACEHILRSSSY	chrysalises
ACEHIMMOPRT	metamorphic
ACEHIMNORSS	marchioness
ACEHIMNOSYY	hyoscyamine
ACEHIMOOSTT	homeostatic
ACEHIMOPRST	atmospheric
ACEHIMORRYZ	mycorrhizae
ACEHIMORTTX	thermotaxic
ACEHIMPSSTY	metaphysics
ACEHIMPSTTY	sympathetic
ACEHIMRSSST	Christmases
ACEHINNPSSU	paunchiness
ACEHINNRSSU	raunchiness
ACEHINNTTUU	unauthentic
ACEHINOPRRS	chairperson
ACEHINOPRRT	chiropteran
ACEHINOPRTU	neuropathic
ACEHINRSSST	starchiness
ACEHINSSSTT	cattishness
ACEHIOOPSTT	osteopathic
ACEHIORSSTY	case history
ACEHIORSTTW	Crosthwaite
ACEHIPRRSST	strip-search
ACEHIQRRSUY	squirearchy
ACEHLLMRSSY	charmlessly
ACEHLLMSSTY	matchlessly
ACEHLMOSSST	stomachless
ACEHLNNRTTY	trenchantly
ACEHLNOPRTY	lycanthrope
ACEHLNORSTW	Charlestown
ACEHLOOSSTT	state school
ACEHLPPPRTU	purple patch
ACEHMNOPRSY	prosenchyma
ACEHMOOPPST	compost heap
ACEHMOORTTY	tracheotomy
ACEHMOPRSTU	champertous
ACEHMORSTTU	master touch
ACEHNNSSSTU	staunchness
ACEHOPPRRTT	chart-topper
ACEHOPRRSSY	chrysoprase
ACEHORSSTTT	scattershot
ACEIIIILNVZ	civilianize
ACEIIILMNRZ	criminalize
ACEIIILMPTV	implicative
ACEIIILNOTT	elicitation
ACEIIILPSTT	pietistical
ACEIIIMNNRT	incriminate
ACEIIIMNOST	semiotician
ACEIIIMNSTT	anti-Semitic
ACEIIIQSTUV	acquisitive
ACEIIKLLNTY	kinetically
ACEIIKLLOOR	kilocalorie
ACEIIKLRSTT	rickettsial
ACEIIKNRSSS	airsickness
ACEIILLMMTY	mimetically
ACEIILLMNNU	illuminance
ACEIILLMOTY	meiotically
ACEIILLMPRY	empirically
ACEIILLMSSY	seismically
ACEIILLNRTV	intervallic
ACEIILLNSTT	scintillate
ACEIILLRSTY	eristically
ACEIILMNPRT	planimetric
ACEIILMNSTT	mentalistic
ACEIILMNSUZ	masculinize
ACEIILMRRTT	trimetrical
ACEIILNOPRT	replication
ACEIILNOPTX	explication
ACEIILNOQTU	equinoctial
ACEIILNOTUV	inoculative
ACEIILNPRUY	pecuniarily
ACEIILNPTUV	inculpative
ACEIILNRRUV	curvilinear
ACEIILNRSTT	clarinetist
ACEIILNRSTU	unrealistic
ACEIILNRTTY	intricately
ACEIILPRRTU	picture rail
ACEIILPRSTT	peristaltic
ACEIILPRSTZ	plasticizer
ACEIILPRTUY	peculiarity
ACEIILRTTVY	verticality
ACEIIMNNORS	Micronesian
ACEIIMNNRST	manneristic
ACEIIMNOPRT	imprecation
ACEIIMNORST	creationism
ACEIIMNORTT	interatomic, metrication
ACEIIMNORTZ	romanticize
ACEIIMNOSTZ	monasticize
ACEIIMNPRRU	pericranium
ACEIIMNPSSU	impuissance
ACEIIMNRRSU	cinerariums
ACEIIMNRSTU	insectarium
ACEIIMNSSTT	semanticist
ACEIINNNOST	incensation
ACEIINNNOTU	enunciation
ACEIINNOPTT	pectination
ACEIINNORRT	incinerator
ACEIINNORTT	interaction
ACEIINOORTX	excoriation
ACEIINOPRTT	crepitation
ACEIINORSTT	creationist, reactionist
ACEIINORTTX	extrication
ACEIINPPRTT	precipitant
ACEIINPRTTY	antipyretic, pertinacity
ACEIJKLOPTT	pilot-jacket
ACEIJLPRSUY	special jury
ACEIKKLNPTY	penalty kick

ACEIKKRRSTT kick-starter
ACEIKLLLRSV Clarksville
ACEIKLPPRRY prickly pear
ACEIKMNORST section-mark
ACEILLLMNOR lamellicorn
ACEILLLMOPY polemically
ACEILLLNRUU unicellular
ACEILLLRTUY cellularity
ACEILLMNNOT non-metallic
ACEILLMNRUY numerically
ACEILLMNSUY masculinely
ACEILLMRRUY mercurially
ACEILLNOPTU cupellation
ACEILLNOSTY sectionally
ACEILLNRSTY crystalline
ACEILLOPPSY episcopally
ACEILLOPRTY pre-coitally
ACEILLOQUVY equivocally
ACEILLRSTTY crystallite
ACEILLRSTYZ crystallize
ACEILLRTUVY lucratively
ACEILMMNOTY metonymical
ACEILMMNOUZ communalize
ACEILMMORTT recommittal
ACEILMMRSTY symmetrical
ACEILMNOOPS scopolamine
ACEILMNOOPW policewoman
ACEILMNRTTU curtailment
ACEILMNSSSU musicalness
ACEILMORRTY calorimetry
ACEILNNNOSS nonsensical
ACEILNNNOTT continental
ACEILNNOOPT Neoplatonic
ACEILNNRTUY uncertainly
ACEILNNSSTY incessantly
ACEILNOOPRR incorporeal
ACEILNOOPRT neotropical, percolation
ACEILNOORRT correlation
ACEILNOPRRY prince royal
ACEILNOPSTU speculation
ACEILNOPTUX exculpation
ACEILNOQUUV unequivocal
ACEILNORSTT intercostal
ACEILNORSUX excursional
ACEILNORTUV countervail
ACEILNOSTUY tenaciously
ACEILNRRRTU intercrural
ACEILNRRTUV ventricular
ACEILOOPPRS polariscope
ACEILOORSTY oral society
ACEILOPRRTT protractile
ACEILOPRTVY proactively
ACEILOPRTXY explicatory
ACEILORSUVY veraciously
ACEILORTVYY viceroyalty
ACEIMMORRTU crematorium
ACEIMMOTTUV commutative
ACEIMMPRSSU supremacism
ACEIMNNNOTT containment
ACEIMNNOORY oneiromancy
ACEIMNOORTX axonometric
ACEIMNORRTY craniometry
ACEIMOOPRTW atomic power
ACEIMOORTVY ovariectomy
ACEIMOPRRTY cryptomeria, imprecatory
ACEIMPRSSTU supremacist
ACEIMSSSTTY systematics
ACEINNNNSSU uncanniness
ACEINNNOSTT Constantine
ACEINNOOTTV connotative
ACEINNORSTT transection
ACEINNOSTTY encystation
ACEINNPTUUV nuncupative
ACEINNRRRUY cinerary urn
ACEINNRSSSW scrawniness
ACEINNRTTUY uncertainty
ACEINOOOPRT cooperation
ACEINOOPRRT incorporate, procreation
ACEINOORRTT retroaction
ACEINOORTUV overcaution
ACEINOOSSST iconostases
ACEINOPRRTU Puerto Rican
ACEINOPRSSS prosaicness
ACEINORRTTY contrariety
ACEINORSTTV contrastive
ACEINPPRSSS scrappiness
ACEINPRSSTU sprauncicst
ACEINRSSSSU narcissuses
ACEIOOPRRTV corporative
ACEIOOPRTVV provocative
ACEIOOQRTUV equivocator
ACEIOPRRSTT triceratops
ACEJKLLRSSU Jack Russell
ACEKKMORSTT stock market
ACEKMORRSST market cross
ACEKMRSSTTY track system
ACELLLMORUY molecularly
ACELLMPRTTU trumpet call
ACELLNOSSSU callousness
ACELLNRTTUY reluctantly
ACELLOOPRRY corporeally
ACELLOORRST roller-coast
ACELLOORSTU slate colour
ACELMOPSTUY costume play
ACELMRSTUUU musculature
ACELNNNOOOS loose cannon
ACELNNOOPVX planoconvex
ACELNNRSTTU translucent
ACELNORSUVY cavernously
ACELNOSSTTU sans culotte
ACELNOSTTTU talent scout
ACELOOPRRTT protectoral
ACELOOPRRTY corporately
ACELOORRSTW slow reactor
ACELOORRTUW watercolour
ACELOPRSTTT scatter plot
ACELOPRTUXY exculpatory
ACEMMNOORTT commentator
ACEMMNOPRTT compartment
ACEMNOOPRST compensator
ACEMOOPRSSS compass rose
ACEMORSSTTU Scoutmaster
ACENOORRSTV conservator
ACENOOSTTTW cotton waste
ACENOPRRSTU Procrustean
ACENOPRRTTU counterpart
ACENORSSSUU raucousness
ACENORSTTUY country seat

ACENOSSSUUV	vacuousness
ACEORSSSSSY	syssarcoses
ACFFGIIKNRT	trafficking
ACFFGIINRST	traffic sign
ACFFGINOSTU	suffocating
ACFFIIILMOS	officialism
ACFFIIINOOT	officiation
ACFFIILLNOY	officinally
ACFFINOOSTU	suffocation
ACFGIIINNST	significant
ACFGIINSTTU	fungistatic
ACFGILOSUUY	fugaciously
ACFGINRSSTU	surf-casting
ACFHIMORRST	ostrich farm
ACFHIOPRSTY	factory ship
ACFHOOPRSTY	factory shop
ACFIIINNOTU	unification
ACFIILLMMSU	musical film
ACFIILLNOTY	fictionally
ACFIILLRSUY	surficially
ACFIILMNORU	californium
ACFIILMORST	formalistic
ACFIIMNOORT	formication
ACFIIMNORST	informatics
ACFIINNOORT	fornication
ACFIINORTUY	unificatory
ACFIKKPSSUU	kick up a fuss
ACFILMNNOTU	malfunction
ACFILNOTTUU	fluctuation
ACFILORSTUY	fractiously
ACFINNOOTTU	confutation
ACFINNORSTW	Francistown
ACFINNORTUY	functionary
ACFLLMNOORY	conformally
ACGGIIKKLNO	goal-kicking
ACGGILNOORS	goalscoring
ACGGILOSTWY	Glasgow City
ACGHHILOOPR	holographic
ACGHHINOPRY	ichnography
ACGHHIOPRRY	chirography
ACGHHNOOPRR	chronograph
ACGHHOOPRRY	chorography
ACGHIILMORT	algorithmic, logarithmic
ACGHIKMOPRY	kymographic
ACGHILLMOOO	homological
ACGHILLOOOR	horological
ACGHILNOOTU	touch-in-goal
ACGHIMNOOPR	gramophonic, monographic, nomographic
ACGHINOOPRY	iconography
ACGHINOPRYZ	zincography
ACGHINPRSTW	watch spring
ACGHIOOPPRT	topographic
ACGHIOPPRTY	pictography, typographic
ACGHIOPRSTY	hypogastric
ACGHIRSSTTW	twitch grass
ACGHIRSTTTU	straight-cut
ACGHMOOPRSY	cosmography
ACGIIJNORST	jargonistic
ACGIILLLLOY	illogically
ACGIILLNOOS	sinological
ACGIILLNOOT	colligation
ACGIILLNTUV	victualling
ACGIILLOORV	virological
ACGIILNNOOT	cognitional
ACGIILNPSST	slip casting
ACGIIMNOSST	agnosticism
ACGIINNNOST	incognisant
ACGIINNNOTZ	incognizant
ACGIINNOSTW	wainscoting
ACGIINORRTY	tragic irony
ACGIJJKMNPU	jumping jack
ACGIJLNOTUY	conjugality
ACGIJNNOOTU	conjugation
ACGIKKNOSTT	stocktaking
ACGILLMNOOO	monological
ACGILLMOOOP	pomological
ACGILLMOORS	oscillogram
ACGILLMOOTY	climatology
ACGILLMOOYZ	zymological
ACGILLNOOOS	nosological
ACGILLNOOOT	ontological
ACGILLOOOPS	posological
ACGILLOOOPT	topological
ACGILLOOPTY	typological
ACGILLOTYYZ	zygotically
ACGIMNNOORT	morning coat
ACGIMNOORRT	motor racing
ACGIMNOORST	gastronomic
ACGINNORRSY	carryings-on
ACGINOOPRTU	action group
ACGINOORRTU	corrugation
ACGINOORSTY	cosignatory
ACGLLNOOOVY	volcanology
ACGLLNOOUVY	vulcanology
ACGLMNNOOUY	agony column
ACGMOOPRRTU	compurgator
ACGMOOPRSSY	gyrocompass
ACGNOORSSTT	cotton grass
ACGRRSSSUVY	scurvy grass
ACHHIILLPTY	ithyphallic
ACHHILOPRSS	scholarship
ACHHINSSTUZ	schizanthus
ACHHIOPRTTY	trichopathy
ACHHIORSTUY	ichthyosaur
ACHHNOOSTTU	autochthons
ACHHOPPSTYY	psychopathy
ACHIIILPRSV	civil parish
ACHIIINPSST	Hispanicist
ACHIILLMSWY	whimsically
ACHIILMOSTT	Thomistical
ACHIILMPSSY	physicalism
ACHIILNRSTY	Christianly
ACHIILOOPPR	coprophilia
ACHIILOPSST	sophistical
ACHIILPSSTY	physicalist
ACHIILPSTYY	physicality
ACHIIMNORST	harmonistic
ACHIIMORRRS	Morris chair
ACHIINNRSTU	unchristian
ACHIINSSTTT	satin stitch
ACHILLMOOPR	allomorphic
ACHILMORRYZ	mycorrhizal
ACHILNNOPSY	non-physical
ACHILNOORRT	chlorinator
ACHIMOPPPSU	hippocampus
ACHIMRSSSTY	Christmassy
ACHIOOPRTTU	autotrophic

ACHIOOPSTTT	photostatic
ACHIOPPRSTY	saprophytic
ACHIOPRRSTU	curatorship
ACHKLNRSUYY	Krasnyy Luch
ACHLLNORSUY	unscholarly
ACHLLOOPRST	chloroplast
ACHLMMOOORS	chromosomal
ACHLNOPRTYY	lycanthropy
ACHMMOPPSTU	stomach pump
ACHOPRSTUXY	choux pastry
ACIIILMNOPT	implication
ACIIILMNRTY	criminality
ACIIILNNNOT	inclination
ACIIILRSTTU	ritualistic
ACIIINNOTTT	nictitation
ACIIINOQSTU	acquisition
ACIILLLNOOS	collisional
ACIILLLOPTY	politically
ACIILLMNOOS	colonialism
ACIILLMNOOT	collimation
ACIILLMNPUY	municipally
ACIILLMOSUY	maliciously
ACIILLNNSTT	scintillant
ACIILLNOOST	colonialist, oscillation
ACIILLNOPTU	unpolitical
ACIILLNOVVY	convivially
ACIILLNPPRY	principally
ACIILLOPRTY	pictorially
ACIILLPRSTU	pluralistic
ACIILLQUYZZ	quizzically
ACIILMNNOTU	culmination
ACIILMNOOPT	compilation
ACIILMNSSTU	masculinist
ACIILMNSTUY	masculinity
ACIILMOPRRY	primary coil
ACIILMSTTUU	mutualistic
ACIILNNOOTU	inoculation
ACIILNNOPTU	inculpation
ACIILNNSTTU	instinctual
ACIILNOSSTU	unsocialist
ACIILNOTTUV	cultivation
ACIILNOTUVY	univocality
ACIILOPRRST	scriptorial
ACIILORSSST	scissor-tail
ACIILORSUVY	vicariously
ACIILOSUVVY	vivaciously
ACIIMMNNOOT	commination
ACIIMMNORST	romanticism
ACIIMMNOSST	monasticism
ACIIMMNSSTU	numismatics
ACIIMNOORSU	acrimonious
ACIIMNORSTT	romanticist
ACIINNOOPTT	action point
ACIINNORRTU	Iron Curtain
ACIINNORTUV	incurvation
ACIINOOPRST	anisotropic
ACIINOOSSST	iconostasis
ACIINOPRTTU	unpatriotic
ACIINORSTTU	rustication
ACIINRTTTUY	taciturnity
ACIIOPRTTVY	proactivity
ACIIOPSSSTT	psittacosis
ACIJNNOORTU	conjuration
ACIKOOPRRTY	prokaryotic
ACILLMNOORY	moronically
ACILLMNOPTY	compliantly
ACILLMNSUUY	unmusically
ACILLMOOSTY	osmotically
ACILLNNOTUY	continually
ACILLNOOOPT	local option
ACILLNPTUYY	untypically
ACILLOORSTY	oscillatory
ACILMMMNOSU	communalism
ACILMMNOOTY	commonality
ACILMMNOSTU	communalist
ACILMMNOTUY	communality
ACILMMORSSU	commissural
ACILMORSTUY	customarily
ACILMRSTUUY	muscularity
ACILNNOOOST	consolation
ACILNOOORTU	colouration
ACILNOPRTUY	inculpatory
ACILNORSSTU	ultrasonics
ACILNPTTUUY	punctuality
ACILOOPRRTY	corporality
ACILOORSTUY	atrociously
ACILOORSUVY	voraciously
ACIMMNOORTY	comminatory
ACIMMNOOTTU	commutation
ACIMMOPSTTY	symptomatic
ACIMNOOORTU	auction room
ACIMNOOOSTT	somatotonic
ACIMNOOPTTU	computation
ACIMOOPRRST	corporatism
ACINNNNOOST	inconsonant
ACINNNOOOTT	connotation
ACINNNOPTUU	nuncupation
ACINNOOPRTT	contraption
ACINNOOPSTY	syncopation
ACINNOPTTUU	punctuation
ACINOOOPRRT	corporation
ACINOOOPRTV	provocation
ACINOOPRRST	conspirator
ACINOOPRRTT	protraction
ACINOOPRRTU	procuration
ACINOORRSUV	carnivorous
ACIOOPPRSTT	potato crisp
ACIOOPRRSTT	corporatist
ACIORSSSSSY	syssarcosis
ACLLMNOORUY	monocularly
ACLLMOORRST	storm-collar
ACLLMOORSUY	clamorously
ACLLMOSTUUU	altocumulus
ACLLNNORTUY	nocturnally
ACLMNOORRST	arms control
ACLNNNOOSTY	consonantly
ACLNOOORSTY	consolatory
ACLNOOPRRSU	proconsular
ACLNOORRSUY	rancorously
ACLOOPRSUXY	xylocarpous
ACLOORRSTUW	straw colour
ACMMNOORSTU	consummator
ACMNOOOPRSU	monocarpous
ADDDDENNOSS	odds and ends
ADDDDNOOSSS	odds and sods
ADDDEEHNNRU	underhanded
ADDDEEHNSTU	sudden death
ADDDEENRSSU	unaddressed
ADDDEFGORRT	draft dodger
ADDDEGGLOPY	doggy-paddle

ADDDEGHINPU	pudding-head
ADDDEGORRSS	dodder-grass
ADDDENOORWW	dawn redwood
ADDDERSSTTU	star-studded
ADDDILQSTUY	diddly-squat
ADDEEEEHLLV	level-headed
ADDEEEGGILN	leading edge
ADDEEEGHPSW	wedge-shaped
ADDEEEHHNRT	three-handed
ADDEEEHIKNS	hide-and-seek
ADDEEEHLLPW	paddle wheel
ADDEEEHLLSW	swelled head
ADDEEEHMPTY	empty-headed
ADDEEELLPST	pedestalled
ADDEEGHHILT	light-headed
ADDEEGHILPY	pig-headedly
ADDEEGHNORW	wrong-headed
ADDEEGHOORT	good-hearted
ADDEEGIIRTV	Great Divide
ADDEEGILMNR	large-minded
ADDEEGIOSSS	dog's disease
ADDEEGJMNTU	adjudgement
ADDEEGNORUY	Younger Edda
ADDEEGNRSSU	guardedness
ADDEEHHLOTY	hot-headedly
ADDEEHHNRTU	thunderhead
ADDEEHIKNRT	kind-hearted
ADDEEHLORSS	saddle-horse
ADDEEHMNPTY	empty-handed
ADDEEHNORTW	downhearted
ADDEEHPRRSS	hard-pressed
ADDEEILLSVW	well advised
ADDEEILRRVY	daredevilry
ADDEEIMRSTU	desideratum
ADDEEINOPRT	depredation
ADDEEMNNNRU	undermanned
ADDEEMOORRT	made to order
ADDEEMRSSTU	mustard seed
ADDEENPRSUU	unpersuaded
ADDEEOPRRTY	depredatory
ADDEFFHLNOY	offhandedly
ADDEFFIISST	distaff side
ADDEFHINSSS	faddishness
ADDEFIIMOTW	midwife toad
ADDEGGHORTU	god-daughter
ADDEGGIIIRT	digitigrade
ADDEGGILNRY	degradingly
ADDEGHHINRT	right-handed
ADDEGHNORTU	dreadnought
ADDEGILMNNY	demandingly, maddeningly
ADDEGIMNNNU	undemanding
ADDEGINNOSU	undiagnosed
ADDEGLNRUUY	unguardedly
ADDEGNOORTU	good-natured
ADDEHHNORST	short-handed
ADDEHIILMOT	thalidomide
ADDEHILNOPR	philodendra
ADDEHILNORS	Rhode Island
ADDEHILNSSS	laddishness
ADDEHILOPSU	diadelphous
ADDEHINORTY	dehydration
ADDEHLOPRSU	shoulder pad
ADDEHLORSTT	stadtholder
ADDEIIINTUV	individuate
ADDEILLMMNS	small-minded
ADDEILNSUVY	unadvisedly
ADDEIMNOORS	rose diamond
ADDEIOOPPSU	pseudopodia
ADDELLNORRY	dandy roller
ADDELLNORVY	Dolly Varden
ADDELMNOTUU	unmodulated
ADDELMOORTU	demodulator
ADDELNNRTUY	redundantly
ADDELNNTUUY	undauntedly
ADDEMNOOORT	rodomontade
ADDGGHILNNO	dog-handling
ADDGHILLNNO	landholding
ADDGHILNOOR	road-holding
ADDGHNORTUW	down draught
ADDHLOOORYY	Holy Rood Day
ADDILMNORTY	dirty old man
ADDLOOQSTUY	doodly-squat
ADDNNOPSSUW	ups and downs
ADEEEEFGHRT	feather edge
ADEEEEGGRST	desegregate
ADEEEELLNVV	needle valve
ADEEEFILNRT	deferential
ADEEEFNRSSV	vas deferens
ADEEEFNRSTT	fenestrated
ADEEEGGLLNO	golden eagle
ADEEEGGLMOR	George Medal
ADEEEGGNNOT	engaged tone
ADEEEGILMNR	legerdemain
ADEEEGIMNRR	gendarmerie
ADEEEGIMNTZ	demagnetize
ADEEEGINNRT	tragedienne
ADEEEGLLNRT	legal tender
ADEEEGMNNRT	derangement
ADEEEGNOTXY	deoxygenate
ADEEEHIMPSZ	de-emphasize
ADEEEHIRSTW	weather side
ADEEEHLLORS	leaseholder
ADEEEHMORST	homesteader
ADEEEHNOPRT	open-hearted
ADEEEHNRRSU	unrehearsed
ADEEEHPPRTY	deep therapy
ADEEEHPRSST	spreadsheet
ADEEEHRRTTU	true-hearted
ADEEEIILMVZ	medievalize
ADEEEILLMNS	linseed meal
ADEEEILLMRS	Emerald Isle
ADEEEILMSSY	Lyme disease
ADEEEILSUXZ	desexualize
ADEEEIMNRTT	determinate
ADEEEIMPRTT	premeditate
ADEEEINNRTV	Venetian red
ADEEEIORRTT	deteriorate
ADEEEIRRSTV	re-advertise
ADEEEKLLLRW	lake-dweller
ADEEEKLRRST	deerstalker
ADEEELLLPSW	well pleased
ADEEELLMRYY	medley relay
ADEEELLNSWY	Wensleydale
ADEEELLSSTT	tessellated
ADEEELMMNRT	entrammeled
ADEEELMNNOW	needlewoman
ADEEELNNRSS	learnedness
ADEEELNRSST	relatedness
ADEEELNRSSX	relaxedness

ADEEELNRTTU launderette
ADEEELNSSTX exaltedness
ADEEELPRSTY desperately
ADEEEMOSTWW meadowsweet
ADEEENRSSSV adverseness
ADEEEOPRRSW road sweeper
ADEEFFIINRT differentia
ADEEFGIINNR fine-grained
ADEEFGILNNY deafeningly
ADEEFGINNRR rangefinder
ADEEFGIRTVY gravity feed
ADEEFHLLRTU full-hearted
ADEEFHOOTVY heavy-footed
ADEEFHORSTT soft-hearted
ADEEFILPRSS self-despair
ADEEFIOPSST safe deposit
ADEEFLLOORR floor leader
ADEEFLLORVW well-favored
ADEEFLRSSSU self-assured
ADEEFMORRTT reformatted
ADEEFNRRRST transferred
ADEEFOOPRRR proof-reader
ADEEFPRSTTU superfatted
ADEEGGGIRRV gravedigger
ADEEGGIINRS disagreeing
ADEEGGILRVY aggrievedly
ADEEGGLORTW waterlogged
ADEEGGMORUY demagoguery
ADEEGGNORRV Garden Grove
ADEEGHINRST near-sighted
ADEEGHIRRST sight-reader
ADEEGHLNORS golden share
ADEEGHMOPRR demographer
ADEEGHNNPRW grand-nephew
ADEEGHNORSY hydrogenase
ADEEGHNORTY hydrogenate
ADEEGIILNNR leading-rein
ADEEGILLNRS resignalled
ADEEGILLNRY legendarily
ADEEGILNNOT leading note, leading tone
ADEEGILNNRY endearingly
ADEEGILNNST disentangle
ADEEGILNPST pedestaling
ADEEGIMMNRU medium-range
ADEEGJLMNTU judgemental
ADEEGLNOSTT Golden State
ADEEGLNRTUU unregulated
ADEEGMNNORY danger money
ADEEGMNRRRY gerrymander
ADEEHHLORRS shareholder
ADEEHHNOPRT heptahedron
ADEEHHNORSX hexahedrons
ADEEHILLNOT endothelial
ADEEHILNOPT elephantoid
ADEEHILNORT lion-hearted
ADEEHILNPRR philanderer
ADEEHIRRRSS hairdresser
ADEEHIRRRSW washer-drier
ADEEHIRRSTW Harris tweed
ADEEHKLORST stakeholder
ADEEHKMNORT mother-naked
ADEEHLLNOSV love handles
ADEEHLLNOSW swollen head
ADEEHLMNOTT mentholated
ADEEHLNNRST Netherlands
ADEEHLPPRSU pedal-pusher
ADEEHNNOPRT pentahedron
ADEEHNORRTT tetrahedron
ADEEHNOSSTW stonewashed
ADEEHNSTUUX unexhausted
ADEEHRRRSWY washer-dryer
ADEEIIKNPSS pink disease
ADEEIILLNRT inter-allied
ADEEIILMMSV medievalism
ADEEIILMMTY immediately
ADEEIILMSTV medievalist
ADEEIILNNOT delineation
ADEEIILNRST residential
ADEEIIMMNPT impedimenta
ADEEIIMNSST disseminate
ADEEIINRTVY evidentiary
ADEEILLMNNR ill-mannered
ADEEILLMRSV silver medal
ADEEILLPPRR ill-prepared
ADEEILMNNST enlisted man
ADEEILMNORT endometrial
ADEEILMNRST streamlined
ADEEILMNRTT detrimental
ADEEILMOORT meteoroidal
ADEEILNNPUX unexplained
ADEEILNORRT old retainer
ADEEILNRSTY sedentarily
ADEEILNRUWY unweariedly
ADEEILNSTTT dilettantes
ADEEILPRSSU displeasure
ADEEILRRSVV slave-driver
ADEEIMMNORS misdemeanor
ADEEIMMNOSU eudaemonism
ADEEIMNNRTT determinant, detrainment
ADEEIMNNTTU edutainment
ADEEIMNOPRT predominate
ADEEIMNRSTY sedimentary
ADEEINNRSSU unreadiness
ADEEINNRTTV inadvertent
ADEEINOPRST desperation
ADEEINORTTU deuteration
ADEEINOSTTT detestation
ADEEINQRTUV verd-antique
ADEEINSSTTU unsteadiest
ADEEJMNRRRY Jerrymander
ADEEKLOPRSU loudspeaker
ADEELLLNNPW well-planned
ADEELLNNRUY unlearnedly
ADEELLNRTUV untravelled
ADEELMMNRTU untrammeled
ADEELNOORST aldosterone
ADEELNOORUV Nuevo Laredo
ADEELNOOSST at loose ends
ADEELNOPRRS alderperson
ADEEMMNORTY dynamometer
ADEEMNNNSSU mundaneness
ADEEMNNOOOW wood anemone
ADEEMNOPPRR name-dropper
ADEEMNORSTT demonstrate
ADEEMNPTTTU unattempted
ADEEMNRRRWY merry andrew
ADEEMOPPRSU purpose-made
ADEENNNRTTU undertenant

ADEENRRSTTU understater
ADEENRSSTUV adventuress
ADEFFILLMMM flimflammed
ADEFFILNRTU fault-finder
ADEFFIORSST disafforest
ADEFGILLNOS self-loading
ADEFGILNRSY lady's finger
ADEFGKNOORS godforsaken
ADEFGLORSTZ glazed frost
ADEFHIKOSST kiss of death
ADEFHILMSTY ham-fistedly
ADEFHILOORR foolhardier
ADEFHINNOSU unfashioned
ADEFIILLSUV visual field
ADEFIILMNPU unamplified
ADEFIILNOOT defoliation
ADEFIILNQUU unqualified
ADEFIILSSTY satisfiedly
ADEFIIMNRSU Freudianism
ADEFIINSSTU unsatisfied
ADEFILLORUV ill-favoured
ADEFILMNOSU sulfonamide
ADEFILNOORT defloration
ADEFILSSTTU distasteful
ADEFIMNOORT deformation
ADEFIMNORWW window frame
ADEFKLOPRSW powder flask
ADEFLLNOSST dental floss
ADEFLNOORRS fool's errand
ADEFLNORUUV unflavoured
ADEFLOOPSTY splay-footed
ADEFNORRSSW forwardness, frowardness
ADEFORRSTTU astroturfed
ADEGGGILYZZ zigzaggedly
ADEGGHILNRT right-angled
ADEGGIINNRW wide-ranging
ADEGGILNNOT goaltending
ADEGGIMOPSU pedagoguism
ADEGGINOSTY steady-going
ADEGGNORRST strong grade
ADEGHHILNNP helping hand
ADEGHHINNTU headhunting
ADEGHHINRRT right-hander
ADEGHHIRSTW High Steward
ADEGHHLNORU rough-handle
ADEGHIILNST ladies' night
ADEGHIILNTV living death
ADEGHILLNNS handselling
ADEGHIMNRST hamstringed
ADEGHINNNRU running head
ADEGHINNSSS dashingness
ADEGHMNORRT grandmother
ADEGHNNORUY younger hand
ADEGHORRSSU Horse Guards
ADEGIIKNNOS indigo snake
ADEGIILNNRW line drawing
ADEGIILNOSV video signal
ADEGIILNPSS displeasing
ADEGIILNSST sliding seat
ADEGIIMNOSS misdiagnose
ADEGIIMNPST die-stamping
ADEGIIMNRTT readmitting
ADEGIIMNTTU unmitigated
ADEGIINNORT denigration
ADEGIINNOST designation
ADEGIINNTUV undeviating
ADEGIINORSZ disorganize
ADEGIINRRWW wiredrawing
ADEGIINRTTU ingratitude
ADEGIKMNRSS dressmaking
ADEGIKNNRTU undertaking
ADEGILLOSSU gladioluses
ADEGILNNSSU languidness
ADEGILNOPSU Douglas pine
ADEGILNORSY grandiosely
ADEGILNOSTW long-waisted
ADEGILNPRTY panty girdle
ADEGILNRRWY rewardingly
ADEGILNSTTY settling day
ADEGIMNORRZ gormandizer
ADEGIMNORSU gourmandise
ADEGINNORUZ unorganized
ADEGINNPRTY pending tray
ADEGINNRRUW unrewarding
ADEGINORRTY denigratory
ADEGKLMOSSS smoked glass
ADEGLMOORTY dermatology
ADEGLNORSSU serous gland
ADEGLNORSUY dangerously
ADEGMMMNOOR monogrammed
ADEGNORRTUW groundwater
ADEGNORSTTU ground state
ADEGNORSTUW waste ground
ADEHHIILPRT diphtherial
ADEHHILMNSU human shield
ADEHHIMOORR haemorrhoid
ADEHHIOPPST diphosphate
ADEHHIORRSS horseradish
ADEHHLMRTTY delta rhythm
ADEHHNORTTU the hat round
ADEHHOOSTWW who-does-what
ADEHIIMNRTU antheridium
ADEHIIOPRSS diaphoresis
ADEHIIORSTT historiated
ADEHILLMMRR hammer drill
ADEHILLNRST disenthrall
ADEHILLOOPR haloperidol
ADEHIMMPPUY happy medium
ADEHIMORSTU diathermous
ADEHINNNSSU unhandiness
ADEHINNRSTU untarnished
ADEHINNRSUV unvarnished
ADEHINNRTTW handwritten
ADEHINORRRS Radnorshire
ADEHINORRTY rehydration
ADEHINOSSSW shadowiness
ADEHINRSTTW withstander
ADEHIPRSSTW stewardship
ADEHIPRSTTW sharp-witted
ADEHJMNOOOR Mohenjo-Daro
ADEHLLLMORS smallholder
ADEHLLLORST stallholder
ADEHNOORTTW down-to-earth
ADEHOPRSSTW shop steward
ADEIIILMNSV semi-invalid
ADEIIILMSST dissimilate
ADEIIINNTTU uninitiated
ADEIIIOPSTV diapositive
ADEIIIPSSTV dissipative

ADEIILLLOPS ellipsoidal
ADEIILLORTY editorially
ADEIILMNNOS dimensional
ADEIILMSSTU dissimulate
ADEIILNORSV diversional
ADEIILRRTTY irritatedly
ADEIIMMNSTU mediastinum
ADEIIMNOPSS impassioned
ADEIIMNORSS readmission
ADEIIMOPPTW meadow pipit
ADEIIMRSTTX taxidermist
ADEIINNNOTT indentation
ADEIINNOOPT opinionated
ADEIINNOSTT destination
ADEIINOPRTT partitioned, trepidation
ADEIINOPRTU repudiation
ADEIINOPRTV deprivation
ADEIINOPSST Passiontide
ADEIINORTTX extradition
ADEIINPRSTY stipendiary
ADEIINQSTTU equidistant
ADEIKNPPRSS sand-skipper
ADEILLORSST ill-assorted, Tordesillas
ADEILLOSVWW swallow-dive
ADEILMNNORT modern Latin
ADEILMNTTUU unmutilated
ADEILNNSTUU uninsulated
ADEILNOOPRT periodontal
ADEILNPPRST spider plant
ADEILNQSSSU squalidness
ADEILNRSTWZ Switzerland
ADEILNSSTUY sustainedly
ADEILOPRRTY predatorily
ADEIMMNNOPU pandemonium
ADEIMNNOORT denominator
ADEIMNNOPRT predominant
ADEIMNNQRUU quadrennium
ADEIMNOTTUV unmotivated
ADEIMNRRTUY rudimentary
ADEIMNRSTTT transmitted
ADEIMNRSTUV adventurism
ADEINNOOPRT ponderation
ADEINNORSTU trades union
ADEINNPRRTY dinner party
ADEINNSSTUU unsustained
ADEINOOPRTT deportation
ADEINRRSSTU understairs
ADEINRSTTUV adventurist
ADEIOPPRRSV disapprover
ADEJMNNORTU adjournment
ADELLMNORUU lunar module
ADELLMNOTUW wall-mounted
ADELLNNNOOP London plane
ADELLNSSTUY dauntlessly
ADELLOOPRRT petrodollar
ADELMNOORTY demonolatry
ADELMNORSTW Westmorland
ADELNOOPRSW snow leopard
ADELNOPPTUU unpopulated
ADELOOPRRST postal order
ADELOPPRSUU dual-purpose
ADELOPRRRSY Lord's Prayer
ADEMMMNORSU memorandums
ADEMMNNOUYY Maundy money
ADEMNNOPTWY down payment
ADEMNOORRRR random error
ADENNOPRRST transponder
ADENNOPRSTU pentandrous
ADENOORTTUU out-and-outer
ADENORRSTTU tetrandrous
ADENORSSSUU arduousness
ADENORSSTUW outwardness
ADENORSTUUV adventurous
ADENPRRSSUY sand spurrey
ADENPRSSSUU unsurpassed
ADENRSSTUWY dusty answer
ADENRSTTUUY nature study
ADEOOPRSTTU tetrapodous
ADEPPRRSTUW dust-wrapper
ADFFGNORSTU ground staff
ADFFHINOSST stand-offish
ADFGIINNRSU fund-raising
ADFGIINQRSU firing squad
ADFGILNNOST soft landing
ADFGILNQSUY flying squad
ADFGINORRWW wing forward
ADFHHNOOSSW show of hands
ADFHILLOORY foolhardily
ADFHINOPSSU soup and fish
ADFIIIMNNTU ad infinitum
ADFIILLLRRZ frill lizard
ADFLMOORSUW world-famous
ADFMOORRTUW outward form
ADFOOPPRRRW prop forward
ADGGGHIILNN hang-gliding
ADGGLNORSSU ground glass
ADGHHHIILOY high holiday
ADGHHIINRTT hard-hitting
ADGHHILNOPT diphthongal
ADGHHOPRRYY hydrography
ADGHIINNRTW handwriting
ADGHIKNORRW hard-working
ADGHINNNNRU running hand
ADGHIOPRTTY dittography
ADGIIINNNOT indignation
ADGIILMNRSY disarmingly
ADGIILNNNTY indignantly
ADGIILNOTUV divulgation
ADGIILOORST radiologist
ADGIILOOSTU audiologist
ADGIILOPRTY prodigality
ADGIINORSTY grandiosity
ADGIKNNOORT Gordian knot
ADGILMNOSUW guildswoman
ADGIMMNORSU gourmandism
ADGIMNOORRW drawing room
ADGINNOSTTU outstanding
ADGINOPRSTT trading post
ADGNNOORSUY androgynous
ADHHOORRTXY hydrothorax
ADHILMNOOSW old-womanish
ADHILNNORST North Island
ADHILNOSSTU South Island
ADHINOOORTT orthodontia
ADIIILMNTUV diminutival
ADIIILNOOTZ idolization
ADIIILNOQTU liquidation
ADIIIMNORTT intimidator
ADIIIMOSSTT mastoiditis
ADIIINOOTXZ oxidization

ADIIINOPSST dissipation
ADIIINORSVY divisionary
ADIILLNOQRU quadrillion
ADIILLOSSTY disloyalist
ADIILMNNOST mandolinist
ADIILMOPSTT diplomatist
ADIIMORSTUU auditoriums
ADIINOPSTTU disputation
ADIIOOPRSUV avoirdupois
ADIIOPSTTUY audio typist
ADILNNOSSTY dissonantly
ADILNOPRSSU Old Prussian
ADILOSSSUUY assiduously
ADINRSTTTUY transit-duty
ADLNOOPRSUY polyandrous
ADNOORSUUYY you and yours
AEEEEFFMRRZ freeze-frame
AEEEEFGGLRU feeler gauge
AEEEEFGILPR life peerage
AEEEEGLMSST telemessage
AEEEEGRRRSV reverse gear
AEEEEHLRTTT leatherette
AEEEELLSVVV sleeve-valve
AEEEENRSVWY New Year's Eve
AEEEEPRRSTV perseverate
AEEEFFLOPPT toffee apple
AEEEFFNRRST transfer fee
AEEEFGIKNPS safe keeping
AEEEFGIRRRT refrigerate
AEEEFHINRRT hereinafter
AEEEFHLRSST featherless
AEEEFILNRRT referential
AEEEFLLNNTT flannelette
AEEEFLLNRSW self-renewal
AEEEFLRSSTU featureless
AEEEGGIKMNP gamekeeping
AEEEGGILNOZ genealogize
AEEEGGIRSTV segregative
AEEEGGNNRRT Gretna Green
AEEEGHIKNST heat-seeking
AEEEGHLPRRT telegrapher
AEEEGHNPRTW great-nephew
AEEEGHNPRTY gene therapy
AEEEGHORRTT theatregoer
AEEEGILMMRR lammergeier
AEEEGILMNRR greenmailer
AEEEGILNRRZ generalizer
AEEEGILNRVZ evangelizer
AEEEGIMNNST steam engine
AEEEGIMNRRT regerminate
AEEEGIMNSST metagenesis
AEEEGINORTT renegotiate
AEEEGINPRRT peregrinate
AEEEGINRRTT reintegrate
AEEEGKNOOPR orange pekoe
AEEEGLMMRRY lammergeyer
AEEEGLMNNRT enlargement
AEEEGLORRVY overeagerly
AEEEGMNNRRU green manure
AEEEGMNNRSS germaneness
AEEEGNORRRT regenerator
AEEEHHLORST shoe leather
AEEEHHLPTTT heptathlete
AEEEHILNNPT elephantine
AEEEHILPTTZ telepathize
AEEEHILRTTY ethereality
AEEEHILSSTT telesthesia
AEEEHIMPRSZ re-emphasize
AEEEHINSTTZ anesthetize
AEEEHLLMPRY ephemerally
AEEEHLMPPRT pamphleteer
AEEEHLNPTTT pentathlete
AEEEHLPRRWY prayer wheel
AEEEHNPRSST parentheses
AEEEHPRRSTU superheater
AEEEIILNRRT inertia reel
AEEEIIRRTTV reiterative
AEEEILNORRS Sierra Leone
AEEEILNRRTT interrelate
AEEEILNRRTV reverential
AEEEILNRTXZ externalize
AEEEILPRRTT preliterate
AEEEILRRSUW leisurewear
AEEEIMNPRTT intemperate
AEEEIMNRSTT Eastern Time
AEEEIMNRTTX exterminate
AEEEIMNRTUV enumerative
AEEEIMPRTTV temperative
AEEEIMQRRTU marqueterie
AEEEINNRRTT entertainer
AEEEINOPRUZ Europeanize
AEEEINORRTT reorientate
AEEEINORTVX exonerative
AEEEINPRTTV penetrative
AEEEINSSSVV evasiveness
AEEEJLMSSTY lese-majesty
AEEEKLLOSTX exoskeletal
AEEEKLLPRSW sleepwalker
AEEELLORTTT teetotaller
AEEELMMNNPT empanelment
AEEELMNNSTV enslavement
AEEELMNOSTV stove-enamel
AEEELMPRTTY temperately
AEEELMRSSSU measureless
AEEELNNRSST eternalness
AEEELNOPPVY pay envelope
AEEELNPQRUY pearly queen
AEEELORSTUY see you later
AEEELPQRSTU plateresque
AEEELRSTTUV street value
AEEEMMNPRTT temperament
AEEEMMNRSTU measurement
AEEEMNNNRST ensnarement
AEEEMNNRTTY tenementary
AEEEMNOSSSW awesomeness
AEEEMNRSTTT restatement
AEEEMORRSUV overmeasure
AEEEMPRRTTU temperature
AEEENNRSSST earnestness
AEEEPPPRRTW water-pepper
AEEEQRSSTTU sequestrate
AEEFFGRSTTU suffragette
AEEFFILORTW water of life
AEEFFILOSTT state of life
AEEFFLNRSSU fearfulness
AEEFFLNSSTU fatefulness
AEEFGGGLLTU left luggage
AEEFGHILNRT half-integer
AEEFGHORRTT heterograft
AEEFGILLNSS self-sealing

AEEFGILNPRT	finger-plate
AEEFGILSSTU	fatigueless
AEEFGIMNRTZ	fragmentize
AEEFGINRRRT	refrigerant
AEEFGIORTUV	overfatigue
AEEFGMNNRTT	engraftment
AEEFGOOPRRS	greaseproof
AEEFHHIKNST	sheath knife
AEEFHHORSTU	house-father
AEEFHLLMNST	mantelshelf
AEEFHLMNORU	funeral home
AEEFHLNSSTU	hatefulness
AEEFIILNNRT	inferential
AEEFIILOTVX	exfoliative
AEEFIILPRTV	private life
AEEFILLNPRU	funeral pile
AEEFILLNRST	self-reliant
AEEFILOPRRT	proliferate
AEEFILPPRRT	filter-paper
AEEFIMNNRRT	refrainment
AEEFIMOPRRT	imperforate
AEEFIMORRTV	reformative
AEEFIOPRRTV	perforative
AEEFKLNSSUW	wakefulness
AEEFKLORRWW	welfare work
AEEFLLORRST	forestaller
AEEFLMORRTU	reformulate
AEEFLMRSSTY	self-mastery
AEEFLNPRRSY	parsley fern
AEEFLNPRRUY	funeral pyre
AEEFLNRSSTU	tearfulness
AEEFLRRSSTT	self-starter
AEEFMNORRSY	Freemasonry
AEEFMORRSTY	term of years
AEEFNNOPRSS	profaneness
AEEFNORRSVW	war of nerves
AEEFNRRRRST	transferrer
AEEGGHORTUY	gauge theory
AEEGGIINORS	seigniorage
AEEGGIINRRT	retiring age
AEEGGIKLNOP	goalkeeping
AEEGGILNOST	genealogist
AEEGGINNOOR	neo-Georgian
AEEGGINORST	segregation
AEEGGINQSTU	gigantesque
AEEGGIRRTTU	regurgitate
AEEGHHITVWY	heavyweight
AEEGHIILMNS	Hegelianism
AEEGHILNPRS	generalship
AEEGHILRRTW	weathergirl
AEEGHIPPRTW	paperweight
AEEGHIPRRRS	serigrapher
AEEGHIRSTTY	straight eye
AEEGHKNOPRS	gopher snake
AEEGHLORSUZ	hazel-grouse
AEEGHLRRSTU	slaughterer
AEEGHMOPTTY	gametophyte
AEEGHMORSTY	games theory
AEEGHNPRSTV	stevengraph
AEEGIILLNSV	Gainesville
AEEGIILLSTV	legislative
AEEGIILLTTU	aiguillette
AEEGIILNNOR	legionnaire
AEEGIILNORZ	regionalize
AEEGIILNRSU	seigneurial
AEEGIIMNRTV	germinative
AEEGIINNRVW	wine vinegar
AEEGIINPTYZ	Egyptianize
AEEGIINRTTV	integrative, vinaigrette
AEEGIINSTTV	investigate
AEEGIJKNRRT	tear-jerking
AEEGILLMNNW	well-meaning
AEEGILLNNTY	inelegantly
AEEGILLNRVY	revealingly
AEEGILLRSTU	legislature
AEEGILMNNRT	realignment
AEEGILMNNSS	meaningless
AEEGILMNORU	minor league
AEEGILNNRUV	unrevealing
AEEGILNRSTV	everlasting
AEEGIMNOTTW	witenagemot
AEEGIMNSSTU	mutagenesis
AEEGIMSSTTU	guesstimate
AEEGINNRSTV	evening star
AEEGINORRRZ	reorganizer
AEEGINORRTT	interrogate
AEEGIOPRRTV	prerogative
AEEGKORSSWW	sewage works
AEEGLLMNNTY	gentlemanly
AEEGLLMNSTY	segmentally
AEEGLLNNOOS	Los Angeleno
AEEGLLOPSWY	Yellow Pages
AEEGLMNNOTW	gentlewoman
AEEGLMNOOPR	prolegomena
AEEGLMNORSU	long measure
AEEGLMNPPTU	nutmeg-apple
AEEGLNORRSY	solar energy
AEEGMMOPRRR	reprogramme
AEEGMNORRTV	overgarment
AEEGMNRTTUY	tegumentary
AEEGNNRSSST	strangeness
AEEGNOORRTV	governorate
AEEGNOSSSSU	gaseousness
AEEGOPRRSTT	report stage
AEEHHILNRTU	unhealthier
AEEHHILNSST	healthiness
AEEHHILRTTW	therewithal, whitleather
AEEHHILRTWW	wherewithal
AEEHHIPSSTY	hypesthesia
AEEHHIRSTWW	whitewasher
AEEHHMORRTT	earth mother
AEEHHMORSTV	harvest home
AEEHHNORSTT	hearthstone
AEEHIIKNSST	kinesthesia
AEEHIINPRST	traineeship
AEEHIKLLLRW	killer whale
AEEHIKPPRSS	speakership
AEEHILLPRSV	Sharpeville
AEEHILNPPRS	planisphere
AEEHILNPSSS	shapeliness
AEEHILNRSST	earthliness
AEEHILNRTUZ	Lutheranize
AEEHILPSTTT	telepathist
AEEHILSSTTT	stealthiest
AEEHIMNSTTY	amethystine
AEEHIMRSTTV	harvest mite
AEEHIMRSTTX	hexametrist
AEEHIMRTTTW	white matter
AEEHINPRSST	parenthesis
AEEHINSSSTY	synesthesia

AEEHIOOPSTZ	apotheosize
AEEHIORTTVX	exhortative
AEEHIPPRRSS	periphrases
AEEHIPPSTUX	exhaust pipe
AEEHKLLRRST	rathskeller
AEEHKMPRRTY	hypermarket
AEEHLLMSSSY	shamelessly
AEEHLLNORTY	lonely heart
AEEHLLPSSSY	shapelessly
AEEHLLRSSTY	heartlessly
AEEHLMNNRTT	enthralment
AEEHLMOSSTV	steam shovel
AEEHLMOSTTY	stately home
AEEHLNPSSSS	haplessness
AEEHLOOPRRT	heteropolar
AEEHLPPRRTU	purple heart
AEEHLRRTTTU	turret lathe
AEEHMMNRTUX	xeranthemum
AEEHMNORSUY	Yeoman Usher
AEEHMORRRTT	earth tremor
AEEHMORRSTW	whoremaster
AEEHMORSSTU	housemaster
AEEHNNOPRSW	answerphone
AEEHNOPRSTU	house-parent
AEEHNORRSST	enarthroses
AEEHNORRSTT	northeaster
AEEHNORRTWW	weather-worn
AEEHORRSSTU	house arrest
AEEHORSSTTU	southeaster
AEEHRSSSTUU	thesauruses
AEEIIILMPRZ	imperialize
AEEIILLMMPR	milliampere
AEEIILMMORZ	memorialize
AEEIILMORTV	meliorative
AEEIILMRRST	semi-trailer
AEEIILNNPTT	penitential
AEEIILNNRRT	interlinear
AEEIILNNRTZ	internalize
AEEIILNNSST	inessential
AEEIILNORTZ	orientalize
AEEIILNRSST	inertialess
AEEIILNSTTX	existential
AEEIILNTTVV	ventilative
AEEIILRSSTW	saltirewise
AEEIILRTTVY	iteratively
AEEIINNTTTV	inattentive
AEEIINOPRTV	inoperative
AEEIINORRTT	reiteration
AEEIIPRTVVW	private view
AEEIKMNSTTU	minute steak
AEEIKNOPSSW	Passion Week
AEEIKNPPRSV	paperknives
AEEIKNQSSSU	squeakiness
AEEIKNRSSST	streakiness
AEEIKOPRRST	perestroika
AEEILLLMPRT	pearl millet
AEEILLMPRXY	exemplarily
AEEILLNNPRY	perennially
AEEILLNRSST	literalness
AEEILLNSSTY	essentially
AEEILLOORTV	alto-relievo
AEEILLPRSTV	silver plate
AEEILLRSTVY	versatilely
AEEILMNNSTT	sentimental
AEEILMNORST	salinometer
AEEILMNPRST	sempiternal
AEEILMNPTTU	penultimate
AEEILMNSSSS	aimlessness
AEEILMNSSWY	Wesleyanism
AEEILMOPRRT	polarimeter
AEEILMORSWY	wearisomely
AEEILMOSTTT	teetotalism
AEEILMSTTTU	statute mile
AEEILNNNPRT	inner planet
AEEILNNOPTX	exponential
AEEILNNOSTX	extensional
AEEILNNSSTU	unessential
AEEILNNSSTY	insensately
AEEILNOPRSZ	personalize
AEEILNOPRTT	interpolate
AEEILNORRSV	reversional
AEEILNPRSTT	interseptal
AEEILNPSTTV	septivalent
AEEILNPSVXY	expansively
AEEILNQRRTU	quarter-line
AEEILNRRTUZ	neutralizer
AEEILNRSSSS	airlessness
AEEILNRSTUX	intersexual
AEEILNRTTXY	externality
AEEILNSSSTT	stateliness
AEEILNTTTVY	attentively, tentatively
AEEILNTTUVY	eventuality
AEEILOPPRTT	toilet paper
AEEILOPRTVX	explorative
AEEILOPRTVY	operatively
AEEILORTTTW	toilet water
AEEILPPRRSV	silver paper
AEEILPRSTUV	superlative
AEEILPRSVVY	pervasively
AEEILRRRSTT	terrestrial
AEEILRSSTVY	assertively
AEEIMMNNPRT	impermanent
AEEIMMNOPRR	Roman Empire
AEEIMNNNOQU	menaquinone
AEEIMNNNRTT	entrainment
AEEIMNNORTU	enumeration, mountaineer
AEEIMNNOSTT	maisonnette
AEEIMNOPRST	impersonate
AEEIMNOPRSU	Europeanism
AEEIMNSSSSV	massiveness
AEEIMOPRRTV	vaporimeter
AEEIMORRSTU	temerarious
AEEIMQRSTTU	marquisette
AEEIMSSTTYZ	systematize
AEEINNOORTX	exoneration
AEEINNOPRTT	penetration
AEEINNOTTUV	eventuation
AEEINNOTTUX	extenuation
AEEINORRSST	reassertion
AEEINORRSTV	reservation
AEEINORTVXY	over-anxiety
AEEINPRSSTT	Esperantist
AEEINPRSSTU	septenarius
AEEINPSSSSV	passiveness
AEEINRSSTUV	unassertive
AEEIOPPRRTX	expropriate
AEEIORRSTTV	restorative
AEEIORSSTTX	stereotaxis
AEEIPPRSSTU	tissue paper

AEEIPRRSSTT stripteaser
AEEIPRRSTUZ pasteurizer
AEEJNORRTUV rejuvenator
AEEKLLORRST roller skate
AEEKLLORSTT Elektrostal
AEEKLLPRSSW Kepler's laws
AEEKLMORRTW metalworker
AEEKMMNORTY money market
AEEKMPRRSTU supermarket
AEEKNORSTVW weaver's knot
AEEKNPRRSTU supertanker
AEELLLMOTWY yellow metal
AEELLLMRSTT small letter
AEELLMNORTT reallotment
AEELLMORRST steamroller
AEELLNORSTW stonewaller
AEELLNPRTVY prevalently
AEELLNSSSSW lawlessness
AEELLOPRTUV pole-vaulter
AEELLPPRTUY perpetually
AEELLSSSTTY tastelessly
AEELMNNPRTY permanently
AEELMNNRSTU mental nurse
AEELMNRSTVW West Malvern
AEELMOPRSTT postal meter
AEELMOQRRSU quarrelsome
AEELMPRRTUY prematurely
AEELNOPPRTT rotten apple
AEELNOPRSSS salesperson
AEELNOPRTTU outer planet
AEELNOSSSUZ zealousness
AEELNPRRSST partnerless
AEELNSSTTUW sweet sultan
AEELOORSUVZ overzealous
AEELOPPPTVV poppet-valve
AEELOPRRSTY pearl-oyster
AEELOPSTTUX expostulate
AEEMNNOQRSU Normanesque
AEEMNNORSTT stone marten
AEEMNNRSSTV menservants
AEEMNOPRSTU pentamerous
AEEMNOPRTVY overpayment
AEEMNORRSTT remonstrate
AEEMNORSSTT easternmost
AEEMOPRRTXY extemporary
AEEMORRSTTU tetramerous
AEEMORRSTVY overmastery
AEENNNOOPRU non-European
AEENNNPRTTU unrepentant
AEENNOPRRTU neuropteran
AEENOOPSTTW new potatoes
AEENOPRRSTT paternoster
AEENOQRRTTU quarter note, quarter-tone
AEENORTTUXY extenuatory
AEEOOPSTTTW sweet potato
AEEOPPRRRTT perpetrator
AEEOPPRRTTU perpetuator
AEEOPRRRSTW tree sparrow
AEEPPPSTTTU puppet state
AEFFHILRSTY sheriffalty
AEFFHINRSSS raffishness
AEFFIIMNORR foraminifer
AEFFILLMMMR flimflammer
AEFFKNRRRTU frankfurter
AEFGGHIRSTT stage fright
AEFGGILNRSS finger glass
AEFGHILORRT Fort Raleigh
AEFGHLOPRXY flexography
AEFGHORSTTU sought after
AEFGIIINRRS fire-raising
AEFGIIKLNRW fire-walking
AEFGIILNRSS self-raising
AEFGIINNPRT finger-paint
AEFGIKLLLNW fell walking
AEFGIKLNNRW walking fern
AEFGILLLNNN flannelling
AEFGILLNRST finger-stall
AEFGILLNRTY falteringly
AEFGILNNOOR gonfalonier
AEFGILNNRTU unfaltering
AEFGILNNSSU gainfulness
AEFGILNPPST self-tapping
AEFGINORRSU graniferous
AEFGINRRSTU transfigure
AEFHHLLLTUY healthfully
AEFHHLLNTUU unhealthful
AEFHILLSSTY faithlessly
AEFHILNNRST lantern fish
AEFHLMMORSY flash memory
AEFHLMNRSSU harmfulness
AEFIILLNNTU influential
AEFIILNOOTX exfoliation
AEFIILOPRRW prairie wolf
AEFIIMNORTV informative
AEFIINNOSTT infestation, sinfonietta
AEFIINNRSTT transfinite
AEFIINOPRTX prefixation
AEFIINORSTT fire station
AEFIKNNRRST transfer ink
AEFILLLMMOR lamelliform
AEFILLLORTV Alfortville
AEFILLNOORS saloon rifle
AEFILMNOSTU filamentous
AEFILMORRUZ formularize
AEFILMORTVY formatively
AEFILMPRSUY superfamily
AEFILNNPSSU painfulness
AEFILNOOPST point of sale
AEFILNORSTW satinflower
AEFILNORSUY nefariously
AEFILOOPRST fore-topsail
AEFILOPPSTV pop festival
AEFIMNNOOTT fomentation
AEFIMNOORRT reformation
AEFINNNOPTU fountain pen
AEFINNRRRST transferrin
AEFINOOPRRT perforation
AEFINOORSTT forestation
AEFINORSSWW sinews of war
AEFINORTUUV unfavourite
AEFIOPPRSST pair of steps
AEFKLLOORRW floorwalker
AEFLLLNTTUY flatulently
AEFLLLOPRUW all-powerful
AEFLLLSSTUY faultlessly
AEFLLMRSTUY masterfully
AEFLLNPSSUY playfulness
AEFLLORSSUV flavourless
AEFLLPRRUYY prayerfully

AEFLMOORSUV	flavoursome
AEFLNOOPSTU	teaspoonful
AEFLNORTTUY	fortunately
AEFMNORRRST	transformer
AEFMNORRRTY	ternary form
AEFMNORRTTT	front matter
AEFMOOPPRRT	tamper-proof
AEFMOOPRSTT	fore-topmast
AEFMOORRRTY	reformatory
AEFNNORSTTU	fast neutron
AEFNNORTTUU	unfortunate
AEFNOSSSTUU	fatuousness
AEGGHHILOTV	high voltage
AEGGHIILNNT	nightingale
AEGGHIINNRT	ingathering
AEGGHIIRRRT	hair-trigger
AEGGHIMNOSU	gaming house
AEGGHINSSSW	waggishness
AEGGHIRSSTT	stage rights
AEGGHMNORTU	Grangemouth
AEGGIIKNSST	kissing gate
AEGGIILNNRS	resignaling
AEGGIINRTTU	ingurgitate
AEGGILNNOPR	ranging-pole
AEGGILRSSTT	straggliest
AEGGIMNRSST	gangsterism
AEGGINNNRRU	running gear
AEGGINORRVZ	overgrazing
AEGGINPSTUY	paying guest
AEGHHILNPRT	higher plant
AEGHHILNSTT	slant height
AEGHHILOPRY	heliography
AEGHHINORST	high treason
AEGHHINSSTU	haughtiness
AEGHHIOPSST	hostageship
AEGHHLOPRSU	ploughshare
AEGHHMOPRRT	thermograph
AEGHHNOPRTY	ethnography
AEGHHOTTUVW	thought-wave
AEGHIILLNRS	hellraising
AEGHIIMNRST	time-sharing
AEGHIIPPRST	epigraphist
AEGHIKLNOSW	walking shoe
AEGHILLMPRT	lamplighter
AEGHILLPTUW	all-up weight
AEGHILMNPPT	pamphleting
AEGHILNNSTU	Lengshuitan
AEGHILNOOTZ	anthologize
AEGHILNSSST	ghastliness
AEGHIMNNRST	garnishment
AEGHIMNORTV	earth-moving
AEGHIMOPRSS	seismograph
AEGHINNRTTT	tenant right
AEGHINNSSTU	naughtiness
AEGHLNOOORR	gonorrhoeal
AEGHLOOPRSY	phraseology
AEGHLRRSSSY	sherry glass
AEGHMNOOPRR	monographer
AEGHNOOPSTU	pathogenous
AEGHNOPRSTY	stenography
AEGHNORSTTU	hart's tongue
AEGHOOPPRRT	topographer
AEGHOPPRRRY	reprography
AEGHOPPRRSS	grasshopper
AEGHOPPRRTY	petrography, typographer
AEGHRSSTTTU	thrust stage
AEGIIILNORS	seigniorial
AEGIIINORTV	originative
AEGIIKLLNRT	giant-killer
AEGIIKMMNOV	movie-making
AEGIILLMMMR	milligramme
AEGIILLMSVY	vigesimally
AEGIILLNOST	legislation
AEGIILLNTVY	genitivally
AEGIILLSTVY	vestigially
AEGIILMNNOT	Maginot Line
AEGIILMNORS	regionalism
AEGIILMNTUV	lignum vitae
AEGIILNORST	regionalist
AEGIILNORSV	oversailing
AEGIILNRSUZ	singularize
AEGIILNRTTY	integrality
AEGIIMMMNUW	minimum wage
AEGIIMMORRR	mirror image
AEGIIMMRSTU	magisterium
AEGIIMNNORT	germination
AEGIIMNNORV	Merovingian
AEGIIMNSTTW	time-wasting
AEGIIMPRSTU	epigastrium
AEGIINNOOTT	negotiation
AEGIINNORST	resignation
AEGIINNORTT	integration
AEGIINNPRST	sign-painter
AEGIINNSTTW	wine tasting
AEGIINPPRTW	wire-tapping
AEGIINRSSTW	waitressing
AEGIJLNRUUV	jugular vein
AEGIKLNOPRW	rope-walking
AEGIKMMNNOY	moneymaking
AEGIKMMNRRY	merrymaking
AEGILLMMNRT	trammelling
AEGILLMNNTY	lamentingly
AEGILLMOOPS	megalopolis
AEGILLMRSST	millet-grass
AEGILLNNRUV	unravelling
AEGILLNOPRY	role-playing
AEGILLNORTT	reallotting
AEGILLNQRRU	quarrelling
AEGILLRRRUY	irregularly
AEGILMNNNUY	unmeaningly
AEGILMNOPRU	pelargonium
AEGILMNOSTU	ligamentous
AEGILMOOSSY	semasiology
AEGILNNNPPR	pre-planning
AEGILNNOSTU	langoustine
AEGILNNPRTY	trying-plane
AEGILNNSSST	lastingness
AEGILNORSTW	signal tower
AEGILNQRUVY	quaveringly
AEGILNRRSTY	arrestingly
AEGILOOTTUZ	tautologize
AEGIMMOPRSU	gemmiparous
AEGIMNNNRTU	running mate
AEGIMNORSSU	ignoramuses
AEGINNNORSU	unreasoning
AEGINNOOTXY	oxygenation
AEGINNOPSST	passing note
AEGINNOPSTV	paving stone

AEGINNOSSUU sanguineous
AEGINNPRSSS sparingness
AEGINNRRSTU unarresting
AEGINOPPRTV voting paper
AEGINOPRTUX expurgation
AEGINPRRSTW spring water
AEGINRRSTUV invert sugar
AEGIPRRSSSV viper's grass
AEGLLNOOPTY planetology
AEGLNNPRTUY repugnantly
AEGNNOPSTUY pentagynous
AEGNORSTTUY tetragynous
AEGOORRRTUV rotogravure
AEGOPRRTUXY expurgatory
AEGORSSSTUU stegosaurus
AEHHIIMPSSS Messiahship
AEHHIKNSSSW hawkishness
AEHHILLNTUY unhealthily
AEHHIMMMRST Hammersmith
AEHHIMOPRTY hypothermia
AEHHINNOPTY hyphenation
AEHHIORTTTW whitethroat
AEHHLLOPTTY thallophyte
AEHHLOPPSYY hypophyseal
AEHHMOOOPTY homoeopathy
AEHHNOORRYY Hooray Henry
AEHHOOPPRST phosphorate
AEHHRRSTTUW waterthrush
AEHIILLPSTT philatelist
AEHIILOPSTZ hospitalize
AEHIIMNRSTT martinetish
AEHIINOPRRS parishioner
AEHIIPPRRSS periphrasis
AEHIKMNSSSW mawkishness
AEHIKNNSSSV knavishness
AEHILLOPRST hospitaller
AEHILMNORTW mother-in-law
AEHILMNOTTY methylation
AEHILMNPSSY misshapenly
AEHILMNRSTU Lutheranism
AEHILMNRTTU thermal unit
AEHILMQSSUY squeamishly
AEHILNNSSUW sunshine law
AEHILNOSTTW West Lothian
AEHILNPRRTY platyrrhine
AEHILNSSSSV slavishness
AEHILOPPRTW white poplar
AEHILOPPSST apostleship
AEHILORSTVY overhastily
AEHILORTTWW with a trowel
AEHIMNNNSSS mannishness
AEHIMNOPPRS ropemanship
AEHIMNOPRST misanthrope
AEHIMNORSTU house martin
AEHIMOOSSST homeostasis
AEHIMORSTTX thermotaxis
AEHIMPPRSTU hippeastrum
AEHIMPRSTYZ sympathizer
AEHINNPPSSU unhappiness
AEHINNPSSSS Spanishness
AEHINOORSTT anorthosite
AEHINOORTTX exhortation
AEHINOPRSST senatorship
AEHINOPRSTT antistrophe
AEHINOPSSTT stephanotis
AEHINORRSST enarthrosis
AEHINORSSTT throatiness
AEHINPPRRST partnership
AEHINPSSSSW waspishness
AEHINQSSSSU squashiness
AEHINRSSSTW swarthiness
AEHIOPPRRST praetorship
AEHIOPSSTYZ hypostasize
AEHIOPSTTYZ hypostatize
AEHIPPPRSSS ship's papers
AEHJNOORRST Trojan Horse
AEHKLLNSSTY thanklessly
AEHLLLMOOPR allelomorph
AEHLLLOOSWW swallow-hole
AEHLLMOOSTY loathsomely
AEHLLNOSSSW shallowness
AEHLMNOQSSU lemon squash
AEHMNOORSTV harvest moon
AEHNNPRSSSU unsharpness
AEHNOOPRRTT orthopteran
AEHNORSTUWY unseaworthy
AEHOOPRRSTT trap-shooter
AEHOORRTTXY exhortatory
AEHOQRRRTUU quarter-hour
AEIIILLMNOR millionaire
AEIIILLMNST sillimanite
AEIIILMMPRS imperialism
AEIIILMNNOT elimination
AEIIILMNRST ministerial
AEIIILMPRST imperialist
AEIIILMRRSV verisimilar
AEIIILMTTVY imitatively
AEIIIMNOTTZ itemization
AEIIIMNRTUZ miniaturize
AEIIINNORTT itineration
AEIIINNSTUV insinuative
AEIIKLLOPRT realpolitik
AEIIKLMNPRS marlinspike
AEIILLLOOTV volatile oil
AEIILLMSSTT satellitism
AEIILLNNRTY triennially
AEIILLNOTVY inviolately
AEIILLNPTVY plaintively
AEIILLNRSTV silver Latin
AEIILLOORTV alto-rilievo
AEIILLRRSTT artillerist
AEIILMMORST memorialist
AEIILMMORTZ immortalize
AEIILMNNOPS Minneapolis
AEIILMNNOTY myelination
AEIILMNOORT melioration
AEIILMNORST orientalism
AEIILMNORTY eliminatory
AEIILMNOSTT testimonial
AEIILMNOSTV love-in-a-mist
AEIILMNPRRY preliminary
AEIILMNPTTY impatiently
AEIILMPSSVY impassively
AEIILMQTTUY quality time
AEIILMRRSTT trimestrial
AEIILMSTTUV stimulative
AEIILNNNOST intensional
AEIILNNNOTT intentional
AEIILNNOTTV ventilation
AEIILNNPRST interspinal

AEIILNNRTTY	internality
AEIILNNSSST	saintliness
AEIILNOPRSV	previsional
AEIILNORSSV	LaserVision
AEIILNORSTT	orientalist
AEIILNORTTT	toilet-train
AEIILNORTTU	elutriation
AEIILNQRTUZ	tranquilize
AEIILNRSSTV	trivialness
AEIILNRSSTW	sister-in-law
AEIILORRRTT	territorial
AEIILPRSSST	peristalsis
AEIILPRTTVY	partitively
AEIILRSTTVY	versatility
AEIIMMMNNST	immanentism
AEIIMMNNSSW	Weismannism
AEIIMMNNSTT	immanentist
AEIIMNNORST	inseminator, nitrosamine
AEIIMNNORTT	termination
AEIIMNNORTV	vermination
AEIIMOPPRRT	impropriate
AEIIMRRTTUV	triumvirate
AEIINNNORTV	innervation
AEIINNNOSVV	non-invasive
AEIINNNOTTT	inattention
AEIINNNQQUU	quinquennia
AEIINNOORTT	orientation
AEIINOPRRST	respiration
AEIINOPRRTT	partitioner, repartition
AEIINOPRTTX	extirpation
AEIINOPRTTY	petitionary
AEIINORRSVY	revisionary
AEIINORRTTY	anteriority
AEIINPSTVXY	expansivity
AEIIOOPRRST	a posteriori
AEIIOPRSTVY	positive ray
AEIKKLMNORW	workmanlike
AEIKLNNOPPS	plain-spoken
AEILLMNNSTT	installment
AEILLMNOORW	mineral wool
AEILLMNOOTY	emotionally
AEILLMNOTTW	little woman
AEILLMNTTUV	multivalent
AEILLNNOOTV	non-volatile
AEILLNNOSTY	tensionally
AEILLNOOTUV	evolutional
AEILLNOPTTY	potentially
AEILLNORSSY	sensorially
AEILLNOSSSY	silly season
AEILLNRSUVY	universally
AEILLNSUUXY	unisexually
AEILLORTTUV	ultraviolet
AEILMMNORTY	momentarily
AEILMNNNSSU	unmanliness
AEILMNNOOTU	unemotional
AEILMNNOPRT	minor planet
AEILMNNOSSW	womanliness
AEILMNNRTTU	nutrimental
AEILMNOORRT	linear motor
AEILMNOOSTT	molestation
AEILMNORTVY	normatively
AEILMOPRRSU	leprosarium
AEILMOPRRTY	polarimetry, temporarily
AEILMOPRTTY	temporality
AEILMOPRTXY	proximately
AEILMPPRSTU	litmus paper
AEILNNOPRSU	unipersonal
AEILNNORRTY	non-literary
AEILNNORSTY	royal tennis
AEILNNRSTTY	transiently
AEILNNRSTUY	saturninely
AEILNOOPRTX	exploration
AEILNOPRSTY	personality
AEILNOPSSSS	passionless
AEILNORRSTU	serrulation
AEILOOPRRRT	reportorial
AEILOPPRRUZ	popularizer
AEILOPRSTTW	water pistol
AEILOSTUVXY	vexatiously
AEIMMNRSSSU	summariness
AEIMMORSTTU	tautomerism
AEIMMSSSTTY	systematism
AEIMNNOPPTT	appointment
AEIMNNORSTU	mensuration
AEIMNNSSTTU	sustainment
AEIMNOPRTTU	importunate, permutation
AEIMNRRSTTT	transmitter
AEIMOORSTTU	auto-erotism
AEIMPRRTTUY	prematurity
AEIMSSSTTTY	systematist
AEINNNNOSTY	Tennysonian
AEINNOOPRST	personation
AEINNOOSTTT	ostentation
AEINNOPSTTY	spontaneity
AEINNORSTUV	intravenous
AEINNOSSSUX	anxiousness
AEINNRSSSSU	Russianness
AEINOOPPRRT	reapportion
AEINOOPRTTX	exportation
AEINOORRSTT	restoration
AEINOORSUVX	over-anxious
AEINOPPRSTT	poster paint
AEINOPRSSSV	vasopressin
AEINOQRSTUY	questionary
AEINORSSSUV	savouriness, variousness
AEINQRSTUWW	squaw winter
AEIOPPRRRTY	proprietary
AEIOPRRRSTY	respiratory
AEIOPRRRTTU	portraiture
AEIOPRRTTUV	vituperator
AEIPPRSTUUV	suppurative
AEKLOPRRSTW	plasterwork
AEKLOPRRSUV	Pervouralsk
AEKMNOOPSSW	spokeswoman
AELLMSSTTYY	tally system
AELLNNOSUXY	non-sexually
AELLOOPRSTW	wool-stapler
AELLOPRSSUX	solar plexus
AELLORSTTTU	statute roll
AELMMRSSTUU	summersault
AELMNOPRRSU	supernormal
AELMNORSTUW	Ulsterwoman
AELMOPSSTUY	sympetalous
AELMORSSSTY	solar system
AELMPRSTYYY	mystery play
AELNNNOOPRS	non-personal

AELNNNOPRTW town planner
AELNNSSSUUU unusualness
AELNOPPSTTY penalty spot
AELNOPRSSSU parlousness
AELNOPRSTTY oyster-plant
AELNPRRSUUY superlunary
AELOOPRRTXY exploratory
AELPPRSTUWY water supply
AEMNNORRSTT remonstrant
AEMNOOPRSTY trypanosome
AEMNOORSSSU amorousness
AEMNOPPRRTY property man
AENNOOPRSSS parson's nose
AENNOOPSSTU spontaneous
AENNOPPRSST Prestonpans
AENNORRSTTU neutron star
AENOPRRRSTT transporter
AENORRSTTTU sternutator
AENPPRSSSTU suppressant
AEOOPPPRRTY party-pooper
AEOPPPPRRTY party popper
AEOPPRRTTVY poverty trap
AEOPPRRTTXY property tax
AFFIINOSTUX suffixation
AFFILNORSTU insufflator
AFFLLLNORTU full-frontal
AFGGHILOORT Goliath frog
AFGHHHIINOS high fashion
AFGHHIILNTU highfalutin
AFGHIILRSTY fairy lights
AFGHILMOPRY filmography
AFGHIPPTTUU put up a fight
AFGIIINNRTU infuriating
AFGIIKLLMNT talking film
AFGIILLNNUY unfailingly
AFGIINNNORU Finno-Ugrian
AFGIINPRRTY firing party
AFGIINSSTUU ignis fatuus
AFGILNORTUU fulguration
AFGILNRSTTY flying start
AFGINOOPRST pair of tongs
AFGINRRSTTU frustrating
AFHIIINNSST satln flnlsh
AFHINORRSTU sharon fruit
AFHLNOOOPRU lap of honour
AFHMNNOOORU man of honour
AFIIIILNNTV infinitival
AFIIILMNNST infantilism
AFIIILNNTTY infantility
AFIIIPRSSTY fissiparity
AFIILLMORTW Fort William
AFIILMNNOTU fulmination
AFIILMNORTY informality
AFIILNORRTT infiltrator
AFIILORSTTU flirtatious
AFIIMNNOORT information
AFIIMNOORSU omnifarious
AFIIMORSTUV favouritism
AFIINNORSTX transfixion
AFIIOPRSSSU fissiparous
AFILLMOOPRT oil platform
AFILMNOORTU formulation
AFILMNORTUY fulminatory
AFIMNOORRTY informatory
AFINNORSSTU transfusion
AFINOOPPRST Port of Spain
AFINORRSTTU frustration
AGGHHIIKNNR high-ranking
AGGHIIJMNTU thingumajig
AGGHIILOOST hagiologist
AGGHMMOPRSY sphygmogram
AGGIIKNRSSS grass skiing
AGGIILNNOYZ agonizingly
AGGIINNOPRT pig-ignorant
AGGILLMORRU glamour girl
AGGILLNNOPY long-playing
AGGILLNNOST long-lasting
AGGIMMNOPRR programming
AGGINOPSSTT staging post
AGHHIILQTUY high-quality
AGHHIIMNRST nightmarish
AGHHIIRSSTT straightish
AGHHILOPRTY lithography
AGHHIMNRSTU human rights
AGHHMNOPRYY hymnography
AGHHMOPRTYY mythography
AGHHNOOPPRY phonography
AGHHOOPPRTY photography
AGHHOOPRRTY orthography
AGHHOPPRSYY hypsography
AGHIIILMNTU humiliating
AGHIIILNPSS sailing ship
AGHIIKLLLNW hillwalking
AGHIILLNOOP philologian
AGHIILMNOOS hooliganism
AGHIILNRSTY hairstyling
AGHIILNRSVY ravishingly
AGHIINNOSST astonishing
AGHIINPRSTY pharyngitis
AGHIKLNOPST talking shop
AGHILNOOSTT anthologist
AGHILNORRWY harrowingly
AGHILOOPSTT pathologist
AGHIMNNRSTY Granny Smith
AGHIMNOPRST prognathism
AGHINOORSTW shooting war
AGHINOPRSTT parting shot
AGHINOPSSST passing shot
AGHIORSTTTU straight-out
AGHJNOOORST John o' Groats
AGHLOOPPSUY polyphagous
AGHLOOPSUXY xylophagous
AGHNOOPPRRY pornography
AGHNOOPRSTU prognathous
AGIIIILLNNT initialling
AGIIIKLLNNP painkilling
AGIIILLMNST mailing list
AGIIILMNSTV vigilantism
AGIIILNNOPT oil painting
AGIIILNNORS original sin
AGIIILNORTV invigilator
AGIIILNORTY originality
AGIIILNPSST salpingitis
AGIIILNRSTV virginalist
AGIIILNSTTW waiting list
AGIIIMMNORT immigration
AGIIINNOORT origination
AGIIINNOSTT instigation
AGIIKKNNRST skating rink
AGIIKMNNPRT printmaking

AGIILMNSTTU	stimulating
AGIILNPRTWY	playwriting
AGIILNRSTUY	singularity
AGIIMMNNTTU	manumitting
AGIIMMORRTY	immigratory
AGIIMNOORTW	waiting room
AGIIMNRSTTW	arm-twisting
AGIINNOPRTZ	patronizing
AGIINOORRTV	invigorator
AGIINORSTTT	tritagonist
AGIKLLNPRSY	sparklingly
AGIKLNORTUW	walking tour
AGIKMNNORSS	king's ransom
AGILLMNNOOU	monolingual
AGILLNPRSWY	sprawlingly
AGILLNRSTTY	startlingly
AGILMNORSST	storm-signal
AGILMOOPRTY	primatology
AGILNNPRSUY	unsparingly
AGILNNRUVYY	unvaryingly
AGILNOPPRVY	approvingly
AGILOOPRSTT	patrologist
AGILOORSSTT	astrologist
AGILOORSSYY	Assyriology
AGILOOSTTTU	tautologist
AGIMMNOORST	mooring-mast
AGIMNNORRST	morning star
AGINNOOPPTU	oppugnation
AGINNPPRSTU	unstrapping
AGINOOOPRRT	prorogation
AGINOOPRSTT	protagonist
AGINOORRSUV	granivorous
AGLLLOOPTTY	polyglottal
AGLLMOORSUY	glamorously
AGLLOOPSTTT	glottal stop
AGLLORRSUUY	garrulously
AGLMNOORSUU	unglamorous
AGLMNOORTYY	laryngotomy
AGLMOOOSTTY	stomatology
AGLMOOPRRTU	promulgator
AGLMOORRTYY	martyrology
AGLOOOSTTUU	tautologous
AGNOOPRRSSW	song sparrow
AHHILNOORTU	holothurian
AHHIMNOPSSW	showmanship
AHHLLNOPTXY	xanthophyll
AHIIILMNOTU	humiliation
AHIIIMNNOSY	Nishinomiya
AHIILLNOSTT	hill station
AHIILLORSUY	hilariously
AHIILMOPSST	hospitalism
AHIILOPSTTY	hospitality
AHIILRSSTTY	hairstylist
AHIIMNNRRTU	antirrhinum
AHIIMNOOOSU	homoiousian
AHIIMOOPPPT	hippopotami
AHIKKOORRSW	kwashiorkor
AHIKLMOORSW	workaholism
AHIKMNOPRSW	workmanship
AHILLMOPRTU	prothallium
AHILLOPSTXY	phyllotaxis
AHILMNPPRST	shrimp plant
AHILNOPRSTY	rhinoplasty
AHILOPPRSXY	prophylaxis
AHIMNOOPSTT	taphonomist
AHIMNOORRSU	honorariums
AHIMNOPRSTY	misanthropy
AHIMNOPSSSS	Spanish moss
AHINNOPSSTW	Spanish Town
AHINOOPSSTX	saxophonist
AHKNNOPSSSY	shanks's pony
AHKNOOTUWWY	you-know-what
AHLMOOPRSUY	amorphously
AHLOPRRSTUU	sulphurator
AHMNNOOPRTT	Northampton
AHMNOOPSTTU	Southampton
AHQRSSTTTUU	squat thrust
AIIILNOTVX	lixiviation
AIIILLLNPTU	lilliputian
AIIILLNOTTT	titillation
AIIILNNOOTZ	lionization
AIIILNNOTTU	intuitional
AIIILNOTTUZ	utilization
AIIIMNRSTTU	miniaturist
AIIIMPSSTVY	impassivity
AIIINNNOSTU	insinuation
AIIINNOPRST	inspiration
AIIKLRSTUVV	survival kit
AIIKNRSSSTT	Sanskritist
AIILLMMNOTU	multinomial
AIILLMNORTU	illuminator
AIILLNNOOPT	pollination
AIILLNRSSTY	sinistrally
AIILLPRSTUY	spiritually
AIILMMORTTY	immortality
AIILMNNNOTT	non-militant
AIILMNNORTY	non-military
AIILMNOOSTZ	solmization
AIILMNOSTTU	stimulation
AIILMRSSUVV	survivalism
AIILNNORTTU	nutritional
AIILNOOPRSV	provisional
AIILNOOPTTY	optionality
AIILNOPRTUY	unipolarity
AIILNOPSTTU	stipulation
AIILNOSTTYZ	stylization
AIILNPRSTUU	unspiritual
AIILNQRTTUY	tranquility
AIILRSSTUVV	survivalist
AIIMMNNOSSU	manumission
AIIMMNSSTTU	numismatist
AIIMNNOOSTU	antimonious
AIIMNOOPRTT	importation
AIIMOPPRRSU	primiparous
AIINNOOOTZZ	ozonization
AIINNOORRST	iron rations
AIINOPRRSTY	inspiratory
AIINOPRRTTU	parturition
AIINOPRSSST	inspissator
AIINORRTTTU	trituration
AIIOOPPRRTT	propitiator
AIIOPRRSTTT	portraitist
AIKNOORSTTW	workstation
AILLLMNOOPP	lollipop man
AILLLNOPTUU	pullulation
AILLMOPSSSY	plasmolysis
AILLNOORSTY	torsionally
AILLNOPRSUU	nulliparous
AILLNORTUVY	voluntarily
AILLNPPSTUY	suppliantly

AILLNRTUUXY	luxuriantly
AILLORRSTTU	illustrator
AILMNNOSUUY	unanimously
AILMNOOOPRT	promotional
AILMNOPRTTY	importantly
AILMNORSTUV	voluntarism
AILMOPRSTUU	multiparous
AILMORSTTUY	stimulatory
AILNNOOPSTU	Postal Union
AILNNORTUVY	involuntary
AILNOOPSTTU	postulation
AILNOPPSTTU	post-nuptial
AILNOPSTTUU	pustulation
AILNORSTTUV	voluntarist
AILNORSUUVY	unsavourily
AILNRSSTUUU	laurustinus
AILOOPRSUVY	oviparously
AILORSTTTUY	statutorily
AIMMOORRSTU	moratoriums
AIMMOOSSTXY	myxomatosis
AIMNNOOSTUU	mountainous
AIMNNOPRTTU	unimportant
AINOOPRRSTT	prostration
AINOPPRSTUU	suppuration
AINORRSSTUU	susurration
AJMMNPQTUUU	quantum jump
AKLNNOOOPTZ	zooplankton
ALLNOPPRUUY	unpopularly
ALMNNOOSUYY	anonymously
ALMNOORSTTU	salmon trout
ALMNOPRSSTY	sportsmanly
ALNNORSTUYY	tyrannously
ALOPRRSTUUY	rapturously
AMNNOOOPPRT	ma non troppo
AMNOOPRSSTW	sportswoman
AMNOOPSSSST	Samson's post
AMOOPRRRTTY	protomartyr
ANOOOPRRTTY	protonotary
BBBEGIIINNW	winebibbing
BBBELRRTUUY	butyl rubber
BBCCEEHKLOR	breech-block
BBCDEEIIKLW	Wicked Bible
BBCDEHIRRTU	butcher-bird
BBCEEEKLORZ	breeze-block
BBCEEHHIRRT	breech birth
BBCEELNOOST	cobblestone
BBCEIILLLPU	public libel
BBCEILMOSTU	combustible
BBCEJKOORST	stockjobber
BBCEKLORSTU	blockbuster
BBCELMORSTU	cluster bomb
BBCGIMOORRY	borborygmic
BBDDEELLOOU	blue-blooded
BBDDEGILNOS	bobsledding
BBDDEILLNOU	double-blind
BBDDEILORUY	bodybuilder
BBDEEELOUYY	blue-eyed boy
BBDEEHHLOOY	hobbledehoy
BBDEFFLLOUU	double bluff
BBDELNRSSUU	blunderbuss
BBDGIIKNNOO	bookbinding
BBEEGIILLNR	gibberellin
BBEEGILMRSU	submergible
BBEEILLLRTY	Liberty Bell
BBEEILMRSSU	submersible
BBEEINRRSSU	rubberiness
BBEENORRSYY	boysenberry
BBEGGGILNOW	begging bowl
BBEGIINSSSU	big business
BBEGINOSSSU	gibbousness
BBEHIIILLOP	bibliophile
BBEHIKLORST	hobble skirt
BBEHINOSSSY	yobbishness
BBEHLORSTTU	bottle-brush
BBELLNOTTUY	belly button
BBEMNNOORTU	neutron bomb
BBFIIMNOOSS	fission bomb
BBGHINNRSUU	burning bush
BBGIILLNQUY	quibblingly
BBGILMNOTUX	tumbling-box
BBGMOORRSUY	borborygmus
BBHIIILLOPY	bibliophily
BCCCEIILLPY	bicycle clip
BCCDEEHKLOU	double-check
BCCDEILNOTU	conductible
BCCEEEEFINN	beneficence
BCCEEEHOPPR	copper beech
BCCEEEIKLLT	click beetle
BCCEEILLLOT	collectible
BCCEEINRSTY	cybernetics
BCCEFFIKLOO	office block
BCCEFIIPSSU	subspecific
BCCEHKKLOST	sketch-block
BCCEIILNNOV	convincible
BCCEIINOOOT	biocoenotic
BCCEIINOORT	necrobiotic
BCCEIKLMORR	rock-climber
BCCEILMPPUY	bicycle pump
BCCEINOOPPR	corn-cob pipe
BCCHHOORSTT	Scotch broth
BCCIIILPSTU	publicistic
BCCLNORTUUY	country club
BCDDDEFOORR	Bedford cord
BCDDDELLOOO	cold-blooded
BCDDEEEILNS	descendible
BCDDEEIIRTT	direct debit
BCDDEHLOTUU	double Dutch
BCDEEEIINNT	Benedictine
BCDEEHILNPT	pitchblende
BCDEEHMNOTU	debouchment
BCDEEIIIMNO	biomedicine
BCDEEIILNRS	discernible
BCDEEIILRRU	irreducible
BCDEEIIMRSS	misdescribe
BCDEEIINNOT	benediction
BCDEEIMNRSU	disencumber
BCDEEINORTY	benedictory
BCDEGHILMOU	much obliged
BCDEGHNRRSU	bergschrund
BCDEHKNOORR	broken chord
BCDEHKOOTTU	buck-toothed
BCDEIIILRTY	credibility
BCDEIILNRSY	discernibly
BCDEIILRRUY	irreducibly
BCDEIKLOQUU	double quick
BCDEILNNORR	blind corner
BCDEKLOORSU	bloodsucker
BCDELMNOSUU	muscle-bound
BCDELOORSSU	double-cross
BCDEOORRRSS	cross-border

BCDGIIKMNOR mockingbird
BCDGILLLOPU bulldog clip
BCDHHIOOPRY hydrophobic
BCDHIILNSTT blind stitch
BCDIILOOPTY body politic
BCDIINRTUUY rubicundity
BCDIIORRSSS scissor-bird
BCDILLNOORU colour-blind
BCEEEELNNOV benevolence
BCEEEFILPRT perfectible
BCEEEGMNRSU submergence
BCEEEHNNQSU Queen's Bench
BCEEEILPPRT perceptible
BCEEEILPRTX excerptible
BCEEELLMRSU cerebellums
BCEEENQSSUU subsequence
BCEEFIIKNST sick benefit
BCEEFINOSTT cost-benefit
BCEEGHMOOSU gobemouches
BCEEHHNOOPT technophobe
BCEEHINNRSU Chinese burn
BCEEHINORRS Breconshire
BCEEHIOORRS seborrhoeic
BCEEHKLRRUY huckleberry
BCEEIJLLLPU Jubilee clip
BCEEIJOTVZ objectivize
BCEEIJLOTVY objectively
BCEEIKOORSV service book
BCEEILMNPUY public enemy
BCEEILNORTV convertible
BCEEILPPRTY perceptibly
BCEEILPSSTU susceptible
BCEEINSSSTU subsistence
BCEEIPRRSSU superscribe
BCEEJLSSSTU subjectless
BCEEKKLNNOU knuckle-bone
BCEEKLLMOPT temple block
BCEELMNRTUY recumbently
BCEELNOOSST obsolescent
BCEEOPRRRTU cub reporter
BCEFFKORSTU buffer stock
BCEFIIOPRST fibre optics
BCEGHHIMOWY High Wycombe
BCEGIINRTTU butter-icing
BCEGILMOORY embryologic
BCEHHIIMRTT timber hitch
BCEHIIIMNRS Hibernicism
BCEHIIIOSTT bioethicist
BCEHIILRRSV silver birch
BCEHILOPSUU public house
BCEHKOPRRTU pork butcher
BCEHLMOPTYY B-lymphocyte
BCEHLORRSYY chrysoberyl
BCEHMOORTTY thrombocyte
BCEIIJMOSTV objectivism
BCEIIJOSTTV objectivist
BCEIIJOTTVY objectivity
BCEIIKLLRST billsticker
BCEIILLOSTY bellicosity
BCEIILMSSUU umbilicuses
BCEIINOOOSS biocoenosis
BCEIINOORSS necrobiosis
BCEIIORSSTY Bossier City
BCEIJNSTUUV subjunctive
BCEIKOOPRTU picture book
BCEILLMOORS solo climber
BCEILLORSSU brucellosis
BCEILMNRSSU crumbliness
BCEILMOOPSS compossible
BCEILMORTUU microtubule
BCEILNORTVY convertibly
BCEILOPRRTU corruptible
BCEILPPRSUU public purse
BCEILPSSTUY susceptibly
BCEIORSTTUV obstructive
BCEKKOOOORY cookery book
BCEKKOORRST stockbroker
BCEKLMOSSTY block system
BCEKRRSTUUY scrub turkey
BCELORSTUUU tuberculous
BCELSTTTTUU scuttlebutt
BCEOOOPRSST stroboscope
BCGHIINNORT Birchington
BCGILMNOOOW combing wool
BCGILNOPRUW public wrong
BCGILOOORYY cryobiology
BCHHIIMORTY biorhythmic
BCHHIOOOPPT photophobic
BCHKLORSTTU thrust block
BCHNOORSSTU hot cross bun
BCHPRSSTUUY scrub typhus
BCIIIILMSTY miscibility
BCIIIILNTVY vincibility
BCIILLORSSS scissor-bill
BCIILMMNOUU cumulonimbi
BCIILMOSSTY symbolistic
BCIJNNOOTUX box junction, junction box
BCIKLOPRSUW public works
BCILMOSTTUU custom-built
BCINOORRTTU contributor
BCINOORSTTU obstruction
BDDDEEEGLOU double-edged
BDDDEEILOSU double-sided
BDDDEEINRRU underbidder
BDDDEFILLNO blindfolded
BDDEEEIMNRT debridement
BDDEEGIMOSU disembogued
BDDEEGLLORU dole-bludger
BDDEEIINOST disobedient
BDDEEKNORYY donkey derby
BDDEFLLLOOU full-blooded
BDDEGIIMNNN mind-bending
BDDEGINRUWY ruby wedding
BDDEHINRRTU thunderbird
BDDEINRSTUU undisturbed
BDDELMMOUUY double dummy
BDDELNNOUUY unboundedly
BDDELNOTUUY undoubtedly
BDDENNOTUUY bounden duty
BDEEEEIIMRR Biedermeier
BDEEEHIKRSW bewhiskered
BDEEEIILRSV disbeliever
BDEEEILMNTV bedevilment
BDEEEILOSTW boiled sweet
BDEEEILPRSS depressible
BDEEEILSSTW wildebeests
BDEEEIMMRRS disremember
BDEEEIMORRR embroiderer
BDEEELLLOVW well-beloved

BDEEELNSSSS	blessedness
BDEEFILLRSU	self-builder
BDEEFLLNORU	bell-founder
BDEEGGHIIRW	weighbridge
BDEEGIILLNR	ill breeding
BDEEGIILLNV	bedevilling
BDEEGIILNRW	bewildering
BDEEGIMOSSU	disembogues
BDEEGINNRTU	reed bunting
BDEEGINORTU	outbreeding
BDEEHIINNPU	Dien Bien Phu
BDEEHILLOUX	double helix
BDEEHILMNSU	unblemished
BDEEHIMNOOT	ethmoid bone
BDEEHLLMTUW	well-thumbed
BDEEHLMORUY	double rhyme
BDEEIILNSST	distensible
BDEEIILPRSS	dispersible
BDEEILLMOOS	loose-limbed
BDEEILLNPRS	spellbinder
BDEEILMNOTY	molybdenite
BDEEILMRRTU	tumble-drier
BDEEILORSTU	turbo-diesel
BDEEIMMNRUX	mixed number
BDEEINNSSSU	business end
BDEEIOORSXY	deoxyribose
BDEELLOOSSV	blood vessel
BDEELMNOORW	demon bowler
BDEELMRRTUY	tumble-dryer
BDEELNORTUY	double entry
BDEENPRRTUU	unperturbed
BDEEOOPRTTU	torpedo tube
BDEFGINOORY	foreign body
BDEFHILMNOS	Flemish bond
BDEFILORSTU	double first
BDEFIMNOORS	bosom friend
BDEGGIINRSW	swing-bridge
BDEGHILNNOS	English bond
BDEGIINNRST	bird-nesting
BDEGILNNNUY	unbendingly
BDEHHOOORRT	brotherhood
BDEHIIINNTU	uninhibited
BDEHIILORST	boiled shirt
BDEHIILPRSU	shipbuilder
BDEHIKLNOOY	blind hookey
BDEHIKLNOTU	doublethink
BDEHILLOOTT	tooth-billed
BDEHILNPSUU	unpublished
BDEHILOOPRY	hyperboloid
BDEHIMOORSU	rhomboideus
BDEHLNORTTU	thunderbolt
BDEIIIILNSV	indivisible
BDEIIIILNTY	inedibility
BDEIIILMSSS	dismissible
BDEIILMRSUU	subdelirium
BDEIKNORSTU	strike-bound
BDEILLLNORR	roller blind
BDEILLOSTUX	billets-doux
BDEIMMNOPRU	Premium Bond
BDEINOSSSUU	dubiousness
BDEKLOOORRY	orderly book
BDELLLOOSSY	bloodlessly
BDELLNOSSUY	boundlessly
BDELLOSSTUY	doubtlessly
BDFGIIKNORS	king of birds
BDFGILLOOOS	bill of goods
BDFKOOOORSW	book of words
BDGHIIMMNRU	hummingbird
BDGIILMNNOW	mind-blowing
BDGIILNNORT	Bridlington
BDGIILNOTUU	outbuilding
BDGIIMMNNNU	mind-numbing
BDGINOOPPPY	body-popping
BDIIIILNSVY	indivisibly
BDIIINOSSUV	subdivision
BDIIMNORTUY	moribundity
BDIIORRSTTU	distributor
BEEEEGILRTT	tiger beetle
BEEEGIINNOR	bioengineer
BEEEGILLNPS	spelling-bee
BEEEGILLNRT	belligerent
BEEEGILLRTT	little grebe
BEEEGILMNTU	beguilement
BEEEGINNNRZ	benzene ring
BEEEGLNORTT	bottle green, greenbottle
BEEEHILLMRS	embellisher
BEEEHILLNOR	helleborine
BEEEHLLRSTT	shelter belt
BEEEHLMRRTY	treble rhyme
BEEEILNNORV	non-believer
BEEEILNPRTV	preventible
BEEEILPRRSS	repressible
BEEEILPRSSX	expressible
BEEEIMMMRRS	misremember
BEEEIRSTTTW	bitter-sweet
BEEELMNNNOT	ennoblement
BEEELNOSTTU	snout-beetle
BEEENOPPRTY	teeny-bopper
BEEENOPPRWY	weeny-bopper
BEEENORSSSV	verboseness
BEEFGIINNTT	benefitting
BEEFGLLOORW	globeflower
BEEFHIORRSU	herbiferous
BEEFIKNRTTU	butter knife
BEEGGILSSTU	suggestible
BEEGHHLNRSU	Helensburgh
BEEGHINNORR	herringbone
BEEGIILLNRV	Bingerville
BEEGIILNNUV	unbelieving
BEEGIIOORSU	bourgeoisie
BEEGIKKNOOP	bookkeeping
BEEGILLMNOW	embowelling
BEEGILLNSST	best-selling
BEEGIMNOSTT	misbegotten
BEEGIPRRSTU	Pietersburg
BEEHILMNOOP	mobile phone
BEEHIMNOORT	theobromine
BEEHKNOORSU	house-broken
BEEHLMNORUW	whole number
BEEHLORRSST	brotherless
BEEHOPRRSTT	stepbrother
BEEIILMPRSS	impressible, permissible
BEEIILNSSSV	visibleness
BEEIIRRTTUV	retributive
BEEIKLLNOTT	Klein bottle
BEEILLLNTUY	ebulliently
BEEILLRRRTU	bull terrier
BEEILMMNORT	embroilment

BEEILNNOSTW	tennis elbow
BEEILNOPRSS	responsible
BEEILNOQSSU	obliqueness
BEEILNPSSSU	suspensible
BEEILNRSSTT	brittleness
BEEILOSSSVY	obsessively
BEEINRSSTTU	butteriness
BEEINRSSTUV	subservient
BEEJLNOSSSS	joblessness
BEEKMNOORRY	money broker
BEEKOOPRRRW	power-broker
BEELLLLOWYY	yellow-belly
BEELLNOSSUV	volubleness
BEELMOORSTU	some trouble, troublesome
BEELPRSSTUU	supersubtle
BEENQRSSSUU	brusqueness
BEERRRSTTUU	surrebutter
BEFGHILLRTU	bullfighter
BEFGIILNTTY	befittingly
BEFGIINNTTU	unbefitting
BEFHLLORRTU	full brother
BEFHLMORTUU	rule of thumb
BEFHLOORRTW	froth-blower
BEFIIILLTXY	flexibility
BEFIMORRSUU	umbriferous
BEFINORSSSU	fibrousness
BEFLLOOPRTU	bulletproof
BEGGIILLNNR	bell-ringing
BEGGIILLNUY	beguilingly
BEGGILNOOVX	boxing glove
BEGGINOORRS	Bognor Regis
BEGHHIIRTTW	birthweight
BEGHILNORUY	neighbourly
BEGHINOPSTT	betting shop
BEGHINOSUUY	house-buying
BEGHORSSTTU	ghostbuster
BEGIIIILLTY	eligibility
BEGILLMNRTY	tremblingly
BEGILNORSWW	swing bowler
BEGILNQRSUU	burlesquing
BEGINNNNOTU	unbonneting
BEHHIMORRTT	birth mother
BEHIIIOPRTV	prohibitive
BEHIIKLMNOS	Shibin el Kom
BEHIILPRSTY	Liberty ship
BEHIIMNPRRS	brine shrimp
BEHIINPRSTU	tribuneship
BEHIINRSSST	Britishness
BEHIKNOOSSS	bookishness
BEHIKOOSTTX	textbookish
BEHILLNSSSU	bullishness
BEHILLRSTTU	bullshitter
BEHILMOPRSY	hyperbolism
BEHILORSSTU	shirt blouse
BEHINOORSSS	boorishness
BEHINRSSSTU	brutishness
BEHIOORRSUV	herbivorous
BEHKRRSTUUY	brush turkey
BEHMNOORTUU	Bournemouth
BEHOORRSSTX	boxer shorts
BEIIILMMORZ	immobilizer
BEIIILMNRST	libertinism
BEIIILMQRUU	equilibrium
BEIIILNSSTY	sensibility
BEIIILQRSTU	equilibrist
BEIILLORTUV	blue vitriol
BEIILMPRSSY	permissibly
BEIILNOSSSU	biliousness
BEIINORRTTU	retribution
BEIKKLNPSUY	sky-blue pink
BEIKLNOSTTT	ink-blot test
BEILLLLOSUY	libellously
BEILLMPSTUU	submultiple
BEILLNORSVW	Brownsville
BEILLNOSSSU	bull session
BEILLORSSTT	stilbestrol
BEILMPRRSTU	rumble strip
BEILNOPRSSY	responsibly
BEILOPRRSTU	protrusible
BEILORSTUVY	obtrusively
BEINOOSSSUV	obviousness
BEINORSSUVV	bons viveurs
BEINORSTUUV	unobtrusive
BEINSSTTTUU	substituent
BEIORRRTTUY	retributory
BEKNNNOSTUW	unbeknownst
BELLNRTTUUY	turbulently
BELNOOSTUUY	bounteously
BELOOPRSTTU	trouble spot
BEMOOPRRSTY	Port Moresby
BENOPRSSTTU	press-button
BERRSSTTTUU	trustbuster
BFFGINOSTUX	stuffing box
BFGIIILNTUY	fungibility
BFILLNOTUUY	bountifully
BGGIIIKNTTU	Bukittinggi
BGGILLMNRUY	grumblingly
BGHIIINOPRT	prohibiting
BGHIIINRRTV	virgin birth
BGHIIKNOPSS	king's bishop
BGHIINOPPWY	whipping boy
BGHIMNPTTUU	tub-thumping
BGHINOOOSTX	shooting box
BGIIILLLTUY	gullibility
BGIILLNOPST	billposting
BGIILOORSTT	tribologist
BGIKNNOSTUY	King's bounty
BGILLMNSTUY	stumblingly
BGILMNNOOOT	Bloomington
BGINNNOSTUW	snow bunting
BGLOOOORYYZ	bryozoology
BHIIINOOPRT	prohibition
BHIIIOPRSTU	triphibious
BHIIOOPRRTY	prohibitory
BIIILOPSSTY	possibility
BIIKNOORSSV	Novosibirsk
BIILLOOSUVY	obliviously
BIIMNOOSTUX	moxibustion
BILMOPSTUUY	bumptiously
BILNOOOSUXY	obnoxiously
BIMNOPSSTUU	subsumption
BIMORSSTUUU	rumbustious
BIOOOPPRRSU	opprobrious
BMMNOTTTUUY	tummy button
CCCCKKLOOOU	cuckoo clock
CCCDEEIINNO	coincidence
CCCDEHINOSY	synecdochic
CCCDIIIOOSS	coccidiosis
CCCDILOOPSU	diplococcus

CCCEEEENRSX	excrescence
CCCEEFLLNOU	flocculence
CCCEEFOORSS	fresco secco
CCCEEIILMST	eclecticism
CCCEEIINRTV	civic centre
CCCEENNORRU	concurrence
CCCEENNORST	concrescent
CCCEFIINOPS	conspecific
CCCEILORSST	Celtic cross
CCCEIMNOOPU	pneumococci
CCCEIMPRSTU	circumspect
CCCEINNOTTU	Connecticut
CCCHILMOTYY	cyclothymic
CCCIIMMOORS	microcosmic
CCCIIMOOPRS	microscopic
CCCIOOPSSTY	cystoscopic
CCDDEEENORS	decrescendo
CCDDELNNOUU	unconcluded
CCDEEEEINNR	Nicene Creed
CCDEEEFHIKN	chicken feed
CCDEEEGINOT	genetic code
CCDEEEIINRS	iridescence
CCDEEENRRST	Red Crescent
CCDEEHILPSY	psychedelic
CCDEEHINORS	Second Reich
CCDEEHIORTT	ricochetted
CCDEEIIINST	insecticide
CCDEEIIRRST	directrices
CCDEEILNOTY	conceitedly
CCDEEILRRSS	dress circle
CCDEELLLOTY	collectedly
CCDEELLNOTU	uncollected
CCDEELNNORY	concernedly
CCDEELNNOTY	connectedly
CCDEENNNORU	unconcerned
CCDEENNNOTU	unconnected
CCDEENORRTU	uncorrected
CCDEIILOORT	crocidolite
CCDEIMNOORS	microsecond
CCDEINNNOUV	unconvinced
CCDENORSSTU	conductress
CCDENORSTTU	deconstruct
CCDFLMOOORT	cold comfort
CCDGIIKNSSU	sucking-disc
CCDHHILLOOS	schoolchild
CCDHILOOPYY	hypocycloid
CCDHIOORTTW	witch doctor
CCDHIOOSTUU	studio couch
CCDHMMNOOOR	common chord
CCDKMOSUUVY	Muscovy duck
CCEEEEILLRT	electric eel
CCEEEEILRTY	electric eye
CCEEEEINPRT	centrepiece
CCEEEFHIKNR	neckerchief
CCEEEFHIRTV	hectic fever
CCEEEFLNORS	florescence
CCEEEGINNRS	nigrescence
CCEEEGINOTT	ectogenetic
CCEEEGINRVY	vicegerency
CCEEEGNNORV	convergence
CCEEEGNRSTU	turgescence
CCEEEHHLOST	cheesecloth
CCEEEHINNOR	incoherence
CCEEEHIRSST	screechiest
CCEEEIINPPR	percipience

CCEEEILSTWY	sweet cicely
CCEEEINNNOV	convenience
CCEEEINOPRV	preconceive
CCEEEINOSTX	coexistence
CCEEEINPRSU	pure science
CCEEEINRRST	Cirencester
CCEEEINRSTV	vitrescence
CCEEELORTTU	electrocute
CCEEENNOQSU	consequence
CCEEENPRSTU	putrescence
CCEEFFIINOT	coefficient
CCEEFHNRRUV	French curve
CCEEFIIMNNU	munificence
CCEEFILNOST	self-conceit
CCEEFILOOPR	police force
CCEEGHHKRRU	Greek Church
CCEEGINOTTY	cytogenetic
CCEEGLLORSV	clever clogs
CCEEGNNOOST	cognoscente
CCEEGNNORVY	convergency
CCEEGNOORRT	concert-goer
CCEEHHKORRY	choke cherry
CCEEHIIKNRW	chicken wire
CCEEHINNORY	incoherency
CCEEHINORTT	theocentric
CCEEHKLLLOS	cockleshell
CCEEHMOPTYY	phycomycete
CCEEHNORSTU	touch screen
CCEEIILNNRR	inner circle
CCEEIILNOSS	soil science
CCEEIILORST	isoelectric
CCEEIILRTTY	electricity
CCEEIIMNNOS	omniscience
CCEEIIMNOSV	misconceive
CCEEIKLMORT	mole cricket
CCEEILNNOTV	conventicle
CCEEILNORST	electronics, stone circle
CCEEILPPRTU	peptic ulcer
CCEEIMNOORT	econometric
CCEEIMNRSTU	music centre
CCEEINNOQTU	cinquecento
CCEEINNOSSS	conciseness
CCEEINNOSST	consistence
CCEEINORRTU	Eurocentric
CCEEINOSTUV	consecutive
CCEEIOPRSTU	Euro-sceptic
CCEEMNNNORT	concernment
CCEENORRSST	correctness
CCEFFIINSUY	sufficiency
CCEFFINOORW	Crown Office
CCEFGIKLNOS	self-cocking
CCEFHHILSTU	hectic flush
CCEFHIIMORS	microfiches
CCEFIIIPSTY	specificity
CCEFIINNOPS	non-specific
CCEFIINOPRY	proficiency
CCEFIORRSUU	cruciferous
CCEGGILNOOY	gynecologic
CCEGHIINORT	ricocheting
CCEGINNNOTY	contingency
CCEGINNOOST	cognoscenti
CCEGINORRRU	reoccurring
CCEHHHORSUU	house church
CCEHHINRSSU	churchiness
CCEHHIOSSTT	schottische

CCEHIILNOPR	necrophilic	**CDDDEEEINSS**	decidedness
CCEHIINPRST	sphincteric	**CDDDEEENNSU**	undescended
CCEHILNOORT	Technicolor	**CDDDEEIIRST**	discredited
CCEHILNOPTY	polytechnic	**CDDDEEILNUY**	undecidedly
CCEHIMNOORT	homocentric	**CDDEEEENPRT**	precedented
CCEHIMOOPRT	ectomorphic	**CDDEEEIPRTU**	decrepitude
CCEHINNRSSU	crunchiness	**CDDEEENNOPS**	despondence
CCEHINOPRTY	pyrotechnic	**CDDEEENNOPT**	codependent
CCEHKLOSTTU	shuttlecock	**CDDEEFILNSU**	self-induced
CCEHKMOORTU	Cockermouth	**CDDEEHLNSUU**	unscheduled
CCEIIINSSTT	scientistic	**CDDEEIINORT**	rodenticide
CCEIIKLRSTY	city slicker	**CDDEEILTUVY**	deductively
CCEIIKNSSTT	stick insect	**CDDEEINPRTU**	unpredicted
CCEIILMORST	cliometrics	**CDDEENNOPSY**	despondency
CCEIIMOORST	sociometric	**CDDEENORSSW**	crowdedness
CCEIIMORSTV	viscometric	**CDDEENRRTUY**	eddy current
CCEIIOPRRTY	reciprocity	**CDDEFIIKLST**	fiddlestick
CCEIJNNOTUV	conjunctive	**CDDEFIIMOST**	discomfited
CCEIKLNOPRU	cupro-nickel	**CDDEHIILMNR**	childminder
CCEILMOORTU	coulometric	**CDDEIILPPSS**	slipped disc
CCEILNORRTY	incorrectly	**CDDEIKOPSTT**	spotted dick
CCEIMMNOORR	common crier	**CDDEILNOOTY**	dicotyledon
CCEINNOOSTU	consecution	**CDDEILNOSSU**	undisclosed
CCEINNOPRRW	Crown prince	**CDDEINSSSUU**	undiscussed
CCEINNOSSTY	consistency	**CDDELLLMOOY**	mollycoddle
CCEJNNORTUU	conjuncture	**CDEEEEFFLNS**	self-defence
CCELLNSTUUY	succulently	**CDEEEEFLNSS**	defenceless
CCELNOOOOPS	colonoscope	**CDEEEEHKRRT**	three-decker
CCELORSSSUU	succourless	**CDEEEEINPRX**	experienced
CCENORRSTTU	reconstruct	**CDEEEFHIMNR**	chemin de fer
CCEOOOPPRST	proctoscope	**CDEEEFILTVY**	defectively
CCEOOOPRRSS	coprocessor	**CDEEEFLNRST**	self-centred
CCFIIINORUX	crucifixion	**CDEEEFNPRTU**	unperfected
CCFIILNNOOT	confliction	**CDEEEGILNXY**	exceedingly
CCGGHHINORU	churchgoing	**CDEEEGINORZ**	derecognize
CCGHILNORSY	scorchingly	**CDEEEHLNOTU**	touch-needle
CCGHIOOPRSY	hygroscopic	**CDEEEHNOSTT**	second teeth
CCGIIINRRTU	ring circuit	**CDEEEHRSTTW**	wretchedest
CCGINOSTTTU	cost-cutting	**CDEEEHSSSTU**	duchesse set
CCHIIILMORT	microlithic	**CDEEEIIOPPR**	period piece
CCHIIILNOPS	silicon chip	**CDEEEILNOST**	deselection
CCHIIMNOOPR	microphonic	**CDEEEILORTT**	lie detector
CCHIIMOORTT	trichotomic	**CDEEEILPTVY**	deceptively
CCHIIMORSTW	microswitch	**CDEEEINPRUV**	unperceived
CCHILMOOPRY	polychromic	**CDEEEINSSTX**	excitedness
CCHILMOPTYY	lymphocytic	**CDEEEIRSSTT**	discreetest
CCHIMMNOOOR	monochromic	**CDEEELLORVW**	well covered
CCHIORSSSTT	cross stitch	**CDEEELNPRTY**	precedently
CCIIMMNOSTU	communistic	**CDEEEMMNORR**	recommender
CCIINOPRTTY	nyctitropic	**CDEEENNOPRS**	respondence
CCIJNNNOOTU	conjunction	**CDEEENORRTT**	retrocedent
CCIKLMNOOTU	coconut milk	**CDEEEOPRRSS**	predecessor
CCILNNOOTUW	town council	**CDEEFFIKNST**	stiff-necked
CCILNOOPRSY	cyclosporin	**CDEEFFNOSTU**	sound effect
CCILNOOSSUY	consciously	**CDEEFHIKLOY**	field hockey
CCIMNNOOPTU	compunction	**CDEEFIILNTY**	deficiently
CCINNOOSSUU	unconscious	**CDEEFIIMNOX**	fixed income
CCINOOPSSUU	conspicuous	**CDEEFIINPSU**	unspecified
CCINOORRSTT	constrictor	**CDEEFIINRTU**	uncertified, unrectified
CCKMMNOOOST	common stock	**CDEEFILLTUY**	deceitfully
CCKNOORRTUY	country rock	**CDEEFILNNTU**	uninflected
CCLNNOOORWY	Crown Colony	**CDEEFILNORT**	field-cornet
CCLNOOOPSY	colonoscopy	**CDEEFILNORY**	eco-friendly
CCNOORRSTTU	constructor	**CDEEFILOSST**	close-fisted
CCNOORTTUUY	county court	**CDEEFINORRT**	Fredericton

CDEEFLLOORS self-colored
CDEEFLNOSSY confessedly
CDEEFNORSTT soft-centred
CDEEFOORRTU tour de force
CDEEFOPRRTW word-perfect
CDEEGGINTTU cutting edge
CDEEGGLORSS cross-legged
CDEEGHLNOPR golden perch
CDEEGNOSSSU second-guess
CDEEHIINNOS Indo-Chinese
CDEEHIINNST indehiscent
CDEEHIKNTVY kidney vetch
CDEEHIMNORT endothermic
CDEEHIOQSTU discotheque
CDEEHNOORSU echo sounder
CDEEIILNORT dereliction
CDEEIILRTTT credit title
CDEEIIMORTU eudiometric
CDEEIINORRT redirection
CDEEIINRSTV viridescent
CDEEIINRTTU incertitude
CDEEIIPRSTV descriptive
CDEEIKLNNOO nickelodeon
CDEEILNNQUY delinquency
CDEEILNORTY reconditely
CDEEILNRUVY curly endive
CDEEILSTUVY seductively
CDEEIMMORTT recommitted
CDEEIMNNRST discernment
CDEEIMNORTV divorcement
CDEEIMOOSTX sextodecimo
CDEEINOPRTV open verdict
CDEEINORRTU reintroduce
CDEEINPRSUU superinduce
CDEEIORRSVY rediscovery
CDEEIORRTXY ex-directory
CDEEIRRRSVW screwdriver
CDEEIRSTTUV destructive
CDEEKLLOSTW well-stocked
CDEEKNOORSS crookedness
CDEELMNOPTU uncompleted
CDEELNNOTTY contentedly
CDEELNRTTUU uncluttered
CDEEMNOOPUY compound eye
CDEENNOPRSY respondency
CDEENNOQRUU unconquered
CDEENNORTUV unconverted
CDEENNOSTTU uncontested
CDEENOPRSSU unprocessed
CDEENOPRTTU unprotected
CDEENPSSTUU unsuspected
CDEEOOPRRUV overproduce
CDEEOPPRSTW crow-stepped
CDEFFIORTUY duty officer
CDEFGINOSSU defocussing
CDEFHIOOPRT pitched roof
CDEFIINORTU countrified
CDEFILNNOTY confidently
CDEFIMNNORU unconfirmed
CDEFINNNOTU unconfident
CDEFINORTUY countryfied
CDEFLNOOORS second floor
CDEGGLRSUUY sculduggery
CDEGHHHIIPT high-pitched
CDEGHINOSST second sight
CDEGIINNORS considering
CDEGIMNORRU corrigendum
CDEGMORRSUY dog's mercury
CDEGNOORRUV ground cover
CDEHIIINNOR enchiridion
CDEHIIKTTTW thick-witted
CDEHIILOOTT theodolitic
CDEHIIMOOTZ dichotomize
CDEHIIMOSTT Methodistic
CDEHIINOOTZ citizenhood
CDEHILPRTUU pulchritude
CDEHIMNOOPR endomorphic
CDEHIMNORST Christendom
CDEHIMORRTY hydrometric
CDEHIORTTUY youth credit
CDEHKLOORST stockholder
CDEHOOORRST horse-doctor
CDEIIILNSUV uncivilised
CDEIIILNUVZ uncivilized
CDEIIIMMSTU mediumistic
CDEIIINORTX nitric oxide
CDEIIINSTTV distinctive
CDEIIIOPRTY periodicity
CDEIIISSTUV vicissitude
CDEIIJNSTUV disjunctive
CDEIIKQTTUW quick-witted
CDEIILLMNOS millisecond
CDEIILLOORV cod liver oil
CDEIILLOSUY deliciously
CDEIILLPTUY pellucidity
CDEIILNOSTU unsolicited
CDEIILNRTUY incredulity
CDEIILNTUVY inductively
CDEIILOPSSU pediculosis
CDEIILOSTUV declivitous
CDEIIMNORST modernistic
CDEIIMOSTTY domesticity
CDEIIMPPRUY cypripedium
CDEIIMSTTWY Midwest City
CDEIINNOORT conditioner, recondition
CDEIINNOSTU discontinue
CDEIINOPRST description, discerption
CDEIJNRSTUU disjuncture
CDEILNOORUU unicoloured
CDEILNOPSST split second
CDEILNORSUU incredulous
CDEILOORRTU tricoloured
CDEIMMNOPSU compendiums
CDEIMMNOTTU uncommitted
CDEIMNOOPSU compendious
CDEINNOPRST nondescript
CDEINNORTUV uncontrived
CDEINOOPSST endoscopist
CDEINORSTTU destruction
CDEINORSTUY countryside
CDEIOPRRTUW word-picture
CDEIORSSTUY discourtesy
CDEIORSSUWW widow's cruse
CDEKKNOOORR door knocker
CDELLLOSSUY cloudlessly
CDELLNORSUY scoundrelly
CDELLOOOPRT protocolled
CDELLOPRRUW crowd-puller
CDELLORSUUY credulously
CDELNNOSTUU unconsulted

CDELOOORTUW	tow-coloured
CDENOPRRTUU	uncorrupted
CDEOOPRRSSW	word-process
CDEOPRRRUWY	curry powder
CDFFIILLTUY	difficultly
CDFGHLLOOOT	cloth of gold
CDFGIILNNOY	confidingly
CDFINNOSTUY	dysfunction
CDGHILNOOPP	clodhopping
CDGHILOOORY	orchidology
CDGIIKNSTTU	sitting duck
CDGILOORTTY	troglodytic
CDGINOPRSTU	crop dusting
CDGNOORSTUY	God's country
CDHHIILOPRY	hydrophilic
CDHIINORSTU	third cousin
CDHIIOOPRST	chiropodist
CDHIMOOOSTU	dichotomous
CDHINOOORTT	orthodontic
CDHINOOPRSY	hydroponics
CDIIIJNOSUU	injudicious
CDIIINNOSTT	distinction
CDIIJLOSUUY	judiciously
CDIIJNNOSTU	disjunction
CDIILOPSTUU	duplicitous
CDIIMMNNOOU	condominium
CDIKLNOPSSU	spondulicks
CDIKNOOPRST	Port Dickson
CDILLOOORSU	solid colour
CDILLORSUUY	ludicrously
CDILOOORUUU	dourougcouli
CEEEEEGHNRS	green cheese
CEEEEEGMNRR	re-emergence
CEEEEEPRRRT	treecreeper
CEEEEHHRRST	three cheers
CEEEEHLMNOS	lemon cheese
CEEEEILNORT	electioneer
CEEEEIMNNPR	pre-eminence
CEEEEINRRRV	irreverence
CEEEEIRRSTV	service tree
CEEEEJNRSUV	rejuvenesce
CEEEENNRRTV	nerve centre
CEEEENPPRST	Peter's pence
CEEEFFHOOSU	coffee house
CEEEFFIINTV	ineffective
CEEEFFILTVY	effectively
CEEEFFLNOSS	offenceless
CEEEFGINNRR	refringence
CEEEFGLLNST	self-neglect
CEEEFHIIPRS	speechifier
CEEEFHNRRTV	trench fever
CEEEFIILRRT	electrifier
CEEEFIKQRUZ	quick-freeze
CEEEFILRSSV	self-service
CEEEFLPRSST	self-respect
CEEEFLRRTUY	cruelty-free
CEEEFMNNORT	enforcement
CEEEFNPRSST	perfectness
CEEEGGNORRR	greengrocer
CEEEGIINOPR	epeirogenic
CEEEGINOSST	ectogenesis
CEEEGLLNOOP	open college
CEEEHHKLNOP	heckelphone
CEEEHIKNTTT	kitchenette
CEEEHILORTT	heteroclite
CEEEHIMNRTU	hermeneutic
CEEEHIORRSV	heroic verse
CEEEHLLNORW	New Rochelle
CEEEHLLRSSY	cheerlessly
CEEEHLMORST	chrome steel
CEEEHLOPRST	Cleethorpes
CEEEHOPRSTV	Cherepovets
CEEEIIKLNTT	telekinetic
CEEEIILNRSV	service line
CEEEIIMNNPT	impenitence
CEEEIINNNRT	internecine
CEEEIINNNST	insentience
CEEEIKLLNST	nickel steel
CEEEILLSTVY	selectively
CEEEILMORTV	velocimeter
CEEEILNOPRT	pre-election
CEEEILNOPST	Pleistocene
CEEEILNORST	reselection
CEEEILNSTUV	unselective
CEEEILPRTVY	receptively
CEEEILRSSVY	recessively
CEEEILRSTVY	secretively
CEEEILSSVXY	excessively
CEEEILTUVXY	executively
CEEEIMMNRTX	cement mixer
CEEEIMMPSUU	museum piece
CEEEINNOPRV	provenience
CEEEINNOSTV	venesection
CEEEINNRSSS	sincereness
CEEEINORTUX	executioner
CEEEINOSTVX	coextensive
CEEEINPRSSS	preciseness
CEEEINPRSST	persistence
CEEEINPRTUV	unreceptive
CEEEIPPRSTV	perspective
CEEEJNNSTUV	juvenescent
CEEEKMNORSS	smokescreen
CEEEKORSTTW	sweet rocket
CEEELLLNTXY	excellently
CEEELLORSTY	electrolyse
CEEELLORTTY	electrolyte
CEEELMMOTTU	telecommute
CEEELMNOSSW	welcomeness
CEEELMORRST	sclerometer
CEEELOPRRST	pre-selector
CEEELOPRTTY	electrotype
CEEELORRTTV	cover letter
CEEEOOPRSST	stereoscope
CEEEPPRRSST	preceptress
CEEFFHIIORS	Irish coffee
CEEFFHINRRS	French fries
CEEFFIIINNT	inefficient
CEEFFIILLOS	slice of life
CEEFFIILNTY	efficiently
CEEFFIITTVY	effectivity
CEEFFILNOOR	line of force
CEEFFILRSTY	self-certify
CEEFGINNRRY	refringency
CEEFGINORRU	reconfigure
CEEFGLNORTU	genuflector
CEEFHHNORTT	thenceforth
CEEFIINNORT	reinfection
CEEFIINSSTV	fictiveness
CEEFIIPRSSU	superficies
CEEFIKKNOPT	pocket knife

CEEFIKOOPRW piece of work
CEEFIKORRST strike force
CEEFILMPRTY imperfectly
CEEFILNORSU fluorescein
CEEFIMNNNOT confinement
CEEFINNQRUY infrequency
CEEFINORRSV five-corners
CEEFINORTTU counterfeit
CEEFLNNOSTT self-content
CEEFLNORSTU fluorescent
CEEFLOORRSU foreclosure
CEEFLORRSUU resourceful
CEEGGOORRSS George Cross
CEEGHIKNPSS King's speech
CEEGHIMNOOT homogenetic
CEEGHINOPST pigeon-chest
CEEGHINRSST sight-screen
CEEGIINPRST string-piece
CEEGILNOPTY polygenetic
CEEGIMNNOOT monogenetic
CEEGIMNORST egocentrism
CEEGINNOOTT ontogenetic
CEEGINOORST oestrogenic
CEEGIOPRRTU picturegoer
CEEGLNNORTU electron gun
CEEGMNOORYY grey economy
CEEGNNOORSU congenerous
CEEHHIIMPRS hemispheric
CEEHHILNOPT technophile
CEEHHIORSVW whichsoever
CEEHHMORSTT home stretch
CEEHIIINORS chinoiserie
CEEHIILLNST Hellenistic
CEEHIIMPSTU euphemistic
CEEHIINOPTZ phoneticize
CEEHIKNSSST sketchiness
CEEHILLNOST clothes line
CEEHILMNORT thermocline
CEEHILOPRST electorship
CEEHILPRSTU lectureship
CEEHKLNOSUY honeysuckle
CEEHLLOORST cholesterol
CEEHLLORSUY lecherously
CEEHLOOPRRS pre-schooler
CEEHMNOORRT chronometer
CEEHNORTTUY youth centre
CEEHOOPSSTT stethoscope
CEEHORRSTTV overstretch
CEEHORRTTYY erythrocyte
CEEIIINRSTT intercities
CEEIIKNRSST ricketiness
CEEIILMPRSY imprecisely
CEEIILMRTUV vermiculite
CEEIILNNRSY insincerely
CEEIILNPRST princeliest
CEEIILSTTVY selectivity
CEEIIMNNPTY impenitency
CEEIIMNNRST reminiscent
CEEIIMOPTTV competitive
CEEIIMORSST esotericism
CEEIIMRRRTW crime writer
CEEIINORSTV insectivore
CEEIINOSSTT seicentoist
CEEIIORSSTT esotericist
CEEIIPRTTVY receptivity
CEEIIRRSTTV restrictive
CEEIKLNORRT interlocker
CEEIKMMOSUY Mickey Mouse
CEEIKNOSTTT stockinette
CEEIKNPRSTY persnickety
CEEIKORRTTV rover ticket
CEEILLMNNTY inclemently
CEEILLMRSSY mercilessly
CEEILLOSSVY voicelessly
CEEILLPRSSY pricelessly
CEEILLSUVXY exclusively
CEEILMNNSTU luminescent
CEEILMOORRT colorimeter
CEEILNNNOOV non-violence
CEEILNOORRT intercooler
CEEILNPRSST split-screen
CEEILNPRSTU cluster pine
CEEILNPRSTY presciently
CEEILNQSTUY quiescently
CEEILRRSTUU sericulture
CEEILRRSUVY recursively
CEEILRSUVXY excursively
CEEIMNNOOPT omnipotence
CEEIMNNOPTT incompetent
CEEIMNNORTT metric tonne
CEEIMNNORTU countermine
CEEIMNNSTTU intumescent
CEEIMNOORSU ceremonious
CEEIMNOOSYZ economy-size
CEEIMNRRTTU recruitment
CEEIMOORRSV room service
CEEIMOPRSSV compressive
CEEIMOPRTUZ computerize
CEEINNNOSTT consentient
CEEINNOORRT reconnoiter, reconnoitre
CEEINNPRRST screen print
CEEINOOPSTY open society
CEEINOPRRTT interceptor
CEEINOPRSTU persecution
CEEINORRSST intercessor
CEEINORRSTU intercourse
CEEINOSSSTU necessitous
CEEINOSSSTV costiveness
CEEINPRSSTY persistency
CEEINRRSSTW winter cress
CEEIOPPRSTV prospective
CEEIOPRSTTY stereotypic
CEEIPQRSTUU picturesque
CEEIRSTTVVY Civvy Street
CEEJLNORSWW crown jewels
CEEKMNOOPTY pocket money
CEEKOORRRTT retro-rocket
CEELLMNOUWY unwelcomely
CEELMNNOSTU locum tenens
CEELMNOPRUZ crumple zone
CEELMNOPSTY splenectomy
CEELMNOPTTY competently
CEELMNSTTUY tumescently
CEELNORSTUW stone curlew
CEELNRRRTUY recurrently
CEEMMMNOORT common metre
CEEMMNNOOSS common sense
CEEMMOOPRTT Comptometer
CEEMNNNOTTT contentment
CEEMNNRSTTU encrustment

CEEMNOORTUV countermove
CEEMNOPRRTU procurement
CEEMNOPRSTT contretemps
CEEMNORRSTT storm centre
CEENNOORRST cornerstone
CEENOOPRRST Poets' Corner
CEENOQSSTUU Queen's Scout
CEENORSTTTU stonecutter
CEEOOPRSSTY stereoscopy
CEEOPRRSSTT protectress
CEEOPRRSTUY persecutory
CEERRRSTTUU restructure
CEFFFINOORT front office
CEFFGIIKLNS King's Cliffe
CEFFHIOORSU office hours
CEFFHIRSSTT festschrift
CEFFHOOORSW show of force
CEFFINRSSSU scruffiness
CEFGHILMRTY mercy flight
CEFGHIORTUV gift voucher
CEFGIIINPRX price-fixing
CEFGIKLLNOS self-locking
CEFGIKLMNOS self-mocking
CEFGILLNOSS self-closing
CEFGINORSSU refocussing
CEFGNOORRST strong force
CEFHIIISSTT fetishistic
CEFHILLRTUY filthy lucre
CEFHINRSTUW Schweinfurt
CEFHKORSTUU future shock
CEFHLLOORSU flesh colour
CEFIIIKNNSS finickiness
CEFIKNNOTUY function key
CEFILMORSUU culmiferous
CEFILNOORRT fire-control
CEFILNOORTU counterfoil
CEFILOORSUY ferociously
CEFILORRSUW furrow-slice
CEFIOPRRSUU cupriferous
CEFLLNOORST self-control
CEFLMOORSST comfortless
CEFLOOOPRSU fluoroscope
CEFNOPRRTUY perfunctory
CEGHHIORRTU higher court
CEGHIILNRST Christingle
CEGHIILNRTT chitterling
CEGHIINNRST christening
CEGHILLNOOY lichenology
CEGHILNORTY hectoringly
CEGHIMNOOPR morphogenic
CEGHIMORRTY hygrometric
CEGHINORRST torch singer
CEGHINORSSU grouchiness
CEGHIOOPRST geostrophic
CEGHLNOOPST sponge cloth
CEGIIJLNORY rejoicingly
CEGIIKLNNSY sickeningly
CEGIIKLNSST single stick
CEGIILLNNST stencilling
CEGIILMNOST closing time
CEGIILNOTVY cognitively
CEGIILOOPST geopolitics
CEGIIMMNNOU immunogenic
CEGIIMNOORT goniometric
CEGIINNOORT recognition
CEGIINRSSTY synergistic
CEGILLMNOWY welcomingly
CEGILLNNOSU counselling
CEGILMNNOUW unwelcoming
CEGILNOOSTY Scientology
CEGIMNNNOST consignment
CEGIMNOOPRU income group
CEGIMOOORRV microgroove
CEGINNNNSSU cunningness
CEGINNOOPST coping stone
CEGINNORSTU countersign
CEGINOORRTY recognitory
CEGLMMOORYY myrmecology
CEGLNNORTUY congruently
CEGORRRSUYY cryosurgery
CEHHIIILLOT heliolithic
CEHHIILOTTY ichthyolite
CEHHIINPRTT pinch-hitter
CEHHILMRSUY helichrysum
CEHHIMRSTUY eurhythmics
CEHHIOPRRST Christopher
CEHHLMOOSTT clothes-moth
CEHHLOOOSSU schoolhouse
CEHHMNORSSY synchromesh
CEHHMOOPRTY phytochrome
CEHIIINPSTZ citizenship
CEHIIJPSSTU justiceship
CEHIIKKNNST kitchen-sink
CEHIIKNSSST kitschiness
CEHIILMNTTU multi-ethnic
CEHIILOOPRT heliotropic
CEHIILPRSTU spherulitic
CEHIIMNOPST phoneticism
CEHIIMNORST thermionics
CEHIIMOSSUV mischievous
CEHIINNSSTZ chintziness
CEHIINOOPRS ionospheric
CEHIINOPSTT phoneticist
CEHIIOPRRST prehistoric
CEHIIOPRSVY viceroyship
CEHIIOSSSVY vichyssoise
CEHIKLLNORT kitchen roll
CEHIKMRSSTU hucksterism
CEHIKNOPSTU soup kitchen
CEHIKNORSWY corn whiskey
CEHIKNPSSSU puckishness
CEHILLNNOPU Punchinello
CEHILMOOPPR pleomorphic
CEHILMOOPRS pleochroism
CEHILMORTTY thermolytic
CEHILNOOQRU chloroquine
CEHILNOSSST coltishness
CEHIMMOOPRS mesomorphic
CEHIMOOPRTT photometric
CEHIMOOPTTY mythopoetic
CEHIMOOSSST schistosome
CEHIMOPPRST coppersmith
CEHIMOPRSTY hypsometric
CEHINNNPRRU pinch-runner
CEHINNORSYZ synchronize
CEHINOOPRRS coronership
CEHINOOPRSW co-ownership
CEHINOORSTT short notice
CEHINORSTUY shire county
CEHINRRSSSU currishness

CEHIOOOPPRT photocopier
CEHIOOOPPST photocopies
CEHIOPRSSTT prosthetics
CEHLLLOPRSY sclerophyll
CEHLMOPTTYY T-lymphocyte
CEHLNNOOSTU Nelson touch
CEHMMOOORSX X chromosome
CEHMMOOORSY Y chromosome
CEHMNOORRTY chronometry
CEHMOOSSTUU custom house
CEHMOPRSTYY psychometry
CEHNNOSSTUU uncouthness
CEHOOPSSTTY stethoscopy
CEIIILLNSST illicitness
CEIIILLPTTY ellipticity
CEIIILNNPTY incipiently
CEIIIMNOPRS imprecision
CEIIIMPSSST pessimistic
CEIIINNRSTY insincerity
CEIIINNSTTV instinctive
CEIIINOSTVV vivisection
CEIIINPRSTV inscriptive
CEIIKLLPSTT lickspittle
CEIIKLNPRSS prickliness
CEIIKLQRSUV quicksilver
CEIIKNRSSST tricksiness
CEIILLNSUVY inclusively
CEIILMSSUVX exclusivism
CEIILNRTUUV viniculture
CEIILOOPPRT pleiotropic
CEIILORSSTT sclerotitis
CEIILRTTUUV viticulture
CEIILSSTUVX exclusivist
CEIILSTUVXY exclusivity
CEIIMNOOPTT competition
CEIIMNOPSUU impecunious
CEIIMNORSTU neuroticism
CEIIMNOSTTU Teutonicism
CEIIMOPRSST semi-tropics
CEIINNNNOTT incontinent
CEIINORRSTT restriction
CEIINOSSSUV viciousness
CEIINOSSTUX Six Counties
CEIINRRSTUZ scrutinizer
CEIINRSTTUV instructive
CEIIOPPRSTU precipitous
CEIIORRRSTT terroristic
CEIIORSSSSW scissorwise
CEIIORSTUVY voyeuristic
CEIIPPRSTUY perspicuity
CEIKLMOORST mortise lock
CEIKLNNSSUU unluckiness
CEIKLOPPRSS slipper sock
CEIKNNORSTU countersink
CEILLLNOOOV violoncello
CEILLLOSUVY collusively
CEILMOOOPST cosmopolite
CEILMOOPPST compost pile
CEILMOOPSTY compositely
CEILMOORRTY colorimetry
CEILMOPRTUU pomiculture
CEILNNNOTTY continently
CEILNNOORTU contour line
CEILNOPRRTW triple crown
CEILNORSSTU courtliness
CEILOOPRTTY proteolytic
CEILOORRSTU terricolous
CEILOORRSVY corrosively
CEILOPRRSTU trouser-clip
CEIMMNORSSU consumerism
CEIMMOOPRRS compromiser
CEIMNOOPRSS compression
CEIMNOOPRTY mycoprotein
CEIMNOORSTU coterminous
CEIMNOPRSSU prosceniums
CEIMNOPSTUV consumptive
CEIMNORSSTU consumerist, misconstrue
CEINNOORSSU connoisseur
CEINNOOSTTU contentious
CEINNORSTTU court tennis, tennis court
CEINNORTTUY intercounty
CEINNOSTTTU constituent
CEINOOPPRTT protopectin
CEINOOPRSTU prosecution
CEINOOPSSSU copiousness
CEINOPQRSTU Cinque Ports
CEINOPRSSSU supersonics
CEINORRSSSU cursoriness
CEINORSSSUU curiousness
CEINOSSSSUV viscousness
CEINOSSSTUV viscountess
CEIOOOPRRTZ Proterozoic
CEIOORRSUUV over-curious
CEIOPPRSSUU perspicuous
CEIOPRRSTUX prosecutrix
CEIPPRRSSTU superscript
CELLMOOPRRT comptroller
CELLNNOOPTU pollen count
CELLNRTTUUY truculently
CELLOORTUVY courtly love
CELMNOORTUU monoculture
CELNNOOORTT tone control
CELNOOPPRUY reply coupon
CELNOOPRTTU counterplot
CELOORSTUUY courteously
CELORSTTUUW two cultures
CEMMNOOPRTT comportment
CENOORRSTVY controversy
CENOPRRRSUY corn spurrey
CENORSTTUWY West Country
CFFHILMNOTU fifth column
CFFIIJNNOOT coffin-joint
CFFIILOOSUY officiously
CFGHIIKNSSU sucking-fish
CFGHIILLNNY flinchingly
CFGHIILNNNU unflinching
CFGHIILNPTY fly-pitching
CFGHIMNOORT forthcoming
CFGILNNOSUY confusingly
CFGINOSTUUY young fustic
CFHILOORSST first school
CFIILMORSTU formulistic
CFIINORSSTU first cousin
CFILLNOORST Fort Collins
CFILMOOPPRY microfloppy
CFILNOOPRSY scorpion fly
CFLLLOORUUY colourfully
CFLNORSUUUU furunculous

CGGHHIIIKKN	high-kicking
CGGIIIKNPST	pigsticking
CGHHILNOOST	night school
CGHHILOOTYY	ichthyology
CGHIIILRSTV	civil rights
CGHIILOOPSY	physiologic
CGHILOOPSTY	phycologist
CGHILOORSTY	Christology
CGHIMNOORST	shortcoming
CGHIMOOPRYZ	zygomorphic
CGHINNOPRTU	hunting crop
CGHINOPTTUY	touch-typing
CGHIOOORSTT	Ostrogothic
CGHKOORSTTW	growth stock
CGIIIKLNOPT	politicking
CGIIILNSSTU	linguistics
CGIIIMNOSTV	cognitivism
CGIIINOSTTV	cognitivist
CGIILLOSSTY	syllogistic
CGIILMMNOOU	immunologic
CGIILMNOORY	criminology
CGIILNNNSUU	cunnilingus
CGIILNNORRU	curling iron
CGIILNNOTTU	linocutting
CGIILNNPRSU	curling pins
CGIILOOOSST	sociologist
CGIINNORTUY	incongruity
CGIINOPRTWY	copywriting
CGIKLNOORSU	King's colour
CGIKNOOSTTV	voting stock
CGILLNNOORT	controlling
CGILLNNOOSY	consolingly
CGILLOOPTTY	polyglottic
CGILMNNOSUY	consumingly
CGILMOOOSST	cosmologist
CGILMOOSSTU	muscologist
CGIMNOOOSST	cosmogonist
CGINNOORSUU	incongruous
CGINOORSSTV	cross-voting
CGINOORSTUU	outsourcing
CGLNOORSUUY	congruously
CHHIILOOPPS	philosophic
CHHIIMRTTYY	rhythmicity
CHHIMMOOOPR	homomorphic
CHHLLLOOPRY	chlorophyll
CHHMORRSSTY	cross-rhythm
CHIIIMORSST	historicism
CHIIINORSST	trichinosis
CHIIIORSSTT	historicist
CHIIIORSTTY	historicity
CHIIOOPRTTX	thixotropic
CHIIOPPRRTY	porphyritic
CHIIORRSSTY	scirrhosity
CHIKNOORRTU	honour-trick
CHILMOOPPRY	polymorphic
CHILOORSTUU	ulotrichous
CHIMMNOOOPR	monomorphic
CHIMNNORSSY	synchronism
CHIMNOOPRRS	prochronism
CHINOOORSSU	isochronous
CHIOOOPPRTT	phototropic
CHIOOPPRRST	proctorship
CHIOOPPRSTY	sporophytic
CHIOPSTTTUY	touch-typist
CHKOOOPRSST	shock troops
CHMOOOPRSTY	psychomotor
CHNNOORRSTY	synchrotron
CHNNOORSSUY	synchronous
CHRRRRSUUYY	hurry-scurry
CIIILLMOPTY	impoliticly
CIIILOPSSST	solipsistic
CIIIMNORTTU	micturition
CIIINNOPRST	inscription
CIIINOOSTTY	isotonicity
CIIINOPSSTZ	Spinozistic
CIIINORSTUY	incuriosity
CIILLOORSTT	torticollis
CIILNOOPSTU	liposuction
CIILNOPSTUU	punctilious
CIILNORSUUY	incuriously
CIIMMNNOOTU	comminution
CIIMNOOOPST	composition
CIIMOPRRSTU	scriptorium
CIIMOPRSTUY	promiscuity
CIINNORSTTU	instruction
CIINOOPSSTY	pinocytosis
CIIOOPRSSUV	piscivorous
CIKNOOPRUWY	pick-your-own
CILLMOOQSUU	colloquiums
CILLMOORTUU	multicolour
CILLOORRTVY	victory roll
CILNNOOOTUV	convolution
CILNNOOSUUY	innocuously
CIMNNOOPSTU	consumption
CIMNOORSSTU	consortiums
CIMNOPPSTUU	suction pump
CIMOOPRSSUU	promiscuous
CIMOPRSSTUU	scrumptious
CLLNOOSUUVV	convolvulus
CNNNNOOTUUU	uncount noun
DDDDEEEEFIL	fiddle-de-dee
DDDEEFIOSST	eisteddfods
DDDEEGLPRRU	drug peddler
DDDEEIILMSZ	middle-sized
DDDEEINORSS	dodderiness
DDDEFHLNORU	hundredfold
DDDEHLOOORT	toddlerhood
DDDENNOORTW	downtrodden
DDEEEFILLNW	well-defined
DDEEEGHIRRT	third degree
DDEEEGIOSTU	outside edge
DDEEEHILLSV	dishevelled
DDEEEHMOPTU	deep-mouthed
DDEEEILNRUV	undelivered
DDEEEINNNPT	independent
DDEEEINNPRT	interdepend
DDEEELLNOWW	well-endowed
DDEEELLORRW	well-ordered
DDEEELLRSSW	well-dressed
DDEEELNNPTY	dependently
DDEEELNOPUV	undeveloped
DDEEENOSSTV	devotedness
DDEEENRRSSU	unredressed
DDEEFFGLLLU	full-fledged
DDEEFHINRUV	five hundred
DDEEFLLNOUW	well-founded
DDEEGGIIRUU	Guide Guider
DDEEGHHOPRS	shepherd dog
DDEEGHILLTY	delightedly
DDEEGHLNOOR	Golden Horde

DDEEGILLNOO golden oldie
DDEEGILNOWW window ledge
DDEEGINNRSU undersigned
DDEEGLNORRU ground elder
DDEEGNOPRSU ground speed
DDEEHILRSSS dress shield
DDEEIIKLNNX index-linked
DDEEIILNPSS spindle side
DDEEIIMMSUZ medium-sized
DDEEIINRRST disinterred
DDEEIIQSTUU disquietude
DDEEILMNPUY unimpededly
DDEEILNNOTU tunnel diode
DDEEILNOSVZ devil's dozen
DDEEINSSSTU studiedness
DDEEIOSSWWW widow's weeds
DDEELLNORTW well-trodden
DDEELLNORUW well-rounded
DDEFFIILNTY diffidently
DDEFGIIILNY dignifiedly
DDEFGIIINNU undignified
DDEFHNORRUU four hundred
DDEFLNNOUUY unfoundedly
DDEGGIINNRW wedding ring
DDEGHIIMNRT right-minded
DDEGHILOTUY gilded youth
DDEGHIMNOTU tough-minded
DDEGIILMSUY misguidedly
DDEGIINSSUU undisguised
DDEGILMNOST dislodgment
DDEGILNRSTU disgruntled
DDEGILSSTUY disgustedly
DDEGINORSWW winged words
DDEGINPSTUU suet pudding
DDEGNNORRUU underground
DDEHHIIOPRT diphtheroid
DDEHIINRSSW widdershins
DDEHINORSTW short-winded
DDEHLMOOTUU loud-mouthed
DDEIIIMNOVV modi vivendi
DDEIIKNRRRV drink-driver
DDEIILLOPSS ill-disposed
DDEIKNNRSUW wunderkinds
DDEILNNOOPR London pride
DDEILNOSSUV undissolved
DDEILNSTUUY unstudiedly
DDEILORSTTY distortedly
DDEINORSTTU undistorted
DDELNNOORRY Londonderry
DDFGHILNNOU fundholding
DDFGILNOOOR folding door
DDGIIINNORV divining rod
DDGIIKLMNPU milk pudding
DDGIILNOORS sliding door
DDGILMNPPUU plum pudding
DDGINNOORSU sounding rod
DEEEEHILRSW side-wheeler
DEEEEHIMPRS ephemerides
DEEEEIMNRRT redetermine
DEEEELOPRRV redeveloper
DEEEEMOPRST speedometer
DEEEENNSTUW unsweetened
DEEEFFGILNS self-feeding
DEEEFFLOOTT fleet-footed
DEEEFFNOOST toffee-nosed
DEEEFFNORSX sex offender
DEEEFGILNSS self-seeding
DEEEFGIRRST first-degree
DEEEFHLNSSU heedfulness
DEEEFILNSTV field events, self-evident
DEEEFILNSVY defensively
DEEEFLLORRW elderflower
DEEEFLNNSSU needfulness
DEEEFLORRTX retroflexed
DEEEFMNNRTU unfermented
DEEEFMNRRSU referendums
DEEEGINNNRV never-ending
DEEEGINNOSS endogenesis
DEEEGINQSUU Queen's Guide
DEEEGLLNOSV long-sleeved
DEEEGLORRSU guelder rose
DEEEGLORRSV gold reserve
DEEEHHPRSSS shepherdess
DEEEHILLOSW oiled wheels
DEEEHLNNORT Heldentenor
DEEEHLNRSTU unsheltered
DEEEHMOPRTT hot-tempered
DEEEIIMRRST semi-retired
DEEEIINNPTX inexpedient
DEEEIINSSTZ desensitize
DEEEILLMPRT ill-tempered
DEEEILLNNST sentinelled
DEEEILLNRSS elderliness
DEEEILMMNUV mendelevium
DEEEILNNOPT needlepoint
DEEEILNPRST spindle tree
DEEEILNPTXY expediently
DEEEILORSTU deleterious
DEEEINPRRTT interpreted
DEEEINPRTUX expenditure
DEEEINRRSST retiredness
DEEEINRRSSV vine-dresser
DEEEINRSSTW dessert wine
DEEEIPPRSST sidestepper
DEEELLPPRXY perplexedly
DEEELMNNORY moneylender
DEEELMNOPTV development
DEEELMNOTVV devolvement
DEEELNNPRST resplendent
DEEELNNRSSS slenderness
DEEELNNSSSS endlessness
DEEELOOPRVV overdevelop
DEEELPRRTVY pervertedly
DEEEMNNORST endorsement
DEEEMSSTWYY Dewey system
DEEENOPRSUX underexpose
DEEENPRSSUX unexpressed
DEEENQRSTUU unrequested
DEEENRRSTTT trendsetter
DEEEORRTTVX extroverted
DEEEPRRSSST prestressed
DEEEPRRSSUU supersedure
DEEFFIINNRT indifferent
DEEFFILNRTY differently
DEEFFINSSSU diffuseness
DEEFGGIOPTT pettifogged
DEEFGHILLST self-delight
DEEFGHIORST foresighted
DEEFGIINNRX index finger

DEEFGIINSST fidgetiness
DEEFGILNNSY self-denying
DEEFGILNNUY unfeignedly
DEEFIIIMNNR indemnifier
DEEFIILNRST friendliest
DEEFIKLORRW fieldworker
DEEFILMNNRU Dunfermline
DEEFILMOPSS self-imposed
DEEFILPRRVY perfervidly
DEEFILRSUUZ desulfurize
DEEFINRRTTT drift-netter
DEEFLLNOSSU dolefulness
DEEFLNOSTVY seventyfold
DEEFLOPRSSY professedly
DEEFMNOPRRU unperformed
DEEFNOPRTUY type founder
DEEGGLNOOOS golden goose
DEEGHHIOPRW high-powered
DEEGHIILNSV disheveling
DEEGHILLNWY wheedlingly
DEEGHILNNUY unheedingly
DEEGHINRTUW underweight
DEEGHLLLNOO golden hello
DEEGHLNRSST dress length
DEEGHNORSTU groundsheet
DEEGIIINSTV indigestive
DEEGIIKLLNS sliding keel
DEEGIILSTVY digestively
DEEGIINNNTW twin-engined
DEEGILLMNOR remodelling
DEEGILMNTUV divulgement
DEEGILNORUV over-indulge
DEEGILNRSVY deservingly
DEEGILNRTVY divergently
DEEGINNRSUV undeserving
DEEGJLRSSUU Judges' Rules
DEEGLLMOORW well-groomed
DEEGLLNORUV ground level
DEEGLNOSSSS godlessness
DEEHHLOORSU householder
DEEHHOPRRSY hydrosphere
DEEHIIMPRSU hesperidium
DEEHIINNPSZ denizenship
DEEHILLORTT title-holder
DEEHILMNOTU endothelium
DEEHINORTUZ untheorized
DEEHINOSSSU hideousness
DEEHINRRSSU hurriedness
DEEHKOOPRRT red-hot poker
DEEHLMNORST Delmenhorst
DEEHLNORRTW nether world
DEEHLNRSSTU thunderless
DEEHMNOOPTU open-mouthed
DEEHNOOORSW wooden horse
DEEHOORRSUV hors d'oeuvre
DEEIIIKKNNX Nikkei index
DEEIIKLLMSS semi-skilled
DEEIIKMMMSS semi-skimmed
DEEIILLLRVY lily-livered
DEEIILLPPQU ill-equipped
DEEIILMNSST limitedness
DEEIILNSTUW unwieldiest
DEEIILRSSSV sllversides
DEEIIMMNRST determinism
DEEIIMNRRST irredentism
DEEIIMNRSTT determinist
DEEIIMNRTTT intermitted
DEEIINNNOTT intentioned
DEEIINNSSTT dissentient
DEEIINPRSTY serendipity
DEEIINRRSTT irredentist
DEEIINRSSTT disinterest
DEEIIOPSTUX expeditious
DEEIKLOOPRT torpedo-like
DEEILLQRRSU squirrelled
DEEILMNOPST despoilment
DEEILNNORVY non-delivery
DEEILNOPTUX unexploited
DEEILNORRSS orderliness
DEEILNSSSTT stiltedness
DEEILOPPPTY polypeptide
DEEILORRSSW World Series
DEEILQRRRSU red squirrel
DEEIMMNORTU endometrium
DEEIMNNNOTU unmentioned
DEEIMNNORST indorsement
DEEIMNOPRRT red orpiment
DEEIMNOPRSY money spider
DEEIMNPRSSU unimpressed
DEEINNNORST non-resident
DEEINNOPSST pointedness
DEEINNOSTTU tendentious
DEEINNPRSTU superintend
DEEINNSSTUW unwitnessed
DEEINORRTTV introverted
DEEINOSSSTU tediousness
DEEINOSSSUV deviousness
DEEINRRRTUW underwriter
DEEIOPPPRRR proper pride
DEEIRRSSTTV driver's test
DEEKNNNRSSU drunkenness
DEELMMNOPSU noms de plume
DEELMNORTTY tormentedly
DEELORSTUXY dexterously
DEENNSSSTTU stuntedness
DEENOPRRRTU under-report
DEENOPSSSSU unpossessed
DEENOPSSSTT spottedness
DEENORRSTUY understorey
DEENOSSSTUU duteousness
DEEORSSSTTU stressed out
DEFFGINNNOU unoffending
DEFFHHIOORS sheriffhood
DEFFIINORSU rediffusion
DEFFIINORTU unfortified
DEFFILLLNUU unfulfilled
DEFGHIISTTT tight-fisted
DEFGHILOOTT light-footed
DEFGHIOORTT right-footed
DEFGIILNNSW self-winding
DEFGIILNPRS Springfield
DEFGILSSSTU self-disgust
DEFHIILORRY horrifiedly
DEFHINNRSUU unfurnished
DEFHINPRSTT spendthrift
DEFHIOORRSX Oxfordshire
DEFHLLMOTUU full-mouthed
DEFHLMOOTUU foul-mouthed
DEFIIIMNSTY misidentify
DEFIIJNSTUU unjustified

DEFIILLMNOR	ill-informed
DEFILMNNSSU	mindfulness
DEFILNSSTUU	dutifulness
DEFILOOORST	foot soldier
DEFILOPRSST	field sports
DEFILRSSSTU	distressful
DEFIOOORRSU	odoriferous
DEFKLNOOORU	unlooked-for
DEFLLNORUWY	wonderfully
DEFNOOPRSTU	profoundest
DEFNOPRTUYY	type foundry
DEGGHILNOST	long-sighted
DEGGIILNNSY	designingly
DEGGILOOPRS	sloop-rigged
DEGGKLRSUUY	skulduggery
DEGHIILPPTT	tight-lipped
DEGHINNRSTU	underthings
DEGHINOPSTT	potting shed
DEGHINOSSTU	doughtiness
DEGHLMOOOTY	methodology
DEGHNOOOSTT	honest-to-God
DEGHNOORSUY	hydrogenous
DEGHNORRTUW	undergrowth
DEGIIILNPRV	piledriving
DEGIIINNOST	indigestion
DEGIIINQSTU	disquieting
DEGIIKNRSTW	writing desk
DEGIILNRTVY	divertingly
DEGIINRSTTV	driving test
DEGIJMMNSTU	misjudgment
DEGILLNNTUY	indulgently
DEGILLNOPRY	deploringly
DEGILNNORWY	wonderingly
DEGILNNOSSU	ungodliness
DEGILNOPSTW	spot-welding
DEGILNORUVY	devouringly
DEGILOOPRTY	pteridology
DEGINOPRSST	top dressing
DEGKOPRRRSU	Krugersdorp
DEGLLNOOPRY	prolongedly
DEGLLNORSUW	groundswell
DEGLNOPRSUY	golden syrup
DEGNNOORSTU	stoneground
DEHHIILMNOT	helminthoid
DEHHLNOSTUU	sleuth-hound
DEHHOOOPPRT	prophethood
DEHIIKNNNST	thin-skinned
DEHIILMNPSU	delphiniums
DEHIILOPRSS	soldiership
DEHIINSTTUW	Whitsuntide
DEHILLMORUU	ill-humoured
DEHILNOSSST	doltishness
DEHILNOSSTY	dishonestly
DEHILNOSTTW	thistledown
DEHILNRRUUY	unhurriedly
DEHINNNOSSS	donnishness
DEHINOPRRST	third person
DEHINPRSSSU	prudishness
DEHINPSSTTU	studentship
DEHIOOOPPRT	photoperiod
DEHLNOOPRSY	polyhedrons
DEHMOOPPRSU	pseudomorph
DEHNORRSSTU	undershorts
DEHOOOPRTTW	tooth powder
DEIIINNPSSS	insipidness

DEIIINPRTTY	intrepidity
DEIIKKLMMMS	skimmed milk
DEIILLMNTUY	unlimitedly
DEIILLORSUY	deliriously
DEIILMPRSTW	limp-wristed
DEIILNNTUVY	uninvitedly
DEIILOPRSTW	low-spirited
DEIILOSSTUY	seditiously
DEIIMNOPRTV	improvident
DEIIMNORTTT	intromitted
DEIIMQRTTUU	tertium quid
DEIINOSTTTU	destitution
DEIKNNOOSSW	Kinnesswood
DEIKNRSTUYY	key industry
DEILLMOOSUY	melodiously
DEILLMRSTUY	dusty miller
DEILLNORSSW	worldliness
DEILLNORSUY	unsoldierly
DEILLORSTUY	desultorily
DEILLORSWWY	worldly-wise
DEILLOSSTUY	dissolutely
DEILMNOOSUU	unmelodious
DEILMNPRTUY	imprudently
DEILNNSTTUY	unstintedly
DEILNOPRTVY	providently
DEILPRRSSUY	surprisedly
DEIMMNNOPTU	impoundment
DEIMMRSSTYY	dissymmetry
DEIMNOORRRS	minor orders
DEIMNOSSSSY	syndesmosis
DEIMOPPRTTU	promptitude
DEINOOPRSTY	ponderosity
DEINPRRSSUU	unsurprised
DEIOOPRRRSW	orris-powder
DEKLLOOPRST	roll-top desk
DELLNOPSUUY	pendulously
DELLNOSSSUY	soundlessly
DELMOOORRRY	orderly room
DELMORRSUUY	murderously
DELNOOPRSUY	ponderously
DELOPPRRSSU	Lord's Supper
DELOPPRRTUY	purportedly
DEMNOSSSTUY	sound system
DENNNOSSSUU	unsoundness
DENNOOOOPSW	wooden spoon
DENNOOPRSSU	unsponsored
DENOPPRSTUU	unsupported
DFGGGHIINOT	dogfighting
DFGGINOOPRR	drop-forging
DFGIIKNNNSU	sinking fund
DFGIILNOORS	sliding roof
DFGIINNRSUW	windsurfing
DFGLNOOORRU	ground floor
DFGNOORRSTU	ground frost
DFGOOOPRRUX	Oxford Group
DFHLOOORSST	Lord of hosts
DFHMOOORTUW	word of mouth
DFIILLLMNOO	millionfold
DFILLMNNUUY	unmindfully
DFILLNTUUUY	undutifully
DFILRSSTTUU	distrustful
DGGHIIILNRT	riding light
DGGIIILLNRR	drilling rig
DGGIILMNNSU	mud-slinging
DGGIKLNOOOO	good-looking

DGHIIINSSTU distinguish
DGHIIMNNSTU midnight sun
DGHILOORSTY hydrologist
DGIIILOORST iridologist
DGIKNNORRST strong drink
DGIKNOOORWW woodworking
DGILOOPRSTT proglottids
DGINNOORTUW woodturning
DGINNORRSUU surrounding
DHHIOOPRTYY hypothyroid
DHHMNOOOSTU smooth hound
DHHNOOOSTTU houndstooth
DHIILMOOORS Moorish idol
DHIMOOOSTTW wisdom tooth
DHINNOOORSU Orion's hound
DHNOOORTUXY unorthodoxy
DIIIILLQTUY illiquidity
DIIILLNOSSU disillusion
DIIILNOSSUY insidiously
DIIILNOSUVY invidiously
DIIINOOPSST disposition
DIILNOOSSTU dissolution
DIILNOPSSTY spondylitis
DIINORSSTUU industrious
DIMNOORSTWW storm window
DIOOPQQRSUU quid pro quos
DLOOOPRRSTV Lord Provost
EEEEEGKNPRR greenkeeper
EEEEFLLMNTU fuel element
EEEEFLNNSTW sweet fennel
EEEEFLRSTTT Fleet Street
EEEEGLNNSST genteelness
EEEEGNPPPRR green pepper
EEEEHKOPRSU housekeeper
EEEEHNNSTTV seventeenth
EEEEHORRSVW wheresoever
EEEEIINRTVW interviewee
EEEEIMNPRSW minesweeper
EEEEKOPRRST storekeeper
EEEELNPRSST repleteness
EEEEMNRSSTX extremeness
EEEEPPPRSTW sweet pepper
EEEFFHILRTW whiffletree
EEEFFILLRST self-fertile
EEEFGIKLNSS self-seeking
EEEFGILLNSS feelingless
EEEFGJLNRUV jungle fever
EEEFGLLNSSU gleefulness
EEEFHIKNRRT freethinker
EEEFHILNSSY fish-eye lens
EEEFHILRRSW Ferris wheel
EEEFHLORRTU rule of three
EEEFHMNRRST refreshment
EEEFHOORRTT theretofore
EEEFILLRSST self-sterile
EEEFILLRVXY reflexively
EEEFINSSSTV festiveness
EEEFLLORVWY yellow fever
EEEFMOORRRV forevermore
EEEGGHORTTT get-together
EEEGGIINNNR engineering
EEEGGIINNRV Vereeniging
EEEGGILOSTV gigot sleeve
EEEGGMNNORT engorgement
EEEGHILNNRT enlightener
EEEGHINNOSU engine house
EEEGIIKMNPT timekeeping
EEEGIILNTVW televiewing
EEEGILNNNRT green linnet
EEEGILNRSTW swingletree
EEEGINNNSSU genuineness
EEEGINNORVW overweening
EEEGINNRRTW wintergreen
EEEGLLOTVVV velvet glove
EEEGLNOORVY venereology
EEEGLNOPRRV green plover
EEEGLNRRTTU green turtle
EEEGNORRSTU tree surgeon
EEEGRRRSTUY tree surgery
EEEHHILLLNP philhellene
EEEHHILPPTW Hepplewhite
EEEHHNPRSTY hypersthene
EEEHIINNPPR epinephrine
EEEHILNPRRS replenisher
EEEHILPPRTW whippletree
EEEHILRSSTV shirtsleeve, theirselves
EEEHIMNRSST smithereens
EEEHINPSSSV peevishness
EEEHIPPPRTW white pepper
EEEHLLRSSST shelterless
EEEHLNNOSST nonetheless
EEEHMMORRTT thermometer
EEEHMNOQRTU queen mother
EEEHMOPRRST spherometer
EEEHOORSSVW whosesoever
EEEIIKLNSST telekinesis
EEEIINNPSVX inexpensive
EEEIINRRTVW interviewer
EEEIIORRTXZ exteriorize
EEEIKLNOSTZ skeletonize
EEEIKRRRSTY Skye terrier
EEEILLRSSSU leisureless
EEEILMMNPRT implementer
EEEILMNNNTV enlivenment
EEEILMNNPRT Inner Temple
EEEILMNNTTT entitlement
EEEILMNSSTU unseemliest
EEEILNNQSSU queenliness
EEEILNPRRTT teleprinter
EEEILNPRSTW winter sleep
EEEILNPSVXY expensively
EEEILNRTTVY retentively
EEEILNSSSUV elusiveness
EEEILNSTVXY extensively
EEEILOSTTVW sweet violet
EEEIMMNNSSS immenseness
EEEIMNNNTTW entwinement
EEEIMNNRRTT reinterment
EEEIMNOSSTV emotiveness
EEEIMNQQRUU quinquereme
EEEIMNQRRTU requirement
EEEIMOPRTXZ extemporize
EEEINNNSSST intenseness
EEEINNPRSTT presentient
EEEINNPSSSV pensiveness
EEEINPPPRSS pepperiness
EEEINPRRRST enterpriser
EEEINPRRRTT interpreter, reinterpret
EEEINPRRSST intersperse
EEEINPRRSSU purse-seiner

EEEINPRSTTX	pre-existent
EEEINRRSTWZ	westernizer
EEEINRSSSTV	restiveness
EEEKKLNOSTY	skeleton key
EEEKLNOOSTX	exoskeleton
EEEKLORRSTW	steelworker
EEELLLNPRTY	repellently
EEELLLPSSSY	sleeplessly
EEELLNRSSVY	nervelessly
EEELLNSSSSY	senselessly
EEELMNNOPTV	envelopment
EEELMORRSSS	remorseless
EEELNSSSSSU	uselessness
EEELNSSSSSX	sexlessness
EEELPRRSSTT	letterpress
EEELRSSTTUX	textureless
EEEMMNOPRTW	empowerment
EEEMNNPRSTT	presentment
EEEMNORSTUV	venturesome
EEEMNPRSSSU	supremeness
EEEMNPRSTTY	empty-nester
EEEMORRSTTY	stereometry
EEFFFHHLOST	off-the-shelf
EEFFGHIIRRT	firefighter
EEFFGILNRSU	glue-sniffer
EEFFGLLNTUY	effulgently
EEFFIINNOSV	inoffensive
EEFFILLPPTU	fipple flute
EEFFILNOSVY	offensively
EEFFLNRSSTU	fretfulness
EEFGGIOPRTT	pettifogger
EEFGHIILRRT	firelighter
EEFGIINNRRT	interfering
EEFGILLNNUY	unfeelingly
EEFGILNNOUX	genuflexion
EEFGILNRSSV	self-serving
EEFGILPRSTU	prestigeful
EEFGIMMORSU	gemmiferous
EEFGINNORSS	foreignness
EEFGINORSSV	forgiveness
EEFGINPRRSV	spring fever
EEFGLLNRTUY	refulgently
EEFGLLOORXY	reflexology
EEFGLLRRTUY	regretfully
EEFGMNOORTT	forget-me-not
EEFHIIKNRST	Kentish fire
EEFHILNSSSS	selfishness
EEFHILOSUWY	housewifely
EEFHIORSTTT	the rest of it
EEFHIORSUWY	housewifery
EEFHKOOSSUY	House of Keys
EEFHLLNPSSU	helpfulness
EEFHLNOPSSU	hopefulness
EEFHMORRRTU	furthermore
EEFHNOORRST	foreshorten
EEFIIINNRST	intensifier
EEFIILRTVXY	reflexivity
EEFIINOPRRS	personifier
EEFIKLLNOWY	Yellowknife
EEFILLLMNTU	mellifluent
EEFILLMORSU	melliferous
EEFILLNOSSX	flexionless
EEFILMORTUV	fluviometer
EEFILNNRTTU	interfluent
EEFILNORSSW	floweriness
EEFILOOPRRT	profiterole
EEFILOORSST	loosestrife
EEFINRSSTUV	furtiveness
EEFIOPRSSTU	pestiferous
EEFLLNRSTUY	resentfully
EEFLLOPRSUY	reposefully
EEFLMNOSSSU	fulsomeness
EEFLNNSSTUU	tunefulness
EEFLNPSSSUU	suspenseful
EEFLNRSSSTU	restfulness
EEFLNSSSTUZ	zestfulness
EEFLOOPRRWW	flower power
EEFLORRSTTU	self-torture
EEFNOPRSSSU	profuseness
EEGGHIINSST	sightseeing
EEGGILLNNTY	negligently
EEGGILORSUY	egregiously
EEGGIMNOOTT	go-to-meeting
EEGGNOOPRST	progestogen
EEGHHIILNST	high-tensile
EEGHHILRTWW	wheelwright
EEGHHIPPRST	high-stepper
EEGHHIPRRST	right sphere
EEGHIINNSTW	white ensign
EEGHIINSSTW	weightiness
EEGHIKNOPPS	shopkeeping
EEGHILNNSSS	Englishness
EEGHILNNSST	lengthiness
EEGHILOORSY	heresiology
EEGHILRSTTT	street light
EEGHIMNOORZ	homogenizer
EEGHIMNOOTY	homogeneity
EEGHIMOORST	isogeotherm
EEGHINNPTWY	pennyweight
EEGHINNSSTU	sight unseen
EEGHINORRTV	overnighter
EEGHLOOPRTY	herpetology
EEGHMNOOOSU	homogeneous
EEGHMNOORRW	whoremonger
EEGHNOORSST	green shoots
EEGIILLNNTT	intelligent
EEGIILMNNRT	intermingle
EEGIILNNNST	sentineling
EEGIIMMNNPT	impingement
EEGIIMNNNRS	minnesinger
EEGIIMNNOPT	opening time
EEGIIMNRSTV	time-serving
EEGIINNQRUV	virgin queen
EEGIINNRSTT	interesting
EEGIINNRTTW	wire netting
EEGIINOPRTV	progenitive
EEGILLLSSUY	guilelessly
EEGILLMOOST	teleologism
EEGILLOOSTT	teleologist
EEGILMOOTYZ	etymologize
EEGILNNNRTU	unrelenting
EEGILNNRSTY	single entry
EEGILNOPSSY	polygenesis
EEGILNORSVY	sovereignly
EEGILOPRSTT	poltergeist
EEGIMNNOOSS	monogenesis
EEGIMNNOTTW	town meeting
EEGIMNNRRTU	interregnum
EEGINNOOSST	ontogenesis
EEGINOORRTU	rouge-et-noir

EEGINOPRRTU	progeniture
EEGINORRSTT	register ton
EEGINORRSTU	terrigenous
EEGINORSTVY	sovereignty
EEGINPRSTTU	guttersnipe
EEGINPSTTTY	typesetting
EEGIOPRRSSV	progressive
EEGKLLMNSUU	muskellunge
EEGKORRSTUW	guest worker
EEGLMOOORTY	meteorology
EEGLNOOSUXY	exogenously
EEGLNSSSSTU	gutlessness
EEGLOPPPTUV	glove puppet
EEGLOQRSTUY	grotesquely
EEGMNNORSST	engrossment
EEGMNOPRRTU	regroupment
EEGNOOORSTU	erotogenous
EEGPRRSSTTU	gutter press
EEHHILLNSSS	hellishness
EEHHILMOPRT	thermophile
EEHHILOPRST	lithosphere
EEHHIOPSTYZ	hypothesize
EEHHIORSSTW	white horses
EEHHMMOOORT	homoeotherm
EEHHMMOORTY	homeothermy
EEHHMOORSTU	house-mother
EEHHNORSTUU	house-hunter
EEHHOOPPRST	photosphere
EEHIILLLTTW	little while
EEHIILMPSTU	epitheliums
EEHIIMPPRRS	premiership
EEHIINRRSST	inheritress
EEHIKMNNOSY	monkeyshine
EEHILMPRRTY	triple rhyme
EEHILNOPSTT	telephonist
EEHILNOSTTV	novelettish
EEHILOPRSST	priest's hole
EEHIMOPPRRS	emperorship
EEHIMOPRSTU	hemipterous
EEHINNOOPTT	thiopentone
EEHINNOSSSU	heinousness
EEHINOPSTVY	hypotensive
EEHINPSSSTT	pettishness
EEHINRSSSTU	hirsuteness
EEHINRSSTYZ	synthesizer
EEHIORSSTTU	housesitter
EEHIORSTTWY	oyster white
EEHIPRRSSUV	herpesvirus
EEHIPRSSTTU	trusteeship
EEHLLLRSTTU	turtle shell
EEHLLMOOSWY	wholesomely
EEHLMMOOPRS	pommel horse
EEHLMNOOSUW	unwholesome
EEHLMNOTTVW	twelvemonth
EEHLOOPRSVW	power shovel
EEHLOPRRSTU	reupholster, upholsterer
EEHLRSSSTTU	shutterless
EEHMMOOPRRT	emperor moth
EEHMMORRTTY	thermometry
EEHMMORSSUU	summer house
EEHMNNOOORY	honeymooner
EEHMOPRRSTT	short temper
EEHNOOPRSTY	stereophony
EEHNOPQSTUY	Pythonesque
EEHNORRSTTW	northwester
EEHOOPPRRST	troposphere
EEHOOPRRSTU	porterhouse
EEHOOPRSTTT	photosetter
EEHORSSTTUW	southwester
EEIIIMNNSTU	einsteinium
EEIIINNSSTV	insensitive
EEIIINORRTZ	interiorize
EEIIJNRSSTT	jitteriness
EEIIKLLNNNS	Enniskillen
EEIIKLLNSTU	unlikeliest
EEIIKLNNRTU	interleukin
EEIILLNRSTY	resiliently
EEIILLPPRST	pipistrelle
EEIILLPRSTU	spirituelle
EEIILLPRSTV	spirit level
EEIILMNOSUZ	emulsionize
EEIILMNRSSS	miserliness
EEIILNNPRRT	line printer
EEIILNNSTVY	intensively
EEIILNNTVVY	inventively
EEIILNRSSSV	silveriness
EEIILNSSTVY	sensitively
EEIILQRSTUY	requisitely
EEIILQSTUXY	exquisitely
EEIIMNNPRTT	impertinent
EEIINNNORTV	reinvention
EEIINNNTUVV	uninventive
EEIINNORRST	reinsertion
EEIINNPRRWZ	prizewinner
EEIINPPRRST	printer's pie
EEIINRSTTUV	investiture
EEIIOPPRSTV	prepositive
EEIIOPRSTTU	repetitious
EEIIORRTTXY	exteriority
EEIIRSTTTUV	restitutive
EEIKMNORSSS	irksomeness
EEILLLOPRWY	yellow peril
EEILLMNOPRT	Montpellier
EEILLMPPRSY	slippery elm
EEILLMPRTUX	multiplexer
EEILLNNPSSY	pennilessly
EEILLNOPQTU	equipollent
EEILLNOSSSY	noiselessly
EEILLNPSSSY	spinelessly
EEILLNPSTTY	pestilently
EEILLOPSVXY	explosively
EEILLPRSUVY	repulsively
EEILMNNOTVV	involvement
EEILMNOOSST	emotionless
EEILMOPRTUV	pluviometer
EEILNNOPSSS	pensionless
EEILNNOSSST	tensionless
EEILNNPRTTY	pertinently
EEILNNSSSSS	sinlessness
EEILNOPRTVY	poverty line
EEILNOSSTVY	ostensively
EEILNSSSSTW	witlessness
EEILOPRSTYZ	proselytize
EEIMMMNOORT	memento mori
EEIMMNOPRTV	improvement
EEIMMNPRSST	impressment
EEIMMPRSUVV	sempervivum
EEIMNNNORTV	environment
EEIMNNOOSSS	noisomeness
EEIMNNOPRST	omnipresent

EEIMNNORSSV	mons Veneris
EEIMNNOSSSW	winsomeness
EEIMNNPSSTU	septenniums
EEIMNOPRSTU	peritoneums
EEIMNORTTZZ	mezzotinter
EEIMNPPPRTY	pepperminty
EEIMNPRRTTY	entry permit
EEIMNRSSTTW	Westminster
EEIMOOPRTVW	motive power
EEIMOPPRSSU	superimpose
EEIMPPRSTUV	presumptive
EEINNNOSTTX	non-existent
EEINNOSSTTU	sententious
EEINNQSSTUU	unquietness
EEINOORRTTX	extortioner
EEINOPRSTTU	pretentious
EEINOPSSSTU	piteousness
EEINORRSTUV	enterovirus
EEINORSSSSU	seriousness
EEINOSSSTUZ	outsizeness
EEINPRRRTTU	interrupter
EEINPRTTTWY	typewritten
EEIOOPPSSTX	opposite sex
EEIOPRRSSSU	superioress
EEIPPRSSSUV	suppressive
EEKKNOPRRTY	pony-trekker
EEKLMNNOSTU	smoke-tunnel
EEKLNNORSSW	lesser-known
EEKMNNPSSTU	unkemptness
EEKNOORRSTW	stoneworker
EEKOOPRRSTW	power stroke
EELLLMNOOWY	lemon yellow
EELLLOORRTW	roller towel
EELLNOPSTUY	plenteously
EELLNORRSTW	Western roll
EELLNPRTUUV	pulverulent
EELLOPRSSWY	powerlessly
EELLORRSTTY	storyteller
EELMOPRRSTT	storm petrel
EELNNSSSSSU	sunlessness
EELNOOPPPRY	polypropene
EELNOOPPSTW	townspeople
EELNOORRSUY	erroneously
EELNOPRSTYY	polystyrene
EELNOPSSSST	toplessness
EELOPPPRRSU	purple prose
EELOPPRSSSU	purposeless
EELOPRRSSUW	low pressure
EELORRSSSTU	trouserless
EEMNNRSTTTU	entrustment
EEMNOORSTTY	enterostomy
EEMNORSSTTW	westernmost
EEMOPSSTTUU	tempestuous
EENNOORSSSU	onerousness
EENNOORSTTT	rotten-stone
EENNOPRSTWW	Newport News
EENNORSSSUV	nervousness
EENNOSSSTUU	tenuousness
EEOOPPRRSTY	prose poetry
EEOOPRRSSSS	repossessor
EEOPQRSSTTU	request stop
EFFFGINORUU	figure of fun
EFFFLLORTUY	effortfully
EFFGHHHIIRS	High Sheriff
EFFGIINRRST	first finger
EFFGILLNOST	tellings-off
EFFGLLORTUY	forgetfully
EFFHHIIPRSS	sheriffship
EFFHLORRSUU	four-flusher
EFFHOOOPSTT	photo-offset
EFFILLLMNTU	fulfillment
EFFILOORRSU	floriferous
EFGGHIINNRT	frightening
EFGGHIIRRST	triggerfish
EFGGLOOORST	footslogger
EFGHHIILOPR	high profile
EFGHHOORTTU	forethought
EFGHIIILNNS	fishing line
EFGHIILNOST	line of sight
EFGHIILNSST	flightiness
EFGHIILORTT	right-to-life
EFGHINORSSU	surgeonfish
EFGHIORRSTU	right of user
EFGHLLNOORT	floor-length
EFGHNNOSUUY	honey fungus
EFGIILLMORU	florilegium
EFGIILLNTTW	well-fitting
EFGIILMNNOT	filet mignon
EFGIILMNSTT	filmsetting
EFGIILNPSTY	self-pitying
EFGIINNNRRU	running fire
EFGIINNPRRT	fingerprint
EFGIINNSSTT	fittingness
EFGILLLORWY	gillyflower
EFGILLMNRUY	flying lemur
EFGINORRSUU	ferruginous
EFGIOPRSSUY	gypsiferous
EFGNNOORTTU	unforgotten
EFHIILORSTY	life history
EFHIINRSSTT	thriftiness
EFHILLNSSUY	unselfishly
EFHILLOSTWW	wolf whistle
EFHILLSSSTY	shiftlessly
EFHILNOOSSS	foolishness
EFHILNSSSUW	wishfulness
EFHIMORRSTX	sixth-former
EFHINOPPSSS	foppishness
EFHIORRSTTT	thrift store
EFHLLLNPUUY	unhelpfully
EFHLNOOOPRR	forlorn hope
EFHLNRSSTUU	hurtfulness
EFHMORRSTTU	furthermost
EFHOOOPRRSW	showerproof
EFIIILNRTTY	infertility
EFIIINORRTY	inferiority
EFIIKRRSSTT	first strike
EFIILNNOOPS	self-opinion
EFIILNPSSTU	pitifulness
EFIINNORSTU	interfusion
EFIINOOPTVW	point of view
EFIKLLNSSSU	skilfulness
EFILLLMOSUU	mellifluous
EFILLLNPTUY	plentifully
EFILLNOOSUY	feloniously
EFILLRSSTUY	fruitlessly
EFILNSSSTUW	wistfulness
EFILOOPRRSU	proliferous
EFILOPPRSTU	life-support
EFILPRSTUUY	superfluity
EFIMNOORSSU	somniferous

EFINNNNSSUU	unfunniness
EFINOPRRSST	first person
EFINORSSSTW	frowstiness
EFINORSSSUU	furiousness
EFIOPRSSTTU	petits fours
EFIOSSSSTTU	soft tissues
EFLLNNTUUUY	untunefully
EFLLNOSSSUU	soulfulness
EFLLNRSTUUY	unrestfully
EFLLNSSSTUU	lustfulness
EFLLRSSSTUY	stressfully
EFLNNOORRSS	forlornness
EFLOPPRSSTU	self-support
EFLOPRSSUUU	superfluous
EFNNNORRRTU	front runner
EFOOPRSSTUY	pussyfooter
EGGGILNNOOS	gone gosling
EGGGINOPRRU	ginger group
EGGHHHIILRT	highlighter
EGGHHIILTTW	lightweight
EGGHIILNNWY	whingeingly
EGGHIINPSSS	piggishness
EGGHIINRRTW	right-winger
EGGHILLNRRU	herring gull
EGGHLNOORSW	hornswoggle
EGGHNOORTUU	rough tongue
EGGIIINPRVZ	prize-giving
EGGIILLNNRY	lingeringly
EGGIILNNSWY	swingeingly
EGGIINNNORT	ringing tone
EGGIJLNOOTT	toggle joint
EGGILLLNRUY	gruellingly
EGGILLNORWY	gloweringly
EGGILMMOOST	gemmologist
EGGINNNOOSS	ongoingness
EGGLNOOORTY	gerontology
EGHHIINNOST	high tension
EGHHILMOPRY	high polymer
EGHHILNNORS	English horn
EGHHILOSSTU	house lights
EGHHIORSTTW	short weight
EGHHLOSSTTU	thoughtless
EGHIILLNRSV	shrivelling
EGHIILLNSWW	wishing-well
EGHIILLOOPZ	philologize
EGHIILNPRSY	perishingly
EGHIILNRSSS	girlishness
EGHIILNRSVY	shiveringly
EGHIILNRTWY	witheringly
EGHIILNSSST	sightliness
EGHIIMNRRST	miner's right
EGHIINNORVY	virgin honey
EGHIKMNNOTY	night monkey
EGHILLMOSTY	lightsomely
EGHILLSSSTY	sightlessly
EGHILMNOORT	moonlighter
EGHILMOOTYZ	mythologize
EGHILNOOSTT	ethnologist
EGHILNOSSST	ghostliness
EGHILORSTUY	righteously
EGHINNNOSST	nothingness
EGHINORRTTW	intergrowth
EGHINORSSSU	roguishness
EGHINORSTUU	unrighteous
EGHINPRSSTU	uprightness
EGHIORRSTTW	ghost writer
EGHLLORTUWW	well-wrought
EGHOORRTUVW	overwrought
EGIIIKNNOTY	ignition key
EGIIILLMNPR	imperilling
EGIIILMNORS	religionism
EGIIILNNNRT	interlining
EGIIILNORST	religionist
EGIIILNQSTU	quislingite
EGIIILORRSU	irreligious
EGIIILORSTY	religiosity
EGIIINNOPRT	pre-ignition
EGIIKLMNOPS	pigeon's milk
EGIIKLNOOSY	kinesiology
EGIILLMNPSS	misspelling
EGIILLNNSSW	willingness
EGIILLNORTU	guillotiner
EGIILLNPRUW	wirepulling
EGIILLORSUY	religiously
EGIILMNPRSY	simperingly
EGIILMOOSST	semiologist
EGIILNNOSUY	ingeniously
EGIILNNQRUY	enquiringly
EGIILNORSUU	unreligious
EGIILNQRRSU	squirreling
EGIILNQRUVY	quiveringly
EGIILNRTTTY	titteringly
EGIIMNNRTTU	unremitting
EGIINNNNSSW	winningness
EGIINNNPRRS	inner-spring
EGIINNPRSSS	springiness
EGIINNRSSST	stringiness
EGIINNRSSTU	unresisting
EGIINOPRSSU	serpiginous
EGIINORSTUV	vertiginous
EGIINPRTTWY	typewriting
EGIIOPRSSTU	prestigious
EGIKLLNNORS	snorkelling
EGIKNNNOSSW	knowingness
EGILLLOOVXY	vexillology
EGILLLSSTUY	guiltlessly
EGILLNORTVY	revoltingly
EGILMNOORTY	terminology
EGILMNPRSUY	presumingly
EGILMNRTTUY	mutteringly
EGILMOOSTTY	etymologist
EGILNNNRUVY	unnervingly
EGILNNOSUUY	ingenuously
EGILNNRSTTY	stringently
EGILNNRSTUY	unrestingly
EGILNOOOPST	stool-pigeon
EGILNOORSTU	neurologist
EGILNOPRRVY	reprovingly
EGILNPSTTUY	upsettingly
EGILOOORSTY	soteriology
EGILOOOSSTT	osteologist
EGILOOPRSTT	petrologist
EGILOOPSSTT	pestologist
EGIMNNOORRY	ironmongery
EGIMNNPRSUU	unpresuming
EGINNNOPRRU	running rope
EGINNNORRSU	running sore
EGINNOORSTU	nitrogenous
EGINNOPRSTY	trypsinogen
EGINOOPRRSS	progression

EGMMNOORRRU rumormonger
EGNNOOPRSUY young person
EGNOOOPRSSU sporogenous
EHHIINRSSTW withershins
EHHILOOPPRS philosopher
EHHIMMOOORT homoiotherm
EHHINORSSSW whorishness
EHHIOOPPRST phosphorite
EHHIOOPRRSW hero-worship
EHHIOOPRSST ship-to-shore
EHHIOOPSSTT theosophist
EHHIOPSSTTY hypothesist
EHHLOOSTTUY youth hostel
EHHOPPRRTYY hypertrophy
EHIIILNPPPS Philippines
EHIIIPRSTTW white spirit
EHIIKLNSTTY kittenishly
EHIILMOOTTZ lithotomize
EHIILMRSSTV silversmith
EHIILNOOPST oenophilist
EHIILOOPTTX toxophilite
EHIIMNPSSSW wimpishness
EHIINNSSSSW swinishness
EHIINPRSSST spinsterish
EHIINRSSSTT thirstiness
EHIJNNNOSTU honest Injun
EHIKLMSSTTU musk thistle
EHILLMRSSTY mirthlessly
EHILMMNOSTY semi-monthly
EHILMNPSSSU lumpishness
EHILMORSSTY thermolysis
EHILNOSSSTU loutishness
EHILNSSSSTY stylishness
EHILOOPRSST horse-pistol
EHILOOPRSUX xerophilous
EHILOPSSTTW whistle-stop
EHIMNNORSTU nourishment
EHIMNOOPSTY Monophysite
EHIMNORRSTU mother's ruin
EHINNOOPSTY hypotension
EHINOORRTUZ true horizon
EHINORSTTUW unworthiest
EHLLOOOOPPT loop-the-loop
EHLLORSSTWY worthlessly
EHLLORTTTTU truth to tell
EHLMNOPPSYY nympholepsy
EHLMNOPTUWY New Plymouth
EHLMOOOSTTY toothsomely
EHLOPRSSUUU sulphureous
EHMNNOORSTU hunter's moon
EHMNOORSTWY money's-worth
EHMOOOPRSTU homopterous
EHMOORSTTUY Oystermouth
EHNNOOPRTTW twopenn'orth
EHNOOORSTUW Rowton house
EHOOPPRSSTW show-stopper
EIIIINQSTUV inquisitive
EIIILMPRTVY primitively
EIIILNTTUVY intuitively
EIIILORSSST listeriosis
EIIIMNORSSV revisionism
EIIIMNORSVX vision mixer
EIIINOPRSTT peritonitis
EIIINOQRSTU requisition
EIIINORSSTV revisionist
EIIINSSTTVY sensitivity
EIIIOPRSSTT periostitis
EIIIRSSTTVY resistivity
EIIKKNORSSS Kirk-session
EIILLLMSSTY limitlessly
EIILLMMNNSU millenniums
EIILLMPSUVY impulsively
EIILLNOSSTX sextillions
EIILLOOQSUZ soliloquize
EIILMMNOPSS Simple Simon
EIILMOPRSUY imperiously
EIILNNSSTTY insistently
EIILNOOPPRT lipoprotein
EIILNOPPRTT triple point
EIILNRSTUVY intrusively
EIIMNNOOPRT premonition
EIIMNNOPSTU pneumonitis
EIIMNOOPRRT Portmeirion
EIIMNOPSSSU impiousness
EIIMNRRTTTY Trinity term
EIIMOORRSTU meritorious
EIIMOPPRRTY impropriety
EIIMOPRSSST prestissimo
EIIMOPSTTUY impetuosity
EIIMORRSTUZ moisturizer
EIINOOPPRST preposition
EIINOOPRRSV provisioner
EIINOPRRSTY iron pyrites
EIINOPRSSUV supervision
EIINORRSSST sinistrorse
EIINORSTTTU restitution
EIIOPRRSTUY superiority
EIKLOPRSSTT split stroke
EILLLPPSTUY split pulley
EILLMOPRTUX multiplexor
EILLNOPSSTY pointlessly
EILLORRTTTY lily-trotter
EILMNNOPRTY prominently
EILMNOOOPRZ monopolizer
EILMOORRSWY worrisomely
EILMOPRSSTY proselytism
EILMOPSTUUY impetuously
EILMORSTTUY multi-storey
EILNOOPRSST portlonless
EILNOOPRSSV silver spoon
EILNOORSSST torsionless
EILNOOSSTTU solution set
EILNOPRSUUY penuriously
EILNOQRTUVY ventriloquy
EILOOPRRSTY posteriorly
EILOOPRSSTY proteolysis
EILOPPRRSTW slipperwort
EILOPPRSUVY purposively
EIMNNOOSSSU ominousness
EIMNOOPRRTY premonitory
EIMNOOQSTTU mosquito net
EIMNOPPRSTU presumption
EIMOOPRSTTT optometrist
EIMOORRSUVV vermivorous
EINNOOPPRTU inopportune
EINNOOSSSUX noxiousness
EINNOQRSTUU non sequitur
EINNORSSSUU ruinousness
EINNOSSSSUU sinuousness
EINOORRSTTU senior tutor

EINOORSSSTU riotousness
EINOPPRSSST stroppiness
EINOPPRSSSU suppression
EINOPRRRTTU interruptor
EINOPSSTTTY stenotypist
EIOPRRSSUVY supervisory
EIORRSSTTUU trouser suit
EKKOOPPRSVY Prokopyevsk
EKLNOOPSTUY outspokenly
EKNNNNOSSUW unknownness
EKNOOPRRSTT porter's knot
ELLMNNOOSTY somnolently
ELLMORSTUUY tremulously
ELLOQRSUUUY querulously
ELMMNOOSTUY momentously
ELMMOPSSSTY symptomless
ELMNOPPSUYY money supply
ELNNOORSTUW slow neutron
ELNOOOPRRTY poltroonery
ELNOOPPRTUY opportunely
ELNORSSTUUY strenuously
ELOPPRSSSTU supportless
EMNNNOORTUV Mount Vernon
EMNOOPPSSSU pompousness
EMOOOPRRSST mosstrooper
EMORRSTTUYY mystery tour
FFGGHIIINTT fighting fit
FFGHILLRTUY frightfully
FGGHIINOPTT fighting-top
FGGIIKKNNOS King of Kings
FGGIILNORVY forgivingly
FGGIINNORUV unforgiving
FGGNNOOOSSS Song of Songs
FGHIILLOPTW pillow-fight
FGHIILNOPST shoplifting
FGHIIMNORSW worm-fishing
FGHIINNRSSU furnishings
FGHIINOPSTT fitting shop, shopfitting
FGHILNORTTY fortnightly
FGIILNNTTUY unfittingly
FGINOORSUUV fungivorous
FGINOORTTTX foxtrotting
FGIOORRSUUV frugivorous
FHHIINOOPST photo finish
FHHIORRSSTT short shrift
FHIILNRTTUY unthriftily
FHIIOPRSTTW with-profits
FHIKNOOPRRS shrink-proof
FHILLOOOPRS floor polish
FIIIMOPRSTT stipitiform
FIILOORSSVY fossil ivory
FIIOOPPRRST proof spirit
FIIRTTTTTUU tutti-frutti
FIKLLLNSUUY unskilfully
FILLOORSUVY frivolously
FILMRSSTTUU mistrustful
FIMOORSTUXY sixty-fourmo
FLLOORRSUWY sorrowfully
GGGIILNNNSU gunslinging
GGHIIKKNNST king's knight
GGHIILLNSTY slightingly
GGHLMOOPSYY sphygmology
GGIIINNRSTW signwriting
GGIINNORSTW songwriting
GGILNNNNORU long-running
GHHINNNORTU hunting horn
GHHIORSTTWY sightworthy
GHHMNNOOOPT monophthong
GHIIKLNNRSY shrinkingly
GHIIKLNTTTY tightly-knit
GHIIKNNNPTU hunting pink
GHIIKNNNRSU unshrinking
GHIILLLNRTY thrillingly
GHIILLOOPST philologist
GHIILNNPSUY punishingly
GHIILNOPSTY philogynist
GHIILOOSSTT histologist
GHIINOPPPTW whipping-top
GHIINOPPRSW worshipping
GHIJMNOPSUW showjumping
GHIKNNNOOTW know-nothing
GHIKNNOOPRU pruning hook
GHIKNOSSTUY sky-shouting
GHILMNOOSTY hymnologist
GHILMOOSTTY mythologist
GHILNOOOPST phonologist
GHILNOOORTY ornithology
GHILNOOPSTY hypnologist
GHILOOOPRTY oligotrophy
GHIMNOOPSYY physiognomy
GHINOORRTUW wrought iron
GIIIINNPRST inspiriting
GIIIKLMNNSS missing link
GIIILLOSTUY litigiously
GIIILNNPRSY inspiringly
GIIILNNSSTY insistingly
GIIIMNNOOSU ignominious
GIIINNNPRSU uninspiring
GIIINOOPSTV ovipositing
GIIKLNNNUWY unwinkingly
GIILLLLMNOR rolling mill
GIILLLNNUWY unwillingly
GIILLMNNSUY unsmilingly
GIILLMNOOST limnologist
GIILLMNOPRY imploringly
GIILLNNSTUY insultingly
GIILLNOPPPP pill-popping
GIILLOOOPST oligopolist
GIILMNOPRSY promisingly
GIILNNPTUYY unpityingly
GIILNNTTUWY unwittingly
GIIMMNPPPRU pump-priming
GIIMNNOPRSU unpromising
GIIMNOORSTT sitting room
GIIMOORRRST rigor mortis
GIINNNOOPRS spring onion
GIINNNOPPST spinning top
GIINNNOPSTW winning post
GIINNOPRRST ripsnorting
GIINOPRRSUU pruriginous
GIINRTTTTYY nitty-gritty
GIKLNNNOUWY unknowingly
GIKLNOOPRVY provokingly
GIKMMNOOORS smoking room
GIKNNNNORTU running knot
GILLLMNOSUU slumgullion
GILLNOSTUUY glutinously
GILMMNRRUUY murmuringly
GILNNNOPSSU nonplussing
GILNRSTTTUY struttingly

GIMMNNOOORR	morning room
GIMMNNRRUUU	unmurmuring
GINNOOPRSTT	strong point
HHMNOOOOPSU	homophonous
HHOOOPPRSSU	phosphorous
HIILLOQRSUY	liquorishly
HIILMNNOOPY	hypolimnion
HIILMOOSTTT	lithotomist
HIILNORTTYY	Holy Trinity
HIILOPRSTTY	lithotripsy
HIIMMOOPRSS	isomorphism
HIIMMOPRRST	trimorphism
HIIMNOOPRST	monitorship
HILNOOPSTXY	xylophonist
HILNOORSSTU	honours list
HIMMOOOPRSZ	zoomorphism
HIMOOOPRSSU	isomorphous
HIMOOPRRSTU	trimorphous
HIMOORTTTWY	thirty-two-mo
HINNOOOPRTU	honour point
HINOOPPRSSS	sponsorship
HIOOPPRSSTV	provostship
HLLMOPSSUYY	symphyllous
HLNOOOPPSUY	polyphonous
HORRSTTTUWY	trustworthy
IIIIMMPRSTV	primitivism
IIIIMNSTTUV	intuitivism
IIIIMPPSSSS	Mississippi
IIIIMPRSTTV	primitivist
IIIINNOQSTU	inquisition
IIIINSTTTUV	intuitivist
IIILLMNOPST	pointillism
IIILLMNOSSU	illusionism
IIILLNNOQTU	quintillion
IIILLNOPSTT	pointillist
IIILLNOSSTT	tonsillitis
IIILLNOSSTU	illusionist
IIINNNORTTU	innutrition
IIINNOSTTTU	institution
IIINOOOPSTV	oviposition
IIJLNORSUUY	injuriously
IILLNNOOOPP	opinion poll
IILLOOQSSTU	soliloquist
IILLORSSTUU	illustrious
IILMOORTTUY	utility room
IILOOPRRSVY	provisorily
IIMNOPRTTUY	importunity
IIMOOPRSSTT	soroptimist
IINOOOPPRST	proposition
IINOOPPSSTU	supposition
IINOPPQRTUY	propinquity
IINOPRRRSTU	stirrup iron
ILLOPSSUWWY	pussy willow
ILLORSUUUXY	luxuriously
ILNOOOPSSUY	poisonously
ILNOOORSTUY	notoriously
IMNOOPPRSTU	opportunism
IMNOORSSTTY	monstrosity
IMOOPPRSTTU	pittosporum
IMOPSSTTUUY	sumptuosity
IMPPPRRSTUU	stirrup pump
INOOPPRSTTU	opportunist
INOOPPRTTUY	opportunity
INOPPTTTUUU	input-output
IOOPPRSSTUY	suppository
IOOPRRSTTTU	prostitutor
LLNOOORRUWY	roll-your-own
LMNOORSSTUY	monstrously
LMOPSSTUUUY	sumptuously
LOORRSTTUUY	torturously
MOOOPRRSSTT	storm troops

TWELVE LETTERS

AAAAAALMRSTT taramasalata
AAAAABBNRRST Santa Barbara
AAAAABCDLMNS Canada balsam
AAAAAGHIKKMR Kakamigahara
AAAABCCHILNN Bacchanalian
AAAABCEILMNR Arabian camel
AAAABDGILMOV viola da gamba
AAAABDIINRSU Saudi Arabian
AAAABEELRSTU tabulae rasae
AAAABGGILLNS basal ganglia
AAAACCCCIRTU acciaccatura
AAAACDELMMRT marmalade cat
AAAACDELMNVY naval academy
AAAACDIILPRS paradisaical, paradisiacal
AAAACEINRRSV caravanserai
AAAACELLLLPP alla cappella
AAAACGIMMNRT anagrammatic
AAAACIMNRSST antimacassar
AAAADDDDGLNZ Dalandzadgad
AAAADHNPRRUU Anuradhapura
AAAADILMNNRS salamandrian
AAAAEGGLNPRU paralanguage
AAAAEGNRTVXZ extravaganza
AAAAEHILMSST thalassaemia
AAAAEIMMNRRT armamentaria
AAAAFINNORST Fianarantsoa
AAAAGILMMNOT amalgamation
AAAAILLPRRSS sarsaparilla
AAAAILNRSSTU Australasian
AAAAINNNORTV Antananarivo
AAABBCEGIRRY baby carriage
AAABBCILLRRY barbarically
AAABBCILLSTY sabbatically
AAABCCGILNNT balancing act
AAABCDEHNOTY Daytona Beach
AAABCDKLNNST Black and Tans
AAABCEHILLPT alphabetical
AAABCEHLOPPR approachable
AAABCEILLNRT trial balance
AAABCEILLRWY cable railway
AAABCEKLNTTU unattackable
AAABCELMMNNU ambulance man
AAABCGIINNRT Cantabrigian
AAABCGINSTTY Batangas City
AAABCHHIIKRS Bakhchisarai
AAABCHIINRVY Baranavichiy
AAABCKLLRTWY wallaby track
AAABDDEGIMNR brain-damaged
AAABDDJNNORY Darby and Joan
AAABDEMRSSSS ambassadress
AAABDGHMNRSS smash-and-grab
AAABDIILPTTY adaptability
AAABDILLOOPR paraboloidal
AAABDNRRSSST Stars and Bars
AAABEEGILMRR marriageable
AAABEEGLMNNU unmanageable
AAABEELLNPPU unappealable
AAABEELNPPSU unappeasable
AAABEGKLLMRY Gamlakarleby
AAABEGLMNNUY unmanageably
AAABEHIKPPPT Phi Beta Kappa
AAABEIIJNRSZ Azerbaijanis
AAABEIILMNNT maintainable
AAABEILLMNOT balletomania
AAABEILLNSSU unassailable
AAABEILNNTTU unattainable
AAABEINNSSST San Sebastian
AAABELLLPRRS parallel bars
AAABELLNNSUY unanalysable
AAABELLNNUYZ unanalyzable
AAABELLNRSTT translatable
AAABELNOOPTY palaeobotany
AAABEMNORTTW water-boatman
AAABFILMRRSS friar's balsam
AAABIIILLTVY availability
AAABIILLPTTY palatability
AAABIKLNNNOT national bank
AAABILLNSSUY unassailably
AAABILNNTTUY unattainably
AAABLLMOPPRS balsam poplar
AAACCDDEIMNR candid camera
AAACCDEEIMRY academic year
AAACCDEILLMY academically
AAACCDEILMNO decalcomania
AAACCDEILMRU camera lucida
AAACCDHILSTU cactus dahlia
AAACCDHNRRSY cash and carry
AAACCDIIPRST aspartic acid
AAACCDIIRRTT tartaric acid
AAACCEHILNUV Huancavelica
AAACCEHIPTTY heat capacity
AAACCEIINPTT incapacitate
AAACCEIIPTTV capacitative
AAACCEINNQTU acquaintance
AAACCHILLNRY anarchically
AAACCHILNPTY anaphylactic
AAACCHIRRRSU churrascaria
AAACCIINNPTT incapacitant
AAACCILORSTU accusatorial
AAACCKMORSTT staccato mark
AAACDDEGNRUV advance guard
AAACDDEILNSV Aladdin's cave
AAACDEEHNRSS Saracen's head
AAACDEELNRRY calendar year
AAACDEGNOORY Cagayan de Oro

AAACDEINOTVX tax avoidance
AAACDEINRSTT tradescantia
AAACDGIIMMRT diagrammatic
AAACDGIIMPRT paradigmatic
AAACDHOOPPRR approach road
AAACDIINNNSV Scandinavian
AAACDILLMRTY dramatically
AAACDILNNOTV vacationland
AAACDIMRRSTY satyric drama
AAACDLRSTUWY casualty ward
AAACEEENPPRR reappearance
AAACEEGNRTVX extravagance
AAACEEILMNOR American aloe
AAACEERRSTTU sauce tartare, tartare sauce
AAACEFIMNORR Afro-American
AAACEFINSTTT fantasticate
AAACEGGGLOTU galactagogue
AAACEGHLNNOT Chalatenango
AAACEGILMMNO megalomaniac
AAACEGIMNPRT paramagnetic
AAACEGMNORRT actor-manager
AAACEGNRTVXY extravagancy
AAACEHILMMTT mathematical
AAACEHIPRRTT patriarchate
AAACEHKNSSTW Saskatchewan
AAACEHLNPSTT capstan lathe
AAACEIILMNRT Latin America
AAACEIJLMNTY Calamity Jane
AAACEILMNNPR American plan
AAACEILMOOST osteomalacia
AAACEILNORTU aeronautical
AAACEILNSTTT Caltanisetta
AAACFGILNNRU lingua franca
AAACFIINRRTT anti-aircraft
AAACGIIMNSTT anastigmatic
AAACGILLLNOY analogically
AAACGILLLNVY galvanically
AAACGILMNRTU natural magic
AAACHIIKPPRT apparatchiki
AAACHIKPPRST apparatchiks
AAACHILMNRST charlatanism
AAACHIPPRRST paraphrastic
AAACIILNNOTZ canalization
AAACIILNNRRT intracranial
AAACILLLMPST small capital
AAACILLLNTYY analytically
AAACILLMNOTY anatomically
AAACILLMORTY aromatically
AAACILLNOPRY paranoically
AAACILMMNNOO monomaniacal
AAACIMNNOTTU catamountain
AAACLMMOPSTY mycoplasmata
AAACMNOORRTV motor caravan
AAADDDEEILNV dead-and-alive
AAADDEEGGLNU dead language
AAADDEGILNNR land drainage
AAADDEGINSTV disadvantage
AAADDILLMNPS Aladdin's lamp
AAADDILMNORS salamandroid
AAADDLMNPRST lamp standard, standard lamp
AAADEFKLRRUW Kafr el Dauwar
AAADEGILNRTV landgraviate
AAADEGIMQRSU Quadragesima
AAADEGNOSTUV advantageous
AAADEHLNRTTU natural death
AAADEHNRRTTW death warrant
AAADEIIMNNST East Indiaman
AAADEILMNNRS salamandrine
AAADEINOPRTT readaptation
AAADGIILLORT gladiatorial
AAADGIMNRSTV avant-gardism
AAADGINRSTTV avant-gardist
AAADGLMMMNRY mammary gland
AAADGLNQRRUU quadrangular
AAADGLOORSVW Avogadro's law
AAADIILLMNPS Palladianism
AAADILLNSSTY All Saints' Day
AAADILNRSSSU Russian salad
AAAEEGGLMNTU metalanguage
AAAEEGGMNRST stage manager
AAAEEGINNRSX sexagenarian
AAAEEGMNNPRT permanganate
AAAEEHIMNTTZ anathematize
AAAEEHIPRSST paraesthesia
AAAEEILLNPRT Earl Palatine
AAAEFGHILLRS false gharial
AAAEFHIMRRSZ Mazar-e-Sharif
AAAEGHLOPPRY palaeography
AAAEGIJLNPTY Petaling Jaya
AAAEGILLMNRY managerially
AAAEGINNNNOR nonagenarian
AAAEGNNRRSTT Narragansett
AAAEHIILLMPT epithalamial
AAAEHMOPRRTY aromatherapy
AAAEIILNQRTU equalitarian
AAAEILMNOPPR paralipomena
AAAEILMRRTTX extramarital
AAAEILNPPRRS prelapsarian
AAAEINRRSTWY sanitary ware
AAAELLOOWWZZ Zelazowa Wola
AAAELQQRSUUV quaquaversal
AAAEMMRRSSTT master-at-arms
AAAENOPRSUYY pay-as-you-earn
AAAFHHLMNORT half-marathon
AAAGGIOPPRTU appoggiatura
AAAGHHNNSSUY Shuangyashan
AAAGHIRSTTWY straightaway
AAAGIILNNOTV navigational
AAAGILLLORRT grallatorial
AAAGILLPRSXY spiral galaxy
AAAGILNNNPRT rataplanning
AAAHHHHNORSS Rosh Hashanah
AAAHIIMNNRTU humanitarian
AAAIILMPRRTY paramilitary
AAAIILNNOSTZ nasalization
AAAIILNOPRST aspirational
AAAIILNORTTT totalitarian
AAAIIMMNRSST Samaritanism
AAAIKLNNOPRT national park
AAAILLNOSTTU salutational
AAAILMNORTTU maturational
AAAILNOPRSTY paralysation
AAAILNORSTTU salutatorian
AAAINORSSSST assassinator
AAALLLLOOOPZ lollapalooza
AAALLMNOPRRY paranormally
AAALNORRRTWY royal warrant
AABBBDEERTTY battered baby

AABBCDEKLLNU black and blue
AABBCDFHIRSS scabbard-fish
AABBCEEEKLNY black-eye bean
AABBCEEGHITW cabbage white
AABBCEEHLNRU unbreachable
AABBCEGIKKNR back-breaking
AABBCEGKKNSU skunk-cabbage
AABBCEHNRSTY baby-snatcher
AABBCIIILMNO bibliomaniac
AABBCIILLNRY rabbinically
AABBDIILLRRS bar billiards
AABBDILMNOSU subabdominal
AABBEEELNRSS bearableness
AABBEEHLNRTU unbreathable
AABBEEILLRVZ verbalizable
AABBEEKLNNOR non-breakable
AABBEIINORTV abbreviation
AABBEILNNOTU unobtainable
AABBEILRTTTU attributable
AABBEINRRRTW rabbit warren
AABBHIIILTTY habitability
AABCCCDIIISS abscisic acid
AABCCCDIINOR carbonic acid
AABCCCDIIORS ascorbic acid
AABCCDEIILRT bactericidal
AABCCDEIKNRR crack-brained
AABCCDEILLSY decasyllabic
AABCCDKKLORW drawback lock
AABCCEEHLNRT carte blanche
AABCCEELNPTU unacceptable
AABCCEELORST obstacle race
AABCCEIINNSV Sabin vaccine
AABCCEILLLNU incalculable
AABCCEILLMOV clavicembalo
AABCCEINORTV active carbon
AABCCEIRRTUU bureaucratic
AABCCEKKLRRT black tracker
AABCCELNORTT contractable
AABCCELNPTUY unacceptably
AABCCENOORSU carbonaceous
AABCCGIKKNRT backing track
AABCCILLLNUY incalculably
AABCCILOOPRS carbolic soap
AABCCINRSTTU subantarctic
AABCCKLNRRTU blackcurrant
AABCCLNOOPTT tobacco plant
AABCDDDEEKLS saddlebacked
AABCDDEJLORS Jacob's ladder
AABCDDEKLRRW bladderwrack
AABCDEEEKLPY black-eyed pea
AABCDEEIILNR ineradicable
AABCDEELLLNW well-balanced
AABCDEELLLSY decasyllable
AABCDEELLNRT ballet dancer
AABCDEGGNNOS eggs and bacon
AABCDEGIKNNR break-dancing
AABCDEHORRTY carbohydrate
AABCDEIILNRY ineradicably
AABCDEINOSTU subdiaconate
AABCDEKLLOPR black leopard
AABCDEKNRSSW backwardness
AABCDELMNRSU candelabrums
AABCDELOPPRR clapperboard
AABCDELRSTTY abstractedly
AABCDENOPRSW bow and scrape
AABCDEOPRRRS scraperboard
AABCDGHINRTU Dutch bargain
AABCDGIKLMOR block diagram
AABCDGINNORT carbon dating
AABCDGINORST broadcasting
AABCDGKLLRUY blackguardly
AABCDIILLLOY diabolically
AABCDKMNOOSW backwoodsman
AABCEEEELLRS cable release
AABCEEEFFILN ineffaceable
AABCEEEFIRTT acetate fibre
AABCEEEGHLNX exchangeable
AABCEEEGHLRR rechargeable
AABCEEEHLLNW balance wheel
AABCEEEHLNST balance sheet
AABCEEEHLRRS researchable
AABCEEFFILNY ineffaceably
AABCEEFIPRRT prefabricate
AABCEEGGPRRT carpet-bagger
AABCEEGHLNNU unchangeable
AABCEEHLMNRT merchantable
AABCEEHLNRSU unsearchable
AABCEEHLOPRR reproachable
AABCEEIKMNRT cabinetmaker
AABCEEILLMMT emblematical
AABCEEILMNSS amicableness
AABCEEILPRTT beta particle
AABCEEIMRRRR barrier cream
AABCEEINORTX exacerbation
AABCEEKLNPST space blanket
AABCEELLNOOT oblanceolate
AABCEELMNOTU uncome-at-able
AABCEFGLMNOR fromage blanc
AABCEFIILLSS classifiable
AABCEFIILLTY beatifically
AABCEFLNRSTU blast furnace
AABCEGHLNNUY unchangeably
AABCEGIKLNNR clearing bank
AABCEGILLMNR all-embracing
AABCEHHNOOPR arachnophobe
AABCEHIILTTY teachability
AABCEHILNRTU uncharitable
AABCEHIRRRRS crash barrier
AABCEHKLNPRT Black Panther
AABCEHKMNNRT merchant bank
AABCEHKMPRRS spark chamber
AABCEHLMNORS elasmobranch
AABCEHLNRSUY unsearchably
AABCEHMNOOPP Pompano Beach
AABCEHOPRSSU habeas corpus
AABCEIILLNPP inapplicable
AABCEIILMMRS bicameralism
AABCEIILRTTY traceability
AABCEILLNUVZ vulcanizable
AABCEILLTTUV cultivatable
AABCEILMNOPR incomparable
AABCEILMORRT barometrical
AABCEILMORVW microwavable
AABCEILNNOST sanctionable
AABCEINRRSTT scatterbrain
AABCEIORSTTT bacteriostat
AABCEKNORTTU back-to-nature
AABCFIKLLSSY black salsify
AABCGHIILOPR biographical
AABCGIKLNPPS backslapping

AABCHIINOOTT	cohabitation
AABCHILNRTUY	uncharitably
AABCIIILNPTY	incapability
AABCIILLNPPY	inapplicably
AABCIILRTTTY	tractability
AABCILLLLSYY	syllabically
AABCILMNOPRY	incomparably
AABCLLOOORRT	collaborator
AABCLNORSTUY	constabulary
AABCMNNNOOTT	non-combatant
AABDDDENRRST	Standardbred
AABDDEEILLLN	dead-ball line
AABDDEEKNRVY	Vandyke beard
AABDDEFOORRT	board of trade
AABDDELMNORS	old man's beard
AABDDGHORRTU	draughtboard
AABDDGINORRW	drawing board
AABDEEEGILRS	disagreeable
AABDEEELNRSS	readableness
AABDEEGILRSY	disagreeably
AABDEEHHRRSY	haberdashery
AABDEEHLRRTY	rehydratable
AABDEEHORRTW	weatherboard
AABDEEILRTTX	extraditable
AABDEEKORRST	skateboarder
AABDEELNOPRS	leopard's bane
AABDEFFLNORU	unaffordable
AABDEFGILLMO	balm of Gilead
AABDEFLLNNOR	flannelboard
AABDEGGLNOST	Gladstone bag
AABDEGGLNOUY	body language
AABDEGHILNSS	Bangladeshis
AABDEGIIMSTU	disambiguate
AABDEHHIRRST	hair's breadth
AABDEILNNOTT	national debt
AABDEIMRRSSS	disembarrass
AABDELNNOPRU	unpardonable
AABDELOPRRST	plasterboard
AABDENNNOPRT	broad pennant
AABDENNORTUV	over-abundant
AABDGIILNORS	boardsailing, sailboarding
AABDHLNNRSSU	slash-and-burn
AABDIIILSTVY	advisability
AABDLNNOPRUY	unpardonably
AABEEEGLMPRS	gas-permeable
AABEEEGLTVWX	vegetable wax
AABEEEHKRRRT	heartbreaker
AABEEELMNNSS	amenableness
AABEEELMNSST	tameableness
AABEEELNPRTU	unrepeatable
AABEEFGILRRR	irrefragable
AABEEFHINRRT	feather-brain
AABEEFLLRSTY	self-betrayal
AABEEFLMOSTV	movable feast
AABEEFLNRRST	transferable
AABEEGGLMORT	mortgageable
AABEEGILMNTZ	magnetizable
AABEEGLNNTUW	Blaenau Gwent
AABEEGMMORRU	Oberammergau
AABEEHIILRTT	rehabilitate
AABEEHLRRSTY	breathalyser
AABEEHLRRTYZ	breathalyzer
AABEEILLLNPP	inappellable
AABEEILLNRUZ	unrealizable

AABEEILLOPRT	parietal lobe
AABEEILMMRSU	immeasurable
AABEEILMRRSS	Lesser Bairam
AABEEILNOPRT	parietal bone
AABEEILNRRST	restrainable
AABEEILNRSSV	variableness
AABEEKLLRTTW	Bakewell tart
AABEEKLMNRRU	unremarkable
AABEEKLMNRTU	unmarketable
AABEELLLNNTV	Van Allen belt
AABEELLOPSTT	table-top sale
AABEELMNNRST	table manners
AABEELMNORUV	manoeuvrable
AABEELMNRSUU	unmeasurable
AABEELNNORSU	unreasonable
AABEELNNOSSU	unseasonable
AABEELNNRRUW	urban renewal
AABEELNNRSUW	unanswerable
AABEELNPSSSS	passableness
AABEELRRTUUV	travel bureau
AABEENNRRSTU	subterranean
AABEFFIILRTW	water bailiff
AABEFFLORTUW	water buffalo
AABEFGILRRRY	irrefragably
AABEFHLMNOTU	unfathomable
AABEFIILNOPS	saponifiable
AABEFIILNQTU	quantifiable
AABEFLLMMNNO	non-flammable
AABEFLNORUUV	unfavourable
AABEGHIKNRTT	breathtaking
AABEGHIMNTTW	bantamweight
AABEGIILMNNU	unimaginable
AABEGIILSTTY	stageability
AABEGIINRRTT	Great Britain
AABEGIINSSUU	Guinea-Bissau
AABEGIKKMNST	basket-making
AABEGILNNSSU	unassignable
AABEGIMNRRTT	battering ram
AABEGLLRSSTU	Glauber's salt
AABEGLMMOPRR	programmable
AABEHILNQSUV	vanquishable
AABEHILNSSTU	habitualness
AABEHILOPSST	base hospital
AABEHLOPPSTU	alphabet soup
AABEHMORRRST	harbormaster
AABEIIILLNTY	alienability
AABEIILLLMTY	malleability
AABEIILLNRTY	learnability
AABEIILLSUVZ	visualizable
AABEIILPRSTY	separability
AABEIKLMNSTU	unmistakable
AABEIKNORSTT	station break
AABEIKNPRRUV	Peruvian bark
AABEILLMNTVY	ambivalently
AABEILLNRRTU	turbellarian
AABEILLPRRTY	Liberal Party
AABEILMMRSUY	immeasurably
AABEILMMRSUZ	summarizable
AABEILMNNTUV	unambivalent
AABEILNPRRST	transpirable
AABEINNNORST	non-abstainer
AABEINSSTTTU	substantiate
AABEKLMNRRUY	unremarkably
AABEKLMORRTU	labour market
AABELLORSTTY	battles royal

AABELMNRSTTU	transmutable	**AACCDEILLNTY**	accidentally
AABELMNRSUUY	unmeasurably	**AACCDEINNTUV**	unvaccinated
AABELMOPRRTU	perambulator	**AACCDEKMPUUV**	vacuum-packed
AABELNNORSUY	unreasonably	**AACCDELLLTUY**	calculatedly
AABELNNOSSUY	unseasonably	**AACCDELLNRSU**	Della Cruscan
AABELNNRSUWY	unanswerably	**AACCDEMNORSS**	random-access
AABELNOPRSST	transposable	**AACCDFIILMSU**	sulfamic acid
AABELNSTTTUU	unstatutable	**AACCDGIILMTU**	glutamic acid
AABELORRSTTY	solar battery	**AACCDGINRRRY**	card-carrying
AABFFGLORSSU	buffalo grass	**AACCDHHIILPT**	phthalic acid
AABFGIIILTTY	fatigability	**AACCDIIILMPT**	palmitic acid
AABFHLMNOTUY	unfathomably	**AACCDIIIMRTU**	muriatic acid
AABFIILLMMTY	flammability	**AACCDIILNOTU**	claudication
AABFIILLOTTY	floatability	**AACCDIKLNORU**	Carolina duck
AABFLLMNOTYY	flamboyantly	**AACCEEEILRTV**	accelerative
AABFLNORUUVY	unfavourably	**AACCEEELPSSU**	escape clause
AABGHIINNRSW	brainwashing	**AACCEEFGHMNO**	game of chance
AABGHIKKNRSS	basking shark	**AACCEEHIRRTZ**	characterize
AABGIIILNTVY	navigability	**AACCEEIILLPR**	capercaillie
AABGIILLNOOT	obligational	**AACCEEIILPRZ**	capercailzie
AABGIILLNRTZ	trailblazing	**AACCEEILNORT**	acceleration
AABGIILMNNUY	unimaginably	**AACCEELPPSSU**	space capsule
AABGILNORSUV	labour-saving	**AACCEFHLRRTU**	characterful
AABHIIILNOTT	habilitation	**AACCEGHILLOP**	glacial epoch
AABHIIILRSSZ	bilharziasis	**AACCEGHILMOR**	agrochemical
AABHIIINNOTT	inhabitation	**AACCEGHILOOR**	archaeologic
AABHIILNNRTY	labyrinthian	**AACCEHHIILRR**	hierarchical
AABIIILNOSST	assibilation	**AACCEHHILPRT**	heptarchical
AABIIILNRTTY	trainability	**AACCEHILLMNY**	mechanically
AABIIINQRTUU	ubiquitarian	**AACCEHILPRTY**	archetypical
AABIINNOORTT	anti-abortion	**AACCEHILRRTT**	tetrarchical
AABIINNORTUZ	urbanization	**AACCEHLMOPRY**	macrocephaly
AABIINOORRTZ	arborization	**AACCEIILLNRT**	anticlerical
AABIKLMNSTUY	unmistakably	**AACCEIIMRSUU**	amicus curiae
AABILLLNOORT	trial balloon	**AACCEILLMSTU**	miscalculate
AABILLMRSUXY	submaxillary	**AACCEILLNNOT**	cancellation
AABILNSSTTUV	substantival	**AACCEILLNOSS**	neoclassical
AABILOPRRSTU	supraorbital	**AACCEILLPRSS**	preclassical
AABIMNORSTTU	masturbation	**AACCEILLSTTY**	ecstatically
AABINOOPRRTY	probationary	**AACCEILMNOPS**	complaisance
AABLMMNNOSTU	somnambulant	**AACCEILMOOST**	osteomalacic
AABLNSTTTUUY	unstatutably	**AACCEILMTUUV**	accumulative
AABMNNOOTTUW	man about town	**AACCEILNORVY**	clairvoyance
AABMORRSTTUY	masturbatory	**AACCEILNRRTT**	recalcitrant
AACCCEEENPRT	reacceptance	**AACCEILNRTUY**	inaccurately
AACCCEEHILTT	catechetical	**AACCEINNORST**	transoceanic
AACCCEEKMRRR	cream cracker	**AACCEINNOTTU**	accentuation
AACCCEFIINOP	Pacific Ocean	**AACCEINORRRT**	incarcerator
AACCCEHIRSTT	catachrestic	**AACCEIOPRTVY**	overcapacity
AACCDDEHIIRS	disaccharide	**AACCELNNOOPV**	planoconcave
AACCDDEHKLNY	cack-handedly	**AACCFIIINOPT**	pacification
AACCDDIILLTY	didactically	**AACCFIILMOPT**	fait accompli
AACCDDIIOTTU	autodidactic	**AACCFIINPRST**	transpacific
AACCDEEFHHTT	hatchet-faced	**AACCFIIOPRTY**	pacificatory
AACCDEEHHIKS	sick headache	**AACCFINNORSS**	San Francisco
AACCDEEHKRTW	cracked wheat	**AACCGHHIPRTY**	tachygraphic
AACCDEEILLMP	decimal place	**AACCGHIILLOR**	oligarchical
AACCDEEILLMS	decimal scale	**AACCGHIILLPR**	calligraphic
AACCDEELNORS	accelerandos	**AACCGHIOPRRT**	cartographic
AACCDEHIINOT	ethanoic acid	**AACCGILLOOST**	scatological
AACCDEHINORS	archdiocesan	**AACCHIILMSST**	schismatical
AACCDEHIPSST	dispatch case	**AACCHIILPRTT**	critical path
AACCDEHNORRY	archdeaconry	**AACCHIINNNOT**	cachinnation
AACCDEIIILNT	dialectician	**AACCHILLLOTY**	catholically
AACCDEIKNOPT	action-packed	**AACCHIMNOPRT**	panchromatic

AACCHIMOOPRT apochromatic
AACCHINNORTY cachinnatory
AACCHINOOSTT coach station
AACCHIOPRSTT catastrophic
AACCIIILPSTT capitalistic
AACCIILLLMTY climatically
AACCIILLMSSS classicalism
AACCIILLSSST classicalist
AACCIILLSSTY classicality
AACCIILMRSST critical mass
AACCIILNRTUY inarticulacy
AACCIILNTTTY Atlantic City
AACCIILPRTTY practicality
AACCIINNOPRR Capricornian
AACCIIORRSTT aristocratic
AACCIIRRSTTU caricaturist
AACCILLLNOVY volcanically
AACCILLNOOSY occasionally
AACCILLNORTY narcotically
AACCILLORSTY Socratically
AACCILLOSTUY acoustically
AACCILMNOTUU accumulation
AACCILNOOPTU occupational
AACCILNRSTUU lunar caustic
AACCINOORSTT castor action
AACCLLRSSSTY crystal class
AACCOOOSSTTT coast to coast
AACDDDEEHLOR dodecahedral
AACDDDEIMORU Ciudad Madero
AACDDEEEHLTY acetaldehyde
AACDDEEFHNOT dance of death
AACDDEEFINRU fricandeaued
AACDDEGNNNOS song and dance
AACDDEIIJTUV adjudicative
AACDDELOORTV Lord Advocate
AACDDENNNOOR Andean condor
AACDDIIJNOTU adjudication
AACDDIKMNNRU mandarin duck
AACDDLNORSTY Scotland Yard
AACDEEEFFINT decaffeinate
AACDEEFHLMSY shamefacedly
AACDEEHLLNST Shetland lace
AACDEEHLNSST scandal sheet
AACDEEHRRRTU Auchterarder
AACDEEILNOST de-escalation
AACDEFIILPTX fixed capital
AACDEGILLNNP landing place
AACDEGINNPRS parascending
AACDEHILLLRY heraldically
AACDEHIMNRTY diathermancy
AACDEHIOPSTV advocateship
AACDEIIIPRST parasiticide
AACDEIILNNRX cranial index
AACDEIILNRTU clairaudient
AACDEIIMRSTY Armistice Day
AACDEIINNORT deracination
AACDEIINOPTT decapitation
AACDEIINOTTV deactivation
AACDEIIOSSST disassociate
AACDEIJLLTVY adjectivally
AACDEILLMNOY demoniacally
AACDEILLNOSW disallowance
AACDEILLNPTY pedantically
AACDEILMMORT melodramatic
AACDEILNOSTT anecdotalist
AACDEIMNORSY aerodynamics
AACDEIMOOSTU diatomaceous
AACDEIMORRTV overdramatic
AACDEINNOSSY Ascension Day
AACDEINNQTUU unacquainted
AACDEINOSSTU unassociated
AACDELLORSTY sacerdotally
AACDELPPRSTU custard apple
AACDEMMNOPPR Command Paper
AACDEMMORSTU costume drama
AACDENORRSTW narrowcasted
AACDFFIINRTY affinity card
AACDFGILNNRT landing craft
AACDFIIILNNT infanticidal
AACDGHIINNPP handicapping
AACDGHIIOPRR radiographic
AACDGHILNNPU launching pad
AACDGHILNNRS crash landing
AACDGHIOPRRY cardiography
AACDGIILLOOR radiological
AACDGIILRSTU gradualistic
AACDGILLMOTY dogmatically
AACDGILOOPST capital goods
AACDHIILNPRS cardinalship
AACDHILMRRUY hydraulic ram
AACDHIMRSSTY Christmas Day
AACDHINOPQRU quadraphonic
AACDHLLNOPSW slow handclap
AACDIIINORTV divarication
AACDIILLSSTY sadistically
AACDIILNNRTY tyrannicidal
AACDIINNORRT doctrinarian
AACDIKNNPPSS spick and span
AACDILLNORSY sardonically
AACDILLNSTYY dynastically
AACDILLOPRSY sporadically
AACDLLNOSSUY scandalously
AACEEEFHLOPS chapel of ease
AACEEEFLMRRX reflex camera
AACEEEGHNRTX exchange rate
AACEEEIRRSSU air-sea rescue
AACEEENPRSVY severance pay
AACEEEPSSTTT cassette tape
AACEEFFINOTT affectionate
AACEEFGORSTT state of grace
AACEEFILMRTT lattice frame
AACEEGGILLNO genealogical
AACEEGHIMNTT team-teaching
AACEEGHNPRTX part exchange
AACEEGHRRRTT Great Charter
AACEEGILLORR large calorie
AACEEGILNRRV vicar-general
AACEEGIMNPTT magnetic tape
AACEEGIMNRST East Germanic
AACEEGLLPTTU cattle-plague
AACEEGLNRTVY travel agency
AACEEHHRRTTW weather chart
AACEEHIINSTT aesthetician
AACEEHILMTTT metathetical
AACEEHINTTTU authenticate
AACEEHKMNRRS snake charmer
AACEEHLNOPRT another place
AACEEHLNPTTU Pentateuchal
AACEEHMNRTTT reattachment
AACEEHNNPPST happenstance

AACEEIILPRTZ	recapitalize
AACEEIINRSTZ	sectarianize
AACEEIIPPRTV	appreciative
AACEEILMPPRS	pre-eclampsia
AACEEILNNRRV	cranial nerve
AACEEILNORRT	recreational
AACEEILPRTTU	recapitulate
AACEEIMRRTTT	tartar emetic
AACEEIOPRSTT	ectoparasite
AACEEIRRRRTW	Water-carrier
AACEEKLNQSUY	squeaky clean
AACEELMORSSU	coal measures
AACEELNRSTUW	nuclear waste
AACEELPRRTTY	plate tracery
AACEEMOPRTTV	caveat emptor
AACEENNPPRTU	appurtenance
AACEENNPRRST	transparence
AACEENNPRRTT	carpenter ant
AACEFFILNORV	naval officer
AACEFFMORTTT	matter of fact
AACEFFORSTTY	safety factor
AACEFGHIRSTT	straight face
AACEFGIINNPT	face-painting
AACEFIIILTTV	facilitative
AACEFIILNOTZ	factionalize
AACEFIINORRT	rarefication
AACEFILOPRSS	pair of scales
AACEFIORRSTU	surface-to-air
AACEFMNRRTUU	manufacturer
AACEGGHILOPR	geographical
AACEGHHIMORR	haemorrhagic
AACEGHHPRRTY	tachygrapher
AACEGHIILPPR	epigraphical
AACEGHILLPRR	calligrapher
AACEGHILMOOT	haematologic
AACEGHIMNOPR	anemographic, phanerogamic
AACEGHNOOPRY	oceanography
AACEGHOPRRRT	cartographer
AACEGIIINRRT	geriatrician
AACEGIILLNRT	interglacial
AACEGIILLOOT	aetiological
AACEGIILPRRS	slip-carriage
AACEGIIMMPRT	epigrammatic
AACEGIINNPTV	cave painting
AACEGILLMNTY	magnetically
AACEGILLNOSU	gallinaceous
AACEGILLORSU	argillaceous
AACEGILMNNRT	magic lantern
AACEGILNSSUV	saving clause
AACEGIMNORSU	graminaceous
AACEGIMNOSTY	gynecomastia
AACEGINNOORT	octogenarian
AACEGINNORTT	octane rating
AACEGINPPRRT	tracing paper
AACEGLNNORRU	canon regular, regular canon
AACEGLNORTTU	congratulate
AACEHHIILMOP	haemophiliac
AACEHIILLOPT	palaeolithic
AACEHIILLRTY	hieratically
AACEHIILMRTT	arithmetical
AACEHIILNTTT	antithetical
AACEHIINPTTT	antipathetic
AACEHIINRRST	Christian era
AACEHILLLTTY	athletically
AACEHILLMPTY	empathically, emphatically
AACEHILLMTTY	thematically
AACEHILLPRSY	seraphically
AACEHILLPTTY	pathetically
AACEHILLRTTY	theatrically
AACEHILMNPRU	alphanumeric
AACEHILMOPRT	metaphorical
AACEHILMPSTY	metaphysical
AACEHILNRSSW	Charles's Wain
AACEHIMPRSTT	metaphrastic
AACEHLMORSST	scholar's mate
AACEHMNNRSTU	transhumance
AACEHMNNRTVY	merchant navy
AACEHMNORRST	stream-anchor
AACEHPRRRTTY	charter party
AACEIIINPTTV	anticipative
AACEIILLMNTU	nautical mile
AACEIILMNTTT	Atlantic Time
AACEIILNOPPS	episcopalian
AACEIILNPRTT	antiparticle
AACEIILNRTTU	inarticulate
AACEIIMNNOPT	emancipation
AACEIIMNRSST	Cartesianism, sectarianism
AACEIIMRTTVX	active matrix
AACEIINOPPRT	appreciation
AACEIINORTTV	reactivation
AACEIINPRSTT	pancreatitis
AACEIJKRSTTT	straitjacket
AACEIJLLMSTY	majestically
AACEIKLLSTTY	Salt Lake City
AACEIKLMNOPT	kleptomaniac
AACEILLLLMTY	metallically
AACEILLLMORS	small calorie
AACEILLMMTUY	immaculately
AACEILLMNSTY	semantically
AACEILLNOORT	reallocation
AACEILLNOSTT	castellation
AACEILLOPRTY	operatically
AACEILLRTTUY	articulately
AACEILMMRSTY	asymmetrical
AACEILMNOSTU	emasculation
AACEILNOPRTY	action replay
AACEILNORTVY	clairvoyante
AACEILOPRRTY	tropical year
AACEILOPRSTT	spectatorial
AACEILRSTTTU	straticulate
AACEILRTTTVY	attractively
AACEIMNNOOPT	companionate
AACEIMNOPRTY	emancipatory
AACEINNNORST	non-sectarian
AACEINOPSSTT	space station
AACEINRTTTUV	unattractive
AACEIOPPRRTY	appreciatory
AACEIOPRRRTV	prevaricator
AACEJKLNNORT	jack-o'-lantern
AACEJKOOPTTT	jacket potato
AACEKNNORSTU	cantankerous
AACELLLLORTY	collaterally
AACELLNNOOPR	coronal plane
AACELLNORWYY	canary yellow
AACELLNRRUVY	vernacularly
AACELMNORSTW	scarlet woman

AACELMORSTUY	emasculatory
AACENNPRRSTY	transparency
AACENORRRSTW	narrowcaster
AACFGGILNRTY	grafting clay
AACFGIIINOST	gasification
AACFHIILLSTW	Wichita Falls
AACFHINORSTU	South African
AACFIIILLRTY	artificially
AACFIIILNOTT	facilitation
AACFIIIMNORT	ramification
AACFIIINORTT	ratification
AACFIILMNOST	factionalism
AACFIILNOOTZ	focalization
AACFIINOSSTT	satisfaction
AACFILLLOSUY	fallaciously
AACFILLNORTY	fractionally
AACFILMORSTT	stalactiform
AACFIORSSTTY	satisfactory
AACGGHHIIOPR	hagiographic
AACGGHIILLOO	hagiological
AACGGIILLNTY	gigantically
AACGHILLOOPT	pathological
AACGHILNOPPR	planographic
AACGHILOOPRR	orographical
AACGHIMRTTUU	thaumaturgic
AACGHINOPPRT	pantographic
AACGHINOPRRU	uranographic
AACGHLMOOPRY	pharmacology
AACGHOOPSSTU	scatophagous
AACGIIILPRST	plagiaristic
AACGIILNNORV	Carlovingian
AACGIIMPRSTT	pragmatistic
AACGIINNOSTT	antagonistic
AACGILLMORSY	orgasmically
AACGILLOOPRT	patrological
AACGILLOORST	astrological
AACGILLOOTTU	tautological
AACGILLOPSST	optical glass
AACGILLORSTY	orgastically
AACGILLRRTUU	agricultural
AACGILMNORST	marginal cost
AACGILNNOOTV	long vacation
AACGIMMOPRRT	programmatic
AACGINOPPRTU	group captain
AACGLMOOSTUU	glaucomatous
AACGLNNORTTU	congratulant
AACHHIIMNPRS	chairmanship
AACHHILMOPTY	hypothalamic
AACHIILMOPRS	parochialism
AACHIILOPRTY	parochiality
AACHIILORRST	tailor's chair
AACHIIMPRRST	patriarchism
AACHIKLMOOTY	Oklahoma City
AACHILLMNORY	harmonically
AACHILLNORTU	hallucinator
AACHILMNORTY	lachrymation
AACHILOPSTTY	hypostatical
AACHIMMNNOPY	nymphomaniac
AACHIMNOPRRS	parachronism
AACHIMOOPRST	chromatopsia
AACHINOPRTTU	naturopathic
AACHLLNNNOTY	nonchalantly
AACHLMORRTYY	lachrymatory
AACHMOORSTTU	trachomatous
AACHNOOSTTVY	anchovy toast
AACIIINNOPTT	anticipation
AACIIINNOTTV	inactivation, vaticination
AACIIINSSTTT	statistician
AACIILLNNOTT	cantillation
AACIILLNOOTZ	localization
AACIILLRSTTY	artistically
AACIILMMORSS	commissarial
AACIILMNNOTU	calumniation
AACIILNNOTTY	National City
AACIILNOOTVZ	vocalization
AACIILNOPTTU	capitulation
AACIILNORTTU	articulation
AACIILNRSTTU	naturalistic
AACIILORSUVY	avariciously
AACIIMMORSST	commissariat
AACIIMNNORST	animatronics
AACIIMOTTTUY	automaticity
AACIINNNNOTU	annunciation
AACIINNOOTZ	canonization
AACIINOORRTT	ratiocinator
AACIINOPRTTY	anticipatory
AACIIOORSSTX	toxocariasis
AACIIOPPRRTT	participator
AACILLLNOPTY	Platonically
AACILLLOOPRT	allotropical
AACILLLRTVWY	cavalry twill
AACILLMNORTY	romantically
AACILLMNOSTY	monastically
AACILLMOSTUY	calamitously
AACILLNNRTYY	tyrannically
AACILLNOOTVY	vocationally
AACILLNPSTYY	synaptically
AACILLPRRTUY	particularly
AACILMNOOPRT	proclamation
AACILMNOORST	astronomical
AACILMNORTUY	calumniatory
AACILMORRTTU	court martial
AACILNOSTTUU	auscultation
AACILOPRTTUY	capitulatory
AACIMMOPSTTY	asymptomatic
AACIMNNOOPWY	companionway
AACIMNNOORTT	contaminator
AACIMOORSSST	sarcomatosis
AACINORSSTTU	astronautics
AACLLNNORTUY	connaturally
AACLMOOPRRTY	proclamatory
AACLNNOPRTTU	contrapuntal
AACLNPRSTTYY	cryptanalyst
AACLORSTTUUY	auscultatory
AADDDEEGHINN	hidden agenda
AADDDEEHHLRY	hard-headedly
AADDDGLNORST	gold standard
AADDEEFHILNT	life-and-death
AADDEEHNSSWY	Ash Wednesday
AADDEFNNOSSU	safe and sound
AADDEGNOPRRU	parade ground
AADDEIMNRSTT	standard time
AADDEINRRSTZ	standardizer
AADDELLMNORS	salmon-ladder
AADDENNSTUVY	Advent Sunday
AADDGHINNRST	hardstanding
AADDHIILOPSY	paid holidays
AADDIIILNOPT	dilapidation
AADDIILLNOTY	additionally

AADEEEGHRRTT great-hearted
AADEEEHHRTVY heavy-hearted
AADEEEILRRSY sidereal year
AADEEELNNRWZ New Zealander
AADEEFHINRTT faint-hearted
AADEEFHOSSTT heads of state
AADEEFILLMRT Fleet Admiral
AADEEGGGIRST disaggregate
AADEEGIILNNR radial engine
AADEEGKMNRRT market garden
AADEEHILNQRU harlequinade
AADEEHLMRSTY headmasterly
AADEEHLNPTTY death penalty
AADEEHQRRSTU headquarters
AADEEILLNTUV unalleviated
AADEEILMMPST semipalmated
AADEEILNQTUY inadequately
AADEEILNRTUZ denaturalize
AADEEIMMNNST misdemeanant
AADEEIMQSTUV desquamative
AADEEINOPRST endoparasite
AADEEJLNNRTW lantern-jawed
AADEELLLNPRU unparalleled
AADEELLNPRTT plattelander
AADEELLRZZZZ razzle-dazzle
AADEELMNPRTT departmental
AADEEMNNRTUX extramundane
AADEEMNORRWY Yeoman Warder
AADEENRSSTUY Easter Sunday
AADEEPPQRRSU squared paper
AADEFFIIILST disaffiliate
AADEFFIILNTU unaffiliated
AADEFGILNORT deflagration
AADEFGNOORRT frontage road
AADEFHILLMRS field marshal
AADEFHINNOTU fountainhead
AADEFILNORTY deflationary
AADEGGILNNOT ganglionated
AADEGGILNNST landing stage
AADEGHILLLOY legal holiday
AADEGHILNORU Dun Laoghaire
AADEGHIOPRRR radiographer
AADEGIILLNNP plain dealing
AADEGIILPQRU quadriplegia
AADEGIIMMNST diamagnetism
AADEGIINPRRR Grand Prairie
AADEGILLNPRV all-pervading
AADEGILNSSST stained glass
AADEGINNNOOS sage and onion
AADEGINNSTVW standing wave
AADEGINOPPRZ propagandize
AADEGINPPRRW drawing paper
AADEGLLNNSUY auld lang syne
AADEGLNPRSST star-spangled
AADEGOPRSTTU postgraduate
AADEHHIILLPP Philadelphia
AADEHIIINRTT Titian-haired
AADEHIILMRTW white admiral
AADEHIKLMORY holidaymaker
AADEHILMNPRS aldermanship
AADEHIOPRRTY radiotherapy
AADEIIILNOTZ idealization
AADEIILLNOTY ideationally
AADEIILLNUVV vaudevillian
AADEIILNNOST desalination
AADEIILNNTUV antediluvian
AADEIILNORTV derivational
AADEIILNRSTT interstadial
AADEIIMNRSTT administrate
AADEIINNNORW Neo-Darwinian
AADEIINNORST Tardenoisian
AADEIKLMNRTW milk and water
AADEILNNNORR noradrenalin
AADEILNORTTU adulteration
AADEILNQRTUV quadrivalent
AADEILNRTUVY valetudinary
AADEIMNOQSTU desquamation
AADEIMNORSTU Suriname toad
AADEINNORTTU denaturation
AADEJLNORRTU trade journal
AADEKLNOPRRV Overland Park
AADELLLNPRSW spandrel wall
AADELMNNRTUU ultramundane
AADELMORSSYY Lady Mayoress
AADELNNNPSTU sun and planet
AADELNNRSTTU untranslated
AADEMNNPRSUU supramundane
AADEMOQRSTUY desquamatory
AADFFFHLNOST stand-off half
AADFFKLNORRW flank forward
AADFILNNOOTU foundational
AADFINNOOSTU soda fountain
AADGGILMMNOR Mid Glamorgan
AADGHHIMNNRT right-hand man
AADGHIINPRSU guardianship
AADGIIIMPRRV primigravida
AADGIILNNORT national grid
AADGIMNOPPRS propagandism
AADGIMNPRSTT trading stamp
AADGINOORSTY Rogation Days
AADGINOPPRST propagandist
AADHILMNOORY Roman holiday
AADHINPRSSTY Danish pastry
AADHIOOPSSWY whoops-a-daisy
AADHKNOOSSTU Thousand Oaks
AADHLORSTUYY Holy Saturday
AADIIILNNOPS Indianapolis
AADIIILNNOTV invalidation
AADIILMNOQRU quadrinomial
AADIILNOOSTV vasodilation
AADIINNOPRTT radiant point
AADIINOOTTUX autoxidation
AADIINORRTTY traditionary
AADIINOSSTTV idiot savants
AADIINPRRSTT rapid transit
AADIIRRSSTUV Stradivarius
AADILNNOORSV Lisdoonvarna
AADILNOPPRST postprandial
AADILOORSTVY vasodilatory
AADINNORSTTU transudation
AADLMNNORUWY laundrywoman
AADMNOQRSUUU quadrumanous
AADNORRSTTUY transudatory
AAEEEELLMNSV mean sea level
AAEEEFHMNPRT mean free path
AAEEEFLRSTTW welfare state
AAEEEGGIRTVX exaggerative
AAEEEGGLNNRT agent-general
AAEEEGGLRSZZ Zalaegerszeg
AAEEEGLLNRSV raglan sleeve

AAEEEHILSSTT	telaesthesia
AAEEEHINSTTZ	anaesthetize
AAEEEHLLNPST	elephant seal
AAEEELOPRTTU	Poet Laureate
AAEEENPRSSST	separateness
AAEEFFGLNRST	general staff
AAEEFGILMTTU	metal fatigue
AAEEFHILRRTU	heart failure
AAEEFHLMRSSU	half measures
AAEEFHLORSSV	half-seas-over
AAEEFIILRSSZ	laissez-faire
AAEEFILNPRVY	five-year plan
AAEEFMNNRRTT	tenant farmer
AAEEFNNPRSST	snap-fastener
AAEEGGGGLLRT	raggle-taggle
AAEEGGIMNRTV	Gram-negative
AAEEGGINORTX	exaggeration
AAEEGGMORRTT	mortgage rate
AAEEGHILNNPT	panel heating
AAEEGHILNRRT	grain leather
AAEEGHLRSSTW	weather-glass
AAEEGILNNORT	generational
AAEEGILNOTTV	vegetational
AAEEGILNPPRT	gelatin paper
AAEEGILNRRST	sterling area
AAEEGILRSSUV	liver sausage
AAEEGIMNTTUV	augmentative
AAEEGIMPSSTU	Septuagesima
AAEEGINNSTUX	exsanguinate
AAEEGJLMNORR	major general
AAEEGLMNORTV	galvanometer
AAEEGLMNRRTV	Great Malvern
AAEEGLNOOPTT	goat-antelope
AAEEGLOPRSSS	opera glasses
AAEEGNNNNRXY	granny annexe
AAEEHHIMPRTT	amphitheater, amphitheatre
AAEEHHIPSSTY	hypaesthesia
AAEEHHORRTTT	heart-to-heart
AAEEHIIKNSST	kinaesthesia
AAEEHIILRTVX	exhilarative
AAEEHILPRSTU	laureateship
AAEEHIMNNPRS	arsphenamine
AAEEHINNRSTU	neurasthenia
AAEEHINPPRRT	heir apparent
AAEEHINRTVWZ	Hertzian wave
AAEEHINSSSTY	synaesthesia
AAEEHINSSTTT	anaesthetist
AAEEHIRRSSTY	East Ayrshire
AAEEHMNORSUW	warehouseman
AAEEIIKKLLTW	walkie-talkie
AAEEIILLMRSS	Marseillaise
AAEEIILLRTTV	alliterative
AAEEIILMORTV	ameliorative
AAEEIINNRRTV	veterinarian
AAEEILLLRSSZ	laissez-aller
AAEEILLMNPST	planetesimal
AAEEILLNORTV	revelational
AAEEILLNRSTW	artesian well
AAEEILLPRSVV	all-pervasive
AAEEILMNRRTW	mineral water
AAEEILMORRST	alstroemeria
AAEEILNORTUV	re-evaluation
AAEEILOPRRTT	proletariate
AAEEIMNNRTTT	reattainment
AAEEIMNPPRTT	apparent time
AAEEIMNPRSTV	private means
AAEEINOPRSTT	entoparasite
AAEEINOPRSTX	exasperation
AAEEINOQTUVW	wave equation
AAEEINORSSTV	asseveration
AAEEINRRSSWW	war-weariness
AAEELLNPRRTY	parenterally
AAEELMMNRTTT	maltreatment
AAEELNNOPPRU	European plan
AAEELNNPSSST	pleasantness
AAEELPQRRTTU	quarter-plate
AAEELQRSSSTU	least squares
AAEEMNNPPRSW	newspaperman
AAEEMNNPRTWY	permanent way
AAEEMNORSSTW	Western Samoa
AAEEMNRSTTTY	testamentary
AAEENNPRSTUU	superannuate
AAEERRRSTTUU	restaurateur
AAEFFGIMORRS	fromage frais
AAEFFQRRSTTU	quarterstaff
AAEFGHHIILNT	faith healing
AAEFGHILLNRT	half-integral
AAEFGHLLNNPR	flannelgraph
AAEFGIKLMNRW	walking frame
AAEFGILLLNOT	flagellation
AAEFGLLLORTY	flagellatory
AAEFGLMNOORR	floor manager
AAEFGNOPRSST	front passage
AAEFHHLOSUWY	halfway house
AAEFHILNRSTW	fathers-in-law
AAEFHIOPRRSS	pair of shears
AAEFIILMORRV	overfamiliar
AAEFILLNSSSY	self-analysis
AAEFILMNRRST	fraternalism
AAEFILNORRTY	reflationary
AAEFILNQRRTU	quarter-final
AAEFLLOPPRSV	self-approval
AAEFLNOQRRTU	quartern loaf
AAEGGGILNNSU	sign language
AAEGGHHIOPRR	hagiographer
AAEGGHMNOPRT	magnetograph
AAEGGHOPRSSU	rough passage
AAEGGINRSTTT	starting gate
AAEGGMNPRSTU	mustang grape
AAEGHHIILMNR	higher animal
AAEGHHIKNRST	earth-shaking
AAEGHILNNOOT	halogenation
AAEGHIMMNPSS	gamesmanship
AAEGHIMNRRTW	heart-warming
AAEGHIMORRRT	metrorrhagia
AAEGHLLNNOTT	ten-gallon hat
AAEGHLMNRSTU	manslaughter
AAEGHNOPRRRU	uranographer
AAEGHNOQRSSU	orange squash
AAEGIILLNNPS	plane sailing
AAEGIILLNOTZ	legalization
AAEGIILNNPVW	plain weaving
AAEGIINNOPRT	repagination
AAEGIINOQSTU	giant sequoia
AAEGIKNNOORV	kangaroo vine
AAEGILLNNTTY	tangentially
AAEGILLRRRUW	guerrilla war
AAEGILNNRRWY	early warning
AAEGILNNSTUY	nauseatingly

AAEGIMNNOTTU	augmentation
AAEGIMNRRSTT	transmigrate
AAEGIMRRSTTU	magistrature
AAEGINRRSSTU	Great Russian
AAEGLLNORTTY	tetragonally
AAEGLMORSSUU	megalosaurus
AAEGMOPPSSTT	postage stamp
AAEHHIINRSTU	hiatus hernia
AAEHHIKNRRSS	Hare Krishnas
AAEHHILMOPTX	exophthalmia
AAEHHIMRRRRS	marsh harrier
AAEHIILMMPTU	epithalamium
AAEHIILNORTX	exhilaration
AAEHIKNOSTTV	Stakhanovite
AAEHILMNPSSS	salesmanship
AAEHILMRSTUY	amateurishly
AAEHIMMRSSTU	shamateurism
AAEHIPPRRSST	star sapphire
AAEIIILMSSTV	assimilative
AAEIILLLPTVY	palliatively
AAEIILLMMRTY	immaterially
AAEIILLNORTT	alliteration
AAEIILMNNOTT	alimentation
AAEIILMNOORT	amelioration
AAEIILMNPTUV	manipulative
AAEIILMOPRRT	imperatorial
AAEIILMRTTUV	multivariate
AAEIILNNOPTZ	penalization
AAEIILNNORTZ	nationalizer
AAEIILNOQTUZ	equalization
AAEIILNORRTZ	rationalizer
AAEIILNORSTT	Aristotelian
AAEIIMNOSSTV	avitaminoses
AAEIINNRSSST	sanitariness
AAEIINOPRRTT	repatriation
AAEIINOPRTTX	expatriation
AAEIINQTTTUV	quantitative
AAEILLLMRTTU	multilateral
AAEILLLNORTY	relationally
AAEILLLNRTUY	unilaterally
AAEILLMNNOUV	nominal value
AAEILLMNNSUY	semi-annually
AAEILLMNRRTY	artilleryman
AAEILLMPRRTY	premaritally
AAEILLMPRRXY	premaxillary
AAEILLOQRTUY	equatorially
AAEILMNORSTV	malversation
AAEILMNPRSTU	planetariums
AAEILMNRSSTT	mistranslate
AAEILNNNPSVY	Pennsylvania
AAEILNNOPTTX	explantation
AAEILNNRSTTU	Saint-Laurent
AAEILNOPSSTY	passionately
AAEILNPRSSTT	plaster saint
AAEILPPQRTUY	quality paper
AAEIMNOOOOPT	onomatopoeia
AAEIMNPSSTTU	Asti spumante
AAEINNOPRSXY	expansionary
AAEINNORSSTU	Austronesian
AAEIPPRRSTTV	private parts
AAEKLMORRTWW	low water mark
AAEKNOQRRSUW	narrow squeak
AAELLMNNORTY	ornamentally
AAELLMRRTUXY	extramurally
AAELLNNPSTUY	unpleasantly
AAELMMNNORRU	Roman numeral
AAELMNNNORTU	unornamental
AAELMNNORTTU	ultramontane
AAELMNPQSTUU	quantum leaps
AAELMOOPRSTZ	spermatozoal
AAELMORSSSUU	elasmosaurus
AAELNNPRRSTT	transplanter
AAELNNPRSTUY	unpleasantry
AAELNORSTTVX	Levant storax
AAELNPRRSTUU	supernatural
AAELNPRSSTUY	sunray pleats
AAELNRSSSTTW	stalwartness
AAELOOPRRTTX	extrapolator
AAEMNNNORSTT	transmontane
AAEMNNOORTUY	neuroanatomy
AAEMNOOPRSTZ	spermatozoan
AAEMNOPRSTTU	portmanteaus
AAEMNOPRTTUX	portmanteaux
AAEOPPRSSTTU	passepartout
AAFFMPRRUUZZ	Muzzaffarpur
AAFIIILNNOTZ	finalization
AAFIILMMNNOT	inflammation
AAFIILNNORTY	inflationary
AAFILMMNOORT	malformation
AAFILMMNORTY	inflammatory
AAFILNNOOSTW	law of nations
AAGGGGILLLNY	lallygagging
AAGGIIINNRTT	ingratiating
AAGGIIKLLNSS	galligaskins
AAGGIKNQRSSU	quaking-grass
AAGHHIMNOWWY	highwaywoman
AAGHIILLRTWY	light railway
AAGHIILMNRST	animal rights
AAGHIPRRSTTY	stratigraphy
AAGHLOOPPRRY	polarography
AAGHOOPPRSSU	saprophagous
AAGIIILLNNPS	plain sailing
AAGIIINNNOTV	invagination
AAGIIINNORTT	ingratiation
AAGIILLLTWWY	willy wagtail
AAGIILLNNPTW	wall painting
AAGIILLNNUVY	unavailingly
AAGIILNNRSUY	sanguinarily
AAGIILNPPRSY	appraisingly
AAGIIMNNNPRZ	marzipanning
AAGIINNOORTZ	organization
AAGIINNORTUU	inauguration
AAGIINPRSTUU	Tupi-Guaranis
AAGILLMNTUWY	mulligatawny
AAGILLNPRSYY	paralysingly
AAGILLNRRTUY	triangularly
AAGILOOPRSTY	parasitology
AAGIMNNOOTTU	mountain goat
AAGIMNNRRSTT	transmigrant
AAGINNOOSTTW	station wagon
AAGINORRTUUY	inauguratory
AAGOPRRRSSSW	sparrow-grass
AAHHINOPRSTT	Parthian shot
AAHHLMOPSTUY	hypothalamus
AAHIIILNNNOT	annihilation
AAHIIMNNOTUZ	humanization
AAHIINOPSTXY	asphyxiation
AAHIINPPRSST	partisanship
AAHIKMMNPRSS	marksmanship
AAHIKMNOSSTV	Stakhanovism

AAHIKNOSSTTV Stakhanovist
AAHILLNNOPSY Pollyannaish
AAHILLNNOPTY antiphonally
AAHILMMOPRTU prothalamium
AAHILMNOOPRT prothalamion
AAHIMNOOPRSS anamorphosis
AAIIILMNOSST assimilation
AAIIILMNOSTZ Islamization
AAIIILMPRTTY impartiality
AAIIILNNOSTZ salinization
AAIIILNNOTTV invitational
AAIIILNNOTTZ Latinization
AAIIILNOTTVZ vitalization
AAIIILORSTTV visitatorial
AAIIIMMNOTXZ maximization
AAIIIMNNRSTU Unitarianism
AAIIIMNOSSTV avitaminosis
AAIIINNOSTTZ sanitization
AAIIINORSTTZ satirization
AAIILLLNNPTY plantain lily
AAIILLNNOSTT installation
AAIILLNORRTY irrationally
AAIILMNNOPTT implantation
AAIILMNNOPTU manipulation
AAIILMNOORTZ moralization
AAIILMNOOTTV motivational
AAIILMNOSSTV salvationism
AAIILMORSSTY assimilatory
AAIILNNNOOTT intonational
AAIILNNNOOTV innovational
AAIILNNORSTT transitional
AAIILNOOPPST appositional
AAIILNOOPRTZ polarization
AAIILNOORSTZ solarization
AAIILNOORTVZ valorization
AAIILNOOTTTZ totalization
AAIILNORRTUZ ruralization
AAIILNOSSTTV salvationist
AAIILNPTTVYY nativity play
AAIILNRSTTTU titular saint
AAIIMNNOORTZ romanization
AAIIMNOORTTZ amortization
AAIINNOQTTUZ quantization
AAIINNORSTTU instauration
AAIINOOPRTVZ vaporization
AAIKMNQRTTUY quantity mark
AAILLMNNOPSY Pollyannaism
AAILLMNOPRTT all-important
AAILLMNOTTUY mutationally
AAILLMNRRTUY intramurally
AAILLNOORTTY rotationally
AAILMNOPRTUY manipulatory
AAILNOOPRSTT rat-tail spoon
AAINNORSTTUU unsaturation
AAINOOORTTTU autorotation
AAIOOPPPRRRT appropriator
AALLMOOPPRST protoplasmal
ABBBCEEHLNOT technobabble
ABBBCEHLOPSY psychobabble
ABBBCIILLTUY clubbability
ABBBDELORYZZ bobby-dazzler
ABBBEESTTTUY test-tube baby
ABBBEGHIILNS Bible-bashing
ABBBEHLMORTU blabbermouth
ABBBGINRRSSU brass rubbing
ABBCCILMNOOV volcanic bomb
ABBCDDGIKLNU dabbling duck
ABBCEEJKMORT bomber jacket
ABBDDEEEHLPS pebble-dashed
ABBDEEFLORSS self-absorbed
ABBDEEGIILRY Bailey bridge
ABBDEEGILNRU unbridgeable
ABBDEGNRRSUU garden suburb
ABBDEHIILRYZ hybridizable
ABBDEILLMRRU umbrella bird
ABBDENRRTTUY brandy butter
ABBDGIILNOTU boat-building
ABBDILMOOPSS bomb disposal
ABBDILOORRST Bristol board
ABBEEEILLNUV unbelievable
ABBEEFLOORTW Tower of Babel
ABBEEILLNUVY unbelievably
ABBEEILMRRSU reimbursable
ABBEEILOPQRU equiprobable
ABBEELNORSUV unobservable
ABBEELORRRSU rabble-rouser
ABBEENNOTWWY Newtownabbey
ABBEIMNNRRUY binary number
ABBELLLRSTUU tubular bells
ABBGHIILOPRY bibliography
ABCCCEHIILNY bicycle chain
ABCCDEEELPST bespectacled
ABCCDEEHKORR checkerboard
ABCCDEHILMNO chemical bond
ABCCDEHILORU coachbuilder
ABCCDEHLMORU cloud chamber
ABCCDHILNSUW club sandwich
ABCCDIIORRTU circuit board
ABCCEEEHLNRT treble chance
ABCCEEEILLNT table licence
ABCCEEELNORT concelebrate
ABCCEEENORRS arborescence
ABCCEEGINNRU buccaneering
ABCCEEHINRSU buccaneerish
ABCCEEIILNSS inaccessible
ABCCEEILLNOR reconcilable
ABCCEELNNORT concelebrant
ABCCEHIIMNOS biomechanics
ABCCEHILLRUY cherubically
ABCCEHLOOOTX chocolate box
ABCCEIIILRTZ criticizable
ABCCEIILNOOT coenobitical
ABCCEIILNSSY inaccessibly
ABCCEIINRRSU cabin cruiser
ABCCEIKLORRT erratic block
ABCCEILMMNOU communicable
ABCCEILNORTT contractible
ABCCEILORSTU scrobiculate
ABCCEKLMNOOY black economy
ABCCILLOOSTY octosyllabic
ABCCILMMNOUY communicably
ABCCKLNORTUY Black Country
ABCDDEEHNOOR Redondo Beach
ABCDDGIKLNPU black pudding
ABCDDHIILSTU Buddhistical
ABCDEEEHILPR decipherable
ABCDEEEHLORR breech-loader
ABCDEEELNRTU uncelebrated
ABCDEEELNTTU undetectable
ABCDEEFILNOS Beaconsfield

ABCDEEGGLMRS scrambled egg
ABCDEEGIKNOR code-breaking
ABCDEEHOQRRU chequerboard
ABCDEEIILLMN medicine ball
ABCDEEIILLNN indeclinable
ABCDEEILMNSS dissemblance
ABCDEEILMOST domesticable
ABCDEEILNORS considerable
ABCDEEILORSV discoverable
ABCDEEKKLNRU bare-knuckled
ABCDEELNORRU unrecordable
ABCDEELNTTUY undetectably
ABCDEEMNRRSU sacred number
ABCDEFLOORRU forced labour
ABCDEFMOPRUU fume cupboard
ABCDEGHIILNR childbearing
ABCDEGHIKORS shock-brigade
ABCDEGILLNNY belly dancing
ABCDEHHLOOOR bachelorhood
ABCDEHNRRRYY cherry brandy
ABCDEIINNSTZ citizens' band
ABCDEILNORSY considerably
ABCDEILNOSTU discountable
ABCDEINOOPRS proboscidean
ABCDEINRSSSU business card
ABCDELLNOOST second ballot
ABCDELMNOOPU compoundable
ABCDELOOPRUV cupboard love
ABCDGHIINRTW birdwatching
ABCDIINOOPRS proboscidian
ABCDILNOOPTY Platonic body
ABCEEEELPRTT carpet beetle
ABCEEEENPRRT carpenter bee
ABCEEEFFIORR office-bearer
ABCEEEFNRSST benefactress
ABCEEEHLNRSS Aschersleben
ABCEEELMNORT electron beam
ABCEEELNNORU renounceable
ABCEEEMNNRTU cetane number
ABCEEFIILLNY beneficially
ABCEEFINORST sorbefacient
ABCEEGHMRRSU surge chamber
ABCEEGILLLNO eco-labelling
ABCEEGILNORZ recognizable
ABCEEHLNNQUU unquenchable
ABCEEHMMNNRT embranchment
ABCEEHMRSTTU butcher's meat
ABCEEHNOPRTW Newport Beach
ABCEEIILLNPX inexplicable
ABCEEIILNNNT bicentennial
ABCEEIILNRTX inextricable
ABCEEIILPPRT precipitable
ABCEEILNNOTU unnoticeable
ABCEEILNOSSS sociableness
ABCEEINNORSV inobservance
ABCEEIOPRSST step aerobics
ABCEEJKLMRTU lumber-jacket
ABCEELLMSTTU lamb's lettuce
ABCEELLNOOST console table
ABCEELLORSTT secret ballot
ABCEELLRSSSU Brussels lace
ABCEELOPRSTU prosecutable
ABCEEMNNORTU octane number
ABCEENOPRRTU protuberance
ABCEEOOPRRRT baroreceptor
ABCEFHORRRTT craft-brother
ABCEFIILOPRT optical fibre
ABCEFILOPRTY cap of liberty
ABCEGHIILNSS Basic English
ABCEGHIKLLNS black English
ABCEGHILLORR bachelor girl
ABCEGHLORRSU Charlesbourg
ABCEGHORRRTU turbocharger
ABCEGIKLNRRW kerb-crawling
ABCEGILLNOOO Boolean logic
ABCEGILMNOST single combat
ABCEGILNORYZ recognizably
ABCEGILNPRUY burying place
ABCEGILOORTY bacteriology
ABCEGINRRTTU carburetting
ABCEHHILLPTU public health
ABCEHHILOPRS bachelorship
ABCEHHINOOPT technophobia
ABCEHIJKNOTX jack-in-the-box
ABCEHIKNRSSS brackishness
ABCEHILLOPRY hyperbolical
ABCEHILSTTTY chastity belt
ABCEHIRRRRSU crush barrier
ABCEHKLRSSUW swashbuckler
ABCEHKNORSTU sea buckthorn
ABCEHLNNQUUY unquenchably
ABCEIIILLRST liberalistic
ABCEIIILTTXY excitability
ABCEIIIMNORT biometrician
ABCEIILLNPXY inexplicably
ABCEIILMNOPT incompatible
ABCEIILNRTXY inextricably
ABCEIILOORST borosilicate
ABCEIILORSTT cristobalite
ABCEIILORTVY revocability
ABCEIILPRSTY plebiscitary
ABCEIIMMNSTU ambient music
ABCEIINORRRS sonic barrier
ABCEIINORSTT obstetrician
ABCEIIRSTTUW water biscuit
ABCEILLNNOOS inconsolable
ABCEILMMNOTU incommutable
ABCEILMNOPRU pre-Columbian
ABCEILNNOTUY unnoticeably
ABCEIMMNORTU atomic number
ABCEIMNNOPTY tympanic bone
ABCELLLNOORT controllable
ABCELLLOOSTY octosyllable
ABCELLNNOOSU unconsolable
ABCELNOPRRUU unprocurable
ABCELNORSTTU counterblast
ABCEMOOPSSSW bow-compasses
ABCENORSSSSU scabrousness
ABCENOSSTUUU subcutaneous
ABCFFHOORRSU Coff's Harbour
ABCFLNOOORRU fluorocarbon
ABCGIILLLOOY biologically
ABCHIIKLOSTY shockability
ABCHIMORSSTX Christmas box
ABCIIIILRSTY irascibility
ABCIIIKLSTTY stickability
ABCIIILNRTUY incurability
ABCIILMNOPTY incompatibly
ABCIILNNOTUY connubiality
ABCIILNOPPRY principal boy

ABCIILORRTUY	orbicularity
ABCILLLMOSYY	symbolically
ABCILLLOPSYY	polysyllabic
ABCILLMNOOSY	monosyllabic
ABCILLNNOOSY	inconsolably
ABCILLNOSSUY	subsonically
ABCILMMNOSTU	noctambulism
ABCILMMNOTUY	incommutably
ABCILMMPSSUU	musical bumps
ABCILMNNOOSU	no-claim bonus
ABCILMNOSTTU	noctambulist
ABCILOOPRRTU	public orator
ABCIMNORSSTU	obscurantism
ABCIMNORSTUU	rambunctious
ABCINORSSTTU	obscurantist
ABCLLLNOORTY	controllably
ABCLLNNOOSUY	unconsolably
ABCOOOORRRRT	corroborator
ABDDDEEEHLOU	double-headed
ABDDEEEHLLTU	bullet-headed
ABDDEEEHLORU	double header
ABDDEEELLORU	double-dealer
ABDDEEELNNPU	undependable
ABDDEEFGILNS	false bedding
ABDDEEGGLORU	double dagger
ABDDEEGINRRR	gardener-bird
ABDDEEGLLOUZ	double-glazed
ABDDEEHLLLUY	bull-headedly
ABDDEEIMNNST	absent-minded
ABDDEGILNNPT	bedding plant
ABDDEILNOOST	bloodstained
ABDDGIINNPSU	pudding basin
ABDDGLNOOORS	dragon's blood
ABDDIIIJNNRY	Yindjibarndi
ABDDNOORTUUW	outward bound
ABDEEEEILMRR	irredeemable
ABDEEEELMNRU	unredeemable
ABDEEEFIILNS	indefeasible
ABDEEEFIRTTW	battered wife
ABDEEEGLRRSW	sedge warbler
ABDEEEIILMRR	irremediable
ABDEEEIILRTV	deliberative
ABDEEEILLRTY	deliberately
ABDEEEILMNRT	determinable
ABDEEEILMRRY	irredeemably
ABDEEEKLORRR	broker-dealer
ABDEEELMNTTT	battlemented
ABDEEELMNTZZ	bedazzlement
ABDEEFHILMRT	half-timbered
ABDEEFIIILNT	identifiable
ABDEEFIILNSY	indefeasibly
ABDEEGGLNORU	double-ganger
ABDEEGHILSTU	East Budleigh
ABDEEGKLLNOW	knowledgable
ABDEEHILMRTW	marbled white
ABDEEHILNPRT	elephant-bird
ABDEEHLNORTU	leather-bound
ABDEEHLNOVYY	heavenly body
ABDEEHNORTUW	weather-bound
ABDEEIIILTTV	debilitative
ABDEEIIKLRST	East Kilbride
ABDEEIILMRRY	irremediably
ABDEEIILNORT	deliberation
ABDEEILMNOPR	imponderable
ABDEEILMRSSS	disassembler
ABDEEILPRSTU	disreputable
ABDEEIMMPPRU	paid-up member
ABDEEIMOPPRR	bromide paper
ABDEEKNORRRS	banker's order
ABDEELLLORRR	rollerblader
ABDEELMNORST	demonstrable
ABDEENORSSTU	obdurateness
ABDEFFHLORSU	shuffle-board
ABDEFGHIOORT	right of abode
ABDEFGILNOTT	floating debt
ABDEFIIILNTY	identifiably
ABDEGHIRRSTT	straight-bred
ABDEGIKNOPRW	baking powder
ABDEGILLLNNY	belly landing
ABDEGINORRTT	batting order
ABDEGJNSTUUU	unsubjugated
ABDEGLNORTTU	battleground
ABDEHHLMOORR	rhombohedral
ABDEHHNOSSUU	house-husband
ABDEHIIILMNS	diminishable
ABDEHIILSSST	disestablish
ABDEHILMNNST	blandishment
ABDEHILNOORS	dishonorable
ABDEHLMMOUWY	double whammy
ABDEHNORUYZZ	honey buzzard
ABDEIIILMNSS	inadmissible
ABDEIIILNOTT	debilitation
ABDEIIILRSTY	desirability
ABDEIILNPSTU	indisputable
ABDEIILNRTUY	endurability
ABDEIILORSTU	sub-editorial
ABDEILLOPRRX	pillar-box red
ABDEILMNOPRY	imponderably
ABDEILPRSTUY	disreputably
ABDEIMORSTUX	ambidextrous
ABDEINORRRSU	sound barrier
ABDEINRTTTUU	unattributed
ABDEKNNORVWY	Vandyke brown
ABDELMNORSTY	demonstrably
ABDELNPQRUUY	pulque brandy
ABDEMOORRTTW	bottom drawer
ABDFGIILLLNO	bill of lading
ABDFIILNNRUU	infundibular
ABDFIILNOOOV	bioflavonoid
ABDGGIILNNOR	bridging loan
ABDGHINOOSWX	shadow-boxing
ABDGIILOOORY	radiobiology
ABDGIINNOORR	ironing board
ABDGILNORRUU	burial ground
ABDGIMNNNORU	mourning-band
ABDGINNNORRU	running-board
ABDGINNOORSW	snowboarding
ABDHHINPSSSU	ship's husband
ABDHLLNNOORW	brown holland
ABDIIIILNTUY	inaudibility
ABDIIILMNSSY	inadmissibly
ABDIIILRSSUY	subsidiarily
ABDIIIRSSTUY	subsidiarity
ABDIILNPSTUY	indisputably
ABDIIRRSTTUY	distributary
ABEEEGILLOTV	vegetable oil
ABEEEGILNORT	renegotiable
ABEEEHKLRSTT	bletherskate
ABEEEHKORRRS	horsebreaker
ABEEEHKORRSU	housebreaker

ABEEEIKLLNSS likeableness
ABEEEILLNRSS reliableness
ABEEEILLNSSV liveableness
ABEEEILMNPRT impenetrable
ABEEEIMMNSST semi-basement
ABEEEIMNQSTU mesquite bean
ABEEEINRRTTV invertebrate
ABEEELLMRRTU umbrella tree
ABEEELMNNORV lemon verbena
ABEEELNSSSSS baselessness
ABEEELQRSSTU sequestrable
ABEEEORRRRTV reverberator
ABEEEPRRSTTY presbyterate
ABEEFFILNRSU insufferable
ABEEFGOPRTUY age of puberty
ABEEFIILLMSU emulsifiable
ABEEFIILLRTZ fertilizable
ABEEFIILNRUV unverifiable
ABEEFLLMSSSY self-assembly
ABEEGGIILNOR globigerinae
ABEEGGILNRSS beggarliness
ABEEGHLORSTT East Bergholt
ABEEGIKNPSTU speaking-tube
ABEEGILNNSST tangibleness
ABEEGINOPRST pigeon-breast
ABEEGINORRTT bitter orange
ABEEGLNNORUV ungovernable
ABEEHHOORSST horseshoe bat
ABEEHIILMPRS imperishable
ABEEHIKLRSTT blatherskite
ABEEHILLMORT thermolabile
ABEEHILPPRSU sapphire blue
ABEEHILPRSST pre-establish
ABEEHILRRSTW Welsh rarebit
ABEEHLLRSSTY breathlessly
ABEEHLMORSTT thermostable
ABEEHLORSTTW bottle-washer
ABEEIILLRSTZ sterilizable
ABEEIILMNNRT interminable
ABEEIILMNRTX intermixable
ABEEIILMPRTY permeability
ABEEIILNOPTT petitionable
ABEEIILNPSST pitiableness
ABEEIILNRTVY venerability
ABEEIILNRTWY renewability
ABEEIILORTTV obliterative
ABEEIKLLLMRU umbrella-like
ABEEILLMNPRU umbrella pine
ABEEILLMNSSY assembly line
ABEEILLNNRUV invulnerable
ABEEILLORRSV irresolvable
ABEEILLPRUVZ pulverizable
ABEEILLRSTVY livery stable
ABEEILMNPRTY impenetrably
ABEEILMNRRSU serial number
ABEEILMOPRTZ problematize
ABEEILNOQSTU questionable
ABEEILNSSSTU suitableness
ABEEILOORSSV basso-relievo
ABEEILPRRSTY presbyterial
ABEEILRRSTTW water blister
ABEEIMNRSTTU steam turbine
ABEEINORRTTV vertebration
ABEEINPRRSTY Presbyterian
ABEEIPRRTTUV perturbative
ABEEKLMORRTU troublemaker
ABEEKLNORSSW workableness
ABEEKMRRSTUY buyer's market
ABEEKORRSSTT breaststroke
ABEELLMNOPUY unemployable
ABEELLMOOPRT temporal lobe
ABEELLNORSTW snowball tree
ABEELLNORSUV unresolvable
ABEELLORSTUW water-soluble
ABEELMMNNOTZ emblazonment
ABEELNNSSSTU unstableness
ABEELNOPRSST portableness
ABEELNOSSSTU absoluteness
ABEELNOSSTUV solvent abuse
ABEELOORSTUZ absolute zero
ABEEMMRRSSTU breastsummer
ABEEMNQRRSUU square number
ABEENPRTTTUU peanut butter
ABEENRSSSSTU abstruseness
ABEFFGGHIOTT gift of the gab
ABEFFIIILNTY ineffability
ABEFFILNRSUY insufferably
ABEFGIKNOSST king of beasts
ABEFGILNORUV unforgivable
ABEFHHILLLOT bill of health
ABEFILNOPRTU unprofitable
ABEFKNOORRST transfer-book
ABEFLNOSSSTU boastfulness
ABEFLNOSSSUU fabulousness
ABEGGHIOOPRY biogeography
ABEGGIILLNOR globigerinal
ABEGGIILNORS globigerinas
ABEGHHKORRTU breakthrough
ABEGHJNNORSU Johannesburg
ABEGIINRSSSU agribusiness
ABEGIKLNNOOR book learning
ABEGILLLNOWY bowling alley
ABEGILLNOOST balneologist
ABEGILLNOSTT losing battle
ABEGIMMNORTU Mount Gambier
ABEGINOQRTUU bouquet garni
ABEGLLLOSSSU soluble glass
ABEGLNNORUVY ungovernably
ABEHIIILRTTY heritability
ABEHIILLNORV hobnail liver
ABEHIILMPRSY imperishably
ABEHIILNNRTY labyrinthine
ABEHIILNOPST inhospitable
ABEHIIMORSUV behaviourism, misbehaviour
ABEHIIORSTUV behaviourist
ABEHIKLNNRSU unshrinkable
ABEHILNNPSUU unpunishable
ABEHILNOPTYZ hypnotizable
ABEHILNORRTW brother-in-law
ABEHLMOPSSSY assembly shop
ABEHLORRSTTY erythroblast
ABEHNORSTTUU hunt saboteur
ABEIIILLLRTY illiberality
ABEIIILLNNRT brilliantine
ABEIIJLNOTYY enjoyability
ABEIIKMNNOTU mountain bike
ABEIILLLMPTU multipliable
ABEIILLORTTY tolerability
ABEIILMMORTY memorability

ABEIILMNNRTY interminably
ABEIILMORTVY removability
ABEIILMPTTTY temptability
ABEIILNNTTUY untenability
ABEIILNOORTT obliteration
ABEIILNRRRTY interlibrary
ABEIILOORSSV basso-rilievo
ABEIILOQRRTU equilibrator
ABEIIMNOORTV overambition
ABEIIMNRSTUU subminiature
ABEIIMOQRSTU Barquisimeto
ABEIINRRSTTW brain-twister
ABEIKNPRSSSU business park
ABEILLNNRUVY invulnerably
ABEILLNORRTU interlobular
ABEILLOPRRVY proverbially
ABEILLRRSTUY treasury bill
ABEILMOSSTUY abstemiously
ABEILNOQSTUY questionably
ABEILNORSSUY Byelorussian
ABEILNORTTXY exorbitantly
ABEILNPRSSUU Prussian blue
ABEIMNRSSTYY binary system
ABEINOOPRRST reabsorption
ABEINOPRRTTU perturbation
ABELLLLOPSYY polysyllable
ABELLLMNOOSY monosyllable
ABELMMOORSSY assembly room
ABELMNORSTUU surmountable
ABELNORSSTUU nebulous star
ABFGHIIMNORT habit-forming
ABFGILNORUVY unforgivably
ABFIIILLNORT fibrillation
ABFIIILNNOTU infibulation
ABFILNOPRTUY unprofitably
ABFLLLOOOOPT football pool
ABGGILLNOSSW glass-blowing
ABGGILNNRSSU burning-glass
ABGHHOORSSTU thorough bass
ABGHIIMMNSTW swimming bath
ABGHIINNNOSU union-bashing
ABGHILNOSSTT shot-blasting
ABGIIIILNTTY ignitability
ABGIIILLMNSU bilingualism
ABGIILLMRSUW Williamsburg
ABGIILLOORTY obligatorily
ABGIMNNOOSUU non-ambiguous
ABHIIKMNNPRS brinkmanship
ABHIILMOPSUY amphibiously
ABHIILNOPSTY inhospitably
ABHIINOPRSTV vibraphonist
ABHIMNNORRTU Northumbrian
ABIIIILRRTTY irritability
ABIIILLPSTUY plausibility
ABIIILMMOTVY immovability
ABIIILMMTTUY immutability
ABIIILMNOOST abolitionism
ABIIILMNOOTZ mobilization
ABIIILNOOSTT abolitionist
ABIIILNPRTTY printability
ABIIILNRSTUY insurability
ABIIILOPTTVY pivotability
ABIILLLMNSUY subliminally
ABIILNORSSUU insalubrious
ABIIMNORSTTU tambourinist
ABIINOOORTTZ robotization
ABILLLNOOOPT pilot balloon
ABILLORSSUUY salubriously
ABILMMMNOSSU somnambulism
ABILMMNOSSTU somnambulist
ABILMNORSTUY subnormality
ABIMNORSSTTU nimbostratus
ABIMOOOQSTTU mosquito-boat
ABINOORRTTUW rainbow trout
ABKKLNOOPRRY Brooklyn Park
ABLMOSSSTTUY status symbol
ABNOORRSSTUU brontosaurus
ACCCCDIIINSU succinic acid
ACCCCEIILRRT Arctic Circle
ACCCDEEIRSST direct access
ACCCEEEELNRS recalescence
ACCCEEEINQSU acquiescence
ACCCEEEINSTX exact science
ACCCEEIILSST ecclesiastic
ACCCEEILLLTY eclectically
ACCCEGIINNOR carcinogenic
ACCCEHINORTT technocratic
ACCCEHKLORTW clock-watcher
ACCCEIJMNRTU circumjacent
ACCCEIMNNOOT concomitance
ACCCEIMNRSTU circumstance
ACCCGHINOSTU casting couch
ACCCHHIILLOT chalcolithic
ACCCHIIOPRRT chiropractic
ACCCHIIOPRSZ schizocarpic
ACCCHIKOSSTT shock tactics
ACCCIIILLOSS loci classici
ACCCIILNNOTY anticyclonic
ACCCIILNOOST iconoclastic
ACCCILLLNOYY cyclonically
ACCCIMNNOOTY concomitancy
ACCDDEHINOOP dodecaphonic
ACCDDEIIIOPR periodic acid
ACCDDEIILLNO Old Icelandic
ACCDDEIINORT endocarditic
ACCDEEEFFKLR freckle-faced
ACCDEEEHLMNY chance-medley
ACCDEEEHLSSU duchesse lace
ACCDEEEKSSTT cassette deck
ACCDEEENORST deconsecrate
ACCDEEFILLMS Macclesfield
ACCDEEILNOPY encyclopedia
ACCDEEILORVY over-delicacy
ACCDEEINNNST incandescent
ACCDEEINNORT concertinaed
ACCDEEINORTX exotic dancer
ACCDEELMORTT clotted cream
ACCDEELNOPRS corpse-candle
ACCDEELOOPRU Cape Coloured
ACCDEENOSSUU succedaneous
ACCDEGHORTUU Dutch courage
ACCDEGIILRSY lysergic acid
ACCDEGNNORRT concert grand
ACCDEHHNRRUW churchwarden
ACCDEHILMOPS accomplished
ACCDEHIOORSU orchidaceous
ACCDEHIORSTV scratch video
ACCDEHLNNORR corn chandler
ACCDEIIILLNO linoleic acid
ACCDEIIILNST insecticidal

ACCDEIILLOPY epicycloidal
ACCDEIILMOUX calcium oxide
ACCDEIILNNOT coincidental
ACCDEIILORST social credit
ACCDEIINORTT direct action
ACCDEILLNOTY occidentally
ACCDEIMNORTU undemocratic
ACCDEMNOSTUU unaccustomed
ACCDENNORTUY country dance
ACCDFIIILMNU fulminic acid
ACCDFIIINOOT codification
ACCDHILOORSU chlorous acid
ACCDHINOTTUU Dutch auction
ACCDIINOORST accordionist
ACCDINOORRTT contradictor
ACCDLNNOORTY concordantly
ACCEEEHILPSV space vehicle
ACCEEEHILRRT electric hare
ACCEEENORRST reconsecrate
ACCEEFGIIMNN magnificence
ACCEEFIIPRRT fire practice
ACCEEFLNORRU nuclear force
ACCEEGHNNORX corn exchange
ACCEEGINNORS recognisance
ACCEEGINNORZ recognizance
ACCEEHIILNPT encephalitic
ACCEEHILMOPS mesocephalic
ACCEEHILRRST Richter scale
ACCEEHIRRTTU architecture
ACCEEHLMNRSY sclerenchyma
ACCEEHMNNORT encroachment
ACCEEHNOSTTT contact sheet
ACCEEIINNORT interoceanic
ACCEEIINPPRT precipitance
ACCEEIINRSTV sciatic nerve
ACCEEILLLRTY electrically
ACCEEILLMNUY ecumenically
ACCEEILLSSSU Celsius scale
ACCEEILMNORS moral science
ACCEEILMPPRT pre-eclamptic
ACCEEILNRTTY tetracycline
ACCEEIMNOTTY actinomycete
ACCEEIORSTTT stereotactic
ACCEELNNOSTV convalescent
ACCEELNNRSTU translucence
ACCEELPRRWYY creepy-crawly
ACCEEMNORTTU accouterment, accoutrement
ACCEENOPRRSU precancerous
ACCEFFIIJKNO jack-in-office
ACCEFGIIINNS significance
ACCEFIILLPSY specifically
ACCEFIILLRST self-critical
ACCEGIIJRSTU gastric juice
ACCEGIILMOST cleistogamic
ACCEGIINNNOZ incognizance
ACCEGILLLOOY ecologically
ACCEGILLNOOR necrological
ACCEGILNNORT Anglocentric
ACCEGILNORSU lacing course
ACCEGILNOSUW wages council
ACCEGINNNOVY conveyancing
ACCEGNOORRTY gerontocracy
ACCEHIILLMRY chimerically
ACCEHIILLNST callisthenic
ACCEHIILMOOR heroi-comical
ACCEHIILNOPR necrophiliac
ACCEHIILNSST calisthenics
ACCEHIILNTTY technicality
ACCEHIKMNSTY chimney stack
ACCEHILLLORY cholerically
ACCEHILMOPRY microcephaly
ACCEHILNNNOT non-technical
ACCEHILNOOOT echolocation
ACCEHILOPRTY chalcopyrite
ACCEHIMNORRS Cornish cream
ACCEHIMNORST mechatronics
ACCEHIMORTTT thermotactic
ACCEHINNNOPT pantechnicon
ACCEHINRSSST scratchiness
ACCEHIOPSTVY psychoactive
ACCEHKLOOSVZ Czechoslovak
ACCEHLNOPSUY cynocephalus
ACCEHMNORRTU countermarch
ACCEHMOPSTUU moustache cup
ACCEIIILNOTV conciliative
ACCEIIILPSST specialistic
ACCEIIKKMNRS camiknickers
ACCEIILLLNTY enclitically
ACCEIILMMORT microclimate
ACCEIILMORRT calorimetric
ACCEIILMRRSU semicircular
ACCEIILNRRSY acrylic resin
ACCEIILNRSST criticalness
ACCEIILORRTV overcritical
ACCEIIMNORRT craniometric
ACCEIIMORRTT meritocratic
ACCEIINORTUX excruciation
ACCEIINPPRTY precipitancy
ACCEIIPPRSTY perspicacity
ACCEILLMMORY commercially
ACCEILLMNOOY economically
ACCEILLMOSTY cosmetically
ACCEILLNOTTY tectonically
ACCEILLOPRRY reciprocally
ACCEILMMNORU uncommercial
ACCEILMNNOOU uneconomical
ACCEILMNORTU counter-claim
ACCEILNNNOOT connectional
ACCEILNNOOPT conceptional
ACCEILNNOOSS concessional
ACCEILNNOOTV convectional
ACCEILNOORRT correctional
ACCEILNOSSSU successional
ACCEINNNNOOS inconsonance
ACCEINNOORST consecration
ACCEINOOPRTU reoccupation
ACCEIOOPRRRT reciprocator
ACCELLMNOPTY complacently
ACCELLNOPTUY conceptually
ACCELMNOOSSY economy class
ACCELMOOSTTY cyclostomate
ACCELNNRSTUY translucency
ACCELNOOPPRY cyclopropane
ACCENNOORRTT concentrator
ACCENOORRSTY consecratory
ACCENOPRRSTU counterscarp
ACCFIIMNNOSU Confucianism
ACCFIINNOOST confiscation
ACCFIINNOSTU Confucianist

ACCFILLNOOTU	flocculation
ACCFILNOORUW	council of war
ACCFINOORSTY	confiscatory
ACCGHHIOOPRR	chorographic
ACCGHIIKNORR	rocking chair
ACCGHIINOOPR	iconographic
ACCGHIIOPPRT	pictographic
ACCGHILLOOPY	phycological
ACCGHIMOOPRS	cosmographic
ACCGIILLOOOS	sociological
ACCGILLMOOOS	cosmological
ACCGILMNOOOS	cosmogonical
ACCGILNORTUY	granulocytic
ACCHHIIOPRTT	trichopathic
ACCHHIOPPSTY	psychopathic
ACCHIIINSTUV	chauvinistic
ACCHIILOPRTY	hypocritical
ACCHIIMMORST	chromaticism
ACCHIIMOORST	isochromatic
ACCHIIMORRTT	trichromatic
ACCHIIMORTTY	chromaticity
ACCHIIOPRSTY	physiocratic
ACCHILLNNOOO	non-alcoholic
ACCHILLOPTTY	phyllotactic
ACCHILOOOPRS	horoscopical
ACCHILOOPSSY	psychosocial
ACCHILOPPRTY	prophylactic
ACCHIOOPRRRT	chiropractor
ACCIIILNNOOT	conciliation
ACCIIINRSSST	narcissistic
ACCIILLNRTUY	uncritically
ACCIILMNOOPT	complication
ACCIILNOORTY	conciliatory
ACCIILOOPPRS	polariscopic
ACCIILOPRSUY	capriciously
ACCIIMOOPRTT	compatriotic
ACCIINNOOOST	consociation
ACCIJLNNOTUV	conjunctival
ACCIJNNOOTTU	joint account
ACCIJNNOSTUV	conjunctivas
ACCILLMNOOSU	malocclusion
ACCILMNNOOUW	councilwoman
ACCIMMNOORTU	communicator
ACCIMNOOSTUU	contumacious
ACCINNOPRTTT	contact print
ACCKMNOOPSTY	stock company
ACCMNORSTUUU	autumn crocus
ACCNOOPRSTTT	contact sport
ACDDDEEHNOOR	dodecahedron
ACDDEEEFLSTU	self-educated
ACDDEEEHIMST	semi-detached
ACDDEEELLTUW	well-educated
ACDDEEFIIRTT	trade deficit
ACDDEEHINNRS	Dresden china
ACDDEEHLLNOR	candleholder
ACDDEEIINORT	rededication
ACDDEELLOORV	collared dove
ACDDEENNOSTV	second advent
ACDDEFNNNOOR	cannon fodder
ACDDEGHIMNRW	wedding march
ACDDEGHINRSU	undischarged
ACDDEGHNRSSU	grand duchess
ACDDEGIILLNO	dialling code
ACDDEHILRSTT	ladder stitch
ACDDEHILSSTT	saddle stitch
ACDDEHINOORS	deoch an doris
ACDDEIILNORU	radionuclide
ACDDEIINNOTV	non-addictive
ACDDEIINORST	endocarditis
ACDDEILLMOUY	duodecimally
ACDDEILRSTTY	distractedly
ACDDEINPRSTY	candy-striped
ACDDHIMNORYY	hydrodynamic
ACDDHINOORRS	doch an dorris
ACDDILNORSTY	discordantly
ACDDOOORRRUY	corduroy road
ACDEEEEHKLPP	apple-cheeked
ACDEEEGINRTT	cigarette end
ACDEEEGKLLRT	ledger-tackle
ACDEEEGLNOOU	eau de Cologne
ACDEEEGNNRRT	garden centre
ACDEEEHINRUV	underachieve
ACDEEEHMNOSS	damson cheese
ACDEEEILNORT	deceleration
ACDEEEILNRTZ	decentralize
ACDEEEILNRUZ	denuclearize
ACDEEEILNSST	delicateness, delicatessen
ACDEEEILORTV	over-delicate
ACDEEEIMNNOR	earned income
ACDEEEINNRTV	inadvertence
ACDEEEINRSSV	disseverance
ACDEEELNNTTY	antecedently
ACDEEEMNNRRT	remand centre
ACDEEENPRRST	centre spread
ACDEEEOPRRRT	tape recorder
ACDEEFFILNNS	self-financed
ACDEEFFLNTUY	unaffectedly
ACDEEFHHIKNR	handkerchief
ACDEEFHIIRST	fireside chat
ACDEEFHNORRW	henceforward
ACDEEFILMTTU	multifaceted
ACDEEFILOPPR	pride of place
ACDEEFLMMNOO	female condom
ACDEEFNRRSUU	undersurface
ACDEEFOORRRT	terraced roof
ACDEEGGINRRT	greeting card
ACDEEGHILRST	clear-sighted
ACDEEGHLLNNU	unchallenged
ACDEEGILNORS	close-grained
ACDEEGILNRSY	decreasingly
ACDEEGINRSSS	dressing case
ACDEEGNNOSTT	decongestant
ACDEEHHIMORT	hemichordate
ACDEEHIMNRRS	merchandiser
ACDEEHINNPRT	prentice hand
ACDEEHKMRSTU	Deutsche Mark
ACDEEHNNOPRU	unchaperoned
ACDEEIILLMPY	epidemically
ACDEEIILLNTY	indelicately
ACDEEIILLTTY	dietetically
ACDEEIIMNRTY	intermediacy
ACDEEIINNTUV	denunciative
ACDEEIINOPRT	depreciation
ACDEEIINTTUX	inexactitude
ACDEEIJKNNRT	dinner jacket
ACDEEIKLLNPT	nickel-plated
ACDEEIKLOOPS	kaleidoscope
ACDEEILLMNRY	endermically
ACDEEILLNNOS	declensional

ACDEEILLNRSY cylinder seal
ACDEEILMNPST displacement
ACDEEILNNNOU non-Euclidean
ACDEEILNRSTT decentralist
ACDEEILORTVY decoratively
ACDEEIMNNOPR predominance
ACDEEINNRTVY inadvertency
ACDEEINOORRT redecoration
ACDEEIOPPRTU propaedeutic
ACDEEIOPRRTY depreciatory
ACDEEJKKNOTY donkey jacket
ACDEEKMPRRSU muck-spreader
ACDEELNOOSSS closed season
ACDEELOPRRRY record player
ACDEEMNOPPTY appendectomy
ACDEENNNOTUV uncovenanted
ACDEENNNRSTT transcendent
ACDEENNNRTUY undertenancy
ACDEENNORSTU second nature
ACDEFFIINOST disaffection
ACDEFHIINRSS disfranchise
ACDEFHOORSSU house of cards
ACDEFIILMRTY family credit
ACDEFIILNNOT confidential
ACDEFIILNSSU unclassified
ACDEFIINNSTT disinfectant
ACDEFIINNSTU unsanctified
ACDEFILLLOTU folliculated
ACDEFLMNOOPU compound leaf
ACDEGHHILLOP Lochgilphead
ACDEGHIMOPRS demographics
ACDEGHINORSS cross-heading
ACDEGHINPRSY physic garden
ACDEGHIOPRRS discographer
ACDEGIIKMNST magnetic disk
ACDEGIILLNSS sliding scale
ACDEGIILPQRU quadriplegic
ACDEGIINRRRV racing driver
ACDEGIINRRTT credit rating
ACDEGILLOOTY dialectology
ACDEGILNNOST long distance
ACDEGINNORTU undercoating
ACDEGINORRSS cross-grained
ACDEHHILNPRS ship chandler
ACDEHIIMORST radiochemist
ACDEHIKLPRST chalk-striped
ACDEHILLMOTY methodically
ACDEHILMNOTU unmethodical
ACDEHIMNRRSS scrimshander
ACDEHINNOPSW open sandwich
ACDEHINNRSTW Sandwich tern
ACDEHINOORSS icosahedrons
ACDEHIOOPRST orthopaedics
ACDEHMOOORRY Maroochydore
ACDEIIILNTVY indicatively
ACDEIIILRTVY veridicality
ACDEIIIMNNOT nicotinamide
ACDEIIIMNNRS incendiarism
ACDEIIIMNRST discriminate
ACDEIIINPPST appendicitis
ACDEIIIOPRTY aperiodicity
ACDEIIIOSSTV dissociative
ACDEIIIPRRST pericarditis
ACDEIIKLRSTT Lake District
ACDEIILLNNTY incidentally
ACDEIILLOPRY periodically
ACDEIILLOPSY episodically
ACDEIILMNOPT decimal point
ACDEIILRRTUV diverticular
ACDEIIMNORST dominatrices
ACDEIIMNOSTU miseducation
ACDEIINNNOTU denunciation
ACDEIINNORTT indoctrinate
ACDEIINOORTV coordinative
ACDEIINOOTTX detoxication
ACDEIINOSTTU educationist
ACDEIKLMRTTU multi-tracked
ACDEIKMNNORT one-track mind
ACDEIKNORSTT stock-in-trade
ACDEIKORSTTU outside track
ACDEILLMOSTY domestically
ACDEILLOPSTY despotically
ACDEILMNOPRU unproclaimed
ACDEILMNOSUY mendaciously
ACDEILMRSTXY mixed crystal
ACDEILNNORTW ancient world
ACDEILNNOTWW lancet window
ACDEILNOOSST disconsolate
ACDEILNOPPPY Iceland poppy
ACDEILNORSSW cowardliness
ACDEILNTTUUV uncultivated
ACDEILOOPRRT particolored
ACDEILOORRUV varicoloured
ACDEIMMNNOOT commendation
ACDEIMMOOORR Air Commodore
ACDEIMNNNOOT condemnation
ACDEIMNORRRS morris dancer
ACDEINNNOOST condensation
ACDEINNNOSTU unsanctioned
ACDEINNNOSTY Innocents' Day
ACDEINNORTUY denunciatory
ACDEINOPSSTT distance post
ACDEINORSTTU discount rate
ACDEIORRSTUV radius vector
ACDELLOPRRUY procedurally
ACDELNOORTYY cotyledonary
ACDELOPRRTTY protractedly
ACDEMMNOORTY commendatory
ACDEMNNOORTY condemnatory
ACDENNPTTUUU unpunctuated
ACDFGIINNNOT fondant icing
ACDFGIKLNOOT floating dock
ACDFIIIINNOT nidification
ACDFIIIMNOOT modification
ACDFIIMOORTY modificatory
ACDGHHIOPRRY hydrographic
ACDGHIIOPRTT dittographic
ACDGHILLOORY hydrological
ACDGIIINRSTV visiting card
ACDGIILOORST cardiologist
ACDGILMMNNOY commandingly
ACDGILMNOORR corn marigold
ACDGINOOOPRT gonadotropic
ACDHHIILNTWY wild hyacinth
ACDHHINOOPRY hypochondria
ACDHHINOOTWY wood hyacinth
ACDHIILRTUYY hydraulicity
ACDHIIMMORST dichromatism
ACDHIIMNOORT mitochondria
ACDHIINORRSW Windsor chair

ACDHIIOPRSTT dictatorship
ACDHINOOPQRU quadrophonic
ACDHINOPSSTT pitch-and-toss
ACDHIORSSTTY hydrostatics
ACDHLNOOSSUY Sunday school
ACDHLOORSSYY Holy Cross Day
ACDIIILNPRSY disciplinary
ACDIIINOOSST dissociation
ACDIILLMNPTU multiplicand
ACDIILMNOPTU undiplomatic
ACDIILMNPSTU platinum disc
ACDIILNOOQTU coloquintida
ACDIINNOOORT coordination
ACDIINORSSYY idiosyncrasy
ACDILMNOSSUU musical sound
ACDILMNSSTYY syndactylism
ACDILNOOORST consolidator
ACDILNOOPRTU productional
ACDILORSTTUY tridactylous
ACDINNORSTTU transduction
ACDINOOQRSTU conquistador
ACDLNOSSTUYY syndactylous
ACDLOOOPRSTT postdoctoral
ACEEEEFFMNTZ Zeeman effect
ACEEEEFMNPRR map reference
ACEEEEFNRRSS carefreeness
ACEEEEGIKNPP peacekeeping
ACEEEEGILPTX epexegetical
ACEEEEHLPSST steeplechase
ACEEEELMNRTT trace element
ACEEEELNORTT coelenterate
ACEEEENPRRSV perseverance
ACEEEFILLNRS self-reliance
ACEEEFIOPRTW piece of water
ACEEEFLNPSSU peacefulness
ACEEEFLNSSSS facelessness
ACEEEFLRRSTV scarlet fever
ACEEEFNNRRST transference
ACEEEGHIKMNS cheesemaking
ACEEEGHINNRS search engine
ACEEEGHINPRS cheese-paring
ACEEEGIKNRRT racketeering
ACEEEGNNRRUY unregeneracy
ACEEEHHILLLS Achilles heel
ACEEEHHLNRTT health centre
ACEEEHILMRST hermetic seal
ACEEEHILSTTT telaesthetic
ACEEEHIMNQTU cinematheque
ACEEEHIORRVV overachiever
ACEEEHMORTTT cathetometer
ACEEEHNOORRS one-horse race
ACEEEHORRSTU terrace house
ACEEEIJNOSTT ejection seat
ACEEEILLNPST license plate
ACEEEILNNNSV Valenciennes
ACEEEIMMNNPR impermanence
ACEEEIMNNPRT intemperance
ACEEEIMNRSVX ex-serviceman
ACEEEINRSSTV creativeness
ACEEEIPPPRTV apperceptive
ACEEEIPRRTUV recuperative
ACEEEKNNNRTT Tennant Creek
ACEEELLOPRTT electroplate
ACEEELNNSTVY evanescently
ACEEELNOTXYY oxyacetylene
ACEEELNRSSSS carelessness
ACEEEMNNNRTT entrancement
ACEEENNRRTTY tercentenary
ACEEENNRSTXY sexcentenary
ACEEENRRRSTU return crease
ACEEFFFGILNS self-effacing
ACEEFFGHILNO change of life
ACEEFFGLLOST staff college
ACEEFFILTTUY effectuality
ACEEFFINOPTT patent office
ACEEFFINOTTU effectuation
ACEEFGILLNNS self-cleaning
ACEEFGILNRST self-catering
ACEEFGLNRSSU gracefulness
ACEEFGNNOOST age of consent
ACEEFHIIKMNN knife machine
ACEEFHIINSST chieftainess
ACEEFHINNOSU finance house
ACEEFHLOPRRS self-reproach
ACEEFHLOPRST chapel of rest
ACEEFHOPPRST part of speech
ACEEFIILNQTU liquefacient
ACEEFIILQTUV liquefactive
ACEEFIKNNNRS frankincense
ACEEFILLNRTY frenetically
ACEEFILNORST self-creation
ACEEFILOPRRT prefectorial
ACEEFIMPRRTU picture frame
ACEEFINORSSU surface noise
ACEEFINPRTTU putrefacient
ACEEFINPSTTU stupefacient
ACEEFIPRTTUV putrefactive
ACEEFLOPPRST craftspeople
ACEEFMNORSST centre of mass
ACEEGGHINNRR change-ringer
ACEEGHILNOSU chaise longue, chaise lounge
ACEEGHINNORX ion-exchanger
ACEEGHINOPTT pathogenetic
ACEEGHIRRSST cash register
ACEEGHLLNSSY changelessly
ACEEGHLNRTUY legacy-hunter
ACEEGHMNNORY money changer
ACEEGHNOPRRS scenographer
ACEEGHNOPSTX post exchange
ACEEGHPRRRSU supercharger
ACEEGIILNNPT palingenetic
ACEEGIILNSTV evangelistic
ACEEGIIMMNNT magnetic mine
ACEEGIIMNORT geometrician
ACEEGIKMSSST message stick
ACEEGIKNNRRV nerve-racking
ACEEGILLLOOT teleological
ACEEGILLLOTY collegiately
ACEEGILMNOPT magnetic pole
ACEEGILNPRST resting place
ACEEGILNPSTT place setting
ACEEGILQRRSU squirrel cage
ACEEGIMNORTY atomic energy
ACEEGIMNRSTW West Germanic
ACEEGINNRSTV ingravescent
ACEEGINNSSTX exactingness
ACEEGLLOOOPY paleoecology
ACEEGLMNOORT conglomerate
ACEEHHIOPRTT heteropathic

ACEEHHIPRRSU hire purchase
ACEEHHIPSTTY hypaesthetic
ACEEHHKNPPRU Kerenhappuch
ACEEHHLLORTT leathercloth
ACEEHHLNORSU charnel house
ACEEHHLORRSY charley horse
ACEEHHMOPRTY chemotherapy
ACEEHHOPRSTU chapter house
ACEEHIIKNSTT kinaesthetic
ACEEHIILNPST encephalitis
ACEEHIIMSSTT aestheticism
ACEEHIINORTT theoretician
ACEEHIINRSTW white arsenic
ACEEHIINSTUU haute cuisine
ACEEHILLMORS hemerocallis
ACEEHILLMRTY hermetically
ACEEHIMNSSTT chastisement
ACEEHIMRSSTV Christmas Eve
ACEEHIMRSTTU music theatre
ACEEHINNOSST inchoateness
ACEEHINNRSTU neurasthenic
ACEEHINORUUV nouveau riche
ACEEHINSSTTY synaesthetic
ACEEHIOPRTTU eutrophicate
ACEEHIPRSTTU therapeutics
ACEEHKLMORTW water hemlock
ACEEHLLOORSV school leaver
ACEEHLLRRRUY cherry laurel
ACEEHLMNNOTU luncheon meat
ACEEHLNOOPPR anchorpeople
ACEEHLPSSTTU space shuttle
ACEEHNNOPRRT Northern Cape
ACEEHOPPRRRS sharecropper
ACEEHORTTUUU haute couture
ACEEIILLRTTV verticillate
ACEEIILMRSTY semi-literacy
ACEEIILNOSTZ sectionalize
ACEEIIMMRSTT meristematic
ACEEIIMNNORT enantiomeric
ACEEIIMNPRSU Epicureanism
ACEEIINNORTZ containerize
ACEEIINNRTUV renunciative
ACEEIINORSTV evisceration
ACEEIKLLTTTT kittle-cattle
ACEEIKNNRSTT tennis racket
ACEEIKNOSSTT season ticket
ACEEIKNPRTTY necktie party
ACEEILLLNTTU intellectual
ACEEILLMMRSY mesmerically
ACEEILLMNORY ceremonially
ACEEILLMNSTY centesimally
ACEEILLMORTY meteorically
ACEEILLNNORT crenellation
ACEEILLNRSUV surveillance
ACEEILLOPRSS solar eclipse
ACEEILLOPSTT total eclipse
ACEEILLORSTY esoterically
ACEEILLRTTUY reticulately
ACEEILMMNPST misplacement
ACEEILMNNOTV nomenclative
ACEEILMNPRST prince's metal
ACEEILNNRRTU internuclear
ACEEILNOPPRT perceptional
ACEEILNOPRRT electron pair
ACEEILNOPRSS precessional
ACEEILOPPRRT preceptorial
ACEEILPPRSTV perspectival
ACEEIMMMNOTT committee man
ACEEIMMNNPRY impermanency
ACEEIMNOPSTV compensative
ACEEIMNORSSX cross-examine
ACEEIMNORSVW servicewoman
ACEEINNRRTTY tricentenary
ACEEINOORRTV overreaction
ACEEINOPPPRT apperception
ACEEINOPRRTU recuperation
ACEEINOPRSTT inspectorate
ACEEINORRSSY recessionary
ACEEINORSTVV conservative
ACEEINORTUXY executionary
ACEEIPRRRTUV river capture
ACEEJKKMNOTY monkey-jacket
ACEEKPRRTTUY Turkey carpet
ACEELLMMNOPT complemental
ACEELLPPRTUY perceptually
ACEELMNNORTU nomenclature
ACEELMNOOSTU lomentaceous
ACEELMNOPTTU outplacement
ACEELMORSSST Maltese cross
ACEELMPRRTUU permaculture
ACEELNOPRRUW nuclear power
ACEELNORTUUV countervalue
ACEELNSSSSTT tactlessness
ACEELOQRRSTU close-quarter
ACEELPSSTUUY eucalyptuses
ACEEMMNORSTU commensurate
ACEEMNNNNOTU announcement
ACEEMNNORRST remonstrance
ACEEMOPRSTTY spermatocyte
ACEENNOORTUV tonneau cover
ACEENOPRSTUU percutaneous
ACEEOOPRRTTT protectorate
ACEEOOPRRTTX expectorator
ACEFFFFHIOST Chief of Staff
ACEFFFFIORST staff officer
ACEFFFIMOORS office of arms
ACEFFIIILMOS semi-official
ACEFFILNNSSU fancifulness
ACEFFORRSUUU furfuraceous
ACEFGHIINRTW fire-watching
ACEFGHILOPRX flexographic
ACEFGIIILMNS facsimileing
ACEFGIIKNNRV carving knife
ACEFGIILLNOT legal fiction
ACEFGILNRSUY flying saucer
ACEFGLLNRUUY ungracefully
ACEFHIIMNRTU fruit machine
ACEFHLNSSTUW watchfulness
ACEFHMNNNORR Norman French
ACEFHNORSTTU countershaft
ACEFHORRSSTU rhesus factor
ACEFIIILNOTT felicitation
ACEFIIILNOTZ fictionalize
ACEFIIINORTV verification
ACEFIILLNNOT inflectional
ACEFIILLRRTY terrifically
ACEFIILMNORR informercial
ACEFIILNOQTU liquefaction
ACEFIILORTUV curvifoliate
ACEFIILSTTVY self-activity

ACEFIIMNORTV confirmative
ACEFIINOORTV vociferation
ACEFIINOPRTT petrifaction
ACEFILLNORSY forensically
ACEFILNNOOSS confessional
ACEFILORRRTY refractorily
ACEFINNOTUVW wave function
ACEFINOORRTT torrefaction
ACEFINOPRTTU putrefaction
ACEFINOPSTTU stupefaction
ACEFINOSSSTU factiousness
ACEFLLMOOPRW camp follower
ACEFLLOORSSU false colours
ACEFLOOPRSST float process
ACEFNOPRRSST craftsperson
ACEGGIILLNSS glass ceiling
ACEGGIILNNST single-acting
ACEGGIKRSSTW swagger stick
ACEGGILLLOOY geologically
ACEGGIMNORTY gyromagnetic
ACEGGINNOORT congregation
ACEGHHINOPRT ethnographic
ACEGHHOOPRRR chorographer
ACEGHHOOPRRY choreography
ACEGHIILLNYY hygienically
ACEGHIIMOTTW atomic weight
ACEGHILLNNOU hallucinogen
ACEGHILLNOOT ethnological
ACEGHILMOPYY hypoglycemia
ACEGHILNNNTY enchantingly
ACEGHILNOPRV graphic novel
ACEGHILOPRXY lexicography
ACEGHIMOPTTY gametophytic
ACEGHINNRSTU Gunter's chain
ACEGHINOOPRR iconographer
ACEGHINOPRST stenographic
ACEGHIOPPRRR reprographic
ACEGHIOPPRRT petrographic
ACEGHIORRSST rags-to-riches
ACEGHIRRSTTT garter stitch
ACEGHLMNOOUY human ecology
ACEGHMOOPRRS cosmographer
ACEGHOPPRRST spectrograph
ACEGIIILLMTY illegitimacy
ACEGIIINSTTV negativistic
ACEGIIKKMNTY mickey-taking
ACEGIILLLOTY collegiality
ACEGIILLMOOS semiological
ACEGIILLNRRV Invercargill
ACEGIILLOOPT geopolitical
ACEGIILLOSTY egoistically
ACEGIILNNOTY congeniality
ACEGIILNNRSY increasingly
ACEGIILORSSU sacrilegious
ACEGIINOOTTX excogitation
ACEGIKLNORSS cross-linkage
ACEGILLMOORT metrological
ACEGILLMOOTY etymological
ACEGILLNNOTY congenitally
ACEGILLNOORU neurological
ACEGILLNORSY early closing
ACEGILLNORVW wallcovering
ACEGILLOOOST osteological
ACEGILLOOPRT petrological
ACEGILLOOPST pestological
ACEGILMMOPSY Olympic Games
ACEGILNNNRTY entrancingly
ACEGILNOOPRT organoleptic
ACEGILNOOPTU unapologetic
ACEGILOOPSST escapologist
ACEGILORSTTU gesticulator
ACEGIMNNORSU cousin german
ACEGIMNPRSUU measuring cup
ACEGINORSSSU graciousness
ACEGLNOOPRSY laryngoscope
ACEGLOORSUUY courageously
ACEHHIILNOPT technophilia
ACEHHIINOPRT hierophantic
ACEHHILMOPTX exophthalmic
ACEHHILOOPST theosophical
ACEHHILOPTTY hypothetical
ACEHHIMNPRST merchant ship
ACEHHIMOOOPT homoeopathic
ACEHHINOPRTT theanthropic
ACEHHKOPRSTY shock therapy
ACEHHMORSTTY chrestomathy
ACEHHNOOSTTU autochthones
ACEHIIINRSTZ Christianize
ACEHIIKRRSWW Warwickshire
ACEHIILLSTTY theistically
ACEHIILMNNTT anthelmintic
ACEHIILNPPRS planispheric
ACEHIINPRRST pre-Christian
ACEHIINSSTTU enthusiastic
ACEHIINTTTUY authenticity
ACEHIIOPSSTT sophisticate
ACEHIIPPRRST periphrastic
ACEHIKMNRRSS scrimshanker
ACEHIKRRSSSW kirschwasser
ACEHILLLOSUY hellaciously
ACEHILLLPTYY phyletically
ACEHILLMNNTU multichannel
ACEHILLNOPST plain clothes
ACEHILLNOPTY phonetically
ACEHILLNORUY unheroically
ACEHILLOPRUY euphorically
ACEHILLORRTY rhetorically
ACEHILLRSTYY hysterically
ACEHILMSSTTZ schmaltziest
ACEHILNNNSSS clannishness
ACEHILNOPPTY phenotypical
ACEHILNPPRTT pitcher plant
ACEHILNPSSSY physicalness
ACEHIMOORTTY atomic theory
ACEHIMOPRSST atmospherics
ACEHIMORSTTT thermostatic
ACEHIMRSSTTW master switch
ACEHINOOSTUU auction house
ACEHINRRTTUW white currant
ACEHKMRRSSTT stretch marks
ACEHLLLPRSUY sepulchrally
ACEHLLMNOPSY shell company
ACEHLLMORSYY lachrymosely
ACEHLLORRSTY orchestrally
ACEHLMMNOOTW commonwealth
ACEHLMNOORSY close harmony
ACEHLMNOPRSY prosenchymal
ACEHLMOORSST schoolmaster
ACEHLOOPSTUY polychaetous
ACEHLOPSSUXY psychosexual

ACEHMNORRRTT trench mortar
ACEHMOORRTTY cherry tomato
ACEHMOORSTTY tracheostomy
ACEHMOPSSTTU stomach upset
ACEHNNOOPRRS anchorperson
ACEHOORRRSTT orchestrator
ACEIIILLRSTT literalistic
ACEIIILMNPUZ municipalize
ACEIIILNSTTY inelasticity
ACEIIILRSTTV relativistic
ACEIIILRSTVV revivalistic
ACEIIIMNPRSS precisianism
ACEIIINNNORT incineration
ACEIIJLLSTUY Jesuitically
ACEIILLLLPTY elliptically
ACEIILLLNSUV all-inclusive
ACEIILLMNSST miscellanist
ACEIILLMOSTY semiotically
ACEIILLNORTY collinearity
ACEIILMMNRST mercantilism
ACEIILMNOSST sectionalism
ACEIILMNRSTT mercantilist
ACEIILMOPPSS episcopalism
ACEIILMOPRRT polarimetric
ACEIILMOPRST semi-tropical
ACEIILMRRTUY mercuriality
ACEIILNNNRTU internuncial
ACEIILNOORTZ creolization
ACEIILNOPRST inspectorial
ACEIILNORTTU reticulation
ACEIILNOSSTT sectionalist
ACEIILNOSTUV vesiculation
ACEIILNRSTTT clarinettist
ACEIILNRSTVV civil servant
ACEIILOQTUVY equivocality
ACEIILPRRSUY superciliary
ACEIILRRSSTU surrealistic
ACEIILRRTTTY retractility
ACEIIMNPTTUY pneumaticity
ACEIIMNRSSTU insectariums
ACEIINNNORTU renunciation
ACEIINNOTTUV continuative
ACEIINOOQTUV equivocation
ACEIINOORTXZ exorcization
ACEIINOPRRTT practitioner
ACEIINOPRSTU pertinacious
ACEIINORRSTW contrariwise
ACEIIOPPRRTT precipitator
ACEIIORTTVVY overactivity
ACEIKLOORRSW social worker
ACEILLMMNNOY mnemonically
ACEILLMNTUVY multivalency
ACEILLMORTUY molecularity
ACEILLMSSTYY systemically
ACEILLMTUUVY cumulatively
ACEILLNOPRTY entropically
ACEILLNORTUY neurotically
ACEILLNOSTTU scutellation
ACEILLOPTUVY copulatively
ACEILLRRSTUU sericultural
ACEILMMMNOSS commensalism
ACEILMMNOSTY commensality
ACEILMNNOOPT componential
ACEILMNOPSTY plastic money
ACEILNNNOOTV conventional
ACEILNOOPRSS processional
ACEILNOOPRTT lactoprotein
ACEILNOORTUY elocutionary
ACEILNORSUXY exclusionary
ACEILNOSTTUV consultative
ACEILOOPRRTV velociraptor
ACEILOOPRRTY corporeality
ACEILOORSTYY Royal Society
ACEILOPRRSUY precariously
ACEILOQSSUUY sequaciously
ACEIMMNOPRSU Paris commune
ACEIMMORRSTU crematoriums
ACEIMNNOOPST companion set, compensation
ACEIMNNOOTUY caution money
ACEIMNNOPRTU unimportance
ACEIMNOOOOPT onomatopoeic
ACEIMNORSSTV conservatism
ACEIMNSSTTUY unsystematic
ACEIMPRRRSTW writer's cramp
ACEINNOOPRTT pernoctation
ACEINNOORSTV conservation, conversation
ACEINNOOSTTT contestation
ACEINNORRSST contrariness
ACEINNORRTUY renunciatory
ACEINNORSTTU encrustation
ACEINOPPRRTU Port-au-Prince
ACEINOPSSSSU spaciousness
ACEINOPSSSTU captiousness
ACEINORRSUXY excursionary
ACEINOSSSTUU cautiousness
ACEIOOPRRRRT troop carrier
ACEIOOQRTUVY equivocatory
ACEIOORSTUUV overcautious
ACEIORRSSTTU resuscitator
ACEJKOPRSSTT sports jacket
ACEKMMMNOORT Common Market
ACEKMNORRTUY rockumentary
ACELLMOPSUUU plumulaceous
ACELLNNOSSUY consensually
ACELLNOOPRSU porcellanous
ACELLNOTTUXY contextually
ACELMMNOSTUY consummately
ACELMNOOPRTT contemplator
ACELMNOORSST Montes Claros
ACELNNPRTTUY century plant
ACELNNRSSUUU ranunculuses
ACELNOOPRSTU proconsulate
ACELOPRRSTTU court plaster
ACEMMMOOORRT commemorator
ACEMMNOOPRRY Common Prayer
ACEMMPRSSSTU mass spectrum
ACEMNOOPRRTY contemporary
ACEMNOOPRSTY compensatory
ACENOOQRTTTU quattrocento
ACENOORRSTVY conservatory
ACEOPRRSSSTT sportscaster
ACFFGGHIILNN cliffhanging
ACFFGHIILRTT traffic light
ACFFIILLNOUY unofficially
ACFFLOOORRTY factory floor
ACFGIIILNOTU uglification
ACFGINOOORRT organ of Corti
ACFHIIIMNOTU humification

ACFHILLORRY horrifically
ACFIIIILNOTV vilification
ACFIIIINNOTV vinification
ACFIIIINOTVV vivification
ACFIIILNOTTY fictionality
ACFIIINNOOTT notification
ACFIIINOOSST ossification
ACFIIINOPRTU purification
ACFIIINOPTTY typification
ACFIIINORTTV vitrifaction
ACFIILLLOPRY prolifically
ACFIILLNOPTY pontifically
ACFIILNNNOOT non-fictional
ACFIILOSTTUY factitiously
ACFIIMNNOORT confirmation
ACFIIOPRRTUY purificatory
ACFILLNNOTUY functionally
ACFILMNOTUYY county family
ACFIMNNOOORT conformation
ACFIMNOORRTY confirmatory
ACFRRSTUUUUY usufructuary
ACGGHILNNNUY unchangingly
ACGGIILLOOST glaciologist
ACGGIILNNORS carol-singing
ACGGLLLOSUUU glaucous gull
ACGHHHIOPTYY ichthyophagy
ACGHHIILOPRT lithographic
ACGHHINOOPPR phonographic
ACGHHIOOPPRT photographic
ACGHHIOOPRRT orthographic
ACGHHIOPPRSY hypsographic
ACGHIILLLOOP philological
ACGHIILLLOOT lithological
ACGHIILLOOST histological
ACGHIILLPRTY triglyphical
ACGHIINPRSTY scintigraphy
ACGHIIOPPRRS spirographic
ACGHILLMOOTY mythological
ACGHILLNOOOP phonological
ACGHILLOOPRS oscillograph
ACGHILOPRSTY stylographic
ACGHIMMNORRW worm charming
ACGHIMNNORTW morning watch
ACGHINOOOSTT shooting coat
ACGHINOOPPRR pornographic
ACGHINOPPRST shopping cart
ACGHINOPPRTT chart-topping
ACGHIOOPSSTY phagocytosis
ACGHKLOPPUYY happy-go-lucky
ACGHOOOPPRSU coprophagous
ACGHOPPRRTYY cryptography
ACGIIILLLOTY illogicality
ACGIIKKLNSTW walking stick
ACGIILLLMNOO limnological
ACGIILLLOSTY logistically
ACGIILLLRTUY liturgically
ACGIILMNOSUU mucilaginous
ACGIILNOORST craniologist
ACGIIMORRTVY microgravity
ACGIINNOSTTW wainscotting
ACGIKLNORSSW working class
ACGILLLNNOOY non-logically
ACGILLLOOOYZ zoologically
ACGILLOOOPRT tropological
ACGILNOOSTUY contagiously
ACGILNOPRRSS Coral Springs
ACGILNOPSUUY pugnaciously
ACGILNORSUUY ungraciously
ACGIMMOOPRRR microprogram
ACGIMNOOPRTU compurgation
ACGKORSSSSTU tussock grass
ACGLLNOORSUY clangorously
ACGMOOPRRTUY compurgatory
ACGMOOPRSTUY cryptogamous
ACHHIILMNOPR philharmonic
ACHHIIMNOPPS championship
ACHHIIMOSTTY stichomythia
ACHHIIMOSTYZ schizothymia
ACHHILLMRTYY rhythmically
ACHHILMNRTUY unrhythmical
ACHHNNOOOPRY onychophoran
ACHIIILMSTWY whimsicality
ACHIIIMNPSSU musicianship
ACHIIINRSTTY Christianity
ACHIILLLOSTY holistically
ACHIILLORSTY historically
ACHIILNNOORT chlorination
ACHIILNOPRST rhinoplastic
ACHIILNORSTU unhistorical
ACHIIMNOPRST misanthropic
ACHIINNNORST non-Christian
ACHIINOPSSWX coxswainship
ACHIIPRSSTTY psychiatrist
ACHIKMORTUUV kurchatovium
ACHILLNOPTYY hypnotically
ACHILLORSUVY chivalrously
ACHILNORSUUV unchivalrous
ACHILOOPTTV photovoltaic
ACHIMNOPPSSY ship's company
ACHINOPRSSTY Cornish pasty
ACHIOPRSSSTY astrophysics
ACHLLMNOOORS normal school
ACHNNOORSSUY asynchronous
ACIIIILMRSTT militaristic
ACIIIILNOTVZ civilization
ACIIILMNNOST nominalistic
ACIIILMNPTUY municipality
ACIIILNOOSTT coalitionist, solicitation
ACIIILNOPRTT triplication
ACIIILNOTVVY conviviality
ACIIILNPPRTY principality
ACIIILQTUYZZ quizzicality
ACIIIMNORSTV Victorianism
ACIIINNOOTTX intoxication
ACIIINOPSSUU inauspicious
ACIIINPRRTTU antipruritic
ACIIJLNORSTU journalistic
ACIILLNNOOPT non-political
ACIILLNOOSTY isotonically
ACIILLNOPRVY provincially
ACIILLNRTUUV vinicultural
ACIILLOOPSTY isotopically
ACIILLOQTUXY quixotically
ACIILLOSSUVY lasciviously
ACIILLRTTUUV viticultural
ACIILMNSTUUY unmusicality
ACIILNNOOOTZ colonization
ACIILNNOOSTU inosculation
ACIILNNOSTUY insouciantly

ACIILNOORSST	consistorial
ACIILNOPPSTU	supplication
ACIILNORSSSS	nail scissors
ACIILNOSTUUY	incautiously
ACIILOPSSUUY	auspiciously
ACIILPRSTTUU	apiculturist
ACIILRSTTUUV	aviculturist
ACIIMNOPRTTU	protactinium
ACIINNNOOTTU	continuation
ACIINNOOPSTT	constipation
ACIINNORSTTU	incrustation
ACILLLLOOQUY	colloquially
ACILLMNNOPSU	spinal column
ACILLMORSUUY	miraculously
ACILLNOPSTYY	synoptically
ACILLOOPSTTY	post-coitally
ACILLOOQSUUY	loquaciously
ACILLPRRSTUY	scripturally
ACILMMNNOOTT	non-committal
ACILMNOOOPST	cosmopolitan
ACILMOOPPRST	protoplasmic
ACILMOPPRSUU	popular music
ACILNNNOSTTY	inconstantly
ACILNNOOSTTU	consultation
ACILNPRRSTUU	unscriptural
ACILOOPPRSTT	protoplastic
ACILOOPPRTTY	prototypical
ACILOPPRSTUY	supplicatory
ACILORRRSTUV	curvirostral
ACILORSSSTTU	tourist class
ACIMMMNOPRUU	cuprammonium
ACIMMNNOOSTU	consummation
ACIMNOOOPRST	compo rations
ACINNNORSTTU	unconstraint
ACINOOOPRRRT	incorporator
ACINOOPRRSTT	cartoon strip
ACIORRRSSTTU	cirrostratus, stratocirrus
ACLLLPRSTUUY	sculpturally
ACLLRRSTTUUY	structurally
ACMNNOORTUWY	countrywoman
ACMNOPRSTTUY	trust company
ACNOPRRTTUYY	country party
ADDDDEEEHLMU	muddle-headed
ADDDDEEEHNRU	dunderheaded
ADDDDEEFFILL	fiddle-faddle
ADDDEEEHNOOW	wooden-headed
ADDDEEFIOSTU	eisteddfodau
ADDDEFIIOOTV	food additive
ADDDFGGINORT	draft dodging
ADDEEEFGNNOR	Garden of Eden
ADDEEEFHLNRY	free-handedly
ADDEEEHLNNVY	even-handedly
ADDEEEIIRSTV	desiderative
ADDEEEKLNOOY	Yankee Doodle
ADDEEELLNTTW	well-attended
ADDEEELNPTXY	extended-play
ADDEEELORRSS	sealed orders
ADDEEELRRTTY	red-letter day
ADDEEFFNRSTU	understaffed
ADDEEFHLLNTY	left-handedly
ADDEEFHLMORY	formaldehyde
ADDEEFLNRSSU	dreadfulness
ADDEEFNORSSW	word-deafness
ADDEEGHILNNS	single-handed
ADDEEGINPPSU	pease pudding
ADDEEGJMNTUY	Judgement Day
ADDEEGNORSTU	adder's tongue
ADDEEHIKNPSY	kidney-shaped
ADDEEHLNNOPY	open-handedly
ADDEEHMNOTTU	mutton-headed
ADDEEHOPRRTU	proud-hearted
ADDEEILMMNNR	mild-mannered
ADDEEILNRSST	desert island
ADDEEINNRRTU	undertrained
ADDEEINRSTUV	unadvertised
ADDEEJLLSTUW	well-adjusted
ADDEELNOSSTT	staddle-stone
ADDEENNRRSTU	understander
ADDEFGILRRSU	disregardful
ADDEFHILNOOS	old-fashioned
ADDEFHILOPST	feldspathoid
ADDEFIILMNRY	fair-mindedly
ADDEFILMRSTU	field mustard
ADDEFLNNNOUW	Newfoundland
ADDEGHHHILNY	high-handedly
ADDEGHHOORTU	daughterhood
ADDEGHIINRRT	third reading
ADDEGILNOPRS	spring-loaded
ADDEGINNRRUW	underdrawing
ADDEHHLORRSU	hard shoulder
ADDEIILLLSVY	ill-advisedly
ADDEIILNQTUU	unliquidated
ADDEIIMNOOPR	modi operandi
ADDEILMNOOTU	demodulation
ADDEILMNOPRS	promised land
ADDEIMMMRSUY	Midsummer Day
ADDEIMNNORRW	narrow-minded
ADDEINRRSUVY	Sunday driver
ADDFHIIMORTY	hydatidiform
ADDFHLNOOSTU	thousandfold
ADDFIILLNSUY	disdainfully
ADDGHIMNOORU	rough diamond
ADDGIILNSSTU	studding-sail
ADDGKMNOOOOR	Komodo dragon
ADDIIILLNUVY	individually
ADDILNOORRRY	Lord Ordinary
ADEEEEEFLNOY	eye of a needle
ADEEEEFNRSTT	defenestrate
ADEEEEGINRTV	degenerative
ADEEEEGLNRTY	degenerately
ADEEEEGRRRSV	reserve grade
ADEEEFFIINRT	differentiae
ADEEEFHILSSV	self-adhesive
ADEEEFINPRRR	referred pain
ADEEEFLNOPRT	plea of tender
ADEEEFNNOSST	tone-deafness
ADEEEGGNRSTU	unsegregated
ADEEEGHLMMRS	sledgehammer
ADEEEGILOPRS	grapeseed oil
ADEEEGIMNRST	disagreement
ADEEEGIMNRTZ	demagnetizer
ADEEEGINNORT	degeneration
ADEEEGINRRTT	redintegrate
ADEEEGMNNNRT	endangerment
ADEEEGNOQRUW	queen dowager
ADEEEHHLORTW	wholehearted
ADEEEHIMNRTT	hereditament
ADEEEHINSSSV	adhesiveness
ADEEEHLNNRRT	Netherlander

ADEEEIILMNRZ	demineralize
ADEEEIILMRST	sidereal time
ADEEEIILSSSW	Weil's disease
ADEEEIIMMRST	semidiameter
ADEEEIIMNRTT	intermediate
ADEEEILLMMOS	Mademoiselle
ADEEEILMNORT	radio-element
ADEEEILNPRRT	interpleader
ADEEEINPRSTT	predestinate
ADEEEKLLMRSS	Skelmersdale
ADEEELLLRTVW	well-traveled
ADEEELLMMNRT	entrammelled
ADEEELLMNNRW	well-mannered
ADEEELLMNOSV	dolman sleeve
ADEEELLPPRRW	well-prepared
ADEEELNOSSST	desolateness
ADEEELOPPRST	tradespeople
ADEEEMNORSST	moderateness
ADEEENOPPRRT	preponderate
ADEEENPPRRSS	preparedness
ADEEENPRRTUV	peradventure
ADEEEOPPRRSV	eavesdropper
ADEEERRRSTTT	street trader
ADEEFFIILNRT	differential
ADEEFGHILNRS	hard feelings
ADEEFGILLSSS	field glasses
ADEEFGINNRST	free-standing
ADEEFGINORRT	foreign trade
ADEEFHILLNOT	lie of the land
ADEEFIILMPPR	preamplified
ADEEFILNNSST	inflatedness
ADEEFILNORTV	over-inflated
ADEEFLLORUVW	well-favoured
ADEEFLLPRSTU	apfelstrudel
ADEEFLMSSTUY	feudal system
ADEEFMORRSTT	terms of trade
ADEEFNOPRRTU	unperforated
ADEEGGHINRSS	edging shears
ADEEGGHIRSTT	straight-edge
ADEEGGIILNRT	trailing edge
ADEEGGIQRRSU	square-rigged
ADEEGHHILRTT	light-hearted
ADEEGHIMNOST	homesteading
ADEEGHINNRRT	heart-rending
ADEEGHNORSTT	dragon's teeth
ADEEGHOPRRSW	hedge sparrow
ADEEGHPRSTTU	stepdaughter
ADEEGIINRSTT	disintegrate
ADEEGIJNNRWW	wandering Jew
ADEEGIKLLLNW	lake-dwelling
ADEEGIKNNRRT	kindergarten
ADEEGILLNPST	pedestalling
ADEEGILNORTU	deregulation
ADEEGINNRRTW	winter garden
ADEEGKNNNRSU	sunken garden
ADEEGLLRRSSY	regardlessly
ADEEGLNNORSY	General Synod
ADEEGLORRRTY	retrogradely
ADEEGMMOPRRR	reprogrammed
ADEEGMNNRRTU	undergarment
ADEEGNOORRVW	wood engraver
ADEEGNPRTUUX	unexpurgated
ADEEHHIKNRRS	headshrinker
ADEEHHLOOTTW	toothed whale
ADEEHHMNOOSU	house and home
ADEEHHNNPTUY	unhyphenated
ADEEHHNOPRST	heptahedrons
ADEEHIILRRTY	hereditarily
ADEEHILORSTU	tousle-haired
ADEEHIMNPPRS	misapprehend
ADEEHIMRSSST	headmistress
ADEEHINORSTU	house-trained
ADEEHMNNOSSS	handsomeness
ADEEHNNOPRST	pentahedrons
ADEEHNORRSTT	tetrahedrons
ADEEHNORSTTY	stony-hearted
ADEEHORSTTTU	stout-hearted
ADEEIIILMRTZ	demilitarize
ADEEIIILORTZ	editorialize
ADEEIILLNTVY	evidentially
ADEEIILMMNPT	impedimental
ADEEIILMTTVY	meditatively
ADEEIILNPRST	presidential
ADEEIILRTVVY	derivatively
ADEEIIMNNOTV	denominative
ADEEIIMNRRTY	intermediary
ADEEIINORSTT	disorientate
ADEEIINRRSTY	residentiary
ADEEIINRRTVW	water-diviner
ADEEIKMNRSSS	semi-darkness
ADEEILLNNRST	lantern slide
ADEEILLOSTVW	old wives' tale
ADEEILMMORTY	immoderately
ADEEILNNTTUV	unventilated
ADEEILNOPPRT	lepidopteran
ADEEILNRRSTY	restrainedly
ADEEILORRSTW	water soldier
ADEEIMMNORSU	misdemeanour
ADEEIMNRSTUV	misadventure
ADEEINNOOPRU	Indo-European
ADEEINNRRSTU	unrestrained
ADEEINNSSSTU	unsteadiness
ADEEINSSTTTU	United States
ADEEJMNRSTTU	readjustment
ADEEKNORSSYY	donkey's years
ADEELLMMNRTU	untrammelled
ADEELLMORUZZ	muzzle-loader
ADEELMNOSTTT	Old Testament
ADEELNPPRRUY	unpreparedly
ADEELNRSTTUY	Sunday letter
ADEELRSSSSTY	lady's tresses
ADEEMNNNORTU	unornamented
ADEEMNNPRSUU	supermundane
ADEEMNNPRTUY	underpayment
ADEENNOPPRRT	preponderant
ADEENORSSTUW	sweet and sour
ADEFFHORSSTT	short-staffed
ADEFFLLOOTTY	flat-footedly
ADEFGHHILNOT	height of land
ADEFGHHIOORT	hair of the dog
ADEFGHILRSTY	far-sightedly
ADEFGIILLNPY	playing field
ADEFGIIMMNRX	mixed farming
ADEFGIINRRST	first reading
ADEFGINOOPRR	proof-reading
ADEFHHLNRSTU	thunderflash
ADEFHILLTTWY	half-wittedly
ADEFHILOORST	foolhardiest
ADEFIIILNNOT	definitional
ADEFIILLMNSU	seminal fluid

ADEFIILNOSTT deflationist
ADEFIILNPRSU Freudian slip
ADEFIINNQTUU unquantified
ADEFILMNNOSS manifoldness
ADEFLLNRTUUY fraudulently
ADEFLMNORTUU unformulated
ADEFLRRSTTUY frustratedly
ADEFOORSSTTW Sword of State
ADEGGHIILLNT leading light
ADEGGIINNRRV driving range
ADEGGINNORRR organ-grinder
ADEGHHILNORS shareholding
ADEGHHOPRRRY hydrographer
ADEGHHORRSTU draught horse
ADEGHIILMTTY daylight time
ADEGHIINRRSS hairdressing
ADEGHIMNOPRY Phrygian mode
ADEGHINORRST horse-trading
ADEGHINRSSTU draughtiness
ADEGHLLNORST stranglehold
ADEGHNOPRSTU sharp-tongued
ADEGIIILLOTV village idiot
ADEGIIILNRTT interdigital
ADEGIILLMNSY misleadingly
ADEGIILLNNOT dialling tone
ADEGIILLNNTU dentilingual
ADEGIILMNORZ demoralizing
ADEGIILNPRSY despairingly
ADEGIINOORRT granodiorite
ADEGIINOORTT Rogationtide
ADEGIJKNNOST standing joke
ADEGILLNORUZ lounge lizard
ADEGILOORRTY derogatorily
ADEGIMNNOPPR name-dropping
ADEGIORRSSWW grass widower
ADEHHILLOOWY whole holiday
ADEHHILLPPSU philadelphus
ADEHHINNORTY hither and yon
ADEHHLMORRTY hydrothermal
ADEHHOPRRTYY hydrotherapy
ADEHIIIMRTTZ mithridatize
ADEHIILMOSSY hemodialysis
ADEHIILNSTTT dilettantish
ADEHIIMNORSZ disharmonize
ADEHIKLMNNOY milk and honey
ADEHILMNOPSU sulphonamide
ADEHILMNORSU malnourished
ADEHILNOOSSY one's holidays
ADEHILOPRSTU triadelphous
ADEHIMMNNOST admonishment
ADEHINNQSUUV unvanquished
ADEHINORSTUU unauthorised
ADEHINORTUUZ unauthorized
ADEHINQRRSTU hindquarters
ADEHIOOPRSTT orthopaedist
ADEHIOPSTTTY typhoid state
ADEHKLMORRSU shoulder mark
ADEHKNNOORTV overhand knot
ADEHLLNOOSTW Shetland wool
ADEHLMNOOPSU monadelphous
ADEHLNNOPSTY Shetland pony
ADEIIILMNOTT delimitation
ADEIIILORSTT editorialist
ADEIIIMNORTZ dimerization
ADEIIIMNOSTV deviationism
ADEIIINNOOTZ deionization
ADEIIINOSTTV deviationist
ADEIIINTTTUZ attitudinize
ADEIILLNPRUV Liverpudlian
ADEIILMNSTTT dilettantism
ADEIILNNORTY inordinately
ADEIILNOOPST despoliation
ADEIILNOPRTV providential
ADEIILNORSST dilatoriness
ADEIIMMNNRSU Indian summer
ADEIIMMNOORT immoderation
ADEIIMNNNOOT denomination
ADEIIMNNOOTZ demonization
ADEIIMNNORSW Neo-Darwinism
ADEIIMNNOSTU mountainside
ADEIIMNNRSTT distrainment
ADEIIMNOOTTV demotivation
ADEIIMNORSST disseminator
ADEIINNOPSST dispensation
ADEIINNORRSS ordinariness
ADEIINNORSTW Neo-Darwinist
ADEIINORRSVY diversionary
ADEIINORSSTT dissertation
ADEIINOSTTUV adventitious
ADEIIOOOPRST radioisotope
ADEILLLNRTUY ill-naturedly
ADEILLNPRTUY prudentially
ADEILLOSTTUW low latitudes
ADEILLPPRSSY lady's slipper
ADEILNOOPPTU depopulation
ADEILNOPRRSU superordinal
ADEILOPRRSUY Lady Superior
ADEIMMOPRSUY praseodymium
ADEIMNNQRSUU quadrenniums
ADEIMOOOPTTV optative mood
ADEIMOOPRSTZ spermatozoid
ADEINNSSSTTW witness-stand
ADEINOORSUVY Douay version
ADEJLORSSSTU loss adjuster
ADELLNORSSUY slanderously
ADELLORSTUUY adulterously
ADEMNOORRSTT demonstrator
ADEMOPRRSSTU superstardom
ADENNORSSTUW untowardness
ADFFGIILNNTU fault-finding
ADFGGILNNORY flying dragon
ADFGHOOPRRTU draught-proof
ADFGIILLNRYZ flying lizard
ADFHIMNOOORU maid of honour
ADFIIILNNOST disinflation
ADFIIILNOTUZ fluidization
ADFIILNOORTU fluoridation
ADFIILOSSTUY fastidiously
ADGGGILNNORU Grand Guignol
ADGGHIINNNPS Pingdingshan
ADGGILNNNOST long-standing
ADGHIKLNORSW world-shaking
ADGHILLLMNOS smallholding
ADGHLMNOOPUY Plough Monday
ADGIIIMNNTT intimidating
ADGIIINOTTZ digitization
ADGIIIMNOSSS misdiagnosis
ADGIILLNNOTU longitudinal
ADGIILNNPRST landing strip
ADGIINNOPRTW word-painting

ADGIINOPPRSV	disapproving
ADGILNNOSTUY	astoundingly
ADGIMNNOOOST	Santo Domingo
ADGIMNNOORST	standing room
ADGINNNNPRUU	up and running
ADGLNNOORTUW	long-drawn-out
ADGOOOPRSSTU	gastropodous
ADGOOPRRSTUV	provost guard
ADHHIOPRSTTY	hydropathist
ADHHLORSTUYY	Holy Thursday
ADHIIIMMRSTT	mithridatism
ADHIILMNOPRU	dolphinarium
ADHILLNOSTUY	outlandishly
ADHNOORRTUWY	unroadworthy
ADIIIIMNNOTT	intimidation
ADIIILLMRSSY	dissimilarly
ADIIILLNOSTT	distillation
ADIIILLNOSVY	divisionally
ADIIIMNORTTY	intimidatory
ADIIINORSTTT	traditionist
ADIILLMOPRRY	primordially
ADIILLNOQRSU	quadrillions
ADIILLNOSSUY	sinusoidally
ADIILLNRSTUY	industrially
ADIILLORSTTY	distillatory
ADIILMNOPRST	palindromist
ADIILMORSSTU	dissimulator
ADIILMORSSUY	Moulay Idriss
ADIILNOORSTT	distortional
ADIILNORSTTU	stridulation
ADIILOQRSTUX	liquid storax
ADIIOPSSTTUU	disputatious
ADILLLLOOPPY	lollipop lady
ADILORSSSTUY	disastrously
ADMNOOOPRRTY	Dartmoor pony
AEEEEFHNORTV	tree of heaven
AEEEEGHLPRST	telegraphese
AEEEEGINRRTV	regenerative
AEEEEGNNRRTU	unregenerate
AEEEEHLPRSVY	heavy sleeper
AEEEEKLMRRTT	telemarketer
AEEEELPRRSSS	press release
AEEEFFILMNTY	effeminately
AEEEFGIINNRT	retaining fee
AEEEFHHIRTTW	white feather
AEEEFHINRRTT	thereinafter
AEEEFHINRSST	featheriness
AEEEFIKLNPTT	palette knife
AEEEFILLTTVY	Fayetteville
AEEEFILNPRRT	preferential
AEEEFIMNRTTV	fermentative
AEEEFLLNSSSS	leaflessness
AEEEFLNRSSSS	fearlessness
AEEEFLORSTTW	telesoftware
AEEEFLRRSTUV	reverse fault
AEEEFMNORSSS	fearsomeness
AEEEGGHLNSTT	snaggle-teeth
AEEEGHKLPRTY	telegraph key
AEEEGHNRRSTW	news-gatherer
AEEEGIKLNNNW	Wankel engine
AEEEGILMNSTZ	segmentalize
AEEEGILNOPTV	negative pole
AEEEGILNRSST	single-seater
AEEEGILTTVVY	vegetatively
AEEEGIMNNSTV	envisagement
AEEEGINNORRT	regeneration
AEEEGINNSSTV	negativeness
AEEEGINORSTV	seronegative
AEEEGINORTTV	revegetation
AEEEGIRRSTTV	tergiversate
AEEEGLMNNNTT	entanglement
AEEEGMMNORTT	magnetometer
AEEEGMMNOSSS	gamesomeness
AEEEGMNNRRSS	messenger RNA
AEEEGMNNRSTT	estrangement
AEEEGMOPRSTT	postage meter
AEEEHHNOTTXY	ethoxyethane
AEEEHILMPRTY	ephemerality
AEEEHILNNSSV	heavenliness
AEEEHILNRSST	leatheriness
AEEEHILRSTTW	weather-tiles
AEEEHIMNNOPP	epiphenomena
AEEEHIMORTTV	movie theatre
AEEEHINPPRSV	apprehensive
AEEEHINPRSTZ	parenthesize
AEEEHKNOPPRS	speakerphone
AEEEHKPPPRRS	pepper shaker
AEEEHLLNNRTW	lantern-wheel
AEEEHLORSTUX	heterosexual
AEEEHMNNSTTW	enswathement
AEEEHNOPRRTT	heteropteran
AEEEHQRRRTTU	three-quarter
AEEEIILMRSTT	semi-literate
AEEEIILNPRTX	experiential
AEEEILLMMNST	elementalism
AEEEILLMNRTY	elementarily
AEEEILLNPRTT	interpellate
AEEEILMNPRTX	experimental
AEEEILNRTTVY	inveterately
AEEEIMNNPRTZ	permanentize
AEEEIMNRRTUV	remunerative
AEEEIMORSTTV	overestimate
AEEEINPRSTTV	presentative
AEEEINPRTTVV	preventative
AEEEIPRRSTVV	preservative
AEEEKLNOOPRS	saloon-keeper
AEEEKLRRSTTW	streetwalker
AEEELLORRRSV	role reversal
AEEELMNNSSSS	namelessness
AEEELMNORSYY	eleemosynary
AEEELNRSSSST	tearlessness
AEEEMNNPRSTT	permanent set
AEEEMNNSTTTW	New Testament
AEEEMNPRRTTT	pretreatment
AEEEMNRSSSST	reassessment
AEEFFGHIRRTU	father figure
AEEFFLLRSTTY	self-flattery
AEEFGHHILRTT	feather-light
AEEFGHINRSST	sergeant-fish
AEEFGIKRRSTU	figure skater
AEEFGIORRRRT	refrigerator
AEEFGLNRSSTU	gratefulness
AEEFHHIKKLRS	Kafr el Sheikh
AEEFHIKNRSSS	freakishness
AEEFHILNRSST	fatherliness
AEEFHILOSTTT	the least of it
AEEFHLLRRSTU	fuller's earth
AEEFHLMNSSSU	shamefulness
AEEFHLMORRTW	flame-thrower
AEEFHLOOSTTT	athlete's foot

AEEFHOOPRRTW weatherproof
AEEFHORSTTTU fourth estate
AEEFHPRRRRSY Harpers Ferry
AEEFIILMPPRR preamplifier
AEEFIKLNNSTY Stanley knife
AEEFIKNNNRST Frankenstein
AEEFILMNORRT interfemoral
AEEFILNRSTVV snifter-valve
AEEFIMNNORTT fermentation
AEEFIMOPRRTV performative, preformative
AEEFINNORSTT fenestration
AEEFINNOSTUX soixante-neuf
AEEFKNNORSSS forsakenness
AEEFLLNSSSSW flawlessness
AEEFLMNORSTT forestalment, man of letters
AEEFLMOPRRUV marvel of Peru
AEEFLNSSSTTU tastefulness
AEEFLNSSSTUW wastefulness
AEEFLOPQRSUW pasque flower
AEEFMNNOOSSW woman of sense
AEEFMORRRSTY term for years
AEEFOOPRRRTW waterproofer
AEEFOOPRRSST professorate
AEEFOQRRRSTU forequarters
AEEGGGINNNSS engagingness
AEEGGHINORTT theatergoing, theatregoing
AEEGGIINNSTV negative sign
AEEGGILRSSVY aggressively
AEEGGIMMNOST geomagnetism
AEEGGINNTTTW wetting agent
AEEGGINRSSUV unaggressive
AEEGHHIRTTTW weathertight
AEEGHHNOPRRT ethnographer
AEEGHILLMMRT hellgrammite
AEEGHILNNRTY hearteningly
AEEGHILNORTW watering hole
AEEGHILORRUV heliogravure
AEEGHILPRSTT telegraphist
AEEGHINOPSST pathogenesis
AEEGHINPRSST sergeantship
AEEGHINPTTVY heavy petting
AEEGHINRRSTT straightener
AEEGHIPRSSTW stage whisper
AEEGHLNOPRSY selenography
AEEGHMOOPRRT meteorograph
AEEGHMOORSTU heterogamous
AEEGHNOPRRST stenographer
AEEGHOPPRRRR reprographer
AEEGHOPPRRRT petrographer
AEEGHOPRRSTY stereography
AEEGIIILLMTT illegitimate
AEEGIIILMTTZ legitimatize
AEEGIIILNRRV Virginia reel
AEEGIILLMTTY legitimately
AEEGIILNNPSS palingenesis
AEEGIINNNRTT entertaining
AEEGIINORRTV reinvigorate
AEEGIINPRRTV privateering
AEEGIKLMNRST single market
AEEGIKMNPRRT parking meter
AEEGIKNRSTUY key signature
AEEGILLMNRTY regimentally
AEEGILMMNNRT entrammeling
AEEGILMNNTTU integumental
AEEGILMNRRSV German silver
AEEGILNNORRT rote learning
AEEGILNNPRST single parent
AEEGILNNRTTY entreatingly
AEEGIMNNOSTT segmentation
AEEGIMNNRSST reassignment
AEEGIMNORRSU rose geranium
AEEGIMNRRSST mastersinger, sister german
AEEGIMORSSTU Aigues-Mortes
AEEGINNNSSSU sanguineness
AEEGINOPRRRT peregrinator
AEEGLLMNOPSY splenomegaly
AEEGLLPRRSSY press gallery
AEEGLLPRRSUU spurge laurel
AEEGLMNNORTV governmental
AEEGMMNORTTY magnetometry
AEEGNNORRSTY roentgen rays
AEEHHILMMNTU helianthemum
AEEHHILNSTTU unhealthiest
AEEHHILOPRTY heliotherapy
AEEHHIMNPRSW New Hampshire
AEEHHIMPRRTY hyperthermia
AEEHHLMMOORT homeothermal
AEEHHLNOSTVY heavenly host
AEEHHNOORSSW snowshoe hare
AEEHIIKNPRSY hyperkinesia
AEEHIINORTTZ etherization
AEEHIJNPRSST serjeantship
AEEHIKLLMNRU humane killer
AEEHIKMQRRSU requiem shark
AEEHILLPPRRY peripherally
AEEHILNSSSTT stealthiness
AEEHILOPRTTV private hotel
AEEHILRSTVWY white slavery
AEEHILSTUVXY exhaustively
AEEHIMNOPRTZ promethazine
AEEHIMNORRSS horse marines
AEEHIMOPRSSV overemphasis
AEEHINNOPPRS apprehension
AEEHINOPSSTV top-heaviness
AEEHIOPPSTTV stove-pipe hat
AEEHIOPRSTUV private house
AEEHIPRRSTTW weatherstrip
AEEHIPRSTTTU therapeutist
AEEHKMNOOPST Keetmanshoop
AEEHLLMMORWY yellowhammer
AEEHLLMNNOPY phenomenally
AEEHLLMNNRTT enthrallment
AEEHLLMORTXY exothermally
AEEHLMNRSSSS harmlessness
AEEHLMORSTTW Tower Hamlets
AEEHLMPRRSUU superhumeral
AEEHLNOPRTUY polyurethane
AEEHMMOOPRST metamorphose
AEEHMNNOPRTY hymenopteran
AEEHMNORSSUY Yeoman Ushers
AEEHMORRSSTU short measure
AEEHMORSSTUV harvest mouse
AEEHNNORRSTT north-eastern
AEEHNORSSTTU south-eastern
AEEHNRRSTTUU treasure hunt
AEEHOPRRSSTT stratosphere

AEEIIKLLLRRS	serial killer
AEEIIKLLMNSS	Milanese silk
AEEIIKLMNPRS	marline-spike
AEEIIKMNNSSY	Keynesianism
AEEIILLLRTTY	illiterately
AEEIILLMMMRT	milliammeter
AEEIILLMSTWW	sweet william
AEEIILLNOSST	essential oil
AEEIILLNPSTT	pestilential
AEEIILLRRTVY	irrelatively
AEEIILMNOOTZ	emotionalize
AEEIILMNSSST	essentialism
AEEIILMPRTVY	imperatively
AEEIILNNPRTY	perenniality
AEEIILNOPRTT	repetitional
AEEIILNOPTTZ	potentialize
AEEIILNRRSST	literariness
AEEIILNRSUVZ	universalize
AEEIILNSSSTT	essentialist
AEEIILNSSTTY	essentiality
AEEIILOPTTVX	exploitative
AEEIIMNSSSTW	Siamese twins
AEEIINNPRTTY	penitentiary
AEEIINNRRTTU	intrauterine
AEEIINORRSTV	inverse ratio
AEEIIPRTTUVV	vituperative
AEEIJLOPRTVY	pejoratively
AEEIJNNORTUV	rejuvenation
AEEIKMNNSSST	mistakenness
AEEILLLSTUVY	televisually
AEEILLMNRTTT	ill-treatment
AEEILLNOSSTT	tessellation
AEEILLNOSSTV	volatileness
AEEILLNQSTUY	sequentially
AEEILLNQTUVY	equivalently
AEEILLNRRSTT	interstellar
AEEILLNRRTVY	irrelevantly
AEEILLNSSSUV	allusiveness
AEEILLTTTTTT	tittle-tattle
AEEILMNNNRSS	mannerliness
AEEILMNRSSST	masterliness
AEEILMNSSTTU	ultimateness
AEEILMPPRSTU	perpetualism
AEEILNNNOSST	non-essential
AEEILNNPSSSS	painlessness
AEEILNOPRSSX	expressional
AEEILNPRRRST	laser printer
AEEILPPRRSTY	parsley-piert
AEEILPRSSUVY	persuasively
AEEIMMNRSTTT	mistreatment
AEEIMMNSSTTT	misstatement
AEEIMNNORRTU	remuneration
AEEIMNORRSST	marine stores
AEEIMNORRTTX	exterminator
AEEIMRRSSTTW	wire mattress
AEEIMRSSTTYZ	systematizer
AEEINNOPRSTT	presentation
AEEINNOPSSTT	state pension
AEEINNPRRRTU	intrapreneur
AEEINOORTTTX	extortionate
AEEINOPPRRTT	perpetration
AEEINOPPRTTU	perpetuation
AEEINOPPSSST	appositeness
AEEINOPRRSTV	preservation
AEEINORRRSVY	reversionary

AEEINPRRSSTX	express train
AEEINPRSSUUV	unpersuasive
AEEINRSSTTTV	transvestite
AEEIORRSTTVY	variety store
AEEIPPRRSSTV	private press
AEEIPPRRTTTT	pitter-patter
AEEKLLORRRST	roller skater
AEEKLLORSTWY	yellow streak
AEEKLMNRSSUW	lukewarmness
AEEKMNOPRRTY	Monterey Park
AEEKMORRSSTT	master stroke
AEELLLMNOTVY	malevolently
AEELLLORTTWY	yellow rattle
AEELLMNPPSTU	supplemental
AEELMNPRRSTU	premenstrual
AEELMSSSTUWY	sweet alyssum
AEELNOPRSSTY	stone parsley
AEELNORRRSTT	retrosternal
AEELNORRRSTU	sale or return
AEELNORSTUXY	extraneously
AEELNRRSSTVY	transversely
AEELQSSTTUUY	statuesquely
AEEMMNORSSSU	summer season
AEEMNOORTUUV	outmanoeuvre
AEENNORSSSUV	ravenousness
AEENNOSSSSUU	nauseousness
AEENOORSSTTT	Rosetta Stone
AEENOPRSSSTT	statesperson
AEENOPRSTTTY	petty treason
AEENORRSSTXY	extrasensory
AEENORRSTTUY	treasury note
AEEOPQRSSUUU	superaqueous
AEEOPRRSTTTU	tetrapterous
AEEOQRRSSTTU	sequestrator
AEEORRRTTTUW	water torture
AEFFGILLLMOR	flagelliform
AEFFHILNSSTU	faithfulness
AEFFILLMMMRY	flimflammery
AEFFILRRSSTU	first refusal
AEFFMMOORRTT	matter of form
AEFGHHINORTY	Fotheringhay
AEFGHHOORRTU	thoroughfare
AEFGHHOORTTU	aforethought
AEFGHHORTTTU	afterthought
AEFGIILRTUVY	figuratively
AEFGIINPPSWW	wife-swapping
AEFGILLMNNUY	meaningfully
AEFGILLNRTTY	flatteringly
AEFGILLNSSUW	wineglassful
AEFGILLOPRTY	profligately
AEFGILNNRTTU	unflattering
AEFGIMNNORRT	morning after
AEFGIMNORRTT	reformatting
AEFGINNNNOTT	non-fattening
AEFGINNRRRST	transferring
AEFGLLNRTUUY	ungratefully
AEFGOORRRSTY	agroforestry
AEFHILMORRST	marsh trefoil
AEFHKLNNSSTU	thankfulness
AEFHLLMNNOTU	flannel-mouth
AEFHLNRSSTUW	wrathfulness
AEFHNOOORRSS	rose of Sharon
AEFHOOPRRSTT	shatter-proof
AEFIIILMNSST	semi-finalist
AEFIIIMNNOTZ	feminization

AEFIILLMORTW water milfoil
AEFIILNORTTX exfiltration
AEFIIMMRSSTT misfit stream
AEFIIMNNNOTT infotainment
AEFILMMNNOOT monofilament
AEFILMNOORTV informal vote
AEFILNOOOSTT neat's-foot oil
AEFILNOOPRSS professional
AEFILNOOPRTV flavoprotein
AEFILNRRSSTT transfer list
AEFILOOPRRRT proliferator
AEFILOOPRRSS professorial
AEFILOPRRSTT self-portrait
AEFIMNNORRST frontiersman
AEFIMNOOPRRT preformation
AEFINNRRTUUV furniture van
AEFINOORSTUV favourite son
AEFLLNNSSUUW unlawfulness
AEFLLOOPRSSY fool's parsley
AEFLNPRSTUVY Venus flytrap
AEFMOOPRRRTY performatory
AEGGGILNRSTY staggeringly
AEGGGILNRSWY swaggeringly
AEGGHIPPRRTY trigger-happy
AEGGHLNOOSTT snaggle-tooth
AEGGHOOOPRYZ zoogeography
AEGGIILLNNRS resignalling
AEGGIJMNRSUU measuring jug
AEGGILORRSUY gregariously
AEGGIMNNORRW warmongering
AEGGINNPRSSS graspingness
AEGGLNORTUUV vulgar tongue
AEGHHILNORTW Higher Walton
AEGHHILOPRRT lithographer
AEGHHIMORSTT home straight
AEGHHIPRSUWY superhighway
AEGHHMNOPRRY hymnographer
AEGHHMOPRRTY mythographer, thermography
AEGHHOOPPRRT photographer
AEGHHOOPRRRT orthographer
AEGHIILNSTTY hesitatingly
AEGHIILRRSST serial rights
AEGHIINNORST training shoe
AEGHIINNSTTU unhesitating
AEGHIKNNRRTT knight errant
AEGHILMNNOSW Englishwoman
AEGHILMNNSTU languishment
AEGHILNRSTTY shatteringly
AEGHILQRRTTU quarter-light
AEGHIMMNOPRY hemp agrimony
AEGHIMNORSUW house-warming
AEGHINOPRRSW power-sharing
AEGHINRRSSTT heartstrings
AEGHINRSSSTT straightness
AEGHIRSSSTTT states' rights
AEGHLLMOPRRS shell program
AEGHLMNNOORS longshoreman
AEGHLMOORTUY rheumatology
AEGHLORSSTUU slaughterous
AEGHMNOOOPTT photomontage
AEGHNNOOPRTY anthropogeny
AEGHNOOPPRRR pornographer
AEGHOOPRRTUV photogravure
AEGHOPPRRTUY group therapy
AEGIIILMNOTT legitimation
AEGIIINNPRSW awe-inspiring
AEGIIINORTVV invigorative
AEGIIINRSTVW West Virginia
AEGIILLNPRVY prevailingly
AEGIILMMNNST misalignment
AEGIILMNOPRT primogenital
AEGIILMNORST mineralogist
AEGIILNNNSSU ungainliness
AEGIILNNSTTY lying-in-state
AEGIILNPPTYZ appetizingly
AEGIILNPRSTT ear-splitting
AEGIILNRSTVV vestal virgin
AEGIILRRRTUY irregularity
AEGIIMNNOPRT impregnation
AEGIIMNNOPTT pigmentation
AEGIIMOPRSTV Gram-positive
AEGIINNNRSTT intransigent
AEGIINNPPSTU unappetising
AEGIINNPPTUZ unappetizing
AEGIINNQRTUY inquiry agent
AEGIINORRSTT registration
AEGIINORSTTV investigator
AEGIINPPRRTW writing paper
AEGIKLMNORTW metalworking
AEGILLMRSTTU metallurgist
AEGILLNNOSTW stonewalling
AEGILLNNPSUY unpleasingly
AEGILLNOSTUY gelatinously
AEGILMMNRSTY stammeringly
AEGILMNNNNOT non-alignment
AEGILMNNOQTU magniloquent
AEGILMNRRSTW arm-wrestling
AEGILNNRSTTY astringently
AEGILNNRUVWY unwaveringly
AEGILNNRUWYY unwearyingly
AEGILNRRSSUY reassuringly
AEGILOORSTTT teratologist
AEGIMPPRRRST strippergram
AEGINNNRRTUW running water
AEGINOORRRTT interrogator
AEGINOPRRTVW private wrong
AEGINOPRSTWY staying power
AEGLLNOOOPTY paleontology
AEGLMNOOPTUY pneumatology
AEGLOORSTUUY outrageously
AEGMMNOPSSUU magnum opuses
AEGNORRRSSST transgressor
AEGOOPSSTTUY steatopygous
AEHHILNOPPRT philanthrope
AEHHILOPSTTU thiosulphate
AEHHIMNOPRSS horsemanship
AEHHLMOOPSTX exophthalmos
AEHHLMOPSTUX exophthalmus
AEHHLOOOPPRT lophophorate
AEHHNOPPRTYY hypnotherapy
AEHHOOPRRSST sharpshooter
AEHIILNOPRST relationship
AEHIILPRRSTT hair-splitter
AEHIIMNRSTTT martinettish
AEHIINNOPRTT trephination
AEHIINOORTTZ theorization
AEHIINOPRRST prehistorian
AEHIINRSSTUW White Russian
AEHIIRRSSTTW shirtwaister

AEHIKMNORRSY Yorkshireman
AEHILLMORSTY isothermally
AEHILMNOOPSU anemophilous
AEHILMNORSTW mothers-in-law
AEHILMOOPRST photorealism
AEHILOOPRSTT photorealist
AEHIMMMOPRST metamorphism
AEHIMMNNNOOT man in the moon
AEHIMNNOOPRT enantiomorph
AEHIMNNOOSSU mansion house
AEHIMNNOPPSU one-upmanship
AEHIMNNOSSSW womanishness
AEHIMNNOSSTT astonishment
AEHIMOOOSSST homoeostasis
AEHIMOPPRRST primrose path
AEHINNPPSSSS snappishness
AEHINNQSSSTU squash tennis
AEHINOOPRRTT prototherian
AEHINOOSSTTU station house
AEHINOPRSTTY attorneyship
AEHIOOPPRSTZ apostrophize
AEHIOPQRSSTU quaestorship
AEHIOPRRSTWY praiseworthy
AEHJMOOPPRRT major prophet
AEHLLMOOSUXY homosexually
AEHLLOOQRSUW hollow square
AEHLMNPRSUUY superhumanly
AEHLNOPSSTUY polyanthuses
AEHMNOOPRTUX pneumothorax
AEHNOOPRRSSU sarrusophone
AEHNORRSSSTY synarthroses
AEHOOPRRSSUW house sparrow
AEIIILLMNTUV illuminative
AEIIILMNRSST militariness
AEIIILNRSTTT interstitial
AEIIILPRSTUZ spiritualize
AEIIIMMNSSTT anti-Semitism
AEIIIMNNNOST insemination
AEIIIMNOSTTZ Semitization
AEIIIMNRSTTV ministrative
AEIIINNRSTTV intransitive
AEIIKKNORSSY karyokinesis
AEIIKNRSSTTY stay-in strike
AEIILLLLMMSY millesimally
AEIILLMMMORY immemorially
AEIILLNQRTUZ tranquillize
AEIILLRSTTUV illustrative
AEIILMMNOOST emotionalism
AEIILMNOOSTT emotionalist
AEIILMNOOTTY emotionality
AEIILMNOPRSS impressional
AEIILMNRSSUV universalism
AEIILMNRTUVY ruminatively
AEIILMNSTTUY simultaneity
AEIILMPRTTTU multipartite
AEIILNNNQUU quinquennial
AEIILNNOOTVZ novelization
AEIILNNOPSTT salient point
AEIILNOOPSTX expositional
AEIILNOOPTTX exploitation
AEIILNOPPSTY inappositely
AEIILNOPTTTY potentiality
AEIILNORSSST solitariness
AEIILNORSSUV Russian olive
AEIILNQRRTUZ tranquilizer
AEIILNQTTUVY quantitively
AEIILNRSSSTW sisters-in-law
AEIILNRSSTUV universalist
AEIILNRSTTVY transitively
AEIILNRSTUVY universality
AEIILNSTUUXY unisexuality
AEIILPRRTTTY tripartitely
AEIIMMNNOTTU Mountain Time
AEIIMMNOORTZ memorization
AEIIMNNNOORT renomination
AEIIMNNOOTTZ monetization
AEIIMNNOPSSX expansionism
AEIIMNNORSST Nestorianism
AEIIMNNOTUVW Mountain View
AEIIMNRSSSTV transmissive
AEIINNOPSSTX expansionist
AEIINOPPRRST perspiration
AEIINOPRTTUV vituperation
AEIJLMORRTUY majority rule
AEIKMNNRSTTU Turkmenistan
AEIKMNOQRSTU question mark
AEIKMNPRRRST printer's mark
AEIKMRSSSSTT taskmistress
AEILLLLPRRRT pralltriller
AEILLMNOPRSY impersonally
AEILLMNORSSV silver salmon
AEILLMNPRSUU superluminal
AEILLMPRSTTU multiple star
AEILLNNORTTY intolerantly
AEILLNORRTTY torrentially
AEILLPPRSUUV visual purple
AEILMNNOOPST Neoplatonism
AEILMNNRSTTU instrumental
AEILMNOOPRTT metropolitan
AEILMNOSSTUU simultaneous
AEILMOORSTTT stromatolite
AEILNNOOPSTT Neoplatonist
AEILNOOOPRRT poor relation
AEILNOOPPRTU repopulation
AEILNOOPRRSS responsorial
AEILNOOPRRTT interpolator
AEILNOORTUVY evolutionary
AEILNPPRRTUY Tyrian purple
AEILOPRRTUVZ pulverizator
AEILOPRSSSUU plesiosaurus
AEIMNNORSTTU menstruation
AEIMNOOPRRST impersonator
AEIMNOPRSSTU reassumption
AEIMNRSSSTTV transvestism
AEINNNOPRSTT transpontine
AEINNORSTTTU sternutation
AEINNOSSTTTU sustentation
AEINOOPRSTTT protestation
AEINOOPRSTTW power station
AEINOOSSTTTU ostentatious
AEINOPRRRSST star prisoner
AEINOPRRSTTT train-spotter
AEINRSSSTTTV transvestist
AEIOOOOPPPRS prosopopoeia
AEIOOPPRRRTX expropriator
AEIOPPRRRSTY perspiratory
AEJMMOPRRTTU trumpet major
AELLLMORSUVY marvellously
AELLMMNNOTUY monumentally
AELLMNOOOSSS Solomon's seal

AELLPRSSUUUV surplus value
AELMNNORRSTT storm lantern
AELMNOOOPSTU monopetalous
AELOOORRTTVY levorotatory
AEMNNOORSSTY stonemasonry
AEMNOOOPRSTZ spermatozoon
AEMNOOOPRTTT Ottoman Porte
AEMNOORRRSTT remonstrator
AEMOOPRSSTUW water opossum
AEMPRRSSTTUU superstratum
AENOOPRSSSUV vaporousness
AENORRSTTTUY sternutatory
AEOOOPRRRTTU tour operator
AFFGIILLMMMN flimflamming
AFFHILLNTUUY unfaithfully
AFFIILNNOSTU insufflation
AFGGGILLNNUY unflaggingly
AFGGHHIILNTU highfaluting
AFGGIILNRTYY gratifyingly
AFGIIKNOPRTT profit-taking
AFGIILLOSTUY flagitiously
AFGIILNSSTYY satisfyingly
AFGIIMNOPRRT profit margin
AFGIINNSSTUY unsatisfying
AFGIKNOORSTT toasting-fork
AFGIMNORRSTY transmogrify
AFHKLLNNTUUY unthankfully
AFHNOOORRSUW honours of war
AFIIILMNNOST inflationism
AFIIILNNORTT infiltration
AFIIILNNOSTT inflationist
AFIILMORSTUU multifarious
AFIILNNOORTU fluorination
AFIINOPRSSTU passion fruit
AFLNOOPPRRTU popular front
AGGHHIIKNSWY King's highway
AGGHHMOPPRSY sphygmograph
AGGHIIKLNPRT parking light
AGGHIIKNNSTV thanksgiving
AGGHILMNNRSY rhyming slang
AGGHILOOPRST graphologist
AGGHLOPPRTYY glyptography
AGGIIINNORTV invigorating
AGGIINNOPRSW growing pains
AGGIKLLNOOSS looking-glass
AGGIKLNPPRSU sparking plug
AGHHILNOPRTT triphthongal
AGHHIOPPRSYY physiography
AGHHOOPPSTUY phytophagous
AGHIIINNPRST training ship
AGHIIKLLMNRS shilling-mark
AGHILMNOOOOT homologation
AGHILORSSTWW whitlow-grass
AGHIMNOOPRST monographist
AGHIMOPRSTUY hypogastrium
AGHINOOPRSTT trap-shooting
AGHINOORSSTT shooting star
AGHLNOOOPRTY anthropology
AGHMNOOPRTYY pharyngotomy
AGIIIILNNOTV invigilation
AGIIILLMNNTU illuminating
AGIIILNRRTTY irritatingly
AGIIINNOORTV invigoration
AGIIKLMNSTTU multitasking
AGIIKLNNOPTT talking point
AGIILLLMNTUU multilingual
AGIILLLNNUUY unilingually
AGIILLMNORYZ moralizingly
AGIILLNNORUY unoriginally
AGIILLOPSSSS salpiglossis
AGIILNNNORRS snarling iron
AGIILNOORSUV vainglorious
AGIILNOPRRRY rip-roaringly
AGIIMNNRSTTT transmitting
AGIKMNNOORWW working woman
AGIKNOPRRTWY working party
AGILLNOOPSTY palynologist
AGILMNNSSUUY unassumingly
AGILMNOOPRTU promulgation
AGILNNNNOPTW town planning
AGILNNOOOPRT prolongation
AGILNPRSSSUY surpassingly
AGILOOPPRSTY papyrologist
AGILORSTTUUY gratuitously
AGINNOORRSTW garrison town
AGINOOPPPRTY party-pooping
AGINOPRSSTTT starting post
AGINORRSSTUU stranguríous
AGLLMOOPSUYY polygamously
AGLLNOORSUUY languorously
AGLMMNOOOSUY monogamously
AHHIILOPPSST hospital ship
AHHILLLLSSYY shilly-shally
AHHILNOPPRTY philanthropy
AHHINNOPRSTT strophanthin
AHIILMMPRSTU triumphalism
AHIILMPRSTTU triumphalist
AHIIMNNOORSU inharmonious
AHIINNNOOPSS Spanish onion
AHIKLOORTTUW kilowatt-hour
AHILLNOORTYZ horizontally
AHILMNOORSUY harmoniously
AHILMNPRTTUY triumphantly
AHILNOPRSTUU sulphuration
AHILOOPPRSSU saprophilous
AHIMNNOORSUU unharmonious
AHIMOOPPPSTU hippopotamus
AHINNOPRSSTU Sinanthropus
AHINOOPSSSTU sousaphonist
AHINORRSSSTY synarthrosis
AHNOOOPRRTTY prothonotary
AIIIIMMNNOTZ minimization
AIIILLMNNOTU illumination
AIIILLNNOSTT instillation
AIIILMNOOSST isolationism
AIIILMPRSSTU spiritualism
AIIILNOOSSTT isolationist
AIIILNRSSTTY sinistrality
AIIILPRSSTTU spiritualist
AIIILPRSTTUY spirituality
AIIIMMNNOTUZ immunization
AIIIMNNORSTT ministration
AIIIMNOOPTTZ optimization
AIIIMNOSSTTU situationism
AIIINNNOOTUZ unionization
AIIINNOPSSST inspissation
AIIINOOPPRTT propitiation
AIIINOPRRTTT tripartition
AIIINOPRSTTT partitionist
AIIINOSSTTTU situationist

AIIINRSTTTVY	transitivity
AIIKMNNOPRSS	Parkinsonism
AIILLLNOOTVY	volitionally
AIILLLNOSUVY	villainously
AIILLNNOOTUV	involutional
AIILLNOOPSTY	positionally
AIILLNORSTTU	illustration
AIILLNQRTTUY	tranquillity
AIILMNNNOOTU	mountain lion
AIILMNNORTTU	malnutrition
AIILMNOPRSTT	trampolinist
AIILNOOOPPST	oppositional
AIILNORRSTTY	transitorily
AIILOPRSUVVY	viviparously
AIILORSSTTTW	tailor's twist
AIIMMNOTTUUY	autoimmunity
AIIMNNORSSST	transmission
AIIMNOOORTTZ	motorization
AIIMNOOPRSSU	parsimonious
AIIMNOOQSTTU	misquotation
AIIMOOPPRRRT	impropriator
AIIOOPPRRTTY	propitiatory
AIKLLLMMOPRS	Plimsoll mark
AILLMNNOOPRY	pronominally
AILLNOOOPSST	saloon pistol
AILLNOOPTTYY	polytonality
AILMNORSTUVY	voluntaryism
AILNOOOPPRRT	proportional
AILNOPPRTUUY	unpopularity
AILNORSTTUVY	voluntaryist
AILOOPRRSUUY	uproariously
AILOORRSTTUY	traitorously
AIMNNOOPRSSU	pons asinorum
AIMOORRRTWWY	two-way mirror
AKMOOORSSUUY	Yamoussoukro
ALMNOOOSTUUY	autonomously
BBBBBEEHLLUU	hubble-bubble
BBBEELLRRTUU	rubber bullet
BBBEELMMORUY	bubble memory
BBCCEEHLOPST	Scotch pebble
BBCEEEHORSUY	breeches-buoy
BBCEEHILNPRU	Bible-puncher
BBCELLLOOSWY	collywobbles
BBCENOORRSTU	broncobuster
BBCGIJKNOOST	stockjobbing
BBCGIKLNOSTU	blockbusting
BBCHIIIILLOP	bibliophilic
BBDDGIILNOUY	body-building
BBDEEEELORTW	beetle-browed
BBDEEGGKLOOO	gobbledegook
BBDEEILLOORU	double boiler
BBDEELLMOOTT	bell-bottomed
BBDEELLOOSUU	double obelus
BBDEGGKLOOOY	gobbledygook
BBDEGHMNOORY	hydrogen bomb
BBDEHLOOORRT	blood brother
BBEEGMNORRUY	money-grubber
BBEEGNOPRRSU	sponge rubber
BBEEHILMPRTU	Bible-thumper
BBEEILMNORSW	women's libber
BBEFIIIIKNRS	bikini briefs
BBEGGHIILNOS	bobsleighing
BBEHINNOSSSS	snobbishness
BBEILNOSSSUU	bibulousness
BBENNORSSSTU	stubbornness
BCCCEHIIKKNR	chicken brick
BCCCEIIMRRSU	circumscribe
BCCCEINNOTTU	cubic content
BCCDEEIJORTT	direct object
BCCEEEHKRRRY	checkerberry
BCCEEEILLRTU	electric blue
BCCEEEILNNOS	noble science
BCCEEELNOOSS	obsolescence
BCCEEHNORRSS	cross-bencher
BCCEHHINOOPT	technophobic
BCCEHNNOOORT	corn on the cob
BCCEHNOOOPRS	bronchoscope
BCCEHORSTTTU	butterscotch
BCCEILMOORTY	motor bicycle
BCCEILOPRSTU	public sector
BCCGIIKLMNOR	rock-climbing
BCCHILLOOPSU	public school
BCCHNOOOPRSY	bronchoscopy
BCCINOOSSSUU	subconscious
BCCIOOOPRSST	stroboscopic
BCDDEEEIINOS	disobedience
BCDDEEEKLORU	double-decker
BCDDEELLLOOR	red blood cell
BCDDEGINORSS	cross-bedding
BCDEEEFIILNT	indefectible
BCDEEEKORRST	stockbreeder
BCDEEEMNNRUU	unencumbered
BCDEEFHIILNT	child benefit
BCDEEFIIKLRR	brickfielder
BCDEEIILPRST	discerptible
BCDEEIIOPPRR	bodice-ripper
BCDEEILLOORR	Border collie
BCDEEILOPRRU	reproducible
BCDEEILRSTTU	destructible
BCDEEINPRRSU	unprescribed
BCDEGIINOPRY	body piercing
BCDEIIILRTUY	reducibility
BCDEIILNORTU	introducible
BCDEIILNPUUZ	unpublicized
BCDEILOPRRUY	reproducibly
BCDELNORTUUU	culture-bound
BCDENORSTTUU	unobstructed
BCDGIKLNOOSU	bloodsucking
BCDGIKNOOSTY	body stocking
BCDIORSSSSUY	cross-subsidy
BCEEEEEHKNRS	knee-breeches
BCEEEEGHRRSU	cheeseburger
BCEEEEGILLNR	belligerence
BCEEEFILNNTY	beneficently
BCEEEGILLNRY	belligerency
BCEEEIKOORSX	exercise book
BCEEEINRSSUV	subservience
BCEEEIRRRSVY	service-berry
BCEEENPPRSTU	pre-pubescent
BCEEFHIORRST	before Christ
BCEEFHNNORRT	frontbencher
BCEEGIMNNOSS	becomingness
BCEEHIKNNRTU	Kitchener bun
BCEEHLLNOSST	Stellenbosch
BCEEHOORSSTU	creosote bush
BCEEIILLRSTT	belletristic
BCEEIJLSTUVY	subjectively
BCEEIJNNOOTV	non-objective
BCEEILMNOPTT	contemptible
BCEEILMOPRSS	compressible

BCEEIMMOSTTU	subcommittee
BCEEIMNOPRRY	pre-embryonic
BCEEINRSSUVY	subserviency
BCEEJLNOOSST	object lesson
BCEEKLLORSTT	block letters
BCEEKNOPRSTU	Purbeck stone
BCEELMMORSUY	cumbersomely
BCEELNOORTVY	conveyor belt
BCEELOORSUVW	obscure vowel
BCEFFHINOSUV	bunch of fives
BCEFGIILPRUU	public figure
BCEGHIILNTWY	bewitchingly
BCEGIIILNORR	incorrigible
BCEGIKKLNOOR	booking clerk
BCEGIKLNOSTU	bluestocking
BCEGILMNNOUY	unbecomingly
BCEGILNOOOOY	biocoenology
BCEHIIMORSTY	biochemistry
BCEHIINOSTTY	biosynthetic
BCEHIKNSSSSU	bush sickness
BCEHIMOORSTW	witches' broom
BCEHIMORSTWW	West Bromwich
BCEIIILLRTVY	civil liberty
BCEIIJMSSTUV	subjectivism
BCEIIJSSTTUV	subjectivist
BCEIIJSTTUVY	subjectivity
BCEIIKLLNRTU	clinker-built
BCEIINORTTUV	contributive
BCEIKLORRSTW	writer's block
BCEIKNNRSUWW	New Brunswick
BCEILLLMNOOP	Colonel Blimp
BCEILMNOPTTY	contemptibly
BCEILORSSTUU	tuberculosis
BCEINNNOSTTU	subcontinent
BCEMNORSSSUU	cumbrousness
BCERRSSTTUUU	substructure
BCGIIILMNNOR	climbing iron
BCGIIILNORRY	incorrigibly
BCGIILLMNOOS	solo climbing
BCGIILMOOORY	microbiology
BCGIILOOOOSY	sociobiology
BCGIKKNOORST	stockbroking
BCHHIMOOORRT	orthorhombic
BCHIIIOPSSTY	biophysicist
BCHIIIPSSSTU	ship's biscuit
BCHILNOORRTT	birth control
BCIIILPPRSTU	public spirit
BCIINNOORTTU	contribution
BCIINOPRSSTU	subscription
BCILMMNOSUUU	cumulonimbus
BCINOORRTTUY	contributory
BDDDEEFIILUZ	fluidized bed
BDDDEILMNOOY	bloody-minded
BDDEEEEFILMN	feeble-minded
BDDEEEEFNNRR	fender bender
BDDEEEFINNRU	unbefriended
BDDEEEFLMNTU	befuddlement
BDDEEEILLRWY	bewilderedly
BDDEEEILMOSW	disemboweled
BDDEEEINNSST	indebtedness
BDDEEFHIORRS	Bedfordshire
BDDEEGGINOOR	good breeding
BDDEEIKNNORW	broken-winded
BDDEEILMOSUX	mixed doubles
BDDEGHNNOORY	hydrogen bond
BDDELMOORRUY	bloody murder
BDDEMOORSTUY	study-bedroom
BDDFGIILNORY	forbiddingly
BDEEEEMMNRRU	unremembered
BDEEEFIILNNS	indefensible
BDEEEGIILNTV	diving beetle
BDEEEHLORRRT	elder brother
BDEEEIIRSVWY	bird's-eye view
BDEEEILMNRTW	bewilderment
BDEEFIILNNSY	indefensibly
BDEEGHHIINRS	Denbighshire
BDEEGIIILNST	indigestible
BDEEGLMNNORU	golden number
BDEEHILORSUU	housebuilder
BDEEHLLORSTU	shoulder-belt
BDEEIIILNRTV	indivertible
BDEEIIRRSTTU	redistribute
BDEEIJLRRRUY	jerry-builder
BDEEILMMORUW	medium bowler
BDEEILNPRRSY	spindle-berry
BDEEIMNRSSTU	disbursement
BDEEINNORSTV	inverted snob
BDEELNORSUVY	unobservedly
BDEFGILNOORY	forebodingly
BDEFHNOOORTU	debt of honour
BDEFLLMOOTTU	full-bottomed
BDEFLNOSSTUU	doubtfulness
BDEGGGILNRUY	begrudgingly
BDEGGIIMNOSU	disemboguing
BDEGHHINOOOR	neighborhood
BDEGHHOORRTU	thoroughbred
BDEGHIILMNTU	midnight blue
BDEGIIILLNNU	building line
BDEGIIILNSTU	building site
BDEGIIILNSTY	indigestibly
BDEGIINNRSST	bird's-nesting
BDEGILLNNRUY	blunderingly
BDEGILLNOOTT	bloodletting
BDEHHMNOOORR	rhombohedron
BDEHMOOORRTU	mouthbrooder
BDEIIIILLNTY	indelibility
BDEIIILNRTVY	indivertibly
BDEIIIORSTVY	biodiversity
BDEIIIRSTTUV	distributive
BDEIILLNOSSU	indissoluble
BDEIILORSSUU	subdelirious
BDEILNNPRSSU	purblindness
BDEIOORSTUVY	vitreous body
BDFGHILLOOSW	goldfish bowl
BDFGIINORTUY	fruiting body
BDGGGIILMNNO	mind-boggling
BDGHIIILNPSU	shipbuilding
BDGHIIORRUVY	hybrid vigour
BDGIILLNNOOT	blind tooling
BDGIILNRSTUY	disturbingly
BDHILOORSTTY	bloodthirsty
BDIIIIILSTVY	divisibility
BDIIILLNOSUY	libidinously
BDIIINORSTTU	distribution
BDIILLNOSSUY	indissolubly
BEEEEEFLMNNT	enfeeblement
BEEEEFHINORR	hereinbefore
BEEEEKLMNRRT	knee-trembler
BEEEELMMNTZZ	embezzlement
BEEEELNOSTTX	sexton beetle

BEEEFGLNOSTT self-begotten
BEEEGGGIRRUV veggie burger
BEEEGILRSSTU Geissler tube
BEEEGIMNPRSU Supreme Being
BEEEGIMRRTTT timber-getter
BEEEGJMNPRUU bungee jumper
BEEEHIIKLPSW Selebi-Phikwe
BEEEHIINNRTT terebinthine
BEEEHLNOOPTX telephone box
BEEEIILRRRSV irreversible
BEEEILLMNTTT belittlement
BEEEILNNSSSS sensibleness
BEEEILNRRSST terribleness
BEEEILOPPRST tribespeople
BEEEIMMNRTTT embitterment
BEEEINNNORTZ nitrobenzene
BEEELLNNOTVY benevolently
BEEELNOOSSST obsoleteness
BEEFGIINNRRT birefringent
BEEFILMNNOOT Bloemfontein
BEEFLLOOTTUW Woulfe bottle
BEEFLNRTTTUY butterfly net
BEEGGIIOOOOW boogie-woogie
BEEGGILNNORW bowling green
BEEGHOOPRRTU Peterborough
BEEGIIILLLNT intelligible
BEEGIILNNPUX inexpungible
BEEGLMORRUUX Luxembourger
BEEGLNNOOTTY only-begotten
BEEGLOORRTTT globe-trotter
BEEHIIINORTX exhibitioner
BEEHILLLRSVY Beverly Hills
BEEHILMOOPTZ phlebotomize
BEEHILNORRSS horribleness
BEEHILOORRSU broiler house
BEEHILORRSTY liberty horse
BEEHINOPQSSU queen's bishop
BEEHKNOORRST honest broker
BEEHLORRRTWY whortleberry
BEEIIILMRRSS irremissible
BEEIIILRRSST irresistible
BEEIIKLNSSSU businesslike
BEEIILRRRSVY irreversibly
BEEILLLORSUY rebelliously
BEEILLNNSTUW news bulletin
BEEILMOPRSTU Sublime Porte
BEEILPPRSSSU suppressible
BEEILRSSUVVY subversively
BEEINNNOOQUZ benzoquinone
BEEKMNNNOOTY bonnet monkey
BEEKNNNORSSU unbrokenness
BEELNNOSSSUU nebulousness
BEELNQSSTUUY subsequently
BEENNOQSTUUY Queen's bounty
BEEOOPRRSSTU obstreperous
BEFGHIINNORT Bonfire Night
BEFIIMNOOPRS pisiform bone
BEFILLNSSSSU blissfulness
BEFLNRTTTUUY butterfly nut
BEGGHIINNORU neighbouring
BEGGHIINOTWX boxing weight
BEGGIILNNOSS obligingness
BEGIIIILLLTY illegibility
BEGIIILLLNTY intelligibly
BEGIILLLNTTY belittlingly
BEGIILOOOSTX exobiologist
BEGIINORRSVW virgin's bower
BEGIKNOOPRRW power-broking
BEGILMOORSTY embryologist
BEGILNOOORUY neurobiology
BEGILNPRRTUY perturbingly
BEHIINOSSSTY biosynthesis
BEHILLMMRSTU miller's thumb
BEHILMOOPSTT phlebotomist
BEHINOSSSSUW show business
BEHLOOORSTTU troubleshoot
BEHNNORTTUUY bounty hunter
BEIIILLNOSUZ insolubilize
BEIIILMQRSUU equilibriums
BEIIILRRSSTY irresistibly
BEIILMSSSUVY submissively
BEIINNOOPRTW brownie point
BEIISSTTTUUV substitutive
BEILLOORSSTT stilboestrol
BEILMNRSTTUU butter muslin
BEILNOPRSSTY spiny lobster
BEILOOQSSUUY obsequiously
BEILOORSSTUY boisterously
BEILOPPRSTUU purpose-built
BEOOORRSTTUU tuberous root
BFGGHIILLNTU bullfighting
BFGHIILLORST Bill of Rights
BFIIIILNSTUY infusibility
BGGGHIILNNTU lightning bug
BGGHHIILRSTT bright lights
BGGHHLOOORUU Loughborough
BGGIILNNOSWW swing bowling
BGHHILLOORSU Hillsborough
BGHIIILLNPPS shipping-bill
BGHIILNOOPRT birthing pool
BGHILLNNSUUY unblushingly
BGHILLNOOOPT polling booth
BGHILOOOOPTY photobiology
BGIIILNNOOPT boiling point
BGIIKLLNNNUY unblinkingly
BGILLORSUUUY lugubriously
BIIIIILNSTVY invisibility
BIIILLNOSTUY insolubility
BIIKOOORSSTV visitors' book
BIILOQSTUUUY ubiquitously
BIINOSSTTTUU substitution
CCCCEEENNORS concrescence
CCCCEENOORRU co-occurrence
CCCCEIILMRRU circumcircle
CCCDEEILNOPY encyclopedic
CCCEEENORRRU reoccurrence
CCCEEHILORTY heterocyclic
CCCEEHKNORTU countercheck
CCCEEIINRTTY eccentricity
CCCEEILMNOTY Metonic cycle
CCCEGIIMNNOO meningococci
CCCEHINOPRTT concert pitch
CCCEIILOSUVY vicious cycle
CCCEIINNOOST conic section
CCCEINNOPSTU concupiscent
CCCEINNSSSTU succinctness
CCCEIOOPRSTT streptococci
CCCEMNOOPSUU pneumococcus
CCCHHHIRRSTU Christchurch
CCCHHHLOORSU church school

CCCIIIMNORSU circumcision
CCCIIIMORRTU microcircuit
CCCIIKLRSTTY trick cyclist
CCDDEEENNOPY codependency
CCDDEEHILNRT child-centred
CCDDEEINNOST disconnected
CCDEEEEMNSTU detumescence
CCDEEEENORRT retrocedence
CCDEEEFIILNV civil defence
CCDEEEHIINNS indehiscence
CCDEEEHIPRST direct speech
CCDEEEHNOSTU escutcheoned
CCDEEEIINRSV viridescence
CCDEEENRRSTU recrudescent
CCDEEHNOSTTU conduct sheet
CCDEEIILLNOV ill-conceived
CCDEEILNNORU unreconciled
CCDEEIORRTTU correctitude
CCDEELLOOPSU close-coupled
CCDEELOOPPRS close-cropped
CCDEGIMNNOOS second coming
CCDEIIIIRSTV recidivistic
CCDEIILNNOTY coincidently
CCDEILNOTUVY conductively
CCDEINNOOSSU second cousin
CCDIINOTTUVY conductivity
CCDINOOOPRTU co-production
CCDNNNOOORTU non-conductor
CCEEEEFIKLPR fleece-picker
CCEEEEHRSTTU cheese-cutter
CCEEEEJNNSUV juvenescence
CCEEEELLRRVV clever-clever
CCEEEFIILNSS life sciences
CCEEEFIILRRT electric fire
CCEEEFLNORSU fluorescence
CCEEEHIIMNPY chimney piece
CCEEEHKLLPRS spell-checker
CCEEEIIMNNRS reminiscence
CCEEEILLORTV recollective
CCEEEILMNNRT encirclement
CCEEEILMNNSU luminescence
CCEEEILOPRST secret police
CCEEEIMNNOPT incompetence
CCEEEIMNNSTU intumescence
CCEEEIMOPSTU costume piece
CCEEEINNORSU neuroscience
CCEEEINORSSV coerciveness
CCEEELOOPRST electroscope
CCEEEMMMNNOT commencement
CCEEENNORSST concreteness
CCEEFFIIINNY inefficiency
CCEEFFIIKOTT ticket office
CCEEFGIILNRT Celtic fringe
CCEEFHIPPRTT perfect pitch
CCEEFIINPSSS specificness
CCEEFINNOORT confectioner
CCEEGILLOOSY ecclesiology
CCEEGINOSTTY cytogenetics
CCEEHIILNORT heliocentric
CCEEHIKPRRRY cherry picker
CCEEHINNORTT ethnocentric
CCEEHKLOORST electro-shock
CCEEHLMOORSU colour scheme
CCEEIIILRSVV civil service
CCEEIILLOTVZ collectivize
CCEEIIMNORSV misconceiver
CCEEIINNNNOT incontinence
CCEEILLLOTVY collectively
CCEEILLNOORT recollection
CCEEILLORTTY electrolytic
CCEEILOPRRTY pyroelectric
CCEEILORRTVY correctively
CCEEILSSSUVY successively
CCEEIMNNOPTY incompetency
CCEEIMNOORST econometrics
CCEEINNNOORT reconnection
CCEEINNNORTT interconnect
CCEEIOOPRSST stereoscopic
CCEEKNORSSSU cocksureness
CCEELMNNOTUY locum tenency
CCEENORRRUUY Euro-currency
CCEEOOPPRSST spectroscope
CCEFFINNOORR coffin corner
CCEFIIINNSTU unscientific
CCEFILMNRTUU circumfluent
CCEFKLOOORUW cuckoo flower
CCEFLLSSSUUY successfully
CCEFLNSSSUUU unsuccessful
CCEGGINNNOOR going concern
CCEGHIINORTT ricochetting
CCEGIINNOOTY oncogenicity
CCEGIKLNORST costing clerk
CCEHHIILNOPT technophilic
CCEHIINOORRT rhinocerotic
CCEHILNOORTU technicolour
CCEHILNOOSUU council house
CCEHIMNOORRT chronometric
CCEHIMOPRSTY psychometric
CCEHINOPRSTY pyrotechnics
CCEHIOOPSSTT stethoscopic
CCEHIORRTTYY erythrocytic
CCEHKLORSTUU culture shock
CCEHNNOPRTUU counterpunch
CCEIIKKSTTWY sticky wicket
CCEIILLMOSTV collectivism
CCEIILLOSTTV collectivist
CCEIILLOTTVY collectivity
CCEIILMOORRT colorimetric
CCEIILNNOSUV inconclusive
CCEIILPRSTUU pisciculture
CCEIINNOTTVY connectivity
CCEIINORSTTV constrictive
CCEIINRSSTTY syncretistic
CCEILLNOSUVY conclusively
CCEILLOOOPSS oscilloscope
CCEILOOPRSUY precociously
CCEINNOSTTUY constituency
CCEINOOPRSSU preconscious
CCEINOORSSST cross-section
CCEINORSTTUV constructive
CCELNNORRTUY concurrently
CCEOOPPRSSTY spectroscopy
CCEORSSSSTUY success story
CCFGGHIIKNOT cockfighting
CCGHILNOOOST conchologist
CCGIILNNNOVY convincingly
CCGIINNNNOUV unconvincing
CCGIKLNOOSTU cucking-stool
CCGILMNOORTY motorcycling
CCHHIIMOSTYZ schizothymic

CCHHIKOSSTWY Scotch whisky
CCHHIMOOOPRT photochromic
CCHIIOOPRSTY hypocoristic
CCHIIORRSTTU short circuit
CCHIOOPPRSTY psychotropic
CCHLNOOOSTUY county school
CCIILNNNSTUU cunnilinctus
CCIILNOPRUVY Privy Council
CCIILORSTUUY circuitously
CCIIMOOPRSST microscopist
CCIINNOOPRST conscription
CCIINNOORSTT constriction
CCIKLNOORSUW works council
CCILMOORSTTY motorcyclist
CCILMORRSUUU cirrocumulus
CCIMNOOPSTUU compunctious
CCIMNORSTUUY country music
CCINNOORSTTU construction
CCNOORRSSTUY cross-country
CDDDDEEEEGKL deckled-edged
CDDDEEFIIOST eisteddfodic
CDDDEEFILNOS second fiddle
CDDEEEEGNORS second-degree
CDDEEEEINNNP independence
CDDEEEGIMOOS geodesic dome
CDDEEEINNNPY independency
CDDEEHIMORTT direct method
CDDEEHLOORRR record holder
CDDEEIILMMNO middle-income
CDDEEIJNPRUU unprejudiced
CDDEEILMORSU middle course
CDDEEINNORSU unconsidered
CDDEEINORSUV undiscovered
CDDEELLNOORT decontrolled
CDDEEMNNOTUU undocumented
CDDEFLNNOOUY confoundedly
CDDEGIIINRST discrediting
CDDEHILLMOOS middle school
CDDEHILNOSSS cloddishness
CDDEHLLOORSU cold shoulder
CDDEHLNORTUU thundercloud
CDDEIINNOSTU discontinued
CDDELMNOORSU scoundreldom
CDDEMNNOOPUU uncompounded
CDDGHILNOPTU pudding cloth
CDDMNOOOPRUW compound word
CDEEEEFGLLNO Golden Fleece
CDEEEEFILNSV self-evidence
CDEEEEFILRSV self-deceiver
CDEEEEIIRRVW wide receiver
CDEEEEILLRVW well received
CDEEEEILRRST Red Leicester
CDEEEELNNPRS resplendence
CDEEEENPRSSU supersedence
CDEEEFFIINNR indifference
CDEEEFHILRST chesterfield
CDEEEFIJLNTU fuel-injected
CDEEEGIILNOS geodesic line
CDEEEGIKLNRS single-decker
CDEEEHIMNPRT decipherment
CDEEEHNRSSTW wretchedness
CDEEEIILMRST semi-derelict
CDEEEIINNPXY inexpediency
CDEEEIINSSSV decisiveness
CDEEEILNQSTU deliquescent
CDEEEIMNORTT mine-detector
CDEEEINNNORS non-residence
CDEEEINRSSST discreetness, discreteness
CDEEEIRRSSSV service dress
CDEEELNNPRSY resplendency
CDEEELNPTUXY unexpectedly
CDEEELNRSSSW endless screw
CDEEEMNNNOTU denouncement
CDEEFFFIILOR field officer
CDEEFFIIINOV divine office
CDEEFFIMNOOT domino effect
CDEEFGILNORZ freezing cold
CDEEFGIOOOPS piece of goods
CDEEFHLNOOOV cloven-hoofed
CDEEFIILNORT line of credit
CDEEFILNNNOT non-inflected
CDEEFILNNNUU uninfluenced
CDEEFLLOORSU self-coloured
CDEEFLNOOOTV cloven-footed
CDEEFLRSSTTU self-destruct
CDEEFOORRSTU tours de force
CDEEGIILLPRV pelvic girdle
CDEEGIILRRTY triglyceride
CDEEGIKNOPRR pecking order
CDEEGINNORUZ unrecognized
CDEEHHKLLOSS shell-shocked
CDEEHIKLORTT ticket-holder
CDEEHIOPRRRS recordership
CDEEHLMOOSTU close-mouthed
CDEEHLNORSTU underclothes
CDEEIIILNSVY indecisively
CDEEIIILOPTZ depoliticize
CDEEIIINNSTV disincentive
CDEEIILMNRSY semicylinder
CDEEIILNOPRT predilection
CDEEIILNRSTY indiscreetly, iridescently
CDEEIILOPSTV velocipedist
CDEEIILPRTVY predictively
CDEEIIMNOPRV improvidence
CDEEIIMNOSTU eudemonistic
CDEEIINNRSST indirectness
CDEEILMNOOPX complexioned
CDEEILOORRSV versicolored
CDEEILRRSTTY restrictedly
CDEEIMMNOOXY mixed economy
CDEEINNOPRRT drop-in centre
CDEEINRRSTTU unrestricted
CDEEIOPRRTUV reproductive
CDEEKKLNNRUU knuckle under
CDEELOOORRSU rose-coloured
CDEEMOOPRRSS decompressor
CDEENNOOPRSS second person
CDEENNOOPRST corespondent
CDEENNRRRTUU undercurrent
CDEENOORSSSU decorousness
CDEEORRRSSSS cross-dresser
CDEFHINNORWW French window
CDEFIIINNOST disinfection
CDEFIIMORSTU discomfiture
CDEGHIMMNOOT night-commode
CDEGHINNOOSU echo-sounding
CDEGIILNNRSY discerningly
CDEGIINNNRSU undiscerning

CDEGINNORSST second string
CDEGINOORRVW overcrowding
CDEGLMNORUUY curmudgeonly
CDEHHIIIPRTT diphtheritic
CDEHHIILNSSS childishness
CDEHHIOPRSTT short-pitched
CDEHIIILPPSS discipleship
CDEHIIINNORS enchiridions
CDEHIIKKNNST thick-skinned
CDEHIILLOPRW chilli powder
CDEHIINNRSTT herd instinct
CDEHIIOPRRST directorship
CDEHIKKLLSTU thick-skulled
CDEHILLOOOST old school tie
CDEHILLOOPRY policyholder
CDEHIORRTTWY creditworthy
CDEHLMMNOOOR commonholder
CDEIIIILNNPS indiscipline
CDEIIILNNPSU undiscipline
CDEIIILNTVVY vindictively
CDEIIIMNORST misdirection
CDEIIINNORST indiscretion
CDEIIINNORTT interdiction
CDEIILMMNOOR melodic minor
CDEIILMRTUUV diverticulum
CDEIILNNPPRU unprincipled
CDEIILRSSUVY discursively
CDEIIMMNOOSS decommission
CDEIIMNORSTU reductionism
CDEIINNNOOSX disconnexion
CDEIINNOOPRT precondition
CDEIINNOSSTU discontinues
CDEIINNSSSTT distinctness
CDEIINOOPRST periodontics
CDEIINORRTTY interdictory
CDEIINORSTTU reductionist
CDEILLOPRSTU portcullised
CDEILMNORSSU scoundrelism
CDEILNOORSUY indecorously
CDEILOPRTUVY productively
CDEIMMNOOPTU compound time
CDEIMOOPRSSU discomposure
CDEINNRSTTUU uninstructed
CDEINOOPRRTU reproduction
CDEINOPRTUUV unproductive
CDEIOORSSTUU discourteous
CDEKNORRSTUW wonder-struck
CDELLNNOORTU uncontrolled
CDELLNOOTUVY convolutedly
CDELNNOOPRUY pronouncedly
CDELNOOOSTUY cotyledonous
CDENRRSTTUUU unstructured
CDFGIIIMNOST discomfiting
CDFGILNOORTY flying doctor
CDGGIKLLNUUY ugly duckling
CDGHIILNOORS riding school
CDGHIKLNOOST stockholding
CDGHILNOOPPU cloud-hopping
CDGIKLNOOSTU ducking-stool
CDHHIILLMNOR Richmond Hill
CDHINOOORSTT orthodontics
CDIIIJNORSTU jurisdiction
CDIIILNNSTTY indistinctly
CDIIMMNNSTTU Nunc Dimittis
CDIILLORSUUY ridiculously
CDIIMMNOOOSU incommodious
CDIINNOORTTU introduction
CDIIOPRTTUVY productivity
CDILMMOOOSUY commodiously
CDILOOORSUUU dourouculis
CDINOORRTTUY introductory
CEEEEELNPRST telepresence
CEEEEFFNRSTV effervescent
CEEEEFHRRSTZ chest freezer
CEEEEFILLSTV self-elective
CEEEEFILNNST life sentence
CEEEEFINNRRT interference
CEEEEGHMNORS cheesemonger
CEEEEGIMNNRY grey eminence
CEEEEHKOORRS Cherokee rose
CEEEEHNOPRRY honeycreeper
CEEEEHNORSVW whencesoever
CEEEEHNPQSSU Queen's Speech
CEEEEIINNPRX inexperience
CEEEEIKKPRTW wicketkeeper
CEEEEILPRSTV pre-selective
CEEEEINPRSTX pre-existence
CEEEEIORRSVX over-exercise
CEEEEIPRRRSV reserve price
CEEEELMORRTT electrometer
CEEEFFINNOTV non-effective
CEEEFFLNORST efflorescent
CEEEFGHIIOPT piece of eight
CEEEFHINRSST scene-shifter
CEEEFHLNRRTT French letter
CEEEFHLNRSSU cheerfulness
CEEEFIIMPRTV imperfective
CEEEFILLLMNU mellifluence
CEEEFILLRTVY reflectively
CEEEFILNPRSV splenic fever
CEEEFILNRTUV unreflective
CEEEFKLNSSSS fecklessness
CEEEGGINOPRR Prince George
CEEEGGNORRRY greengrocery
CEEEGIILLNNT intelligence
CEEEGINNPRRT Prince Regent
CEEEGINOOSTT osteogenetic
CEEEHHIINSTW Chinese white
CEEEHIIPRRSV receivership
CEEEHILLOPRT electrophile
CEEEHIMNNPRT encipherment
CEEEHIMNPSWY chimney sweep
CEEEHIMNRSTU hermeneutics
CEEEHINOSSSV cohesiveness
CEEEHIPRRSTW speech-writer
CEEEHKNOSSTY Cheyne-Stokes
CEEEHLLPSSSY speechlessly
CEEEHLMOORSW hero's welcome
CEEEHLNNOTTU luncheonette
CEEEHMNNNRTT entrenchment
CEEEHMNNRRTT retrenchment
CEEEIILLNTTV intellective
CEEEIIMNNPRT impertinence
CEEEIINPRTTV interceptive
CEEEIIPRRSTV irrespective
CEEEILLLMNSU selenium cell
CEEEILLNOPQU equipollence
CEEEILNOORTU Euro-election
CEEEILNOPRST pre-selection
CEEEILNRRSSV silver screen

CEEEILNRRSTV	client-server
CEEEILPPRTVY	perceptively
CEEEILPRSTVY	respectively
CEEEIMNNOPRS	omnipresence
CEEEIMNPPSTY	type specimen
CEEEINNNOSTX	non-existence
CEEEINNORSSV	overniceness
CEEEINNQSSTU	quintessence
CEEEINPPRTUV	unperceptive
CEEEINRRRSTW	screenwriter
CEEEIORRSSTV	retrocessive
CEEEIPRRSSUV	repercussive
CEEEJOPRRTTX	export reject
CEEEKKNOSTTW	ten-week stock
CEEEKLNRSSSS	recklessness
CEEELLNNORST	electron lens
CEEELLNSSSSU	cluelessness
CEEELLOPRTXY	electroplexy
CEEELLORRSTY	electrolyser
CEEELMMORTTU	telecommuter
CEEELMNOPSST	completeness
CEEELMORRTTY	electrometry
CEEELOPRRTTY	electrotyper
CEEELORRSSSU	resourceless
CEEEMNNNORTU	renouncement
CEEEMNOPRSSS	mesne process
CEEEMOPRRSTT	spectrometer
CEEENNPRTUUV	venepuncture
CEEFFHIOORSU	house officer
CEEFFIKOORRW	office worker
CEEFFIOPRTTY	petty officer
CEEFFLNORSSU	forcefulness
CEEFGHIIMRRT	crime fighter
CEEFGILNNOTU	genuflection
CEEFGILNNRTU	unreflecting
CEEFGLLLNTUY	neglectfully
CEEFHKMORRTU	motherfucker
CEEFIILRTTVY	reflectivity
CEEFIIMNOPRT	imperfection
CEEFIINOPRST	frontispiece
CEEFILMNRSSU	mercifulness
CEEFLLPRSTUY	respectfully
CEEFLMNOPSTT	self-contempt
CEEFLNOQRUWY	low frequency
CEEFLNOQSSTU	self-conquest
CEEGGILNOSSY	glycogenesis
CEEGHIINOSTT	histogenetic
CEEGHILNOPTY	phylogenetic
CEEGHIMORSTY	geochemistry
CEEGHINOORTT	orthogenetic
CEEGHKOOPPRT	pocket gopher
CEEGIINNSSTX	excitingness
CEEGIINOPRTV	precognitive
CEEGIINOSSTT	geoscientist
CEEGIKLLNOPS	glockenspiel
CEEGILLNNNOR	Lincoln green
CEEGINNOORTV	covering note
CEEGMNOORRST	costermonger
CEEHHIILLLNP	philhellenic
CEEHHIMMOORT	homeothermic
CEEHHIMPRRTY	hyperthermic
CEEHHLOORSST	clothes horse
CEEHHMOOPRRS	chromosphere
CEEHHOOPPRSS	phosphoresce
CEEHIIKNPRTY	hyperkinetic
CEEHIILLNPRS	spine-chiller
CEEHIINPPRST	prenticeship
CEEHIKKLNTUW	white-knuckle
CEEHIKMNOSSS	homesickness
CEEHILMOORTV	motor vehicle
CEEHILNNORTY	incoherently
CEEHIMMORRTT	thermometric
CEEHIMNOOSTU	Home Counties
CEEHINNNPPRY	penny-pincher
CEEHINOOPRST	stereophonic
CEEHINOORRSS	rhinoceroses
CEEHINRSSSTT	stretchiness
CEEHIOPRSTUX	executorship
CEEHKMNNORWY	monkey wrench
CEEHLMOOPRTU	thermocouple
CEEHMOPRRSTY	psychrometer
CEEHMORSTTYY	hysterectomy
CEEHNNOORSTU	Southern Cone
CEEIIIMNPPRT	impercipient
CEEIIINNSSSV	incisiveness
CEEIIJNNORTT	interjection
CEEIIJNORSTT	rejectionist
CEEIIKKLNPRW	winkle-picker
CEEIIKLLNRSV	nickel silver
CEEIILLNNOTT	intellection
CEEIILMNNORT	inclinometer
CEEIILNNPRSS	princeliness
CEEIILNPPRTY	percipiently
CEEIILNPSSTX	explicitness
CEEIIMNOSSSS	secessionism
CEEIIMOPRSSU	semi-precious
CEEIIMORRSTU	meretricious
CEEIIMORSSTV	viscosimeter
CEEIINNNNOTV	inconvenient
CEEIINNOPRTT	interception
CEEIINNORSST	intercession
CEEIINNORSTT	intersection
CEEIINOPRSTT	receptionist
CEEIINORSSTT	resectionist
CEEIINOSSSST	secessionist
CEEIIPPRRSTV	prescriptive
CEEIIPPRTTVY	perceptivity
CEEIJLOPRTVY	projectively
CEEIJNORRTTY	interjectory
CEEIKLMNPPRU	pumpernickel
CEEIKLNOSSSV	lovesickness
CEEILLMNOPTY	incompletely
CEEILLNOPQUY	equipollency
CEEILLORSSTY	electrolysis
CEEILMOOPRYZ	copolymerize
CEEILNNNOTVY	conveniently
CEEILOOPRSTT	coleopterist
CEEILOPRTTVY	protectively
CEEILPRSSUVY	percussively
CEEIMMMNORTT	recommitment
CEEIMNOORSTT	econometrist
CEEIMNORRSTU	Eurocentrism
CEEIMOORRRST	eco-terrorism
CEEINNNOQSTU	inconsequent
CEEINNOORRSV	reconversion
CEEINNORRTTV	interconvert
CEEINNORSSTT	contriteness
CEEINNPRTUUV	venipuncture
CEEINNRRRTTU	intercurrent
CEEINOOPRSTT	stereopticon

CEEINOOPRSTU	counterpoise
CEEINOORRSST	retrocession
CEEINOORRSVV	cover version
CEEINOPRRSSU	repercussion
CEEINOPRSSSU	preciousness
CEEINOPSSSSU	speciousness
CEEINORRRSTU	resurrection
CEEINORRSSTY	intercessory
CEEINORSTTTU	reconstitute
CEEIOORRRSTT	eco-terrorist
CEEKLLNSSSSU	lucklessness
CEEKLLOORTWY	yellow rocket
CEEKLNOOSTTY	cytoskeleton
CEEKNORRSUVW	nervous wreck
CEEKOOPRRSSU	pressure-cook
CEELLNOORTTV	electronvolt
CEELNNOQSTUY	consequently
CEELNOOQRSUU	Queen's colour
CEELOOOPRSTU	coleopterous
CEELOPPRSSST	prospectless
CEEMOPRRSTTY	spectrometry
CEEMOPRRSTUU	Supreme Court
CEENNOOQRSTU	queen consort
CEENNOORRTTU	counter-tenor
CEENOOOPPRSS	snooperscope
CEENOOSSSTUV	covetousness
CEENORSTTUUV	Venture Scout
CEEOOPPRRRSS	pre-processor
CEEOPPRSSSTU	prospectuses
CEFFIIORRST	first officer
CEFFHIORRSTU	sheriff court
CEFFIIINNSTU	insufficient
CEFFIILNSTUY	sufficiently
CEFFIILOOPRT	pilot officer
CEFFIORRSTUU	fructiferous
CEFGIIKLNPTY	flying picket
CEFGIILNOSTT	close-fitting
CEFHHILNOPRS	French polish
CEFHLLLOOOSW	schoolfellow
CEFHLMOOORRS	reform school
CEFIIILNOSTU	infelicitous
CEFIILLOSTUY	felicitously
CEFIILMNNTUY	munificently
CEFIILNOPRSS	prolificness
CEFIILNOPRTY	proficiently
CEFIILNORSST	frictionless
CEFIILNOSTUY	infectiously
CEFILLMNRUUY	unmercifully
CEFILLMOORSY	frolicsomely
CEFILLORRTUU	floriculture
CEFILNNOSSTU	functionless
CEFILOORSUVY	vociferously
CEFKKLOORRSW	clerk of works
CEFLNNORSSSU	scornfulness
CEGGHILOSTTW	toggle switch
CEGHHIILOPRY	hieroglyphic
CEGHHIIRSTUY	high-security
CEGHHILNOSTT	nightclothes
CEGHIIOPSSTY	geophysicist
CEGHIJORSTUU	rough justice
CEGHIKNNOSSS	shockingness
CEGHIKNOORRS	rocking horse
CEGHILNOOORZ	chronologize
CEGHILNOOSTT	technologist
CEGHILOOORST	choreologist
CEGHILOOPSYZ	psychologize
CEGHIMORTUUX	cough mixture
CEGHINNOSSTU	touchingness
CEGHINOORSTU	trichogenous
CEGHKMOORSSU	smoker's cough
CEGIIKLNNRSY	snickeringly
CEGIILLOOSTX	lexicologist
CEGIIMMNORTT	recommitting
CEGIINNOOPRT	precognition
CEGIKLNNOSSU	King's Counsel
CEGIKLNOSSST	stockingless
CEGIKNNOORST	rocking-stone
CEGILLLMNOPY	compellingly
CEGILLMOPTUX	guilt complex
CEGILNNNOTTY	contingently
CEGILNOOORTW	cooling tower
CEGILNOOPRTY	glycoprotein
CEGILNOOSSTY	synecologist
CEGIMORRRSUY	microsurgery
CEGINNNNOSTU	unconsenting
CEGINNNOORTW	conning tower
CEGINNPSSTUU	unsuspecting
CEGINOORRSSV	crossing over
CEGINORRSSTU	string-course
CEGINPRSSTTU	press cutting
CEGLMORSTUUY	ugly customer
CEHHIILMOPRT	thermophilic
CEHHIILOPRST	lithospheric
CEHHILNRSSSU	churlishness
CEHHILOOPRTY	hypochlorite
CEHHILORSTTT	torch-thistle
CEHHIMOPSTTY	phytochemist
CEHHIOOPPRST	photospheric
CEHHIOPPRRTY	hypertrophic
CEHIIIMNSTTT	stitch in time
CEHIIKLNSSST	ticklishness
CEHIILLNNORS	Lincolnshire
CEHIILMNOPRS	necrophilism
CEHIILNOPRST	necrophilist
CEHIILNQSSSU	cliquishness
CEHIILOPSTTY	polytheistic
CEHIIMNOOSTT	monotheistic
CEHIKMOOPRSU	skeuomorphic
CEHILLOPPTYY	polyphyletic
CEHILMNOOPTY	monophyletic
CEHILMNOPPTY	nympholeptic
CEHILMOPRSTU	ostrich plume
CEHILNNOSSSW	clownishness
CEHILOQSTTUY	coquettishly
CEHILORRTTUU	horticulture
CEHIMOOPRRTT	thermotropic
CEHIMOORSTTY	stoichometry
CEHINNORRSYZ	synchronizer
CEHINOPRSTTY	pyrotechnist
CEHINOSSSSTT	Scottishness
CEHIOOPPRRST	tropospheric
CEHIOOPRRSTU	chiropterous
CEHKKOORRSSW	shock-workers
CEHLMMOORSSU	summer school
CEHLMMOOSSTU	smooth muscle
CEHMOOOOPRTY	oophorectomy
CEHMOOSSSTUU	customs house
CEHNOORSTUUY	country house
CEIIILMNPSST	implicitness
CEIIIMNOPRSS	precisionism

CEIIINOPRSST	precisionist	**CFIILLNOOSTU**	solifluction
CEIIJNNOORTT	introjection	**CFILNORSSUUU**	furunculosis
CEIIKLLPSTTY	lickety-split	**CFIMNNOORTUY**	unconformity
CEIIKLSSTWZZ	swizzle-stick	**CGGILNNORSTU**	curling tongs
CEIIKRRSSTUY	security risk	**CGHHIINNTTUW**	witch-hunting
CEIILLNOSTUY	licentiously	**CGHHIINORTUW**	witching hour
CEIILLRSTUUV	silviculture	**CGHIIKKNNOPS**	shocking pink
CEIILMNNOSTY	omnisciently	**CGHIILOOOPRT**	oligotrophic
CEIILMOPRTUV	pluviometric	**CGHIILOORSTT**	trichologist
CEIILNOOSTTU	elocutionist	**CGHIIMNOOPSY**	physiognomic
CEIILNOPRSUY	perniciously	**CGHIIMOOPRTT**	thigmotropic
CEIILNOPRTUY	polyneuritic	**CGHIINOPSTTT**	topstitching
CEIILNOSSSTU	seclusionist	**CGHIKKNNOOPS**	knocking shop
CEIILNOSSTUX	exclusionist	**CGHIKLNNORUW**	working lunch
CEIILOPRSSUU	supercilious	**CGHILNOOORST**	chronologist
CEIIMMNOORSS	commissioner, recommission	**CGHILOOPSSTY**	psychologist
		CGHINORRSSUU	scouring-rush
CEIIMMNOPRTU	minicomputer	**CGIIIMNOSSTY**	misogynistic
CEIIMOORSSTT	sociometrist	**CGIILMOOSSTU**	musicologist
CEIINNNOSSTT	inconsistent, non-scientist	**CGIILOOOSTTX**	toxicologist
		CGIKLLNOORST	rolling stock
CEIINNORRSTU	insurrection	**CGIKNOOPRRST**	King's Proctor
CEIINOOPRRTY	incorporeity	**CGILLNOOOPRT**	protocolling
CEIINOPPRRST	prescription	**CGILMNOOPSSU**	gossip column
CEIINORSSTUX	excursionist	**CGILNOOSTUUY**	contiguously
CEIINOSTTTUV	constitutive	**CGILOOOPRSTT**	proctologist
CEIIOPPRRSTV	proscriptive	**CGILOOPRSTTY**	cryptologist
CEIIPRRRSTTW	scriptwriter	**CGLNOOOPRRTU**	control group
CEIKKMNORSTY	monkey tricks	**CHIIILOPRTTT**	lithotriptic
CEILLMOPSUVY	compulsively	**CHIINOOPPRSW**	whip scorpion
CEILLMOSTUUY	meticulously	**CHIINOPSSTUV**	viscountship
CEILLNOSUVVY	convulsively	**CHIMNOOOSSTU**	monostichous
CEILLOQRSTUV	quill-coverts	**CHKOORRRRSTU**	horror-struck
CEILLRSTUUVY	sylviculture	**CHLMOOOPRSUY**	polychromous
CEILMNOOSTUU	contumelious	**CHMMNOOORSST**	short commons
CEILNNOSSTTY	consistently	**CHNNOORRTTUY**	north country
CEILNOORRTTU	interlocutor	**CIIIIOPSSTTV**	positivistic
CEILNOORSSUY	censoriously	**CIIILLMPTTUY**	multiplicity
CEILNOORSTUW	Low Countries	**CIIKLRTTTUUY**	utility truck
CEILNOSSSSUU	lusciousness	**CIIKNOOPSTTU**	tuck position
CEILNOSSTUUY	incestuously	**CIILLOOSSTUY**	solicitously
CEIMMNOOPSST	compos mentis	**CIILMNOOOPST**	monopolistic
CEIMNNOOPRSU	mispronounce	**CIILOORSTUVY**	victoriously
CEIMNNOORSTU	conterminous	**CIILOPSSSUUY**	suspiciously
CEIMNOPRSTTY	streptomycin	**CIIMOPRRSSTU**	scriptoriums
CEINNOOPRTTU	counterpoint	**CIINNOOSTTTU**	constitution
CEINRRSSSTTU	instructress	**CIINOOPPRRST**	proscription
CEIOPPPRRSTU	support price	**CIINOPSSSUUU**	unsuspicious
CEKORRRRSTTU	terror-struck	**CIJLNORSSTUU**	jurisconsult
CELLLOORSSUY	colourlessly	**CIKLOPPPPRYY**	prickly poppy
CELMOPRSTUUU	corpus luteum	**CILLMOOPRSUY**	compulsorily
CELNOOORRTTW	control tower	**CILLORRSSUUY**	scurrilously
CELNOPRSTUUW	slow puncture	**CILNNOOSTUUY**	continuously
CEMMNNNOOSSU	uncommonness	**CILOPRSSTUUY**	scrupulosity
CEMNOOPSTTUU	contemptuous	**CIMMNNNOOSTU**	non-communist
CEMOOOORRSTT	motor scooter	**CIMNNOOSSTUU**	customs union
CENNOSSSTUUU	unctuousness	**CLLOPRSSUUUY**	scrupulously
CFFHKLNOPSUU	Suffolk punch	**CLNOPRSSUUUU**	unscrupulous
CFGHHIINORST	torch-fishing	**DDDEEENNSSUW**	unweddedness
CFGIILNOOSTV	cost of living	**DDDEEFHILRSU**	Huddersfield
CFGILMNOORTY	comfortingly	**DDDEEIIIMPSY**	epididymides
CFHIINOOPRSS	scorpion fish	**DDDEGILMNORU**	middle ground
CFIIIKNNORST	skin friction	**DDDEHNNOOORR**	rhododendron
CFIIILOSTTUY	fictitiously	**DDDEIIIKRSTV**	divided skirt
CFIIKLLOORST	folkloristic	**DDDEIIKLNTWY**	tiddledywink

DDEEEEFINNSV	defensive end
DDEEEELLRSVW	well-deserved
DDEEEEMNNSST	dementedness
DDEEEENRSSSV	deservedness
DDEEEGILLNSW	well-designed
DDEEEGMOOPRT	good-tempered
DDEEEIKNRTWY	dirty weekend
DDEEEILLMMPT	Middle Temple
DDEEEILMNRTY	determinedly
DDEEEIMNNRTU	undetermined
DDEEEINNOSSS	one-sidedness
DDEEELLMMOSY	meddlesomely
DDEEELNOPRRT	Old Pretender
DDEEELNRSUVY	undeservedly
DDEEENOPRRUW	underpowered
DDEEENORSUVZ	rendezvoused
DDEEFFGLLLUY	fully fledged
DDEEFGIILMNR	middle finger
DDEEFHIIIMRU	dehumidifier
DDEEFIIINNTU	unidentified
DDEEGGINRRSU	designer drug
DDEEGHHOOPRS	Good Shepherd
DDEEGHIILMTW	middleweight
DDEEGHIINTWW	white wedding
DDEEGIILMNNS	single-minded
DDEEGILMNOST	dislodgement
DDEEGILNNSUY	undesignedly
DDEEGLLNORUW	well-grounded
DDEEHIIINRST	disinherited
DDEEIIKLLMNY	like-mindedly
DDEEIILMMNPS	simple-minded
DDEEIKNNRRUW	wunderkinder
DDEEILLOPSSW	well disposed
DDEEILMNNOPY	open-mindedly
DDEEILNNPSSS	splendidness
DDEEILNOPSSS	lopsidedness
DDEEIMNNORUZ	unmodernized
DDEEIMNNOSTW	disendowment
DDEELNNOPSTY	despondently
DDEEMNOOSSTU	outmodedness
DDEFGINNNRUU	underfunding
DDEGGHIINNTW	wedding night
DDEGHHIILMNY	high-mindedly
DDEGHILNRSUY	shudderingly
DDEGHMOOORUU	good-humoured
DDEGILLNNOWY	long-windedly
DDEGILNOORST	dendrologist
DDEGIMNNORST	strong-minded
DDEGINNOPSTU	pudding-stone
DDEGINNORSSW	dressing down
DDEHIIIMNNSU	undiminished
DDEHILNNOOPR	philodendron
DDEIIILPRSTY	dispiritedly
DDEIIJLNOSTY	disjointedly
DDEIIMNOSUVV	modus vivendi
DDEIMOOPPSUU	pseudopodium
DDGHILMNOOOU	hood-moulding
DDGIIIKNNRRV	drink-driving
DDGIILMNOPRU	drip-moulding
DDIIINOORSVW	word division
DEEEEEMNPRTV	even-tempered
DEEEEFFILRRT	filter-feeder
DEEEEHIMNOTV	eventide home
DEEEEHLNSSSS	heedlessness
DEEEEIMNPRRT	predetermine
DEEEELNNSSSS	needlessness
DEEEELPRSSST	pressed steel
DEEEENRRRVVY	Very Reverend
DEEEENRRSSSV	reservedness
DEEEFGLNORSV	self-governed
DEEEFHILRSTW	Wethersfield
DEEEFIINNSST	definiteness
DEEEFLLMOPSY	self-employed
DEEEFLMRRRSU	self-murderer
DEEEFNNQRTUU	unfrequented
DEEEFOPRSTTV	spotted fever
DEEEGHIMMRRT	hedge trimmer
DEEEGHNOPRRT	three-pronged
DEEEGIINNRRV	engine driver
DEEEGIKNNNOY	donkey engine
DEEEGINNRSSS	resignedness
DEEEGINNRSSV	evening dress
DEEEGINRRSTU	unregistered
DEEEGJMNPRTU	prejudgement
DEEEHHILRTTY	diethyl ether
DEEEHHIPPRSS	shepherd's pie
DEEEHILMNSTV	dishevelment
DEEEHLORSSTV	short-sleeved
DEEEHLRRSSSW	Welsh dresser
DEEEHMNNORTT	dethronement
DEEEIINRSSSV	derisiveness
DEEEIINRSSTZ	desensitizer
DEEEILLNRUVY	unrelievedly
DEEEILLPPQUW	well-equipped
DEEEILMOPRYZ	depolymerize
DEEEILNRSTTY	interestedly
DEEEILNSSSUV	delusiveness
DEEEIMNNOPST	semi-deponent
DEEEIMNORRSS	reindeer moss
DEEEIMNORSTT	densitometer
DEEEIMNRSSTV	disseverment
DEEEIMPRRTTT	pretermitted
DEEEINNRSTTU	uninterested
DEEEIPRRSSUZ	depressurize
DEEEJLLOPPRT	jet-propelled
DEEEKLNNOOST	endoskeleton
DEEELMNOPRTY	redeployment
DEEELNORSSSV	resolvedness
DEEELNRRSUVY	unreservedly
DEEEMNORRSTV	Most Reverend
DEEENORSSUVZ	rendezvouses
DEEFFHINRRSU	under-sheriff
DEEFFIILNRRY	friendly fire
DEEFFMOORRSU	four freedoms
DEEFGIIKNNRR	knife-grinder
DEEFHIIIMNSS	semi-finished
DEEFHIINNSSS	fiendishness
DEEFHOPRSTUY	duty-free shop
DEEFIIILNNTY	indefinitely
DEEFIIILNTVY	definitively
DEEFIIINNORT	redefinition
DEEFIILNNRRU	unfriendlier
DEEFIILNNRSS	friendliness
DEEFIILNRSTU	unfertilised
DEEFIILNRTUZ	unfertilized
DEEFIILPPRTT	filter-tipped
DEEFILLMNORW	well-informed
DEEFILLNOSSU	self-delusion
DEEFILLNOSVV	self-involved
DEEFILNOOSTV	self-devotion

DEEFILNRRSUY user-friendly
DEEFILOPRSTT potter's field
DEEFIMNNORSS informedness
DEEFIMOORRRT Order of Merit
DEEFLOORSTUY sure-footedly
DEEFMNOPRRRU underperform
DEEFNNOORSSV overfondness
DEEGGIMNORST disgorgement
DEEGHIILLNSV dishevelling
DEEGHIILNRVW driving wheel
DEEGHIINNSTW winding-sheet
DEEGIILLLNPW pile dwelling
DEEGIILMOOPY epidemiology
DEEGIILNNSSY yieldingness
DEEGIILNPRUV unprivileged
DEEGIILRSSVY digressively
DEEGIIMNSSTU disguisement
DEEGIINOPRST predigestion
DEEGIJMMNSTU misjudgement
DEEGILLNOOOR golden oriole
DEEGILMNNNOY moneylending
DEEGILNOPRRV ringed plover
DEEGILNPRSSY depressingly
DEEGIMNNOPRU deep mourning
DEEGINNNNSSU unendingness
DEEGINNNPRTU unpretending
DEEGINNRSTTT trendsetting
DEEGNOORRSTT Gordon setter
DEEHIIKRSSSW side-whiskers
DEEHIILNSSSV devilishness
DEEHIINPRSST residentship
DEEHILOORRSS horse-soldier
DEEHILPRSUUZ desulphurize
DEEHIMNOORTU time-honoured
DEEHIOPPRTTY pteridophyte
DEEHLNOORSTU shoulder note
DEEHLPRSTTUU sulphuretted
DEEHOORRSSUV hors d'oeuvres
DEEIIIMNRTTV divertimenti
DEEIIINSSSVV divisiveness
DEEIILNNSSUW unwieldiness
DEEIILNRTUUZ underutilize
DEEIIMNNRSTT disinterment
DEEIIMNORTTV divertimento
DEEIINPRSSST spiritedness
DEEIIRRSSSTW weird sisters
DEEIJNORRRSU surrejoinder
DEEIKMNOPRSY spider monkey
DEEIKNORSSVV Severodvinsk
DEEILLNNQTUY delinquently
DEEILLNORRSS slender loris
DEEILLORRSSV silver solder
DEEILMMNOOPT dipole moment
DEEILMNNSSSS mindlessness
DEEILMNOOOPZ demonopolize
DEEILNQRTUUY unrequitedly
DEEILNRSSTUY unresistedly
DEEIMNNORUVY never you mind
DEEINNOQSTUU unquestioned
DEEINPRSSUUV unsupervised
DEEKMNOOPRWY powder monkey
DEEKNOORRRWW wonder-worker
DEELLNORSUVY unresolvedly
DEELMNORSTUY tremendously
DEELNORSSSSW wordlessness
DEELNOSSSSUU sedulousness
DEENNNOSSTUW unwontedness
DEENOOPRSSST dessertspoon
DEFFHIRSSTTU stuffed shirt
DEFFHLNOOPSU pound of flesh
DEFGHHIIILTY high fidelity
DEFGHILLLTUY delightfully
DEFGIILNNUYY unedifyingly
DEFGIINNRTTT drift-netting
DEFGILMNNOOY folding money
DEFHILOPPRST Doppler shift
DEFHLOOORSSU House of Lords
DEFIILOPRSUY perfidiously
DEFILOORSTUY do-it-yourself
DEFINOOOPRRT point of order
DEFIOORRSSUU sudoriferous
DEFNNOOPRSSU profoundness
DEGGGINNRSSU grudgingness
DEGGHILNOOSU lodging house
DEGGHLOOORYY hydrogeology
DEGGINNORSSW dressing gown
DEGGKLLRSUUY skullduggery
DEGHHHILORSU shoulder-high
DEGHHIIIPRST high-spirited
DEGHHIINOPTZ diphthongize
DEGHHIORRTUV drive-through
DEGHHIORSSTT short-sighted
DEGHILNNRTUY thunderingly
DEGHNNOOSTUU hound's-tongue
DEGIIIKLNNNX index-linking
DEGIIINNRRST disinterring
DEGIILLNNUYY unyieldingly
DEGIILLOOSTT deltiologist
DEGIILNNNOSU sounding line
DEGIILNNOSUY indigenously
DEGIINNOSSUU disingenuous
DEGIKNOORRRW working order
DEGILMNOOOST demonologist
DEGILMNOOPRU rope-moulding
DEGILNNORSUY resoundingly
DEGILNOOOSTT deontologist
DEGILOOPRSTT proglottides
DEGIMNNOORUV mourning dove
DEGIMNNORRSS morning dress
DEGIMNOORRSS dressing room
DEGKNOORRSTU ground stroke
DEGLLNORSSUY groundlessly
DEGMNOORRRUY merry-go-round
DEHHHMMORTTY rhythm method
DEHHILNORSST North Shields
DEHHILOSSSTU South Shields
DEHHIOPRRTYY hyperthyroid
DEHIIKLLNOOU unlikelihood
DEHILOOPRRSV overlordship
DEHIMNOOORTY domino theory
DEHINNOOQRUY hydroquinone
DEHINOOPRSST spinsterhood
DEHKLNOORSTU shoulder-knot
DEHLLOOOPRSU shoulder loop
DEHLLOORRTWY other-worldly
DEHLNOORRSUY horrendously
DEHLNORSTUUY thunderously
DEHMNORRSTTU thunderstorm
DEHNOOORSTUW southernwood
DEIIILMNTUVY diminutively

DEIIILMSSSVY	dismissively
DEIIINORSSTV	diversionist
DEIILPRSTUVY	disruptively
DEIINOOPRSTT	periodontist
DEIINOORSTUX	nitrous oxide
DEIIOOPPRRST	poor-spirited
DEIJNPRRSTUU	jurisprudent
DEILLMORTUXY	dolly mixture
DEIMNOPSTUYY	pseudonymity
DEINOOOPPRRT	proportioned
DEINOSSSSTUU	studiousness
DELNOPSSTUUY	stupendously
DEMNOOPSSUUY	pseudonymous
DENNOORSSSUW	wondrousness
DFFGGHIINNTU	fighting fund
DFFIIINOSSTU	diffusionist
DFHNOOOORRUW	word of honour
DGGGILNNRUUY	ungrudgingly
DGGHHIINNOSU	high-sounding
DGGHIILNNORT	lightning rod
DGGHINNOTTUU	doughnutting
DGGIIKNNNORS	drinking song
DGGIILNSSTUY	disgustingly
DGIIIINNOSSV	division sign
DGIIILNNOOSV	long division
DGIILOOPRSUY	prodigiously
DGILMOORSTTY	troglodytism
DGILNOOOOSTT	odontologist
DGINNORRSSUU	surroundings
DGNOOPRRSSTU	sports ground
DHHIILOOPPPS	phospholipid
DHIIMNNOORUY	hydronium ion
DHIMOOPRRSTY	hydrotropism
DHINOOORSTTT	orthodontist
DHLNOOORTUXY	unorthodoxly
DHMMPPTTUUYY	humpty-dumpty
DIIIINOQSSTU	disquisition
EEEEEGKNPRRS	greenskeeper
EEEEEHHLRRTW	three-wheeler
EEEEGIILNPSS	spiegeleisen
EEEEHHKOPSTU	keep the house
EEEEHLMNOPRT	nephelometer
EEEEHLNRRSTW	sternwheeler
EEEEHLNRSSTV	nevertheless
EEEEIMNPRRTX	experimenter
EEEEINNQRSTU	equestrienne
EEEELMNRSTTT	resettlement
EEEELNRSSSST	treelessness
EEEEMNORSTTX	extensometer
EEEENNPRRRTU	entrepreneur
EEEENNSSTWYY	teensy-weensy
EEEENPRRSSSV	perverseness
EEEEPPRRRSSU	peer pressure
EEEFFINSSSUV	effusiveness
EEEFGGINNRRS	green fingers
EEEFGLLNRUVY	revengefully
EEEFGLNNSSUV	vengefulness
EEEFHINRRRSW	Renfrewshire
EEEFHINRSSSV	feverishness
EEEFIIKLLNSS	lifelikeness
EEEFIIMNNNSS	feminineness
EEEFILLNSSSS	lifelessness
EEEFILNRSSTT	self interest
EEEFILNSSTTX	self-existent
EEEFILPRRSSX	express rifle
EEEFLLNSSSSS	selflessness
EEEFLLOOPPRW	flower people
EEEFLNNSSTUV	eventfulness
EEEGGGILLNPV	level pegging
EEEGHIKNOPSU	housekeeping
EEEGHILRTTWW	welterweight
EEEGHIMNOSTU	meeting house
EEEGHINSTTVY	seventy-eight
EEEGHNNRRSTT	strengthener
EEEGHNOORSTU	heterogenous
EEEGHNORSSTT	togetherness
EEEGHOORTTYZ	heterozygote
EEEGIILMNNTV	inveiglement
EEEGIINNORRT	orienteering
EEEGIKMNNNOY	monkey engine
EEEGILRRSSVY	regressively
EEEGINNORSSU	neurogenesis
EEEGINNPSSSW	sweepingness
EEEGINOOSSST	osteogenesis
EEEGINPPPRTU	puppeteering
EEEGIOQRRSTU	grotesquerie
EEEGLNNNSSTU	ungentleness
EEEGMNORSSSU	gruesomeness
EEEGNNORSSSU	generousness
EEEGNOOPRRST	progesterone
EEEGNOORRSUV	overgenerous
EEEHHINPSSSS	sheepishness
EEEHHMOPRRST	thermosphere
EEEHIMNNNRST	enshrinement
EEEHIMORSSTX	heterosexism
EEEHINNOPRRS	reprehension
EEEHINPRSTVY	hypertensive
EEEHIORSSTTX	heterosexist
EEEHLLNOPTYY	polyethylene
EEEHLLNPSSSS	helplessness
EEEHLMNOSSSS	homelessness
EEEHLNOPSSSS	hopelessness
EEEHLOPRSTTW	potter's wheel
EEEHMNNNORTT	enthronement
EEEHMOORRSTU	heteromerous
EEEHMOORRSTW	meteor shower
EEEHOPRRSSTZ	herpes zoster
EEEIILPRTTVY	repetitively
EEEIIMNRSSTT	mesenteritis
EEEIINNNRTTV	intervenient
EEEIINPRRTTV	interpretive
EEEIINPRSSVX	inexpressive
EEEIIPQRRSTU	prerequisite
EEEILLLOPPTT	little people
EEEILMNNPRTY	pre-eminently
EEEILMNNSSSU	unseemliness
EEEILMNSSSST	timelessness
EEEILMOORVZZ	mezzo-relievo
EEEILNPRTVVY	preventively
EEEILNRRRTVY	irreverently
EEEILNRSSSST	tirelessness
EEEILNRSSSTW	Western Isles
EEEILPRRSSVY	repressively
EEEILPRSSVXY	expressively
EEEILRRRTTTW	letter-writer
EEEIMNNPRSTT	presentiment
EEEIMNNPRSTU	supereminent
EEEIMNNRSTTV	reinvestment
EEEIMNORSSST	tiresomeness
EEEIMNORSSTT	sensitometer

EEEIMNPRRSST	misrepresent
EEEIMOORRSST	stereoisomer
EEEIMOPRSTUX	time exposure
EEEIMORSVWWY	worm's-eye view
EEEINNPRSSTX	inexpertness
EEEINNPRSTUV	supervenient
EEEINOORRTVX	overexertion
EEEINRSSSSTV	Seven Sisters
EEEJLLORSWYY	yellow jersey
EEELLLNRSSTY	relentlessly
EEELLNOSSSSV	lovelessness
EEELLOPPPRWY	yellow pepper
EEELMMNOPRTY	re-employment
EEELMNNOOSSS	lonesomeness
EEELMNNSTTTU	unsettlement
EEELMOPPRRTT	teleprompter
EEELNNSSSSTU	tunelessness
EEELNORSSSTU	resoluteness
EEELNRSSSSST	restlessness
EEEMPRSSTTXY	expert system
EEENOORSSTTT	testosterone
EEEOOPRRSUVX	overexposure
EEFFGGIINNRR	fringing reef
EEFFLLORSSTY	effortlessly
EEFGGIOPRTTY	pettifoggery
EEFGHIIKNNRT	freethinking
EEFGHIILNRRT	Freightliner
EEFGHIILRTTW	weightlifter
EEFGHIIPRRTZ	prizefighter
EEFGHILNOSTW	flowing sheet
EEFGHILNRRSY	refreshingly
EEFGHIMORRTU	mother figure
EEFGIILLNRTT	little finger
EEFGIIMNNNRT	infringement
EEFHHMMMOOOR	home from home
EEFHIKNORRTW	knife-thrower
EEFHILNOPPST	slip of the pen
EEFIIIIMNNST	semi-infinite
EEFIIINNNSST	infiniteness
EEFIIMNORSSU	seminiferous
EEFILMORSTTU	flitter-mouse
EEFILNNQRTUY	infrequently
EEFILNOORRTX	retroflexion
EEFILNORRSST	frontierless
EEFILNPSSSTU	spitefulness
EEFIMNOPRSST	mesne profits
EEFKLMNOORWY	monkey flower
EEFLLMORRSUY	remorsefully
EEFLLNNTUUVY	uneventfully
EEFLMNORRSUU	unremorseful
EEFLMNORSSSS	formlessness
EEFLNOPRSSUW	powerfulness
EEFNNNOOPRUY	fourpenny one
EEGGGGHMRRUU	hugger-mugger
EEGGHIINNRTT	teething ring
EEGGIILNNRSS	gingerliness
EEGGILSSTUVY	suggestively
EEGGINNPRRSS	spring greens
EEGGINNPRTTU	putting green
EEGGINSSTUUV	unsuggestive
EEGGNOORSSSU	gorgeousness
EEGHHHORRTTU	therethrough
EEGHHIPRRSSU	high pressure
EEGHIINOSSST	histogenesis
EEGHIINRSTUX	extinguisher
EEGHIKNNQSTU	queen's knight
EEGHIKNRRSTU	hunger strike
EEGHILLSSTWY	weightlessly
EEGHILMNORVW	overwhelming
EEGHILNOPPST	teleshopping
EEGHILNOPSSY	phylogenesis
EEGHIMMRSTUW	summer-weight
EEGHIMNOSSTY	mythogenesis
EEGHINNOPSSY	hypnogenesis
EEGHINOORSST	orthogenesis
EEGHINOPSSTY	phytogenesis
EEGHLLOOPRST	hot gospeller
EEGHLNRSSSTT	strengthless
EEGHLOOORSTU	heterologous
EEGHMNOORTTU	mother tongue
EEGHNOOORSTU	heterogonous
EEGHOORSTUYZ	heterozygous
EEGIILLLNPPS	sleeping pill
EEGIILLNNNST	sentinelling
EEGIILLNORSS	religionless
EEGIILNORRTV	green vitriol
EEGIILNPSSTU	sleeping suit
EEGIINNNOPST	piston engine
EEGIINNPRRST	enterprising
EEGIINNPRRTT	interpreting
EEGIINNRRTTY	eternity ring
EEGILLNNPSUY	unsleepingly
EEGILLNOOSST	selenologist
EEGILLNPPRXY	perplexingly
EEGILLNRSTWY	swelteringly
EEGILLNRSUYY	Guernsey lily
EEGILLOOPSST	speleologist
EEGILMOOPPSS	goose pimples
EEGILMOOPSTY	epistemology
EEGILNNRSSST	sterlingness
EEGILNOORRSW	lower regions
EEGILNORSTUV	silver tongue
EEGILQRRRSUY	grey squirrel
EEGIMNNRRSTU	interregnums
EEGINNNRRSSU	unerringness
EEGINNPRRSTU	turnip greens
EEGINOOPRRVW	overpowering
EEGINOOPRSSS	sporogenesis
EEGINOPPRRSU	upper regions
EEGINORSSSUV	grievousness
EEGINOSSSUUX	exiguousness
EEGLMNNOOOPR	prolegomenon
EEGLMNORSSSS	gormlessness
EEGLNNORSUUY	ungenerously
EEGNNOORRSUU	neurosurgeon
EEGNORRRSUUY	neurosurgery
EEHHIINSSSTV	thievishness
EEHHIIOOSSUU	housie-housie
EEHHILLNOPTY	theophylline
EEHHINRSSSSW	shrewishness
EEHHIOPRSTYZ	hypothesizer
EEHHLLOPRTYY	heterophylly
EEHHOOOSSTUU	house-to-house
EEHHOOSSUUYY	housey-housey
EEHIIIRRRRST	Irish terrier
EEHIIKNPRSSY	hyperkinesis
EEHIILNPRSTY	prehensility
EEHIILNRSSSV	liverishness
EEHILMNORSST	motherliness
EEHILNNPSTWY	penny whistle

EEHIMOOPRTTT	photoemitter
EEHINNOORTVZ	event horizon
EEHINNOPRSTY	hypertension
EEHLNRSSSSTU	ruthlessness
EEHLOPRRSTUY	reupholstery
EEHMNNOOORRU	neurohormone
EEHMNOOORSTU	heteronomous
EEHMNRRRSUYY	nursery rhyme
EEHNNORRSTTW	north-western
EEHNORSSTTUW	south-western
EEHOOPPSTTTY	phototypeset
EEIIKLLNNSSU	unlikeliness
EEIIKLOORSTT	tortoise-like
EEIILMNNPTTY	impenitently
EEIILMNNSSTU	untimeliness
EEIILMNOPSST	impoliteness
EEIILMOORVZZ	mezzo-rilievo
EEIILMPRSSVY	impressively, permissively
EEIILNPPRSSS	slipperiness
EEIILNPRSSST	priestliness
EEIILNPSSSST	pitilessness
EEIILNRSSSST	sisterliness
EEIILOOPPSTV	positive pole
EEIILOSSTTTU	toilet tissue
EEIIMNNRTTTT	intermittent
EEIIMNOQSTTU	question time
EEIIMNPRRSTT	misinterpret
EEIIMNPRSSUV	unimpressive
EEIIMNPRSTTY	sempiternity
EEIIMNRRTTUX	intermixture
EEIINNNORTTV	intervention
EEIINNRSSSST	sinisterness
EEIINOPRRSSV	irresponsive
EEIINOPSSSTV	positiveness
EEIINORRSTVV	introversive
EEIINORRTTVV	introvertive
EEIINPRRTTUV	interruptive
EEIIOOPRSSTV	seropositive
EEIIPPRRRSTW	wire stripper
EEIIPRSSTVXY	expressivity
EEIKLMNNOSTY	Milton Keynes
EEIKOPRRRSTW	worker priest
EEILLMOSSTVY	motivelessly
EEILLNNOSSSV	slovenliness
EEILLNNOSSUV	unloveliness
EEILLNSSSSST	listlessness
EEILLORRSTUY	irresolutely
EEILLRSSSSTY	resistlessly
EEILMNOOSSST	toilsomeness
EEILMNORSTUV	volunteerism
EEILMOPPRRTY	peremptorily
EEILMORSSSTU	moistureless
EEILNNOOPSVX	non-explosive
EEILNOPRSSSU	perilousness
EEILNOPRSSVY	responsively
EEILNOQSSSTU	questionless
EEILNPRSSTTY	persistently
EEILNPSSSUVY	suspensively
EEILOPPRSSVY	oppressively
EEILOPRRSTYZ	proselytizer
EEILOPSSSSVY	possessively
EEIMNNNOPRSY	money spinner
EEINNOOPQSTU	open question
EEINNOPRSSUV	unresponsive
EEINNOPRSTUV	supervention
EEINOOPPSSST	oppositeness
EEINOOPRSSSS	repossession
EEINOORRRSTV	retroversion
EEINOORRSTVX	extroversion
EEINOORSSSTU	interosseous
EEINOPRSSSSU	supersession
EEINOPRSSSTV	sportiveness
EEINOPRSSSUV	perviousness, previousness
EEINORSSSTUV	vitreousness
EEIOPPRRRSST	proprietress
EEIPRRSSSTUU	pressure suit
EEKLMNOPUYZZ	monkey-puzzle
EEKLNOORTTUV	true-love knot
EEKNNOORSTTT	Stoke-on-Trent
EEKNOOPPRSSS	spokesperson
EELLNOPSSSST	plotlessness
EELLNOSSSSSU	soullessness
EELMMNNOPTUY	unemployment
EELMOPRRSTTY	stormy petrel
EELNOPSSSSST	spotlessness
EEMNNOOPPSTT	postponement
EEMNNOORSSSU	enormousness
EEMNNOOSSSUV	venomousness
EEMNNORSSSUU	numerousness
EEMOOOPPRTTU	moto perpetuo
EENNOOPRSTTY	none-so-pretty
EENNOSSSSSUU	sensuousness
EENNRRRSSUUY	nursery nurse
EENNTTTTWWYY	twenty-twenty
EENOOPRRSTUU	neuropterous
EEOOPPRRSSTU	preposterous
EEPPRRTTTTYY	pretty-pretty
EFFGGHIIINRT	fire-fighting
EFFGGIILNNSU	glue-sniffing
EFFILNRSSTUU	fruitfulness
EFGGGIINOPTT	pettifogging
EFGGHHIINRTT	night fighter
EFGGHIILNRST	self-righting
EFGHHILNTTTW	Twelfth Night
EFGHIINRRSTT	first-nighter
EFGHIKOORRSY	Yorkshire fog
EFGHILNRSSTU	rightfulness
EFGHLNOOPUUY	young hopeful
EFGIILLMORSU	florilegiums
EFGIILNORSUV	griseofulvin
EFGIILNRRTYY	terrifyingly
EFGIINORRSTV	virgin forest
EFGILNPSTUYY	stupefyingly
EFGINNOOORTT	Grootfontein
EFGLNNORSSUW	wrongfulness
EFHHILLOOOSY	holy of holies
EFHILLMNORTU	run-of-the-mill
EFHILLRSSTTY	thriftlessly
EFHILMNRSSTU	mirthfulness
EFHINNOORSSU	sunshine roof
EFHLLNOSSSTU	slothfulness
EFHLNOSSTUUY	youthfulness
EFHLNRSSTTUU	truthfulness
EFIIIKLNTTUY	utility knife
EFIIILNNOOSV	line of vision
EFIIIMNNNTUY	unfemininity
EFIIINOPRSTW	spirit of wine
EFIIJLNOOPRU	oil of juniper

EFIILMNORSUU luminiferous
EFIILMOPRSVY oversimplify
EFIIMMNOPSST post-feminism
EFIIMNOPSSTT post-feminist
EFIIOPRRSTUY pyritiferous
EFIOOOPRRSSU soporiferous
EFIOORRRSSTU rostriferous
EFLLOOSTUUUV luteofulvous
EFLLOPPRSUUY purposefully
EFLMNNORSSUU mournfulness
EFLNRSSSTTUU trustfulness
EGGGIILNNRSY sniggeringly
EGGHHIINPPST high-stepping
EGGHHINSSSTU thuggishness
EGGHIIKLNNSS King's English
EGGHIINPRSSS priggishness
EGGHILNSSSSU sluggishness
EGGIILLMMNRY glimmeringly
EGGIILLNRTTY glitteringly
EGGILLLNORVY grovellingly
EGGILOOPSTTY Egyptologist
EGGIMNOOPRSS gossip monger
EGHHILNOSSSU ghoulishness
EGHHIMNOOPPS home shopping
EGHHINNOSTUU house-hunting
EGHHMORRTTUY merry thought
EGHHNOORSSTU thoroughness
EGHIIKLNNSST knightliness
EGHIILMMNRSY shimmeringly
EGHIILMNPRWY whimperingly
EGHIILNOTTWZ twilight zone
EGHILMOORTYZ mythologizer
EGHILNOOPRST phrenologist
EGHILOOPPSST psephologist
EGHIMNOOORSU rooming house
EGHIMNORSSTW women's rights
EGHINOOPRRSV governorship
EGHINOOPSTTT photosetting
EGHINORRRSTT night terrors
EGHINORSSTTU outrightness
EGIIILLNNRSV silver lining
EGIIIMNNRTTT intermitting
EGIIIMNOPSTU impetiginous
EGIIINNNPRWZ prizewinning
EGIIINOPSSTV positive sign
EGIIKLNPPRRS klipspringer
EGIIKNNRSSST strikingness
EGIIKNOPPPRS skipping rope
EGIILLLNNSVY snivellingly
EGIILLMNPTUX multiplexing
EGIILLNNOPST selling point
EGIILLNQRRSU squirrelling
EGIILMNNNPSU spinning mule
EGIILMNNOPTT melting point
EGIILMOOSSST seismologist
EGIIMNNOPSSS imposingness
EGIIMNOOPRRT primogenitor
EGIIMNOORRST Risorgimento
EGIKKNNOPRTY pony-trekking
EGIKLLMNOORY Kremlinology
EGILLNNOORST rolling stone
EGILLNORSTTY storytelling
EGILLOORSUWW willow grouse
EGILMNNORTTY tormentingly
EGILMNOOOSTT entomologist
EGILMNOORSTU numerologist
EGILNNNOSSUV unlovingness
EGILNNRSUVWY unswervingly
EGILNOORSSSU gloriousness
EGILNOPRSTTY protestingly
EGILNRSTTTUY stutteringly
EGIMNOORRTTY trigonometry
EGINNOPRSTTU unprotesting
EGINNRSSSTTU trustingness
EGINOORRSSSU rigorousness
EGINOORSSSUV vigorousness
EGKNNOORSSTU surgeon's knot
EGMMNOORRRUU rumour-monger
EHHHIMRRSTTU hermit thrush
EHHIILOOPPSZ philosophize
EHHILMRSSSTU missel thrush
EHHILMRSSTTU mistle thrush
EHHINOOOPPRS siphonophore
EHIIILORTTVW white vitriol
EHIIIMNPRSST ministership
EHIIKLMOOPRT poikilotherm
EHIIKNSSSSTT skittishness
EHIILLMNPSTU phillumenist
EHIILLNOSTTX sextillionth
EHIILLOPSTWW will-o'-the-wisp
EHIILMOOPRST heliotropism
EHIILOPRRTTT lithotripter
EHIIMNPRSTUX xiphisternum
EHIINORSTTUY Trinity House
EHIIOPRRSSTV servitorship
EHIKLORSTTUW Turkish towel
EHILLMOPPSTU multiple shop
EHILMMOOPPRS pleomorphism
EHILNOOPSUUY euphoniously
EHILNSSSSTTU sluttishness
EHIMMORRSSTT short-termism
EHIMNOOPPRRT minor prophet
EHINNORSSTUW unworthiness
EHINOOOPSSST photo session
EHIOPRRSSUVY surveyorship
EHLLMORSSUUY humourlessly
EHMNNOORRSTT northernmost
EHMNOORSSSUU humorousness
EHMNOORSSTTU southernmost
EHMNOORSSTUY honour system
EHOOOPRRSTTU orthopterous
EIIIJMNOOSSV Mission Viejo
EIIIMNNORSST intermission
EIIIMNOOPRST reimposition
EIIIMPRTTTVY permittivity
EIILLLLMNOPS Plimsoll line
EIILLNORSSSU illusoriness
EIILLPRSSSTY spiritlessly
EIILMNOOSTUV evolutionism
EIILMOOPPRST pleiotropism
EIILMOPRSUVY imperviously
EIILMRSTTUVY multiversity
EIILNNNOSTUV tunnel vision
EIILNOOOPPST pole position
EIILNOORRSTU irresolution
EIILNOOSTTUV evolutionist
EIILNOPRSTUY polyneuritis
EIIMMNNOPRST imprisonment
EIIMMOOPRSTV over-optimism
EIIMNNNQQUUU quinquennium

EIIMNNOOPRST	premonitions
EIIMNNORTTTT	intromittent
EIINNOORRSTV	introversion
EIINNOPRRTTU	interruption
EIINNOPRSSTU	interspinous
EIINOORSTTTX	extortionist
EIINOPRSSTTU	superstition
EIIOOPPSSTTV	postpositive
EIIOOPRRSTTY	posteriority
EIKLLNOSSSSU	skull session
EILLMNOOSSTY	motionlessly
EILMNNOOPTTY	omnipotently
EILMNNOSSSUU	luminousness
EILMOPPRSTUU	multi-purpose
EILMOPSSSSTY	spoils system
EILMORSSTUYY	mysteriously
EILOPPRSTUVY	supportively
EIMNOOOPPRRT	proper motion
EIMNOORSSSTU	timorousness
EIMOPRSSSSTT	postmistress
EINOORSSSUUX	uxoriousness
EINOPPRSTUUV	unsupportive
EINOPRRRTTUY	interruptory
EINOPRRSSTTW	winter sports
EINOPRSSSSUU	spuriousness
EINORSSSTUUV	virtuousness
EIOOOOPRSSST	osteoporosis
EIOPRRRSSTTW	sports writer
EKKNNOOSTUVZ	Novokuznetsk
ELNOOPPSSSUU	populousness
ELNOOPRSTTUY	portentously
ELNORSSSSTUU	lustrousness
ELOOPPRRSSUY	prosperously
ELOORRSSTTUY	stertorously
EMMNOOOPRSSU	monospermous
EMOOOPRRRSTT	storm trooper
EMOPPRSSTUUU	presumptuous
ENNOOORSSSSU	sonorousness
ENOOPPRRSSST	sportsperson
ENOOPPRRSSUU	unprosperous
ENOORSSSTTUU	tortuousness
FFGGHHIIINST	fighting fish
FFGIILLLNNUU	unfulfilling
FFGILNOPTTUY	off-puttingly
FFILLNRTUUUY	unfruitfully
FFLLOOSSTTYY	softly-softly
FGGHIIINTTTT	tight-fitting
FGHHILORRTTY	forthrightly
FGHHLLOTTUUY	thoughtfully
FGHIIIORSTTV	right of visit
FGHIILLNSTUY	insightfully
FGHIILNORRYY	horrifyingly
FGIILMNORTYY	mortifyingly
FGIILMNSTYYY	mystifyingly
FGIKNOOPRSST	sport of kings
FGILOORSTTUU	futurologist
FHIIIMNORRRS	mirror finish
FHILLOPRSUWY	worshipfully
FHLLNRTTUUUY	untruthfully
FIIILLOOORTV	oil of vitriol
FIILMMORTTUY	multiformity
FILOORSTTUUY	fortuitously
GGHHIINOSSTT	sighting shot
GGHHILNRSTUY	highly strung
GGHIIINNNNSY	singing hinny
GGHIILNNNRTU	running light
GGIIILNNRTUY	intriguingly
GGIIMNNNORRU	mourning ring
GGILMNNOORRY	morning glory
GHHILOOPRSUY	hygrophilous
GHHMNPRRSTUY	sprung rhythm
GHIIKLNNNTUY	unthinkingly
GHIILNNORSUY	nourishingly
GHIILOOPSSTY	physiologist
GHIINNOOORST	shooting iron
GHIINOPPPSTW	whipping post
GHIKNOORRSUW	working hours
GHILMOOOPRST	morphologist
GHILNOPRSTTU	Port Sunlight
GHIMNOOPSSTY	gymnosophist
GHINOOPPSSTW	show-stopping
GHMOOOPRSUYZ	zygomorphous
GIIIKNNRSST	stinking iris
GIIIMNNOSVX	vision mixing
GIIILNNNTUVY	uninvitingly
GIIIMNNORTTT	intromitting
GIILLNOORSUY	ingloriously
GIILMMNOOPSW	swimming pool
GIILMMNOOSTU	immunologist
GIILMNNOPSUY	unimposingly
GIILNNNSTTUY	unstintingly
GIILNPRRSSUY	surprisingly
GIINNNOPRTTU	turning point
GIINNNORSSTU	unison string
GIINNPRRSSUU	unsurprising
GILLMOOPSTTY	polyglottism
GILNNOPRSTUY	unsportingly
GILNOPPRSTUY	supportingly
GILOOOPRSTTY	protistology
GLLNOOSTTUUY	gluttonously
HHILMMOOPRSY	hylomorphism
HHIMMMOOOPRS	homomorphism
HHIOOTTTUUWW	tu-whit tu-whoo
HHMMOOOOPRSU	homomorphous
HHMMOOOTTTUU	mouth-to-mouth
HIIIILMNPSST	philistinism
HIILLOOPPRWW	whippoorwill
HIIOOPRSSTUV	virtuosoship
HILMMOOPPRSY	polymorphism
HIMMMNOOOPRS	monomorphism
HIMOOOPPRSTT	phototropism
HLMOOOPPRSUY	polymorphous
HLMOOPSSTUUY	posthumously
HMMNOOOOPRSU	monomorphous
IIIIMMMNNPYY	miminy-piminy
IIIIMMNNNPYY	niminy-piminy
IIIIMNNOSTTU	intuitionism
IIIINNOSTTTU	intuitionist
IIILLLMMNOTU	multimillion
IIILLNNOQSTU	quintillions
IIILNOQSTUUY	iniquitously
IIIMNNOORSST	intromission
IIINNORSTTTU	nutritionist
IIINNORSTTUU	innutritious
IILMNOOSTUVY	voluminosity
IILNORSTTUUY	nutritiously
IILOOPPRSTUY	propitiously
IINNOOOPPTTT	point-to-point
IINOOOPPSSTT	postposition
IINOOPPRSTUU	unpropitious

IINOOPRSTTTU prostitution
IIOOPPSSSTUU suppositious
ILLMNOOSUUVY voluminously
ILMNOOORSUVY omnivorously
ILOPRSTTUVYY topsy-turvily
INNNOOOOPSSU non-poisonous
KKMNOOOOSSVV Novomoskovsk
LLMOSTTUUUUY tumultuously
LLOOPSTUUUVY voluptuously
LMNNOOOOSTUY monotonously
LMNNOOSSUYYY synonymously